Strategic Brand Management

Building, Measuring, and Managing Brand Equity

Strategic Brand Management

Building, Measuring, and Managing Brand Equity

Fifth Edition

Kevin Lane Keller

Tuck School of Business
Dartmouth College

Vanitha Swaminathan

Katz Graduate School of Business
University of Pittsburgh

 Pearson

Vice President, Business, Economics, and UK
   Courseware: Donna Battista
Director of Portfolio Management:
   Stephanie Wall
Executive Portfolio Manager: Lynn M. Huddon
Editorial Assistant: Rachel Chou
Vice President, Product Marketing:
   Roxanne McCarley
Senior Product Marketer: Becky Brown
Product Marketing Assistant: Marianela Silvestri
Manager of Field Marketing, Business Publishing:
   Adam Goldstein
Field Marketing Manager: Nicole Price
Vice President, Production and Digital Studio,
   Arts and Business: Etain O'Dea

Director, Production and Digital Studio, Business
   and Economics: Ashley Santora
Managing Producer, Business: Melissa Feimer
Content Producer: Michelle Zeng
Operations Specialist: Carol Melville
Design Lead: Kathryn Foot
Full Service Project Management: Ana Diaz-Caneja/
   Bhanuprakash Sherla, Pearson CSC
Interior Design: Pearson CSC
Cover Design: Pearson CSC
Cover Art: wowomnom/Shutterstock
Printer/Binder: LSC Communications
Cover Printer: LSC Communications

Microsoft and/or its respective suppliers make no representations about the suitability of the information contained in the documents and related graphics published as part of the services for any purpose. All such documents and related graphics are provided "as is" without warranty of any kind. Microsoft and/or its respective suppliers hereby disclaim all warranties and conditions with regard to this information, including all warranties and conditions of merchantability, whether express, implied or statutory, fitness for a particular purpose, title and non-infringement. In no event shall Microsoft and/or its respective suppliers be liable for any special, indirect or consequential damages or any damages whatsoever resulting from loss of use, data or profits, whether in an action of contract, negligence or other tortious action, arising out of or in connection with the use or performance of information available from the services.

The documents and related graphics contained herein could include technical inaccuracies or typographical errors. Changes are periodically added to the information herein. Microsoft and/or its respective suppliers may make improvements and/or changes in the product(s) and/or the program(s) described herein at any time. Partial screen shots may be viewed in full within the software version specified.

Microsoft® and Windows® are registered trademarks of the Microsoft Corporation in the U.S.A. and other countries. This book is not sponsored or endorsed by or affiliated with the Microsoft Corporation.

Cataloging-in-Publication Data is available on file at the Library of Congress.

1 19

ISBN 10:   0-13-489249-6
ISBN 13: 978-0-13-489249-8

Dedication

This book is dedicated to
the memories of my father and mother
with much love, respect, and admiration.
—KLK

This book is dedicated to the memory of
my father, to my mother, and to my family,
with much love and gratitude.
—VS

BRIEF CONTENTS

CONTENTS

PREFACE

WHAT IS THE BOOK ABOUT?

This book deals with brands—why they are important, what they represent to consumers, and what firms should do to manage them properly. As many business executives now recognize, perhaps one of the most valuable assets a firm has are the brands it has invested in and developed over time. Although brands may represent invaluable intangible assets, creating and nurturing a strong brand poses considerable challenges.

The chief purpose of this book is to provide a comprehensive and up-to-date treatment of the subjects of brands, brand equity, and *strategic brand management*—the design and implementation of marketing programs and activities to build, measure, and manage brand equity. One of the book's important goals is to provide managers with concepts and techniques to improve the long-term profitability of their brand strategies. We incorporate current thinking and developments on these topics from both academics and industry participants, and combine a comprehensive theoretical foundation with enough practical insights to assist managers in their day-to-day and long-term brand decisions. And we draw on illustrative examples and case studies of brands marketed in the United States and all over the world.

We address three important questions:

1. How can we create brand equity?
2. How can we measure brand equity?
3. How can we sustain brand equity to expand business opportunities?

What's Different about This Book?

Although a number of excellent books have been written about brands, no book has really maximized breadth, depth and relevance to the greatest possible extent. We developed a framework that provides a definition of brand equity, identified sources and outcomes of brand equity, and provided tactical guidelines about how to build, measure, and manage brand equity. The framework approaches branding from the perspective of the consumer; it is called *customer-based brand equity*.

Who Should Read the Book?

A wide range of people can benefit from reading this book:

- Students interested in increasing both their understanding of basic branding principles and their exposure to classic and contemporary branding applications and case studies
- Managers and analysts concerned with the effects of their day-to-day marketing decisions on brand performance
- Senior executives concerned with the longer-term prosperity of their brand franchises and product or service portfolios
- All marketers interested in new ideas with implications for marketing strategies and tactics

The perspective we adopt is relevant to any type of organization (public or private, large or small), and the examples cover a wide range of industries and geographies.

NEW TO THIS EDITION

As we all know, the world of marketing is undergoing a radical transformation. The growth of digital and mobile technologies has given consumers the ability to connect with each other at warped speed and on a scale that has never been witnessed before. The access to information in today's world is unparalleled, and brand marketers are using a plethora of new digital channels to connect with consumers, creating exciting new opportunities along with daunting new challenges for brands.

NEW: A Greater Focus on Digital Branding

Against this backdrop, the new edition has taken a fresh look at branding paradigms and practices through a digital lens, while retaining aspects of traditional brand management that continue to be important and relevant. We have achieved this both by updating existing material and adding new examples with a view toward incorporating the latest developments. More important, a whole new **Chapter 7** titled **"Branding in the Digital Era"** has been written. This chapter provides an overview of the key changes that have transformed the world of branding, has integrated a variety of new case studies to highlight these changes, and has proposed a novel way of assessing impact of brands on consumers using the metric of brand engagement. This chapter also provides a comprehensive overview of the major digital channels, and discusses their pros and cons.

NEW Examples and Boxes in Chapters 1–16

We also highlight the many changes to the brand management function and have incorporated updated content throughout all the chapters, adding new material on important examples or topics about brands as listed in the following section:

NEW EXAMPLES AND BOXES IN FIFTH EDITION

Chapter	Brand and/or Topic
1: Brands and Brand Management	**New Examples:** Adobe, Airbnb, Lady Gaga, LaCroix
	New Brand Focus: Unlocking the Secrets of Digital Native Brands
2: Customer-Based Brand Equity and Brand Positioning	**New Example:** Annie's Homegrown, Netflix
3: Brand Resonance and Brand Value Chain	**New Branding Brief:** How Digital-Platform-Based Brands Create Customer Engagement
4: Choosing Brand Elements to Build Brand Equity	**New Examples:** JetBlue, Method, StarKist's Charlie
	New Branding Briefs: Do-Overs with Brand Makeovers; The Battle over Trademarks
5: Designing Marketing Programs to Build Brand Equity	**New Example:** Yeti Is the Cooler Brand
	New Branding Brief: Chew on This: Milk Bone Brushing Chews Connected with Customers
	New Science of Branding: Research on Omnichannel
6: Integrating Marketing Communications to Build Brand Equity	**New Examples:** Tide, Grey Goose
7: Branding in the Digital Era (NEW!)	**New Examples:** Pepsi's Ad Misfire, Tough Mudder, John Deere – *Furrow* Magazine
	New Branding Briefs: Campaigning Using Clicks with Google AdWords; Igniting a Digital Firestorm, On Being Social in China; Shaving the Price of Razors; The Phenomenal Rise of Amazon; Turning Flight Delays into Marketing Opportunities
	New Science of Branding: Is Co-Creation of Products and Brands Always Good; Drivers of Brand Engagement
	New Brand Focus: Understanding How Online Word-of-Mouth Influences Brands and Brand Management
8: Leveraging Secondary Brand Associations to Build Brand Equity	**New Example:** Grey Goose
	New Branding Brief: Rachael Ray's Nutrish

Chapter	Brand and/or Topic
9: Developing a Brand Equity Measurement and Management System	**New Example:** Domino's Pizza
	New Branding Brief: How Taco Bell Uses Data-Driven Social Media Marketing to Engage Its Customers
10: Measuring Sources of Brand Equity: Capturing Customer Mind-Set	**New Branding Briefs:** Gatorade's Social Media Command Center; How P&G Innovates Using Qualitative Research Data; Netnography as a Digital Research Technique; Understanding Attribution Modeling
11: Measuring Outcomes of Brand Equity: Capturing Market Performance	**New Brand Focus:** Financial Perspectives on Brands and the Brand Value Chain
12: Designing and Implementing Brand Architecture Strategies	**New Examples:** GE, L.L.Bean, Philips, Toms Shoes
	New Branding Briefs: Google: Expanding Beyond Search; Netflix: Evolving a Brand Architecture to Grow the Brand
	New Brand Focus: Corporate Social Responsibility and Brand Strategy
13: Introducing and Naming New Products and Brand Extensions	**New Examples:** Coke Zero
	New Brand Focus: Apple: Creating a Tech Megabrand
14: Managing Brands Over Time	**New Examples:** Chobani, Febreze, JC Penney, Pabst, Volkswagen
	New Branding Brief: Patagonia
	New Science of Branding: Understanding Brand Crises
15: Managing Brands Over Geographic Boundaries and Market Segments	**New Example:** Häagen-Dazs Global Brand, Levi Strauss, Nielsen's Spectra Behaviorstages, Campbell's Soup, Lenovo in China
	New Branding Brief: Marketing to Bicultural Consumers Using Bilingual Advertising
16: Closing Observations	**New Section:** New Capabilities for Brand Marketers

In addition, we have updated nearly all the existing cases, removed outdated cases, and have provided new insights and information where applicable. Our focus on new digitally focused brands, as well as brands that have undergone major transformations, has allowed us to provide in-depth timelines on innovative brands and companies including Amazon, Google, Apple, Mountain Dew, Harley Davidson, and Burberry. These timelines will help the reader trace key developments in the history of these brands.

NEW Topics in Branding

The book also attempts to provide some insights into new topics relating to branding. Examples of new topics include:

- Attribution modeling
- Social listening
- Netnography as a research technique
- Influencer marketing
- Online brand engagement
- New capabilities for brand marketers
- Digital platform brands
- Digital native vertical brands
- Marketing to bicultural consumers
- Managing brand crises in the social media era

SOLVING TEACHING AND LEARNING CHALLENGES

The book is aimed at both students who are focusing on brand management as it relates to a career, and those students who are intellectually curious about the topic. The key challenges in teaching and learning surrounding this course can be framed as four questions that are posed by students:

1. How are these concepts relevant to the real world?
2. How do we know that this is true? Do we have any evidence that this phenomenon exists or is true?
3. How can the frameworks proposed here be useful to a practicing manager in decision-making?
4. How can the instructor ensure that students apply their critical-thinking skills in evaluating the frameworks in this book?

We have two features that address the real-world applicability of our chapters. These are in-text examples and Branding Briefs. **In-text examples** connect to key ideas in the section, and typically highlight a specific brand or an issue that a brand is facing.

ANNIE'S HOMEGROWN

Annie's Homegrown has successfully created a brand image by advertising that its food can help you live the good life. "Choose Good" is the theme across their ads which concludes with "Good can be hard, but Good can also be easy." Annie's stated mission is to make the world healthier and happier through nourishing and healthy foods and by a healthy code of conduct in all that they do and how they treat people and the planet.

Annie's has the second largest market share in the boxed pasta market next only to Kraft. It also has made inroads into various categories such as frozen pizza, crackers, salad dressing, and the condiment market. So, how did Annie's Homegrown carve out a unique position in a market dominated by large corporations such as Kraft? Annie's Homegrown's focus on corporate social responsibility was the right focus at the right time, and it resonated with the shifting consumers' interest in sustainability and corporate social responsibility. Its packaging consisted of faux-handwritten letters from founder Annie Withey and was made of recycled paper.[25] Annie's flavors such as "Organic Peace Pasta & Parmesan," in a tie-dye box, had a unique feel to them. The signature brand character 'Bernie the Bunny' made the brand seem warm and lovable.[26] Their Web site featured 3-minute videos dedicated to American family farms. Thus, in many different ways, Annie's Homegrown married comfort foods with ethical values, which resonated with its consumers, including themes such as supporting small, family farmers and social commitments like college scholarships for students studying sustainable agriculture, and so on.

In 2014, Annie's Homegrown was acquired by General Mills for $820 million. Despite its acquisition, Annie's has maintained its positioning and values, and has branched out into other product categories (e.g., cereal). Of note is that this acquisition by General Mills is part of a general trend by big food manufacturers—such as Coca-Cola, Kellogg's, and General Mills—of acquiring small brands with healthy, environmentally aware positioning. Following the acquisition, Annie's Homegrown has retained its small but stable market share in the increasingly popular segment of clean, environmentally aware, and healthy foods.[27]

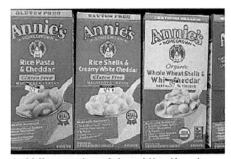

Annie's Homegrown has crafted a special brand image by focusing its positioning on nourishing and healthy foods that can help customers live the good life.

Branding Briefs are slightly longer real-world case scenarios that provide a more in-depth look into a brand's strategy, with a view toward enhancing students' understanding regarding a particular topic by bringing key concepts to life.

BRANDING BRIEF 5-1
Yeti Is the "Cooler" Brand

Yeti is a manufacturer of high-quality and expensive coolers that have become status symbols for members of its core target audience, such as hunters and fishers. The brand is known for its authentic messaging, and its coolers range in price from a low of $250 to thousands of dollars. Its best-selling models are small and medium-sized hardcase coolers that fit in the back of a truck or car. Yeti is credited with reinventing this category and for creating an aspirational brand among its target audiences.

A key marketing challenge that the brand has had to overcome is the high sticker price associated with a mundane product (i.e., coolers). So, what are the keys to Yeti's success? The coolers actually work; they keep ice cold for days. However, Yeti needed to convince customers of the value of the product and, to do so, relied on professional endorsements from well-known individuals in hunting and fishing communities. Yeti used some traditional print advertising and placed these endorsement ads in hunting and fishing programs on Outdoor Channel, along with marketing on specialized networks such as Sportsman, World Fishing Network, and so forth. Its credibility got a further boost when the company received an endorsement from the Interagency Grizzly Bear Committee that the coolers were "grizzly proof."

To build awareness among its target audiences, Yeti has also made considerable investments in social media. To further create excitement for the brand, Yeti invested in apparel and merchandise, such as branded hats, T-shirts, and bottle openers, and included these with every cooler purchased, ensuring increased buzz about its products. The company has also invested significantly in data analytics to personalize the content audiences receive, based on historical data on prior purchase behavior, favorite outdoor adventures, and so on. Yeti also ensures that the varying touchpoints are well-orchestrated to provide a unified experience. By relying on a combination of traditional and nontraditional approaches, combining online and offline advertising, and deploying personalized marketing approaches, Yeti has been successful in creating an aspirational brand.

The Yeti brand of coolers is seen as a status symbol, thanks to high quality, authentic messaging and the use of nontraditional/social media marketing.

The Yeti brand grew from $5 million to $450 million in 2016 and is now facing a new set of challenges. Competition in the high-end cooler market has increased with the entry of brands such as Igloo's Sportsman, Orion 45, and Cabela's Polar Cap. Therefore, the company has to work extremely hard to maintain its appeal and authenticity. To do so, Yeti has become more deliberate in its use of social media marketing. For example, it produces and distributes short videos that glorify the outdoors. By depicting rugged and intrepid outdoorsy types such as a legendary Rio Grande Valley fly fisherman or a female Grand Canyon river guide navigating the great outdoors, these movies (posted on its Web site) are intended to retain the interest of hunters and fishers who are core targets of the brand, even though the brand has grown beyond these audiences. Yeti products are only featured briefly in these videos. The brand also posts fan-submitted photos of wildlife and outdoors

---

Another frequently encountered question from students is as follows: How do we know that these brands have any effect on consumers? What is the evidence for this? To address this question, we have incorporated **The Science of Branding**. These sections appear throughout the textbook and highlight the latest academic research on a topic. We use jargon-free language to enhance the accessibility of the material to all types of audiences, e.g., academic, practitioner, and consultant.

 ### THE SCIENCE OF BRANDING 7-1
Is Co-Creation of Brands and Products Always Good?

What are the implications of social media from a consumer's standpoint? Are consumers, in fact, motivated to participate in co-creation of brands and products? When does consumer co-creation of brands and products benefit a firm? On the positive side, research has shown that co-creation can increase loyalty by promoting feelings of psychological ownership and makes consumers feel empowered. Furthermore, the amount of effort consumers put in and the enjoyment they experience from participating in co-creating a product can lead to greater consumer preference for the co-created product itself.

While co-creation can positively influence consumers' preferences for the products that they are helping to co-create, not all consumers are equally willing to participate or benefit from such involvement. Similarly, the benefits to brands are also uneven and depend on various factors. In an advertising setting, researchers have shown that co-creation can benefit brands when viewers' ability to scrutinize messages is low, when the identities of the ad creators and viewers are similar, or when viewers are highly loyal to the brand. In product categories in which quality is extremely important or with luxury products, co-creation efforts are less successful. Moreover, when consumers' cultural orientations include a high belief in power distance (or the belief in inequality or hierarchy), their propensity to purchase co-created products is also lower.

These findings indicate that brand marketers should tread carefully when implementing mechanisms that allow for consumer participation. While there appear to be many benefits, there are also significant downsides if the co-creation efforts involve the wrong product categories or customer groups.

Sources: C. Fuchs, E. Prandelli, and M. Schreier, "The Psychological Effects of Empowerment Strategies on Consumers' Product Demand," *Journal of Marketing* 74, no. 1 (2010): 65–79; Christoph Fuchs, and Martin Schreier, "Customer Empowerment in New Product Development," *Journal of Product Innovation Management* 28, no. 1 (2011): 17–32; Christoph Fuchs, Emanuela Prandelli, Martin Schreier, and Darren W. Dahl, "All That Is Users Might Not Be Gold: How Labeling Products as User Designed Backfires in the Context of Luxury Fashion Brands," *Journal of Marketing* 77, no. 5 (2013): 75–91; Debora Thompson, and Prashant Malaviya, "Consumer-Generated Ads: Does Awareness Co-Creation Help or Hurt Persuasion?" *Journal of Marketing* 77, no. 3 (May 2013): 33–47; Martin Schreier, Christoph Fuchs, and Darren W. Dahl, "The Innovation Effect of User Design: Exploring Consumers' Innovation Perceptions of Firms Selling Products Designed by Users," *Journal of Marketing* 76, no. 5 (2012): 18–32; N. Franke, and M. Schreier, "Why Customers Value Self-Designed Products: The Importance of Process Effort and Enjoyment," *Journal of Product Innovation Management* 27, no. 7 (2010): 1020–1031; Susan Fournier, and Jill Avery, "The Uninvited Brand," *Business Horizons* 54, no. 3 (2011): 193–207; Neeru Paharia and Vanitha Swaminathan, "Who Is Wary of Cocreation? The Hazards of Empowering Power-Distant and Conservative Consumers," working paper, Georgetown University.

Each chapter contains a **Brand Focus** appendix that delves into detail on specific branding-related topics such as brand audits, private labels, legal issues, etc.

BRAND FOCUS 9.0
Sample Rolex Brand Audit

For over a century, Rolex has remained one of the most recognized and sought-after luxury brands in the world. In 2017, the BrandZ Top 100 Most Valuable Global Brands (which is a ranking by Kantar Millward Brown, or KMB), the world's most valuable watch brand is Rolex, which has an estimated brand value of $8.053 billion.[39] The estimate is based on a complicated formula combining financial information and consumer surveys. KMB interviews three million consumers in more than 50 global markets about 100,000 different brands. It uses data from Bloomberg and Kantar Worldpanel to analyze companies' financial and business performance.

To be clear, Rolex is not among KMB's Top 100 brands. (A brand needed a value of at least $11.3 billion to make that list.) Rolex appears in the report on the BrandZ Luxury Top 10 list, where it holds the #5 position (see table below). Rolex is the only one of the top 10 luxury brands whose sole product is watches. No other watches-only brand is included in the BrandZ report.

A thorough audit can help pinpoint opportunities and challenges for Rolex, whose brand equity has been historically strong, as much is at stake.

"The name of Rolex is synonymous with quality. Rolex—with its rigorous series of tests that intervene at every stage—has redefined the meaning of quality."

—**www.rolex.com**

BACKGROUND

History

Rolex was founded in 1905 by a German named Hans Wilsdorf and his brother-in-law, William Davis, as a watch-making company, Wilsdorf & Davis, with headquarters in London, England. Wilsdorf, a self-proclaimed perfectionist, set out to improve the mainstream pocket watch right from the start. By 1908, he had created a timepiece that kept accurate time but was small enough to be worn on the wrist. That same year, Wilsdorf trademarked the name "Rolex" because he thought it sounded like the noise a watch made when it was wound. Rolex was also easy to pronounce in many different languages.

"A" certificate after passing the world's toughest timing test, which included testing the watch at extreme temperature levels.

Twelve years later, Wilsdorf developed and patented the now-famous Oyster waterproof case and screw crown. This mechanism became the first true protection against water, dust, and dirt. To generate publicity for the watch, jewelry stores displayed fish tanks in their windows with the Oyster watch completely submerged in it. The Oyster was put to the test on October 7, 1927, when Mercedes Gleitze swam the English Channel wearing one. She emerged 15 hours later with the watch functioning perfectly, much to the amazement of the media and public. Gleitze became the first of a long list of "ambassadors" that Rolex has used to promote its wristwatches.

Over the years, Rolex has pushed innovation in watches to new levels. In 1931, the firm introduced the Perpetual self-winding rotor mechanism, eliminating the need to wind a watch. In 1945, the company invented the first watch to display a number date at the 3 o'clock position and named it the Datejust. In 1953, Rolex launched the Submariner—the first diving watch that was water-resistant and pressure-resistant to 100 meters. The sporty watch appeared in various James Bond movies in the 1950s and became an instant symbol of prestige and durability.

For decades, Swiss-made watches owned the middle and high-end markets, remaining virtually unrivaled until the invention of the quartz watch in 1969. Quartz watches kept more accurate time, were less expensive to make, and quickly dominated the middle market. Within 10 years, quartz watches made up approximately half of all watch sales worldwide.[40] Joe Thompson, editor of *Modern Jeweler*, a U.S. trade publication, explained, "By 1980, people thought the mechanical watch was dead."[41]

Rolex proved the experts wrong. The company would not give in to the quartz watch rage. In order to survive, however, Rolex was forced to move into the high-end market exclusively—leaving the middle to the quartz people—and create a strategy to defend and build its position there. More recently, the watch industry has undergone a significant change with the introduction of smart watches, e.g., Apple Watch, which combine the functionality of a watch with many features of a smartphone.

DEVELOPING EMPLOYABILITY SKILLS

Brand management is undergoing a transformation, and the chapters in this book have shone a spotlight on various aspects of brand management and the shifting roles of brand managers. Many of the skills that are needed to manage brands are also skills that are required in leadership roles within companies and organizations. We highlight a few of these critical skills needed in Chapter 16 of the book.

INSTRUCTOR TEACHING RESOURCES

This program comes with the following teaching resources.

Supplements available to instructors at www.pearsonhighered.com	Features of the Supplement
Instructor's Manual authored by Christy Ashley from The University of Rhode Island	• Chapter-by-chapter summaries • Examples and activities not in the main book • Teaching outlines • Teaching tips • Solutions to all questions and problems in the book
PowerPoints	Slides include all the graphs, tables, and equations in the textbook. PowerPoints meet accessibility standards for students with disabilities. Features include, but are not limited to: • Keyboard and screen reader access • Alternative text for images • High color contrast between background and foreground colors

ACKNOWLEDGEMENTS

Kevin Lane Keller

I have been gratified by the acceptance of the first four editions of *Strategic Brand Management*. It has been adopted by numerous universities and used by scores of marketing executives around the world. The success of the text is, in large part, due to the help and support of others whom I would like to acknowledge and thank.

My first thanks—and a big one—goes to Vanitha Swaminathan who agreed to become a co-author on this new edition. She has done a superb job leading the revision effort and updating the book in so many interesting and important ways. I am very much indebted to her scholarship and love of branding, which is reflected in everything that she does.

The Pearson team on the fifth edition was a huge help in the revision—many thanks to Ana Diaz-Caneja, Lynn Huddon, Maya Lane, Michelle Zeng, and Stephanie Wall.

I have learned much about branding in my work with industry participants, who have unique perspectives on what is working and not working (and why) in the marketplace. Our discussions have enriched my appreciation for the challenges in building, measuring, and managing brand equity and the factors affecting the success and failure of brand strategies.

I have benefited from the wisdom of my colleagues at the institutions where I have held academic positions: Dartmouth College, Duke University, the University of California at Berkeley, Stanford University, the Australian Graduate School of Management, and the University of North Carolina at Chapel Hill.

I have learned a lot about branding from my co-authors on various projects. Special thanks to David Aaker for joining me in the early pursuit of brand research. He was an insightful and inspiring research partner who always made it fun. Over the years, the doctoral students I advised, including Sheri Bridges, Christie Brown, Jennifer Aaker, Meg Campbell, and Sanjay Sood, have helped in my branding pursuits in a variety of useful ways.

Finally, thanks go to my wife, Punam Anand Keller, and two daughters, Carolyn and Allison, for their continual patience and understanding.

Vanitha Swaminathan

I would like to express my sincere thanks to Kevin Lane Keller for inviting me to be a co-author on the fifth edition of *Strategic Brand Management*. Kevin is an intellectual giant and visionary in marketing and his ideas have had far-reaching impact on the field. His ability to organize complex ideas into easily accessible frameworks is unparalleled, and I greatly benefitted from his thoughtful input and guidance. It has truly been a privilege and a pleasure to work with him on this revision.

My thanks also to the Pearson team (Stephanie Wall, Lynn Huddon, Michelle Zeng, and Emily Tamburri) for keeping us on track with the revision, and for the help they provided along the way. A special note of thanks to Angela Urquhart and her team for the skillful and timely copyediting help, and to Maya Lane for handling the permissions.

I would like to thank the various students who helped me with background research on the new case studies in the book, including Jeff Chojnicki, Emma Delaney, Katie Denshaw, Tessa Drinkwater, Julian Ferrante, Ethan Guswiler, Robert Innis, Anirudh Kothari, Madeline Brierly Manning, Kaylee Philbrick, Zach Serbin, and Nicole Vivian Sloan. Thanks also to Jeff Godish, Christian Hughes, Sayan Gupta, Leah Belman, and Rabia Bayer for reviewing chapters of the book. My grateful thanks to Teresa Abney, Andy Seagram, and Francesca Van Gorp for copyediting help, and to Natalia Fenton and Elizabeth Sismour for reviewing chapters. A note of thanks to Emma Delaney for help on the millennial and multicultural material. Additional research assistance from Dartmouth undergraduates Jordan Siegal, Charlie Lebens, Jake Johnson, and Richard Newsome-White is also greatly appreciated.

A special acknowledgment to my collaborator and friend, Professor Zeynep Gurhan-Canli, who shares my enthusiasm for research on branding, and to my mentors, Professor Srinivas Reddy, Professor Atul Parvatiyar, and Professor Jagdish Sheth. I sincerely thank my co-authors and the doctoral students that I have advised over the years. You have helped shape my scholarship and my research over the years and, for that, I am very grateful.

I am also thankful to the University of Pittsburgh and my colleagues in the Department of Marketing and Business Economics, where I've spent a majority of my academic life. A special note of thanks to Dean Assad for enabling my vision of a *Center for Branding* at the Katz School of Business.

Most importantly, I would like to extend my gratitude to my family. My heartfelt thanks go to my parents and sister for their support of my education and career. I also am most grateful to my husband Jaideep, my son Nikhil, and my daughter Meghna for their continual encouragement, love, and enthusiastic support—they have all contributed significantly to helping me complete this book in a timely fashion.

ABOUT THE AUTHORS

KEVIN LANE KELLER is the E. B. Osborn Professor of Marketing at the Tuck School of Business at Dartmouth College. Professor Keller has degrees from Cornell, Carnegie-Mellon, and Duke universities. At Dartmouth, he teaches MBA courses on marketing management and strategic brand management and lectures in executive programs on those topics.

Previously, Professor Keller was on the faculty at Stanford University, where he also served as the head of the marketing group. Additionally, he has been on the faculty at the University of California at Berkeley and the University of North Carolina at Chapel Hill, been a visiting professor at Duke University and the Australian Graduate School of Management, and has two years of industry experience as a marketing consultant for Bank of America.

Professor Keller's general area of expertise lies in marketing strategy and planning, and branding. His specific research interest is in how understanding theories and concepts related to consumer behavior can improve marketing and branding strategies. His research has been published in three of the major marketing journals—the *Journal of Marketing*, the *Journal of Marketing Research*, and the *Journal of Consumer Research*. He also has served on the editorial review boards of those journals. With over 120 published papers, his research has been widely cited and has received numerous awards.

He has served as a consultant and advisor to marketers for some of the world's most successful brands, including Accenture, American Express, Disney, Ford, Intel, Levi Strauss, L.L. Bean, Nike, Procter & Gamble, and Samsung. Additional brand-consulting activities have been with other top companies such as Allstate, Beiersdorf (Nivea), BJs, BlueCross BlueShield, Campbell, Capital One, Caterpillar, Colgate, Combe, Eli Lilly, ExxonMobil, General Mills, GfK, Goodyear, Hasbro, Heineken, Intuit, Irving Oil, Johnson & Johnson, Kodak, Mayo Clinic, MTV, Nordstrom, Ocean Spray, Red Hat, SAB Miller, Serta, Shell Oil, Starbucks, Time Warner Cable, Unilever, and Young & Rubicam. He has served as an expert witness for a wide variety of firms. He has also served as an academic trustee for the Marketing Science Institute and as their executive director from 2013 to 2015.

A popular and highly sought-after speaker, he has made keynote speeches and conducted marketing seminars to top executives in a variety of forums. Some of his senior management and marketing training clients have included such diverse business organizations as AT&T, Cisco, Coca-Cola, Deutsche Telekom, ExxonMobil, Fidelity, GE, Google, Hershey, Hyundai, IBM, Macy's, Microsoft, Nestle, Novartis, PepsiCo, S.C. Johnson, and Wyeth. He has lectured all over the world, from Seoul to Johannesburg, from Sydney to Stockholm, and from Sao Paulo to Mumbai.

Professor Keller is currently conducting a variety of studies that address strategies to build, measure, and manage brand equity. In addition to *Strategic Brand Management*, which has been heralded as the "bible of branding," he is also the co-author (with Philip Kotler) of the all-time best-selling introductory marketing textbook, *Marketing Management*, now in its fifteenth edition.

An avid sports, music, and film enthusiast, in his so-called spare time he has helped to manage and market, as well as serve as executive producer for, one of Australia's great rock and roll treasures, The Church, along with American power-pop legends Tommy Keene and Dwight Twilley. He also serves on the board of directors for The Doug Flutie, Jr. Foundation for Autism and the Lebanon Opera House. Professor Keller lives in Etna, New Hampshire, with his wife, Punam (also a Tuck marketing professor), and his two daughters, Carolyn and Allison.

VANITHA SWAMINATHAN is Thomas Marshall Professor of Marketing at the Katz Graduate School of Business, University of Pittsburgh. She is the director of the Katz Center for Branding. Her research focuses on branding strategy and the conditions that foster consumer-brand relationships. Additionally, her research investigates how firms can successfully design brand strategies—such as co-branding, brand extensions, brand acquisitions, marketing alliances— to strengthen customer loyalty as well as to firm up stock market performance. More recently, her focus is on understanding how brand managers can leverage the power of social media to build stronger relationships with customers.

Professor Swaminathan has published in various leading marketing and management journals including *Journal of Marketing, Journal of Marketing Research, Journal of Consumer Research, Marketing Science,* and *Strategic Management Journal.* She is currently serving as area editor of *Journal of Marketing,* and has served as associate editor for the *Journal of Consumer Psychology.* She has won awards for her research, including the Lehmann award for the best dissertation-based article and *Journal of Advertising's* Best Paper Award, and has been selected as Marketing Science Institute's Young Scholar. Professor Swaminathan serves as a president of *American Marketing Association*'s Academic Council (2018–2019) and currently serves on the *American Marketing Association*'s Academic Council for the period 2014–2020.

Professor Swaminathan's research and commentaries on branding and digital marketing are quoted in various international media outlets such as *Forbes, Washington Post, The Miami Herald, Los Angeles Times, U.S. News & World Report, NPR, Sirius Radio, Science Daily, Slate, Pittsburgh Post-Gazette, Economic Times (India), Frontline (India), BBC Brasil (UK),* and *Último.* She has worked with companies such as The Hershey Company, Kraft Heinz, StarKist, AC Nielsen, GlaxoSmithKline, and Procter & Gamble on marketing and branding consulting projects. She has also extensively worked with small businesses on advising them regarding their digital marketing efforts.

Professor Swaminathan lives in Pittsburgh, PA, with her husband Jaideep (who is on the faculty at the University of Pittsburgh School of Medicine), and their children, Nikhil and Meghna.

Brands and Brand Management

1

Learning Objectives

After reading this chapter, you should be able to

1. Define "brand," state how brand differs from a product, and explain what brand equity is.
2. Summarize why brands are important.
3. Explain how branding applies to virtually everything.
4. Describe the main branding challenges and opportunities.
5. Identify the steps in the strategic brand management process.

A brand can be a person, organization, place, or firm.

PREVIEW

Ever more firms and other organizations have realized that one of their most valuable assets is the brand names associated with their products or services. In our increasingly complex world, all of us, as individuals and as business managers, face more choices with less time to make them. Thus, a strong brand's ability to simplify decision making, reduce risk, and set expectations is invaluable. Creating strong brands that deliver on that promise, and maintaining and enhancing the strength of those brands over time, is a management imperative.

This text will help you reach a deeper understanding of how to achieve those branding goals. Its basic objectives are:

1. To explore the important issues in planning, implementing, and evaluating brand strategies.
2. To provide appropriate concepts, theories, models, and other tools to make better branding decisions.

We place particular emphasis on understanding psychological principles at the individual and firm level in order to make better decisions about brands. Our objective is to be relevant for any type of organization regardless of its size, nature of business, or profit orientation.[1]

With these goals in mind, this first chapter defines what a brand is. We consider the functions of a brand from the perspective of both consumers and firms and discuss why brands are important to both. We look at what can and cannot be branded and identify some strong brands. The chapter concludes with an introduction to the concept of brand equity and the strategic brand management process. Brand Focus 1.0 at the end of the chapter traces the historical origins of branding.

WHAT IS A BRAND?

Branding has been around for centuries as a means to distinguish the goods of one producer from those of another. The word *brand* is derived from the Old Norse word *brandr,* which means "to burn," as brands were and still are the means by which owners of livestock mark their animals to identify them.[2]

According to the American Marketing Association (AMA), a ***brand*** is a "name, term, sign, symbol, or design, or a combination of them, intended to identify the goods and services of one seller or group of sellers and to differentiate them from those of competition." Technically speaking, then, whenever a marketer creates a new name, logo, or symbol for a new product, he or she has created a brand.

However, many practicing managers refer to a brand as more than that—as something that has created a certain amount of awareness, reputation, prominence, and so on, in the marketplace. It is the difference between a commodity and a distinctive offering that constitutes a brand. Thus, we can make a distinction between the AMA definition of a "brand" with a small *b* and the industry's concept of a "Brand" with a big *B*. The difference is important for us because disagreements about branding principles or guidelines often revolve around what we mean by the term.

Brand Elements

Thus, the key to creating a brand, according to the AMA definition, is to be able to choose a name, logo, symbol, package design, or other characteristic that identifies a product and distinguishes it from others. These different components of a brand that identify and differentiate it are ***brand elements***. We will see in Chapter 4 that brand elements come in many different forms.

For example, consider the variety of brand name strategies. Some companies, like General Electric and Samsung, use their names for essentially all their products. Other manufacturers assign new products individual brand names that are unrelated to the company name, like Procter & Gamble's (P&G) Tide, Pampers, and Pantene product brands. Retailers create their own brands based on their store name or some other means; for example, Macy's has its own Alfani, INC, and Charter Club brands.

Brand names themselves come in many different forms.[3] There are brand names based on people's names, like Estée Lauder cosmetics, Porsche automobiles, and Orville Redenbacher popcorn; names based on places, like Santa Fe cologne, Chevrolet Tahoe SUV, and British Airways; and names based on animals or birds, like Mustang automobiles, Dove soap, and Greyhound buses. In the category of "other," we find Apple computers, Diamond foods, and Shell gasoline.

Some brand names use words with inherent product meaning, like Lean Cuisine, Ocean Spray 100% Juice Blends, and Ticketron, or suggesting important attributes or benefits, like DieHard auto batteries, Mop & Glo floor cleaner, Beautyrest mattresses, and the TripAdvisor travel Web site and online community. Other names are made up and include prefixes and suffixes that sound scientific, natural, or prestigious, like Lexus automobiles, Pentium microprocessors, and Visteon auto supplies.

Not just names, but also other brand elements like logos and symbols can be based on people, places, things, and abstract images. In creating a brand, marketers have many choices about the number and nature of the brand elements they use to identify their products.

Brands versus Products

How do we contrast a brand and a product? A ***product*** is anything we can offer to a market for attention, acquisition, use, or consumption that might satisfy a need or want. Thus, a product may be a physical good like a cereal, tennis racquet, or automobile; or a service such as an airline, bank, or insurance company. A product could also be a retail outlet like a department store, specialty store, or supermarket; a person such as a political figure, social media celebrity, entertainer, or professional athlete; an organization like a nonprofit, trade organization, or arts group; or a place including a city, state, or country; or even an idea like a political or social cause. This very broad definition of product is the one we adopt in this book. We'll discuss the role of brands in some of these different categories in more detail later in this chapter and in Chapter 16.

We can define five levels of meaning for a product:[4]

1. The ***core benefit level*** is the fundamental need or want that consumers satisfy by consuming the product or service.
2. The ***generic product level*** is a basic version of the product containing only those attributes or characteristics absolutely necessary for its functioning but with no distinguishing features. This is essentially a stripped-down, no-frills version of the product that adequately performs the product function.
3. The ***expected product level*** is a set of attributes or characteristics that buyers normally expect and agree to when they purchase a product.
4. The ***augmented product level*** includes additional product attributes, benefits, or related services that distinguish the product from competitors.
5. The ***potential product level*** includes all the augmentations and transformations that a product might ultimately undergo in the future.

Figure 1-1 illustrates these different levels in the context of an air conditioner. In many markets, most competition takes place at the product augmentation level, because most firms can successfully build satisfactory products at the expected product level. Harvard's Ted Levitt argued that "the new competition is not between what companies produce in their factories but between what they add to their factory output in the form of packaging, services, advertising, customer advice, financing, delivery arrangements, warehousing, and other things that people value."[5]

A brand is, therefore, more than a product, because it can have dimensions that differentiate it in some way from other products designed to satisfy the same need. These differences may be rational and tangible—related to product performance of the brand—or more symbolic, emotional, and intangible—related to what the brand represents.

Extending our previous example, a branded product may be a physical good like Kellogg's Corn Flakes cereal, Prince tennis racquets, or Ford Mustang automobiles; a service such as Delta Airlines, Bank of America, or Allstate insurance; a digital good or service such as Match.com, Spotify, or iTunes. It could be an online or offline store like Amazon, Bloomingdale's department store, Body Shop specialty store, or Safeway supermarket; a person such as Oprah Winfrey, Taylor Swift, or Tom Hanks; a place like the city of London, state of California, or country of Australia; an organization such as the American Red Cross, American Automobile Association, or the Rolling Stones; or an idea like corporate responsibility, free trade, or freedom of speech.

Some brands create competitive advantages with product performance. For example, brands such as Gillette, Merck, and others have been leaders in their product categories for decades, due,

Level	Air Conditioner
1. Core Benefit	Cooling and comfort.
2. Generic Product	Sufficient cooling capacity (BTU per hour), an acceptable energy efficiency rating, adequate air intakes and exhausts, and so on.
3. Expected Product	*Consumer Reports* states that, for a typical large air conditioner, consumers should expect at least two cooling speeds, expandable plastic side panels, adjustable louvers, removable air filter, vent for exhausting air, environmentally friendly R-410A refrigerant, power cord at least 60 inches long, one-year parts-and-labor warranty on the entire unit, and a five-year parts-and-labor warranty on the refrigeration system.
4. Augmented Product	Optional features might include electric touch-pad controls, a display to show indoor and outdoor temperatures and the thermostat setting, an automatic mode to adjust fan speed based on the thermostat setting and room temperature, a toll-free 800 number for customer service, and so on.
5. Potential Product	Silently running, completely balanced throughout the room, and completely energy self-sufficient.

FIGURE 1-1

Examples of Different Product Levels

in part, to continual innovation. Steady investments in research and development have produced leading-edge products, and sophisticated mass marketing practices have ensured rapid adoption of new technologies in the consumer market. A number of media organizations rank firms on their ability to innovate. Figure 1-2 lists 10 innovative companies that showed up on many of those lists in 2017.

Other brands create competitive advantages through non-product-related means. For example, Coca-Cola, Chanel No. 5, and others have been leaders in their product categories for decades by understanding consumer motivations and desires and creating relevant and appealing images surrounding their products. Often, these intangible image associations may be the only way to distinguish different brands in a product category.

FIGURE 1-2

Ten Firms Rated Highly on Innovation

Source: Based on Fast Company's 2018 List of Most Innovative Companies.

1. Apple

2. Netflix

3. Square

4. Tencent

5. Amazon

6. Patagonia

7. CVS Health

8. *The Washington Post*

9. Spotify

10. NBA

Brands, especially strong ones, carry a number of different types of associations, and marketers must account for all of them when making marketing decisions. The marketers behind some brands have learned this lesson the hard way. Branding Brief 1-1 describes the problems Coca-Cola encountered in the introduction of "New Coke" when it failed to account for all the different aspects of the Coca-Cola brand image.

Not only are there many different types of associations to link to the brand, but there are many different means to create them—the entire marketing program can contribute to consumers' understanding of the brand and how they value it as well as other factors outside the control of the marketer.

By creating perceived differences among products through branding and by developing a loyal consumer franchise, marketers create value that can translate to financial profits for the firm. The reality is that the most valuable assets many firms have may not be tangible ones, such as plant and equipment and real estate, but *intangible* assets such as management skills, marketing,

BRANDING BRIEF 1-1
Coca-Cola's Branding Lesson

One of the classic marketing mistakes occurred in April 1985 when Coca-Cola replaced its flagship cola brand with a new formula. The motivation behind the change was primarily a competitive one. Pepsi-Cola's "Pepsi Challenge" promotion had posed a strong challenge to Coke's supremacy over the cola market. Starting initially just in Texas, the promotion involved advertising and in-store sampling showcasing consumer blind taste tests between Coca-Cola and Pepsi-Cola. Invariably, Pepsi won these tests. Fearful that the promotion, if expanded nationally, could take a big bite out of Coca-Cola's sales, especially among younger cola drinkers, Coca-Cola felt compelled to act.

Coca-Cola's strategy was to change the formulation of Coke to more closely match the slightly sweeter taste of Pepsi. To arrive at a new formulation, Coke conducted taste tests with an astounding number of consumers—190,000! The findings from this research clearly indicated that consumers "overwhelmingly" preferred the taste of the new formulation to the old one. Brimming with confidence, Coca-Cola announced the formulation change with much fanfare.

Consumer reaction was swift but, unfortunately for Coca-Cola, negative. In Seattle, retired real estate investor Gay Mullins founded the "Old Cola Drinkers of America" and set up a hotline for angry consumers. A Beverly Hills wine merchant bought 500 cases of "Vintage Coke" and sold them at a premium. Meanwhile, back at Coca-Cola headquarters, roughly 1,500 calls a day and literally truckloads of mail poured in, virtually all condemning the company's actions. Finally, after several months of slumping sales, Coca-Cola announced that the old formulation would return as "Coca-Cola Classic" and join "New" Coke in the marketplace (see the accompanying photo).

The New Coke debacle taught Coca-Cola a very important, albeit painful and public, lesson about its brand. Coke clearly is not just seen as a beverage or thirst-quenching refreshment by consumers. Rather, it seems to be viewed as more of an American icon, and much of its appeal lies not only in its ingredients but also in what it represents in terms of Americana, nostalgia, and its heritage and relationship with consumers. Coke's brand image certainly has emotional components, and consumers have a great deal of strong feelings for the brand.

The epic failure of New Coke taught Coca-Cola a valuable lesson about branding.
Source: Al Freni/Time & Life Pictures/Getty Images

Although Coca-Cola made a number of other mistakes in introducing New Coke (both its advertising and its packaging probably failed to clearly differentiate the brand and communicate its sweeter quality), its biggest slip was losing sight of what the brand meant to consumers in its totality. The *psychological* response to a brand can be as important as the *physiological* response to the product. At the same time, American consumers also learned a lesson—just how much the Coke brand really meant to them. As a result of Coke's marketing fiasco, it is doubtful that either side will take the other for granted from now on.

Sources: Patricia Winters, "For New Coke, 'What Price Success?'" *Advertising Age*, March 20, 1989, S1–S2; Jeremiah McWilliams, "Twenty-Five Years Since Coca-Cola's Big Blunder," *Atlanta Business News*, April 26, 2010; Abbey Klaassen, "New Coke: One of Marketing's Biggest Blunders Turns 25," April 23, 2010, www.adage.com.

financial and operations expertise, and, most importantly, the brands themselves. Steve Jobs, the cofounder and CEO of Apple, famously said, "It's a complicated and noisy world, and we're not going to get a chance to get people to remember much about us." That chance to make a memory, he says, is the essence of brand marketing.[6] Jobs went on to argue:

> Our customers want to know, "Who is Apple and what is it that we stand for? Where do we fit in this world?" What we're about isn't making boxes for people to get their jobs done, though we do that well. We do that better than almost anybody in some cases. But Apple's about something more than that: Apple, at the core, its core value, is we believe that people with passion can change the world for the better. That's what we believe.

This value was also recognized by John Stuart, CEO of Quaker Oats from 1922 to 1956, who famously said, "If this company were to split up I would give you the property, plant and equipment and I would take the brands and the trademarks and I would fare better than you."[7] Let's see why brands are so valuable.

WHY DO BRANDS MATTER?

The obvious question is, why are brands important? What functions do they perform that make them so valuable to marketers? We can take a couple of perspectives to uncover the value of brands to both customers and firms themselves. Figure 1-3 provides an overview of the different roles that brands play for these two parties. We will begin by discussing consumers.

Consumers

As with the term *product*, this book uses the term **consumer** broadly to encompass all types of customers, including individuals as well as organizations. To consumers, brands provide important functions. Brands identify the source or maker of a product and allow consumers to assign responsibility to a particular manufacturer or distributor. Most important, brands take on special meaning to consumers. Because of past experiences with the product and its marketing program over the years, consumers find out which brands satisfy their needs and which ones do not. As a result, brands provide a shorthand device or means of simplification for their product decisions.[8]

If consumers recognize a brand and have some knowledge about it, then they do not have to engage in a lot of additional thought or processing of information to make a product decision. Thus, from an economic perspective, brands allow consumers to lower the search costs for products both internally (regarding how much they have to think) and externally (regarding how much they have to look around). Based on what they already know about the brand—its quality, product characteristics, and so forth—consumers can make assumptions and form reasonable expectations about what they may *not* know about the brand.

The meaning imbued in brands can be quite profound, allowing us to think of the relationship between a brand and the consumer as a type of bond or pact. Consumers offer their trust and loyalty with the implicit understanding that brands will behave in certain ways and provide

Consumers
Identification of source of product
Assignment of responsibility to product maker
Risk reducer
Search cost reducer
Promise, bond, or pact with maker of product
Symbolic device
Signal of quality

Manufacturers
Means of identification to simplify handling or tracing
Means of legally protecting unique features
Signal of quality level to satisfied customers
Means of endowing products with unique associations
Source of competitive advantage
Source of financial returns

FIGURE 1-3
Roles That Brands Play

them utility through consistent product performance and appropriate pricing, promotion, and distribution programs and actions. To the extent that consumers realize advantages and benefits from purchasing brands, and as long as they derive satisfaction from product consumption, they are likely to continue to buy them.

These benefits may not be purely functional in nature. Brands can serve as symbolic devices, allowing consumers to project their self-image. Certain brands are associated with certain types of people and thus reflect different values or traits. Consuming such products is a means by which consumers can communicate to others—or even to themselves—the type of person they are or would like to be.[9]

Some branding experts believe that for some people, certain brands even play a religious role of sorts and substitute for religious practices and help reinforce self-worth.[10] The cultural influence of brands is profound, and much interest has been generated in recent years in understanding the interplay between consumer culture and brands.[11]

Brands can also play a significant role in signaling certain product characteristics to consumers. Researchers have classified products and their associated attributes or benefits into three major categories: search goods, experience goods, and credence goods.[12]

- For *search goods* like grocery produce, consumers can evaluate product attributes like sturdiness, size, color, style, design, weight, and ingredient composition by visual inspection.
- For *experience goods* like automobile tires, consumers cannot assess product attributes like durability, service quality, safety, and ease of handling or use so easily by inspection, and actual product trial and experience is necessary.
- For *credence goods* like insurance coverage, consumers may rarely learn product attributes.

Given the difficulty of assessing and interpreting product attributes and benefits for experience and credence goods, brands may be particularly important signals of quality and other characteristics to consumers for these types of products.[13]

Brands can reduce the risks in product decisions. Consumers may perceive many different types of risks in buying and consuming a product:[14]

- *Functional risk:* The product does not perform up to expectations.
- *Physical risk:* The product poses a threat to the physical well-being or health of the user or others.
- *Financial risk:* The product is not worth the price paid.
- *Social risk:* The product results in embarrassment from others.
- *Psychological risk:* The product affects the mental well-being of the user.
- *Time risk:* The failure of the product results in an opportunity cost of finding another satisfactory product.

Consumers can certainly handle these risks in a number of ways, but one way is obviously to buy well-known brands, especially those with which consumers have had favorable past experiences. Thus, brands can be a very important risk-handling device, especially in business-to-business settings where risks can sometimes have quite profound implications.

In summary, to consumers, the special meaning that brands take on can change their perceptions and experiences with a product. The identical product may be evaluated differently depending on the brand identification or attribution it carries. Brands take on unique, personal meanings to consumers that facilitate their day-to-day activities and enrich their lives. As consumers' lives become more complicated, rushed, and time-starved, the ability of a brand to simplify decision-making and reduce risk is invaluable.

Firms

Brands also provide a number of valuable functions to their firms.[15] Fundamentally, they serve an identification purpose, to simplify product handling or tracing. Operationally, brands help organize inventory and accounting records. A brand also offers the firm legal protection for unique features or aspects of the product. A brand can retain intellectual property rights, giving legal title to the brand owner.[16] The brand name can be protected through registered trademarks; manufacturing processes can be protected through patents; and packaging can be protected through copyrights and designs. These intellectual property rights ensure that the firm can safely invest in the brand and reap the benefits of a valuable asset.

Company	Brand Value (in $ billions)	Total Value (in $ billions)	Brand Value as a Percentage of Overall Value
Apple	184.1	868.88	21%
Google	141.7	729.1	19%
Microsoft	79.9	659.9	12%
Coca-Cola	69.7	195.5	36%
Amazon	64.7	563.5	11%
Samsung	56.2	300	19%
Toyota	50.3	188.2	27%
Facebook	48.2	420.8	11%
Mercedes	47.8	79.3	60%
IBM	46.8	142	33%

We've seen that these investments in the brand can endow a product with unique associations and meanings that differentiate it from other products. Brands can signal a certain level of quality so that satisfied buyers can easily choose the product again.[17] This brand loyalty provides predictability and security of demand for the firm and creates barriers of entry that make it difficult for other firms to enter the market.

Although manufacturing processes and product designs may be easily duplicated, lasting impressions in the minds of individuals and organizations from years of marketing activity and product experience may not be so easily reproduced. One advantage that brands such as Crest toothpaste, Nike shoes, and Levi's jeans have is that consumers have literally grown up with them. In this sense, branding can be seen as a powerful means to secure a competitive advantage.

In short, to firms, brands represent enormously valuable pieces of legal property, capable of influencing consumer behavior, being bought and sold, and providing the security of sustained future revenues.[18] For these reasons, huge sums, often representing large multiples of a brand's earnings, have been paid for brands in mergers or acquisitions. Mergers and acquisitions allow companies to seek out undervalued brands that can be combined with existing product portfolios of acquirers, resulting in higher earnings and profit performance for firms.

The price premium paid for many companies is clearly justified by the opportunity to earn and sustain extra profits from their brands, as well as by the tremendous difficulty and expense of creating similar brands from scratch. Figure 1-4 highlights the value of a brand as a percentage of a firm's overall value (as measured by its stock market value) for a selected set of top brands. As can be seen in the figure, most of the value of a firm can be accounted for by its intangible assets and goodwill, and as much as 60 percent of intangible assets can be supplied by brands.

CAN ANYTHING BE BRANDED?

Brands clearly provide important benefits to both consumers and firms. An obvious question, then, is, how are brands created? How do you "brand" a product? Although firms provide the impetus for brand creation through their marketing programs and other activities, ultimately *a brand is something that resides in the minds of consumers*. A brand is a perceptual entity rooted in reality, but it is more than that—it reflects the perceptions and perhaps even the idiosyncrasies of consumers.

To brand a product, it is necessary to teach consumers "who" the product is—by giving it a name and using other brand elements to help identify it—as well as what the product does and why consumers should care. In other words, marketers must give consumers a *label* for the product ("here's how you can identify the product") and provide *meaning* for the brand ("here's what this particular product can do for you, and why it's special and different from other brand name products").

Branding creates mental structures and helps consumers organize their knowledge about products and services in a way that clarifies their decision making and, in the process, provides value to the firm. *The key to branding is that consumers perceive differences among brands in a product category*. These differences can be related to attributes or benefits of the product or service itself, or they may be related to more intangible image considerations.

When consumers are deciding between alternatives, brands can play an important decision-making role. *Accordingly, marketers can benefit from branding whenever consumers are in a choice situation*. Given the myriad choices consumers make each and every day—commercial and otherwise—it is no surprise how pervasive branding has become. Branding Brief 1-2 considers how even one-time commodities have been branded.

We can recognize the universality of branding by looking at some different product applications in the categories we defined previously—physical goods, services, retail stores, online businesses, people, organizations, places, and ideas. For each of these different types of products, we will review some basic considerations and look at examples. (We consider some of these special cases in more detail in Chapter 16.)

BRANDING BRIEF 1-2
Branding Commodities

A *commodity* is a product so basic that it cannot be physically differentiated from competitors in the minds of consumers. Over the years, a number of products that at one time were seen as essentially commodities have become highly differentiated as strong brands have emerged in the category. Some notable examples are coffee (Maxwell House), salt (Morton), bath soap (Ivory), flour (Gold Medal), beer (Budweiser), oatmeal (Quaker), pickles (Vlasic), bananas (Chiquita), chickens (Perdue), pineapples (Dole), and even water (Perrier).

These products became branded in various ways. The key success factor in each case, however, was that consumers became convinced that all the product offerings in the category were not the same, and that meaningful differences existed. In some instances, such as with produce, marketers convinced consumers that a product was *not* a commodity and could actually vary appreciably in quality. In these cases, the brand was seen as ensuring uniformly high quality in the product category on which consumers could depend. In other cases, like Perrier bottled mineral water, because product differences were virtually nonexistent, brands have been created by image or other non product-related considerations.

One of the best examples of branding a commodity in this fashion is diamonds. De Beers Group added the phrase "A Diamond Is Forever" as the tagline in its ongoing ad campaign in 1948. The diamond supplier, which was founded in 1888 and currently has about a 33 percent market share, wanted to attach more emotion and symbolic meaning to the purchase of diamond jewelry. "A Diamond Is Forever" became one of the most recognized slogans in advertising and helped fuel a diamond jewelry industry that's now worth nearly $25 billion per year in the United States alone.

After years of successful campaigns that helped generate buzz for the overall diamond industry, De Beers began to focus on its proprietary brands. Its 2009 campaign highlighted its new Everlon line. Partly in reaction to the recession, De Beers's marketing also began to focus on the long-term value and staying power of diamonds; new campaigns included the slogans "Fewer Better

De Beers' classic tagline "A Diamond Is Forever" has withstood the test of time.

Things" and "Here Today, Here Tomorrow." In fact, the slogan captured the sentiment that De Beers was hoping to instill through their ad campaign and discouraged people from reselling their diamonds. As this example illustrates, brands can be created by image or other non product-related considerations. With De Beers, the brand conveys powerful emotions and symbolic value (eternal love).

Sources: Theodore Levitt, "Marketing Success Through Differentiation—of Anything," *Harvard Business Review* (January–February 1980): 83–91; Sandra O'Loughlin, "Sparkler on the Other Hand," *Brandweek*, April 19, 2004; Blythe Yee, "Ads Remind Women They Have *Two* Hands," *The Wall Street Journal*, August 14 2003; Lauren Weber, "De Beers to Open First U.S. Retail Store," *Newsday*, June 22, 2005; "De Beers Will Double Ad Spending," *MediaPost*, November 17, 2008, https://blog.hubspot.com/marketing/diamond-de-beers-marketing-campaign, accessed April 7, 2018.

Physical Goods

Physical goods are traditionally associated with brands and include many of the best-known and highly regarded consumer products, like Mercedes-Benz, Nescafé, and Sony. More and more companies selling industrial products or durable goods to other companies are recognizing the benefits of developing strong brands. Brands have begun to emerge among certain types of physical goods that never supported brands before. We provide a brief history of branding in The Science of Branding 1-1 section.

Branding has been adopted in a variety of industries. Let us consider the role of branding in industrial "business-to-business" products and technologically intensive "high-tech" products.

Business-to-Business Products.   The business-to-business (B2B) market makes up a huge percentage of the global economy. Some of the world's most accomplished and respected brands belong to business marketers, such as ABB, Caterpillar, DuPont, FedEx, General Electric, Hewlett-Packard, IBM, Intel, Microsoft, Oracle, SAP, and Siemens.

THE SCIENCE OF BRANDING 1-1
History of Branding

Branding, in one form or another, has been around for centuries. Branding, or at least trademarks, can be traced back to ancient pottery and stonemason's marks, which were applied to handcrafted goods to identify their source. Pottery and clay lamps were sometimes sold far from the shops where they were made, and buyers looked for the stamps of reliable potters as a guide to quality. Subsequently, in another example of branding, an English law passed in 1266 requiring bakers to put their mark on every loaf of bread sold.

When Europeans began to settle in North America, they brought the convention and practice of branding with them. The makers of patent medicines and tobacco manufacturers were early U.S. branding pioneers. By the early 1800s, manufacturers had packed bales of tobacco under labels such as Smith's Plug and Brown and Black's Twist. In the late 1800s and early 1900s, mass-produced merchandise in packages largely replaced locally produced merchandise sold from bulk containers. The development and management of these brands was largely driven by the owners of the firm and their top-level management. For example, the first president of National Biscuit was involved heavily in the 1898 introduction of Uneeda Biscuits, the first nationally branded biscuit. H. J. Heinz built up the Heinz brand name through production innovations and spectacular promotions. Coca-Cola became a national powerhouse due to the efforts of Asa Candler, who actively oversaw the growth of the extensive distribution channel. By 1915, manufacturer brands had become well established in the United States on both a regional and national basis.

The onset of the Great Depression in 1929 posed new challenges to manufacturer brands. Greater price sensitivity swung the pendulum of power in the favor of retailers who pushed their own brands and dropped nonperforming manufacturer brands. During this time, P&G put the first brand management system into place, whereby each of their brands had a manager assigned only to that brand who was responsible for its financial success. In the brand management system, a brand manager took "ownership" of a brand. A brand manager was responsible for developing and implementing the annual marketing plan for his or her brand, as well as identifying new business opportunities. The brand manager might be assisted, internally, by representatives from manufacturing, the sales force, marketing research, financial planning, research and development, personnel, legal, and public relations and, externally, by representatives from advertising agencies, research suppliers, and public relations agencies.

Between 1940 and 1980, the pent-up demand for high-quality brands led to an explosion of sales. Personal income grew as the economy took off, and market demand intensified as the rate of population growth exploded. Demand for national brands soared, fueled by a burst of new products and a receptive and growing middle class. Firm after firm during this time period adopted the brand management system.

The merger and acquisitions boom of the mid-1980s raised the interest of top executives and other board members as to the financial value of brands. With this realization came an appreciation of the importance of managing brands as valuable intangible assets. At the same time, more different types of firms began to see the advantages of having a strong brand and the corresponding disadvantages of having a weak brand. The last two decades have seen an explosion in the interest and application of branding as more firms have embraced the concept.

Branding in the twenty-first century has witnessed an increase in the use of data-driven marketing approaches, and an increasing reliance on digital channels for both communication and distribution. As discussed in Brand Focus 1.0, the growth of digital native brands such as Warby Parker and Bonobos has created a new model for brands to go direct to consumers. As more and more different kinds of products are sold or promoted directly to consumers, the adoption of modern marketing practices and branding has spread further.

Sources: Adapted from George S. Low and Ronald A. Fullerton, "Brands, Brand Management, and the Brand Manager System: A Critical-Historical Evaluation," *Journal of Marketing Research* 31 (May 1994): 173–190; Hal Morgan, *Symbols of America* (Steam Press, 1986); Steven Wolfe Pereira, "Are You Building a 21st Century Brand?," Advertising Age.com, March 5, 2018, http://adage.com/article/quantcast/building-a-21st-century-brand/312554/.

Business-to-business branding creates a positive image and reputation for the company as a whole. Creating such goodwill with business customers is thought to lead to greater selling opportunities and more profitable relationships. A strong brand can provide valuable reassurance and clarity to business customers who may be putting their company's fate—and perhaps their own careers!—on the line. A strong business-to-business (B2B) brand can thus provide a strong competitive advantage.

Some B2B firms, however, carry the attitude that purchasers of their products are so well-informed and professional that brands don't matter. However, savvy business marketers reject that reasoning and recognize both the importance of their brand and how they must execute well in a number of areas to gain marketplace success.

Boeing, which manufactures everything from commercial airplanes to satellites, implemented the "One Firm" brand strategy to unify all its different operations with a one-brand culture. The strategy was based in part on a "triple helix" representation: (1) Enterprising Spirit (*why* Boeing does what it does), (2) Precision Performance (*how* Boeing gets things done), and (3) Defining the Future (*what* Boeing achieves as a firm).[19]

Another example of successful business-to-business branding is Cisco. Cisco, the network communications equipment manufacturer, sought growth by directing considerable research and marketing resources at an underserved market: small- and medium-sized business (SMB) customers. Cisco conducted customer research that segmented the overall SMB market into four tiers by networking expenditure and purchase patterns. Tier 1 and Tier 2 companies, which view networking as the core of their business, made up 30 percent of the SMB space but accounted for 75 percent of total networking expenditures. Tier 3 and Tier 4 companies made up 70 percent of the market but were hesitant to invest heavily in networking technology. Based on this understanding of the market, Cisco was able to target these segments with products and services designed specifically for them. The Science of Branding 1-2 describes some additional, important guidelines for business-to-business branding.

THE SCIENCE OF BRANDING 1-2
Understanding Business-to-Business Branding

Business-to-Business (B2B) purchase decisions are complex and often high risk; therefore, branding plays an important role in B2B markets. Six specific guidelines (developed in greater detail in later chapters) can be defined for marketers of B2B brands.

1. **Ensure the entire organization understands and supports branding and brand management.** Employees at all levels and in all departments must have a complete, up-to-date understanding of the vision for the brand and their role in supporting it. A particularly crucial area is the sales force; personal selling is often the profit driver of a business-to-business organization. The sales force must be properly aligned so that the department can more effectively leverage and reinforce the brand promise. If branding is done right, the sales force can ensure that target customers recognize the brand's benefits sufficiently to pay a price commensurate with the brand's potential value.

2. **Adopt a corporate branding strategy if possible and create a well-defined brand hierarchy.** Because of the breadth and complexity of the product or service mix, companies selling business-to-business are more likely to emphasize corporate brands (such as Cisco, GE, and Caterpillar). Ideally, they will also create straightforward sub-brands that combine the corporate brand name with descriptive product modifiers,

such as with DellEMC or GE. If a company has a distinctive line of business, however, a more clearly differentiated sub-brand may need to be developed, such as the IBM Services division, which focuses on applying technology to help clients. This division is further segmented into two subdivisions called IBM Global Business Services to provide infrastructure and technology support services, and IBM Global Technology Services, to serve the information technology services needs of their clients, and to help provide artificial intelligence capabilities to their clients.

3. **Frame value perceptions.** Given the highly competitive nature of business-to-business markets, marketers must ensure that customers fully appreciate how their offerings are different. *Framing* occurs when customers are given a perspective or point of view that allows the brand to "put its best foot forward." Framing can be as simple as making sure customers realize all the benefits or cost savings offered by the brand, or becoming more active in shaping how customers view the economics of purchasing, owning, using, and disposing of the brand in a different way. Framing requires understanding how customers currently think of brands and choose among products and services, and then determining how they *should* ideally think and choose.

4. **Link relevant non-product-related brand associations.** In a business-to-business setting, a brand may be differentiated on the basis of factors beyond product performance, such as having superior customer service or well-respected customers or clients. Other relevant brand imagery might relate to the size or type of firm. For example, Microsoft and Oracle might be viewed as "aggressive" companies, whereas Apple and Google might be seen as "innovative." Imagery may also be a function of the other organizations to which the firm sells. For example, customers may believe that a company with many customers is established and a market leader.

5. **Find relevant emotional associations for the brand.** B2B marketers too often overlook the power of emotions in their branding. Emotional associations related to a sense of security, social or peer approval, and self-respect can also be linked to the brand and serve as key sources of brand equity. That is, reducing risk to improve customers' sense of security can be a powerful driver of many decisions and thus, an important source of brand equity. Being seen as someone who works with other top firms may inspire peer approval and personal recognition within the organization; and, beyond respect and admiration from others, a business decision-maker may just feel more satisfied by working with top organizations and brands.

6. **Segment customers carefully both within and across companies.** Finally, in a business-to-business setting, different customer segments may exist both within and across organizations. Within organizations, different people may assume the various roles in the purchase decision process: initiator, user, influencer, decider, approver, buyer and gatekeeper. Across organizations, businesses can vary according to industry and company size, technologies used and other capabilities, purchasing policies, and even risk and loyalty profiles. Brand building must keep these different segmentation perspectives in mind in building tailored marketing programs.

7. **Leverage digital techniques and social media marketing approaches.** In a business-to-business setting, digital marketing can play an increasingly important role in allowing companies to target current and potential customers in an efficient manner. Incorporating digital channels into the overall marketing effort can help optimize a promotional mix. Specifically, LinkedIn, Twitter, and Facebook are among the most popular social media tools that are used by business-to-business marketers to showcase their products and engage with their audience. In addition to its usefulness as a lead generation tool, social media can also allow companies to engage with their audiences and strengthen their relationships with current customers. Content marketing is another effective way of connecting with consumers, and B2B companies are increasingly using video content to engage with their audiences.

Sources: James C. Anderson and James A. Narus, *Business Market Management: Understanding, Creating, and Delivering Value*, 3rd ed. (Upper Saddle River, NJ: Prentice Hall, 2009); Kevin Lane Keller and Frederick E. Webster, Jr., "A Roadmap for Branding in Industrial Markets," *Journal of Brand Management*, 11 (May 2004): 388–40; Philip Kotler and Waldemar Pfoertsch, *B2B Brand Management* (Berlin–Heidelberg, Germany: Springer, 2006); Kevin Lane Keller, "Building a Strong Business-to-Business Brand," in *Business-to-Business Brand Management: Theory, Research, and Executive Case Study Exercises*, in *Advances in Business Marketing & Purchasing* series, Volume 15, ed. Arch Woodside (Bingley, UK: Emerald Group Publishing Limited, 2009), 11–31; Kevin Lane Keller and Philip Kotler, "Branding in Business-to-Business Firms," in *Business to Business Marketing Handbook*, eds. Gary L. Lilien and Rajdeep Grewal (Northampton, MA: Edward Elgar Publishing, 2012); IBM.Com, (2017), "IBM Delivers First Cognitive Services Platform to Transform Business," https://www-03.ibm.com/press/us/en/pressrelease/52781.wss, accessed May 2, 2018; Dave Chaffey, "Using Social Media Marketing in B2B Markets?," www.smartinsights.com/b2b-digital-marketing/b2b-social-media-marketing/b2bsocialmediamarketing/, accessed May 1, 2018; Douglas Burdett, "The 3 Social Media Networks That Are Best for B2B Marketing," www.artillerymarketing.com/blog/bid/195560/the-3-social-media-networks-that-are-best-for-b2b-marketing, accessed May 1, 2018; Olsy Sorokina, "9 B2B Social Media Marketing Tips for Social Media Managers," February 12, 2015, https://blog.hootsuite.com/b2b-social-media-marketing-tips/, accessed May 1, 2018.

High-Tech Products.   Many technology companies have struggled with branding. Managed by technologists, these firms often lack any kind of brand strategy and sometimes see branding as simply naming their products. In many of their markets, however, financial success is no longer driven by product innovation alone, or by the latest and greatest product specifications and features. Marketing skills are playing an increasingly important role in the adoption and success of high-tech products. The Branding Brief 1-3 depicts how marketing of high-tech products utilizes many of the principles of branding, while highlighting certain key criteria for success, and uses the Adobe brand transformation as a context.

The speed and brevity of technology product life cycles create unique branding challenges. Trust is critical, and customers often buy into companies as much as products. Marketing budgets may be small, although high-tech firms' adoption of classic consumer marketing techniques has increased expenditures on marketing communications.

Services

Although strong service brands like American Express, British Airways, Ritz-Carlton, Merrill Lynch, and Federal Express have existed for years, the pervasiveness of service branding and its sophistication have accelerated in the past decade.

Role of Branding with Services.   One of the challenges in marketing services is that they are less tangible than products and more likely to vary in quality, depending on the particular person

BRANDING BRIEF 1-3
Adobe

Adobe is a worldwide leader in multimedia and creativity software, well-known for Photoshop, an image editing software, Acrobat Reader, the Portable Document Format (PDF), the Adobe Creative Suite, and subsequently, Adobe Creative Cloud. Adobe achieved record annual revenue of $7.3 billion in 2017 and was recognized that year as being among the fastest growing brands on *Interbrand's Best Global Brands* survey. According to this survey, Adobe's brand valuation of $9 billion in 2017 represented an 19% growth in brand value over the previous year. What are the keys to Adobe's success? Adobe's focus on innovation and emphasis on being customer-centric has allowed it to develop a portfolio of products which are simultaneously innovative yet customer-friendly. In addition, Adobe has shown that excellent design is a key part of technology product marketing. Adobe's advertising and promotional campaigns to support these products have connected with audiences at an emotional level. As an example, in the aftermath of Hurricane Harvey, a number of homes and communities were devastated, and victims sadly lost their cherished photos. Under Adobe's "The Future Is Yours" campaign, high school students in Texas, working with volunteer organizations, embarked on a project in which they used Adobe products to restore family photos of victims, returning them in a form that was actually even better than new. In these and other ways, Adobe has used a novel and well-executed brand strategy to strengthen relationships with its customers and generate profits for the firm.

Adobe's focus on customer-focused innovation is key to its success in brand-building.

Sources: Interbrand's Best Global Brands 2017, https://www.interbrand .com/best-brands/best-global-brands/2017/ranking/, accessed September 29, 2018; Tim Nudd, "Ad of the Day: Adobe's Delightful Ads Imagine if Bob Ross Had Painted on an iPad," February 17, 2016, www.adweek .com/brand-marketing/ad-dayadobe-honors-bob-ross-fun-and-funny-digital-paintingtutorials-169689/; Jack Alexander, "Students Help Digitally Restore Photos for Hurricane Harvey Victims," *Fstoppers*, January 31, 2018, https://fstoppers.com/photoshop/students-help-digi-tally-restore-photos-hurricane-harvey-victims-216824.

or people providing them. For that reason, branding can be particularly important to service firms as a way to address intangibility and variability problems. Brand symbols may also be especially important, because they help make the abstract nature of services more concrete. Brands can help identify and provide meaning to the different services provided by a firm. For example, branding has become especially important in financial services to help organize and label the myriad new offerings in a manner that consumers can understand.

For a service firm like Mayflower, dependable, high-quality service is critical.

Source: Bohemian Nomad Picturemakers/Getty Images

Branding a service can also be an effective way to signal to consumers that the firm has designed a particular service offering that is special and deserving of its name. For example, British Airways not only brands its premium business class service as "Club World"; it also brands its regular coach service as "World Traveller," a clever way to communicate to the airline's regular passengers that they are also special in some way and that their patronage is not taken for granted. Branding has clearly become a competitive weapon for services.

Professional Services.   Professional services firms such as Accenture (consulting), Goldman Sachs (investment banking), and Ernst & Young (accounting) offer specialized expertise and support to other businesses and organizations. Professional services branding is an interesting combination of B2B branding and traditional consumer services branding.

Corporate credibility is key in terms of expertise, trustworthiness, and likability. Variability is more of an issue with professional services because it is harder to standardize the services of a consulting firm than those of a typical consumer services firm (like Mayflower movers or Orkin pest control). Long-term relationships are crucial; losing one customer can be disastrous if it is a big enough account.

One big difference in professional services is that individual employees have a lot more of their own equity in the firm and are often brands in their own right! The challenge is, therefore, to ensure that their words and actions help build the corporate brand and not just their own. Ensuring that the organization retains at least some of the equity that employees (especially senior ones) build is thus crucial, in case any of them leave.

Referrals and testimonials can be powerful when the services offered are highly intangible and subjective. Emotions also play a big role in terms of sense of security and social approval. Switching costs can be significant and pose barriers to entry for competitors, but clients do have the opportunity to bargain and will often do so to acquire more customized solutions.

Retailers and Distributors

To retailers and other channel members distributing products, brands provide a number of important functions. Brands can generate consumer interest, patronage, and loyalty in a store, as consumers learn to expect certain brands and products. To the extent "you are what you sell," brands help retailers create an image and establish positioning. Retailers can also create their own brand image by attaching unique associations to the quality of their service, their product assortment and merchandising, and their pricing and credit policy. Finally, the appeal and attraction of brands, whether manufacturers' brands or the retailers' own brands, can yield higher price margins, increased sales volumes, and greater profits.

Retailers can introduce their own brands by using their store name, creating new names, or some combination of the two. Many distributors, especially in Europe, have actually introduced their own brands, which they sell in addition to—or sometimes even instead of—manufacturers' brands. Products bearing these *store brands* or *private label* brands offer another way for retailers to increase customer loyalty and generate higher margins and profits.

In 2016, store brand dollar sales volume amounted to about 118.1 billion U.S. dollars, which is about 15 percent of the overall consumer packaged goods sales in the United States.[20] In Britain, five or six grocery chains selling their own brands account for roughly half the country's food and packaged-goods sales, led by Sainsbury and Tesco.[21] Several U.S. retailers also emphasize their own brands. (Chapter 5 considers store brands and private labels in greater detail.)

The Internet has transformed retailing in recent years as retailers have adopted a "bricks and clicks" approach to their business or, in many cases, become pure-play online retailers, operating only on the Web. Regardless of the exact form, to be competitive online, many retailers have had to improve their online service by making customer service agents available in real time, shipping products promptly, providing tracking updates, and adopting liberal return policies.

Digital Brands

Some of the strongest brands in recent years have been born online. Amazon, Google, Facebook, and Twitter are notable examples. That wasn't always the case. At the onset of the Internet, many online marketers made serious—and sometimes fatal—mistakes. Some oversimplified the branding process, equating flashy or unusual advertising with building a brand. Although such marketing efforts sometimes caught consumers' attention, more often than not, they failed to create awareness of what products or services the brand represented, why those products or services were unique or different, and most important, why consumers should visit their Web site.

Online marketers now realize the realities of brand building. First, as for any brand, it is critical to create unique aspects of the brand on some dimension that is important to consumers, such as convenience, price, or variety. At the same time, the brand needs to perform satisfactorily in other areas, such as customer service, credibility, and personality. For instance, customers increasingly began to demand higher levels of service both during and after their Web site visits.

Successful digital brands have been well positioned and have found unique ways to satisfy consumers' unmet needs. Brand Focus 1.0 presents an in-depth look at the phenomenon of digital native vertical brands—that is, brands that are born online, and go direct to consumers. By offering unique features and services to consumers, the best online brands are able to avoid extensive advertising or lavish marketing campaigns, relying more on word-of-mouth and publicity.

- Hulu enables consumers to watch videos of their past and present favorite TV programs at their own convenience.
- Spotify allows customers to customize online radio stations with bands and genres they enjoy, while learning about other music they might also like.
- Online encyclopedia Wikipedia provides consumers with extensive, constantly updated, user-generated information about practically everything.

Airbnb is an example of how to build a successful online brand.

AIRBNB

Airbnb is a company which began in 2008 and has, within a decade, built up a massive platform used by 40 million people. The company matches individuals looking to rent out spaces for brief periods with travelers and tourists looking for a temporary place to stay. Airbnb reportedly has a revenue of $900 million per year, 2,000 employees, and a service spanning 34,000 cities. Although some argue that it is in competition with hotel chains, the company does not believe that its growth has limited the business that typically goes to hotels.

An internal study undertaken at Airbnb quantified the impact of brand-building on an enterprise. The company's CMO was a previous executive at Coca-Cola and brought a greater understanding of the value of emotional connection in driving brand value to a technology firm. The underlying assumption that Airbnb had to overcome was the mindset that brand strength cannot deliver value, and technology alone is a driver of value. Through its research, Airbnb has been able to overcome that barrier, and the result was its ability to build a strong brand.[22]

Airbnb used storytelling to convey its message, and its content was focused on the people who owned the homes listed, as well as the travelers who go there. They describe how these connections are important to the brand's value, and how the brand itself makes it possible. Airbnb also created a brand magazine called Pineapple which was described as a platform for stories that Airbnb's extended family intended to share. This publication allows readers to see how people live and create connections in cities today.[23]

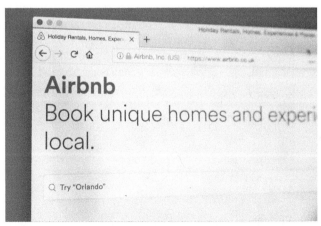

Airbnb uses storytelling to convey its message and to build a
strong emotional connection with its customers.

Online brands also learned the importance of off-line activities to draw customers to Web sites. This could involve introducing new products sold offline or gaining access to brick-and-mortar distribution channels. For example, the Echo (an Amazon product), is offered to consumers in brick-and-mortar locations. Amazon's acquisition of Whole Foods provided it with an opportunity to gain access to physical locations. Home page Web addresses, or URLs, began to appear on all collateral and marketing material. Partnerships became critical as online brands developed networks of online partners and links. They also began to target specific customer groups—often geographically widely dispersed—for whom the brand could offer unique value propositions. As we will describe more in Chapter 6, Web site designs have finally begun to maximize the benefits of interactivity, customization, and timeliness and the advantages of being able to inform, persuade, and sell all at the same time.

People and Organizations

When the product category is people or organizations, the naming aspect of branding, at least, is generally straightforward. These often have well-defined images that are easily understood and liked (or disliked) by others. That's particularly true for public figures such as politicians, entertainers, and professional athletes. All these compete in some sense for public approval and acceptance, and all benefit from conveying a strong and desirable image.

That's not to say that only the well-known or famous can be thought of as a brand. Certainly, one key for a successful career in almost any area is that coworkers, superiors, or even important people outside your company or organization know who you are and recognize your skills, talents, attitude, and so forth. By building up a name and reputation in a business context, you are essentially creating your own brand.[24] The right awareness and image can be invaluable in shaping

LADY GAGA

Lady Gaga is among the most glamorous and outrageous celebrity brands in recent times. Her unique musical talent, over-the-top performances, and attention-getting fashion choices have earned her a large fan following, and a No. 25 position on the Forbes Celebrity 100 list.[25] Lady Gaga became prominent in the late 2000s with a powerful voice and a style that seemed to simultaneously enthrall and shock her fans. Whether it is her meat-inspired dresses, or her arrival at a Grammy Awards show emerging from an egg shell, or a performance where she smeared herself in blood, this artist created a special brand. Her live performances feature elaborate sets, and her antics are intended to create an experience like no other. Unlike other celebrities, despite her outrageous costumes and her controversial moments, she is not apologetic, and is very much in control of her brand and her message. It is this clarity of mission and message that attracts a large following. Lady Gaga also remains in close touch with her fans and followers, continually thanking them for their support and encouragement. At her live performances, she often goes out of her way to give shout-outs to fans by name, and invites them backstage to meet with her. Lady Gaga engages in storytelling throughout her performances, describing what or who inspired her various songs.[26] Lady Gaga updates her looks and remains current, in order to maintain her novelty and appeal to her audiences. Lady Gaga is also in the process of extending her brand. Among her brand extensions, Lady Gaga is in the process of launching her own beauty brand called "Haus Beauty,"[27] along with a line of pet products, including grain-free, organic food for pets.[28]

Lady Gaga is among the best-known celebrity brands, thanks to her musical talent, unique style, and social media savvy, all of which have resulted in a loyal base of followers.

the way people treat you and interpret your words, actions, and deeds.[29] Lady Gaga is one such celebrity whose personal brand offers numerous lessons for marketers.

Similarly, organizations often take on meanings through their programs, activities, and products. Nonprofit organizations such as the Sierra Club, the American Red Cross, and Amnesty International have increasingly emphasized marketing. The children's advocate nonprofit UNICEF has initiated a number of marketing activities and programs through the years.

UNICEF

UNICEF launched its "Tap Project" campaign in 2007, which asked diners to pay $1 for a glass of New York City tap water in restaurants, with the funds going to support the organization's clean water programs. That was the first time UNICEF had run a consumer campaign in over 50 years. The UNICEF logo was featured on the Barcelona soccer team's jersey from 2006 to 2011 under an arrangement in which the team donated $2 million annually to the organization.

UNICEF launched another consumer campaign in the UK in February 2010. This five-year "Put it Right" campaign features celebrity ambassadors for the organization and aims to protect the rights of children. One of UNICEF's most successful corporate relationships has been with IKEA. The partnership, which also emphasizes children's rights, was established in 2000 and encompasses direct donations from IKEA and an annual toy campaign, the sales from which directly benefit UNICEF programs.[30] In 2016, IKEA partnered with UNICEF and launched the "Let's Play for Change" initiative, which hopes to raise funds and promote the role of play in helping young children reach optimal brain development.[31]

Nonprofit organizations like UNICEF need strong brands and modern marketing practices to help them fundraise and satisfy their organizational goals and mission.
Source: ton koene/Alamy Stock Photo

Sports, Arts, and Entertainment

A special case of marketing people and organizations as brands exists in the sports, arts, and entertainment industries. Sports marketing has become highly sophisticated in recent years, employing traditional packaged-goods techniques. No longer content to allow win–loss records to dictate attendance levels and financial fortunes, many sports teams are marketing themselves through a creative combination of advertising, promotions, sponsorship, direct mail, digital, and other forms of communication. By building awareness, image, and loyalty, these sports franchises are able to meet ticket sales targets regardless of what their team's actual performance might turn out to be. Brand symbols, and logos in particular, have become an important financial contributor to professional sports through licensing agreements.

Branding plays an especially valuable function in the arts and entertainment industries that bring us movies, television, music, and books. These offerings are good examples of experience goods: prospective buyers cannot judge quality by inspection and must use cues such as the particular people involved, the concept or rationale behind the project, and word-of-mouth and critical reviews.

Think of a movie as a product whose "ingredients" are the plot, actors, and director.[32] Certain movie franchises such as *James Bond*, *Transformers*, and *Star Wars* have established themselves as strong brands by combining all these ingredients into a formula that appeals to consumers and allows the studios to release sequels (essentially brand extensions) that rely on the title's initial popularity. For years, some of the most valuable movie franchises have featured recurring characters or ongoing stories, and many successful recent films have been sequels. Their success is due to the fact that moviegoers know from the title, the actors, producers, directors, and other contributors that they can expect a certain experience—a classic application of branding.

HARRY POTTER

With its ability to transcend its original format—books—the *Harry Potter* film series has been likened to the *Star Wars* franchise. All seven of the popular novels were turned into blockbuster movies. In the first year it launched Harry Potter toys, Mattel saw $160 million in sales. And in 2010, Universal Studios opened a Florida theme park based on the Harry Potter stories that has become a major attraction for fans of the franchise. The Harry Potter empire has been praised for its attention to core marketing techniques—a good product, emotional involvement of its consumers, word-of-mouth promotion, "tease" marketing, and brand consistency. Several estimates have pegged the Harry Potter brand to be worth $25 billion as of 2016,[33] which includes $7 billion in movie sales, and an equivalent amount in books. Beyond these, Mattel and Hasbro have collectively earned around $7 billion in toys and games relating to the Potter franchise. NBC Universal acquired the TV rights to the Harry Potter and Fantastic Beasts movies until 2025 from Warner Bros. for as much as $250 million. Other companies such as Johnson & Johnson, Coca-Cola, Fossil Group, and Electronic Arts have made various products featuring the Harry Potter trademark. Harry Potter also has spawned numerous line extensions, which provide new ways for customers to experience the Harry Potter brand. For example, in addition to the Harry Potter theme park, the brand also has a show on Broadway. These extensions allow the brand to retain its cache, which at the same time refreshes its image in consumers' minds. Taken together, it looks like the Harry Potter brand is likely to continue for quite some time into the future.

Few brands have generated as much worldwide consumer loyalty—and profits—as *Harry Potter*.
Source: WARNER BROS. PICTURES/Album/Newscom

BRANDING BRIEF 1-4
Place Branding

Branding is not limited to vacation destinations. Countries, states, and cities, large and small, are beginning to brand their respective images as they try to draw visitors or encourage relocation. Some notable early examples of place branding include "Virginia Is For Lovers" and "Shrimp on the Barbie" (Australia). Now virtually every physical location, area, or region considers place branding.

Las Vegas ran its hugely successful "What Happens Here, Stays Here" campaign beginning in 2003. The ads were meant to sell Las Vegas as an experience. In 2008, the city took a different route, selling Vegas differently and in more practical terms in light of the economy. Las Vegas was the scene of a tragic mass shooting in 2017, one that caused sorrow and suffering to a large number of people. In the immediate aftermath of the tragedy, the city used a new tagline, with the theme "Vegas Strong," to remind consumers about the strength and resilience of the city, while encouraging visitors to keep coming back. In 2018, Las Vegas reverted to the "What Happens Here, Stays Here" campaign, based on marketplace input suggesting that customers wanted "their Vegas back."

Branding countries to increase appeal to tourists is also a growing phenomenon. Some recent success stories include Spain's use of a logo designed by Spanish artist Joan Miró, the "Incredible India" campaign, and New Zealand's marketing of itself in relation to

The Lord of the Rings movie franchise. Some other tourist slogans include "Essential Costa Rica. My Choice, Naturally" for Costa Rica and "A Curious Place" for Belize. Future Brand, a brand consultancy and research company, ranks countries on the strengths of their respective brands. In 2017, it deemed the top five country brands to be Switzerland, Canada, Japan, Sweden, and New Zealand.

Sources: Roger Yu, "Cities Use Destination Branding to Lure Tourists," *USA Today*, February 12, 2010; Yana Polikarpov, "Visitors Bureau Lures Tourists to 'Happy' San Diego," *Brandweek*, April 23, 2009; Liz Benston, "Will Vegas Advertising That Worked Before, Work Again?," *Las Vegas Sun*, September 27, 2009; Sean O'Neill, "Careful with Those Tourist Slogans," *Budget Travel*, September 24, 2009; John Cook, "Packaging a Nation," *Travel + Leisure*, January 2007; Forbes.com, "Top 25 Country Brands," www.forbes.com/pictures/efkk45lgim/5-new-zealand/#12d5581e7b58, accessed April 11, 2018; Katie Richards, "MGM's First Ad Following the Las Vegas Shootings Draws Swift Criticism on Social," *Adweek*, October 18, 2017, www.adweek.com/brandmarketing/mgms-first-ad-following-the-las-vegasshootings-draws-swift-criticism-on-social/; Richard Velotta, "Las Vegas 'What Happens Here, Stays Here' Ads Revived," *Review Journal*, January 3, 2018, www.reviewjournal.com/business/tourism/las-vegas-what-happens-here-stays-here-ads-revived/.

A strong brand is valuable in the entertainment industry because of the fervent feelings that brands generate as a result of pleasurable past experiences. A new album release from Robert Plant would probably not cause much of a ripple in the marketplace, even if it were marketed as coming from a founding member of the band Led Zeppelin. If it were to actually be released and marketed under the Led Zeppelin name, however, greater media attention and higher sales would be virtually guaranteed.

Geographic Locations

Increased mobility of both people and businesses and growth in the tourism industry have contributed to the rise of place marketing. Cities, states, regions, and countries are now actively promoted through advertising, direct mail, and other communication tools. These campaigns aim to create awareness and a favorable image of a location that will entice temporary visits or permanent moves from individuals and businesses alike. Although the brand name is usually preordained by the name of the location, there are a number of different considerations in building a place brand, some of which are considered in Branding Brief 1-4.

Ideas and Causes

Finally, numerous ideas and causes have been branded, especially by nonprofit organizations. They may be captured in a phrase or slogan and even be represented by a symbol, such as AIDS ribbons. By making ideas and causes more visible and concrete, branding can provide much value. As Chapter 12 describes, marketing increasingly relies on sophisticated marketing practices to inform or persuade consumers about the issues surrounding a cause.

WHAT ARE THE STRONGEST BRANDS?

It is clear from these examples that virtually anything can be and has been branded. Which brands are the strongest, that is, the best known or most highly regarded? Figure 1-5 reveals Interbrand's ranking of the world's 25 most valuable brands in 2017 based on its brand valuation methodology (see Chapter 11), as published in its annual "Best Global Brands" report.[34]

We can easily find some of the best-known brands by simply walking down a supermarket aisle. It's also easy to identify a number of other brands with amazing staying power that have

2017 Rank	Brand	Sector	Brand Value	Change in Brand Value
1	Apple	Technology	184,154$m	+3%
2	Google	Technology	141,703$m	+6%
3	Microsoft	Technology	79,999$m	+10%
4	Coca-Cola	Beverages	69,733$m	−5%
5	Amazon	Retail	64,796$m	+29%
6	Samsung	Technology	56,249$m	+9%
7	Toyota	Automotive	50,291$m	−6%
8	Facebook	Technology	48,188$m	+48%
9	Mercedes	Automotive	47,829$m	+10%
10	IBM	Business Services	46,829$m	−11%
11	GE	Diversified	44,208$m	+3%
12	McDonald's	Restaurants	41,533$m	+5%
13	BMW	Automotive	41,521$m	0%
14	Disney	Media	40,772$m	+5%
15	Intel	Technology	39,459$m	+7%
16	Cisco	Technology	31,930$m	+3%
17	Oracle	Technology	27,466$m	+3%
18	Nike	Sporting Goods	27,021$m	+8%
19	Louis Vuitton	Luxury	22,919$m	−4%
20	Honda	Automotive	22,696$m	+3%
21	SAP	Technology	22,635$m	+6%
22	Pepsi	Beverages	20,491$m	+1%
23	H&M	Apparel	20,488$m	−10%
24	Zara	Apparel	18,573$m	+11%
25	Ikea	Retail	18,472$m	+4%

FIGURE 1-5

Twenty-Five Most Valuable Global Brands

Sources: Based on Interbrand, "The 100 Most Valuable Global Brands," 2017.

been market leaders in their categories for decades. Brands are still among the most valuable assets that can be owned by a firm.

As noted in Figure 1-4, as much as 60 percent of the value of a firm could be attributed to intangible assets such as brands. Many brands endure the test of time. For example, many brands that were number one in the United Kingdom in 1933 remain strong today: Hovis bread, Stork margarine, Kellogg's Corn Flakes, Cadbury's chocolates, Gillette razors, Schweppes mixers, Brooke Bond tea, Colgate toothpaste, and Hoover vacuum cleaners. Many of these brands have evolved over the years, however, and made a number of changes. Most of them barely resemble their original forms.

At the same time, some seemingly invincible brands, including Montgomery Ward, Polaroid, and Xerox, have run into difficulties and seen their market preeminence challenged or even lost. Although some of these failures are related to factors beyond the control of the firm, such as technological advances or shifting consumer preferences, in other cases, the blame could probably be placed on the action or inaction of the marketers behind the brands. Some failed to account for changing market conditions and continued to operate with a "business as usual" attitude or, perhaps even worse, recognized that changes were necessary but reacted inadequately or inappropriately.

Clearly, maintaining brand relevance and differentiation is important to the success of a brand. The Science of Branding 1-3 provides some academic insights into brand relevance and brand differentiation and summarizes novel views of various authors on these topics.

The bottom line is that any brand—no matter how strong at one point in time—is vulnerable and susceptible to poor brand management. The next section discusses why it is so difficult to manage brands in today's environment. Brand Focus 1.0 at the end of the chapter describes a new type of entity in branding—that is, digital native vertical brands, which are born online, and then later go direct to consumers. It is likely that this type of brand could present a unique set of challenges and opportunities, as companies begin to leverage the power of digital marketing to strengthen their bonds with customers.

THE SCIENCE OF BRANDING 1-3
On Brand Relevance and Brand Differentiation

The Importance of Brand Relevance to Winning in the Marketplace

Brand relevance is a key concept and can make the difference in winning and keeping customers in the marketplace. Differentiation is also key to brand equity and is at the heart of what makes a brand successful. Both relevance and differentiation are important to the models proposed in this book, and in other models of brand-building and brand equity described later in this book—for example, Young and Rubicam's Brand Asset Valuator framework. Despite their importance in various brand-building models, relevance and differentiation have been the subject of many alternative interpretations and perspectives. We first describe Aaker's perspective on brand relevance. We then review Sharp and his colleagues' arguments, which provide a contrast to some of the ideas regarding the role of differentiation and its importance to brand equity.

Aaker defines brand relevance as involving multiple stages. First, a person chooses a category, then selects a set within the category, for further consideration. In a subsequent stage, a brand is chosen because of its differential strength on a functional attribute, or its ability to convey some emotional or self-expressive benefits. Finally, brand evaluation is based on a user's experience.

It should be noted that brand relevance as developed by Aaker—although not inconsistent—is certainly not identical to the traditional notion of brand relevance. Brand relevance traditionally refers to whether or not a brand is worth considering by consumers because they feel that it provides some personally useful benefits. In Aaker's view, brand relevance combines both category choice and brand choice stages, and envisions the brand as having a critical role to play in the category choice stage as well as in the brand choice stage. A brand with a high degree of awareness is likely to generate awareness about a category as a whole.

For example, Uber, which began in 2009, became well-known as a ridesharing service which can be conveniently accessed via a mobile app. Three years later, competing brand Lyft was introduced as another ride service. Uber's prominence within the ride service category no doubt attracted new competitors. Still, Uber's position as a first mover allowed it to become an exemplar brand and dominate the category which it helped to develop, thereby increasing its relevance. The same is true of other innovative companies and brand names such as Airbnb, Zappos, and Tesla,

each of which radically reinvented the categories they were in, and became dominant players. In line with this, Aaker argues as follows: "Brand preference can also affect brand relevance. If a brand is preferred because of a compelling brand proposition, a strong personality, a satisfying user experience, and a positive customer relationship, then it will affect the consideration set and may well influence or drive attitudes toward the category or subcategory."

The innovativeness of a brand's product or service offerings may determine whether they are a dominant player within a category or subcategory. Brands with high awareness and strong image can raise the prominence of the category that they are in, thus increasing the likelihood that the category is chosen, and that they enter the consideration set. Aaker believes this type of "brand relevance" is a critical success factor in today's environment.

Growth Strategies, and the Role of Niche versus Mass Marketing

The work of Sharp et al. on *How Brands Grow* offers unconventional advice for managers and provides evidence from various packaged goods sectors to support their arguments. Two key points made in the book are: (1) Sharp et al. criticize the overemphasis on loyalty and retention, in place of acquisition of new customers, and offer that acquisition is probably more important. They support this argument by further suggesting that differences between large and small brands are accounted for by differences in penetration rather than differences in average buying. Data from categories such as shampoo and laundry detergents is used to support this. (2) Sharp et al. argue that there is too much emphasis on brand differentiation and argue that it does not translate into distinctiveness of customer profiles across major brands. According to the authors, the lack of difference in buyer profiles across major competitors must mean that differentiation is not working. Instead, they advocate that brands focus their attention on developing a consistent theme and message—that is, more on mass marketing, than niche marketing.

Niche marketing involves focusing marketing efforts on a specific subset of the market, which has specific needs; in contrast, mass marketing involves appealing to the entire market with a standardized product, distribution approach, and advertising campaign. Which of these is more effective? Are there conditions which favor one versus another? Brand marketers may need to ask a series of key questions, the answers to which will determine whether or not a mass marketing or niche marketing strategy will be more appropriate for a given category and within a specific stage of the brand's life cycle. These questions include:

1. Is there a compelling value proposition that can appeal to a specific segment of the population?

2. Is this target segment willing to pay a price premium over an undifferentiated product?

3. Related, is it cost-effective to engage with niche markets rather than offer an undifferentiated product to a larger audience?

4. What are the competitive advantages to a mass marketing strategy versus a niche strategy? Are there incumbents in the market that are using one or the other approach? Does the company's resources and culture support a mass marketing or a niche marketing approach?

Sources: David A. Aaker, *Brand Relevance: Making Competitors Irrelevant* (John Wiley & Sons, 2010); Byron Sharp, John Gerard Dawes, Jennifer Therese Romaniuk, and John Scriven, *How Brands Grow: What Marketers Don't Know* (Oxford University Press, 2010); Frederick F. Reichheld, *The Loyalty Effect* (Boston: Harvard Business School Press, 1996).

BRANDING CHALLENGES AND OPPORTUNITIES

Although brands may be as important as ever to consumers, in reality, *brand management may be more difficult than ever.* Let's look at some recent developments that have significantly complicated marketing practices and pose challenges for brand managers (see Figure 1-6).[35]

Unparalleled Access to Information and New Technologies

Technology has produced the ability to access vast amounts of information about almost any topic. Algorithms—such as Google search—act as a mediator between those who seek answers and the answers themselves. Marketers are able to gain access to search terms as a window into the minds of consumers, and search advertising has evolved to leverage this deeper understanding of consumers' needs and wants, as revealed in their searches on the Internet for more information.

As technology grows and expands and becomes embedded in the physical world, search for information will be a facet, even in the physical world.[36] For example, museums may embrace new digital tools to enhance the museum experience in many ways. Some of the new technologies in museums may include augmented reality to enhance the visitor experience, feature a smart assistant that provides supplemental information about artwork and delivers this to a smartphone, or 3D technology that allows consumers to reproduce, hold, and feel an accurate replica of an object.[37] Over time, as these technologies become more standard, brand marketers may find opportunities to utilize these innovative features in designing better brand experiences for their customers.

Downward Pressure on Prices

As search costs of information become lower, it is easier for consumers to compare prices and switch to the cheapest alternative with just a few clicks. This trend could encourage greater commodification of products and services, and the availability of third-party comparison shopping Web sites (e.g., Kayak, Vayama for travel) further makes it difficult for brands to retain their ability to differentiate and charge premiums.[38]

Unparalleled Access to Information and New Technologies
Downward Pressure on Prices
Ubiquitous Connectivity and Consumer Backlash
Sharing Information and Goods
Unexpected Sources of Competition
Disintermediation and Reintermediation
Alternative Sources of Information about Product Quality
Winner-Takes-All Markets
Media Transformation
Customer Centricity

FIGURE 1-6

Challenges to Brand Builders

The Met and other museums use technology to help transform the museum experience.

Source: Sherbien Dacalanio/Pacific Press/Light-Rocket/Getty Images

Ubiquitous Connectivity and the Consumer Backlash

The growth of digital technology has provided consumers the ability to connect with each other throughout the day, using technologies such as multimedia mobile services. As connectivity increases, it also lowers consumers' attention and makes them more vulnerable to intrusions. As a result, a backlash may develop as consumers increasingly resist marketers' attempts to gain access to them, and various types of software may become available to combat the intrusiveness of communications. Apple recently introduced a technology that would prevent mobile phones from receiving text messages while consumers are driving. Ad blocking services have been around for some time, offering a unique way for consumers to escape from intrusive ads. Thus, while marketers can gain unparalleled access to consumers, consumers may become protective of their time and find ways of escaping this unwanted attention.

Sharing Information and Goods

New technologies have made it increasingly possible for consumers to share information and goods with each other. This trend has resulted in two related types of phenomena. Social media platforms have become vehicles for consumers to meet and share information with each other. These platforms offer various types of features to allow consumers to become online friends and share information in various formats (pictures, text, videos, etc.). Consumers are increasingly producers of content. Social platforms such as Facebook and Instagram are enablers of online social interactions, allowing users to post updates about their daily whereabouts and activities. Platforms such as YouTube have furthered the ability of consumers to broadcast content of various forms—text, audio, video—to a global audience.

The opportunity offered by these platforms is that they enable marketers to gain very precise information about their target audiences, including political views and entertainment preferences, which allows for a 360-degree view of a consumer. However, these platforms have increasingly faced intense scrutiny by regulatory agencies, concerned about the privacy implications of unbridled access to customer data. Also, in the United States, social media companies have traditionally not had to obtain permissions for use of customer data. Facebook has, in recent times, faced a lot of scrutiny from lawmakers about its use of detailed customer information and the subsequent legal consequences.[39] In Europe, privacy laws are already in place that require companies to gain explicit permission prior to their using consumer data for marketing purposes.

Due to the increased availability of travel search sites such as Kayak (with easy access to pricing information), travel brands have to increasingly differentiate themselves with other attributes such as quality and service.

Social media platforms have unprecedented access to customers' media and browsing habits, entertainment preferences, etc., thereby providing marketers with a unique ability to target their offerings with greater precision.

Other types of platforms are enabling sharing of specific types of goods. Napster allows for peer-to-peer file sharing, whereas platforms such as Airbnb, Zipcar, and Uber allow individuals with certain goods (homes for rent or cars for rides) to share these consumers with other consumers, in return for a fee.

Unexpected Sources of Competition

The dynamics of the digital world are such that it can be easier for companies to enter into new categories without having to face the barriers to entry (e.g., the need for a well-established system for distribution) that typically exist in the physical world. This means that new competitors may crop up in unexpected places, and a digital brand has to remain vigilant for new sources of competition.[40] For example, when Amazon Movies began offering streaming services to its customers, it came into direct competition with incumbents such as Netflix and Apple iTunes.

Disintermediation and Reintermediation

The rapid rise of the Internet has been accompanied by two trends—disintermediation and reintermediation. *Disintermediation* refers to the reduction or elimination of intermediaries from the channel of distribution, including entities such as agents, brokers, and wholesalers.

The sharing economy has witnessed the rise of companies such as Zipcar and Airbnb, which allow individuals with certain goods (cars, homes) to rent these to other customers in return for a fee.

Online review sites (TripAdvisor, Yelp) have become powerful platforms that allow customers to share word-of-mouth and learn about product quality quickly, causing the decline of traditional advisory services (e.g., travel agents).

For example, the travel industry has witnessed a significant decline in the need for travel agencies that once offered advisory services and helped make bookings in return for a small fee or commission. *Reintermediation* refers to the introduction of new intermediaries that perform some of the same functions or have additional roles in the channel of distribution. There has also been a significant growth of a new class of intermediaries who focus on providing reviews to help in consumer decision-making. These information intermediaries—that is, infomediaries—include online review sites such as Yelp, online consumer guides (ConsumerReports .com), influential bloggers, and so on. As an example of reintermediation, the online Web site TripAdvisor offers some of the services that travel agencies used to provide and acts as a valuable resource for travelers.

Alternative Sources of Information about Product Quality

The growth of the Internet and availability of vast amounts of information about products and brands online suggests that there are many new ways in which consumers can learn about product quality. Figure 1-7 displays some of the ways consumers now collect information. As more consumer decision-making is based on online word-of-mouth and reviews, there is reduced information asymmetry between producer and consumer.[41] This increase in information on product quality certainly has reduced the reliance on brands as signals of quality.

There is no doubt that the growth of the Internet and availability of online reviews and information has transformed the role of brands in some ways. Rather than act merely as a signal of quality, brands now have to do much more. They have to be translators of trends, acting on information about changing customer tastes and desires almost instantaneously. Further, given the speed with which consumers can learn about actual quality (or what has been called by some as "absolute value"), it is also very important that brands invest a great deal in creating exceptional customer experiences that are worthy of buzz. We highlight several such examples later in the book.

Winner-Takes-All Markets

The availability of information about product quality in vast quantities suggests that consumers are likely to become much more quality sensitive. Brands which are market leaders within categories (i.e., brands which are seen as having high quality to consumers) are likely to be chosen at an even greater rate. Since unambiguous quality information is available for a low cost, consumers will gravitate towards brands that are seen as having the highest average quality with the lowest variance. This will speed up the exit of brands that do not occupy a leadership position in a category. Thus, brands will be under greater pressure to deliver a high quality product or have a dominant position within the market on a particular aspect—for example,

Source of Information	Percentage of Respondents Rating the Source as Credible
Friends and Family	83%
Television Advertising	63%
Newspaper Advertising	60%
Magazine Advertising	58%

FIGURE 1-7

How Credible Are Consumer Information Sources?

Source: Andrew McCaskill, "Recommendations from Friends Remain Most Credible Form of Advertising Among Consumers; Branded Websites Are the Second-Highest-Rates Form," Press Room, September 28, 2015.

price and after sale services. Such winner-take-all competitive outcomes, typical of sports and entertainment industries, are likely to become increasingly common in other industries as well.[42] This phenomenon has also been documented across a variety of other industries such as airlines, automobiles, petroleum producers, the European semiconductor industry, baby foods, and so on, where it has been shown that three major players typically dominate any given industry.[43] We expect that the time taken to achieve this state of dominance by the three major players will be significantly reduced in the future, and the shakeout of weaker players will take place at an accelerated pace, due to the wide availability of product quality information at a relatively low cost.

Media Transformation

Another important change in the marketing environment is the erosion or fragmentation of traditional advertising media and the emergence of interactive and nontraditional media, promotion, and other communication alternatives. For several reasons related to media cost, clutter, and fragmentation—as outlined in Chapter 6—marketers have become disenchanted with traditional advertising media, especially network television. We further explore the implications of fragmentation of media for digital and social channels in Chapter 7.

The percentage of the communication budget devoted to traditional advertising has shrunk over the years. In its place, marketers are spending more on nontraditional forms of communication. These newer communication options, which include the use of social media platforms for advertising (generating online word-of-mouth through online social influencers), are increasingly very effective.

Consider how P&G has dramatically changed its marketing communications in recent years. The one-time queen of daytime TV soap operas—the company produced the shows and ran ads during the broadcasts—P&G has dramatically overhauled the way it markets its brands. It no longer airs any soap operas and puts more emphasis on social media instead. The company sells Pampers diapers on Facebook, offers an iPhone application for Always feminine products that allows women to track menstrual cycles and ask questions, and uses social media to sell its traditionally male-targeted Old Spice personal care products.[44]

A good example of a relatively new brand which effectively leverages newer forms of communication to strengthen bonds with their customers is LaCroix.

LACROIX

LaCroix (pronounced La-CROY) is an American brand of sparkling water with no artificial sweeteners, sugars, or sodium and available in a variety of natural flavors marketed as LaCroix (with flavors such as pure, lime, orange, berry), and its two sub-brands, LaCroix Cúrate (including flavors such as Melón Pomelo, Kiwi Sandía, and Muré Pepino), and LaCroix NiCola (with its flavor LaCola, which is a natural cola essence sparking water).[45] LaCroix is distributed by the Sundance Beverage Company, a subsidiary of National Beverage Corp. LaCroix markets to its target audience by positioning itself as an "all occasion" beverage.[46]

There are many elements of LaCroix's marketing which have fueled the brand's success, including its positioning, use of social media marketing to generate buzz, and its use of non traditional advertising and social influencers to build awareness and engagement. The brand has positioned itself as a healthier alternative to carbonated beverages, which has been particularly attractive to millennial populations, who are focused on healthy eating. LaCroix's packaging indicates that it has no calories, no sugars, no artificial ingredients, no genetically modified organisms, and no added phosphoric acid in its beverages, making this a viable alternative to carbonated beverages among very health-conscious consumers.

LaCroix has distinguished itself by focusing more on social media marketing rather than traditional advertising. This represents a big departure from norms, particularly in the beverage category. It has focused its efforts on those social media channels where its target population (i.e., millennials) are likely to spend time, particularly channels such as Instagram. The brand also elevates brand engagement by creating a sense of community around the LaCroix brand. The brand maintains engagement by acknowledging all comments made on social media by its members. It promotes social media engagement by connecting to trending themes and topics as they emerge on social media. The LaCroix brand employs a wide range of marketing approaches to gain attention and engagement from its consumers. In order to further appeal to health-conscious consumers, in a Challenge campaign the brand encouraged consumers to swap a can of diet or sugary soda for LaCroix for 40 days and then to post stories and share photos about their experience in social media venues.[47] The colorful packaging and the consumer-sponsored stories allows the brand itself to "sparkle" on social media venues such as Instagram. This also lends the brand a great deal of authenticity and discovery.[48]

Finally, LaCroix has effectively leveraged micro-influencers on social media to help drive customer engagement.[49] It also has associated its brand with various fitness programs. For example, it became a sponsor of the month-long clean-eating campaign called the Whole30 program. LaCroix uses its hashtags such as #LaCroixlove and #LiveLaCroix to encourage followers to distribute its cocktail and mocktail recipes. While many brands only focus on online influencers, LaCroix's unique approach is its encouragement of microinfluencers (or influencers with smaller followings, but higher engagement). For example, when influencer Kelly Fox posted photos of LaCroix to her 2,500-plus followers, the brand sent her vouchers for cases of LaCroix.[50]

LaCroix's unique positioning as a healthier alternative to traditional beverages and its effective use of social media advertising are key factors enabling its success in the marketplace.

The Importance of Customer-Centricity

The growth of digital channels and ubiquitous connectivity has ushered in an era in which product quality information is easily available online. This suggests that brand equity can be vulnerable to destruction if product and service claims are not verified by actual experience. Review forums can quickly reveal the quality of products, and consumers can learn about product quality from their peers and online word-of-mouth. Any negative news about brands can be amplified and destroy brand value quickly. This profound shift in the previously held central role of product in creating brand value has had significant implications for brand marketers. In turn, brands have shifted their emphasis to becoming more customer-centric in their marketing, focusing instead on customer issues and concerns, as it relates to their everyday lives and society at large.

THE BRAND EQUITY CONCEPT

Marketers clearly face a number of competitive challenges, and some critics feel the response of many has been ineffective or, worse, has further aggravated the problem. In the rest of this book, we present theories, models, and frameworks that accommodate and reflect marketing's new challenges in order to provide useful managerial guidelines and suggest promising new directions for future thought and research. We introduce a "common denominator" or unified conceptual framework, based on the concept of brand equity, as a tool to interpret the potential effects of various brand strategies.

One of the most popular and potentially important marketing concepts to arise in recent years is ***brand equity***. Its emergence, however, has meant both good news and bad news to marketers. The good news is that brand equity has elevated the importance of the brand in marketing strategy and provided focus for managerial interest and research activity. The bad news is that, confusingly, the concept has been defined a number of different ways for a variety of purposes. No common viewpoint has emerged about how to conceptualize and measure brand equity.

Fundamentally, branding is all about endowing products and services with the power of brand equity. Despite the many different views, most observers agree that brand equity consists of the marketing effects uniquely attributable to a brand. That is, brand equity explains why different outcomes result from the marketing of a branded product or service than if it were not branded. That is the view we take in this book. As a stark example of the transformational power of branding, consider the auction sales in Figure 1-8. Without such celebrity associations, it is doubtful that any of these items would cost more than a few hundred dollars at a flea market.[51]

Branding is all about creating differences. Most marketing observers also agree with the following basic principles of branding and brand equity:

- Differences in outcomes arise from the "added value" endowed to a product in part as a result of past marketing activity for the brand.
- This value can be created for a brand in many different ways.
- Brand equity provides a common denominator for interpreting marketing strategies and assessing the value of a brand.
- There are many different ways in which the value of a brand can be manifested or exploited to benefit the firm (in terms of greater proceeds or lower costs or both).

Fundamentally, the brand equity concept reinforces how important the brand is in marketing strategies. Chapters 2 and 3 in Part II of the book provide an overview of brand equity and a blueprint for the rest of the book. The remainder of the book addresses in much greater depth how to build brand equity (Chapters 4–8 in Part III), measure brand equity (Chapters 9–11 in Part IV), and manage brand equity (Chapters 12–15 in Part V). The concluding Chapter 16 in Part VI provides some additional applications and perspectives.

FIGURE 1-8

Notable Recent Auction Sales

Source: Zoe Henry, "8 Famous Items That Sold for Ridiculous Amounts of Money," April 8, 2016.

- J.K. Rowling's chair sold for $394,000.

- *Casablanca* piano sold for $3.4 million.

- *Wizard of Oz* Lion costume sold for $3 million.

- John Lennon's guitar sold for $2.4 million.

- Andy Warhol's wig sold for $10,800.

- Keith Moon's (drummer for the band *The Who*) - drum set sold for nine times its estimated value for $252,487.

- Buddy Holly's glasses sold for $80,000.

- Justin Timberlake's unfinished French toast from breakfast was sold on eBay for $1,025.

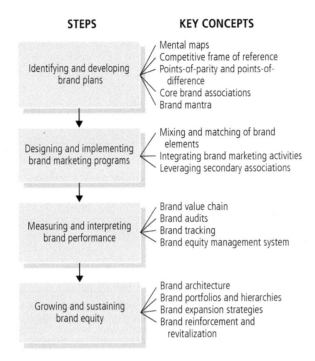

STEPS   **KEY CONCEPTS**

FIGURE 1-9
Strategic Brand
Management Process

The remainder of this chapter provides an overview of the strategic brand management process that helps pull all these various concepts together.

STRATEGIC BRAND MANAGEMENT PROCESS

Strategic brand management involves the design and implementation of marketing programs and activities to build, measure, and manage brand equity. In this text, we define the *strategic brand management process* as having four main steps (see Figures 1-9):

1. Identifying and developing brand plans
2. Designing and implementing brand marketing programs
3. Measuring and interpreting brand performance
4. Growing and sustaining brand equity

Let's briefly highlight each of these four steps.[52]

Identifying and Developing Brand Plans

The strategic brand management process starts with a clear understanding of what the brand is to represent and how it should be positioned with respect to competitors.[53] Brand planning, as described in Chapters 2 and 3, uses the following three interlocking models.

- The *brand positioning model* describes how to guide integrated marketing to maximize competitive advantages.
- The *brand resonance model* describes how to create intense loyalty and strong customer relationships with customers.
- The *brand value chain* is a means to trace the value creation process for brands, to better understand the financial impact of brand marketing expenditures and investments.

Designing and Implementing Brand Marketing Programs

As Chapter 2 outlines, building brand equity requires properly positioning the brand in the minds of customers and achieving as much brand resonance as possible. In general, this knowledge-building process will depend on three factors:

1. The initial choices of the brand elements making up the brand and how they are mixed and matched;

2. The marketing activities and supporting marketing programs and the way the brand is integrated into them; and
3. Other associations indirectly transferred to or leveraged by the brand as a result of linking it to some other entity (such as the company, country of origin, channel of distribution, or another brand).

Some important considerations of each of these three factors are as follows.

Choosing Brand Elements.   The most common brand elements are brand names, URLs, logos, symbols, characters, packaging, and slogans. The best test of the brand-building contribution of a brand element is what consumers would think about the product or service if they knew only its brand name or its associated logo or other element. Because brand elements have different advantages, marketing managers often use a subset of all the possible brand elements or even all of them. Chapter 4 examines in detail the means by which the choice and design of brand elements can help to build brand equity.

Integrating the Brand into Marketing Activities and the Supporting Marketing Program.   Although the judicious choice of brand elements can make some contribution to building brand equity, the biggest contribution comes from marketing activities related to the brand. This text highlights only some particularly important marketing program considerations for building brand equity. Chapter 5 addresses new developments in designing marketing programs as well as issues in product strategy, pricing strategy, and channels strategy. Chapter 6 addresses issues in communications strategy. Chapter 7 provides an overview of the digital landscape, along with an in-depth assessment of the pros and cons of different digital and social media channels.

Leveraging Secondary Associations.   The third and final way to build brand equity is to leverage secondary associations. Brand associations may themselves be linked to other entities that have their own associations, creating these secondary associations. For example, the brand may be linked to certain source factors, such as the company (through branding strategies), countries or other geographical regions (through identification of product origin), and channels of distribution (through channel strategy), as well as to other brands (through ingredients or co-branding), characters (through licensing), spokespeople (through endorsements), sporting or cultural events (through sponsorship), or some other third-party sources (through awards or reviews).

Because the brand becomes identified with another entity, even though this entity may not directly relate to the product or service performance, consumers may *infer* that the brand shares associations with that entity, thus, producing indirect or secondary associations for the brand. In essence, the marketer is borrowing or leveraging some other associations for the brand to create some associations of the brand's own and thus, help build its brand equity. Chapter 8 describes the means of leveraging brand equity.

Measuring and Interpreting Brand Performance

To manage their brands profitably, managers must successfully design and implement a brand equity measurement system. A ***brand equity measurement system*** is a set of research procedures designed to provide timely, accurate, and actionable information for marketers so that they can make the best possible tactical decisions in the short run and the best strategic decisions in the long run. As described in Chapter 9, implementing such a system involves three key steps—conducting ***brand audits***, designing ***brand tracking*** studies, and establishing a ***brand equity management system***.

The task of determining or evaluating a brand's positioning often benefits from a brand audit. A ***brand audit*** is a comprehensive examination of a brand to assess its health, uncover its sources of equity, and suggest ways to improve and leverage that equity. A brand audit requires understanding sources of brand equity from the perspective of both the firm and the consumer.

Once marketers have determined the brand positioning strategy, they are ready to put into place the actual marketing program to create, strengthen, or maintain brand associations. ***Brand tracking studies*** collect information from consumers on a routine basis over time, typically through quantitative measures of brand performance on a number of key dimensions marketers can identify in the brand audit or other means. Chapters 10 and 11 describe a number of measures to operationalize brand performance.

A *brand equity management system* is a set of organizational processes designed to improve the understanding and use of the brand equity concept within a firm. Three major steps help implement a brand equity management system: creating brand equity charters, assembling brand equity reports, and defining brand equity responsibilities.

Growing and Sustaining Brand Equity

Maintaining and expanding on brand equity can be quite challenging. Brand equity management activities take a broader and more diverse perspective of the brand's equity—understanding how branding strategies should reflect corporate concerns and be adjusted, if at all, over time or over geographical boundaries or multiple market segments.

Defining Brand Architecture.   The firm's brand architecture provides general guidelines about its branding strategy and which brand elements to apply across all the different products sold by the firm. Two key concepts in defining brand architecture are brand portfolios and the brand hierarchy. The *brand portfolio* is the set of different brands that a particular firm offers for sale to buyers in a particular category. The *brand hierarchy* displays the number and nature of common and distinctive brand components across the firm's set of brands. Chapter 12 reviews a three-step approach to brand architecture and how to devise brand portfolios and hierarchies. Chapter 13 concentrates on the topic of brand extensions in which an existing brand is used to launch a product into a different category or subcategory.

Managing Brand Equity over Time.   Effective brand management also requires taking a long-term view of marketing decisions. A long-term perspective of brand management recognizes that any changes in the supporting marketing program for a brand may, by changing consumer knowledge, affect the success of future marketing programs. A long-term view also produces proactive strategies designed to maintain and enhance customer-based brand equity over time and reactive strategies to revitalize a brand that encounters some difficulties or problems. Chapter 14 outlines issues related to managing brand equity over time.

Managing Brand Equity over Geographic Boundaries, Cultures, and Market Segments. Another important consideration in managing brand equity is recognizing and accounting for different types of consumers when developing branding and marketing programs. International factors and global branding strategies are particularly important in these decisions. In expanding a brand overseas, managers need to build equity by relying on specific knowledge about the experience and behaviors of those market segments. Chapter 15 examines issues related to broadening of brand equity across market segments.

REVIEW

This chapter began by defining a brand as a name, term, sign, symbol, or design, or some combination of these elements, intended to identify the goods and services of one seller or group of sellers and to differentiate them from those of competitors. The different components of a brand (brand names, logos, symbols, package designs, and so forth) are brand elements. A brand is distinguished from a product, which is defined as anything that can be offered to a market for attention, acquisition, use, or consumption that might satisfy a need or want. A product may be a physical good, service, retail store, person, organization, place, or idea.

A brand is a product, but one that adds other dimensions that differentiate it in some way from other products designed to satisfy the same need. These differences may be rational and tangible—related to product performance of the brand—or more symbolic, emotional, or intangible—related to what the brand represents. Brands themselves are valuable intangible assets that need to be managed carefully. Brands offer a number of benefits to customers and the firms.

The key to branding is that consumers perceive differences among brands in a product category. Marketers can brand virtually any type of product by giving the product a name and attaching meaning to it in terms of what it has to offer and how it differs from competitors. A number of branding challenges and opportunities faced by present-day marketing managers were outlined related to changes in customer attitudes and behavior, competitive forces, marketing efficiency and effectiveness, and internal company dynamics.

The strategic brand management process has four steps:

1. Identifying and developing brand plans
2. Designing and implementing brand marketing programs
3. Measuring and interpreting brand performance
4. Growing and sustaining brand equity.

The remainder of the book outlines these steps in detail.

DISCUSSION QUESTIONS

1. What do brands mean to you? What are your favorite brands and why? Check to see how your perceptions of brands might differ from those of others.
2. Who do you think has the strongest brands? Why? What do you think of the Interbrand list of the 25 strongest brands in Figure 1-5? Do you agree with the rankings? Why or why not?
3. Can you think of anything that cannot be branded? Pick an example that was not discussed in each of the categories provided (services; retailers and distributors; people and organizations; sports, arts, and entertainment) and describe how each is a brand.
4. Can you think of yourself as a brand? What do you do to "brand" yourself?
5. What do you think of the new branding challenges and opportunities that were listed in the chapter? Can you think of any other issues?

BRAND FOCUS 1.0
Unlocking the Secrets of Digital Native Brands

Digitally native vertical brands (DNVB) are brands that originate on the Web and primarily interact with customers via digital channels. A key feature of these brands is that they go direct to consumers. Examples of successful DNVBs include Warby Parker, Dollar Shave Club, and Bonobos, which are known to have disrupted the status quo in their respective industries. This section focuses on some of the key learnings from studying digital native brands, and implications for brand management.

The term "digital native vertical brands" was coined by Andy Dunn (founder of Bonobos) and they are typically brands which interact and transact with consumers primarily on the Web. They are also characterized by tight distribution control, although they may use partnerships to extend to brick–and–mortar stores.[54] This growth in digital native brands is understandable if we consider the growth of e-commerce in general. Overall, e-commerce is expected to grow more than 50 percent between 2015 and 2020 and reach up to $23 billion, and is expected to account for 17 percent of all retail sales by 2022.[55] Direct-to-consumer retail is expected to reach a sales of $16 billion in 2020, growing from $6.6 billion in 2015. The rapid pace of growth in e-commerce (with an average annual growth of 9.3 percent),[56] the dominance of Amazon, and the parallel rise of direct-to-consumer retail have provided conditions that are ripe for digital branding to become key to future success.

A few characteristics of successful DNVBs include the following:

1. A relentless focus on customer acquisition, and investment in various marketing strategies to reach a large number of potential consumers.
2. Direct sourcing of raw materials.
3. Enhancing the customer experience by combining unique product offerings with exceptional customer service and user experience.
4. Engaging and building strong ties with customers through social media, online communities, and social influencers.
5. Direct distribution to consumers.

Going direct offers four primary advantages to these firms. First, it enables them to gain affinity to consumers and gather feedback about product and service offerings, which allows them to stay closer to customers than competitors who use indirect channels of distribution. Second, going direct allows these companies to rely less on Amazon, in particular, and provides significant cost advantages induced by eliminating retail markups.[57] Third, it allows them to control the customer experience end-to-end, making them more agile and responsive to customer issues. Fourth, it also allows them better control over their message and to develop a more authentic and consumer-focused brand.[58]

While it is unclear whether digitally native brands will reach the scale and success of traditional brands born out of the more traditional consumer packaged goods-type brand system, some key statistics point to their success.[59] Digital native brands are quicker to open new stores than traditional brands. For example, within 10 years of being in business Warby Parker had 61 stores relative to Nike, which had just one in a comparable period of its first 10 years. Digital native brands are not as profitable or independent as traditional brands; however, because of access to larger amounts of venture capital funding, digital native brands reach $100 million in sales faster than their predecessors or more traditional brands.[60]

A related trend is that a number of digital native brands have extended into brick-and-mortar stores. Rather than treating these stores as opportunities to sell to customers, the stores typically are inventory-free, but they serve to showcase the product offerings. In some cases, the store can customize the product to individual customers' needs and wants (as we describe in the upcoming Warby Parker example), which further strengthens customer engagement with the brand. Even when there is in-store selling involved, the process is much simpler, with sales people who are equipped with mobile checkout tools to make the experience more seamless. We next present an in-depth analysis of Warby Parker.

Warby Parker: The Future Is So Bright

Warby Parker is a manufacturer and retailer of eyeglasses, sunglasses, and gift cards. It was incorporated in 2009, and is based in New York City. It has showrooms in California, Florida, Georgia, Illinois, Louisiana, Massachusetts, New York, Oklahoma, Pennsylvania, Tennessee, Texas, and Virginia.[61] As of 2018, Warby Parker had a total revenue of $30.2 million and employed 679 personnel globally. Its founders (and co-CEOs) Neil Blumenthal and David Gilboa, along with cofounders Andrew Hunt and Jeffrey Raider, took a simple idea to create among the fastest-growing digital brands in the world. How did they do it?

The concept for Warby Parker began when one of the founders lost a pair of $700 glasses, and this personal experience led the founders to question why eyeglasses were so expensive, and why (at the time of its founding) they were not available online. Warby Parker (whose name was based on the characters from unpublished Jack Kerouac writings) is based on the simple premise that you could have eyeglasses ordered online and delivered to your doorstep.[62] Eyeglasses from Warby Parker typically cost $95, and the company donates one pair as a charitable donation for each pair sold. Within a year of their launch, the company had sold 20,000 pairs, far exceeding their sales target for the year, and suggested that the company had hit upon a winning product in the marketplace.

The eyewear industry is traditionally dominated by offline retailers, and many of the brands offered within retail outlets are owned by the offline company Luxottica. Luxottica owned many leading brand names in the eyewear industry including Oakley, Ray-Ban, and the Luxottica brand.[63] Luxottica also owned the major retail outlets of LensCrafters, Pearle Vision, and Sunglass Hut. In addition, Luxottica licensed various brand names, such as Anne Klein, Chanel, Ralph Lauren, and Coach eyewear. Due to a merger with Essilor, EssilorLuxottica's combined revenue in 2016 was $16 billion and a valuation of $50 billion. Taken together, Luxottica is a formidable competitor with a dominant presence in the industry.[64] How did Warby Parker manage to establish itself as a credible alternative to traditional brands sold by the industry leader Luxottica?

Warby Parker—a digital native brand—established itself as a credible lifestyle brand and an alternative to traditional eyewear companies within a relatively short period of time.

Against this background of a dominant competitor, and high prices for eyeglasses, Warby Parker positioned itself as a lifestyle brand, with unique product offerings suited to the tastes of the millennial generation, an appealing price point, and exceptional customer service. The brand enables customers to try on glasses virtually, and customer service personnel are available to provide feedback on how the glasses look. It also gives the customer the option of ordering up to five pairs they can try on at home, and choose the one they like best. The brand also differentiated itself by incorporating a broader purpose and social mission. Additionally, the company leveraged the power of social media and online social influencers to generate word-of-mouth. A number of buzz-worthy events allowed Warby Parker to become well-known, such as its participation in New York's Fashion Week, when it invited models to the New York Public Library and had them wear Warby Parker's glasses. Warby Parker also understood the importance of customer service early on and paid careful attention to customer issues. In addition to its online presence, Warby Parker slowly expanded their physical presence. Warby Parker's physical retail outlets have an appealing ambiance, customizing capabilities in-store, and well-trained salespeople, all of which make these locations excellent complements to their Web site.

Finally, one further key to success of DNVB's is the focus on hiring and training of the right kind of employees. This investment in employees is critical given that DNVBs employees are in many cases directly interacting with consumers. For example, another digital native brand called Bonobos is focused on custom-fit clothing for men.[65] The company has outstanding service but credits its people-centric culture for its success. The founder and CEO, Andy Dunn, helped create a unique corporate culture, which was youthful and energetic, and hired employees that were empathetic, self-aware, and filled with positive energy. The rationale for their employee-centric culture is summarized by their CEO Andy Dunn as follows: "If your team loves the brand, there's a good chance that your customers will love the brand, because people don't want to work on something that they're not proud of. That's where that culture becomes really precious."[66] Bonobos has made employee satisfaction a key focus area and has created a "Chief People Officer" to improve teamwork and leadership among its employees.

Given the appeal and success of digital native brands such as Warby Parker and Bonobos, it is likely that the future will belong to digital native brands. According to David Bell, the founders' former marketing professor at Wharton Business School, "If you went to your kitchen, your bedroom, your bathroom, your living room, and you went through all the stuff that was in there—it could all be Warby-ed."[67]

More broadly, branding has become part of the everyday vernacular and it is not uncommon to hear people of all walks of life talk about branding and branding concepts. Although the interest in branding has many positive consequences, people don't always seem to understand how branding works or apply branding concepts correctly. This is particularly true, given the changes taking place with the growth of digital marketing and social media marketing. For branding success, an appreciation of and aptitude for using appropriate branding concepts—a focus of this book—is critical.

NOTES

1. For general background and in-depth research on a number of branding issues, consult the *Journal of Brand Management* and *Journal of Brand Strategy*, Henry Stewart publications.
2. Interbrand Group, *World's Greatest Brands: An International Review* (New York: John Wiley, 1992).
3. Adrian Room, *Dictionary of Trade Greatest Brands: An International Review* (New York: John Wiley, 1992); Adrian Room, *Dictionary of Trade Name Origins* (London: Routledge & Kegan Paul, 1982).
4. The second through fifth levels are based on a conceptualization in Theodore Levitt, "Marketing Success Through Differentiation—of Anything," *Harvard Business Review* (January–February 1980): 83–91.
5. Theodore Levitt, "Marketing Myopia," *Harvard Business Review* (July–August 1960): 45–56.
6. Drake Baer, "Timeless Branding Lessons From A Young Steve Jobs," *Fast Company*, August 12, 2013, https://www.fastcompany.com/3015526/timeless-branding-lessons-from-a-young-steve-jobs.
7. Thomas J. Madden, Frank Fehle, and Susan M. Fournier, "Brands Matter: An Empirical Demonstration of the Creation of Shareholder Value through Brands," *Journal of the Academy of Marketing Science* 34, no. 2 (2006): 224–235; Frank Fehle, Susan M. Fournier, Thomas J. Madden, and David G. Shrider, "Brand Value and Asset Pricing," *Quarterly Journal of Finance & Accounting* 47, no. 1 (2008): 59–82.
8. Jacob Jacoby, Jerry C. Olson, and Rafael Haddock, "Price, Brand Name, and Product Composition Characteristics as Determinants of Perceived Quality," *Journal of Consumer Research* 3, no. 4 (1971): 209–216; Jacob Jacoby, George Syzbillo, and Jacqueline Busato-Sehach, "Information Acquisition Behavior in Brand Choice Situations," *Journal of Marketing Research* 11 (1977): 63–69.
9. Susan Fournier, "Consumers and Their Brands: Developing Relationship Theory in Consumer Research," *Journal of Consumer Research* 24, no. 3 (1997): 343–373.
10. Susan Fournier, "Consumers and Their Brands: Developing Relationship Theory in Consumer Research," *Journal of Consumer Research* 24, no. 3 (1997): 343–373; Aric Rindfleisch, Nancy Wong, and James E. Burroughs, "God and Mammon: The Influence of Religiosity on Brand Connections," in *The Connected Customer: The Changing Nature of Consumer and Business Markets*, eds. Stefan H. K. Wuyts, Marnik G. Dekimpe, Els Gijsbrechts, and Rik Pieters (Mahwah, NJ: Lawrence Erlbaum, 2010), 163–201; Ron Shachar, Tülin Erdem, Keisha M. Cutright, and Gavan J. Fitzsimons, "Brands: The Opiate of the Nonreligious Masses?," *Marketing Science* 30 (January–February 2011): 92–110.
11. For an excellent example of the work being done on culture and branding, consult the following: Grant McCracken, *Culture and Consumption II: Markets, Meaning and Brand Management* (Bloomington, IN: Indiana University Press, 2005) and Grant McCracken, *Chief Culture Officer: How to Create a Living, Breathing Corporation* (New York: Basic Books, 2009). For a broader discussion of culture and consumer behavior, see Eric J. Arnould and Craig J. Thompson, "Consumer Culture Theory (CCT): Twenty Years of Research," *Journal of Consumer Research* 31 (March 2005): 868–882.
12. Philip Nelson, "Information and Consumer Behavior," *Journal of Political Economy* 78 (1970): 311–329; and Michael R. Darby and Edi Karni, "Free Competition and the Optimal Amount of Fraud," *Journal of Law and Economics* 16 (April 1974): 67–88.
13. Allan D. Shocker and Richard Chay, "How Marketing Researchers Can Harness the Power of Brand Equity." Presentation to New Zealand Marketing Research Society, August 1992.
14. Ted Roselius, "Consumer Ranking of Risk Reduction Methods," *Journal of Marketing* 35 (January 1971): 56–61.
15. Leslie de Chernatony and Gil McWilliam, "The Varying Nature of Brands as Assets," *International Journal of Advertising* 8 (1989): 339–349.
16. Constance E. Bagley and Diane W. Savage, *Managers and the Legal Environment: Strategies for the 21st Century*, 6th ed. (Mason, OH: Southwestern-Cengage Learning, 2010).
17. Tülin Erdem and Joffre Swait, "Brand Equity as a Signaling Phenomenon," *Journal of Consumer Psychology* 7, no. 2 (1998): 131–157.
18. Charles Bymer, "Valuing Your Brands: Lessons from Wall Street and the Impact on Marketers," ARF Third Annual Advertising and Promotion Workshop, February 5–6, 1991.
19. Elisabeth Sullivan, "Building a Better Brand," *Marketing News* 15 (September 2009): 14–17.
20. "Total Store Brand Dollar Sales Volume in the United States from 2013 to 2016 (in billion U.S. dollars)," Statista, accessed April 7, 2018, www.statista.com/statistics/627597/total-store-brand-dollar-sales-in-the-us/.

21. Stewart Hodgson (2017), "Quintessentially British brands: It's not just branding, it's Marks & Spencer branding," November 30, 2017, http://fabrikbrands.com/marks-and-spencer-branding/, accessed September 26, 2019.

22. Leigh Gallagher, "The Education of Brian Chesky," *Fortune*, June 26, 2015, http://fortune.com/brian-chesky-airbnb, accessed October 21, 2018; Robert Safian, "What Airbnb Has Discovered About Building A Lasting Brand," *Fast Company*, April 18, 2017, https://www.fastcompany.com/40407506/what-airbnb-has-discovered-about-building-a-lasting-brand, accessed October 21, 2018.

23. Jarom McDonald, "How Airbnb and Apple Build Their Brands with Storytelling Marketing," *Lucidpress*, February 17, 2016, www.lucidpress.com/blog/how-airbnb-and-apple-use-storytelling-marketing-to-build-their-brands.

24. David Lidsky, "Me Inc.: the Rethink," *Fast Company*, March 2005, 16.

25. "Lady Gaga," Profile, Forbes, www.forbes.com/profile/lady-gaga/, accessed October 21, 2018.

26. Denise Lee Yohn, "Lady Gaga Is Still Schooling Marketers," *Forbes*, July 15, 2014, www.forbes.com/sites/deniselyohn/2014/07/16/lady-gaga-is-still-schooling-marketers/#6ed46d6e7c29.

27. Marci Robin, "Lady Gaga Is Launching Her Own Makeup Brand, Called 'Haus Beauty'," *Allure*, May 9, 2018, www.allure.com/story/lady-gaga-makeup-brand-haus-beauty.

28. Shira Karsen, "Lady Gaga's Newest Venture Is Four-Legged Friendly," *Billboard*, May 28, 2015, www.billboard.com/articles/columns/pop-shop/6582885/lady-gaga-pet-products-miss-asia-kinney-dog.

29. University professors are certainly aware of the power of the name as a brand. In fact, one reason many professors choose to have students identify themselves on exams by numbers of some type instead of by name is so they will not be biased in grading by their knowledge of which student's exam they are reading. Otherwise, it may be too easy to give higher grades to those students the professor likes or, for whatever reason, expects to have done well on the exam.

30. UNICEF, www.unicef.org; Ariel Schwartz, "The UNICEF TAP Project Charges Cash for Tap Water to Raise Funds, Awareness," *Fast Company*, March 22, 2011; "UNICEF Aims to 'Put It Right' with a Five-Year Plan to Raise £55m," *Mail Media Centre*, February 6, 2010; Rosie Baker, "UNICEF Brings Campaign to London Streets," *Marketing Week*, February 15, 2010; IKEA, www.ikea.com.

31. "IKEA & IKEA Foundation, UNICEF and Partners Launch the 'Let's Play for Change' Initiative for Children," *Unicef*, November 17, 2016, www.unicef.org/corporate_partners/index_93336.html.

32. Joel Hochberg, "Package Goods Marketing vs. Hollywood," *Advertising Age*, January 20, 1992.

33. Katie Meyer, "Harry Potter's $25 Billion Magic Spell," *Time*, April 6, 2016, http://time.com/money/4279432/billion-dollar-spell-harry-potter/, accessed October 21, 2018; Nick Wells and MarkFahey, "Harry Potter and the $25 Billion Franchise," *CNBC*, October 13, 2016, www.cnbc.com/2016/10/13/harry-potter-and-the-25-billion-franchise.html.

34. For an illuminating analysis of top brands, see Francis J. Kelley III and Barry Silverstein, *The Breakaway Brand: How Great Brands Stand Out* (New York; McGraw-Hill, 2005).

35. Allan D. Shocker, Rajendra Srivastava, and Robert Ruekert, "Challenges and Opportunities Facing Brand Management: An Introduction to the Special Issue," *Journal of Marketing Research* 31, no. 2 (May 1994): 149–158.

36. John Deignton and Leora Kornfeld, "Interactivity's Unanticipated Consequences for Marketers and Marketing." *Journal of Interactive Marketing* 23, no. 1 (2009): 4–10.

37. Steve Lohr, "Museums Morph Digitally," *The New York Times*, October 26, 2014, www.nytimes.com/2014/10/26/arts/artsspecial/the-met-and-other-museums-adapt-to-the-digital-age.html.

38. Martin Hirt and Paul Willmott, "Strategic Principles for Competing in the Digital Age," *McKinsey Quarterly*, May 2014, www.mckinsey.com/business-functions/strategy-and-corporate-finance/our-insights/strategic-principles-for-competing-in-the-digital-age.

39. The Times Editorial Board, "Facebook Finally Steps Up on Privacy. Now It's Congress's Turn," *Los Angeles Times*, April 8, 2018, www.latimes.com/opinion/editorials/la-ed-facebook-privacy-rights-20180406-story.html.

40. Martin Hirt and Paul Willmott (2014), "Strategic principles for competing in the digital age," https://www.mckinsey.com/business-functions/strategy-and-corporate-finance/our-insights/strategic-principles-for-competing-in-the-digital-age.

41. Itamar Simonson and Emanuel Rosen, *Absolute Value: What Really Influences Customers in the Age of (Nearly) Perfect Information* (New York: Harper Collins, 2014).

42. Ronnie Phillips, "Rock and Roll Fantasy?: The Reality of Going from Garage Band to Superstardom" (Berlin: *Springer Science & Business Media*). *ISBN 9781461459002*; Randy R. Grant, John C. Leadley, and Zenon X. Zygmont *The Economics of Intercollegiate Sports* (Singapore: World Scientific Publishing Co Inc.). *ISBN 9789814583398*.

43. Jagdish Sheth and Rajendra Sisodia. *The Rule of Three: Surviving and Thriving in Competitive Markets* (New York: Simon and Schuster, 2002).

44. Dan Sewell, "Procter & Gamble Moves from Soap Operas to Social Media," *USA Today*, December 11, 2010.

45. "Nutritional FAQs," LaCroix, accessed April 29, 2018, www.lacroixwater.com/nutritional-faqs/.

46. "Meridan Success Story: 8, LaCroix," Meridian Associates Inc., accessed April 29, 2018, www.meridianai.com/success_product_lacroix.html.

47. Mike Esterl, "LaCroix Bubbles Up in Sparkling Water Brand Competition," *The Wall Street Journal*, April 7, 2016, www.wsj.com/articles/lacroix-bubbles-up-in-sparkling-water-brand-competition-1460047940.

48. Tanya Dua, "The LaCroix Guide to Tapping 'Micro-influencers'," *Digiday*, May 18, 2016, https://digiday.com/marketing/the-lacroix-guide-micro-influencers/.

49. Ibid.

50. Ibid.

51. Jem Aswad, "Single Michael Jackson Glove Sold for over $300K," *Rolling Stone*, December 6, 2010; Jerry Garrett, "Putting a Price on Star Power," *The New York*

Times, January 28, 2011; Christies, www.christies.com; For an academic treatment of the topic, see George E. Newman, Gil Diesendruck, and Paul Bloom, "Celebrity Contagion and the Value of Objects," *Journal of Consumer Research* 38 (August 2011): 215–228.

52. For discussion of some other approaches to branding, see David A. Aaker, *Managing Brand Equity* (New York: Free Press, 1991); David A. Aaker, *Building Strong Brands* (New York: Free Press, 1996); David A. Aaker and Erich Joachimsthaler, *Brand Leadership* (New York: Free Press, 2000); Jean-Noel Kapferer, *Strategic Brand Management,* 2nd ed. (New York: Free Press, 2005); Scott M. Davis, *Brand Asset Management* (New York: Free Press, 2000); Giep Franzen and Sandra Moriarty, *The Science and Art of Branding* (Armonk, NY: M. E. Sharpe, 2009). For an overview of current research findings, see *Brands and Brand Management: Contemporary Research Perspectives,* eds. Barbara Loken, Rohini Ahluwalia, and Michael J. Houston (New York: Taylor and Francis, 2010) and *Kellogg on Branding,* eds. Alice M. Tybout and Tim Calkins (Hoboken, NJ: John Wiley & Sons, 2005).

53. For a very practical brand-building guide, see David Taylor and David Nichols, *The Brand Gym,* 2nd ed. (West Sussex, UK: John Wiley & Sons, 2010).

54. Juliet Carnoy, "The Rise of the Digitally Native Vertical Brand," *The Huffington Post,* February 28, 2017, www.huffingtonpost.com/entry/the-rise-of-the-digitally-native-vertical-brand_us_58b4c830e4b0658fc20f9965.

55. Daniel Keyes, "E-Commerce Will Make Up 17% of All U.S. Retail Sales by 2022-And One Company Is The Main Reason." *Business Insider,* August 11, 2017, www.businessinsider.com/e-commerce-retail-sales-2022-amazon-2017-8.

56. "The Top 25 Digitally Native Vertical Brands 2017," ANA, accessed May 17, 2018, www.ana.net/getfile/24698.

57. "A Guide to Building Digitally Native Vertical Brands," *TechStyle Fashion Group,* January 5, 2018, https://techstylefashiongroup.com/guide-building-digitally-native-vertical-brands/.

58. Tom Foster, "Over 400 Startups Are Trying to Become the Next Warby Parker. Inside the Wild Race to Overthrow Every Consumer Category," *Inc. Magazine,* May 2018, www.inc.com/magazine/201805/tom-foster/direct-consumer-brands-middleman-warby-parker.html.

59. Richie Siegel, "Will the Digitally Native Brand Building Playbook Produce Results?," *Business of Fashion,* November 29, 2017, www.businessoffashion.com/articles/opinion/op-ed-will-the-digital native-brand-building-playbook-produce-results.

60. Ibid.

61. Capital IQ, www.capitalIQ.com.

62. "A Guide to Building Digitally Native Vertical Brands," *TechStyle Fashion Group,* January 5, 2018, https://techstylefashiongroup.com/guide-building-digitally-native-vertical-brands/.

63. Ana Gotter, "What Your Brand Can Learn from Warby Parker's Massive Success," *Pixlee,* www.pixlee.com/blog/what-your-brand-can-learn-from-warby-parkers-massive-success/; Claire Cain Miller, "Defying Conventional Wisdom to Sell Glasses Online," *The New York Times,* January 16, 2011, www.nytimes.com/2011/01/17/technology/17glasses.html.

64. Chad Bray and Elizabeth Paton, "Luxottica, Owner of Ray-Ban, in $49 Billion Merger With Essilor," *The New York Times,* January 16, 2017, www.nytimes.com/2017/01/16/business/dealbook/luxottica-essilor-merger.html.

65. Barbara Thau, "Why a Store You've Likely Never Heard of Hints at Retail's Future," *Forbes,* July 8, 2015, www.forbes.com/sites/barbarathau/2015/07/08/bonobos/#370a6528359b.

66. Sarah Lawson, "Bonobos Just Hired a New Chief People Officer to Scale Company Culture," *Fast Company,* September 25, 2015, www.fastcompany.com/3051429/bonobos-just-hired-a-new-chief-people-officer-to-scale-company-culture.

67. Tom Foster, "Over 400 Startups Are Trying to Become the Next Warby Parker. Inside the Wild Race to Overthrow Every Consumer Category," *Inc. Magazine,* May 2018, www.inc.com/magazine/201805/tom-foster/direct-consumer-brands-middleman-warby-parker.html.

Customer-Based Brand Equity and Brand Positioning

2

Learning Objectives

After reading this chapter, you should be able to

1. Define customer-based brand equity.
2. Outline the sources and outcomes of customer-based brand equity.
3. Identify the four components of brand positioning.
4. Describe the guidelines in developing a good brand positioning.
5. Explain brand mantras and how they should be developed.

Starbucks' unique brand positioning helped to fuel its phenomenal growth.
Source: AP Photo/Ted S. Warren

PREVIEW

Chapter 1 introduced some basic notions about brands, particularly brand equity, and the roles they play in marketing strategies. Part II of the text explores how to develop brand strategies. Great brands are not accidents. They are a result of thoughtful and imaginative planning. Anyone building or managing a brand must carefully develop and implement creative brand strategies.

To aid in that planning, three tools or models are helpful. Like the famous Russian nesting *matryoshka* dolls, the three models are interconnected and, in turn, become larger in scope: the first model is a component in the second model; the second model, in turn, is a component in the third. Combined, the three models provide crucial micro and macro perspectives on successful brand building. These are the three models:

1. *Brand positioning model* describes how to establish competitive advantages in the minds of customers in the marketplace;
2. *Brand resonance model* describes how to take these competitive advantages and create intense, active, loyalty relationships with customers for brands; and
3. *Brand value chain model* describes how to trace the value creation process to better understand the financial impact of marketing expenditures and investments to create loyal customers and strong brands.

Collectively, these three models help marketers devise branding strategies and tactics to maximize profits and long-term brand equity and track their progress along the way. This chapter develops the brand positioning model; Chapter 3 reviews the brand resonance and brand value chain models.

This chapter begins, however, by more formally examining the brand equity concept, introducing one particular view—the concept of customer-based brand equity—that will serve as a useful organizing framework for the rest of the book.[1] We will consider the sources of customer-based brand equity to provide the groundwork for our discussion of brand positioning.

Positioning requires defining our desired or ideal brand knowledge structures and establishing points-of-parity and points-of-difference to establish the right brand identity and brand image. Unique, meaningful points-of-difference (PODs) provide a competitive advantage and the "reason why" consumers should buy the brand. On the other hand, some brand associations can be roughly as favorable as those of competing brands, so they function as points-of-parity (POPs) in consumers' minds—and negate potential points-of-difference for competitors. In other words, these associations are designed to provide "no reason why not" for consumers to choose the brand.

The chapter then reviews how to identify and establish brand positioning and create a brand mantra, a shorthand expression of the positioning.[2] We conclude with Brand Focus 2.0 and an examination of the many benefits of creating a strong brand.

CUSTOMER-BASED BRAND EQUITY

Two questions often arise in brand marketing: What makes a brand strong? How do you build a strong brand? To help answer both, we introduce the concept of customer-based brand equity (CBBE). Although a number of useful perspectives concerning brand equity have been put forth, the CBBE concept provides a unique point of view on what brand equity is and how it should best be built, measured, and managed.

Defining Customer-Based Brand Equity

The CBBE concept approaches brand equity from the perspective of the consumer—whether the consumer is an individual or an organization, or an existing or prospective customer. Understanding the needs and wants of consumers and organizations and devising products and programs to satisfy them are at the heart of successful marketing. In particular, marketers face two fundamentally important questions: What do different brands mean to consumers? How does the brand knowledge of consumers affect their response to marketing activity?

The basic premise of the CBBE concept is that the power of a brand lies in what customers have learned, felt, seen, and heard about the brand as a result of their experiences over time. In other words, the power of a brand lies in what resides in the minds and hearts of customers. The challenge for marketers in building a strong brand is ensuring that customers have the right type of experiences with products and services and their accompanying marketing programs so that the desired thoughts, feelings, images, beliefs, perceptions, opinions, and experiences become linked to the brand.

We formally define *customer-based brand equity* as the differential effect that brand knowledge has on customer response to the marketing of that brand. A brand has positive customer-based brand equity when customers react more favorably to a product and the way it is marketed when the brand is identified than when it is not (say, when the product is attributed to a fictitious name or is unnamed). Thus, customers might be more accepting of a new brand extension for a brand with positive customer-based brand equity, less sensitive to price increases and withdrawal of advertising support, or more willing to seek the brand in a new distribution channel. On the other hand, a brand has negative customer-based brand equity if customers react less favorably to marketing activity for the brand compared with an unnamed or fictitiously named version of the product.

Let's look at the three key ingredients to this definition: (1) "differential effect," (2) "brand knowledge," and (3) "customer response to marketing." First, brand equity arises from differences in customer response. If no differences occur, then the brand-name product can essentially be classified as a commodity or a generic version of the product. Competition, most likely, would then just be based on price. Second, these differences in response are a result of customer knowledge about the brand, that is, what they have learned, felt, seen, and heard about the brand as a result of their experiences over time. Thus, although strongly influenced by the marketing activity of the firm, brand equity ultimately depends on what resides in the minds and hearts of existing and prospective customers. Third, customers' differential responses, which make up brand equity, are reflected in perceptions, preferences, and behavior related to all aspects of brand marketing—for example, including choice of a brand, recall of copy points from an ad, response to a sales promotion, and evaluations of a proposed brand extension. Brand Focus 2.0 provides a detailed account of these advantages, as summarized in Figure 2-1.

The simplest way to illustrate what we mean by customer-based brand equity is to consider one of the typical results of product sampling or comparison tests. In blind taste tests, two groups of individuals sample a product: one group knows which brand it is, the other doesn't. Invariably, the two groups have different opinions despite consuming the same product.

When consumers report different opinions about branded and unbranded versions of identical products—which almost invariably happens—it must be the case that knowledge about the brand, created by whatever means (past experiences, marketing activity for the brand, or word of mouth), has somehow changed customers' product perceptions. This result has occurred with virtually every type of product—conclusive evidence that customer perceptions of product performance are highly dependent on their impressions of the brand that goes along with it. In other words, clothes may seem to fit better, a car may seem to drive more smoothly, and the wait in a bank line may seem shorter, depending on the particular brand involved.

Brand Equity as a Bridge

Thus, according to the customer-based brand equity concept, consumer knowledge drives the differences that manifest themselves in terms of brand equity. This realization has important managerial implications. For one thing, brand equity provides marketers with a vital strategic bridge from their past to their future.

Improved perceptions of product performance
Greater loyalty
Less vulnerability to competitive marketing actions
Less vulnerability to marketing crises
Larger margins
More inelastic consumer response to price increases
More elastic consumer response to price decreases
Greater trade cooperation and support
Increased marketing communication effectiveness
Possible licensing opportunities
Additional brand extension opportunities

FIGURE 2-1

Marketing Advantages
of Strong Brands

Brands as a Reflection of the Past.   Marketers should consider all the dollars spent on manufacturing and marketing products each year not so much as expenses but as investments in what consumers saw, heard, learned, felt, and experienced about the brand. If not properly designed and implemented, these expenditures may not be good investments, in that they may not have created the right knowledge structures in consumers' minds, but we should consider them investments nonetheless.

Thus, the *quality* of the investment in brand building is the most critical factor, not the *quantity* beyond some minimal threshold amount. In fact, it is possible to overspend on brand building if money is not being spent wisely. Conversely, as we will see throughout the book, some brands are considerably outspent but amass a great deal of brand equity through marketing activities that create valuable, enduring memory traces in the minds of consumers, as has been the case with Netflix.

NETFLIX

From a DVD mailing business to producing top-notch original content and streaming services across devices, Netflix is competing with major studios and is now focusing its marketing activities around getting consumers to watch its growing portfolio of original content.[3] Netflix has adopted a few marketing strategies that have been key to its success. Netflix's ability to identify and understand customers' needs is a distinct capability that Netflix has leveraged effectively. In order to deliver original programming, Netflix tracks when, how, and what content or programming consumers like to watch, which then allows them to create new content that is explicitly tailored to consumers' tastes and behaviors. Its success with original hit shows such as *Black Mirror* and *Stranger Things* can be attributed, in part, to the firm's ability to use technology in novel ways to promote the shows and engage with the audience. For example, to promote *Stranger Things*, it created an app which allowed users to create content using a web tool. Likewise, the company used an app called RateMe to accompany the show *Black Mirror*. It is no wonder that Netflix is hugely successful, and at the close of 2016, had 93.8 million subscribers, adding 20 million in 2016 alone. Netflix has developed such a strong relationship with its customers that the brand name has become a verb—the phrase "Netflix Binge" has become part of the national vocabulary, to refer to binge-watching on Netflix.

Binge-watching on Netflix has become a popular entertainment pastime, and "Netflix binge" has become a part of our everyday vocabulary.

Brands as a Direction for the Future.   The brand knowledge that marketers create over time dictates appropriate and inappropriate future directions for the brand. Consumers will decide, based on their brand knowledge, where they think the brand should go and grant permission (or not) to any marketing action or program. Thus, the true value and future prospects of a brand rest with consumers and their knowledge about the brand.

No matter how we define brand equity, though, its value to marketers as a concept ultimately depends on how they use it. Brand equity can offer focus and guidance, providing a means to interpret past marketing performance and design future marketing programs. Everything the firm does can either enhance or detract from brand equity. Those marketers who build strong brands have embraced the concept and use it to its fullest as a means of clarifying, communicating, and implementing their marketing actions.

DISCOVERY CHANNEL

The Discovery Channel was launched with the motto "Explore Your World" and well-defined brand values of adventure, exploration, science, and curiosity. After a detour to reality programming featuring crime and forensics shows and biker and car content, the channel returned to its mission of producing high-quality work that the company could be proud of and that was beneficial for people and sustainability of the environment.[4] The Discovery Channel is seen as a dominant cable channel (ranked in the top five cable channels within the United States), with popular shows such as *Shark Week, MythBusters, and Gold Rush,* with a particular appeal to certain segments of consumers (e.g., men aged 35–54).[5] In another effort to strengthen its relationships with its customers, and to reaffirm the brand's commitment to the environment, Discovery leveraged the power of its popular show *Shark Week*—an annual show dedicated to sharks—to advocate for donations to an ocean conversation organization called Oceana.[6] Today, the Discovery Channel cumulatively reaches 94 million households within the United States.[7] Internationally, the Discovery Channel has more than 3 billion global cumulative viewers in more than 220 countries and territories.[8]

Other factors can influence brand success, and brand equity has meaning for other constituents besides customers, such as employees, suppliers, channel members, media, and the government.[9] Nevertheless, success with customers is often crucial for success for the firm, so the next section considers brand knowledge and CBBE in more detail.

MAKING A BRAND STRONG: BRAND KNOWLEDGE

From the perspective of the CBBE concept, brand knowledge is the key to creating brand equity, because it creates the differential effect that drives brand equity. What marketers need, then, is an insightful way to represent how brand knowledge exists in consumer memory. An influential model of memory developed by psychologists is helpful for this purpose.[10]

The ***associative network memory model*** views memory as a network of nodes and connecting links, in which nodes represent stored information or concepts, and links represent the strength of association between the nodes. Any type of information—whether it is verbal, abstract, or contextual—can be stored in the memory network.

Using the associative network memory model, let's think of brand knowledge as consisting of a brand node in memory with a variety of associations linked to it. Brand knowledge has two components: brand awareness and brand image. ***Brand awareness*** is related to the strength of the brand node or trace in memory, which we can measure as the consumer's ability to identify the brand under different conditions.[11] It is a necessary, but not always a sufficient, step in building brand equity. Other considerations, such as the image of the brand, often come into play.

Brand image has long been recognized as an important concept in marketing.[12] Although marketers have not always agreed about how to measure it, one generally accepted view is that, consistent with our associative network memory model, ***brand image*** is consumers' perceptions about a brand, as reflected by the brand associations held in consumer memory.[13] In other words, brand associations are the other informational nodes linked to the brand node in memory and contain the meaning of the brand for consumers. Associations come in all forms and may reflect characteristics of the product or aspects independent of the product.

For example, if someone asked you what came to mind when you thought of the Apple brand, what would you say? You might reply with associations such as well-designed, easy to use, leading-edge technology, and so forth. Figure 2-2 displays some commonly mentioned associations for Apple that consumers have expressed in the past.[14] The associations that came to *your* mind make up your brand image for Apple. Through breakthrough products and skillful marketing, Apple has been able to achieve a rich brand image made up of a host of brand associations. Many are likely to be shared by a majority of consumers, so we can refer to *the* brand image of Apple, but at the same time, we recognize that this image varies, perhaps even considerably, depending on the consumer or market segment.

Other brands, of course, carry a different set of associations. For example, McDonald's marketing program attempts to create brand associations in consumers' minds between its products and quality, service, cleanliness, and value. McDonald's rich brand image probably also includes strong associations to Ronald McDonald, golden arches, for kids, and convenient—as well as perhaps

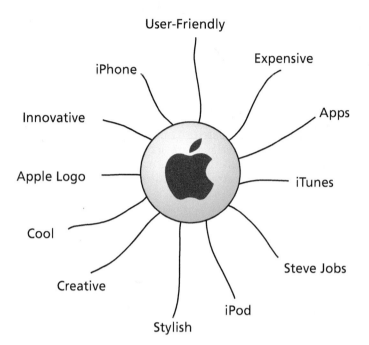

FIGURE 2-2

Possible Associations with the Apple Brand Name

Source: Staff/MCT/News-com; Hyoryung Nam, Yogesh V. Joshi, and P. K. Kannan, "Harvesting Brand Information from Social Tags," *Journal of Marketing* 81, no. 4 (2017): 88–108.

potentially negative associations, such as fast food. Whereas Mercedes-Benz has achieved strong associations to performance and status, Volvo has created a strong association to safety. We'll return in later chapters to the different types of associations and how to measure their strength.

SOURCES OF BRAND EQUITY

What causes brand equity to exist? How do marketers create it? Customer-based brand equity occurs when the consumer has a high level of awareness and familiarity with the brand and holds some strong, favorable, and unique brand associations in memory. In some cases, brand awareness alone is enough to create favorable consumer response, for example, in low-involvement decisions when consumers are willing to base their choices on mere familiarity. In most other cases, however, the strength, favorability, and uniqueness of brand associations play a critical role in determining the differential response that makes up brand equity. If customers perceive the brand as only representative of the product or service category, then they will respond as if the offering were unbranded.

Thus, marketers must also convince consumers that there are meaningful differences among brands. Consumers must not think all brands in the category are the same. Establishing a positive brand image in consumer memory—strong, favorable, and unique brand associations—goes hand-in-hand with creating brand awareness to build customer-based brand equity. Let's look at both these sources of brand equity.

Brand Awareness

Brand awareness consists of brand recognition and brand recall performance:

- **Brand recognition** is consumers' ability to confirm prior exposure to the brand when given the brand as a cue. In other words, when they go to the store, will they be able to recognize the brand as one to which they have already been exposed?
- **Brand recall** is consumers' ability to retrieve the brand from memory when given the product category, the needs fulfilled by the category, or a purchase or usage situation as a cue. In other words, consumers' recall of Kellogg's Corn Flakes will depend on their ability to retrieve the brand when they think of the cereal category or of what they should eat for breakfast or a snack, whether at the store when making a purchase or at home when deciding what to eat.

Research reveals that many consumer decisions are made at the point of sale, where the brand name, logo, packaging, and so on, will be physically present and visible; hence, brand recognition is very important. If consumer decisions are mostly made in settings away from the point of purchase, on the other hand, then brand recall will be more important.[15] For this reason, creating brand recall is critical for service and online brands: Consumers must actively seek the brand and therefore be able to retrieve it from memory when appropriate.

Note, however, that even though brand recall may be less important at the point of purchase, consumers' brand evaluations and choices will still often depend on what else they recall about the brand given that they are able to recognize it there. As is the case with most information in memory, we are generally more adept at recognizing a brand than at recalling it.

Advantages of Brand Awareness.   What are the benefits of creating a high level of brand awareness? There are three—learning advantages, consideration advantages, and choice advantages.

Learning Advantages.   Brand awareness influences the formation and strength of the associations that make up the brand image. To create a brand image, marketers must first establish a brand node in memory, the nature of which affects how easily the consumer learns and stores additional brand associations. The first step in building brand equity is to register the brand in the minds of consumers. If the right brand elements are chosen, the task becomes easier.

Consideration Advantages.   Consumers must consider the brand whenever they are making purchase decisions to fulfill or satisfy a need. Raising brand awareness increases the likelihood that the brand will be a member of the *consideration set*, the handful of brands that receive serious consideration for purchase.[16] Much research has shown that consumers are rarely loyal to only one brand but instead have a set of brands they would consider buying and another—possibly smaller—set of brands they actually buy on a regular basis. Because consumers typically consider only a few brands for purchase, making sure that the brand is in the consideration set also makes other brands less likely to be considered or recalled.[17]

Choice Advantages.   The third advantage of creating a high level of brand awareness is that it can affect choices among brands in the consideration set, even if there are essentially no other associations to those brands.[18] For example, consumers have been shown to adopt a decision rule in some cases to buy only more familiar, well-established brands.[19] Thus, in low-involvement decision settings, a minimum level of brand awareness may be sufficient for product choice, even in the absence of a well-formed attitude.[20]

One influential model of attitude change and persuasion, the elaboration-likelihood model, is consistent with the notion that consumers may make choices based on brand awareness considerations when they have low involvement. Low involvement results when consumers lack either purchase motivation (they don't care about the product or service), purchase ability (they don't know anything else about the brands in a category), or purchase opportunity (they don't have the time or face some other constraint such that they cannot make a more deliberate or thoughtful brand choice).[21]

1. **Consumer purchase motivation:** Although products and brands may be critically important to marketers, choosing a brand in many categories is not a life-or-death decision for most consumers. For example, despite millions of dollars spent in television advertising over the years to persuade consumers of product differences, 40 percent of consumers surveyed believed all brands of gasoline were about the same or did not know which brand was best. A lack of perceived differences among brands in a category is likely to leave consumers unmotivated about the choice process.

2. **Consumer purchase ability:** Consumers in some product categories just do not have the necessary knowledge or experience to judge product quality even if they so desired. The obvious examples are products with a high degree of technical sophistication, like telecommunications equipment with state-of-the-art features. However, consumers may be unable to judge quality even in low-tech categories. Consider the college student who has not really had to cook or clean before, shopping the supermarket aisles in earnest for the first time, or a new manager forced to make an expensive capital purchase for the first time. The reality is that product quality is often highly ambiguous and difficult to judge without a great deal of prior experience and expertise. In such cases, consumers will use whichever shortcut or *heuristic* they can come up with to make their decisions in the best manner possible. Sometimes, they simply choose the brand with which they are most familiar and aware.

3. **Consumer purchase opportunity:** Even if consumers want to make a good brand choice and know enough to be able to do so, they still may not be able to make a highly involved decision because they lack the time, energy, or some other factor necessary to do so. The marketplace itself may present certain barriers to prevent detailed decision-making. For whatever reason, if consumers do not have the opportunity to engage in deliberate, thoughtful evaluation of brand offerings, they may rely on heuristics such as brand awareness to arrive at a brand choice.

Establishing Brand Awareness.   How do you create brand awareness? In the abstract, creating brand awareness means increasing the familiarity of the brand through repeated exposure, although this is generally more effective for brand recognition than for brand recall. That is, the more a consumer experiences the brand by seeing it, hearing it, or thinking about it, the more likely he or she is to strongly register the brand in memory.

Thus, anything that causes consumers to experience one of a brand's element—its name, symbol, logo, character, packaging, or slogan, including advertising and promotion, sponsorship and event marketing, publicity and public relations, and outdoor advertising—can increase familiarity and awareness of that brand element. And the more elements marketers can reinforce, usually the better. For instance, in addition to its name, Intel has used the "Intel

---

E*TRADE

In re-branding E*TRADE, the firm initially ran campaigns featuring the wisecracking E*Trade baby and was known for cheeky marketing. The ads were showcased in high profile media spots during Super Bowl broadcasts between 2008 and 2013. As the brand became more established, E*Trade shifted its strategy and redefined its advertising goals from just developing brand recognition to focusing more on lead generation and on reinforcing loyalty of existing customers.[22] While the baby provided the brand with desirable attributes such as fun, approachability, and likability, it was important to change the advertising to signal the evolution of the brand. They branded themselves as a sober, wiser adviser. E*TRADE was seeking a competitive advantage by building old-fashioned "high touch" relationships, which was ironic as it rose to fame as a technology-driven disruptor. The advertising campaign began to focus on a new type of investor, one who was confident, self-directed and independent or what the brand called a "Type-E" customer.[23] Today, E*TRADE's advertisements began to downplay the jokes and depicted its customers as cautious planners who leave nothing to chance. As the CEO of E*TRADE puts it: "We want to grow with investors and educate them, help them get smarter. As long as that happens, it's good for the bottom line."[24]

The wisecracking E*TRADE baby featured in humorous television commercials together with advertising placement during Super Bowl games helped to generate a high level of brand awareness for E*TRADE.

Inside" logo and its distinctive symbol as well as its famous four-note jingle in television ads to enhance awareness.

Repetition increases recognizability, but improving brand recall also requires linkages in memory to appropriate product categories or other purchase or consumption cues. A slogan or jingle creatively pairs the brand and the appropriate cues (and, ideally, the brand positioning as well, helping build a positive brand image). Other brand elements like logos, symbols, characters, and packaging can also aid recall.

The way marketers pair the brand and its product category, such as with an advertising slogan, helps to determine the strength of product category links. For brands with strong category associations, like Ford cars, the distinction between brand recognition and recall may not matter much—consumers thinking of the category are likely to think of the brand. In competitive markets or when the brand is new to the category, it is more important to emphasize category links in the marketing program. Strong links between the brand and the category or other relevant cues may become especially important over time if the product meaning of the brand changes through brand extensions, mergers, or acquisitions.

ANNIE'S HOMEGROWN

Annie's Homegrown has successfully created a brand image by advertising that its food can help you live the good life. "Choose Good" is the theme across their ads which concludes with "Good can be hard, but Good can also be easy." Annie's stated mission is to make the world healthier and happier through nourishing and healthy foods and by a healthy code of conduct in all that they do and how they treat people and the planet.

Annie's has the second largest market share in the boxed pasta market next only to Kraft. It also has made inroads into various categories such as frozen pizza, crackers, salad dressing, and the condiment market. So, how did Annie's Homegrown carve out a unique position in a market dominated by large corporations such as Kraft? Annie's Homegrown's focus on corporate social responsibility was the right focus at the right time, and it resonated with the shifting consumers' interest in sustainability and corporate social responsibility. Its packaging consisted of faux-handwritten letters from founder Annie Withey and was made of recycled paper.[25] Annie's flavors such as "Organic Peace Pasta & Parmesan," in a tie-dye box, had a unique feel to them. The signature brand character 'Bernie the Bunny' made the brand seem warm and lovable.[26] Their Web site featured 3-minute videos dedicated to American family farms. Thus, in many different ways, Annie's Homegrown married comfort foods with ethical values, which resonated with its consumers, including themes such as supporting small, family farmers and social commitments like college scholarships for students studying sustainable agriculture.

In 2014, Annie's Homegrown was acquired by General Mills for $820 million. Despite its acquisition, Annie's has maintained its positioning and values and has branched out into other product categories (e.g., cereal). Of note is that this acquisition by General Mills is part of a general trend by big food manufacturers—such as Coca-Cola, Kellogg's, and General Mills—of acquiring small brands with healthy, environmentally aware positioning. Following the acquisition, Annie's Homegrown has retained its small but stable market share in the increasingly popular segment of clean, environmentally aware, and healthy foods.[27]

Annie's Homegrown has crafted a special brand image by focusing its positioning on nourishing and healthy foods that can help customers live the good life.

Many marketers have attempted to create brand awareness through so-called shock advertising, using bizarre themes. For example, online retailer Outpost.com used ads featuring gerbils shot from cannons, wolverines attacking marching bands, and preschoolers having the brand name tattooed on their foreheads. The problem with such approaches is that they invariably fail to create strong category links because the product is just not prominent enough in the ad. They also can generate a fair amount of ill will. Often coming across as desperate measures, they rarely provide a foundation for long-term brand equity. In the case of Outpost.com, most potential customers did not have a clue what the company represented.

Brand Image

Creating brand awareness by increasing the familiarity of the brand through repeated exposure (for brand recognition) and forging strong associations with the appropriate product category or other relevant purchase or consumption cues (for brand recall) is an important first step in building brand equity. Once a sufficient level of brand awareness is created, marketers can put more emphasis on crafting a brand image.

Creating a positive brand image takes marketing programs that link strong, favorable, and unique associations to the brand in memory. Brand associations may be either brand attributes or benefits. **Brand attributes** are those descriptive features that characterize a product or service. **Brand benefits** are the personal value and meaning that consumers attach to the product or service attributes.

Consumers form beliefs about brand attributes and benefits in different ways. The definition of customer-based brand equity, however, does not distinguish between the source of brand associations and the manner in which they are formed; all that matters is their strength, favorability, and uniqueness. This means that consumers can form brand associations in a variety of ways other than marketing activities: from direct experience; from online social media; through information from other commercial or nonpartisan sources, such as *Consumer Reports* or other media vehicles; from word of mouth; and by assumptions or inferences consumers make about the brand itself, its name, logo, or identification with a company, country, channel of distribution, or person, place, or event.

Marketers should recognize the influence of these other sources of information by both managing them as well as possible and by adequately accounting for them in designing communication strategies. Consider how Annie's Homegrown originally built its brand equity.

In short, to create the differential response that leads to customer-based brand equity, marketers need to make sure that some strongly held brand associations are not only favorable but also unique and distinct from competing brands. Unique associations help consumers choose the brand. To choose which favorable and unique associations to strongly link to the brand, marketers carefully analyze the consumer and the competition to determine the best positioning for the brand. Let's consider some factors that, in general, affect the strength, favorability, and uniqueness of brand associations.

Strength of Brand Associations.   The more deeply a person thinks about product information and relates it to existing brand knowledge, the stronger the resulting brand associations will be. Two factors that strengthen association to any piece of information are its personal relevance and the consistency with which it is presented over time. The particular associations we recall and their salience will depend not only on the strength of association but also on the retrieval cues present and the context in which we consider the brand.

In general, direct experiences create the strongest brand attribute and benefit associations and are particularly influential in consumers' decisions when they accurately interpret them. Word-of-mouth is likely to be especially important for restaurants, entertainment, banking, and personal services. Starbucks, Google, Red Bull, and Amazon are all classic examples of companies that created amazingly rich brand images without the benefit of intensive advertising programs. Mike's Hard Lemonade sold its first 10 million cases without any advertising because it was a discovery brand fueled by word-of-mouth.[28]

On the other hand, company-influenced sources of information, such as advertising, are often likely to create the weakest associations and, thus, may be the most easily changed. To overcome this hurdle, marketing communication programs use creative communications that cause consumers to elaborate on brand-related information and relate it appropriately to existing knowledge. They expose consumers to communications repeatedly over time and ensure that many retrieval cues are present as reminders.

Favorability of Brand Associations.   Marketers create favorable brand associations by convincing consumers that the brand possesses relevant attributes and benefits that satisfy their needs and wants, such that they form positive overall brand judgments. Consumers will not hold all brand associations to be equally important, nor will they view them all favorably or value them all equally across different purchase or consumption situations. Brand associations may be situation- or context-dependent and vary according to what consumers want to achieve in that purchase or consumption decision.[29] An association may thus be valued in one situation but not another.[30]

For example, the associations that come to mind when consumers think of FedEx may be fast, reliable, and convenient, with purple and orange packages. The color of the packaging may matter little to most consumers when choosing an overnight delivery service, although it may perhaps play an important brand awareness function. Fast, reliable, and convenient service may be more important, but even then, only in certain situations. A consumer who needs delivery only may consider less expensive options, like USPS Priority Mail, which may take one to two days.

Uniqueness of Brand Associations.   The essence of brand positioning is that the brand has a sustainable competitive advantage or unique selling proposition that gives consumers a compelling reason why they should buy it.[31] Marketers can make this unique difference explicit through direct comparisons with competitors, or they may highlight it implicitly. They may base it on performance-related or nonperformance-related attributes or benefits.

Although unique associations are critical to a brand's success, unless the brand faces no competition, it will most likely share some associations with other brands. One function of shared associations is to establish category membership and define the scope of competition with other products and services.[32]

A product or service category can also share a set of associations that include specific beliefs about any member in the category, as well as overall attitudes toward all members of the category. These beliefs might include many of the relevant performance-related attributes for brands in the category, as well as more descriptive attributes that do not necessarily relate to product or service performance, like the color of a product, such as red for ketchup.

Consumers may consider certain attributes or benefits prototypical and essential to all brands in the category, and a specific brand an exemplar and most representative.[33] For example, they might expect a running shoe to provide support and comfort and to be built well enough to withstand repeated wearing, and they may believe that Asics, New Balance, or some other leading brand best represents a running shoe. Similarly, consumers might expect an online retailer to offer easy navigation, a variety of offerings, reasonable shipping options, secure purchase procedures, responsive customer service, and strict privacy guidelines, and they may consider Amazon, Wayfair, or some other market leader to be the best example of an online retailer.

Because the brand is linked to the product category, some category associations may also become linked to the brand, either specific beliefs or overall attitudes. Product category attitudes can be a particularly important determinant of consumer response. For example, if a consumer thinks that all brokerage houses are basically greedy, and that brokers are in it for themselves, then he or she probably will have similarly unfavorable beliefs about and negative attitudes toward any particular brokerage house, simply by virtue of its membership in the category.

Thus, in almost all cases, some product category associations will be shared with all brands in the category. Note that the strength of the brand associations to the product category is an important determinant of brand awareness.[34]

IDENTIFYING AND ESTABLISHING BRAND POSITIONING

Having developed the CBBE concept in some detail as background, we next outline how marketers should approach brand positioning.

Basic Concepts

Brand positioning is at the heart of marketing strategy. It is the "act of designing the company's offer and image so that it occupies a distinct and valued place in the target customer's mind."[35]

As the name implies, positioning means finding the proper location in the minds of a group of consumers or market segment, so that they think about a product or service in the right or desired way to maximize potential benefit to the firm. Good brand positioning helps guide marketing strategy by clarifying what a brand is all about, how it is unique, and how it is similar to competitive brands, and why consumers should purchase and use it.

Deciding on a positioning requires determining a frame of reference (by identifying the target market and the nature of competition) and the optimal points-of-parity and points-of-difference brand associations. In other words, marketers need to know (1) who the target consumer is, (2) who the main competitors are, (3) how the brand is similar to these competitors, and (4) how the brand is different from them. We will talk about each of these.

Target Market

Identifying the consumer target is important because different consumers may have different brand knowledge structures and different perceptions and preferences for the brand. Without this understanding, it may be difficult for marketers to say which brand associations should be strongly held, favorable, and unique. Let's look at defining and segmenting a market and choosing target market segments.

A *market* is the set of all actual and potential buyers who have sufficient interest in, income for, and access to a product. *Market segmentation* divides the market into distinct groups of homogeneous consumers who have similar needs and consumer behavior, and who thus require similar marketing programs and tactics. Market segmentation requires making trade-offs between costs and benefits. The more finely segmented the market, the more likely that the firm will be able to implement marketing programs that meet the needs of consumers in any one segment. That advantage, however, can be offset by the greater costs of reduced standardization.

Segmentation Bases.   Figures 2-3 and 2-4 display some possible segmentation bases for consumer and business-to-business markets, respectively. We can classify these bases as descriptive or customer-oriented (related to what kind of person or organization the customer is) or as behavioral or product-oriented (related to how the customer thinks of or uses the brand or product).

Behavioral segmentation bases are often most valuable in understanding branding issues because they have clearer strategic implications. For example, defining a benefit segment

FIGURE 2-3

Consumer Segmentation Bases

Behavioral
User status
Usage rate
Usage occasion
Brand loyalty
Benefits sought

Demographic
Income
Age
Sex
Race
Family

Psychographic
Values, opinions, and attitudes
Activities and lifestyle

Geographic
International
Regional

FIGURE 2-4

Business-to-Business Segmentation Bases

Nature of Good
Kind
Where used
Type of buy

Buying Condition
Purchase location
Who buys
Type of buy

Demographic
SIC code
Number of employees
Number of production workers
Annual sales volume
Number of establishments

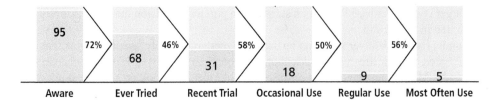

FIGURE 2-5
Hypothetical Examples
of Funnel Stages and
Transitions

makes it clear what should be the ideal point-of-difference or desired benefit with which to establish the positioning. Take the toothpaste market. One research study uncovered four main segments:[36]

1. **The Sensory segment:** Seeking flavor and product appearance
2. **The Sociables:** Seeking brightness of teeth
3. **The Worriers:** Seeking decay prevention
4. **The Independent segment:** Seeking low prices.

Given this market segmentation scheme, marketing programs could be put into place to attract one or more segments. For example, Close-Up initially targeted the first two segments, whereas Crest primarily concentrated on the third. Taking no chances, Aquafresh was introduced to go after all three segments, designing its toothpaste with three stripes to dramatize each of the three product benefits. With the success of multipurpose toothpastes such as Colgate Total, virtually all toothpaste brands now offer products that emphasize multiple performance benefits.

Other segmentation approaches build on brand loyalty in some way. The classic funnel model traces consumer behavior in terms of initial awareness through brand-most-often-used. Figure 2-5 shows a hypothetical pattern of results. For the purposes of brand building, marketers want to understand both (1) the percentage of target market that is present at each stage and (2) factors facilitating or inhibiting the transition from one stage to the next. In the hypothetical example, a key bottleneck appears to be converting those consumers who have never tried the brand to those who recently tried, as less than half (46 percent) "convert." To convince more consumers to consider trying the brand again, marketers may need to raise brand salience or make the brand more acceptable in the target consumer's repertoire.

Marketers often segment consumers by their behavior. For example, a firm may target a certain age group, but the underlying reason is that they are particularly heavy users of the product, are unusually brand loyal, or are most likely to seek the benefit the product is best able to deliver. For example, many credit card companies target specific groups—students, seniors—with particular benefits. Discover credit cards for students offers cash back on purchases made in product categories that will appeal to students such as gas stations, grocery stores, restaurants, and so on. They also offer Good Grades rewards for those who maintain a GPA of 3.0 or higher. Similarly, Barclaycard Arrival Plus is a credit card aimed at seniors who like to travel. Cardholders earn double miles with every purchase made, which can then be applied toward travel expenses.[37]

In some cases, however, broad demographic descriptors may mask important underlying differences.[38] A fairly specific target market of women aged 40 to 54 may contain a number of very different segments who require totally different marketing mixes (think Celine Dion versus Courtney Love). Millennials consist of a variety of different subsegments which can be distinguished based on their attitudes and lifestyles. For example, one study contrasted Pro-Millenials (those aged 22–34) who lived in the New Heartland (midwestern, southwestern, southeastern parts of the United States) and found that there are stark differences between this group and the Coastal Pro-Millenials who live on the east or west coasts of the United States. They have different values and interests and, as such, can be treated as different segments altogether.[39]

The main advantage of demographic segmentation bases is that the demographics of traditional media vehicles are generally well-known from consumer research; as a result, it has been easier to buy media on that basis. Newer ways of profiling customers on behavioral or media usage bases have merged, reducing the emphasis on pure demographic segmentation. Increasingly, it is possible to target consumers based on which stage of the purchase decision they are currently in. This is illustrated in Figure 2-5.

For example, Facebook advertising can be used to hypertarget highly specific targets that are distinguished based on their lifestyles, political orientation, their support of various social causes (e.g., Black Lives Matter), and so on. It was this capability that Facebook provided that allowed Russian bots to target various groups of individuals during the 2016 U.S. presidential election, with various news stories (some of which were considered "fake news") that would be aligned with their stated interests, potentially with a view to influencing their thoughts and perceptions regarding various social issues.

Criteria.   A number of criteria have been offered to guide segmentation and target market decisions, such as the following:[40]

- **Identifiability:** Can we easily identify the segment?
- **Size:** Is there adequate sales potential in the segment?
- **Accessibility:** Are specialized distribution outlets and communication media available to reach the segment?
- **Responsiveness:** How favorably will the segment respond to a tailored marketing program?

The obvious overriding consideration in defining market segments is profitability. In many cases, profitability can be related to behavioral considerations. Developing a segmentation scheme with direct customer lifetime value perspectives can be highly advantageous. To improve the long-term profitability of their customer base, drugstore chain CVS considered the role of beauty products for its customers at three distinct stages of life, producing the following hypothetical profiles or personas:[41]

- Caroline, a single 20-something, is relatively new to her career and still has an active social life. She is an extremely important beauty customer who visits the chain once a week. Her favorite part of shopping is getting new beauty products, and she looks to CVS to help her cultivate her look at a price she can afford.
- Caroline will grow into Vanessa, the soccer mom with three children; she may not be as consumed with fashion as she once was, but preserving her youthful appearance is still a major priority. She squeezes in trips to the store en route to or from work or school, and convenient features such as drive-through pharmacies are paramount for Vanessa.
- Vanessa becomes Sophie. Sophie isn't much of a beauty customer, but she is CVS's most profitable demographic—a regular pharmacy customer who actively shops the front of the store for key OTC items.

CVS Pharmacy may sell different products to multiple segments of customers, and these segments may represent customers who are in varying stages of life.

Nature of Competition

At least implicitly, deciding to target a certain type of consumer often defines the nature of competition, because other firms have also decided to target that segment in the past or plan to do so in the future, or because consumers in that segment already may look to other brands in their purchase decisions. Competition takes place on other bases, of course, such as channels of distribution. Competitive analysis considers a whole host of factors—including the resources, capabilities, and likely intentions of various other firms—in order for marketers to choose markets where consumers can be profitably served.[42]

Indirect Competition.   One lesson stressed by many marketing strategists is not to define competition too narrowly. Research on noncomparable alternatives suggests that even if a brand does not face direct competition in its product category, and does not share performance-related attributes with other brands, it can still share more abstract associations and face indirect competition in a more broadly defined product category.[43]

Competition often occurs at the benefit level rather than the attribute level. Thus, a luxury good with a strong hedonic benefit like stereo equipment may compete as much with a vacation as with other durable goods like furniture. A maker of educational software products may be implicitly competing with all other forms of education and entertainment, such as books, videos, television, magazines, and mobile apps. For these reasons, branding principles are now being used to market a number of different categories as a whole—for example, banks, furniture, carpets, bowling, and trains, to name just a few.

Unfortunately, many firms narrowly define competition and fail to recognize the most compelling threats and opportunities. For example, sales in the apparel industry often have been stagnant in recent years as consumers have decided to spend on home furnishings, electronics, and other products that better suit their lifestyle.[44] Leading clothing makers may be better off considering the points-of-differences of their offerings not so much against other clothing labels as against other discretionary purchases.

As Chapter 3 outlines, products are often organized in consumers' minds in a hierarchical fashion, meaning that marketers can define competition at a number of different levels. Take Dr. Pepper soft drink, as an example: At the product type level, it competes with flavored soft drinks; at the product category level, it competes with all soft drinks; and at the product class level, it competes with all beverages.

Multiple Frames of Reference.   It is not uncommon for a brand to identify more than one frame of reference. This may be the result of broader category competition or the intended future growth of a brand, or it can occur when the same function can be performed by different types of products. For example, Canon EOS Rebel digital cameras compete with digital cameras from Nikon, Kodak, and others, but also with photo-taking cell phones. Their advantages against cell phones—such as easy photo sharing on social networks like Facebook or the ability to shoot high-definition video for sharing—would not necessarily be an advantage at all against other digital camera brands.[45]

As another example, Starbucks can define very distinct sets of competitors, which would suggest very different POPs and PODs as a result:

1. Quick-serve restaurants and convenience shops (McDonald's and Dunkin', previously known as Dunkin' Donuts). Intended PODs might be quality, image, experience, and variety; intended POPs might be convenience and value.
2. Supermarket brands for home consumption (Nescafé and Folgers). Intended PODs might be quality, image, experience, variety, and freshness; intended POPs might be convenience and value.
3. Local cafés. Intended PODs might be convenience and service quality; intended POPs might be quality, variety, price, and community.

Note that some POPs and PODs are shared across competitors; others are unique to a particular competitor. Under such circumstances, marketers have to decide what to do. There are two main options. Ideally, a robust positioning could be developed that would be effective across the multiple frames somehow. If not, then it is necessary to prioritize and choose the most relevant set of competitors to serve as the competitive frame. One thing that is crucial though is to be careful to not try to be all things to all people—that typically leads to ineffective lowest common denominator positioning.

Finally, note that if there are many competitors in different categories or subcategories, it may be useful to either develop the positioning at the categorical level for all relevant categories (quick-serve restaurants or supermarket take-home coffee for Starbucks) or with an exemplar from each category (Dunkin' or Nescafé for Starbucks).

Points-of-Parity and Points-of-Difference

The target and competitive frame of reference chosen will dictate the breadth of brand awareness and the situations and types of cues that should become closely related to the brand. Once marketers have fixed the appropriate competitive frame of reference for positioning by defining the customer target market and the nature of competition, they can define the basis of the positioning itself. Arriving at the proper positioning requires establishing the correct points-of-difference and points-of-parity associations.

Points-of-Difference Associations.   ***Points-of-difference (PODs)*** are formally defined as attributes or benefits that consumers strongly associate with a brand, positively evaluate, and believe that they could not find to the same extent with a competitive brand.[46] Although different types of brand associations are possible, we can broadly classify candidates as either functional, performance-related considerations or as abstract, imagery-related considerations.

Consumers' actual brand choices often depend on the perceived uniqueness of brand associations. Swedish retailer IKEA took a luxury product—home furnishings and furniture—and made it a reasonably priced alternative for the mass market. IKEA supports its low prices by having customers serve themselves and deliver and assemble their own purchases. IKEA also gains a point-of-difference through its product offerings. As one commentator noted, "IKEA built their reputation on the notion that Sweden produces good, safe, well-built things for the masses. They have some of the most innovative designs at the lowest cost out there."[47] As another example, consider Subaru, discussed in Branding Brief 2-1 below.

Points-of-difference may rely on performance attributes (Tesla's autopilot can change lanes without driver assistance) or performance benefits (Apple products have unique retina display that

BRANDING BRIEF 2-1
Subaru Finds Its Groove

By 1993, Subaru was selling only 104,000 cars annually in the United States, down 60 percent from its earlier peak. Cumulative U.S. losses approached $1 billion. Advertised as "Inexpensive and Built to Stay That Way," Subaru was seen as a me-too car that was undifferentiated from Toyota, Honda, and all their followers. To provide a clear, distinct image, Subaru decided to sell only all-wheel-drive in its passenger cars. After upgrading its luxury image—and increasing its price—Subaru sold more than 187,000 cars by 2004. Following the updating of its brand image, the company launched its "Share the Love" ad campaign, which focused on the fun, adventure, and experiences the vehicles afford and the strong passion and loyalty its customers have for the brand. With its "Share the Love Event," Subaru's unique emotional play for relatively upscale buyers who value freedom and frugality paid off in the 2008–2010 recession, when it bucked the industry tide to experience record sales.

More recently, in order to improve its appeal, and to reverse its relatively flat sales, Subaru targeted four segments of customers that were shown to account for more than 50% of its sales. These included teachers and educators, healthcare professionals, IT professionals, and outdoorsy types. Research further uncovered

a fifth segment who liked the Subaru brand because it was good for outdoor trips and hauling, without being as large as a truck or an SUV. Out of this customer insight, and the realization that this was a target market that no marketing campaign was speaking to, Subaru developed various marketing programs that targeted lesbian customers through specific media buys and ad campaigns with taglines which held a special meaning for this target audience (e.g., the tagline "Get Out and Stay Out," which could pertain to Subaru's ability to help explore the outdoors, or subtly communicate to the intended target of gays/lesbians regarding their coming out). By identifying a unique target audience that no one was targeting overtly, Subaru was able to attain significant market share and ensure customer loyalty.

Sources: Jeff Green and Alan Ohnsman, "At Subaru, Sharing the Love Is a Market Strategy," *Bloomberg Businessweek*, May 24–30, 2010, 18–20; Jean Halliday, "Subaru of America: An America's Hottest Brands Case Study," *Advertising Age*, November 16, 2009; "Love Guru: How Tim Mahoney Got Subaru Back on Track," *Brandweek*, September 13, 2010; "Subaru Announces Third Annual Share the Love Event," *PR Newswire*, November 8, 2010; Alex Mayyasi, "How Subarus Came to Be Seen as Cars for Lesbians," *The Atlantic*, June 22, 2016.

ensures picture clarity). In other cases, PODs come from imagery associations (e.g., the luxury and status imagery of Louis Vuitton) or may pertain to both performance and imagery (e.g., Singapore Airlines advertising itself as a "A Great Way to Fly"). Many top brands attempt to create a point-of-difference on overall superior quality, whereas other firms become the low-cost provider of a product or service.

Thus, a host of different types of PODs are possible. PODs are generally defined in terms of consumer benefits. These benefits often have important underlying proof points or *reasons to believe (RTBs)*. These proof points can come in many forms: functional design concerns (a unique shaving system technology, leading to the benefit of a closer electric shave); key attributes (a unique tread design, leading to the benefit of safer tires); key ingredients (contains fluoride, leading to the benefit of prevents dental cavities); or key endorsements (recommended by more audio engineers, leading to the benefit of superior music fidelity).[48] Having compelling proof points and RTBs are often critical to the deliverability aspect of a POD.

Points-of-Parity Associations. **Points-of-parity associations (POPs)**, on the other hand, are not necessarily unique to the brand but may, in fact, be shared with other brands. There are three types: category, competitive, and correlational.

Category points-of-parity represent necessary—but not necessarily sufficient—conditions for brand choice. They exist minimally at the generic product level and are most likely at the expected product level. Thus, consumers might not consider a bank truly a *bank* unless it offered a range of checking and savings plans; provided safety deposit boxes, traveler's checks, and other such services; and had convenient hours, automated teller machines, and online banking capabilities. Category POPs may change over time because of technological advances, legal developments, and consumer trends, but these attributes and benefits are like "greens fees" to play the marketing game.

Competitive points-of-parity are those associations designed to negate competitors' points-of-difference. In other words, if a brand can break even in those areas where its competitors are trying to find an advantage and can achieve its own advantages in some other areas, the brand should be in a strong—and perhaps unbeatable—competitive position.

Correlational points-of-parity are those potentially negative associations that arise from the existence of other, more positive associations for the brand. One challenge for marketers is that many of the attributes or benefits that make up their POPs or PODs are inversely related. In other words, in the minds of consumers, if your brand is good at one thing, it can't be seen as also good on something else. For example, consumers might find it hard to believe a brand is inexpensive and at the same time of the highest quality. Figure 2-6 displays some other examples of negatively correlated attributes and benefits.

Moreover, individual attributes and benefits often have both positive and negative aspects. A long heritage could be seen as a positive attribute because it can suggest experience, wisdom, and expertise. On the other hand, it could be a negative attribute because it might imply being old-fashioned and not contemporary and up-to-date. Below, we consider strategies to address these trade-offs.

Points-of-Parity versus Points-of-Difference. POPs are important because they can undermine PODs; unless certain POPs can be achieved to overcome potential weaknesses, PODs may not even matter. For the brand to achieve a point-of-parity on a particular attribute or benefit, a sufficient number of consumers must believe that the brand is good enough on that dimension.

Low price versus high quality
Taste versus low calories
Nutritious versus good tasting
Efficacious versus mild
Powerful versus safe
Strong versus refined
Ubiquitous versus exclusive
Varied versus simple

FIGURE 2-6

Examples of Negatively Correlated Attributes and Benefits

There is a zone or range of tolerance or acceptance with POPs. The brand does not have to be seen as *literally* equal to competitors, but consumers must feel that it does sufficiently well on that particular attribute or benefit so that they do not consider it to be a negative or a problem. Assuming consumers feel that way, they may then be willing to base their evaluations and decisions on other factors potentially more favorable to the brand.

Points-of-parity are easier to achieve than points-of-difference, where the brand must demonstrate clear superiority. Often, the key to positioning is not so much achieving a POD as achieving necessary, competitive, and correlational POPs.

POSITIONING GUIDELINES

The concepts of points-of-difference and points-of-parity can be invaluable tools to guide positioning. Two key issues in arriving at the optimal competitive brand positioning are (1) defining and communicating the competitive frame of reference and (2) choosing and establishing points-of-parity and points-of-difference.[49]

Defining and Communicating the Competitive Frame of Reference

A starting point in defining a competitive frame of reference for a brand positioning is to determine category membership. With which products or sets of products does the brand compete? As noted earlier, choosing to compete in different categories often results in different competitive frames of reference and different POPs and PODs.

The product's category membership tells consumers about the goals they might achieve by using a product or service. For highly established products and services, category membership is not a focal issue. Customers are aware that Coca-Cola is a leading brand of soft drink, Kellogg offers a leading brand of cereal (e.g., Kellogg's Corn Flakes), McKinsey is a leading strategy consulting firm, and so on.

There are many situations, however, in which it is important to inform consumers of a brand's category membership. Perhaps the most obvious is the introduction of new products, where the category membership is not always apparent.

Sometimes consumers know a brand's category membership but may not be convinced the brand is a true, valid member of the category. For example, when Chobani first introduced its Greek Yogurt, consumers were not convinced that it legitimately belonged with other yogurts on the market. Similarly, when Yuengling introduced its light lager, it was of a noticeably darker color than other light beers on the market. Yuengling used this darker color and taste to set itself apart from other light beers, a fact that allowed the brand to stake out a unique position in the market. Still, these types of brands may need to work hard to convince customers of its category membership.

Brands are sometimes affiliated with categories in which they do not hold membership rather than with the one in which they do. This approach is a viable way to highlight a brand's point-of-difference from competitors, provided that consumers know the brand's actual membership. For example, Bristol-Myers Squibb ran commercials at one time for its Excedrin aspirin acknowledging Tylenol's perceived consumer acceptance for aches and pains, but touting the Excedrin brand as "the Headache Medicine." With this approach, however, it is important that consumers understand what the brand is, and not just what it is *not*.

The preferred approach to positioning is to inform consumers of a brand's membership before stating its point-of-difference in relationship to other category members. Presumably, consumers need to know what a product is and what function it serves before they can decide whether it dominates the brands against which it competes. For new products, separate marketing programs are generally needed to inform consumers of membership and to educate them about a brand's point-of-difference. For brands with limited resources, this implies the development of a marketing strategy that establishes category membership prior to one that states a point-of-difference. Brands with greater resources can develop concurrent marketing programs, one of which features membership and the other, the point-of-difference. Efforts to inform consumers of membership and points-of-difference in the same ad, however, are often ineffective.

There are three main ways to convey a brand's category membership: communicating category benefits, comparing to exemplars, and relying on a product descriptor.

Communicating Category Benefits.   To reassure consumers that a brand will deliver on the fundamental reason for using a category, marketers frequently use benefits to announce category membership. Thus, industrial motors might claim to have power, and analgesics might announce their efficacy. These benefits are presented in a manner that does not imply brand superiority but merely notes that the brand possesses them as a means to establish category POPs. Performance and imagery associations can provide supporting evidence. A cake mix might attain membership in the cake category by claiming the benefit of great taste and might support this benefit claim by possessing high-quality ingredients (performance) or by showing users delighting in its consumption (imagery).

Exemplars.   Well-known, noteworthy brands in a category can also be used as exemplars to specify a brand's category membership. When Tommy Hilfiger was an unknown designer, advertising announced his membership as a great American designer by associating him with Geoffrey Beene, Stanley Blacker, Calvin Klein, and Perry Ellis, who were recognized members of that category at that time. The National Pork Board successfully advertised for over two decades that pork was "the Other White Meat," riding the coattails of the popularity of chicken in the process.[50]

Product Descriptor.   The product descriptor that follows the brand name is often a very compact means of conveying category origin. For example, USAir changed its name to US Airways, according to CEO Stephen Wolf, as part of the airline's attempted transformation from a regional carrier with a poor reputation to a strong national or even international brand. The argument was that other major airlines had the word *airlines* or *airways* in their names rather than *air,* which was felt to be typically associated with smaller, regional carriers.[51] Consider these two examples:

- When Campbell's launched its V8 Splash beverage line, it deliberately avoided including the word "carrot" in the brand name despite the fact that carrot was the main ingredient. The name was chosen to convey healthful benefits but to avoid the negative perception of carrots.[52]
- California's prune growers and marketers have attempted to establish an alternative name for their product, "dried plums," because prunes were seen by the target market of 35- to 50-year-old women as "a laxative for old people."[53]

Establishing a brand's category membership is usually not sufficient for effective brand positioning. If many firms engage in category-building tactics, the result may even be consumer confusion. For example, in the context of streaming television/video services, Sling, Roku, and so on, are newcomers that are reinventing the way in which television is watched. In trying to redefine the category, they are up against more established players such as Netflix, Amazon Prime, and even Hulu. A sound positioning strategy requires marketers to specify not only the category but also how the brand dominates other members of its category. Developing compelling points-of-difference is thus critical to effective brand positioning.[54]

Choosing Points-of-Difference

A brand must offer a compelling and credible reason for choosing it over the other options. In determining whether an attribute or benefit for a brand can serve as point-of-difference, there are three key considerations. The brand association must be seen as desirable, deliverable, and differentiating. These three considerations for developing an optimal positioning align with the three perspectives on which any brand must be evaluated, namely, the consumer, the company, and the competition. *Desirability* is determined from the consumer's point of view, *deliverability* is based on a company's inherent capabilities, and *differentiation* is determined relative to the competitors.

To function as a POD, consumers ideally would see the attribute or benefit as highly important, feel confident that the firm has the capabilities to deliver it, and be convinced that no other brand could offer it to the same extent. If these three criteria are satisfied, the brand association should have sufficient strength, favorability, and uniqueness to be an effective POD. Each of these three criteria has a number of considerations, which we look at next.

Desirability Criteria.   Target consumers must find the POD personally relevant and important. Brands that tap into growing trends with consumers often find compelling PODs. For example, Apple & Eve's pure, natural fruit juices have ridden the wave of the natural foods movement to find success in an increasingly health-minded beverage market.[55]

Just being different is not enough—the differences must matter to consumers. For example, at one time a number of brands in different product categories (colas, dishwashing soaps, beer, deodorants, gasoline) introduced clear versions of their products to better differentiate themselves.

The "clear" association has not seemed to be of enduring value or to be sustainable as a point-of-difference. In most cases, these brands experienced declining market share or disappeared altogether.

Deliverability Criteria.   The deliverability of an attribute or benefit brand association depends on both a company's actual ability to make the product or service (feasibility) as well as its effectiveness in convincing consumers of its ability to do so (communicability), as follows:[56]

- *Feasibility:* Can the firm actually supply the benefit underlying the POD? The product and marketing must be designed in a way to support the desired association. It is obviously easier to convince consumers of some fact about the brand that they were unaware of or may have overlooked than to make changes in the product and convince consumers of the value of these changes. As noted above, perhaps the simplest and most effective approach is to point to a unique attribute of the product as a proof point or reason-to-believe. Thus, Mountain Dew may argue that it is more energizing than other soft drinks and support this claim by noting that it has a higher level of caffeine. On the other hand, when the point-of-difference is abstract or image based, support for the claim may reside in more general associations to the company that have been developed over time. Thus, Chanel No. 5 perfume may claim to be the quintessential elegant, French perfume and support this claim by noting the long association between Chanel and haute couture.
- *Communicability:* The key issue in communicability is consumers' perceptions of the brand and the resulting brand associations. It is very difficult to create an association that is not consistent with existing consumer knowledge, or that consumers, for whatever reason, have trouble believing in. What factual, verifiable evidence or proof points can marketers communicate as support, so that consumers will actually believe in the brand and its desired associations? These reasons-to-believe are critical for consumer acceptance of a potential POD. Any claims must pass legal scrutiny too. The manufacturers of pomegranate-based products, POM Wonderful and POMx supplements, were the target of FTC's scrutiny and a lawsuit which challenged their claim that pomegranate juice had the ability to treat, prevent, or reduce the risk of heart disease and alleviate the risk of prostate cancer. Later, these claims were judged unsubstantiated, and the courts ruled that POM Wonderful's claims misled consumers.[57]

Differentiation Criteria.   Finally, target consumers must find the POD distinctive and superior. When marketers are entering a category in which there are established brands, the challenge is to find a viable, long-term basis for differentiation. Is the positioning preemptive, defensible, and difficult to attack? Can the brand association be reinforced and strengthened over time? If these are the case, the positioning is likely to last for years.

Sustainability depends on internal commitment and use of resources as well as external market forces. In order to establish itself as a market leader in cloud computing and analytics solutions, IBM targeted small and medium sized businesses, particularly in overseas markets.[58] The strategy of exploring new markets with few competitors has been termed "Blue Ocean Strategy."[59]

Establishing Points-of-Parity and Points-of-Difference

The key to branding success is to establish both points-of-parity *and* points-of-difference. Branding Brief 2-2 describes how the two major U.S. political parties have applied basic branding and positioning principles in their pursuit of elected office.

In creating both POPs and PODs, one of the challenges in positioning is the inverse relationships that may exist in the minds of many consumers. Unfortunately, as noted above, consumers typically want to maximize both the negatively correlated attributes and benefits. To make things worse, competitors often are trying to achieve their point-of-difference on an attribute that is negatively correlated with the point-of-difference of the target brand.

Much of the art and science of marketing is knowing how to deal with trade-offs, and positioning is no different. The best approach, clearly, is to develop a product or service that performs well on both dimensions. Gore-Tex, for example, was able to overcome the seemingly conflicting product image of breathable and waterproof through technological advances.

Several additional ways exist to address the problem of negatively correlated POPs and PODs. The following three approaches are listed in increasing order of effectiveness—but also increasing order of difficulty.

BRANDING BRIEF 2-2
Positioning Politicians

The importance of marketing has not been lost on politicians, and, although there are a number of different ways to interpret their words and actions, one way to interpret campaign strategies is from a branding perspective. For example, consultants to political candidates stress the importance of having "high name ID" or, in other words, a high level of brand awareness. In major races, at least 90 percent awareness is desired. Consultants also emphasize "positives–negatives"—voters' responses when asked whether they think positively or negatively of a candidate. A 3:1 ratio is desired (and 4:1 is even better). This measure corresponds to brand attitude in marketing terms.

The last three decades of presidential campaigns are revealing about the importance of properly positioning a politician. George H. W. Bush ran a textbook presidential campaign in 1988. The objective was to move the candidate to the center of the political spectrum and make him a safe choice, and to move his Democratic opponent, Massachusetts governor Michael Dukakis, to the left and make him seem more liberal and a risky choice.

In 1992, the new Democratic candidate, Bill Clinton, was a fierce campaigner who ran a focused effort to create a key point-of-difference on one main issue—the economy. Rather than attempting to achieve a point-of-parity on this issue, Bush, who was running for reelection, campaigned on other issues such as family values. By conceding a key point-of-difference to the Democrats and failing to create a compelling one of their own, Bush and the Republicans were defeated handily.

Failing to learn from their mistakes, the Republicans ran a meandering campaign in 1996 and their presidential candidate, Bob Dole, lost decisively to the incumbent Bill Clinton. The closeness of the 2000 election between Al Gore and George W. Bush reflected the failure of either candidate to create a strong point-of-difference with the electorate. There was a similarly tight election in 2004 because neither George W. Bush nor John Kerry was successful at carving out a strong position in voters' minds.

The 2008 presidential election, however, was another textbook application of branding as Barack Obama ran a very sophisticated and modern marketing campaign. Republican candidate John McCain attempted to create a point-of-difference on experience and traditional Republican values; Obama sought to create a point-of-difference on new ideas and hope. The Obama campaign team effectively hammered his message home. Multimedia tactics combined offline and online media as well as free and paid media. In addition to traditional print, broadcast, and outdoor ads, social media like Facebook, Meetup, YouTube, and Twitter and long-form videos were employed so people could learn more about Obama and the passion others had about the candidate. Even Obama's slogans ("Yes We Can" and "Change We Can Believe In") and campaign posters (the popular stencil portrait of Obama in solid red, white, and pastel and dark shades of blue with the word "PROGRESS," "HOPE," or "CHANGE" prominently below) became iconic symbols, and Obama breezed to victory.

The 2016 presidential campaign ushered in a new era of politics. President Donald J. Trump was elected in a surprise win against Hillary Clinton, in an election that caught many pundits and pollsters by surprise. As a presidential candidate, Donald Trump focused his points-of-differentiation on his being an outsider, and his platform was to end the status quo in Washington, DC. Further, Trump's message and style of delivery were highly effective among his target audience, specifically middle income, white, blue-collar voters living in Rust Belt states, who felt that Trump understood their pain. This can be contrasted with his opponent, candidate Hillary Clinton, whose campaign points of differentiation rested on her prior experience in politics. Many of Trump's supporters were unable to connect with candidate Hillary Clinton both at the message level as well as on an emotional level. Trump's campaign promise "Make America Great Again" (the Twitter hashtag #MAGA) was a simple positioning statement, and interpreted by many as a rallying cry for a return to the days of economic prosperity for the intended target groups. The slogan was used multiple times, and it was often presented alongside emotion-laden rallies that played to what the audience wanted to hear. The use of social media (primarily Twitter) and campaign rallies afforded candidate Trump a free platform for the spread of his ideas. In this sense, Donald Trump's campaign may be seen as a great example of the importance of understanding your customer, emphasizing a particular set of PODs (which were viewed favorably by the intended target audience), and building a brand around it. Hillary Clinton won the popular vote across the United States; however, Trump's election win was made possible due to his winning a larger number of votes in the electoral college.

Sources: "Gore and Bush Are Like Classic Brands," *The New York Times*, July 25, 2000, B8; Michael Learmonth, "Social Media Paves Way to White House," *Advertising Age*, March 30, 2009, 16; Noreen O'Leary, "GMBB," *AdweekMedia*, June 15, 2009, 2; John Quelch, "The Marketing of a President," *Harvard Business School Working Knowledge*, November 12, 2008; Steven Ma, "Lessons from Donald Trump's Marketing Campaign Success," https://sparkflow.co/7-lessons-donald-trumps-marketing-campaign-success/, accessed February 28, 2018; Gil Press, "6 Trump Marketing Lessons," November 11, 2016, www.forbes.com/sites/gilpress/2016/11/11/6-trump-marketing-lessons/#322bbeef68e1, accessed February 28, 2018.

Separate the Attributes.   An expensive but sometimes effective approach is to launch two different marketing campaigns, each devoted to a different brand attribute or benefit. These campaigns may run concurrently or sequentially. For example, Head & Shoulders met success in Europe with a dual campaign in which one ad emphasized its dandruff removal efficacy while another ad emphasized the appearance and beauty of hair after its use. The hope is that consumers will be less critical when judging the POP and POD benefits in isolation, because the negative correlation might be less apparent. The downside is that two strong campaigns have to be developed—not just one. Moreover, if the marketer does not address the negative correlation head-on, consumers may not develop as positive an association as desired.

Leverage Equity of Another Entity.   Brands can link themselves to any kind of entity that possesses the right kind of equity—a person, other brand, event, and so forth—as a means to establish an attribute or benefit as a POP or POD. Self-branded ingredients may also lend some credibility to a questionable attribute in consumers' minds.

MILLER LITE

When Philip Morris bought Miller Brewing, its flagship High Life brand was not competing particularly well, leading the company to decide to introduce a light beer. The initial advertising strategy for Miller Lite was to ensure parity with a necessary and important consideration in the category by stating that it "tastes great," while at the same time creating a point-of-difference with the fact that it contained one-third fewer calories (96 calories versus 150 calories for conventional 12-ounce full-strength beer) and was thus "less filling." The point-of-parity and point-of-difference were somewhat conflicting, as consumers tend to equate taste with calories. To overcome potential consumer resistance to this notion, Miller employed credible spokespeople, primarily popular former professional athletes who would presumably not drink a beer unless it tasted good. These athletes were placed in amusing situations in ads where they debated which of the two product benefits—"tastes great" or "less filling"—was more descriptive of the beer, creating valuable points-of-parity and points-of-difference. The ads ended with the clever tag line "Everything You've Always Wanted in a Beer and Less." More recently, Miller Lite's ad campaign is focusing on its PODs against its competitor, Bud Light. Miller's new advertisements show a Miller Lite can set on top of a Bud Light coaster, while a voiceover plugs Lite as brewed with "more taste, less calories, and half the carbs" and concludes with the tag line "Holds True." The "Holds True" message is meant to convey multiple meanings, including "holding to the authentic original light beer, with minimalist graphics on its packaging," creating valuable points of parity and points of difference. Miller Lite is emphasizing its POD of taste relative to competition; the Lite beer also has 14 fewer calories than Bud Light making this a lesser, more subtle POD. Overall, Miller Lite's original advertising campaign provides an example of how a brand can leverage the equity of well-liked celebrities to lend credibility to one of its negatively correlated benefits. However, this is neither costless nor riskless. Chapter 8 reviews these considerations in detail and outlines the pros and cons of leveraging equity.

Redefine the Relationship.   Finally, another potentially powerful but often difficult way to address the negative relationship between attributes and benefits in the minds of consumers is to convince them that, in fact, the relationship is positive. Marketers can achieve this by providing consumers with a different perspective and suggesting that they may be overlooking or ignoring certain factors or other considerations. Apple offers another classic example.

Although difficult to achieve, such a strategy can be powerful because the two associations can become mutually reinforcing. The challenge is to develop a credible story with which consumers can agree.

Straddle Positions

Occasionally, a company will be able to straddle two frames of reference with one set of points-of-difference and points-of-parity. In these cases, the points-of-difference in one category become points-of-parity in the other and vice versa. For example, Accenture defines itself as the company that combines (1) strategic insight, vision, and thought leadership and (2) information technology expertise in developing client solutions. This strategy permits points-of-parity with its two main competitors, McKinsey and IBM, while simultaneously achieving points-of-difference. Specifically, Accenture has a point-of-difference on technology and execution with respect to McKinsey and a point-of-parity on strategy and vision. The reverse is true with respect to IBM: technology and execution are points-of-parity, but strategy and vision are points-of-difference. Another brand that has successfully employed a straddle positioning is BMW.

While a straddle positioning often is attractive as a means of reconciling potentially conflicting consumer goals and creating a best-of-both-worlds solution, it also carries an extra burden. If the points-of-parity and points-of-difference with respect to both categories are not credible, consumers may not view the brand as a legitimate player in either category. Many of the new tablet brands (e.g., iPad, Kindle) introduced smaller versions that ended up looking

APPLE

When Apple launched the Macintosh computer in the 1980s—back in the early days of personal computing—its key point-of-difference was that it was user friendly. Many consumers valued ease of use—especially those who bought personal computers for the home—because in a pre-Windows world, the DOS PC operating system was complex and clumsy. One drawback with that association for Apple, however, was that customers who bought personal computers for business applications inferred that if a personal computer was easy to use, then it also must not be very powerful—and power was a key choice consideration in the business market. Recognizing this potential problem, Apple ran a clever ad campaign with the tag line "The Power to Be Your Best," in an attempt to redefine what being a powerful computer meant. The message behind the ads was that because Apple was easy to use, people in fact did just that—they used them!—a simple but important indication of power. In other words, the most powerful computers were ones that people actually used.

Apple has worked hard through the years to convince consumers that its computer products are powerful and easy to use.
Source: Piero Cruciatti/Alamy Stock Photo

like larger phones (or were called "phablets"). These products that unsuccessfully tried to straddle categories ranging from smartphones to laptop computers provide a vivid illustration of this risk.

Updating Positioning over Time

The previous section described some positioning guidelines that are especially useful for launching a new brand. With an established brand, an important question is how often to update its positioning. As a general rule, positioning should be fundamentally changed very infrequently, and only when circumstances significantly reduce the effectiveness of existing POPs and PODs.

Positioning, however, will evolve over time to better reflect market opportunities or challenges. A point-of-difference or point-of-parity may be refined, added, or dropped as situations dictate. One common market opportunity that often arises is the need to deepen the meaning of the brand to permit further expansion—*laddering*. One common market challenge is how to respond to competitive actions that threaten an existing positioning—*reacting*. We consider the positioning implications of each in turn.

Laddering.   Although identifying PODs to dominate competition on benefits that are important to consumers provides a sound way to build an initial position, once the target market attains a basic understanding of how the brand relates to alternatives in the same category, it may be necessary to deepen the meanings associated with the brand positioning. It is often useful to explore underlying consumer motivations in a product category to uncover the relevant associations. For example, Maslow's hierarchy maintains that consumers have different priorities and levels of needs.[60]

BMW

When BMW first made a strong competitive push into the U.S. market in the early 1980s, it positioned the brand as being the only automobile that offered both luxury *and* performance. At that time, U.S. luxury cars like Cadillac were seen by many as lacking performance, and U.S. performance cars like the Chevy Corvette were seen as lacking luxury. By relying on the design of its cars, its German heritage, and other aspects of a well-designed marketing program, BMW was able to simultaneously achieve (1) a point-of-difference on performance and a point-of-parity on luxury with respect to luxury cars and (2) a point-of-difference on luxury and a point-of-parity on performance with respect to performance cars. The clever slogan, "The Ultimate Driving Machine," effectively captured the newly created umbrella category—luxury performance cars.

BMW's "Ultimate Driving Machine" slogan nicely captures the brand's dual features of luxury and performance.
Source: BMW AG

From lowest to highest priority, they are as follows:

1. Physiological needs (food, water, air, shelter, sex)
2. Safety and security needs (protection, order, stability)
3. Social needs (affection, friendship, belonging)
4. Ego needs (prestige, status, self-respect)
5. Self-actualization (self-fulfillment).

According to Maslow, higher-level needs become relevant once lower-level needs have been satisfied. The Science of Branding below highlights a study which links benefits associated with brand names to a hierarchy of values which align with Maslow's hierarchy of needs. This study points to stark differences across brands and categories in what constitutes a brand's appeal to its customers.

Marketers have also recognized the importance of higher-level needs. For example, ***means-end chains*** have been devised as a way of understanding higher-level meanings of brand characteristics. A means-end chain takes the following structure: attributes (descriptive features that characterize a product) lead to benefits (the personal value and meaning attached to product attributes), which, in turn, lead to values (stable and enduring personal goals or motivations).[61]

In other words, a consumer chooses a product that delivers an attribute (A) that provides benefits or has certain consequences (B/C) that satisfy values (V). For example, in a study of salty snacks, one respondent noted that a flavored chip (A) with a strong taste (A) would mean that she would eat less (B/C), not get fat (B/C), and have a better figure (B/C), all of which would enhance her self-esteem (V).

THE SCIENCE OF BRANDING 2-1

Brand Values Pyramid

A recent study by authors Almquist, Senior, and Bloch propose a set of brand values, which is then organized in a pyramid ranging from functional at the bottom of the pyramid to social impact at the top of the pyramid. The authors identify 30 separate elements of brand positioning, which follow Maslow's hierarchy of needs and can be categorized into functional, emotional, life-changing, and social impact. The data collected to support this idea suggests that companies that perform well on more than four elements of value have more loyal customers, and higher net promoter scores, as well as four times higher revenue growth. Examples of these brands include Apple, USAA, TOMS, and Amazon. Further, pure-play retailers such as Amazon which demonstrate extraordinary growth rates are shown to have strengths in eight different elements of value.

We next highlight the different aspects of the building blocks of value, as described by Almquist et al., across the four levels of the brand value pyramid, regrouped as functional, emotional benefits, life-changing values, and social impact.

Functional: Time and money savings (e.g., reduces effort, avoids hassles, reduces cost), providing basic benefits (quality, variety), and generates efficiencies and convenience in daily life (simplifies, informs, connects, integrates, organizes).

Emotional: Self-enhancement (e.g., reduces anxiety, nostalgia, badge value, attractiveness) and hedonic benefits and rewards (e.g., fun/entertainment, therapeutic value, wellness).

Life-changing values: Includes motivation, investment for the future, affiliation/belonging, provides hope, and self-actualization.

Social impact: Includes self-transcendence.

The above elements of the value pyramid vary greatly with respect to their importance across different categories. While quality is seen as important to influencing consumer advocacy across the board, the authors also found that sensory appeal was important to success in food and beverages, while providing access was

important in financial services. Brand names such as Zappos were found to excel on saving time and avoiding hassles (functional benefits), but also was seen as twice as good at delivering those benefits than traditional competitors. Netflix had scores three times higher than its competitors (i.e., traditional TV service providers) on reduction of cost, therapeutic value, and nostalgia.

In order to improve on value delivery to customers, companies may add benefits to their existing products. The authors note that Vanguard's addition of a low-fee automated advice platform may have been motivated by its desire to keep its clients better informed and also to reduce risk. The addition of Apple Pay to iPhone's many features allows customers to make payments a seamless part of their buying experience. Similarly, Amazon Prime offers unlimited two-day shipping for a flat fee during the year, which eliminates hassles and reduces costs of paying for shipping throughout the year. Amazon's streaming services offer access to a large collection of programming, thereby increasing the fun/entertainment value delivered by the brand. Recently, Almquist et al. extended the idea of a value hierarchy to a business-to-business setting as well, and they provided a set of value drivers that could be used in marketing B2B brands. Thus, the framework proposed by Almquist et al. is a useful way of thinking about how value is delivered to customers across a broad range of categories and is also firmly rooted in Maslow's hierarchy of needs.

Sources: Eric Almquist, John Senior, and Nicolas Bloch, " The Elements of Value" *Harvard Business Review*, September 2016, https:/hbr .org/2016/09/the-elements-of-value, accessed February 1, 2016; Mike Owen, "How to Create Value for Customers? A New Model Gives Useful Pointers and Adds to Existing Insights about Customer Value Marketing," November 21, 2016, https://stratminder.wordpress.com/2016/11/21/how-to-create-value-for-customers-a-new-model-gives-useful-pointers-and-adds-to-existing-insights-about-customer-value-marketing/, accessed March 5, 2018; Eric Almquist, Janie Cleghorn, Lori Sherer, "The B2B Elements of Value," *Harvard Business Review*, March–April 2018, https:// hbr.org/2018/03/the-b2b-elements-of-value, accessed March 5, 2018.

Laddering thus progresses from attributes to benefits to more abstract values or motivations. In effect, laddering repeatedly asks what the implication of an attribute or benefit is for the consumer. Failure to move up the ladder may reduce the strategic alternatives available to a brand.[62] For example, P&G introduced low-sudsing Dash detergent to attract consumers who used front-loading washing machines. Many years of advertising Dash in this manner made this position impenetrable by other brands. Dash was so associated with front-loaders, however, that when this type of machine went out of fashion, so did Dash, despite the fact that it was among P&G's most effective detergents, and despite significant efforts to reposition the brand.

Some attributes and benefits may lend themselves to laddering more easily than others. For example, the Betty Crocker brand appears on a number of different baking products and is characterized by the physical warmth associated with baking. Such an association makes it relatively easy to talk about emotional warmth and the joy of baking or the good feelings that might arise from baking for others across a wide range of baking-related products.

Thus, some of the strongest brands deepen their points-of-difference to create benefit and value association—for example, Volvo and Michelin (safety and peace of mind), Intel (performance and compatibility), Marlboro (Western imagery), Coke (Americana and refreshment),

Disney (fun, magic, family entertainment), Nike (innovative products and peak athletic performance), and BMW (styling and driving performance).

As a brand becomes associated with more and more products and moves up the product hierarchy, the brand's meaning will become more abstract. At the same time, it is important that the proper category membership and POPs and PODs exist in the minds of consumers for any particular products sold under the brand name, as discussed in Chapter 11.

Reacting.   Competitive actions are often directed at eliminating points-of-difference to make them points-of-parity or to strengthen or establish new points-of-difference. Often, competitive advantages exist for only a short period of time before competitors attempt to match them.

DISCOVER

Discover introduced an all-in-one credit card with various features that were unique for a period of time.[63] For example the Discover card had a modern blue metallic finish and had various features such as $0 Fraud Liability Guarantee, which meant that cardmembers were not responsible for unauthorized charges to their account. Further, Discover added features such as allowing card members to choose their own due dates and allowing them to pay until midnight of the due date. Various online management tools including mobile apps and email reminders allowed customers to keep track of their accounts. In this way, Discover effectively leveraged its advertising campaign "It Pays to Discover."[64] However, its differentiating features were quickly replicated by its aggressive rivals Visa and Mastercard, and some of their once-innovative features are now considered standard in the industry.

Discover Credit Card introduced an all-in-one credit card featuring unique benefits that were later replicated by its rivals.

When a competitor challenges an existing POD or attempts to overcome a POP, there are essentially three main options for the target brand—from no reaction to moderate to significant reactions.

- **Do nothing.** If the competitive actions seem unlikely to recapture a POD or create a new POD, then the best reaction is probably to just stay the course and continue brand-building efforts.
- **Go on the defensive.** If the competitive actions appear to have the potential to disrupt the market some, then it may be necessary to take a defensive stance. One way to defend the positioning is to add some reassurance in the product or advertising to strengthen POPs and PODs.
- **Go on the offensive.** If the competitive actions seem potentially quite damaging, then it might be necessary to take a more aggressive stance and reposition the brand to address the threat. One approach might be to launch a product extension or ad campaign that fundamentally changes the meaning of the brand.

A brand audit can help marketers assess the severity of the competitive threat and the appropriate competitive stance, as described in Chapter 9.

Developing a Good Positioning

A few final comments are useful to help guide positioning efforts. First, a good positioning has a foot in the present and a foot in the future. It needs to be somewhat aspirational so that the brand has room to grow and improve. Positioning on the basis of the current state of the market is not forward-looking enough, but, at the same time, the positioning cannot be so removed from the current reality that it is essentially unobtainable. The real trick in positioning is to strike just the right balance between what the brand is and what it could be.

Second, a good positioning is careful to identify all relevant points-of-parity. Too often, marketers overlook or ignore crucial areas where the brand is potentially disadvantaged to concentrate on areas of strength. Both are obviously necessary as points-of-difference will not matter without the requisite points-of-parity. One good way to uncover key competitive points-of-parity is to role-play competitor's positioning and infer their intended points-of-difference. Competitor's PODs will, in turn, become the brand's POPs. Consumer research into the trade-offs in decision-making that exist in the minds of consumers can also be informative.

Third, a good positioning should reflect a consumer point of view in terms of the benefits that consumers derive from the brand. It is not enough to advertise that you are the "largest wireless network"—as Verizon has claimed in its U.S. advertising. An effective POD should make clear *why* that it so desirable to consumers. In other words, what benefits would a consumer get from that unique attribute? Does that mean Verizon can be used by more customers in more places, or does the wider coverage lead to other benefits such as the ability to charge lower prices due to economies of scale? Those benefits, if evident, should become the basis for the positioning, with the proof point or RTB being the attribute of the largest wireless network.

Finally, as we will develop in greater detail with the brand resonance model in the next chapter, it is important that a duality exists in the positioning of a brand such that there are rational and emotional components. In other words, a good positioning contains points-of-difference and points-of-parity that appeal both to the head and the heart.

DEFINING A BRAND MANTRA

Brand positioning describes how a brand can effectively compete against a specified set of competitors in a particular market. In many cases, however, brands span multiple product categories, and therefore, may have multiple distinct—yet related—positionings. As brands evolve and expand across categories, marketers will want to craft a brand mantra that reflects the essential heart and soul of the brand.

Brand Mantras

To better establish what a brand represents, marketers will often define a brand mantra.[65] A **brand mantra** is a short, three- to five-word phrase that captures the irrefutable essence or spirit of the brand positioning. It's similar to brand essence or core brand promise, and its purpose is to ensure that all employees and external marketing partners understand what the brand most fundamentally is to represent to consumers so they can adjust their actions accordingly. For example, McDonald's brand mission is to be their customers' favorite place and way to eat and drink nicely captures its brand essence and core brand promise.

Brand mantras are powerful devices. They can provide guidance about what products to introduce under the brand, what ad campaigns to run, and where and how the brand should be sold. They may even guide the most seemingly unrelated or mundane decisions, such as the look of a reception area and the way employees answer the phone. In effect, brand mantras create a mental filter to screen out brand-inappropriate marketing activities or actions of any type that may have a negative bearing on customers' impressions of a brand.

Brand mantras help the brand present a consistent image. Any time a consumer or customer encounters a brand—in any way, shape, or form—his or her knowledge about that brand may change and affect the equity of the brand. Given that a vast number of employees come into contact with consumers, either directly or indirectly, their words and actions should consistently reinforce and support the brand meaning. Marketing partners like ad agency members may not even recognize their role in influencing equity. The brand mantra signals its meaning and importance to the firm, as well as the crucial role of employees and marketing partners in its management. It also provides memorable shorthand as to what are the crucial considerations of the brand that should be kept most salient and top-of-mind.

Designing a Brand Mantra. What makes a good brand mantra? Two high-profile and successful examples of brand mantras come from two powerful brands, Nike and Disney, as described in Branding Briefs 2-3 and 2-4. Brand mantras must economically communicate what the brand is and what it is *not.* The Nike and Disney examples show the power and utility of a well-designed brand mantra. These examples help suggest what might characterize a good brand mantra. In the case of Nike and Disney, the brand mantras are essentially structured the same way, with three terms, as follows:

	Emotional Modifier	**Descriptive Modifier**	**Brand Function**
Nike	Authentic	Athletic	Performance
Disney	Fun	Family	Entertainment

BRANDING BRIEF 2-3
Nike Brand Mantra

A brand with a keen sense of what it represents to consumers is Nike. Nike has a rich set of associations with consumers, revolving around such considerations as its innovative product designs, its sponsorships of top athletes, its award-winning advertising, its competitive drive, and its irreverent attitude. Internally, Nike marketers adopted a three-word brand mantra of "authentic athletic performance" to guide their marketing efforts. Thus, in Nike's eyes, its entire marketing program—its products and how they are sold—must reflect the key brand values conveyed by the brand mantra.

Nike's brand mantra has had profound implications for its marketing. In the words of ex-Nike marketing gurus Scott Bedbury and Jerome Conlon, the brand mantra provided the "intellectual guard rails" to keep the brand moving in the right direction and to make sure it did not get off track somehow. Nike's brand mantra has even affected product development. Over the years, Nike has expanded its brand meaning from "running shoes" to "athletic shoes" to "athletic shoes and apparel" to "all things associated with athletics (including equipment)."

Each step of the way, however, it has been guided by its "authentic athletic performance" brand mantra. For example, as Nike rolled out its successful apparel line, one important hurdle for the products was that they should be innovative enough through material, cut, or design to truly benefit top athletes. The revolutionary moisture-wicking technology of their Dri-Fit apparel line left athletes drier and more comfortable as they perspired. At the same time, the company has been careful to avoid using the Nike name to brand products that did not fit with the brand mantra, like casual "brown" shoes.

When Nike has experienced problems with its marketing program, they have often been a result of its failure to figure out how to translate its brand mantra to the marketing challenge at hand. For example, in going to Europe, Nike experienced several false starts until realizing that "authentic athletic performance" has a different meaning over there and, in particular, has to involve soccer in a major way. Similarly, Nike stumbled in developing its

Nike's brand mantra of "authentic athletic performance" is exemplified by athletes such as Roger Federer.
Source: Jean Catuffe, PacificCoastNews/Newscom

All Conditions Gear (ACG) outdoors shoes and clothing sub-brand, which attempted to translate its brand mantra into a less competitive arena.

BRANDING BRIEF 2-4

Disney Brand Mantra

Disney developed its brand mantra in response to its incredible growth through licensing and product development during the mid-1980s. In the late 1980s, Disney became concerned that some of its characters, like Mickey Mouse and Donald Duck, were being used inappropriately and becoming overexposed. To investigate the severity of the problem, Disney undertook an extensive brand audit. As part of a brand inventory, it first compiled a list of all Disney products that were available (licensed and company manufactured) and all third-party promotions (complete with point-of-purchase displays and relevant merchandising) from stores across the country and all over the world. At the same time, Disney launched a major consumer research study—a brand exploratory—to investigate how consumers felt about the Disney brand.

The results of the brand inventory revealed some potentially serious problems: the Disney characters were on so many products and marketed in so many ways that in some cases it was difficult to discern the original rationale behind the deal. The consumer study only heightened Disney's concerns. Because of the broad exposure of the characters in the marketplace, many consumers had begun to feel that Disney was exploiting its name. In some cases, consumers felt that the characters added little value to products and, worse yet, involved children in purchase decisions that they would typically ignore.

Because of its aggressive marketing efforts, Disney had written contracts with many of the park participants for copromotions or licensing arrangements. Disney characters were selling everything from diapers to cars to McDonald's hamburgers. Disney

learned in the consumer study, however, that consumers did not differentiate between all the product endorsements. "Disney was Disney" to consumers, whether they saw the characters in films, records, theme parks, or consumer products. Consequently, *all* products and services that used the Disney name or characters had an impact on Disney's brand equity. Consumers reported that they resented some of these endorsements because they felt that they had a special, personal relationship with the characters and with Disney that should not be handled so carelessly.

As a result of the brand audit, Disney moved quickly to establish a brand equity team to better manage the brand franchise and more carefully evaluate licensing and other third-party promotional opportunities. One of the mandates of this team was to ensure that a consistent image for Disney—reinforcing its key brand associations—was conveyed by all third-party products and services. To facilitate this supervision, Disney adopted an internal brand mantra of "fun family entertainment" to serve as a screening device for proposed ventures.

Opportunities that were not consistent with the brand mantra—no matter how appealing—were rejected. For example, Disney was approached to cobrand a mutual fund in Europe that was designed as a way for parents to save for the college expenses of their children. The opportunity was declined despite the consistent family association, because Disney believed that a connection with the financial community or banking suggested other associations that were inconsistent with its brand image (mutual funds are rarely intended to be entertaining!).

Disney's brand mantra of "fun family entertainment" gave marketers "guard rails" to help avoid brand-inconsistent actions.
Source: Todd Anderson/Handout/Getty Images

The **_brand functions_** term describes the nature of the product or service or the type of experiences or benefits the brand provides. It can range from concrete language that reflects the product category itself, to more abstract notions (such as Nike's and Disney's), where the term relates to higher-order experiences or benefits that a variety of different products could deliver. The **_descriptive modifier_** further clarifies its nature. Thus, Nike's performance is not just any kind (not artistic performance, for instance) but only athletic performance; Disney's entertainment is not just any kind (not adult-oriented) but only family entertainment (and arguably an additional modifier, "magical," could add even more distinctiveness). Combined, the brand function term and descriptive modifier help to delineate the brand boundaries. Finally, the **_emotional modifier_** provides another qualifier—how exactly does the brand provide benefits and in what ways?

Brand mantras don't necessarily have to follow this exact structure, but they should clearly delineate what the brand is supposed to represent and therefore, at least implicitly, what it is not. Several additional points are worth noting.

1. Brand mantras derive their power and usefulness from their collective meaning. Other brands may be strong on one, or perhaps even a few, of the brand associations making up the brand mantra. For the brand mantra to be effective, no other brand should singularly excel on all dimensions. Part of the key to both Nike's and Disney's success is that for years, no other competitor could really deliver on the promise suggested by their brand mantras as well as they did.
2. Brand mantras typically are designed to capture the brand's points-of-difference, that is, what is unique about the brand. Other aspects of the brand positioning—especially the brand's points-of-parity—may also be important and may need to be reinforced in other ways.
3. For brands facing rapid growth, a brand functions term can provide critical guidance as to appropriate and inappropriate categories into which to extend. For brands in more stable categories, the brand mantra may focus more on points-of-difference as expressed by the functional and emotional modifiers, perhaps not even including a brand functions term.

Implementing a Brand Mantra.   Brand mantras should be developed at the same time as the brand positioning. As we've seen, brand positioning typically is a result of an in-depth examination of the brand through some form of brand audit or other activities. Brand mantras may benefit from the learning gained from those activities, but, at the same time, require more internal examination and involve input from a wider range of company employees and marketing staff. Part of this internal exercise is actually to determine the different means by which each and every employee currently affects brand equity, and how he or she can contribute in a positive way to a brand's destiny. The importance of internal branding is reinforced in The Science of Branding 2-2.

Marketers can often summarize the brand positioning in a few sentences or a short paragraph that suggests the ideal core brand associations consumers should hold. Based on these core brand associations, a brainstorming session can attempt to identify PODs, POPs, and different brand mantra candidates. In the final brand mantra, the following considerations should come into play:

- **Communicate:** A good brand mantra should both define the category (or categories) of the business to set the brand boundaries and clarify what is unique about the brand.
- **Simplify:** An effective brand mantra should be memorable. That means it should be short, crisp, and vivid. A three-word mantra is ideal because it is the most economical way to convey the brand positioning.
- **Inspire:** Ideally, the brand mantra should also stake out ground that is personally meaningful and relevant to as many employees as possible. Brand mantras can do more than inform and guide; they can also inspire, if the brand values tap into higher-level meaning with employees as well as consumers.

Regardless of how many words make up the mantra, however, there will always be a level of meaning beneath the brand mantra itself that will need to be articulated. Virtually any word may have many interpretations. For example, the words "fun," "family," and "entertainment" in Disney's brand mantra can each take on multiple meanings, leading Disney to drill deeper to provide a stronger foundation for the mantra. Two or three short phrases were therefore added later to clarify each of the three words.

THE SCIENCE OF BRANDING 2-2
Branding Inside the Organization

Brand mantras point out the importance of internal branding—making sure that members of the organization are properly aligned with the brand and what it represents. Much of the branding literature has taken an external perspective, focusing on strategies and tactics that firms should take to build or manage brand equity with customers. Without question, at the heart of all marketing activity is the positioning of a brand and the essence of its meaning with consumers.

Equally important, however, is positioning the brand internally.[66] For service companies especially, it's critical that all employees have an up-to-date and deep understanding of the brand. Recently, a number of companies have put forth initiatives to improve their internal branding.

One of the fastest growing and most successful restaurant chains in the United States, Panda Express, devotes significant resources to internal training and development for employees. Besides services training, privately owned Panda Express supports the personal improvement efforts of its staff—controlling weight, working on communications skills, jogging, and attending seminars—in the belief that healthier, happier employees increase sales and profitability.

Singapore Airlines also invests heavily in employee training: new recruits receive four months of training, twice as long as the industry average. The company also spends about $70 million a year on retraining each of its 14,500 existing employees. Training focuses on deportment, etiquette, wine appreciation, and cultural sensitivity. Cabin crew learn how to interact differently with Japanese, Chinese, and U.S. passengers as well as the importance of communicating at eye level and not "looking down" at passengers.

Companies need to engage in continual open dialogue with their employees. Branding should be perceived as participatory. Some firms have pushed B2E (business-to-employee) programs through corporate intranets and other means. Disney is seen as so successful at internal branding that its Disney Institute holds seminars on the "Disney Style" of creativity, service, and loyalty for employees from other companies.

In short, for both motivating employees and attracting external customers, internal branding is a critical management priority.

Sources: Karl Taro Greenfeld, "The Sharin' Huggin' Lovin' Carin' Chinese Food Money Machine," *Bloomberg Businessweek*, November 28, 2010, 98–103; Loizos Heracleous and Joachen Wirtz, "Singapore Airlines' Balancing Act," *Harvard Business Review*, July–August 2010, 145–149; James Wallace, "Singapore Airlines Raises the Bar for Luxury Flying," www.seattlepi.com, January 16, 2007. For some seminal writings in the area, see Hamish Pringle and William Gordon, *Brand Manners: How to Create the Self-Confident Organization to Live the Brand* (New York: John Wiley & Sons, 2001); Thomas Gad, *4-D Branding: Cracking the Corporate Code of the Network Economy* (London: Financial Times Prentice Hall, 2000); Nicholas Ind, *Living the Brand: How to Transform Every Member of Your Organization into a Brand Champion*, 2nd ed. (London, UK: Kogan Page, 2004); Scott M. Davis and Kenneth Dunn, *Building the Brand-Driven Business: Operationalize Your Brand to Drive Profitable Growth* (San Francisco: Jossey-Bass, 2002); Mary Jo Hatch and Make Schultz, *Taking Brand Initiative: How Companies Can Align Strategy, Culture, and Identity Through Corporate Branding* (San Francisco, CA: Jossey-Bass, 2008); Andy Bird and Mhairi McEwan, *The Growth Drivers: The Definitive Guide to Transforming Marketing Capabilities* (West Sussex, UK: John Wiley & Sons, 2012).

REVIEW

Customer-based brand equity is the differential effect that brand knowledge has on consumer response to the marketing of that brand. A brand has positive customer-based brand equity when customers react more favorably to a product and the way it is marketed when the brand is identified than when it is not.

We can define brand knowledge in terms of an associative network memory model, as a network of nodes and links wherein the brand node in memory has a variety of associations linked to it. We can characterize brand knowledge in terms of two components: brand awareness and brand image. Brand awareness is related to the strength of the brand node or trace in memory, as reflected by consumers' ability to recall or recognize the brand under different conditions. It has both depth and breadth. The depth of brand awareness measures the likelihood that consumers can recognize or recall the brand. The breadth of brand awareness measures the variety of purchase and consumption situations in which the brand comes to mind. Brand image is consumer perceptions of a brand as reflected by the brand associations held in consumers' memory.

Customer-based brand equity occurs when the consumer has a high level of awareness and familiarity with the brand and holds some strong, favorable, and unique brand associations in memory. In some cases, brand awareness alone is sufficient to result in more favorable consumer response—for example, in low-involvement decision settings where consumers are willing to base their choices merely on familiar brands. In other cases, the strength, favorability, and uniqueness of the brand associations play a critical role in determining the differential response making up the brand equity.

Deciding on a positioning requires determining a frame of reference (by identifying the target market and the nature of competition), the optimal points-of-parity and points-of-difference brand associations, and an overall brand mantra as a summary. First, marketers need to understand consumer behavior and the consideration sets that consumers adopt in making brand choices. After establishing this frame of reference, they can then turn to identifying the best possible points-of-parity and points-of-difference.

Points-of-difference are those associations that are unique to the brand, strongly held, and favorably evaluated by consumers. Marketers should find points-of-difference associations that are strong, favorable, and unique based on desirability, deliverability, and differentiation considerations, as well as the resulting anticipated levels of sales and costs that might be expected with achieving those points-of-difference.

Points-of-parity, on the other hand, are those associations that are not necessarily unique to the brand but may, in fact, be shared with other brands. Category points-of-parity associations are necessary to be a legitimate and credible product offering within a certain category. Competitive points-of-parity associations negate competitors' points-of-differences. Correlational points-of-parity negate any possible disadvantages or negatives that might also arise from a point-of-difference.

Finally, a brand mantra is an articulation of the heart and soul of the brand, a three- to five-word phrase that captures the irrefutable essence or spirit of the brand positioning and brand values. Its purpose is to ensure that all employees and all external marketing partners understand what the brand is, most fundamentally, in order to represent it with consumers.

The choice of these four ingredients determines the brand positioning and the desired brand knowledge structures.

DISCUSSION QUESTIONS

1. Apply the categorization model to a product category other than beverages. How do consumers make decisions whether or not to buy the product, and how do they arrive at their final brand decision? What are the implications for brand equity management for the brands in the category? How does it affect positioning, for example?

2. Pick a category basically dominated by two main brands. Evaluate the positioning of each brand. Who are their target markets? What are their main points-of-parity and points-of-difference? Have they defined their positioning correctly? How might it be improved?

3. Consider a book store in your area. What competitive frames of reference does it face? What are the implications of those frames of reference for its positioning?

4. Can you think of any negatively correlated attributes and benefits other than those listed in Figure 2-6? Can you think of any other strategies to deal with negatively correlated attributes and benefits?

5. What do you think of the brand values pyramid suggested by Bain & Company consultants in The Science of Branding 2-1? How would you apply the framework to a particular brand? Do you think this set of elements yields any unique insights relative to the traditional Maslow's hierarchy of needs?

BRAND FOCUS 2.0
The Marketing Advantages of Strong Brands

Customer-based brand equity occurs when consumer response to marketing activity differs when consumers know the brand and when they do not. How that response differs will depend on the level of brand awareness and how favorably and uniquely consumers evaluate brand associations, as well as the particular marketing activity under consideration.

A number of benefits can result from a strong brand, both in terms of greater revenue and lower costs.[67] For example, one marketing expert categorizes the factors creating financial value for strong brands into two categories: factors related to growth (a brand's ability to attract new customers, resist competitive activity, introduce line extensions, and cross international borders) and factors related to profitability (brand loyalty, premium pricing, lower price elasticity, lower advertising/sales ratios, and trade leverage).[68]

This brand focus feature considers in detail some of the benefits to the firm of having brands with a high level of awareness and a positive brand image.[69]

Greater Loyalty and Less Vulnerability to Competitive Marketing Actions and Crises

Research shows that different types of brand associations—if favorable—can affect consumer product evaluations, perceptions of quality, and purchase rates.[70] This influence may be especially apparent with difficult-to-assess experience goods[71] and as the uniqueness of brand associations increases.[72] In addition, familiarity with a brand has been shown to increase consumer confidence, attitude toward the brand, and purchase intention,[73] and to mitigate the negative impact of a poor trial experience.[74]

For these and other reasons, one characteristic of brands with a great deal of equity is that consumers feel great loyalty to them. Some top brands have been market leaders for years despite significant changes in both consumer attitudes and competitive activity over time. Through it all, consumers have valued these brands enough to stick with them and reject the overtures of competitors, creating a steady stream of revenues for the firm. Research also shows that brands with large market shares are more likely to have more loyal customers than brands with small market shares, a phenomenon called *double jeopardy*.[75] One study found that brand equity was strongly correlated (.75) with subsequent market share and profitability.[76]

A brand with a positive brand image also is more likely to successfully weather a brand crisis or downturn in the brand's fortunes.[77] Perhaps the most compelling example is Johnson & Johnson's (J&J) Tylenol brand. The brand focus feature describes how J&J contended with a tragic product-tampering episode in the early 1980s. Despite seeing its market share drop from 37 percent to almost zero overnight and fearing Tylenol would be written off as a brand with no future, J&J was able to regain virtually all lost market share for the brand through its skillful handling of the crisis and a good deal of brand equity. More recently, two automobile brands—that is, Toyota, and perhaps to a lesser extent, Volkswagen—have successfully weathered crises that posed significant threats to their brand equity.

The lesson is that effective handling of a marketing crisis requires swift and sincere action, an immediate admission that something has gone wrong, and assurance that an effective remedy will be put in place. The greater the brand equity, the more likely that these statements will be credible enough to keep customers understanding and patient as the firm sets out to solve the crisis. Without some underlying brand equity, however, even the best-laid plans for recovery may fall short with a suspicious or uninformed public.[78] Finally, even absent a crisis, a strong brand offers protection in a marketing downturn or when the brand's fortunes fall.

Larger Margins

Brands with positive customer-based brand equity can command a price premium.[79] Moreover, consumers should also have a fairly inelastic response to price increases and elastic responses to price decreases or discounts for the brand over time.[80] Consistent with this reasoning, research has shown that consumers loyal to a brand are less likely to switch in the face of price increases and more likely to increase the quantity of the brand purchased in

the face of price decreases.[81] In a competitive sense, brand leaders draw a disproportionate amount of share from smaller-share competitors.[82] At the same time, market leaders are relatively immune to price competition from these small-share brands.[83]

In a classic early study, Intelliquest explored the role of brand name and price in the decision purchase of business computer buyers.[84] Survey respondents were asked, "What is the incremental dollar value you would be willing to pay over a 'no-name' clone computer brand?" IBM commanded the greatest price premium, followed by Compaq and Hewlett-Packard. Some brands had negative brand equity; they actually received negative numbers. Clearly, according to this study, brands had specific meaning in the personal computer market that consumers valued and were willing to pay for.

It is noteworthy that there is a contradictory trend that is currently taking hold in that a brand's loyal customers often have higher leverage and, therefore, expect to enjoy lower prices than those with less loyal status. One published study examined this phenomenon of willingness to pay less among a firm's most loyal customers.[85] This is particularly true in larger purchases and in business-to-business transactions in which salespeople are often willing to provide greater discounts in price negotiations to their more loyal customers. One way to ensure that loyal customers are rewarded in ways other than price discounts may be to offer different rewards—for example, free gifts or customer service, to ensure loyal customers don't receive steep discounts. Salespeople can be trained not to give away large discounts, and higher quality brands can afford to maintain price by emphasizing the quality difference accompanying choice of their brand.

Greater Trade Cooperation and Support

Wholesalers, retailers, and other middlemen in the distribution channel play an important role in the selling of many products. Their activities can thus facilitate or inhibit the success of the brand. If a brand has a positive image, retailers and other middlemen are more likely to respond to the wishes of consumers and actively promote and sell the brand.[86] Channel members are also less likely to require any marketing push from the manufacturer and will be more receptive to manufacturers' suggestions to stock, reorder, and display the brand,[87] as well as to pass through trade promotions, demand smaller slotting allowances, give more favorable shelf space or position, and so on. Given that many consumer decisions are made in the store, the possibility of additional marketing push by retailers is important.

Increased Marketing Communication Effectiveness

A host of advertising and communication benefits may result from creating awareness of and a positive image for a brand. One well-established view of consumer response to marketing communications is the hierarchy of effects models. These models assume that consumers move through a series of stages or mental states on the basis of marketing communications—for example, exposure to, attention to, comprehension of, yielding to, retention of, and behaving on the basis of a marketing communication.

A brand with a great deal of equity already has created some knowledge structures in consumers' minds, increasing the likelihood that consumers will pass through various stages of the hierarchy. For example, consider the effects of a positive brand image on the persuasive ability of advertising: Consumers may be more likely to notice an ad, may more easily learn about the brand and form favorable opinions, and may retain and act on these beliefs over time.

Familiar, well-liked brands are less susceptible to interference and confusion from competitive ads,[88] are more responsive to creative strategies such as humor appeals,[89] and are less vulnerable to negative reactions due to concentrated repetition schedules.[90] In addition, panel diary members who were highly loyal to a brand increased purchases when advertising for the brand increased.[91] Other advantages associated with more advertising include increased likelihood of being the focus of attention and increased brand interest.[92]

Because strong brand associations exist, lower levels of repetition may be necessary. For example, in a classic study of advertising weights, Anheuser-Busch ran a carefully conducted field experiment in which it varied the amount of Budweiser advertising shown to consumers in different matched test markets.[93] Seven different advertising expenditure levels were tested, representing increases and decreases from the previous advertising expenditure levels: minus 100 percent (no advertising), minus 50 percent, 0 percent (same level), plus 50 percent, plus 100 percent (double the level of advertising), plus 150 percent, and plus 200 percent. These expenditure levels were run for one year and revealed that the "no advertising" level resulted in the same amount of sales as the current program. In fact, the 50 percent cut in advertising expenditures actually resulted in an increase in sales, consistent with the notion that strong brands such as Budweiser do not require the same advertising levels, at least over a short period of time, as a less well-known or well-liked brand.[94]

Similarly, because of existing brand knowledge structures, consumers may be more likely to notice sales promotions, direct mail offerings, or other sales-oriented marketing communications and respond favorably. For example, several studies have shown that promotion effectiveness is asymmetric in favor of a higher-quality brand.[95]

Possible Licensing and Brand Extension Opportunities

A strong brand often has associations that may be desirable in other product categories. To capitalize on this value, as discussed in Chapter 8, a firm may choose to license its name, logo, or other trademark item to another company for use on its products and merchandise, in return for a royalty fee. The rationale for the licensee (the company obtaining the rights to use the trademark)

is that consumers will pay more for a product because of the recognition and image lent by the trademark. As we outline in Chapter 11, one leading valuation firm (i.e., Brand Finance) uses royalty rates as a way of measuring the value of a brand.

As will be outlined in Chapter 12, a **brand extension** occurs when a firm uses an established brand name to enter a new market. A *line extension* uses a current brand name to enter a new market segment in the existing product class, say, with new varieties, new flavors, or new sizes.

Academic research has shown that well-known and well-regarded brands can extend more successfully and into more diverse categories than other brands.[96] In addition, the amount of brand equity has been shown to be correlated with the highest- or lowest-quality member in the product line for vertical product extensions.[97] Research has also shown that positive symbolic associations may be the basis of these evaluations, even if overall brand attitude itself is not necessarily high.[98]

Brands with varied product category associations through past extensions have been shown to be especially extendable.[99] As a result, introductory marketing programs for extensions from an established brand may be more efficient than others.[100] Several studies have indicated that extension activity has aided (or at least did not dilute) brand equity for the parent brand. For instance, brand extensions strengthened parent brand associations, and "flagship brands" were highly resistant to dilution or other potential negative effects caused by negative experiences with an extension.[101] Research has also found evidence of an ownership effect, whereby current owners generally had more favorable responses to brand line extensions.[102] Finally, extensions of brands that have both high familiarity and positive attitudes have been shown to receive higher initial stock market reactions than other brands.[103]

Other Benefits

Brands with positive customer-based brand equity may provide other advantages to the firm not directly related to the products themselves, such as helping the firm to attract or motivate better employees, generate greater interest from investors, and garner more support from shareholders.[104] In terms of the latter, several research studies have shown that brand equity can be directly related to corporate stock price.[105]

NOTES

1. Kevin Lane Keller, "Conceptualizing, Measuring, and Managing Customer-Based Brand Equity," *Journal of Marketing* 57, no. 1 (January 1993): 1–29.
2. Much of this chapter is based on Kevin Lane Keller, Brian Sternthal, and Alice Tybout, "Three Questions You Need to Ask About Your Brand," *Harvard Business Review* 80, no. 9 (September 2002): 80–89.
3. Danya Sargen, "Marketing Takeaways from Netflix's Content Strategy," *American Marketing Association*, www.ama.org/publications/MarketingNews/Pages/netflix-content-strategy.aspx; Dennis Williams, "4 Content Marketing Lessons to Learn from Netflix," *Entrepreneur*, May 22, 2017, www.entrepreneur.com/article/294050.
4. Kevin Lane Keller, "Discovery Channel Looks to Bring New Energy, Focus to Brand Identity," *Art & Business in Motion*, August 26, 2011, www.dennytu.wordpress.com; Dan Butcher, "Discovery Channel Launches Cross-Network Ad Campaign with Microsoft," *Mobile Marketer*, April 26, 2009; www.dsc.discovery.com.
5. Rick Kissell, "Ratings: Discovery Channel Delivers Biggest May Ever," *Variety*, June 5, 2015, http://variety.com/2015/tv/ratings/ratings-discovery-channel-best-ever-1201513568/.
6. US News.com, "Discovery Channel Asks Shark Week Viewers to Be Donors, Too," *U.S. News & World Report*, June 19, 2017,

7. Broadcastingcable.com, "Cable Network Coverage Area Household Universe Estimates: January 2016," *Broadcasting & Cable*, 2016, www.broadcastingcable.com/content/cable-network-coverage-area-household-universe-estimates-january-2016/153590.

8. "Business & Brands," Discovery, accessed February 2, 2018, https://corporate.discovery.com/businesses-and-brands/.

9. Richard Jones, "Finding Sources of Brand Value: Developing a Stakeholder Model of Brand Equity," *Journal of Brand Management* 13, no. 1 (October 2005): 10–32.

10. John R. Anderson, *The Architecture of Cognition* (Cambridge, MA: Harvard University Press, 1983); Robert S. Wyer Jr. and Thomas K. Srull, "Person Memory and Judgment," *Psychological Review* 96, no. 1 (1989): 58–83.

11. John R. Rossiter and Larry Percy, *Advertising and Promotion Management* (New York: McGraw-Hill, 1987).

12. Burleigh B. Gardner and Sidney J. Levy, "The Product and the Brand," *Harvard Business Review* 33, no. 2 (March–April 1955): 33–39.

13. H. Herzog, "Behavioral Science Concepts for Analyzing the Consumer," in *Marketing and the Behavioral Sciences,* ed. Perry Bliss (Boston: Allyn & Bacon, 1963), 76–86; Joseph W. Newman, "New Insight, New Progress for Marketing," *Harvard Business Review* 35, no. 6 (November–December 1957): 95–102.

14. Jim Joseph, "How Do I Love Thee, Apple? Let Me Count the Ways," *Brandweek*, May 24, 2010; Michael Learmonth, "Can the Apple Brand Survive Without Steve Jobs?," *Advertising Age*, January 14, 2009; Miguel Helft and Ashlee Vance, "Apple Passes Microsoft as No. 1 in Tech," *The New York Times*, May 26, 2010; Sarah Vizard, "Why Apple is looking to shift brand perceptions to become more than just 'the iPhone maker'," *Marketing Week*, January 27, 2016, www.marketingweek.com/2016/01/27/why-apple-is-looking-to-shift-brand-perceptions-to-become-more-than-just-the-iphone-maker/; Hyoryung Nam, Yogesh V. Joshi, and P. K. Kannan, "Harvesting Brand Information from Social Tags," *Journal of Marketing* 81, no. 4 (2017): 88–108.

15. James R. Bettman, *An Information Processing Theory of Consumer Choice* (Reading, MA: Addison-Wesley, 1979); John R. Rossiter and Larry Percy, *Advertising and Promotion Management* (New York: McGraw-Hill, 1987).

16. William Baker, J. Wesley Hutchinson, Danny Moore, and Prakash Nedungadi, "Brand Familiarity and Advertising: Effects on the Evoked Set and Brand Preference," in *Advances in Consumer Research,* Vol. 13, ed. Richard J. Lutz (Provo, UT: Association for Consumer Research, 1986), 637–642; Prakash Nedungadi, "Recall and Consumer Consideration Sets: Influencing Choice without Altering Brand Evaluations," *Journal of Consumer Research* 17, no. 3 (December 1990): 263–276.

17. For seminal supporting memory research, see Henry L. Roediger, "Inhibition in Recall from Cuing with Recall Targets," *Journal of Verbal Learning and Verbal Behavior* 12, no. 6 (1973): 644–657; and Raymond S. Nickerson, "Retrieval Inhibition from Part-Set Cuing: A Persisting Enigma in Memory Research," *Memory and Cognition* 12, no. 6 (November 1984): 531–552.

18. Rashmi Adaval, "How Good Gets Better and Bad Gets Worse: Understanding the Impact of Affect on Evaluations of Known Brands," *Journal of Consumer Research* 30, no. 3 (December 2003): 352–367.

19. Jacob Jacoby, George J. Syzabillo, and Jacqeline Busato-Schach, "Information Acquisition Behavior in Brand Choice Situations," *Journal of Consumer Research* 3, no. 4 (1977): 209–216; Ted Roselius, "Consumer Ranking of Risk Reduction Methods," *Journal of Marketing* 35, no. 1 (January 1977): 56–61.

20. James R. Bettman and C. Whan Park, "Effects of Prior Knowledge and Experience and Phase of the Choice Process on Consumer Decision Processes: A Protocol Analysis," *Journal of Consumer Research* 7, no. 3 (December 1980): 234–248; Wayne D. Hoyer and Steven P. Brown, "Effects of Brand Awareness on Choice for a Common, Repeat-Purchase Product," *Journal of Consumer Research* 17, no. 2 (September 1990): 141–148; C. W. Park and V. Parker Lessig, "Familiarity and Its Impact on Consumer Biases and Heuristics," *Journal of Consumer Research* 8, no. 2 (September 1981): 223–230.

21. Richard E. Petty and John T. Cacioppo, *Attitudes and Persuasion: Classic and Contemporary Approaches.* (Boulder, CO: Westview, 1996).

22. Shareen Pathak, "It's Official: E-Trade Is Ending Its Super Bowl Streak," *Ad Age*, December 11, 2013, http://adage.com/article/special-report-super-bowl/e-trade-ends-super-bowl-streak/245630/.

23. Jeff Beer, After The Baby: E-Trade Trades Its Long-Running Campaign For "Type-E" Personalities, Kevin Spacey," *Fast Company*, April 3, 2014, www.fastcompany.com/3028672/after-the-baby-e-trade-trades-its-long-running-campaign-for-type-e-personalities-kevin-space.

24. Matthew Heimer, "How E*Trade Came Back from a Wipeout," *Fortune,* May 20, 2016, http://fortune.com/2016/05/20/etrade-online-investing/.

25. Jesse Dorris, "The Cheese Stands Alone," *Slate*, October 21, 2013, www.slate.com/articles/business/when_big_businesses_were_small/2013/10/annie_s_homegrown_profits_how_the_company_recast_selling_out_as_buying_in.html.

26. Ted Mininni, "Annie's Hops into Consumers' Hearts, Minds and Hands," *Design Force*, June 18, 2012, www.designforceinc.com/annies-homegrown-packaging-as-advertising.

27. David Gianatasio, "Annie's Homegrown Says Its Food Can Help You Live the 'Good' Life," *Adweek,* October 14, 2015, www.adweek.com/brand-marketing/annies-homegrown-says-its-food-can-help-you-live-good-life-167553/.

28. Heather Landi, "When Life Gives You Lemons," *Beverage World*, November 2010, 18–22.

29. George S. Day, Allan D. Shocker, and Rajendra K. Srivastava, "Customer-Oriented Approaches to Identifying Products-Markets," *Journal of Marketing* 43, no. 4 (Fall 1979): 8–19.

30. K. E. Miller and J. L. Ginter, "An Investigation of Situational Variation in Brand Choice Behavior and Attitude," *Journal of Marketing Research* 16, no. 1 (February 1979): 111–123.

31. David A. Aaker, "Positioning Your Brand," *Business Horizons* 25 (May/June 1982): 56–62; Al Ries and Jack Trout, *Positioning: The Battle for Your Mind* (New York: McGraw-Hill, 1979); Yoram Wind, *Product Policy: Concepts, Methods, and Strategy* (Reading, MA: Addison-Wesley, 1982).

32. Dipankar Chakravarti, Deborah J. MacInnis, and Kent Nakamoto, "Product Category Perceptions, Elaborative Processing and Brand Name Extension Strategies," in *Advances in Consumer Research* 17, eds. M. Goldberg, G. Gorn, and R. Pollay (Ann Arbor, MI: Association for Consumer Research, 1990): 910–916; Mita Sujan and James R. Bettman, "The Effects of Brand Positioning Strategies on Consumers' Brand and Category Perceptions: Some Insights from Schema Research," *Journal of Marketing Research* 26, no. 4 (November 1989): 454–467.

33. Joel B. Cohen and Kanul Basu, "Alternative Models of Categorization: Towards a Contingent Processing Framework," *Journal of Consumer Research* 13, no. 4 (March 1987): 455–472; Prakash Nedungadi and J. Wesley Hutchinson, "The Prototypicality of Brands: Relationships with Brand Awareness, Preference, and Usage," in *Advances in Consumer Research,* Vol. 12, eds. Elizabeth C. Hirschman and Morris B. Holbrook (Provo, UT: Association for Consumer Research, 1985), 489–503; Eleanor Rosch and Carolyn B. Mervis, "Family Resemblance: Studies in the Internal Structure of Categories," *Cognitive Psychology* 7, no. 4 (October 1975): 573–605; James Ward and Barbara Loken, "The Quintessential Snack Food: Measurement of Prototypes," in *Advances in Consumer Research,* Vol. 13, ed. Richard J. Lutz (Provo, UT: Association for Consumer Research, 1986), 126–131.

34. Prakash Nedungadi and J. Wesley Hutchinson, "The Prototypicality of Brands"; Ward and Loken, "The Quintessential Snack Food."

35. Phillip Kotler and Kevin Lane Keller, *Marketing Management,* 14th ed. (Upper Saddle River, NJ: Prentice Hall, 2012).

36. Russell I. Haley, "Benefit Segmentation: A Decision-Oriented Research Tool," *Journal of Marketing* 32, no. 3 (July 1968): 30–35.

37. Maryalene LaPonsie, "3 Best Rewards Credit Cards for Seniors," *U.S. News*, August 13, 2015, https://money.usnews.com/money/retirement/articles/2015/08/13/3-best-rewards-credit-cards-for-seniors.

38. Also, it may be the case that the actual demographic specifications given do not fully reflect consumers' underlying perceptions. For example, when the Ford Mustang was introduced, the intended market segment was much younger than the ages of the customers who actually bought the car. Evidently, these consumers felt or wanted to feel younger psychologically than they really were.

39. Paul Jankowski, "Which Group of Millenials Are You Targeting," https://www.forbes.com/sites/pauljankowski/2018/05/09/which-group-of-millennials-are-you-targeting/, accessed August 21, 2018.

40. Ronald Frank, William Massey, and Yoram Wind, *Market Segmentation* (Englewood Cliffs, NJ: Prentice Hall, 1972); Malcolm McDonald and Ian Dunbar, *Market Segmentation: How to Do It, How to Profit from It* (Oxford, UK: Elsevier Butterworth-Heinemann, 2004).

41. Kevin Lane Keller. "CVS' Goal: Attract Customers for Life," *DSN Retailing Today*, May 23, 2005; Kevin Lane Keller. "Women Making a Difference at CVS," *Chain Drug Review*, April 18, 2005.

42. A complete treatment of this material is beyond the scope of this chapter. Useful reviews can be found in any good marketing strategy text. For example, see David A. Aaker, *Strategic Market Management,* 9th ed. (New York: John Wiley & Sons, 2011) or Donald R. Lehmann and Russell S. Winer, *Product Management,* 4th ed. (New York: McGraw-Hill/Irwin, 2005).

43. James R. Bettman and Mita Sujan, "Effects of Framing on Evaluation of Comparable and Noncomparable Alternatives by Expert and Novice Consumers," *Journal of Consumer Research* 14, no. 2 (September 1987): 141–154; Michael D. Johnson, "Consumer Choice Strategies for Comparing Noncomparable Alternatives," *Journal of Consumer Research* 11, no. 3 (December 1984): 741–753; C. Whan Park and Daniel C. Smith, "Product Level Choice: A Top-Down or Bottom-Up Process?" *Journal of Consumer Research* 16, no. 3 (December 1989): 289–299.

44. Teri Agins, "As Consumers Find Other Ways to Splurge, Apparel Hits a Snag," *The Wall Street Journal*, February 4, 2005, A1, A6.

45. Isaac Arnsdorf, "The Best Shot: Cell or Camera?," *The Wall Street Journal*, June 23, 2010.

46. Patrick Barwise and Sean Meehan, *Simply Better: Winning and Keeping Customers by Delivering What Matters Most* (Cambridge, MA: Harvard Business School Press, 2004).

47. Richard Heller, "Folk Fortune," *Forbes*, September 4, 2000, 66–69; Lauren Collins, "House Perfect," *New Yorker*, October 3, 2011.

48. Leonora Polansky, Personal correspondence, June 16, 2011.

49. Interestingly, when Miller Lite was first introduced, the assumption was that the relevant motivation underlying the benefit of "less filling" for consumers was that they could drink more beer. Consequently, Miller targeted heavy users of beer with a sizable introductory ad campaign concentrated on mass-market sports programs. As it turned out, the initial research showed that the market segment they attracted was more the moderate user—older and upscale. Why? The brand promise of "less filling" is actually fairly ambiguous. To this group of consumers, "less filling" meant that they could drink beer and stay mentally and physically agile (sin with no penalty!). From Miller's standpoint, attracting this target market was an unexpected but happy outcome because it meant that there would be less cannibalization with their more mass-market High Life brand. To better match the motivations of this group, there were some changes in the types of athletes in the ads, such as using ex-bullfighters to better represent mental and physical agility.

50. Robert Klara, "'The Other White Meat' Finally Cedes Its Place in the Pen," *Brandweek*, March 4, 2011.

51. Richard A. Melcher, "Why Zima Faded So Fast," *Business Week,* March 10, 1997, 110–114.

52. Keith Naughton, "Ford's 'Perfect Storm,'" *Newsweek*, September 17, 2001, 48–50.

53. Elizabeth Jensen, "Campbell's Juice Scheme: Stealth Health," *The Wall Street Journal,* April 18, 1997, B6.

54. David A. Aaker, *Brand Relevance: Making Competitors Irrelevant* (San Francisco: John Wiley & Sons, 2011).

55. Heather Landi, "Good to the Core," *Beverage World,* August 2010, 35–42.

56. For a thorough examination of how an organization can improve its marketing capabilities, see Andy Bird and Mhairi McEwan, *The Growth Drivers: The Definitive Guide to Transforming Marketing Capabilities* (West Sussex, UK: John Wiley & Sons, 2012).

57. Chloe Sorvino, "The Verdict: POM Wonderful Misled Its Customers, A Blow to Its Billionaire Owners," *Forbes,* May 2, 2016, www.forbes.com/sites/chloesorvino/2016/05/02/the-verdict-pom-wonderful-misled-its-customers-a-blow-to-its-billionaire-owners/#56ae05024b94; Goeffrey Mohan, "Pom Wonderful case not wonderful enough, Supreme Court says" *L.A. Times,* May 4, 2016, www.latimes.com/business/la-fi-pom-wonderful-20160503-snap-story.html.

58. Lalatendu Mehra, "IBM Cloud Eyes 'Small Business,'" *The Hindu,* May 12, 2017, www.thehindu.com/todays-paper/tp-business/ibm-cloud-eyes-small-business/article18587190.ece.

59. W. Chan Kim and Renee Mauborgne. "How to create uncontested market space and make the competition irrelevant." *Harvard Business Review* 4, no. 13 (2005): 1–2.

60. Abraham Maslow, *Motivation and Personality,* 2nd ed. (New York: Harper & Row, 1970).

61. Thomas J. Reynolds and Jonathan Gutman, "Laddering Theory: Method, Analysis, and Interpretation," *Journal of Advertising Research* (February/March 1988): 11–31; Thomas J. Reynolds and David B. Whitlark, "Applying Laddering Data to Communications Strategy and Advertising Practice," *Journal of Advertising Research* (July/August 1995): 9–17.

62. Brian Wansink, "Using Laddering to Understand and Leverage a Brand's Equity," *Qualitative Market Research* 6, no. 2 (2003): 111–118.

63. Lance Cothern, "Bold Move by Discover—The Discover it™ Credit Card," *Money Manifesto,* January 9, 2014, www.moneymanifesto.com/bold-move-by-discover-the-discover-it-credit-card-2793/.

64. *Business Wire,* "Discover Launches Game-Changing New "it" Credit Card," January 2, 2013, accessed February 1, 2018.

65. Marco Vriens and Frenkel Ter Hofstede, "Linking Attributes, Benefits, and Consumer Values," *Marketing Research* 12, no. 3 (Fall 2000): 3–8.

66. Kevin Lane Keller, "Brand Mantras: Rationale, Criteria, and Examples," *Journal of Marketing Management* 15, no. 1-3 (1999): 43–51.

67. Brand Focus 2.0 is based in part on Steven Hoeffler and Kevin Lane Keller, "The Marketing Advantages of Strong Brands," *Journal of Brand Management* 10, no. 6 (August 2003): 421–445.

68. Ian M. Lewis, "Brand Equity or Why the Board of Directors Needs Marketing Research," paper presented at the ARF Fifth Annual Advertising and Promotion Workshop, February 1, 1993.

69. The following sections review seminal research in each of the areas. For more recent research on these topics, see Philip Kotler and Kevin Lane Keller, *Marketing Management,* 15th ed. (Upper Saddle River, NJ: Prentice Hall, 2016).

70. Peter A. Dacin and Daniel C. Smith, "The Effect of Brand Portfolio Characteristics on Consumer Evaluations of Brand Extensions," *Journal of Marketing Research* 31, no. 2 (May 1994): 229–242; George S. Day and Terry Deutscher, "Attitudinal Predictions of Choices of Major Appliance Brands," *Journal of Marketing Research* 19, no. 2 (May 1982), 192–198; W. B. Dodds, K. B. Monroe, and D. Grewal, "Effects of Price, Brand, and Store Information on Buyers' Product Evaluations," *Journal of Marketing Research* 28, no. 3 (August 1991): 307–319; France Leclerc, Bernd H. Schmitt, and Laurette Dube, "Foreign Branding and Its Effects on Product Perceptions and Attitudes," *Journal of Marketing Research* 31, no. 5 (1994): 263–270; Akshay R. Rao and K. B. Monroe, "The Effects of Price, Brand Name, and Store Name on Buyers' Perceptions of Product Quality: An Integrative Review," *Journal of Marketing Research* 26, no. 3 (August 1989): 351–357.

71. B. Wernerfelt, "Umbrella Branding as a Signal of New Product Quality: An Example of Signaling by Posting a Bond," *Rand Journal of Economics* 19, no. 3 (1988): 458–466; Tullin Erdem, "An Empirical Analysis of Umbrella Branding," *Journal of Marketing Research* 35, no. 8 (1998): 339–351.

72. Fred M. Feinberg, Barbara E. Kahn, and Leigh McAllister, "Market Share Response When Consumers Seek Variety," *Journal of Marketing Research* 29, no. 2 (May 1992): 227–237.

73. Michel Laroche, Chankon Kim, and Lianxi Zhou, "Brand Familiarity and Confidence as Determinants of Purchase Intention: An Empirical Test in a Multiple Brand Context," *Journal of Business Research* 37, no. 2 (1996): 115–120.

74. Robert E. Smith, "Integrating Information from Advertising and Trial," *Journal of Marketing Research* 30, no. 2 (May 1993): 204–219.

75. Andrew S. C. Ehrenberg, Gerard J. Goodhardt, and Patrick T. Barwise, "Double Jeopardy Revisited," *Journal of Marketing* 54, no. 3 (July 1990): 82–91.

76. Ipsos-ASI, January 30, 2003.

77. Rohini Ahluwalia, Robert E. Burnkrant, and H. Rao Unnava, "Consumer Response to Negative Publicity: The Moderating Role of Commitment," *Journal of Marketing Research* 37, no. 2 (May 2000): 203–214; Narij Dawar and Madam M. Pillutla, "Impact of Product-Harm Crises on Brand Equity: The Moderating Role of Consumer Expectations," *Journal of Marketing Research* 37, no. 2 (May 2000): 215–226.

78. Susan Caminit, "The Payoff from a Good Corporate Reputation," *Fortune,* February 10, 1992, 74–77.

79. Deepak Agrawal, "Effects of Brand Loyalty on Advertising and Trade Promotions: A Game Theoretic Analysis with Empirical Evidence," *Marketing Science* 15, no. 1 (1996): 86–108; Chan Su Park and V. Srinivasan, "A Survey-Based Method for Measuring and Understanding Brand Equity and Its Extendability," *Journal of Marketing Research* 31, no. 2 (May 1994): 271–288; Raj Sethuraman, "A Model of How Discounting High-Priced Brands Affects the Sales of Low-Priced Brands,"

Journal of Marketing Research 33, no. 4 (November 1996): 399–409.

80. Hermann Simon, "Dynamics of Price Elasticity and Brand Life Cycles: An Empirical Study," *Journal of Marketing Research* 16, no. 4 (November 1979): 439–452; K. Sivakumar and S. P. Raj, "Quality Tier Competition: How Price Change Influences Brand Choice and Category Choice," *Journal of Marketing* 61, no. 3 (July 1997): 71–84.

81. Lakshman Krishnamurthi and S. P. Raj, "An Empirical Analysis of the Relationship Between Brand Loyalty and Consumer Price Elasticity," *Marketing Science* 10, no. 2 (Spring 1991): 172–183. See also, Garrett Sonnier and Andrew Ainsle, "Estimating the Value of Brand-Image Associations: The Role of General and Specific Brand Image," *Journal of Marketing Research* 48, no. 3 (June 2011): 518–531; William Boulding, Eunkyu Lee, and Richard Staelin, "Mastering the Mix: Do Advertising, Promotion, and Sales Force Activities Lead to Differentiation?" *Journal of Marketing Research* 31, no. 2 (May 1994): 159 172. See also Vinay Kanetkar, Charles B. Weinberg, and Doyle L. Weiss, "Price Sensitivity and Television Advertising Exposures: Some Empirical Findings," *Marketing Science* 11, no. 4 (Fall 1992): 359–371.

82. Greg M. Allenby and Peter E. Rossi, "Quality Perceptions and Asymmetric Switching Between Brands," *Marketing Science* 10, no. 3 (Summer 1991): 185–204; Rajiv Grover and V. Srinivasan, "Evaluating the Multiple Effects of Retail Promotions on Brand Loyal and Brand Switching Segments," *Journal of Marketing Research* 29, no. 1 (February 1992): 76–89; Gary J. Russell and Wagner A. Kamakura, "Understanding Brand Competition Using Micro and Macro Scanner Data," *Journal of Marketing Research* 31, no. 2 (May 1994): 289–303.

83. Albert C. Bemmaor and Dominique Mouchoux, "Measuring the Short-Term Effect of In-Store Promotion and Retail Advertising on Brand Sales: A Factorial Experiment," *Journal of Marketing Research* 28, no. 2 (May 1991): 202–214; Robert C. Blattberg and Kenneth J. Wisniewski, "Price-Induced Patterns of Competition," *Marketing Science* 8, no. 4 (Fall 1989): 291–309; Randolph E. Bucklin, Sunil Gupta, and Sangman Han, "A Brand's Eye View of Response Segmentation in Consumer Brand Choice Behavior," *Journal of Marketing Research* 32, no. 1 (February 1995): 66–74; K. Sivakumar and S. P. Raj, "Quality Tier Competition: How Price Change Influences Brand Choice and Category Choice," *Journal of Marketing* (1997): 71–84.

84. Kyle Pope, "Computers: They're No Commodity," *The Wall Street Journal,* October 15, 1993, B1.

85. Jan Wieseke, Sascha Alavi and Johannes Habel," Willing to Pay More, Eager to Pay Less, The Role of Customer Loyalty in Price Negotiations." Journal of Marketing 78, no. 6 (2014): 17–27.

86. Peter S. Fader and David C. Schmittlein, "Excess Behavioral Loyalty for High-Share Brands: Deviations from the Dirichlet Model for Repeat Purchasing," *Journal of Marketing Research* 30, no. 11 (1993): 478–493; Rajiv Lal and Chakravarthi Narasimhan, "The Inverse Relationship Between Manufacturer and Retailer Margins: A Theory," *Marketing Science* 15, no. 2 (1996): 132–151; Mark S. Glynn, "The Moderating Effect of

Brand Strength in Manufacturer-Reseller Relationships," *Industrial Marketing Management* 39, no. 8 (2010): 1226–1233.

87. David B. Montgomery, "New Product Distribution: An Analysis of Supermarket Buyer Decisions," *Journal of Marketing Research* 12, no. 3 (1978): 255–264.

88. Robert J. Kent and Chris T. Allen, "Competitive Interference Effects in Consumer Memory for Advertising: The Role of Brand Familiarity," *Journal of Marketing* 58, no. 3 (July 1994): 97–105.

89. Amitava Chattopadyay and Kunal Basu, "Humor in Advertising: The Moderating Role of Prior Brand Evaluation," *Journal of Marketing Research* 27, no. 4 (November 1990): 466–476; D. W. Stewart and David H. Furse, *Effective Television Advertising: A Study of 1000 Commercials* (Lexington, MA: D.C. Heath, 1986); M. G. Weinburger and C. Gulas, "The Impact of Humor in Advertising: A Review," *Journal of Advertising* 21, no. 4 (1992): 35–60.

90. Margaret Campbell and Kevin Lane Keller, "Brand Familiarity and Ad Repetition Effects," *Journal of Consumer Research* 30, no. 2 (September 2003), 292–304.

91. S. P. Raj, "The Effects of Advertising on High and Low Loyalty Consumer Segments," *Journal of Consumer Research* 9, no. 1 (June 1982): 77–89.

92. Ravi Dhar and Itamar Simonson, "The Effect of the Focus of Comparison on Consumer Preferences," *Journal of Marketing Research* 29, no. 4 (November 1992): 430–440; Karen A. Machleit, Chris T. Allen, and Thomas J. Madden, "The Mature Brand and Brand Interest: An Alternative Consequence of Ad-Evoked Affect," *Journal of Marketing* 57, no. 4 (October 1993): 72–82; Itamar Simonson, Joel Huber, and John Payne, "The Relationship between Prior Brand Knowledge and Information Acquisition Order," *Journal of Consumer Research* 14, no. 4 (March 1988): 566–578.

93. Russell L. Ackoff and James R. Emshoff, "Advertising Research at Anheuser-Busch, Inc. (1963–1968)," *Sloan Management Review* 16, no.2 (Winter 1975): 1–15.

94. These results should be interpreted carefully, however, as they do not suggest that large advertising expenditures did not play an important role in creating equity for the brand in the past, or that advertising expenditures could be cut severely without some adverse sales consequences at some point in the future.

95. See Robert C. Blattberg, Richard Briesch, and Edward J. Fox, "How Promotions Work," *Marketing Science* 14, no. 3 (1995): G122–G132. See also Bart J. Bronnenberg and Luc Wathieu, "Asymmetric Promotion Effects and Brand Positioning," *Marketing Science* 15, no. 4 (1996): 379–394. This study shows how the relative promotion effectiveness of high- and low-quality brands depends on their positioning along both price and quality dimensions.

96. David A. Aaker and Kevin Lane Keller, "Consumer Evaluations of Brand Extensions," *Journal of Marketing* 54, no. 1 (1990): 27–41; Kevin Lane Keller and David A. Aaker, "The Effects of Sequential Introduction of Brand Extensions," *Journal of Marketing Research* 29, no. 1 (February 1992): 35–50; A. Rangaswamy, R. R. Burke, and T. A. Oliva, "Brand Equity and the Extendibility of Brand Names," *International Journal of Research in Marketing* 10, no. 3 (1993): 61–75.

97. Taylor Randall, Karl Ulrich, and David Reibstein, "Brand Equity and Vertical Product Line Extent," *Marketing Science* 17, no. 4 (1998): 356–379.

98. Srinivas K. Reddy, Susan Holak, and Subodh Bhat, "To Extend or Not to Extend: Success Determinants of Line Extensions," *Journal of Marketing Research* 31, no. 5 (1994): 243–262; C. Whan Park, Sandra Milberg, and Robert Lawson, "Evaluation of Brand Extensions: The Role of Product Feature Similarity and Brand Concept Consistency," *Journal of Consumer Research* 18, no. 9 (1991): 185–193; Susan M. Broniarcysyk and Joseph W. Alba, "The Importance of the Brand in Brand Extension," *Journal of Marketing Research* 31, no. 5 (1994): 214–228.

99. Peter A. Dacin and Daniel C. Smith, "The Effect of Brand Portfolio Characteristics on Consumer Evaluations of Brand Extensions," *Journal of Marketing Research* 31, no. 2 (May 1994): 229–242; Keller and Aaker, "The Effects of Sequential Introduction of Brand Extensions"; Daniel A. Sheinin and Bernd H. Schmitt, "Extending Brands with New Product Concepts: The Role of Category Attribute Congruity, Brand Affect, and Brand Breadth," *Journal of Business Research* 31, no. 1 (1994): 1–10.

100. Roger A. Kerin, Gurumurthy Kalyanaram, and Daniel J. Howard, "Product Hierarchy and Brand Strategy Influences on the Order of Entry Effect for Consumer Packaged Goods," *Journal of Product Innovation Management* 13, no. 1 (1996): 21–34.

101. Maureen Morrin, "The Impact of Brand Extensions on Parent Brand Memory Structures and Retrieval Processes," *Journal of Marketing Research* 36, no. 4 (November 1999): 517–525; John Roedder, Barbara Loken, and Christopher Joiner, "The Negative Impact of Extensions: Can Flagship Products Be Diluted?" *Journal of Marketing* 62, no. 1 (January 1998): 19–32; Daniel A. Sheinin, "The Effects of Experience with Brand Extensions on Parent Brand Knowledge," *Journal of Business Research* 49, no. 1 (2000): 47–55.

102. Amna Kirmani, Sanjay Sood, and Sheri Bridges, "The Ownership Effect in Consumer Responses to Brand Line Stretches," *Journal of Marketing* 63, no. 1 (January 1999): 88–101.

103. Vicki R. Lane and Robert Jacobson, "Stock Market Reactions to Brand Extension Announcements: The Effects of Brand Attitude and Familiarity," *Journal of Marketing* 59, no. 1 (1995): 63–77.

104. Douglas E. Hughes and Michael Ahearne, "Energizing the Reseller's Sales Force: The Power of Brand Identification," *Journal of Marketing* 74, no. 4 (July 2010): 81–96; V. Kumar and Denish Shah, "Can Marketing Lift Stock Prices?," *MIT Sloan Management Review* 52, no. 4 (Summer 2011): 24–26.

105. David A. Aaker and Robert Jacobson, "The Financial Information Content of Perceived Quality," *Journal of Marketing Research* 31, no. 5 (1994): 191–201; David A. Aaker and Robert Jacobson, "The Value Relevance of Brand Attitude in High-Technology Markets," *Journal of Marketing Research* 38, no. 4 (November 2001): 485–493; M. E. Barth, M. Clement, G. Foster, and R. Kasznik, "Brand Values and Capital Market Valuation," *Review of Accounting Studies* 3, no. 1–2 (1998): 41–68.

3

Brand Resonance and the Brand Value Chain

Learning Objectives

After reading this chapter, you should be able to

1. Define brand resonance.
2. Describe the steps in building brand resonance.
3. Define the brand value chain.
4. Identify the stages in the brand value chain.
5. Contrast brand equity and customer equity.

Corona used its strong brand imagery of "beach in a bottle" to become the leading U.S. import beer.

Source: AP Photo/Amy Sancetta

PREVIEW

Chapter 2 outlined in detail the concept of customer-based brand equity and introduced a brand positioning model based on the concepts of points-of-parity and points-of-difference. We next broaden our discussion to consider the two other interlinking models, which all together make up the brand planning system.

We first present the **brand resonance model**, which describes how to create intense, active loyalty relationships with customers. The model considers how brand positioning affects what consumers think, feel, and do and the degree to which they resonate or connect with a brand. After discussing some of the main implications of that model, we consider how brand resonance and these loyalty relationships, in turn, create brand equity or value.

The **brand value chain model** is a means by which marketers can trace the value creation process for their brands to better understand the financial impact of their marketing expenditures and investments. Based in part on the customer-based brand equity (CBBE) concept developed in Chapter 2, it offers a holistic, integrated approach to understanding how brands create value.

Brand Focus 3.0 at the end of the chapter provides a detailed overview of the topic of customer equity.

BUILDING A STRONG BRAND: THE FOUR STEPS OF BRAND BUILDING

The brand resonance model looks at building a brand as a sequence of steps, each of which is contingent on successfully achieving the objectives of the previous one. The steps are as follows:

1. Ensure identification of the brand with customers and an association of the brand in customers' minds with a specific product class, product benefit, or customer need.
2. Firmly establish the totality of brand meaning in the minds of customers by strategically linking a host of tangible and intangible brand associations.
3. Elicit the proper customer responses to the brand.
4. Convert brand responses to create brand resonance and an intense, active loyalty relationship between customers and the brand.

These four steps represent a set of fundamental questions that customers invariably ask about brands—at least implicitly. The four questions (with corresponding brand steps in parentheses) are:

1. Who are you? (brand identity)
2. What are you? (brand meaning)
3. What about you? What do I think or feel about you? (brand responses)
4. What about you and me? What kind of association and how much of a connection would I like to have with you? (brand relationships)

Notice the ordering of the steps in this **branding ladder**, from identity to meaning to responses to relationships. That is, we cannot establish meaning unless we have created an identity; responses cannot occur unless we have developed the right meaning; and we cannot forge a relationship unless we have elicited the proper responses.

To provide some structure, let us think of establishing six **brand building blocks** with customers that we can assemble in a pyramid, with significant brand equity only resulting if brands reach the top of the pyramid. This brand-building process is illustrated in Figures 3-1 and 3-2. We will look at each of these steps and corresponding brand building blocks and their subdimensions in the following sections. As will become apparent, building blocks up the left side of the pyramid represent a more rational route to the brand-building, whereas building blocks up the right side of the pyramid represent a more emotional route. Most strong brands are built by going up both sides of the pyramid.

Brand Salience

Achieving the right brand identity means creating brand salience with customers. **Brand salience** measures various aspects of the awareness of the brand and how easily and often the brand is evoked under various situations or circumstances. To what extent is the brand top-of-mind and

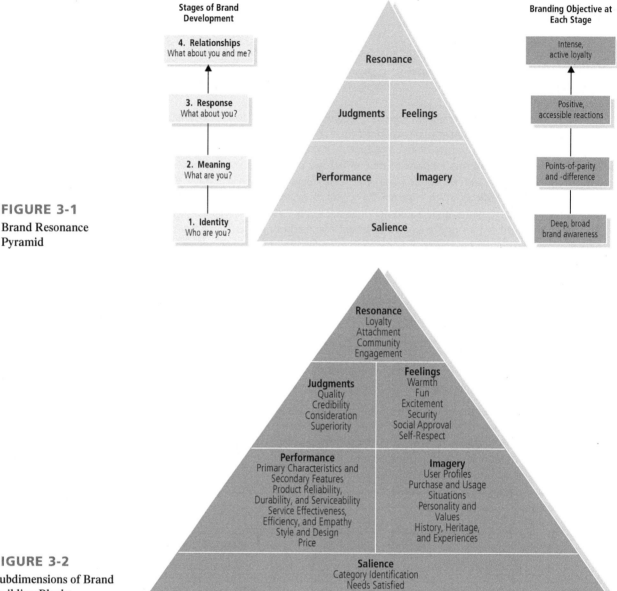

FIGURE 3-1

Brand Resonance
Pyramid

FIGURE 3-2

Subdimensions of Brand
Building Blocks

easily recalled or recognized? What types of cues or reminders are necessary? How pervasive is this brand awareness?

We have said that brand awareness refers to customers' ability to recall and recognize the brand under different conditions and to link the brand name, logo, symbol, and so forth, to certain associations in memory. In particular, building brand awareness helps customers understand the product or service category in which the brand competes and what products or services are sold under the brand name. It also ensures that customers know which of their "needs" the brand—through these products—is designed to satisfy. In other words, what basic functions does the brand provide to customers?

Breadth and Depth of Awareness.   Brand awareness thus gives the product identity by linking brand elements to a product category and associated purchase and consumption or usage situations. The *depth* of brand awareness measures how likely it is for a brand element to come to mind and the ease with which it does so. A brand we easily recall has a deeper level of brand awareness than one that we recognize only when we see it. The *breadth* of brand awareness measures the range of purchase and usage situations in which the brand element comes to mind and depends to a large extent on the organization of brand and product knowledge in memory.[1] To see how this works, consider the breadth and depth of brand awareness for Tropicana orange juice.

TROPICANA

Consumers should at least recognize the Tropicana brand when it is presented to them. Beyond that, consumers should think of Tropicana whenever they think of orange juice, particularly when they are considering buying orange juice. Ideally, consumers would think of Tropicana whenever they were deciding which type of beverage to drink, especially when seeking a "tasty but healthy" beverage. Thus, consumers must think of Tropicana as satisfying a certain set of needs whenever those needs arise. One of the challenges for any provider of orange juice is to link the product to usage situations beyond the traditional one of breakfast—hence, the industry campaign to boost consumption of Florida orange juice that used the slogan "It's Not Just for Breakfast Anymore."

For Tropicana, it is important that consumers think of the brand in other consumption situations beyond breakfast.
Source: Keri Miksza

Product Category Structure.   As the Tropicana example suggests, to fully understand brand recall, we need to appreciate ***product category structure***, or how product categories are organized in memory. Typically, marketers assume that products are grouped at varying levels of specificity and can be organized in a hierarchical fashion.[2] Thus, in consumers' minds, a product hierarchy often exists, with product class information at the highest level, product category information at the second-highest level, product type information at the next level, and brand information at the lowest level.

The beverage market provides a good setting to examine issues in category structure and the effects of brand awareness on brand equity. Figure 3-3 illustrates one hierarchy that might exist in consumers' minds. According to this representation, consumers first distinguish between flavored and nonflavored beverages (water). Next, they distinguish between nonalcoholic and alcoholic flavored beverages. They further distinguish nonalcoholic beverages into hot drinks like coffee or tea, and cold drinks like milk, juices, and soft drinks. Alcoholic beverages are distinguished by whether they are wine, beer, or distilled spirits. We can make even further distinctions. For example, we can divide the beer category into no-alcohol, low-alcohol (or "light"), and full-strength beers, and divide full-strength beers by variety (ale or lager), brewing method (ice or dry), serving style (draft or bottle), price and quality (discount, premium, or super-premium), source or origin (imported versus domestic), and so on.

The organization of the product category hierarchy that generally prevails in memory will play an important role in brand awareness, brand consideration, and consumer decision-making. For example, consumers often make decisions in a top-down fashion, first deciding whether to have

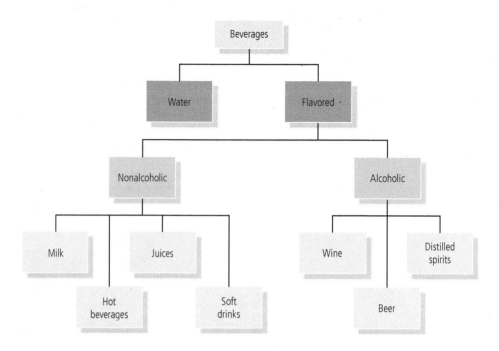

FIGURE 3-3

Beverage Category Hierarchy

water or some type of flavored beverage. If the consumer chooses a flavored drink, the next decision would be whether to have an alcoholic or a nonalcoholic drink. Finally, consumers might then choose a particular brand within the product category in which they are interested.

The *depth* of brand awareness will influence the likelihood that the brand comes to mind, whereas the *breadth* of brand awareness describes the different types of situations in which the brand might come to mind. In general, soft drinks have great breadth of awareness in that they come to mind in a variety of different consumption situations. A consumer may consider drinking one of the different varieties of Coke virtually any time, anywhere. Other beverages, such as alcoholic beverages, milk, and juices, have much more limited perceived consumption situations.

Strategic Implications.   The product hierarchy shows us that not only the depth of awareness matters, but also the breadth. In other words, the brand must not only be top-of-mind and have sufficient mindshare, but it must also do so at the right times and places.

Breadth is an oft-neglected consideration, even for brands that are category leaders. For many brands, the key question is not *whether* consumers can recall the brand but *where* they think of it, *when* they think of it, and how *easily* and how *often* they think of it. Many brands and products are ignored or forgotten during possible usage situations. For those brands, the best route for improving sales may be not to try to improve consumer attitudes but, instead, increasing brand salience and the breadth of brand awareness and situations in which consumers would consider using the brand to drive consumption and increase sales volume.

Tax preparer H&R Block makes a concerted effort to make sure its brand is top-of-mind at all times, reminding consumers that tax-pertinent events happen all year round, such as when taking

---

CAMPBELL'S SOUP

Ads for Campbell's soup through the years have sometimes emphasized taste, with its longtime advertising slogan "Mmm, Mmm, Good," or nutrition, with "Never Underestimate the Power of Soup." Part of Campbell's challenge in increasing sales may lie not so much in the consumer attitudes these slogans address as with memory considerations and the fact that people do not think of using or eating soup as often as they should for certain meal occasions. In 2010, Campbell launched a new ad campaign, "It's Amazing What Soup Can Do," showcasing the soup as an indispensable food for any occasion—paired with a variety of foods; poured over meat, pasta, or rice as a sauce; or used as an ingredient in a recipe.

Creating a communication program for those consumers who already have a favorable attitude toward the brand that will help them remember it in more varied consumption settings may be the most profitable way to grow the Campbell's soup franchise.[4] Campbell's has continued to evolve this theme in its advertising campaigns. Recently, Campbell's Soup has depicted real families as well as real weather patterns to tie in soup consumption with various events in consumers' lives. For example, one ad depicts a mom in a grocery store with her kids when she hears the weather forecast about an impending storm. Upon hearing this, she gets extra cans of soup so that she can add to her stock at home. In this way, the new tagline "Made for Real, Real Life," aligns well with the company's corporate purpose of "real food that matters for life's moments."[5] Expanding the range of occasions that Campbell's is consumed helps reinforce how Campbell's Soup is viewed by consumers and allows the company to increase the breadth of brand awareness.

Campbell Soup's best growth prospect might be just to remind consumers of more situations in which they could eat soup.

Source: Campbell Soup Company

---

clients out to dinner, buying a new laptop computer or looking for a new job.[3] Consider the brand salience challenges for Campbell's soup.

In other words, it may be harder to try to *change* existing brand attitudes than to *remind* people of their existing attitudes toward a brand in additional, but appropriate, consumption situations.

A highly salient brand is one that has both depth and breadth of brand awareness, such that customers always make sufficient purchases as well as always think of the brand across a variety of settings in which it could be employed or consumed. Brand salience is an important first step in building brand equity but is usually not sufficient. For many customers in many situations, other considerations, such as the meaning or image of the brand, also come into play.

Creating brand meaning includes establishing a brand image—what the brand is characterized by and should stand for in the minds of customers. Brand meaning is made up of two major categories of brand associations related to performance and imagery. These associations can be formed directly, from a customer's own experiences and contact with the brand, or indirectly, through advertising or by some other source of information, such as word of mouth.

The next section describes the two main types of brand meaning—brand performance and brand imagery—and the subcategories within each of those two building blocks.

Brand Performance

The product itself is at the heart of brand equity because it is the primary influence on what consumers experience with a brand, what they hear about a brand from others, and what the firm can tell customers about the brand in their communications. Designing and delivering a product that fully satisfies consumer needs and wants is a prerequisite for successful marketing, regardless of whether the product is a tangible good, service, organization, or person. To create brand loyalty and resonance, marketers must ensure that consumers' experiences with the product at least meet, if not surpass, their expectations. As Chapter 1 noted, numerous studies have shown that high quality brands tend to perform better financially and yield higher returns on investment.

SUBWAY

Subway zoomed to the top as the biggest-selling quick-serve restaurant through a clever positioning of offering healthy, good-tasting sandwiches. This straddle positioning allowed the brand to create a POP on taste and a POD on health concerning quick-serve restaurants such as McDonald's and Burger King, but, at the same time, a POP on health and a POD on taste with respect to health food restaurants and cafés. One of Subway's highly successful product launches was the $5 footlong sandwich. Dreamed up by a franchise operator in Miami, the idea quickly took hold and was the perfect solution for hungry, cash-starved consumers during the recession. This strong performance and value message has allowed Subway to significantly expand its market coverage and potential customer base.[6]

Brand performance describes how well the product or service meets customers' more functional needs. How well does the brand rate on objective assessments of quality? To what extent does the brand satisfy utilitarian, aesthetic, and economic customer needs and wants in the product or service category?

Brand performance transcends the product's ingredients and features to include dimensions that differentiate the brand. Often, the strongest brand positioning relies on performance advantages of some kind, and it is rare that a brand can overcome severe performance deficiencies. Five important types of attributes and benefits often underlie brand performance, as follows:[7]

1. **Primary ingredients and supplementary features.** Customers often have beliefs about the levels at which the primary ingredients of the product operate (low, medium, high, or very high), and about special, perhaps even patented, features or secondary elements that complement these primary ingredients. Some attributes are essential ingredients necessary for a product to work, whereas others are supplementary features that allow for customization and more versatile, personalized usage. Of course, these vary by product or service category.

2. **Product reliability, durability, and serviceability.** *Reliability* measures the consistency of performance over time and from purchase to purchase. *Durability* is the expected economic life of the product, and *serviceability*, the ease of repairing the product if needed. Thus, perceptions of product performance are affected by factors such as the speed, accuracy, and care of product delivery and installation; the promptness, courtesy, and helpfulness of customer service and training; and the quality of repair service and the time involved.

3. **Service effectiveness, efficiency, and empathy.** Customers often have performance-related associations with service. *Service effectiveness* measures how well the brand satisfies

customers' service requirements. *Service efficiency* describes the speed and responsiveness of service. Finally, *service empathy* is the extent to which service providers are seen as trusting, caring, and having the customer's interests in mind.

4. **Style and design.** The design has a functional aspect regarding how a product works that affects performance associations. Consumers also may have associations with the product that goes beyond its functional aspects to more aesthetic considerations such as its size, shape, materials, and color involved. Thus, performance may also depend on sensory aspects such as how a product looks and feels, and perhaps even what it sounds or smells like.

5. **Price.** The pricing policy for the brand can create associations in consumers' minds about how relatively expensive (or inexpensive) the brand is, and whether it is frequently or substantially discounted. Price is a particularly important performance association because consumers may organize their product category knowledge in terms of the price tiers of different brands.[8]

Brand Imagery

The other main type of brand meaning is brand imagery. Brand imagery depends on the extrinsic properties of the product or service, including how the brand attempts to meet customers' psychological or social needs. It is the way people think about a brand abstractly, rather than what they think the brand actually does. Thus, imagery refers to more intangible aspects of the brand, and consumers can form imagery associations directly from their own experience or indirectly through advertising or by some other source of information, such as word of mouth. Many kinds of intangibles can be linked to a brand, but four main ones are:

1. User profiles
2. Purchase and usage situations
3. Personality and values
4. History, heritage, and user experiences.

For example, take a brand with rich brand imagery such as Nivea in Europe, makers of many different skin care and personal care products. Some of its more notable intangible associations include: (1) family/shared experiences/maternal, (2) multipurpose, (3) classic/timeless, and (4) childhood memories.

User Imagery.   One set of brand imagery associations is about the type of person or organization who uses the brand. This imagery may result in customers' mental image of actual users or more aspirational, idealized users. Consumers may base associations of a typical or idealized brand user on descriptive demographic factors or more abstract psychographic factors. Demographic factors might include the following:

- **Gender.** Venus razors and Secret deodorant have feminine associations, whereas Gillette razors and Axe deodorant have more masculine associations.[9]
- **Age.** Pepsi and Under Armour shoes have tried to position themselves as fresher and younger in spirit than Coca-Cola and Nike, respectively.
- **Race.** Goya foods and the Univision television network have a strong identification with the Hispanic market.
- **Income.** Sperry's shoes, Polo shirts, and BMW automobiles became associated with "yuppies"—young, affluent, urban professionals.

Psychographic factors might include attitudes toward life, careers, possessions, social issues, or political institutions; for example, a brand user might be seen as iconoclastic or as more traditional and conservative.

In a business-to-business setting, user imagery might relate to the size or type of organization. For example, buyers might see Microsoft as an aggressive company and Cisco as a technology leader. User imagery may focus on more than characteristics of just one type of individual and center on broader issues regarding perceptions of a group as a whole. For example, customers may believe that a brand is used by many people and therefore view the brand as popular or a market leader.

Purchase and Usage Imagery.   A second set of associations tells consumers under what conditions or situations they can or should buy and use the brand. Associations can relate to type of channel, such as department stores, specialty stores, or the Internet; to specific stores, such as Macy's, Foot Locker, or Nordstrom; and to ease of purchase and associated rewards (if any).

Associations to a typical usage situation can relate to the time of day, week, month, or year to use the brand; location—for instance, inside or outside the home; and type of activity during which to use the brand—formal or informal. For a long time, pizza chain restaurants had strong associations to their channels of distribution and the manner by which customers would purchase and eat the pizza—Domino's was known for delivery, Little Caesar for takeout, and Pizza Hut for dine-in service—although in recent years, each of these major competitors has made inroads in the traditional markets of the others.

Brand Personality and Values.   Through consumer experience or marketing activities, brands may take on personality traits or human values and, like a person, appear to be modern, old-fashioned, lively, or exotic.[10] Five dimensions of brand personality (with corresponding subdimensions) are sincerity (down-to-earth, honest, wholesome, and cheerful), excitement (daring, spirited, imaginative, and up-to-date), competence (reliable, intelligent, successful), sophistication (upper class and charming), and ruggedness (outdoorsy and tough).[11]

How does brand personality get formed? Any aspect of a brand may be used by consumers to infer brand personality. One research study found that consumers perceived nonprofit companies as being warmer than for-profit companies, but less competent. Further, consumers were less willing to buy a product made by a nonprofit than a for-profit company because of their perception that the firm lacked competence, but those purchasing misgivings disappeared when perceptions of the competency of the nonprofit were improved, for example, by a credible endorsement such as from *The Wall Street Journal*.[12]

Although any aspect of the marketing program may affect brand personality, marketing communications and advertising may be especially influential because of the inferences consumers make about the underlying user or usage situation depicted or reflected in an ad. For example, advertisers may imbue a brand with personality traits through anthropomorphization and product animation techniques; through personification and the use of brand characters; and through user imagery, such as the preppy look of Abercrombie & Fitch models.[13] More generally, the actors in an ad, the tone or style of the creative strategy, and the emotions or feelings evoked by the ad can affect brand personality. Once brands develop a personality, it can be difficult for consumers to accept information they see as inconsistent with that personality.[14]

Still, user imagery and brand personality may not always be in agreement. When performance-related attributes are central to consumer decisions, as they are for food products, for example, brand personality and user imagery may be less closely related. Differences between personality and imagery may arise for other reasons, too. For example, early in its U.S. brand development, Perrier's brand personality was sophisticated and stylish, whereas its actual user imagery was not as flattering or subdued but flashy and trendy.

When user and usage imagery are important to consumer decisions, however, brand personality and imagery are more likely to be related, as they are for cars, beer, liquor, cigarettes, and cosmetics. Thus, consumers often choose and use brands that have a brand personality consistent with their self-concept, although in some cases, the match may be based on consumers' desired, rather than their actual, image.[15] These effects may also be more pronounced for publicly consumed products than for privately consumed goods because the signaling aspect of a brand may be more important under those conditions.[16] Consumers who are high self-monitors and sensitive to how others view them are more likely to choose brands whose personalities fit the consumption situation.[17]

User and usage imagery is often an issue in these highly competitive categories. One company looking to sharpen its brand personality and user imagery is Hyatt Hotels.

Brand History, Heritage, and Experiences.   Finally, brands may take on associations to their past and certain noteworthy events in the brand's history. These types of associations may recall distinctly personal experiences and episodes or past behaviors and experiences of friends, family, or others. They can be highly personal and individual, or more well-known and shared by many people. For example, there may be associations to aspects of the brand's marketing program, the color of the product or look of its package, the company or person that makes the product and the country in which it is made, the type of store in which it is sold, the events for which the brand is a sponsor, and the people who endorse the brand. Retro-themed packaging and retro advertising have become an often-used strategy by brands who want to appeal to older audiences, particularly baby boomers.

HYATT

Hyatt Hotels has built an emotional connection with its customers through branding itself in unique ways across a portfolio of different offerings. Hyatt's strategy for building strong customer relationships is by specializing each hotel within its portfolio to focus on a specific customer segment, and by ensuring that the hotel stay is tailored to meet the needs of that segment. For example, Park Hyatt is one of the high-end hotels within the Hyatt portfolio which focuses on providing rare and intimate experiences to the luxury traveler, while at the same time, doing it in an understated way. Grand Hyatt, by contrast, is a more traditional luxury hotel offering larger-than-life experiences at its various locations. Hyatt Place and Hyatt House are targeting the ambitious customer, who is a multitasker. The advertising for Hyatt Place and Hyatt House leverages the idea of ambition and focuses on consumers who do not want to settle. The ad campaign features real people who do not want to settle in their lives, such as a former college football player turned professional opera singer. By moving beyond features and functionality, the Hyatt Place and Hyatt House advertising is hoping to improve its appeal to its customers. In these ways, each of the hotels within the Hyatt lineup has a unique mission and delivery that capitalizes on its knowledge of what a particular subsegment is looking for and delivers exceptional experiences to that particular segment in hopes of building an emotional connection with its customers.[18]

Grand Hyatt is a more traditional luxury hotel offering larger-than-life experiences at its various locations, and occupies an important place in the Hyatt portfolio of hotels.

Source: EQRoy/Shutterstock.

These types of associations can help create strong points-of-difference. In the midst of the recent major recession, Northern Trust used the fact that it was more than 130 years old and had weathered many financial downturns through the years to reinforce trust and stability to its wealthy clientele.[19] In any case, associations to history, heritage, and experiences draw upon more specific, concrete examples that transcend the generalizations that make up the usage imagery. In the extreme case, brands become iconic by combining all these types of associations into what is, in effect, a myth, tapping into enduring consumer hopes and dreams.[20] The overall service or customer experience associated with a brand can also become integral to its overall brand image. The Science of Branding 3-1 outlines some examples of great customer experiences becoming integral to a brand's image.

Some different types of associations related to either performance or imagery may become linked to the brand. We can characterize the brand associations making up the brand image and meaning according to three important dimensions—strength, favorability, and uniqueness—that provide the key to building brand equity. Successful results on these three

THE SCIENCE OF BRANDING 3-1
How Customer Experiences Define a Brand

Amazon is ranked as among the most relevant brands according to one consulting firm's Brand Relevance Index. It also has been known for its ability to deliver exceptional customer experiences in the retail sector. Amazon's customer experience has been carefully developed through attention to detail regarding all aspects of the customer journey, which translates into a focus on various aspects of order placement, product delivery, product returns, and so on. One key facet of its customer experience is investing in technologies, such as cheap tablets and smart speakers that it can install in customers' homes, which becomes a way for Amazon to develop a richer understanding of customer needs and behaviors.

Alexa is Amazon's voice service which powers Amazon's Echo smart speakers. The advent of digital voice services such as Alexa represents the slow ramping up of the customer experience by large technology firms. Amazon's Alexa uses machine learning and artificial intelligence to know customers' needs, preferences, and behaviors which allows them to guide the customer experience as they shop on Amazon or interact with Apple devices. Another investment in a seamless customer experience is Amazon's Prime service, which, for a low price of $79, allows customers to enjoy free two-day shipping throughout the year. Prime customers outspend regular customers of Amazon by more than $700 per year, which makes them extremely valuable customers, accounting for almost 50 percent of Amazon's customer base. Thus, Amazon Prime is yet another weapon in Amazon's ever-growing arsenal of ways to make the customer experience seamless and friction-free.

This phenomenon is by no means unique to Amazon and Apple. Companies such as Uber, Lyft, Spotify, Dropbox, Grubhub, TripAdvisor, and Zappos are examples of other digital-only brands that have redefined the customer experience and transformed it into a seamless, one-of-a-kind experience. This type of customer experience is integral to the essence of these digital brands. While technology is a key enabler of what the customer experiences when interacting with these brands, a second key ingredient is also empathy. One story captures the essence of how Zappos' customer experience is seen as exceptional.

It is said that a Zappos customer accidentally packaged his wife's jewelry in a spare Zappos box during a move; the wife,

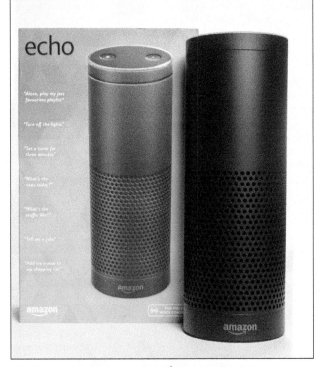

Alexa is a digital voice service that has enabled Amazon to gain unique insights into customers' needs, preferences, and behaviors.

unaware that the jewelry was in the box, shipped the box to Zappos. The Zappos employee, upon receiving the box, immediately recognized the error and, rather than mail the contents back, made a flight booking and hand-delivered the contents of the box to the couple, ensuring a happy ending to what otherwise could have been a disastrous situation for the couple. In doing so, and by empowering their employees to act on their behalf and to keep customers' needs at the center of all that they do, Zappos has been successful in gaining a loyal customer base.

Southwest Airlines is another company that is often lauded for its exceptional dedication to improving the customer experience. One key is its systems and processes for customer service combined with employee empowerment. For example, one passenger on a Southwest Airlines flight found that her suitcase (which had been checked in during a flight) arrived with a damaged handle. The passenger was expecting the usual mountain of paperwork that accompanies a typical claim that accompanies damages to baggage. Instead, imagine her surprise when she was escorted into a room with new baggage, was able to choose a replacement bag, and transfer all her contents into the new bag, and walk out of the airport with a new bag to replace the one that broke. By empowering its employees to address customer complaints by investing in systems and processes that could handle typical problem situations, Southwest has redefined the customer experience in the airline industry. In this way, exceptional user experience has become a key component of brand image.

Sources: Megan Webb-Morgan, "Southwest Airlines: A Case Study in Great Customer Service," February 22, 2017, accessed February 1, 2018; Southwest Airlines Co. (2018) "Southwest Airlines Again Among Fortune's Top10 World's Most Admired Companies," January 19, 2018, *PR Newswire*, accessed February 1, 2018; Shep Hyken, "Southwest Airlines Customer Experience Leads to Loyalty," January 9, 2016, *Forbes.com*, accessed February 1, 2018. Scott Davis, "How Amazon's Brand and Customer Experience Became Synonymous," July 14, 2016, Forbes.com, accessed February 1, 2018; Eric Feinberg, "How Amazon Is Investing In Customer Experience By Reimagining Retail Delivery," January 4, 2018, www.forbes.com/sites/forbescommunicationscouncil/2018/01/04/how-amazon-is-investing-in-customer-experience-by-reimagining-retail-delivery/#3164b3d42c2e, accessed April 5, 2018; Micah Solomon, "Three Wow Customer Service Stories From Zappos, Southwest Airlines and Nordstrom," August 1, 2017, www.forbes.com/sites/micahsolomon/2017/08/01/three-wow-customer-service-stories-from-zappos-southwest-airlines-and-nordstrom/#355076582aba, accessed April 5, 2018.

dimensions produce the most positive brand responses, the underpinning of intense and active brand loyalty.

Creating strong, favorable, and unique associations is a real challenge to marketers, but essential to building customer-based brand equity. Strong brands typically have firmly established favorable and unique brand associations with consumers. Brand meaning is what helps produce **brand responses**, or what customers think or feel about the brand. We can distinguish brand responses as either brand judgments or brand feelings, that is, regarding whether they arise from the head or the heart, as the following sections describe.

Brand Judgments

Brand judgments are customers' personal opinions about and evaluations of the brand, which consumers form by putting together all the different brand performance and imagery associations. Customers may make all types of judgments concerning a brand, but four types are particularly important: judgments about quality, credibility, consideration, and superiority.

Brand Quality. Brand attitudes are consumers' overall evaluations of a brand and often form the basis for brand choice.[21] Brand attitudes generally depend on specific attributes and benefits of the brand. For example, consider Hilton Hotels. A consumer's attitude toward Hilton depends on how much he or she believes the brand is characterized by certain associations that matter to the consumer for a hotel chain, such as location; room comfort, design, and appearance; service quality of staff; recreational facilities; food service; security; prices; and so on.

Consumers can hold a host of attitudes toward a brand, but the most important relate to its perceived quality and to customer value and satisfaction. Perceived quality measures are inherent in many approaches to brand equity. In the annual EquiTrend study by Harris Interactive, 100,000 consumers in the U.S. rate more than 4,000 brands in more than 450 categories ranging from automobiles to technology to news media. The EquiTrend Brand Equity Index is comprised of three key factors— familiarity, quality and consideration—that result in a Brand Equity rating for each brand. Brands that rank highest in equity receive the Harris Poll EquiTrend "Brand of the Year" award in their category.[22]

Brand Credibility. Customers may also form judgments about the company or organization behind the brand. **Brand credibility** describes the extent to which customers see the brand as credible in terms of three dimensions: perceived expertise, trustworthiness, and likability. Is the brand seen as (1) competent, innovative, and a market leader (brand expertise); (2) dependable and keeping customer interests in mind (brand trustworthiness); and (3) fun, interesting, and worth spending time with (brand likability)? In other words, credibility measures whether consumers see the company or organization behind the brand as good at what it does, concerned about its customers, and just plain likable.[23]

FEDEX

From its earliest advertising, "When It Absolutely, Positively Has to Be There Overnight," FedEx has stressed its speed, skill, and dependability in shipping and delivery. Its brand campaign, "Solutions That Matter" launched in 2011, offers the perfect platform to enable FedEx to tell stories about the various ways in which the company solves problems for customers ranging from delivering cargo to printing documents or shipping unusual or special items.[24] The company wants customers to think of it as a trusted partner, with a commitment to reliable but cost-effective shipping all over the world. Its advertising, however, often uses humor and high production values. FedEx ads that run during the Super Bowl are often rated among the most enjoyable by consumers. Recently, FedEx has expanded its customer engagement and service delivery through the use of social media channels such as Facebook and Twitter, thus providing a variety of different ways in which FedEx customers receive service from the company.[25] Also, FedEx uses content marketing via online channels which involve developing and sharing content to build stronger connections with its customers.[26] FedEx's "In the Wild" content marketing campaign encourages its followers on Instagram to take pictures of FedEx vehicles in various locations, and carefully curates the most engaging photos to post them on its Instagram. This approach allowed FedEx to gain a large following on Instagram, and as a result of the campaign the follower-ship grew nearly 400 percent.[27] Through its flawless service delivery and creative marketing communications, FedEx can establish all three dimensions of credibility: expertise, trustworthiness, and likability.[28]

A brand like FedEx is seen as highly credible due to its expertise, trustworthiness, and likability.
Source: Adam Slinger/Alamy

Brand Consideration.   Favorable brand attitudes and perceptions of credibility are important, but not important enough if customers do not consider the brand for possible purchase or use. As Chapter 2 introduced, consideration depends in part on how personally relevant customers find the brand and is a crucial filter regarding building brand equity. No matter how highly they regard the brand or how credible they find it, unless they also give it serious consideration and deem it relevant, customers will keep a brand at a distance and never closely embrace it. Brand consideration depends in large part on the extent to which strong and favorable brand associations can be created as part of the brand image.

Brand Superiority.   Superiority measures the extent to which customers view the brand as unique and better than other brands. Do customers believe it offers advantages that other brands cannot? Superiority is critical to building intense and active relationships with customers and depends to a great degree on the number and nature of unique brand associations that make up the brand image.

Brand Feelings

Brand feelings are customers' emotional responses and reactions to the brand. Brand feelings also relate to the social currency evoked by the brand. What feelings are evoked by the marketing program for the brand or by other means? How does the brand affect customers' feelings about themselves and their relationship with others? These feelings can be mild or intense and can be positive or negative.

For example, Kevin Roberts of Saatchi & Saatchi argues that companies must transcend brands to create "trustmarks"—a name or symbol that emotionally binds a company with the desires and aspirations of its customers—and ultimately "lovemarks." He argues that it is not enough for a brand to be just respected.

> Pretty much everything today can be seen in relation to a love-respect axis. You can plot any relationship—with a person, with a brand—by whether it's based on love or based on respect. It used to be that a high respect rating would win. But these days, a high love rating wins. If I don't love what you're offering me, I'm not even interested.[29]

A passionate believer in the concept, Roberts reinforces the point that trustmarks truly belong to the people who offer the love to the brand, and that an emotional connection is critical.[30]

The emotions evoked by a brand can become so strongly associated that they are accessible during product consumption or use. Researchers have defined *transformational advertising* as advertising designed to change consumers' perceptions of the actual usage experience with the product.[31] Corona Extra overtook Heineken as the leading imported beer in the United States via its "beach in a bottle" advertising. With a tagline "Miles Away from Ordinary," the campaign was designed to transport drinkers—at least mentally—to sunny, tranquil beaches.[32]

More and more firms are attempting to tap into more consumer emotions with their brands. The following are six important types of brand-building feelings:[33]

1. **Warmth:** The brand evokes soothing types of feelings and makes consumers feel a sense of calm or peacefulness. Consumers may feel sentimental, warmhearted, or affectionate about the brand. Many heritage brands such as Welch's jelly, Quaker oatmeal, and Aunt Jemima pancake mix and syrup tap into feelings of warmth.
2. **Fun:** Upbeat types of feelings make consumers feel amused, lighthearted, joyous, playful, cheerful, and so on. With its iconic characters and theme park rides, Disney is a brand often associated with fun. Microsoft's Xbox and YouTube also evoke brand associations linked to fun and entertainment.
3. **Excitement:** The brand makes consumers feel energized and that they are experiencing something special. Brands that evoke excitement may generate a sense of elation, of being alive, or being cool, sexy, and so on. Red Bull is a brand seen by many teens and young adults as exciting.
4. **Security:** The brand produces a feeling of safety, comfort, and self-assurance. As a result of the brand, consumers do not experience worry or concerns that they might have otherwise felt. Allstate Insurance with "You're in Good Hands," State Farm with "Like a Good Neighbor," and Nationwide with "On Your Side" are all insurance brands that have slogans to communicate safety, security and trust to consumers.
5. **Social approval:** The brand gives consumers a belief that others look favorably on their appearance, behavior, and so on. This approval may be a result of direct acknowledgment of the consumer's use of the brand by others or may be less overt and a result of attribution of product use to consumers. To an older generation of consumers, Cadillac is a brand that historically has been a signal of social approval.
6. **Self-respect:** The brand makes consumers feel better about themselves; consumers feel a sense of pride, accomplishment, or fulfillment. A brand like Tide laundry detergent can link its brand to "doing the best things for the family" to many homemakers.

These six feelings can be divided into two broad categories: The first three types of feelings are experiential and immediate, increasing in level of intensity; the latter three types of feelings are private and enduring, increasing in level of gravity.

Although all types of customer responses are possible—driven from both the head and heart—ultimately, what matters is how positive they are. Responses must also be accessible and come to mind when consumers think of the brand. Brand judgments and feelings can favorably affect consumer behavior only if consumers internalize or think of positive responses in their various encounters with the brand.

Brand Resonance

The final step of the model focuses on the ultimate relationship and level of identification that the customer has with the brand.[34] ***Brand resonance*** describes the nature of this relationship and the extent to which customers feel that they are in sync with the brand. Examples of brands with historically high resonance include Harley-Davidson, Apple, and Amazon.

Resonance is characterized in terms of *intensity*, or the depth of the psychological bond that customers have with the brand, as well as the level of *activity* engendered by this loyalty (repeat purchase rates and the extent to which customers seek out brand information, events, and other loyal customers). We can break down these two dimensions of brand resonance into four categories:

1. Behavioral loyalty
2. Attitudinal attachment
3. Sense of community
4. Active engagement

Behavioral Loyalty. We can gauge ***behavioral loyalty*** in terms of repeat purchases and the amount or share of category volume attributed to the brand—that is, the share of category requirements. In other words, how often do customers purchase a brand and how much do they purchase? For bottom-line profit results, the brand must generate sufficient purchase frequencies and volumes.

The lifetime value of behaviorally loyal consumers can be enormous.[35] For example, a loyal General Motors customer could be worth $276,000 over his or her lifetime (assuming 11 or more vehicles bought and word-of-mouth endorsement that makes friends and relatives more likely to consider GM products). Or consider new parents. By spending $100 a month on diapers and wipes for 24 to 30 months, they can create lifetime value of as much as $3,000 for just one baby.

Attitudinal Attachment. Behavioral loyalty is necessary but not sufficient for resonance to occur.[36] Some customers may buy out of necessity—because the brand is the only product stocked or readily accessible, the only one they can afford, or other reasons. Resonance, however, requires a strong personal ***attachment***. Customers should go beyond having a positive attitude to viewing the brand as something special in a broader context. For example, customers with a great deal of attitudinal attachment to a brand may state that they love the brand, describe it as one of their favorite possessions, or view it as a little pleasure that they look forward to.

Prior research has shown that mere satisfaction may not be enough.[37] Xerox found that when customer satisfaction was ranked on a scale of 1 (completely dissatisfied) to 5 (completely satisfied), customers who rated Xerox products and services as "4"—and thus, were satisfied—were six times more likely to defect to competitors than those customers who provided ratings of "5."[38] Creating greater loyalty requires creating deeper attitudinal attachment, through marketing programs and products and services that fully satisfy consumer needs. Attitudinally loyal customers also become brand evangelists, which also helps solidify a brand's equity.[39]

Sense of Community. The brand may also take on a broader meaning to the customer by conveying a sense of ***community***.[40] Identification with a brand community may reflect an important social phenomenon in which customers feel a kinship or affiliation with other people associated with the brand, whether fellow brand users or customers, or employees or representatives of the company. A brand community can exist online or off-line.[41] Branding Brief 3-1 profiles three company-initiated programs to help build brand communities. A stronger sense of community among loyal users can engender favorable brand attitudes and intentions.[42]

Active Engagement   Finally, perhaps the strongest affirmation of brand loyalty occurs when customers are **engaged**, or willing to invest time, energy, money, or other resources in the brand beyond those expended during purchase or consumption of the brand.[43] For example, customers may choose to join a club centered on a brand, receive updates, and exchange correspondence with other brand users or formal or informal representatives of the brand itself. Companies are making it increasingly easy for customers to buy a range of branded merchandise so they can literally express their loyalty.

BMW

BMW's lifestyle business was started 15 years ago as a marketing initiative whose objectives were to broaden the brand's presence and strengthen loyalty. The lifestyle division focuses primarily on selling mobility products, including bicycles and skateboards for kids, and aims for a profit margin (7%) similar to what BMW generates from sales of its automobiles. More than 2,000 products are sold, from €39 ($52) Mini rain boots to the highly regarded €2750 ($3,620) lightweight M Carbon Racer bike from BMW's M performance unit. These are not your run-of-the-mill products, however. BMW's €79 ($105) Snow Racer sled has replaceable metal runners, a suspension-system in the red steering ski, and a horn to warn inattentive passersby. The battery-powered Baby Racer, designed internally by BMW Designworks, comes in three different models and costs €79 ($106). Winner of several design prizes and featured in the Museum of Modern Art in New York, it sells 60,000 units a year. In China, which is now its third-largest market for car sales, BMW opened a store selling merchandise a year before it began assembling cars in the country and had more than 50 BMW stores there by the end of 2012.[44]

Customers may choose to visit brand-related Web sites, participate in chat rooms, or post to discussion forums. In this case, customers themselves became brand evangelists and ambassadors and helped communicate about the brand and strengthen the brand ties of others. Strong attitudinal attachment or social identity or both are typically necessary, however, for active engagement with the brand to occur.

BRANDING BRIEF 3-1
Building Brand Communities

Harley-Davidson

The world-famous motorcycle company sponsors the Harley Owners Group (H.O.G.), which has members in chapter groups all over the world sharing a very simple mission, "To Ride and Have Fun." By 2017, the H.O.G. community had grown to include more than 1 million members at a cost of approximately $49 per year. There are many benefits of belonging to a H.O.G. including Harley-Davidson Customization, subscription to the H.O.G. magazine, roadside assistance, safe rider programs, and access to a Fly & Ride program enabling members to rent Harleys while on vacation.

Over and above these benefits, H.O.G. owners contribute to the Wounded Warriors Project, and can gain access to special (e.g., Iron Elite) communities through the H.O.G. Web site. More important, the community facilitates sharing of Harley experiences among owners of the bike, thereby fostering a greater sense of community and deeper engagement with the brand. The company also maintains an extensive Web site devoted to H.O.G., which includes information about club chapters and events and features a special members-only section.

With 1.2 million members, Harley Owners Group is the quintessential example of a brand community.

Sephora

Sephora has sponsored an online brand community and embedded various features that make this a vibrant community. For example, the brand community for Sephora allows users to

Sephora's online brand community encourages its customers to engage with the brand in various ways.

create customer accounts linked to their social presences and loyalty cards, which allows the company to learn about customers' shopping habits and media consumption behaviors. Sephora's brand community (called *BeautyTalk*) encourages its customers to actively engage with each other off-line as well. Further, Sephora launched a new digital community platform called "Beauty Insiders" which asks participants of the page (which is on the Sephora.com Web site) to design their own personal makeup profile, join groups, participate in Q&A sessions with other Beauty Insiders, and get beauty and makeup advice from experts.

Participants of the Beauty Insider community can trade beauty tips with other users, thereby fostering the network of people with similar interests. There is also an interactive "Beauty Board" in which members can post looks and videos along with product recommendations that can be accessed by others. Community members can also allow others to provide real-time input on purchases as they are being made, and the community is also accessible via the Sephora App. Through these various innovative features, Sephora has built a community of beauty enthusiasts and deepened customer engagement with the brand.

Jeep

In addition to joining the hundreds of local Jeep enthusiast clubs throughout the world, Jeep owners can convene with their vehicles in wilderness areas across the United States as part of the company's official Jeep Jamborees. A tradition since 1953, Jeep Jamborees bring Jeep owners and their families together for two-day off-road adventures in 34 different locations throughout the United States from spring through autumn each year. Trails and obstacles are rated on a 1–10 scale in terms of difficulty. In a new twist, Jeep owners can participate in the "My Jeep Story" digital and social campaign. This campaign allowed Jeep's customers to celebrate the company's seventy-fifth anniversary. This campaign was an example of its broader theme used in its advertising in which it implores its customers to engage with the brand using the tagline, "We Don't Make Jeep, You Do."

The advantage of the "My Jeep Story" campaign was its ability to draw the customer into a conversation with the company about what the brand meant to them. The campaign was activated through various social media channels including Instagram, Facebook, and Twitter. Fans were told to go to the Web site www.jeep.com/myjeepstory to post videos of their stories. This campaign also featured "Story Sessions" in which the brand featured summer fun, military appreciation, etc. By encouraging loyal users to share their brand stories on social media, Jeep increased its engagement with its customers.

Taken together, the case studies of brand community portrayed here have a common theme—they allow their existing customer base to act as brand ambassadors and evangelists for the brand. One firm has developed a metric called "Participation Brand Index" (PBI) to measure how much a brand community is able to harness its members to get involved in the brand. According to their analysis, brands such as Apple score very high on PBI, as do brands such as Amazon, Google, Netflix, and BMW. Jeep is the second-highest rated brand in terms of PBI or the ability of a brand to make customers feel part of a community.

Sources: Mailys Reslinger, "How Does Harley Davidson Gather Its Riders," May 26, 2015, https://potion.social/en/blog/the-phenomenon-of-harley-davidsons-online-community-study-case, accessed February 1, 2018; Jonathan Salem Baskin, "Harley-Davidson Will Be a Case History in Social Branding," July 12, 2013, Forbes.com, accessed February 1, 2018; FCA US LLC (2016), "Jeep Brand Launches Global "My Jeep Story" Digital and Social Campaign," PR Newswire, March 28, 2016, accessed February 1, 2018; Julian Thumm, "Sephora Learns the Importance of Online Brand Communities," October 12, 2015, PowerRetail, accessed February 1, 2018; BusinessWire (2017), "Sephora's New Beauty Insider Community Is Poised to Be the World's Most Trusted and Beauty-Obsessed Social Platform," August 17, 2017, accessed February 1, 2018; PR Newswire, Luttner, Kathryn (2017), "How Brands Like Jeep and Airbnb Get Their Fans to Do Their Marketing for Them," February 15, 2017, www.campaignlive.com/article/brands-jeep-airbnb-fans-marketing/1424286#vQJQpqGS8rUPfFLT.99, accessed February 1, 2018.

In short, brand resonance and the relationships consumers have with brands have two dimensions: *intensity* and *activity*. Intensity measures the strength of the attitudinal attachment and sense of community. Activity tells us how frequently the consumer buys and uses the brand, as well as engages in other activities not related to purchase and consumption.

Brand-Building Implications

The brand resonance model provides a roadmap and guidance for brand building, a yardstick by which brands can assess their progress in their brand-building efforts as well as a guide for marketing research initiatives. With respect to the latter, one model application aids in brand tracking and providing quantitative measures of the success of brand-building efforts (see Chapter 9). Figure 3-4 contains a set of candidate measures for the six brand-building blocks.

The brand resonance model also reinforces some important branding tenets, six of which are particularly noteworthy. We discuss them in the following sections.

I. Salience

What brands of product or service category can you think of?
   (using increasingly specific product category cues)
Have you ever heard of these brands?
Which brands might you be likely to use under the following
   situations . . . ?
How frequently do you think of this brand?

II. Performance

Compared with other brands in the category, how well does this brand
   provide the basic functions of the product or service category?
Compared with other brands in the category, how well does this brand
   satisfy the basic needs of the product or service category?
To what extent does this brand have special features?
How reliable is this brand?
How durable is this brand?
How easily serviced is this brand?
How effective is this brand's service? Does it completely satisfy your
   requirements?
How efficient is this brand's service in terms of speed, responsiveness, and
   so forth?
How courteous and helpful are the providers of this brand's service?
How stylish do you find this brand?
How much do you like the look, feel, and other design aspects of
   this brand?
Compared with other brands in the category with which it competes, are
   this brand's prices generally higher, lower, or about the same?
Compared with other brands in the category with which it competes, do
   this brand's prices change more frequently, less frequently, or about the
   same amount?

III. Imagery

To what extent do people you admire and respect use this brand?
How much do you like people who use this brand?
How well do the following words describe this brand: down-to-earth,
   honest, daring, up-to-date, reliable, successful, upper class, charming,
   outdoorsy?
What places are appropriate to buy this brand?
How appropriate are the following situations to use this brand?
Can you buy this brand in a lot of places?
Is this a brand that you can use in a lot of different situations?
To what extent does thinking of the brand bring back pleasant memories?
To what extent do you feel you grew up with the brand?

IV. Judgments

Quality
What is your overall opinion of this brand?
What is your assessment of the product quality of this brand?
To what extent does this brand fully satisfy your product needs?
How good a value is this brand?

Credibility
How knowledgeable are the makers of this brand?
How innovative are the makers of this brand?
How much do you trust the makers of this brand?
To what extent do the makers of this brand understand your needs?
To what extent do the makers of this brand care about your opinions?
To what extent do the makers of this brand have your interests in mind?

(Continued)

FIGURE 3-4

Possible Measures of
Brand Building Blocks

Credibility (cont.)
How much do you like this brand?
How much do you admire this brand?
How much do you respect this brand?

Consideration
How likely would you be to recommend this brand to others?
Which are your favorite products in this brand category?
How personally relevant is this brand to you?

Superiority
How unique is this brand?
To what extent does this brand offer advantages that other brands cannot?
How superior is this brand to others in the category?

V.   Feelings
Does this brand give you a feeling of warmth?
Does this brand give you a feeling of fun?
Does this brand give you a feeling of excitement?
Does this brand give you a feeling of security?
Does this brand give you a feeling of social approval?
Does this brand give you a feeling of self-respect?

VI.   Resonance
Loyalty
I consider myself loyal to this brand.
I buy this brand whenever I can.
I buy as much of this brand as I can.
I feel this is the only brand of this product I need.
This is the one brand I would prefer to buy/use.
If this brand were not available, it would make little difference to me if I had to use another brand.
I would go out of my way to use this brand.

Attachment
I really love this brand.
I would really miss this brand if it went away.
This brand is special to me.
This brand is more than a product to me.

Community
I really identify with people who use this brand.
I feel as if I almost belong to a club with other users of this brand.
This is a brand used by people like me.
I feel a deep connection with others who use this brand.

Engagement
I really like to talk about this brand to others.
I am always interested in learning more about this brand.
I would be interested in merchandise with this brand's name on it.
I am proud to have others know I use this brand.
I really like to post comments about this brand on social media.
I visit the brand's Facebook page regularly.
I like to visit the Web site for this brand.
Compared with other people, I follow news about this brand closely.

It should be recognized that the core brand values at the bottom two levels of the pyramid—brand salience, performance, and imagery—are typically more idiosyncratic and unique to a product and service category than other brand values.

Customers Own the Brands.   The basic premise of the brand resonance model is that the true measure of the strength of a brand is the way consumers think, feel, and act with respect to that brand.

The strongest brands will be those to which consumers become so attached and passionate that they, in effect, become evangelists or missionaries and attempt to share their beliefs and spread the word about the brand. The power of the brand and its ultimate value to the firm reside with customers.

It is through learning about and experiencing a brand that customers end up thinking, feeling, and acting in a way that allows the firm to reap the benefits of brand equity. Although marketers must take responsibility for designing and implementing the most effective and efficient brand-building marketing programs possible, the success of those marketing efforts ultimately depends on how consumers respond and the actions they take. This response, in turn, depends on the knowledge that has been created in their minds and hearts for those brands.

Don't Take Shortcuts with Brands.   The brand resonance model reinforces the fact that there are no shortcuts in building a brand. A great brand is not built by accident but is the product of carefully accomplishing—either explicitly or implicitly—a series of logically linked steps with consumers. The more explicitly marketers recognize the steps and define them as concrete goals, the more likely they will give them the proper attention and fully realize them so they can provide the greatest contribution to brand-building. The length of time to build a strong brand will therefore be directly proportional to the amount of time it takes to create sufficient awareness and understanding so that firmly held and felt beliefs and attitudes about the brand are formed that can serve as the foundation for brand equity.

The brand-building steps may not be equally difficult. Creating brand awareness is a step that an effectively designed marketing program often can accomplish in a relatively short period of time. Unfortunately, this step is the one that many brand marketers tend to skip in their mistaken haste to quickly establish an image for the brand. It is difficult for consumers to appreciate the advantages and uniqueness of a brand unless they have some sort of frame of reference for what the brand is supposed to do and with whom or what it is supposed to compete. Similarly, consumers cannot have highly positive responses without a reasonably complete understanding of the brand's dimensions and characteristics.

Even if, due to circumstances in the marketplace, consumers actually start a repeated-purchase or behavioral loyalty relationship with a brand without much underlying feeling, judgment, or associations, these other brand-building blocks will have to come into place at some point to create true resonance. That is, although the start point may differ, the same steps in brand-building eventually must occur to create a truly strong brand.

Brands Should Have a Duality.   One important point reinforced by the model is that a strong brand has a duality—it appeals to both the head and the heart. Thus, although there may be two different ways to build loyalty and resonance—going up the left-hand and right-hand sides of the pyramid—strong brands often do both. Strong brands blend product performance and imagery to create a rich, varied, but complementary set of consumer responses to the brand.

By appealing to both rational and emotional concerns, a strong brand provides consumers with multiple access points while reducing competitive vulnerability. Rational concerns can satisfy utilitarian needs, whereas emotional concerns can satisfy psychological or emotional needs. Combining the two allows brands to create a formidable brand position. Consistent with this reasoning, a McKinsey study of 51 corporate brands found that having distinctive physical *and* emotional benefits drove greater shareholder value, especially when the two were linked.[45]

___

MASTERCARD

MasterCard is an example of a brand with much duality, because it emphasizes both the rational advantages of the credit card—its acceptance at establishments worldwide—as well as the emotional advantages—expressed in the award-winning "Priceless" advertising campaign. Ads depict people buying items to achieve both a very practical goal and a more important emotional goal. The first ad, for example, showed a father taking his son to a baseball game. As they made purchases on the way to their seats, superimposed on the screen and in a voiceover were highlighted the different items they bought—tickets, hot dogs, and an autographed baseball—and how much each cost. But, the last item highlighted was not a product but "real conversation with 11-year-old son" and, in this case, the cost was stated as "priceless." The ad ended with the tagline, "There Are Some Things Money Can't Buy; For Everything Else There's MasterCard" and "Accepted at Ballparks Coast-to-Coast." The campaign has been so successful that it has run around the world, with appropriate cultural adaptation. The baseball spot, for example, was redone as a cricket ad for Australia. The campaign has received many awards, including multiple EFFIES from the American Marketing Association for effectiveness.[46] MasterCard has continued to use the Priceless campaign and has brought it into the digital and social media space. In doing so, it has allowed MasterCard to devise interesting promotions using the Priceless themes (e.g., Priceless cities), and to leverage digital channels to strengthen brand engagement.[47]

Brands Should Have Richness.   The level of detail in the brand resonance model highlights the number of possible ways to create meaning with consumers and the range of possible avenues to elicit consumer responses. Collectively, these various aspects of brand meaning and the resulting responses produce strong consumer bonds to the brand. The various associations making up the brand image may be reinforcing, helping strengthen or increase the favorability of other brand associations, or they may be unique, helping add distinctiveness or offset some potential deficiencies. Strong brands thus have both breadth (in terms of duality) and depth (in terms of richness).

At the same time, brands should not necessarily be expected to score highly on all the various dimensions and categories making up each core brand value. Building blocks can have hierarchies in their own right. For example, with respect to brand awareness, typically marketers should first establish category identification in some way before considering strategies to expand brand breadth via needs satisfied or benefits offered. With brand performance, they may wish to first link primary characteristics and related features before attempting to link additional, more peripheral associations.

Similarly, brand imagery often begins with a fairly concrete initial articulation of user and usage imagery that, over time, leads to broader, more abstract brand associations of personality, value, history, heritage, and experience. Brand judgments usually begin with positive quality and credibility perceptions that can lead to brand consideration and then perhaps ultimately to assessments of brand superiority. Brand feelings usually start with either experiential ones (warmth, fun, and excitement) or inward ones (security, social approval, and self-respect.) Finally, resonance again has a clear ordering, whereby behavioral loyalty is a starting point, but attitudinal attachment or a sense of community is almost always needed for active engagement to occur.

Brand Resonance Provides Important Focus.   As Figure 3-1 shows, brand resonance is the pinnacle of the brand resonance model and provides important focus and priority for decision making about marketing. Marketers building brands should use brand resonance as a goal and a means to interpret their brand-related marketing activities. The question to ask is: To what extent is marketing activity affecting the key dimensions of brand resonance—consumer loyalty, attachment, community, or engagement with the brand? Is marketing activity creating brand performance and imagery associations and consumer judgments and feelings that will support these brand resonance dimensions?

Customer Networks Strengthen Brand Resonance.   Although the digital platform (e.g., the customer base of Dropbox's customers) comprising networks of customers is a relatively recent phenomenon, the idea that customer networks can be a resource for building brand resonance has been around for a long time. For example, companies such as Amway have leveraged customer-to-customer interactions to strengthen their brands for years.

In recent years, a number of digital native brands have relied on networks of customer relationships to generate many positive outcomes including attracting new customers and deepening relationships with existing customers. Recruiting new customers through referrals is more effective as customers have been shown to be more receptive to information and behaviors that are shared by peers than those received from traditional advertising.[48] Further, the platform can become a valuable resource for companies to launch various initiatives in conjunction with customers.

For example, this could include co-creation of both products and branded content allowing for companies to interact with users that form part of the platform at a high level. The process of co-creation also increases the identification of customers with the brand, strengthening consumer-brand resonance.[49] Branding Brief 3-2 highlights how two platform-based digital native brands

BRANDING BRIEF 3-2
How Digital Platform-Based Brands Create Customer Engagement

Grubhub

Against a crowded and chaotic food delivery landscape, Grubhub has managed to carve out a unique space for its brand, and that space has been growing. Grubhub is a digital food delivery service which began operating in 2004. Following its merger with Seamless (a competitor) in 2013, the brand is available in more than 1,000 cities within the United States and has partnered with a network of 44,000 restaurants delivering 267,000 orders daily to more than 7 million active users.

So, what are the keys to Grubhub's success? The company's keys to success are its portfolio of diverse restaurants and how it generates a deep understanding of its customers' eating behaviors. To leverage these advantages, the company has four main strategies that it uses. First, it promotes the establishments that form part of Grubhub's network, thereby generating goodwill for the restaurants while, at the same time, balancing the needs of diners and their food experience. The transfer of goodwill and brand associations that comes with co-opting customers' favorite local restaurants ultimately benefits Grubhub and contributes to its brand equity. Second, it taps into the data accumulated across multiple customer purchases and touchpoints to create personalized experiences across the entire customer decision journey. Third, Grubhub redefined its mission from merely delivering food to creating quality experiences and moments that are crucial to stronger customer–brand relationships. This focus on high quality delivery, in addition to being a takeout service, enables Grubhub to maintain high standards throughout the experience. Fourth, it segments users into different personas in ways which allow Grubhub to customize the takeout and delivery experience to meet the diverse needs of its audiences. These strategies have been effective in helping Grubhub communicate with potential new customers and in retaining existing customers.

TripAdvisor

TripAdvisor is the world's largest travel site and boasts upward of $1.2 billion in revenue with a large roster of participants. TripAdvisor has four main strategies that it uses. First, the company believes in developing a deep understanding of customers, their motivations, and pain points. In doing so, the company tries to go beyond the data and develops an empathetic view of what the customer is looking for as they interact with the travel site, whether it's booking a business trip or buying tickets for a honeymoon. Second, TripAdvisor includes the customer in brand conversations by asking community participants to provide insights into why they use TripAdvisor, and encourages them to offer their opinions online. TripAdvisor also encourage its travel partners to promote TripAdvisor as part of their own marketing activities, thereby maximizing the brand's exposure. Third, TripAdvisor has learned to leverage technology to maximize return-on-investment (ROI). Its marketing department consists of data scientists and engineers who are continuously optimizing its online expenditures to ensure that the 350 million monthly visitors are able to interact and engage with the brand. Fourth,

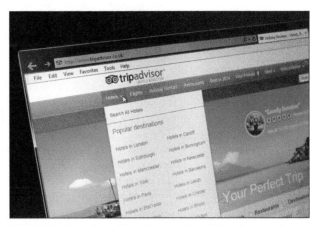

Digital platform-based brands—such as TripAdvisor—have leveraged the power of technology and data-driven insights to create value for their customers.

TripAdvisor also personalizes its communications after taking into account the insights generated from its customer interactions and transactions data. For example, just before a customer embarks on a trip, TripAdvisor knows that its mobile app will be of great value to the customer, particularly features such as "near me now" that allow customers to find nearby restaurants to eat at. The company has utilized information from prior searches and introduced MyTrips—a feature which allows TripAdvisor to personalize its service to each individual customer. By further leveraging the power of its mobile app, TripAdvisor has been very effective in building customer engagement. In addition to these features, TripAdvisor also experiments with adding unique content that will promote engagement among its travel-oriented customers. TripAdvisor has been revising its brand strategy from being known as the brand trusted for reviews to a brand where a customer can find the lowest price and find the right hotel. In these ways, TripAdvisor—a digital platform—has been able to continuously evolve its brand, create brand value, and build enduring consumer-brand relationships.

Sources: Zach Brooke, "Grubhub Aims to Redefine Food Delivery with Rebrand," *Marketing News Weekly*, May 24, 2016, https://www.ama .org/publications/eNewsletters/Marketing-News-Weekly/Pages/grubhub-aims-to-redefine-food-delivery-with-rebrand---.aspx, accessed February 1, 2018; Alison Griswold, "Grubhub Is Fending Off Copycats by Doubling Down on Delivery," March 14, 2016, https://qz.com/637471/grubhub-is-chasing-silicon-valleys-delivery-success-story/, accessed February 28, 2018; Jessica Wohl, "Pho, Anyone? Grubhub Suggests People Try Something New," November 14, 2017, http://adage.com/article/cmo-strategy/grubhub-suggests-people/311295/, accessed February 28, 2018; Corinne Bagish, "The Marketing Savvy Powering TripAdvisor's Global Growth," December 21, 2015, Marketo.com, accessed February 2, 2018; "8 Interesting Things We Learned from TripAdvisor's Recent Brand Strategy Update," June 13, 2017, www.siteminder.com/r/hotel-distribution/hotel-metasearch/8-things-learned-tripadvisor-brand-strategy-update/, accessed February 28, 2018.

(i.e., Grubhub and TripAdvisor) leverage the strength of their platform to build consumer-brand relationships and strong brand resonance.

It is virtually impossible, however, for consumers to experience an intense, active loyalty relationship with *all* the brands they purchase and consume. Thus, some brands will be more meaningful to consumers than others, because of the nature of their associated product or service, the characteristics of the consumer, and so on. Some brands have more resonance potential than others. When it is difficult to create a varied set of feelings and imagery associations, marketers might not be able to obtain the deeper aspects of brand resonance like active engagement. Nevertheless, by taking a broader view of brand loyalty, they may be able to gain a more holistic appreciation for their brand and how it connects to consumers. And by defining the proper role for the brand, they should be able to obtain higher levels of brand resonance.

THE BRAND VALUE CHAIN

Developing a strong positioning and building brand resonance are crucial marketing goals. To better understand the ROI of marketing investments, however, another tool is necessary. The **brand value chain** is a structured approach to assessing the sources and outcomes of brand equity and the manner by which marketing activities create brand value.[50] It recognizes that many different people within an organization can affect brand equity and need to be aware of relevant branding effects. The brand value chain thus provides insights to support brand managers, chief marketing officers, managing directors, and chief executive officers, all of whom may need different types of information.

The brand value chain has several basic premises. Consistent with the brand resonance model, it assumes that the value of a brand ultimately resides with customers. Based on this insight, the model next assumes that the brand value creation process begins when the firm invests in a marketing program targeting actual or potential customers (stage 1). The associated marketing activity then affects the customer mind-set—what customers know and feel about the brand—as reflected by the brand resonance model (stage 2). This mind-set, across a broad group of customers, produces the brand's performance in the marketplace—how much and when customers purchase, the price that they pay, and so forth (stage 3). Finally, the investment community considers this market performance—and other factors such as replacement cost and purchase price in acquisitions—to arrive at an assessment of shareholder value in general and a value of the brand in particular (stage 4).

The model also assumes that a number of linking factors intervene between these stages. These linking factors determine the extent to which value created at one stage transfers or "multiplies" to the next stage. Three sets of multipliers filter and moderate the transfer between the marketing program and the three value stages: the program quality multiplier, the marketplace conditions multiplier, and the investor sentiment multiplier. The brand value chain model is summarized in Figure 3-5. Next, we describe the value stages and multiplying factors in more detail and look at examples of both positive and negative multiplier effects.

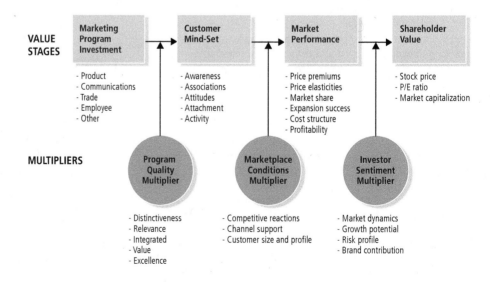

FIGURE 3-5
Brand Value Chain

Value Stages

Brand value creation begins with marketing activity by the firm.

Marketing Program Investment.   Any marketing program investment that can contribute to brand value development, intentionally or not, falls into this first value stage. Chapters 4–8 outline many such marketing activities, like product research, development, and design; trade or intermediary support; marketing communications including advertising, promotion, sponsorship, direct and digital marketing, personal selling, publicity, and public relations; and employee training. Of course, a big investment does not guarantee success. The ability of a marketing program investment to transfer or multiply farther down the chain depends on *qualitative* aspects of the marketing program and the program quality multiplier.

Program Quality Multiplier.   The ability of the marketing program to affect the customer mind-set will depend on its quality. Throughout the book, we review a number of different means to judge the quality of a marketing program. One handy way to remember some key considerations is through the acronym DRIVE, as follows:

1. **Distinctiveness:** How unique is the marketing program? How creative or differentiating is it?
2. **Relevance:** How meaningful is the marketing program to customers? Do consumers feel the brand is one they should seriously consider?
3. **Integrated:** How well integrated is the marketing program at one point in time and over time? Do all aspects combine to create the biggest impact with customers as possible? Does the marketing program relate effectively to past marketing programs and properly balance continuity and change, evolving the brand in the right direction?
4. **Value:** How much short-run and long-run value does the marketing program create? Will it profitably drive sales in the short run? Will it build brand equity in the long run?
5. **Excellence:** Is the individual marketing activity designed to satisfy the highest standards? Does it reflect state-of-the art thinking and corporate wisdom as success factors for that particular type of marketing activity?

Not surprisingly, a well-integrated marketing program, carefully designed and implemented to be highly relevant and unique, is likely to achieve a greater return on investment from marketing program expenditures. For example, despite being outspent by such beverage brand giants as Coca-Cola, Pepsi, and Budweiser, the California Milk Processor Board was able to reverse a decades-long decline in consumption of milk in California through the well-designed and executed "Got Milk?" campaign.

On the other hand, numerous marketers have found that expensive marketing programs do not necessarily produce sales unless they are well conceived. For example, through the years, brands such as Michelob, Minute Maid, 7 Up, and others have seen their sales slide despite sizable marketing expenditures because of poorly targeted and delivered marketing campaigns.

Customer Mind-Set.   In what ways have customers been changed as a result of the marketing program? How have those changes manifested themselves in the customer mind-set?

Remember, the customer mind-set includes everything that exists in the minds of customers with respect to a brand: thoughts, feelings, experiences, images, perceptions, beliefs, and attitudes. In its totality, the brand resonance model captures a wide range of aspects of the customer mind-set. To provide a concise summary, a shorter "5 As" list can highlight important measures of the customer mind-set as suggested by the resonance model:

1. **Brand Awareness:** The extent and ease with which customers recall and recognize the brand and can identify the products and services with which it is associated.
2. **Brand Associations:** The strength, favorability, and uniqueness of perceived attributes and benefits for the brand. Brand associations often represent key sources of brand value, because they are the means by which consumers feel brands satisfy their needs.
3. **Brand Attitudes:** Overall evaluations of the brand in terms of its quality and the satisfaction it generates.

4. **Brand Attachment:** The degree of loyalty the customer feels toward the brand. A strong form of attachment, *adherence*, is the consumer's resistance to change and the ability of a brand to withstand bad news like a product or service failure. In the extreme, attachment can even become *addiction.*

5. **Brand Activity:** The extent to which customers use the brand; talk to others about the brand; seek out brand information, promotions, and events, and so on.

These five dimensions can be easily related to the brand resonance model (awareness relates to salience, associations relate to performance and imagery, attitudes relate to judgments and feelings, and attachment and activity relate to resonance). As in the resonance model, an obvious hierarchy exists in the dimensions of value: awareness supports associations, which drive attitudes that lead to attachment and activity. Brand value is created at this stage when customers have (1) deep, broad brand awareness; (2) appropriately strong, favorable, and unique points-of-parity and points-of-difference; (3) positive brand judgments and feelings; (4) intense brand attachment and loyalty; and (5) a high degree of brand activity.

Creating the right customer mind-set can be critical in terms of building brand equity and value. For example, AMD and Cyrix found that achieving performance parity with Intel's micro-processors did not return benefits in 1998, when original equipment manufacturers were reluctant to adopt the new chips because of their lack of a strong brand image with consumers. Moreover, success with consumers may not translate to success in the marketplace unless other conditions also prevail. The ability of this customer mind-set to create value at the next stage depends on external factors we call the marketplace conditions multiplier, as follows.

Marketplace Conditions Multiplier. The extent to which value created in the minds of customers affects market performance depends on factors beyond the individual customer. Three such factors are:

1. **Competitive superiority:** How effective are the marketing investments of competing brands?
2. **Channel and other intermediary support:** How much brand reinforcement and selling effort is being put forth by various marketing partners?
3. **Customer size and profile:** How many and what types of customers are attracted to the brand? Are they profitable?

The value created in the minds of customers will translate to favorable market performance when competitors fail to provide a significant threat, when channel members and other intermediaries provide strong support, and when a sizable number of profitable customers are attracted to the brand.

The competitive context faced by a brand can have a profound effect on its fortunes. For example, Nike and McDonald's have benefited in the past from the prolonged marketing woes of their main rivals, Reebok and Burger King, which both have suffered from numerous reposition-ings and management changes. On the other hand, MasterCard has had to contend for the past decade with two strong, well-marketed brands in Visa and American Express, and consequently, has faced an uphill battle gaining market share despite its well-received "Priceless" ad campaign, as described earlier in this chapter.

Market Performance. We saw in Chapter 2 that the customer mind-set affects how custom-ers react in the marketplace in six main ways. The first two relate to price premiums and price elasticities. How much extra are customers willing to pay for a comparable product because of its brand? And how much does their demand increase or decrease when the price rises or falls? A third outcome is market share, which measures the success of the marketing program in driving brand sales. Collectively, the first three outcomes determine the direct revenue stream attributable to the brand over time. Brand value is created with higher market shares, greater price premiums, and more elastic responses to price decreases and inelastic responses to price increases.

The fourth outcome is brand expansion, the success of the brand in supporting line and cat-egory extensions and new product launches into related categories. This dimension captures the brand's ability to add enhancements to the revenue stream. The fifth outcome is cost structure or, more specifically, reduced marketing program expenditures thanks to the prevailing customer mind-set. When customers already have favorable opinions and knowledge about a brand, any aspect of the marketing program is likely to be more effective for the same expenditure level; alternatively, the same level of effectiveness can be achieved at a lower cost because ads are more memorable, sales calls more productive, and so on. When combined, these five outcomes lead to brand profitability, the sixth outcome.

The ability of the brand value created at this stage to reach the final stage in terms of stock market valuation again depends on external factors, this time according to the investor sentiment multiplier.

Investor Sentiment Multiplier.   Financial analysts and investors consider a host of factors in arriving at their brand valuations and investment decisions. Among them are the following:

- **Market dynamics:** What are the dynamics of the financial markets as a whole (interest rates, investor sentiment, supply of capital)?
- **Growth potential:** What is the growth potential or prospects for the brand and the industry in which it operates? For example, how helpful are the facilitating factors and how inhibiting are the hindering external factors that make up the firm's economic, social, physical, and legal environment?
- **Risk profile:** What is the risk profile for the brand? How vulnerable is the brand to those facilitating and inhibiting factors?
- **Brand contribution:** How important is the brand to the firm's brand portfolio?

The value the brand creates in the marketplace is most likely fully reflected in shareholder value when the firm is operating in a healthy industry without serious environmental hindrances or barriers, and when the brand contributes a significant portion of the firm's revenues and appears to have bright prospects.

The obvious examples of brands that benefited from a strong market multiplier—at least for a while—were the numerous dot-com brands at the turn of the century, such as Pets.com, eToys, Boo.com, and Webvan. The huge premium placed on their (actually negative) market performance, however, quickly disappeared—and in some cases, so did the whole company! Sometimes, the entry of strong competitors could threaten the existence of a business. For example, Dropbox was a pioneer in offering online storage solutions, but advances in cloud computing have created numerous strong rivals, including Google, Apple, and Microsoft, all of which now offer file storage applications and the ability to sync with other apps within their portfolio.[51]

On the other hand, many firms have lamented what they perceive as undervaluation by the market. For example, repositioned companies such as Corning have found it difficult to realize what they viewed as their true market value due to lingering investor perceptions from their past. Corning's heritage was in dishes and cookware; its more recent emphasis is on telecommunications, flat panel displays, and the environmental, life sciences, and semiconductor industries.

Shareholder Value.   Based on all available current and forecasted information about a brand, as well as many other considerations, the financial marketplace formulates opinions and assessments that have very direct financial implications for the brand value. Three particularly important indicators are the stock price, the price/earnings multiple, and overall market capitalization for the firm. Research has shown that not only can strong brands deliver greater returns to stockholders, they can do so with less risk.[52]

Implications

According to the brand value chain, marketers create value first by making shrewd investments in their marketing program and then by maximizing, as much as possible, the program, customer, and market multipliers that translate that investment into bottom-line financial benefits. The brand value chain thus provides a structured means for managers to understand where and how value is created and where to look to improve that process. Certain stages will be of greater interest to different members of the organization.

Brand and category marketing managers are likely to be interested in the customer mind-set and the impact of the marketing program on customers. Chief marketing officers (CMOs), on the other hand, are likely to be more interested in market performance and the impact of customer mind-set on actual market behaviors. Finally, a managing director or CEO is likely to focus on shareholder value and the impact of market performance on investment decisions.

The brand value chain has a number of implications. First, value creation begins with the marketing program investment. Therefore, a necessary—but not sufficient—condition for value creation is a well-funded, well-designed, and well-implemented marketing program. It is rare that marketers can get something for nothing.

Second, value creation requires more than the initial marketing investment. Each of the three multipliers can increase or decrease market value as it moves from stage to stage. In other words, value creation also means ensuring that value transfers from stage to stage. Unfortunately, many factors that can inhibit value creation may be largely out of the marketer's hands, like investors' industry sentiment. Recognizing the uncontrollable nature of these factors is important to help put in perspective the relative success or failure of a marketing program to create brand value. Just as sports coaches cannot be held accountable for unforeseen circumstances such as injuries to key players and financial constraints that make it difficult to attract top talent, so marketers cannot necessarily be held accountable for certain market forces and dynamics.

Third, as we outline in Chapters 9–11, the brand value chain provides a detailed roadmap for tracking value creation that can make marketing research and intelligence efforts easier. Each of the stages and multipliers has a set of measures by which we can assess it. In general, there are three main sources of information, and each taps into one value stage and one multiplier. The first stage, the marketing program investment, is straightforward and can come from the marketing plan and budget. We can assess both customer mind-set and the program quality multiplier with quantitative and qualitative customer research. Market performance and the marketplace conditions multiplier appear in market scans and internal accounting records. Finally, we can estimate shareholder value and the investor sentiment multiplier through investor analysis and interviews.

Modifications to the brand value chain can expand its relevance and applicability. First, there are a number of feedback loops. For example, stock prices can have an important effect on employee morale and motivation. Second, in some cases, the value creation may not occur sequentially. For example, stock analysts may react to an ad campaign for the brand—either personally or in recognition of public acceptance—and factor those reactions directly into their investment assessments. Third, some marketing activities may have only very diffuse effects that manifest over the long term. For example, cause-related or social responsibility marketing activity might affect customer or investor sentiment slowly over time. Fourth, both the mean and the variance of some brand value chain measures could matter. For example, a niche brand may receive very high marks but only across a very narrow range of customers.

REVIEW

Brand planning is aided by three interlocking models that can both qualitatively guide and interpret possible marketing actions as well as quantitatively measure marketing effects (see Figure 3-6). Chapter 2 introduced the brand positioning model. This chapter described in detail the second and third brand-planning tools—the brand resonance and brand value chain models.

The brand resonance model lists a series of steps for building a strong brand: (1) establishing the proper brand identity, (2) creating the appropriate brand meaning, (3) eliciting the right brand responses, and (4) forging appropriate brand relationships with customers. Specifically, according to this model, building a strong brand requires establishing breadth and depth of brand awareness; creating strong, favorable, and unique brand associations; eliciting positive, accessible brand responses; and forging intense, active brand relationships. Achieving these four steps, in turn, means establishing six brand-building blocks: brand salience, brand performance, brand imagery, brand judgments, brand feelings, and brand resonance.

The strongest brands excel on all six of these dimensions and thus fully execute all four steps of building a brand. In the brand resonance model, the most valuable brand-building block, brand resonance, occurs when all the other core brand values are completely "in sync" with respect to customers' needs, wants, and desires. In other words, brand resonance reflects

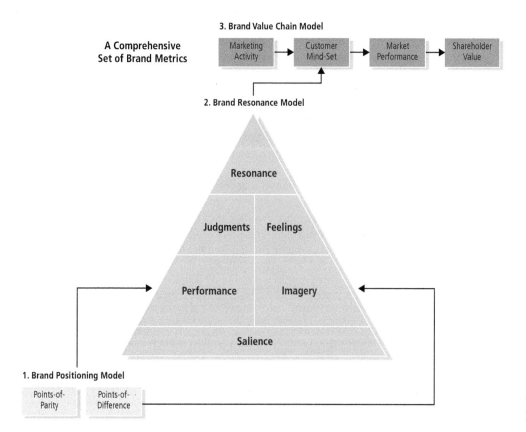

FIGURE 3-6
The Brand Planning
Models

a completely harmonious relationship between customers and the brand. With true brand resonance, customers have a high degree of loyalty marked by a close relationship with the brand and actively seek means to interact with the brand and share their experiences with others. Firms that are able to achieve resonance and affinity with their customers should reap a host of valuable benefits, such as greater price premiums and more efficient and effective marketing programs.

Thus, the basic premise of the brand resonance model is that the true measure of the strength of a brand depends on how consumers think, feel, and act with respect to that brand. Achieving brand resonance requires eliciting the proper cognitive appraisals and emotional reactions to the brand from customers. That, in turn, necessitates establishing brand identity and creating the right meaning in terms of brand performance and brand imagery associations. A brand with the right identity and meaning can make a customer believe it is relevant and "my kind of product." The strongest brands will be those to which consumers become so attached and passionate that they, in effect, become evangelists or missionaries and attempt to share their beliefs and spread the word about the brand.

The brand value chain is a means to trace the value creation process for brands to better understand the financial impact of brand marketing expenditures and investments. Taking the customers' perspective of the value of a brand, the brand value chain assumes that the brand value creation process begins when the firm invests in a marketing program targeting actual or potential customers. Any marketing program investment that potentially can be attributed to brand value development falls into this category, for example, product research, development, and design; trade or intermediary support; and marketing communications.

The marketing activity associated with the program then affects the customer mind-set with respect to the brand—what customers know and feel about the brand. The customer mind-set includes everything that exists in the minds of customers with respect to a brand: thoughts, feelings, experiences, images, perceptions, beliefs, and attitudes. Consistent with the brand resonance model, five key dimensions that are particularly important measures of the customer mind-set are brand awareness, brand associations, brand attitudes, brand attachment, and brand activity or experience.

The customer mind-set affects how customers react or respond in the marketplace in a variety of ways. Six key outcomes of that response are price premiums, price elasticities, market share, brand expansion, cost structure, and brand profitability. Based on a thorough understanding of the brand's past, current, and future prospects, as well as other factors, the financial marketplace then formulates opinions and makes various assessments that have direct financial implications for the value of the brand. Three particularly important indicators are the stock price, the price/earnings multiple, and overall market capitalization for the firm.

The model also assumes that a number of linking factors intervene between these stages. These linking factors determine the extent to which value created at one stage transfers or multiplies to the next stage. Thus, there are three sets of multipliers that moderate the transfer between the marketing program and the subsequent three value stages: the program multiplier, the customer multiplier, and the market multiplier.

Once marketers have determined the brand planning, they can put into place the actual marketing program to create, strengthen, or maintain brand associations. Chapters 4–8 in Part III of the text describe some of the important marketing issues in designing brand-building marketing programs.

DISCUSSION QUESTIONS

1. Pick a brand. Attempt to identify its sources of brand equity. Assess its level of brand awareness and the strength, favorability, and uniqueness of its associations.
2. Which brands do you have the most resonance with? Why?
3. Can every brand achieve resonance with its customers? Why or why not?
4. Pick a brand. Assess the extent to which the brand is achieving the various benefits of brand equity.
5. Which companies do you think do a good job managing their customers? Why?
6. Can you think of digital platforms (such as TripAdvisor, Airbnb) that have built a strong brand presence? Can you identify key factors contributing to their success?

BRAND FOCUS 3.0
Creating Customer Value

Many firms are now more carefully defining the financial value of prospective and actual customers and devising marketing programs to optimize that value. Customer–brand relationships are the foundation of brand resonance and building a strong brand. Marketers have long recognized the importance of adopting a strong consumer and customer orientation. The customer-based brand equity concept certainly puts that notion front and center, making it clear that the power of a brand resides in the minds and hearts of consumers and customers.

Too many firms, however, still find themselves paying the price for lacking a customer focus. Even the biggest firms can stumble. For example, companies such as Apple, Samsung, and GE have been consistent in their efforts to focus on customers. Others have not been as successful in maintaining a customer focus. For instance, at one time Hewlett Packard (HP) had a track record of success. After the year 2000, the innovative market leader became more of a market follower, which focused on efficiencies and cost-cutting. Successive changes

of CEOs at HP did not alleviate its problems, and the lack of customer-focused innovation really hurt the company's fortunes significantly.[53]

HP is not alone in recognizing the financial value of customer experiences. Many firms are now more carefully defining the financial value of prospective and actual customers and devising marketing programs to optimize that value.

Customer Equity

Many firms have introduced customer relationship marketing programs to improve customer interactions. Some marketing observers encourage firms to formally define and manage the value of their customers. The concept of customer equity can be useful in that regard. Although we can define customer equity in different ways, one definition calls it "the sum of lifetime values of all customers."[54] Customer lifetime value (CLV) is affected by revenue and by the cost of customer acquisition, retention, and cross-selling. What are these concepts and approaches? See next page.

Blattberg and Deighton.   Blattberg and Deighton have defined customer equity as the optimal balance between what marketers spend on customer acquisition and what they spend on customer retention.[55] They calculated customer equity as follows:

> We first measure each customer's expected contribution toward offsetting the company's fixed costs over the expected life of that customer. Then, we discount the expected contributions to a net present value at the company's target rate of return for marketing investments. Finally, we add together the discounted, expected contributions of all current contributions.

The authors observe that a focus on either customer acquisition or on customer retention alone may be misplaced. Instead they argue that a focus on maximizing customer equity may offer more direction to managers. Maximizing customer equity would require a judicious balance of acquisition and retention efforts.

Blattberg and Deighton offer eight guidelines as a means of maximizing customer equity:

1. Invest in highest-value customers first.
2. Transform product management into customer management.
3. Consider how add-on sales and cross-selling can increase customer equity.
4. Look for ways to reduce acquisition costs.
5. Track customer equity gains and losses against marketing programs.
6. Relate branding to customer equity.
7. Monitor the intrinsic retainability of your customers.
8. Consider writing separate marketing plans—or even building two marketing organizations—for acquisition and retention efforts.

Rust, Zeithaml, and Lemon.   Rust, Zeithaml, and Lemon define customer equity as the discounted lifetime values of a firm's customer base.[56] According to their view, customer equity is made up of three components and key drivers:

- **Value equity:** Customers' objective assessment of the utility of a brand based on perceptions of what is given up for what is received. Three drivers of value equity are quality, price, and convenience.
- **Brand equity:** Customers' subjective and intangible assessment of the brand, above and beyond its objectively perceived value. Three key drivers of brand equity are customer brand awareness, customer brand attitudes, and customer perception of brand ethics.
- **Relationship equity:** Customers' tendency to stick with the brand, above and beyond objective and subjective assessments of the brand. Four key drivers of relationship equity are loyalty programs, special recognition and treatment programs, community-building programs, and knowledge-building programs.

Note that this definition of brand equity differs from the customer-based brand equity definition proposed in this text, which puts the focus on the beneficial differential response to marketing activity that strong brands produce.

These authors propose that the three components of customer equity vary in importance by company and industry. For example, they suggest that brand equity will matter more with low-involvement purchases involving simple decision processes (like facial tissues), when the product is highly visible to others, when experiences associated with the product can be passed from one individual or generation to the next, or when it is difficult to evaluate the quality of a product or service prior to consumption. On the other hand, value equity will be more important in business-to-business settings, whereas retention equity will be more important for companies that sell a variety of products and services to the same customer.

Rust and colleagues advocate customer-centered brand management to firms with the following directives that, they maintain, go against current management convention:

1. Make brand decisions subservient to decisions about customer relationships.
2. Build brands around customer segments, not the other way around.
3. Make your brands as narrow as possible.
4. Plan brand extensions based on customer needs, not component similarities.
5. Develop the capability and the mind-set to hand off customers to other brands in the company.
6. Take no heroic measures to try to save ineffective brands.
7. Change how you measure brand equity to make individual-level calculations.

Kumar and Colleagues.   In a series of studies, Kumar and his colleagues explore a number of questions concerning customer lifetime value and how firms should allocate their marketing spending to customer acquisition and retention efforts.[57] The authors show that marketing contacts across various channels influence CLV nonlinearly. Customers who are selected on the basis of their lifetime value provide higher profits in future periods than do customers selected on the basis of several other customer-based metrics. Kumar and his colleagues show how each customer varies in his or her lifetime value to a firm, and how customer lifetime value computations require different approaches depending on the business application. They also demonstrate how their framework, which incorporates projected profitability of customers in the computation of lifetime duration, can be superior to traditional methods such as the recency, frequency, and monetary value framework and past customer value.

Linking Customer Equity to Shareholder Value.
A series of studies have aimed to link the notion of customer equity to a firm's value on the stock market. Gupta, Lehmann, and Stuart showed the feasibility of using a firm's customer equity—the sum of CLVs over all customers—to derive a firm's stock market capitalization. A study by Kumar and Shah also corroborated the link between customer equity and firm value.[58] Another study proposed that customer equity can function as a proxy for market capitalization, demonstrating the validity of this approach using an in-depth case study of Netflix.[59] Further, research has proposed a new metric called customer referral value (CRV), which is born out of the notion that the value of customers to a firm is not entirely based on the transactions of customers alone, but also in their ability to drive word-of-mouth.[60]

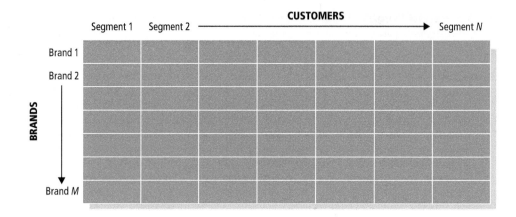

FIGURE 3-7
Brand and Customer
Management

Relationship of Customer Equity to Brand Equity.
Brand equity management can be related to customer equity management in different ways. One way to reconcile the two points of view is to think of a matrix where all the brands and sub-brands and variants that a company offers are rows, and all the different customer segments or individual customers that purchase those brands are columns (see Figure 3-7). Effective brand and customer management would necessarily take into account both the rows and the columns to arrive at optimal marketing solutions. In fact, scholars have proposed that co-managing brand equity and customer equity could lead to rich rewards.[61]

Differences between the Two Points of View.
As they have been developed conceptually and put into practice, however, the two perspectives tend to emphasize different aspects (see Figure 3-8). The customer equity perspective puts much focus on the bottom-line financial value created by customers. Its clear benefit is the quantifiable measures of financial performance it provides. In its calculations, however, the customer equity perspective largely ignores some of the important advantages of creating a strong brand, such as the ability of a strong brand to attract higher quality employees, elicit stronger support from channel and supply chain partners, create growth opportunities through line and category extensions and licensing, and so on.

The customer equity perspective also tends to be less prescriptive about specific marketing activities beyond general recommendations toward customer acquisition, retention, and cross-selling. The customer equity perspective does not always fully account for competitive response and the resulting moves and countermoves, nor does it fully account for social network effects, word of mouth, and customer-to-customer recommendations.

Thus, customer equity approaches can overlook the option value of brands and their potential impact on revenues and costs beyond the current marketing environment. Brand equity, on the other hand, tends to put more emphasis on strategic issues in managing brands and how marketing programs can be designed to create and leverage brand awareness and image with customers. It provides much practical guidance for specific marketing activities.

With a focus on brands, however, managers do not always develop detailed customer analyses in terms of the brand equity they achieve with specific consumers or groups of consumers and the resulting long-term profitability that is created. Brand equity approaches could benefit from sharper segmentation schemes.

Reconciling the Two Points of View. There is no question that customer equity and brand equity are related. In theory, both approaches can be expanded to incorporate the

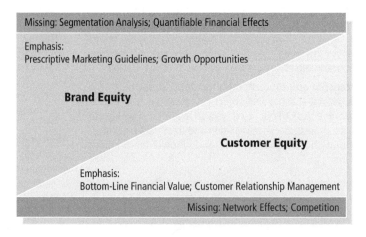

FIGURE 3-8
Brand Equity versus
Customer Equity

other point of view and they are clearly inextricably linked. Customers drive the success of brands, but brands are the necessary touchpoint that firms have to connect with their customers. Customer-based brand equity maintains that brands create value by eliciting differential customer response to marketing activities. The higher price premiums and increased levels of loyalty engendered by brands generate incremental cash flows.

Many of the actions that will increase brand equity will increase customer equity, and vice versa. In practice, customer equity and brand equity are complementary notions in that they tend to emphasize different considerations. Brand equity tends to put more emphasis on the "front end" of marketing programs and intangible value potentially created by marketing programs; customer equity tends to place more emphasis on the "back end" of marketing programs and the realized value of marketing activities in terms of revenue.

The two concepts go hand in hand: customers need and value brands, but a brand ultimately is only as good as the customers it attracts. As evidence of this duality, consider the role of the retailer as a middleman between firms and consumers.

Retailers clearly recognize the importance of both brands and customers. A retailer chooses to sell those brands that are the best bait for those customers it wants to attract. Retailers essentially assemble brand portfolios to establish a profitable customer portfolio. Manufacturers make similar decisions, developing brand portfolios and hierarchies to maximize their customer franchises.

But effective brand management is critical, and it is a mistake to ignore its important role in developing long-term profit streams for firms. Some marketing observers have perhaps minimized the challenge and value of strong brands to overly emphasize the customer equity perspective, for example, maintaining that "our attitude should be that brands come and go—but customers . . . must remain."[62] Yet that statement can easily be taken to the logical, but opposite, conclusion: "Through the years, customers may come and go, but strong brands will endure." Perhaps the main point is that both are really crucial, and the two perspectives can help improve the marketing success of a firm. The customer-based brand equity concept is an attempt to do just that.

NOTES

1. Elizabeth Cowley and Andrew A. Mitchell, "The Moderating Effect of Product Knowledge on the Learning and Organization of Product Information," *Journal of Consumer Research* 30 (December 2003): 443–454.

2. Mita Sujan and Christine Dekleva, "Product Categorization and Inference Making: Some Implications for Comparative Advertising," *Journal of Consumer Research* 14, no. 3 (December 1987): 372–378.

3. Elaine Wong, "For H&R Block's CMO, It's Tax Time Year-Round," *Brandweek*, August 23, 2009, https://www.adweek.com/brand-marketing/hr-blocks-cmo-its-tax-time-year-round-106300/, accessed October 24, 2018.

4. Campbell Soup Company, "Campbell Launches 'It's Amazing What Soup Can Do' Ad Campaign to Promote Campbell's US Soup Brands," *Business Wire*, September 7, 2010, https://www.businesswire.com/news/home/20100907006087/en/Campbell-Launches_"It's-Amazing-Soup-Do"-Ad; Al Lewis, "Soup's Suffering Sales," *The Wall Street Journal*, September 12, 2010; Elaine Wong, "Campbell Gets Happy in 100 Mil. Push," *Brandweek*, September 7, 2010.

5. Jessica Wohl, "Campbell Soup "Shows 'Real, Real Life' in New Brand Campaign," *Advertising Age*, October 5, 2015, http://www.adageindia.in/marketing/cmo-strategy/campbell-soup-shows-real-real-life-in-new-brand-campaign/articleshow/49227670.cms.

6. Chip Heath and Dan Heath, *Made to Stick: Why Some Ideas Survive and Others Die* (New York: Random House, 2007); Matthew Boyle, "The Accidental Hero," *Businessweek*, November 5, 2009, https://www.bloomberg.com/news/articles/2009-11-05/the-accidental-hero

7. David Garvin, "Product Quality: An Important Strategic Weapon," *Business Horizons* 27, no. 3 (May–June 1984): 40–43; Philip Kotler and Kevin Lane Keller, *Marketing Management*, 14th ed. (Upper Saddle River, NJ: Prentice Hall, 2012).

8. Robert C. Blattberg and Kenneth J. Wisniewski, "Price-Induced Patterns of Competition," *Marketing Science* 8, no. 4 (Fall 1989): 291–309; Raj Sethuraman and V. Srinivasan, "The Asymmetric Share Effect: An Empirical Generalization on Cross-Price Effects," *Journal of Marketing Research* 39, no. 3 (August 2002): 379–386.

9. Bianca Grohmann, "Gender Dimensions of Brand Personality," *Journal of Marketing Research* 46, no. 1 (February 2009): 105–119.

10. Joseph T. Plummer, "How Personality Makes a Difference," *Journal of Advertising Research* 24, no. 6 (December 1984/January 1985): 27–31.

11. See Jennifer Aaker, "Dimensions of Brand Personality," *Journal of Marketing Research* 34, no. 3 (August 1997): 347–357.

12. Jennifer Aaker, Kathleen Vohs, and Cassie Mogilner, "Nonprofits Are Seen as Warm and For-Profits as Competent: Firm Stereotypes Matter," *Journal of Consumer Research* 37, no. 2 (August 2010): 277–291.

13. Jennifer L. Aaker, "Dimensions of Brand Personality." *Journal of Marketing Research* 34, no. 3 (1997): 347–356; Susan Fournier, "Consumers and Their Brands: Developing Relationship Theory in Consumer Research," *Journal of Consumer Research* 24, no. 3 (1997): 343–373.

14. Gita Venkataramani Johar, Jaideep Sengupta, and Jennifer L. Aaker, "Two Roads to Updating Brand Personality Impressions: Trait Versus Evaluative Inferencing,"

Journal of Marketing Research 42, no. 4 (November 2005): 458–469; see also Alokparna Basu Monga and Loraine Lau-Gesk, "Blending Cobrand Personalities: An Examination of the Complex Self," *Journal of Marketing Research* 44, no. 3 (August 2007): 389–400.

15. M. Joseph Sirgy, "Self-Concept in Consumer Behavior: A Critical Review," *Journal of Consumer Research* 9, no. 3 (December 1982): 287–300; Lan Nguyen Chaplin and Deborah Roedder John, "The Development of Self-Brand Connections in Children and Adolescents," *Journal of Consumer Research* 32, no. 1 (June 2005): 119–129; Lucia Malär, Harley Krohmer, Wayne D. Hoyer, and Bettina Nyffenegger, "Emotional Brand Attachment and Brand Personality: The Relative Importance of the Actual and the Ideal Self," *Journal of Marketing* 75, no. 4 (July 2011): 35–52; Alexander Chernev, Ryan Hamilton, and David Gal, "Competing for Consumer Identity: Limits to Self-Expression and the Perils of Lifestyle Branding," *Journal of Marketing* 75, no. 3 (May 2011): 66–82.

16. Timothy R. Graeff, "Consumption Situations and the Effects of Brand Image on Consumers' Brand Evaluations," *Psychology & Marketing* 14, no. 1 (1997): 49–70; Timothy R. Graeff, "Image Congruence Effects on Product Evaluations: The Role of Self-Monitoring and Public/Private Consumption," *Psychology & Marketing* 13, no. 5 (1996): 481–499. See also, Ji Kyung Park and Deborah Roedder John, "Got to Get You into My Life: Do Brand Personalities Rub Off on Consumers?," *Journal of Consumer Research* 37, no. 4 (December 2010): 655–669.

17. Jennifer L. Aaker, "The Malleable Self: The Role of Self-Expression in Persuasion," *Journal of Marketing Research* 36, no. 2 (1999): 45–57. See also, Vanitha Swaminathan, Karen Stilley, and Rohini Ahluwalia, "When Brand Personality Matters: The Moderating Role of Attachment Styles," *Journal of Consumer Research* 35, no. 6 (April 2009): 985–1002.

18. Sarah Steimer, "Recap: Why Hyatt Is Making an Emotional Connection with Customers and Differentiating Its Properties," October 6, 2016, Marketing News Weekly, accessed February 1, 2018; Katie Richards, "Hyatt Celebrates All the Business Travelers Who Never Settle in New Integrated Campaign," www.adweek.com/brand-marketing/hyatt-celebrates-all-businesstravelers-who-never-set2016), tle-new-integrated-campaign-173323/, accessed February 27, 2018; Tanya Gazdik, "Hyatt Launches First Dual-Branded Effort," September 12, 2016, www.mediapost.com/publications/article/284368/hyatt-launches-first-dual-brandedeffort.html, accessed February 28, 2018.

19. Northern Trust, "Top Performers: World's Most Admired Companies," *Fortune*, August 16, 2010, 16.

20. Douglas B. Holt, *How Brands Become Icons* (Cambridge, MA: Harvard Business School Press, 2004). Holt has a number of other thought-provoking pieces, including "Why Do Brands Cause Trouble? A Dialectical Theory of Consumer Culture and Branding," *Journal of Consumer Research* 29, no. 1 (June 2002): 70–90; Douglas B. Holt and Craig J. Thompson, "Man-of-Action Heroes: The Pursuit of Heroic Masculinity

in Everyday Consumption," *Journal of Consumer Research* 31, no. 2 (September 2004): 425–440.

21. William L. Wilkie, *Consumer Behavior,* 3rd ed. (New York: John Wiley & Sons, 1994).

22. "Equitrend," The Harris Poll, www.theharrispoll.com/equitrend/#.

23. For an insightful examination of credibility and the related concept of truth, see Lynn Upshaw, *Truth: The New Rules for Marketing in a Skeptical World* (New York: AMACOM, 2007).

24. Stuart Elliott, "Delivered Just in Time for Kickoff," *The New York Times,* September 7, 2011, www.nytimes.com/2011/09/08/business/media/fedex-to-introduce-new-campaign.html.

25. Ekaterina Walter, "The Big Brand Theory: How FedEx Achieves Social Customer Service Success," *Social Media Today*, May 28, 2013, www.socialmediatoday.com/content/big-brand-theory-how-fedex-achieves-social-customer-service-success.

26. Andrea Fryrear, "A Content Success Story: How FedEx Operations Now Delivers a Better Customer Experience," *Content Marketing Institute*, August 16, 2017, http://contentmarketinginstitute.com/2017/08/fedex-content-operations/.

27. Izea, "15 Top B2C Content Marketing Examples," *IZEA*, August 28, 2017, https://izea.com/2017/08/28/b2c-content-marketing-examples/.

28. Elaine Wong, "FedEx Rolls with Changes in Global Campaign," *Brandweek*, October 29, https://www.adweek.com/brand-marketing/fedex-rolls-changes-global-campaign-106604/; Elaine Wong, "CPG Brands Top Most Trusted List," *Brandweek*, February 22, 2010, https://www.adweek.com/brand-marketing/cpg-brands-top-most-trusted-list-107079/, accessed October 23, 2018.

29. Alan M. Webber, "Trust in the Future," *Fast Company*, September 2000, 210–220.

30. Kevin Roberts, *Lovemarks: The Future Beyond Brands* (New York: Powerhouse Books, 2004).

31. For seminal research, see William D. Wells, "How Advertising Works," unpublished paper, 1980; Christopher P. Puto and William D. Wells, "Informational and Transformational Advertising: The Differential Effects of Time," in *Advances in Consumer Research* 11, ed. Thomas C. Kinnear (Ann Arbor, MI: Association for Consumer Research, 1983), 638–643; Stephen J. Hoch and John Deighton, "Managing What Consumers Learn from Experience," *Journal of Marketing* 53, no. 2 (April 1989): 1–20; for a current application, see also Gillian Naylor, Susan Bardi Kleiser, Julie Baker, and Eric Yorkston, "Using Transformational Appeals to Enhance the Retail Experience," *Journal of Retailing* 84, no. 1 (April 2008): 49–57.

32. Elizabeth Olson, "Corona Light Sets Sights on a Younger Party Crowd," *The New York Times*, August 1, 2010, https://www.nytimes.com/2010/08/02/business/media/02adco.html.

33. Lynn R. Kahle, Basil Poulos, and Ajay Sukhdial, "Changes in Social Values in the United States During the Past Decade," *Journal of Advertising Research* (February/March 1988): 35–41.

34. For a stimulating and comprehensive set of readings, see Deborah J. MacInnis, C. Whan Park, and Joseph R. Priester, eds. *Handbook of Brand Relationships* (Armonk, NY: M. E. Sharpe, 2009).

35. Greg Farrell, "Marketers Put a Price on Your Life," *USA Today,* July 7, 1999, 3B.

36. Arjun Chaudhuri and Morris B. Holbrook, "The Chain of Effects from Brand Trust and Brand Affect to Brand Performance: The Role of Brand Loyalty," *Journal of Marketing* 65, no. 2 (April 2001): 81–93.

37. Thomas A. Stewart, "A Satisfied Customer Is Not Enough," *Fortune,* July 12, 1997, 112–113.

38. Thomas O. Jones and W. Earl Sasser Jr. "Why Satisfied Customers Defect," *Harvard Business Review* (November–December 1995): 88–99.

39. Faith Logan, "Are Your Customers 'Attitudinally-Loyal' and Why Should You Care?," *CBC,* September 28, 2017, www.cbcads.com/attitudinal-loyalty/.

40. James H. McAlexander, John W. Schouten, and Harold F. Koenig, "Building Brand Community," *Journal of Marketing* 66, no. 1 (January 2002): 38–54; Albert Muniz and Thomas O'Guinn, "Brand Community," *Journal of Consumer Research* 27, no. 4 (March 2001): 412–432.

41. Gil McWilliam, "Building Stronger Brands Through Online Communities," *MIT Sloan Management Review* 41, no. 3 (Spring 2000): 43–54.

42. Rene Algesheimer, Utpal M. Dholakia, and Andreas Hermann, "The Social Influence of Brand Community: Evidence from European Car Clubs," *Journal of Marketing* 69, no. 3 (July 2005): 19–34.

43. Rob Walker, *Buying In* (New York: Random House, 2008).

44. Chris Reiter, "For Luxury Automakers, Selling Toys Is No Game," *Bloomberg Businessweek,* November 29–December 5, 2010, 26–28; Markus Seidel, "BMW Uses Lifestyle Products as a Strategic Differentiating Factor in the Automotive Industry," *PDMA Visions,* July 2004, 24–25; BMW, www.shopbmwusa.com.

45. Nikki Hopewell, "Generating Brand Passion," *Marketing News,* May 15, 2005, 10.

46. "Creative: Inside Priceless MasterCard Moments," *Adweek,* April 12, 1999; Marc De Swaan Arons, "MasterCard—Finding a Compelling Global Positioning," *All About Branding,* August 6, 2005; www.effie.org.

47. Giselle Abramovich, "Three Lessons from MasterCard's 'Priceless' Campaign," *CMO,* August 21, 2013, www.cmo.com/features/articles/2013/8/19/three_lessons_from_m.html#gs.jICbWtI.

48. The Nielsen Company, "Under the Influence: Consumer Trust in Advertising." *Nielson,* September 17, 2013, www.nielsen.com/us/en/insights/news/2013/under-the-influence-consumer-trust-in-advertising.html.

49. Darren W. Dahl, Christoph Fuchs, and Martin Schreier. "Why and When Consumers Prefer Products of User-Driven Firms: A Social Identification Account," *Management Science* 61, no. 8 (2014): 1978–1988; Roderick J. Brodie, Linda D. Hollebeek, Biljana Jurić, and Ana Ilić, "Customer Engagement: Conceptual Domain, Fundamental Prepositions, and Implications For Research," *Journal of Service Research* 14, no. 3 (2011): 252–271.

50. Kevin Lane Keller and Don Lehmann, "How Do Brands Create Value?," *Marketing Management* 12, no. 3 (May/June 2003): 26–31. See also R. K. Srivastava, T. A. Shervani, and L. Fahey, "Market-Based Assets and Shareholder Value," *Journal of Marketing* 62, no. 1 (1998): 2–18; and M. J. Epstein and R. A. Westbrook, "Linking Actions to Profits in Strategic Decision Making," *MIT Sloan Management Review* (Spring 2001): 39–49. In terms of related empirical insights, see Manoj K. Agrawal and Vithala Rao, "An Empirical Comparison of Consumer-Based Measures of Brand Equity," *Marketing Letters* 7, no. 3 (1996): 237–247; and Walfried Lassar, Banwari Mittal, and Arun Sharma, "Measuring Customer-Based Brand Equity," *Journal of Consumer Marketing* 12, no. 4 (1995): 11–19.

51. Miguel Helft, "Dropbox Under Siege—But It's Not Slowing Down," July 29, 2015, Forbes.com, https://www.forbes.com/sites/miguelhelft/2015/07/29/dropbox-is-under-siege-but-its-not-slowing-down/#51ea99d9141b

52. Thomas J. Madden, Frank Fehle, and Susan Fournier, "Brands Matter: An Empirical Demonstration of the Creation of Shareholder Value Through Branding" *Journal of the Academy of Marketing Science,* 34(2): 224–235.

53. Ira Kalb, "Everything at Hewlett-Packard Started to Go Wrong When Cost-Cutting Replaced Innovation," *Business Insider,* May 27, 2012, www.businessinsider.com/heres-where-everything-at-hewlett-packard-started-to-go-wrong-2012-5.

54. Roland T. Rust, Valarie A. Zeithamal, and Katherine N. Lemon, "Customer-Centered Brand Management," *Harvard Business Review* (September 2004), 110–118.

55. Robert C. Blattberg and John Deighton, "Manage Marketing by the Customer Equity Test," *Harvard Business Review* (July–August 1996). See also Robert C. Blattberg, Gary Getz, and Jacquelyn S. Thomas, *Customer Equity: Building and Managing Relationships as Valuable Assets* (Boston, MA: Harvard Business School Press, 2001); Robert Blattberg and Jacquelyn Thomas, "Valuing, Analyzing, and Managing the Marketing Function Using Customer Equity Principles," in *Kellogg on Marketing,* ed. Dawn Iacobucci (New York: John Wiley & Sons, 2001).

56. Roland T. Rust, Valarie A. Zeithaml, and Katherine N. Lemon, *Driving Customer Equity* (New York: Free Press, 2000); Roland T. Rust, Valarie A. Zeithaml, and Katherine N. Lemon, "Customer-Centered Brand Management," *Harvard Business Review* (September 2004), 110–118.

57. W. Reinartz, J. Thomas, and V. Kumar, "Balancing Acquisition and Retention Resources to Maximize Profitability," *Journal of Marketing* 69, no. 1 (January 2005): 63–79; R. Venkatesan and V. Kumar, "A Customer Lifetime Value Framework for Customer Selections and Resource Allocation Strategy," *Journal of Marketing* 68, no. 4 (October 2004): 106–125; V. Kumar, G. Ramani, and T. Bohling, "Customer Lifetime Value Approaches and Best Practice Applications," *Journal of Interactive Marketing* 18, no. 3 (Summer 2004): 60–72; J. Thomas, W. Reinartz, and V. Kumar, "Getting the Most Out of All Your Customers,"

Harvard Business Review (July–August 2004): 116–123; W. Reinartz and V. Kumar, "The Impact of Customer Relationship Characteristics on Profitable Lifetime Duration," *Journal of Marketing* 67, no. 1 (2003): 77–99.

58. Sunil Gupta, Donald R. Lehmann, and Jennifer Ames Stuart, "Valuing Customers," *Journal of Marketing Research* 41, no. 1 (2004): 7-18; V. Kumar and Denish Shah, "Expanding the Role of Marketing: From Customer Equity to Market Capitalization," *Journal of Marketing* 73, no. 6 (2009): 119–136.

59. Thomas Shoutong Zhang, "Firm Valuation from Customer Equity: When Does It Work and When Does It Fail?," *International Journal of Research in Marketing* 33, no. 4 (2016): 966–970.

60. J. Viswanathan Kumar, Andrew Petersen, and Robert P. Leone. "How Valuable Is Word of Mouth?" *Harvard Business Review* 85, no. 10 (2007): 139; J. Viswanathan Kumar, Andrew Petersen, and Robert P. Leone. "Driving Profitability by Encouraging Customer Referrals: Who, When, and How," *Journal of Marketing* 74, no. 5 (2010): 1–17.

61. Anita Luo, Donald R. Lehmann, and Scott A. Neslin, "Co-managing Brand Equity and Customer Equity," In V. Kumar and Denish Shah (Eds.), *Handbook of Research on Customer Equity in Marketing* (pp. 363–381). Cheltenham, UK: Edward Elgar Publishing, 2015.

62. Roland T. Rust, Valarie A. Zeithamal, and Katherine N. Lemon, "Customer-Centered Brand Management," *Harvard Business Review* (September 2004): 110–118.

Choosing Brand Elements to Build Brand Equity

4

Learning Objectives

After reading this chapter, you should be able to

1. Identify the different types of brand elements.
2. List the general criteria for choosing brand elements.
3. Describe key tactics in choosing different brand elements.
4. Explain the rationale for "mixing and matching" brand elements.
5. Highlight some of the legal issues surrounding brand elements.

A brand symbol like the Energizer Bunny can reinforce key brand associations and be used in a variety of different communication applications.

Source: Paul Martinka/ Polaris/Newscom

PREVIEW

Brand elements, sometimes called brand identities, are those trademarkable devices that serve to identify and differentiate the brand. The main ones are brand names, URLs, logos, symbols, characters, spokespeople, slogans, jingles, packages, and signage. The customer-based brand equity model suggests that marketers should choose brand elements to enhance brand awareness; facilitate the formation of strong, favorable, and unique brand associations; or elicit positive brand judgments and feelings. The test of the brand-building ability of a brand element is what consumers would think or feel about the product *if they knew only that particular brand element* and not anything else about the product and how else it would be branded or marketed. A brand element that provides a positive contribution to brand equity conveys or implies certain valued associations or responses.

This chapter considers how marketers choose brand elements to build brand equity. After describing the general criteria for choosing brand elements, we consider specific tactical issues for each of the different types of brand elements and finish by discussing how to choose the best brand elements to build brand equity. Brand Focus 4.0 at the end of the chapter highlights some legal issues for branding.

CRITERIA FOR CHOOSING BRAND ELEMENTS

In general, there are six criteria for brand elements (with more specific subchoices for each, as shown in Figure 4-1):

1. Memorability
2. Meaningfulness
3. Likability
4. Transferability
5. Adaptability
6. Protectability

1. **Memorability**
   Easily recognized
   Easily recalled

2. **Meaningfulness**
   Descriptive
   Persuasive

3. **Likability**
   Fun and interesting
   Rich visual and verbal imagery
   Aesthetically pleasing

4. **Transferability**
   Within and across product categories
   Across geographic boundaries and cultures

5. **Adaptability**
   Flexible
   Updatable

6. **Protectability**
   Legally
   Competitively

FIGURE 4-1

Criteria for Choosing
Brand Elements

The first three criteria—memorability, meaningfulness, and likability—are the marketer's offensive strategy and build brand equity. The latter three—transferability, adaptability, and protectability—however, play a defensive role for leveraging and maintaining brand equity in the face of different opportunities and constraints. Let's consider each of these general criteria.

Memorability

A necessary condition for building brand equity is achieving a high level of brand awareness. Brand elements that promote that goal are inherently memorable and attention-getting and therefore facilitate recall or recognition in purchase or consumption settings. For example, a brand of propane gas cylinders named Blue Rhino featuring a powder-blue animal mascot with a distinctive yellow flame is likely to stick in the minds of consumers.

Meaningfulness

Brand elements may take on all kinds of meaning, with either descriptive or persuasive content. We saw in Chapter 1 that brand names could be based on people, places, animals or birds, or other things or objects. Two particularly important criteria are how well the brand element conveys the following:

- *General information about the function of the product or service:* Does the brand element have descriptive meaning and suggest something about the product category, the needs satisfied or benefits supplied? How likely is it that a consumer could correctly identify the product category for the brand based on any one brand element? Does the brand element seem credible in the product category?
- *Specific information about particular attributes and benefits of the brand:* Does the brand element have persuasive meaning and suggest something about the particular kind of product, or its key points-of-difference attributes or benefits? Does it suggest something about some aspect of the product performance or the type of person who might use the brand?

The first dimension is an important determinant of brand awareness and salience; the second, of brand image and positioning.

Likability

Independent of its memorability and meaningfulness, do customers find the brand element aesthetically appealing?[1] Is it likable visually, verbally, and in other ways? Brand elements can be rich in imagery and inherently fun and interesting, even if not always directly related to the product.

A memorable, meaningful, and likable set of brand elements offers many advantages because consumers often do not examine much information in making product decisions. Descriptive and persuasive elements reduce the burden on marketing communications to build awareness and link brand associations and equity, especially when few other product-related associations exist. Often, the less concrete the possible product benefits are, the more important is the creative potential of the brand name and other brand elements to capture intangible characteristics of a brand.

Transferability

Transferability measures the extent to which the brand element adds to the brand equity for new products or in new markets for the brand. There are several aspects to this criterion.

First, how useful is the brand element for line or category extensions? In general, the less specific the name, the more easily it can be transferred across categories. For example, Amazon was chosen as a brand name because it refers to a massive South American river and, as a name, can be appropriate for a large retail store. Books "R" Us obviously would not have afforded the same flexibility if Amazon had chosen that name to describe its original line of business.

Second, to what extent does the brand element add to brand equity across geographic boundaries and market segments? To a large extent, this depends on the cultural content and linguistic

Although it can be difficult to judge the accuracy of some reports of past marketing failures, here are some of the more widely cited global branding failures reported over the years.

1. When Braniff translated a slogan touting its upholstery, "Fly in leather," it came out in Spanish as "Fly naked."

2. Coors put its slogan, "Turn it loose," into Spanish, where it was read as "Suffer from diarrhea."

3. Chicken magnate Frank Perdue's line, "It takes a tough man to make a tender chicken," sounds much more interesting in Spanish: "It takes a sexually stimulated man to make a chicken affectionate."

4. When Pepsi started marketing its products in China, it translated the slogan "Pepsi Brings You Back to Life" pretty literally. In Chinese it really meant, "Pepsi Brings Your Ancestors Back from the Grave."

5. Clairol introduced the "Mist Stick," a curling iron, into Germany only to find out that mist is slang for manure in German.

6. Japan's Mitsubishi Motors had to rename its Pajero model in Spanish-speaking countries because the term related to masturbation.

7. Toyota Motor's MR2 model dropped the number in France because the combination sounded like a French swearword.

FIGURE 4-2
Global Branding Mishaps

qualities of the brand element. One of the main advantages of nonmeaningful, synthetic names like Exxon is that they transfer well into other languages.

The difficulties or mistakes that even top marketers have encountered in translating their brand names, slogans, and packages into other languages and cultures over the years have become legendary. As an example, Microsoft was challenged when launching its Vista operating system in Latvia, because the name means "chicken" or "frumpy woman" in the local language.[2] Figure 4-2 includes some of the more notorious mishaps.[3] To avoid such complications, companies must review all their brand elements for cultural meaning before introducing the brand into a new market.

Adaptability

The fifth consideration for brand elements is their adaptability over time. Because of changes in consumer values and opinions, or simply because of a need to remain contemporary, most brand elements must be updated. The more adaptable and flexible the brand element, the easier it is to update it. For example, logos and characters can be given a new look or a new design to make them appear more modern and relevant.

MICHELIN MAN

Michelin recently launched a newer, slimmer version of its famous Michelin Man (whose real name is Bibendum). A company press release notes, "thinner and smiling, Michelin Man will look like the leader he is, with an open and reassuring manner." Michelin has used the character to promote its brand values of research, safety, and environmentalism for more than 100 years. In 2000, Michelin Man was voted the "greatest logo in history" in a competition sponsored by the *Financial Times*. In a 2009 global campaign that features the character as a hero, the Michelin Man—which has been the exclusive focus of Michelin advertising since 2001—moved from a "more passive endorser to a more active problem solver." Reinforced by the slogan "The Right Tire Changes Everything," the new ad campaign emphasized the role tires play in people's everyday lives.[4] Michelin ads have since evolved to focus on real-world scenarios[5] in which the Michelin Man's presence is large and meaningful, invoking emotion with a positive influence on the scene to express a benefit for the customer.[6]

The Michelin Man—whose actual name is Bibendum—has served as the centerpiece of the tire brand's advertising for years.

Source: Michelin, North America

THE SCIENCE OF BRANDING 4-1
Counterfeit Business Is Booming

From Calloway golf clubs to Louis Vuitton handbags, counterfeit versions of well-known brands are everywhere. The current size of the counterfeit market is estimated to be $600 billion, representing costs of $460 billion annually to U.S. businesses. The fakes are soaking up profits faster than multinationals can squash counterfeiting operations, and they're getting tougher and tougher to distinguish from the real thing. The difference can be as subtle as lesser-quality leather in a purse or fake batteries inside a cell phone. And counterfeiters can produce fakes cheaply by cutting corners on safety and quality, as well as by avoiding paying for marketing, R&D, or advertising.

It's not just luxury items and consumer electronics that are being copied. The World Health Organization has raised concerns about instances of life-saving drugs such as antimalaria drugs to everyday antibiotics or birth control medicines that are counterfeited. Those drugs not only purloin pharmaceutical industry profits, but they also present a danger to anyone who takes them because they are manufactured under inadequate safety controls.

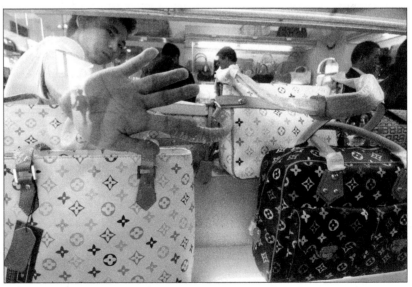

A popular target for counterfeiters who turn out fakes like these, Louis Vuitton uses legal means to vigorously defend its trademarks.

Source: Iain Masterton/Alamy Stock Photo

Counterfeiting has become increasingly sophisticated and pervasive, with many counterfeits being sold online. The unregulated nature of Internet retailing has exacerbated this problem.

To avoid being detected, counterfeiters are knocking off smaller brands that do not have the resources to fight back, focusing on fewer high-end brands, and increasing prices on fake goods sold over the Web to counter consumer suspicions.

The U.S. Trade Representative's office now publishes an annual "notorious markets" list of the worst sites—physical and online—for piracy and counterfeiting. These days, 63 percent of counterfeit goods in the United States come from China. Other sources are Turkey, Singapore, Thailand, and India, and several countries in Southeast Asia (Philippines and Indonesia) and Latin America (Ecuador, Paraguay, and Argentina).

The operations are financed by such varied sources as businessmen who invest in facilities in Asian countries for export, local entrepreneurs, and criminal networks. One study showed that most of the counterfeits are bought and sold online, and some online retailers such as Aliexpress (a Web site linked to Alibaba.com), Facebook, Tokopedia, and Amazon have become unintentional middlemen in the market for counterfeits. In fact, according to the study conducted by RedPoints, a brand protection firm based in Barcelona, 18 percent of the merchandise in AliExpress is fake, although this number is disputed by the retailer.

The replication process has also sped up as counterfeiters have honed their engineering skills and increased their speed. Chinese factories can now copy a new model of a golf club in less than a week. Producing counterfeit goods is as profitable as trading in illegal drugs but does not carry the same risk. In many countries, convicted counterfeiters get off with a fine of a few thousand dollars. It is widely believed that China is the key to stemming the counterfeit trade.

Some companies have decided to target the end users of knockoff products, hoping manufacturers will eventually be forced to get a license and pay royalties. And some patent holders are beginning to get creative and target anyone on the supply chain who knowingly ignores counterfeit businesses. Louis Vuitton has partnered with New York City landlords to prevent the sale of counterfeit Louis Vuitton goods by tenants on notorious knockoff hot spot Canal Street. Because the business of counterfeiting thrives on globalization, experts say that all many companies can do for now is to slow, not stop, the counterfeiters.

Advances in artificial intelligence and machine learning have both helped and hurt counterfeiting. On the one hand, counterfeiters can use the power of technology to hasten the process of counterfeiting products as well as digital goods (such as music or movies). In turn, brand protection firms and agencies are employing machine learning and artificial intelligence to quickly spot counterfeits and fakes on various online and e-commerce Web sites. For example, Entrupy and Red Points use machine learning to develop a classification algorithm which can help distinguish counterfeits from real products with a great deal of accuracy, and then issue a certificate of authenticity.

Interestingly, some provocative academic research shows that fake products are not uniformly bad for companies. Although some consumers may initially feel pleased at buying a fake handbag, for example, many ultimately realize the fake cannot replace the genuine item. While some who cannot afford to buy genuine luxury items may always buy fakes, other consumers will find that buying a counterfeit motivates them to later buy the real thing. Research has also shown that the positive effect of counterfeits is most pronounced for high-fashion products (such as women's high-leg boots and dress shoes), shoes tailored to young customers, and high-end products of brands not yet well-known at the time of counterfeiter entry.

Sources: Robert Klara, "Counterfeit Goods Are a $460 Billion Industry, and Most Are Bought and Sold Online," February 3, 2017, www.adweek.com/brand-marketing/counterfeit-goods-are-a-460-billion-industry-and-most-are-bought-and-sold-online/, accessed March 16, 2018; Billy Bambrough, "World's Largest Producers of Fake Goods Revealed as Value of Counterfeit Goods Nears Half a Trillion Dollars Per Year," April 18, 2016, www.cityam.com/239107/worlds-largest-producers-of-fake-goods-revealed-as-value-of-counterfeit-goods-nears-half-a-trillion-dollars-per-year-, accessed March 16, 2018; Andrew Tarantola, "Counterfeiters Are Using AI and Machine Learning to Make Better Fakes," November 10, 2017, www.engadget.com/2017/11/10/counterfeit-ai-machine-learning-forgery/, accessed March 16, 2018. Julia Boorstin, "Louis Vuitton Tests a New Way to Fight the Faux," *Fortune,* May 16, 2005; Robert Klara, "The Fight Against Fakes," *Brandweek*, June 27, 2009; Stephanie Clifford, "Economic Indicator: Even Cheaper Knockoffs," *The New York Times*, July 31, 2010; Doug Palmer, "U.S. Calls China's Baidu 'Notorious Market'," *Reuters*, February 28, 2011; Renée Richardson Gosline, "Rethinking Brand Contamination: How Consumers Maintain Distinction When Symbolic Boundaries Are Breached," working paper, MIT Sloan School of Management, 2009; Keith Wilcox, Hyeong Min Kim, and Sankar Sen, "Why Do Consumers Buy Counterfeit Luxury Brands?," *Journal of Marketing Research*, 46 (April 2009): 247–259; Young Jee Han, Joseph C Nunes, and Xavier Drèze, "Signaling Status with Luxury Goods: The Role of Brand Prominence," *Journal of Marketing* 74 (July 2010): 15–30; Katherine White and Jennifer J. Argo, "When Imitation Doesn't Flatter: The Role of Consumer Distinctiveness in Responses to Mimicry," *Journal of Consumer Research* 38 (December 2011): 667–680; Yi Qian, "Counterfeiters: Foes or Friends? How Counterfeits Affect Sales by Product Quality Tier," *Management Science* 60, no. 10 (2014): 2381–2400.

Protectability

The sixth and final general consideration is the extent to which the brand element is protectable—both in a legal and a competitive sense. Marketers should (1) choose brand elements that can be legally protected internationally, (2) formally register them with the appropriate legal bodies, and (3) vigorously defend trademarks from unauthorized competitive infringement. The necessity of legally protecting the brand is dramatized by the billions of dollars in losses in the United States alone from unauthorized use of patents, trademarks, and copyrights, as described in The Science of Branding 4-1.

Another consideration is whether the brand is competitively protectable. If a name, package, or other attribute is too easily copied, much of the uniqueness of the brand may disappear. For example, consider the once red-hot ice-beer category. Although Molson Ice was one of the early entries in the category, it quickly lost its pioneering advantage when Miller Ice and what later became Bud Ice were introduced. Marketers need to reduce the likelihood that competitors can create a derivative based on the product's own elements.

OPTIONS AND TACTICS FOR BRAND ELEMENTS

Consider the advantages of "Apple" as the name of a personal computer. Apple was a simple but well-known word that was distinctive in the product category—which helped develop brand awareness. The meaning of the name also gave the company a "friendly shine" and warm brand personality. It could also be reinforced visually with a logo that would transfer easily across geographic and cultural boundaries. Finally, the name could serve as a platform for sub-brands like the Macintosh, aiding the introduction of brand extensions. As Apple illustrates, a well-chosen brand name can make an appreciable contribution to the creation of brand equity.

What would an ideal brand element be like? Consider brand names—perhaps the most central of all brand elements. Ideally, a brand name would be easily remembered, highly suggestive of both the product class and the particular benefits that serve as the basis of its positioning, inherently fun or interesting, rich with creative potential, transferable to a wide variety of product and geographic settings, enduring in meaning and relevant over time, and strongly protectable both legally and competitively.

Unfortunately, it is difficult to choose a brand name—or any brand element, for that matter—that satisfies all these criteria. The more meaningful the brand name, for example, the more difficult it may be to transfer it to new product categories or translate it to other cultures. This is one reason why it is preferable to have multiple brand elements. Let's look at the major considerations for each type of brand element.

Brand Names

The brand name is a fundamentally important choice because it often captures the central theme or key associations of a product in a very compact and economical fashion. Brand names can be an extremely effective shorthand means of communication.[7] Whereas an advertisement lasts half a minute, and a sales call could run to hours, customers can notice the brand name and register its meaning or activate it in memory in just a few seconds.

Because it is so closely tied to the product in the minds of consumers, however, the brand name is also the most difficult element for marketers to change. One study conducted by U.K. research firm Millward Brown suggested that replacing a brand name could result in an immediate drop in sales of 5 to 20 percent and the new brand image may not be as strong as the previous one.[8] So, companies systematically research names before making a choice. Still, it is possible to make serious mistakes, even if inadvertently, in brand name selection. For example, a Silicon Valley start-up called Bodega caused a significant stir when they introduced their company to the public. Bodega is a term referring to a corner store, and the company was selling a vending machine replacement that would actually replace neighborhood bodegas. This type of cultural misappropriation could be harmful to the future of a brand or a company.

Is it difficult to come up with a brand name? Ira Bachrach, a well-known branding consultant, has noted that, although there are 140,000 words in the English vocabulary, the average U.S. adult recognizes only 20,000; Bachrach's consulting company, NameLab, sticks to the 7,000 words that make up the vocabulary of most television programs and commercials.

Although that may seem to allow many choices, each year tens of thousands of new brands are registered as legal trademarks. Arriving at a satisfactory brand name for a new product can be a painfully difficult and prolonged process. After realizing that most of the desirable brand names are already legally registered, many a frustrated executive has lamented that "all the good ones are taken."

Naming Guidelines.   Selecting a brand name for a new product is certainly an art and a science. Brand names come in many different forms. They may be descriptive of the product function (Sleep Inn), be evocative of a certain feature (Quicken Loans), convey personality (Snapple), be completely synthetic and made up (Verizon), or reflect the founder (Dyson), among other brand name strategies (see Figure 4-3). Like any brand element, brand names

Descriptive
Sleep Inn

Evocative
Quicken Loans

Personality
Snapple

Synthetic
Verizon

Founder
Dyson

FIGURE 4-3
Brand Name Taxonomy

must be chosen with the six general criteria of memorability, meaningfulness, likability, transferability, adaptability, and protectability in mind.

Brand Awareness.   Brand names that are simple and easy to pronounce or spell, familiar and meaningful, and different, distinctive, and unusual can obviously improve brand awareness.[9]

Simplicity and Ease of Pronunciation and Spelling.   Simplicity reduces the effort consumers have to make to comprehend and process the brand name. Short names often facilitate recall because they are easy to encode and store in memory—consider Aim toothpaste, Apple computer, Raid pest spray, Bold laundry detergent, Suave shampoo, Off insect repellent, Jif peanut butter, Ban deodorant, and Bic pens. Marketers can shorten longer names to make them easier to recall. For example, over the years Chevrolet cars have also become known as "Chevy," Budweiser beer has become "Bud," and Coca-Cola is also "Coke."[10]

To encourage word-of-mouth exposure that helps build strong memory links, marketers should also make brand names easy to pronounce. Also keep in mind that rather than risk the embarrassment of mispronouncing a difficult name like Hyundai automobiles, Shiseido cosmetics, or Façonnable clothing, consumers may avoid pronouncing it altogether.

Brands with difficult-to-pronounce names have an uphill battle because the firm has to devote so much of its initial marketing effort to teaching consumers how to pronounce the name. Polish vodka Wyborowa (pronounced VEE-ba-ro-va) was supported by a print ad to help consumers pronounce the brand name—a key factor for success in the distilled spirits category, where little self-service exists and consumers usually need to ask for the brand in the store.[11]

Ideally, the brand name should have a clear, understandable, and unambiguous pronunciation and meaning. However, the way a brand is pronounced can affect its meaning, so consumers may take away different perceptions if ambiguous pronunciation results in different meanings. One research study showed that certain hypothetical products with brand names that were acceptable in both English and French, such as Vaner, Randal, and Massin, were perceived as more "hedonic" (providing pleasure) and were better liked when pronounced in French than in English.[12]

Pronunciation problems may arise from not conforming to linguistic rules. Although Honda chose the name "Acura" because it was associated with words connoting precision in several languages, it initially had some trouble with consumer pronunciation of the name (AK-yur-a) in the U.S. market, perhaps in part because the company chose not to use the phonetically simpler English spelling of Accura (with a double *c*).

To improve pronounceability and recallability, many marketers seek a desirable cadence and pleasant sound in their brand names.[13] For example, brand names may use alliteration (repetition of consonants, such as in Coleco), assonance (repetition of vowel sounds, such as in Ramada Inn), consonance (repetition of consonants with intervening vowel change, such as in Hamburger Helper), or rhythm (repetition of the pattern of syllable stress, such as in Better Business Bureau). Some words employ onomatopoeia—words composed of syllables that when pronounced generate a sound strongly suggestive of the word's meaning, like Sizzler restaurants, Cap'n Crunch cereal, Ping golf clubs, and Schweppes carbonated beverages.

Familiarity and Meaningfulness.   The brand name should be familiar and meaningful so it can tap into existing knowledge structures. It can be concrete or abstract in meaning. Because the names of people, objects, birds, animals, and inanimate objects already exist in memory, consumers have to do less learning to understand their meanings as brand names.[14] Links form more easily, increasing memorability.[15] Thus, when a consumer sees an ad for the first time for a car called "Fiesta," the fact that the consumer already has the word stored in memory should make it easier to encode the product name and thus improve its recallability.

To help create strong brand-category links and aid brand recall, the brand name may also suggest the product or service category, as do Netflix streaming service for videos, TripAdvisor travel advisory Web site, and Ticketron ticket selling service. Brand elements that are highly descriptive of the product category or its attribute and benefits can be quite restrictive, however.[16] For example, it may be difficult to introduce a soft drink extension for a brand called Juicy Juice.

Differentiated, Distinctive, and Unique.   Although choosing a simple, easy-to-pronounce, familiar, and meaningful brand name can improve recallability, to improve brand recognition, on the other hand, brand names should be different, distinctive, and unusual. As Chapter 2 noted, recognition depends on consumers' ability to discriminate between brands, and more complex brand names are more easily distinguished. Distinctive brand names can also make it easier for consumers to learn intrinsic product information.[17]

A brand name can be distinctive because it is inherently unique, or because it is unique in the context of other brands in the category.[18] Distinctive words may be seldom-used or atypical words for the product category, like Apple computers; unusual combinations of real words, like Toys"R"Us; or completely made-up words, such as Cognos or Luxottica. Even made-up brand names, however, have to satisfy prevailing linguistic rules and conventions—for example, try to pronounce names without vowels such as Blfft, Xgpr, or Msdy!

Here, too, there are trade-offs. Even if a distinctive brand name is advantageous for brand recognition, it also has to be credible and desirable in the product category. A notable exception is Smucker's jelly, which has tried to turn the handicap of its distinctive—but potentially dislikable—name into a positive through its slogan, "With a Name Like Smucker's, It Has to Be Good!"

Brand Associations.   Because the brand name is a compact form of communication, the explicit and implicit meanings consumers extract from it are important. In naming a new peer-to-peer communication technology, the founders landed on the descriptive "Sky peer-to-peer" which they decided to shorten to Skyper. When the corresponding Web address Skyper.com was not available, they shortened it again to the much more user-friendly Skype.[19]

The brand name can be chosen to reinforce an important attribute or benefit association that makes up its product positioning (see Figure 4-4). Besides performance-related considerations, brand names can also communicate more abstract considerations, such as Joy dishwashing liquid, Caress soap, and Obsession perfume. Consider the reasoning behind the name of Colgate's new mini toothbrush.

ColorStay lipsticks
Head & Shoulders shampoo
Close-Up toothpaste
SnackWell reduced fat snacks
DieHard auto batteries
Mop & Glo floor wax
Lean Cuisine low-calorie frozen entrees
Shake'n Bake chicken seasoning
Sub-Zero refrigerators and freezers
Cling-Free static buildup remover
Facebook social network
Dropbox cloud storage

FIGURE 4-4

Sample Suggestive Brand Names

COLGATE WISP

Famed brand-identity firm Lexicon has developed some successful brand names, such as BlackBerry, Dasani, Febreze, OnStar, Pentium, Scion, Lucid, and Swiffer. To develop a name for a new disposable mini toothbrush from Colgate, the firm went through a careful development process. The center of the disposable toothbrush held a dab of special toothpaste that made rinsing unnecessary and brushing on the go possible. Deciding to focus on the lightness, softness, and gentleness of the product, Lexicon's global network of 70 linguists in 50 countries brainstormed metaphors and sounds that conveyed lightness. One name—Wisp—jumped out at company founder David Placek. Subsequent consumer research validated its positive connotations, and a new name was born.[20]

A descriptive brand name should make it easier to link the reinforced attribute or benefit.[21] Consumers will find it easier to believe that a laundry detergent "adds fresh scent" to clothes if it has a name like "Blossom" than if it is called something neutral like "Circle."[22] However, brand names that reinforce the initial positioning of a brand may make it harder to link new associations to the brand if it later has to be repositioned.[23] For example, if a laundry detergent named Blossom is positioned as "adding fresh scent," it may be more difficult to reposition the product later, if necessary, and add a new brand association that it "fights tough stains." Consumers may find it more difficult to accept or just too easy to forget the new positioning when the brand name continues to remind them of other product considerations.

With sufficient time and the proper marketing programs, however, this difficulty can sometimes be overcome. Southwest Airlines no longer stands for airline service just in Texas and the southwestern United States, which it once did. Such marketing maneuvers can be a long and expensive process, however. Imagine the difficulty of repositioning brands such as "I Can't Believe It's Not Butter!" or "Gee, Your Hair Smells Terrific!"—both are real brands! Thus, it is important when choosing a meaningful name to consider the possibility of later repositioning and the necessity of linking other associations.

Meaningful names are not restricted to real words. Consumers can extract meaning, if they so desire, even from made-up or fanciful brand names. For example, one study of computer-generated brand names containing random combinations of syllables found that "whumies" and "quax" reminded consumers of breakfast cereal and that "dehax" reminded them of laundry detergent.[24] Thus, consumers were able to extract at least some product meaning from these essentially arbitrary names when instructed to do so. Nevertheless, consumers are likely to extract meaning from highly abstract names only when they are sufficiently motivated.

Marketers generally devise made-up brand names systematically, basing words on combinations of morphemes. A *morpheme* is the smallest linguistic unit having meaning. There are 7,000 morphemes in the English language, including real words like "man" and prefixes, suffixes, or roots. For example, Nissan's Sentra automobile is a combination of two morphemes suggesting "central" and "sentry."[25] By combining carefully chosen morphemes, marketers can construct brand names that have some relatively easily inferred or implicit meaning.

Brand names raise a number of interesting linguistic issues.[26] Figure 4-5 contains an overview of different categories of linguistic characteristics, with definitions and examples. Even individual letters can contain meaning that may be useful in developing a new brand name. The letter *X* became popular (e.g., ESPN's X Games and Nissan's Xterra SUV) because *X* represents "extreme," "on the edge," and "youth."[27] Research has shown that in some instances, consumers prefer products with brand names bearing some of the letters from their own name (Jonathan may exhibit a greater-than-expected preference for a product named Jonoki).[28]

The sounds of letters can take on meaning as well.[29] For example, some words begin with phonemic elements called *plosives*, like the letters *b, c, d, g, k, p,* and *t*, whereas others use *sibilants*, which are sounds like *s* and soft *c*. Plosives escape from the mouth more quickly than sibilants and are harsher and more direct. Consequently, they are thought to make names more specific and less abstract, and to be more easily recognized and recalled.[30] On the other hand, because sibilants have a softer sound, they tend to conjure up romantic, serene images and are often found in the names of products such as perfumes—think of Chanel, Ciara (by Revlon), and Shalimar and Samsara (Guerlin).[31]

One study found a relationship between certain characteristics of the letters of brand names and product features: As consonant hardness and vowel pitch increased in hypothetical brand names for toilet paper and household cleansers, consumer perception of the harshness of the

Characteristics	Definitions and/or Examples
Phonetic Devices	
Alliteration	Consonant repetition (Coca-Cola, PayPal)
Assonance	Vowel repetition (Kal Kan)
Consonance	Consonant repetition with intervening vowel changes (Weight Watchers, Best Buy)
Masculine rhyme	Rhyme with end-of-syllable stress (Max Pax)
Feminine rhyme	Unaccented syllable followed by accented syllable (American Airlines)
Weak/imperfect/slant rhyme	Vowels differ or consonants similar, not identical (Black & Decker)
Onomatopoeia	Use of syllable phonetics to resemble the object itself (Wisk)
Clipping	Product names attenuated (Chevy)
Blending	Morphemic combination, usually with elision (Aspergum, Duracell, Facebook)
Initial plosives	/b/, /c-hard/, /d/, /g-hard/, /k/, /p/, /q/, /t/ (Bic)
Orthographic Devices	
Unusual or incorrect spellings	Kool-Aid, Google, Lyft
Abbreviations	7 Up for Seven Up
Acronyms	Amoco
Morphologic Devices	
Affixation	Jell-O
Compounding	Janitor-in-a-Drum
Semantic Devices	
Metaphor	Amazon was named after the world's largest river to symbolize scale, and to support the tagline "Earth's largest bookstore"
Metonymy	Application of one object or quality for another (Midas)
Synecdoche	Substitution of a part for the whole (Red Lobster)
Personification/pathetic fallacy	Humanizing the nonhuman, or ascription of human emotions to the inanimate (Betty Crocker)
Oxymoron	Conjunction of opposites (Easy-Off)
Paranomasia	Pun and word plays (Hawaiian Punch)
Semantic appositeness	Fit of name with object (Bufferin)

FIGURE 4-5

Brand Name Linguistic Characteristics

product also increased.[32] The actual font or logotype used to express the brand name may also change consumer impressions.[33]

Brands are not restricted to letters alone.[34] Alphanumeric names may include a mixture of letters and digits (WD-40), a mixture of words and digits (Formula 409), or mixtures of letters or words and numbers in written form (Saks Fifth Avenue). They can also designate generations or relationships in a product line like BMW's 3, 5, and 7 series.

Naming Procedures. A number of different procedures or systems have been suggested for naming new products. Most marketers adopt a procedure something along the following lines.[35]

1. **Define objectives.** First, define the branding objectives in terms of the six general criteria we noted earlier, and in particular, define the ideal meaning the brand should convey. Recognize the role of the brand within the corporate branding hierarchy and how it should relate to other brands and products (we will discuss this in Chapter 12). In many cases, existing brand

names may serve, at least in part. Finally, understand the role of the brand within the entire marketing program and the target market.

2. **Generate names.** With the branding strategy in place, next, generate as many names and concepts as possible. Any potential sources of names are valid: company management and employees; existing or potential customers (including retailers or suppliers if relevant); ad agencies, professional name consultants, and specialized computer-based naming companies. Tens, hundreds, or even thousands of names may result from this step.

3. **Screen initial candidates.** Screen all the names against the branding objectives and marketing considerations identified in step 1, and apply the test of common sense to produce a more manageable list. For example, General Mills starts by eliminating the following:

   • Names that have unintentional double meaning
   • Names that are unpronounceable, already in use, or too close to an existing name
   • Names that have obvious legal complications
   • Names that represent an obvious contradiction of the positioning

   Next, General Mills runs in-depth evaluation sessions with management personnel and marketing partners to narrow the list to a handful of names, often conducting a quick-and-dirty legal search to help screen out possible problems.

4. **Study candidate names.** Collect more extensive information about each of the final 5 to 10 names. Before spending large amounts of money on consumer research, it is usually advisable to do an extensive international legal search. Because this step is expensive, marketers often search on a sequential basis, testing in each country only those names that survived the legal screening from the previous country.

5. **Research the final candidates.** Next, conduct consumer research to confirm management expectations about the memorability and meaningfulness of the remaining names. Consumer testing can take all forms. Many firms attempt to simulate the actual marketing program and consumers' likely purchase experiences as much as possible.[36] Thus, they may show consumers the product and its packaging, price, or promotion so that they understand the rationale for the brand name and how it will be used. Other aids in this kind of research are realistic three-dimensional packages and concept boards or low-cost animatic advertising using digital techniques. Marketers may survey many consumers to capture differences in regional or ethnic appeal. They should also factor in the effects of repeated exposure to the brand name and what happens when the name is spoken versus written.

6. **Select the final name.** Based on all the information collected from the previous step, management should choose the name that maximizes the firm's branding and marketing objectives and then formally register it.

Some segment of consumers or another will always have at least some potentially negative associations with a new brand name. In most cases, however, assuming they are not severe, these associations will disappear after the initial marketing launch. Some consumers will dislike a new brand name because it is unfamiliar or represents a deviation from the norm. Marketers should remember to separate these temporal considerations from more enduring effects. Here is how a new airline arrived at its name.[37]

JETBLUE

Traditionally, airlines use descriptive names that evoke specific geographic origins, like American, or broad geographic reach, like United. In launching a new airline with a fresh concept—stylish travel for the budget-minded flier—JetBlue decided it needed an evocative name, but not one that sounded like an airline. Working with its ad agency, Merkley & Partners, and brand consultant, Landor, the company generated a list of candidate names—Fresh Air, Taxi, Egg, and It. The name Blue, suggesting peaceful clear skies, quickly became a favorite, but trademark lawyers noted that it would be impossible to protect the name without a distinctive qualifier. The first candidate, TrueBlue, went by the wayside when it was found to also be the name of a car rental agency. JetBlue emerged as the best substitute and the brand was born. JetBlue has also leveraged the "jet" portion of its brand name with its optimistic "jetting" campaign, which occurred during the economic downturn and was a response to difficult times in the airline industry. The ads served to distinguish JetBlue and its "maverick" approach to service. Its "TrueBlue" loyalty program cleverly leverages the second half of its name.[38]

JetBlue has used evocative brand imagery and a strong customer focus to build its brand.

Source: Mark Waugh/Alamy Stock Photo

URLs

URLs (uniform resource locators) specify locations of pages on the Web and are also commonly referred to as ***domain names***. Anyone wishing to own a specific URL must register and pay for the name. As companies clamored for space on the Web, the number of registered URLs increased dramatically. Every three-letter combination and virtually all words in a typical English dictionary have been registered. The sheer volume of registered URLs often makes it necessary for companies to use coined words for new brands if they wish to have a Web site for the brand. For example, when Andersen Consulting selected its new name, it chose the coined word "Accenture" in part because the URL www.accenture.com had not been registered.

Another issue facing companies with regard to URLs is protecting their brands from unauthorized use in other domain names.[39] A company can sue the current owner of the URL for copyright infringement, buy the name from the current owner, or register all conceivable variations of its brand as domain names ahead of time.

In 2010, cybersquatting cases reached record levels. *Cybersquatting* or *domain squatting,* as defined by government law, is registering, trafficking in, or using a domain name with bad-faith intent to profit from the goodwill of a trademark belonging to someone else. The cybersquatter then offers to sell the domain to the person or company who owns a trademark contained within the name at an inflated price. Under such cases, trademark holders sue for infringement of their domain names through the World Intellectual Property Organization (an agency of the UN).[40] A number of companies—such as Panasonic, Avon, and Hertz—were targets of cybersquatting, and in certain cases, even had to eventually pay large sums of money to buy back the domain names.

In 2010, the Academy Awards filed a lawsuit against GoDaddy alleging that 57 domains which had cybersquatting issues were sold by GoDaddy. Domain names such as 2011Oscars.com had confusingly similar names to the Academy Awards' own domain name, and allowed GoDaddy to profit from individuals who parked on these domains and collected revenue. Ultimately, the courts ruled in favor of GoDaddy since it did not "possess the requisite bad faith intent to profit" from their sales. Many regarded this as a landmark ruling in the cybersquatting space because it suggests that brands may not be able to reasonably expect a third-party to "police" a brand's trademark.[41] Another example of trademark infringement of Louis Vuitton follows.

LOUIS VUITTON VERSUS LOUIS VUITON DAK

A South Korean fried chicken restaurant recently lost a trademark battle with designer Louis Vuitton, after the restaurant's name of Louis Vuiton Dak was judged to be too similar to Louis Vuitton. The restaurant's logo and packaging closely mirrored the designer's iconic imagery. Initially, after Louis Vuitton filed a lawsuit against the restaurant, the courts ordered the restaurant to desist and threatened a 500,000 won-per-day fine for noncompliance.[42] The restaurant was ultimately hit with another 14.5 million won (which translates to about $12,500) fine for noncompliance, after changing their name immediately after the first ruling to LOUISVUI TONDAK. Many brands can avoid similarly expensive legal battles by avoiding mirroring their brand closely after another, even if the products and purchase channels have nothing in common.

Cybersquatting has recently morphed into another type of deceptive practice called spoofing—a practice in which scam artists set up fraudulent Web sites which use variants of a brand's name to set up a series of URLs in order to attract unsuspecting actors and encourage them to spend money. These sorts of fraudulent Web sites are said to be worth $460 billion annually, which is much larger than the stated size of the personal $264 billion that eMarketer estimated is the value of the online personal luxury goods market in 2016. A related study conducted by cybersecurity research firms suggested that the names of eight luxury brands (i.e., Chanel, Gucci, Cartier, Prada, Givenchy, Hermès, Burberry, and Louis Vuitton) appeared in various forms in 538 different domains, many of which were deemed fraudulent.[43]

The practice of spoofing relies on consumers' inattention to minor variations in domain names including misspellings or additional letters included (e.g., Hermes-bag.us, Givvenchy. com, or Chamel.us). The preponderance of these Web sites also suggests a variety of ways in which these sites can defraud customers including stealing credit card information or selling knockoffs.[44] From a brand marketer's perspective, the instances of cybersquatting and spoofing seem to be growing over time. For instance, in 2016, the World Intellectual Property Organization (WIPO) reported a 16 percent increase in cybersquatting disputes, of which 9 percent involved fashion brand names. As an example, Hugo Boss alone filed 42 domain name disputes in 2016.

Another version of spoofing that occurs is fraudulent e-mails that are sent on behalf of the brand to unsuspecting customers to obtain credit card information. These phishing attempts can be extremely harmful to a brand's reputation, as they can destroy consumer trust and harm a brand's reputation. Brand names such as eBay, Paypal, and Amazon have been targeted in phishing attempts by online scammers and thieves.[45]

How can a brand name guard against these types of Internet hoaxes and scams which threaten to dilute a brand's equity? A phased approach may be worth considering, beginning with a "cease and desist letter" to request counterfeiters to stop infringing on their trademark. Failure to comply could result in litigation under existing laws such as the Anticybersquatting Consumer Protection Act (ACPA), Uniform Domain-Name Dispute-Resolution Policy (UDRP), and so on. Regardless, continuous vigilance to prevent counterfeiters from destroying a brand's trust and reputation is needed against the backdrop of the increasing prevalence of counterfeiting.[46]

Logos and Symbols

Although the brand name typically is the central element of the brand, visual elements also play a critical role in building brand equity and especially brand awareness. *Logos* have a long history as a means to indicate origin, ownership, or association. For example, families and countries have used logos for centuries to visually represent their names (think of the Hapsburg eagle of the Austro-Hungarian Empire).

Logos range from corporate names or trademarks (word marks with text only) written in a distinctive form, to entirely abstract designs that may be completely unrelated to the word mark, corporate name, or corporate activities.[47] Examples of brands with strong word marks and no accompanying logo separate from the name include Coca-Cola, Dunhill, and Kit Kat. Examples of abstract logos include the Mercedes star, Rolex crown, CBS eye, Nike swoosh, and Olympic rings. These nonword mark logos are also often called *symbols*.

Many logos fall between these two extremes. Some are literal representations of the brand name, enhancing brand meaning and awareness, such as the Arm and Hammer, American Red

Cross, and Apple logos. Logos can be quite concrete or pictorial like the American Express centurion, the Land O'Lakes Native American, the Morton salt girl with umbrella, and Ralph Lauren's polo player. Certain physical elements of the product or company can become a symbol, as did the Goodyear blimp, McDonald's golden arches, and the Playboy bunny ears. Many technology brands use logos to convey information about brand benefits, such as the WhatsApp logo featuring a landline phone in a speech bubble or the Amazon logo featuring a smile under the wordmark to convey service and to highlight its ability to supply a broad range of goods from A to Z.

Like names, abstract logos can be quite distinctive and thus recognizable. Nevertheless, because abstract logos may lack the inherent meaning present with a more concrete logo, one danger is that consumers may not understand what the logo is intended to represent without a significant marketing initiative to explain its meaning. Consumers can evaluate even fairly abstract logos differently depending on the shape.

Benefits.   Logos and symbols are often easily recognized and can be a valuable way to identify products, although consumers may recognize them but be unable to link them to any specific product or brand. Many insurance firms use symbols of strength (the Rock of Gibraltar for Prudential and the stag for Hartford) or security (the "good hands" of Allstate, the hard hat of Fireman's Fund, and the red umbrella of Travelers).

Another branding advantage of logos is their versatility: Because they are often nonverbal, logos transfer well across cultures and over a range of product categories. For example, corporate brands often develop logos in order to confer their identity on a wide range of products and to endorse different sub-brands. Marketers must think carefully, however, as to how prominent the brand name and logo should be on any product, especially more luxury ones.[48]

Abstract logos offer advantages when the full brand name is difficult to use for any reason. In the United Kingdom, for example, National Westminster Bank created a triangular device as a logo because the name itself was long and cumbersome and the logo could more easily appear as an identification device on checkbooks, literature, signage, and promotional material. The logo also uses the shortened version of the company name, NatWest.[49]

Finally, unlike brand names, logos can be easily adapted over time to achieve a more contemporary look. For example, in 2000, John Deere revamped its deer trademark for the first time in 32 years, making the animal appear to be leaping up rather than landing. The change was intended to "convey a message of strength and agility with a technology edge."[50]

One study of logos associated with top 100 brand names aimed to uncover some common themes.[51] Findings of this study revealed some interesting patterns. Nearly half of all logos used a single color, and a third used either red or blue; additionally, 23 percent used black and white, and more than half of all logos featured a horizontal aspect ratio. To enhance their appeal to customers, some brands have changed their logos in recent years. For instance, Instagram, Uber and Google have all attempted to change their logos.

One logo research study also analyzed the impact of the change in logos on "branding seconds" for each logo.[52] A branding second was defined as the percentage of people who saw the logotype multiplied by the average time spent on it. Uber, Paypal, and Google demonstrated the highest lift in branding seconds of nearly 50 percent between the old and the new logos. In contrast, Airbnb's logo change registered only a 9 percent lift in branding seconds.

Regardless of the reason for doing it, changing a logo is not cheap. According to branding experts, engaging a firm for four to six months to create a symbol or remaking an old one for a big brand "usually costs $1 million."[53]

Characters

Characters represent a special type of brand symbol—one that takes on human or real-life characteristics. Brand characters typically are introduced through advertising and can play a central role in ad campaigns and package designs. Some are animated characters like the Pillsbury Doughboy, Peter Pan peanut butter, and numerous cereal characters, such as Tony the Tiger and Snap, Crackle, and Pop. Others are live-action figures like Juan Valdez (Colombian coffee) and Ronald McDonald. In the Branding Brief 4-1, we highlight the role of StarKist's Charlie the Tuna in helping further enhance the brand's presence.

BRANDING BRIEF 4-1
StarKist's Charlie the Tuna

StarKist is the largest tuna brand in the United States, with a full range of canned and pouched yellowfin, albacore, and skipjack tuna. The brand's packaging features the image of its iconic mascot, Charlie the Tuna, a brand character that has stayed with the brand since 1961. StarKist is owned by the Dongwon Group of South Korea (and was previously owned by Heinz and Del Monte Foods), and Charlie the Tuna has been an integral to the growth and transformation of the StarKist Tuna brand into a market leader within its category. The blue talking tuna with bifocals is credited with enabling StarKist to achieve an astounding 90 percent brand awareness and high brand loyalty, while at the same time allowing the brand to weather ups and downs in the popularity of the category.

Charlie the Tuna was featured in commercials for StarKist as a hipster wearing a beret and coke-bottle glasses. Charlie believed that he was so hip and cultured that he was the perfect tuna for StarKist, but was always rejected with a note attached to a fish hook which said, "Sorry, Charlie," and that StarKist was not looking for tuna with good taste, but rather for tuna that tasted good. "Sorry, Charlie" became closely associated with StarKist and also a part of the popular vernacular in America. All commercials ended with Charlie telling the viewers "Tell 'em Charlie sent you."

A brief overview of trends in the industry can help showcase how the StarKist brand has grown and changed over the years. StarKist was a market share leader in the category of canned tuna, commanding an overall dollar market share in the tuna category of 47 percent by 2017. Brands such as Bumblebee and Chicken of the Sea are market followers, with an average market share of 23 percent and 11 percent respectively. Much of StarKist's dominance has to do with recent introductions in flavored pouches (e.g., Tuna Creations) in a variety of flavors.

With the growth of health and wellness as a key consideration, there has also been a steady increase in sales of goods that are placed at the perimeter of the store (typically fresh foods). In addition, a second trend has been the growing popularity of ethnic flavors in foods, including habanero, wasabi, Cajun, sriracha, and so on. In response to the shift in preference for healthy food options, as well as the growing popularity of ethnic and spicy flavors, StarKist responded by introducing flavored tuna pouches. Flavored pouches represented an easy and convenient alternative to existing foods, combining the health benefits of tuna along with taste in one affordable meal solution. Another benefit has been the availability of spicy flavors. The shift away from cans and the convenience of pouches has increased the brand's appeal among millenials and also among many segments of on-the-go consumers (e.g., busy moms, young professionals, etc.). These factors helped propel the growth of StarKist Tuna, and StarKist tuna pouches grew at a cumulative annual growth rate of 12 percent between 2014 and 2017. StarKist Flavored Pouch tuna grew to account for 88 percent of the dollar market share of the pouch category. This allowed StarKist to quickly reaffirm its position as a market leader, and helped reverse the declining sales trend.

What is the role of Charlie the Tuna in the success of StarKist's line extension? According to authors Hosani et al., line

Charlie the Tuna is a legendary mascot for the StarKist brand of tuna and among the most recognized U.S. brand characters.

and brand extensions can help build and sustain a brand character, and extending the brand character to new product lines can also help maintain the visibility of the brand and generate new revenue sources. As the tuna pouch became more popular, StarKist retained its No. 1 brand in the tuna category and in the millennials. StarKist also introduced a new celebrity endorser Candace Cameron Bure (successful mom, actress, author), who was featured in commercials alongside Charlie. Both were helpful in launching StarKist's on-the-go lifestyle StarKist Creations pouches. StarKist's Tuna & Salmon Creations single-serve pouches are meant to ease the challenge of having tasty meal options fit into a busy lifestyle. The ads featured both Candace Cameron Bure and Charlie dropping in (quite literally) on a hook to chat with Bure and offer some tasty lunch options. In sum, Charlie the Tuna's role now is to be brand spokefish, a *brand ambassador* who brings "innovative mealtime solutions" via meals on-the-go, flavors, and introducing different seafood species and proteins. By being a friendly and approachable character, Charlie has become famous and is honored as being among the most recognized brand characters in the United States. For example, in 2017, Charlie was named to Advertising Week's 2017 Madison Walk of Fame alongside some of the most legendary mascots.

Sources: James Wright (2015), "The Top 25 North American Seafood Suppliers," June 4, 2015, www.seafoodsource.com/news/supply-trade/the-top-25-north-american-seafood-suppliers?content%5Bb1a7c925-1ed6-4bc4-ab97-58e281440ce3%5D=21, accessed March 19, 2018; Theresa Lindeman, "ToonSeum Helps StarKist's Charlie the Tuna Celebrate 50th Year," February 17, 2011, www.postgazette.com/business/businessnews/2011/02/17/ToonSeum-helps-StarKist-s-Charlie-the-Tuna-celebrate-50th-year/stories/201102170333, accessed March 19, 2018; "2017 Dollar Share Nielsen Report for Tuna, All US XAOC; Top Seafood Suppliers in North America, 2015," *Market Share Reporter.* Ed. Robert S. Lazich and Virgil L. Burton, III. 28th ed. Farmington Hills, MI: Gale, 2018; *Business Insights: Global*, December 3, 2017; Sameer Hosany, Girish Prayag, Drew Martin, and Wai-Yee Lee, "Theory and Strategies of Anthropomorphic Brand Characters from Peter Rabbit, Mickey Mouse, and Ronald McDonald, to Hello Kitty," *Journal of Marketing Management* 29, no. 1–2 (2013): 48–68; G. Sylvia, "Actress Candace Cameron Bure Stars Alongside Brand Icon Charlie the Tuna in Two New Ads Promoting Brand's Tuna & Salmon Creations," February 8, 2017, www.adstasher.com/2017/02/candace-cameron-bure-stars-charlie-tuna-ads.html, accessed March 19, 2018; http://starkist.com/charlie/all-about-charlie.

Benefits.   Because they are often colorful and rich in imagery, brand characters tend to be attention getting and quite useful for creating brand awareness. Brand characters can help brands break through marketplace clutter as well as help communicate a key product benefit. For example, Maytag's Lonely Repairman helped reinforce the company's key "reliability" product association for decades.

The human element of brand characters can enhance likeability and help create perceptions of the brand as fun and interesting.[54] A consumer may more easily form a relationship with a brand when the brand has a human or other character presence. Characters avoid many of the problems that plague human spokespeople—they do not grow old or demand pay raises. An interesting exception occurred, however, when Aflac fired the human voice to its famed duck character, comedian Gilbert Gottfried, after he posted some controversial remarks on Twitter that made light of the fallout from the earthquake and tsunami in Japan.[55]

Finally, because brand characters do not typically have direct product meaning, they may also be transferred relatively easily across product categories. For example, Aaker notes that "the Keebler's elf identity (which combines a sense of home-style baking with a touch of magic and fun) gives the brand latitude to extend into other baked goods—and perhaps even into other types of food where homemade magic and fun might be perceived as a benefit."[56] Popular characters also often become valuable licensing properties, providing direct revenue and additional brand exposure.

Cautions.   There are some cautions and drawbacks to using brand characters. Brand characters can be so attention-getting and well-liked that they dominate other brand elements and actually *dampen* brand awareness.

EVEREADY

When Ralston Purina introduced its drumming pink bunny that "kept going . . . and going . . . and going" in ads for the Eveready Energizer battery, many consumers were so captivated by the character that they paid little attention to the name of the advertised brand. As a result, they often mistakenly believed that the ad was for Eveready's chief competitor, Duracell. Eveready had to add the pink bunny to its packages, promotions, and other marketing communications to create stronger brand links. Through its concerted marketing efforts through the years, however, the Energizer Bunny has now achieved iconic status. Many marketing experts view the character as the "ultimate product demo"

The Energizer Bunny has become a symbol of longevity and determination, and has helped showcase key brand attributes, i.e., long-lived batteries, in an inventive, fresh way.

because of how effectively it showcases the product's unique selling proposition—long-lived batteries—in an inventive, fresh way. As the company's CEO noted, "The message of the Energizer Bunny has remained consistent over the last two decades; he speaks to longevity, determination and perseverance." The bunny celebrated its 27th anniversary in 2016, having achieved several milestones, including 95 percent awareness among consumers and an entry in the Oxford English Dictionary. Perhaps the greatest compliment, however, is how often everyone from politicians to sport stars have used the Energizer Bunny to describe their own staying power.[57]

Characters often must be updated over time so that their image and personality remain relevant to the target market. Japan's famous Hello Kitty character, which became a multibillion dollar product and license powerhouse, was able to maintain its appeal and revive its brand image through a broad set of licensing agreements ranging from paper towels to airplanes, and through a marketing strategy which is focused around niche markets.[58]

In general, the more realistic the brand character, the more important it is to keep it up-to-date. One advantage of fictitious or animated characters is that their appeal can be more enduring and timeless than that of real people. Branding Brief 4-2 describes the efforts by General Mills to evolve the Betty Crocker character over time. Finally, some characters are so culturally specific that they do not travel well to other countries.

Slogans

Slogans are short phrases that communicate descriptive or persuasive information about the brand. They often appear in advertising but can play an important role in packaging and in other aspects of the marketing program. When Snickers advertised, "Hungry? Grab a Snickers," the slogan also appeared on the candy bar wrapper itself.

Slogans are powerful branding devices because, like brand names, they are an extremely efficient, shorthand means to build brand equity. They can function as useful "hooks" or "handles" to help consumers grasp the meaning of a brand—what it is and what makes it special.[59] They are an indispensable means of summarizing and translating the intent of a marketing program in a few short words or phrases. For example, State Farm Insurance's "Like a Good Neighbor, State Farm Is There" has been used for decades to represent the brand's dependability and aura of friendship.

Benefits. Some slogans help build brand awareness by playing off the brand name in some way, as in "The Citi Never Sleeps." Others build brand awareness even more explicitly by making strong links between the brand and the corresponding product category, like when Lifetime would advertise that it was "Television for Women." Most important, slogans can help reinforce the brand positioning as in "Staples. That Was Easy." For HBO, a slogan was critical to conveying its unique positioning.

BRANDING BRIEF 4-2
Updating Betty Crocker

In 1921, Washburn Crosby Company, makers of Gold Medal flour, launched a picture puzzle contest. The contest was a huge success—the company received 30,000 entries—and several hundred contestants sent along requests for recipes and advice about baking. To handle those requests, the company decided to create a spokesperson. Managers chose the name Betty Crocker because "Betty" was a popular, friendly sounding name and "Crocker" was a reference to William G. Crocker, a well-liked, recently retired executive. The company merged with General Mills in 1928, and the newly merged company introduced the *Betty Crocker Cooking School of the Air* as a national radio program. During this time, Betty was given a voice and her signature began to appear on nearly every product the company produced.

In 1936, the Betty Crocker portrait was drawn by artist Neysa McMein as a composite of some of the home economists at the company. Prim and proper, Betty was shown with pursed lips, a hard stare, and graying hair. Her appearance has been updated a number of times over the years (see the accompanying figure) and has become more friendly, although she has never lost her reserved look.

Prior to a makeover in 1986, Betty Crocker was seen as honest and dependable, friendly and concerned about

FIFTY YEARS OF BETTY CROCKER

One advantage of characters—they can be timeless. Although Betty Crocker is over 75 years old, she still looks 35!

Source: The Advertising Archives/Alamy Stock Photo

customers, and a specialist in baked goods, but also out-of-date, old and traditional, a manufacturer of "old standby products," and not particularly contemporary or innovative. The challenge was to give Betty a look that would attract younger consumers but not alienate older ones who remembered her as the stern homemaker of the past. There needed to be a certain fashionableness about her—not too dowdy and not too trendy, since the new look would need to last for 5 to 10 years. Her look also needed to be relevant to working women. Finally, for the first time, Betty Crocker's look was also designed to appeal to men, given the results of a General Mills study that showed that 30 percent of U.S. men at the time sometimes cooked for themselves.

A few years later, Betty Crocker received another update. This ultramodern model, the current one, was the work of a committee that selected images of 75 women of many different races to create a computerized composite. This seventh makeover seemed to have taken—although Betty Crocker was now close to 75, she didn't look a day over 35! Although the Betty Crocker name is on 200 or so products, her visual image has been largely replaced by the red spoon symbol and signature on package fronts, and she appears only on cookbooks, advertising, and online via her Facebook and Twitter accounts and a mobile app downloaded

by millions. By 2017, Betty Crocker had over 5 million followers on Facebook and an impressive YouTube presence with over 23 million views for her baking and cooking instructional videos. Betty has remained among the most recognized brand names even among younger millennial audiences. In many ways, Betty Crocker may be thought of as one of the earliest examples of exceptional content marketing, as she continues to evolve and engage with her consumer base, thereby forging a stronger connection with her customer base.

Sources: Charles Panati, *Panati's Extraordinary Origins of Everyday Things* (New York: Harper & Row, 1989); Milton Moskowitz, Robert Levering, and Michael Katz, *Everybody's Business: A Field Guide to the 400 Leading Companies in America* (New York: Doubleday/Currency, 1990); "FYI Have You Seen This Person?," *Minneapolis–St. Paul Star Tribune*, October 11, 2000; Susan Marks, *Finding Betty Crocker: The Secret Life of America's First Lady of Food* (New York: Simon & Schuster, 2005); General Mills, "Betty Crocker Celebrates 90th Birthday," November 18, 2011, https://www.businesswire.com/news/home/20111118005153/en/Betty-Crocker-Celebrates-90th-Birthday, accessed October 26, 2018; Nyla Smith, "The Brand Story of Betty Crocker (and What We Can Learn from It)," November 24, 2017, www.nvision-that.com/design-from-all-angles/the-brand-story-of-betty-crocker, accessed April 25, 2018.

HBO

As a pay-TV channel, HBO has always needed to convince viewers it was worth paying extra money for. More than just a pay movie channel, HBO has a tradition of broadcasting original, edgy programming such as *Sex and the City*, *The Sopranos*, and *Entourage* that would not be found on free channels. To highlight its most compelling point-of-difference and brand essence, HBO developed a clever slogan in 1996: "It's Not TV, It's HBO." Externally, the slogan gave viewers a point of reference to understand and categorize the brand. Internally, the slogan gave employees a clear vision and goal to keep in mind: No matter what they did, it should never look like ordinary TV.[60]

The clever slogan "It's Not TV, It's HBO" reinforces how the cable network with shows like Entourage is different from other networks.

Source: AF archive/Alamy Stock Photo

Slogans often become closely tied to advertising campaigns and serve as taglines to summarize the descriptive or persuasive information conveyed in the ads. DeBeers's "A Diamond Is Forever" tagline communicates that diamonds bring eternal love and romance and never lose value. Dollar Shave Club's slogan "Shave Time. Shave Money" is closely linked to its positioning as a cost-effective solution to meet consumers' shaving needs. Slogans can be more expansive and more enduring than just ad taglines, though campaign-specific taglines may help reinforce the message of a particular campaign instead of the brand slogan for a certain period.

For example, through the years, Nike has used taglines specific to ad campaigns for events or sports such as "Prepare for Battle" and "Quick Can't Be Caught" (basketball); "Write the Future" (World Cup); "My Better Is Better" (multisport); and "Here I Am" (women) instead of the well-known brand slogan, "Just Do It." Such substitutions can emphasize that the ad campaign represents a departure of some kind from the message conveyed by the brand slogan, or just a means to give the brand slogan a rest so that it remains fresh.

Designing Slogans.   Some of the most powerful slogans contribute to brand equity in multiple ways.[61] They can play off the brand name to build both awareness *and* image, such as "Maybe She's Born with It, Maybe It's Maybelline" for Maybelline cosmetics; or "The Big Q Stands for Quality" for Quaker State motor oil.

Slogans also can contain product-related messages and other meanings. Consider the historical Champion sportswear slogan, "It Takes a Little More to Make a Champion." The slogan could be interpreted regarding product performance, meaning that Champion sportswear is made with a little extra care or with extra-special materials, but it could mean that Champion sportswear is associated with top athletes. This combination of superior product performance and aspirational user imagery is a powerful platform on which to build brand image and equity. Benetton has had an equally strong slogan on which to build brand equity ("United Colors of Benetton").

Updating Slogans.   Some slogans become so strongly linked to the brand that it becomes difficult to introduce new ones (take the famous slogan quiz in Figure 4-7 and check the accompanying footnote to see how many slogans you can correctly identify). Marketers of 7UP tried a number of different successors to the popular "Uncola" slogan—including "Freedom of Choice," "Crisp and Clean and No Caffeine," "Don't You Feel Good About 7UP," and "Feels So Good Coming Down," and for more than five years, the somewhat edgy "Make 7UP Yours." The slogan changed again when 7UP asked consumers to "Mix It Up a Little" featuring 7UP as an essential ingredient for a variety of different uses, including baking, cooking, use in drinks, and so on.[62]

A slogan that becomes so strongly identified with a brand can box it in. Or successful slogans can take on lives of their own and become public catch phrases (like Wendy's "Where's the Beef?" in the 1980s, "Got Milk?" spoofs in the 2000s), but there can also be a downside to this kind of success: the slogan can quickly become overexposed and lose specific brand or product meaning.

Once a slogan achieves such a high level of recognition and acceptance, it may still contribute to brand equity, but probably as more of a reminder of the brand. Consumers are unlikely to consider what the slogan means thoughtfully after seeing or hearing it too many times. At the same time, a potential difficulty arises if the slogan continues to convey some product meaning that the brand no longer needs to reinforce. In this case, by not facilitating the linkage of new, desired brand associations, the slogan can become restrictive and fail to allow the brand to be updated as much as desired or necessary.

Because slogans are perhaps the easiest brand element to change over time, marketers have more flexibility in managing them. In changing slogans, however, they must do the following:

1. Recognize how the slogan is contributing to brand equity, if at all, through enhanced awareness or image.
2. Decide how much of this equity enhancement, if any, is still needed.
3. Retain the needed or desired equities still residing in the slogan as much as possible while providing whatever new twists of meaning are necessary to contribute to equity in other ways.

1._____ Reach Out and Touch Someone

2._____ Have It Your Way

3._____ Just Do It

4._____ When It Absolutely, Positively Has to Be There Overnight

5._____ Drivers Wanted

6._____ Don't Leave Home Without It

7._____ Like a Rock

8._____ Because I'm Worth It

9._____ The Ultimate Driving Machine

10._____ When You Care Enough to Send the Very Best

11._____ Capitalist Tool

12._____ The Wonder Drug That Works Wonders

13._____ No More Tears

14._____ Melts in Your Mouth, Not in Your Hands

15._____ We Try Harder

16._____ The Antidote for Civilization

17._____ Where Do You Want to Go Today?

18._____ Let Your Fingers Do the Walking

19._____ Breakfast of Champions

20._____ Fly the Friendly Skies

Answers: (1) Bell Telephone; (2) Burger King; (3) Nike; (4) Federal Express; (5) Volkswagen; (6) American Express; (7) Chevrolet; (8) L'Oreal; (9) BMW; (10) Hallmark; (11) Forbes magazine; (12) Bayer aspirin; (13) Johnson's Baby Shampoo; (15) M&M's; (16) Club Med; (17) Microsoft; (18) Yellow Pages; (19) Wheaties; and (20) United Airlines.

FIGURE 4-7
Famous Slogans Quiz

Sometimes modifying an existing slogan is more fruitful than introducing a new slogan with a completely new set of meanings. However, there are times when the slogan change is part of a broader repositioning, in which case a dramatic change in slogan can help signal a shift in the positioning of the brand. For example, Cover Girl abandoned its slogan from the well-received "Easy, Breezy, Beautiful Cover Girl" to "I Am What I Make Up," as part of a larger repositioning strategy based on the realization that there are no set standards for beauty, and that makeup can be viewed as a tool for self-expression and personal transformation.[63] Dockers switched its slogan from the well-received "Nice Pants" to "One Leg at a Time" in the late 1990s before reverting to the previous slogan when recognizing it had given up too much built-up equity.

Jingles

Jingles are musical messages written around the brand. Typically composed by professional songwriters, they often have enough catchy hooks and choruses to become almost permanently registered in the minds of listeners—sometimes whether they want to or not! During the first half of the twentieth century, when broadcast advertising was confined primarily to the radio, jingles were important branding devices.

We can think of jingles as extended musical slogans, and in that sense, classify them as a brand element. Because of their musical nature, however, jingles are not nearly as transferable as other brand elements. They can communicate brand benefits, but they often convey product meaning in a nondirect and fairly abstract fashion. Thus, the potential associations they might create for the brand are most likely to relate to feelings and personality and other intangibles.

Jingles are perhaps most valuable in enhancing brand awareness. Often, they repeat the brand name in clever and amusing ways that allow consumers multiple encoding opportunities. Consumers are also likely to mentally rehearse or repeat catchy jingles after the ad is over, providing even more encoding opportunities and increasing memorability.

A well-known jingle can serve as an advertising foundation for years. The familiar "Give Me a Break" jingle for Kit Kat candy bars has been sung in ads since 1988 and has helped make the brand the sixth best-selling chocolate candy bar in the United States.[64] There was an uproar when, after two decades, the U.S. Army switched from its familiar "Be All That You Can Be" to "Army of One." Finally, the distinctive four-note signature to Intel's ads echoes the company's slogan "In-tel In-side." Although the jingle seems simple, the first note alone is a mix of 16 sounds, including a tambourine and a hammer striking a brass pipe.[65]

Packaging

Packaging is the activities of designing and producing containers or wrappers for a product. Like other brand elements, packages have a long history. Early humans used leaves and animal skin to cover and carry food and water. Glass containers first appeared in Egypt as early as 2000 B.C. Later, the French emperor Napoleon awarded 12,000 francs to the winner of a contest to find a better way to preserve food, leading to the first crude method of vacuum packing.[66]

From the perspective of both the firm and consumers, packaging must achieve several objectives:[67]

- Identify the brand.
- Convey descriptive and persuasive information.
- Facilitate product transportation and protection.
- Assist in at-home storage.
- Aid product consumption.

Marketers must choose the aesthetic and functional components of packaging correctly to achieve marketing objectives and meet consumers' needs. Aesthetic considerations govern a package's size and shape, material, color, text, and graphics. Innovations in printing processes now permit eye-catching and appealing graphics that convey elaborate and colorful messages on the package at the "moment of truth"—the point of purchase.[68]

Functionally, structural design is crucial. For example, innovations over the years have resulted in food packages that are resealable, tamperproof, and more convenient to use—easy to hold, easy to open, or squeezable. Consider these General Mills packaging innovations: Yoplait Go-Gurt's yogurt in a tube packaging concept was a huge hit with kids and their parents; packaging for Betty Crocker Warm Delights showcased a microwavable (two minutes), convenient, single-serve dessert treat; and Green Giant Valley Fresh Steamers uses materials that withstand microwave cooking temperatures to offer steamable vegetables with sauce.[69]

Benefits.   Often, one of the strongest associations consumers have with a brand is inspired by the look of its packaging. For example, if you ask the average consumer what comes to mind when he or she thinks of Heineken beer, a common response is a "green bottle." The package can become an important means of brand recognition and convey or imply information to build or reinforce valuable brand associations. Molson's beer sales increased by 40 percent in the United States after the company modified the bottle's back labels to include cheeky "ice-breakers" for bar patrons such as "On the Rebound," "Sure, You Can Have My Number," and "Fairly Intimidated by Your Beauty." Buoyed by that success, they later introduced "Answer Honestly" bottle back labels that gave drinkers challenging choices to mull over.[70]

Structural packaging innovations can create a point-of-difference that permits a higher margin. New packages can also expand a market and capture new market segments. Packaging changes can have an immediate impact on customer shopping behavior and sales: a redesign of Häagen-Dazs ice cream packaging increased flavor shoppability by 21 percent; General Mills saw an increase in sales of 80 percent after redesigning Bisquick Shake n' Pour package to improve its ergonomics and by creating a "smooth, curvy form that reinforces the brand equity"; and a redesign on the packaging for Jimmy Dean's Biscuit Sandwiches led to an increase of 13 percent in household penetration.[71]

One of the major packaging trends of recent years is to make both bigger and smaller packaged versions of products (as well as portions) to appeal to new market segments.[72] Jumbo sizes have been successfully introduced for hot dogs, pizzas, English muffins, frozen dinners, and beer. Also, certain lighter versions of packaging are being introduced, and sustainable packaging is being used, both of which mirror changing consumers' priorities with regard to packaging.[73]

Packaging the Right Content. Innovations in packaging have always been important to brand management. One particular innovation has been the integration of content marketing or advertising themes into the packaging. A key reason for this trend is that the 75 million millennial population has begun tuning out traditional advertising. Brands which can incorporate thematic content into their packaging are therefore better able to communicate their message to consumers, which then becomes the basis for stronger consumer-brand relationships. Examples of brands that successfully incorporated thematic content on their packaging are provided next.

Kashi Kashi's new look for its cereal boxes, featuring stories from behind the brand to foster a more personal connection and to highlight its commitment to healthy food that makes a positive impact on the world.[74] In addition to featuring a new design with cleaner lines and more vivid colors, Kashi incorporated stories about how the food was made and where it came from. As an example, the Kashi Organic Promise Sprouted Grains Cereal featured a story of Peggy Sutton, whose sprouted flours are used to create the product. Further, Kashi also directs readers of its packaging story to visit the Web site to watch a video version of the same story.[75] In another example of storytelling, Kashi Dark Cocoa Karma Shredded Wheat Biscuits features the story of Wyoming-based farmer Newton Russell, who was one of the first farmers to pilot the Certified Transitional protocol (an initiative to help farmers transition fields from conventional to organic). In this way, Kashi is reinventing the role of packaging as a key touchpoint that can showcase the brand's own story.

Chipotle Chipotle has also incorporated content into its packaging through a partnership with author Jonathan Safran. This partnership involved a "Cultivating Thought" series in which written content was featured on cups and bags that their meals were served on. Various celebrities such as Sarah Silverman and Toni Morrison were responsible for contributing content.[76]

This approach helped showcase Chipotle as a brand which cared to maintain high ethical standards for where it sourced its ingredients and how it delivered from farm to table. Chipotle has thus elevated its brand in consumers' eyes by upholding high standards for ingredient and food quality, and has also strengthened its appeal by utilizing its packaging to deliver engaging content to its customers.

Snickers Snickers chocolate bars have had a successful advertising campaign based on the idea that people are transformed in undesirable ways when they are hungry. Symptoms of hunger

Kashi's packaging serves as an opportunity for the brand to engage in brand storytelling.

include being cranky, irritable, forgetful, and dramatic. While taglines from this ad campaign—"You're Not You When You're Hungry" and "Who Are You When You're Hungry?"—have been closely linked to the brand, Snickers took this concept to the next level by creating twenty-one customized bar packages, which feature these symptoms. Although swapping out the brand name for these symptoms may be viewed as risky by some, it helped make this brand appear cool and edgy.

These innovations in packaging highlight a key to successful brand management—ensuring that every touchpoint with consumers is used to reinforce a key brand message in such a way as to ensure consistency and coherence in all marketing efforts.

Packaging at the Point of Purchase.   The right packaging can create strong appeal on the store shelf and help products stand out from the clutter. This is critical when you realize that the average supermarket shopper can be exposed to 20,000 or more products in a shopping visit that may last less than 30 minutes and include many unplanned purchases. Many consumers may first encounter a new brand on the supermarket shelf or in the store. Because few product differences exist in some categories, packaging innovations can provide at least a temporary edge on the competition.

For these reasons, packaging is a particularly cost-effective way to build brand equity.[77] It is sometimes called the "last five seconds of marketing" as well as "permanent media" or "the last salesman." Walmart looks at packaging critically and tests whether consumers understand the brand promise behind the package within three seconds and up to 15 feet from the shelf. Note that consumer exposure to packaging is not restricted to the point of purchase and moments of consumption, because brand packages often can play a starring role in advertising.

Packaging Innovations.   Packaging innovations can both lower costs and improve demand. One important supply-side goal for many firms is to redesign packages and employ more recyclable materials to lower the use of paper and plastic. Toward that goal, U.S. food, beverage, and consumer product manufacturers reported that they had eliminated 1.5 billion pounds of packaging between 2005 and 2011, with another 2.5 billion pounds expected to be avoided by 2020, representing an overall reduction of 19 percent in total average U.S. packaging weight.[78] Likewise, many consumer-packaged goods are being marketed in flexible packaging (as opposed to rigid packaging), again reflecting changing consumer trends.[79]

On the demand side, in mature markets especially, package innovations can provide a short-term sales boost. The beverage industry, in general, has been characterized by some packaging innovations. For example, following the lead of Snapple's wide-mouth glass bottle, Arizona iced teas and fruit drinks in oversize (24-ounce), pastel-colored cans with a southwestern motif became a $300 million brand in a few years with no marketing support beyond point-of-purchase and rudimentary outdoor ads, designed in-house.[80]

Package Design.   An integral part of product development and launch, package design has become a more sophisticated process. In the past, it was often an afterthought, and colors, materials, and so forth were often chosen fairly arbitrarily. For example, legend has it that Campbell's famous soup is red and white because one executive at the company liked the uniforms of Cornell University's football team!

These days, specialized package designers bring artistic techniques and scientific skills to package design in an attempt to meet the marketing objectives of a brand. These consultants conduct detailed analyses to break down the package into several different elements.[81] They decide on the optimal look and content of each element and choose which elements should be dominant in any one package—whether the brand name, illustration, or some other graphical element—and how the elements should relate to each other. Designers can also decide which elements should be shared across packages and which should differ (and how).

Designers often refer to the "shelf impact" of a package—the visual effect the package has at the point of the purchase when consumers see it in the context of other packages in the category. For example, "bigger and brighter" packages are not always better when competitors' packages are also factored in.[82] Given enough shelf space, however, manufacturers can create billboard effects with their brand to raise their prominence and impact. General Mills deliberately "tiled" graphical elements of their packaging so that some of their mega-brands with multiple varieties such as Cheerios, Nature Valley Granola Bars, and Progresso Soup would stand out.[83]

Although packaging is subject to some legal requirements, such as nutrition information on food products, there is plenty of scope for improving brand awareness and forming brand associations. Perhaps one of the most important visual design elements for a package is its color.[84] Some package designers believe that consumers have a "color vocabulary" when it comes to products and expect certain types of products to have a particular look.

For example, it would be difficult to sell milk in anything but a white carton, club soda in anything but a blue package, and so forth. At the same time, certain brands are thought to have "color ownership" such that it would be difficult for other brands to use a similar look. Here is how some experts see the brand color palette:[85]

- *Red:* Ritz crackers, Folgers coffee, Colgate toothpaste, Target retailer, and Coca-Cola soft drinks.
- *Orange:* Tide laundry detergent, Wheaties cereal, Home Depot retailer, and Stouffer's frozen dinners.
- *Yellow:* Kodak film, Juicy Fruit chewing gum, McDonald's restaurants, IKEA retailers, Cheerios cereal, Lipton tea, and Bisquick biscuit mix.
- *Green:* Del Monte canned vegetables, Green Giant frozen vegetables, Walmart retailers, Starbucks coffee, BP retail gasoline, and 7 Up lemon-lime soft drink.
- *Blue:* IBM technology and services, Ford automobiles, Windex cleaner, Downy fabric softener, and Pepsi soft drinks.

Packaging color can affect consumers' perceptions of the product itself.[86] For example, the darker the orange shade of a can or bottle, the sweeter consumers believe the drink inside to be. Color is thus a critical element of packaging. Like other packaging design elements, the color should be consistent with information conveyed by other aspects of the marketing program.

Packaging Changes.   Although packaging changes can be expensive, they can be cost-effective compared with other marketing communication costs. Firms change their packaging for a number of reasons:[87]

- *To signal a higher price, or to more effectively sell products through new or shifting distribution channels.* For instance, Kendall Oil redid its package to make it more appealing to do-it-yourselfers when it found more of its sales coming from supermarkets and hardware stores rather than service stations.
- *When a significant product line expansion would benefit from a common look.* For example, Planters nuts, Weight Watchers foods, and Stouffer's frozen foods.
- *To accompany a new product innovation to signal changes to consumers.* To emphasize the brand's "green" heritage, Stevia redesigned the packaging on its SweetLeaf product, changing the look and the size and promoting the 100 percent recycled materials used in its manufacture.[88]
- *When the old package just looks outdated.* Kraft updated its macaroni and cheese packaging in 2010—the first time in more than 10 years—to better underscore the brand's core equities (happiness, smiles, and joy) through a "noodle smile" symbol as well as to unify its three sub-brands.[89]

Packaging changes have accelerated in recent years as marketers have sought to gain an advantage wherever possible. Greater competition has led companies to change their boxes more frequently, both on a short-term promotional basis and longer-term look to put forth a more dynamic image.

In making a packaging change, marketers need to recognize its effect on the original or current customer franchise for the brand.[90] Under these circumstances, marketers must not lose the key package equities that have been built up. Branding Brief 4-3 describes some setbacks marketers have faced updating packaging and other brand elements in recent years.

To identify or confirm key package equities, consumer research is usually helpful (see Branding Brief 4-3). If packaging recognition is a critical consumer success factor for the brand, however, marketers must be especially careful. It would be a mistake to change the packaging so significantly that consumers do not recognize it in the store. Retailers' opinions can also be important too.

Some marketing observers consider packaging important enough to be the "fifth P" of the marketing mix. Packaging can play an important role in building brand equity directly, through points-of-difference created by functional or aesthetic elements of the packaging, or indirectly through the reinforcement of brand awareness and image.[91]

PUTTING IT ALL TOGETHER

Each brand element can play a different role in building brand equity, so marketers "mix and match" to maximize brand equity.[92] For example, meaningful brand names that are visually represented through logos are easier to remember with than without such reinforcement.[93]

BRANDING BRIEF 4-3
Do-Overs with Brand Makeovers

With more markets characterized by intense competition, rapidly changing products, and increasingly fickle customers, many marketers are looking at makeovers to breathe new life into their brands. Logos, symbols, packaging, and even brand names are being updated to create greater meaning, relevance, and differentiation. Unfortunately, in an increasingly networked world, consumer reaction to changes to any brand element—both pro and con—can be quickly spread. Here are some high-profile examples and the challenges and difficulties their brand makeovers encountered.

Tropicana.   In February 2009, Pepsi introduced a dramatic overhaul to its category-leading orange juice. Gone was the visual image of an orange with a straw protruding from it (designed to evoke freshness); in its place was a close-up image of a glass of orange juice and the phrase "100% Orange." Consumer reaction was swift and largely negative. Customers complained about being unable to differentiate between the company's pulp-free, traditional, and other juice varieties. Even worse, customers also felt the look was too generic. Facing online fury, and with the words "ugly," "stupid," and "bargain brand" ringing in their ears, Pepsi capitulated. Announcing that it had "underestimated the deep emotional bond" consumers had with the original packaging, the company reverted to the old versions after only six weeks.

The Gap.   Another brand walking into a digital brand-makeover firestorm, The Gap actually asked for it. After unexpectedly unveiling a new logo (the word *Gap* in a basic black Helvetica font with a small blue square over the upper-right hand portion of the p), the company asked consumers on its Facebook page for comments and further logo ideas. Feedback was far from kind, and after enduring a long week of criticism, Gap management announced that "We've heard loud and clear that you don't like the new logo" and reverted to its iconic white text logo and unique brand font.

Starbucks has evolved its logo to keep up with changes in its positioning over time.

Gatorade and Pepsi.   Around the same time as the Tropicana makeover, Pepsi also completely overhauled its Gatorade brand as well as its classic Pepsi product lineup. Gatorade's makeover included introducing a whole new system of thirst quenchers and fluid restoration for before (Prime 01), during (Perform 02), and after (Recover 03) exercise. The new brand goal was to reach athletes in a wide range of sports and experience levels while positioning itself as the one-stop source for hydration and other needs before, during, and after their workouts. Pepsi's makeover included a new logo—a white band in the middle of the Pepsi circle that appeared to loosely form a smile. Both brand makeovers received some negative feedback and the products experienced sluggish sales afterwards, although several factors may have contributed, including the severe recession.

Lessons.   When changing a well-received or even iconic brand element—a character, logo, or packaging—two issues are key.

One, the new brand element must be inherently highly regarded. Part of the problems some brands have run into is that their new logos or packaging are just not that appealing to consumers, leading the consumer to wonder why a change needed to be made. Two, regardless of the inherent appeal of a new brand element, changes are hard for consumers and should be handled carefully and patiently.

No wonder Starbucks went to great pains in 2010 to carefully explain the rationale of its logo makeover, its fourth since the brand was created in 1971. The change was prompted by the company's fortieth anniversary and the new directions it was considering, which would take the brand outside the coffee category. Founder Howard Schultz explained that the iconic green Siren in the center of the logo was made more prominent—by dropping the words "Starbucks Coffee"—to reflect new business lines and new international markets. Like many brand makeovers, it initially met mixed public reaction.

The bold decision to move away from coffee in its logo seems appropriate. Currently, Starbucks is associated with a wide variety of different products including coffee, tea, pastries, ready-to-drink beverages, and coffee brewing equipment. Starbucks defines its mission as nurturing and inspiring the human spirit, and it proposes to achieve its mission by delivering coffee to its customers across many different neighborhoods.

Sources: Linda Tischler, "Never Mind!" Pepsi Pulls Much-Loathed Tropicana Packaging," *Fast Company*, February 23, 2009; Stuart Elliott, "Tropicana Discovers Some Buyers Are Passionate About Packaging," *The New York Times*, February 23, 2009; Patrick Conlon, "Tropicana to Abandon Much-Maligned Juice Carton," *The Wall Street Journal*, February 24, 2009, https://www.wsj.com/articles/SB123544345146655887; Tim Nudd, "People Not Falling in Love with New Gap Logo," *Adweek*, October 6, 2010, https://www.adweek.com/creativity/people-not-falling-love-new-gap-logo-12126/, accessed October 26, 2018; Christine Birkner, "Minding the Gap: Retailer Caught in Logo Fiasco," *Marketing News*, October 21, 2010; Natalie Zmuda, "What Went Into the Update Pepsi Logo," *Advertising Age*, October 27, 2008; Jeremiah Williams, "PepsiCo Revamps Formidable Gatorade Franchise After Rocky 2009," *Atlanta Journal-Constitution*, March 23, 2010; Valarie Bauerlein, "Gatorade's 'Mission': Sell More Drinks," *The Wall Street Journal*, September 13, 2010; Julie Jargon, "Starbucks Drops Coffee from Logo," *The Wall Street Journal*, January 6, 2011; Sarah Skidmore, "Starbucks Gives Logo a New Look," *Associated Press*, January 5, 2011; Matt Cannon, "Brand Stories: The Evolution of Starbucks," February 24, 2015, www.worksdesigngroup.com/brand-redesign-evolution-starbucks/, accessed October 26, 2018; Starbucks, 2016. Company information available at: www.starbucks.com/about-us/company-information, accessed April 22, 2018.

The entire set of brand elements makes up the ***brand identity***, the contribution of all brand elements to awareness and image. The cohesiveness of the brand identity depends on the extent to which the brand elements are consistent. Ideally, marketers choose each element to support the others, and all can be easily incorporated into other aspects of the brand and the marketing program.

Some strong brands have a number of valuable brand elements that directly reinforce each other. For example, consider Charmin toilet tissue. Phonetically, the name itself conveys softness. The brand character, Mr. Whipple, and the brand slogan, "Please Don't Squeeze the Charmin," also help reinforce the key point-of-difference for the brand of "softness."

Brand names characterized by rich, concrete visual imagery often can yield powerful logos or symbols. Wells Fargo, a large California-based bank, has a brand name rich in Western heritage that can be exploited throughout its marketing program. Wells Fargo has adopted a stagecoach as a symbol and has named individual services to be thematically consistent, for example, creating investment funds under the Stagecoach Funds brand umbrella.

Although the actual product or service itself is critical in building a strong brand, the right brand elements can be invaluable in developing brand equity. Method Products is a prime example of the payoffs from getting both correct.

METHOD

Celebrating its tenth anniversary in 2011 and still one of the fastest-growing companies in the United States, Method Products is the brainchild of former high school buddies Eric Ryan and Adam Lowry. The company took a big supermarket category—cleaning and household products—and literally and figuratively turned things upside down by taking a completely fresh approach. Ryan and Lowry designed a sleek, uncluttered dish soap container that also had a functional advantage—the bottle, shaped like a chess piece, was built to let soap flow out the bottom, so users would never have to turn it upside down. This signature product, with its pleasant fragrance, was designed by award-winning industrial designer Karim Rashid. By creating a line of nontoxic, biodegradable household cleaning products with bright colors and sleek designs totally unique to the category, Method has surpassed $100 million in annual revenues. Although it is available in such desirable retail outlets as Target and Lowe's, the company believes its marketing must work harder to express the brand positioning given its limited advertising budget. In addition to its attractive packaging, the company is capitalizing on growing interest in green products by emphasizing its nontoxic, nonpolluting ingredients. It is also developing a strong brand personality as hip, modern, and somewhat irreverent as reflected by its slogan, "People Against Dirty."[94]

Method built a highly successful line of cleaning products by paying attention to what was inside the bottle as well as outside.
Source: Sheila Fitzgerald/Shutterstock

REVIEW

Brand elements are those trademarkable devices that identify and differentiate the brand. The main ones are brand names, URLs, logos, symbols, characters, slogans, jingles, and packages. Brand elements can both enhance brand awareness and facilitate the formation of strong, favorable, and unique brand associations.

Six criteria are particularly important. First, brand elements should be inherently memorable, easy to recognize, and easy to recall. Second, they should be inherently meaningful to convey information about the nature of the product category, the particular attributes and benefits of a brand, or both. The brand element may even reflect the brand personality, user or usage imagery, or feelings for the brand. Third, the information conveyed by brand elements does not necessarily have to relate to the product alone and may simply be inherently appealing or likable. Fourth, brand elements can be transferable within and across product categories to support line and brand extensions, and across geographic and cultural boundaries and market segments. Fifth, brand elements should be adaptable and flexible over time. Finally, they should be legally protectable and, as much as possible, competitively defensible. Brand Focus 4.0 outlines some of the key legal considerations in protecting the brand.

Because different brand elements have different strengths and weaknesses, marketers "mix and match" to maximize their collective contribution to brand equity. Figure 4-8 offers a critique of different brand elements according to the six key criteria.

	Brand Element				
Criterion	Brand Names and URLs	Logos and Symbols	Characters	Slogans and Jingles	Packaging and Signage
Memorability	Can be chosen to enhance brand recall and recognition	Generally more useful for brand recognition	Generally more useful for brand recognition	Can be chosen to enhance brand recall and recognition	Generally more useful for brand recognition
Meaningfulness	Can reinforce almost any type of association, although sometimes only indirectly	Can reinforce almost any type of association, although sometimes only indirectly	Generally more useful for non-product-related imagery and brand personality	Can convey almost any type of association explicitly	Can convey almost any type of association explicitly
Likability	Can evoke much verbal imagery	Can provoke visual appeal	Can generate human qualities	Can evoke much verbal imagery	Can combine visual and verbal appeal
Transferability	Can be somewhat limited	Excellent	Can be somewhat limited	Can be somewhat limited	Good
Adaptability	Difficult	Can typically be redesigned	Can sometimes be redesigned	Can be modified	Can typically be redesigned
Protectability	Generally good, but with limits	Excellent	Excellent	Excellent	Can be closely copied

FIGURE 4-8
Critique of Brand Element Options

DISCUSSION QUESTIONS

1. Pick a brand. Identify all its brand elements and assess their ability to contribute to brand equity according to the choice criteria identified in this chapter.
2. What are your favorite brand characters? Do you think they contribute to brand equity in any way? How? Can you relate their effects to the customer-based brand equity model?
3. What are some other examples of slogans not listed in the chapter that make strong contributions to brand equity? Why? Can you think of any "bad" slogans? Why do you consider them to be so?
4. Choose a package of any supermarket product. Assess its contribution to brand equity. Justify your decisions.
5. Can you think of some general guidelines to help marketers mix and match brand elements? Can you ever have "too many" brand elements? Which brand do you think does the best job of mixing and matching brand elements? How do online channels and offline channels differ in their use of brand elements?

BRAND FOCUS 4.0

Legal Branding Considerations

According to the U.S. Patents and Trademarks Office, a trademark is a word, phrase, symbol, or design that effectively distinguishes one party's goods from another.[95] These could pertain to services as well and are typically defined based on usage. Based on this definition, firms should carefully manage their trademarks to ensure that their brand assets are adequately protected. According to Dorothy Cohen, a trademark strategy could include all the following aspects:[96]

- *Trademark planning:* requires selecting a valid trademark, adopting and using the trademark, and engaging in search and clearance processes.
- *Trademark implementation:* requires effectively using the trademark in enacting marketing decisions, especially with respect to promotional and distributional strategies.
- *Trademark control:* requires a program of aggressive policing of a trademark to ensure its efficient usage in marketing

activities, including efforts to reduce trademark counterfeiting and to prevent the trademark from becoming generic, as well as instituting suits for infringement of the trademark.

This Brand Focus highlights a few key legal branding considerations. For more comprehensive treatments, it is necessary to consider other sources.[97]

Counterfeit and Imitator Brands

Why is trademark protection of brand elements such as brand names, logos, and symbols such an important brand management priority? Virtually any product is fair game for illegal counterfeiting or questionable copycat mimicking—from Nike apparel to Windows software, and from Similac baby formula to ACDelco auto parts.[98]

Also, some products attempt to gain market share by imitating successful brands. These copycat brands may mimic any one of the possible brand elements, such as brand names or packaging. For example, Calvin Klein's popular Obsession perfume and cologne has had to withstand imitators such as Compulsion, Enamoured, and Confess, whose package slogan proclaimed, "If you like Obsession, you'll love Confess."

Many copycat brands are put forth by retailers as store brands, putting national brands in the dilemma of protecting their trade dress by cracking down on some of their best customers. Complicating matters is the fact that if challenged, many private labels contend, with some justification, that they should be permitted to continue labeling and packaging practices that have come to identify entire categories of products rather than a single national brand.[99] In other words, certain packaging looks may become a necessary point-of-parity in a product category. A common victim of brand cloning, Contac cold medication underwent its first packaging overhaul in 33 years to better prevent knockoffs as well as update its image.

In recent years, and as noted earlier, Chinese manufacturers of branded goods may use some of their excess capacity to manufacture branded goods that bear a strong resemblance to the products they already make for their Western clients.[100] As an example, a manufacturer of accessories and branded goods for Marc Jacobs, Prada, and Coach can have its own manufactured products, which bear a striking similarity to the luxury brands that they manufacture. Whether these are derivative designs or blatant knockoffs, there is a spectrum of imitation, which poses significant challenges from a trademark standpoint. Many national brand manufacturers are also responding through legal action. For national brands, the key is proving that brand clones are misleading consumers, who may think that they are buying national brands. The burden of proof is to establish that an appreciable number of reasonably acting consumers are confused and mistaken in their purchases.[101] In such cases, many factors might be considered by courts in determining the likelihood of confusion, such as the strength of the national brand's mark, the relatedness of the national brand and brand clone products, the similarity of the marks, evidence of actual confusion, the similarity of marketing channels used, the likely degree of buyer care, the brand clone's intent in selecting the mark, and the likelihood of expansion of the product lines.

Simonson provides an in-depth discussion of these issues and methods to assess the likelihood of confusion and "genericness" of a trademark. He stresses the importance of recognizing that consumers may vary in their level or degree of confusion, and

that it is difficult, as a result, to identify a precise threshold level above which confusion occurs. He also notes how survey research methods must accurately reflect the consumers' state of mind when engaged in marketplace activities.[102]

Historical and Legal Precedence

Simonson and Holbrook have made some provocative observations about and connections between appropriation and dilution, making the following points.[103] They begin by noting that legally, a brand name is a "conditional-type property"—protected only after it has been used in commerce to identify products (goods or services) and only in relation to those products or to closely related offerings. To preserve a brand name's role in identifying products, the authors note, federal law protects brands from actions of others that may tend to cause confusion concerning proper source identification.

By contrast with the case of confusion, Simonson and Holbrook identify **trademark appropriation** as a developing area of state law that can severely curtail even those brand strategies that do not "confuse" consumers. They define appropriation in terms of enhancing the image of a new offering via the use of some property aspect of an existing brand. That is, appropriation resembles theft of an intangible property right. They note that the typical argument to prevent imitations is that, even in the absence of confusion, a weaker brand will tend to benefit by imitating an existing brand name. Jerre Swann similarly argues that "the owner of a strong, unique brand should thus be entitled, incipiently, to prevent impairment of the brand's communicative clarity by its substantial association with another brand, particularly where there is an element of misappropriation."[104]

Simonson and Holbrook also summarize the legal concept of **trademark dilution**:

> Protection from "dilution"—a weakening or reduction in the ability of a mark to clearly and unmistakably distinguish the source—arose in 1927 when a legal ruling declared that "once a mark has come to indicate to the public a constant and uniform source of satisfaction, its owner should be allowed the broadest scope possible for the 'natural expansion of his trade' to other lines or fields of enterprise."

They observe that two brand-related rights followed: (1) the right to preempt and preserve areas for brand extensions and (2) the right to stop the introduction of similar or identical brand names, even in the absence of consumer confusion, to protect a brand's image and distinctiveness from being diluted.

Dilution can occur in three ways: blurring, tarnishment, and cybersquatting.[105] **Blurring** happens when the use of an existing mark by a different company in a different category alters the "unique and distinctive significance" of that mark. **Tarnishment** is when a different company employs the mark in order to degrade its quality, such as in the context of a parody or satire. **Cybersquatting** occurs when an unaffiliated party purchases an Internet "domain name consisting of the mark or name of a company for the purpose of relinquishing the right to that domain name to the legitimate owner for a price."[106]

New American laws register trademarks for only 10 years (instead of 20); to renew trademarks, firms must prove they are using the name and not just holding it in reserve. The Trademark

Law Revision Act of 1988 allowed entities to apply for a trademark based on their "intent to use" it within 36 months, eliminating the need to have an actual product in the works. To determine legal status, marketers must search trademark registrations, brand name directories, phone books, trade journals and advertisements, and so forth. As a result, the pool of potentially available trademarks have shrunk.[107]

The remainder of this Brand Focus describes some of the particular issues involved with two important brand elements: brand names and packaging.

Trademark Issues Concerning Names

Without adequate trademark protection, brand names can become legally declared generic, as was the case with *vaseline, victrola, cellophane, escalator,* and *thermos.* For example, when Bayer set out to trademark the "wonder drug" acetylsalicylic acid, they failed to provide a "generic" term or common descriptor for the product and provided only a trademark, Aspirin. Without any other option available in the language, the trademark became the common name for the product. In 1921, a U.S. district court ruled that Bayer had lost all its rights in the trademark. Other brand names have struggled to retain their legal trademark status—for example, Band-Aids, Kleenex, Scotch Tape, Q-Tips, and Jell-O. Xerox spends $100,000 a year explaining that you don't "Xerox" a document, you photocopy it.[108]

Legally, the courts have created a hierarchy for determining eligibility for registration. In descending order of protection, these categories are as follows (with concepts and examples in parentheses):

1. **Fanciful:** a made-up word with no inherent meaning (e.g., Kodak)

2. **Arbitrary:** actual word but not associated with the product (e.g., Camel)

3. **Suggestive:** actual word evocative of product feature or benefit (e.g., Eveready)

4. **Descriptive:** common word protected only with secondary meaning (e.g., Ivory)

5. **Generic:** a word synonymous with the product category (e.g., Aspirin)

Thus, fanciful names are the most easily protected, but at the same time are less suggestive or descriptive of the product itself, suggesting the type of trade-off involved in choosing brand elements. Generic terms are never protectable. Marks that are difficult to protect include those that are surnames, descriptive terms, or geographic names or those that relate to a functional product feature. Marks that are not inherently distinctive, and thus, are not immediately protectable, may attain trademark protection if they acquire secondary meaning.

Secondary meaning refers to a mark gaining a meaning other than the older (primary) meaning. The secondary meaning must be the meaning the public usually attaches to the mark and that indicates the association between the mark and goods from a single source. Secondary meaning is usually proven through extensive advertising, distribution, availability, sales volume, length and manner of use, and market share.[109] Secondary meaning is necessary to establish trademark protection for descriptive marks, geographic terms, and personal names.

Trademark Issues Concerning Packaging

In general, names and graphic designs are more legally defensible than shapes and colors. The issue of legal protection of the color of packaging for a brand is a complicated one. One federal appeals court in San Francisco ruled that companies cannot get trademark protection for a product's color alone.[110] However, a Supreme Court ruling later overturned that ruling, arguing that the interpretation of a trademark, according to the Lanham Act, could be broad. The court ruled against a small Chicago manufacturer that makes the green-gold padding used by dry cleaners and garment makers on machines that press clothes; the manufacturer had filed suit against a competitor that had started selling padding of the same hue. In rejecting protection for the color alone, the court said manufacturers with distinctively colored products can rely on existing law that protects "trade dress" related to the overall appearance of the product: "Adequate protection is available when color is combined in distinctive patterns or designs or combined in distinctive logos."

Color is one factor, but not a determinative one, under a trade dress analysis. This ruling differed from a landmark ruling in 1985 arising from a suit by Owens-Corning Fiberglass Corporation, which sought to protect the pink color of its insulation. A Washington court ruled in the corporation's favor. Other courts have made similar rulings, but at least two other appeals courts in other regions of the country have subsequently ruled that colors cannot be trademarked. Note that these trademark rulings apply only when color is not an integral part of the product. However, when the color acquires a "secondary meaning" by being closely linked to a product, it can be trademarked, and the trademark typically pertains to a particular shade of color which can be used and within a specific product category. John Deere has trademarked the green and yellow colors that appears in its logo, Target has a trademark for the red color, and Tiffany has trademarked its distinctive blue. At the same time, the way in which the color is linked to a product also matters. In a landmark lawsuit between Christian Louboutin and Yves. St. Laurent, regarding the former's use of the color red, the courts ruled that Christian Louboutin could trademark the red sole (which was typical of the shoes made by this brand), but other shoe manufacturers (including YSL) had the right to sell a shoe that was entirely red.[111]

Trademark law varies in its emphasis across different areas of the world. For example, the European Union has laid down the following factors to consider while assessing the existence of trademark dilution: (1) the degree of similarity between the marks; (2) nature of goods or services for the trademarks registered; (3) the level of reputation of the earlier mark; (4) the degree of distinctive character of the earlier mark; and (5) the probability of the existence of a likelihood of confusion among consumers. There are some differences in how trademark laws in China are enforced. Unlike the United States, China observes a first-to-file system in connection with trademark registrations. As such, the first party to file an application for a trademark is given priority. This contrasts with the U.S. system. In the United States, it is not registration, but the actual use of a trademark that creates rights and priority over others—that is, the system favors entities that are the first to use a mark in commerce. China's first-to-file system poses problems for some brand owners because there is no way for brand owners to block applicants who are bad-faith trademark applicants who intend to engage in trademark squatting.[112]

NOTES

1. Bernd H. Schmitt and Alex Simonson, *Marketing Aesthetics: The Strategic Management of Brands, Identity, and Image* (New York: Free Press, 1997).

2. Nick Farrell, "Latvians Laugh at Vista," *The Inquirer*, September 8, 2006, https://www.theinquirer.net/inquirer/news/1035505/latvians-laugh-vista, accessed October 21, 1018.

3. For some provocative discussion, see Matt Haig, *Brand Failures* (London: Kogan Page, 2003) and www.snopes.com, accessed October 26, 2018.

4. Eleftheria Parpis, "Michelin Gets Pumped Up," *Brandweek*, October 6, 2009, https://www.adweek.com/brand-marketing/michelin-gets-pumped-106498/, accessed October 26, 2018; Roger Parloff, "Michelin Man: The Inside Story," *Fortune*, September 19, 2005, https://money.cnn.com/magazines/fortune/fortune_archive/2005/09/19/8272906/, accessed October 26, 2018; Brent Marcus, "Brand Icons Get an Online Facelift," *iMedia Connection*, May 30, 2007, www.imediaconnection.com.

5. Anna Lee, "Michelin Ad to Air During Super Bowl," *Greenville News*, February 4, 2017, www.greenvilleonline.com/story/news/local/2017/02/04/michelin-ad-air-during-super-bowl/97498280/.

6. Dale Buss, " 'Michelin Man' Bibendum Slims Down in Brand Refresh," June 19, 2017, http://www.brandchannel.com/2017/06/19/michelin-rebrand-061917/, accessed June 22, 2018; https://www.michelin.com/eng/media-room/press-and-news/michelin-news/Passion/Bibendum-a-new-style-to-better-communicate2.

7. For a stimulating treatment of brand naming, see Alex Frankel, *Word Craft* (New York: Crown, 2004).

8. Robert Klara, "11 Brand Names That Simply Couldn't Survive the Times, "*Adweek*, March 18, 2015, www.adweek.com/brand-marketing/11-brand-names-simply-couldnt-survive-times-163440/.

9. An excellent overview of the topic, some of which this section draws on, can be found in Kim R. Robertson, "Strategically Desirable Brand Name Characteristics," *Journal of Consumer Marketing* 6, no. 4 (1989): 61–71.

10. Interestingly, GM sent a memo to its headquarter Chevrolet employees in June 2010 telling them, for the sake of brand consistency, to stop using the Chevy nickname, a move many branding experts criticized for not reflecting consumer desires. Richard S. Chang, "Backtracking, GM Says Please, Call It a Chevy," *The New York Times*, June 10, 2010, https://www.nytimes.com/2010/06/11/automobiles/11CHEVY.html, accessed October 26, 2018.

11. Later, after meeting with some success in the UK, Wyborowa launched an ad campaign based again on its name. Themed "There is No V in Wodka," it was based on the fact that in Poland, where vodka originated, the spirit is called wodka! "Wyborowa Campaigns for No V in Wodka," *Harpers Wine & Spirits Trades Review*, June 6, 2008.

12. Frances Leclerc, Bernd H. Schmitt, and Laurette Dube, "Foreign Branding and Its Effects on Product Perceptions and Attitudes," *Journal of Marketing Research* 31, no. 2 (May 1994): 263–270. See also M. V. Thakor and B. G. Pacheco, "Foreign Branding and Its Effect on Product Perceptions and Attitudes: A Replication and Extension in a Multicultural Setting," *Journal of Marketing Theory and Practice* 5, no. 1 (Winter 1997): 15–30.

13. Eric Yorkston and Geeta Menon, "A Sound Idea: Phonetic Effects of Brand Names on Consumer Judgments," *Journal of Consumer Research* 31, no. 1 (June 2004): 43–51; Richard R. Klink, "Creating Brand Names with Meaning: The Use of Sound Symbolism," *Marketing Letters* 11, no. 1 (2000): 5–20.

14. Kim R. Robertson, "Recall and Recognition Effects of Brand Name Imagery," *Psychology and Marketing* 4 (1987): 3–15.

15. Robert N. Kanungo, "Effects of Fittingness, Meaningfulness, and Product Utility," *Journal of Applied Psychology* 52, no. 4 (1968): 290–295.

16. Kevin Lane Keller, Susan Heckler, and Michael J. Houston, "The Effects of Brand Name Suggestiveness on Advertising Recall," *Journal of Marketing* 62, no. 1 (January 1998): 48–57.

17. Luk Warlop, S. Ratneshwar, and Stijn M. J. van Osselaer, "Distinctive Brand Cues and Memory for Product Consumption Experiences," *International Journal of Research in Marketing* 22, no. 1 (2005): 27–44.

18. Daniel J. Howard, Roger A. Kerin, and Charles Gengler, "The Effects of Brand Name Similarity on Brand Source Confusion: Implications for Trademark Infringement," *Journal of Public Policy & Marketing* 19, no. 2 (Fall 2000): 250–264.

19. Rob Lammle, "How Etsy, eBay, Reddit Got Their Names," *CNN*, April 22, 2001, www.cnn.com.

20. Dan Heath and Chip Heath, "How to Pick the Perfect Brand Name," Fast Company, January 3, 2011, https://www.fastcompany.com/1702256/how-pick-perfect-brand-name, accessed October 26, 2018; Lexicon Branding, www.lexiconbranding.com; Ciulla Association, www.ciulla-assoc.com.; "Colgate's Portable Wisp Targets Young, On-the-Go Consumers," *Schneider Associates*, April 21, 2009, www.launchpr.com.

21. William L. Moore and Donald R. Lehmann, "Effects of Usage and Name on Perceptions of New Products," *Marketing Science* 1, no. 4 (1982): 351–370.

22. Yih Hwai Lee and Kim Soon Ang, "Brand Name Suggestiveness: A Chinese Language Perspective," *International Journal of Research in Marketing* 20, no. 4 (December 2003): 323–335.

23. Kevin Lane Keller, Susan E. Heckler, and Michael J. Houston, "Effects of Brand Name Suggestiveness on Advertising Recall." *American Marketing Association* 62, no. 1 (1988): 48–57, https://www.jstor.org/stable/1251802.

24. Robert A. Peterson and Ivan Ross, "How to Name New Brands," *Journal of Advertising Research* 12, no. 6 (December 1972): 29–34.

25. Robert A. Mamis, "Name-Calling," *Inc.*, July 1984, https://www.inc.com/magazine/19840701/8838.html, accessed October 26, 2018.

26. Tina M. Lowrey, L. J. Shrum, and Tony M. Dubitsky, "The Relationship Between Brand-Name Linguistic

Characteristics and Brand-Name Memory," *Journal of Advertising* 32, no. 3 (2003): 7–17; Tina M. Lowrey and L. J. Shrum, "Phonetic Symbolism and Brand Name Preference," *Journal of Consumer Research* 34, no. 3 (October 2007): 406–414.

27. Michael McCarthy, "Xterra Discovers Extra Success," *USA Today*, February 26, 2001, 4B.

28. C. Miguel Brendl, Amitava Chattopadyhay, Brett W. Pelham, and Mauricio Carvallo, "Name Letter Branding: Valence Transfers When Product Specific Needs Are Active," *Journal of Consumer Research* 32, no. 3 (December 2005): 405–415.

29. Jennifer J. Argo, Monica Popa, and Malcolm C. Smith, "The Sound of Brands," *Journal of Marketing* 74, no. 4 (July 2010): 97–109.

30. Bruce G. Vanden Bergh, Janay Collins, Myrna Schultz, and Keith Adler, "Sound Advice on Brand Names," *Journalism Quarterly* 61, no. 4 (1984): 835–840; Bruce G. Vanden Bergh, Keith E. Adler, and Lauren Oliver, "Use of Linguistic Characteristics with Various Brand-Name Styles," *Journalism Quarterly* 65, no. 2 (1987): 464–468.

31. Daniel L. Doeden, "How to Select a Brand Name," *Marketing Communications* (November 1981): 58–61.

32. Timothy B. Heath, Subimal Chatterjee, and Karen Russo, "Using the Phonemes of Brand Names to Symbolize Brand Attributes," in *The AMA Educator's Proceedings: Enhancing Knowledge Development in Marketing,* eds. William Bearden and A. Parasuraman (Chicago: American Marketing Association, August 1990).

33. John R. Doyle and Paul A. Bottomley, "Dressed for the Occasion: Font-Product Congruity in the Perception of Logotype," *Journal of Consumer Psychology* 16, no. 2, 2006: 112–123. See also Pamela W. Henderson, Joan L. Giese, and Joseph A. Cote, "Impression Management Using Typeface Design," *Journal of Marketing* 68, no. 4 (October 2004): 60–72; Terry L. Childers and Jeffrey Jass, "All Dressed Up with Something to Say: Effects of Typeface Semantic Associations on Brand Perceptions and Consumer Memory," *Journal of Consumer Psychology* 12, no. 2 (2002): 93–106.

34. Much of this passage is based on Teresa M. Paiva and Janeen Arnold Costa, "The Winning Number: Consumer Perceptions of Alpha-Numeric Brand Names," *Journal of Marketing* 57 , no. 3 (July 1993): 85–98. See also, Kunter Gunasti and William T. Ross Jr., "How and When Alphanumeric Brand Names Affect Consumer Preferences," *Journal of Marketing Research* 47, no. 6 (December 2010): 1177–1192.

35. Beth Snyder Bulik, "Tech Sector Ponders: What's in a Name?" *Advertising Age,* May 9, 2005, https://adage .com/article/news/tech-sector-ponders-a/103129/, accessed October 26, 2018.

36. John Murphy, *Brand Strategy* (Upper Saddle River, NJ: Prentice Hall, 1990), 79.

37. Alex Frankel, "The New Science of Naming," *Business 2.0,* December 1, 2004 (Business 2.0), https://money .cnn.com/magazines/business2/business2_archive/2004/, accessed October 26, 2018; Chuck Slater, "Project Runway," *Fast Company*, October 2010, 170–174.

38. Brett Snyder, "How JetBlue Tends to Its Brand," *CBS,* July 14, 2010, www.btnet.com; Cliff Medney, "Flying Sucks. They Know," *Brandweek*, June 16, 2008, Vol. 49 Issue 24, p. 30. Rupal Parekh, "How JetBlue Became

One of the Hottest Brands in America, *Advertising Age,* July 6, 2010, https://adage.com/article/cmo-strategy/ jetblue-hottest-brands-america/144799/, accessed October 26, 2018; JetBlue, www.jetblue.com.

39. Matthew Hicks, "Order Out of Chaos," *eWeek,* July 1, 2001, www.eweek.com/it-management/order-out-of-chaos, accessed October 26, 2018.

40. Anticybersquatting Consumer Protection Act (ACPA), November 29, 1999; "Cybersquatting Hits Record Level, WIPO Center Rolls Out New Services," March 31, 2011, www.wpio.int; Evan Brown and Brian Beckham, "Internet Law in the Courts," *Journal of Internet Law* 12, no. 7 (May 2009): 24–26.

41. Trademark Infringement, "9 Nasty Trademark Trademark Infringement Cases — and How to Avoid Them (2016)," *TrademarkNow*, September 6, 2016, www.trademarknow.com/blog/9-nasty-trademark-infringement-cases-and-how-to-avoid-them; PCT Law Group, "Trademark Violation by Cybersquatter Is Not GoDaddy's Problem," *PCT Law* Group, April 29, 2015, http://pctlg.com/trademark-violation-cybersquatter-godaddys-problem-2/, accessed October 26, 2018; Philiop Corwin, "GoDaddy Hit with Another Trademark Infringement Suit—A Hint of Things to Come?" *Internet Commerce*, February 25, 2014, www.internetcommerce .org/godaddy_tm_infringement_lawsuits/.

42. "Louis Vuitton Fried Chicken's Owner Fined in South Korea," *The Star*, April 19, 2016, www .thestar.com.my/news/regional/2016/04/19/ louis-vuitton-fried-chicken-owner-fined-in-skorea/.

43. Robert Klara, "Luxury Brands Just Got One More Reason to Hate the Internet: Spoofing," *Adweek*, September 5, 2017, http://www.adweek.com/brand-marketing/luxury-brands-just-got-one-more-reason-to-hate-the-internet-spoofing/, accessed March 17, 2018.

44. Ibid.

45. Florian Malecki, "Fight the Phishers: Stop E-Mail Spoofers Trashing Your Brand's Reputation," *Tech Radar*, February 20, 2015, www.techradar.com/news/world-of-tech/management/fight-the-phishers-stop-email-spoofers-trashing-your-brand-s-reputation-1285401.

46. Gerald Levine, "Understanding the Legal Options Used to Fight Cybersquatting," *Network World*, January 14, 2015, www.networkworld.com/article/2868398/ security0/understanding-the-legal-options-used-to-fight-cybersquatting.html.

47. John Murphy, *Brand Strategy* (Upper Saddle River, NJ: Prentice Hall, 1990), 79.

48. Young Jee Han, Joseph C. Nunes, and Xavier Drèze, "Signaling Status with Luxury Goods: The Role of Brand Prominence," *Journal of Marketing* 74, no. 4 (July 2010): 15–30.

49. Murphy, *Brand Strategy*.

50. Michael McCarthy, "More Firms Flash New Badge," *USA Today,* October 4, 2000, B3.

51. Steve Douglas, "Top 100 Brands & Their Logos," Top 100 Brand Logos, The Logo Factory, accessed March 15, 2018, www.thelogofactory.com/top-100-brand-logos/; Katie Richards, "Here's What the Most Popular Brands' Logos Have in Common," July 15, 2015, https://www.adweek.com/brand-marketing/heres-what-most-popular-brands-logos-have-common-165884/, accessed October 6, 2018.

52. Jean Templin, "Were This Year's Most Controversial Logo Changes Effective?," September 29, 2016, https://conversionxl.com/blog/logo-study/, accessed October 6, 2018.

53. Michael McCarthy, "More Firms Flash New Badge," USA Today, October 4, 2000, B3; Natalie Zmuda, "What Went into the Updated Pepsi Logo," *Advertising Age*, October 27, 2008, https://adage.com/article/news/pepsi-s-logo-update/132016/, accessed October 26, 2018.

54. Dorothy Pomerantz and Lacey Rose, "America's Most Loved Spokescreatures," *Forbes*, March 18, 2010, https://www.forbes.com/2010/03/18/tony-tiger-woods-doughboy-cmo-network-spokescreatures.html#57a097187002, accessed October 26, 2018.

55. Andrew Ross Sorkin, "The Aflac Duck Will Quack Again," *The New York Times*, March 22, 2011.

56. David A. Aaker, *Building Strong Brands* (New York: Free Press, 1996), 203.

57. Jim Salter, "Still Going and Going: Energizer Bunny Enters His 20th Year," *Associated Press*, November 29, 2008, www.sandiegouniontribune.com/sdut-energizer-bunny-112908-2008nov29-story.html, accessed October 26, 2018; Energizer, http://www.energizer.com/; AdAge, "The Energizer Bunny: Ad Age Advertising Century: Icons," AdAge, March 29, 1999, https://adage.com/article/special-report-the-advertising-century/energizer-bunny/140174/, accessed October 26, 2018.

58. Sophia Yan, "How Hello Kitty Built A Massive Business Empire" *CNN*, August 21, 2015, http://money.cnn.com/2015/08/20/news/hello-kitty-sanrio-business/index.html.

59. Claudiu V. Dimotfe, "Consumer Response to Polysemous Brand Slogans," *Journal of Consumer Research* 33, no. 4 (March 2007): 515–522.

60. Allen Adamson, *BrandSimple* (New York: Palgrave Macmillan, 2007); Melissa Grego, "It's Not Just Any Network Executive," *Broadcasting & Cable*, February 15, 2010, Vol. 140 Issue 7, p. 20.

61. Claudiu V. Dimofte and Richard F. Yalch, "Consumer Response to Polysemous Brand Slogans," *Journal of Consumer Research* 33, no. 4 (March 2007): 515–522.

62. "New 7 Up Campaign Asks Consumers to "Mix It UP"," *BevNET*, February 13, 2017, www.bevnet.com/news/2017/new-7up-campaign-asks-consumers-mix; "7 Up TV Commercial, 'Do More with 7 Up: Taco Tuesday' Featuring Beth Dover," accessed April 23, 2018, www.ispot.tv/ad/wvKF/7up-do-more-with-7up-taco-tuesday-featuring-beth-dover.

63. Jenna Rosenstein, "Covergirl Is Being Revamped—See Their New Slogan and Logo," October 10, 2017, www.harpersbazaar.com/beauty/a12815826/covergirl-relaunch/.

64. The classic lyrics are:
Gimme a break,
Gimme a break,
Break me off a piece o' that
Kit Kat bar
That chocolatey taste is gonna make your day,
Everywhere you go you hear the people say
Gimme a break,
Gimme a break,
Break me off a piece o' that
Kit Kat bar

65. Dirk Smillie, "Now Hear This," *Forbes*, December 25, 2000, 234.

66. Nancy Croft, "Wrapping Up Sales," *Nation's Business* (October 1985): 41–42.

67. Susan B. Bassin, "Value-Added Packaging Cuts Through Store Clutter," *Marketing News*, September 26, 1988, 21.

68. Raymond Serafin, "Packaging Becomes an Art," *Advertising Age*, August 12, 1985, 66.

69. Pan Demetrakakes, "Packaging Innovator of the Decade," *Food and Beverage Packaging*, April 1, 2009, https://www.packagingstrategies.com/publications/3/editions/1113, accessed October 26, 2018.

70. Nate Nickerson, "How About This Beer Label: 'I'm in Advertising!,'" *Fast Company*, March 2004, 43; Coors Brewing Co., "Coors Brewing Company Reveals 2008 Advertising," *Business Wire*, April 8, 2008, https://www.businesswire.com/news/home/20080408005888/en/Coors-Brewing-Company-Reveals-2008-Advertising, accessed October 26, 2018.

71. Stephanie Hildebrandt, "A Taste-full Redesign," *Brand Packaging*, July/August 2010, digital.bnpmedia.com/allarticle/6029/43952/43952/allarticle.html, accessed October 26, 2018; Pan Demetrakakes, "Packaging Innovator of the Decade," *Food and Beverage Packaging*, April 1, 2009, https://www.packagingstrategies.com/publications/3/editions/1113, accessed October 26, 2018. Elaine Wong, "IRI Summit: How Sara Lee Beefed Up Jimmy Dean Brand," *Brandweek*, March 23, 2010, https://www.adweek.com/brand-marketing/iri-summit-how-sara-lee-beefed-jimmy-dean-brand-107202/, accessed October 26, 2018.

72. Eben Shapiro, "Portions and Packages Grow Bigger and Bigger," *The Wall Street Journal*, October 12, 1993, B1.

73. Rachel Arthur, "Molson Coors Sees Changing Consumer Preferences In Beer Packaging, Cuts Packaging Weight By 21%," *Beveragedaily.com*, August 18, 2015, www.beveragedaily.com/Article/2015/08/18/Molson-Coors-sees-changing-consumer-preferences-in-beer-packaging-cuts-packaging-weight-by-21.

74. Rick Lingle, "Natural Storytelling Helps Redefine Kashi Packaging," *Packaging Digest*, August 8, 2016, www.packagingdigest.com/packaging-design/natural-storytelling-redefines-kashi-packaging1608.

75. Rachel Parker, "Stories That Sell Packaging," *BXP*, September 26, 2016, www.bxpmagazine.com/article/stories-sell-packaging.

76. Mike Whitney, "3 Brands That Are Bringing Content Marketing to Their Packaging," *Mainstreethost*, December 5, 2015, www.mainstreethost.com/blog/brands-bringing-content-marketing-to-their-packaging/.

77. Alecia Swasy, "Sales Lost Their Vim? Try Repackaging," *The Wall Street Journal*, October 11, 1989, B1.

78. Supermarket News Staff, "CPGs Cutting 4 Billion Pounds of Packaging," *Supermarket News*, March 17, 2011, https://www.supermarketnews.com/latest-news/cpgs-cutting-4-billion-pounds-packaging, accessed October 26, 2018; Rachel Arthur, "Molson Coors Sees Changing Consumer Preferences In Beer Packaging, Cuts Packaging Weight By 21," *Beveragedaily.com*, August 18, 2015, www.beveragedaily.com/

Article/2015/08/18/Molson-Coors-sees-changing-consumer-preferences-in-beer-packaging-cuts-packaging-weight-by-21.

79. Kevin Keating, "Consumer Demand and Manufacturing Costs Drive Flexible Packaging Trends," *PKG Branding*, May 30, 2017, www.pkgbranding.com/blog/consumer-demand-and-manufacturing-costs-drive-flexible-packaging-trends.

80. Gerry Khermouch, "John Ferolito, Don Vultaggio," *Brandweek,* November 14, 1994, Vol. 35 Issue 44, p. 57.

81. For some academic perspectives on package design, see Ulrich R. Orth and Keven Malkewitz, "Holistic Package Design and Consumer Brand Impressions," *Journal of Marketing* 72, no. 3 (May 2008): 64–81.

82. For an interesting discussion, see Margaret C. Campbell and Ronald C. Goodstein, "The Moderating Effect of Perceived Risk on Consumers' Evaluations of Product Incongruity: Preference for the Norm," *Journal of Consumer Research* 28, no. 3 (December 2001): 439–449.

83. Pan Demetrakakes, "Packaging Innovator of the Decade," *Food and Beverage Packaging*, April 1, 2009, https://www.packagingstrategies.com/publications/3/editions/1113, accessed October 26, 2018.

84. For an interesting application of color to brand names, see Elizabeth G. Miller and Barbara E. Kahn, "Shades of Meaning: The Effect of Color and Flavor Names on Consumer Choice," *Journal of Consumer Research* 32, no.1 (June 2005): 86–92.

85. Michael Purvis, president of Sidjakov, Berman, and Gomez, as quoted in Carla Marinucci, "Advertising on the Store Shelves," *San Francisco Examiner,* October 20, 1986, C1–C2; Angela Bright, "Why Color Matters," *Beneath the Brand*, December 13, 2010, www.talentzoo.com/beneath-the-brand/blog_news.php?articleID=8810, accessed October 26, 2018.

86. Lawrence L. Garber Jr., Raymond R. Burke, and J. Morgan Jones, "The Role of Package Color in Consumer Purchase Consideration and Choice," MSI-Report 00–104 (Cambridge, MA: Marketing Science Institute, 2000); Ronald Alsop, "Color Grows More Important in Catching Consumers' Eyes," *The Wall Street Journal,* November 29, 1984, 37.

87. Bill Abrams and David P. Garino, "Package Design Gains Stature as Visual Competition Grows," *The Wall Street Journal,* March 14, 1979, 48.

88. Ann Marie Mohan, "Established Stevia Brand Refreshes Packaging for Greater Green Mileage," *Packaging World*, October 10, 2010, https://www.packworld.com/article/package-design/graphic/established-stevia-brand-refreshes-packaging-greater-green-mileage, accessed October 26, 2018.

89. Jim George, "Kraft Says 'Smile' with Updated Macaroni & Cheese," Packaging World, April 10, 2011, https://www.packworld.com/article/applications/food/dairy/kraft-says-smile-updated-macaroni-cheese, accessed October 26, 2018.

90. Lawrence L. Garber Jr., Raymond R. Burke, and J. Morgan Jones, "The Role of Package Color in Consumer Purchase Consideration and Choice," MSI-Report 00-104 (Cambridge, MA: Marketing Science Institute, 2000).

91. See also Peter H. Bloch, "Seeking the Ideal Form—Product Design and Consumer Response," *Journal of Marketing* 59, no. 3 (1995): 16–29; Peter H. Bloch, Frederick F. Brunel, and T. J. Arnold, "Individual Differences in the Centrality of Visual Product Aesthetics: Concept and Measurement," *Journal of Consumer Research* 29, no. 4 (2003): 551–565; Priya Raghubir and Aradna Krishna, "Vital Dimensions in Volume Perception: Can the Eye Fool the Stomach?" *Journal of Marketing Research* 36, no. 3 (August 1999): 313–326; Valerie Folkes, Ingrid Martin, and Kamal Gupta, "When to Say When: Effects of Supply on Usage," *Journal of Consumer Research* 20, no. 3 (December 1993): 467–477; Valerie Folkes and Shashi Matta, "The Effects of Package Shape on Consumers' Judgment of Product Volume: Attention as Mental Containment," *Journal of Consumer Research* 31, no. 2 (September 2004): 390–401.

92. Alina Wheeler, *Designing Brand Identity: An Essential Guide for the Whole Branding Team*, 3rd ed. (Hoboken, NJ: John Wiley & Sons, 2009).

93. Terry L. Childers and Michael J. Houston, "Conditions for a Picture Superiority Effect on Consumer Memory," *Journal of Consumer Research* 11, no. 2 (September 1984): 551–563; Kathy A. Lutz and Richard J. Lutz, "Effects of Interactive Imagery on Learning: Application to Advertising," *Journal of Applied Psychology* 62, no. 4 (1977): 493–498.

94. Jessica Shambora, "David vs. Goliath: Method vs. Clorox," *Fortune*, November 15, 2010, Vol. 162 Issue 8, p. 55; Stuart Elliott, "A Clean Break with Staid Detergent Ads," *The New York Times*, Ilana DeBare, "Cleaning Up without Dot-coms: Belittled Entrepreneurs Choose Household Products Over the High-Tech Industry and Become Highly Successful," *San Francisco Chronicle*, October 8, 2006, https://www.sfgate.com/business/article/Cleaning-up-without-dot-coms-Belittled-2468573.php, accessed October 26, 2018; "Marketers of the Next Generation," *Brandweek,* April 17, 2006, 30.

95. USPTO.Gov, "Trademark, Patent or Copyright," accessed April 22, 2018, www.uspto.gov/trademarks-getting-started/trademark-basics/trademark-patent-or-copyright.

96. Dorothy Cohen, "Trademark Strategy," *Journal of Marketing* 50, no. 1 (January 1986): 61–74; Dorothy Cohen, "Trademark Strategy Revisited," *Journal of Marketing* 55, no. 3 (July 1991): 46–59.

97. For example, see Judy Zaichkowsky, *Defending Your Brand Against Imitation* (Westpoint, CO: Quorom Books, 1995); Judy Zaichkowsky, *The Psychology Behind Trademark Infringement and Counterfeiting* (Mahwah, NJ: Lawrence Erlbaum Associates, 2006); Jerre B. Swann, Sr., David Aaker, and Matt Reback, "Trademarks and Marketing," *The Trademark Reporter* 91 (July–August 2001): 787; and a series of articles by Ross D. Petty in the *Journal of Brand Management*, e.g., "Naming Names: Part Three—Safeguarding Brand Equity in the United States by Developing a Family of Trademarks," *Journal of Brand Management* 17, no. 8 (2010): 561–567.

98. David Stipp, "Farewell, My Logo A Detective Story Counterfeiting Name Brands Is Shaping Up As the Crime of the 21st Century. It Costs U.S. Companies $200 Billion A Year," *Fortune*, May 13, 1996, pp. 128–140, archive.fortune.com/magazines/fortune/fortune_archive/1996/05/13/212869/index.htm, accessed October 26, 2018.

99. Paul F. Kilmer, "Tips for Protecting Brand from Private Label Lawyer," *Advertising Age,* December 5, 1994, 29, https://adage.com/article/news/tips-protecting-brand-private-label-lawyer/89040/, accessed October 26, 2018.

100. Melissa Twigg, "China's Factory Brands: Clones or Clever Business?," *Business of Fashion,* June 31, 2016, www.businessoffashion.com/articles/global-currents/chinas-factory-brands-clones-counterfeits-copycats-business.

101. Greg Erickson, "Seeing Double," *Brandweek,* October 17, 1994, 31–35.

102. Itamar Simonson, "Trademark Infringement from the Buyer Perspective: Conceptual Analysis and Measurement Implications," *Journal of Public Policy & Marketing* 13, no. 2 (Fall 1994): 181–199.

103. Alex Simonson and Morris Holbrook, "Evaluating the Impact of Brand-Name Replications on Product Evaluations," working paper, Marketing Department, Seton Hall University, 1994.

104. Jerre B. Swann, "Dilution Redefined for the Year 2000," *Houston Law Review* 37 (2000): 729.

105. For a detailed discussion of dilution, see Jerre B. Swann, "Dilution Redefined for the Year 2002," *The Trademark Reporter* 92 (May/June 2002): 585–613. See also Maureen Morrin and Jacob Jacoby, "Trademark Dilution: Empirical Measures for an Elusive Concept," *Journal of Public Policy & Marketing* 19, no. 2 (Fall 2000): 265–276; Maureen Morrin, Jonathan Lee, and Greg M. Allenby, "Determinants of Trademark Dilution," *Journal of Consumer Research* 33, no. 2 (September 2006): 248–257; and Chris Pullig, Carolyn J. Simmons, and Richard G. Netemeyer, "Brand Dilution: When Do New Brands Hurt Existing Brands?" *Journal of Marketing* 70, no. 2 (April 2006): 52–66.

106. J. Thomas McCarthy, *McCarthy on Trademarks and Unfair Competition,* 4th ed. (Deerfield, IL: Clark Boardman Callaghan, 1996).

107. Alex Frankel, "Name-o-rama," *Wired,* June 1, 1997, https://www.wired.com/1997/06/es-namemachine/, accessed October 26, 2018.

108. Constance E. Bagley, *Managers and the Legal Environment: Strategies for the 21st Century,* 2nd ed. (Minneapolis, MN: West, 1995).

109. Garry Schuman, "Trademark Protection of Container and Package Configurations—A Primer," *Chicago Kent Law Review* 59 (1982): 779–815.

110. Junda Woo, "Product's Color Alone Can't Get Trademark Protection," *The Wall Street Journal,* January 5, 1994, B8.

111. Alexi Tzatsev, "10 Colors That Might Get You Sued," Business Insider, September 29, 2012, https://www.businessinsider.com/colors-that-are-trademarked-2012-9, accessed August 19, 2018.

112. Joyce Lee, "International Report—China's Continued Trademark Reforms," *iAm-Media,* February 17, 2018, www.iam-media.com/reports/Detail.aspx?g=9d87b306-085d-474c-ab54-72ed13f4ac2b.

Designing Marketing Programs to Build Brand Equity

5

Learning Objectives

After reading this chapter, you should be able to

1. Identify some of the new perspectives and developments in marketing.
2. Describe how marketers enhance product experience.
3. Explain the rationale for value pricing.
4. List some of the direct and indirect channel options.
5. Summarize the reasons for the growth in private labels.

Part of John Deere's success is its well-conceived and executed product, pricing, and channel strategies.

Source: John Crowe/Alamy Stock Photo

PREVIEW

This chapter considers how marketing activities in general—and product, pricing, and distribution strategies in particular—build brand equity. How can marketers integrate these activities to enhance brand awareness, improve the brand image, elicit positive brand responses, and increase brand resonance?

Our focus is on designing marketing activities from a branding perspective. We will consider how the brand itself can be effectively integrated into the marketing program to create brand equity. Of necessity, we leave a broader perspective on marketing activities to basic marketing management texts.[1] We begin by considering some key developments in designing marketing programs. After reviewing product, pricing, and channel strategies, we conclude by considering private label brands in Brand Focus 5.0.

NEW PERSPECTIVES ON MARKETING

The strategy and tactics behind marketing programs have changed dramatically in recent years as firms have experienced enormous shifts in their external marketing environments. As outlined in Chapter 1, changes in the economic, technological, political–legal, sociocultural, and competitive environments have forced marketers to embrace new approaches and philosophies. Some of these changes include[2]

- Rapid technological developments;
- Greater customer empowerment;
- Fragmentation of traditional media;
- Growth of digital and mobile marketing options;
- Channel transformation and disintermediation;
- Increased competition and industry convergence;
- Globalization and growth of developing markets;
- Heightened sustainability concerns, with an increased emphasis on corporate social responsibility; and
- Greater empowerment of consumers because of their ability to influence opinions through social media and word of mouth.

These changes, as well as others such as privatization and regulation, have combined to give customers and companies new capabilities with important implications for the practice of brand management (see Figure 5-1). Marketers are increasingly abandoning the mass-market strategies that built brand powerhouses in the twentieth century to implement new approaches for a new

Consumers

Can wield substantially more customer power.

Can purchase a greater variety of available goods and services.

Can obtain a great amount of information about practically anything.

Can more easily interact with marketers in placing and receiving orders.

Can interact with other consumers and compare notes on products and services.

Companies

Can operate a powerful new information and sales channel with augmented geographic reach to inform and promote their company and its products.

Can collect fuller and richer information about their markets, customers, prospects, and competitors.

Can facilitate two-way communication with their customers and prospects, and facilitate transaction efficiency.

Can send ads, coupons, promotions, and information by e-mail to customers and prospects who give them permission.

Can customize their offerings and services to individual customers.

Can improve their purchasing, recruiting, training, and internal and external communication.

FIGURE 5-1

The New Capabilities of
the New Economy

marketing era. Even marketers in staid, traditional categories and industries are rethinking their practices to go beyond "business as usual."

CLIF BAR

Started in 1990 by avid cyclist Gary Erickson and named to honor his father, CLIF Bar set out to offer a better-tasting energy bar with wholesome ingredients. With little advertising support, the company grew in popularity through the years via word of mouth and public relations. The Clif Bar product line also grew to include dozens of flavors and varieties, including White Chocolate Macadamia, Peanut Toffee Buzz, Maple Nut, and Chocolate Almond Fudge.[3] Some of these flavors were formulated especially for women and children and featured healthful ingredients, such as brown rice syrup and barley malt instead of refined white flour. Behind Clif Bar products is a strong socially and environmentally responsible corporate message, with many ingredients being organically grown (or certified as being organically grown) or grown sustainably.[4]

Clif Bar is active in its local community and known for its passionate employees, who are allowed to do volunteer work on company time. It relies on biodiesel-powered vehicles and supports the construction of farmer- and Native American-owned wind farms through carbon offsets. Its nontraditional marketing activities focus on athletic sponsorships and public events. To broaden its appeal, Clif Bar launched its "Meet the Moment"™ campaign in which participants provide stories and photos of inspirational athletic adventures. The campaign continues to this day, and the Adventure Challenge described on Clif Bar packaging urges consumers to go on an adventure and spread the word on social media using the #MeetTheMoment.[5] The unique integrated marketing campaign features a fully interactive Web site and mobile applications for iPhone and Android systems and touches consumers on a personal level. To further extend its base of customers, Clif Bar also launched the Luna line of bars, which are designed for women's nutritional and energy needs. The Luna brand is further bolstered through its sponsorship of an annual festival called Lunafest, which focuses on films by, about, and for women.

All these marketing efforts have paid off: by 2016, Clif Bar had a 15 percent market share of the nutritional health bar category and far exceeded the market share of large packaged goods manufacturers such as General Mills and Kellogg's. In addition, it exports to more than 18 countries in Asia, Europe, and Australia, with a growth rate of more than 20 percent annually.[6]

CLIF Bar uses a mix of nontraditional and social media advertising to maintain its market share and to build customer engagement.

Source: Editorial Image, LLC/Alamy Stock Photo

INTEGRATING MARKETING

Today's marketplace affords many different means by which products and services and their corresponding marketing programs can build brand equity. Channel strategies, communication strategies, pricing strategies, and other marketing activities can all enhance or detract from brand equity. The customer-based brand equity model provides some useful guidance to interpret these effects. One implication of the conceptualization of customer-based brand equity is that the *manner* in which brand associations are formed does not matter—only the resulting awareness and strength, favorability, and uniqueness of brand associations are important.

The bottom line is that brand equity can be built in many different ways. Unfortunately, many firms are also attempting to build their brand equity in the marketplace. Creative and original thinking is necessary to create fresh new marketing programs that break through the noise in the marketplace to connect with customers. Marketers are increasingly trying a host of unconventional means to build brand equity, as demonstrated in the Branding Brief 5-1 regarding the brand, Yeti.

BRANDING BRIEF 5-1
Yeti Is the "Cooler" Brand

Yeti is a manufacturer of high-quality and expensive coolers that have become status symbols for members of its core target audience, such as hunters and fishers. The brand is known for its authentic messaging, and its coolers range in price from a low of $250 to thousands of dollars. Its best-selling models are small and medium-sized hardcase coolers that fit in the back of a truck or car. Yeti is credited with reinventing this category and for creating an aspirational brand among its target audiences.

A key marketing challenge that the brand has had to overcome is the high sticker price associated with a mundane product (i.e., coolers). So, what are the keys to Yeti's success? The coolers actually work; they keep ice cold for days. However, Yeti needed to convince customers of the value of the product and, to do so, relied on professional endorsements from well-known individuals in hunting and fishing communities. Yeti used some traditional print advertising and placed these endorsement ads in hunting and fishing programs on Outdoor Channel, along with marketing on specialized networks such as Sportsman, World Fishing Network, and so forth. Its credibility got a further boost when the company received an endorsement from the Interagency Grizzly Bear Committee that the coolers were "grizzly proof."

To build awareness among its target audiences, Yeti has also made considerable investments in social media. To further create excitement for the brand, Yeti invested in apparel and merchandise, such as branded hats, T-shirts, and bottle openers, and included these with every cooler purchased, ensuring increased buzz about its products. The company has also invested significantly in data analytics to personalize the content audiences receive, based on historical data on prior purchase behavior, favorite outdoor adventures, and so on. Yeti also ensures that the varying touchpoints are well-orchestrated to provide a unified experience. By relying on a combination of traditional and non-traditional approaches, combining online and offline advertising, and deploying personalized marketing approaches, Yeti has been successful in creating an aspirational brand.

The Yeti brand of coolers is seen as a status symbol, thanks to high quality, authentic messaging and the use of nontraditional/social media marketing.

The Yeti brand grew from $5 million in 2009 to $450 million in 2016 and is now facing a new set of challenges. Competition in the high-end cooler market has increased with the entry of brands such as Igloo's Sportsman, Orion 45, and Cabela's Polar Cap. Therefore, the company has to work extremely hard to maintain its appeal and authenticity. To do so, Yeti has become more deliberate in its use of social media marketing. For example, it produces and distributes short videos that glorify the outdoors. By depicting rugged and intrepid outdoorsy types such as a legendary Rio Grande Valley fly fisherman or a female Grand Canyon river guide navigating the great outdoors, these movies (posted on its Web site) are intended to retain the interest of hunters and fishers who are core targets of the brand, even though the brand has grown beyond these audiences. Yeti products are only featured briefly in these videos. The brand also posts fan-submitted photos of wildlife and outdoors on its Instagram page. Thus, using effective storytelling allows Yeti to connect with customers at an emotional level, which allows the brand to build enduring consumer–brand relationships.

Sources: Ashley Rodriguez, "How Yeti Made a Cooler an Aspirational Brand," October 6, 2014, http://adage.com/article/cmo-strategy/high-priced-yeti-coolers-aspirational-brand/295243/, accessed March 10, 2018; Salesforce.com, "YETI Coolers Launches New Digital Shopping Experience on Salesforce Commerce Cloud," January 16, 2018, www.prnewswire.com/news-releases/yeti-coolers-launches-new-digital-shopping-experience-on-salesforce-commerce-cloud-300582825.html, accessed March 1, 2018; Hunter Atkins, "Why Is Yeti Coolers Producing Really Cool Movies?," April 20, 2016, www.forbes.com/sites/hunteratkins/2016/04/20/why-is-yeti-coolers-producing-really-cool-movies/#424bbc823f7e, accessed March 1, 2018; Michael Shea, "Ice-Chest Throwdown," March 25, 2016, www.fieldandstream.com/articles/fishing/2016/03/ice-chest-throwdown-12-top-end-coolers-ranked-and-reviewed, accessed March 10, 2018.

Creativity must not sacrifice a brand-building goal, however, and marketers must orchestrate programs to provide seamlessly integrated solutions and personalized experiences for customers that create awareness, spur demand, and cultivate loyalty.

Personalizing Marketing

The rapid expansion of the Internet and continued fragmentation of mass media have brought the need for personalized marketing into sharp focus. Many pundits maintain that the modern economy celebrates the power of the individual consumer. To adapt to the increased consumer desire for personalization, marketers have embraced concepts such as experiential marketing and relationship marketing. Branded experiences are playing an increasingly important role in helping forge a personal connection with consumers, and the next section provides an overview along with some examples of the role of experiences in building consumer–brand relationships.

Experiential Marketing.   *Experiential marketing* promotes a product not only by communicating a product's features and benefits but also by connecting it with unique and interesting consumer experiences. One marketing commentator describes experiential marketing this way: "The idea is not to sell something, but to demonstrate how a brand can enrich a customer's life."[7]

Pine and Gilmore, pioneers on the topic, argued more than a decade ago that we are on the threshold of the "Experience Economy," a new economic era in which all companies must orchestrate memorable events for their customers.[8] They made the following assertions:

- If you charge for stuff, then you are in the *commodity business.*
- If you charge for tangible things, then you are in the *goods business.*
- If you charge for the activities you perform, then you are in the *service business.*
- If you charge for the time that customers spend with you, then and only then are you in the *experience business.*

Citing a range of examples from Disney to AOL, they maintain that salable experiences come in four forms: entertainment, education, aesthetic, and escapist.

Columbia University's Bernd Schmitt, another pioneering expert on the subject, notes that "experiential marketing is usually broadly defined as any form of customer-focused marketing activity, at various touchpoints, that creates a sensory-emotional connection to customers."[9] Figure 5-2 displays a scale developed by Schmitt and his colleagues to measure experiences and its dimensions. Their study respondents rated Lego, Victoria's Secret, iPod, and Starbucks as the most experiential brands.[10]

Meyer and Schwager describe a customer experience management (CEM) process that involves monitoring three different patterns: past patterns (evaluating completed transactions), present patterns (tracking current relationships), and potential patterns (conducting inquiries in the hope of unveiling future opportunities).[11] Brands are investing in unique experiences that allow consumers to enjoy memorable experiences without feeling that they are being marketed to. For example, the U.S. drive-in restaurant Sonic used the Coachella Arts and Music Festival to showcase its milkshakes and smoothies. Recognizing that purchases made at the festival are typically posted on Instagram, Sonic created a unique square milkshake featuring premium flavors and ingredients, expecting

Victoria's Secret has been praised for its success in creating an experiential brand.

Source: Louis Johnny/SIPA/Newscom

SENSORY	This brand makes a strong impression on my visual sense or other senses.
	I find this brand interesting in a sensory way.
	This brand does not appeal to my senses.
AFFECTIVE	This brand induces feelings and sentiments.
	I do not have strong emotions for this brand.
	This brand is an emotional brand.
BEHAVIORAL	I engage in physical actions and behaviors when I use this brand.
	This brand results in bodily experiences.
	This brand is not action oriented.
INTELLECTUAL	I engage in a lot of thinking when I encounter this brand.
	This brand does not make me think.
	This brand stimulates my curiosity and problem solving.

FIGURE 5-2

Brand Experience Scale

Source: Based on J. Joško Brakus, Bernd H. Schmitt, and Lia Zarantonello, "Brand Experience: What Is It? How Is It Measured? Does It Affect Loyalty?," *Journal of Marketing* 73 (May 2009): 52–68.

consumers to share the unique product on Instagram.[12] The company also used geo-fencing to allow festivalgoers to place orders using the "Shop Now" button.

Another example of branded experiences is the programs launched by Van Cleef & Arpels into the world of jewelry and watchmaking.[13] In 2012, this well-known jewelry design house launched a program for people interested in learning more about the secret world of jewelry and watchmaking. The program was intended to increase knowledge and help the public gain a better understanding of the crafts behind jewelry making. The company created various four-hour classes given in French and English around three broad themes: *Savoir-Faire* (know-how), Art History of Jewels, and the Universe of Gemstones.[14] In these classes, guests learn how to appreciate design and craftsmanship and are guided through the process of creating fine works. In this way, the brand reinforces quality perceptions and enables customers to obtain new information about the brand, thereby making it seem more accessible.

More generally, the advantages of these experiences are threefold. First, they help expand brand awareness among new segments of consumers (e.g., arts and music festivalgoers). Second, they build brand buzz by encouraging participants to share their experiences on social media, thus helping to increase social media engagement. For example, promoting its milkshakes at Coachella increased the Sonic brand's Instagram followers by 11,000 and generated 26,000 likes.[15] Third, these types of experiences can help reshape consumers' perceptions of the brand. For example, the Van Cleef & Arpels programs on jewelry making helped shape the audiences' perception of the value of different products within the category and reinforced the brand's positioning as a high-quality product.

Relationship Marketing.   Marketing strategies must transcend the actual product or service to create stronger bonds with consumers and maximize brand resonance. As we described previously, an important distinction with brand experiences is that experiences allow brands to focus on topics of interest to their key target audiences (rather than the brand itself), which drives engagement and increases resonance.[16] Analogously, the role of relationship marketing is to put customers' needs front and center of everything that is done in marketing.

This broader set of activities is sometimes called *relationship marketing* and is based on the premise that current customers are the key to long-term brand success.[17] Relationship marketing attempts to provide a more holistic, personalized brand experience to create stronger consumer ties. It expands both the depth and the breadth of brand-building marketing programs.

The following are just a few of the basic benefits relationship marketing provides:[18]

- Acquiring new customers can cost five times as much as satisfying and retaining current customers.
- The average company loses 10 percent of its customers each year.

- A 5 percent reduction in the customer defection rate can increase profits by 25 to 85 percent, depending on the industry.
- The customer profit rate tends to increase over the life of the retained customer.

We outline three concepts that can be helpful in relationship marketing: mass customization, personalization/one-to-one marketing, and permission marketing.

Mass Customization.   The concept behind mass customization—namely, making products to fit customers' exact specifications—is an old one, but new digital-age technology now enables companies to offer customized products on a previously unheard-of scale. By going online, customers can communicate their preferences directly to the manufacturer, which, by using advanced production methods, can assemble the product for a price comparable to that of a non-customized item.

In an age defined by the pervasiveness of mass-market goods, mass customization enables consumers to distinguish themselves with even basic purchases. Mass customization is not restricted to products; many service organizations, such as banks, have developed customer-specific services, with the aim to improve the personal nature of the service experience with more service options, more customer-contact personnel, and longer service hours.[19]

With the advent of social media and the availability of vast troves of customer data (e.g., click-stream data, including Web site traffic and engagement metrics), companies are in an excellent position to tailor offerings to individual customers, in a highly targeted way. However, companies must also evolve their offerings to tap into real value or emotional drivers that influence customer purchases.[20] One way to do this is to involve customers in the purchase process, and customers are now in a position to co-create their offerings with firms. For example, Nike enables customers to put their own personalized message on a pair of shoes with the NIKEiD program. At the NIKEiD Web site, visitors can make a customized shoe by selecting the size, width, and color scheme and affixing an eight-character personal ID to their creation. Then, they can share their shoes with others to admire.[21]

Another feature that has ramped up in recent times is the emphasis on location-based marketing, in which companies tailor and customize their offerings depending on where customers live. With this approach, the Spartan Race organization (which sponsors races in various locations) was able to target its e-mail marketing to recipients' locations and saw an increase of 50 percent in Web site traffic, a 25 percent increase in new users, and a 13 percent improvement in conversions.[22] An example of a highly successful relationship marketing program comes from Tesco, the United Kingdom's largest grocer.

With NIKEiD, customers can customize their shoes and share their creations with others online.

Source: Getty Images/Getty Images for Nike

TESCO

Celebrating its 15th anniversary in 2010, Tesco Clubcard is one of the world's most successful retail loyalty schemes. Each of the 10 million members in the program has a unique "DNA profile" based on the products he or she buys. Products themselves are classified on up to 40 dimensions—such as package size, healthy, own label, eco-friendly, and ready-to-eat—to facilitate this customer categorization. In exchange for providing their purchase information and basic demographic information, members receive a variety of purchase benefits across a wide range of products and services beyond what is sold in the stores. Tracking customers' purchases in the program, in turn, helps Tesco uncover price elasticities, offer targeted promotions, and improve marketing efficiency. By also strengthening customer loyalty, the Clubcard program has been estimated to generate cumulative savings to Tesco of more than £350 million. The range of products, the nature of merchandising, and even the location of Tesco's convenience stores all benefit from the use of these customer data to develop tailored solutions. Tesco has introduced several Clubcard program innovations through the years, including key fobs and newly designed cards issued in 2008.[23] Despite these innovations, Tesco went through a period of losses, and customers lost trust in the brand. However, the company began turning around through a relentless focus on the customer, by cutting prices, and by improving customer service.[24] Investments in digital channels and reduced emphasis on television advertising have also been key changes to Tesco's marketing.

Tesco's Clubcard is the centerpiece of one of the world's most successful retail loyalty programs.
Source: Kevin Britland/Alamy Stock Photo

Permission Marketing. *Permission marketing*, the practice of marketing to consumers only after gaining their express permission, is another influential perspective on how companies can break through the clutter and build customer loyalty. A pioneer on the topic, Seth Godin, has noted that marketers can no longer employ "interruption marketing" or mass-media campaigns featuring magazines, direct mail, billboards, radio and television commercials, and the like because consumers have come to expect—but not necessarily appreciate—these interruptions.[25] Seth defined "permission marketing" as anticipated (people look forward to hearing from you), personal (messages pertain directly to individuals), and relevant (the focus of the effort is of interest to the prospect).[26]

Given the large number of marketing communications that bombard consumers every day, Godin argues that if marketers want to attract a consumer's attention, they first need to get his or her permission with some type of inducement—a free sample, a sales promotion or discount, a contest, and so on. By eliciting consumer cooperation in this manner, marketers *might* develop stronger relationships with consumers so that they will want to receive further communications in the future. Those relationships will develop, however, only if marketers respect consumers' wishes, and if consumers express a willingness to become more involved with the brand.[27]

E-mail is one of the main tools permission marketers employ, even though social media is increasingly being used to send information to interested prospects. With the help of large databases and advanced software, companies can store gigabytes of customer data and process this information to send targeted, personalized marketing messages to customers. For example, Facebook Connect is an application that allows users to interact with various Web sites through their Facebook account. Users can also post updates to their Facebook page while using a third-party Web site or app. These features make Facebook Connect a source of information about users to marketers, giving advertisers more access to user information. This technology also allows brands to establish permission-based relationships with their users on their own Web sites. When users are comfortable with sharing information with social networking sites, they are more likely to share information with Web sites linked through Facebook Connect.[28]

Godin identifies five steps to effective permission marketing:[29]

1. **Situational permission:** Prospects permit the company to access their personal information.
2. **Brand trust:** Prospects allow the company to provide for their needs.
3. **Personal relationship:** Prospects offer information based on a personal relationship with the provider's organization.
4. **Incentive-based permission:** Incentives such as points or free prizes are used to maintain permission to access customer data.
5. **Intravenous permission:** Customers become dependent on the company, and the supplier controls the supply of certain goods or services.

Across each of these stages, brands should carefully manage their relationships with customers to ensure they are not misusing the permissions granted to them by the customer. The U.K.-based bank Mondo was noted for its carefully worded, low-pressure marketing offer to its customers in return for gaining their permission to market to them. The statement read "We'll only send you an email when we've got something interesting to show, or something cool for you to try."[30]

Permission marketing poses significant risks to marketers. Many public interest groups as well as the U.S. Federal Trade Commission (FTC) are penalizing companies that collect data on customers without explicitly obtaining permission from them. For example, in 2014, the FTC filed a lawsuit against television manufacturer Vizio, alleging that the company was automatically tracking what consumers were watching and relaying it back to its services, without clearly informing consumers or obtaining consent.[31] Furthermore, Vizio turned all that information into profit, by selling consumers' viewing histories (including highly identifiable and personal information such as IP addresses) to data aggregators and advertisers. Vizio used the term "Smart Interactivity" to describe the tracking behavior to customers. The company eventually agreed to pay $2.2 million to settle the charges.[32] These types of instances show that establishing consumer permissions and obtaining consent should be a high priority for brands.

According to survey data, consumers are generally aware of data privacy issues associated with online vendors. According to one global survey, 55 percent of the consumers surveyed had decided against buying something because of privacy concerns, while another survey of consumers in specific industries, such as financial services, indicates that 84 percent of respondents are concerned about the security of their personal data.[33] More ad blockers are being downloaded today than previously, and search engines such as DuckDuckGo (which promises not to track users) are growing in popularity, suggesting that permission marketing has entered a new phase. Some critics have argued that in this new era, brands should relinquish control over consumers' personal data and allow users to control how their data will be used.[34] Others have argued for more customer-friendly approaches to data management in which consumers opt-in to have their data shared with marketers, as opposed to the opt-out model (in which the system defaults to sharing information). Regarding these developments, *participation marketing* or *engagement marketing* may replace the *permission marketing* era, as marketers and consumers increasingly try to work together to find how firms can best satisfy consumer goals.[35]

Search engines such as DuckDuckGo are popular among consumers who care about privacy because they do not track customers' browsing behavior.

Reconciling the Different Marketing Approaches

These and other different approaches to personalization help to reinforce important marketing concepts and techniques. From a branding standpoint, they are particularly useful means of both eliciting positive brand responses and creating brand resonance to build customer-based brand equity. Mass customization and one-to-one and permission marketing are all potentially effective ways to get consumers more actively engaged with a brand.

According to the customer-based brand equity model, however, these various approaches emphasize different aspects of brand equity. For example, mass customization and one-to-one and permission (or participation) marketing are particularly effective at creating greater relevance, stronger behavioral loyalty, and attitudinal attachment. Conversely, experiential marketing is particularly effective at establishing brand imagery and tapping into a variety of feelings as well as helping build brand communities. Despite potentially different areas of emphasis, all four approaches can build stronger consumer–brand bonds.

An implication of these new approaches is that the traditional "marketing mix" concept and the notion of the "4 Ps" of marketing—product, price, place (or distribution), and promotion (or marketing communications)—may not fully describe modern marketing programs or the many activities, such as loyalty programs or pop-up stores that may not necessarily fit neatly into one of those designations. Nevertheless, firms still need to make decisions about what exactly they are going to sell, how (and where) they are going to sell it, and at what price. In other words, firms must still devise product, pricing, and distribution strategies as part of their marketing programs.

The specifics of how they set those strategies, however, have changed considerably. We turn next to these topics and highlight a key development in each area, recognizing that there are many other important areas beyond the scope of this text. With product strategy, we emphasize the role of extrinsic factors; with pricing strategy, we focus on value pricing; and with channel strategy, we concentrate on channel integration.

PRODUCT STRATEGY

The product itself is the primary determinant of what consumers experience with a brand, what they hear about a brand from others, and what the firm can tell customers about the brand. At the heart of a great brand is invariably a great product.

Designing and delivering a product or service that fully satisfies consumer needs and wants is a prerequisite for successful marketing, regardless of whether the product is a tangible good, service, or organization. For brand loyalty to exist, consumers' experiences with the product must at least meet, if not surpass, their expectations. After considering how consumers form their opinions of the quality and value of a product, we consider how marketers can go beyond the actual product to enhance product experiences and add additional value before, during, and after product use.

Perceived Quality

Perceived quality is customers' perceptions of the overall quality or superiority of a product or service compared with alternatives and with respect to its intended purpose. Achieving a satisfactory level of perceived quality has become more difficult for companies as continual product improvements over the years have led to heightened consumer expectations.[36]

A wealth of research has tried to understand how consumers form their opinions about quality. The specific attributes of product quality can vary from category to category. Nevertheless, consistent with the brand resonance model from Chapter 3, research has identified the following general dimensions: primary ingredients and supplementary features; product reliability, durability, and serviceability; and style and design.[37] Consumer beliefs about these characteristics often define quality and, in turn, influence attitudes and behavior toward a brand. Product quality depends not only on functional product performance but broader performance considerations as well, such as speed, accuracy, and care of product delivery and installation; the promptness, courtesy, and helpfulness of customer service and training; and the quality of repair service.

Brand attitudes may also depend on more abstract product imagery, such as the symbolism or personality reflected in the brand. These "augmented" aspects of a product are often crucial to its equity. Finally, consumer evaluations may not correspond to the perceived quality of the product and may be formed by less thoughtful decision making, such as simple heuristics and decision rules based on brand reputation or product characteristics such as color or scent.

Managing Customers Post-Purchase

To achieve the desired brand image, product strategies should focus on both purchase *and* consumption. A great deal of marketing activity is devoted to finding ways to encourage trial and repeat purchases by consumers. Perhaps the strongest and potentially most favorable associations, however, come from actual product experiences—what Procter & Gamble calls the "second moment of truth" (the "first moment of truth" occurs at purchase).

Unfortunately, too little marketing attention is devoted to finding new ways for consumers to truly appreciate the advantages and capabilities of products. Perhaps in response to this oversight, one notable trend in marketing is the emphasis on the post-purchase phase of the consumer decision-making process. Marketing in this phase is sometimes referred to as *aftermarketing*—that is, the marketing activities that occur *after* customer purchase. Innovative design, thorough testing, quality production, and effective communication—through mass customization or any other means—are without question the most important considerations in enhancing product consumption experiences that build brand equity.

Post-purchase marketing or aftermarket is particularly important in the context of e-commerce. Companies such as Zappos have made their mark primarily through their aftermarketing efforts, which involves integrating their support operations with an e-commerce platform, to ensure seamless integration across the two. Also, ensuring that the company's contact information is accessible and support is available to customers across a multitude of channels (e.g., phone, web, live chat) is critical to enhancing customers' post-purchase experience.[38]

User Manuals.   Instruction or *user manuals* for many products are too often an afterthought, put together by engineers who use overly technical terms and convoluted language. As a result, consumers' initial product experiences may be frustrating or, even worse, unsuccessful. Even if consumers can figure out how to use the product's basic functions, they may not learn to appreciate some of its more advanced features, which are usually highly desirable and possibly unique to the brand.

To enhance consumers' consumption experiences, marketers must develop user manuals or help features that clearly and comprehensively describe both what the product or service can do and how consumers can realize these benefits. With increasing globalization, writing easy-to-use instructions has become even more important because they often require translation into multiple languages.[39] Manufacturers are spending more time designing and testing instructions to make them as user-friendly as possible.

User manuals increasingly may need to appear in online and multimedia formats to most effectively demonstrate product functions and benefits. Intuit, makers of the Quicken personal finance management software package, routinely sends researchers home with first-time buyers to check that its software is easy to install and to identify any sources of problems that might arise. Corel software adopts a similar "Follow Me Home" strategy and also has "pizza parties" at the company where marketing, engineering, and quality assurance teams analyze the market research together so that marketing does not just hand down conclusions to other departments.[40]

Customer Service Programs.   However, aftermarketing is more than the design and communication of product instructions. As one expert in the area notes, "The term 'aftermarketing' describes a necessary new mindset that reminds businesses of the importance of building a lasting relationship with customers, to extend their lifetimes. It also points to the crucial need to better balance the allocation of marketing funds between conquest activities (like advertising) and retention activities (like customer communication programs)."[41] Customer service plays an important role in the post-purchase phase. Investments in customer service offer multiple benefits, including the ability to connect with customers and gain valuable feedback.

One study examined Twitter data on customer service interactions in the airline and wireless carrier industry and found that when customers had interacted with a brand's customer service representative on Twitter, they were significantly more willing to choose the brand from a set of

Sephora is an example of a company that uses its online community of users to provide customer service.

Source: Patti McConville/Alamy Stock Photo

competitors and were also willing to pay more for the brand. In the airline industry, for example, these same customers were willing to pay $9 more than those who had not interacted with a customer service representative on social media.[42] Customer service agents who added initials or signatures to their responses were able to elicit an even better response, and customers were willing to pay a premium of $14 after their interactions.

Bad customer service, on the other hand, can create significant negative publicity and with the help of social media, has the potential to go viral and damage the reputation of the company. American Airlines was subject to ridicule on the Internet when it responded to a sarcastic customer complaint which began with the word "congratulations." Without having read the complaint fully, American Airlines customer service mistook this message for a compliment and responded with a canned message thanking the customer for their support. In fact, the message went on to complain about the company. Incidents like this can tarnish a brand's customer service reputation because of the speed with which they can spread on the Internet.[43]

In recent years, to strengthen ties with customers, companies are turning to brand communities to help enhance the support provided to customers and quickly resolve technical issues. Nearly half of all companies with brand communities can reduce customer support costs by 10 to 25 percent.[44] A good example of this is Sephora's community Beauty Talk, which allows users to post questions and share ideas about Sephora products. Brand enthusiasts are fully engaged with helping answer questions asked about Sephora beauty products by others in the online community. In this way, Sephora has effectively used its online branded community as a vehicle for enhancing customer service. Microsoft's Xbox community is another example of a brand community that helps with customer service. The community is made up of Xbox enthusiasts who are often involved in providing support on Xbox forums, creating YouTube videos, and providing product feedback. These enthusiasts often have achieved a minimum game score to qualify to become a brand ambassador and are rewarded with games, branded merchandise, and the like.

Companies can also gain significant benefits from cross-selling and up-selling following good customer service. Post-purchase marketing can include the sale of complementary products that help make up a system or, in any other way, enhance the value of the core product. Printer manufacturers such as Hewlett-Packard derive much of their revenue from high-margin post-purchase items such as ink-jet cartridges, laser toner cartridges, and paper specially designed for PC printers. The average owner of a home PC printer spends more on consumables over the life of the machine than on the machine itself.[45]

Aftermarketing can be an important determinant of profitability. According to a McKinsey & Co. study across 30 industries, the provision of aftermarket services, such as parts, repair, maintenance, and digital services, resulted in earnings of 25 percent, compared to 10 percent for new equipment.[46] Aftermarket sales are strongest when customers are locked into buying from the company that sold them the primary product, due to service contracts, proprietary technology or patents, or unique service expertise.[47] The percentage of original equipment manufacturer products sold with a service contract reflects the *attach rate* or the *share of lifetime*—that is, the percentage of a product's lifetime in which the manufacturer is the primary service provider. Together, the attach rate and the share of lifetime determine the lifetime penetration, which contributes to aftermarket profitability.[48]

Loyalty Programs.   *Loyalty* or *frequency programs* have become a popular means by which marketers can create stronger ties to customers.[49] Their purpose is "identifying, maintaining, and increasing the yield from a firm's 'best' customers through long-term, interactive, value-added relationships."[50] Firms in all kinds of industries—most notably the airlines—have established loyalty programs through different mixtures of specialized services, newsletters, premiums, and incentives. Often, they include extensive co-branding arrangements or brand alliances. With the growth of mobile commerce and digital payments (e.g., PayPal and Apple Pay), loyalty programs can be integrated into e-commerce transactions quite easily. Branded apps can be used to maintain relationships with customers, administer loyalty programs, and allow customers to transact with the firm. For example, in addition to helping customers make payments, the Starbucks app keeps track of rewards for customer loyalty, thereby aiding in brand building.[51]

In 1981, American Airlines founded the first airline loyalty program, Advantage. This frequent-flier program rewarded the airline's top customers with free trips and upgrades based on mileage flown. Many companies in addition to the airlines introduced loyalty programs in the intervening years because they often yield positive results.[52] Loyalty programs reduce defection rates and increase retention, and the value created by the loyalty program creates switching costs for consumers, reducing price competition among brands. To get discounts, however, consumers must typically hand over personal data, raising privacy concerns.

The appeal to marketers is clear as well. Most loyalty marketers employ sophisticated databases and software to determine which customer segments to target with a given program. However, loyalty programs are increasingly finding it difficult and costly to maintain, given the proliferation of such programs. Companies must constantly update the program to attract new customers and prevent other companies in their category from developing "me-too" programs.[53] Suggestions and complaints from top customers deserve careful consideration, because they can lead to improvements in the program. Because they typically represent a large percentage of business, top customers must also receive better service and more attention. It is also helpful if the program is easy to use and offers immediate rewards when customers sign up. After they become members, many companies also try to make customers "feel special" by, for example, sending them birthday greetings, special offers, or invitations to special events.

The product is at the heart of brand equity. Product strategy entails choosing both the tangible and intangible benefits the product will embody and marketing activities that consumers desire and the marketing program can deliver. A range of possible associations can be linked to the brand— some functional and performance related, and some abstract and imagery related. Perceived quality and perceived value are particularly important brand associations that often drive consumer decisions.

PRICING STRATEGY

Price is the one revenue-generating element of the traditional marketing mix, and price premiums are among the most important benefits of building a strong brand. This section considers the different price perceptions that consumers might form and the different pricing strategies firms might adopt to build brand equity. The increasingly competitive retail environment and the increasing dominance of online retailing have posed significant pricing challenges for many brands. The Science of Branding 5-1 outlines key insights generated from research on pricing.

THE SCIENCE OF BRANDING 5-1

Understanding Consumer Price Perceptions

Economists traditionally assumed that consumers were "price takers" who accepted prices as given. However, as Ofir and Winer note, consumers often actively process price information, interpreting prices from knowledge acquired from past purchasing experience, formal corporate communications (e.g., advertising), informal communications with friends or family members, and point-of-purchase or online information. Consumers' purchase decisions are based on perceived prices and not on the marketer's stated value. Understanding how consumers arrive at their perceptions of prices is thus an important marketing priority.

A wealth of research has shown that surprisingly few consumers can recall specific prices of products accurately, though they may have a fairly good idea of the relevant range of prices. When examining or considering price, however, consumers often compare it with internal frames of reference (prices they remember) or external frames of reference (a posted "regular retail price"). Internal reference prices occur in many forms, including the following:

- "Fair price" (what the product should cost)
- Typical price
- Last price paid
- Upper-bound price (the most consumer would pay)
- Lower-bound price (the least consumer would pay)
- Competitive prices
- Expected future price
- Usual discounted price

When one or more of these frames of reference comes to mind, consumers' perceived price can vary from the stated price.

Most research on reference prices has found that "unpleasant surprises," such as a higher stated price than the perceived price, have a greater impact on purchase likelihood than pleasant surprises.

Alternative pricing strategies also affect consumers' perceptions of prices. For example, research has shown that a relatively expensive item can seem less expensive if the price is broken down into smaller units (a $500 annual membership seems pricier than "less than $50 a month"). One reason prices often end with the number nine (e.g., $49.99) is that consumers process prices in a left-to-right manner rather than holistically or by rounding. This effect is more pronounced when competing products' prices are numerically and psychologically close together. Another study shows that package size affects perceived quality, such that consumers believe that the identical product in a smaller package, by influencing perceptions of unit prices, is seen to be of higher quality than if in a larger package.

Sources: Chezy Ofir and Russell S. Winer, "Pricing: Economic and Behavioral Models," in *Handbook of Marketing*, eds. Bart Weitz and Robin Wensley (New York: Sage Publications, 2002): 5–86; John T. Gourville, "Pennies-a-Day: The Effect of Temporal Reframing on Transaction Evaluation," *Journal of Consumer Research* 24, no. 4 (March 1998): 395–408; Manoj Thomas and Vicki Morwitz, "Penny Wise and Pound Foolish: The Left-Digit Effect in Price Cognition," *Journal of Consumer Research* 26 (June 2005): 54–64; Eric Anderson and Duncan Simester, "Mind Your Pricing Cues," *Harvard Business Review* 81, no. 9 (September 2003): 96–103; Tridib Mazumdar, S. P. Raj, and Indrajit Sinha, "Reference Price Research: Review and Propositions," *Journal of Marketing* 69 (October 2005): 84–102; Yan, Dengfeng, Jaideep Sengupta, and Robert S. Wyer. "Package Size and Perceived Quality: The Intervening Role of Unit Price Perceptions." *Journal of Consumer Psychology* 24, no. 1 (2014): 4–17.

Consumer Price Perceptions and Setting Prices

Choosing a pricing strategy to build brand equity means determining

- A method for setting current prices, and
- A policy for choosing the depth and duration of promotions and discounts.

There are many different approaches to setting prices, and the choice depends on various considerations. This section highlights a few of the most important issues as they relate to brand equity.[54]

Factors related to the costs of making and selling products and the relative prices of competitive products are important determinants in pricing strategy. Increasingly, however, firms are putting greater importance on consumer perceptions and preferences. Consumers perceptions of pricing are based on price tiers in a category.[55] For example, Figure 5-3 shows the price tiers that resulted from a study of the ice cream market.[56] In that market, as the figure shows, the price is also related to quality.

Within any price tier is a range of acceptable prices, called *price bands*, that indicate the flexibility and breadth marketers can adopt in pricing their brands. Some companies sell multiple brands to better compete in multiple categories. Figure 5-4 displays clothing offerings from PVH Corp. (formerly Phillips-Van Heusen) that, at one time, covered a wide range of prices and corresponding retail outlets.[57]

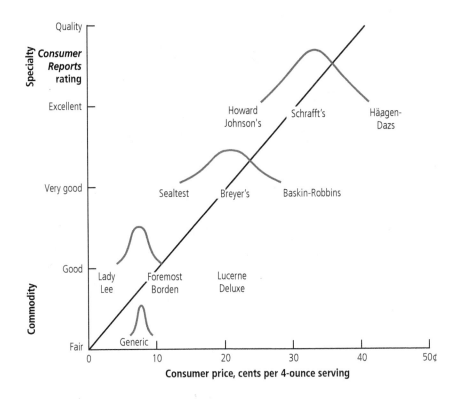

FIGURE 5-3

Price Tiers in the Ice Cream Market

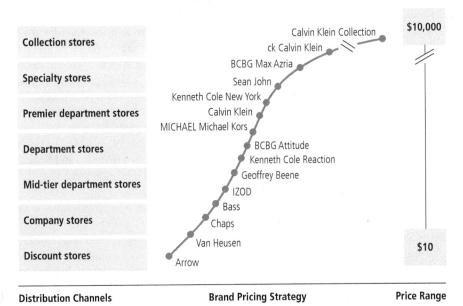

FIGURE 5-4

Services Provided by Channel Members

Source: Reprinted from Donald Lehmann and Russell Winer, *Product Management,* 2nd ed. (Burr Ridge, IL: Irwin, 1997), Figure 13-8 on p. 379. © The McGraw-Hill Companies.

Consumer associations of perceived value are often an important factor in purchase decisions. Thus, many marketers have adopted *value-based pricing strategies* in an attempt to sell the right product at the right price to meet consumer wishes better, as described in the next section. Consumers may have price perceptions and may infer the quality of a product by its price. An integral component of the perceived value of a product is the cost of a product. Costs here are not restricted to the actual monetary price but may reflect opportunity costs of time, energy, and any psychological involvement on the part of the consumer.[58]

In addition to value-based pricing, consumers' price perceptions can be shaped by other ways pricing is implemented. Two other types of pricing strategies are described next. One pricing approach is the razor-and-blades pricing model. For example, in this approach, the Gillette Pro-Glide razor costs approximately $10 online, but after purchasing the razor, customers are locked in because of the proprietary blade technology and razor-blade interface.

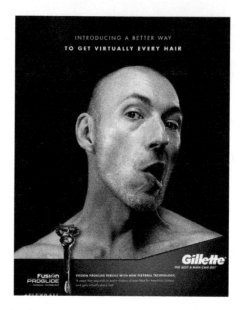

Famous athletes and celebrities, such as NBA player Tony Parker, WWE wrestler John Cena, and TV sportscaster Erin Andrews, have promoted Gillette's latest Fusion ProGlide razor and its innovative performance features.

Source: The Advertising Archives/Alamy Stock Photo

Even customers with a limited budget become bound to buying the product because the initial price for the durable component is very accessible.[59] Several other industries have used the razor-and-blades pricing model. For example, in the traditional printer pricing model, the printer itself is priced at an accessible low rate, while the printer manufacturer makes a profit on selling cartridges. The razor-and-blades pricing model has begun losing its appeal however, as consumers have increasingly expressed frustration at being locked into a single system. In response, companies are moving away from constraints imposed on customers in the post-purchase phase. For example, Epson printer has introduced the new model Ecotank, which replaces the printer cartridge (which is typically expensive) with a large, refillable ink tank.[60]

In another variation of the pricing approach is the freemium model, in which many start-up companies first launch a free service. Companies such as Dropbox, LinkedIn, and Spotify have all grown to prominence by using the freemium model.[61] After building a large installed base, those who use the freemium model then promote a premium tier, which has a price attached to it. For example, Dropbox, a file-sharing and cloud storage service, provides customers with 2 GB of free storage and then charges customers for additional storage. Customers can get additional storage by providing referrals. Dropbox Plus offers one terabyte of space and additional features for approximately $9.99 per month. Dropbox has more than 500 million total users, which points to the success of the freemium model.[62] A 2 to 5 percent conversion rate of free to premium customers is considered average across companies embracing the freemium model.[63] Despite its apparent advantages, companies need to be cognizant that this model could potentially weaken the company if the cost of servicing customers for free turns out to be too high, relative to the number of premium customers who form part of the installed base. To ensure a healthy mix of free and premium customers, companies should work to provide good value for their premium customers and to clarify the value proposition relative to that for free customers. For this model to be effective, firms must ensure sufficient conversion among free customers to the premium-pricing tier.

Another pricing model that companies have used in recent years is pay-as-you-wish pricing. For example, Panera Cares Community Cafes operate under this model.[64] The pricing strategy can dictate how consumers categorize the price of the brand (as low, medium, or high) and how firm or flexible they think the price is, based on how deeply or frequently it is discounted.

In short, the price has complex meanings and can play multiple roles in consumers' decision making. As you have seen, The Science of Branding 5-1 provided insights into how consumers perceive and process prices as part of their shopping behavior. Marketers need to understand all price perceptions that consumers have of a brand, to uncover quality and value inferences and to discover any price premiums that exist.

Many firms are now employing a value-pricing approach to setting prices and an everyday-low-pricing (EDLP) approach to determining their discount pricing policy over time. Let's look at both.

Value Pricing.   The objective of *value pricing* is to uncover the right blend of product quality, product costs, and product prices that fully satisfy the needs and wants of consumers and the profit targets of the firm. Marketers have employed value pricing in various ways for years, sometimes learning the hard way that consumers will not pay price premiums that exceed their perceptions of the value of a brand.

In today's challenging new climate, several firms have been successful in adopting a value-pricing strategy. Southwest Airlines combined low fares with no-frills service to become a powerful force in the airline industry. The success of this and other firms has dramatized the potential benefits of implementing a value-pricing strategy.

As you might expect, companies can select among any number of opinions when adopting a value-based pricing approach. In general, however, a successful value-pricing strategy should strike the proper balance among three key components:

- Product design and delivery,
- Product costs, and
- Product prices.

In other words, the right kind of product must be made the right way and sold at the right price. We examine each of these three elements in the following section. A brand that has experienced great success in recent years by balancing this formula is Hyundai.

HYUNDAI

Taking a page from the Samsung playbook, Korean upstart automaker Hyundai is trying to do to Toyota and Honda what Samsung successfully did to Sony—provide an affordable alternative to a popular market leader. Like Samsung, Hyundai has adopted a well-executed value-pricing strategy that combines advanced technology, reliable performance, and attractive design with lower prices. Hyundai's 10-year or 100,000-mile powertrain warranty programs and positive reviews from car analysts such as J.D. Power provided additional reassurance to potential buyers of the quality of the products and the company's stability. Hyundai's current Assurance program is centered on a new Trade-In Value Guarantee that preserves the market value of a new Hyundai by guaranteeing to customers at the time of purchase exactly how much it would be worth two, three, or four years from purchase date.[65] Hyundai has also moved to make pricing more transparent and to streamline purchasing, in addition to allowing customers to return their cars if the mileage is under 300 miles.[66] In this way, Hyundai is certainly ahead of the curve in understanding the importance of pricing in the overall strategy of a company or brand.

Hyundai has a strong value proposition, anchored by its 10-year or 100,000-mile warranty.

Source: Hyundai Motor America

Product Design and Delivery.   The first key to a successful value-pricing strategy is the proper design and delivery of the product. Product value can be enhanced through many types of well-conceived and well-executed marketing programs, such as those covered in this and other chapters of the book. Proponents of value pricing note that the concept does not mean selling stripped-down versions of products at lower prices. Consumers are willing to pay premiums when they perceive added value in products and services. Some companies (e.g., Apple) have been able to *increase* prices by skillfully introducing new or improved "value-added" products. Still other companies (e.g., Gillette) have coupled well-marketed product innovations and improvements with higher prices (or using a tiered pricing system) to strike an acceptable balance for at least some market segments.

With the advent of the Internet, many critics predicted that customers' ability to perform extensive, assisted online searches would result in only low-cost providers surviving. In reality, the advantages of creating strong brand differentiation have led to price premiums for brands sold online just as much as for those sold offline. For example, though undersold by numerous book and music sellers online, Amazon.com was able to maintain market leadership, eventually forcing low-priced competitors such as Books.com and others out of business.[67]

Product Costs.   The second key to a successful value-pricing strategy is to lower costs as much as possible. Meeting cost targets invariably requires finding additional cost savings through productivity gains, outsourcing, material substitution (less expensive or less wasteful materials), product reformulations, and process changes such as automation or other factory improvements.[68] As one marketing executive once put it:

> The customer is only going to pay you for what he perceives as real value-added. When you look at your overhead, you've got to ask yourself if the customer is really willing to pay for that. If the answer is no, you've got to figure out how to get rid of it or you're not going to make money.[69]

> Firms must be able to develop business models and cost structures to support their pricing plans.

Product Prices.   The third key to a successful value-pricing strategy is to understand exactly how much value consumers perceive in the brand and, thus, the extent to which they will pay a premium over product costs.[70] Myriad techniques are available to estimate these consumer value perceptions. Perhaps the most straightforward approach is to directly ask consumers their perceptions of price and value in different ways.

The price suggested by estimating perceived value can often be a starting point for marketers in determining actual marketplace prices, adjusting by cost and competitive considerations as necessary.

Communicating Value.   Combining these three components in the right way to create value is crucial. Just delivering good value, while necessary, is not sufficient for achieving pricing success—consumers need to understand and appreciate the value of the brand. In many cases, that value may be obvious—the product or service benefits are clear, and comparisons with competitors are easy. In other cases, however, the value may not be obvious, and consumers may too easily default to purchasing from lower-priced competitors. Marketers may then need to engage in marketing communications to help consumers better recognize the value. In some cases, the solution may simply require straightforward communications that expand on the value equation for the brand, such as stressing quality over price. For example, take a premium-priced brand such as Procter & Gamble's Pantene. It faces pressure from many competing brands, but especially private label and store and discount brands that may cost much less. In tough times, even small cost savings may matter to penny-pinching consumers. Assume a bottle of Pantene cost a $1 more than its main competitors but could be used for up to 100 shampoos. In that case, the price difference is really only one cent *per shampoo*. By framing the purchase decision in terms of cost per shampoo, P&G could then advertise, "Isn't it worth a penny more to get a better-looking head of hair?" In other cases, it may involve "framing" and convincing consumers to think about their brand and product decisions differently.

Price Segmentation.   At the same time, consumers may have differing value perceptions, and therefore, could—and most likely should—receive varying prices. Price segmentation sets and adjusts prices for appropriate market segments. Starbucks similarly has raised the prices of some of its specialty beverages while charging less for some basic drinks.[71]

Partly because of wide adoption of the Internet, firms are increasingly employing *yield management principles* or *dynamic pricing*, such as those adopted by airlines to vary their prices for distinct market segments and value perceptions. Two examples include the following:

- Allstate Insurance embarked on a yield management pricing program, assessing drivers' credit history, demographic profile, and other factors to better match automobile policy premiums to customer risk profiles.[72]
- To better compete with scalpers and online ticket brokers such as StubHub, concert giant Ticketmaster has begun implementing more efficient variable pricing schemes based on demand that charge higher prices for the most sought-after tickets and lower prices for less-desirable seats for sporting events and concerts.[73]

With the advent of digital and social media channels, it is increasingly easy for brands and companies to alter their pricing on a minute-to-minute basis, making it easier to implement yield management practices.

Everyday Low Pricing. *Everyday low pricing (EDLP)* has received increased attention as a means of determining price discounts and promotions over time. EDLP avoids the sawtooth pattern of alternating price increases and decreases or discounts in favor of a more consistent set of "everyday" base prices on products. In many cases, these EDLP prices are based on the value-pricing considerations we noted previously.

The P&G Experience. In the early 1990s, Procter & Gamble made a well-publicized conversion to EDLP.[74] By reducing list prices on half its brands and eliminating many temporary discounts, P&G reported that it saved $175 million in 1991, or 10 percent of its previous year's profits. Advocates of EDLP argue that maintaining consistently low prices on major items every day helps build brand loyalty, fend off private-label inroads, and reduce manufacturing and inventory costs.[75]

Even strict adherents of EDLP, however, see the need for some types of price discounts over time. When P&G encountered some difficulties in the late 1990s, it altered its value-pricing strategy in some segments and reinstated selected price promotions. More recently, P&G has adopted a more fluid pricing strategy in reaction to market conditions.[76] Management felt confident about the strength of some of the firm's popular premium-priced brands—such as Fusion ProGlide, Crest 3D products, and Old Spice body wash—and did not feel the need to discount price.

Reasons for Price Stability. Why, then, do firms seek greater price stability? Although trade promotions are supposed to result in discounts on products only for a certain length of time and in a certain geographic region, that is not always the case. With *forward buying*, retailers order more product than they plan to sell during the promotional period so that they can later obtain a larger margin by selling the remaining goods at the regular price after the promotional period has expired. With *diverting*, retailers pass along or sell the discounted products to retailers outside the designated selling area.

From a manufacturer's perspective, these retailer practices can lead to excess demand during the promotion period but result in slack capacity when the promotion period ends, costing them millions of dollars. On the demand side, many marketers believe that the seesaw of high and low prices on products train consumers to wait until the brand is discounted or on special to buy it, thus eroding its perceived value.

Summary

To build brand equity, marketers must determine strategies for setting prices and then adjusting them, if at all, over the short and long run. Increasingly, these decisions will reflect consumer perceptions of value. Value pricing strikes a balance among product design, product costs, and product prices. From a brand equity perspective, consumers must find the price of the brand appropriate and fair, given the benefits they receive from the product and its relative advantages over competitive offerings, among other factors. Everyday low pricing is a complementary pricing approach to determine the nature of price discounts and promotions over time that maintains consistently low, value-based prices on major items on a day-to-day basis.

There is always tension between lowering prices on the one hand and increasing consumer perceptions of product quality on the other. Academic researchers Lehmann and Winer believe that, though marketers commonly use price reductions to improve perceived value, in reality, discounts are often a more expensive way to add value than brand-building marketing activities.[77] Their argument is that the lost revenue from a lower margin on each item sold is often much greater than the additional cost of value-added activities, primarily because many of these costs are fixed and spread over *all* the units sold, as opposed to the per unit reductions that result from lower prices.

CHANNEL STRATEGY

The manner by which a product is sold or distributed can have a profound impact on the equity and ultimate sales success of a brand. *Marketing channels* refer to "sets of interdependent organizations involved in the process of making a product or service available for use or consumption."[78] Channel strategy includes the design and management of intermediaries such as wholesalers, distributors, brokers, and retailers. Let's look at how channel strategy can contribute to brand equity.[79]

Channel Design

Many possible channel types and arrangements exist, broadly classified into direct and indirect channels. *Direct channels* mean selling through personal contacts from the company to prospective customers by mail, phone, electronic means, in-person visits, and so forth. *Indirect channels* sell through third-party intermediaries, such as agents or broker representatives, wholesalers or distributors, and retailers or dealers.

Increasingly, winning channel strategies will be those that can develop "integrated shopping experiences" that combine physical stores, Internet, phone, and catalogs. For example, consider the wide variety of direct and indirect channels by which Nike sells its shoes, apparel, and equipment products.[80]

- *Branded Nike Stores:* Nike Stores, located in prime shopping avenues in metropolitan centers around the globe, offer a complete range of Nike products and serve as showcases for the latest styles. Each store consists of individual shops or pavilions that feature shoes, clothes, and equipment for a different sport (e.g., tennis, jogging, biking, or water sports) or different lines within a sport (e.g., three basketball shops and two tennis shops). Each shop develops its own concepts with lights, music, temperature, and multimedia displays. Nike is also experimenting with newer, smaller stores that target specific customers and sports (a running-only store in Palo Alto, California, a soccer-only store in Manchester, England).

Nike uses a variety of marketing channels for different purposes. Its Niketown stores have been very useful as a brand-building tool.
Source: AP Photo/Marcio Jose Sanchez

- *NikeStore.com:* Nike's e-commerce site allows consumers to place Internet orders for a range of products or to custom-design some products through NIKEiD.[81]
- *Outlet stores:* Nike's outlet stores feature discounted Nike merchandise.
- *Retail:* Nike products are sold in retail locations such as shoe stores, sporting goods stores, department stores, and clothing stores.
- *Catalog retailers:* Nike's products appear in numerous shoe, sporting goods, and clothing catalogs.
- *Specialty stores:* Nike equipment from product lines such as Nike Golf is often sold through specialty stores such as golf pro shops.

A wealth of research has considered the pros and cons of selling through various channels. Although the decision ultimately depends on the relative profitability of the different options, some more specific guidelines have been proposed. For example, one study on industrial products shows that direct channels may be preferable when product information needs are high, product customization is high, product quality assurance is important, purchase lot size is of concern, and logistics are paramount. Conversely, indirect channels may be preferable when a broad assortment is essential, availability is critical, and after-sales service is of great value. Exceptions to these generalities exist, especially depending on the market segments.[82]

From the standpoint of consumer shopping and purchase behaviors, channels can often blend three key factors: information, entertainment, and experiences.

- Consumers may learn about a brand and what it does and why it is different or special.
- Consumers may also be entertained by the means through which the channel permits shopping and purchases.
- Consumers may be able to participate in and experience channel activities.

Rarely will a manufacturer use only a single type of channel. More likely, the company will choose a hybrid channel design with multiple channel types.[83]

OMNICHANNEL INTEGRATION

Omnichannel is a multichannel sales approach that provides the customer with an integrated experience, across all channels, whether it be shopping online from a laptop or tablet, by Smartphone, or within a store.[84] Each touchpoint turns into a direct or indirect experience of the customer with the brand. One study suggests that omnichannel customers (or the customers who used multiple touchpoints) spend 10 percent more than other customers, implying that companies should pay special attention to omnichannel customers.[85]

Some examples of how companies are integrating online and offline channels are worth noting.[86] Several brands and companies are investing in augmented reality (AR) technology to help bridge the online and offline worlds. For example, Ikea uses an augmented reality app to help buyers visualize how their furniture would look in their home. The virtual rendition allows Ikea to help customers select the right furniture. A related approach involves providing consumers with apps that can help illustrate a product or service. Sherwin-Williams has a Colorsnap visualizer that allows consumers to visualize the right color paint for a room.

Another approach is to permit customers to place orders online for easy pickup at the store. Nearly 8 in 10 large retailers has a retailer app, and retailers such as Kohl's and Wal-Mart have been providing the buy-online-pick-up-in-store option as a service. This option can increase retail sales; for example, a UPS study indicates that among those who use the in-store pickup option, 44 percent end up making a new purchase when they are picking up their purchase.[87]

A related approach to integrating the online and offline strategies is to use Bluetooth beacons to send push notifications when shoppers enter a store or when they are nearby. For example, Macy's and American Eagle are using beacons with the Shopkick app to notify shoppers of promotions and offers available when they enter a store. As another example, Home Depot first rolled out its app in 2014; the app automatically switches to an "in-store" mode when consumers enter, allowing them to pull up features such as the "product locator" tool. By using location-based technology, the app automatically detects which store users are in, giving them a map to specific products located near their exact position.[88]

Some brands are particularly well-known for their ability to integrate online and offline marketing strategies. One often cited example is Disney. Disney uses the My Disney Experience tool to help customers plan their entire theme park trip, including the attractions they might want to see and the estimated wait time. The MagicBand program acts as a hotel room key, photo storage device, and a food ordering tool. By integrating across all customer touchpoints through the MagicBand and the My Disney Experience tool, Disney is able to provide seamless integration across all customer experiences. Another example is Starbucks, which uses its app and rewards card as a way to integrate across multiple channels. Any changes the customer makes in one venue get updated across all channels, in real time, allowing for seamless integration of the customer experience.

An often-repeated concern with the growing integration of online and offline is that customers are using their mobile devices in-store to search for better prices elsewhere, a practice called *showrooming*. Alternatively, customers seek information online and purchase offline, in a practice called *webrooming*. One study showed that shoppers who searched online for information were also the same shoppers who spent 13 percent more in-store than those who did not engage in online searches.[89] Furthermore, with the increasing blurring of online and offline channels, many brick-and-mortar retailers (e.g., H&M and Macy's) are investing in beacon technology. This technology allows for proximity-based marketing, such that customers receive a coupon tailored specifically to them based on their browsing history, purchase behavior, and demographics while in the store. While customers tend to be receptive to such targeted offers, they are also increasingly concerned about the use of their personal data for these promotions.[90] Brands should be mindful of delivering value to customers with every single interaction, particularly those touchpoints that bring the customer directly in contact with the brand at various moments of truth. The Science of Branding 5-2 highlights findings from research on how marketing in omnichannel environments can impact brand as well as firm outcomes.

THE SCIENCE OF BRANDING 5-2
Research on Omnichannel

An omnichannel differs from its counterpart, the multichannel, in that it includes more channels and the boundaries between channels are increasingly blurred.[91] Various studies have examined the implications of this omnichannel environment on retailers and, consequently, the brand. Researchers examined the impact of omnichannel retail operations (buying online and picking up in store) on profitability and argued that implementation of this practice may not always be profitable across all product categories because it may be less cost-effective.

It is common for brick-and-mortar stores to add an online channel or branded app to increase the number of customer touchpoints. Some digital native brands have also embraced offline channels to build relationships with their customers. Researchers Bell and colleagues[92] studied the phenomenon by examining the impact of WarbyParker.com (a digital-first company) introducing showrooms. Their findings suggest that the addition of showrooms confers branding benefits, which in turn increase credibility, resulting in higher profitability for both online and offline channels, by generating positive spillover. The highest cost-to-serve customers in online channels were the first to migrate to offline channels, and the cost of product returns also reduced. Pauwels and Neslin[93] examined the impact of adding brick-and-mortar stores to a retailer's already existing catalog and Internet channels and found a 20 percent increase in revenue overall from the addition of physical stores.

Ailawadi and Farris[94] provided a framework for managing distribution and highlighted the importance of distribution breadth and depth in understanding the role of the supplier (or brand) on retailers, and vice versa. They also suggested a new set of metrics for understanding the effectiveness of online channels, including percentage of a product category's search volume (PCSV) and rank of a branded app in an app store, as new metrics to consider in conjunction with traditional metrics for brick-and-mortar stores, such as the percentage of ACV (all commodity volume).

Sources: Fei Gao, and Xuanming Su, "Omnichannel Retail Operations with Buy-Online-and-Pick-Up-in-Store," *Management Science* 63, no. 8 (2016): 2478–2492; David R. Bell, Santiago Gallino, and Antonio Moreno, "How to Win in an Omnichannel World," *MIT Sloan Management Review* 56, no. 1 (2014): 45; David R. Bell, Santiago Gallino, and Antonio Moreno, "Offline Showrooms in Omnichannel Retail: Demand and Operational Benefits," *Management Science* 64, no. 4 (April 2018): 1629–1651; United Parcel Service of America, "UPS Pulse of the Online Shopper: A Customer Experience Study," https://pressroom.ups.com/mobile0c9a66/assets/pdf/pressroom/white%20paper/UPS_2017_POTOS_media%20executive%20summary_FINAL.pdf, accessed March 11, 2018; Peter C. Verhoef, P. K. Kannan, and J. Jeffrey Inman, "From Multi-Channel Retailing to Omni-Channel Retailing: Introduction to the Special Issue on Multi-Channel Retailing," *Journal of Retailing* 91, no. 2 (2015): 174–181; Koen Pauwels, and Scott A. Neslin, "Building with Bricks and Mortar: The Revenue Impact of Opening Physical Stores in a Multichannel Environment," *Journal of Retailing* 91, no. 2 (2015): 182–197.

The goal is to maximize channel coverage and effectiveness while minimizing channel cost and conflict. Because marketers use both direct and indirect channels, let's consider the brand equity implications of the two major channel design types.

Indirect Channels

Indirect channels can consist of different types of intermediaries, but we concentrate on retailers. Retailers tend to have the most visible and direct contact with customers and therefore have the greatest opportunity to affect brand equity. As we outline in greater detail in Chapter 8, consumers may have associations with any retailer based on product assortment, pricing and credit policy, and quality of service, among other factors. Through the products and brands they stock and the means by which they sell, retailers strive to create their own brand equity by establishing awareness and strong, favorable, and unique associations.

At the same time, retailers can have a profound influence on the equity of the brands they sell, especially regarding the brand-related services they can support or help create. The term "Moments of Truth," which was introduced by P&G in 2005, describes what happens before, during, and after a purchase.[95] FMOT, or first moment of truth, reflects the first time a customer views a product (e.g., on the retail shelf).[96] The retail channel has an impact on FMOT, as it impacts how consumers perceive their interaction with the brand. Sometimes, there are spillover effects from the retailer to the brand itself, when consumers make assumptions such as "this store only sells good-quality, high-value merchandise, so this particular product must also be good quality and high value."

Push and Pull Strategies.   In addition to the indirect avenue of image transfer, retailers can directly affect the equity of the brands they sell. Their methods of stocking, displaying, and selling products can enhance or detract from brand equity, suggesting that manufacturers must take an active role in helping retailers add value to their brands. Online retailers—notably Amazon.com—also exerts a great deal of clout over manufacturers and consumers, by making available information about product reviews. This creates greater pressure on marketers to ensure that their product and service quality is consistently high. In recent years, shopper marketing has become even more important in ensuring that customers obtain value with their purchases.

Though defined differently by various people at its core, *shopper marketing* emphasizes collaboration between manufacturers and retailers on in-store marketing, such as brand-building displays, sampling, promotions, and other in-store activities designed to capitalize on a retailer's capabilities. Although digital channels pose tremendous challenges to brick-and-mortar retailers, many consumers still like to touch and feel products in the store.

Because of greater competition for shelf space among what many retailers find are increasingly undifferentiated brands, retailers have gained power and are now in a better position to set the terms of trade with manufacturers. Increased power means that retailers can command more frequent and lucrative trade promotions. Even more dramatic, however, is the shift in power to consumers. With the proliferation of online retailers, and the low search costs associated with locating information about prices and availability online, consumers are increasingly shopping via the Internet. Thus, no retailer is immune to the challenges posed to the traditional brick-and-mortar retail from digital channels.

One way for manufacturers (and even retailers) to regain some of their lost leverage is to create strong brands through some of the brand-building tactics described in this book—for example, selling innovative and unique products, properly priced and advertised, that consumers demand. In this way, consumers may ask or even pressure retailers to stock and promote manufacturers' products.

By devoting marketing efforts to the end consumer, a manufacturer is said to employ a *pull strategy*, as consumers use their buying power and influence over retailers to "pull" the product through the channel. Alternatively, marketers can devote their selling efforts to the channel members themselves, providing direct incentives for them to stock and sell products to end consumers. This approach is called a *push strategy*, because the manufacturer is attempting to reach the consumer by "pushing" the product through each step of the distribution chain. Although certain brands seem to emphasize one strategy more than the other (push strategies are usually associated with more selective distribution and pull strategies with broader, more intensive distribution), the most successful marketers—brands such as Colgate, Tide, and Folgers—skillfully blend push *and* pull strategies.

Channel Support.   A variety of services provided by channel members can enhance the value to consumers of purchasing and consuming a brand name product (see Figure 5-4). Although firms are increasingly providing some of the services themselves through toll-free numbers and Web sites, establishing a "marketing partnership" with retailers may, nevertheless, be critical to ensuring proper channel support and the execution of these various services. It is important for firms to keep up with new retailer capabilities to ensure they garner as much support as possible. For example, one new retail trend is the growth of augmented reality and virtual reality as a feature of retail showrooms. The Bay Area Neiman Marcus features touchscreen mirrors that provide a 360-degree view of an outfit that a customer may be interested in. In another twist, Rebecca

Minkoff's dressing rooms in New York's SoHo outlet are "smart" dressing rooms that allow customers to use a digital wall to place orders for drinks or request help from an employee.[97]

Manufacturers can take steps to keep retail partners happy and prevent breaks in the supply chain. Resellers often invest significant amounts of money in maintaining their facilities and paying sales staff. To compensate them, manufacturers can offer dealers exclusive access to new products, or branded variants, as described later. Experts also advise that manufacturers stick to fixed prices when they offer products directly to consumers. If they do offer large discounts, they should offer them at outlet malls, where they will not confuse customers.

Manufacturers also can support their distributors by educating them about their products so the retail partners can shape an effective sales force. The Branding Brief 5-2 describes how Milk-Bone dog chew from Big Heart Pet Brands used shopper marketing to build brand awareness.

BRANDING BRIEF 5-2

Chew on This: How Milk-Bone Brushing Chews Connected with Customers

According to research conducted by Big Heart Pet Brands' research team, although most pet owners ought to know how to brush their dog's teeth, few actually knew how to do it, and those who did know how to do it thought it was an unpleasant task. The company wanted to introduce a new dental treat called Milk-Bone Brushing Chews. The marketing challenge was to get people to fall in love with a task they did not know about or did not like doing.

Big Heart Pet Brands had ambitious targets for the launch of Milk-Bone Brushing Chews—it wanted to grow the dental category by more than 10 percent and to increase trial for the new product at major retailers. The key target audience was pet owners who felt responsible for their dog's health and would use the treat to reinforce a bond. A key shopper marketing challenge was that at mass merchants and grocers, the focus was more on food, whereas at a specialty store such as PetSmart, there were too many different product choices.

The company used a well-defined shopper marketing strategy to strengthen awareness. In addition to creating awareness through free-standing inserts, veterinary outreach, and displays inside clinics, the company created signage and an endcap in retail stores such as Target to support the effort. They also employed retailer-specific programs. To build buzz, the company allowed pre-shopping on Walmart.com. At Target, the Cartwheel app

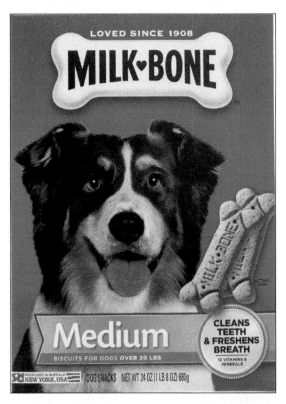

Milk-Bone used a shopper marketing strategy to create awareness for a new type of product—a dental treat that also helps brush your dog's teeth.

Source: Keith Homan/Alamy Stock Photo

(which gives 5 to 50 percent off certain items when shopping in store at Target) and Target's pet prescription service were brought into the effort. For PetSmart, the company held a Dental Day event to educate employees so that they could serve as brand ambassadors.

The campaign was a success, and the company met its sales goal for the launch, with the category growing at 10 percent, per its goal. The marketing campaign was based on the idea that Milk-Bone Brushing Chews is the only dental treat that dogs would love. Shoppers (and their dogs) loved the idea, and trial and repeat for the new product met and exceeded the target. The shopper marketing campaign won an Effie award for its effectiveness in 2015.

Source: Shoppermarketingmag.com, "Effie Case Study: Milk-Bone Brushing Chews Shopper Marketing Launch Campaign," May 18, 2015, https://shoppermarketingmag.com/effie-case-study-milk-bone-brushing-chews-shopper-marketing-launch-campaign, accessed March 15, 2018; Kristina Manllos, "Milk-Bone Gets into the Teeth Brushing Business," April 18, 2014, www.adweek.com/brand-marketing/milk-bone-gets-teeth-brushing-business-157067/, accessed March 15, 2018; Effie Worldwide, Inc., "Milk-Bone Brushing Chews," November 12, 2015, accessed March 15, 2018.

Ultimately, companies must share the power to make decisions with their retail distributors and also recognize that these dealers' success benefits them as well. In many markets, dealers have captured a greater percentage of retail sales, so manufacturers must keep them happy and profitable if they want the benefits of a smooth supply chain relationship. Two important components of partnership strategies are retail segmentation activities and cooperative advertising programs.

Retail Segmentation.   Retailers are "customers" too. Because of their different marketing capabilities and needs, retailers may need to be divided into segments or even treated individually so that they will provide the necessary brand support.[98] Consider how the following packaged goods companies have customized their marketing efforts to particular retailers. Frito-Lay developed a tailored supply chain system for its corn chip and potato chip markets, making fast and broad distribution possible, reducing stock-outs, and creating better-turning store displays for its various retail customers. SC Johnson has leveraged customized market research insights to develop unique category management solutions to its strategic retail customers.

Retailers may require different product mixes, special delivery systems, customized promotions, or even their own branded version of the products. With its growth and dominance as an online retailer, Amazon.com has many guidelines for customizing marketing efforts. With its crowded marketplace, Amazon strives to provide accurate product information so that customers who look for specific features can find the product. Amazon also has a "Buy Box" feature, which is a white box on the side of its product detail page where customers can add items to their shopping carts. This highly competitive feature is typically only available to the most competitively priced products in a category, and it exerts a great deal of impact on customers' buying decisions. Amazon has an algorithm that decides which brands to feature in the Buy Box to maximize customer value.[99]

Branded variants are branded items in a diverse set of durable and semidurable goods categories that are not directly comparable to other items carrying the same brand name.[100] Manufacturers create branded variants in many ways, including making changes in color, design, flavor, options, style, stain, motif, features, and layout. For example, portable stereo "boom boxes" from brands such as Sony, Panasonic, and Toshiba came in a broad assortment, varying in speaker size, total weight, number of audio controls, recording features, and SKU number.

Branded variants are a means to reduce retail price competition because they make direct price comparisons by consumers difficult. Thus, different retailers may be given varying items or models of the same brand to sell. Shugan and his colleagues show that, as the manufacturer of a product offers more branded variants, a greater number of retail stores carry the product, and these stores offer higher levels of retail service for these products.[101]

Cooperative Advertising.   One relatively neglected means of increasing channel support is well-designed cooperative advertising programs. Traditionally, with co-op advertising, a manufacturer pays for a portion of the advertising that a retailer runs to promote the manufacturer's product.

Amazon has a "Buy Box" feature on the side of its product detail page highlighting the most competitively priced products in a category; and this has a great deal of impact on consumers' buying decisions.

To be eligible to receive co-op funds, the retailer usually must follow the manufacturer's stipulations about the nature of brand exposure in the ad. Manufacturers generally share the cost of the advertising on a percentage basis up to a certain limit, though it is usually 50–50. The total amount of cooperative advertising funds the manufacturer provides to the retailer is usually based on a percentage of dollar purchases made by the retailer from the manufacturer.[102] The rationale behind cooperative advertising for manufacturers is that it concentrates some of the communication efforts at the local level where they may have more relevance and selling impact with consumers.

Summary.   In eliciting channel support, manufacturers must be creative in the way they develop marketing and merchandising programs aimed at channel members. They should consider how channel activity can encourage trial purchase and communicate or demonstrate product information, to build brand awareness and image and to elicit positive brand responses.

Direct Channels

For some of the reasons we have already noted, manufacturers may choose to sell directly to consumers. Let's examine some of the brand equity issues of selling through direct channels.

Company-Owned Stores.   To gain control over the selling process and build stronger relationships with customers, some manufacturers are introducing their own retail outlets, as well as selling their products directly to customers through various means. These channels can take many forms, the most complex of which, from a manufacturer's perspective, is company-owned stores. Hallmark, Goodyear, and others have sold their own products in their own stores for years. They have eventually been joined by several other firms, including some of the largest marketers around.

Brands of all kinds have created their own stores, such as Bang & Olufsen audio equipment, OshKosh B'gosh children's wear, and Dr. Martens boots and shoes, but not all company stores are large structures with an extensive inventory. One recent trend is the launching of pop-up stores—temporary stores that blend retail and event marketing.[103] Pop-up shops are likely to be a significant source of commerce and can range upwards of $8 billion in value.[104] For example, in 2010, the online eyewear retailer Warby Parker opened a pop-up store that involved a big yellow bus traveling across America and stopping in select cities to set up shop. This retail adventure was called Class Trip. In another effort, the company created kiosks in hotels called the Readery, in which it paired its 1960s eyewear with vintage accessories.[105] Other digital native brands are also increasingly embracing brick-and-mortar outlets to build high-touch relationships with customers. For example, Greats, a digital native luxury sneaker company, opened retail outlets in Los Angeles and New York, and this trend is seen in store openings of various digital native brands including Everlane, Glossier, Bonobos, and Casper.[106]

Temporary pop-up stores have given marketers a creative way to generate consumer interest and involvement.

Source: Andrew H. Walker/ Getty Images for Target

Company stores provide many benefits.[107] Primarily, they are a means to showcase the brand and all its different product varieties in a manner not easily achieved through normal retail channels. For example, Nike might find its products spread all across department stores and athletic specialty stores. These products may not be displayed in a logical, coordinated fashion, and certain product lines may not even be stocked. By opening its own stores, Nike was able to effectively put its best foot forward by showing the depth, breadth, and variety of its branded products. Company stores can provide the added benefit of functioning as a test market to gauge consumer response to alternative product designs, presentations, and prices, allowing retailers to keep their fingers on the pulse of consumers' shopping habits.

A disadvantage of company stores is that some companies lack the skills, resources, or contacts to operate effectively as a retailer. For example, Disney Store, started in 1987, sells exclusive Disney-branded merchandise, ranging from toys and videos to collectibles and clothing, priced from $3 to $3,000. Disney views the stores as an extension of the "Disney experience," referring to customers as "guests" and employees as "cast members," just as it does in its theme parks. The growth of online shopping has posed challenges for Disney stores as well, and the company has begun experimenting with redesigning its stores to seem more like its theme park, through the addition of video screens that help showcase Disney movies, Disney parades, and so on.[108]

Another issue with company stores is the potential conflict between existing retail channels and distributors. In many cases, however, company stores can be a means of bolstering brand image and building brand equity rather than as direct sales devices. For example, Nike views its stores as essentially advertisements and tourist attractions. The company reports that research studies have confirmed that Nike stores enhanced the Nike brand image by presenting the full scope of its sports and fitness lines to customers and "educating them" on the value, quality, and benefits of Nike products. The research also revealed that though only about 25 percent of visitors actually made a purchase at a Niketown store, 40 percent of those who did not buy during their visit eventually purchased Nike products from some other retailer.

These manufacturer-owned stores can also be considered a means of hedging bets with retailers that continue to push their own labels. With one of its main distributors, JCPenney, pushing its own Arizona brand of jeans, Levi's can protect its brand franchise to some extent by establishing its own distribution channel. Nevertheless, many retailers and manufacturers are dancing around the turf issue, avoiding head-on clashes in establishing competitive distribution channels. Manufacturers, in particular, have been careful to stress that their stores are not a competitive threat to their retailers but rather a "showcase" that can help sell merchandise for any retailer carrying their brand.

Store-within-a-Store.   In addition to creating their own stores, some marketers—such as Nike, Polo, and Levi Strauss (with Dockers)—are attempting to create their own shops within major department stores. More common in other parts of the world such as Asia, these approaches can offer the dual benefits of appeasing retailers—and perhaps even allowing them to benefit from the retailer's brand image—while allowing the firm to retain control over the design and implementation of the product presentation at the point of purchase.[109]

The store-within-a-store concept can take hold through actual leasing arrangements or less formal arrangements in which branded mini-stores are used. For retailers, these arrangements help drive foot traffic and acquire new capabilities quickly. For smaller brands, such as Murray's Cheese Shop, which has an arrangement with the Kroger Co., they allow for quick distribution growth.

Retailers are also combining with other retailers to gain similar benefits.[110] Sears partnered with the much trendier retailer Forever 21 to upgrade its image and also established in-store leases with Edwin Watts Golf Shops, uniform apparel seller Work 'N Gear, and Whole Foods organic foods grocer. Macy's has partnered with Sunglass Hut, maternity apparel brand Destination Modernity, and the U.K. toiletries brand Lush. Recently, Best Buy expanded its store-within-a-store program to increase retail space for brands such as Sony, Samsung, and Microsoft.[111]

Other Means.   Finally, another channel option is to sell directly to consumers by phone, mail, or electronic means. Retailers have sold their goods through catalogs for years. Many mass marketers, especially those that also sell through their own retail stores, are increasingly using direct selling, a successful long-term strategy for brands such as Mary Kay and Avon. These vehicles not only help sell products but also contribute to brand equity by increasing consumer awareness of the range of products associated with a brand and increasing consumer understanding of the key benefits of those products. Marketers can execute direct marketing efforts in many ways, such as through catalogs, videos, physical sites, or the Internet, all of which are opportunities to engage in a dialogue and establish a relationship with consumers.

Online Strategies

The advantages of having both a physical brick-and-mortar channel and a virtual online retail channel are becoming clearer to many firms. Integrated channels allow consumers to shop when and how they want. Many consumers value the convenience of ordering from companies online or over the phone and picking up the physical product at their local store rather than having it shipped. They also want to be able to return merchandise at a store even if they originally bought it and had it shipped outside the store.[112]

Many consumers also like the convenience of being able to access their online accounts inside the store and use Internet kiosks to research purchase decisions in the store itself.[113] The influence of the Internet extends outside the store as well. A Forrester research report estimated that 16 percent of all store sales were influenced by consumers initially searching on the web outside the store.[114]

Integrating channels benefits manufacturers, retailers, and consumers. Figure 5-5 shows an analysis of JCPenney's channel mix, which reveals that its most profitable customers were those who shopped multiple channels. Similarly, a Deloitte study reported that multichannel shoppers spent 82 percent more in each transaction than those who shopped only in one store.[115]

The Boston Consulting Group concluded that multichannel retailers were able to acquire customers at half the cost of Internet-only retailers, citing several advantages for the multichannel retailers:[116]

- They have market clout with suppliers.
- They have established distribution and fulfillment systems (e.g., L.L.Bean and Land's End).
- They can cross-sell between Web sites and stores (e.g., Gap and Barnes & Noble).

Multichannel product manufacturers can realize many of these same advantages. Recognizing the power of integrated channels, many Internet-based companies are also engaging in "physical world" activities to boost their brand. For example, Yahoo! opened a promotional store in New York's Rockefeller Center, and eTrade.com opened a flagship own-brand financial center on New York's Madison Avenue as well as mini-centers and kiosks in Target stores.

Summary

Channels are the means by which companies distribute their products to consumers. Channel strategy to build brand equity includes designing and managing direct and indirect channels to build brand awareness and improve the brand image. Direct channels can enhance brand equity by allowing consumers to better understand the depth, breadth, and variety of the products associated with the brand, as well as any distinguishing characteristics. Indirect channels can influence brand equity through the actions and support of intermediaries such as retailers, as well as the transfer of any associations these intermediaries might have with the brand.

FIGURE 5-5

JCPenney Customer Channel Value Analysis

Source: Customer Values Analysis, Doublecheck (2004). Courtesy of Abacus Direct, LLC.

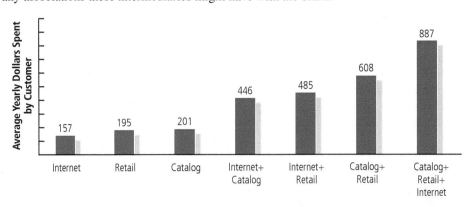

Direct and indirect channels offer varying advantages and disadvantages that marketers must thoughtfully combine, both to sell products in the short run and to maintain and enhance brand equity in the long run. As is often the case with branding, the key is to mix and match channel options so that they collectively realize these goals. Thus, it is important to assess each possible channel option regarding its direct effect on product sales and brand equity, as well as its indirect effect through interactions with other channel options.

REVIEW

Marketing activities and programs are the primary means through which companies build brand equity. The brand-building of product, pricing, channel, and communication strategies must be put into place. In terms of product strategies, both tangible and intangible aspects of the brand will matter. Successful brands often create strong, favorable, and unique brand associations, with both functional and symbolic benefits. Although perceived quality is often at the heart of brand equity, consumers may have a wide range of associations with the brand.

Marketers are personalizing their consumer interactions through experiential and relationship marketing. Experiential marketing promotes a product by not only communicating a product's features and benefits but also connecting it with unique and interesting consumer experiences. Relationship marketing includes marketing activities that deepen and broaden the way consumers think about and act toward the brand. Mass customization, one-to-one marketing, and permission marketing are all means of getting consumers more actively engaged with the product or service. Aftermarketing and loyalty programs are also ways to help create holistic, personalized buying experiences.

For pricing strategies, marketers should fully understand consumer perceptions of value. Increasingly, firms are adopting value-based pricing strategies to set prices and everyday-low-pricing strategies to guide their discount pricing policy over time. Value-based pricing strategies attempt to properly balance product design and delivery, product costs, and product prices. Everyday-low-pricing strategies establish a stable set of "everyday" prices and introduce price discounts very selectively.

Regarding channel strategies, marketers need to match brand and store images appropriately to maximize the leverage of secondary associations, integrate push strategies and shopper marketing activities for retailers with pull strategies, and consider a range of direct and indirect distribution options. In the next chapter, we consider how to develop integrated marketing communication programs to build brand equity.

DISCUSSION QUESTIONS

1. Have you had any experience with a brand that has done a great job in relationship marketing, permission marketing, experiential marketing, or one-to-one marketing? What did the brand do? Why was it effective? Could others learn from that?
2. Think about the products you own. Assess their product design. Critique their aftermarketing efforts. Are you aware of all the products' capabilities? Identify a product whose benefits you may not be fully capitalizing on. What improvements would you suggest?
3. Choose a product category. Profile all the brands in the category in terms of pricing strategies and perceived value. If possible, review the brands' pricing histories. Have these brands set and adjusted prices properly? What would you do differently?
4. Visit a department store and evaluate the in-store marketing effort. Which categories or brands seem to be receiving the biggest in-store push? What unique in-store merchandising efforts do you see?
5. Take a trip to a supermarket and observe the extent of private-label brands. In which categories do you believe private labels might be successful? Why?

BRAND FOCUS 5.0
Private-Label Strategies and Responses

This appendix considers the issue of private labels or store brands. After portraying private-label branding strategies, it describes how major manufacturers' brands have responded to their threat.

PRIVATE LABELS

Although different terms and definitions are possible, **private labels** can be defined as products marketed by retailers and other members of the distribution chain. Private labels can be called **store brands** when they actually adopt the name of the store itself in some way (such as Safeway Select). Private labels should not be confused with **generics**, whose simple black-and-white packaging typically provides no information about who made the product.

Private-label brands typically cost less to make and sell than the national or manufacturer brands with which they compete. Thus, the appeal to consumers of buying private labels and store brands often are the cost savings involved; the appeal to retailers of selling private labels and store brands is that their gross margin is often 25 percent to 30 percent—nearly twice that of national brands.

The history of private labels is one of many ups and downs. The first private-label grocery products in the United States were sold by the Great Atlantic and Pacific Tea Company (later known as A&P), which was founded in 1863. During the first half of the twentieth century, several store brands were successfully introduced. Under competitive pressure from the sophisticated mass-marketing practices adopted by large packaged-goods companies in the 1950s, private labels fell out of favor with consumers.

Because the appeal of private labels to consumers has traditionally been their lower cost, the sales of private labels generally have been highly correlated with personal disposable income. The recession of the 1970s saw the successful introduction of low-cost, basic-quality, and minimally packaged generic products that appealed to bargain-seeking consumers. During the subsequent economic upswing, though, the lack of perceived quality eventually hampered sales of generics, and many consumers returned to national or manufacturers' brands.

To better compete in today's marketplace, private-label makers have begun improving quality and expanding the variety of their private-label offerings to include premium products. In recognition of the power of bold graphics, supermarket retailers have been careful to design attractive, upscale packages for their own premium branded products. Because of these and other actions, private-label sales have recently made some major inroads in new markets. Retailers value private labels for their profit margins and their means of differentiation to drive customer loyalty. Retailer Target has introduced a steady stream of exclusives through the years, such as its stylish Mossimo apparel and Michael Graves houseware brands.[117]

Private-Label Status

The major recession that began in 2008 heightened interest once again in private labels. Given retailers' success in improving private-label quality and developing cohesive branding and marketing programs, many critics wondered whether this time, things would be different, and sales would not drop after the end of the recession.[118]

In the United States, private-label goods have accounted for roughly 16 to 17 percent of total supermarket dollar volume. In other countries, these percentages are often quite higher, on average twice as much. For example, Western Europe dominates the market for private labels in the supermarket, with the biggest being Switzerland at 45 percent, Germany at 30 percent, Spain at 26 percent, and Belgium at 25 percent.[119]

Private labels in the United Kingdom make up over a third of sales at grocery stores, in part because the grocery industry is more concentrated. Two of the largest UK grocery chains are Tesco and Sainsbury.[120]

- Tesco, with the brand slogan "Every Little Helps," has a number of its own private-label brands, ranging from Value to Finest, and has its own lifestyle brands, such as Organic, Free Form, and Healthy Living, positioned as "Making Life Taste Better."

- Sainsbury's originally used its name to introduce a wide variety of fruit, vegetables, grocery, and household products, later expanding to clothing, housewares, and other nonsupermarket products. Sainsbury's own brand products are categorized into one of three quality tiers; for example, the lasagna range is comprised of the Basics sub-brand for "good," the core, Sainsbury's label line for "better," and the premium "Taste the Difference" line for "best." Sainsbury's began a major overhaul of these various brand lines in 2010.

The private-label appeal is widespread. In supermarkets, private-label sales have always been strong in product categories such as dairy goods, vegetables, and beverages. More recently, private labels have been successful in previously "untouchable" categories such as cigarettes, disposable diapers, and cold remedies. *Consumer Reports* conducted a study on private labels published in September 2010. Key findings included the facts that 84 percent of U.S. consumers have purchased a store brand, and 93 percent of store-brand shoppers indicated that they would continue to purchase private labels even as the economy recovered.[121]

Nevertheless, some categories have not seen a strong private-label presence. Many shoppers, for example, still seem unwilling to trust their hair, complexion, or dental care to store brands. Private labels also have been relatively unsuccessful in categories such as candy, cereal, pet foods, baby food, and beer.

One implication that can be drawn from this pattern of product purchases is that consumers are more selective in what they buy, no longer choosing to purchase only national brands. For less important products in particular, consumers seem to feel "that the very best is unnecessary, and good is good enough." Categories that are particularly vulnerable to private-label advances are those in which there are little perceived quality difference among brands in the eyes of a sizable group of consumers, for example, over-the-counter pain relievers, bottled water, plastic bags, paper towels, and dairy products.

Private-Label Branding Strategy

Although the growth of private labels has been interpreted by some as a sign of the decline of brands, the opposite conclusion may, in fact, be more valid: private-label growth could be seen in some ways as a consequence of cleverly designed branding strategies. In terms of building brand equity, the key point-of-difference for private labels in consumers' eyes has always been "good value," a desirable and transferable association across many product categories. As a result, private labels can be extremely broad, and their name can be applied across many diverse products.

As with national brands, implementing a value-pricing strategy for private labels requires determining the right price and product offering. For example, one reported rule of thumb is that the typical "no-name" product has to sell for at least 15 percent less than a national brand, on average, to be successful. The challenge for private labels has been to determine the appropriate product offering.

Specifically, to achieve the necessary points-of-parity, or even to create their own points-of-difference, private labels have been improving quality, and, as a result, are now aggressively positioning against even national brands. In its September 2010 study, *Consumer Reports* conducted taste tests in 21 categories comparing the two and found that national brands won seven times, private labels won three times, with the rest resulting in a tie. *Consumer Reports* concluded that consumers could cut their costs by as much as half by switching to a store brand.[122]

Many supermarket chains have introduced their own premium store brands, such as Safeway Select, Vons's Royal Request, and Ralph's Private Selection. For example, A&P positioned its premium Master Choice brand to fill the void between the mass-market national brands and the upscale specialty brands it sells. It has used the brand across a wide range of products, such as teas, pasta, sauces, and salad dressings. Trader Joe's offers 2,000 private-label products—only 10 percent of what would be found in a typical supermarket—but creates a fun, roomy atmosphere for bargain seekers wanting the best in gourmet-style foods, health food supplements, and wines.[123]

Sellers of private labels are also adopting more extensive marketing communication programs to spread the word about their brands. For example, Walgreens launched its first national advertising campaign for Walgreens-branded health and wellness products in February 2011. The campaign emphasized the durability and quality of the Walgreens-brand products, using the store's 26,000 pharmacists as endorsers.[124] Loblaws has been a pioneer in marketing its private-label brands.

Loblaws

Loblaws is Canada's largest food distributor. In 1978, Loblaws was the first store in Canada to introduce generics, reflecting a carefully crafted strategy to build an image of quality and high value in six areas. By 1983, Loblaws carried more than 500 generic products that accounted for 10 percent of store sales. This success was due to innovative marketing, low costs, and a large network of suppliers. In 1984, Loblaws chose to introduce a private-label brand, President's Choice, which was designed to offer unique value through exceptional quality and moderate prices. These categories ranged from basic supermarket categories such as chocolate chip cookies, colas, and cereals to more exotic categories such as Devonshire custard from England and gourmet Russian mustard. These products also used distinctive and attractive packaging with modern lettering and colorful labels and names ("decadent" cookies, "ultimate" frozen pizza, and "too good to be true" peanut butter). In terms of marketing communications, Loblaws put into place a strong promotional program with much in-store merchandising. Loblaws also introduced its *Insider's Report,* a quarterly publication featuring its own store brands and offering consumers shopping tips.[125]

Major Brand Response to Private Labels

Procter & Gamble's value-pricing program was one strategy to combat competitive inroads from private labels and other brands. To compete with private labels, a number of different other tactics also have been adopted by marketers of major national or manufacturer brands (see Figure 5-6).

First, marketers of major brands have attempted to decrease costs and reduce prices to negate the primary point-of-difference of private labels and achieve a critical point-of-parity. In many categories, prices of major brands had crept up to a point at which price premiums over private labels were 30 to 50 percent or even 100 percent. In those categories in which consumers make frequent purchases, the cost savings of "trading down" to a private label brand were, therefore, quite substantial.

In instances in which major brands and private labels are on an equal footing with regard to price, major brands often compete well because of other favorable brand perceptions that

Decrease costs.

Cut prices.

Increase R&D expenditures to improve products and identify new product innovations.

Increase advertising and promotion budgets.

Eliminate stagnant brands and extensions and concentrate efforts on a smaller number of brands.

Introduce discount "fighter" brands.

Supply private-label makers.

Track store brands' growth and compete market-by-market.

FIGURE 5-6

Major Brand Response to Private Labels

consumers might have. Procter & Gamble, Colgate, and Unilever cut prices on a number of old standbys during the recent recession to help fend off private-label competition.

One problem faced by marketers of major brands is that it can be difficult to lower prices even if they so desire. Supermarkets may not pass along the wholesale price cuts they are given. Moreover, marketers of major brands may not want to alienate retailers by attacking their store brands too forcefully, especially in zero-sum categories in which their brands could be easily replaced.

Besides these various pricing moves to achieve points-of-parity, marketers of major brands have used other tactics to achieve additional points-of-difference to combat the threat of private labels. They have increased R&D expenditures to improve products and identify new product innovations, as was the case with Kimberly-Clark and its Kleenex brand.[126]

Kleenex

Kleenex has dominated the facial tissue category for years, currently holding 46 percent market share. In recent years, with the economic downturn, more consumers are switching to less-expensive store brands as private labels in the category have increased quality to provide a more viable alternative. Kimberly-Clark—maker of Kleenex—chose to respond through product innovation. The average home purchases facial tissues about eight times a year and contains four boxes at any point in time. Increasingly, those boxes are not placed inside a decorative cover. Much of that is due to Kimberly-Clark's innovative efforts to improve the design aesthetics of the Kleenex box. Oval-shaped packages and embossed wallpaper-like patterns have been introduced as well as seasonal offerings. An oval package with a pattern of Christmas lights was introduced that actually flickered when a tissue was taken out. To boost summer sales—when revenue typically drops by as much as 60 percent from the winter months—new packages were launched that resembled wedges of fruit such as watermelon, orange, and lime. Through all these packaging innovations, Kimberly-Clark hopes to keep Kleenex differentiated as the market leader.

Marketers of major brands have also increased advertising and promotion budgets. They have also tracked store-brand growth more closely than in the past and are competing on a market-by-market basis. Marketers of major brands have also adjusted their brand portfolios. They have eliminated stagnant brands and extensions and concentrated their efforts on smaller numbers of brands. They have introduced discount "fighter" brands that are specially designed and promoted to compete with private labels.

Marketers of major brands have also been more aggressive about legally protecting their brands. For example, Unilever filed suit against global supermarket giant Ahold alleging trademark and trade dress (the design and visual appearance of the product and package) infringement across four of its European margarine brands. Unilever also filed suit against Lipton iced tea and Bertolli olive oil, maintaining that their packaging looked too similar to its own brands.[127]

One controversial move by some marketers of major brands is actually to supply private-label makers. For example, Sara Lee, Del Monte, and Birds Eye have all supplied products—sometimes lower in quality—to be used for private labels in the past. Other marketers, however, criticize this "if you can't beat 'em, join 'em" strategy, maintaining that these actions, if revealed, may create confusion or even reinforce a perception by consumers that all brands in a category are essentially the same.

Future Developments

Many marketers feel that the brands most endangered by the rise of private labels are second-tier brands that have not been as successful at establishing a clear identity as market leaders have. For example, in the laundry detergent category, the success of a private-label brand such as Walmart's Ultra Clean is more likely to come at the expense of brands such as Oxydol, All, or Fab rather than market leader Tide. Highly priced, poorly differentiated, and undersupported brands are especially vulnerable to private-label competition.

At the same time, if nothing else, retailers will need the quality and image that goes along with well-researched, efficiently manufactured, and professionally marketed major brands, because of consumer demand. The rise of private label brands by e-commerce companies support this idea. Recent developments in private labels includes the creation of an e-commerce brand called *Uniquely J*, which is a private brand owned by Jet.com (which, in turn, is owned by Wal-Mart Stores). Another e-commerce giant, Amazon.com, has entered the fray with many private-label brands.[128] Its brand Happy Belly has grown significantly primarily due to its ability to promote its products through its deals platform and Amazon's existing loyal customer base. Following its acquisition of Whole Foods Market, Amazon began selling 365 on the Amazon.com Web site, which allowed it to expand its appeal. Amazon launched its private-label brand Wickedly Prime, and the boxes feature the Amazon "smile" in the brand's logo, and the product packaging says that it is "Distributed by Amazon Fulfillment Services."[129] The Wickedly Prime brand is available to Amazon Prime members, and it targets millennials and foodies with a range of products such as popcorn, tortilla chips, and so on.[130] Amazon has made significant inroads in terms of market share across a variety of categories including speakers (such as Amazon Echo), baby wipes (such as Amazon Elements), and batteries (such as AmazonBasics).[131] Thanks to its acquisitions of brands across various categories, Amazon now has more than 70 private-label launches or acquisitions of thriving private-label brands, Amazon's business is expected to generate added revenues of $25 billion by 2022.[132] While traditional private-label brands aimed to be cheap, utilitarian alternatives to national brands, recent private-label brands have developed their own identities. For example, Amazon's Wickedly Prime popcorn touts that it is expertly crafted in Chicago. These, along with the strides made by private label brands in bolstering quality, suggest that the lines between private label and national brands are increasingly blurring.

NOTES

1. Philip Kotler and Kevin Lane Keller, *Marketing Management,* 14th ed. (Upper Saddle River, NJ: Prentice Hall, 2012).
2. Ibid.
3. Scott S. Smith, "Gary Erickson Guided Clif Bar's Rise by Taking the Road Less Traveled," *Investor's Business Daily,* April 24, 2017, www.investors.com/news/management/leaders-and-success/gary-erickson-guided-clif-bars-rise-by-taking-the-road-less-traveled/, accessed October 30, 2018.
4. Ibid.
5. Kelsi Hashtag Marx, "Lessons from Clif Bar's #MeetTheMoment Campaign," *Simply Measured,* January 13, 2015, https://simplymeasured.com/blog/hashtag-lessons-from-clif-bars-meetthemoment-campaign/#sm.0001oftwtwoewf8g10y7pyckc62m4, accessed October 30, 2018.
6. Renée Frojo, "Clif Bar CEO Has Company Revenue and Employee Count Growing," *San Francisco Business Times,* November 10, 2016, www.bizjournals.com/sanfrancisco/news/2016/11/10/most-admired-kevin-cleary-clif-bar-revenue-growth.html; "Top Nutritional Health Bar Brands, 2016," in *Market Share Reporter,* edited by Robert S. Lazich and Virgil L. Burton, III, 28th ed., Gale, 2018. *Gale Directory Library,* http://link.galegroup.com/apps/doc/EJPGFJ606041841/GDL?u=upitt_main&sid=GDL&xid=19347d0f, accessed October 30, 2018.
7. Peter Post, "Beyond Brand—The Power of Experience Branding," *ANA/The Advertiser,* October/November 2000.
8. B. Joseph Pine and James H. Gilmore, *The Experience Economy: Work Is Theatre and Every Business a Stage* (Cambridge, MA: Harvard University Press, 1999).
9. Bernd H. Schmitt and David L. Rogers, *Handbook on Brand and Experience Management* (Northampton, MA: Edward Elgar Publishing, 2008); Bernd H. Schmitt, *Customer Experience Management: A Revolutionary Approach to Connecting with Your Customers* (Hoboken, NJ: John Wiley & Sons, 2003); Bernd H. Schmitt, *Experiential Marketing: How to Get Customers to Sense, Feel, Think, Act, and Relate to Your Company and Brands* (New York: Free Press, 1999): 53–67.
10. Liz Zarantonello and Bernd H. Schmitt, "Using the Brand Experience Scale to Profile Consumers and Predict Consumer Behaviour," *Journal of Brand Management* 17, no. 7 (June 2010): 532–540.
11. Christopher Meyer and Andre Schwager, "Understanding Customer Experience," *Harvard Business Review,* February 1, 2007, https://hbr.org/product/understanding-customer-experience/R0702G-PDF-ENG, accessed October 30, 2018.
12. Nikki Gililand, "Five Innovative Examples of Food & Drink Brand Experiences," *Econsultancy,* August 31, 2017, https://econsultancy.com/blog/69389-five-innovative-examples-of-food-drink-brand-experiences, accessed March 14, 2018.
13. Michelle Greenwald, "The 3 Best Global Brand Experiences: Guinness, Van Cleef & Arpels, Samsung," *Forbes,* June 6, 2016, www.forbes.com/sites/michellegreenwald/2016/06/06/3-of-the-best-global-brand-experiences-guinness-van-cleef-arpels-samsung/#372e3de04df3, accessed October 30, 2018.
14. Harpersbazaararabia.com, "D3 Jewels: Van Cleef & Arpels Announces Arrival of L'ECOLE In The Middle East," *Harper's Bazaar Arabia,* April 12, 2017, www.harpersbazaararabia.com/fashion/watches-jewellery/d3-jewels-van-cleef-arpels-announces-arrival-of-l%E2%80%99ecole-in-the-middle-east, accessed March 15, 2018.
15. Nikki Gililand, "Five Innovative Examples of Food & Drink Brand Experiences," August 31, 2017, https://econsultancy.com/blog/69389-five-innovative-examples-of-food-drink-brand-experiences, accessed March 14, 2018.
16. Keith Bendes, "The Key to Extending the ROI of Brand Experiences," *Forbes,* January 16, 2018, www.forbes.com/sites/forbescommunicationscouncil/2018/01/16/the-key-to-extending-the-roi-of-brand-experiences/2/#1306a0ca3a9e.
17. Jennifer Aaker, Susan Fournier, and S. Adam Brasel, "When Good Brands Do Bad," *Journal of Consumer Research* 31, no. 1 (June 2004): 1–16; Pankaj Aggarwal, "The Effects of Brand Relationship Norms on Consumer Attitudes and Behavior," *Journal of Consumer Research* 31, no. 1 (June 2004): 87–101; Pankaj Aggarwal and Sharmistha Law, "Role of Relationship Norms in Processing Brand Information," *Journal of Consumer Research* 32, no. 3 (December 2005): 453–464.
18. Frederick F. Reichheld, *The Loyalty Effect* (Boston, MA: Harvard Business School Press, 1996); Robert W. Palmatier, Rajiv P. Dant, Dhruv Grewal, and Kenneth R. Evans, "Factors Influencing the Effectiveness of Relationship Marketing: A Meta-Analysis," *Journal of Marketing* 70, no. 4 (October 2006): 136–153.
19. Roland T. Rust, Christine Moorman, and Peter R. Dickson, "Getting Returns from Service Quality: Revenue Expansion, Cost Reduction, or Both?," *Journal of Marketing* 66, no. 4 (October 2002): 7–24.
20. Jenna Gross, "Take It Personal: Relationship Marketing in the Age of Digital," *Forbes,* February 5, 2018, www.forbes.com/sites/forbesagencycouncil/2018/02/05/take-it-personal-relationship-marketing-in-the-age-of-digital/3/#985053c55015, accessed October 30, 2018.
21. Dave Sloan, "5 Signs That Customer Co-creation Is a Trend to Watch," July 19, 2010, Venture Beat, https://venturebeat.com/2010/07/19/5-signs-that-customer-co-creation-is-a-trend-to-watch/, accessed October 30, 2018.
22. Rob Boehring, "45 Examples of Personalized Marketing That Really Work," *Rewardstream,* https://rewardstream.com/blog/45-examples-personalized-marketing-really-work/, accessed October 30, 2018.
23. Sallie Burnett, "Tesco Revamps Loyalty Program," *Customer Insight Group,* September 20, 2010, https://www.customerinsightgroup.com/loyaltyblog/loyal-customers-in-britain-the-tesco-story; Mary-Louise Clews, "Tesco Unveils Plan for Next Generation of Loyalty Card," *Marketing Week* 32, no. 16 (2009): 73. Zoe Wood and Teena Lyons, "Clubcard Couple Head for Checkout at Tesco," *The Guardian,* October 29, 2010, https://www.theguardian.com/business/2010/oct/29/tesco-clubcard-couple-depart.
24. Sarah Vizard "How the Tesco Brand Recovered from Crisis," *Marketing Week,* April 18, 2016, www.marketingweek.com/2016/04/18/how-the-tesco-brand-bounced-back-from-crisis/, accessed October 30, 2018.

25. Seth Godin, *Permission Marketing: Turning Strangers into Friends, and Friends into Customers* (New York: Simon & Schuster, 1999).

26. Jeffrey K. Rohrs, Seth Godin's 'Permission Marketing' Turns 15," *Forbes*, April 30, 2014, www.forbes.com/sites/onmarketing/2014/04/30/seth-godins-permission-marketing-turns-15/#61b3b24958e4, accessed October 30, 2018.

27. Susan Fournier, Susan Dobscha, and David Mick, "Preventing the Premature Death of Relationship Marketing," *Harvard Business Review* 76, no. 1 (January–February 1998): 42–51; Erwin Danneels, "Tight-Loose Coupling with Customers: The Enactment of Customer Orientation," *Strategic Management Journal* 24, no. 6 (2003): 559–576.

28. David A. Yovanno, "Why Permission Marketing Is the Future of Online Advertising," *Mashable*, February 3, 2011, https://mashable.com/2011/02/03/permission-marketing-social-data/#nHU4PwNGtuq1, accessed October 30, 2018.

29. Seth Godin, *Permission Marketing: Turning Strangers into Friends, and Friends into Customers* (New York: Simon & Schuster, 1999); Andy Kulina and Morgan Beard, "The Importance of Permission Marketing in the Digital Age," *TSYS*, www.tsys.com/Assets/TSYS/downloads/wp_the-importance-of-permission-marketing-in-the-digital-age.pdf, accessed March 20, 2018.

30. Andy Kulina and Morgan Beard, "The Importance of Permission Marketing in the Digital Age," www.tsys.com/Assets/TSYS/downloads/wp_the-importance-of-permission-marketing-in-the-digital-age.pdf, accessed March 20, 2018.

31. Lesley Fair, " What Vizio Was Doing Behind the TV Screen," *Federal Trade Commission*, February 6, 2017, www.ftc.gov/news-events/blogs/business-blog/2017/02/what-vizio-was-doing-behind-tv-screen, accessed October 30, 2018.

32. FTC.gov, "VIZIO to Pay $2.2 Million to FTC, State of New Jersey to Settle Charges It Collected Viewing Histories on 11 Million Smart Televisions Without Users' Consent," *Federal Trade Commission*, February 6, 2017, www.ftc.gov/news-events/press-releases/2017/02/vizio-pay-22-million-ftc-state-new-jersey-settle-charges-it, accessed October 30, 2018.

33. WARC.com, "Consumers' Privacy Concerns Grow," *WARC*, January 25, 2017, www.warc.com/NewsAndOpinion/News/38101; KPMG.com, "Companies That Fail to See Privacy as a Business Priority Risk Crossing the 'Creepy Line'," November 6, 2016, https://home.kpmg.com/sg/en/home/media/press-releases/2016/11/companies-that-fail-to-see-privacy-as-a-business-priority-risk-crossing-the-creepy-line.html, accessed October 30, 2018.

34. Marie Stafford and Elizabeth Cherian, "Consumer Data: Pass Control of Data to the Customer," *WARC*, May 2016, www.warc.com/content/article/admap/consumer_data_pass_control_of_data_to_the_customer/107364, accessed October 30, 2018.

35. Michael Nutley, "Participation Marketing Starts When Customers Talk Back," *CMO*, September 26, 2014, www.cmo.com/features/articles/2014/9/26/participation_market.html#gs.BHkObcUNeel.

36. Stratford Sherman, "How to Prosper in the Value Decade," *Fortune,* November 30, 1992, 91.

37. David Garvin, "Product Quality: An Important Strategic Weapon," *Business Horizons* 27, no. 3 (May–June 1985): 40–43; Philip Kotler, *Marketing Management,* 10th ed. (Upper Saddle River, NJ: Prentice Hall, 2000).

38. Ross Beyeler, "Keeping the Flame Alive: 5 Strategies for the Post-purchase Relationship," *The Future of Customer Engagement and Commerce*, March 6, 2015, www.the-future-of-commerce.com/2015/03/06/keeping-the-flame-alive-5-strategies-for-the-post-purchase-relationship/.

39. Jessica Mintz, "Using Hand, Grab Hair. Pull," *The Wall Street Journal,* December 23, 2004, B1, B5.

40. Jacqueline Martense, "Get Close to Your Customers," *Fast Company,* August 2005, 37.

41. Terry Vavra, *Aftermarketing: How to Keep Customers for Life Through Relationship Marketing* (Chicago, IL: Irwin Professional Publishers, 1995).

42. Wayne Huang, John Mitchell, Carmel Dibner, Andrea Ruttenberg, and Audrey Tripp, "How Customer Service Can Turn Angry Customers into Loyal Ones," *Harvard Business Review*, January 16, 2018, https://hbr.org/2018/01/how-customer-service-can-turn-angry-customers-into-loyal-ones.

43. Isabella Steele, "Don't Try This at Work: 15 Social Media Mistakes and Bad Customer Service Examples to Avoid at All Costs," November 6, 2017, www.comm100.com/blog/social-media-customer-service-mistakes.html.

44. Michael Brenner, "5 Examples of Brilliant Brand Communities That Are Shaping the Online World," *Comm100*, May 1, 2017, https://marketinginsidergroup.com/content-marketing/5-examples-brilliant-brand-communities-shaping-online-world/.

45. Clif Edwards, "HP Gets Tough on Ink Counterfeiters," *Bloomberg BusinessWeek*, May 28, 2009, https://www.bloomberg.com/news/articles/2009-05-28/hp-gets-tough-on-ink-counterfeiters; Tom Spring, "Why Do Ink Cartridges Cost So Much?," *PCWorld,* September 3, 2003, https://www.pcworld.idg.com.au/article/27024/why_do_ink_cartridges_cost_much_/, accessed October 30, 2018.

46. Aditya Ambadipudi, Alexander Brotschi, Markus Forsgren, Florent Kervazo, Hugues Lavandier, and James Xing, "Industrial Aftermarket Services: Growing the Core," *McKinsey & Company*, July 2017, www.mckinsey.com/industries/advanced-electronics/our-insights/industrial-aftermarket-services-growing-the-core.

47. Michael Bean, "Developing an Aftermarket Strategy," *Forio's Forum*, June 29, 2003.

48. Aditya Ambadipudi, Alexander Brotschi, Markus Forsgren, Florent Kervazo, Hugues Lavandier, and James Xing "Industrial Aftermarket Services: Growing the Core," July 2017, www.mckinsey.com/industries/advanced-electronics/our-insights/industrial-aftermarket-services-growing-the-core, accessed March 15, 2018.

49. Kevin Lane Keller, "Loyal, My Brand, to Thee," *Promo,* October 1, 1997; Arthur Middleton Hughes, "How Safeway Built Loyalty—Especially among Second-Tier Customers," *Target Marketing,* March 1, 1999, https://www.targetmarketingmag.com/article/how-safeway-built-loyaltyespecially-among-second-tier-customer-28212/all/, accessed October 30, 2018; Laura Bly, "Frequent Fliers Fuel a Global Currency," *USA Today,* April 27, 2001, p. 36.

50. Frequency Marketing, accessed December 10, 2011, www.frequencymarketing.com.

51. Alex McCeachern, "A History of Loyalty Programs, and How They Have Changed," *Smile.io*, November 24, 2017, https://blog.smile.io/a-history-of-loyalty-programs.

52. James L. Heskett, W. Earl Sasser Jr., and Leonard A. Schlesinger, *The Service Profit Chain* (New York: Simon & Schuster, 1997); Michael Lewis, "The Influence of Loyalty Programs and Short-Term Promotions on Customer Retention," *Journal of Marketing Research* 41, no. 3 (August 2004), 281–292; Yuping Liu, "The Long-Term Impact of Loyalty Programs on Consumer Purchase Behavior and Loyalty," *Journal of Marketing* 71, no. 4 (October 2007): 19–35.

53. Elizabeth Holmes, "Why Pay Full Price?," *The Wall Street Journal*, May 5, 2011, https://www.wsj.com/articles/SB10001424052748703834804576301221367302288, accessed October 30, 2018.

54. For a more detailed and comprehensive treatment of pricing strategy, see Thomas T. Nagle and Reed K. Holden, *The Strategy and Tactics of Pricing: A Guide to Profitable Decision-Making,* 5th ed. (Upper Saddle River, NJ: Prentice Hall, 2011); Kent B. Monroe, *Pricing: Making Profitable Decisions*, 3rd ed. (New York: McGraw-Hill/Irwin, 2002); Robert J. Dolan and Hermann Simon, *Power Pricing* (New York: Free Press, 1997).

55. Robert C. Blattberg and Kenneth Wisniewski, "Price-Induced Patterns of Competition," *Marketing Science* 8, no. 4 (Fall 1989): 291–309.

56. Elliot B. Ross, "Making Money with Proactive Pricing," *Harvard Business Review* 63, no. 6 (November–December 1984): 145–155.

57. www.pvh.com/annual_pdfs/pdf_2004/corp_strategy.pdf. All brands in the figure are registered trademarks of Phillips-Van Heusen or its licensors.

58. Phillip Kotler and Kevin Lane Keller, *Marketing Management,* 12th ed. (Upper Saddle River: NJ: Prentice Hall, 2006).

59. Anirudh Dhebar, "Razor-and-Blades Pricing Revisited," *Business Horizons* 59, no. 3 (2016): 303–310.

60. Consumer Reports.com, "Can Epson EcoTank Printers Deliver Cheap Ink?," *Consumer Reports*, August 4, 2015, www.consumerreports.org/cro/news/2015/08/epson-ecotank-printers-deliver-cheap-ink/index.htm.

61. Vineet Kumar, "Making 'Freemium' Work," *Harvard Business Review*, (May 2014): 2–4.

62. "Number of registered Dropbox users from April 2011 to March 2016 (in millions), Statista, www.statista.com/statistics/261820/number-of-registered-dropbox-users/, accessed October 30, 2018.

63. Vineet Kumar, "Making 'Freemium' Work," *Harvard Business Review*, 92, no. 5 (May 2014): 2–4.

64. Panera Bread Foundation, "Panera Cares," accessed March 3, 2018, http://paneracares.org/.

65. Alan Ohnsman and Seonjin Cha, "Restyling Hyundai for the Luxury Market," *Bloomberg BusinessWeek*, December 28, 2009, https://www.bloomberg.com/news/articles/2009-12-28/restyling-hyundai-for-the-luxury-market; Hannah Elliott, "Best New-Car Incentives," *Forbes*, February 3, 2010, https://www.forbes.com/2010/02/03/new-car-incentives-lifestyle-vehicles-cash-back-deals_slide_8.html?thisspeed=25000#4c13e52932b0; Alex Taylor III, "Hyundai Smokes the Competition," *Fortune*, January 18, 2010, 62–71; David Kiley, "Hyundai Gains with Marketing Blitz," *Bloomberg*

BusinessWeek, September 17, 2009, https://www.bloomberg.com/news/articles/2009-09-17/hyundai-gains-with-marketing-blitz, accessed October 30, 2018; Moon Ihlwan and David Kiley, "Hyundai Floors It in the U.S.," *BusinessWeek*, February 27, 2009, 30–31.

66. Vignesh Vijayenthran, "Hyundai Looks to Make Car Buying Easier Via Transparent Pricing, Full Refunds," *Motor Authority*, October 11, 2017, www.motorauthority.com/news/1113197_hyundai-looks-to-make-car-buying-easier-via-transparent-pricing-full-refunds.

67. Peter Coy, "The Power of Smart Pricing," *BusinessWeek,* April 10, 2000, https://www.bloomberg.com/news/articles/2000-04-09/the-power-of-smart-pricing, accessed October 30, 2018.

68. Allan J. Magrath, "Eight Timeless Truths about Pricing," *Sales & Marketing Management* (October 1989): 78–84.

69. Thomas J. Malott, CEO of Siemens, which makes heavy electrical equipment and motors, quoted in Stratford Sherman, "How to Prosper in the Value Decade," *Fortune,* November 30, 1992, https://money.cnn.com/magazines/fortune/fortune_archive/1992/11/30/77188/index.htm, accessed October 30, 2018.

70. For a discussion of the pros and cons of customer value mapping (CVM) and economic value mapping (EVM), see Gerald E. Smith, and Thomas T. Nagle, "Pricing the Differential," *Marketing Management,* May/June 2005, 28–32.

71. Claire Cain Miller, "Will the Hard-Core Starbucks Customer Pay More? The Chain Plans to Find Out," *The New York Times*, August 20, 2009, https://www.nytimes.com/2009/08/21/business/21sbux.html, accessed October 30, 2018.

72. Adrienne Carter, "Telling the Risky from the Reliable," *BusinessWeek*, August 1, 2005, 57–58.

73. Ben Sisario, "Ticketmaster Plans to Use a Variable Pricing Policy," *The New York Times*, April 18, 2011, https://www.nytimes.com/2011/04/19/business/19pricing.html, accessed October 30, 2018.

74. Alecia Swasy, "In a Fast-Paced World, Procter & Gamble Sets Its Store in Old Values," *The Wall Street Journal,* September 21, 1989, A1; Zachary Schiller, "The Marketing Revolution at Procter & Gamble," *BusinessWeek,* July 25, 1988, 72; Bill Saporito, "Behind the Tumult at P&G," *Fortune,* March 7, 1994, 74–82; Zachary Schiller, "Procter & Gamble Hits Back," *BusinessWeek,* July 19, 1993, https://www.bloomberg.com/news/articles/1993-07-18/procter-and-gamble-hits-back, accessed October 30, 2018; Zachary Schiller, "Ed Artzt's Elbow Grease Has P&G Shining," *BusinessWeek,* October 10, 1994, https://www.bloomberg.com/news/articles/1994-10-09/ed-artzts-elbow-grease-has-p-and-g-shining, accessed October 30, 2018; Zachary Schiller, "Make It Simple: That's P&G's New Marketing Mantra and It's Spreading," *BusinessWeek*, September 9, 1996, https://www.bloomberg.com/news/articles/1996-09-08/make-it-simple, accessed October 30, 2018; "Investor's Business Daily, "Executive Update Value Pricing Plan Helps Push Products," *Investor's Business Daily,* August 30, 1995. For an interesting analysis, see Kusum L. Ailawadi, Donald R. Lehmann, and Scott A. Neslin, "Market Response to a Major Policy Change in the Marketing Mix: Learning from P&G's Value Pricing Strategy," *Journal of Marketing* 65, no. 1 (2001): 71–89.

75. Richard Gibson, "Broad Grocery Price Cuts May Not Pay," *The Wall Street Journal,* May 7, 1993, B1.

76. Ellen Byron, "P&G Puts Up Its Dukes Over Pricing," *The Wall Street Journal*, April 30, 2010, https://www.wsj.com/articles/SB100014240527487043023045752137 80586525548; Jack Neff and E. J. Schultz, "P&G, Colgate, Clorox to Raise Prices, Marketing Spending," *Advertising Age*, February 25, 2011, http://adage.com/article/news/p-g-colgate-clorox-raise-prices-marketing-spending/149116/.

77. Donald R. Lehmann and Russell S. Winer, *Product Management*, 4th ed. (New York: McGraw-Hill, 2007).

78. Phillip Kotler and Kevin Lane Keller, *Marketing Management,* 12th ed. (Upper Saddle River, NJ: Prentice Hall, 2006).

79. For a more detailed and comprehensive treatment of channel strategy, see Anne T. Coughlan, Erin Anderson, Louis W. Stern, and Adel I. El-Ansary, *Marketing Channels,* 7th ed. (Upper Saddle River, NJ: Prentice Hall, 2006).

80. Erik Siemers, "Nike Veers from Large Niketown Format," *Portland Business Journal*, May 16, 2010, https://www.bizjournals.com/portland/stories/2010/05/17/story9.html, accessed October 30, 2018; Mark Brohan, "Nike's Web Sales Flourish in Fiscal 2010," *Internet Retailer*, June 30, 2010, https://www.digitalcommerce360.com/2010/06/30/nikes-web-sales-flourish-fiscal-2010/.

81. Danny Wong, "NIKEiD Makes $100M+: Co-Creation Isn't Just a Trend," *The Huffington Post*, July 20, 2010, www.huffingtonpost.com/danny-wong/nikeid-makes-100m-co-crea_b_652214.html.

82. V. Kasturi Rangan, Melvyn A. J. Menezes, and E. P. Maier, "Channel Selection for New Industrial Products: A Framework, Method, and Applications," *Journal of Marketing* 56, no. 3 (July 1992): 69–82.

83. Rowland T. Moriarty and Ursula Moran, "Managing Hybrid Marketing Systems," *Harvard Business Review* 68 (Nov/Dec 1990): 146–155, https://hbr.org/1990/11/managing-hybrid-marketing-systems, accessed October 30, 2018.

84. Arius Agius, "7 Outstanding Examples of Omni-Channel Experience," December 13, 2017, https://blog.hubspot.com/customer-success/omni-channel-experience, accessed March 10, 2018.

85. Emma Sopadjieva, U. Dholakia, and Beth Benjamin, "A Study of 46,000 Shoppers Shows That Omnichannel Retailing Works," *Harvard Business Review* 3 (2017), https://hbr.org/2017/01/a-study-of-46000-shoppers-shows-that-omnichannel-retailing-works.

86. OroInc.com, "5 Great Examples of Integrating Online and Offline Marketing," *ORO Inc.*, September 13, 2017, https://oroinc.com/orocrm/blog/5-great-examples-integrating-online-offline-marketing.

87. United Parcel Service of America, "UPS Pulse of the Online Shopper: A Customer Experience Study," https://pressroom.ups.com/mobile0c9a66/assets/pdf/pressroom/white%20paper/UPS_2017_POTOS_media%20executive%20summary_FINAL.pdf, accessed March 11, 2018.

88. Nicki Gilliland, "How Retailers Are Using Geofencing to Improve In-store CX," *Econsultancy*, January 17, 2018, www.econsultancy.com/blog/69727-how-retailers-are-using-geofencing-to-improve-in-store-cx.

89. Emma Sopadjieva, U. Dholakia, and Beth Benjamin, "A Study of 46,000 Shoppers Shows That Omnichannel Retailing Works," *Harvard Business Review* 3 (2017), https://hbr.org/2017/01/a-study-of-46000-shoppers-shows-that-omnichannel-retailing-works.

90. T. L. Stanley, "5 Trends That Are Radically Reshaping Shopper Marketing," *Adweek*, June 19, 2016, www.adweek.com/brand-marketing/5-trends-are-radically-reshaping-shopper-marketing-171960/, accessed March 18, 2018.

91. Peter C. Verhoef, P. K. Kannan, and J. Jeffrey Inman, "From Multi-Channel Retailing to Omni-Channel Retailing Introduction to the Special Issue on Multi-Channel Retailing," *Journal of Retailing* 91, no. 2 (2015), 174–181.

92. David R. Bell, Santiago Gallino, and Antonio Moreno, "Offline Showrooms in Omnichannel Retail: Demand and Operational Benefits," *Management Science* 64, no. 4 (2017), 1629–1651.

93. Koen Pauwels and Scott A. Neslin, "Building with Bricks and Mortar: The Revenue Impact of Opening Physical Stores in a Multichannel Environment," *Journal of Retailing* 91, no. 2 (2015): 182–197.

94. Kusum L. Ailawadi and Paul W. Farris, "Managing Multi- and Omnichannel Distribution: Metrics and Research Directions," *Journal of Retailing* 93, no. 1 (2017): 120–135.

95. Think with Google, "Zero Moment of Truth (ZMOT)," accessed March 18, 2018, www.thinkwithgoogle.com/marketing-resources/micro-moments/zero-moment-truth/.

96. Ship Hyken, "The New Moment of Truth In Business," *Forbes*, April 19, 2016, www.forbes.com/sites/shephyken/2016/04/09/new-moment-of-truth-in-business/#400c203238d9, accessed October 30, 2018.

97. Edgar Elvarez, "How Rebecca Minkoff Uses Tech to Make Her Fashion Stores Stand Out," *Engadget*, December 25, 2016, www.engadget.com/2016/12/25/rebecca-minkoff-tech-stores/, accessed October 30, 2018.

98. For a discussion of CRM issues with multichannel retailers, see Jacquelyn S. Thomas and Ursula Y. Sullivan, "Managing Marketing Communications," *Journal of Marketing* 69, no. 4 (October 2005): 239–251.

99. Eyal Lanxner, "The Amazon Buy Box: How It Works for Sellers, and Why It's So Important," *Big Commerce*, www.bigcommerce.com/blog/win-amazon-buy-box/#what-is-the-amazon-buy-box, accessed October 25, 2018.

100. Steven M. Shugan, "Branded Variants," *Research in Marketing,* AMA Educators' Proceedings, Series no. 55 (Chicago: American Marketing Association, 1989), 33–38. Shugan cites alarm clocks, answering machines, appliances, baby items, binoculars, dishwashers, luggage, mattresses, microwaves, sports equipment, stereos, televisions, tools, and watches as examples.

101. Mark Bergen, Shantanu Dutta, and Steven M. Shugan, "Branded Variants: A Retail Perspective," *Journal of Marketing Research* 33 (February 1995): 9–21. Chen, Yuxin, and Tony Haitao Cui, "The Benefit of Uniform Price for Branded Variants," working paper, Kellogg School of Management, Northwestern University, 2011.

102. George E. Belch and Michael A. Belch, *Introduction to Advertising and Promotion* (Chicago: Irwin, 1995).

103. Matthew Townsend, "The Staying Power of Pop-Up Stores," *Bloomberg BusinessWeek*, November 11, 2010, thinkwithgoogle.com/marketing-resources/micro-moments/zero-moment-truth/, accessed October 30, 2018; Keith Mulvihill, "Pop-Up Stores Become Popular for New York Landlords," *The New York Times*, June 22, 2010, accessed October 30, 2018.

104. Humayun Khan, "Pop-Ups & the Future of Retail," accessed March 18, 2018, www.shopify.com/guides/ultimate-guide-to-pop-up-shops/the-future-of-retail.

105. Ibid.

106. Ann-Marie Alcántara, "Why These 2 Niche Ecommerce Brands Are Opening Up More Brick-and-Mortar Stores," *Adweek*, April 19, 2018, www.adweek.com/digital/why-these-2-ecommerce-brands-are-opening-up-more-brick-and-mortar-stores/.

107. Mary Kuntz, "These Ads Have Windows and Walls," *BusinessWeek,* February 27, 1995, 74.

108. Brooks Barnes, "Disney Reimagines Its Stores to Be More Like a Vacation," *The New York Times*, September 26, 2017, www.nytimes.com/2017/09/26/business/media/disney-stores.html, accessed October 30, 2018.

109. Kinshuk Jerath and Z. John Zhang, "Store Within a Store," *Journal of Marketing Research* 47, no. 4 (August 2010): 748–763.

110. Kit R. Roane, "Stores Within Stores: Retail's Savior?," *CNN Money*, January 24, 2011, http://archive.fortune.com/2011/01/24/news/companies/retail_stores_inside_stores.fortune/index.htm, accessed October 31, 2018.

111. Daphne Howland, "Store-within-a-Store: Brick-and-Mortar's 'Godfather Strategy'," *Retail Dive*, April 6, 2015, www.retaildive.com/news/store-within-a-store-brick-and-mortars-godfather-strategy/382275/.

112. *The Economist* (US), "Clicks, Bricks, and Bargains," *The Economist*, December 3, 2005, 57–58, https://www.economist.com/business/2005/12/01/clicks-bricks-and-bargains, accessed October 31, 2018.

113. eMarketer, "Catering to Multichannel Consumers," September 8, 2008, https://www.emarketer.com/Article/Catering-Multichannel-Consumers/1006516, accessed October 31, 2018.

114. Tamara Mendelsohn, "The Web's Impact on In-Store Sales: U.S. Cross-Channel Sales Forecast, 2006 To 2012," *Forrester Research*, May 2007, https://www.forrester.com/report/The+Webs+Impact+On+In Store+Sales+US+CrossChannel+Sales+Forecast+200 6+To+2012/-/E-RES42084#.

115. Chloe Rigby, "Multichannel Shoppers Spend 82% More," *InternetRetailing*, December 14, 2010, https://internetretailing.net/themes/themes/multichannel-shoppers-spend-82-more-6965, accessed October 31, 2018.

116. *The Economist*, "The Real Internet Revolution," August 19, 1999, https://www.economist.com/business/1999/08/19/the-real-internet-revolution, accessed October 31, 2018; Scott A. Neslin and Venkatesh Shankar, "Key Issues in Multichannel Customer Management: Current Knowledge and Future Directions," Journal of Interactive Marketing 23 (February 2009), 70–81, https://ssrn.com/abstract=2061792; Jie Zhang, Paul W. Farris, John W. Irvin, Tarun Kushwaha, Thomas J. Steenburgh, and Barton A. Weitz, "Crafting Integrated Multichannel Retailing Strategies," *Journal of Interactive Marketing*, 24 no. 2 (May 2010): 168–180; Jill Avery, Thomas J. Steenburgh, John Deighton, and Mary Caravella, "Adding Bricks to Clicks: Predicting the Patterns of Cross-Channel Elasticities Over Time," *Journal of Marketing* 76, no. 3 (May 2012): 96–111.

117. Lorrie Grant, "Retailers Private Label Brands See Sales Growth Boom," *USA Today*, April 15, 2004.

118. Noreen O'Leary, "New & Improved Private Label Brands," *Adweek*, October 22, 2007, https://www.adweek.com/brand-marketing/new-improved-private-label-brands-90737/, accessed October 31, 2018.

119. George Anderson, "Private Labels: The Global View," www.retailwire.com, October 2010.

120. "Tesco and Sainsbury's Expand Private Label Beverages," www.storebrandsdecisions.com, August 3, 2010; J. Sainsbury plc, "Sainsbury's Announces Its Biggest Ever Own-Label Revamp with Launch of 'by Sainsbury's'," May 11, 2011, https://web.archive.org/web/20110724182241/http://www.jsainsburys.co.uk/index.asp?PageID=424&section=&Year=Latest&NewsID=1535, accessed October 31, 2018.

121. *Consumer Reports*, "Latest Taste Tests Find Some Store Brands at Least as Good as National Brands," September 7, 2010, https://www.consumerreports.org/media-room/press-releases/2010/09/latest-taste-tests-find-some-store-brands-at-least-as-good-as-national-brands/, accessed October 31, 2018.

122. Ibid.

123. Irwin Speizer, "The Grocery Store That Shouldn't Be," *Fast Company*, February 2004, 31; Beth Kowitt, "Inside the Secret World of Trader Joe's," *Fortune*, August 23, 2010, http://archive.fortune.com/2010/08/20/news/companies/inside_trader_joes_full_version.fortune/index.htm, accessed October 31, 2018.

124. Tanzina Vega, "Walgreens Launches Campaign to Push Store-Brand Products," *The New York Times*, February 10, 2011, https://www.nytimes.com/2011/02/11/business/media/11adco.html, accessed October 31, 2018.

125. Mary L. Shelman and Ray A. Goldberg, "Loblaw Companies Limited," Case 9–588–039 (Boston, MA: Harvard Business School, 1994); Gordon H. G. McDougall and Douglas Snetsinger, "Loblaws," in *Marketing Challenges*, 3rd ed., eds. Christopher H. Lovelock and Charles B. Weinberg (New York: McGraw-Hill, 1993), 169–185; "Loblaw Launches a New Line of Discount Store Brands," www.storebrandsdecisions.com, February 16, 2010; Marina Strauss, "Loblaws Takes Aim at Rivals, *The Globe and Mail*, February 10, 2010, https://www.theglobeandmail.com/globe-investor/loblaw-takes-aim-at-rivals/article4306384/, accessed October 31, 2018.

126. Andrew Adam Newman, "A Sharp Focus on Design When the Package Is Part of the Product," *The New York Times*, July 8, 2010, https://www.theglobeandmail.com/globe-investor/loblaw-takes-aim-at-rivals/article4306384/, accessed October 31, 2018.

127. Jack Neff, "Marketers Put Down Foot on Private-Label Issue," *Advertising Age*, April 4, 2005, https://www.theglobeandmail.com/globe-investor/loblaw-takes-aim-at-rivals/article4306384/, accessed October 31, 2018, 14.

128. Sarah Halzack, "Retail's Secret Weapon Is the Private Label," *Bloomberg*, October 24, 2017, www.bloomberg.com/gadfly/articles/2017-10-24/private-label-brands-retail-s-new-secret-weapon, accessed June 4, 2018.

129. Sarah Perez, "Amazon Launches Its Newest Private Label, Wickedly Prime," *Tech Crunch*, December 23, 2016, https://techcrunch.com/2016/12/23/amazon-launches-its-newest-private-label-wickedly-prime/.

130. Ibid.

131. Ibid.

132. Thomas Franck, "Amazon's Flourishing Private Label Business to Help Stock Rally Another 20%, Analyst Says," *CNBC*, June 4, 2018, www.cnbc.com/2018/06/04/suntrust-amazons-private-label-business-to-help-stock-rally-20-percent.html.

6

Integrating Marketing Communications to Build Brand Equity

Learning Objectives

After reading this chapter, you should be able to

1. Describe some of the changes in the new media environment.
2. Outline the major marketing communication options.
3. Describe some of the key tactical issues in evaluating different communication options.
4. Identify the choice criteria in developing an integrated marketing communication program.
5. Explain the rationale for mixing and matching communication options.

Ford launched its new Fiesta model in the United States with a combination of events, traditional media, and a heavy dose of social media.

Source: P. Cox/Alamy Stock Photo

184

PREVIEW

The preceding chapter described how various marketing activities and product, price, and distribution strategies can contribute to brand equity. This chapter considers the final, and perhaps most flexible, element of marketing programs. *Marketing communications* are the means by which companies attempt to inform, persuade, and remind consumers—directly or indirectly—about the brands they sell. In a sense, marketing communications represent the voice of the brand and are a means by which the brand can establish a dialogue and build relationships with consumers. Although advertising is often a central element of a marketing communications program, it is usually not the only element—or even the most important one—for building brand equity. Figure 6-1 displays some of the common marketing communication options for the consumer market.

Designing marketing communication programs is a complex task. We begin by describing the rapidly changing media landscape and the new realities in marketing communications. To provide necessary background, we next evaluate how the major communication options contribute to brand equity and some of their main costs and benefits. We conclude by considering how to mix and match communication options—that is, how to employ a range of communication options in a coordinated or integrated fashion—to build brand equity. We consider some of what we have learned about advertising in Brand Focus 6.0. For the sake of brevity, we will not consider specific marketing communication issues such as media scheduling, budget estimation techniques, and research approaches or the topic of personal selling.[1]

Media advertising
Television
Radio
Newspaper
Magazines

Direct response advertising
Mail
Telephone
Broadcast media
Print media
Computer-related
Media-related

Place advertising
Billboards and posters
Movies, airlines, and lounges
Product placement
Point of purchase

Point-of-purchase advertising
Shelf talkers
Aisle markers
Shopping cart ads
In-store radio or TV

Trade promotions
Trade deals and buying allowances
Point-of-purchase display allowances
Push money
Contests and dealer incentives
Training programs
Trade shows
Cooperative advertising

Consumer promotions
Samples
Coupons
Premiums
Refunds and rebates
Contests and sweepstakes
Bonus packs
Price-offs

Digital marketing
Search
Display
Social Media (Facebook, Twitter)
E-mail
Video
Blogs

Event marketing and sponsorship
Sports
Arts
Entertainment
Fairs and festivals
Cause-related

Mobile
SMS & MMS messages
Ads
Location-based services

Publicity and public relations
Word-of-mouth
Personal selling

FIGURE 6-1
Marketing Communications Options

THE NEW MEDIA ENVIRONMENT

Although advertising and other communication options can play different roles in the marketing program, one important purpose they all serve is to contribute to brand equity. According to the customer-based brand equity model, marketing communications can contribute to brand equity in a number of different ways: by creating awareness of the brand; linking points-of-parity and points-of-difference associations to the brand in consumers' memory; eliciting positive brand judgments or feelings; and facilitating a stronger consumer–brand connection and brand resonance. In addition to forming the desired brand knowledge structures, marketing communication programs can provide incentives eliciting the differential response that makes up customer-based brand equity.

The flexibility of marketing communications comes in part from the number of different ways they can contribute to brand equity. At the same time, brand equity helps marketers determine how to design and implement a variety of marketing communication options. In this chapter, we consider how to develop marketing communication programs to build brand equity. We will assume the other elements of the marketing program have been properly put into place. Thus, the optimal brand positioning has been defined—especially in terms of the desired target market—and product, pricing, distribution, and other marketing program decisions have largely been made.

Complicating the picture for marketing communications programs, however, is that fact that the media environment has changed dramatically in recent years. Traditional advertising media such as television, radio, magazines, and newspapers seem to be losing their grip on consumers due to increased competition for consumer attention. The digital revolution offers a host of new ways for consumers to learn and talk about brands with companies or with each other.

Challenges in Designing Brand-Building Communications

The new media environment has further complicated marketers' perennial challenge to build effective and efficient marketing communication programs. Skillfully designed and implemented marketing communications programs require careful planning and a creative knack. Let us first consider a few useful tools to provide some perspective.

Perhaps the simplest—but most useful—way to judge any communication option is by its ability to contribute to brand equity. For example, how well does a proposed ad campaign contribute to brand awareness or to creating, maintaining, or strengthening certain brand associations? Does a sponsorship cause consumers to have more favorable brand judgments and feelings? To what extent does an online promotion encourage consumers to buy more of a product? To what extent and at what price does an online promotion encourage consumers to buy more of a product? Figure 6-2 displays a simple three-step model for judging the effectiveness of advertising or any communication option to build brand equity.

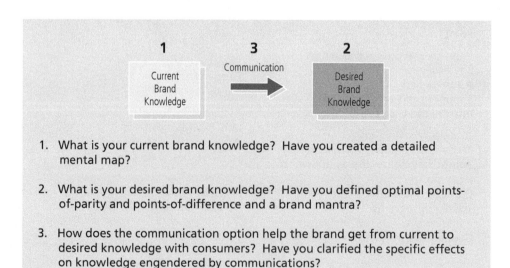

FIGURE 6-2

Simple Test for Marketing
Communication
Effectiveness

Information Processing Model of Communications.   To provide some perspective, let's consider in more depth the process by which marketing communications might affect consumers. Several models have been put forth over the years to explain communications and the steps in the persuasion process—recall the discussion on the hierarchy of effects model from Brand Focus 2.0. For example, for a person to be persuaded by any form of communication (a TV advertisement, newspaper editorial, or blog posting), the following six steps must occur:[2]

1. **Exposure:** A person must see or hear the communication.
2. **Attention:** A person must notice the communication.
3. **Comprehension:** A person must understand the intended message or arguments of the communication.
4. **Yielding:** A person must respond favorably to the intended message or arguments of the communication.
5. **Intentions:** A person must plan to act in the desired manner of the communication.
6. **Behavior:** A person must actually act in the desired manner of the communication.

You can appreciate the challenge of creating a successful marketing communications program when you realize that each of the six steps must occur for a consumer to be persuaded. If there is a breakdown or failure in any step along the way, then successful communication will not result. For example, consider the potential pitfalls in launching a new advertising campaign:

1. A consumer may not be exposed to an ad because the media plan missed the mark.
2. A consumer may not notice an ad because of a boring and uninspired creative strategy.
3. A consumer may not understand an ad because of a lack of product category knowledge or technical sophistication, or because of a lack of awareness and familiarity about the brand itself.
4. A consumer may fail to respond favorably and form a positive attitude because of irrelevant or unconvincing product claims.
5. A consumer may fail to form a purchase intention because of a lack of an immediate perceived need.
6. A consumer may fail to actually buy the product because he or she does not remember anything from the ad when confronted with the available brands in the store.

To show how fragile the whole communication process is, assume that the probability of *each* of the six steps being successfully accomplished is 50 percent—most likely an extremely generous assumption. The laws of probability suggest that the likelihood of all six steps successfully occurring, assuming they are independent events, is $0.5 \times 0.5 \times 0.5 \times 0.5 \times 0.5 \times 0.5$, which equals 1.5625 percent. If the probability of each step's occurring, on average, were a more pessimistic 10 percent, then the joint probability of all six events occurring is .000001. In other words, only 1 in 1,000,000! No wonder advertisers sometimes lament the limited power of advertising.

One implication of the information processing model is that, to increase the odds for a successful marketing communications campaign, marketers must attempt to increase the likelihood that each step occurs. For example, from an advertising standpoint, the ideal ad campaign would ensure that:

1. The right consumer is exposed to the right message in the right place and at the right time.
2. The creative strategy for the advertising causes the consumer to notice and attend to the ad but does not distract from the intended message.
3. The advertisement properly reflects the consumer's level of understanding about the product and the brand.
4. The ad correctly positions the brand in terms of desirable and deliverable points-of-difference and points-of-parity.
5. The ad motivates consumers to consider the purchase of the brand.
6. The ad creates strong brand associations to all these stored communication effects so that they can have an effect when consumers are considering making a purchase.

Marketers need to design and execute marketing communication programs carefully if they are to have the desired effects on consumers.

Role of Multiple Communications

How much and what kinds of marketing communications are necessary? Economic theory suggests placing dollars into a marketing communications budget and across communication options according to marginal revenue and cost. For example, the communication mix would be optimally distributed when the last dollar spent on each communication option generated the same return.

Because such information may be difficult to obtain, however, other models of budget allocation emphasize more observable factors such as stage of brand life cycle, objectives and budget of the firm, product characteristics, size of the budget, and media strategy of competitors. These factors are typically contrasted with the different characteristics of the media.

For example, marketing communication budgets tend to be higher when there is low channel support, much change in the marketing program over time, many hard-to-reach customers, more complex customer decision making, differentiated products and nonhomogeneous customer needs, and frequent product purchases in small quantities.[3]

Besides these efficiency considerations, different communication options also may target various market segments. For example, advertising may attempt to bring new customers into the market or attract competitors' customers to the brand, whereas promotions might attempt to reward loyal users of the brand.

Invariably, marketers will employ multiple communications to achieve their goals. In doing so, they must understand how each communication option works and how to assemble and integrate the best set of choices. The following section presents an overview and critique of four major marketing communication options from a brand-building perspective.

THREE MAJOR MARKETING COMMUNICATION OPTIONS

We contend that, in the future, there will be four vital ingredients to the best brand-building communication programs: (1) advertising and promotion, (2) interactive marketing, and (3) events and experiences. We consider each in turn.

Advertising

Advertising is any paid form of nonpersonal presentation and promotion of ideas, goods, or services by an identified sponsor. Although it is a powerful means of creating strong, favorable, and unique brand associations and eliciting positive judgments and feelings, advertising is controversial because its specific effects are often difficult to quantify and predict. Nevertheless, a number of studies using very different approaches have shown the potential power of advertising on brand sales. As Chapter 1 noted, the latest recession provided numerous examples of brands benefiting from increased advertising expenditures. Some prior research studies are consistent with that view.[4]

Given the complexity of designing advertising—the number of strategic roles it might play, the sheer number of specific decisions to make, and its complicated effect on consumers—it is difficult to provide a comprehensive set of detailed managerial guidelines. Different advertising media clearly have different strengths, however, and therefore, are best suited to play certain roles in a communication program. Brand Focus 6.0 provides some empirical generalizations about advertising. Now we'll highlight some key issues about each type of advertising medium in turn.

Television.　Television is a powerful advertising medium because it allows for sight, sound, and motion and reaches a broad spectrum of consumers. Virtually all U.S. households have televisions, and the average American watches five hours of television per day, and this includes both live television and DVR.[5] Approximately 50 percent of households within the U.S. now have access to streaming services from Netflix, Amazon Prime, or Hulu, suggesting a big shift in how television is being watched.[6]

Pros and Cons.　From a brand equity perspective, television advertising has two particularly important strengths. First, it can be an effective means of vividly demonstrating product attributes and persuasively explaining their corresponding consumer benefits. Second, TV advertising can be a compelling means for dramatically portraying user and usage imagery, brand personality, emotions, and other brand intangibles.

On the other hand, television advertising has its drawbacks. Because of the fleeting nature of the message and the potentially distracting creative elements often found in a TV ad, consumers can overlook product-related messages and the brand itself. Moreover, the large number of ads and nonprogramming material on television creates clutter that makes it easy for consumers to ignore or forget ads. A large number of channels creates fragmentation, and the widespread existence of digital video recorders gives viewers the means to skip commercials.

Another important disadvantage of television ads is the high cost of production and placement. In 2016, for example, a 30-second spot to air during the popular show *Walking Dead* —with a viewership of 16 million—was $400,000.[7] The cost of one TV spot on the NCAA Men's Basketball Game final on CBS was a whopping $1.55 million, for viewership of 21 million. A 30-second spot on a primetime broadcast television show typically costs over $112,000.[8] Although the price of TV advertising has skyrocketed, the share of the primetime audience for the major networks has steadily declined. By any number of measures, the effectiveness of any one television ad, on average, has diminished.

Nevertheless, properly designed and executed TV ads can affect sales and profits. For example, over the years, one of the most consistently successful TV advertisers has been Tide. Tide's television advertising success is highlighted in the box below.

TIDE

Tide is among the most-advertised brands in the United States with ad spend approaching $200 million dollars.[9] In 2018, the television ad for Tide shown during the Super Bowl garnered the largest number of tweets. Tide's advertising during the Super Bowl made every ad look like an ad for Tide.

How did Tide manage to do this? Procter & Gamble Co. (which owns Tide) ran four ads totaling one minute and thirty seconds that attempted to make every Super Bowl ad look like a Tide ad—by mimicking typical themes found in all the ads. For example, the brand used Isiah Mustafah reprising his role as the Old Spice guy, a reasonably believable pharmaceutical ad, and even a Clydesdale (which typically appears in every Budweiser commercial during Superbowl) being shown in a Tide ad. By injecting clever humor into their ads, Tide was able to capture a lot of the audience's attention.

Sources: Jack Neff, "Tide Is Everywhere with Campaign to Own All Super Bowl Ads," http://adage.com/article/special-report-super-bowl/t/312249/, accessed March 25, 2018; Jack Neff, "Tide Is Back in the Super Bowl, with a Couple Things It Hopes You Forget," January 30, 2018, http://adage.com/article/special-report-super-bowl/tide-back-super-bowl-a-couple-big-things-forget-pods-tambor/312143/, accessed March 6, 2018.

P&G, who has been cutting advertising budgets to minimize ineffective spending, recently shifted $100 million of its advertising funds away from digital, arguing that some hyper-targeting has not been very effective in generating reach.[10] This has also coincided with a time when television networks have been making a more aggressive case that marketers have indeed been allocating too much of their budgets to digital marketing.

Further clarity on the effectiveness of digital marketing to brand-building is needed to help marketers understand the optimal allocations of online and offline advertising. With increasing focus on creating single-source data (one which combines consumer purchase histories with data on multiple media including television, print, radio, digital, and social media), the ability to understand and evaluate the effectiveness of different media and channels will be greater. To that end, many marketers are investing in attribution modeling—which allows marketers to assess the contribution made by each advertising medium—as is discussed further in Chapter 10.

Guidelines.   In designing and evaluating an advertising campaign, marketers should distinguish the ***message strategy*** or positioning of an ad (what the ad attempts to convey about the brand) from its ***creative strategy*** (the way the ad expresses the brand claims). Designing effective advertising campaigns are both an art and a science: The artistic aspects relate to the creative strategy of the ad and its execution; the scientific aspects relate to the message strategy and the brand claim information the ad contains. Thus, as Figure 6-3 describes, the two main concerns in devising an advertising strategy is as follows:

- Defining the proper positioning to maximize brand equity
- Identifying the best creative strategy to communicate or convey the desired positioning

DEFINE POSITIONING TO ESTABLISH BRAND EQUITY

Competitive frame of reference
Nature of competition
Target market

Point-of-parity attributes or benefits
Category
Competitive
Correlational

Point-of-difference attributes or benefits
Desirable
Deliverable
Differentiating

IDENTIFY CREATIVE STRATEGY TO COMMUNICATE POSITIONING CONCEPT

Informational (benefit elaboration)
Problem–solution
Demonstration
Product comparison
Testimonial (celebrity or unknown consumer)

Transformational (imagery portrayal)
Typical or aspirational usage situation
Typical or aspirational user of product
Brand personality and values

Motivational ("borrowed interest" techniques)
Humor
Warmth
Sex appeal
Music
Fear
Special effects

FIGURE 6-3

Factors in Designing
Effective Advertising
Campaigns

Source: Based in part on an insightful framework put forth in John R. Rossiter and Larry Percy, Advertising and Promotion Management, 2nd ed. (New York: McGraw-Hill, 1997).

Chapter 3 described some issues with respect to positioning strategies to maximize brand equity. Creative strategies tend to be either largely *informational*, elaborating on a specific product-related attribute or benefit, or largely *transformational*, portraying a specific nonproduct-related benefit or image.[11] These two general categories each encompass several different specific creative approaches.

Regardless of which general creative approach marketers take, however, certain motivational or "borrowed interest" devices can attract consumers' attention and raise their involvement with an ad. These devices include cute babies, frisky puppies, popular music, well-known and liked celebrities, amusing situations, provocative sex appeals, and fear-inducing threats. Many believe such techniques are necessary for the new media environment characterized by low-involvement consumer processing and much competing ad and programming clutter.

Unfortunately, these attention-getting tactics are often *too* effective and distract from the brand or its product claims. Thus, the challenge in arriving at the best creative strategy is figuring out how to break through the clutter to attract the attention of consumers but still deliver the intended message.

Television advertising for brands increasingly leverages live events (e.g., sporting events such as Super Bowl) to garner greater attention and elevate advertising effectiveness.

What makes an effective TV ad?[12] Fundamentally, a TV ad should contribute to brand equity in some demonstrable way, for example, by enhancing awareness, strengthening a key association or adding a new association, or eliciting a positive consumer response. Earlier, we identified six broad information-processing factors as affecting the success of advertising: consumer targeting, the ad creative, consumer understanding, brand positioning, consumer motivation, and ad memorability.

Although managerial judgment using criteria such as these can and should be employed in evaluating advertising, research also can play a productive role. Advertising strategy research is often invaluable in clarifying communication objectives, target markets, and positioning alternatives. To evaluate the effectiveness of message and creative strategies, ***copy testing*** is often conducted, in which a sample of consumers is exposed to candidate ads and their reactions are gauged in some manner.

Unfortunately, copy-testing results vary considerably depending on exactly how tests are conducted. Consequently, the results must be interpreted as only one possible data point that should be combined with managerial judgment and other information in evaluating the merits of an ad. Copy testing is perhaps most useful when managerial judgment reveals some fairly clear positive and negative aspects to an ad, and is, therefore, somewhat inconclusive. In this case, copy-testing research may shed some light on how these various conflicting aspects "net out" and collectively affect consumer processing.

Regardless, copy-testing results should not be seen as a means of making a "go" or "no go" decision; ideally, they should play a diagnostic role in helping to understand *how* an ad works.

Future Prospects.   Although doubts have been raised about the future of television and traditional mass marketing advertising, it is clear that they are not going away anytime soon. Some key facts to keep in mind about TV advertising follow.

A great deal of television advertising is now focused on live TV events including various awards shows such as the Academy Awards and Grammys and sporting events such as the Olympic Games and World Cup Soccer. In the United States, National Football League (NFL) games are extremely popular, culminating in the Super Bowl. Some marketers focus their television advertising around these live events.[13]

According to David Christopher, CMO of AT&T Mobility, "TV, at least in the foreseeable future, is always going to have a place in big brands' media mixes. Every medium has a place in your mix. We think about it as video, not TV. That's how we buy it and how we think about it."[14]

Most of the impact of digital channels has been on the newspaper, magazine, and radio industries. Television advertising still offers a unique medium for advertising. Television advertising has evolved to include ads served during shows streamed on cable and broadcast channels, streaming apps, and Hulu. Although reports vary about how much time-shifting takes place, one analysis suggests that, in 2017, among adults 35 years and older, time-shifted television watching now accounts for 34 percent of the number of hours of television watched each week.[15] Among millennials, this number is much higher, and they watch 55 percent of their content on time-shifted formats.[16]Ads aired during shows that are streamed via Hulu which are viewed on large screens may be thought of as television, but are technically classified as digital advertising.[17]

Radio.   Radio is a pervasive medium: According to Nielsen research, 270 million, or 90 percent of the U.S. population, listen to the radio at least weekly.[18] The main advantage to radio is flexibility—stations are highly targeted, ads are relatively inexpensive to produce and place, and short closings allow for quick responses. Companies such as Comcast, T-Mobile, and Berkshire Hathaway are among the highest spenders in the United States on radio advertising.[19]

Radio is a particularly effective medium in the morning and can effectively complement or reinforce TV ads. Radio also enables companies to achieve a balance between broad and localized market coverage. One recent industry study claimed that $1 spent on radio advertising returns $12 in purchases for consumer-packaged goods companies.[20] Obvious disadvantages of radio, however, are the lack of visual image and the relatively passive nature of consumer processing that results. Several brands, however, have effectively built brand equity with radio ads.

MOTEL 6

One notable radio ad campaign is for Motel 6, the nation's largest budget motel chain, which was founded in 1962 when the "6" stood for $6 a night. After finding its business fortunes hitting bottom in 1986 with an occupancy rate of only 66.7 percent, Motel 6 made some marketing changes, including the launch of a radio campaign of humorous 60-second ads featuring folksy contractor-turned-writer Tom Bodett. Containing the clever tagline "We'll Leave the Light on for You," the campaign is credited with a rise in occupancy and a revitalization of the brand that continues to this day.[21] Keeping the same ad format, Motel 6's latest ad campaign still features Tom Bodett who riffs about millennials. The Motel 6 radio ad campaign has withstood the test of time for nearly three decades, a remarkable feat for a brand.[22]

Using the clever slogan, "We'll Leave the Light on for You," radio—complemented by magazine ads like this—has been a highly effective brand-building medium for Motel 6.
Source: Ken Wolter/Shutterstock

What makes an effective radio ad?[23] Radio has been less studied than other media. Because of its low-involvement nature and limited sensory options, advertising on the radio often must be fairly focused. For example, the advertising pioneer David Ogilvy believed four factors were critical:[24]

1. Identify your brand early in the commercial.
2. Identify it often.
3. Promise the listener a benefit early in the commercial.
4. Repeat it often.

Nevertheless, radio ads can be extremely creative. Some see the lack of visual images as a plus because they feel the clever use of music, sounds, humor, and other creative devices can tap into the listener's imagination in a way that creates powerfully relevant and liked images.

Print.   Print media has taken a huge hit in recent years as more and more consumers choose to collect information and seek entertainment online. In response, publishers are doing their own digital innovation in the form of iPad apps and a stronger Internet presence.

Print media does offer a stark contrast to broadcast media. Most importantly, because they are self-paced, magazines and newspapers can provide detailed product information. At the same time, the static nature of the visual images in print media makes it difficult to provide dynamic presentations or demonstrations. Another disadvantage of print advertising is that it can be a fairly passive medium.

Pros and Cons.   The two main print media—magazines and newspapers—have many of the same advantages and disadvantages. Magazines are particularly effective at building user and usage imagery. They can also be highly engaging: one study showed that consumers are more likely to view magazine ads as less intrusive, more truthful, and more relevant than ads in other media and are less likely to multitask while reading.[25]

Newspapers, however, are more timely and pervasive. Daily newspapers in the United States have about 35 million subscribers, but the numbers of subscribers are declining each year.[26] On the other hand, although advertisers have some flexibility in designing and placing newspaper ads, poor reproduction quality and short shelf life can diminish some of the possible impacts of newspaper advertising. These are disadvantages that magazine advertising usually does not share.

Although print advertising is particularly well suited to communicate product information, it can also effectively communicate user and usage imagery. Fashion brands such as Calvin Klein, Ralph Lauren, and Guess have also created strong nonproduct associations through print advertising. Some brands attempt to communicate both product benefits and user or usage imagery in their print advertising, for example, car makers such as Ford, Volkswagen, and Volvo or cosmetics makers such as Maybelline and Revlon.

One of the longest-running and perhaps most successful print advertising campaigns ever is for Absolut vodka.[27]

ABSOLUT

In 1980, Absolut was a tiny brand, selling 100,000 nine-liter cases a year. Research pointed out a number of liabilities for the brand: the name was seen as too gimmicky; the bottle shape was ugly, and bartenders found it hard to pour; shelf prominence was limited; and there was no credibility for a vodka brand made in Sweden. Michel Roux, president of Carillon (Absolut's importer), and TBWA (Absolut's New York ad agency) decided to use the oddities of the brand—its quirky name and bottle shape—to create brand personality and communicate quality and style in a series of creative print ads. Each ad in the campaign visually depicted the product in an unusual fashion and verbally reinforced the image with a simple, two-word headline using the brand name and some other word in a clever play on words. For example, the first ad showed the bottle prominently displayed, crowned by an angel's halo, with the headline "Absolut Perfection" appearing at the bottom of the page. Follow-up ads explored various themes (seasonal, geographic, celebrity artists) but always attempted to put forth a fashionable, sophisticated, and contemporary image. By 2001, Absolut had become the leading imported vodka in the United States, and by 2006, it was the third-largest premium spirits brand in the world, with sales of 9.8 million nine-liter cases. Facing slowing sales in 2007, however, the firm launched its first new campaign in 25 years, "In an Absolut World." Later ads expanded the meaning of an "Absolut World" to include special, offbeat, or unusual events, people, and things by including celebrities such as Kate Beckinsale and Zooey Deschanel.[28] Overall, Absolut's ad campaign represents one of the finest examples of the use of print advertising for brand-building purposes.

Absolut's new print ad campaign has returned to a creative strategy that emphasizes the product's packaging and appearance. This ad featured artist Dave Kinsey.

Source: monticello/Shutterstock

Guidelines.   What makes an effective print ad? The evaluation criteria we noted earlier for television advertising apply, but print advertising has some special requirements and rules. For example, research on print ads in magazines reveals that it is not uncommon for two-thirds of a magazine audience to not even notice any one particular print ad, or for only 10 percent or so of the audience to read much of the copy of any one ad. Many readers only glance at the most visible elements of a print ad, making it critical that an ad communicates clearly, directly, and consistently in the ad illustration and headline. Finally, many consumers can easily overlook the brand name if it is not readily apparent. We can summarize the creative guidelines for print ads in three simple criteria: clarity, consistency, and branding.

Direct Response.   In contrast to advertising in traditional broadcast and print media, which typically communicates to consumers in a nonspecific and nondirective manner, **direct response** uses mail, telephone, Internet, and other contact tools to communicate with or solicit a response from specific customers and prospects. Direct response can take many forms and is not restricted to solicitations by mail, telephone, or even within traditional broadcast and print media.

Direct mail remains popular, and more than 100 million U.S. adults made a catalog purchase in 2016.[29] Marketers are exploring other options, however. One increasingly popular means of direct marketing is infomercials, formally known as direct response TV marketing.[30] In a marketing sense, infomercials attempt to combine the sell of commercials with the draw of educational information and entertainment. We can, therefore, think of them as a cross between a sales call and a television ad. According to Infomercial DRTV, a trade Web site, infomercials are typically 28 minutes and 30 seconds long with an average cost in the $150,000 to $250,000 range (although production can cost as little as $75,000 and as much as $500,000).[31]

Starting with infomercials, although now moving online and also employing social media, many infomercial products are now showing up in stores carrying little "As Seen on TV" signs.

Brands such as Apple, Nissan, Discover Card, Nikon, and the U.S. Navy have all employed some form of direct response on television.[32] Some of the best-known infomercial campaigns have garnered millions of dollars in sales revenue. For example, Nutrisystem (the nutrition management system) had $545.5 million in revenue in 2016 and had $1.7 billion in market value in 2017, and a large part of their success is owed to infomercials.[33] Another infomercial success story is the Snuggie, which had $400 million in revenue in 2015.[34]

Guidelines.   The steady growth of direct marketing in recent years is a function of technological advances like the ease of setting up toll-free numbers and Web sites; changes in consumer behavior, such as the increased demand for convenience; and the needs of marketers, who want to avoid wasteful communications to nontarget customers or customer groups. The advantage of direct response is that it makes it easier for marketers to establish relationships with consumers.

Direct communications through electronic or physical newsletters, catalogs, and so forth allow marketers to explain new developments with their brands to consumers on an ongoing basis as well as allow consumers to provide feedback to marketers about their likes and dislikes and specific needs and wants. By learning more about customers, marketers can fine-tune marketing programs to offer the right products to the right customers at the right time. Direct marketing is often seen as a key component of relationship marketing—an important marketing trend we reviewed in Chapter 5. Some direct marketers employ what they call **precision marketing**—combining data analytics with strategic messages and compelling colors and designs in their communications.[35]

As the name suggests, the goal of direct response is to elicit some type of behavior from consumers; given that, it is easy to measure the effects of direct marketing efforts—people either respond or they do not. The disadvantages to direct response, however, are intrusiveness and clutter. To implement an effective direct marketing program, marketers need the three critical ingredients of (1) developing an up-to-date and informative list of current and potential future customers, (2) putting forth the right offer in the right manner, and (3) tracking the effectiveness of the marketing program. To improve the effectiveness of direct marketing programs, many marketers are embracing database marketing, as highlighted by The Science of Branding 6-1.

THE SCIENCE OF BRANDING 6-1
The Importance of Database Marketing

Formally, ***database marketing*** has been defined as "managing a computerized relational database, in real time, of comprehensive, up-to-date, relevant data on customers, inquiries, prospects and suspects, to identify our most responsive customers for the purpose of developing a high quality, long-standing relationship of repeat business by developing predictive models which enable us to send desired messages at the right time in the right form to the right people—all with the result of pleasing our customers, increasing our response rate per marketing dollar, lowering our cost per order, building our business, and increasing our profits."

Regardless of the particular means of direct marketing, database marketing can help create targeted communication and marketing programs tailored to the needs and wants of specific consumers. When customers place orders, send in a coupon, fill out a warranty card, or enter a sweepstakes, database marketers collect their names and information about their attitudes and behavior, which they compile in a comprehensive database.

Database marketing is generally more effective at helping firms retain existing customers than in attracting new ones. Many marketers believe it makes more sense the higher the price of the product and the more often consumers buy it. Database marketing is often at the heart of a successful loyalty rewards program. Best Western uses both online and mail outlets to contact its program participants and relies on database information to improve the relevance and timeliness of its messages.

Database marketing pioneers include a number of financial services firms and airlines. Even packaged-goods companies, however, are exploring the possible benefits of database marketing. For example, Procter & Gamble created a database to market Pampers disposable diapers, allowing it to send out individualized birthday cards for babies and reminder letters to parents to move their child up to the next size. Combining this effort with a well-developed helpline and Web site and in-store couponing, P&G is creating interactive, individualized, value-added contacts.

Database management tools will become a priority to marketers as they attempt to track the lifetime value (LTV) of customers. Some database marketing activities that can occur through the application of LTV analysis include predictive modeling, multiple campaign management, targeted promotions, up-selling, cross-selling, segmentation, churn management, multichannel management, product personalization, and acquisition and retention management.

Sources: Robert C. Blattberg, Byung-Do Kim, and Scott A. Neslin, *Database Marketing: Analyzing and Managing Customers* (New York: Springer Science + Business, 2008); James Tenser, "'Behavior-Activated Research' Benefits P&G's Pampers Brand," www.cpgmatters.com; Thomas Haire, "Best Western Melds Old and New," *Response*, March 2009.

Place. The last category of advertising is also often called "nontraditional," "alternative," or "support" advertising, because it has arisen in recent years as a means to complement more traditional advertising media. ***Place advertising***, also called ***out-of-home advertising***, is a broadly defined category that captures advertising outside traditional media. Increasingly, ads and commercials are showing up in unusual spots, sometimes as parts of experiential marketing programs.

The rationale is that, because traditional advertising media—especially television advertising—are becoming less effective, marketers are better off reaching people in other environments, such as where they work, play, and, of course, shop. According to the Outdoor Advertising Association of America, out-of-home advertising accounted for $7.3 billion in ad expenditures in 2015.[36] Some of the options include billboards and posters; movies, airlines, lounges, and other places; product placement; and point-of-purchase advertising. Top advertisers that use outdoor ads include McDonald's restaurant, Apple, Anheuser-Busch, Geico, Sprint, Coca-Cola, Universal Pictures, Verizon, Citi, and Walt Disney Pictures.[37] Outdoor advertising can help augment and reinforce advertising through more traditional media such as television, digital, and print.

Billboards and Posters.   Billboards have a long history but have been transformed over the years and now employ colorful, digitally produced graphics, backlighting, sounds, movement, and unusual—even three-dimensional—images to attract attention. The medium has improved in terms of effectiveness (and measurability), technology (some billboards are now digitized), and provide a good opportunity for companies to sync their billboard strategies with mobile advertising.

Billboard-type poster ads are now showing up everywhere in the United States each year to increase brand exposure and goodwill. Transit ads on buses, subways, and commuter trains have been around for years and have now become a valuable means to reach working women. Street furniture (bus shelters, kiosks, and public areas) has also become a fast-growing area. In Japan, cameras and sensors are being added to signs and electronic public displays so that—combined with cell-phone technology—they can become more interactive and personalized.[38] In Times Square, Coca-Cola launched a billboard featuring a robotic 3D ad with 1760 LED screens, which was particularly high in visual appeal.[39]

Oscar Mayer's Wienermobile, with its two Hotdoggers drivers, tour the country and make appearances at various events.

Source: Leila Navid/ZUMA Press Inc/Alamy Stock Photo

Billboards do not even necessarily have to stay in one place. Marketers can buy ad space on billboard-laden trucks that are driven around all day in marketer-selected areas. Oscar Mayer sends seven "Wienermobiles" traveling across the country each year. New York City became the first major city to allow its taxi cabs to advertise via onboard television screens.

Advertisers can now buy space in stadiums and arenas and on garbage cans, bicycle racks, parking meters, airport luggage carousels, elevators, gasoline pumps, the bottom of golf cups, airline snacks, and supermarket produce in the form of tiny labels on apples and bananas. Leaving no stone unturned, advertisers can even buy space in toilet stalls and above urinals, which, according to research studies, office workers visit an average of three to four times a day for roughly four minutes per visit. At Chicago O'Hare airport, digital commercials are now being shown in 150 bathroom mirrors above lavatory sinks.[40] Figure 6-4 displays some of the most successful outdoor advertisers.

FIGURE 6-4

Obie Hall of Fame Winners (as selected by the Outdoor Advertising Association of America)

Chick-fil-A (2006)

Walt Disney Company (2007)

Altoids (2008)

Absolut (2009)

MINI Cooper (2010)

Cracker Barrel Old Country Store (2011)

Maker's Mark (2012)

ESPN (2013)

Gap (2014)

HBO (2015)

Corona Extra (2016)

Warner Brothers (2017)

MillerCoors (2018)

Movies, Airlines, Lounges, and Other Places.   Increasingly, advertisers are placing traditional TV and print ads in unconventional places. Companies such as Whittle Communication and Turner Broadcasting have tried placing TV and commercial programming in classrooms, airport lounges, and other public places. Airlines now offer media-sponsored audio and video programming that accepts advertising (*USA Today Sky Radio* and *National Geographic Explorer*). Movie theater chains such as Loews Cineplex now run 30-, 60-, or 90-second ads on 2,000-plus screens. Although the same ads that appear on TV or in magazines often appear in these unconventional places, many advertisers believe it is important to create specially designed ads for these out-of-home exposures to better meet consumer expectations.

Ad placement in unconventional places (e.g., movie theaters, airport lounges, and other places) constitutes another approach to increase effectiveness of advertising.

Product Placement.   Many major marketers pay fees of $50,000 to $100,000 and even higher so their products can make cameo appearances in movies and on television, with the exact fee depending on the amount and nature of the brand exposure. This practice got a boost in 1982, when—after Mars declined an offer for the use of its M&M's brand—sales of Reese's Pieces increased 65 percent after the candy appeared prominently in the blockbuster movie *E.T.: The Extraterrestrial.*[41] More recently, hit shows such as *Breaking Bad* have been targets for product placement, as advertisers benefit from the exposure they get through the show's popularity.[42] With streaming services becoming increasingly popular, it is possible that product placement can also be personalized to the target's location as well as shopping history and preferences.

Among the brands with the highest number of product placements are Mercedes Benz, Apple, and Pepsi.[43] Marketers combine product placements with special promotions to publicize a brand's entertainment tie-ins and create "branded entertainment." For example, Beats headphones uses its product placement in movies such as *Avengers* to connect with its target audience and reinforce its positioning at the high end. Beats also uses product placement in music videos, appropriately enough, but also with leading athletes at major sporting events.[44]

Point of Purchase.   Myriad possibilities have emerged in recent years as ways to communicate with consumers at the point of purchase. In-store advertising includes ads on shopping carts, cart straps, aisles, or shelves, as well as promotion options such as in-store demonstrations, live sampling, and instant coupon machines.[45] Stores like Marshall's, TJ Maxx, Nordstrom Rack, Sephora, and Victoria's Secret all use physical displays to create a path for customers to wind down on their way to check out; these physical displays showcase small items that cost significantly less. Similarly, Best Buy practices point-of-purchase marketing within its stores by allowing customers to try out the latest version of PlayStation or Xbox.[46]

The appeal of point-of-purchase advertising lies in the fact that, as numerous studies have shown, consumers in many product categories make the bulk of their final brand decisions in the store. In-store media are designed to increase the number and nature of spontaneous and planned buying decisions. One company placing ads on the entryway security panels of major retail chains reported that the advertised brands experienced an average increase in sales of 20 percent over the four-week period in which their ads appeared.[47]

Guidelines.   Nontraditional or place media present some interesting options for marketers to reach consumers in new ways. Advertisements now can appear virtually any place where consumers have a few spare minutes or even seconds and thus, enough time to notice them. The main advantage of nontraditional media is that they can reach a very precise and captive audience in a cost-effective and increasingly engaging manner.

Because the audience must process out-of-home ads quickly, however, the message must be simple and direct. In fact, outdoor advertising is often called the "15-second sell." In noting how out-of-home aligns with twenty-first-century consumers, one commentator observed that, with people on-the-go and wanting content in short bursts, "Billboards are the original tweets—you get a quick image or piece of knowledge then move on."[48] In that regard, strategically, out-of-home advertising is often more effective at enhancing awareness or reinforcing existing brand associations than at creating new ones.

The challenge with nontraditional media is demonstrating their reach and effectiveness through credible, independent research. Another danger of nontraditional media is a consumer backlash against overcommercialization. Perhaps because of the sheer pervasiveness of advertising, however, consumers seem to be less bothered by nontraditional media now than in the past.

Consumers must be favorably affected in some way to justify the marketing expenditures for nontraditional media, and some firms offering ad placement in supermarket checkout lines, fast-food restaurants, physicians' waiting rooms, health clubs, and truck stops have suspended business at least in part because of lack of consumer interest. The bottom line, however, is that there will always be room for creative means of placing the brand in front of consumers—the possibilities are endless.

Promotion

Although they do very different things, advertising and promotion often go hand-in-hand. **Sales promotions** are short-term incentives to encourage trial or usage of a product or service.[49] Marketers can target sales promotions to either the trade or end consumers. Like advertising, sales promotions come in all forms. Whereas advertising typically provides consumers a *reason* to buy, sales promotions offer consumers an *incentive* to buy. Thus, sales promotions are designed to do the following:

- Change the behavior of the trade so that they carry the brand and actively support it.
- Change the behavior of consumers so that they buy a brand for the first time, buy more of the brand, or buy the brand earlier or more often.

Analysts maintain that the use of sales promotions grew as a business practice for a number of reasons. Brand management systems with quarterly evaluations were thought to encourage short-term solutions, and an increased need for accountability seemed to favor communication tools like promotions, whose behavioral effects are more quickly and easily observed than the often "softer" perceptual effects of advertising. Economic forces worked against advertising effectiveness as ad rates rose steadily despite what marketers saw as an increasingly cluttered media environment and fragmented audience. Consumers were thought to be making more in-store decisions, and to be less brand loyal and more immune to advertising than in the past. Many mature brands were less easily differentiated. On top of it all, retailers became more powerful.

For all these reasons, some marketers began to see consumer and trade promotions as a more effective means than advertising to influence the sales of a brand. There clearly are advantages to sales promotions. Consumer sales promotions permit manufacturers to price discriminate by effectively charging different prices to groups of consumers who vary in their price sensitivity. Besides conveying a sense of urgency to consumers, carefully designed promotions can build brand equity through information or actual product experience that helps to create strong, favorable, and unique associations. Sales promotions can encourage the trade to maintain full stocks and actively support the manufacturer's merchandising efforts.

One interesting finding by researchers examining purchase behavior across 23 product categories and four supermarket chains showed that instant reward programs—a reward for consumers that is given immediately based on fixed spending—can increase the number of shopping trips made by consumers, whereas bonus premiums—a nonprice premium that is attached to the purchase of a brand—can increase a brand's market share within a category and also make consumers more likely to buy within a category.[50]

On the other hand, from a consumer behavior perspective, there are some disadvantages of sales promotions, such as decreased brand loyalty and increased brand switching, decreased quality perceptions, and increased price sensitivity. Besides inhibiting the use of franchise-building advertising or other communications, diverting marketing funds into coupons or other sales promotion leads to reductions in research and development budgets and staff. Perhaps most importantly, the widespread discounting arising from trade promotions may have led to the increased importance of price as a factor in consumer decisions, breaking down traditional brand loyalty patterns.

Another disadvantage of sales promotions is that, in some cases, they may merely subsidize buyers who would have purchased the brand anyway. Interestingly, the more affluent, educated, suburban, and ethnically Caucasian a household is, the more likely it is to use coupons, mainly because its members are more likely to read newspapers where the vast majority of coupons appear. Another drawback to sales promotions is that new consumers attracted to the brand may attribute their purchase to the promotion and not to the merits of the brand per se and, as a result, may not repeat their purchase when the promotional offer is withdrawn. As an example, when JCPenney withdrew its coupon offers in 2012, it saw a 23 percent decline in sales.[51] Finally, retailers have come to expect and now demand trade discounts. The trade may not actually provide the agreed-upon merchandising and take advantage of promotions by engaging in nonproductive activities such as forward buying (stocking up for when the promotion ends) and diversion (shipping products to areas where the promotion was not intended to go).[52]

Promotions have a number of possible objectives.[53] With consumers, objectives may target new category users, existing category users, and/or existing brand users. With the trade, objectives may center on distribution, support, inventories, or goodwill. Next, we consider some specific issues related to consumer and trade promotions.

Consumer Promotions. Consumer promotions are designed to change the choices, quantity, or timing of consumers' product purchases. Although they come in all forms, we distinguish between customer franchise-building promotions like samples, demonstrations, and educational material, and noncustomer franchise-building promotions such as price-off packs, premiums, sweepstakes, and refund offers.[54] Customer franchise-building promotions can enhance the attitudes and loyalty of consumers toward a brand—in other words, affect brand equity.

For example, sampling is a means of creating strong, relevant brand associations while also perhaps kick-starting word-of-mouth among consumers. Marketers are increasingly using sampling at the point of use, growing more precise about where and how they deliver samples to maximize brand equity. For a $10 monthly subscription, one new firm, Birchbox, sends consumers a box of deluxe-size samples from such notable beauty brands as Benefit, Kiehl's, and Marc Jacobs. Members can go to the Web site to collect more information, provide feedback, and earn points for full-sized products. The beauty brands like the selectivity and customer involvement of the promotion.[55]

Thus, marketers increasingly judge sales promotions by their ability to contribute to brand equity as well as generate sales. Creativity is as critical to promotions as it is to advertising or any other form of marketing communications. The Promotion Marketing Association (PMA) bestows Reggie awards to recognize "superior promotional thinking, creativity, and execution across the full spectrum of promotional marketing."

Promotion strategy must reflect the attitudes and behavior of consumers. The percentage of coupons consumers redeem dropped steadily for years—in part due to the clutter of coupons that were increasingly being distributed. In 2016, there were 305 billion coupons distributed in the United States.[56] Free-standing inserts (FSIs) accounted for 89 percent of all redeemed coupons, and their value exceeded 545 million dollars in 2017.[57] Although redemption rates for coupons delivered from FSIs are fairly low (0.5–2 percent), the redemption rates for e-mail coupons is higher at 2.7 percent.[58] One area of promotional growth is in-store coupons, which marketers have increasingly turned to given that their redemption rates far exceed those of traditional out-of-store coupons. Another growing area is digital coupons, and 55 percent of adults in the United States used a digital coupon in 2016, and mobile coupon redemption rate is 10 percent. [59] One survey of 30,000 Web shoppers showed that 83 percent receive coupons by advertisers via e-mail, 66 percent by social media, 48 percent by mobile app or push notification, and 44 percent through word of mouth from others.[60]

GROUPON

Groupon launched in 2008 as a company offering a new marketing vehicle to businesses. By leveraging the Internet and e-mail, the company helps businesses use promotions as a form of advertisement. Specifically, Groupon maintains a large base of subscribers who receive a humorously worded daily deal—a specific percentage or dollar amount off the regular price—for a specific branded product or service. Through these e-mail discounts, Groupon offers three benefits to businesses: increased consumer exposure to the brand, the ability to price discriminate, and the creation of a "buzz factor." For these benefits, Groupon takes a 40 to 50 percent cut in the process. Many promotions are offered on behalf of local retailers such as spas, fitness centers, and restaurants, but Groupon also manages deals on behalf of national brands such as Gap, Southwest Airlines, and FTD. As of 2017, Groupon had 49.5 million unique customers and had a sales revenue of 2.84 billion dollars.[61] Groupon now faces several competitors in the market it helped create, including LivingSocial, RetailMeNot, and so on.

Companies such as Groupon and LivingSocial have been trying to disrupt the sales promotion industry by creating a platform that customers would use to buy all types of coupons. The issue with these platforms is that they are seen as more beneficial to customers than the merchants/retailers. The merchants typically experience a decline in traffic, as customers typically stockpile in advance to avail themselves of the coupons.[62]

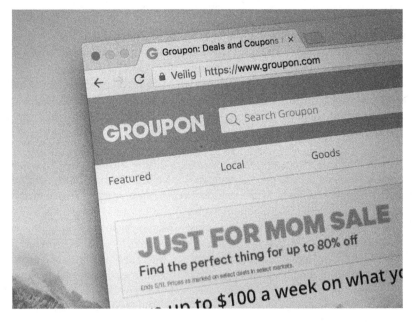

Groupon is an online marketplace which connects its subscribers with local merchants through a variety of promotional offers.
Source: Jarretera/Shutterstock

Trade Promotions. Trade promotions are often financial incentives or discounts given to retailers, distributors, and other channel members to stock, display, and in other ways facilitate the sale of a product through slotting allowances, point-of-purchase displays, contests and dealer incentives, training programs, trade shows, and cooperative advertising. Trade promotions are typically designed either to secure shelf space and distribution for a new brand, or to achieve more prominence on the shelf and in the store. Shelf and aisle positions in the store are important because they affect the ability of the brand to catch the eye of the consumer; placing a brand on a shelf at eye level may double sales over placing it on the bottom shelf.[63]

Because of a large amount of money spent on trade promotions, there is increasing pressure to make trade promotion programs more effective. Many firms are failing to see the brand-building value in trade promotions and are seeking to reduce and eliminate as much of their expenditures as possible.

Online Marketing Communications

The first decade of the twenty-first century has seen a headlong rush by companies into the world of interactive, online marketing communications. With the pervasive incorporation of the Internet into everyday personal and professional lives, marketers are scrambling to find the right places to be in cyberspace. The main advantages to marketing on the Web are the low cost and the level of detail and degree of customization it offers. Online marketing communications can accomplish almost any marketing communication objective and are especially valuable in terms of solid relationship building. We provide a detailed description of digital communications in Chapter 7.

Events and Experiences

As important as online marketing is to brand management, "real world" events and experiences play an equally important role. Brand building in the virtual world must be complemented with brand building in the real or physical world. Events and experiences range from an extravagant multimillion dollar sponsorship of a major international event to a simple local in-store product demonstration or sampling program. What all these different kinds of events and experiences share is that, one way or another, the brand engages the consumers' senses and imagination, changing brand knowledge in the process.

Experiences can take all forms and are limited only by the marketers' imagination. To create awareness of insights generated from Facebook's IQ platform, it created an event series called IQ Live which launched a kickoff event in New York with a 500-guest gathering. It also had events in Chicago and New York, which helped bring Facebook's data insights to life in a fun and personal way. To do this, as an example, in the New York event, they created a stage which was inspired by Madison Square Garden. The stage was covered in Astroturf, and included a model newsstand and a café. This everyday setting was based on IQ's major findings that Facebook is a platform allowing users to share their life's big moments.[64] As another example, consider Grey Goose.

GREY GOOSE

Grey Goose has used events as part of its experiential marketing strategy to connect with luxury consumers, with a goal of creating a stronger connection among consumers for the vodka brand.[65] Grey Goose (and the brand's owner Bacardi) used experiential marketing to overcome this challenge by using pop-up stores (called *Boulangerie Francois*) that featured and served bread made from the same French wheat used to make Grey Goose vodka.[66] This French bakery style pop-up store will offer drinks, pastries, and other foods to consumers, and at the location, they step through a secret door featuring a beach scene.

The campaign was supported by social media and public relations. For instance, Bacardi targeted journalists and influencers by sending them baskets of "Grey Goose Bread" along with jams made with each of the Grey Goose flavors, and at the boulangerie, a French baker explained the story behind the brand while serving customers. The campaign was a massive success with 229 pieces of coverage, 18.9 million digital reach, and 708m PR opportunity-to-see (OTS).[67]

Grey Goose has used experiential marketing in an effecive way to connect with luxury consumers.

Formally, *event marketing* can be defined as public sponsorship of events or activities related to sports, art, entertainment, or social causes. According to one survey of B2B, B2C, and nonprofit companies, 79 percent of those polled (based on a sample size of 931 respondents), saw events as important to their business. The survey highlighted various reasons that event marketing is used, such as educating customers, generating leads, and receiving donations. Companies such as EventBrite and Meetup.com have allowed companies to organize events seamlessly, thus providing a boost to event marketing.[68] Additionally, 80 percent of marketers believe that event marketing is key to the success of their business, with technology including event management software, mobile event apps, marketing automation systems, software integration, live-streaming, social media, social walls, augmented reality, and the like, acting as major facilitators of event marketing.[69] Nearly 20 percent of a business-to-business marketers' budget comprises of event marketing.[70]

Global sponsorship spending was approximately $62.7 billion globally in 2017, and a vast majority of these expenditures were in the following categories: sports, entertainment, causes, arts festivals and fairs.[71] Once employed mostly by cigarette, beer, and auto companies, sports marketing is now being embraced by virtually every type of company. Moreover, seemingly every sport—from dogsled racing to fishing tournaments and from tractor pulls to professional beach volleyball—now receives corporate backing of some kind. Chapter 8 examines the issues of event marketing and sponsorship in terms of the secondary associations that they bring to the brand.

Rationale.   Event sponsorship provides a different kind of communication option for marketers. By becoming part of a special and personally relevant moment in consumers' lives, sponsors can broaden and deepen their relationship with their target market. Marketers report a number of reasons why they sponsor events:[72]

- **To identify with a particular target market or lifestyle:** Marketers can link their brands to events popular with either a select or broad group of consumers. They can target customers geographically, demographically, psychographically, or behaviorally, according to the sponsored events. In particular, marketers can choose events based on attendees' attitudes and usage of certain products or brands. No athletic event in the United States attracts more "pentamillionaires"—those with a net worth of more than $5 million—than the U.S. Open tennis tournament. Perhaps it is no surprise that its sponsors include luxury brands such as American Express, Chase, Westin, and Grey Goose, which largely target affluent customers.[73]
- **To increase awareness of the company or product name:** Sponsorship often offers sustained exposure to a brand, a necessary condition for building brand recognition. By skillfully choosing sponsorship events or activities, marketers can enhance identification with a product and thus, also brand recall.
- **To create or reinforce consumer perceptions of key brand image associations:** Events themselves have their own associations that help to create or reinforce brand associations. Seiko has been the official timer of the Olympics and other major sporting events for years. Subaru believes there is a match in interests between skiing events and potential buyers of its all-wheel-drive vehicles.
- **To enhance corporate image dimensions:** Sponsorship is a soft sell and a means to improve perceptions that the company is likable, prestigious, and so forth. Marketers hope consumers will credit the company for its sponsorship and favor it in later product choices. Mountain Dew created the multicity Dew Tour, in which athletes compete in different skateboarding, BMX, and freestyle motocross events to reach and make a favorable impression with the coveted, but fickle, 12- to 24-year-old target market. The Dew Tour now includes events under the themes of City, Beach, and Mountain. The brand also created a digital platform called Green-Label.com, whose mission is to support young artists and musicians, and currently traffic to this Web site exceeds visitors to the Mountain Dew.com Web site.[74] Mountain Dew also encourages its employees to participate in these events, thereby allowing employees and consumers to connect and to generate deeper employee engagement.
- **To create experiences and evoke feelings:** Events can be part of an experiential marketing program. The feelings engendered by an exciting or rewarding event may indirectly link to the brand. Marketers can also use the Web to provide further event support and additional experiences.
- **To express commitment to the community or on social issues:** Often called *cause-related marketing*, sponsorships dedicated to the community or to promote social issues create corporate tie-ins with nonprofit organizations and charities (see Chapter 12). For over 23 years, Colgate-Palmolive has sponsored the Starlight Children's Foundation, which grants wishes to young people who are critically ill.
- **To entertain key clients or reward key employees:** Many events have lavish hospitality tents and other special services or activities that are available only for sponsors and their guests. For example, Bank of America's golf tournament sponsorship includes special events for clients. Involving clients with the event in these and other ways can engender goodwill and establish valuable business contacts. From an employee perspective, events can build participation and morale or create an incentive.

- **To permit merchandising or promotional opportunities:** Many marketers tie in contests or sweepstakes, in-store merchandising, and direct response or other marketing activities with their event. Warner-Lambert sponsors the "Taste of Chicago" promotion in part so it can gain shelf space in stores and participate in retailer co-op advertising.

Despite these potential advantages, there are some potential disadvantages to sponsorship. The success of an event can be unpredictable and out of the sponsor's control. There can be much clutter in sponsorship. Finally, although many consumers will credit sponsors for providing necessary financial assistance to make an event possible, some consumers may still resent the commercialization of events through sponsorship.

Guidelines. Developing successful event sponsorship means choosing the appropriate events, designing the optimal sponsorship program, and measuring the effects of sponsorship on brand equity.

Choosing Sponsorship Opportunities.

Because of the huge amount of money involved and numerous event opportunities, many marketers are thinking more strategically about the events with which they will get involved and the manner by which they will do so.

There are some potential guidelines for choosing events. First, the event must meet the marketing objectives and communication strategy defined for the brand. That is, the audience delivered by the event must match the target market of the brand. Moreover, the event must have sufficient awareness, possess the desired image, and be capable of creating the desired effects with that target market. Of particular concern is whether consumers make favorable attributions to the sponsor for its participation.

An "ideal event" might be one whose audience closely matches the ideal target market, that generates much favorable attention, that is unique but not encumbered with many sponsors, that lends itself to ancillary marketing activities, and that reflects or even enhances the brand or corporate image of the sponsor. Adding digital and social activations can help bring the event to life and help generate positive buzz or word-of-mouth surrounding the event.

Of course, rather than linking themselves to an event, some sponsors create their own. Branding Brief 6-1 describes how cable sports network ESPN created the X Games to appeal to a market segment not easily attracted by traditional sports. More and more firms are also using their names to sponsor the arenas, stadiums, and other venues that actually hold the events. American Express Community Stadium is in the U.K., the American Airlines Arena in Dallas, and Heinz Field in Pittsburgh. Staples paid $100 million over 20 years to name the downtown Los Angeles arena where the NBA Lakers and Clippers and the NHL Kings play, and where concerts and other events are also held. Although stadium naming rights can command high fees, its direct contribution to building brand equity is primarily in creating brand recognition, not brand recall, and marketers can expect it to do little for brand image except perhaps to convey a certain level of scope and size.

Designing Sponsorship Programs.

Many marketers believe that the marketing program accompanying a sponsorship is what ultimately determines its success. A sponsor can strategically identify itself at an event in various ways, including banners, signs, and programs. For more significant and broader impact, however, sponsors typically supplement such activities with samples, prizes, advertising, retail promotions, publicity, and so forth. Marketers often note that the budget for related marketing activities should be at least two to three times the amount of the sponsorship expenditure.

BRANDING BRIEF 6-1

Brand Building via the X Games

Although the action sports industry contains a variety of high-energy and sometimes potentially high-risk sports, it is largely defined by various forms of skateboarding, snowboarding, surfing, and BMX biking. Action sports are increasingly seen as mainstream in terms of legitimacy, participation, public interest, and sponsor/business investment. They have become increasingly profitable, with skate, snow and surf gear, apparel, and accessories categories contributing to the sports apparel industry. GoPro, the tiny video maker has transformed the action sports industry as athletes can wear these cameras as they do their incredible stunts whether they are trail cyclists, big wave surfers, half pipe snowboarders, kite boarders, or Tough Mudder racers. These incredible feats are then uploaded to YouTube, and have caused many of these action sports to become more mainstream. GoPro had a sales revenue of $1.18 billion in 2017.

ESPN's X Games, begun as a biannual event in 1995, remain at the forefront of the industry. They are ESPN's largest owned and operated property and are regarded as the gold standard in the action sports world. While the public initially saw the X Games as "the circus coming to town" or as a showcase for death-defying stunts and tricks, people have begun to realize that the riders are legitimate athletes in a sustainable business. Viewers 18 and younger, especially, have grown up with the X Games and consider it their own Olympics.

X Games quickly grew into a franchise and has successfully launched a variety of brand extensions in consumer products and home entertainment and touches all seven continents. ESPN believes the evolution and growth of all elements of the X Games have positioned it well for continued successes—in brand perception and relevance, live event attendance, record-setting broadcast viewership and ratings, increased sponsor investment, and overall popularity and incorporation into the mainstream.

X Games has many sponsors including Harley-Davidson, Jeep, LifeProof, Monster Energy, and Geico, which have sponsored it over a number of years. Newer brands such as Netflix and Great Clips joined the list of prominent sponsors in 2018. In return for sponsorship rights, brands gain a significant media presence during the X Games telecasts, in addition to prominent positions on social media platforms and access to VIP experiences during the games. Figure 6-5 provides sponsorship details for the X Games.

The X Games held its sixteenth consecutive Winter X Games in Aspen in 2017. During this event, the X Games viewership

The X Games, which have become an annual event focused on action sports, have become an excellent opportunity for advertisers to reach out to and engage a younger, athletic consumer.
Source: ZUMA Press, Inc./Alamy Stock Photo

through WatchESPN grew significantly by 32 percent, with 16 million minutes of X Games events being viewed. The Facebook page for X Games gained 23,000 likes, and the X Games Aspen's Snapchat story had 6.5 million users. Globally, X Games Aspen was televised in 215 countries to more than 365 million homes. The four-day and final attendance for Summer X Games in Minneapolis 2017 was about 105,000 attendees.

Despite its exponential growth, the action sports sector is not without its challenges. Chief among these challenges include the warmer winters that have limited action sports during the winter months. The cost of participation has also been steadily increasing, making it difficult for families with children to afford the cost of participating in these sports. These have contributed

FIGURE 6-5

X Games 17 Sponsorship Information

Source: Fay Wells, "ESPN X Games: Launching a New Category," in *Best Practice Cases in Branding*, 4th ed. Kevin Lane Keller and Lowey Sichol (Upper Saddle River, NJ: Pearson, 2013).

Official Sponsors

BFGoodrich—BFGoodrich's national marketing efforts included television spots, print collateral, digital advertising, on-site activations, and competition course signage.

Ford—Ford's national marketing efforts included television spots, print collateral, digital advertising, on-site activations, and competition course signage.

U.S. Navy—The U.S. Navy's national marketing efforts included television spots, print collateral, digital advertising, radio campaigns, on-site activations, and competition course signage.

Red Bull—Red Bull's national marketing efforts included television spots, print collateral, digital ad space, on-site activations, and unique competition course signage.

Event Sponsors

Casio G'zOne Commando—Casio's national marketing efforts included television spots, online advertising, on-site activations, and competition course signage.

Shark Week—Discovery's national marketing efforts included television spots, print collateral, online advertising, on-site activations, and competition course signage.

Mobil 1—Mobil 1's national marketing efforts included television spots, online advertising, radio campaigns, and competition course signage.

Sony—Sony's national marketing efforts included television spots, online advertising, on-site TV displays, and competition course signage.

to these sports to appear inaccessible to many people. Despite these trends, there is a great deal of potential in overseas markets, particularly Europe and Asia; while action sports such as skateboarding have become more mainstream in the United States, in emerging markets like Japan, it is still a growing trend.

Sources: Fay Wells and Kevin Lane Keller (2013), "ESPN X Games—Building a Youth Sports Brand," edited by Lowey Bundy Sichol (Case-Marketing.com); Kevin Gray, "Tiny Camera, Big Impact: How GoPro Transformed Sports," June 27, 2014, www.zdnet.com/article/tiny-camera-big-impact-how-gopro-transformed-sports/, accessed March 30, 2018; www.marketwatch.com/investing/stock/gpro/financials, accessed March 30, 2018; Interview with Rick Alessandri, senior vice president and managing director of ESPN X Game's franchise, November 2008; www.xgamesmediakit.com/read-me/, accessed March 30, 2017; www.xgamesmediakit.com/read-me/, accessed March 30, 2017; Lars Becker, "Action Sports: An Industry Searching for the Way Out of Crisis," June 21, 2016, www.ispo.com/en/trends/id_78182622/action-sports-an-industry-searching-for-the-way-out-of-crisis.html, accessed March 30, 2018; Kaylee Bradstreet, "The State of Skate 2016 Official Report | How Much International Growth Will the Skate Market See?," June 21, 2016, https://www.adventuresportsnetwork.com/transworld-business/state-skate-2016-international-growth/, accessed March 30, 2018; William L. Shankin and John Kuzma, "Buying That Sporting Image," *Marketing Management* (Spring 1992): 65.

Measuring Sponsorship Activities.   There are two basic approaches to measuring the effects of sponsorship activities: the *supply-side method* focuses on potential exposure to the brand by assessing the extent of media coverage, and the *demand-side method* focuses on reported exposure from consumers.

Supply-side methods attempt to approximate the amount of time or space devoted to the brand in media coverage of an event. For example, we can estimate the number of seconds the brand is clearly visible on a television screen, or the column inches of press clippings covering an event that mention the brand. Then, we can translate this measure of potential impressions delivered by an event sponsorship into an equivalent value in advertising dollars, according to the fees associated with actually advertising in the particular media vehicle. Additionally, one can evaluate the extent of incremental traffic to one's Web site based on public relations campaigns, and also examine the impact on social media engagement.

Although supply-side exposure methods provide quantifiable measures, equating media coverage with advertising exposure ignores the content of the respective communications that consumers receive. The advertiser uses media space and time to communicate a strategically designed message. Media coverage and telecasts only expose the brand and do not embellish its meaning in any direct way. Some public relations professionals maintain that positive editorial coverage can be worth 5 to 10 times the advertising equivalency value, but it is rare that sponsorship affords the brand such favorable treatment. Many critics note that TV ads, for example, are carefully designed to persuasively reflect as many positives of the brand as possible. The brand is the "star" of the ad, unlike the case with sponsorship, where the event or game takes center stage and the brand only just appears visually, if it is even noticed.

An alternative measurement approach is the demand-side method, which attempts to identify the effects that sponsorship has on consumers' brand knowledge structures. Thus, tracking or custom surveys can explore the ability of the event sponsorship to affect awareness, attitudes, or even sales. We can identify and survey event spectators after the event to measure recall of the event's sponsor, as well as attitudes and intentions toward the sponsor as a result of the event. We can also conduct internal tracking to see how different aspects of the sales process are impacted.

BRAND AMPLIFIERS

Complementing these four broad sets of marketing communication activities are efforts to engage consumers and the public via word-of-mouth and public relations and publicity. Although they can perform many different functions, they are especially well-suited at amplifying the effects created by other marketing activities.[75]

Public Relations and Publicity

Public relations and publicity relate to a variety of programs and are designed to promote or protect a company's image or its products. *Publicity* is nonpersonal communications such as press releases, media interviews, press conferences, feature articles, newsletters, photographs, films, and tapes. *Public relations* may also include annual reports, fund-raising and membership drives, lobbying, special event management, and public affairs.

The marketing value of public relations received a big boost in 1983 when public relations firm Burson-Marsteller's skillful handling of Johnson & Johnson's Tylenol product tampering incident was credited with helping to save the brand. Brand Focus 11.0 provides a comprehensive account of that landmark campaign. Around that time, politicians also discovered the power of campaign sound bites that were picked up by the press as a means of broad, cost-efficient candidate exposure.

Marketers now recognize that although public relations are invaluable during a marketing crisis, it can also be an important part of any marketing communications program. In 2018, PRWeek awarded Frito-Lay the Campaign of the Year award for their work on the Tostitos Party Safe Bag, which doubled as a breathalyzer-like alcohol detector. In order to generate publicity, the brand partnered with Mothers Against Drunk Driving (MADD), a well-known advocacy group for preventing drunk driving. It also partnered with Uber to offer $10 off any Uber ride on Super Bowl Sunday, by using the codes on the back of the Tostitos bag. To strengthen its appeal to NFL fans, the brand partnered with sports celebrity Delanie Walker, who previously underwent a personal tragedy due to drunk driving. The nature of the campaign and its unusual focus made it a huge success with 13 million views generated, without even a single commercial being aired. More than 30,000 Uber rides were given during the promotion.[76]

Word-of-Mouth

Publicity and PR often serve another important role—they get people talking. Word-of-mouth is a critical aspect of brand building as consumers share their likes, dislikes, and experiences with brands and with each other.[77] The power of word-of-mouth is the credibility and relevance it often brings. Study after study has shown that the most trusted source of product information is friends and families.

If marketers do their job right and create marketing programs that offer consumers superior delivery of desired benefits, people will write and talk about the brand, amplifying any marketing effects. In effect, a buzz has been created among consumers. Companies are attempting to create this consumer word-of-mouth through various techniques such as *influencer marketing*.[78]

In Chapter 7, we provide a deeper assessment of influencer marketing, which refers to the practice of using social influencers to spread word-of-mouth about a product or a brand. Although it is a sponsored form of word-of-mouth (social influencers typically get paid by the company either via cash or free products), its influence on consumer decision-making has been increasing.

DEVELOPING INTEGRATED MARKETING COMMUNICATION PROGRAMS

We have examined in depth some of the communication options available to marketers. Chapter 7 offers a deep dive into online and digital channels. Now, we consider how to develop an integrated marketing communication (IMC) program by choosing the best set of options and managing the relationships between them.[79] Integrated marketing communications is regarded as a process of strategically managing stakeholders, content, channels, and results of brand communication programs.[80] Our main theme is that marketers should "mix and match" communication options to build brand equity—that is, choose a variety of communication options that share common meaning and content but also offer different, complementary advantages so that the whole is greater than the sum of the parts.[81]

Integrated marketing communication is shown to drive a brand's financial performance through influencing the effectiveness of communication campaigns and the brand's market-based performance. However, there are several impediments to successfully implementing IMC including miscommunication, compartmentalization of duties, and loss of trust.[82] These are further exacerbated due to the proliferation of new media, and the consequent lowering of attention among consumers who are faced with a tremendous explosion of information.[83] To effectively implement IMC, one approach proposes combining a bottom-up communications matching model—involving the identification of communication options best suited to different stages of the consumer purchase funnel with a top-down communications model—in which a marketing communications program is judged in terms of its ability to drive sales and equity.[84]

Numerous firms are embracing this broad-based approach to developing their communications program. Lululemon, an athletic apparel brand, uses a combination of brand ambassadors, events and out-of-home and social media to build engagement with its consumers. For example, brand ambassadors are used to giving free class events in stores several times per week, while social media influencers show off the product on Instagram, YouTube, and Snapchat; digital video does the heavy lifting; the company did not even run ads until 2017.[85]

Criteria for IMC Programs

In assessing the collective impact of an integrated marketing communication program, the marketer's overriding goal is to create the most effective and efficient communication program possible. Here are six relevant criteria, known as "the 6 Cs" for short:[86]

1. Coverage
2. Contribution
3. Commonality
4. Complementarity
5. Conformability
6. Cost

After considering the concept of coverage and how it relates to the other five criteria, let's look quickly at each in turn.

Coverage.   Coverage is the proportion of the audience reached by each communication option, as well as how much overlap exists among communication options. In other words, to what extent do different communication options reach the designated target market, and the same or different consumers making up that market? As Figure 6-6 shows, the unique aspects of coverage relate to the direct main effects of any communication; the common aspects relate to the interaction or multiplicative effects of two communication options working together. Communication effects from consumer exposure to one communication option can be enhanced when consumers have had prior exposure to a different communication option.

The unique aspect of coverage is the inherent communication ability of a marketing communication option, as suggested by the second criterion, contribution. If there is some overlap in communication options, however, marketers must decide how to design their communication program to reflect the fact that consumers may already have some communication effects in memory before exposure to any particular communication option.

A communication option can either reinforce associations and strengthen linkages that are also the focus of other communication options, or it can address other associations and linkages, as suggested by the third and fourth criteria, commonality and complementarity. Moreover, if less

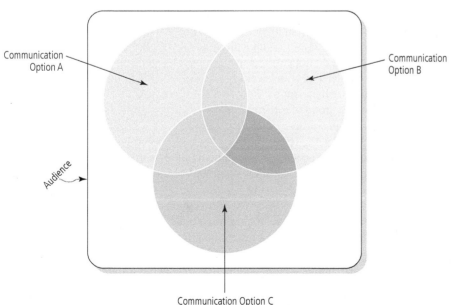

FIGURE 6-6

IMC Audience Communication Option Overlap

than perfect overlap exists—which is almost always the case—marketers can design a communication option to reflect the fact that consumers may or may not have seen other communication options, as suggested by the fifth criterion, conformability. Finally, all of these considerations must be offset by their cost, as suggested by the sixth criterion.

Contribution.   Contribution is the inherent ability of a marketing communication to create the desired response and communication effects from consumers *in the absence of exposure to any other communication option.* In other words, contribution describes the main effects of a marketing communication option in terms of how it affects consumers' processing of a communication and the resulting outcomes. As we noted earlier, marketing communications can play many different roles, like building awareness, enhancing the company's image, eliciting responses, and inducing sales, and the contribution of any marketing communication option will depend on how well it plays that role. Also, as we noted earlier, much prior research has considered this aspect of communications, generating conceptual guidelines and evaluation criteria in the process. Given that overlap with communication options exists, however, marketers must consider other factors, as follows.

Commonality.   Regardless of which communication options marketers choose, they should coordinate the entire marketing communication program to create a consistent and cohesive brand image in which brand associations share content and meaning. The consistency and cohesiveness of the brand image are important because the image determines how easily consumers can recall existing associations and responses and how easily they can link additional associations and responses to the brand in memory.

Commonality is the extent to which *common* information conveyed by different communication options shares meaning across communication options. Most definitions of IMC emphasize only this criterion—sending target audiences the same consistent message across communication options.

In general, we learn and recall information that is consistent in meaning more easily than unrelated information—though the unexpectedness of inconsistent information sometimes can lead to more elaborate processing and stronger associations than consistent information.[87] Nevertheless, with inconsistent associations and a diffuse brand image, consumers may overlook some associations, or, because they are confused about the meaning of the brand, form less strong and less favorable new associations.

Therefore, in the long run, marketers should design different communication elements and combine them so that they work effectively together to create a consistent and cohesive brand image. The more abstract the association to be created or reinforced by marketing communications, the more likely it would seem that we could effectively reinforce it in different ways across heterogeneous communication options.[88]

For example, if the association we desire is "contemporary," then there may be a number of different ways we can make a brand seem modern and relevant. On the other hand, if our desired association is a concrete attribute, say, "rich chocolate taste," then it may be difficult to convey it in communication options that do not permit explicit product statements, such as sponsorship.

Take Heineken, for example. The brand seeks to achieve a strong premium image and positioning in its communications. Heineken's "Walk-In Fridge" campaign started as a video and then a TV ad that first showed a group of girlfriends jumping up and down and shrieking with joy when one of them gets a walk-in wardrobe closet, followed by a group of guys equally ecstatic over a walk-in refrigerator lined with Heineken. Heineken next placed gigantic cardboard boxes labeled "Walk-In Fridge" all over Amsterdam as if put out in the trash. Finally, Heineken placed real walk-in fridges at various beer festivals, allowing groups of friends to mimic the ad and video and upload their own video to YouTube.[89]

Finally, another commonality issue is the extent of execution consistency across communication options—that is, the extent to which we convey nonproduct-related information in different communication options. The more coordinated execution information is, the more likely it is that this information can serve as a retrieval cue to other communication effects.[90] In other words, if a symbol is established in one communication option, like a feather in a TV ad for a deodorant to convey mildness and softness, then marketers can use it in other communications to help trigger the knowledge, thoughts, feelings, and images stored in memory from exposure to a previous communication.

Complementarity.   Communication options are often more effective when used in tandem. *Complementarity* describes the extent to which *different* associations and linkages are emphasized across communication options. The ideal marketing communications program would ensure that the communication options chosen are mutually compensatory and reinforcing to create desired consumer knowledge structures.

Marketers might most effectively establish different brand associations by capitalizing on those marketing communication options best suited to eliciting a particular consumer response or establishing a particular type of brand association. For example, some media, like sampling and other forms of sales promotion, are demonstrably better at generating trial than engendering long-term loyalty. Research with some industrial distributors has shown that follow-up sales efforts generate higher sales productivity when firms have already exposed customers to its products at a trade show.[91]

The Science of Branding 6-2 describes how communication options may need to be explicitly tied together to capitalize on complementarity to build brand equity.

THE SCIENCE OF BRANDING 6-2
Coordinating Media to Build Brand Equity

For brand equity to be built, it is critical that communication effects created by advertising be linked to the brand. Often, such links are difficult to create. Television ads, in particular, do not "brand" well. There are a number of reasons why:

- Competing ads in the product category can create interference and consumer confusion as to which ad goes with which brand.

- "Borrowed interest" creative strategies and techniques—humor, music, special effects, sex appeals, fear appeals, and so on—may grab consumers' attention, but result in the brand being overlooked in the process.

- Delaying brand identification or providing few brand mentions may raise processing intensity but direct attention away from the brand.

- Limited brand exposure time in the ad may allow little opportunity for the elaboration of existing brand knowledge.

- Consumers may not have any inherent interest in the product or service category or may lack knowledge of the specific brand.

- A change in advertising strategy may make it difficult for consumers to easily relate new information to existing brand knowledge.

Strategies to Strengthen Communication Effects

For a variety of reasons, advertising may "succeed" in the sense that communication effects are stored in memory, yet "fail" at the same time in that these communication effects are not accessible when critical brand-related decisions were made.

To address this problem, one common tactic marketers employ is to make the brand name and package information prominent in the ad. Unfortunately, this increase in brand emphasis means that communication effects and brand associations are less likely to be able to be created by the ad and stored in consumer memory. In other words, although consumers are better able to recall the advertised brand, there is *less* other information about the brand actually to recall. Three potentially more effective strategies are brand signatures, ad retrieval cues, and media interactions.

Brand Signatures

Perhaps the easiest way to increase the strength of brand links to communication effects is to create a more powerful and compelling brand signature. The **brand signature** is the manner by which the brand is identified in a TV or radio ad or displayed within a print or digital ad. The brand signature must creatively engage the consumer and cause him or her to pay more attention to the brand itself, and, as a consequence, increase the strength of brand associations created by the ad.

An effective brand signature often dynamically and stylistically provides a seamless connection to the ad as a whole. For example, the famous "Got Milk?" campaign always displayed that tagline or slogan in a manner fitting the ad (in flames for the "yuppie in hell" ad or primary-school print for the "school lunchroom bully" ad). As another example, the introductory "Intel Inside" ad campaign always ended with a swirling image from which the Intel Inside logo dramatically appeared, in effect stamping the end of the ad with Intel Inside in an "in your face" manner.

Ad Retrieval Cues

Another effective tactic to use **advertising retrieval cues**—visual or verbal information uniquely identified with an ad that is evident when consumers are making a product or service decision. The purpose is to maximize the probability that consumers who have seen or heard the cued ad will retrieve the communication effects stored in long-term memory. Ad retrieval cues may consist of a key visual, a catchy slogan, or any unique advertising element that serves as an effective reminder to consumers. For example, Eveready featured a picture of its pink bunny character on packages of Energizer batteries to reduce consumer confusion with Duracell.

Media Interactions

Finally, digital, print and radio reinforcement of television ads (in which the video and audio components of a TV ad serve as the basis for the respective type of ads) can be an effective means to leverage existing communication effects from TV ad exposure and more strongly link them to the brand. Cueing a TV ad with an explicitly linked digital, radio, or print ad can create similar or even enhanced processing outcomes that can substitute for additional TV ad exposures. Moreover, a potentially useful, although rarely employed, media strategy is to run explicitly linked digital, print, or radio ads *prior* to (or concurrently with) the accompanying TV ad. The digital, print, and radio ads, in this case, function as teasers and increase consumer motivation to process the complete television ad consisting of both audio and video components. Conversely, TV ads can also encourage audiences to engage with the brand via social media, but advertising a Web link or a link to a campaign (e.g., a Twitter handle), where consumers can find more information. One research study by Joo and colleagues found that television advertising for financial services advertising increased the likelihood that audiences conducted branded keyword searches for a given advertised brand (rather than generic searches), confirming the potential for media interactions in ad campaigns.

Sources: Raymond R. Burke and Thomas K. Srull, "Competitive Interference and Consumer Memory for Advertising," *Journal of Consumer Research* 15, no. 1 (June 1988): 55–68; Kevin Lane Keller, "Memory Factors in Advertising: The Effect of Advertising Retrieval Cues on Brand Evaluations," *Journal of Consumer Research* 14, no. 3 (February 1987): 316–333; Robert J. Kent and Chris T. Allen, "Competitive Interference Effects in Consumer Memory for Advertising: The Role of Brand Familiarity," *Journal of Marketing* 58, no. 3 (July 1994): 97–105; Kevin Lane Keller, Susan Heckler, and Michael J. Houston, "The Effects of Brand Name Suggestiveness on Advertising Recall," *Journal of Marketing* 62, no. 1 (January 1998): 48–57; William E. Baker, Heather Honea, and Cristel Antonia Russell, "Do Not Wait to Reveal the Brand Name: The Effect of Brand-Name Placement on Television Advertising Effectiveness," *Journal of Advertising* 33, no. 3 (Autumn 2004): 77–85; Micael Dahlén and Sara Rosengren, "Brands Affect Slogans Affect Brands? Competitive Interference, Brand Equity and the Brand-Slogan Link," *Journal of Brand Management* 12, no. 3 (February 2005): 151–164; Peter J. Danaher, André Bonfrer, and Sanjay Dhar, "The Effect of Competitive Advertising Interference on Sales for Packaged Goods," *Journal of Marketing Research* 45, no. 2 (April 2008): 211–225; Isaac M. Dinner, Harald J. Van Heerde, and Scott A. Neslin. "Driving Online and Offline Sales: The Cross-channel Effects of Traditional, Online Display, and Paid Search Advertising," *Journal of Marketing Research* 51, no. 5 (2014): 527–545; Mingyu Joo, Kenneth C. Wilbur, Bo Cowgill, and Yi Zhu, "Television Advertising and Online Search," *Management Science* 60, no. 1 (2013): 56–73. Peter J. Danaher and Tracey S. Dagger, "Comparing the Relative Effectiveness of Advertising Channels: A Case Study of a Multimedia Blitz Campaign," *Journal of Marketing Research* 50, no. 4 (August 2013): 517–534.

Conformability.   Conformability refers to the extent that a marketing communication option is robust and effective for different groups of consumers. There are two types of conformability: communication and consumer. The reality of any IMC program is that when consumers are exposed to a particular marketing communication, some consumers will have already been exposed to other marketing communications for the brand, and others will not. The ability of a marketing communication to work at two levels—effectively communicating to both groups—is critically important. We consider a marketing communication option conformable when it achieves its desired effect *regardless* of consumers' past communication history.

Besides this communication conformability, we can also judge a communication option in terms of broader consumer conformability, that is, how well does it inform or persuade consumers who vary on dimensions other than communication history? Communications directed at primarily creating brand awareness, like sponsorship, may be more conformable by virtue of their simplicity.

There seem to be two possible means of achieving this dual communication ability:

1. **Multiple information provision strategy:** Provide different information within a communication option to appeal to the various types of consumers. An important issue here is how information designed to appeal to one target market of consumers will be processed by other consumers and target markets. Issues of information overload, confusion, and annoyance may come into play if communications become burdened with a great deal of detail.
2. **Broad information provision strategy:** Provide information that is rich or ambiguous enough to work regardless of prior consumer knowledge. The important issue here is how potent or successful marketers can make that information. If they attempt to appeal to the lowest common denominator, the information may lack precision and sufficient detail to have any meaningful impact on consumers. Consumers with disparate backgrounds will have to find information in the communication sufficiently relevant to satisfy their goals, given their product or brand knowledge or communications history.

Cost.   Finally, evaluations of marketing communications on all of the preceding criteria must be weighed against their cost to arrive at the most effective *and* efficient communication program.

Using IMC Choice Criteria

The IMC choice criteria can provide some guidance for designing integrated marketing communication programs. Two key steps are evaluating communication options and establishing priorities and trade-offs.

Evaluating Communication Options. We can judge marketing communication options or communication types according to the response and communication effects they can create, as well as how they rate on the IMC choice criteria. The communication types and options have different strengths and weaknesses and raise varying issues.

Several points about the IMC choice criteria are worth noting. First, there are not necessarily any inherent differences across communication types for contribution and complementarity, because each communication type, if properly designed, can play a critical and unique role in achieving those communication objectives. Similarly, all marketing communications appear expensive, although some differences in cost per thousands can prevail. Communication types vary, however, in their breadth and depth of audience coverage, and regarding commonality and conformability according to the number of modalities they employ: The more modalities available with a communication type, the greater its potential commonality and conformability.

Arriving at a final mix requires making decisions on priorities and tradeoffs among the IMC choice criteria as discussed next.

Establishing Priorities and Trade-Offs. The IMC program a marketer adopts, after profiling the various options, will depend in part on how he or she ranks the choice criteria. Because the IMC choice criteria themselves are related, the marketer must also make tradeoffs. The objectives of the marketing communications program, and whether they are short run or long run, will set priorities along with a host of factors beyond the scope of this chapter. We identify three possible tradeoffs with the IMC choice criteria that result from overlaps in coverage.

- **Commonality and complementarity will often be inversely related.** The more various marketing communication options emphasize the same brand attribute or benefit, all else being equal, the less they can effectively emphasize other attributes and benefits.
- **Conformability and complementarity will also often be inversely related.** The more a communication program accounts for differences in consumers across communication options, the less necessary it is that any one type of communication be designed to appeal to many different groups.
- **Commonality and conformability do not share an obvious relationship.** It may be possible, for example, to develop a sufficiently abstract message, like "Brand X is contemporary," to effectively reinforce the brand across multiple communication types including advertising, interactive, sponsorship, and promotions.

REVIEW

This chapter provided conceptual frameworks and managerial guidelines for how marketing communications can be integrated to enhance brand equity. The chapter addressed this issue from the perspective of customer-based brand equity, which maintains that brand equity is fundamentally determined by the brand knowledge created in consumers' minds by the supporting marketing, program. Four main types of communications were identified as being critical: (1) advertising and promotion, (2) interactive marketing, and (3) events and experiences.

A number of specific communication options—broadcast, print, direct response, and place advertising media; consumer and trade promotions; Web sites, online ads, videos, and social media online marketing; and events and experiences—were reviewed in terms of basic characteristics as well as success factors for effectiveness. Brand amplifiers that enhance these effects in the form of publicity and public relations, word-of-mouth, and buzz marketing were also discussed. The chapter also provided criteria as to how different communication options should be combined to maximally build brand equity.

Two key implications emerge from this discussion. First, from the perspective of customer-based brand equity, all possible communication options should be evaluated regarding their ability to affect brand equity. In particular, the CBBE concept provides a common denominator by which the effects of different communication options can be evaluated: Each communication option can be judged in terms of the effectiveness and efficiency by which it affects brand awareness and by which it creates, maintains, or strengthens favorable and unique brand associations. Different communication options have varying strengths and can accomplish differing objectives. Thus, it is important to employ a mix of communication options, each playing a specific role in building or maintaining brand equity.

The second important insight that emerges from the conceptual framework is that the marketing communications program should be put together in a way such that the whole is greater than the sum of the parts. As such, there should be a match among certain communication options so that the effects of any one type of communication option are enhanced by the presence of another option.

In closing, the basic message of this chapter is simple: marketers need to evaluate marketing communication options strategically to determine how they can contribute to brand equity. To do so, marketers need some theoretical and managerial guidelines by which they can determine the effectiveness and efficiency of various communication options both singularly and in combination with other marketing communications. Figure 6-7 provides one philosophy concerning the design, implementation, and interpretation of marketing communication strategies.

1. *Be analytical:* Use frameworks of consumer behavior and managerial decision making to develop well-reasoned communication programs.
2. *Be curious:* Better understand customers by using all forms of research, and always be thinking of how you can create added value for consumers.
3. *Be single-minded:* Focus your message on well-defined target markets (less can be more).
4. *Be integrative:* Reinforce your message through consistency and cuing across all communication options and media.
5. *Be creative:* State your message in a unique fashion; use alternative promotions and media to create favorable, strong, and unique brand associations.
6. *Be observant:* Keep track of competition, customers, channel members, and employees through monitoring and tracking studies.
7. *Be patient:* Take a long-term view of communication effectiveness to build and manage brand equity.
8. *Be realistic:* Understand the complexities involved in marketing communications.

FIGURE 6-7

General Marketing Communication Guidelines: The "Keller Bs"

DISCUSSION QUESTIONS

1. Pick a brand and gather all its marketing communication materials. How effectively has the brand mixed and matched marketing communications? Has it capitalized on the strengths of different media and compensated for their weaknesses at the same time? How explicitly has it integrated its communications program?
2. What do you see as the role of the Internet in building brands? How would you evaluate the Web site for a major brand—for example, Nike, Disney, or Levi's? How about one of your favorite brands?
3. Pick up a current issue of a popular magazine. Which print ad do you feel is the best, and which ad do you feel is the worst based on the criteria described in this chapter?
4. Look at the coupon supplements in a Sunday newspaper. How are they building brand equity, if at all? Try to find a good example and a poor example of brand-building promotions.
5. Choose a popular event. Who sponsors it? How are they building brand equity with their sponsorship? Are they integrating the sponsorship with other marketing communications?

BRAND FOCUS 6.0
Empirical Generalizations in Advertising

In a comprehensive academic endeavor, a number of researchers have worked together to accumulate what they call "empirical generalizations" (EG) of advertising. In putting this research into context, the lead authors Jerry Wind and Byron Sharp note: "Even advertising has scientific laws, empirical patterns that generalize across a wide range of known conditions. These empirical generalizations provide us with benchmarks, predictions, and valuable insights into how the digital revolution may affect advertising."

Empirical generalizations emerge from careful, thoughtful research. The authors are quick to add several caveats. Empirical generalizations are not formal laws themselves, and there may be important exceptions and boundary conditions as to when they operate. Nevertheless, they suggest three possible benefits to having some empirical generalizations: (1) as a starting point in the development of an advertising strategy; (2) as an initial set of tentative rules that management can follow; and (3) as a benchmark, giving management some sense of how much change to expect when advertising is launched or something changes in the advertising environment.

The empirical generalizations they identified can be grouped into four broad topics: return on investment (ROI), 360-degree media planning, value of TV, and creative quality. While digital and social media continues to increase in importance, we feature the research findings in this area in greater detail in Chapter 7. However, we feature some of the research examining cross-media interactions (digital and television, digital and print, and so on), in this overview.

ROI

- Advertising typically has a half-life of three to four weeks. If advertising is to be sales-effective in the long term, it must show immediate sales effects in single-source data.

- Based on the established EG that advertising elasticity is approximately 0.1, net profit is optimized by setting the advertising budget to be 10 percent of gross profit. If the elasticity is 0.15, then the advertising budget should be 15 percent of gross profit, and so on.

- Brand advertising often has a pronounced short-term sales impact (as shown in single-source data). This impact decays over time. The most dramatic influence on short-term effect is creative copy.

- Even with no clicks or minimal clicks, online display advertisements generate lift in site visitation, trademark search queries, and lift in both online and offline sales.

- In-store digital signage featuring "newsworthy" information (e.g., new items, seasonal offers, and promotions) has a markedly favorable impact on sales. This effect is stronger for hedonic (food and entertainment) products.

- TV advertising for consumer services follow a 70:30 rule (70 percent of the efforts create interest, 30 percent create

action). And 90 percent of TV advertising for consumer services dissipates within three months (versus four months for consumer goods).

- If advertising changes by 1 percent, sales or market share will change by about 0.1 percent. (That is, advertising elasticity is 0.1.) The advertising elasticity is higher in Europe relative to the United States, for durables relative to nondurables, in early relative to late stages of the product life cycle, and in print over television.

- There is a greater than 50 percent chance that the typical TV advertising campaign will lose money both short term and long term. The risk of losing money fluctuates over the years, but has been over 50 percent. The average elasticity of TV advertising has fluctuated between 0.043 and 0.163 over the past 25 years.

- The advertising response curve is "convex"—the greatest marginal response is from the first exposures. As the number of cumulative exposures in a period increases, the marginal effect of the advertising drops.

360-Degree Media Planning

- A retail store layout that makes shopping quicker results in increased shopper spending.

- Approximately 20 percent of word-of-mouth (WOM) about brands refers to paid advertising in media. The level and effectiveness of WOM are substantially increased when stimulated, encouraged, and/or supported by advertising, increasing the probability by about 20 percent that a consumer will make a strong recommendation to buy or try a product.

- If the advertisements recently recalled were on traditional media, they were more likely to have left a positive impression than if they were on digital media. If the consumers had a previous positive impression of the brand or product advertised for advertisements recently recalled, the advertisements were more likely to have left a positive impression, regardless of the media.

- Doubling the clutter does not halve the number of advertisements recalled. Advertisements recalled in high clutter are more likable on average.

- Repeat viewing is 38 percent, and this does not alter when a program changes time. Repeat viewing is lower for comedies than police dramas and for low rating shows, but within these program types or ratings levels, repeat viewing remains at a consistent low or high value across time changes.

- Where TV, radio, and magazines (and even special interest ones) claim to attract a specific audience, the target group is typically less than half of the media's total audience, and rival outlets often outperform them in reaching this subsegment.

- Spaced multiple exposures (distributed) produce greater learning than repeated exposures with short intervals (massed). Longer intervals between exposures result in better learning than shorter intervals.

- Television advertising does influence online shopping, and that advertising content plays a key role. Content that is action-focused increased Web site traffic and sales; further information-focus and emotion-focus ad content actually reduced Web site traffic while simultaneously increasing purchases, with a positive net effect on sales. These results imply ad copy is a key factor in driving brand sales.

- The main drivers of sales variation for the studied brand include online owned (10 percent), (un)earned (3 percent), and paid (2 percent) media, which help explain a substantial part of the path to purchase. It is noteworthy that TV advertising (5 percent) explains significantly less than online media.

- Display ads increase search conversion. However, display ads may also increase search clicks, thereby increasing search advertising costs. After accounting for these effects, it has been shown that $1 invested in display and search leads to a return of $1.24 for display and $1.75 for search ads.

- Across six touchpoint types—brand advertising, retailer advertising, in-store communications, word-of-mouth, peer observation (seeing other customers), and traditional earned media such as editorial—in-store communication is, in general, more influential than that of other touchpoints including brand advertising. Further, the findings showcased the importance of retailer, social effects and third-party endorsement in addition to traditional brand advertising in influencing brand consideration.

- The impact of advertising varies based on brand familiarity. Specifically, within-online synergy is higher than online–offline synergy for both familiar brands but not for both unfamiliar brands. Managers of unfamiliar brands may obtain substantial synergy from offline marketing spending, whereas managers of familiar brands can generate more synergy by investing in different online media.

Value of TV

- Over the past 15 years, television advertising has not declined in its effectiveness at generating sales lift and appears to be more effective than either online or print at generating brand awareness and recognition.

- Households with DVRs are similar to non-DVR households in the basic measures of advertising effectiveness (recall and recognition).

- TV still has very high reach. Declining ratings are due to fragmentation (more channels), not to reduced TV viewing levels that are remarkably resilient to social and technological changes and to the emergence of "new media." Average ratings halve if the number of channels doubles. In addition, the double jeopardy law applies to TV channels. Bigger channels have more viewers, and these viewers watch the channel for more hours.

- Despite increase in TV channels and fragmentation of audience, TV appears to retain its perceived clout among target audiences in Asia, Europe, and North America and holds across recent years. While the influence of digital media has grown, it has not caused a corresponding decrease in television's perceived clout.

Creative Quality

- Advertising that communicates a unique selling proposition (USP) outperforms advertising that does not. Ideally, the USP should be based on an important benefit; alternatively and riskier, it could be based on a feature that clearly implies a benefit. It is effective if it is unique in the minds of consumers, even though other brands could make the same claim. However, it is especially effective if it cannot be easily matched by competitors.

- The number of times a brand visually appears in a television commercial increases the degree of correct brand association with that commercial.

- Emotional response to a television advertisement influences both branded engagement (directly) and persuasion (indirectly), and therefore, the likelihood of short-term sales. This pattern holds for TV advertisements across Argentina, Brazil, and Mexico, but the magnitude of effect is different.

Sources: Yoram Wind and Byron Sharp, "Advertising Empirical Generalizations: Implications for Research and Action," *Journal of Advertising Research* 49, no. 2 (June 2009): 246–252. See also Scott Koslow and Gerard J. Tellis, "What Scanner Panel Data Tell Us About Advertising: A Detective Story with a Dark Twist," *Journal of Advertising Research* 51, no. 1 (March 2011): 87–100; Raj Sethuraman, Gerard J. Tellis, and Richard A. Briesch, "How Well Does Advertising Work? Generalizations from Meta-Analysis of Brand Advertising Elasticities," *Journal of Marketing* Research 48, no. 3 (June 2011): 457-471; Paul R. Hoban and Randolph E. Bucklin, "Effects of Internet Display Advertising in the Purchase Funnel: Model-Based Insights from a Randomized Field Experiment," *Journal of Marketing Research* 52, no. 3 (2015): 375–393; Pavel Kireyev, Koen Pauwels, and Sunil Gupta, "Do Display Ads Influence Search? Attribution and Dynamics in Online Advertising," *International Journal of Research in Marketing* 33, no. 3 (2016): 475–490; Shane Baxendale, Emma K. Macdonald, and Hugh N. Wilson, "The Impact of Different Touch Points on Brand Consideration," *Journal of Retailing* 91, no. 2 (2015): 235–253; Jura Liaukonyte, Thales Teixeira, and Kenneth C. Wilbur, "Television Advertising and Online Shopping," *Marketing Science* 34, no. 3 (2015): 311–330; Shuba Srinivasan, Oliver J. Rutz, and Koen Pauwels, "Paths To and Off Purchase: Quantifying the Impact of Traditional Marketing and Online Consumer Activity," *Journal of the Academy of Marketing Science* 44, no. 4 (2016): 440–453; Rajeev Batra and Kevin Lane Keller, "Integrating Marketing Communications: New Findings, New Lessons, and New Ideas," *Journal of Marketing* 80, no. 6 (2016): 122–145; Koen Pauwels, Ceren Demirci, Gokhan Yildirim, and Shuba Srinivasan, "The Impact of Brand Familiarity on Online and Offline Media Synergy," *International Journal of Research in Marketing* 33, no. 4 (2016): 739–753; Jura Liaukonyte, Thales Teixeira, and Kenneth C. Wilbur, "Television Advertising and Online Shopping," *Marketing Science* 34, no. 3 (2015): 311–330.

NOTES

1. To obtain a broader perspective, it is necessary to consult good advertising texts, such as George E. Belch and Michael A. Belch, *Advertising and Promotion: An Integrated Marketing Communications Perspective,* 9th ed. (Homewood, IL: McGraw-Hill, 2012); Thomas C. O'Guinn, Richard J. Seminik, and Chris T. Allen, *Advertising and Integrated Brand Promotion,* 6th ed. (Cincinnati, OH: South-Western, 2012); John R. Rossiter and Larry Percy, *Advertising and Promotion Management,* 2nd ed. (New York: McGraw-Hill/Irwin, 1997).

2. William J. McGuire, "The Nature of Attitudes and Attitude Change," in *The Handbook of Social Psychology,* Vol. 3, 2nd ed., eds. G. Lindzey and E. Aronson (Reading, MA: Addison-Wesley, 1969): 136–314; Robert J. Lavidge and Gary A. Steiner, "A Model for Predictive Measurements of Advertising Effectiveness," *Journal of Marketing* 25, no. 6 (1961): 59–62; Thomas E. Barry and Daniel J. Howard, "A Review and Critique of the Hierarchy of Effects in Advertising," *International Journal of Advertising* 9, no. 2 (1990): 121–135.

3. Thomas C. Kinnear, Kenneth L. Bernhardt, and Kathleen A. Krentler, *Principles of Marketing,* 4th ed. (New York: HarperCollins, 1995).

4. Alexander L. Biel, "Converting Image into Equity," in *Brand Equity and Advertising,* eds. David A. Aaker and Alexander L. Biel (Hillsdale, NJ: Lawrence Erlbaum Associates, 1993): 67–82.

5. David Hinckley, "Average American Watches 5 Hours of TV per Day, Report Shows," *New York Daily News,* March 5, 2014, www.nydailynews.com/lifestyle/average-american-watches-5-hours-tv-day-article-1.1711954.

6. John Koblin, "How Much Do We Love TV? Let Us Count the Ways," *The New York Times,* June 30, 2016, www.nytimes.com/2016/07/01/business/media/nielsen-survey-media-viewing.html.

7. Adage.com, "What It Costs: Ad Prices from TV's Biggest Buys to the Smallest Screens," *AdAge,* April 6, 2015, http://adage.com/article/news/costs-ad-prices-tv-mobile-billboards/297928/.

8. Brian Sternberg, "'Sunday Night Football' Remains Costliest Show," *Advertising Age,* October 26, 2009, http://adage.com/article/ad-age-graphics/tv-advertising-sunday-night-football-costliest-show/139923/.

9. Statista.com, "Procter & Gamble's Advertising Spending on Tide in the United States from 2011 to 2016 (in million U.S. dollars)," www.statista.com/statistics/314855/tide-ad-spend-usa/, accessed March 30, 2018.

10. Alexandra Bruell and Sharon Terlep, "P&G Cuts More Than $100 Million in 'Largely Ineffective' Digital Ads," *The Wall Street Journal,* July 27, 2017, www.wsj.com/articles/p-g-cuts-more-than-100-million-in-largely-ineffective-digital-ads-1501191104.

11. John R. Rossiter and Larry Percy, *Advertising and Promotion Management* (New York: McGraw-Hill Book Company, 1987).

12. The American Marketing Association gives EFFIE awards for advertising campaigns that can demonstrate an impact on sales and profits. They are awarded based on the following subjective criteria: background and strategy (marketing challenge, target insight, campaign objective), creative (idea, link to strategy, and quality of execution), and media (link to market strategy, link to creative strategy), which together account for 70 percent of an ad campaign's score. Proof of results accounts for 30 percent. See www.effie.org.

13. Andrew Nusca, "Why Isn't TV Advertising Dead? It's Complicated," *Fortune,* January 5, 2017, http://fortune.com/2017/01/05/tv-advertising-cmo/.

14. Ibid.

15. Rani Molla, "Millennials Mostly Watch TV after It's Aired," *Recode,* www.recode.net/2017/9/9/16266854/millennials-watch-tv-live-video-on-demand; Nielsen.com, "Connecting With the Cosmos: The Total Audience Media Universe," *Nielson,* March 19, 2015, www.nielsen.com/us/en/insights/news/2015/connecting-with-the-cosmos-the-total-audience-media-universe.html.

16. Rani Molla, "Millennials Mostly Watch TV after It's Aired," www.recode.net/2017/9/9/16266854/millennials-watch-tv-live-video-on-demand, accessed March 27, 2018.

17. Julia Greenberg, "Nope TV Business Isn't Dead, Far from It, Really," May 9, 2016, www.wired.com/2016/05/nope-tv-business-isnt-dead-yet-far-really/, accessed March 30, 2018.

18. The Nielsen Company, "Nielsen Audio," www.nielsen.com/us/en/solutions/capabilities/audio.html; Radio Advertising Bureau, "Why Radio," www.rab.com/why-radio.cfm.

19. "Radio Advertising Spending in the United States from 2012 to 2021 (in billion U.S. dollars)," www.statista.com/statistics/272412/radio-advertising-expenditure-in-the-us/, accessed March 7, 2018.

20. Chris Ariens, "Study Shows That Every $1 Spent on Radio Advertising Returns $12 in Purchase Activity," *AdWeek,* March 6, 2018, www.adweek.com/digital/study-shows-that-every-1-spent-on-radio-advertising-returns-12-in-purchase-activity/.

21. Steve Krajewski, "Motel 6 Keeps Light On," *Adweek,* May 4, 1998, https://www.adweek.com/brand-marketing/motel-6-keeps-light-44593/; "Motel 6 Earns Grand Prize at Radio Mercury Awards," July 1, 2009, www.motel6.com; C. Marcucci, "Mercurys Give the Richards Group Top Honors for Motel 6 Spot," *RBR,* June 18, 2009, https://www.rbr.com/mercurys-give-the-richards-group-top-honors-for-motel-6-spot/, accessed November 2, 2018.

22. Tim Nudd, "30 Years Later, Motel 6 and Tom Bodett Are Still Cranking Out the World's Best Radio Ads," *AdWeek,* April 20, 2017, www.adweek.com/creativity/30-years-later-motel-6-and-tom-bodett-are-still-cranking-out-the-worlds-best-radio-ads/, accessed November 2, 2018.

23. For a comprehensive overview, see Bob Schulberg, *Radio Advertising: The Authoritative Handbook* (Lincolnwood, IL: NTC Business Books, 1990).

24. David Ogilvy, *Ogilvy on Advertising* (New York: Vintage Books, 1983).

25. Magazine Publishers of America, "How Do You Measure a Smile?" *Advertising Age,* September 26, 2005, M6.

26. Statista.com, "Paid Circulation of Daily Newspapers in the United States from 1985 to 2016 (in thousands)," www.statista.com/statistics/183422/paid-circulation-of-us-daily-newspapers-since-1975/, accessed March 25, 2018; Pew Research Center, www.journalism.org/fact-sheet/newspapers/, accessed March 25, 2018.

27. Andrew Kohut, "Internet Gains on Television as Public's Main News Source," *Pew Research Center for the People & Press*, January 4, 2011, http://www.people-press.org/2011/01/04/internet-gains-on-television-as-publics-main-news-source/.

28. Stuart Elliott, "In an 'Absolut World,' a Vodka Could Use the Same Ads for More Than 25 Years," *The New York Times*, April 27, 2007, https://www.nytimes.com/2007/04/27/business/media/27adco.html; Stuart Elliott, "Loved the Ads? Now Pour the Drinks," *The New York Times*, August 27, 2008, https://archive.nytimes.com/query.nytimes.com/gst/fullpage-9C0DE5D61F3CF934A1575BC0A96E9C8B63.html, accessed November 2, 2018; Stuart Elliot Media Decoder, "Absolut Adds Star Power," *The New York Times*, December 1, 2009, https://mediadecoder.blogs.nytimes.com/2009/12/01/absolut-adds-star-power/?mtrref=www.google.com&gwh=5CD91803 24069D5C270BE5A3F94CFF0F&gwt=pay; Absolut Company, "Absolut Inspires a New Movement of Creativity with an Absolut Blank," July 12, 2011, www.absolutcompany.com. Absolut ® Vodka. Absolut country of Sweden vodka and logo, Absolut bottle design and Absolut calligraphy are trademarks owned by the Absolut Company AB.

29. David Gianatasio, "How Blending Art and Commerce Drove Absolut Vodka's Legendary Campaigns," *AdWeek*, September 28, 2015, www.adweek.com/brand-marketing/how-blending-art-and-commerce-drove-absolut-vodka-s-legendary-campaigns-167143/.

30. Lois Brayfield and Lauren Ackerman, "Direct Mail Statistics," The DMA Organization, 2017, https://thedma.org/marketing-insights/marketing-statistics/direct-mail-statistics/.

31. Matt Robinson, "As Seen on TV—and Sold at Your Local Store," *BusinessWeek*, August 1, 2010, 21–22; Lacey Rose, "Shill Shocked," *Forbes*, November 22, 2010, 146–148.

32. Infomercial DRTV, "Infomercial Cost," www.infomercialdrtv.com/infomercial-cost.htm.

33. Tim Hawthorne, "7 Things Brand Advertisers Should Know about DRTV," https://blog.hubspot.com/agency/7-things-brand-advertisers-should-know-about-drtv, accessed May 28, 2018.

34. Lia Sestric, "The Most Profitable As Seen on TV Products of All Time," *GOBankingRanks*, September 30, 2017, www.gobankingrates.com/making-money/profitable-seen-tv-products-time/#2.

35. Courtney Nagle, "Are Infomercial Products Really Worth the Costs?," *Clearpoint*, September 15, 2015, www.clearpoint.org/blog/are-infomercial-products-really-worth-the-costs/.

36. Bruce Britt, "The Medium Gets Larger," *Deliver* 7, no. 2 (April 2011): 15–17; Jeff Zabin and Gresh Brebach, *Precision Marketing: The New Rules for Attracting, Retaining and Leveraging Profitable Customers* (Hoboken, NJ: John Wiley & Sons, Inc., 2004).

37. Outdoor Advertising Association of America, "OAAA: OOH Finished Strong 2015, Looks for Solid 2016 a High," *OAAA*, March 15, 2016, https://oaaa.org/StayConnected/NewsArticles/IndustryRevenue/tabid/322/id/4449/Default.aspx.

38. Outdoor Advertising Association of America, "Out of Home Advertising Up 4.1% in Q2 2016," *OAAA*, September 16, 2006, https://oaaa.org/StayConnected/NewsArticles/IndustryRevenue/tabid/322/id/4616/Default.aspx.

39. Daisuke Wakabayashi, "Billboards That Can See You," *The Wall Street Journal*, September 2, 2010, http://allthingsd.com/20100903/billboards-that-can-see-you/; Emily Steel, "The Billboard That Knows: Ad Industry Experiments with Technologies That Recognize Expressions, Gestures," February 28, 2011, https://www.wsj.com/articles/SB10001424052748704692904576167272357856608, accessed November 2, 2018.

40. Zack Palm, "3D Coca-Cola Ad Gives Billboards a New Look in NYC's Times Square," *PSFK*, August 2017, www.psfk.com/2017/08/3d-coca-cola-ad-give-nyc-times-square.html.

41. Ben Mutzabaugh, "Wash Your Hands, Watch a Commercial," *USA Today*, March 12, 2011, 87–100.

42. David T. Friendly, "Selling It at the Movies," *Newsweek,* July 4, 1983, 46.

43. CBC Radio, "Show Me the Money: The World of Product Placement," *CBC*, August 25, 2015, www.cbc.ca/radio/undertheinfluence/show-me-the-money-the-world-of-product-placement-1.3046933.

44. Abe Sauer, "Announcing the 2016 Brandcameo Product Placement Awards," February 24, 2016, http://brandchannel.com/2016/02/24/2016-brandcameo-product-placement-awards-022416/.

45. Abe Sauer, "Apple and Beats: A Match Made in Product Placement Heaven," *Brand Channel*, March 28, 2014, http://brandchannel.com/2014/05/28/apple-and-beats-a-match-made-in-product-placement-heaven/, accessed June 13, 2018.

46. "Walmart Updates In-Store TV Network," *Promo*, September 8, 2008.

47. Kali Hawlik, "Point of Purchase Marketing: How Retailers Can Optimize POP Areas for Higher Sales," *Shopify*, February 23, 2017, www.shopify.com/retail/point-of-purchase-marketing-how-retailers-can-optimize-pop-areas-for-higher-sales.

48. Michael Applebaum, "Run from Interactive Digital Displays to Traditional Billboards, Out-of-Home Is on an Upswing," *Adweek*, April 15, 2011.

49. For a classic summary of issues related to the type, scope, and tactics of sales promotions design, see John A. Quelch, "Note on Sales Promotion Design," Teaching Note N-589-021 (Boston: Harvard Business School, 1988).

50. Alec Minnema, Tammo H.A. Bijmolt, and Mariëlle C. Non, "The Impact of Instant Reward Programs and Bonus Premiums on Consumer Purchase Behavior," *International Journal of Research in Marketing* 34, no. 1 (March 2017): 194–211, www.sciencedirect .com/science/article/abs/pii/S0167811616300842, accessed November 2, 2018.

51. Lita Epstein, "The Pros & Cons of Using Coupons for Your Business," *Investopedia*, www.investopedia.com/ articles/personal-finance/051815/pros-cons-using- coupons-your-business.asp, accessed November 2, 2018.

52. Andrew Ehrenberg and Kathy Hammond, "The Case against Price-Related Promotions," *Admap* 418 (June 2001): 30–32.

53. John A Quelch, *Note on Sales Promotion Design* (Cambridge, MA: Harvard Business School, 1988).

54. Michael L. Ray, *Advertising and Communication Management* (Upper Saddle River, NJ: Prentice Hall, 1982).

55. Suzy Evans, "Random Samples No More," *Fast Company*, (February 2011): 35.

56. Statista.com, "Total Number of Coupons Distributed in the United States from 2011 to 2016 (in billions)," https://www.statista.com/statistics/630086/total- number-of-coupons-distributed-in-the-us/, accessed November 2, 2018.

57. Statista.com, "Cumulative Value of Free Standing Insert (FSI) Coupons Offered in the United States from 2013 to 2017 (in billion U.S. dollars)," https://www.statista .com/statistics/502230/value-fsi-coupons-usa/, accessed November 2, 2018.

58. Alex Brown, "Study Shows ROI for Mobile Coupon Redemption," https://pointofsale.com/Success-stories/ Study-Shows-ROI-for-Mobile-Coupon-Redemption .html.

59. Brandon Carter, "Coupon Statistics: The Ultimate Collection," November 15, 2017, https://blog .accessdevelopment.com/ultimate-collection-coupon- statistics/, accessed May 9, 2018.

60. Deal Nerd, "Study: How Coupon Codes Are Influencing Online Purchase Decisions," https://www.blippr.com/ about/coupon-code-stats/, accessed November 2, 2018.

61. Statista.com, "Number of Groupon's Active Customers from 2nd Quarter 2009 to 2nd Quarter 2018 (in millions)," https://www.statista.com/statistics/273245/ cumulative-active-customers-of-groupon/, accessed November 2, 2018.

62. Karan Girotra, Simone Marinesi, and Serguei Netessine, "Can Groupon Save Its Business Model?, *Harvard Business Review*, December 26, 2013, https://hbr .org/2013/12/can-groupon-save-its-business-model.

63. John R. Rossiter and Larry Percy, *Advertising and Promotion Management.* (New York: McGraw-Hill Book Company, 1987).

64. Jenny Berg, "How Facebook Made a Data-Focused Event Fun," *BizBash*, July 15, 2015, www.bizbash .com/how-facebook-made-a-data-focused-event-fun/ new-york/story/30738/#.WqPSbmfsZRI.

65. Natalie Mortimer, "Grey Goose Is Deepening Ties to Luxury in Latest 'Fly Beyond' Campaign," *The Drum*, May 19, 2016, www.thedrum.com/news/2016/05/19/ grey-goose-deepening-ties-luxury-latest-fly-beyond- campaign.

66. Jack Simpson, "How Grey Goose Used Experiential Marketing to Tell Its Luxury Story," *Econsultancy*, February 15, 2016, https://econsultancy .com/blog/67513-how-grey-goose-used-experiential- marketing-to-tell-its-luxury-story.

67. Ibid.

68. Edmund Ingham, "Who Are the Major Players Disrupting the Events Industry?," *Forbes*, December 10, 2014, www.forbes.com/sites/edmundingham/2014/12/10/ who-are-the-major-players-disrupting-the-events- industry/2/#11e556c43463.

69. Brandon Rafalson, "Marketing Stats That Point to the Future of the Industry," *Hello Endless*, November 2, 2017, https://helloendless.com/event-marketing-stats/.

70. Ruth P. Stevens, "How to Triple Your Trade Show Marketing Results," *AdAge*, July 31, 2014, http://adage.com/ article/guest-columnists/triple-trade-show-marketing- results/294357/.

71. Statista.com, "Global Sponsorship Spending from 2007 to 2018 (in billion U.S. dollars)," https://www.statista .com/statistics/196864/global-sponsorship-spending- since-2007/, accessed November 2, 2018.

72. See also IEG, "IEG's Guide to Guide to Why Companies Sponsor," http://www.sponsorship.com/Resources/ What-Companies-Sponsor.aspx.

73. U.S. Tennis Association, "Sponsors," U.S. Open, accessed November 2, 2018, www.usopen.org/en_US/ about/sponsors.html.

74. Stan Phelps, "Three Lessons from Mountain Dew on Leveraging Events to Create an Authentic Brand Experience," *Forbes*, October 18, 2014, www.forbes .com/sites/stanphelps/2014/10/18/three-lessons-from- mountain-dew-on-leveraging-events-to-create-an- authentic-brand-experience/#3fb56cda7d27.

75. John E. Hogan, Katherine N. Lemon, and Barak Libai, "Quantifying the Ripple: Word-of-Mouth and Advertising Effectiveness," *Journal of Advertising Research* 44, no. 3 (September 2004): 271–280.

76. PRWeek.com, "PRWeek U.S. Awarded 2018: The Winners," *PRWeek*, March 16, 2018, www.prweek.com/ article/1458806/prweek-us-awards-2018-winners.

77. Jonah Berger and Eric Schwartz, "What Drives Immediate and Ongoing Word-of-Mouth?," *Journal of Marketing Research* 48, no. 5 (October 2011): 869–880.

78. Gerry Khermouch, "Buzz Marketing," *BusinessWeek*, July 30, 2001, https://www.bloomberg.com/news/ articles/2001-07-29/buzz-marketing; Mark Hughes, *Buzzmarketing: Get People to Talk about Your Stuff* (New York: Penguin Books, 2005); Knowledge@Wharton, "What's the Buzz About Buzz Marketing," January 12, 2005, http://knowledge.wharton.upenn.edu/article/whats-the- buzz-about-buzz-marketing/, accessed November 2, 2018.

79. For a review of some academic and practitioner issues with IMC, see Prasad A. Naik, "Integrated Marketing Communications: Provenance, Practice and Principles," in *Handbook of Advertising*, eds. Gerard J. Tellis and Tim Ambler (Thousand Oaks, CA: Sage Publications, 2007); Tom Duncan and Frank Mulhern, eds., "A White Paper on the Status, Scope, and Future of IMC," March 2004, Daniels College of Business at the University of Denver.

80. Mart Ots and Gergely Nyilasy, "Integrated Marketing Communications (IMC): Why Does It Fail?: An Analysis of Practitioner Mental Models Exposes Barriers of IMC Implementation," *Journal of Advertising Research* 55, no. 2 (2015): 132–145; J. Kliatchko, "Revisiting the IMC Construct," *International Journal of Advertising*, 27, no. 1 (2008): 133–160.

81. Prasad A. Naik, Kalyan Raman, and Russ Winer, "Planning Marketing-Mix Strategies in the Presence of Interactions," *Marketing Science* 24, no. 10 (2005): 25–34.

82. Mart Ots, and Gergely Nyilasy, "Integrated Marketing Communications (IMC): Why Does It Fail?: An Analysis of Practitioner Mental Models Exposes Barriers of IMC Implementation," *Journal of Advertising Research* 55, no. 2 (2015): 132–145.

83. Rajeev Batra and Kevin Lane Keller, "Integrating Marketing Communications: New Findings, New Lessons, and New Ideas," *Journal of Marketing* 80, no. 6 (2016): 122–145.

84. Ibid.

85. Jackie Quintana, "5 Companies Who Are Doing Integrated Marketing Right in 2017," *Lonely Brand*, January 7, 2017, https://lonelybrand.com/blog/3-companies-integrated-marketing-right/.

86. This discussion assumes that the marketer has already thoroughly researched the target market and fully understands who they are—their perceptions, attitudes, and behaviors—and therefore knows exactly what needs to be done with them in terms of communication objectives.

87. Susan E. Heckler and Terry L. Childers, "The Role of Expectancy and Relevancy in Memory for Verbal and Visual Information: What Is Incongruency?" *Journal of Consumer Research* 18, no. 4 (March 1992): 475–492; Michael J. Houston, Terry L. Childers, and Susan E. Heckler, "Picture-Word Consistency and the Elaborative Processing of Advertisements," *Journal of Marketing Research* 24, no. 4 (November 1987): 359–369; Thomas K. Srull and Robert S. Wyer, "Person Memory and Judgment," *Psychological Review* 96, no. 1 (1989): 58–83.

88. Michael D. Johnson, "Consumer Choice Strategies for Comparing Noncomparable Alternatives," *Journal of Consumer Research* 11, no. 3 (December 1984): 741–753.

89. David Kiley and Robert Klara, "Heineken's 'Walk-In Fridge'," *Adweek Media*, November 1, 2010, 15.

90. Julie A. Edell and Kevin Lane Keller, "The Information Processing of Coordinated Media Campaigns," *Journal of Marketing Research* 26, no. 2 (May 1989): 149–163; Julie Edell and Kevin Lane Keller, "Analyzing Media Interactions: The Effects of Coordinated Print-TV Advertising Campaigns," *Marketing Science Institute Report*, No. 99-120, http://www.msi.org/reports/analyzing-media-interactions-the-effects-of-coordinated-tv-print-advertisin/, accessed November 2, 2018.

91. Timothy M. Smith, Srinath Gopalakrishna, and Paul M. Smith, "The Complementary Effect of Trade Shows on Personal Selling," *International Journal of Research in Marketing* 21, no. 1 (2004): 61–76.

Branding in the Digital Era

7

Learning Objectives

After reading this chapter, you should be able to

1. Describe changes in marketing and consumer behavior in a digital era.

2. Define brand engagement and understand the brand engagement pyramid and key drivers of brand engagement.

3. Understand digital communications and the various options available.

4. Understand the role of e-mail marketing and Web site optimization as important components of digital marketing strategy.

5. Evaluate the pros and cons of various social media channels (e.g., Facebook and Twitter) as digital marketing tools.

6. Understand ongoing developments within mobile marketing.

7. Develop a broad understanding of influencer marketing approaches and how word-of-mouth and social influence occurs and can be managed.

8. Describe content marketing and its role in creating brand awareness and engagement.

9. Describe changes in brand management organizational structure.

Brand managers are increasingly required to coordinate their communications (message and appearance) across various digital channels and across different devices, as consumers utilize multiple devices and channels to complete their purchase.

219

PREVIEW

In recent times, branding and brand management have undergone a tremendous shift, primarily due to the growth of online and digital marketing as a means of communicating with and selling to consumers. Brands are taking on more and different kinds of meaning, and consumers are playing a bigger and more explicit role in the success—or failure—of those brands. At the same time, marketers know more about consumers than ever and can employ different marketing tactics to reach and influence them.

As consumers increasingly spend time and money in online channels, both marketing and consumer behavior have evolved and changed significantly. We begin our analysis by outlining some of the important changes taking place in both consumer behavior and brand management in the digital area. We then introduce the important topic of brand engagement and profile the wide variety of digital communications that exists for marketers. Finally, we consider some issues around social influence and brand management structure. Brand Focus 7.0 reviews some research findings regarding online word-of-mouth.

KEY ISSUES FOR BRANDING IN THE DIGITAL ERA

In this section, we review a number of important developments with branding in the digital era. To help set the stage, consider the following findings and how they highlight today's rapidly changing marketing landscape and the profound implications for brand marketers:[1]

1. Ninety-seven percent of consumers turn to a search engine like Google when they are buying a product.
2. Ninety-six percent of consumers search for product information using their mobile device.
3. Ninety-five percent of millennials expect brands to have a Facebook presence.
4. Eighty-nine percent of consumers do online research before purchasing in-store.

Table 7-1 summarizes some key digital trends, which are described in detail.

Changes in the Consumer Decision Journey

The traditional consumer decision journey implied a series of systematic stages, including aware-ness, consideration, purchase intention, and purchase. Imagine a couple, Anne and Joe, who are looking for a new refrigerator to replace their old one. In the "old days," they would have driven to the nearest physical outlet, such as Sears, and looked at a few options. After talking to the sales staff about their needs, they might identify and shortlist three models across two brand names. They would then complete their purchase after perhaps conferring with a couple of friends who had recently undergone a similar purchase in the same product category. Mapping their consumer decision journey would have been fairly simple, including predictable steps such as trips to the local retailer and discussions with sales staff within the store.

Due to the dramatic developments in digital marketing and social media, however, Anna and Joe's consumer decision journey today would be significantly different.

Table 7-1 Key Digital Era Trends with Implications for Branding and Brand Management

1. Changes in the consumer decision journey
2. A sharp increase in buying via online retail channels
3. A shift in advertising and promotion expenditures toward digital channels
4. The rise of many-to-many communications
5. A dramatic increase in consumer touchpoints
6. A tremendous increase in data availability
7. The use of digital personalization
8. A loss of control over the brand message and the co-creation of brand meaning
9. The role of user experiences
10. The growth of brands as cultural symbols

Anna and Joe are likely to begin their search for a new refrigerator by going online to get information about the top models and their attribute ratings on any number of review sites, including Amazon reviews, online *Consumer Reports*, and so forth. During this information search phase, a manufacturer such as Samsung may target them with an online ad for refrigerators, based on a Google search algorithm that has been optimized to target individuals who are searching online for information about "purchasing a refrigerator." This exposure to online ads may cause Anna and Joe to focus on a brand they had never purchased before but is offering a large discount on the product during the upcoming holiday (e.g., Memorial Day) weekend. Anna and Joe also post a query on Facebook asking their friends for some recommendations for refrigerator brands, which results in two new recommended brand names. Based on the ads that were served up online and word-of-mouth information from friends on Facebook, Anna and Joe decide to purchase a particular make and model.

They place their order online with Amazon, and while they are placing this order, Amazon's recommendation agent uses a machine-learning algorithm to suggest additional, related products that other people typically buy along with refrigerators, including a microwave oven. Anna has an Amazon account, so she quickly places an order and sets a delivery date for the following week. When the product gets installed on the stated date, Anna and Joe try out the new product. Anna is pleased with her purchase, and she goes on Facebook to thank the two friends for their recommendation. She posts a picture of herself posing next to her new refrigerator and posts a review, along with a Facebook "like" for the product. At the same time, they receive an e-mail from Amazon asking them to rate their customer service experience, which Anna and Joe rate very positively with 5 stars.

Clearly, this depiction of the consumer decision journey in the digital era diverges from previous journeys consumers have undertaken in many important ways. The implications for brand management are also significant. The traditional purchase funnel involves a sequence of steps beginning with awareness and ending with choice; in contrast, the online context produces conditions in which consumers may move through these steps in no particular sequence, with new information about brands impacting the decision journey at any stage.[2] Brand managers should account for the multitude of available online channels that provide consumers with brand information across various stages of decision-making. Figure 7-1 provides an overview of the expanded consumer decision journey that is especially pertinent to an online context.

In response to the aforementioned changes in the consumer decision journey—and its more complex nature—brand managers should equip themselves with information about how the decision journey varies across different segments of consumers. Furthermore, consumers should be encouraged to engage with the brand following a purchase. Given the important post-purchase advocacy that consumers can provide for a brand, marketers should incentivize and encourage consumers to provide positive referrals for the brand. We return to a discussion of the role of word-of-mouth later in this chapter.

FIGURE 7-1

Expanded Consumer Decision Journey

Source: R. Batra and K. L Keller, "Integrating Marketing Communications: New Findings, New Lessons, and New Ideas," *Journal of Marketing* 80, no. 6 (2016): 122–145.

Growth of Online Retailing

In addition to communication channels, the number of online retail options has also multiplied. The popularity of online retailing can be inferred from the following statistics:[3]

1. The value of e-commerce sales will reach $414 billion in 2018.
2. Sixty percent of American adults are happy to not shop in a crowded mall or store.
3. Seventy-one percent of shoppers believe they will get a better deal online than in stores.
4. Forty percent of men and 33 percent of women aged 18 to 34 years say they would ideally "buy everything online."

It is no surprise that online retailers have been phenomenally successful. Amazon alone accounts for 5 percent of all retail sales, with overall sales of $35 billion. The rapid growth in the popularity of online retailing has been accompanied by a decrease in preference for in-store shopping, which has further threatened the existence of many brick-and-mortar retailers, such as Macy's, JCPenney, Walmart, and so on.

Brand managers should therefore find ways of increasing their online appeal and presence and optimize brand experiences online. Online retailers have added many new features to help make online shopping experiences personalized and engaging. Still, many consumers like to visit stores and to touch and feel products—sometimes called *showrooming*—and is often followed by consumers placing an online order (at the lowest available price). Consumers like to visit retail locations, and this reality can serve as a reassurance that not all brick-and-mortar retailers will disappear any time soon.[4] These trends have important implications for managing brands by strategically coordinating online and offline channels.

One of the most prominent success stories in the online retailing context is that of Amazon. As Amazon continues to disrupt retail through its innovations in drone deliveries and acquisitions (e.g., Whole Foods), brands should be mindful of all the changes taking place in online retailing, as these changes can significantly affect how they merchandise and distribute their products. Branding Brief 7-1, which follows, chronicles Amazon's meteoric rise as it has grown to become a dominant player in the online retailing context.

BRANDING BRIEF 7-1

The Phenomenal Rise of Amazon

In 1995, Amazon sold its first book as an online bookseller. At that point in time, no one could have imagined what Amazon would eventually become. From selling a single book to becoming a multinational conglomerate, Amazon has continued to wildly surpass expectations on its path to success.

For two years, Amazon grew its bookstores and was able to issue an IPO in 1997, allowing the company to begin its rapid expansion. During this time, Amazon revealed its new logo, signaling to the marketplace that it desired to sell everything from A to Z. In the period ranging from 2001 to 2004, Amazon began making quarterly profits, launched cloud computing software, and started selling jewelry and shoes for the first time. These expansions were very profitable for Amazon.

In 2005, Amazon launched its membership platform, Amazon Prime, featuring its free two-day shipping in the United States. In 2006, Amazon expanded into the food sector for the first time by launching AmazonFresh, a fresh food delivery service. In 2007, Amazon unveiled its Kindle e-reader, briefly returning to its roots in the book industry. In 2008, Amazon bought Audible, which provides digital audiobooks in downloadable form, thereby expanding Amazon's ability to provide books to its customers in many different formats.

By 2010, Amazon had further expanded into other related segments. For instance, Amazon Studios, an original television studio, launched in 2010. In 2011, Amazon expanded its

Amazon's CEO Jeff Bezos describes Amazon's ability to make quick changes as a key ingredient of its success.

technology offerings when it unveiled its first tablet, the Kindle Fire. In 2013, the company took steps to transform its package-delivery system that had existed until that point with the introduction of drone delivery service. By this point, Amazon had almost completely transformed any previously held notions about what online shopping and shipping would look like in the future.

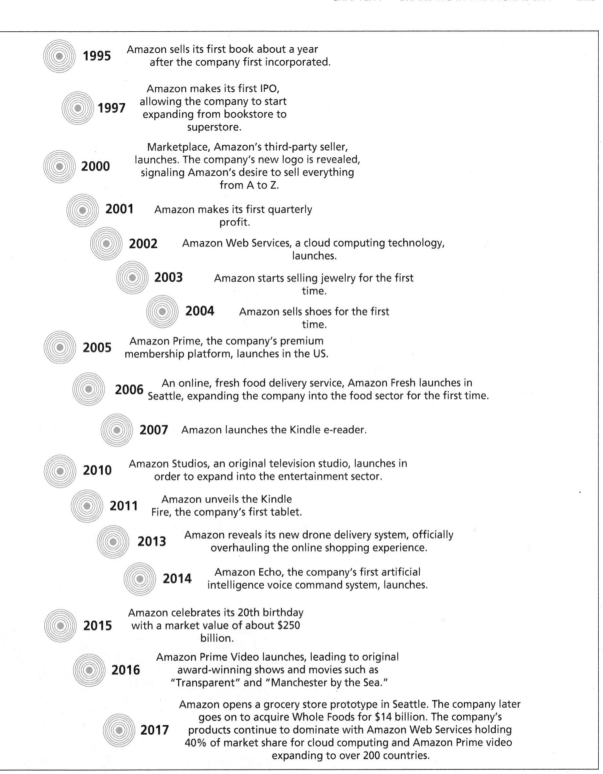

1995 Amazon sells its first book about a year after the company first incorporated.

1997 Amazon makes its first IPO, allowing the company to start expanding from bookstore to superstore.

2000 Marketplace, Amazon's third-party seller, launches. The company's new logo is revealed, signaling Amazon's desire to sell everything from A to Z.

2001 Amazon makes its first quarterly profit.

2002 Amazon Web Services, a cloud computing technology, launches.

2003 Amazon starts selling jewelry for the first time.

2004 Amazon sells shoes for the first time.

2005 Amazon Prime, the company's premium membership platform, launches in the US.

2006 An online, fresh food delivery service, Amazon Fresh launches in Seattle, expanding the company into the food sector for the first time.

2007 Amazon launches the Kindle e-reader.

2010 Amazon Studios, an original television studio, launches in order to expand into the entertainment sector.

2011 Amazon unveils the Kindle Fire, the company's first tablet.

2013 Amazon reveals its new drone delivery system, officially overhauling the online shopping experience.

2014 Amazon Echo, the company's first artificial intelligence voice command system, launches.

2015 Amazon celebrates its 20th birthday with a market value of about $250 billion.

2016 Amazon Prime Video launches, leading to original award-winning shows and movies such as "Transparent" and "Manchester by the Sea."

2017 Amazon opens a grocery store prototype in Seattle. The company later goes on to acquire Whole Foods for $14 billion. The company's products continue to dominate with Amazon Web Services holding 40% of market share for cloud computing and Amazon Prime video expanding to over 200 countries.

FIGURE 7-2

Amazon's Timeline

Sources: Lindsay Deutsch, "20 Years of Amazon: 20 Years of Major Disruptions," *USA Today*, Gannett Satellite Information Network, July 15 2015, www.usatoday.com/story/news/nation-now/2015/07/14/working---amazon-disruptions-timeline/30083935/; James Quinn, "Amazon Timeline: From Internet Bookshop to the World's Biggest Online Retailer," *The Telegraph*, Telegraph Media Group, August 15, 2015, www.telegraph.co.uk/technology/amazon/11801515/Amazon-timeline-from-internet-bookshop-to-the-worlds-biggest-online-retailer.html.

In 2014, Amazon continued to broaden its technology product portfolio by introducing Amazon Alexa (a voice-controlled intelligent personal assistant) and its companion product Amazon Echo. The Amazon Fire TV product, launched in 2014, was designed as a network appliance that would allow consumers to gain access to streaming digital video and audio content. Through the introduction of Amazon Fire, Amazon gained entry into the entertainment sector, which subsequently led to various entertainment service offerings, such as Amazon Prime Video which launched in 2016.

Amazon celebrated its 20th birthday in 2015. Its gift? A market value of about $250 billion. Amazon accomplished an entire lifetime of growth and diversification within its first 20 years, expanding to seemingly every sector possible. It grew from a single bookstore that took four years to earn a profit to a company that dominates in both branding and product offerings. Many of these are huge success stories. Its foray into original programming has earned awards for original shows such as *Transparent*

and *Manchester by the Sea*. Amazon Web Services (AWS) is now widely regarded as a market leader, boasting 40 percent of revenue share worldwide in the cloud computing market. In 2017, Amazon even acquired the grocery store giant Whole Foods for $14 billion, marking its expansion into brick-and-mortar retail.

What is the secret of Amazon's success? Founder and CEO Jeff Bezos describes Amazon's ability to make quick and bold decisions as one of the reasons for its spectacular success. This ability to take on calculated risks was one of the hallmarks of Jeff Bezos' management style as he presided over Amazon's growth. In the two decades since he founded the company, Amazon expanded into new markets by finding creative new ways to identify and deliver customer value. It was able to foresee trends in digitization and mobility and invest in new products (e.g., Amazon Kindle) at exactly the right time. Amazon has been effective in its overseas expansion as well, with offerings such as Amazon Prime Video available in more than 200 countries. Figure 7-2 provides a timeline of key events in Amazon's development over time.

Advertising and Promotions Using Digital Channels

Among the most important changes taking place with the advent of digital channels is the change in how advertising dollars are allocated across online and offline channels. As of 2017, the expenditure on digital media worldwide exceeded the amount spent on traditional television advertising ($209 billion for digital ad spending versus $178 billion for TV advertising worldwide).[5] Furthermore, the growth in digital media is expected to outpace growth in traditional media channels. It has been projected that, by 2020, online channels will be almost 50 percent larger than TV advertising ($113 billion for digital relative to $78 billion for traditional TV advertising budgets).[6] Of particular importance is the rapid increase in mobile advertising spending relative to advertising on a desktop device. Worldwide, mobile advertising accounts for $100 billion in advertising expenditures and nearly half of all digital advertising.[7] Branding Brief 7-2 shows how REI has utilized online channels to reinforce its brand message and create resonance with their customers.

BRANDING BRIEF 7-2

Igniting a Digital Firestorm

The day following Thanksgiving in America, called "Black Friday," is often a day that avid shoppers look forward to getting incredible deals and price promotions, such as a $300 savings on a high-definition television, a $50 discount on a $300 PlayStation, or a 60 percent discount off handbags from Saks Fifth Avenue. Black Friday is a day when bargain hunters can experience a surge of adrenaline as they locate the best deals in town. Malls are full of throngs of frenzied shoppers—who often wait for hours outside for stores to open—hoping to get the best deals and doorbusters. This day officially marks the start of the holiday shopping season, which culminates with Christmas. With plenty of special offers and deals, what's not to love about this special shopping day?

However, Black Friday is not without its detractors and naysayers. Some have protested against this "holiday" because retailers make their employees work during a time when many of them would prefer to be spending time with their families enjoying the Thanksgiving holiday. With many of the deals being available online before they come to the stores, some retailers have made a statement by shutting their stores on Black Friday. REI was among the first to pioneer the "Alternative Black Friday Movement" and became a disruptor by choosing to close all 143 of its stores, distribution centers, and headquarters on Black Friday. The strategy produced very positive PR for the company, and customers and employees applauded the company for its bold move.

REI encouraged its customers to opt-out of Black Friday shopping and, instead, spend the day enjoying the outdoors.

How exactly did REI's Alternative Black Friday work? Instead of the usual Black Friday sales and visits to retail outlets for the occasion, REI's #OptOutside campaign exhorted its employees *and* customers to go outdoors on Black Friday, using a series of billboards, videos, social media posts, and so on, to promote its campaign. The company utilized various digital and social channels to build excitement for its unique #OptOutside campaign.

The results were a major success, and REI increased its mentions on Facebook, Instagram, and Twitter by an astounding 7,000 percent. More than 170 other organizations subsequently decided to close down for Black Friday, and hundreds of parks opened without charging any fees. It is estimated that nearly 1.4 million people spent their day outdoors. Due in part to the online campaign, REI received a record 1 million new memberships in 2015. In-store sales increased by 7 percent, and digital sales grew by almost 23 percent. Given the initial success of this campaign, REI has made #OptOutside an annual event.

REI's Black Friday campaign is an example of how social-media buzz can increase awareness of brand messages. A large part of the success of REI's campaign can be attributed to the tight linkage between its products (i.e., outdoor gear) and the theme of the campaign (i.e., encouraging consumers to go outside). REI used this campaign as an opportunity to demonstrate its understanding of what truly mattered and resonated with its customers and therefore was able to generate greater awareness and engagement among its target customers. This was a bold move on REI's part to show its customers and employees that the company cared more about them than about the money and profits that have become synonymous with the traditional view of Black Friday.

A video for the REI ad for #OptOutside can be found at https://youtu.be/MEVXU4RDUoI.

Sources: "#OptOutside—Will You Go Out With Us?," REI, www.rei.com/blog/news/optoutside-will-you-go-out-with-us; Shep Hyken, "The Alternative Black Friday Movement," *Forbes*, November 26, 2016, www.forbes.com/sites/shephyken/2016/11/26/the-alternative-black-friday-movement/#4ad1cffc6007.

One-to-Many to Many-to-Many Channels

The traditional world of marketing involved brand managers relying on mass media channels, such as TV, print, and radio advertising, to communicate with consumers. The direction of communication was usually from manufacturer to consumer, and limited feedback was provided by consumers to manufacturers in turn. Thus, audiences were generally passive recipients of carefully crafted messages sent by brand marketers. This was particularly true in the case of the traditional one-to-many marketing approach to communications, as depicted in Figure 7-3 (where customers are labeled as A, B, and C).

Over time, the one-to-many channels gave way to a greater emphasis on interactive or one-to-one communications between the brand and the customer (see Figure 7-4). Catalog companies such as L.L.Bean or J.Crew embraced this direct marketing approach by viewing each customer individually. In recent years, these one-to-many and one-to-one channels are being supplemented or even replaced by many-to-many channels, such as Facebook and Twitter, in which consumers have become broadcasters in conversation with one another (many-to-many communications) and have become engaged in a two-way dialogue with brand marketers. This fundamental shift from one-to-many communications to many-to-many communications has led to other significant related trends, including an increase in consumer touchpoints and data availability, which are discussed in the next section.

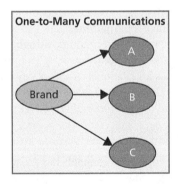

FIGURE 7-3

Traditional Marketing: One-to-Many Communications

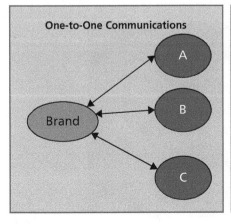

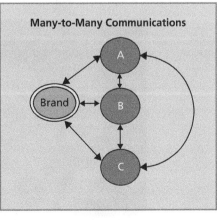

FIGURE 7-4

New Media Environment: Two-Way and Many-to-Many Communications

Increase in Consumer Touchpoints

Meet Anita Berman, senior brand manager for a leading cosmetics brand who works in New York City. Anita started out as a brand assistant for a leading skincare brand nearly 20 years ago. At that time, her life in brand management involved meetings with product development, advertising agencies, R&D, sales force, and the like. She remembers meetings with the rest of the brand team in the late 1990s, when they would brainstorm with the ad agency regarding the brand's ad campaign. At the time, their primary options for advertising included ads on TV and in print (particularly magazines). Anita remembers that this was the time when the Internet was just starting, and there was no such thing as Facebook.

Fast-forward to 2018. Anita's meetings with her brand team still include discussions about product development and getting input from the sales team. However, they now spend a lot of time thinking about a social media and digital marketing strategy for the cosmetics brand that she is managing and its target audience of 18- to 24-year-olds. Anita wonders how best to allocate her advertising budget across various channel options, including TV, display ads on magazine Web sites, social media advertising on Instagram, and video ads on YouTube. They are also launching a mobile app for the brand, which allows her customers to check their appearance and get day-to-day tips on makeup. They have contracted with a weather channel to partner on the mobile app, so that the makeup tips can vary based on where her customers live and the weather on any given day. Anita has to track various metrics such as click-through rates on banner ads, number of impressions, cost-per-click, and so on. They are also launching a social influencer program and are in the process of deciding which social media celebrity would offer the best return on investment.

The growth of digital marketing and social media channels and consumers' ability to communicate with one another have fueled a sharp increase in the number of touchpoints that brand managers have at their disposal to engage with and communicate with their consumers. As noted previously, the traditional model included one-to-many communications, in which the options would be restricted to one-way communications using mass media channels such as TV, print, radio, and so on. Today, brand managers have a dizzying array of digital communication options they can use to connect with consumers, including Facebook, Twitter, Instagram, Pinterest, LinkedIn, and so on. The implication of this increase in media options is growth in the complexity of media planning; brand managers have to orchestrate these various channels to create an integrated strategy across the consumer decision journey. Furthermore, brand managers have to ensure that brands have a unified message and a consistent look and feel across all these platforms. Having a sharply defined brand positioning and clear guidelines on how a brand should be presented and marketed to consumers is an important step in ensuring that the brand has a consistent theme across all channels. Another key concern of brand managers is to understand which channels are producing the greatest return on advertising dollar expenditures. This particular set of tasks—called *attribution modeling*—can be complex and challenging.

Increase in Data Availability

Data, data everywhere! The growth of digital channels has caused a deluge of data, ranging from clickstream data on users' browsing behaviors on companies' Web pages, to data on advertising metrics (e.g., click-through rates and cost per clicks), to information regarding the number of

Brand managers have various digital channels to choose from for placement of ads, including social media venues such as Facebook and Twitter.

Table 7-2 Top Five Brands in Social Media Mentions

Brands (Based on Mentions)	Number of Social Media Mentions Worldwide (2015–2016)[8]
Facebook	60,665,800
Apple	28,858,274
eBay	28,677,175
Amazon	26,001,012
Disney	16,543,436

unique visitors to a brand's Web site. Marketers now have the ability to use information gathered from customers' online behavior to tailor their offerings to customers' needs.[9] Yet this quantity of information can quickly become overwhelming if brands don't invest in tools for transforming all this information into usable bits of knowledge.

With data being so abundant, how can companies gather useful knowledge from the vast stores of information they have access to? Many companies rely on advanced analytics to generate insights from these data. For example, when J.Crew began using clickstream analysis, it generated key insights that increased online sales by 22 percent.[10] Its analysis showed that certain channels (e.g., Facebook, Twitter, Pinterest, and Instagram) yielded customers with the highest engagement. J.Crew also has optimized its presence on Facebook so that audiences can click on featured links and make purchases on the company's Web site.[11] It found that 21 percent of Pinterest users were likely to buy an item in a store after liking it on Pinterest, and this rate was even higher among younger consumers. In ways such as this, insights into the online behaviors of consumers can improve the brand marketer's ability to fine-tune segmentation and targeting strategies and strengthen customer engagement and sales.

Another factor contributing to the vast increase in data availability is the growth in social media conversations taking place on Facebook, Twitter, and so on. These conversations can be effectively mined using advanced analytics to generate important insights into consumers' mindsets and sentiments related to specific brands. To further illustrate the magnitude and scope of this type of data, Table 7-2 lists the top five brands and the number of social media mentions worldwide during 2015–2016, based on a study by NetBase.[12] The nearly 61 million mentions of Facebook and 29 million mentions of Apple represent a wealth of information for brand marketers and provide unique insights into consumers' thoughts and perceptions of their brand. Social media control rooms offer brand marketers the ability to listen to customer conversations and understand trends.

While the availability of data has provided many advantages to brand marketers in targeting consumer segments with specific benefits and offers, there are also downsides to these vast amounts of data. One challenge of data availability has to do with ensuring that customer privacy is preserved. Privacy violations can lower consumers' trust in brands. Brand marketers have to balance their desire to collect, analyze, and use customer data to improve their strategy while avoiding loss in customer trust.

Digital Personalization

Maya, an 18-year-old female college student, likes to shop online and is interested in fashion. She is looking for a new pair of jeans to purchase in time for an upcoming family reunion. While browsing for jeans, she found a yellow dress that she really liked.

The digital ecosystem is complex and offers various new opportunities for brands to engage with customers. Digital personalization is a new trend that uses customer data to develop specific offerings tailored to customer needs.

She almost purchased it and placed it in her shopping cart, but she decided at the last minute that it was too expensive. Although she logged out, the online retailer, which had hired a digital analytics firm to identify patterns of customer behavior, was able to track Maya's abandoned shopping cart along with its contents. As Maya went about her day, she got a text on her mobile phone asking her to unlock a special offer from the same online retailer. This time, Maya could not resist and decided to purchase the dress.

This anecdote describes a familiar scenario to anyone who has shopped online. The idea that the same product can become available at different prices based on expressed customer interest is called *dynamic pricing*. Various online retailers have invested in extensive analytics that allow companies to explicitly target individual consumers with varying offers to try to ensure that they complete the purchase. Marketers now have the ability to offer highly tailored messages relevant to various audiences to potentially elicit higher customer loyalty from a larger segment of people.

The advent of digital tools has ushered in an era of unprecedented personalization, in terms of both product and message.[13] *Digital personalization* has been defined as "the tailoring of messages and offerings to individuals based on their actual behavior." One study found that this ability to personalize can help reduce customer acquisition costs by 50 percent, increase revenues by 5 to 15 percent, and strengthen marketing efficiency by 10 to 30 percent.

Brand managers have access to big data and can utilize it to micro-target consumers at various touchpoints and in different stages of the decision journey. This targeting should take into account various demographic and psychographic aspects of consumers, their online browsing patterns, and their propensity to respond positively to different types of online offers made across various online channels. The data should also show consumers' proximity to brick-and-mortar locations (i.e., the nearest physical retailer) so that these retailers can provide some inducements and price discounts to incentivize purchase.

What are the implications of microtargeting for consumer behavior? While digital personalization offers many advantages from the marketer's perspective, it can also have a downside. Some researchers have suggested consumers may react negatively to personalized offers because of privacy concerns. These negative reactions might be overcome by reminding consumers of various free services and benefits that are provided to them online and by seeking their permission to use their information to target them with personalized offers.[14]

As our anecdote reveals, one way that digital personalization works is by *retargeting* consumers—that is, by targeting consumers with ads for products that they previously browsed but did not buy. One risk with this approach is that customers might react negatively to variable deals or offers and perceive this practice to be unfair. Orbitz was the target of customer outcry when it was discovered that the company was serving up higher prices on hotel rooms when visitors to their Web site used a Mac (versus a PC).[15] Orbitz's actions were based on the observation that Mac users typically spend 30 percent more on a hotel room. Still, the publicity surrounding this revelation led to a loss of reputation for Orbitz. This incident highlights a potential downside of personalizing offers to suit customers' profiles.

Retargeting, or targeting consumers with ads for products that they previously browsed but did not buy, is increasingly used by online retailers to convert browsers to buyers.

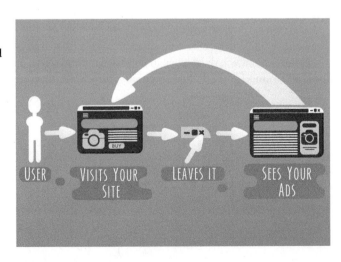

Researchers have shown that, under certain conditions, retargeting is more effective, particularly after consumers visited a product review site and for consumers who are browsing information about the category as a whole.[16] Retargeting is particularly effective because it allows brand marketers to be more focused in their advertising to users who have demonstrated previous interest, thereby allowing firms to strengthen their conversions among customers who visit their Web site. Ideally, an integrated strategy in which customers are targeted with ads using search advertising, display advertising, or content marketing, and are then made the focus of retargeting, helps strengthen the overall effectiveness of a digital marketing campaign.

A primary goal for brand marketers is to understand key triggers that work well with consumers with different profiles and in varying stages of the consumer decision journey. An analytics engine may uncover important nuggets of information (e.g., a job change to a different city or a propensity among consumers to go golfing every Saturday), and these nuggets can be leveraged to target specific offers to customers, in real time, to improve the conversion efficiencies (or the rates at which consumers move from one stage of the decision journey to the next).

One major bank added $300 million in savings by utilizing customer data to better target customers across various stages of the purchase decision process. This was done by specifying the various stages of the banking decision journey—including when customers first browse the Web, when they visit a branch, when they call, and so on—and targeting customers with offers that varied depending on which stage they were in. To undertake such personalization, organizational infrastructure is an important consideration.

To be successful in engaging in digital personalization, organizations must be proficient in prioritizing and identifying the data they need, developing agile teams, and having an effective testing-and-learning process. These key organizational strengths are preconditions for digital personalization at scale. The following points summarize three organizational prerequisites for digital personalization to be successful:[17]

1. Organizations must invest in a customer data warehouse that provides continuous monitoring and feedback regarding customer needs and wants and how well those are being satisfied through company offerings.
2. Organizations must deploy cross-functional teams to understand the customer's decision journey, which may involve a variety of different channels, including the company's Web site, a mobile app, or an in-store experience.
3. Organizations must employ an iterative process of testing and learning to identify what works and what does not.

Loss of Control over Brand Message and Co-Creation of Brand Meaning

The shift to digital has decreased the extent of control that a brand manager has on brand meaning. In the nondigital era, brand managers exercised greater control over their messages that were available through limited channels. With today's many-to-many communications model (see Figure 7-4), the growth and proliferation of large social media platforms, such as Facebook, Twitter, and Instagram, have ushered in an era in which dynamic and real-time conversations are taking place among consumers on a massive scale. Therefore, it behooves marketers to coordinate brand meaning generation on a large scale.[18]

The large number of social media channels available to consumers has reduced the amount of control that a brand can exert on the conversation.

This shift in the role of consumers as co-creators of brand meaning means that brand managers must manage and guide consumer conversations without holding a central or exclusive role as the authors or sources of brand meaning. This is a complex task that is exacerbated by the fact that experiences and stories are being shared in social media, which further decreases the ability of brand marketers to control the conversation. In addition, brand meaning can be shaped by many unexpected forces. For example, one study that provided a novel approach for measuring brand image based on Twitter found that 7UP was closely linked to the brand Smirnoff in social media.[19] The unexpected link to Smirnoff was due to a new cocktail recipe that was gaining favor in social media that included 7UP as a key ingredient.

In summary, the digital age has created conditions in which brand meaning is co-produced by three different but interacting forces:

1. *Firm-generated brand meaning:* Through their online and offline marketing activities and programs, along with other means, firms attempt to shape the meaning of brands with consumers.
2. *Consumer-generated brand meaning:* In the digital age, consumer-to-consumer conversations are enabled through social media platforms (e.g., Facebook and Twitter) that supplement traditional offline word-of-mouth. These conversations, which are taking place on various digital platforms and on a large scale, can significantly shape brand meaning.
3. *Media and cultural influences:* A variety of new entities and channels also play a significant role in co-creating brand meaning. Media channels may themselves contribute to brand meaning. Furthermore, cultural influences are continually evolving and shaping customer conversations and contributing to brand meaning.

Figure 7-5 provides a visual depiction of the role of consumers and firms in co-creating brand meaning, in addition to broader media and cultural influences.

Customer-generated brand meaning can have a powerful impact on how other consumers view a brand and their impact on brand image. The social media megaphone can amplify both negative and positive stories about brands and have a massive impact. For example, when Samsung Galaxy phones were the subject of a recall, the negative social media buzz posed a serious threat to the brand's reputation. In contrast, when Apple launches a new product (i.e., the iPhone XR), social media buzz about the product builds up months before the actual launch.

The challenge for brand managers is to assess how best to coordinate multiple sources of brand meaning in a cohesive manner. They should also be prepared to handle public relations crises in a quick and efficient way to minimize any possible damage to brand reputation. In Chapter 9, we describe the role of social media monitoring as one potential way for brands to keep up with social media conversations.

One important technology-induced change is the ability and willingness of brands to invite consumers to co-create brand meaning in an explicit manner. This involvement may also extend to consumers providing valued input into which product designs brands should choose. Brands may also seek advice on which types of logos work best and even ask consumers to design ads to use in branded campaigns.

Some of these invitations from brands to consumers are structured as contests with one large prize given for a winning submission. For example, the Frito-Lay Doritos' "Crash the Super

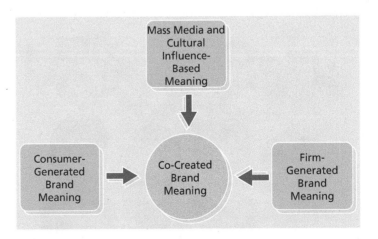

FIGURE 7-5

Sources of Brand Meaning

Bowl" ad contest had a $1 million prize, and the winning ad was aired during the Super Bowl. The contest, which ran from 2006 until 2015, marked one of the first efforts by a big brand name to outsource a part of its advertising to amateur participants via a contest and was seen as a bold and risky move on the brand's part.[20] This approach toward co-creating products and brands has become more prevalent today. Still, there are limits to how much co-creation a brand can engage in, as outlined below in The Science of Branding 7-1.

User Experience Is the Key to Digital Brand Success

Whether its Amazon's easy-to-use interface that allows users to make purchases with a single click, the intuitive appeal of Apple devices that allows even a 5-year-old child to easily operate an iPad, or the elegant simplicity of Google's search engine that is popular all over the world, successful digital brands have mastered the art of making the user experience flow seamlessly and smoothly.[21] These success stories showcase how crucial a seamless user experience is to the success of a digital brand.

Creating an interface that consumers can effortlessly navigate is one part of maximizing user experience. Another key element is to ensure that consumers can seamlessly switch from one device to another, allowing for a smoother user experience. For example, Apple has worked tirelessly to create an ecosystem such that its hardware, software, and peripherals are integrated into a single system that works seamlessly, as one commentator noted:[22]

> Steve Jobs and Apple took end-to-end responsibility for the user experience—something too few companies do. From the performance of the ARM microprocessor in the iPhone to the act of buying that phone in an Apple Store, every aspect of the customer experience was tightly linked together.

THE SCIENCE OF BRANDING 7-1

Is Co-Creation of Brands and Products Always Good?

What are the implications of social media from a consumer's standpoint? Are consumers, in fact, motivated to participate in co-creation of brands and products? When does consumer co-creation of brands and products benefit a firm? On the positive side, research has shown that co-creation can increase loyalty by promoting feelings of psychological ownership and makes consumers feel empowered. Furthermore, the amount of effort consumers put in and the enjoyment they experience from participating in co-creating a product can lead to greater consumer preference for the co-created product itself.

While co-creation can positively influence consumers' preferences for the products that they are helping to co-create, not all consumers are equally willing to participate or benefit from such involvement. Similarly, the benefits to brands are also uneven and depend on various factors. In an advertising setting, researchers have shown that co-creation can benefit brands when viewers' ability to scrutinize messages is low, when the identities of the ad creators and viewers are similar, or when viewers are highly loyal to the brand. In product categories in which quality is extremely important or with luxury products, co-creation efforts are less successful. Moreover, when consumers' cultural orientations include a high belief in power distance (or the belief in inequality or hierarchy), their propensity to purchase co-created products is also lower.

These findings indicate that brand marketers should tread carefully when implementing mechanisms that allow for consumer participation. While there appear to be many benefits, there are also significant downsides if the co-creation efforts involve the wrong product categories or customer groups.

Sources: C. Fuchs, E. Prandelli, and M. Schreier, "The Psychological Effects of Empowerment Strategies on Consumers' Product Demand," *Journal of Marketing* 74, no. 1 (2010): 65–79; Christoph Fuchs and Martin Schreier, "Customer Empowerment in New Product Development." *Journal of Product Innovation Management* 28, no. 1 (2011): 17–32; Christoph Fuchs, Emanuela Prandelli, Martin Schreier, and Darren W. Dahl, "All That Is Users Might Not Be Gold: How Labeling Products as User Designed Backfires in the Context of Luxury Fashion Brands," *Journal of Marketing* 77, no. 5 (2013): 75–91; Debora Thompson and Prashant Malaviya, "Consumer-Generated Ads: Does Awareness Co-Creation Help or Hurt Persuasion?" *Journal of Marketing* 77, no. 3 (May 2013): 33–47; Martin Schreier, Christoph Fuchs, and Darren W. Dahl, "The Innovation Effect of User Design: Exploring Consumers' Innovation Perceptions of Firms Selling Products Designed by Users," *Journal of Marketing* 76, no. 5 (2012): 18–32; N. Franke and M. Schreier, "Why Customers Value Self-Designed Products: The Importance of Process Effort and Enjoyment," *Journal of Product Innovation Management* 27, no. 7 (2010): 1020–1031; Susan Fournier and Jill Avery, "The Uninvited Brand," *Business Horizons* 54, no. 3 (2011): 193–207; Neeru Paharia and Vanitha Swaminathan, "Who Is Wary of Cocreation? The Hazards of Empowering Power-Distant and Conservative Consumers," working paper, Georgetown University.

Apple's extraordinary focus on a seamless user experience both instore, online, and across all its devices, is one of the most important reasons for its success.

This level of utility and convenience that is expected from online brands now translates to the offline world as well. Designing both online and offline interfaces to ensure that Web sites are so simple to navigate that consumers will easily locate what they are looking for or ensuring that a smartphone app is designed to optimize user convenience will be critical to the success of a brand.[23] As American Marketing Association CEO Russ Klein writes, "No industry space is an island. You expect Avis to be as effortless and friction-free as Uber."[24]

Brands as Cultural Symbols

Brands have greater impact as cultural icons than ever before. Brands can help consumers feel a part of something and allow them to signal to and connect with others.[25] As brands become increasingly embedded in consumers' daily online conversations, brand managers must deploy a new set

---

PEPSI'S AD MISFIRE

Kendall Jenner—a supermodel who starred in a Pepsi commercial—inadvertently became the target of controversy following a Pepsi ad campaign. In the commercial, Jenner was featured as leaving a photo shoot to stop a political protest by handing a policeman a can of Pepsi. The ad was the subject of significant backlash from its viewers, who felt that it was inappropriately exploiting a national protest movement—the Black Lives Matter movement—in an attempt to increase Pepsi's own sales. Even though Pepsi quickly pulled the ad to avert further controversy, it had to issue an apology to ensure that its audiences were not offended by Pepsi's "lack of taste" in its choice of advertising themes. Nevertheless, the incident drew criticism on social media from various sources. Notably, Bernice King, daughter of Martin Luther King Jr., issued a scathing criticism, arguing that the ad trivialized the sacrifices of many of the people (such as those of Martin Luther King) involved in civil rights protests.

One Pepsi ad featuring Kendall Jenner became a source of controversy for seemingly trivializing the protests surrounding the Black Lives Matter movement. Pepsi later apologized for the unintentional tone of the ad.

---

of techniques to ensure that brands maintain their cultural relevance.[26] Brand managers should incorporate ways for consumers to "friend" brand names on Facebook, Twitter, and Instagram; they should allow consumers to participate in brand communities and, at the same time, preserve the authenticity of the brand community by embracing a hands-off approach. They should find ways of achieving cultural resonance by presenting an authentic voice and a genuine point of view. Brands whose efforts to reach consumers have any traces of hypocrisy will be subject to parody. For example, Pepsi's ad campaign featuring Kendall Jenner was the subject of much ridicule and criticism in social media.[27]

Pepsi learned the lesson of how quickly a public relations crisis can spread through social media channels. Brands have to be prepared for sudden crises to occur and develop a crisis management plan to ensure that the organization is prepared to address any controversies as they arise.

BRAND ENGAGEMENT

Consumer–brand engagement is an important focus of brand managers, and there is even more emphasis on achieving this in a digital marketing and social media context. As noted in Chapter 2, when customers are *engaged*, they are willing to invest time, energy, money, or other resources in the brand beyond those expended during its purchase or consumption. For example, customers may choose to join a club related to a brand, receive updates, and exchange correspondence with other brand users or formal or informal representatives of the brand itself.

In an online context, consumers engage in a number of activities that go beyond mere purchase, including cross-buying, word-of-mouth and referrals, and posting reviews and blogging about a brand. These customer actions may be described as customer engagement. At the most basic level, consumers engage with firms by donating their own time, money, or other resources that help strengthen their bonds with a brand or firm. This section provides an overview of brand engagement and related issues, including (1) describing the brand engagement pyramid, (2) highlighting brand and non-brand drivers of brand engagement, and (3) reviewing the role of brand boycotts and social movements as specific examples of consumer activism in the digital era.

We distinguish three levels of customer engagement based on the extent to which a customer engages in various types of behaviors:

1. *Low brand engagement:* Low levels of engagement may translate into a higher frequency of purchasing a product or providing positive feedback about a product or service. On a related note, we should recognize that a vast majority of consumers may have no engagement with a brand. This type of consumer may be referred to as being "indifferent" to the brand.
2. *Moderate brand engagement:* Calling a company's 1-800 help line to seek additional information about a product or service or providing the company with some feedback about new flavors may be viewed as moderate brand engagement.
3. *High brand engagement:* Positive forms of high brand engagement include joining a brand community or starting a fan page on Facebook dedicated to a brand, evangelizing by troubleshooting customer complaints on a Web site, helping others find the right product variant to suit their needs, and so on. Companies should foster such evangelizing among their customers by offering various monetary and nonmonetary incentives.

Many consumers of a given brand could engage in these behaviors to varying degrees and be characterized as having low, moderate, and high engagement with the brand. It is worth recognizing, however, that some consumers may also have negative brand engagement. On the negative side, low engagement may involve withdrawing from a brand by lowering purchase frequency, complaining about a product or service, and so on. Stronger negative actions toward the brand may include terminating a service contract, posting a negative review about the brand on a review Web site, or discouraging others from purchasing the product. An even more extreme set of behaviors could involve boycotting a brand or encouraging consumers to join a "brand hate" group on Facebook (e.g., "I Hate Walmart" and "Comcast Sucks"). In a subsequent section, we analyze the role of online channels in fostering social movements and brand boycotts.

Brand Engagement Pyramid

Customers vary in their propensity to engage with firms; therefore, marketers must develop various approaches to strengthen and foster positive brand engagement. Segmenting customers according to their propensity to engage with a firm can be accompanied with segment descriptions based on age, income, expertise, and so on. The resulting brand engagement pyramid can offer insights into who to target and how to market to these segments. Figure 7-6 captures the possible ways a company might segment its customer base according to their level of engagement. The blue arrows reflect brand marketing activities or other influences that are outside the control of the brand marketers; the red arrows reflect the flow of information and influence both within and across different levels of the brand engagement pyramid.

The following set of questions represent some key issues that marketers need to address regarding their customers' level of brand engagement:

1. What is the shape of the brand engagement pyramid? What is the size of the highly positively engaged group? What is the size of the not-very-engaged versus the highly engaged group? How many negatively engaged customers exist and at what levels?
2. Are there any trickle-down effects, such that those who are highly engaged exert influence over those who are less engaged? Are there any influences of the disengaged group on the engaged group, or vice versa? Does a reverse influence of the less engaged on the highly engaged customers harm the brand, and how can marketers stem this direction of influence if it is negative in nature?
3. What are the flows of information (as well as influence) for a given level of engagement? What does this imply for brand loyalty and purchase behavior?
4. Among those who are highly engaged, what are the most efficient means of marketing communications? Similarly, among those who are least engaged, how can marketing communications be leveraged to strengthen engagement?

Branding Brief 7-3 provides insights into how Dollar Shave Club has been able to strengthen engagement among its customers. The Science of Branding 7-2 provides some academically grounded insights into drivers of brand engagement.

Taken together, understanding the different levels of brand engagement and how marketing communications can strengthen brand engagement is critically important. Next, we offer a description of online brand communities, social movements and brand boycotts and brand hate and parody as instances of negative brand engagement and discuss the role of digital media in facilitating such movements.

Negative Brand Engagement

The growth of digital marketing and social media has resulted in greater collaboration and the creation of brand communities among consumers. While these brand communities are generally positively disposed toward brands, they can also become the source of hatred and dissatisfaction with the brand. Facebook pages such as "Comcast Sucks" and "I Hate Apple" command large followings and allow consumers to vent their frustration regarding the brands' failings, including their lack of customer service or high prices.

Sometimes, these communities can present opportunities for brands to redress customer grievances. In fact, a number of companies hire service personnel to act as brand ambassadors to specifically help redress consumers' concerns. These Web sites stand in stark contrast to brand fan pages that often spring up around communities of individuals who are positively disposed toward a brand

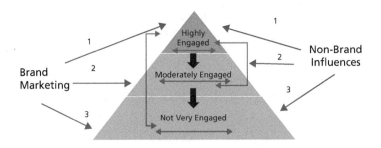

FIGURE 7-6

Brand Engagement
Pyramid

BRANDING BRIEF 7-3
Shaving the Price of Razors

Dollar Shave Club (DSC) is positioned as a convenient and cost-effective alternative to delivering razors and personal grooming products via mail. The company has garnered 3.4 percent of a competitive razor market and has 1.7 million active members per month. Its positioning as a value brand is consistent with its pricing at $1 per month for a package of razors, and customers choose from a variety of subscription services based on their particular needs.

To highlight its value proposition, DSC campaigns effectively leverage humor to increase their social media buzz. DSC's #RazorBurn campaign used humor to poke fun at its competitors, mocking the higher-priced alternatives and inaccessibility of rival products. Their online videos have been watched more than 20 million times, and nearly 50,000 of its highly engaged customers provide referrals to new customers to join DSC each month. For example, the campaign jokes that typical razor companies had blades of such high quality that you could use them for a month. The campaign then featured images of old, "gross" razors with captions such as "Your razor's so old it eats dinner at 4:30."

According to the company, the campaign was successful, resulting in a 24 percent lift in overall social media mentions, with social followers increasing by 6 percent and DSC's Twitter engagement increasing by 31 percent. The keys to online brand engagement for DSC included a clear value proposition, which targeted a felt need among consumers (i.e., alleviating the high prices of personal grooming products), and a very reasonable cost for an online subscription, which offered greater convenience. These benefits resulted in high loyalty toward and brand engagement with the DSC brand.

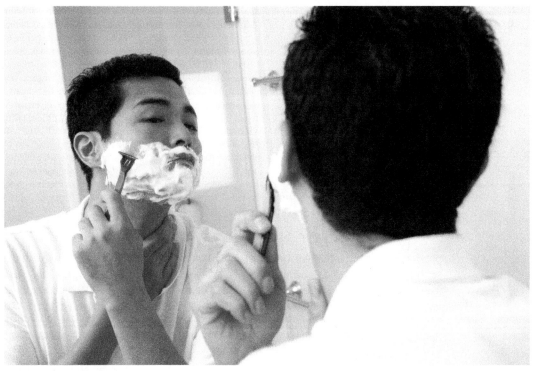

Dollar Shave Club

and typically love a brand. Both brand love and brand hate can become more exaggerated in online communities, as individuals with similar beliefs unite together around their opinions about a brand.

These communities can also become the basis for social movements and brand boycotts—for example, when consumers boycotted retailers that carried merchandise owned by Ivanka Trump. The campaign, #GrabYourWallet, was meant to boycott businesses (e.g., Macy's and Bed Bath & Beyond) that carried Trump-family products as an expression of protest against the perceived ethical failings of the president. In contrast, during the same period, Amazon saw an increase in sales of Ivanka Trump-branded perfume, as supporters of the brand demonstrated their support.

The availability of various means of communicating easily or in a relatively anonymous manner has increased the likelihood of brands being ridiculed and parodied to a greater extent than

THE SCIENCE OF BRANDING 7-2
Drivers of Brand Engagement

What are some factors that drive consumers to exhibit low, moderate, or high levels of brand engagement? According to research findings, brand characteristics, message characteristics, medium characteristics, and consumer characteristics can all drive brand engagement.

- *Brand characteristics:* Certain types of brands have higher engagement. For example, brands that have more symbolic (or nonfunctional) positioning and those with unique or differentiating attributes or associations tend to elicit higher brand engagement. The type of good (whether publicly consumed or private) has also been shown to impact brand engagement, with consumers demonstrating higher engagement for publicly consumed goods.

- *Message characteristics:* Messages pertaining to a brand could include advertising by the brand, content created or curated by the brand and shared via social media, sponsored blogs, or any news item featuring the brand. Characteristics of these messages can impact brand engagement. Message relevance to the consumer can also increase brand engagement. An additional way for brands to engage consumers is to arouse certain emotions via the messages that they post online. For example, research has shown that emotions such as awe and surprise increase consumers' willingness to engage with a brand's message.

- *Medium characteristics:* The size of the audience and the strength of ties between the consumer and the audience (i.e., other consumers) can also change engagement with the brand message. Research has shown that consumers can also be strategic in where they post messages based on the

type of medium. The co-location of brands with other brand names on the same medium or within the same message can also impact perceptions of a given brand by creating a conversation space in which brands vie with each other for customer attention. Therefore, brands may be better off selecting unique or less crowded social media venues or channels, thus improving their ability to be "heard" by consumers.

- *Consumer characteristics:* Several consumer characteristics have also been shown to drive brand engagement, including prior loyalty and identity goals, such as consumers' desire to express themselves or to manage others' impressions of them. Inviting consumers to co-create different aspects of a product or service or advertising can help strengthen engagement, but this only works for certain types of consumers and in certain product categories (see The Science of Branding 7-1).

Sources: Vanitha Swaminathan, Andrew H. Schwartz, and Shawndra Hill, "The Language of Brands: Understanding Brand Image through Text Mining of Social Media Data," (2017), University of Pittsburgh; Oded Netzer, Ronen Feldman, Jacob Goldenberg, and Moshe Fresko, "Mine Your Own Business: Market-Structure Surveillance through Text Mining," *Marketing Science* 31 (May–June 2012): 521–543; Christian Hughes, Vanitha Swaminathan, and Gillian Brooks, "In Blogs We Trust: The Impact of Blogging on Awareness and Brand Engagement," (2018), University of Pittsburgh; Jonah Berger, and Katherine L. Milkman, "What Makes Online Content Viral?," *Journal of Marketing Research* 49 (April 2012): 192–205; Yu-Jen Chen and Amna Kirmani, "Posting Strategically: The Consumer as an Online Media Planner," *Journal of Consumer Psychology* 25 (October 2015): 609–21; Zoey Chen, "Social Acceptance and Word of Mouth: How the Motive to Belong Leads to Divergent WOM with Strangers and Friends," *Journal of Consumer Research* 44 (October 2017): 613–632.

previously. When United Airlines passenger and musician Dave Carroll met with poor customer service from the airline—the airline broke his Taylor guitar during a flight—the musician took to YouTube and created a video called "United Breaks Guitars." The video became a viral sensation and caused the company's stock prices to plunge in the immediate aftermath of the video's release. More recently, the airline was again in the news when one of its passengers was unceremoniously dragged off an airplane and the entire incident was captured on video and posted online.[28]

The social media megaphone has provided consumers with unprecedented power to share information with millions of current and future consumers, thereby shifting considerable power into their hands. The next section offers a closer look at the many channels that are available to brand marketers today to share information and to engage with consumers. Digital communications across a variety of channels—for example, Web site, e-mail, search and banner ads, and influencer marketing using blogs—can complement traditional forms of communication. Each of these channels has unique aspects that are worth considering as marketers embark on a plan to incorporate different digital media. We begin with an overview of three types of communications: paid, owned, and earned channels.

DIGITAL COMMUNICATIONS

In this section, we provide an overview of three types of channels that are available to the digital brand marketer—paid, owned, and earned channels—as first introduced in Chapter 1. A *paid* channel is one in which a marketer typically runs paid advertising, such as Facebook

FIGURE 7-7

Summary of Digital Marketing Communication Channels

advertising, and can also include traditional paid advertising channels, such as TV, print, and so on. Paid (digital) channels include search advertising (e.g., Google AdWords), display advertising, banner advertising, social media advertising (e.g., advertising on Facebook, Twitter, Instagram, and Pinterest), e-mail marketing, and mobile ads (e.g., messaging or in-app advertising). Social media advertising is increasingly shifting toward video ads that are placed on various social media Web sites. *Owned* channels—such as a company's Web site, a YouTube channel, or mobile apps—can be valuable sources of information for consumers about a company's offerings.

Earned channels refer to review sites and reviews posted online that typically do not cost the company anything but create a buzz to help build publicity for the brand, especially if the reviews are positive. Earned channels include social media mentions of a brand or likes and comments in response to a social media post or blog post. These earned channels are valuable real estate on the Internet because they do not cost anything to a brand. Generating sufficient buzz online can be an important contributor to brand engagement and online sales.

Figure 7-7 summarizes the main communication vehicles that are available to digital marketers today. All three—paid, owned, and earned channels—can contribute to brand presence and brand engagement. For example, Warby Parker utilizes its Web site to invite customers to design a unique pair of eyeglasses, which it then delivers to customers. In addition to leveraging the ability of the Internet to offer customization options to its users, Warby Parker has leveraged online social media to build brand engagement and create loyalty. Other brands have utilized digital and social channels to attract younger, millennial consumer segments to their brand, as shown in the example below of the Ford Fiesta. Recently, to call attention to the important

DRIVING GROWTH AMONG MILLENNIALS

Ford's prelaunch "Fiesta Movement" campaign invited 100 handpicked young millennials to live with the Fiesta car for six months. Drivers were chosen based on their online experience with blogging and size and quality of their online social network, as well as a video they submitted about their desire for adventure. After the six months of trial usage, the campaign had drawn 4.3 million YouTube views, more than 500,000 Flickr views, more than 3 million Twitter impressions, and 50,000 potential customers, 97 percent of whom were not already Ford owners.

Ford Fiesta

role of sharing of information by consumers on various social media, some commentators have added *shared media* to paid, owned, and earned channels as a fourth type of communication channel. We describe these various word-of-mouth effects in Brand Focus 7.0 at the end of this chapter.

In summary, a mix of paid, earned, and owned channels can help support a brand's overall marketing strategy. We begin our subsequent discussion by describing the role and importance of two important channel options, company Web sites and e-mail marketing. These two channels are among the most traditional approaches to using digital channels to appeal to customers.

Company Web Sites

As an example of an owned channel, the company's Web site represents a key brand asset and a primary marketing tool in the online context. Consumers often use the Web site as the first place they turn to learn more about a brand. Web sites offer companies the ability to tell their story to their customers and can offer an effective platform for engagement. Company Web sites are particularly crucial to the success of small businesses and in business-to-business settings because they are often the only vehicle of communication between the company and the customer. Company Web sites provide various advantages to marketers, including generating leads, providing contact information, and facilitating customer communications, feedback, and after-sales service.[29]

Companies have to invest time and money, however, in ensuring that the company Web site reflects the look and feel of the brand itself, in addition to ensuring that the content reflects the story they want to tell. Company Web sites should be optimized to make sure that their presence on search engines allows customers to find them quickly. This optimization requires that the content companies provide has high relevancy with respect to the keywords that consumers employ while searching for them, thus maximizing their position in organic searches. We will later describe the nuances of search advertising, which relies on sponsored ads to allow customers to land on company Web sites. Recently, companies have begun making mobile apps available as an option for consumers to access company content via their mobile devices. These are particularly beneficial as they are relatively easy to set up.

E-mail Marketing

E-mail marketing, while sometimes eclipsed by its more glamorous counterparts such as social media advertising, is still the most effective form of communication. Various studies have described the exceptional return on investment of e-mail marketing. For example, one study by the Data & Marketing Association suggests that the median return on investments in e-mail marketing (122 percent) is four times higher than that of other notable communication channels, including social media (28 percent), direct mail (27 percent), and paid search (25 percent).[30] Perhaps due to its high return on investment, studies have shown that marketers intend to spend more on e-mail marketing in the coming years.[31] There are a few key considerations in conducting an effective e-mail campaign, as discussed in the following paragraphs.[32]

Segmenting, Targeting, and Personalization. Segmenting e-mail lists, identifying the right customers to target, and then sending personalized e-mail messages to these targets are exceedingly important to the success of an e-mail campaign.[33] Developing buyer personas that describe each segment's interests and needs often provides the basis for effective targeting. However, not all personalization is equally effective, and much depends on delivering personalized messages that take into account the recipient's unique purchase history or demographic. Merely creating e-mails with the individual's name in the greeting may not result in successful response rates. In fact, individuals may be wary of e-mails listing their first names, as many recipients might suspect that these communications are scams or phishing attempts.

Google's search advertising matches potential customers and companies using search terms provided by users.
Source: Ilesia/123RF

E-mail Structure and Subject Line. Differences in content and structure, as well as the subject line used, have been shown to result in different response rates. Extremely short subject lines (49 characters or less) have been shown to be as effective as subject lines with more than 70 characters. One study tracked more than 900 million e-mails in its analysis and showed that there was no increase in either open rate or click-throughs at the 60- to 70-character length of the subject line.[34] The e-mail campaign conducted by the Obama campaign prior to his election in 2008 showed a significant success rate with short subjects like "Hey" and "Wow."

Timing and Industry Differences. There are many differences in success rates based on *when* (e.g., what day of the week) e-mail campaigns are sent and which industries these e-mail campaigns are used in. Mondays are the most effective for e-mail campaigns, with a 13.3 percent open rate relative to Fridays, which have an 11.9 percent open rate. Among industries, the insurance industry has the highest usage of commercial e-mail, with nearly 94 percent of insurance companies using this channel.

Entertaining and Engaging Content. Having a unique and appealing message is the key to success in e-mail marketing. JetBlue is known for its quirky and attention-grabbing advertising, and it also has developed engaging e-mails to send to its audiences. A recent JetBlue e-mail campaign reminded customers about their one-year anniversary and created fun and engaging content to pique audience attention.[35] Successful engagement can also involve offering unique promotions or providing good value, wrapped in entertaining content.[36]

Testing and Monitoring. Analytics are now available to track the success of all digital campaigns. A company can test and monitor different versions of e-mail campaigns to identify the ones that are working and then optimize the e-mail marketing campaign accordingly.

Search Advertising.   Search advertising is perhaps the largest source of spending among all digital ad formats and is expected to account for $130 billion in advertising spending worldwide by 2019. Branding Brief 7-4 provides an overview of Google AdWords, which represents the most popular product within the search advertising industry.

Advertisers that seek to build a brand can utilize Google search advertising as a brand awareness-building tool. By connecting to category-level keywords and by targeting specific search terms, a new brand can increase the number of consumers who click on their ad and then take them to a landing page with more information. Alternatively, brand marketers can provide specific product-level information to target potential new customers by advertising key aspects of the product (e.g., upcoming promotions or discounts). This type of advertising is geared toward those who are ready to make a purchase or those in later stages of the purchase funnel.[37]

Thus, based on the goals of the advertiser, search advertising can provide a highly targeted approach to advertising. Because advertisers only pay based on actual clicks (also

BRANDING BRIEF 7-4
Campaigning Using Clicks with Google AdWords

The Google AdWords search advertising platform is among the largest digital advertising platforms available. Within the United States, Google search advertising dominates the search advertising space and accounts for almost 78 percent of advertising revenues from search ads. Search advertising continues to increase, with a growth rate of approximately 10 percent in 2017.

How does AdWords work? AdWords can be thought of as a platform that connects buyers and sellers within Google's search engine and complements the organic search results of a particular query. Sponsored search ads typically appear on the right side or the top of the Google home page. For ads to appear at the top of the page or high on the list of search ads, marketers need to bid for particular keywords in an online auction that takes place continuously. The behind-the-scenes online auction makes keywords available for a price, with the price being determined based on demand. Payment to Google is on a cost-per-click basis.

Advertisers typically only pay Google when someone clicks on the ad, so merely serving up an ad on a search engine might drive impressions but not necessarily increase the cost of an ad campaign. The position of an ad on the home page or the rank of the ad plays an important role in its effectiveness: The higher the rank of the ad, the higher is its effectiveness. The ad rank for a given ad is based on the cost-per-click bid on a given keyword and the quality score metric that determines how relevant the ad is to a given user. In general, ad rank is determined by the combination of maximum bid on a given keyword and the quality score associated with the ad. For example, an online shoe retailer such as Zappos may bid on keywords such as "buy shoes online" or "online shoes" so that a search ad will appear when consumers type those keywords into Google's search engine.

Brand marketers must choose keywords carefully by understanding how consumers search for their category or brand. Companies may advertise using branded keywords (e.g., Zappos shoes)

or generic or unbranded keywords (e.g., shoes online). The selection of branded or unbranded keywords is based in part on the extent of brand recognition that already exists. If consumers are not as familiar with a brand and its name, search is more likely to use category-related, unbranded search terms. An example of a search ad for 1-800-Flowers appears in Figure 7-8. The ad is shown in response to a branded search for 1-800-Flowers. In contrast, the second ad is for an unbranded, generic search for "auto insurance."

The success of a search ad depends on the placement of the ad on the Google search page: The higher the placement, the better are the chances of the ad being seen by consumers. In turn, the ad's placement depends on Google's quality score. Google has a proprietary algorithm that assigns a score to each ad based on various factors such as the overall historical performance of a keyword within Google, ad text relevance (i.e., the match between the keywords and the content on the advertiser's landing page), and user experience on the landing page or Web site.

Google offers various ways of targeting consumers, including geo-targeting. Consumers in certain geographic regions can be targeted, and users whose IP addresses are geotagged as belonging to a particular location will be shown an ad. Highly targeted ads that best address a customer's search query are most likely to be clicked on and therefore will ensure a higher success rate, as measured by the *click-through rate.** Impressions are measured based on the number of times an ad is displayed on Google or within a Google network.

*The formula for click-through rate is: $\dfrac{Number\ of\ Clicks}{Number\ of\ Impressions}$.

If an ad generates 50,000 impressions and generates 1,700 clicks, the click-through rate is .034 or 3.4%.

Source: www.emarketer.com; https://support.google.com/adwords/answer/2454010?co=ADWORDS.IsAWNCustomer%3Dfalse&hl=en.

FIGURE 7-8
Google Search
Advertising

known as a cost-per-click advertising model), there is no waste (or comparably fewer wasted dollars relative to traditional ad campaigns) of advertising dollars.[38] As of 2016, the average cost-per-click was $2.14, and the click-through rates were 1.16 percent, with high click-through rates in industries such as dating/personal services (3.4 percent), finance (2.65 percent), business-to-business (2.55 percent), consumer services (2.40 percent), and technology (2.38 percent).[39] In addition to click-through rate, *conversion rate* is another metric used to gauge the success of a search ad: The higher the conversion rate, the more successful is the search ad campaign. Based on how the advertiser defines a conversion, it could involve something as simple as a user requesting further information about a product or could involve an actual sale.

Display Advertising.   Display advertising or banner ads involve the placement of ads in related Web sites. Display advertising is an effective mechanism for reaching a large number of people and for generating impressions. Unlike search advertising, display advertising is monetized on a cost-per-thousand basis and relies on impressions generated by an ad. Banner advertising can be an incredibly efficient awareness-generating tool, enabling brands to advertise on Web sites that are closely linked to a particular target audience. For example, a banner ad on *The Wall Street Journal* Web site alongside an article about financial prudence in *The Wall Street Journal* is a means to target consumers with an interest in financial analysis.

Taken together, search ads and banner or display ads are very effective ways of building an online brand presence. The low cost of purchasing keywords and the high degree of targeting possible makes these types of ads a viable medium for companies with modest advertising budgets or even business-to-business companies that value the direct approach to targeting consumers with their ad message. Next, we provide a closer look at a variety of social media paid channel options available to marketers today.

OVERVIEW OF SOCIAL MEDIA PAID CHANNELS

Social media channels (e.g., Facebook and Twitter) offer unparalleled access to communities of users with similar demographic, geographic, and psychographic characteristics. Social media plays many roles, including (1) establishing a public voice and online presence, (2) amplifying marketing messages, (3) helping monitor and obtain feedback from consumers, and (4) promoting customer engagement. In recent years, various forms of social media advertising have also become available to marketers. These forms of advertising leverage the benefits of social media platforms. Managing social media effectively requires a broad understanding of what social media can accomplish in general, but also understanding how various platforms within social media differ from each other; each social media platform has unique benefits that marketers should be aware of, but each has potential limitations too.

Overall, social media offers a unique way for marketers to promote dialogue with their audiences, gather feedback and insights, and solicit input regarding their products. However, a caveat is in order. As noted previously with regard to the brand engagement pyramid, only some consumers want to get involved with only some of their brands, and even then, maybe only some of the time. Some consumers may view a brand's presence on social media channels as intrusive and imposing on their privacy. Companies should monitor their social media presence to ensure that it is appropriate and welcomed by consumers.

Next, we review the largest social media platforms (see Table 7-3), describing the pros and cons of marketing brands on these platforms and highlighting some examples of campaigns that have successfully leveraged these platforms.

Facebook

If Facebook were a country, it would be the largest country in the world! Facebook's social media platform has 1.6 billion active users, which is larger than China's population of 1.4 billion; stated differently, 1 in 4 persons in the world can be accessed via Facebook, and 80 percent of these users access Facebook via mobile devices.[40] Consider the demographics of Facebook users: 79 percent of American adults have a Facebook account. As a social network, Facebook is particularly influential among young adults, and 88 percent of Americans aged 18 to 29 have a Facebook account.[41] It is also especially popular among females, with 83 percent of females in the United States using Facebook, relative to 75 percent of males. Facebook is also comprised of users who are educated (79 percent of Facebook users in the United States have a college degree) and who live in urban and suburban areas.

Advertising revenue comprises the largest source of revenue for Facebook. In 2017, based on projections by eMarketer, the global ad revenues for Facebook approached $34 billion. In 2017, Facebook's share of the digital ad business in the United States was 21 percent, and 87 percent of Facebook's revenue was from mobile advertising.[42]

Some metrics that are of relevance in assessing the impact of Facebook advertising campaigns include the following:

1. *Reach:* Facebook breaks down reach into organic, paid, and viral. *Organic reach* is the number of people who have seen a post in the news feed, in the ticker, and on the page itself. *Paid reach* is the number of unique people who have seen an ad or a sponsored story. *Viral reach* is the number of unique people who have seen a story about a page published by a friend.
2. *Followers:* The number of Facebook followers is a good metric to capture the reach and popularity of a given message.

Table 7-3 Number of Users across Selected Social Media Venues (January 2017)

Facebook	1.9 billion
Twitter	317 million
Instagram	600 million
Snapchat	300 million
Pinterest	150 million

Sources: "Assets," Facebook, June 10, 2018, https://en.facebookbrand.com/assets; Kathleen Chaykowski, "Pinterest Reaches 150 Million Monthly Users, Boosts Engagement Among Men," *Forbes*, October 13, 2016, https://www.forbes.com/sites/kathleenchaykowski/2016/10/13/pinterest-reaches-150-million-monthly-users/#4cb46f4a732e; "Most Famous Social Network Sites Worldwide as of September 2017, Ranked by Number of Active Users (in millions)," Statista.com, September 2017, https://www.statista.com/statistics/272014/global-social-networks-ranked-by-number-of-users/; "Social Media Logos," Freepik, http://www.flaticon.com/packs/social-media-logos-2.

3. *Likes and shares:* The number of Facebook likes is indicative of customer engagement with a particular message. The number of Facebook shares also indicates how viral a particular message is.

Next, we consider the various pros and cons to advertising on Facebook.

Pros.   Clearly, the large size of the Facebook community provides marketers with a tremendous set of advantages by offering a large marketplace for connecting buyers and sellers. Sellers can instantly generate brand awareness among a large number of globally distributed users by advertising on Facebook. In addition to its ability to generate brand awareness among its users, Facebook's advertising platform provides many features that allow advertisers to target very specific segments of users on a variety of characteristics including age, gender, political orientation, hobbies, interests, and so on. This targeting capability allows advertisers to reach their target audience with a minimum waste of ad dollars. Facebook's direct purchasing feature and instant-play videos allow campaigns to reach more consumers and facilitate direct customer service.

Cons.   One downside of Facebook advertising is the reality that a Facebook post will likely not reach every user who follows the company because users can choose which posts to view. Furthermore, companies like Procter & Gamble have begun stepping away from Facebook as a result of

---

THE TOUGH MUDDER CAMPAIGN

Tough Mudder is a challenging obstacle race for teams, designed in the spirit of British Special Forces. It features 29 different obstacles with creative names such as the Devil's Beard, Shocks on the Rocks, and Funky Monkey. Competitors encounter hazards such as walls, 15-foot planks, ice baths, nightmare monkey bars, greased halfpipes, and electrified army crawls. Funded with $20,000 in seed capital in 2010, Tough Mudder spent its entire $8,000 communication budget at launch on Facebook advertising, which generated plenty of word-of-mouth. By 2013, more than 750,000 competitors were participating in 53 scheduled events. With entry fees of about $155 per person, the company's margin was about 48 percent.

Tough Mudder—a challenging obstacle race—leveraged Facebook advertising to generate word-of-mouth and create awareness.

---

their realization that precision targeting can sometimes produce suboptimal results. For example, when Procter & Gamble tried targeting ads for its Febreze air freshener to pet owners and large households, the company found that sales were stagnant; however, when the target audiences were expanded to anyone older than 18 years of age, sales increased significantly.[43] Social media also carries the risk of a firestorm when users target a company's social network presence due to a company scandal or its position on political or social issues. Further, Facebook and other social media platforms are increasingly under fire because of the possibility that data on consumers is being used without their explicit permission, which in turn, poses both legal and reputational issues for platforms such as Facebook. This has become an increasingly hot-button issue, and one which could potentially harm the future of social media advertising, unless consumers, policymakers, and social media platforms come together to ensure that these concerns about data-sharing and privacy are resolved to everyone's satisfaction.

#LIKEAGIRL

Procter & Gamble launched the #LikeAGirl campaign for its Always feminine hygiene brand in 2015 to expose the effects of the phrase "like a girl" on limiting the possibilities for young women. The campaign was launched with a television advertisement that appeared during the Super Bowl, with both pre- and post-puberty women stating the effects that societal limitations have had on them, whether it be quitting a sports team or not having confidence to take on challenges. The girls then wrote how the effects of the phrase impacted their life on boxes, which they then destroyed. The ad went viral, with #LikeAGirl trending on Twitter after the ad appeared on TV. The ad itself has been viewed more than 80 million times since airing. The Always brand has built on the interest the ad generated and created LikeAGirl confidence summits and an interactive Web site, where feminine care products are sold on the bottom of the page. The ad marks the growing movement among advertisers to support women's empowerment causes, which in turn has led to increased sales in some cases.

Twitter

Twitter is the second largest social medium after Facebook. There are many advantages to Twitter advertising. Every Twitter message (or Tweet) goes directly to followers, and they are easy to create. This allows for direct communication between customer service and customers and shows a brand's personality. However, Twitter is not without its downsides. Twitter is flooded with tweets, making it more difficult for a company's posts to stand out. There is limited visual content, and tweets are constrained to 140 characters (although Twitter increased its limit to 280 characters).[44] The following example of the #LikeAGirl campaign shows how a company can leverage Twitter to increase its brand presence.

Twitter is particularly beneficial in helping resolve customer service issues. Delta Air Lines used a Twitter strategy to improve social interactions with its customers and to provide customer service. The Delta Assist Twitter handle was helpful in connecting the company with its customers. Delta has used the #deltaassist to both listen to customer complaints and respond to issues. A number of other companies followed Delta's lead in making their Twitter account a focus of their customer service enhancement strategy. Beginning in May 2015, Domino's Pizza used Twitter to let customers request delivery of their favorite pizza by tweeting a pizza emoji to the @Dominos Twitter account and by using the hashtag #EasyOrder. More recently, Domino's made the pizza-ordering process even simpler by introducing an app that would do the same.[45] This campaign received significant media coverage, and more than 50 percent of Domino's orders come from digital channels today.

Instagram

Instagram is a platform with about 400 million users that is targeted to a younger audience and typically has higher brand engagement levels than comparable platforms. Its ability to engage its audiences visually (through images and videos) allows for more nontraditional marketing approaches. Instagram's younger, more cynical audience is more likely to see traditional ads negatively and as "too manufactured." Instagram offers the opportunity to reach these users in ways that traditional media cannot. For instance, Samsung implemented a holiday marketing campaign called #SamsungPayItForward that promoted its new mobile payment service. A number of social influencers were engaged to promote this service, which resulted in a series of sponsored Instagram posts showcasing how people used the payment app.[46]

Domino's used Twitter to let customers request delivery of their favorite pizza by using the hashtag #EasyOrder.

Source: James A. Martin, "10 Top Social Media Marketing Success Stories," *CIO.com*, April 28, 2016. www.cio.com/article/3062615/social-networking/10-top-social-media-marketing-success-stories. html#slide7

Pinterest

Pinterest is a medium that allows users to share and post pictures featuring different brands. It is particularly conducive to marketing certain brands that rely on visual imagery. Pinterest's easy-to-create "Buy It" pins on products, as well as its ability to generate more referral traffic than other forms of social media, present significant advantages to brand marketers. However, limitations include its niche content (focus on lifestyle content) and a disproportionate appeal to a female fan base.

Krylon paint is an example of a Pinterest success story when it held its "first-ever Pinterest yard sale." The 127 Yard Sale is the "World's Largest Yard Sale" and happens every August in six states along Highway 127, stretching between Michigan and Alabama.[47] In 2015, Krylon sent its DIY experts to buy 127 seemingly worthless items along the route and transform them into something desirable, listing the resulting items for sale using Pinterest's "Buy It" pin feature. All proceeds from the sale were subsequently donated to charity. As a result of this campaign, Krylon saw a 4,400 percent increase in its following on Pinterest and gained $2.7 million in earned media from a $200,000 budget.

Video

Video has become an important medium for brand building, particularly when brands want to engage in deeper themes and storytelling using their brand. Videos can be paid ads that appear on social networking Web sites such as YouTube or Facebook; in addition, brand videos may appear in owned media channels, such as the company's Web site or other places. There are various examples that demonstrate the power of video advertising to elevate a brand's ability to engage in storytelling. A successful campaign that used video advertising was Nivea's "Second Skin"

Krylon's 127 Yard Sale campaign leveraged Pinterest to create the "World's Largest Yard Sale."

YouTube video. This video featured a mother and her adult son who could not spend Christmas together. The video showed how advanced technology (virtual-reality goggles and a fabric simulating human skin) could help reunite mother and son. By using a nonsales approach and evoking human emotion, the Nivea campaign received considerable buzz with more than 150,000 views. Examples such as Nivea show how video advertising can impact consumers positively by touching them emotionally as much—if not more—than any 60-second commercial.

As another example, the German supermarket chain Edeka created a Christmas-themed video that showed an elderly man alone on Christmas and whose grown children were too busy to visit. The #HeimKommen ad helped highlight the loneliness of older people during the holidays. The

Nivea's Second Skin Ad

Source: James A. Martin, "10 Top Social Media Marketing Success Stories," CIO, April 28, 2016. www.cio.com/article/3062615/social-networking/10-top-social-media-marketing-success-stories.html#slide7

video garnered 33.5 million views within a week, and two weeks later, it had 20 million views and 579,000 shares, making it a successful campaign that raised brand awareness and enhanced brand image.[48]

Video advertising can also be used by luxury brands to feature exclusive video content, helping the brand maintain its upscale or prestige image. For example, in 2016, Burberry became among the first luxury brands to run a Snapchat-Discover-channel ad, which featured a new Burberry fragrance. The video featured exclusive content that was meant to be only available for a brief period in time.[49]

Global Use of Social Media

It is worth noting how social media is a global phenomenon, and many of the techniques presented here are applicable in many parts of the world. One notable exception is in China. Due to government restrictions, Facebook, YouTube, and Twitter are banned in China. Still, the Chinese consumer loves to use social media. We provide a brief review of the top social media platforms in China in Branding Brief 7-5.

BRANDING BRIEF 7-5
On Being Social in China

WeChat (owned by Tencent), often known as the "Facebook of China," is a dominant social media platform. It is an all-in-one messaging app that provides games, online shopping, and other services and has more than 1 billion active monthly users. With 10 million apps, Chinese consumers use WeChat for various daily activities, including booking flights, making investments, shopping, paying taxes, and so on. Brands can also use the WeChat platform to communicate with their customers. For example, brands can leverage WeChat Moments to push messages and other content out to their followers.

Sina Weibo, or **Weibo,** is a micro-blogging platform and is considered a combination of Twitter and Facebook. Users typically use Weibo to upload videos and images, follow individuals, read their posts, and so on. Weibo has 313 million active monthly users and is particularly popular in urban locations.

QQ (also owned by Tencent) is another messaging app that offers its vast installed base of 869 million users various features, including games, shopping, group chats, and voice chats.

Youku is the video-sharing analog of YouTube in China. It offers its users streamed or downloaded movies and TV shows. With 580 million active users, it allows brands to appeal to their audiences via banner ads, branded viral videos, and pause ads.

Baidu Tieba (part of the Chinese search engine company Baidu) offers a communication platform that is tightly connected with the search engine services offered by Baidu. With 660 million active monthly users, it offers businesses (and brands)

Chinese consumers use the popular social media platform WeChat for multiple purposes including playing games, booking flights, and online shopping.

Baidu is the largest search engine in China and the second-largest search enginge in the World.

the ability to create their own forums that users can be directed to based on searches of the brand name on the search engine.

Sources: Laurie Beaver, "WeChat Breaks 700 Million Monthly Active Users," *Business Insider*, April 20, 2016, www.businessinsider.com/ wechat-breaks-700-million-monthly-active-users-2016-4; Lauren Johnson, "5 Things Brands Need to Know about WeChat, China's Mobile Giant," *Adweek*, December 14, 2015, www.adweek.com/ digital/5-things-brands-need-know-about-wechat-chinas-mobile-giant-168588/; Nha Thai, "10 Most Popular Social Media Sites in China," Dragon Social, June 30, 2017. https://www.dragonsocial.net/ blog/social-media-in-china/.

MOBILE MARKETING

Did you know that consumers today may check their mobile phones 150 times a day, and many view smartphones as a "lifeline" or a "butler"? It is not surprising, therefore, that mobile advertising and promotions are expected to grow tremendously in the near future. The global mobile advertising market totaled $141.7 billion in 2017 and is expected to grow to $531 billion in 2024. Various forms of mobile communications (display, search, SMS, among others) together totaled approximately $50 billion in 2017 advertising expenditures in the United States alone. Of these, display advertising accounted for approximately $26 billion in 2017 ad expenditures, and search advertising accounted for $22 billion.[50]

Why is mobile so popular? Clearly, the importance of smartphone devices for information, social interaction, and, to a lesser extent, shopping has contributed to this increase. Consumers in the United States spend more time on their mobile devices (more than 3 hours per day relative to the one hour a day that consumers spent just a few years ago) than on their desktop computers. In particular, consumers (particularly in the United States) spend 42 percent of their time using mobile devices on a single favored app. Social media apps, including Facebook, Google, and You-Tube, are among the most popular apps, reinforcing the notion that mobile is primarily a means of entertainment and communication rather than commerce.[51]

Mobile advertising is particularly helpful in sending timely, location-based messages to customers at the right time and place. This increase in relevance offered by mobile messages—that is, reaching a customer at the right time and place—creates opportunities for developing a vast database of customers' needs and wants based on their responses to mobile advertising and promotions. Because mobile devices are always on, marketers can communicate in real time with their customers. This puts additional pressure on marketers to engage with customers using intuitive interfaces with easy navigation. Mobile ad copy has to be simple and direct to attract the attention of its target audience.

Furthermore, mobile marketing helps engage customers while they are shopping by offering them timely promotions, discounts, and so on. Mobile promotions can vary based on different geographic locations as well as different "dayparts," suggesting that marketers can customize their advertising and promotions to an unparalleled degree. This also means that customers who are targeted with advertising messages and promotions based on their location, time of day, or behavior will find marketing efforts of greater relevance to their purchases.

Messaging Services.   Of the various mobile options available, text messages—specificaly, short messaging service (SMS) and multimedia messaging service (MMS)—can offer customers unique offers based on time and location. SMS marketing has remained popular, as research has shown that 90 percent of messages are read within 3 minutes, and audiences are five times more likely to respond to a text than an e-mail. For example, Reuters used texts to engage with its customers in connection with its Eikon suite of financial products. BMW ran a messaging campaign to remind its customers in Germany of the importance of snow tires during winter.

In-App Advertising.   *In-app advertising* is another way mobile marketing can help brands touch customers. For example, the social media platform Snapchat allows brands to utilize its mobile app to target customers. Taco Bell used Snapchat for its popular "Taco Head" campaign, in which each customer turned themselves into visual tacos and then shared their branded images with their friends. This campaign generated nearly 224 million views in a single day and increased visual engagement three times (up to 24 seconds) relative to regular images (which are typically viewed for 8 seconds).[52] Alternatively, in-game advertising involves delivering messages within mobile games or sponsoring entire games to drive customer engagement. The Starbucks mobile app is another example of how mobile apps can drive customer engagement for brands, as the following example demonstrates.[53]

One example of effective mobile marketing is the Starbucks mobile app, which perfectly blends a store locator, its rewards program, and gift card information. Starbucks uses its mobile app to offer customers incentives such as birthday gifts and free beverages. Each time a purchase is made, customers collect a certain number of stars, which can later be redeemed for free offers. An SMS is sent to customers to complete surveys sent through the phone, which also allows them to earn more points. The mobile-order-and-pay feature allows customers to pay for a beverage ahead of time, prior to picking up the beverage in-store. The Starbucks mobile app has contributed to sales increases of more than 22 percent and has nearly 7 million customers. There are three key lessons from Starbucks' success in mobile marketing: (1) Mobile apps can facilitate companies' learning about their customers' motives; (2) mobile apps can be used to reward customers at appropriate times, thus increasing its effectiveness; and (3) mobile apps can help companies strengthen their bond with customers. Most importantly, Starbucks perfected its mobile payment system over many years, using countless experiments and tests to refine its marketing strategy, suggesting that mobile marketing approaches may need constant testing and learning to ensure they work just right.

Proximity Systems Marketing.   *Proximity systems marketing*, or *geo-fencing*, involves delivering particular advertising messages to mobile users within a defined geographic area. By serving up highly targeted, relevant ads, geo-targeting and proximity systems can benefit companies and customers alike.[54] For example, Campari offered customers in a tightly defined geographic area (an area with many bars) $5 off or a free Lyft ride if they checked a score on an app.[55] Branding Brief 7-6 provides another example of a company, Red Roof Inn, that effectively used location-based targeting.

BRANDING BRIEF 7-6
Turning Flight Delays into Marketing Opportunities

Red Roof Inn's mobile marketing approach of leveraging flight cancellation information to increase reservations is an excellent example of the power of mobile marketing strategies in enabling companies to target customers in real time. Previously, Red Roof Inn was struggling to compete with big-budget hotel chains in the search marketing landscape. Achieving a high ranking in the search ad space was increasingly challenging. There was also competition with searches from travel intermediaries such as Kayak and Vayama.

In this context, Red Roof Inn decided to utilize its limited budget toward a mobile search advertising approach in which it would target only those customers with a high likelihood of conversion. One potential segment of travelers that presented an interesting opportunity were those whose travel plans were disrupted by delays or cancellations (typical of air travel). With an estimated 2 to 3 percent of flights cancelled daily, 500 planes don't take off, and 90,000 passengers get stranded.

Using real-time data and geographical information, along with specific search queries, the company targeted these stranded travelers with specific search queries such as "hotels near O'Hare Airport." The algorithm developed by Red Roof Inn included automatically boosting bids and adjusting ad copy across its various mobile search campaigns. These ads would be displayed when the volume of cancellations exceeded a threshold. As it turned out, 2014 had one of the harshest winters in history, and

the company utilized flight cancellation data to develop an algorithm to automatically target stranded travelers when the volume of flight cancellations was high and during the evenings. The ads showed distances from travelers' airports.

The campaign, beginning in March 2014, demonstrated the effective use of technology and big data to augment search management, such that, despite budget limitations, Red Roof Inn was able to capitalize on specific moments of opportunity—in this case, when a traveler was stranded at an airport and looking for a place to stay. Using a blend of real-time data and mobile search, Red Roof Inn was able to target prospects who were most likely to convert to buyers. Ads that featured the call to action "Stranded at the airport? Come stay with us!" allowed Red Roof Inn to perfectly target consumers who were willing to book a room, increasing Red Roof Inn's bookings by more than 60 percent relative to other campaigns. The precision targeting of more than 400,000 stranded travelers allowed Red Roof Inn to gain first position within the segment of last-minute queries. Overall, Red Roof Inn showed a 375 percent increase in conversion rate, a 650 percent increase in share-of-voice, and a 98 percent increase in click-through rates across all nonbrand campaigns.

Sources: Matt Lawson, "Win Every Micro-Moment with a Better Mobile Strategy," Think with Google, September 2015. www .thinkwithgoogle.com/marketing-resources/micro-moments/

win-every-micromoment-with-better-mobile-strategy/; "Red Roof Inn Turns Flight Cancellations into Customers" Mobile Marketing Association, accessed September 23, 2017, www.mmaglobal .com/case-study-hub/case_studies/view/31739; Rob Petersen, "16 Case Studies of Companies Proving ROI of Big Data," B2C.com, December 27, 2015, www.business2community.com/big-data/16-case-studies-companies-proving-roi-big-data-01408654#ZPCMLZ 1w53LZLPp5.99; Sunil Gupta, "In Mobile Advertising, Timing Is Everything," *Harvard Business Review*, November 4, 2015. https:// hbr.org/2015/11/in-mobile-advertising-timing-is-everything.

One key takeaway from the Red Roof Inn example is the importance of understanding how consumers react to your brand throughout the day and identifying particular moments during the day that present an opportunity to target consumers with specific offerings. The ability to reach consumers at a time and place that is more relevant to their purchasing of a brand with mobile marketing provides marketers with tremendous ability to hypertarget their offerings and to engage their customers to an even higher degree. Push notifications allow a company to notify users about new messages or events even when they are not actively using the app—they can be sent to all users or a particular group of users. For example, Walmart developed a mobile app that allows customers to search, browse, buy, and view rollbacks and locate their nearest store (and for Walmart to send push notifications).[56]

As mobile devices continue to grow in importance to consumers' daily lives, research has also examined how mobile marketing techniques can contribute to added sales. A few key findings from academic research are worth noting:[57]

1. Environments may impact the effectiveness of mobile advertising and promotions. One study found that, counterintuitively, mobile promotions can actually be more effective in crowded areas (e.g., trains), as consumers adaptively focus more on their mobile devices to tune out external noise and distractions.

2. Mobile targeting based on time and location is more effective the closer the promotion is to actual purchase.

3. Targeting consumers who are closer in physical location to competitors' locations produces better results than targeting mobile promotions to consumers who are closer to the company's own locations. Targeting consumers closer to the company's own location with mobile promotions and discounts may result in cannibalizing sales from that location and reducing profitability.

4. Targeting consumers with mobile promotional coupons can boost overall spending, particularly unplanned spending, if the coupon requires consumers to travel farther than their planned path.

INFLUENCER MARKETING AND SOCIAL MEDIA CELEBRITIES

Influencer marketing involves utilizing key influencers, such as bloggers, celebrities, topic experts, and opinion leaders, to provide information and opinions about products and brands.[58] Influencer marketing is expected to account for $5 billion dollars of global marketing expenditure within the next five years.[59] Instagram influencer marketing alone is a $1 billion industry and is forecasted to reach $2 billion by 2019.[60] In 2016, 86 percent of marketers invested in social influencer marketing, and 48 percent of marketing practitioners surveyed indicated that they planned to increase their budgets for influencer marketing in 2017.[61]

Marketers have been utilizing influencers for their brands to a greater extent in recent years because of the results they have seen. Sponsored bloggers and celebrity influencers can often hold greater sway over some consumers than any advertiser can. One study reported that audiences exposed to influencer marketing spent $639,700 more than an audience that had not been exposed.[62] The popularity of influencer marketing also has translated into the success of online social influencers. Some of these online social influencers, such as beauty guru Michelle Phan, can earn up to $3 million per year based on their endorsement of specific brands.[63] Top influencers on YouTube can earn $300,000 per video, while a top Facebook influencer can earn $200,000 per post.[64] There have been a number of studies examining how word-of-mouth influences consumers, particularly as it pertains to online word-of-mouth (we review these studies in Brand Focus 7.0 at the end of the chapter). However, it is worth noting that there is a difference between organic word-of-mouth and sponsored word-of-mouth (which is more consistent with the idea of influencer marketing).

Many brands have leveraged social media celebrities to influence their audiences. For example, Emirates Airlines wanted to use social and digital channels to appeal to American consumers.

Emirates Airlines used key influencers to highlight their experiences with the brand, in order to strengthen their appeal to American consumers.

Emirates hired online influencer and YouTuber Casey Neistat to talk about an upgrade he received from business class to first class on Emirates. This campaign was an instant success, and his video generated more than 27 million views. Mercedes-Benz also used online social influencers with its #MBPhotoPass campaign, in which the company let influencers tell a story using their vehicles. These influencers were given keys to a Mercedes-Benz vehicle and were asked to drive around while taking pictures and curating the brand's Instagram account. One video featured a dog and his owner, and by telling a unique and relevant story about their relationship, this video provided Mercedes with the opportunity to tell a real, genuine story that connected the brand to its audience. The campaign was wildly successful; nearly 1,700 videos were created to tell influencer-based stories, generating 173 million impressions, 2.3 million likes and comments, and $4 million worth of earned media. The ability of influencers to engage in storytelling about brands can thus be a powerful way for brands to connect with their consumers.

Influencer marketing relies a great deal on the authentic tone of the influencer, who that are often, in fact, paid to post information about a brand. Marketers need to exercise caution that the information regarding sponsorship of the influencer's post by the brand is made obvious to the customer. The Federal Trade Commission requires clear and unambiguous language to be made available. Recently, in the United States, the Federal Trade Commission actually sent out letters to more than 90 Instagram influencers, informing them know that their relationships with brands must be disclosed on their social media accounts.[65]

CONTENT MARKETING

What is content marketing? According to the Content Marketing Institute, "Content marketing is a strategic marketing approach focused on creating and distributing valuable, relevant, and consistent content to attract and retain a clearly defined audience—and, ultimately, to drive profitable customer action."[66] Content marketing is a type of marketing that involves the creation and sharing of online material (e.g., videos, blogs, and social media posts) that does not explicitly promote a brand but is intended to stimulate interest in its products or services.[67] Content marketing can be beneficial to companies in appealing to certain groups of people and in achieving specific goals.[68]

Guidelines for Good Content Marketing

A key difference between content marketing and traditional marketing is that consumers typically want to consume the posts that form part of a content marketing campaign.[69] The goal of content marketing is to engage an audience in topics of interest to *them*. Therefore, selling products and services cannot be the primary goal of content marketing.

Understanding buyer needs must always be a starting point for generating good content. This may involve mapping out a buyer's decision journey. Developing a set of buyer personas that depict the typical customer at various stages of the decision journey can also be very helpful. Evolving content that addresses the information needs of different types of consumers at each of these stages is a key task of content marketers. Another key to success in content marketing is excellent storytelling. As Joe Pulizzi, founder and executive director of Content Marketing Institute puts it, "The integration of storytelling and content marketing is now, more than ever, critical for retaining customers and attracting potential leads."[70]

It is important to recognize that content distribution is an extremely important component of the content marketing effort. Much thought must go into the various channels in which content will be distributed. To ensure broad distribution, the strategy for distributing content must involve channels beyond social media sharing and may involve identifying unique ways of disseminating content to ensure audience reach. For example, a blog may be a great way of ensuring that there is a ready and committed audience for content pieces.

A good content strategy has to be integrated with a broader public relations and marketing strategy. The goals of the overall marketing strategy in terms of reaching and engaging the audience should be aligned with the content marketing strategy; doing so can help reach the audience, build a brand, increase brand awareness, generate leads, and ensure sales.[71]

Case Studies

John Deere.   *The Furrow* magazine was launched by John Deere in 1895 by the founder's son, Charles. The magazine was launched as a way of addressing farmers' needs for information regarding soil health, soil conversation, and other topics, and it currently has a circulation of 2 million globally in 40 countries and 12 languages. Unlike other content marketing efforts, John Deere makes its sponsorship of the magazine prominent, as the brand appears in the magazine. Furthermore, the magazine is actually distributed by John Deere dealers. However, the magazine's success has been in large part due to its focus on its customers. According to David Jones, the publication manager for *The Furrow*, "Telling stories that folks enjoy reading—and that they can use in their own operations—has been the recipe since the beginning." The magazine has evolved over years. As a corporate historian for John Deere noted, "Looking back at our archives, you can see the changes, from an advertorial, to a general agriculture journal with farming hints and reprinted articles that look a lot like the *Farmers' Almanac*, to today's magazine that tells farmers how to run their businesses." By maintaining its focus on the target audience—that is, farmers, rather than John Deere's equipment—the magazine has maintained its appeal over the 120+ years of the magazine's history.[72]

Movoto.   Real estate agency Movoto launched a campaign called "Mapping Marvel Origins" with the goal of stimulating comic book fans' interest in regional real estate.[73] An infographic was created that featured the background stories of Marvel characters and showing their birthplaces around the world. The campaign featured 365 stories about Marvel characters that were placed in various outlets such as Yahoo, Mashable, and MTV, among others. The campaign, which effectively leveraged the popularity of Marvel characters, resulted in more than 9,000 shares in social media.

Legal and Ethical Considerations

While content marketing can be effective, it may also give rise to various legal and ethical concerns that marketers should be wary of. In particular, the Federal Trade Commission's rules for sponsorship identification of broadcast content mandate that any piece of content posted by an author who received any reimbursement for the content from a company sponsor must disclose that compensation.[74] Thus, content marketing efforts must walk the fine line between sponsorship of content and ensuring that such sponsorship efforts (particularly in the case of social media promotions and endorsements) are adequately disclosed, to ensure compliance with the law.

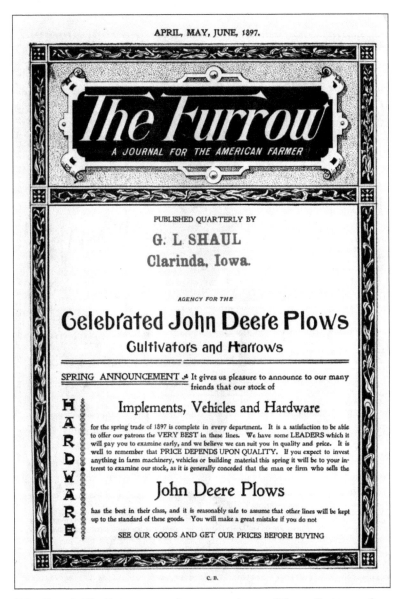

John Deere's *The Furrow* magazine represents one of the earliest uses of content marketing to appeal to consumers.

Source: Kate Gardiner, "The Story Behind 'The Furrow' the World's Oldest Content Marketing," *The Content Strategist*, October 3, 2013. https://contently.com/strategist/2013/10/03/the-story-behind-the-furrow-2/.

THE PROS AND CONS OF PAID CHANNELS AND THE NEED FOR INTEGRATION

Given the plethora of choices available with online and social media channels, brand marketers have to make an effort to create integrated digital media campaigns that leverage the benefits of different social media. For easy reference, Table 7-4 provides a summary of the pros and cons of primary paid channels. Because of similarities in these types of communications, we combine influencer marketing and content marketing. Brand managers can evaluate the pros and cons of different paid options and create campaigns that provide the optimal balance of targeting, reach, conversions, and engagement.

Integrating across channels can also provide significant benefits to storytelling. For example, when the Chicago Cubs won the World Series in 2016, it ended a 108-year long losing streak that began in 1908. To leverage the excitement of the win, Anheuser-Busch used special effects to create a video that had the Cubs' fans' legendary, but deceased, announcer Harry Caray call the victory. Anheuser-Busch created a compelling video that showed its understanding of the city's nostalgia and history; the video contained historic footage of the Cubs playing in various

Table 7-4 Pros and Cons of Primary Paid Channels

Channel	Pros	Cons
E-mail	Less costly, quick and easy to conduct a campaign. Highest return on investment (ROI) among major channel options.	Unsolicited e-mails may lower reputation among customers; e-mails may be viewed as scam.
Search	Allows for hypertargeting of desired target audience and high-quality lead generation; required budgets are small, campaigns have clear ROI metrics.	Competition for certain keywords can drive up budgets; optimization of a campaign is time-consuming; a non-visual (text-only) ad type can limit what the brand can convey.
Display or banner	High reach of banner ads is ideal for building awareness. Flexible style and format.	Lack of control over ad placement, potentially harmful to reputation, could be viewed as spam.
Social media advertising (e.g., Facebook, Twitter, LinkedIn, etc.)	Effective targeting capabilities; on Facebook, it is possible to target based on specific interests, political affiliation, etc.; on LinkedIn, by profession, job titles, etc. Affordable and generally effective. Click-through rates of Facebook ads are 8 times that of normal Web ads. High degree of accessibility to all types of businesses or individuals.	ROI is unknown, and social media ads may be viewed as intrusive by consumers. Optimizing an ad campaign requires constant monitoring and updating. Concerns over privacy may prompt further legislation preventing use of customer information for advertising targeting.
Video advertising (e.g., Facebook video and YouTube video)	Video allows brands to engage customers through sight, sound, and audio.	Targeting may not be as precise; customization or verification is not possible; audience may be too distracted to pay attention.
Sponsored blogging, influencer marketing, and content marketing	Brands can leverage popular social influencers to persuade consumers through sponsored word-of-mouth. High awareness-generating potential; high potential for engaging customers.	Depends on identifying the right influencers with the right appeal. The Federal Trade Commission requires all sponsored bloggers to disclose their sponsorships, thus lowering the effectiveness of word-of-mouth relative to organic word-of-mouth.
In-app (mobile) advertising	Ability to target consumers at the right place and time. Mobile in-app advertising leverages the popularity of mobile devices. Location data allows for precision targeting, particularly of coupons and promotions.	In-app banner ads may not generate the most revenue.

Sources: Evan LePage, "Display Ads, Search Ads, and Social Media Ads: Pros and Cons," *Hootsuite,* June 3, 2015, https://blog.hootsuite.com/display-ads-search-ads-and-social-media-ads/; George Root, "The Pros & Cons of Email Marketing," *Chron,* accessed September 27, 2017, http://smallbusiness.chron.com/pros-cons-email-marketing-1448.html; James Brook, "The Pros and Cons of Facebook and YouTube Video Advertising," *ClickZ,* February 4, 2016, www.clickz.com/the-pros-and-cons-of-facebook-and-youtube-video-advertising/92925/.

close-call games. The brand leveraged social media as well as TV advertising as the Cubs won the game, and over the course of the campaign, the video generated more than 3 million views. This campaign showcases how a brand can wrap a story around its message (in this case, an underdog story) to demonstrate that it understands its customers, thereby creating relevancy.[75]

BRAND MANAGEMENT STRUCTURE

The digital era has also shifted consumer behavior in significant ways, and these changes are important because they help illuminate the shifts taking place in branding and brand management. Brand marketers have to evolve a strategy to address the shifts in advertising spending across a range of digital channels and implement an organizational structure and processes that support the strategy. Various factors for creating a successful strategy have been suggested to organizations to help them to cope with these changes, some of which are described in the following list:

1. Senior management for the organization should be tasked with understanding how products and brands are being researched and viewed online, and how consumers are using these channels to research their products.
2. Cross-functional coordination within the organization is increasingly important for faster decision-making and problem-solving in a more integrated manner.
3. Data-driven decision-making will become the standard operating procedure, and organizations should compete to gain access to the best data available and to use it in the most effective way.

4. A brand or marketing strategy should be viewed as a part of an overall strategy exercise that involves understanding how data is collected, used, and shared within the organization.

5. By acquiring high-quality data about what types of customers are interested in which products, which digital or social media channels they use to access information about the product and brand, and how they feel about different products that are offered in the category, marketers can personalize a given message to an audience based on their behavior. Marketers also have to be aware of how a brand's appeal shifts across various stages of consumer decision-making.

6. The availability of vast amounts of customer data implies that companies can create personalized offerings for their customers. Accessing data on consumers' conversations will help uncover important information that can be useful to brand managers in providing customized offerings (as described in Chapter 5). The social listening industry, with companies such as Crimson Hexagon, Radian6, and Brandwatch, have emerged to address the needs of brand marketers with regard to social monitoring. Several companies (e.g., Gatorade) have installed in-house social monitoring "control rooms" to provide continuous insights to top management regarding conversations about their brand. Chapter 9 provides more insights into the role of social listening and monitoring in decision-making.

7. Understanding how online and offline communications interact and coordinating an online digital channel strategy are important. Even within digital channels, there are many options that go beyond just social media marketing, including e-mail marketing, search and banner advertising, the brand Web site, and so on.

REVIEW

The growth of digital marketing and social media has ushered in a new era with many distinct trends. These trends portend changes that need to be made in how marketers organize their efforts and deliver value to their customers. The wide variety of communication options and the availability of data to target customers with offerings at the right time and place put marketers in a powerful position to engage with customers. These changes also imply that brands will occupy a different role in consumers' lives and have an even greater role as cultural symbols.

DISCUSSION QUESTIONS

1. Select a brand. Conduct an online audit to see how many different channels the brand has a presence in. What are the pros and cons of each of these social media channels for strengthening brand engagement for the brand?

2. This question tests your familiarity with three key concepts that were discussed in the context of search and display advertising: click-through rates (CTR), cost-per-click (CPC), and cost-per-thousand (CPM).
   - Assume a company launched a search advertising campaign that generated 10,000 impressions and 100 clicks. What is the click-through rate of the ad?
     - 100/10,000 = .01, or this can be expressed in percentage terms as .01*100 or 1%.
   - What is the cost-per-click if an ad campaign costing $250 generates 50 clicks?
     - 250/50 = $5 is the cost-per-click (CPC).
   - What is the cost-per-thousand (CPM) if an ad gets 20,000 impressions and the total cost is $100?
     - CPM is $5 (100/20).

3. Highlight some of the issues associated with brand marketers losing control over brand meaning. Are there any benefits to firms intervening to control the conversations taking place in social media? Why or why not?

4. How can brands develop systems to ensure that dynamic information coming in from social media is acted upon quickly? What would this imply for the brand management function?

5. Provide a summary of pros and cons associated with the following: (1) mobile advertising and (2) content marketing. What are some brands that appear to utilize these channels in an effective manner?

BRAND FOCUS 7.0

Understanding How Online Word-of-Mouth Influences Brands and Brand Management

An important trend for brand marketers is that consumers are spending considerable time posting reviews as well as accessing and researching word-of-mouth information posted by others in various blogs and videos (e.g., YouTube), microblogs (Twitter), online forums, and review sites (Amazon reviews) before purchasing a brand. A global survey of 30,000 consumers in more than 60 countries shows that while 60 percent of consumers trusted traditional advertising—including TV, print, and so on—a much larger percentage (83 percent) said that the most credible form of advertising was recommendations from people they knew.

Given the importance of online word-of-mouth (also known as electronic word-of-mouth, or eWOM) as a key factor in consumer decision-making about products/brands, it has received prominent attention in academic research. Researchers have identified the following five aspects of online word-of-mouth that influence overall sentiment and engagement toward a brand and drive sales.

Word-of-Mouth Volume and Valence

Two key factors that impact the influence of online word-of-mouth are the *volume* of word-of-mouth information available online and its *valence* (i.e., how positive or negative the word-of-mouth information is). Not surprisingly, a high volume of word-of-mouth information has been shown to exert a significant impact on sales. Furthermore, researchers have found that negative word-of-mouth information in the form of negative ratings or reviews exerts a greater impact than positive ratings or reviews. Paradoxically, researchers have shown that there is a much larger prevalence of positive information posted online than negative information. Some observers have ascribed this to the prevalence of fake reviews—that is, companies attempt to manipulate what is said about a brand by posting positive reviews themselves.

Word-of-Mouth Venue and Source

In addition to what is being shared, the location of where the information is shared also has an impact. Research has shown that approaches to monitoring online word-of-mouth that ignore the variations in brand sentiment across different social media venues or platforms can lead to misleading conclusions. Instead, it is recommended that measures of brand sentiment incorporate the wide variations that sometimes exist across different social media venues or platforms. This could be the outcome of the type of information shared (e.g., videos versus text), as well as the types of consumers that are attracted to different social media venues (e.g., Facebook and Twitter may command different audiences). Furthermore, researchers have shown that social media venues are important because they correspond to a set of competitor brands that vie for attention on those often crowded venues. Therefore, considering the venue of word-of-mouth is critically important.

Virality and Content of Word-of-Mouth Information

Research has shown that content that evokes emotions such as awe or surprise (i.e., high-arousal content) tends to spread faster than posts that evoke sadness (e.g., low-arousal content). Furthermore, one study has shown that positive content is more likely to spread virally on social media than negative content.

Who and When Are Important in Word-of-Mouth

The timing of online word-of-mouth matters. Word-of-mouth information exerts the greatest impact just before the launch of a new product. Researchers have also shown that only a small percentage of users' social media connections influence their behavior in an online setting, suggesting that there is a benefit to identifying who the key influencers are that impact their followers' brand perceptions.

Online Word-of-Mouth Is Complementary to Other Information Sources

Researchers have distinguished online word-of-mouth effects across paid media (e.g., advertising), owned media (e.g., company Web sites), and earned media (e.g., online reviews). In fact, one study shows that earned media from social media channels exerts a greater impact than traditional earned media. Another study shows that both traditional and social media sources impact each other, creating an "echoverse" of reverberating brand communication information. In short, these researchers suggest that brand marketers should use social media (e.g., Twitter) to personalize customer responses, alongside traditional consumer communication approaches such as press releases and advertising.

Online Word-of-Mouth Can Help with Brand Mapping and Positioning

Research has shown that data from mining online word-of-mouth information can be used to infer various aspects of brand positioning, including how a brand is perceived by its customers and employees, and to map how a brand is positioned relative to its competitors. These insights can provide a valuable tool to brand managers as they track their brand image over time.

Word-of-Mouth Correlates with Referrals, Customer Satisfaction, Sales, and Stock Market Performance

Research has examined whether word-of-mouth correlates with important outcome measures such as customer satisfaction, sales, and stock market performance. Three key findings in this area include the following: (1) word-of-mouth referrals can be more impactful in the long-term than referrals from more traditional sources, (2) negative word-of-mouth has a stronger impact than positive word-of-mouth on sales and stock market returns, and (3) customers acquired through word-of-mouth have stronger loyalty toward brands.

Sources: "Recommendations from Friends Remain Most Credible Form of Advertising among Consumers, Branded Websites Are the Second-Highest-Rated Form," *Nielson*, last modified September 28, 2015. www .nielsen.com/us/en/press-room/2015/recommendations-from-friends-remain-most-credible-form-of-advertising.html; Andrew T. Stephen and Jeff Galak, "The Effects of Traditional and Social Earned Media on Sales: A Study of a Microlending Marketplace," *Journal of Marketing Research* 49, no. 5 (October 2012): 624–639; Rajeev Batra and Kevin Lane Keller, "Integrating Marketing Communications: New Findings, New Lessons, and New Ideas." *Journal of Marketing* 80, no. 6 (2016): 122–145; David Godes and Dina Mayzlin, "Using Online Conversations to Study Word-of-Mouth Communication," *Marketing Science* 23, no. 4 (2004): 545–560; David A. Schweidel and Wendy W. Moe, "Listening In on Social Media: A Joint Model of Sentiment and Venue Format Choice," *Journal of Marketing Research* 51, no. 4 (August 2014): 387–402; Judith Chevalier and Dina Mayzlin (2006), "The Effect of Word of Mouth on Sales: Online Book Reviews," *Journal of Marketing Research* 43, no. 3 (2006), 345–354; Jonah Berger and Katherine L. Milkman, "What Makes Online Content Viral?" *Journal of Marketing Research* 49, no. 2 (2012), 192–205; Jonah Berger and Katherine L. Milkman, "Firm-Created Word-of-Mouth Communication: Evidence from a Field Test," *Marketing Science* 28, no. 4 (2009), 721–39; Kelly Hewett, William Rand, Roland T. Rust, and Harald J. van Heerde, "Brand Buzz in the Echoverse," *Journal of Marketing* 80, no. 3 (May 2016): 1–24; Cait Lamberton and Andrew T. Stephen, "A Thematic Exploration of Digital, Social Media, and Mobile Marketing: Research Evolution from 2000 to 2015 and an Agenda for Future Inquiry," *Journal of Marketing* 80, no. 6 (2016): 146–172; V. Kumar, Vikram Bhaskaran, Rohan Mirchandani, and Milap Shah, "Practice Prize Winner—Creating a Measurable Social Media Marketing Strategy: Increasing the Value and ROI of Intangibles and Tangibles for Hokey Pokey," *Marketing Science* 32, no. 2 (2013): 194–212; Xinxin Li and Lorin M. Hitt, "Self-Selection and Information Role of Online Product Reviews," *Information Systems Research* 19, no. 4 (2008): 456–474; Yong Liu, "Word of Mouth for Movies: Its Dynamics and Impact on Box Office Revenue," *Journal of Marketing* 70, no. 3 (2006): 74–89; Xueming Luo, "Consumer Negative Voice and Firm-Idiosyncratic Stock Returns," *Journal of Marketing* 71, no. 3 (2007): 75–88; Oded Netzer, Ronen Feldman, Jacob Goldenberg, and Moshe Fresko, "Mine Your Own Business: Market-Structure Surveillance through Text Mining," *Marketing Science* 31, no. 3 (2012): 521–543; Vanitha Swaminathan, Andrew H. Schwartz and Shawndra Hill, "The Language of Brands: Understanding Brand Image through Text Mining of Social Media Data," (2017), working paper, University of Pittsburgh; K. Zhang and W.W. Moe, "Bias in your Brand Page? Measuring and Identifying Bias in your Social Media Community," (2017); "The Top 10 Social Media Influences," http://mediakix.com/2017/02/biggest-social-media-influencers-of-all-time-infographic/#gs.AQpuXF8; Seshadri Tirunillai and Gerard J. Tellis, "Mining Marketing Meaning from Online Chatter: Strategic Brand Analysis of Big Data Using Latent Dirichlet Allocation," *Journal of Marketing Research* 51, no. 4 (2014): 463–479; M.Trusov, A.V. Bodapati, and R.E. Bucklin, "Determining Influential Users in Internet Social Networks," *Journal of Marketing Research* 47, no. 4 (2010): 643–658; Michael Trusov, Randolph E. Bucklin, and Koen Pauwels, "Effects of Word-of-Mouth versus Traditional Marketing: Findings from an Internet Social Networking Site," *Journal of Marketing* 73, no. 5 (2009): 90–102; Christophe Van den Bulte, Emanuel Bayer, Bernd Skiera, and Philipp Schmitt, "How Customer Referral Programs Turn Social Capital into Economic Capital," Marketing Science Institute Working Paper Series, (2015): 15–102; Ya You, Gautham G. Vadakkepatt, and Amit M. Joshi, "A Meta-Analysis of Electronic Word-of-Mouth Elasticity," *Journal of Marketing* 79, no. 2 (2015): 19–39; Zhang Kunpeng and Wendy W. Moe, "Bias in Your Brand Page? Measuring and Identifying Bias in Your Social Media Community," Wharton Marketing, January 18, 2017. https://marketing.wharton.upenn.edu/wp-content/uploads/2016/12/Moe-Wendy-PAPER-ver2-Marketing-Camp.pdf.

NOTES

1. Rob Petersen, "50 Amazing Stats and Facts about Online Consumer Behavior Not to Ignore," *Coxblue*, October 2, 2016, https://www.coxblue.com/50-amazing-stats-and-facts-about-online-consumer-behavior-not-to-ignore/.

2. David C. Edelman, "Branding in the Digital Age: You're Spending Your Money in All the Wrong Places," *Harvard Business Review* 88, no. 12 (2010): 62–69.

3. "Online versus Brick and Mortar Retail Shopping: The Statistics," March 15, 2017, https://icrealestate.com/2017/03/online-vs-brick-mortar-retail-shopping-statistics/.

4. Sandy Skrovan, "Why Most Shoppers Still Choose Brick-and-Mortar Stores over E-Commerce," *Retail-Dive*, February 22, 2017, http://www.retaildive.com/news/why-most-shoppers-still-choose-brick-and-mortar-stores-over-e-commerce/436068/.

5. Peter Kafka and Rani Molla, "2017 Was the Year Digital Ad Spending Finally Beat TV," December 4, 2017, https://www.recode.net/2017/12/4/16733460/2017-digital-ad-spend-advertising-beat-tv, accessed Novermber 24, 2018.

6. Dave Chaffey, "Mobile Marketing Statistics Compilation," *SmartInsights*, January 14, 2016, https://www.smartinsights.com/mobile-marketing/mobile-marketing-analytics/mobile-marketing-statistics/.

7. "Mobile Ad Spend to Top $100 Billion Worldwide in 2016, 51% of Digital Market," *eMarketer*, April 2, 2015, http://www.emarketer.com/Article/Mobile-Ad-Spend-Top-100-Billion-Worldwide-2016-51-of-Digital-Market/1012299/.

8. Anthony D. Miyazaki, "Online Privacy and the Disclosure of Cookie Use: Effects on Consumer Trust and Anticipated Patronage," *Journal of Public Policy & Marketing* 27, no. 1 (2008): 19–33.

9. David C. Edelman, "Mastering Digital Marketing," *McKinsey*, June 2014, https://www.mckinsey.com/business-functions/marketing-and-sales/our-insights/mastering-digital-marketing.

10. Deren Baker, "It's Time to Unleash Clickstream Data to Turn Browsers into Buyers," *Marketing Tech*, February 14, 2017, https://www.marketingtechnews.net/news/2017/feb/14/its-time-unleash-clickstream-data-turn-browsers-buyers/.

11. Kara Burney, "J.Crew's Data-Driven Approach to Fashion (and Marketing)," *TrackMaven*, May 21, 2014, https://trackmaven.com/blog/j-crews-data-driven-marketing-approach-fashion/.

12. Ted Starkey, "Which Brands Get the Most Love on Social Media," *Newsday*, July 6, 2016, https://www.newsday.com/business/50-brands-that-get-the-most-love-on-social-media-include-facebook-apple-ebay-disney-amazon-1.11972730.

13. Brian Gregg, Hussein Jalaoui, Joel Maynes, and Gustavo Schuler, "Marketing's Holy Grail: Digital Personalization at Scale," *McKinsey & Company*, November 2016, https://www.mckinsey.com/business-functions/digital-mckinsey/our-insights/marketings-holy-grail-digital-personalization-at-scale.

14. J. H. Schumann, F. von Wangenheim, and N. Groene, "Targeted Online Advertising: Using Reciprocity Appeals to Increase Acceptance Among Users of Free Web Services," *Journal of Marketing* 78, no. 1 (2014): 59–75.

15. Mark Memmott, "Orbitz Shows Mac Users Pricier Hotel Options: Big Deal Or No Brainer?," *NPR*, June 26, 2012, http://www.npr.org/sections/thetwo-way/2012/06/26/155756095/orbitz-shows-mac-users-pricier-hotel-options-big-deal-or-no-brainer.

16. A. Lambrecht, and C. Tucker, "When Does Retargeting Work? Information Specificity in Online Advertising," *Journal of Marketing Research* 50, no. 5 (2013): 561–576.

17. Edwin van Bommel, David Edelman, and Kelly Ungerman, "Digitizing the Consumer Decision Journey," *McKinsey & Company*, June 2014, https://www.mckinsey.com/business-functions/marketing-and-sales/our-insights/digitizing-the-consumer-decision-journey.

18. Vanitha Swaminathan, Andy Schwartz, and Shawndra Hill, "The Language of Brands in Social Media," working paper, University of Pittsburgh (2018).

19. S. Gensler, F. Völckner, Y. Liu-Thompkins, and C. Wiertz, "Managing Brands in the Social Media Environment," *Journal of Interactive Marketing* 27, no. 4 (2013): 242–256.

20. E. J. Schultz, "How 'Crash the Super Bowl' Changed Advertising," *Adage*, January 4, 2016, http://adage.com/article/special-report-super-bowl/crash-super-bowl-changed-advertising/301966/.

21. Jonathan Gabay, "Apple's All-Important UX Lessons," *SmartInsights*, October 4, 2016, http://www.smart-insights.com/user-experience/apples-important-ux-lessons/.

22. Walter Isaacson, "The Real Leadership Lessons of Steve Jobs," *Harvard Business Review*, April 2012, https://hbr.org/2012/04/the-real-leadership-lessons-of-steve-jobs.

23. Ben Davis, "Why the Digital User Experience Is Synonymous with Brand," *Marketing Week*, May 16 2017, https://www.marketingweek.com/2017/05/16/why-user-experience-is-synonymous-with-brand/.

24. Russ Klein, "Make Yourself Useful," *Medium*, August 15, 2017, https://medium.com/@KleinRuss/make-yourself-useful-1bf3097d24db.

25. E. Buechel and Jonah Berger, "Motivations for Consumer Engagement with Social Media," in Consumer *Psychology in a Social Media World*, C. V. Dimofte, C. P. Haugtvedt, and R. F. Yalch, eds, (2016): Routledge, 17.

26. Douglas Holt, "Branding in the Age of Social Media," *Harvard Business Review*, March 2016, https://hbr.org/2016/03/branding-in-the-age-of-social-media.

27. Alexander Smith, "Pepsi Pulls Controversial Kendall Jenner Ad After Outcry," *NBC*, April 5, 2017, https://www.nbcnews.com/news/nbcblk/ pepsi-ad-kendall-jenner-echoes-black-lives-matter-sparks-anger-n742811.

28. Daniella Silva, "David Dao and United Airlines Reach 'Amicable' Settlement After Viral Video Incident," NBC, April 27, 2017, http://www.nbcnews.com/news/us-news/david-dao-united-airlines-reach-settlement-after-viral-video-incident-n752051.

29. Brian Sutter, "Why Every Small Business Needs a Website—Your Company's Most Valuable Marketing Tool," AllBusiness, accessed September 27, 2017, https://www.allbusiness.com/small-business-website-offer-2017-110113-1.html.

30. "Email Marketing Statistics," DMA, https://thedma.org/marketing-insights/marketing-statistics/email-marketing-statistics/.

31. Helen Leggatt, "58% of Marketers to Increase Spend on Email Marketing in 2017," *BizReport*, June 14, 2017, http://www.bizreport.com/2017/06/58-of-marketers-to-increase-spend-on-email-marketing-in-2017.html.

32. Brian Marsh, "Email Marketing Budgets: Spend This Much for 122% ROI [and How to Do It]," *Web Strategies*, May 1, 2017, https://www.webstrategicsinc.com/blog/email-marketing-budgets-spend-this-much-on-email-marketing-for-122-roi.

33. Geoffrey James, "The 17 Essential Rules for Email Marketing," *Inc.*, August 22, 2017, https://www.inc.com/geoffrey-james/the-17-essential-rules-for-email-marketing.html.

34. Kevan Lee, "8 Effective Email Marketing Strategies, Backed by Science," *Bufferapp*, September 20, 2017, https://blog.bufferapp.com/8-effective-email-strategies-backed-by-research.

35. "9 Tips to an Effective Email Marketing Campaign," *Hult Marketing*, June 15, 2015, https://blog.hultmarketing.com/blog/tips-effective-email-marketing-campaign.

36. "8 Fashion E-Commerce Email Marketing Examples," *Referral Saasquatch*, https://www.referralsaasquatch.com/8-fashion-e-commerce-email-marketing-examples/.

37. Mark Irvine, "Google AdWords Benchmarks for YOUR Industry," *WordStream*, December 11, 2017, http://www.wordstream.com/blog/ws/2016/02/29/google-adwords-industry-benchmarks.

38. Jonathan Hochman, "The Cost of Pay-Per-Click (PPC) Advertising—Trends and Analysis," *Hochman Consultants*, February 22, 2017, https://www.hochmanconsultants.com/cost-of-ppc-advertising/.

39. Shannon Greenwood, Andrew Perrin, and Maeve Duggan, "Social Media Update 2016," *Pew Research Center*, November 11, 2016, http://www.pewinternet.org/2016/11/11/social-media-update-2016/.

40. Lucy Handley, "Facebook and Google Predicted to Make $106 Billion from Advertising in 2017, Almost Half of World's Digital Ad Spend," CNBC, March 21, 2017, https://www.cnbc.com/2017/03/21/facebook-and-google-ad-youtube-make-advertising-in-2017.html.

41. "Google and Facebook Tighten Grip on US Digital Ad Market," *eMarketer*, September 21, 2017, https://www.emarketer.com/Article/Google-Facebook-Tighten-Grip-on-US-Digital-Ad-Market/1016494.

42. Marty Swant, "Facebook Raked in $9.16 Billion in Ad Revenue in the Second Quarter of 2017," *Adweek*, July

26, 2017, http://www.adweek.com/digital/facebook-raked-in-9-16-billion-in-ad-revenue-in-the-second-quarter-of-2017/.

43. Garrett Sloane, "Why P&G Decided Facebook Ad Targeting Often Isn't Worth the Money," *Adage*, August 10, 2016, http://adage.com/article/digital/p-g-decided-facebook-ad-targeting-worth-money/305390/; Chantal Tode, "Why Other Brands Will Follow P&G Away from Facebook Targeting," *Mobile Marketer*, August 11, 2016, https://www.mobilemarketer.com/ex/mobilemarketer/cms/news/social-networks/23409.html; Sharon Terlep, and Deepa Seetharaman, "P&G to Scale Back Targeted Facebook Ads," *The Wall Street Journal*, August 17, 2016, http://www.wsj.com/articles/p-g-to-scale-back-targeted-facebook-ads-1470760949.

44. Kurt Wagner, "Twitter Is Testing a Big Change: Doubling the Length of Tweets from 140 to 280 Characters," *Recode*, September 26. 2017, https://www.recode.net/2017/9/26/16364002/twitter-longer-tweets-character-limit-140-280; Yoni Heisler, "Twitter's 280 Character Limit Increased Engagement without Increasing the Average Tweet Length," https://bgr.com/2018/02/08/twitter-characterlimit-280-vs-140-user-engagement/, accessed June 10, 2018.

45. Chris Plante, "New Domino's App Automatically Orders a Pizza When You or Anyone Else Opens iI," *The Verge*, April 6, 2016, https://www.theverge.com/2016/4/6/11377860/dominos-pizza-zero-click-app-easy-order.

46. "How Brands Are Marketing on Instagram This Holiday Season," *Media Kix* December 29, 2015, http://mediakix.com/2015/12/how-brands-are-marketing-on-instagram-this-holiday-season/#gs.X1pD3y.

47. *"A Flashy Night Owl Lamp," video*, https://www.krylon127yardsale.com/projects/.

48. James A. Martin, "10 Top Social Media Marketing Success Stories," *CIO*, April 28, 2016, http://www.cio.com/article/3062615/social-networking/10-top-social-media-marketing-success-stories.html#slide7.

49. Sunil Gupta, "For Mobile Devices, Think Apps, not Ads," *Harvard Business Review*, March 2013, https://hbr.org/2013/03/for-mobile-devices-think-apps-not-ads.

50. Liz Erikson, Louise Herring, and Kelly Ungerman, "Busting Mobile Shopping Myths," *McKinsey*, December 2014, https://www.mckinsey.com/industries/retail/our-insights/busting-mobile-shopping-myths.

51. Tim Peterson, "Snapchat Adopts Facebook-Style Ad, Targeting Like Email, Mobile Device Matching," *Marketing Land*, September 13, 2016, http://marketingland.com/snapchat-adopts-facebook-style-ad-targeting-like-email-mobile-device-matching-191207.

52. Bruce Horovitz, "Snapchat: The Future of Marketing," *QSR*, September 2016, https://www.qsrmagazine.com/technology/snapchat-future-marketing.

53. Chris Chidgey, "Lessons Learned from Successful Mobile Marketing Campaigns," *Gummicube*, March 24, 2016, http://www.gummicube.com/blog/2016/03/mobile-marketing-campaigns/; Brian Roemelle, "Why Is the Starbucks Mobile Payments App So Successful?" *Forbes*, June 13, 2014, https://www.forbes.com/sites/quora/2014/06/13/why-is-the-starbucks-mobile-payments-app-so-successful/#4293fcad3957

54. Robert D. Hof, "Marketing in the Moments, to Reach Customers Online," *The New York Times*, January 17, 2016, http://www.nytimes.com/2016/01/18/business/media/marketing-in-the-moments-to-reach-customers-online.html?_r=0.

55. Alex Samuely, "Campari Unscrews Real-Time Data for Lyft Offer Targeting Bar-Goers," *Mobile Marketer*, June 29, 2015, http://www.mobilemarketer.com/cms/news/strategy/20764.html.

56. Phil Wahba, "Walmart Launches Its Own Mobile Payment System," *Fortune*, December 10, 2015, http://fortune.com/2015/12/10/walmart-mobile-payment/; Julian Chokkattu, "Walmart Pay Is Here to Enhance Your Walmart Shopping Experience," *Digital Trends*, July 6, 2016, http://www.digitaltrends.com/mobile/walmart-pay/; Brielle Jaekel, "Walmart's Take on Mobile Video Ads Increased In-store Sales," *Mobile Marketer*, March 25, 2016, http://www.mobilemarketer.com/cms/news/video/22512.html?utm_referrer=https%3A%2F%2Fwww.google.co.nz%2F.

57. Michelle Andrews, Xueming Luo, Zheng Fang, and Anindya Ghose, "Mobile Ad Effectiveness: Hyper-Contextual Targeting with Crowdedness," *Marketing Science* 35, no. 2 (2015): 218–233; Peter C. Verhoef, Andrew T. Stephen, P. K. Kannan, Xueming Luo, Vibhanshu Abhishek, Michelle Andrews, Yakov Bart, et al., "Consumer Connectivity in a Complex, Technology-Enabled, and Mobile-Oriented World with Smart Products," *Journal of Interactive Marketing* 40 (November 2017): 1–8; Nathan M. Fong, Zheng Fang, and Xueming Luo, "Geo-conquesting: Competitive Locational Targeting of Mobile Promotions," *Journal of Marketing Research* 52, no. 5 (2015): 726–735; Xueming Luo, Michelle Andrews, Zheng Fang, and Chee Wei Phang, "Mobile Targeting," *Management Science* 60, no. 7 (2013): 1738–1756; Zheng Fang, Bin Gu, Xueming Luo, and Yunjie Xu, "Contemporaneous and Delayed Sales Impact of Location-Based Mobile Promotions," *Information Systems Research* 26, no. 3 (2015): 552–564; Alan D. J. Cooke and Peter P. Zubcsek, "The Connected Consumer: Connected Devices and the Evolution of Customer Intelligence," *Journal of the Association for Consumer Research* 2, no. 2 (2017): 164–178; Venkatesh Shankar, Mirella Kleijnen, Suresh Ramanathan, Ross Rizley, Steve Holland, and Shawn Morrissey, "Mobile Shopper Marketing: Key Issues, Current Insights, and Future Research Avenues," *Journal of Interactive Marketing* 34 (2016): 37–48; Michelle Andrews, Jody Goehring, Sam Hui, Joseph Pancras, and Lance Thornswood, "Mobile Promotions: A Framework and Research Priorities," *Journal of Interactive Marketing* 34 (2016): 15–24.

58. Duncan Brown and Nick Hayes, *Influencer Marketing: Who Really Influences Your Customers* (Oxford U.K: Elsevier, 2009).

59. "Influencer Marketing to Be a $5–$10 Billion Market within Next 5 Years," *Mediakix*, http://mediakix.com/2015/12/influencer-marketing-5-10-billion-dollar-market/#gs.D7_aSto.

60. "Instagram Influencer Marketing Is a $1 Billion Dollar Industry," *Mediakix*, http://mediakix.com/2017/03/instagram-influencer-marketing-industry-size-how-big/#gs.nB4resk.

61. "The State of Influencer Marketing 2017: A Look into How Brands and Agencies View the Future of Influencer Marketing," *Linqia*, 2017, http://www.linqia.com/wp-content/uploads/2016/11/The-State-of-Influencer-Marketing-2017_Final-Report.pdf.

62. Bill Sussman, "Influencer Marketing and the Power of Data Science," *Forbes*, July 28, 2017, https://www.forbes.com/sites/forbesagencycouncil/2017/07/28/influencer-marketing-and-the-power-of-data-science/#6e2b351e79a6/.

63. "How Do Instagram Influencers Make Money," *Mediakix*, http://mediakix.com/2016/03/instagram-influencers-making-money/#gs.7mJOc2w; Amanda Pressner Kreuser, "What Influencers Like Michelle Phan and PewDiePie Get Paid," *Inc.*

64. Clare O'Connor, "Earning Power: Here's How Much Top Influencers Can Make on Instagram and YouTube," *Forbes*, April 10, 2017, https://www.forbes.com/sites/clareoconnor/2017/04/10/earning-power-heres-how-much-top-influencers-can-make-on-instagram-and-youtube/#5dc2f5d424db.

65. Kevin Gallagher, "Instagram Influencers Warned by the FTC," *Business Insider*, April 21, 2017, http://www.businessinsider.com/instagram-influencers-warned-by-the-ftc-2017-4.

66. Taylor Oster, "Guest Posting: The Spark Your Marketing Strategy Is Missing," *Influence & Co.*, 2014, https://blog.influenceandco.com/guest-posting-the-spark-your-marketing-strategy-is-missing.

67. Josh Steimle, "What Is Content Marketing?," *Forbes*, September 19, 2014, https://www.forbes.com/sites/joshsteimle/2014/09/19/what-is-content-marketing/#6e7797fd10b9.

68. "Creating a Content Marketing Strategy,"*Marketo*, accessed October 11, 2017, https://www.marketo.com/content-marketing/.

69. Content Marketing, http://www.contentmarketingconf.com/.

70. John Hall, "TheTruth about Content Marketing and What Brands Need to Know," *Forbes*, October 8, 2017, https://www.forbes.com/sites/johnhall/2017/10/08/the-truth-about-content-marketing-and-what-brands-need-to-know/2/#1bb4fb8d7a1d.

71. "What Is Content Marketing,' *Content Marketing Institute*, http://contentmarketinginstitute.com/what-is-content-marketing/.

72. Kate Gardiner, "The Story Behind 'The Furrow' the World's Oldest Content Marketing," *The Content Strategist*, October 3, 2013, https://contently.com/strategist/2013/10/03/the-story-behind-the-furrow-2/.

73. "Marvel Origins Case Study," http://frac.tl/clients/movoto/hero-locations/.

74. Aaron Burstein, "FTC Puts "Influencers' on Notice: Disclose Marketing Relationships in Social Media Posts," *Broadcast Law*, April 26, 2017, http://www.broadcastlawblog.com/articles/payola-and-sponsorship-identification/.

75. Tim Nudd, "Budweiser Ran This Classic '80s Ad with Harry Caray Right after the World Series Ended," *AdWeek*, November 3, 2016, http://www.adweek.com/creativity/budweiser-ran-classic-80s-ad-harry-caray-right-after-world-series-ended-174419/.

Leveraging Secondary Brand Associations to Build Brand Equity

Learning Objectives

After reading this chapter, you should be able to

1. Outline the eight main ways to leverage secondary associations.

2. Explain the process by which a brand can leverage secondary associations.

3. Describe some of the key tactical issues in leveraging secondary associations from different entities.

If Salomon decided to extend from skis to tennis racquets, there are a number of different ways it could leverage secondary brand associations.

Source: Karl Mathis/EPA/Newscom

PREVIEW

The preceding chapters described how we can build brand equity through the choice of brand elements (Chapter 4) or marketing program activities and product, price, distribution, and marketing communication strategies (Chapters 5 and 6). Chapter 7 presented an overview of digital channels that can be leveraged to communicate with consumers. This chapter considers the third means of building brand equity—namely, through leveraging related or secondary brand associations.

Brands themselves may be linked to other entities that have their own knowledge structures in the minds of consumers. Because of these linkages, consumers may assume or infer that some of the associations or responses that characterize the other entities may also be true for the brand. In effect, the brand "borrows" some brand knowledge and, depending on the nature of those associations and responses, perhaps some brand equity from other entities.

This indirect approach to building brand equity is *leveraging secondary brand associations* for the brand. Secondary brand associations may be quite important for creating strong, favorable, and unique associations or positive responses if existing brand associations or responses are deficient in some way. It can also be an effective way to reinforce existing associations and responses freshly and differently.

This chapter considers the different means by which we can leverage secondary brand associations by linking the brand to the following (see Figure 8-1 for a fuller depiction):

1. Companies (through branding strategies)
2. Countries or other geographic areas (through identification of product origin)
3. Channels of distribution (through channel strategy)
4. Other brands (through co-branding)
5. Characters (through licensing)
6. Spokespersons (through endorsements)
7. Events (through sponsorship)
8. Other third-party sources (through awards or reviews)

The first three entities reflect source factors: who makes the product, where the product is made, and where it is purchased. The remaining entities deal with related people, places, or things.

As an example, suppose that Salomon—makers of alpine and cross-country ski bindings, ski boots, and skis—decided to introduce a new tennis racquet called "the Avenger." Although Salomon has been selling safety bindings for skis since 1947, much of its growth was fueled by its diversification into ski boots and the introduction of a revolutionary new type of ski called the Monocoque in 1990. Salomon's innovative, stylish, and top-quality products have led to strong leadership positions.

In creating the marketing program to support the new Avenger tennis racquet, Salomon could attempt to leverage secondary brand associations in several different ways.

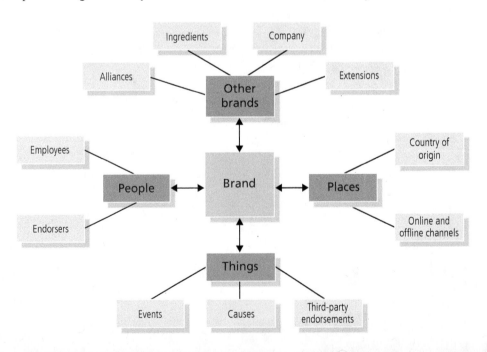

FIGURE 8-1

Secondary Sources of Brand Knowledge

- Salomon could leverage associations to the corporate brand by sub-branding the product—for example, by calling it "Avenger by Salomon." Consumers' evaluations of the new product extension would be influenced by the extent to which they held favorable associations about Salomon as a company or brand because of its skiing products, and how strongly they felt that such knowledge could predict the quality of a Salomon tennis racquet.
- Salomon could try to rely on its European origins (it is headquartered near Lake Annecy at the foot of the Alps), although such a location would not seem to have much relevance to tennis.
- Salomon could try to sell through upscale, professional tennis shops and clubs in hopes that these retailers' credibility would rub off on the Avenger brand.
- Salomon could attempt to co-brand by identifying a strong ingredient brand for its grip, frame, or strings (as Wilson did by incorporating Goodyear tire rubber on the soles of its ProStaff Classic tennis shoes).
- Although it is doubtful that a licensed character could be effectively leveraged, Salomon could attempt to find one or more top professional players to endorse the racquet or could choose to become a sponsor of tennis tournaments, or even the entire professional ATP men's or WTA women's tennis tour. Salomon could create a social influencer campaign using well-known celebrities—such as Novak Djokovic, Serena Williams, Roger Federer—who also command large social media audiences, to help raise awareness of the Avenger brand.
- Salomon could attempt to secure and publicize favorable ratings from third parties, such as *Tennis* magazine.

Thus, independent of the associations created by the racquet itself, its brand name, or any other aspects of the marketing program, Salomon may be able to build equity by linking the brand to other entities in various ways.

This chapter first considers the nature of brand knowledge that marketers can leverage or transfer from other entities, and the process for doing so. We then consider in detail each of the eight different means of leveraging secondary brand associations. The chapter concludes by considering the special topic of Olympic sponsorship in Brand Focus 7.0.

CONCEPTUALIZING THE LEVERAGING PROCESS

Linking the brand to some other entity—some source factor or related person, place, or thing—may create a new set of associations from the brand to the entity, as well as affecting existing brand associations. Let's look at both of these outcomes.

Creation of New Brand Associations

By making a connection between the brand and another entity, consumers may form a mental association from the brand to this other entity and, consequently, to any or all associations, judgments, feelings, and the like linked to that entity. In general, these secondary brand associations are most likely to affect evaluations of a new product when consumers lack either the motivation or the ability to judge product-related concerns. In other words, when consumers either do not care much about or do not feel that they possess the knowledge to choose the appropriate brand, they may be more likely to make brand decisions on the basis of secondary considerations such as what they think, feel, or know about the country from which the product came, the store in which it is sold, or some other characteristic.

Effects on Existing Brand Knowledge

Linking the brand to some other entity may create not only new brand associations to the entity but also affect existing brand associations. This is the basic mechanism. Consumers have some knowledge of an entity. When a brand is identified as linked to that entity, consumers may infer that some of the associations, judgments, or feelings that characterize the entity may also characterize the brand. Several different theoretical mechanisms from psychology predict this type of inference. One is "cognitive consistency"—in other words, in the minds of consumers, what is true for the entity, must be true for the brand.[1]

To describe the process more formally, here are three important factors in predicting the extent of leverage from linking the brand to another entity:

1. *Awareness and knowledge of the entity:* If consumers have no awareness or knowledge of the secondary entity, then obviously, there is nothing they can transfer from it. Ideally, consumers

would be aware of the entity; hold some strong, favorable, and perhaps even unique associations about it; and have positive judgments and feelings about it.

2. *Meaningfulness of the knowledge of the entity:* Given that the entity evokes some positive associations, judgments, or feelings, is this knowledge relevant and meaningful for the brand? The meaningfulness may vary depending on the brand and product context. Some associations, judgments, or feelings may seem relevant to and valuable for the brand, whereas others may seem to consumers to have little connection.

3. *Transferability of the knowledge of the entity:* If some potentially useful and meaningful associations, judgments, or feelings exist regarding the entity and could possibly transfer to the brand, how strongly will this knowledge actually become linked to the brand?

In other words, the basic questions we want to answer about transferring secondary knowledge from another entity are: What do consumers know about the other entity? Does any of this knowledge affect what they think about the brand when it becomes linked or associated in some fashion with this other entity?

Theoretically, consumers can infer any aspect of knowledge from other entities to the brand (see Figure 8-2), although some types of entities are more likely to inherently create or affect certain kinds of brand knowledge than others. For example, events may be especially conducive to the creation of experiences; people may be especially effective for the elicitation of feelings; other brands may be especially well suited for establishing particular attributes and benefits; and so on. At the same time, any one entity may be associated with multiple dimensions of knowledge, each of which may affect brand knowledge directly or indirectly.

For example, consider the effects on knowledge of linking the brand to a cause, such as CVS's "Quit Smoking Together" campaign or AT&T's "It Can Wait" pledge which asked consumers not to text and drive. A cause marketing program could build brand awareness via recall and recognition; enhance brand image in terms of attributes such as brand personality or user imagery like kind and generous; evoke brand feelings like social approval and self-respect; establish brand attitudes such as trustworthy and likable; and create experiences through a sense of community and participation in cause-related activities.

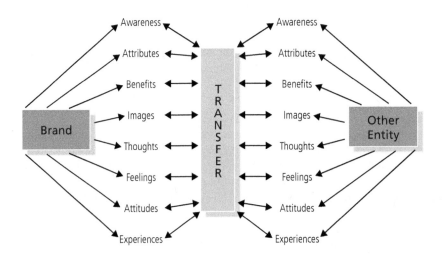

FIGURE 8-2
Understanding Transfer
of Brand Knowledge

CVS's "Quit Smoking
Together" campaign
leveraged a cause to
build the brand's equity.

Judgments or feelings may transfer more readily than more specific associations, which are likely to seem irrelevant or be too strongly linked to the original entity to transfer. As we will see in Chapter 12, the inferencing process depends largely on the strength of the linkage or connection in consumers' minds between the brand and the other entity. The more consumers see the similarity between the entity and the brand, the more likely they will infer similar knowledge about the brand.

Guidelines

Leveraging secondary brand associations may allow marketers to create or reinforce an important point-of-difference or competitive point-of-parity versus competitors. When choosing to emphasize source factors or a particular person, place, or thing, marketers should take into account consumers' awareness of that entity, as well as how the associations, judgments, or feelings for it might become linked to the brand or affect existing brand associations.

Marketers can choose entities for which consumers have some or even a great deal of similar associations. A *commonality* leveraging strategy makes sense when consumers have associations to another entity that are congruent with desired brand associations. For example, consider a country such as New Zealand, which is known for having more sheep than people. A New Zealand sweater manufacturer that positioned its product on the basis of its "New Zealand wool" presumably could more easily establish strong and favorable brand associations because New Zealand may already mean "wool" to many people.

On the other hand, there may be times when entities are chosen that represent a departure for the brand because there are few if any common or similar associations. Such *complementarity* branding strategies can be strategically critical in terms of delivering the desired position. The marketer's challenge here is to ensure that the less congruent knowledge for the entity has either a direct or an indirect effect on existing brand knowledge. This may require skillfully designed marketing programs that overcome initial consumer confusion or skepticism. For example, when the ice cream chain Cold Stone Creamery and coffee shop Tim Horton's embarked on a co-branded partnership where selected stores would feature the other's menu items, the partnership may have caused some questions and doubts. The two companies had similar target customers, but there was little overlap in terms of their menu offerings. However, the complementary offerings also were a particular advantage. While Tim Horton's sales primarily occurred in the morning or the afternoon, Cold Stone's menu offerings were more popular with customers in the evening.

Tim Hortons and Cold Stone Creamery entered into a co-branded partnership to leverage the complementary nature of their product offerings, which were consumed at different times of the day, or dayparts.

Thus, the two combined their complementary daypart offerings, which allowed them to appeal to a broader range of customers. With the success of the partnership, the companies even began offering some joint menu options (e.g., coffee floats).[2]

Even if consumers buy into the association one way or another, leveraging secondary brand associations may be risky because the marketer gives up some control of the brand image. The source factors or related person, place, or thing will undoubtedly have a host of other associations, of which only some smaller set will be of interest to the marketer. Managing the transfer process so that only the relevant secondary knowledge becomes linked to the brand may be difficult. Moreover, this knowledge may change over time as consumers learn more about the entity, and these new associations, judgments, or feelings may or may not be advantageous for the brand. The following sections consider some of the main ways by which we can link secondary brand associations to the brand.

COMPANY

Branding strategies are an important determinant of the strength of association from the brand to the company and any other existing brands. Three main branding options exist for a new product:

1. Create a new brand;
2. Adopt or modify an existing brand;
3. Combine an existing and a new brand.

Existing brands may be related to the corporate brand, say Samsung, or a specific product brand, such as Samsung Galaxy C8 mobile phone. If the brand is linked to an existing brand, as with options 2 and 3, then knowledge about the existing brand may also become linked to the brand.

A corporate or family brand can be a source of much brand equity. For example, a corporate brand may evoke associations of common product attributes, benefits, or attitudes; people and relationships; programs and values; and corporate credibility. Branding Brief 8-1 describes the corporate image campaign for IBM.

Leveraging a corporate brand may not always be useful, however. In fact, in some cases, large companies have deliberately introduced new brands or bought successful niche brands in an attempt to convey a "smaller" image. Examples of the latter strategy—that might even surprise their existing customers!—include Ben and Jerry's (Unilever), Kashi (Kellogg's), Odwalla (Coca-Cola), and Tom's of Maine (Colgate-Palmolive). Clorox paid almost $1 billion for Burt's Bees—famous for beeswax lip balm, lotions, soaps and shampoos—in part because of the market opportunity, but also to better learn about best practices for environmental sustainability, an emerging corporate priority.[3] Anheuser-Busch InBev acquired the successful Midwest craft beer Goose Island in part to better compete with rival MillerCoors's highly successful Blue Moon brand.[4]

BRANDING BRIEF 8-1
IBM Promotes a Smarter Planet

IBM's long tradition as "Big Blue" helped it become one of the world's most successful companies of the twentieth century. Unfortunately, many of the product areas on which this success was built became highly competitive and increasingly commoditized in the new millennium. As a result, IBM decided it needed to radically transform itself from a product-focused company to a value-added, services-oriented company.

IBM Chairman and CEO Sam Palmisano spun off the company's famous personal computer (PC) division and began to invest heavily in software and business consulting. Another critical aspect of the transformation was aligning the public perception of IBM with this new vision. The vision itself—and the

corresponding marketing communications program—was rooted in a basic belief that the world was changing in three significant ways that provided clear direction to IBM's new mission. In other words, the world was becoming:

- Instrumented ("Instrument the world's systems")
- Interconnected ("Interconnect them")
- Intelligent ("Make them intelligent")

IBM wanted to be the leader in each of these three areas. The original name chosen to reflect this new positioning was the very literal "Integrated Intelligent Infrastructure," but further work led to the snappier, more inspiring "Smarter Planet" phrase that also became the slogan for the corporate campaign. The basic premise of the campaign was that every business would become a technology company and be forced to face new and challenging policy changes, especially concerning sustainability, security, and privacy. IBM was positioned to be the ideal partner to assist in these efforts. Given the ambitious scope of the positioning, government officials became the target as much as business leaders.

The "Smarter Planet" positioning had its roots in some of IBM's recent accomplishments. For example, in Stockholm, Sweden, IBM smart traffic systems cut gridlock by 20 percent, reduced emissions by 12 percent, and resulted in a dramatic increase in the use of public transportation. Smart grid projects in various locales had already helped consumers save 10 percent on their bills and reduced peak demand by 15 percent.

With these accomplishments in mind, the initial goal of the "Smarter Planet" campaign was to position IBM as a leader in solving the world's most pressing problems. The "Building a Smarter Planet" campaign was launched with full-page ads in leading newspapers along with TV ads that targeted three groups: business and government leaders in large organizations, IT professionals, and the mid-market. It included a strong digital component, with an expanded IBM Web site and a Smarter Planet blog. Videos were created and distributed across eight of the largest video-sharing sites. IBM also launched a "Smarter Cities" global tour to bring key policy and decision makers together to discuss the topical issues they faced, such as transportation, energy, health care, education, and public safety.

IBM analysts estimated that the Smarter Planet strategy contributed significantly to revenue increases and helped strengthen the brand. IBM's brand tracking revealed increases across the board on a variety of image measures (such as "making the world a better place" and "an expert in how the world works") and overall judgments related to consideration, preference, and the likelihood of doing business. IBM's stock price during the campaign increased by 64 percent, while the Dow index grew only 14 percent over the same time.

In 2009, IBM launched its Smarter Cities campaign, extending its Smarter Planet strategy, to help cities run more efficiently, conserve resources, and improve quality of life for its citizens. It held 100 Smarter Cities Forums around the world to identify ways of transforming life in these cities, making use of interconnected information, and addressing key challenges such as traffic congestion, energy use, and sustainable communities. By 2010, IBM began working with colleges and universities to help give students access to technologies and training to learn new skills and help put them to work in cities around the world. IBM's Smarter Planet initiative showed a revenue growth with $3 billion, across 6,000 client engagements across a variety of areas—including mobile Web, nanotechnology, stream computing, analytics, and cloud computing. IBM used the Smarter Planet initiative to make inroads into several high-growth industries such as health care and oil and gas. During this year, IBM also received the "Gold Global Effie" for its Smarter Planet initiative and was identified by *PRWeek* as the "Corporate Branding Campaign of the Year." In 2011, IBM began using smarter systems to enable reductions of energy utilization and increases in efficiency in designing "smarter buildings."

In 2015, in an apparent shift of strategy, IBM replaced the Smarter Planet brand strategy with a new campaign called "Cognitive Business," which reflects the shift in focus towards cloud computing and data analytics. This shift in strategy was prompted by the emergence of artificial intelligence and big data analytics as important trends that IBM has embraced through its Watson technology. IBM's new data analytics products surrounding cognitive computing has focused on taking vast amounts of data (such as medical data) and producing insights and learnings to improve decision-making. As part of its Cognitive Business campaign, IBM developed ads with spots featuring the voice of IBM's Watson chatting with former *Jeopardy!* champ Ken Jennings and folk-rock legend Bob Dylan. Thus, IBM's Cognitive Business campaign articulates a brand and corporate strategy for IBM in the era of big data, and represents the evolution of the company itself from a focus on using the information to solve modern-day challenges (which formed the basis for the Smarter Planet campaign), to generating data-driven solutions by leveraging the power of computing technology. Figure 8-3 has an excerpt from a talk given by a longstanding IBM executive (now retired) talking about the Smarter Planet campaign.

IBM's "Smarter Planet" positioning has strengthened the corporate brand, benefiting all the company's associated product and services.

Source: Courtesy of International Business Machines Corporation, © International Business Machines Corporation.

FIGURE 8-3

Excerpt from IBM's "Building a Smarter Planet" First Op-Ad Piece

Source: www.ibm.com/ smarterplanet; www.ibm. com. Used with permission of IBM.

Just over a year ago, we began a global conversation about how the planet is becoming smarter. By smarter, we mean that intelligence is being infused into the systems and processes that make the world work—into things no one would recognize as computers: cars, appliances, roadways, power grids, clothes, even natural systems such as agriculture and waterways.

Trillions of digital devices, connected through the Internet, are producing a vast ocean of data. And all this information—from the flow of markets to the pulse of societies—can be turned into knowledge because we now have the computational power and advanced analytics to make sense of it. With this knowledge we can reduce costs, cut waste, and improve the efficiency, productivity and quality of everything from companies to cities.

A year into this new era, the signs of a smarter planet are all around us. Smarter systems are being implemented and are creating value in every major industry, across every region in both the developed and developing worlds. This idea isn't a metaphor, or a vision, or a proposal—it's a rapidly emerging reality.

Sources: Talk given by Jon Iwata, SVP, Marketing & Communications, IBM, at the Tuck School of Business at Dartmouth College, February 10, 2010; "Let's Build a Smarter Planet," 2010 Gold Effie Winner, www .effie.org/-winners/showcase/2010/4625; www.ibm.com/-smarterplanet; www.ibm.com; www-03.ibm.com/ibm/history/ibm100/us/en/icons/ smarterplanet/, accessed December 17, 2017; Kate Kaye (2015), "Tangled Up in Big Blue: IBM Replaces Smarter Planet with . . . Bob Dylan," http://adage.com/article/datadriven-marketing/ibm-replaces-smarter-planet-cognitive-business-strategy/300774/, October 6, 2015, accessed December 17, 2017.

BLUE MOON

Although the U.S. beer market has been in a slowdown in recent years, a bright spot is craft beers, which have been able to combine quality, heritage, and some unique characteristics to command a premium price. Blue Moon was named for the second full moon in a calendar month. Launched in 1995 by Coors in Denver, Colorado, it was positioned as a uniquely flavored, highly drinkable, handcrafted Belgian-style wheat beer. Brewed with oats for creaminess and spiced with orange peel and coriander, Blue Moon's Belgian White is often served with an orange slice. Coors downplays its connection, and the beer is branded as brewed by the "Blue Moon Brewing Company." Deemed the leading craft beer by many, the beer has received extensive marketing support. Its brand slogan—"Artfully Crafted," describing how the beer is made—has also served as the basis for a multimedia communication program. TV and print ads have featured hand-painted images of Blue Moon beer bottles and glasses. Taking the campaign online, a contest gave Blue Moon fans the chance to upload their own "Artfully Crafted" photos to the Photo Crafter tab on the brand's Facebook Web page. An application there transformed the photo into artfully crafted Blue Moon paintings and entered fans into the contest to win prizes.[5] Blue Moon recently won a lawsuit allowing it to continue marketing itself as a craft beer, even though a lawsuit against the brand alleged that it was a mass-marketed brand, which has the support of a large company such as MillerCoors. A judge ruled in the brand's favor, suggesting that its approach of being perceived as a small craft beer brew can be continued in the near future.

Finally, brands and companies are often unavoidably linked to the category and industry in which they compete, sometimes with adverse consequences. Some industries are characterized by fairly divided opinions, but consider the challenges faced by brands in the oil and gas or financial services industries, which consumers have generally viewed in a negative light.[6] By membership in the category in which it competes, an oil company may expect to face a potentially suspicious or skeptical public *regardless* of what it does. Chapters 11 and 12 describe in detail how marketers can leverage the equity of existing brands to launch their new products.

COUNTRY OF ORIGIN AND OTHER GEOGRAPHIC AREAS

Besides the company that makes the product, the country or geographic location from which it originates may also become linked to the brand and generate secondary associations.[7] Many countries have become known for expertise in certain product categories or for conveying a particular type of image.

The world is becoming a "cultural bazaar" where consumers can pick and choose brands originating in different countries, based on their beliefs about the quality of certain types of products from certain countries or the image that these brands or products communicate.[8] Thus, a consumer from anywhere in the world may choose to drink French wine, wear Italian suits, exercise in U.S. athletic shoes, drive a German car, or drink English ale.

Choosing brands with strong national ties may reflect a deliberate decision to maximize product utility and communicate self-image, based on what consumers believe about products from those countries. Some brands can create a strong point-of-difference, in part because of consumers' identification of and beliefs about the country of origin. For example, consider the following strongly linked brands and countries:

Levi's jeans—United States	Toyota—Japan
Chanel perfume—France	Cadbury—England
Foster's beer—Australia	Gucci shoes and purses—Italy
Barilla pasta—Italy	Mont Blanc pens—Switzerland
BMW—Germany	Samsung—South Korea
Ikea—Sweden	

Other geographic associations besides country of origin are possible, such as states, regions, and cities. Three classic U.S. tourism slogans, "I Love New York," "Virginia Is for Lovers," and Las Vegas's "What Happens Here, Stays Here," are for these more specific types of locales.

Puerto Rico rum makers have leveraged their geographical roots to establish a dominant market position.
Source: Bowers/Stringer/Getty Images

Marketers can establish a geographic or country-of-origin association in different ways. They can embed the location in the brand name, such as Idaho potatoes, Real California Milk, Irish Spring soap, or South African Airways, or combine it with a brand name in some way as in Bailey's Irish Cream. Alternatively, they can make the location the dominant theme in brand advertising, as has been the case for Coors with Foster's beer.

Some countries have even created advertising campaigns to promote their products. For example, "Rums of Puerto Rico" advertise that they are the finest-quality rums, leading to a 70 percent share of U.S. brand sales.[9] Other countries have developed and advertised labels or seals for their products.[10] Branding Brief 8-2 describes how New Zealand's launch of its "The New Zealand Way" brand has led to much marketing success for the country.

Because it is typically a legal necessity for the country of origin to appear somewhere on the product or package, associations to the country of origin almost always have the potential to be created at the point of purchase and to affect brand decisions there. The question really is one of relative emphasis, and the role of country of origin or other geographic regions throughout the marketing program. Becoming strongly linked to a country of origin or specific geographic region is not without potential disadvantages. Events or actions associated with the country may color people's perceptions.[11]

BRAND AMERICA

The turn of the century and George W. Bush's presidency coincided with a sharp drop in the image of the United States in the eyes of the world's citizens. A comprehensive analysis by the Pew Research Center in 2008 concluded:

> The U.S. image abroad is suffering almost everywhere. Particularly in the most economically developed countries, people blame America for the financial crisis. Opposition to key elements of American foreign policy is widespread in Western Europe, and positive views of the U.S. have declined steeply among many of America's longtime European allies. In Muslim nations, the wars in Afghanistan and particularly Iraq have driven negative ratings nearly off the charts. The United States earns positive ratings in several Asian and Latin American nations, but usually by declining margins.[12]

One BBC-commissioned poll of 26,000 respondents in the 25 largest countries in 2007 found that roughly half thought the United States had a "mostly negative" influence on the world. A global economic recession, unpopular wars, and disagreements on various social and environmental policies took their toll. Although few global U.S. companies experienced the same erosion in reputation—many people seemed willing to compartmentalize politics and commerce—restoring U.S. image became a popular theme with the presidential election of Barack Obama in 2008. Recognizing the importance of tourism to the U.S. economy—one in nine U.S. jobs is in a travel or tourism-related sector—the U.S. Travel Association has been aggressively marketing visits to the United States to the international travel industry.[13]

More recently, the image of America around the world has dropped significantly. In a Pew Research Survey conducted across more than 40,000 people in 39 countries, only 22 percent of those who participated in the survey indicated confidence in their views of the U.S. President and America's role on the world stage.[14] According to the Pew Research Survey, this was particularly true in the aftermath of the 2016 election of Donald Trump as the President of the United States; President Trump indicated a desire to withdraw from international trade agreements and climate accords. These stances may have contributed to the loss of America's brand image on the world stage.

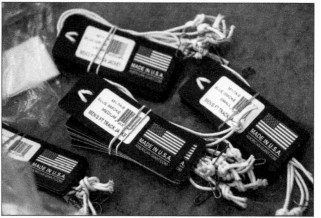

Countries such as the United States can be viewed as brands, and their images can have implications for various industries such as tourism and commerce.

Finally, consider the favorability of a country-of-origin association from both a domestic and a foreign perspective. In the domestic market, country-of-origin perceptions may stir consumers' patriotic notions or remind them of their past. As international trade grows, consumers may view certain brands as symbolically important of their own cultural heritage and identity. Some research found that domestic brands were more strongly favored in collectivistic countries such as Japan and other Asian countries that have strong group norms and ties to family and country. In individualistic societies such as the United States and other Western countries that are more guided by self-interest and personal goals, consumers demand stronger evidence of product superiority.[15]

Patriotic appeals have been the basis of marketing strategies all over the world. However, they can lack uniqueness and even be overused. For example, during the Reagan administration in the 1980s, a number of different U.S. brands in a diverse range of product categories including cars, beer, and clothing used pro-U.S. themes in their advertising, perhaps diluting the efforts of all as a result. In recent years, the debate over outsourcing and offshoring and, tragically, the events of September 11, 2001, raised the visibility of patriotic appeals once again.

BRANDING BRIEF 8-2
Selling Brands the New Zealand Way

In 2013, a Forbes survey of country brands listed New Zealand as the fifth-strongest country brand in the world—ahead of the United States—by brand consultancy FutureBrand's Country Brand Index. The ranking was a credit to the country's remarkable qualities, but also to its concerted marketing program through the years.

Back in 1991, New Zealand began a branding initiative called "The New Zealand Way." The key objectives of the New Zealand Way brand campaign were to reposition New Zealand to reflect its contemporary positioning and undertake a sustained campaign that could be a powerful force to benefit trade and tourism in the global marketplace. The innovative program was owned and funded by the New Zealand Tourism Board, and New Zealand Trade & Enterprise (NZTE, the government's official economic development agency), working with the best businesses across tourism and trade, known as "Brand Partners."

The New Zealand Way brand campaign promoted the country, its tourism and trade products and services, and its famous people, known as "Brand Ambassadors." From this research and focus groups, a fern logo was developed and intellectually protected as a new icon for New Zealand. It represented New Zealand's green provenance and leveraged the well-known existing silver fern used by many sports teams (such as the rugby team the All Blacks) and some industries (such as Anchor butter). From research, a set of brand values were also agreed on by New Zealanders to inform the repositioning.

Buoyed also by publicity from the highly popular *Lord of the Rings* film trilogy, which was filmed there, plus the profile from the America's Cup, which Tourism New Zealand cleverly used for promotion, the number of visitors to the country increased by 50 percent during this time. NZTE chose to focus its branding efforts on international business development reflecting emerging and relevant values for enterprise such as innovation, creativity, and integrity. This complemented the ongoing successes of the primary sector and New Zealand's clean and green environment.

In 2011, the tagline for the tourism campaign was changed to "100% Pure You" with the subline, "It's About Time." The intent was to build on the prior campaign to target people who were actively considering New Zealand for a holiday vacation and to encourage them to travel soon. The "100% Pure" tagline was originally conceived for tourism, but has since become a tagline leveraged by New Zealand across multiple industries, specifically agriculture and food exports, in which "clean, green" is linked to food quality and safety. The country's wine producers have marketed their products' origin as the "clean, green land," while New Zealand's dairy industry has placed advertising in congested London settings, depicting happy cows on spacious, green fields. The success of the campaign resulted in a growing awareness of New Zealand as a destination for travel and resulted in a record number of visitors by 2014, representing a 5 percent growth over the previous year.

The campaign for marketing New Zealand as a destination also involved using digital media channels. To attract tourists, the campaign relied heavily on targeting international travelers who were looking for an outdoors destination with a focus on scenery and nature. Rather than spending on mass media advertising, the company spent money on search engine marketing to identify travelers that sought the types of destinations that New Zealand represented. Further, the company's own Web site NewZealand.com, which attracts about 20 million visits a year, was used to provide information for visitors to learn more about New Zealand. Social media channels such as Facebook and Sina Weibo were used to spread awareness to potential travelers across the world.

New Zealand has benefited from popular films and a concerted marketing effort to build the country brand.
Source: Tourism New Zealand

The campaign also managed the travelers' experiences after they arrived in New Zealand. For instance, the campaign relied on a mobile app to connect people as they visited New Zealand to potential activities and accommodations listings. Using social media platforms, travelers could access stories and images about what was happening in New Zealand, thus helping them by creating travel itineraries and providing information. The goal of these activities was to build strong relationships with customers, and to encourage travelers to New Zealand to spread positive word-of-mouth.

A big component of destination branding involves managing myriad partnerships with other organizations. The destination marketing organization for New Zealand has partnered with airlines, airports, and travel sellers, and it becomes more important as the decision-making path becomes more integrated and people receive advice from different sources. The brand's association with famous movies such as the *Lord of the Rings* trilogy, and additional movies such as *Avatar 2* and *Pete's Dragon* has helped the brand increase awareness among potential audiences. Thanks to the marketing efforts, brand New Zealand has the attributes of a strong brand including high awareness as well as strong, favorable, and unique associations as a travel destination.

Sources: New Zealand, https://ww.newzealand.com; Valarie Tjolle, "Tourism New Zealand Unveils New Digital Marketing Campaign," www.travel-mole.com, February 21, 2011; Grant McPherson, "Branding Debate Goes Beyond Logos," www.nzte.govt.nz, August 23, 2011; Magdalena Florek and Andrea Insch, "The Trademark Protection of Country Brands: Insights from New Zealand," *Journal of Place Management and Development* 1, no. 3 (2008): 292–305; Top 25 Country Brands, *Forbes*, www.forbes.com/pictures/efkk45lgim/5-new-zealand/#7df87b57b580, accessed December 17, 2017; Samantha Skift, "Interview: Tourism New Zealand CEO on Smarter Digital Marketing," March 5, 2015, https://skift.com/2015/03/05/interview-tourism-new-zealand-ceo-on-smarter-digital-marketing/#1, accessed December 17, 2017.

Another challenge with country-of-origin is how consumers actually define it and under what circumstances they care. Many U.S. companies are moving their manufacturing offshore. Although they may still base their headquarters on U.S. soil, some very iconic brands—including Converse, Levi's, Mattel, and Rawlings baseballs—are no longer manufactured in the United States. Some other famous U.S. brands, such as Ben & Jerry's, Budweiser, and Gerber, are owned by foreign corporations.

In an increasingly globally connected world, the concept of country-of-origin is likely to become very confusing at times. Governments in some countries have even taken steps to protect their popular industries. Swiss lawmakers have stipulated that local watchmakers can label their products Swiss-made only if non-Swiss parts equal less than 50 percent of the value of the watch's movement, or motor.[16]

CHANNELS OF DISTRIBUTION

Chapter 5 described how members of the channels of distribution could directly affect the equity of the brands they sell. Let's next consider how retail stores can indirectly affect brand equity through an "image transfer" process because of consumers' associations linked to the retail stores.

Because of associations to product assortment, pricing and credit policy, quality of service, and so on, retailers have their own brand images in consumers' minds. The Science of Branding 8-1 summarizes academic research into the dimensions of retailer images. Retailers create these associations through the products and brands they stock and the means by which they sell them. To more directly shape their images, many retailers aggressively advertise and promote directly to customers.

A consumer may infer certain characteristics about a brand by where it is sold: "If it's sold by Nordstrom, it must be good quality." Consumers may perceive the same brand differently depending on whether it is sold in a store viewed as prestigious and exclusive, or in a store designed for bargain shoppers and having more mass appeal.

THE SCIENCE OF BRANDING 8-1
Understanding Retailers' Brand Images

Like the brands they sell, retailers have brand images that influence consumers and must be carefully constructed and maintained. Academics have identified the following five dimensions of a retailer's brand image.

Access

The location of a store and the distance that consumers must travel to shop are basic criteria in their store choice decisions. Access is a key component in consumers' assessment of total shopping costs, and is especially important for retailers who wish to get a substantial share of wallet from fill-in trips and small-basket shoppers.

Store Atmosphere

Different elements of a retailer's in-store environment, such as color, music, and crowding can influence consumers' perceptions of its atmosphere, whether or not they visit a store, how much time they spend in it, and how much money they spend there. A pleasing in-store atmosphere provides substantial hedonic utility to consumers and encourages them to visit more often, stay longer, and purchase more. Although it improves consumers' perceptions of the quality of merchandise in the store, consumers also tend to associate it with higher prices. An appealing in-store atmosphere also offers much potential in terms of crafting

a unique store image and establishing differentiation. Even if the products and brands stocked by a retailer are similar to those sold by others, the ability to create a strong in-store personality and rich experiences can play a crucial role in building retailer brand equity.

Price and Promotion

A retailer's price image is influenced by attributes, such as average level of prices, how much variation there is in prices over time, the frequency and depth of promotions, and whether the retailer positions itself on a continuum between EDLP (everyday low price) and HILO (high-low promotional) pricing. Consumers are more likely to develop a favorable price image when retailers offer frequent discounts on a large number of products than when they offer less frequent, but steeper, discounts. Further, products that have a high unit price and are purchased more frequently are more salient in determining the retailer's price image. One pricing format does not dominate another, however research has shown that large-basket shoppers prefer EDLP stores, while small-basket shoppers prefer HILO, and it is optimal for HILO stores to charge an average price that is higher than the EDLP. Finally, price promotions are associated with store switching, however the effect is indirect, altering consumers' category purchase decisions while they are in the store rather than their choice of which store to visit.

Cross-Category Assortment

Consumers' perception of the breadth of different products and services offered by a retailer under one roof significantly influences store image. A broad assortment can create customer value by offering convenience and ease of shopping. It is risky to extend too far too soon, but staying too tightly coupled to the current assortment and image may unnecessarily limit the retailer's range of experimentation. The logic and sequencing of a retailer's assortment policy are critical to its ability to successfully expand its meaning and appeal to consumers over time.

Within-Category Assortment

Consumers' perceptions of the depth of a retailer's assortment within a product category are an important dimension of store image and a key driver of store choice. As the perceived assortment of brands, flavors, and sizes increases, variety-seeking consumers will perceive greater utility, consumers with uncertain future preferences will believe they have more flexibility in their choices, and, in general, consumers are more likely to find the item they desire. A greater number of SKUs need not directly translate to better perceptions. Retailers often can reduce the number of SKUs substantially without adversely affecting consumer perceptions, as long as they pay attention to the most preferred brands, the organization of the assortment, and the availability of diverse product attributes.

Online versus Offline Retailer Image

With the growth of e-commerce and online retailing, an important question is how retailers manage their image in online and offline settings. One study examined how incongruity between online and offline retailer brand image impacts consumer attitudes towards a Web site. The study found that any incongruity between online and offline experiences can disrupt the Web site's navigation experience. With the proliferation of digital channels and interfaces (e.g., tablet versus PC versus mobile phone), ensuring a seamless user experience is critical to maintaining retailer image.

Sources: Kusum L. Ailawadi and Kevin Lane Keller, "Understanding Retail Branding: Conceptual Insights and Research Priorities," *Journal of Retailing* 80, no. 4 (December 2004): 331–342; Dennis B. Arnett, Debra A. Laverie, and Amanda Meiers, "Developing Parsimonious Retailer Equity Indexes Using Partial Least Squares Analysis: A Method and Applications," *Journal of Retailing* 79, no. 3 (December 2003): 161–170; Dhruv Grewal and Michael Levy, "Emerging Issues in Retailing Research," *Journal of Retailing* 85, no. 4 (December 2009): 522–526; Myles Landers, Sharon E. Beatty, Sijun Wang, and David L. Mothersbaugh, "The Effect of Online versus Offline Retailer-Brand Image Incongruity on the Flow Experience," *Journal of Marketing Theory and Practice* 23, no. 4 (2015): 370–387.

The transfer of store image associations can be either positive or negative for a brand. For many high-end brands, a natural growth strategy is to expand the customer base by tapping new channels of distribution. Such strategies can be dangerous, however, depending on how existing customers and retailers react. When Vera Wang decided to also distribute her wares through Kohl's, Macy's decided to drop her popular lingerie line. The retailer also cut ties with Liz Claiborne when the fashion brand decided to offer a line called Liz & Co. to JCPenney.[17] Conversely, offering exclusive brands can also negatively harm the retailer. For example, when Sears began offering Rolex, Chanel, Jimmy Choo, Stella McCartney, and other fashion brands on its online marketplace, a number of analysts questioned whether this would be the right strategy for the retailer, because this could dilute the image of the affordable, mass-market Sears brand.[18]

CO-BRANDING

We've noted that through a brand extension strategy, a new product can become linked to an existing corporate or family brand that has its own set of associations. An existing brand can also leverage associations by linking itself to other brands from the same or different company. *Co-branding*—also called brand bundling or brand alliances—occurs when two or more existing brands are combined into a joint product or are marketed together in some fashion.[19] A special case of this strategy is ingredient branding, which we'll discuss in the next section.[20]

Co-branding has been around for years; for example, Betty Crocker paired with Sunkist Growers in 1961 to successfully market a lemon chiffon cake mix.[21] Interest in co-branding as a means of building brand equity has increased in recent years. For example, Hershey's Heath toffee candy bar has not only been extended into several new products—Heath Sensations (bite-sized candies) and Heath Bits and Bits of Brickle (chocolate-covered and plain toffee baking products)—but also has been licensed to a variety of vendors, such as Dairy Queen (with its Blizzard dessert), Ben & Jerry's, and Blue Bunny (with its ice cream bar).

Some other notable supermarket examples of co-branding are Yoplait Trix yogurt, Betty Crocker's brownie mix with Hershey's chocolate syrup, and Kellogg's Cinnabon cereal. In the credit card market, co-branding often links three brands, as in the Shell Gold MasterCard from Citi Cards. With airlines, brand alliances can unite a host of brands, such as Star Alliance, which includes 16 different airlines such as United Airlines, Lufthansa, and Singapore Airlines. Technology brands have also begun partnering with their non-technology counterparts in unique ways to appeal to customers. For example, Nike and Apple co-branded to create a new

Apple and Nike's co-branded partnership increased the appeal of both brands by allowing users to track their fitness goals using an app that could be accessed via their iPhones.

footwear line called Nike+. Apple equipped these shoes with a microchip that helps record users' progress as they activate this feature via their iPhone, and it can record user statistics such as calories burned.[22] Nike and Apple expanded this partnership to the Apple Watch Nike+, which allows users to stream their favorite music from an app called Nike+ Run Club. When launched from their watch, the app can provide in-ear training, and the custom face on the watch provides motivation for wearers with slogans such as "Are We Running Today?" By co-branding with Nike, Apple has increased Apple Watch's appeal to athletes and fitness-minded consumers. In turn, Nike has benefitted from its association with the Apple Watch as it reinforces Nike's associations with fitness and health and allows it to broaden its appeal to regular runners, as well as the aspirational group of fitness enthusiasts.

Figure 8-4 summarizes the advantages and disadvantages of co-branding and licensing. The main advantage of co-branding is that a product may be uniquely and convincingly positioned by virtue of the multiple brands in the campaign. Co-branding can create more compelling points-of-difference or points-of-parity for the brand—or both—than otherwise might have been feasible. As a result, it can generate greater sales from the existing target market as well as additional opportunities with new consumers and channels. When Kraft adds Dole fruit to its popular Lunchables lunch combinations line for kids, it was partly to help address health concerns and criticism from nutrition critics.[23]

Co-branding can reduce the cost of product introduction because it combines two well-known images, accelerating potential adoption. Co-branding also may be a valuable means to learn about consumers and how other companies approach them. In poorly differentiated categories especially, co-branding may be an important means of creating a distinctive product.[24]

The potential disadvantages of co-branding are the risks and lack of control that arise from becoming aligned with another brand in the minds of consumers. Consumer expectations about the level of involvement and commitment with co-brands are likely to be high. Unsatisfactory performance thus could have negative repercussions for both (or all) brands.[25] If the brands are very distinct, consumers may be less sure about what each brand represent.[26] If the other brand has entered into other co-branding arrangements, there also may be a risk of overexposure that would dilute the transfer of any association. It may also result in distraction and a lack of focus on existing brands.

Guidelines

The Science of Branding 8-2 provides some academic insight into how consumers evaluate co-branded products. To create a strong co-brand, both brands should have adequate brand awareness; sufficiently strong, favorable, and unique associations; and positive consumer judgments

Advantages

Borrow needed expertise
Leverage equity you don't have
Reduce cost of product introduction
Expand brand meaning into related categories
   Broaden meaning
   Increase access points
Source of additional revenue

Disadvantages

Loss of control
Risk of brand equity dilution
Negative feedback effects
Lack of brand focus and clarity
Organizational distraction

FIGURE 8-4

Advantages and Disadvantages of Co-Branding and Licensing

THE SCIENCE OF BRANDING 8-2
Understanding Brand Alliances

Brand alliances, which combine two brands in some way, come in all forms. Academic research has explored the effects of co-branding and ingredient branding strategies.

Co-branding

Park, Jun, and Shocker compare co-brands to the notion of "conceptual combinations" in psychology. A conceptual combination ("apartment dog") consists of a modifying concept, or "modifier" (*apartment*) and a modified concept, or "header" (*dog*). Experimentally, Park and his colleagues explored the different ways that Godiva (associated with expensive, high-calorie boxed chocolates), and Slim-Fast (associated with inexpensive, low-calorie diet food) could hypothetically introduce a chocolate cake mix separately or together through a co-brand.

They found that the co-branded version of the product was better accepted than if either brand attempted to extend individually into the cake mix category. They also found that consumers' impressions of the co-branded concept were driven by the header brand—Slim-Fast chocolate cake mix by Godiva was viewed as lower calorie than if the product was called Godiva chocolate cake mix by Slim-Fast; the reverse was true for associations of richness and luxury. Similarly, consumers' impressions of Slim-Fast after exposure to the co-branded concept were more likely to change when it was the header brand than when it was the modifier brand. The findings show how carefully selected brands can be combined to overcome the potential problems of negatively correlated attributes (here, rich taste and low calories).

Simonin and Ruth found that consumers' attitudes toward a brand alliance could influence subsequent impressions of each partner's brands (spillover effects existed), but that these effects also depended on other factors such as product fit or compatibility and brand fit or image congruity. Brands less familiar than their partners contributed less to an alliance but experienced stronger spillover effects than their more familiar partners. Voss and Tansuhaj found that consumer evaluations of an unknown brand from another country was more positive when it was allied with a well-known domestic brand.

Levin and Levin explored the effects of dual branding, which they defined as a marketing strategy in which two brands, usually restaurants, share the same facilities while providing consumers with the opportunity to use either one or both brands. Kumar found that introducing a co-branded extension into a new product category made it less likely that a brand from the new category could turn around and introduce a counterextension into the original product category. LeBar and colleagues found that joint branding helped to increase a brand's perceived differentiation, but also sometimes decreased consumers' perceived esteem for the brand and knowledge about the brand.

Swaminathan and colleagues examined situations when co-branded partnerships featuring two brands with dissimilar (or complementary attribute levels, such as Godiva partnering with Ben & Jerry's) would be preferred by consumers, to those partnerships among similar (or non-complementary) co-branded partners (such as Godiva and Weight Watchers). They argue that

different segments of consumers may evaluate these types of co-branded products favorably, based on their thinking or processing style (linked to different cultural orientations). Under a property-mapping thinking style, complementary co-branded partnerships are evaluated more favorably. When consumers process co-brand information in a relational way, partnerships with similar brands were more favorably evaluated.

Another study examined whether partners in a brand alliance should be similar or dissimilar in brand image, to foster favorable fit perceptions. Van der Lans, van den Bergh, and Dieleman found that conceptual coherence across brands in terms of their brand personalities (e.g., similarities in levels of sophistication in brand personalities) that entered into a co-branded partnership predicted attitudes towards the alliance.

One research study examined the links between international and native brands on perceptions of a co-branded partnership. They found that the prominent partner brand—for example, the brand whose name appears first in the co-branded partnership—exerts a stronger impact on the perceptions of the co-branded product.

A review paper by Newmeyer and colleagues proposes an overarching framework of evaluating co-branded partnerships. They argue that evaluations of co-branded products are influenced by both the structure of the partnership and the constituent brands. The structure could involve how well the two partner brands are integrated as well as exclusivity and duration of the partnership. The consistency of brand images can impact co-brand evaluations as well.

Thus, across various studies, past research has elucidated basic rules for how to choose co-branded partners. Researchers have helped shine a light on how consumers view co-branded partnerships. These rules can help clarify which partnerships are likely to succeed, based on the structure of the partnership itself and the consistency in partners' brand images.

Ingredient Branding

Desai and Keller conducted a laboratory experiment to consider how ingredient branding affected consumer acceptance of an initial line extension, as well as the ability of the brand to introduce future category extensions. They studied two particular types of line extensions, defined as brand expansions: (1) *slot filler expansions*, in which the level of one existing product attribute changed (a new type of scent in Tide detergent), and (2) *new attribute expansions*, in which an entirely new attribute or characteristic was added to the product (cough relief liquid added to LifeSavers candy). They examined two types of ingredient branding strategies by branding the target attribute ingredient for the brand expansion with either a new name as a *self-branded ingredient* (Tide with its own EverFresh scented bath soap) or an established, well-respected name as a *co-branded ingredient* (Tide with Irish Spring scented bath soap).

The results indicated that with slot filler expansions, although a co-branded ingredient eased initial acceptance of the expansion, a self-branded ingredient led to more favorable later extension evaluations. With more dissimilar new attribute expansions, however, a co-branded ingredient led to more favorable evaluations of both the initial expansion and the subsequent extension.

Venkatesh and Mahajan derived an analytical model based on bundling and reservation price notions to help formulate optimal pricing and partner selection decisions for branded components. In an experimental application in the context of a university computer store selling 486-class laptop computers, they showed that at the bundle level, an all-brand Compaq PC with Intel 486 commanded a clear price premium over other alternatives. The relative brand strength of the Intel brand, however, was shown to be stronger in some senses than that of the Compaq brand.

Sources: C. Whan Park, Sung Youl Jun, and Allan D. Shocker, "Composite Branding Alliances: An Investigation of Extension and Feedback Effects," *Journal of Marketing Research* 33, no. 4 (November 1996): 453–466; Bernard L. Simonin and Julie A. Ruth, "Is a Company Known by the Company It Keeps? Assessing the Spillover Effects of Brand Alliances on Consumer Brand Attitudes," *Journal of Marketing Research* 35, no. 2 (1998): 30–42; Piyush Kumar, "The Impact of Cobranding on Customer Evaluation of Brand Counterextensions," *Journal of Marketing* 69, no. 3 (July 2005): 1–18; Kalpesh Desai and Kevin Lane Keller, "The Effects of Ingredient Branding Strategies on Host Brand Extendibility," *Journal of Marketing* 66, no. 1 (January 2002): 73–93; Mrinal Ghosh and George John, "When Should Original Equipment Manufacturers Use Branded Component Contracts with Suppliers?," *Journal of Marketing Research* 46, no. 5 (October 2009): 597–611; Alokparna Basu Monga and Loraine Lau-Gesk, "Blending Cobrand Personalities: An Examination of the Complex Self," *Journal of Marketing Research* 44, no. 3 (August 2007): 389–400; Casey E. Newmeyer, R. Venkatesh, and Rabikar Chatterjee, "Cobranding Arrangements and Partner Selection: A Conceptual Framework and Managerial Guidelines," *Journal of the Academy of Marketing Science* 42, no. 2 (2014): 103–118; Vanitha Swaminathan, Zeynep Gürhan-Canli, Umut Kubat, and Ceren Hayran. "How, When, and Why Do Attribute-Complementary versus Attribute-Similar Cobrands Affect Brand Evaluations: A Concept Combination Perspective," *Journal of Consumer Research* 42, no. 1 (2015): 45–58; Ralf van der Lans, Bram Van den Bergh, and Evelien Dieleman, "Partner Selection in Brand Alliances: An Empirical Investigation of the Drivers of Brand Fit," *Marketing Science* 33, no. 4 (2014): 551–566; Yan Li and Hongwei He, "Evaluation of International Brand Alliances: Brand Order and Consumer Ethnocentrism," *Journal of Business Research* 66, no. 1 (January 2013): 89–97; Philip Kotler and Waldemar Pfoertsch, *Ingredient Branding: Making the Invisible Visible* (New York: Springer, 2010); John Quelch, "How to Brand an Ingredient," October 8, 2007, www.blogs.hbr.org.

and feelings. Thus, a necessary, but not sufficient, condition for co-branding success is that the two brands *separately* have some potential brand equity. The most important requirement is a logical fit between the two brands, so that the combined brand or marketing activity maximizes the advantages of the individual brands while minimizing the disadvantages.[27]

Besides these strategic considerations, marketers must enter into and execute co-branding ventures carefully. They must ensure the right kind of fit in values, capabilities, and goals in addition to an appropriate balance of brand equity. When it comes to execution, marketers need detailed plans to legalize contracts, make financial arrangements, and coordinate marketing programs. As one executive at Nabisco put it, "Giving away your brand is a lot like giving away your child—you want to make sure everything is perfect." The financial arrangement between brands may vary, although typically the company using the other brand will pay some type of licensing fee and/or royalty from sales. The aim is for the licensor and the licensee to benefit from these agreements as a result of the shared equity, increased awareness for the licensor, and greater sales for the licensee.

More generally, brand alliances, such as co-branding, require marketers to ask themselves a number of questions, such as:

- What capabilities do we *not* have?
- What resource constraints do we face (people, time, money)?
- What growth goals or revenue needs do we have?

In assessing a joint branding opportunity, marketers will ask themselves:

- Is it a profitable business venture?
- How does it help to maintain or strengthen brand equity?
- Is there any possible risk of dilution of brand equity?
- Does it offer any extrinsic advantages such as learning opportunities?

One of the highest-profile brand alliances was that of Disney and McDonald's, which had the exclusive global rights from 1996 to 2006 in the fast-food industry to promote everything from Disney movies and videos to TV shows and theme parks. Interestingly, because of concerns that the fast-food industry is fueling childhood obesity, Disney ended its exclusive partnership with McDonald's, although they agreed to continue partnering on some occasional promotions. This example demonstrates some of the downsides of co-branded partnerships, particularly when one partner ceases to be a source of positive brand associations.[28] It may help for brands to consider a potential exit strategy if their partnerships do not work out. However, McDonald's continues to have partnerships with a number of different brands, including leading toy and entertainment companies for its Happy Meals, and other consumer brands such as Kraft's Oreo, Hershey's M&M's, and Rolo brands for its McFlurry dessert.

Ingredient Branding

A special case of co-branding is *ingredient branding*, which creates brand equity for materials, components, or parts that are necessarily contained within other branded products.[29] Some successful ingredient brands over the years include Intel chips, Arm & Hammer Baking Soda, OnStar security service, Oreo cookies, Stainmaster stain-resistant fibers, and Scotchgard fabrics. In a digital setting, ingredient branding is also useful in boosting the attractiveness of the host brand. For example, Apple's CarPlay is a feature that is available in certain automobiles only, and a car such as Fiat 500 may be more attractive to a potential buyer because it is among the shortlist of cars that offer the mobile iOS as an option to its customers.[30]

OnStar security service has built a strong component brand by advertising that its presence in cars is a source of security and safety for passengers.

Ingredient brands attempt to create enough awareness and preference for their product that consumers will not buy a host product that does not contain the ingredient.

From a consumer behavior perspective, branded ingredients are often a signal of quality. In a provocative academic research study, Carpenter, Glazer, and Nakamoto found that the inclusion of a branded attribute ("Alpine Class" fill for a down jacket) significantly affected consumer choices even when consumers were explicitly told that the attribute was not relevant to their decision.[31] Clearly, consumers inferred certain quality characteristics as a result of the branded ingredient.

The uniformity and predictability of ingredient brands can reduce risk and reassure consumers. As a result, ingredient brands can become industry standards and consumers will not want to buy a product that does not contain the ingredient. In other words, ingredient brands can become, in effect, a category point-of-parity. Consumers do not necessarily have to know exactly how the ingredient works—just that it adds value.

Ingredient branding has become more prevalent as mature brands seek cost-effective means to differentiate themselves on the one hand, and potential ingredient products seek means to expand their sales opportunities on the other hand. Corning's Gorilla Glass was sold as a stand-alone product prior to its use by phone manufacturers as a way of preventing phone screens from cracking. After a successful video series, which garnered millions of views, Motorola began touting its use of Gorilla Glass as a key differentiator.[32] Some companies create their own ingredient brands, such as Nike's Dri-Fit technology—a high-performance, microfiber fabric—which, when used in athletic wear, can help keep athletes dry and comfortable; similarly, another example is the ingredient brand EcoBoost that Ford developed for its new engines that improves fuel economy and increases performance.[33] To illustrate the range of alternatives in ingredient branding, consider how Singapore Airlines uses both co-branded and self-branded ingredients in their service delivery.

Thus, as in this example, one product may contain some different branded ingredients. Ingredient brands are not restricted to products and services. For example, through the years, Chevy Camaro has been featured in the movie *Transformers* as the character Bumblebee. In this case,

SINGAPORE AIRLINES

In its Suites class of service, Singapore Airlines offers bedding and tableware from Givenchy as well as new chairs hand stitched by "master Italian craftsman" Poltrona Frau. The First Class SkySuites feature leather seats trimmed with burr wood. The airline offers the Krisworld entertainment system and Givenchy fleece blankets. In the more expensive suites, first, and business classes, customers can enjoy Bose QuietComfort 2 acoustic noise-canceling headphones (economy flyers get Dolby). For its cuisine, Singapore Airlines's meals are prepared by its International Culinary Panel featuring renowned chefs, and premium classes enjoy ethnically branded meals, such as Shahi Thali (suites and first class) and Hanakoireki (business class). All passengers can join the KrisFlyer frequent flyer program.

Singapore Airlines uses a combination of co-branded and self-branded ingredients in branding its services.
Source: Steve Parsons/PA Images/Getty Images

the Chevy Camaro may be seen as an ingredient in the *Transformers* movie. The alliance between Chevy and *Transformers* allowed the brand to gain status as a pop culture icon and increase its visibility with younger audiences.[34] The yellow Chevy Camaro saw an increase in sales of about 10 percent, and sold nearly 80,000 of the yellow cars, most of which was attributable to the co-branding with Transformers. The look of the car also changed to keep up with the movie's sequel releases. For example, during the fourth film, the car was redesigned to appear more aggressive and muscular. Various other models of GM such as Cadillac and the green Corvette Stingray were featured in various roles in the *Transformer* movies, thus generating both awareness and sales for the brands. Another example of co-branding can be found in retail partnerships, as in the exclusive partnership between Barnes & Noble and Starbucks, in which Starbucks has an in-store coffee shop in numerous Barnes & Noble bookstore locations.

The highly successful Transformer movies featured a yellow Chevy Camaro and allowed the company to gain status and build brand awareness.

Advantages and Disadvantages.   The pros and cons of ingredient branding are similar to those of co-branding.[35] From the perspective of the firm making and supplying the ingredient, the benefit of branding its products as ingredients is that by creating consumer pull, the company can generate greater sales at a higher margin. There may also be more stable and broader customer demand and better long-term supplier–buyer relationships. Enhanced revenues may accrue from having two revenue streams—the direct revenue from the cost of the supplied ingredients, as well as possible extra revenue from the royalty rights paid to display the ingredient brand.

From the standpoint of the host product manufacturer, the benefit is in leveraging the equity from the ingredient brand to enhance its own brand equity. On the demand side, the host product brands may achieve access to new product categories, different market segments, and more distribution channels than they otherwise could have expected. On the supply side, the host product brands may be able to share some production and development costs with the ingredient supplier.

Ingredient branding is not without its risks and costs. The costs of a supporting marketing communications program can be high—advertising to sales ratios for consumer products often surpass 5 percent—and many suppliers are relatively inexperienced at designing mass media communications that may have to contend with inattentive consumers and noncooperative intermediaries. As with co-branding, there is a loss of control, because marketing programs for the supplier and manufacturer may have different objectives, and thus, may send different signals to consumers.

Some manufacturers may be reluctant to become supplier dependent or may not believe that the branded ingredient adds value, resulting in a loss of possible accounts. Manufacturers may resent any consumer confusion about what is the "real brand" if the branded ingredient gains too much equity. Finally, the sustainability of the competitive advantage may be somewhat uncertain, because brands that follow may benefit from consumers' increased understanding of the role of the ingredient. As a result, follower brands may have to communicate not so much the importance of the ingredient as for why their particular ingredient brand is better than the pioneer or other brands.

Guidelines.   Ingredient branding programs build brand equity in many of the same ways that conventional branding programs do. Branding Brief 8-3 describes ingredient branding efforts at DuPont, which has successfully introduced many such brands.

BRANDING BRIEF 8-3

Ingredient Branding the DuPont Way

Perhaps one of the most successful ingredient brand marketers of all times is DuPont, which was founded in Delaware as a black-powder manufacturer in 1802 by Frenchman E. I. du Pont de Nemours. Over the years, the company introduced a number of innovative products for use in markets ranging from apparel to aerospace. Many of the company's innovations, such as Lycra and Stainmaster fabrics, Teflon coating, and Kevlar fiber, became household names as ingredient brands in consumer products manufactured by many other companies. Although some have been spun off, the company still maintains a healthy roster of consumer products. It should be noted that both Teflon and Stainmaster have both been spun off and are no longer a part of Dupont (which is now DowDupont). Still, the lessons from ingredient branding based on DuPont's approach are worthy of our attention.

In 2016, DuPont generated some 24.5 billion U.S. dollars of revenue. On August 31, 2017, it merged with The Dow Chemical Company to create DowDuPont Inc., the world's largest chemical company in terms of sales. Following the merger with Dow, the new company DowDuPont has an estimated value of $130 billion and will be organized as three separate companies focusing on agricultural chemicals, materials science, and specialty product industries.

Early on, DuPont learned an important branding lesson the hard way. Because the company did not protect the name of its first organic chemical fiber, nylon, it was not trademarkable and became generic. The brands created by DuPont through the years have been components in a wide variety of products that are marketed to make everyday life better, safer, and healthier. The innovations that DuPont has been known for over the years are a result of its investments in R&D. DuPont has 150 research and development facilities located in China, Brazil, India, Germany, and Switzerland. On average, the DuPont company invested $2 billion annually in a diverse range of technologies and employed more than 10,000 scientists and engineers.

A key question that DuPont constantly confronts is whether to brand a product as an ingredient brand. To address this question, the firm has traditionally applied several criteria, both quantitative and qualitative.

- On the quantitative side, DuPont has a model that estimates the return on investment of promoting a product as an ingredient brand. Inputs to the model include brand resource allocations such as advertising and trade support; outputs relate to favorability ratings and potential sales. The goal of the model is to determine whether branding an ingredient can be financially justified, especially in industrial markets.

- On the qualitative side, DuPont assesses how an ingredient brand can help a product's positioning. If competitive and consumer analyses reveal that conveying certain associations would boost sales, DuPont is more likely to brand the ingredient. For example, one reason that DuPont launched its stain-resistant carpet fiber under the ingredient brand Stainmaster was that the company felt a "tough" association would be highly valued in the market. As noted previously, Stainmaster is no longer owned by DuPont. In 2003, DuPont sold its Invista unit (which included Stainmaster) to Koch Industries for $4.4 billion.

DuPont maintains that an appropriate, effective ingredient branding strategy leads to a number of competitive advantages, such as higher price premiums (often as much as 20 percent), enhanced brand loyalty, and increased bargaining power with other members of the value chain. DuPont employs both push and pull strategies to create its ingredient brands. Consumer advertising creates consumer pull by generating interest in the brand and a willingness to specifically request it. Extensive trade support in the form of co-op advertising, training, and trade promotions creates push by fostering a strong sense of loyalty to DuPont from other members of the value chain. This loyalty helps DuPont negotiate favorable terms from distributors and leads to increased cooperation when new products are introduced.

Another example of an ingredient brand, Kevlar is known for its bulletproof material and protective strength.

Sources: Nigel Davis, "DuPont Innovating a Way Out of a Crisis," www.icis.com, June 23, 2009; Kevin Lane Keller, "DuPont: Managing a Corporate Brand," *Best Practice Cases in Branding*, 3rd ed. (Upper Saddle River, NJ: Pearson Prentice Hall, 2008); "2010 DuPont Annual Review," www.dupont.com; "2013 DuPont Databook," www.dupont.com, accessed December 20, 2017; Wikipedia, https://en.wikipedia.org/wiki/DuPont#cite_note-data-1, accessed December 20, 2017; "Company News; DuPont to Sell Invista Unit for $4.4 Billion," *Bloomberg News*, November 18, 2003, https://www.nytimes.com/2003/11/18/business/company-news-dupont-to-sell-invista-unit-for-4.4-billion.html, accessed October 27, 2018.

Turning to the other side of the equation, what are some specific requirements for successful ingredient branding? In general, ingredient branding must accomplish four tasks:

1. Consumers must first perceive that the ingredient matters to the performance and success of the end product. Ideally, this intrinsic value is visible or easily experienced.
2. Consumers must then be convinced that not all ingredient brands are the same, and that the ingredient is superior. Ideally, the ingredient would have an innovation or some other substantial advantage over existing alternatives.
3. A distinctive symbol or logo must be designed to clearly signal to consumers that the host product contains the ingredient. Ideally, the symbol or logo would function essentially as a "seal" and would be simple and versatile—it could appear virtually anywhere—and credibly communicate quality and confidence to consumers.
4. Finally, a coordinated push and pull program must be put into place such that consumers understand the importance and advantages of the branded ingredient. Often, this will include consumer advertising and promotions and, sometimes in collaboration with manufacturers, retail merchandising and promotion programs. As part of the push strategy, some communication efforts may also need to be devoted to gaining the cooperation and support of manufacturers or other channel members.

LICENSING

Licensing creates contractual arrangements whereby firms can use the names, logos, characters, and so forth of other brands to market their own brands for some fixed fee. Essentially, a firm is "renting" another brand to contribute to the brand equity of its own product. Because it can be a shortcut means of building brand equity, licensing has gained in popularity in recent years. The top 125 global licensors drove more than $184 billion in sales of licensed products in 2010. Perhaps the champion of licensing is Walt Disney.[36]

Entertainment licensing has certainly become big business in recent years. Successful licensors include movie titles and logos, such as *Harry Potter, Transformers,* and *Spider-Man*; comic strip characters such as *Garfield* and *Peanuts*; and television and cartoon characters from *Sesame Street, The Simpsons, SpongeBob SquarePants,* and others. Every summer, marketers spend millions of dollars in movie tie-ins as they look for the next blockbuster franchise.

Licensing can be quite lucrative for the licensor. It has long been an important business strategy for designer apparel and accessories, for example. Designers such as Donna Karan, Calvin Klein, Pierre Cardin, and others command large royalties for the right to use their name on a variety of merchandise such as clothing, belts, ties, and luggage. Throughout three decades, Ralph Lauren became the world's most successful designer, licensing his Ralph Lauren, Double RL, and Polo brands to many different kinds of products. In 2015, Ralph Lauren's earned revenues from licensing

DISNEY CONSUMER PRODUCTS

The Walt Disney Company is recognized as having one of the strongest brands in the world. Much of its success lies in its flourishing television, movie, theme park, and other entertainment ventures. These different vehicles have created a host of well-loved characters and a reputation for quality entertainment. Disney Consumer Products (DCP) is designed to keep the Disney name and characters fresh in the consumer's mind through various lines of business: Disney Toys, Disney Fashion & Home, Disney Food, Health & Beauty, and Disney Stationery. DCP has a long history, which can be traced back to 1929 when Walt Disney licensed the image of Mickey Mouse for use on a children's writing tablet. Disney started licensing its characters for toys made by Mattel in the 1950s. Disney Consumer Products (DCP) ranked as the number-one global licensor in 2015, reporting $52.5 billion in retail sales of licensed merchandise worldwide.[37] DCP's *Star Wars* franchise was the most dominant property of the year at retail, generating $7.2 billion in retail sales in 2015. Marvel's *Avengers, Frozen,* Disney Princess, and "Doc McStuffins" also contributed significantly to licensing revenues. Artists in Disney Licensing's Creative Resources department work closely with manufacturers on all aspects of product marketing, including design, prototyping, manufacturing, packaging, and advertising.

Licensing continues to be an important source of revenue for Disney particularly from the video game developers, publishers, and retailers. According to their 10-K report, "The Consumer Products & Interactive Media segment generates revenue primarily from licensing characters and content from our film, television, and other properties to third parties for use on consumer merchandise, published materials, and in multi-platform games," (pg. 14). Additionally, Disney also has merchandise licensing operations of its own including toys, apparel, stationery, footwear, consumer electronics, and some of the main licensing properties for Disney include Star Wars, Mickey and Minnie, Frozen, Avengers, Disney Princess, etc.[38] Over a five-year period (2010–2015), Disney added a total of $23.9 billion in retail sales of licensed merchandise—thereby retaining Disney's no. 1 position in licensing revenues in the United States—a fact which is indicative of the strength of the Disney brand.

Disney's licensing activities represent an important source of revenue for the company, particularly from video game developers, publishers, and retailers.
Source: Kevin Britland/Alamy Stock Photo

Luxury brands such as Ralph Lauren utilize licensing as an important source of secondary revenue.

were $169 million.[39] Everyone seems to get into the act with licensing. Sports licensing of clothing apparel and other products has grown considerably to become a multibillion-dollar business.

Licensing can also provide legal protection for trademarks. Licensing the brand for use in certain product categories prevents other firms or potential competitors from legally using the brand name to enter those categories. For example, Coca-Cola entered licensing agreements in a number of product areas, including radios, glassware, toy trucks, and clothes, in part as legal protection. As it turns out, its licensing program has been so successful, the company now sells a variety of products bearing the Coca-Cola name directly to consumers.

Licensing certainly carries risks, too. A trademark can become overexposed if marketers adopt a saturation policy. Consumers do not necessarily know the motivation or marketing arrangements behind a product and can become confused or even angry if the brand is licensed to a product that seemingly bears no relation. Moreover, if the product fails to live up to consumer expectations, the brand name could become tarnished.

Guidelines

One danger in licensing is that manufacturers can get caught up in licensing a brand that might be popular at the moment but is only a fad and produces short-lived sales. Because of multiple licensing arrangements, licensed entities can also easily become overexposed and wear out quickly as a result. Sales of Izod Lacoste, with its familiar alligator crest, peaked at $450 million in 1982, but dwindled to an estimated $150 million in shirt sales in 1990 after the brand became overexposed and discount priced.[40] A number of knock-off replicas flooded the market, further exposing the brand, and lowering its value. The name was split into Lacoste and Izod brands, and while Lacoste tried to move upmarket, Izod stayed mid-scale. Ultimately, the brands were sold to separate companies, with Izod being owned by Van Heusen. Subsequently purchased by Phillips-Van Heusen, the brand has been making a comeback as the result of more careful marketing.

Firms are taking a number of steps to protect themselves in their licensing agreements, especially those firms that have little brand equity of their own and rely on the image of their licensor.[41] For example, firms are obtaining licensing rights to a broad range of licensed entities—some of which are more durable—to diversify their risk. Licensees are developing unique new products and sales and marketing approaches so that their sales are not merely a function of the popularity of other brands. Some firms conduct marketing research to ensure the proper match of product and the licensed entity or to provide more precise sales forecasts for effective inventory management.

Corporate trademark licensing is the licensing of company names, logos, or brands for use on various, often unrelated products. For example, in the depths of a financial crisis a number of years ago, Harley-Davidson chose to license its name—synonymous with motorcycles and a certain lifestyle—to a polo shirt, a gold ring, and even a wine cooler. Once it regained firmer financial footing, the company developed a much more concerted strategy, meeting with much success as described in its 10-K report in 2015.

The Company creates an awareness of the Harley-Davidson brand among its customers and the non-riding public through a wide range of products for enthusiasts by licensing the name "Harley-Davidson" and other trademarks owned by the Company. The Company's licensed products include t-shirts, vehicles and vehicle accessories, jewelry, small leather goods, toys, and numerous other products. Although the majority of licensing activity occurs in the U.S., the Company continues to expand these activities in international markets. According to Harley Davidsons' 10-K report in 2015, royalty revenues from licensing, included in Motorcycles segment net revenue, were $46.5 million, $47.1 million, and $58.9 million in 2015, 2014, and 2013, respectively.[42]

Other seemingly narrowly focused brands such as Jeep, Caterpillar, John Deere, and Jack Daniels have also entered a broad portfolio of licensing arrangements.

In licensing their corporate trademarks, firms may have different motivations, including generating extra revenues and profits, protecting their trademarks, increasing their brand exposure, or enhancing their brand image. The profit appeal can be enticing because there are no inventory expenses, accounts receivables, or manufacturing expenses. In an average deal, a licensee pays a corporation a royalty of about 5 percent of the wholesale price of each product, although the actual percentage can vary from 2 percent to 10 percent. As noted in Chapter 5, some firms now sell licensed merchandise through their own catalogs.

As in any co-branded arrangement, however, the risk is that the product will not live up to the reputation established by the brand. Inappropriate licensing can dilute brand meaning with consumers and marketing focus within the organization. Consumers do not care about the financial arrangements behind a particular product or service; if the brand is used, the brand promise must be upheld.

CELEBRITY ENDORSEMENT

Using well-known and admired people for promoting products is a widespread phenomenon with a long marketing history. Even the late U.S. President Ronald Reagan was a celebrity endorser, pitching several different products, including cigarettes, during his acting days. Some U.S. actors or actresses who refuse to endorse products in the United States are willing to do so in overseas markets. For example, rugged American actors Arnold Schwarzenegger (Bwain drink), Brad Pitt (Softbank), and Harrison Ford (Kirin beer) have all done ads for brands in Japan. Although Millward Brown estimates that celebrities show up in 15 percent of U.S. ads, that number jumps to 24 percent for India and 45 percent for Taiwan.[43]

The rationale behind these strategies is that a famous person can draw attention to a brand and shape the perceptions of the brand, by the inferences that consumers make based on the knowledge they have about the famous person. The hope is that the celebrities' fans will also become fans of their products or services. The celebrity must be well enough known to improve awareness, image, and responses for the brand.

In particular, a celebrity endorser should have a high level of visibility and a rich set of potentially useful associations, judgments, and feelings.[44] Ideally, he or she would be credible in terms of expertise, trustworthiness, and likability or attractiveness, as well as having specific associations that carry potential product relevance. One person who has done a remarkable job building and leveraging a highly credible brand is Oprah Winfrey.

OPRAH WINFREY

One of the most successful and valuable person brands in the world is Oprah Winfrey—*Forbes* magazine estimates her net worth at a staggering $3.1 billion.[45] Overcoming a childhood of poverty and other personal challenges and driven by her own motto, "Live Your Best Life," she has parlayed her relentless optimism and drive for self-improvement into an entertainment franchise covering all media markets and corners of the globe. Her empathetic connection with her audience has created a marketing gold mine in the process. Her Harpo production company, shrewdly formed early in her show's syndication life, launched hit spin-off shows for some of her most popular guests such as Dr. Phil, Dr. Oz, Rachael Ray, and design expert Nate Berkus. Her magazine, *O, the Oprah Magazine*, published by Hearst, celebrated fifteen years in 2015, and has a monthly circulation of roughly 18 million.[46] Winfrey has produced Broadway shows, feature films, and television movies and has her own satellite radio station. After ending the 25-year run of her broadcast television show on May 25, 2011, she turned her energy to her new cable channel, OWN. Her television network OWN (Oprah Winfrey Network) was seen by 15.8 million viewers daily in the United States alone, and was eventually sold to Discovery Communications.[47]

Oprah Winfrey's *O* Magazine has a large audience and builds on her popularity as a celebrity.
Source: Getty Images

Winfrey's sincere nature and credibility with her audience have made any product or brand endorsements instant hits—a phenomenon called the "Oprah effect." "Oprah's Book Club" launched many best-sellers (e.g., Toni Morrison's books) and is credited by some with saving the publishing industry. When she bought a 10 percent stake in Weight Watchers, the company's stock soared. Her annual infomercial-like "Favorite Things" show sometimes transformed a low-profile brand into an overnight success. For example, a natural beauty company called Carol's Daughter won millions of dollars in celebrity funding after they appeared on Oprah, and the brand was eventually bought by L'Oréal.[48] Oprah Winfrey announced plans to co-launch a line of packaged foods with Kraft Heinz called "O! That's Good" featuring reasonably priced refrigerated comfort foods such as Baked Potato Soup and Broccoli Cheddar Soup. This product line will both strengthen Oprah Winfrey's forays into health and nutrition and solidify Kraft Heinz's position in healthy refrigerated foods.

Potential Problems

Despite the potential upside of linking a celebrity endorser to a brand, there are some potential problems. First, celebrity endorsers can endorse so many products that they lack any specific product meaning or are seen as opportunistic or insincere. Although NFL star quarterback Peyton Manning has parlayed success on the football field and his "Aw, shucks" personality into endorsement contracts for several different brands—DirectTV, Gatorade, MasterCard, Oreo, Reebok, and Sprint, among others—he runs the risk of overexposure, especially given that so many of his ads run concurrently with the football season.[49] The case study on Rachael Ray Nutrish described in Branding Brief 8-4 highlights this type of risk.

Second, there must be a reasonable match between the celebrity and the product.[50] Many endorsements would seem to fail this test. Despite being featured in their ads, NBA star Kobe Bryant and race car driver Danica Patrick would seem to have no logical connection to Turkish Airlines and the Go Daddy Internet domain registrar and Web hosting company, respectively.

Third, celebrity endorsers can get in trouble or lose popularity, diminishing their marketing value to the brand, or just fail to live up to expectations. Most companies conduct background

BRANDING BRIEF 8-4
Rachael Ray's Nutrish

Rachael Ray's Nutrish is a brand of pet food that is aimed at the super-premium segment of the market. The cat food market in particular has a number of competitors including Nestle's Purina and IAMS which have a dominant presence. Purina sells treats for cats, cat litter, and other non-food-related products. The aim of Rachael Ray's Nutrish is to provide loving, health-conscious cat owners with a super-premium product that cats love by focusing on wholesome, appealing, all-natural ingredients with zero fillers.

In order to convince pet owners of the nutritional benefits of the super-premium cat food, they had to embark on a celebrity endorsement strategy featuring Rachael Ray. Why was Rachael Ray an ideal celebrity for this brand? Rachael Ray was (and still is) among the most recognizable chefs in the world, thanks to her television appearances and shows about cooking. She grew in prominence from being a cooking instructor at a local market to hosting her own show called *30 Minute Meals* on the Food Network. That show was a launching point for several other shows starring Ray including *$40 a Day*, *Rachael Ray's Tasty Travels*, *Rachael Ray's Week in a Day*, and *Rachael vs. Guy: Celebrity Cook-Off*. With these shows, two Daytime Emmy Awards, and multiple Emmy nominations, Rachael Ray was well on her way to becoming a celebrity chef.

In addition to Rachael Ray's celebrity chef status, her philanthropic work surrounding pets made her an ideal celebrity endorser for the brand. Rachael Ray passionately advocated for no-kill pet shelters across the country through her organization *Rachael's Rescue*, and donated $15 million in 2015 for caring for pets in pet shelters across the country. News about pets dying from consuming food made with fillers caused *Rachael Ray's Nutrish* to be launched in 2008 as a no-filler brand to address an unmet need in the market.

The partnership of Rachael Ray with Nutrish gave the brand credibility as a tasty alternative in the pet food market and leveraged key trends in the market. At this time, a growing emphasis on health and wellness among consumers had important implications for the pet food market as well. Many pet owners were caring for their pets in much the same way as humans have cared for their children, which was fueling sales growth in the premium end of the market at a 9 percent rate (relative to a decrease of 6 percent in the value segment). A key customer insight was that pet owners frequently mixed food from their own meals into the pet's bowl. Against this background of "humanization of pets" and growth in super-premium brands, *Rachael Ray's Nutrish* succeeded by allowing pet owners to feel that they are providing the best food for their pets prepared using a recipe from a celebrity chef.

The *Rachael Ray's Nutrish* brand's marketing efforts successfully strengthened the sales of the super-premium segment of the market. The brand increased traffic to the pet food aisle in mass merchandise retail stores by increasing in-store signage and by placing purchase triggers in adjacent aisles. A $40 million ad campaign was created which spanned TV, print media, and digital advertising to target the brand's target audience of ages 35–54 which included busy working moms. The brand also conducted campaigns involving online social

Rachael Ray's Nutrish represents an excellent use of a celebrity endorser for a pet food brand. Rachael Ray is a well-known celebrity chef who is also known for her advocacy of pet shelters through her organization "Rachael's Rescue."

influencers to drive both awareness and trial for the brand. A co-branded partnership with BuzzFeed included videos and sponsored posts with content revolving around cat rescue and adoption. One co-branded video titled "People Who Hate Cats Live with Cats for a Week" generated more than 6.5 million views on YouTube and Facebook, in three weeks following its launch. Nutrish and BuzzFeed also had a co-branded presence at CatConLA, where visitors to the booth had the chance to take home a custom "Caticature"—a caricature of themselves melded with their cat—created by an on-site caricature artist. These activations using digital and social media channels, along with traditional TV and print advertising, and their celebrity endorser strategy, had the intended effect. In 2015, the *Rachael Ray's Nutrish* brand grew at an astounding pace with a 49 percent compound annual growth rate (CAGR), establishing itself as a leading pet food brand; as a result of its success, sales of super-premium dog food in mainstream retailers rose from a negative sales growth of 0.5 percent in 2011 to 13 percent in 2015. Steve Joyce, Ainsworth's vice president of marketing states that, "We attribute this success to the fact that we offer a high-quality pet product at a reasonable price where consumers can purchase our products in traditional grocery stores and mass retailers versus pet specialty stores in addition to consumers connecting with Ray's genuine love of her dog Isaboo, animals, and how much Ray cares about nutrition in general."

Despite the success of the co-branded product, the partnership also has many downsides. The excessive reliance on a single celebrity, Rachael Ray, exposes the brand to risks, in the event that the celebrity loses appeal over time. The strength of the link to Rachael Ray may also prevent the brand from adding new associations with other celebrity endorsers or leveraging other partnerships. The strong link to healthy pet food may prevent the brand from introducing new products aimed at other types of product categories. Therefore, the relationship with Rachael Ray may prevent the brand from growing in other ways, thereby limiting its opportunities in the future.

Sources: Meggen Taylor, "Nutrish: Rachael Ray's Pet Food Comes with a Heaping Dash of Philanthropy," June 20, 2016, www.forbe.com/sites/meggentaylor/2016/06/20/nutrish-rachael-rays-pet-food-comes-with-a-heaping-dash-of-philanthropy/#440e5a2312c9, accessed December 22, 2017; Nielsen.com, "Premiumization Can Teach an Old Pet Food Brand New Tricks," March 15, 2016, www.nielsen.com/us/en/insights/news/2016/premiumization-can-teach-an-old-pet-food-brand-new-tricks.html, accessed December 22, 2017; Tanya Gazdik, "Rachael Ray's Nutrish Pet Food Launches $ 40 Million Campaign," May 6, 2016, www.mediapost.com/publications/article/275164/rachael-rays-nutrish-pet-food-launches-40-millio.html?edition, accessed December 22, 2017.

checks before signing celebs, but that does not guard against bad behavior in the future. A number of spokespeople over the years have run into legal difficulties, personal problems, or controversies of some form that diminished their marketing value, such as Bill Cosby, Lance Armstrong, O.J. Simpson, Martha Stewart, and Michael Jackson.[51] Figure 8-5 is a rogue's gallery of high-profile celebrity endorsement mishaps.

To broaden the appeal and reduce the risks of linking to one celebrity, some marketers have begun to employ several different celebrities or even celebrities who are deceased, and therefore, a known commodity. For example, dead celebrities such as Michael Jackson (who generates $115 million a year), Elvis Presley (who generates $55 million), and Charles Schulz (creator of the *Peanuts* characters, which generates $40 million) continue to generate revenues from licensing and endorsements.[52]

Celebrity & Brand	Mishap
James Garner and Cybil Shepherd for Beef	Both actors were dropped as spokespersons after Garner had heart trouble and Shepherd reported in a magazine interview that she did not eat red meat.
Martina Hingis for Sergio Tacchini	In the midst of a 5-year contract, the one-time women's tennis champ sued the Italian maker of her tennis shoes for $35 million after she claimed they gave her a chronic foot injury.
Michael Vick for Nike, Reebok, Upper Deck, and others	When a dog-fighting conviction led to a prison sentence, pro football star Vick reportedly lost over $50 million in endorsement contracts after being dropped by companies.
Whoopi Goldberg for SlimFast	The comic actress was dropped as an endorser after she made critical comments about then-President George W. Bush during a Democratic fundraiser.
Kobe Bryant for McDonald's, Sprite, and Nutella	The basketball star lost millions in endorsements after being charged with sexual assault.
Kate Moss for H&M, Pepsi, Burberry, and Chanel	The model was dropped as spokesperson by a number of companies after tabloid newspapers showed her using cocaine.
Michael Phelps for Kellogg	The Olympic champion swimmer was dropped after being photographed smoking marijuana.
Tiger Woods for Accenture, Gillette, Gatorade, and AT&T	The golf champion lost numerous endorsements as reports of his serial infidelity emerged.

FIGURE 8-5

Celebrity Endorsement Mishaps

Source: Based on Jack Trout, "Celebs Who Un-Sell Products," *Forbes*, September 13, 2007; Mike Chapman, "Celebrities Moving Products? Not So Much," *Adweek*, June 8, 2011; Steve McKee, "The Trouble with Celebrity Endorsements," *Bloomberg BusinessWeek*, November 14, 2008.

Fourth, many consumers feel celebrities are doing the endorsement only for the money and do not necessarily believe in or even use the brand. Even worse, some feel the fees celebrities earn to appear in commercials add a significant and unnecessary cost to the brand. In reality, celebrities often do not come cheap and can demand millions of dollars for endorsements.

Celebrities also can be difficult to work with and may not willingly follow the marketing direction of the brand. Tennis player Andre Agassi tried Nike's patience when—at the same time he was advertising for Nike—he appeared in commercials for the Canon Rebel camera. In these ads, he looked into the camera and proclaimed "Image Is Everything"— the antithesis of the "authentic athletic performance" positioning that has been the foundation of Nike's brand equity. Winning the French Open, however, put Agassi back in Nike's good graces.

Finally, as noted in Chapter 6, celebrities may distract attention from the brand in ads so that consumers notice the stars but have trouble remembering the advertised brand. PepsiCo decided to drop singers Beyoncé Knowles and Britney Spears from high-profile ad campaigns when they felt the Pepsi brand did not get the same promotion boost from the campaign that the stars were getting.

As we noted in Chapter 7, sometimes brands featuring celebrities could be the subject of controversy, which may lower the standing of the brand and the associated endorser. Kendall Jenner—a supermodel who starred in a Pepsi commercial—inadvertently became the target of controversy following a Pepsi ad campaign. The ad was the subject of significant backlash from its viewers who felt that it was inappropriately exploiting a national protest movement—the Black Lives Matter movement—in an attempt to increase Pepsi's sales, thus causing both the brand and celebrity (i.e., Pepsi and Kendall Jenner) to be the target of negative sentiment.

Kobe Bryant (a famous basketball player) represents one of the many celebrity athletes that Nike used to effectively promote their brand.

Brands can become too reliant on a celebrity. Founder and Chairman Dave Thomas was an effective pitchman for his Wendy's restaurant chain because of his down-home, unpretentious folksy style and strong product focus. Recognized by more than 90 percent of adult consumers, he appeared in hundreds of commercials over a 12-year period until his death in early 2002.[53] The brand struggled for years afterward, however, trying to find the right advertising approach to replace him. The example of Rachael Ray's Nutrish is also a case study that reflects this concern.

Guidelines

To overcome these problems, marketers should strategically evaluate, select, and use celebrity spokespeople. First, choose a well-known and well-defined celebrity whose associations are relevant to the brand and likely to be transferable. For example, despite false starts for his retirement, Brett Favre's rugged, down-to-earth persona fits well for the backyard football games in the "Real. Comfortable. Jeans." Wrangler ads.

Then, there must be a logical fit between the brand and the person.[54] To reduce confusion or dilution, the celebrity ideally will not be linked to many other brands or be overexposed. Popular Hong Kong actor Jackie Chan has been criticized for endorsing too many products— from electric bikes to antivirus software to frozen dumplings and more. Unfortunately, many of the products he has endorsed have run into problems—a shampoo was alleged to contain carcinogens, an auto repair school was hit by a diploma scandal, and makers of both video compact discs and an educational computer went out of business. As one Chinese editorial commented: "He has become the coolest spokesperson in history—a man who can destroy anything!"[55]

Third, the advertising and communication program should use the celebrity in a creative fashion that highlights the relevant associations and encourages their transfer. Dennis Haysbert has played the President of the United States in the TV series *24* and adopted a similarly stately, reassuring tone for his spokesperson role in the "You're in Good Hands" ads for Allstate insurance. William Shatner's humorous Priceline ads take a completely different

Q SCORES

Marketing Evaluations conducts surveys to determine "Q Scores" for a broad range of entertainers and other public figures, such as TV performers, news and sports anchors, and reporters, athletes, and models. Each performer is rated on the following scale: "One of My Favorites," "Very Good," "Good," "Fair," "Poor," and "Never Seen or Heard of Before." The sum of the "Favorite" through "Poor" ratings is "Total Familiar." Because some performers are not very well known, a positive Q Score is a ratio of the "One of My Favorites" rating to the "Total Familiar" rating, and a negative Q Score is a ratio of the sum of "Poor" and "Fair" ratings to the "Total Familiar" rating. Q Scores thus capture how appealing or unappealing a public figure is among those who do know him or her. Q Scores will move around, depending on the fame and fortune of the subject. For example, Steph Curry of the Golden State Warriors, who recently topped LeBron James as the most sought-after National Basketball Association (NBA) star, also boasts of an outsized Q Score of 34 (relative to higher-ranked Kevin Durant who has a Q score of 26, or LeBron James with a Q Score of 29 among sports fans).[56]

---

tack and take advantage of the actor's self-deprecating, campy wit to draw attention to its discount message.

Finally, marketing research must help identify potential endorser candidates and facilitate the development of the proper marketing program, as well as track its effectiveness.

Celebrities themselves must manage their own "brands" to ensure that they provide value. Anyone with a public profile, even if just within the company in which he or she works, should consider how to manage his or her brand image best.[57] Branding Brief 8-5 offers some thoughts

BRANDING BRIEF 8-5
Managing a Person Brand

Although many branding principles apply, there are some important differences between a person brand and a product or service brand. Here are some of the main differences to consider:

1. Person brands are more abstract and intangible but have very rich imagery.
2. Person brands are more difficult to compare because the competition is very broad and often not easily relatable.
3. Person brands can be difficult to control and keep consistent. A person brand can have many facets, and many interactions and experiences with many different people over time, all adding to the complexity of brand management.
4. People may adopt different personas for various situations (such as work versus play) that will affect the dimensionality of their brand.
5. Repositioning a person brand can be tricky because people like to categorize other people, but it is not impossible. Actors and entertainers (such as Mark Wahlberg and Madonna) have changed their images, whereas others (such as Sylvester Stallone and Jim Carrey) have found it more difficult.

As guidelines for managing a person brand, consider the following recommendations:

1. A person brand must manage brand elements. Names can be shortened and nicknames adopted. Even though a person does not necessarily have a logo or symbol, appearance in terms of dress and look can still help to create a brand identity.
2. A person brand is built by the words and actions of that person. Given the intangible nature of a person brand, however,

it is hard to form judgments at one point in time—repeated exposures are usually necessary.

3. A person brand can borrow brand equity through secondary associations such as geographical regions, schools and universities, and so on. A person brand can employ strategic partnerships with other people to enhance brand equity.
4. Credibility is key to a person brand. Trustworthiness is important, but so is likability and appeal in terms of eliciting more emotional responses.
5. Person brands can use multiple media channels—online is especially useful for social networking and community building.
6. A person brand must stay fresh and relevant and properly innovate and invest in key person traits.
7. A person brand should consider optimal positioning in terms of brand potential and associated points-of-parity and points-of-difference. A clear and compelling point-of-difference is especially important to carve out a unique identity in the workplace or market.
8. Brand architecture is simpler for a person brand—sub-branding is less relevant—but brand extensions can occur, for instance when a person adds to his or her perceived capabilities.
9. A person brand must live up to the brand promise at all times. Reputations and brands are built over the years but can be harmed or even destroyed in days. One slip can be devastating and difficult to recover from.
10. A person brand must be a self-advocate and help to shape impressions.

about how person branding works in general and how it differs from more traditional branding for products and services.

Social Influencers as the New Celebrities

Despite its importance, the area of rapid growth has been in the use of social media celebrities for advertising brands. We provided an overview of this phenomenon and described some leading celebrities who have large YouTube followings. Some of these online social influencers such as beauty guru Michelle Phan can earn up to $3 million per year based on their endorsement of specific brands.[58] Top influencers on YouTube can earn $300,000 per video, while a top Facebook influencer can earn $200,000 per post.[59]

In addition to macro-influencers who may command large followings on social media, there are also several noncelebrity or micro-influencers who hold considerable sway on social media. One survey suggested that these micro-influencers may have 10 times more impact on in-store purchases than celebrity influencers,[60] and more than half the respondents suggested that they turned to YouTube reviewers (such as Michelle Phan) to learn more about markets. Today's customers trust regular people like Phan because their endorsements appear to be driven by genuine expertise, and not just money. A survey of 1,470 women found that 86 percent of them wanted product recommendations from real people, and that 58 percent turn to YouTube reviewers to get them. In this way, online social influencers are rapidly taking the place of traditional celebrity endorsement strategies as more authentic ways of connecting with smaller audiences.

SPORTING, CULTURAL, OR OTHER EVENTS

As Chapter 6 described, events have their own set of associations that may become linked to a sponsoring brand under certain conditions. Sponsored events can contribute to brand equity by becoming associated with the brand and improving brand awareness, adding new associations, or improving the strength, favorability, and uniqueness of existing associations.[61]

The main means by which an event can transfer associations is credibility. A brand may seem more likable or perhaps even trustworthy or expert by becoming linked to an event. The extent to which this transfer takes place will depend on which events are selected and how the sponsorship program is designed and integrated into the entire marketing program to build brand equity. Brand Focus 8.0 at the end of the chapter discusses sponsorship strategies for leading companies making major investments in sports marketing.

SPORTS SPONSORSHIPS

Red Bull sponsoring a Major League Soccer team and calling it "The New York Red Bulls." Or, Polo's sponsorship of the U.S. Open, and Campbell's Soup sponsoring the National Football League (and celebrating its athletes).[62] These are examples of brands aligning themselves with various sports to strengthen their own brand equity.

The rationale for sports sponsorships, in general, is that they provide access to specific target audiences. In the case of Red Bull, the partnership with New York Red Bulls makes sense because the audiences for soccer in the United States are represented in the 18–29 segment, a group that represented a key consumer target for Red Bull. Further, both brands (Red Bull and the Major League Soccer team called Metrostars), have associations with attributes such as energetic, fun, and daring, thereby creating synergies in their images. Alternatively, a sports sponsorship may involve a new target audience that has typically not been associated with either a brand or a sport. For instance, CoverGirl's sponsorship of the National Football League was based on the key customer insight that 47 percent of viewers were women.[63]

The partnership can also allow the sport to thrive outside the traditional confines of the game season and elevate it to a lifestyle brand. This is evinced in the case of Merrell, an outdoor gear company which sponsored the Tough Mudder race, which is a twelve-mile obstacle race to challenge the toughest athletes. The partnership was very beneficial to both parties; Merrell is known for its outdoor hiking and running shoes, and was looking for ways of expanding its presence.[64] In line with this, the Tough Mudder brand was also looking to find a way to elevate itself to a lifestyle everyday-brand. Both brands achieved their goals through the partnership. A similar partnership was announced between Reebok and the Spartan Race, which also led to the introduction of the Spartan Race-branded All Terrain shoe series. In this way, sports sponsorships can offer a unique source of brand association transfer and allow brands to be seen by both current and potential target audiences.

THIRD-PARTY SOURCES

Finally, marketers can create secondary associations in several different ways by linking the brand to various third-party sources. For example, the *Good Housekeeping* seal has been seen as a mark of quality for decades, offering product replacement or refunds for defective products for up to two years from purchase. Endorsements from leading magazines like *PC* magazine, organizations like the American Dental Association, acknowledged experts such as film critic Roger Ebert, or carefully selected Elite critics of the online Yelp consumer review site can obviously improve perceptions of and attitudes toward brands.

Third-party sources can be especially credible sources. As a result, marketers often feature them in advertising campaigns and selling efforts. J.D. Power and Associates' well-publicized Customer Satisfaction Index helped to cultivate an image of quality for Japanese automakers in the 1980s, with a corresponding adverse impact on the quality image of their U.S. rivals. In the 1990s, they began to rank quality in other industries, such as airlines, credit cards, rental cars, and phone service, and top-rated brands in these categories began to feature their awards in ad campaigns. Grey Goose vodka cleverly employed a third-party endorsement to drive sales.

GREY GOOSE

Sidney Frank first found success in the liquor industry with a little-known German liqueur, Jägermeister, which he began to market in the United States in the mid-1980s and drove to 700,000 annual cases in sales and market leadership by 2001. Turning his sights to the high-margin super-premium market, Frank decided to create a French vodka that would use water from the Cognac region and be distilled by the makers of Cardin brandy. Branded as "Grey Goose," the product had distinctive packaging—a must in the category—with a bottle taller than competitors that combined clear and frosted glass with a cutaway of geese in flight and the French flag. But perhaps the most important factor in the brand's eventual success was a taste-test result from the Beverage Testing Institute that ranked Grey Goose as the number-one imported vodka. Fueled by exhaustive advertising that trumpeted its big win as "the World's Best-Tasting Vodka," Grey Goose became a top seller. Frank eventually sold Grey Goose Vodka brand to Bacardi in 2004 for a stunning $2.2 billion. Its success continues to this day. Despite the fact that vodka has been characterized as essentially odorless and tasteless, it is consistently ranked as the top brand of vodka brand in consumer loyalty polls on the basis of image, versatility, and smoothness.[65]

Distinctive packaging and taste-test awards have propelled Grey Goose to a leadership position in the vodka category.
Source: Carl Miller/Alamy Stock Photo

REVIEW

This chapter considered the process by which other entities can be leveraged to create secondary associations. These other entities include source factors such as the company that makes a product, where the product is made, and where it is purchased, as well as related people, places, or things. When they link the brand to other entities with their own set of associations, consumers may expect that some of these same associations also characterize the brand.

Thus, independent of how a product is branded, the nature of the product itself, and its supporting marketing program, marketers can create brand equity by "borrowing" it from other sources. Creating secondary associations in this fashion may be quite important if the corresponding brand associations are deficient in some way. Secondary associations may be especially valuable as a means to link favorable brand associations that can serve as points-of-parity or create unique brand associations that can serve as points-of-difference in positioning a brand.

Eight different ways to leverage secondary associations to build brand equity are linking the brand to (1) the company making the product; (2) the country or some other geographic location in which the product originates; (3) retailers or other channel members that sell the product; (4) other brands, including ingredient brands; (5) licensed characters; (6) famous spokespeople or endorsers; (7) events; and (8) third-party sources.

In general, the extent to which any of these entities can be leveraged as a source of equity depends on consumer knowledge of the entity and how easily the appropriate associations or responses to the entity transfer to the brand. Overall credibility or attitudinal dimensions may be more likely to transfer than specific attribute and benefit associations, although the latter can be transferred, too. Linking the brand to other entities, however, is not without risk. Marketers give up some control, and managing the transfer process so that only the relevant secondary associations become linked to the brand may be a challenge.

DISCUSSION QUESTIONS

1. The Boeing Company manufactures different types of aircraft for the commercial airline industry, for example, the 727, 747, 757, 767, 777, and now, the 787 jet models. Is there any way for Boeing to adopt an ingredient branding strategy with its jets? How? What would be the pros and cons?
2. After winning major championships, star players often complain about their lack of endorsement offers. Similarly, after every Olympics, some medal-winning athletes lament their lack of commercial recognition. From a branding perspective, how would you respond to the complaints of these athletes?
3. Think of the country in which you live. What image might it have with consumers in other countries? Are there certain brands or products that are highly effective in leveraging that image in global markets?
4. Which retailers have the strongest image and equity in your mind? Think about the brands they sell. Do they contribute to the equity of the retailer? Conversely, how does that retailer's image help the image of the brands it sells? What is the impact of online versus offline retail storefronts in creating your image of this retailer?
5. Pick a brand. Evaluate how it leverages secondary associations. Can you think of any ways that the brand could more effectively leverage secondary brand associations?
6. Select a social media celebrity. Can you find brand names that could use this celebrity for sponsored posts online? What about a smaller, less known celebrity? How would the effects of these two types of influencers (i.e., large/well-known versus small) vary in terms of their impact on a brand?

BRAND FOCUS 8.0

Going for Corporate Gold at the Olympics

Competition at the Olympics is not restricted to just the athletes. A number of corporate sponsors also vie to maximize the return on their sponsorship dollars. Corporate sponsorship is a significant part of the business side of the Olympics and contributes almost one-third of the revenue of the International Olympic Committee (IOC). Countries themselves compete for the rights to host the Games. Rio de Janeiro, Brazil, won the rights to host the 2016 Games over Chicago, Madrid, and Tokyo.

Corporate Sponsorship

Corporate sponsorship of the Olympics exploded with the commercial success of the 1984 Summer Games in Los Angeles. At that time, many international sponsors, such as Fuji, achieved positive image building and increased market share.

Eleven companies have paid for the highest level of Olympic sponsorship (TOP)—estimated to cost in the neighborhood of $200 million—for exclusive worldwide marketing rights to the Summer, Winter, and Youth Olympic Games: Coca-Cola, Alibaba Group, Atos, Bridgestone, Dow, General Electric (GE), Intel, Omega, Panasonic, P&G, Samsung, Toyota, and Visa.[66] In addition to exclusive worldwide marketing opportunities, partners receive:

- Use of all Olympic imagery, as well as appropriate Olympic designations on products
- Hospitality opportunities at the Olympic Games
- Direct advertising and promotional opportunities, including preferential access to Olympic broadcast advertising
- On-site concessions/franchise and product sale/showcase opportunities
- Ambush marketing protection (discussed later)
- Acknowledgement of their support through a broad Olympic sponsorship recognition program.

Other tiers at lower levels of sponsorship also exist. For example, the Winter Olympics in PyeongChang 2018 included various sponsors such as McDonald's, KT, The North Face, Korean Air, Samsung, and Hyundai, among others.

Besides direct expenditures, companies spent hundreds of millions more on related marketing efforts. A long-time Olympics supporter since the 1976 Summer Games in Montreal, McDonald's always runs a number of promotional campaigns to tie in with its sponsorship. Building on prior McDonald's kids' programs at the Olympic Games in Beijing and Vancouver, McDonald's "Champions of Play for the Olympic Games" brought up to 200 children from around the world to London (each with a guardian) as part of a new global program.

A relative newcomer beginning its sponsorship with the Vancouver Olympics in 2010, Procter & Gamble launched its "Proud Sponsor of Mums (or Moms)" campaign that it extended throughout P&G's sponsorship of the Rio 2016 Olympics. P&G's Olympic Games partnership is the first to cover multiple brands under one sponsor and will span the next 10 years, more than 30 product categories, and 205 National Olympic Committees. The campaign's goals are to raise awareness of and reward mothers' contributions globally, based on customer insight that every athlete is supported by an amazing mom.[67]

Another company in the list of worldwide sponsors is General Electric (GE). In announcing GE's sponsorship, Jeff Immelt,

chairman and CEO, stated, "The Olympic Games provide a unique opportunity to showcase our innovative technologies and services. Hosting a successful Olympic Games is a transformational opportunity for every host city. We are committed to working with the IOC and the local organizing committees to deliver world-class infrastructure solutions and a sustainable legacy to future generations."

GE works closely with host countries, cities, and organizing committees to provide infrastructure solutions for Olympic Games venues including power, water treatment, transportation, and security, and to supply hospitals with ultrasound and MRI equipment to help doctors treat athletes.[68]

Sponsorship ROI

Although several firms have long-term relationships and commitments with the Olympics, in recent years, other long-time sponsors have cut their ties. Kodak ended over a century of sponsorship after the Beijing Olympic Games, and General Motors ended its decades-long support at that time, too. Other TOP partners that chose not to renew after the 2008 Games included Johnson & Johnson, Lenovo, and Manulife.

Although many factors affect the decision to engage in or renew an Olympic sponsorship, its marketing impact is certainly widely debated. For example, one survey of 1,500 Chinese city residents just before the 2008 Beijing Games revealed that only 15 percent could name two of the 12 global sponsors, and just 40 percent could name one: Coca-Cola. After virtually every Olympic Games, surveys show that many spectators at the Games and even avid viewers of the broadcasts mistakenly identify a nonsponsoring company as an official sponsor.[69] Having a tight connection between the products and the Olympic sponsorship helps with improving the return on investment (ROI). As an example, Nike is a brand which symbolizes athletic achievement and therefore should provide a natural way of linking the brand with sponsorship of the Olympic Games.

Ambush Marketing

In some cases, sponsorship confusion may be due to **ambush marketing**, in which advertisers attempt to give consumers the false impression they are Olympic sponsors without paying for the right to do so. The Brand Protection Guidelines for the 2016 Rio Olympics describe this as "any intentional or unintentional attempt to create a false, unauthorized commercial association with a brand or event."[70] Nonsponsoring companies attempt to attach themselves to the Games by, for instance, running Olympic-themed ads that publicize other forms of sponsorship, such as sponsoring a national team, by identifying the brand as an official supplier, or by using current or former Olympians as endorsers.[71]

For the Beijing Games, not only did popular former Chinese gymnastics champion Li Ning light the Olympic cauldron in the opening ceremony, he did so wearing shoes from the sportswear company he had founded. His actions drew tremendous attention to the Li Ning line while the official athletic sponsor, Adidas, which had spent millions on its rights, could only sit and watch. To improve the marketing effectiveness of sponsorship, the Olympic Committee has declared that it will vigorously fight ambush marketing. It has reduced the number of sponsors to avoid clutter.[72]

Containing ambush marketing requires much diligence. For London 2012, online betting company Paddy Power's billboards were the source of the IOC's wrath because of their proclamation that it was the official sponsor of "the largest athletics event in London" that year, which was about an egg-and-spoon race to be held in London, France (as opposed to what some might believe is the London Olympics). In each case, the IOC warned the offending company against employing ambush marketing tactics.[73]

London 2012 Summer Games

Every Olympic Games also presents the opportunity to learn from past successes and mistakes and to run an event that will benefit athletes, spectators, viewers, and sponsors alike. Recognizing the important financial contribution of sponsorship, the London Games were supported by the British government's introduction of extensive anti-ambush legislation. Banned were activities such as sky-writing, flyers, posters, billboards, and projected advertising within 200 meters of any Olympic venue. The government also passed legislation to forbid a variety of words such as "Games," "2012," "Two Thousand and Twelve," and "Twenty Twelve" to be used in combination with words such as, "Gold," "Silver," "Bronze," "London," "Medals," "Sponsor," or "Summer" in an unauthorized manner such that the general public would think there was an association with the London Olympics.[74]

Ticket revenue is also critical to the success of the Olympics, so organizers of the London Games also embarked on a multimillion-dollar advertising campaign, "The Greatest Tickets on Earth," in the hope of raising £500 million from ticket sales. Twelve ads showcased likely Olympic stars, including local favorites gymnast Beth Twiddle and diver Tom Daley. Over half of all tickets to the most popular events, however, were earmarked for corporate sponsors and their employees or guests.[75]

Outside the country, the government also embarked on a "Visit Britain" and "Visit London" promotional campaign to attract tourists. The campaigns set out strategically to emphasize the "timeless," "dynamic," and "genuine" qualities—based on the people, places, and culture—that define the British brand.

City and Country Effects

Another hotly debated Olympics topic is the value of the payback to the host city, region, and country. Bringing an aggressive new sponsorship approach to the Los Angeles Olympics resulted in those Games being a financial success, but other Games since then have been a mixed bag. However, some benefits may be evident for a host country that can be hard to quantify.[76]

One important psychological benefit is civic pride and patriotism for serving as host to such an iconic global sporting event. With a worldwide television audience for two weeks and more, the Games also serve as a huge advertising and public relations opportunity to aid tourism, real estate, and commercial business. The 1992 Barcelona, 2000 Sydney Games, and 2018 PyeongChang Games have enjoyed these broad sets of benefits.

Another often-overlooked benefit is the investment in improving infrastructure that often leads up to hosting the Games. Beijing added new subway lines, highways, an airport to ease transportation, and new parks alongside to add to the scenery, providing some badly needed improvements in transportation and quality of life for residents of the city.

Nevertheless, the financial stakes are high, and only careful planning and execution and the right circumstances can result in success for the Olympics host city, region, and country. The 1976 Montreal and 2004 Athens Games, for example, had a much less positive effect on the host countries. It took Montreal almost 30 years to pay back the $2.7 billion in debt it incurred in hosting the Games.

Summary

Olympic sponsorship remains highly controversial. Many corporate sponsors continue to believe that their Olympic sponsorship yields many significant benefits, creating an image of goodwill for their brand, serving as a platform to enhance awareness and communicate messages, and affording numerous opportunities to reward employees and entertain clients. Others view the Games as overly commercialized, despite the measures undertaken by the IOC and USOC to portray the Olympics as wholesome. In any case, the success of Olympic sponsorship—like that of any sports sponsorship—depends in large part on how well it is executed and incorporated into the entire marketing plan.

NOTES

1. For an examination of lower-level transfer effects, see Claudiu V. Dimofte and Richard F. Yalch, "The Mere Association Effect and Brand Evaluations," *Journal of Consumer Psychology* 21, no. 1 (2011): 24–37.

2. Morgan Williams, "6 Examples of Great Co-Branding," *Altitude Branding*, July 7, 2016, http://altitudebranding.com/6-examples-great-co-branding/.

3. Louise Story, "Can Burt's Bees Turn Clorox Green?," *The New York Times*, January 6, 2008, https://www.nytimes.com/2008/01/06/business/06bees.html, accessed June 20, 2018.

4. Heather Landi, "A-B Gets the Golden Egg," *Beverage World*, April 2011, http://www.nxtbook.com/nxtbooks/idealmedia/bw0411/index.php?startid=8#/8, accessed November 3, 2018.

5. Ab InBev, www.sabmiller.com; "Blue Moon to Raise Awareness through 'Artfully Crafted' Campaign," *The Drum*, June 23, 2011; Brady Walen, "Blue Moon

Artfully Crafted Facebook Photo Contest," June 29, 2011, www.craftedsocialmedia.com; Joseph T. Hallinan, "Craft Beers Have Big Breweries Thinking Small," *The Wall Street Journal*, November 20, 2006, B1, B8.

6. Jeff Smith, "Reputation Winners and Losers: Highlights from Prophet's 2010–2011 U.S. Reputation Study," white paper, March 1, 2011, www.prophet.com.

7. Wai-Kwan Li and Robert S. Wyer Jr., "The Role of Country of Origin in Product Evaluations: Informational and Standard-of-Comparison Effects," *Journal of Consumer Psychology* 3, no. 2 (1994): 187–212.

8. Tülin Erdem, Joffre Swait, and Ana Valenzuela, "Brands as Signals: A Cross-Country Validation Study," *Journal of Marketing* 70, no. 1 (January 2006): 34–49; Yuliya Strizhakova, Robin Coulter, and Linda Price. Branding in a Global Marketplace: The Mediating Effects of Quality and Self-Identity Brand Signals," *International Journal of Research in Marketing* 28, no. 4 (December 2011): 342–351.

9. Karl Greenberg, "Rums of P.R. Effort Promos Brands, Puerto Rico," February 23, 2011, https://www.mediapost.com/publications/article/145540/rums-of-pr-effort-promos-brands-puerto-rico.html, accessed November 3, 2018; Rums of Puerto Rico, "Rums of Puerto Rico Encourages Consumers to 'Just Think, Puerto Rican Rum'," *PR Newswire*, February 23, 2011, https://www.prnewswire.com/news-releases/rums-of-puerto-rico-encourages-consumers-to-just-think-puerto-rican-rum-116757469.html, accessed November 3, 2018.

10. For a broader discussion of "nation branding," see Philip Kotler, Somkid Jatusriptak, and Suvit Maesincee, *The Marketing of Nations: A Strategic Approach to Building National Wealth* (New York: Free Press, 1997); Wally Olins, "Branding the Nation—The Historical Context," *Journal of Brand Management* 9, no. 4 (April 2002): 241–248; and for an interesting analysis in the context of Iceland, see Hlynur Gudjonsson, "Nation Branding," *Place Branding* 1, no. 3 (2005): 283–298.

11. For stimulating and enlightening discussion, see www.strengtheningbrandamerica.com.

12. The Pew Research Center, "Global Public Opinion in the Bush Years (2001–2008)," *Pew Research Center*, December 18, 2008, http://www.pewglobal.org/2008/12/18/global-public-opinion-in-the-bush-years-2001-2008/.

13. John A. Quelch and Katherine E. Jocz, "Can Brand Obama Rescue Brand America?," *Brown Journal of World Affairs* 16, no. 1 (Fall–Winter 2009): 163–178; BBC News, "View of U.S.'s Global Role 'Worse'," January 23, 2007, http://news.bbc.co.uk/2/hi/americas/6286755.stm, accessed November 3, 2018; Alex Y. Vergara, "'Brand America'—How U.S. Tourism Plans to Recover Lost Ground," *Philippine Daily Inquirer*, June 19, 2011; Bill Marriott Jr., "America Needs More Tourists," *Fortune*, June 1, 2011, http://fortune.com/2011/06/01/america-needs-more-tourists/, accessed November 3, 2018.

14. Richard Wike, Bruce Stokes, Jacob Poushter, and Janell Fetterolf, "U.S. Image Suffers as Publics Around World Question Trump's Leadership," *Pew Research* Center, June 26, 2017, www.pewglobal.org/2017/06/26/u-s-image-suffers-as-publics-around-world-question-trumps-leadership/.

15. Zeynep Gurhan-Canli and Durairaj Maheswaran, "Cultural Variations in Country of Origin Effects," *Journal of Marketing Research* 37, no. 3 (August 2000): 309–317.

16. Thomas Mulier, "Clash of the Angry Swiss Watchmakers," *Bloomberg BusinessWeek*, April 28, 2011, https://www.bloomberg.com/news/articles/2011-04-28/clash-of-the-angry-swiss-watchmakers, accessed November 3, 2018.

17. Eric Wilson and Michael Barbaro, "Big Names in Retail Fashion Are Trading Teams," *The New York Times*, March 8, 2008, https://www.nytimes.com/2008/03/08/business/08designers.html, accessed November 3, 2018; Stephanie Rosenbloom, "Liz Claiborne to Be Sold Only at J.C. Penney Stores," *The New York Times*, October 9, 2009, https://www.nytimes.com/2009/10/09/business/09liz.html, accessed November 3, 2018.

18. Robert Passikoff, "Sears Opens Luxury Department Offering Rolex, Chanel, Jimmy Choo, Alaia & Stella McCartney," July 24, 2013, www.forbes.com/sites/robertpassikoff/2013/07/24/sears-opens-luxury-department-offering-rolex-chanel-jimmy-choo-alaia-stella-mccartney/#7efd2566b5cf, accessed November 17, 2017.

19. Akshay R. Rao and Robert W. Ruekert, "Brand Alliances as Signals of Product Quality," *Sloan Management Review* 36, no. 1 (Fall 1994): 87–97; Akshay R. Rao, Lu Qu, and Robert W. Ruekert, "Signaling Unobservable Product Quality through Brand Ally," *Journal of Marketing Research* 36, no. 2 (May 1999): 258–268; Mark B. Houston, "Alliance Partner Reputation as a Signal to the Market: Evidence from Bank Loan Alliances," *Corporate Reputation Review* 5, no. 4 (Winter 2003): 330–342; Henrik Uggla, "The Brand Association Base: A Conceptual Model for Strategically Leveraging Partner Brand Equity," *Journal of Brand Management* 12, no. 2 (November 2004): 105–123.

20. Robin L. Danziger, "Cross Branding with Branded Ingredients: The New Frontier," paper presented at the ARF Fourth Annual Advertising and Promotion Workshop, February 1992.

21. Kim Cleland, "Multimarketer Melange an Increasingly Tasty Option on the Store Shelf," *Advertising Age*, May 2, 1994, https://adage.com/article/news/multimarketer-melange-increasingly-tasty-option-store-shelf/87398/, accessed November 3, 2018.

22. Morgan Williams, "6 Examples of Great Co-Branding," *Altitude Branding*, July 7, 2016, http://altitudebranding.com/6-examples-great-co-branding/.

23. E. J. Schultz, "How Kraft's Lunchables Is Evolving in the Anti-Obesity Era," *Advertising Age*, April 19, 2011, https://adage.com/article/news/kraft-s-lunchables-evolving-anti-obesity-era/227075/, accessed November 3, 2018.

24. Ed Lebar, Phil Buehler, Kevin Lane Keller, Monika Sawicka, et al., "Brand Equity Implications of Joint Branding Programs," *Journal of Advertising Research* 45, no. 4 (2005): 413–425.

25. Nicole L. Votolato and H. Rao Unnava, "Spillover of Negative Information on Brand Alliances," *Journal of Consumer Psychology* 16, no. 2 (2006): 196–202.

26. Ed Lebar, Phil Buehler, Kevin Lane Keller, Monika Sawicka, Zeynep Aksehirli, and Keith Richey, "Brand Equity Implications of Joint Branding Programs," *Journal of Advertising Research* 45, no. 4 (2005): 413–425; Tansev Geylani, J. Jeffrey Inman, and Frenkel Ter Hofstede, "Image Reinforcement or Impairment: The Effects of Co-Branding on Attribute Uncertainty," *Marketing Science*, 27, no. 4 (July–August 2008): 730–744.

27. For general background, see Akshay R. Rao, "Strategic Brand Alliances," *Journal of Brand Management* 5, no. 2 (1997): 111–119; Akshay R. Rao, L. Qu, and Robert W. Ruekert, "Signaling Unobservable Product Quality through a Brand Ally," *Journal of Marketing Research* 36, no. 2 (May 1999): 258–268; Allen D. Shocker, Raj K. Srivastava, and Robert W. Ruekert, "Challenges and Opportunities Facing Brand Management: An Introduction to the Special Issue," *Journal of Marketing Research* 31, no. 2 (May 1994): 149–158; Tom Blackett and Bob Boad, *Co-Branding—The Science of Alliance* (London: Palgrave MacMillan, 1999).

28. Rachel Abramovitz, "Disney Loses its Appetite for Happy Meal Tie-Ins," *LA Times*, May 8, 2006, http://articles.latimes.com/2006/may/08/entertainment/et-mcdonalds8.

29. Philip Kotler and Waldemar Pfoertsch, *Ingredient Branding: Making the Invisible Visible* (New York: Springer, 2010); John Quelch, "How to Brand an Ingredient," October 8, 2007, https://hbr.org/2007/10/how-to-brand-an-ingredient-1, accessed November 3, 2018.

30. Mike May, "What's an Ingredient Brand? Only the Future of Retail," *Magenta*, November 2, 2017, https://magenta.as/whats-an-ingredient-brand-only-the-future-of-retail-4b53eef2ea2e.

31. Gregory S. Carpenter, Rashi Glazer, and Kent Nakamoto, "Meaningful Brands from Meaningless Differentiation: The Dependence on Irrelevant Attributes," *Journal of Marketing Research* 31, no. 3 (August 1994): 339–350. See also Christina Brown and Gregory Carpenter, "Why Is the Trivial Important? A Reasons-Based Account for the Effects of Trivial Attributes on Choice," *Journal of Consumer Research* 26, no. 4 (March 2000): 372–385; Susan M. Broniarczyk and Andrew D. Gershoff, "The Reciprocal Effects of Brand Equity and Trivial Attributes," *Journal of Marketing Research* 41, no. 2 (2003): 161–175.

32. Mike May, "What's an Ingredient Brand? Only the Future of Retail," *Magenta*, November 2, 2017, https://magenta.as/whats-an-ingredient-brand-only-the-future-of-retail-4b53eef2ea2e.

33. Firedrive Marketing Group, "Getting Ingredient Branding Right," *Firedrive Marketing*, www.firedrivemarketing.com/getting-ingredient-branding-right/, accessed December 20, 2017.

34. Marc Graser, "How Chevy's Camaro Changed with the 'Transformers' Franchise," *Variety*, June 26, 2014, http://variety.com/2014/film/news/how-chevy-camaro-changed-with-transformers-franchise-1201242157/.

35. Philip Kotler and Waldemar Pfoertsch, *Ingredient Branding: Making the Invisible Visible* (New York: Springer, 2010); Donald G. Norris, "Ingredient Branding: A Strategy Option with Multiple Beneficiaries," *Journal of Consumer Marketing* 9, no. 3 (1992): 19–31.

36. License! Global, "Top 125 Global Licensors," May 10, 2012, https://www.licenseglobal.com/top-125-global-licensors-0, accessed November 3, 2018; "Disney's 2011 Investor Conference: Disney Consumer Products," *Disney*, accessed February 17, 2011 www.disney.com/investors; Bruce Orwall, "Disney's Magic Transformation?" *The Wall Street Journal*, October 4, 2000.

37. License! Global, "The Top 150 Global Licensors," May 6, 2015, https://www.licenseglobal.com/magazine-article/top-150-global-licensors-1, accessed November 3, 2018.

38. The Walt Disney Company, Fiscal Year 2016 Annual Financial Report, Form 10-K, United States Securities and Exchange Commission.

39. Trefis Team, "Why Have Ralph Lauren's Licensing Revenues Been Declining in Recent Years?," *Forbes*, May 5, 2016, www.forbes.com/sites/greatspeculations/2016/05/05/why-have-ralph-laurens-licensing-revenues-been-declining-in-recent-years/#24f04f317e6a.

40. Teri Agins, "Izod Lacoste Gets Restyled and Repriced," *The Wall Street Journal*, July 22, 1991, B1.

41. Udayan Gupta, "Licensees Learn What's in a Pop-Culture Name: Risk," *The Wall Street Journal*, August 8, 1991, B2.

42. Form 10 K for the year ending December 31, 2017, *Harley-Davidson* http://investor.harley-davidson.com/static-files/98813045-7888-4ad9-8574-8f13991acf26, Accessed June 10, 2018.

43. Cate Doty, "For Celebrities, Ads Made Abroad Shed Some Stigma," *The New York Times*, February 4, 2008, https://www.nytimes.com/2008/02/04/business/media/04japander.html, accessed November 3, 2018;

Dean Crutchfield, "Celebrity Endorsements Still Push Product," *Advertising Age*, September 22, 2010, https://adage.com/article/cmo-strategy/marketing-celebrity-endorsements-push-product/146023/, accessed November 3, 2018.

44. Grant McCracken, "Who Is the Celebrity Endorser? Cultural Foundations of the Endorsement Process," *Journal of Consumer Research* 16, no. 3 (December 1989): 310–321.

45. Sam Dangremond, "How Much Is Oprah Winfrey Actually Worth?," *Town & Country Magazine*, October 16, 2017, www.townandcountrymag.com/society/money-and-power/a12808751/oprah-winfrey-net-worth/.

46. Newswire, "Holland America Line and O, The Oprah Magazine Embark on Exclusive Partnership," *Newswire*, February 9, 2017, www.newswire.ca/news-releases/holland-america-line-and-o-the-oprah-magazine-embark-on-exclusive-partnership-613301673.html.

47. Meg James, "Discovery Buys Majority Stake in OWN from Oprah Winfrey," *LA Times*, December 4, 2017, www.latimes.com/business/hollywood/la-fi-ct-discovery-ups-stake-own-oprah-20171204-story.html.

48. Irina Ivanova, "Oprah's Greatest Product Hits," *Moneywatch*, August 10, 2017, www.cbsnews.com/news/oprah-winfreys-greatest-product-hits/.

49. "Manning's Roster of Endorsements," *USA Today*, November 16, 2006; Curtis Eichelberger, "Colts Victory May Bring Manning $3 Million More in Endorsements," *Bloomberg*, February 5, 2010, www.bloomberg.com.

50. Shekhar Misra and Sharon E. Beatty, "Celebrity Spokesperson and Brand Congruence," *Journal of Business Research* 21, no. 2 (1990): 159–173.

51. Steve McKee, "The Trouble with Celebrity Endorsements," *Bloomberg BusinessWeek*, November 14, 2008, https://www.bloomberg.com/news/articles/2008-11-14/the-trouble-with-celebrity-endorsementsbusinessweek-business-news-stock-market-and-financial-advice, accessed November 3, 2018.

52. Zack O'Malley Greenburg, "The 13 Top-Earning Dead Celebrities of 2015," *Forbes*, October 27, 2015, www.forbes.com/sites/zackomalleygreenburg/2015/10/27/the-13-top-earning-dead-celebrities-of-2015/#ee5210159f72; Jonathan Keehner and Lauren Coleman-Lochner, "In Death, Endorsements Are a Girl's Best Friend," *Bloomberg BusinessWeek*, January 23, 2011; *Brand Week*, "I See Dead People," March 14, 2011, http://archive.commercialalert.org/news/archive/2011/03/i-see-dead-people.

53. John Grossman, "Dave Thomas' Recipe for Success," *Sky*, November 2000, 103–107; Bruce Horvitz, "Wendy's Icon Back at Work," *USA Today*, March 31, 1997, B1–B2.

54. Shekhar Misra and Sharon E. Beatty, "Celebrity Spokesperson and Brand Congruence," *Journal of Business Research* 21, no. 2 (1990): 159–173.

55. David Pierson, "If Jackie Chan Says It's Good—Well, Get a Second Opinion," *Los Angeles Times*, August 23, 2010, http://articles.latimes.com/2010/aug/23/business/la-fi-chan-curse-20100823, accessed November 3, 2018; for a more charitable view of Jackie Chan, see Ron Gluckman, "Kicking It Up for Kids," *Forbes*, July 18, 2011.

56. Sean Deveney, "Kevin Durant Should Rake in Way More Money and Fame with Warriors, Experts Say,"

Sporting News, July 13, 2016, www.sportingnews .com/nba/news/kevin-durant-marketing-value-golden-state-warriors-q-scores-lebron-james-stephen-curry/ 1nlcro7n3kro1dncmmghhn0yt; Dave McMenamin, "23 for 23: Little-Known Facts about LeBron James," *ESPN*, June 4, 2015, www.espn.com/blog/cleveland-cavaliers/post/_/ id/1028/23-for-23-little-known-facts-about-lebron-james.

57. Tom Peters, "A Brand Called You," *Fast Company* 31 (August 1997); Dorie Clark, "Reinventing Your Personal Brand," *Harvard Business Review,* March 2011 Issue, 78–81, https://hbr.org/2011/03/reinventing-your-personal-brand, accessed November 3, 2018.

58. MediaKix, "How Do Instagram Influencers Make Money?," March 2016, http://mediakix.com/2016/03/instagram-influencers-making-money/#gs.G6nEIq0, accessed November 3, 2018; Amanda Pressner Kreuser, "What Influencers Like Michelle Phan and PewDiePie Get Paid," May 26, 2016, https://www.inc.com/amanda-pressner-kreuser/the-pricing-of-fame-what-social-influencers-are-getting-paid.html, accessed November 3, 2018.

59. Clare O'Connor, "Earning Power: Here's How Much Top Influencers Can Make on Instagram and YouTube," *Forbes*, April 10, 2017, https://www.forbes.com/sites/ clareoconnor/2017/04/10/earning-power-heres-how-much-top-influencers-can-make-on-instagram-and-youtube/#3ad16bb224db, accessed November 3, 2018.

60. Matt Roche, "Why Peer-to-Peer Marketing Does More Than Celebrity Endorsements," *Adweek*, August 12, 2016, www.adweek.com/digital/why-peer-to-peer-marketing-does-more-than-celebrity-endorsements/.

61. For general background and in-depth research on a number of sponsorship issues, consult the *Journal of Sponsorship*, a Henry Stewart publication.

62. Michael Sussman, "Brands: How to Score with Sports Sponsorships," *Ad Age*, September 29, 2015, http://adage.com/article/agency-viewpoint/ score-sports-sponsorships/300524/.

63. Ibid.

64. Erin Beresini, "Tough Mudder Partners with Merrell," *Outside*, November 19, 2015. www.outsideonline .com/2036086/tough-mudder-partners-merrell.

65. David Kiley, "World's Best Vodka? It's Anybody's Guess," *Bloomberg BusinessWeek* May 23, 2008, https:// www.bloomberg.com/news/articles/2008-05-23/worlds-best-vodka-its-anybodys-guessbusinessweek-business-news-stock-market-and-financial-advice, accessed November 3, 2018; Adweek Staff, "Vodka," July 1, 2010, https://www.adweek.com/brand-marketing/vodka-106876/, accessed November 3, 2018; BusinessWire, "Grey Goose Vodka Continues to Soar in the U.S. Despite the Economy," *Reuters,* April 6, 2009, https:// www.businesswire.com/news/home/20090406005489/ en/GREY-GOOSE%C2%AE-Vodka-Continues-Soar-U.S.-Economy, accessed November 3, 2018.

66. International Olympic Committee, "The Olympic Partner Programme," https://www.olympic.org/sponsors, accessed November 3, 2018; Ira Boudway, "Olympic Sponsorships Are About to Get More Expensive," *Bloomberg*, September 28, 2007, https://www .bloomberg.com/news/articles/2017-09-28/olympic-sponsorships-are-about-to-get-a-lot-more-expensive.

67. Olympic.org, "P&G Launches "Thank You, Mom" Campaign for Rio 2016," April 27, 2016, accessed December 22, 2017, www.olympic.org/news/p-g-launches-thank-you-mom-campaign-for-rio-2016.

68. The International Olympic Committee, "IOC and GE Extend Partnership to 2020," June 29, 2011, https://www.olympic .org/news/ioc-and-ge-extend-partnership-to-2020.

69. Frederik Balfour and Reena Jana, "Are Olympic Sponsorships Worth It?," *Bloomberg BusinessWeek*, July 31, 2008; Ed Kemp, "Kodak to End 100-Year Olympic Sponsorship Tie," Campaign US, October 17, 2007, https://www.campaignlive.com/article/ kodak-end-100-year-olympic-sponsorship-tie/745530.

70. Dec Saif Gangjee, "How the IOC Ruthlessly Protects the Olympics Brand," *The New Republic*, August 5, 2016, https://newrepublic.com/article/135847/ioc-ruthlessly-protects-olympics-brand; David Wolf, "Let the Ambush Games Begin," *Advertising Age*, August 11, 2008.

71. John Grady, Steve McKelvey, and Matthew J. Bernthal, "From Beijing 2008 to London 2012: Examining Event-Specific Olympic Legislation Vis-à-Vis the Rights and Interests of Stakeholders," *Journal of Sponsorship* 3, no. 2 (February 2010): 144–156;

72. Nicholas Burton and Simon Chadwick, "Ambush Marketing in Sport: An Analysis of Sponsorship Protection Means and Counter-Ambush Measures," *Journal of Sponsorship* 2, no. 4 (September 2009): 303–315.

73. Marina Palomba, "Ambush Marketing and the Olympics 2012," *Journal of Sponsorship* 4, no. 3 (June 2011): 245–252; Dana Ellis, Marie-Eve Gauthier, and Benoit Séguin, "Ambush Marketing, the Olympic and Paralympic Marks Act and Canadian Sports Organisations: Awareness, Perceptions and Impacts," *Journal of Sponsorship* 4, no. 3 (June 2011): 253–271.

74. Kirsten D. Toft, "UK: Ambush Marketing and the London Olympics 2012," August 24, 2009, http://www.mondaq .com/uk/x/84874/Trademark/Ambush+Marketing+And +The+London+Olympics+2012, accessed November 3, 2018; Jacquelin Magnay, "London 2012 Olympics: Government Unveils Plans to Ban Ambush Marketing and Bolster Games Security," *Telegraph*, March 7, 2011; Akshata Rangarajan, "Ambush Marketing & the London Olympics, Slingshot Sponsorship, February 14, 2011, https:// www.slingshotsponsorship.com/ambush-marketing-the-london-olympics/, accessed November 3, 2018.

75. "Olympic Advertising Aims to Sell £500m in Tickets," *Marketing News*, March 21, 2011; Sam Greenhill, "The Freebie Olympics: Corporate Fat Cats Get More Than Half of Top Games Tickets," *Daily Mail*, June 3, 2011, https://www.dailymail.co.uk/news/article-1394064/ London-2012-Olympics-Corporate-fat-cats-half-Games-tickets.html, accessed November 3, 2018; Visit Britain, www.visitbritain.org.

76. Room for Debate: A New York Times Blog, "Do Olympic Host Cities Ever Win?" October 2, 2009, https:// roomfordebate.blogs.nytimes.com/2009/10/02/do-olympic-host-cities-ever-win/, accessed November 3, 2018; PricewaterhouseCoopers, "The Economic Impact of the Olympic Games," *Pricewaterhouse Coopers European Economic Outlook*, June 2004, http://www.pages.drexel.edu/~rosenl/sports%20Folder/ Economic%20Impact%20of%20Olympics%20PWC .pdf, accessed November 3, 2018; H. Preuss (2004), "The Economics of Staging the Olympics: A Comparison of the Games 1972–2008," London: Edward Elgar.

Developing a Brand Equity Measurement and Management System

9

Learning Objectives

After reading this chapter, you should be able to

1. Describe the new accountability in terms of ROMI (Return on Marketing Investment)

2. Create an understanding of analytics dashboards as a tool for monitoring performance and the implications of brand investments

3. Outline the two main steps in conducting a brand audit and how to execute a digital marketing review

4. Describe how to design, conduct, and interpret a tracking study

5. Identify the steps in implementing a brand equity management system.

Marketing analytics dashboards are key tools for tracking a brand's metrics and provide a way for managers to evaluate the effectiveness of their marketing expenditures.

PREVIEW

The previous eight chapters, which made up Parts II and III of the text, described various strategies and approaches to building brand equity. In the next three chapters, which make up Part IV, we take a detailed look at what consumers know and feel about and act toward brands, and how marketers can develop measurement procedures to assess how well their brands are doing.

The customer-based brand equity (CBBE) concept provides guidance about how we can measure brand equity. Given that customer-based brand equity is the differential effect that knowledge about the brand has on customer response to the marketing of that brand, two basic approaches to measuring brand equity present themselves. An *indirect approach* can assess potential sources of customer-based brand equity by identifying and tracking consumers' brand knowledge—all the thoughts, feelings, images, perceptions, and beliefs linked to the brand. A *direct approach*, on the other hand, can assess the actual impact of brand knowledge on consumers' response to different aspects of the marketing program.

The two approaches are complementary, and marketers can and should use both. In other words, for brand equity to provide a useful strategic function and guide marketing decisions, marketers must fully understand the sources of brand equity, how they affect outcomes of interest such as sales, and how these sources and outcomes change, if at all, over time. Chapter 3 provided a framework for conceptualizing consumers' brand knowledge structures. Chapter 10 uses this information and reviews research methods to measure sources of brand equity and the customer mind-set. Chapter 11 reviews research methods to measure outcomes—that is, the various benefits that may result from creating these sources of brand equity.

Before we get into specifics of measurement, this chapter offers some big-picture perspectives of how to think about brand equity measurement and management. Specifically, we will consider how to develop and implement a brand equity measurement system. A *brand equity measurement system* is a set of research procedures designed to provide marketers with timely, accurate, and actionable information about brands, so they can make the best possible tactical decisions in the short run and strategic decisions in the long run. The goal is to achieve a full understanding of the sources and outcomes of brand equity and to be able to relate the two as much as possible.

The ideal brand equity measurement system would provide complete, up-to-date, and relevant information about the brand and its competitors to the right decision makers at the right time within the organization. After providing some context about the heightened need for marketing accountability, we will look in detail at three steps toward achieving that ideal—conducting brand audits, designing brand tracking studies, and establishing a brand equity management system.

THE NEW ACCOUNTABILITY

Although senior managers at many firms have embraced the marketing concept and the importance of brands, they often struggle with questions such as: How strong is our brand? How can we ensure that our marketing activities create value? How do we measure that value?

Virtually every marketing dollar spent today must be justified as both effective and efficient in terms of *return on marketing investment (ROMI)*.[1] This increased accountability has forced marketers to address tough challenges and develop new measurement approaches.

Complicating matters is that, depending on the particular industry or category, some observers believe up to 70 percent (or even more) of marketing expenditures may be devoted to programs and activities that improve brand equity but cannot be linked to short-term incremental profits.[2] Measuring the long-term value of marketing in terms of both its full short-term and long-term impact on consumers is thus crucial for accurately assessing return on investment.

This tension between demonstrating short-term profitability versus investing in long-term value has been exacerbated by the digital economy, with an emphasis on strong long-term customer relationships and networks, rather than immediate profitability. A recent Forbes Marketing Accountability Initiative highlights that many digital companies such as Waze, LinkedIn, Tumblr, and Airbnb are worth billions of dollars in terms of intangible value derived from their strong customer relationships.[3]

Given this shift, marketers need new tools and procedures that clarify and justify the value of their expenditures, beyond ROMI measures tied to short-term changes in sales. In Chapter 3, we introduced the brand resonance model and brand value chain, a structured means to understand how consumers build strong bonds with brands and how marketers can assess the success of their branding efforts. In the remainder of this chapter, we offer several additional concepts and perspectives to help in that pursuit.

CONDUCTING BRAND AUDITS

To learn how consumers think, feel, and act toward brands and products so the company can make informed strategic positioning decisions, marketers should first conduct a brand audit. A *brand audit* is a comprehensive examination of a brand to discover its sources of brand equity. In accounting, an audit is a systematic inspection by an outside firm of accounting records including analyses, tests, and confirmations.[4] The outcome is an assessment of the firm's financial health in the form of a report.

A similar concept has been suggested for marketing. A *marketing audit* is a "comprehensive, systematic, independent, and periodic examination of a company's—or business unit's—marketing environment, objectives, strategies, and activities with a view of determining problem areas and opportunities and recommending a plan of action to improve the company's marketing performance."[5] The process is a three-step procedure in which the first step is agreement on objectives, scope, and approach; the second is data collection; and the third and final step is report preparation and presentation. This is an internally, company-focused exercise to make sure marketing operations are efficient and effective.

On the other hand, a *brand audit* is a more externally, consumer-focused exercise to assess the health of the brand, uncover its sources of brand equity, and suggest ways to improve and leverage its equity. A brand audit requires understanding the sources of brand equity from the perspective of both the firm and the consumer. From the perspective of the firm, what products and services are currently being offered to consumers, and how are they being marketed and branded? From the perspective of the consumer, what deeply held perceptions and beliefs create the true meaning of brands and products?

The brand audit can set strategic direction for the brand, and management should conduct one whenever important shifts in strategic direction are likely.[6] Are the current sources of brand equity satisfactory? Do certain brand associations need to be added, subtracted, or just strengthened? What brand opportunities exist, and what potential challenges exist for brand equity? With answers to these questions, management can put a marketing program into place to maximize sales and long-term brand equity.

Conducting brand audits on a regular basis, such as during the annual planning cycle, allows marketers to keep their fingers on the pulse of their brands. Brand audits are thus particularly useful background for managers as they set up their marketing plans and can have profound implications on brands' strategic direction and resulting performance. Consider Domino's Pizza.

DOMINO'S PIZZA

In late 2009, Domino's was a struggling business in a declining market. Pizza sales were slumping as consumers defected to healthier and fresher dining options at one end or to less expensive burger or sandwich options at the other end. Caught in the middle, Domino's also found its heritage in "speed" and "best in delivery" becoming less important; even worse, it was undermining consumer's perceptions of the brand's taste, the number-one driver of choice in the pizza category. To address the problem, Domino's decided to conduct a detailed brand audit with extensive qualitative and quantitative research. Surveys, focus groups, intercept interviews, social media conversations, and ethnographic research generated a number of key insights. The taste problem was severe—some consumers bluntly said that Domino's tasted more like the box than the pizza. Research also revealed that consumers felt betrayed by a company they felt they no longer knew. A focus on impersonal, efficient service meant that in consumers' minds, there was no Domino's kitchens, no chefs, not even ingredients. Consumers were skeptical of "new and improved" claims and felt companies never admitted they were wrong. Based on these and other insights, Domino's began its brand comeback. Step one—new recipes for crust, sauce, and cheese that resulted in substantially better taste-test scores. Next, Domino's decided not to run from criticism and launched the "Oh Yes We Did" campaign. Using traditional TV and print media and extensive online components, the company made clear that it had listened and responded by creating a better pizza. Documentary-type filming showed Domino's CEO and other executives observing the original consumer research and describing how they took it to heart. Surprise visits were made to harsh critics from the focus groups, who tried the new pizza on camera and enthusiastically praised it. Domino's authentic, genuine approach paid off, with the company doubling its revenue and increasing its stock price by 5,000 percent over the next 8 years.[7]

More recently, Domino's Pizza has reinforced its brand identity through an innovative social media and digital marketing activation strategy. Many of these campaigns have been developed and fine-tuned over time through a process of testing and learning, and observing reactions to various types of activations. For example, a new digital marketing campaign uses face-swapping technology and images to show the joy of a Domino's pizza arriving. Domino's also used Snapchat lenses to let users imitate the TV ad by "boggling" their mouth to show their reactions to a pizza. Overall, Domino's investments in analytics and social media listening have yielded additional rich insights that have helped it improve its appeal to its target audience.[8]

A thorough, insightful brand audit helped to convince Domino's they needed to confront their own perceived flaws head on.
Source: Domino's Pizza LLC

The brand audit consists of two steps: the brand inventory and the brand exploratory. We'll discuss each in turn. Brand Focus 9.0 illustrates a sample brand audit using the Rolex brand as an example.

Brand Inventory

The purpose of the ***brand inventory*** is to provide a current, comprehensive profile of how all the products and services sold by a company are marketed and branded. Profiling each product or service requires marketers to catalogue the following in both visual and written form for each product or service sold: the names, logos, symbols, characters, packaging, slogans, or other trademarks used; the inherent product attributes or characteristics of the brand; the pricing, communications, and distribution policies; and any other relevant marketing activity related to the brand.

Often firms set up a "war room" where all the various marketing activities and programs can be displayed or accessed. Visual and verbal information help to provide a clearer picture. Figure 9-1 shows a wall that software pioneer Red Hat created of all its various ads, brochures, and other marketing materials. Managers were pleasantly surprised when they saw how consistent all the various items were in form, look, and content, although they were left scratching their heads as to why the Red Hat office in Australia had created branded underwear as a promotional gift. Needless to say, the "tighty whities" were dropped after being deemed off-brand.[9]

With the advent of digital marketing and social media, conducting an inventory of digital brand assets has become an important task in the context of conducting a brand inventory. Digital brand assets may consist of all assets pertaining to a brand including images, audio, video, etc., which are deployed online. The digital brand asset inventory may also include various types of content that are linked to a brand including custom YouTube videos, white papers, blog posts, sponsored content, customer guides, licensed news articles, and even musings on social media channels.[10] The burgeoning number of social media channels implies that brand marketers should pay special attention to maintaining the consistency of look and feel of a brand across digital and social media channels.

FIGURE 9-1
Red Hat Brand Wall
Source: Photo courtesy of
Red Hat, Inc.

A digital inventory of brand assets may provide four types of useful insights: (1) Outdated brand accounts that have fallen into disuse, and perhaps need to be closed or updated; (2) Overlapping brand assets which can be merged or deleted, to ensure a more streamlined set of assets; (3) Existing brand accounts with information that is either inaccurate or not up-to-date. For example, brand logos may feature outdated colors or design, which may need to be updated; (4) Particular digital and social media channels where the brand does not have a presence—this could be a starting point for reworking the strategy going forward.

The outcome of the brand inventory—both online and offline—should be an accurate, comprehensive, and up-to-date profile of how all the products and services are branded in terms of which brand elements are employed and how, and the nature of the supporting marketing program. Marketers should also profile competitive brands in as much detail as possible to determine points-of-parity and points-of-difference.

Rationale.   The brand inventory is a valuable first step for several reasons. First, it helps to suggest what consumers' current perceptions may be based on. Consumer associations are typically rooted in the intended meaning of the brand elements attached to them—but not always. The brand inventory, therefore, provides useful information for interpreting follow-up research such as the brand exploratory we discuss next.

Although the brand inventory is primarily a descriptive exercise, it can supply some useful analysis, too, and initial insights into how brand equity may be better managed. For example, marketers can assess the consistency of all the different products or services sharing a brand name. This assessment should also extend to a brand's digital asset inventory. Are the different brand elements used on a consistent basis, or are there many different versions of the brand name, logo, and so forth for the same product—perhaps for no obvious reason—depending on which geographic market it is being sold in, which market segment it is being targeted to, and so forth? Are there consistencies in colors and fonts in online marketing pertaining to the brand? Similarly, are the supporting marketing programs logical and consistent across related brands?

As firms expand their products geographically and extend them into other categories, deviations—sometimes significant in nature—commonly emerge in brand appearance and marketing. A thorough brand inventory should be able to reveal the extent of brand consistency. At the same time, a brand inventory can reveal a lack of perceived differences among various products sharing the brand name—for example, as a result of line extensions—that are designed to differ on one or more key dimensions. Creating sub-brands with distinct positions is often a marketing priority, and a brand inventory may help to uncover undesirable redundancy and overlap that could lead to consumer confusion or retailer resistance.

Brand Exploratory

Although the supply-side view revealed by the brand inventory is useful, actual consumer perceptions, of course, may not necessarily reflect those the marketer intended. Thus, the second step of the brand audit is to provide detailed information about what consumers actually think of the brand by means of the **brand exploratory**. The brand exploratory is research directed to understanding what consumers think and feel about the brand and act toward it in order to better understand sources of brand equity, as well as any possible barriers.

Preliminary Activities. Several preliminary activities are useful for the brand exploratory. First, a number of prior research studies may exist and be relevant. It is important to dig through company archives to uncover reports that may have been buried, and perhaps even long forgotten, but that contain insights and answers to a number of important questions or suggest new questions that may still need to be posed.

Second, it is also useful to interview internal personnel to gain an understanding of their beliefs about consumer perceptions for the brand and competitive brands. Past and current marketing managers may be able to share some wisdom not necessarily captured in prior research reports. The diversity of opinion that typically emerges from these internal interviews serves several functions, increasing the likelihood that useful insights or ideas will be generated, as well as pointing out any inconsistencies or misconceptions that may exist internally for the brand.

Although these preliminary activities are useful, additional research is often required to better understand how customers shop for and use different brands and what they think and feel about them. To allow marketers to cover a broad range of issues and to pursue some in greater depth, the brand exploratory often employs qualitative research techniques as a first step, as summarized in Figure 9-2, followed by more focused and definitive survey-based quantitative research.

Interpreting Qualitative Research. There are a wide variety of qualitative research techniques. Marketers must carefully consider which ones to employ.

.Criteria. Levy identifies three criteria by which we can classify and judge any qualitative research technique: direction, depth, and diversity.[11] For example, any projective research technique varies in terms of the nature of the stimulus information (is it related to the person or the brand?), the extent to which responses are superficial and concrete as opposed to deeper and more abstract (and requiring more interpretation), and the way the information relates to information gathered by other projective techniques.

In Figure 9-2, the tasks at the top of the left-hand list ask very specific questions whose answers may be easier to interpret. The tasks on the bottom of the list ask questions that are much richer but also harder to interpret. Tasks on the top of the right-hand list are elaborate exercises that consumers undertake themselves and that may be either specific or broadly directed. Tasks at the bottom of the right-hand list consist of direct observation of consumers as they engage in various behaviors.

According to Levy, the more specific the question, the narrower the range of information given by the respondent. When the stimulus information in the question is open-ended and responses are freer or less constrained, the respondent tends to give more information. The more abstract and symbolic the research technique, however, the more important it is to follow up with probes and other questions that explicitly reveal the motivation and reasons behind consumers' responses.

Free association	Day/Behavior reconstruction
Adjective ratings and checklists	Photo/Written journal
Confessional interviews	Participatory design
Projective techniques	Consumer-led problem solving
Photo sorts	Real-life experimenting
Archetypal research	Collaging and drawing
Bubble drawings	Consumer shadowing
Story telling	Consumer–product interaction
Personification exercises	Video observation
Role playing	
Metaphor elicitation*	

*ZMET trademark

FIGURE 9-2
Summary of Qualitative Techniques

Ideally, qualitative research conducted as part of the brand exploratory should vary in direction and depth as well as in technique. The challenge is to provide accurate interpretation—going beyond what consumers explicitly state to determine what they implicitly mean. Chapter 10 reviews how to best conduct qualitative research.

Mental Maps and Core Brand Associations.   One useful outcome of qualitative research is a mental map. A ***mental map*** accurately portrays in detail all salient brand associations and responses for a particular target market. One of the simplest means to get consumers to create a mental map is to ask them for their top-of-mind brand associations ("When you think of this brand, what comes to mind?"). The brand resonance pyramid from Chapter 3 helps to highlight some of the types of associations and responses that may emerge from the creation of a mental map.

It is sometimes useful to group brand associations into related categories with descriptive labels. ***Core brand associations*** are those abstract associations (attributes and benefits) that characterize the 5 to 10 most important aspects or dimensions of a brand. They can serve as the basis of brand positioning in terms of how they create points-of-parity and points-of-difference. For example, in response to a Nike brand probe, consumers may list athletes featured in Nike ads such as LeBron James or Serena Williams, whom we could call "top athletes." The challenge is to include all relevant associations while making sure each is as distinct as possible. Figure 9-3 displays a hypothetical mental map and some core brand associations that were created as part of a brand analysis for Music Television (MTV) at one time.

A related methodology, brand concept maps (BCM), elicits brand association networks (brand maps) from consumers and aggregates individual maps into a consensus map.[12] This approach structures the brand elicitation stage of identifying brand associations by providing survey respondents with a set of brand associations used in the mapping stage. The mapping stage is also structured and has respondents use the provided set of brand associations to build an individual brand map that shows how brand associations are linked to each other and to the brand, as well as how strong these linkages are. Finally, the aggregation stage is also structured and analyzes individual brand maps step by step, uncovering the common thinking involved. Figure 9-4 displays a brand concept map for the Mayo Clinic (the subject of Branding Brief 9-3) provided by a sample of patients.

One goal from qualitative, as well as quantitative, research in the brand exploratory is a clear, comprehensive profile of the target market. As part of that process, many firms are literally creating personas to capture their views as to the target market, as summarized in The Science of Branding 9-1.

Conducting Quantitative Research.   Qualitative research is suggestive, but a more definitive assessment of the depth and breadth of brand awareness, and the strength, favorability, and uniqueness of brand associations often requires a quantitative phase of research.

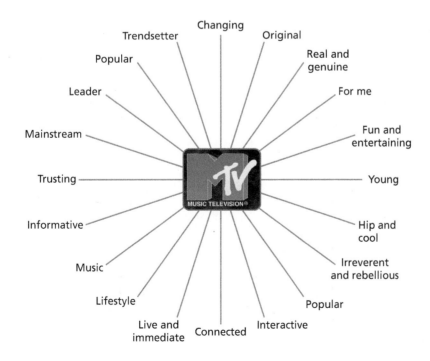

FIGURE 9-3A

Classic MTV Mental Map

Source: MTV logo, MCT/Newscom

Music
What's hot and what's new

Community
Shared experience
(literally and talk value)

Credibility
Expert, trusting,
reality

Modern
Hip, cool

Personality
Irreverent, hip, cool

Spontaneity
Up-to the-minute,
immediate

Accessibility
Relevant, for
everyone

Originality
Genuine, creative

Interactivity
Connected and
participatory

Fluidity
Always changing and evolving

FIGURE 9-3B

Possible MTV Core
Brand Associations

The guidelines for the quantitative phase of the exploratory are relatively straightforward. Marketers should attempt to assess all potentially salient associations identified by the qualitative research phase according to their strength, favorability, and uniqueness. They should examine both specific brand beliefs and overall attitudes and behaviors to reveal potential sources and outcomes of brand equity. And they should assess the depth and breadth of brand awareness by employing various cues. Typically, marketers will also need to conduct similar types of research for competitors to better understand their sources of brand equity and how they compare with the target brand.

Much of the above discussion of qualitative and quantitative measures has concentrated on associations to the brand name—for example, what do consumers think about the brand when given its name as a probe? Marketers should study other brand elements in the brand exploratory as well, because they may trigger other meanings and facets of the brand.

For example, we can ask consumers what inferences they make about the brand on the basis of the product packaging, logo, or other attribute alone, such as, "What would you think about the brand just on the basis of its packaging?" We can explore specific aspects of the brand elements—for instance, the label on the package or the shape of the package itself—to uncover their role in creating brand associations and thus, sources of brand equity. We should also determine which of these elements most effectively represents and symbolizes the brand as a whole.

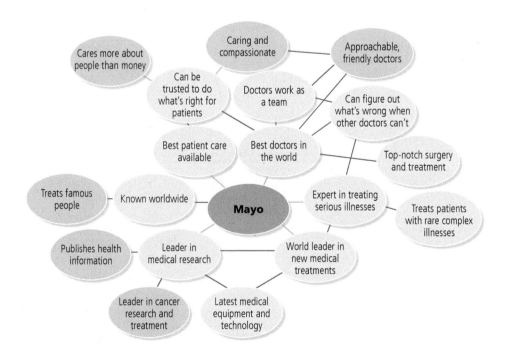

FIGURE 9-4

Sample Mayo Clinic
Brand Concept Map

Digital Marketing Reviews. With the growing importance of digital marketing, a formal digital marketing review can provide important input to a brand audit which could help generate useful insights regarding a brand's online presence. A digital marketing review offers the following benefits:[13]

A brand exploratory can uncover important information about various brand elements, including how a brand's packaging is perceived by consumers.

1. It can highlight whether a brand's digital efforts are received in online channels, relative to competitors.
2. It can help unlock important customer-level insights as well as industry trends, which is made possible due to in-depth analysis of online conversations surrounding a brand. This can be useful in developing a better picture of brand image and brand personality, as it pertains to digital channels.
3. It can provide useful input to brand strategy development and, by providing rich customer insights, the crafting or refinement of the brand positioning.
4. It can act as a health check of a brand's digital marketing and social media strategy, and allow brand managers to introduce course correction measures if the online strategy is seen as inconsistent with the brand's overall strategy.

Ongoing social media conversations can be successfully mined to generate granular insights about topics and themes that are connected with a brand. One way of summarizing the information obtained from a digital marketing review is to focus on the 5 Cs related to brand conversations that surround the brand in various digital channels: (1) conversation channel; (2) conversation source; (3) conversation content; (4) channel-specific engagement; (5) context. Table 9-1 provides more details of each of these.[14]

TABLE 9-1 5 Cs of Online Brand Conversations

Characteristic of Online Brand Conversations	Definition
Conversation channel	A digital review should spotlight *where* the conversation surrounding the brand is taking place (e.g., Facebook, Instagram, Twitter, or YouTube).
Conversation source	A digital review can highlight *who* the source for the conversation is, whether it is consumers, competitors, or third parties/influencers.
Conversation content	Marketers are also using digital reviews to learn about the content of conversations surrounding a brand. Social media content can be both verbal as well as visual, and can be summarized in various ways, including (1) sentiment (positive versus negative); (2) volume of conversation, which can indicate the number of mentions; and (3) topics or themes can be extracted from social media conversations. Word clouds can be useful in summarizing verbal content; the sizes of words in a word cloud typically describe how important they are (larger words in a word cloud are more frequently mentioned), and the colors of the word cloud can be coded to depict positive or negative sentiment. Visual content can be summarized by describing key features, such as images that are typically associated with a brand, as well as content and themes that are typically featured in these images.
Channel-specific engagement	Brand engagement refers to actions taken by consumers, as a response to posts or conversations surrounding a brand, and a digital review can summarize the extent to which a brand elicits engagement (or actions) across different types of channels. For example, the number of Facebook Likes for a brand can help summarize the popularity of a brand on Facebook. Or, number of views on YouTube for a video about the brand can be indicative of consumer engagement with the brand on YouTube. In this way, a summary of engagement metrics for various digital channels can help spotlight the extent of consumer engagement.
Context	The information that has been generated above can be further refined by providing two types of contextual information: (1) how the themes and sentiment for a given brand compare to key competitors; and (2) how the nature of conversations has shifted over time.

Analyzing social media conversations surrounding a brand and tracking these over time offers managers important insights into customers' ongoing thoughts and feelings regarding a brand.

One important outcome of the analysis of these social media conversations is a better understanding of the associations held by consumers toward the brand. As we described in Chapter 7, researchers have shown how brand positioning maps can be constructed by applying natural language processing and machine learning techniques to data on social media conversations surrounding a brand. There are several key benefits associated with this approach, over more traditional survey-based approaches, as social media data costs less to collect and can be more timely. Further, social media data consists of voluntary posts by consumers; therefore, it overcomes typical biases that accompany survey responses obtained from consumers.

On the flip side, brand positioning derived from social media data may only represent a segment of consumers who tend to engage with a brand online; thus, it is more suitable only for those categories where offline consumption is limited. Additionally, social media posting behavior may be driven by consumers' motivations to impress others or project a certain image; therefore, brand posts may reflect such a bias. Despite this, drawing positioning maps based on social media data represents a good way of supplementing data obtained from other (more traditional) approaches.

In summary, a digital marketing review can help shine a light into the mind of the consumer, thus acting as a tool for market research. By tracking brand perceptions over time, periodic digital reviews can help strengthen brand audits. In turn, these insights generated can help managers become more responsive to marketplace trends.

Brand Positioning and the Supporting Marketing Program

Regardless of whether data is derived from social media or traditional survey-based approaches, the brand exploratory is meant to uncover the current knowledge structures for the core brand and its competitors, as well as determining the desired brand awareness and brand image and points-of-parity and points-of-difference. Moving from the current brand image to the desired brand image typically means adding new associations, strengthening existing ones, or weakening or eliminating undesirable ones in the minds of consumers according to the guidelines outlined in Chapter 2.

John Roberts, one of Australia's top marketing academics, sees the challenge in achieving the ideal positioning for a brand as being able to achieve congruence among four key considerations: (1) what customers currently believe about the brand (and find credible), (2) what customers will value in the brand, (3) what the firm is currently saying about the brand, and (4) where the firm would like to take the brand (see Figure 9-5).[15] Because each of the four considerations may suggest or reflect different approaches to positioning, finding a positioning that balances the four considerations as much as possible is key.

A number of different internal management personnel can be part of the planning and positioning process, including brand, marketing research, and production managers, as can relevant outside marketing partners like the marketing research suppliers and ad agency team. Once marketers have a good understanding from the brand audit of current brand knowledge structures for their target consumers and have decided on the desired brand knowledge structures for optimal positioning, they may still want to do additional research testing alternative tactical programs to achieve that positioning.

FIGURE 9-5

John Roberts's
Brand Positioning
Considerations

Source: Used with permission of John Roberts, ANU College of Business and Economics, The Australian National University.

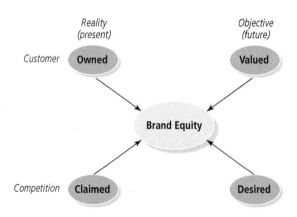

THE SCIENCE OF BRANDING 9-1
The Role of Brand Personas

To crystalize all the information and insights they have gained about their target market(s), researchers can employ personas. **Personas** are detailed profiles of one, or perhaps a few, target market consumers. They are often defined in terms of demographic, psychographic, geographic, or other descriptive attitudinal or behavioral information. Researchers may use photos, images, names, or short bios to help convey the particulars of the persona.

The rationale behind personas is to provide exemplars or archetypes of how the target customer looks, acts, and feels that are as true-to-life as possible, to ensure marketers within the organization fully understand and appreciate their target market and therefore, incorporate a nuanced target customer point of view in all their marketing decision-making. Personas are fundamentally designed to bring the target consumer to life.

A good brand persona can guide several marketing activities. For example, many brands have embraced the idea of buyer personas in developing targeted campaigns. Zipcar's buyer persona revolves primarily around millennial urban dwellers. Zipcar's advertising tone and language is aimed at the millennial world traveler as shown in the tweet using the Twitter handle #WorthTheTrip.

In addition to developing a single communications campaign based on buyer personas, another use of personas is to guide the development of multiple personalized communications that is tailored to different buyer personas. Personas can help focus the personalization efforts by helping drive content creation and content delivery. Analytical tools such as Facebook Insights can help provide detailed descriptions of target audiences including their age, gender, and location (country, city, etc.). Further, different media usage habits of varying buyer personas can dictate the use of different types of online and offline communication channels for delivering advertising and communications.

Although personas can provide a very detailed and accessible perspective on the target market, it can come at a cost. Overly focusing on a narrow slice of the target market can lead to

Buyer personas allow marketers to personalize offers to customers based on typical buying habits and media usage habits.

oversimplification and erroneous assumptions about how the target market as a whole thinks, feels, or acts. The more heterogeneity in the target market, the more problematic the use of personas can be. To overcome the potential problem of overgeneralization, some firms are creating varying levels of personas, such as primary (target consumer), secondary (target consumer with differing needs, targets, goals), and negative (false stereotypes of users).

Sources: Allen P. Adamson, *Brand Digital: Simple Ways Top Brands Succeed in the Digital Age* (New York: Palgrave-MacMillan, 2008); Lisa Sanders, "Major Marketers Get Wise to the Power of Assigning Personas," *Advertising Age*, April 9, 2007, 36; Stephen Herskovitz and Malcolm Crystal, "The Essential Brand Persona: Storytelling and Branding," *Journal of Business Strategy* 31, no. 3 (2010): 21. For additional information on storytelling, see Edward Wachtman and Sheree Johnson, "Discover Your Persuasive Story," *Marketing Management* (March/April 2009): 22–27; Heidi Cohen, "Social Media Personas: What You Need to Know," May 29, 2012, https://heidicohen.com/social-media-personas-what-you-need-to-know/, accessed November 22, 2017.

Zipcar used personas to guide the development of personalized communications that were tailored to different personas.

DESIGNING BRAND TRACKING STUDIES

Brand audits are a means to provide in-depth information and insights essential for setting long-term strategic direction for the brand. But to gather information for short-term tactical decisions, marketers will typically collect less detailed brand-related information through ongoing tracking studies.

Brand tracking studies collect information from consumers on a routine basis over time, usually through quantitative measures of brand performance on a number of key dimensions that marketers can identify in the brand audit or other means. They apply components from the brand value chain to better understand where, how much, and in what ways brand value is being created, offering invaluable information about how well the brand has achieved its positioning.

As more marketing activity surrounds the brand—as the firm introduces brand extensions or incorporates an increasing variety of communication options in support of the brand—it becomes difficult and expensive to research each one. Regardless of how few or how many changes are made in the marketing program over time, marketers need to monitor the health of the brand and its equity, so they can make adjustments if necessary.

Tracking studies thus play an important role by providing consistent baseline information to facilitate day-to-day decision-making. A good tracking system can help marketers better understand a host of important considerations such as category dynamics, consumer behavior, competitive vulnerabilities and opportunities, and marketing effectiveness and efficiency.

What to Track

Chapter 3 provided a detailed list of potential measures that correspond to the brand resonance model, which are candidates for tracking. It is usually necessary to customize tracking surveys, however, to address the specific issues faced by the brand or brands in question. Each brand faces a unique situation that the different types of questions in its tracking survey should reflect.

Product–Brand Tracking.   Tracking an individual branded product requires measuring brand awareness and image, using both recall and recognition measures and moving from more general to more specific questions. Thus, it may make sense to first ask consumers what brands come to mind in certain situations, to next ask for recall of brands on the basis of various product category cues, and to then finish with tests of brand recognition (if necessary).

Moving from general to more specific measures is also a good idea in brand tracking surveys to measure brand image, especially specific perceptions like what consumers think characterizes the brand, and evaluations such as what the brand means to consumers. A number of specific brand associations typically exist for the brand, depending on the richness of consumer knowledge structures, which marketers can track over time.

Given that brands often compete at the augmented product level (see Chapter 1), it is important to measure all associations that may distinguish competing brands. Thus, measures of specific, lower-level brand associations should include all potential sources of brand equity such as performance and imagery attributes and functional and emotional benefits. Benefit associations often represent key points-of-parity or points-of-difference, so it is particularly important to track them as well. Marketers may also want to measure the attribute beliefs that underlie those benefit beliefs to better understand any changes in benefit beliefs for a brand. In other words, changes in descriptive attribute beliefs may help to explain changes in more evaluative benefit beliefs for a brand.

Marketers should assess those key brand associations that make up the potential sources of brand equity on the basis of strength, favorability, and uniqueness *in that order.* Unless associations are strong enough for consumers to recall them, their favorability does not matter, and unless they are favorable enough to influence consumers' decisions, their uniqueness does not matter. Ideally, marketers will collect measures of all three dimensions, but perhaps for only certain associations and only some of the time; for example, favorability and uniqueness may be measured only once a year for three to five key associations.

At the same time, marketers will track more general, higher-level judgments, feelings, and other outcome-related measures. After soliciting their overall opinions, consumers can be asked whether they have changed their attitudes or behavior in recent weeks or months and, if so, why. Branding Brief 9-1 provides an illustrative example of a simple tracking survey for Starbucks.

BRANDING BRIEF 9-1

Sample Brand Tracking Survey

Assume Starbucks is interested in designing a short online tracking survey. How might you set it up? Although there are a number of different types of questions, your tracking survey might take the following form.

Introduction: We're conducting a short online survey to gather consumer opinions about quick-service or coffeehouse chains.

Brand Awareness and Usage

a. What brands of coffeehouse chains are you aware of?

b. At which coffeehouse chains would you consider visiting?

c. Have you visited a coffeehouse chain in the last week? Which ones?

d. If you were to visit a coffeehouse tomorrow, which one would you go to?

e. What are your favorite coffeehouse chains?

We want to ask you some general questions about a particular coffeehouse chain, Starbucks.

Have you heard of this brand? [Establish familiarity.]

Have you ever visited a Starbucks coffeehouse? [Establish trial.]

When I say Starbucks, what are the first associations that come to your mind? Anything else? [List all.]

Brand Judgments

a. We're interested in your overall opinion of Starbucks.

b. How favorable is your attitude toward Starbucks?

c. How well does Starbucks satisfy your needs?

d. How likely would you be to recommend Starbucks to others?

e. How good a value is Starbucks?

f. Is Starbucks worth a premium price?

g. What do you like best about Starbucks? Least?

h. What is most unique about Starbucks?

i. To what extent does Starbucks offer advantages that other similar types of coffeehouses cannot?

j. To what extent is Starbucks superior to other brands in the coffeehouse category?

k. Compared to other brands in the coffeehouse category, how well does Starbucks satisfy your basic needs?

We now want to ask you some questions about Starbucks as a company. Please indicate your agreement with the following statements.

Starbucks Is . . .

a. Innovative

b. Knowledgeable

c. Trustworthy

d. Likable

e. Concerned about their customers

Starbucks uses brand tracking surveys to gather consumer opinions on a periodic basis.

f. Concerned about society as a whole

g. Likable

h. Admirable

Brand Performance

a. We now would like to ask some specific questions about Starbucks. Please indicate your agreement with the following statements.

Starbucks . . .

a. Is convenient to visit for coffee

b. Provides quick, efficient service

c. Has clean facilities

d. Is ideal for the whole family

e. Has delicious coffee

f. Has tasty snacks

g. Has a varied menu

h. Has friendly, courteous staff

i. Offers fun promotions

j. Has a stylish and attractive look and design

k. Has high-quality food

l. Has baristas who prepare excellent coffee

Brand Imagery

a. To what extent do people you admire and respect visit a Starbucks?

b. How much do you like people who frequently visit Starbucks?

c. How well do each of the following words describe Starbucks? Down-to-earth, honest, daring, up-to-date, reliable, successful, upper class, charming, outdoorsy

d. Is Starbucks a coffeehouse chain that you can visit at a variety of different times of the day?

e. To what extent does thinking of Starbucks bring back pleasant memories?

f. To what extent do you feel that you grew up with Starbucks?

Brand Feelings

Does Starbucks give you a feeling of . . .

a. Warmth?

b. Fun?

c. Excitement?

d. Security or confidence?

e. Social approval?

f. Self-respect?

Brand Resonance

a. I consider myself loyal to Starbucks.

b. I buy Starbucks whenever I can.

c. I would go out of my way to visit a Starbucks.

d. I really love Starbucks.

e. I would really miss Starbucks if it went away.

f. Starbucks is special to me.

g. Starbucks is more than a product to me.

h. I really identify with people who go to Starbucks.

i. I feel a deep connection with Starbucks as a company.

j. I really like to talk about Starbucks to others.

k. I am always interested in learning more about Starbucks.

l. I would be interested in merchandise with the Starbucks name on it.

m. I am proud to have others know that I eat at Starbucks.

n. I like to visit the Starbucks Web site.

o. Compared to other people, I follow news about Starbucks closely.

Corporate or Family Brand Tracking.   Marketers may also want to track the corporate or family brand separately or concurrently (or both) with individual products. Besides the measures of corporate credibility we identified in Chapter 2, you can consider other measures of corporate brand associations including the following (illustrated with the Nike corporate brand):

- How well managed is Nike?
- How easy is it to do business with Nike?
- How concerned is Nike with its customers?
- How approachable is Nike?
- How accessible is Nike?
- How much do you like doing business with Nike?
- How likely are you to invest in Nike stock?
- How would you feel if a good friend accepted employment with Nike?

The actual questions should reflect the level and nature of experience your respondents are likely to have had with the company.

When a brand is identified with multiple products, as in a corporate or family branding strategy, one important issue is which particular products the brand reminds consumers of. At the same time, marketers also want to know which particular products are most influential in affecting consumer perceptions about the brand.

To identify these more influential products, ask consumers which products they associate with the brand on an unaided basis ("What products come to mind when you think of the Nike brand?") or an aided basis by listing sub-brand names ("Are you aware of Nike's basketball shoes? Nike Air Max running shoes?"). To better understand the dynamics between the brand and its corresponding products, also ask consumers about their relationship between them ("There are many different products associated with Nike. Which ones are most important to you in formulating your opinion about the brand?").

Assessing the brand image of a corporate brand like Nike may involve understanding which products are associated with the brand.

Economic Indicators
Gross domestic product
Interest rates
Unemployment
Average wage
Disposable income
Home ownership and
  housing debt
Exchange rates, share markets,
  and balance of payments

Retail
Total spent in supermarkets
Change year to year
Growth in house brand

Technology
Computer at home
DVR
Access to and use of Internet
Phones
PDA
Microwaves
Television

Personal Attitudes and Values
Confidence
Security
Family
Environment
Traditional values
Foreigners vs. sovereignty

Media Indicators
Media consumption: total time
  spent watching TV, consuming
  other media
Advertising expenditure: total, by
  media and by product category

Demographic Profile
Population profile: age, sex, income,
  household size
Geographic distribution
Ethnic and cultural profile

Other Products and Services
Transport: own car—how many
Best description of car
Motorbike
Home ownership or renting
Domestic trips overnight in last year
International trips in last two years

Attitude to Brands and Shopping
Buy on price
Like to buy new things
Country of origin or manufacture
Prefer to buy things that have been
  advertised
Importance of familiar brands

FIGURE 9-6
Brand Context Measures

Global Tracking.   If your tracking covers diverse geographic markets—especially in both developing and developed countries—then you may need a broader set of background measures to put the brand development in those markets in the right perspective. You would not need to collect them frequently, but they could provide useful explanatory information (see Figure 9-6 for some representative measures).

BIG DATA AND MARKETING ANALYTICS DASHBOARDS

With the growth of mobile payments, and the rise of networks of data-gathering sensors, there is a sudden availability of troves of data which can enable continuous tracking of customers. For example, MillerCoors previously did not have direct access to consumer-level data, as it traditionally sold its products to licensed merchants. However, with mobile payments, it became possible for MillerCoors to directly track a shopper moving from bar to restaurant to Costco to Target, and then stopping at a convenience store. This capability provides the company with effective ways of optimizing their marketing or communication strategy in real time.

Social media data has also been a source of data that facilitates this trend toward continuous tracking. In fact, McDonald's decision to move to all-day breakfast was based on analysis of Twitter data, which showed that millennials were complaining that breakfast at McDonald's

Brands like MillerCoors can track shoppers who use mobile payments as they move from a bar to a restaurant to a convenience store.

was not available after 10:30 am. By swiftly moving to offer an all-day breakfast menu, McDonald's scored a big hit with millennials—78 percent of them said they visited a McDonald's restaurant at least once a month or more in the quarter following their move to an all-day breakfast.[16]

Marketing Analytics Dashboards

As companies grapple with the tremendous increase in data availability, they are finding significant benefits to investing in data analytics systems and processes within the organization, as well as marketing analytic dashboards, which can communicate important metrics and make them available throughout the organization. Nearly 27 percent of companies are currently using marketing analytics dashboards for improving their branding strategy.[17] In fact, one report suggested that brands planned to increase spending on analytics dashboards in 2015–2017 by 73 percent.[18] The same report highlighted that more than a billion dollars have been invested in data analytics in this time period, with a growth in the number of marketing tech companies to almost 2,000.

Against this backdrop, we describe the benefits of analytic dashboards as a valuable tool to help in decision-making. Different from standard tracking tools, these analytic dashboards provide ways of linking different types of marketing expenditures to outcome variables such as profits. Marketing analytic dashboards can help answer four types of questions: What happened? Why did it happen? What will happen if? What should happen?[19] Stated differently, questions such as the ones listed below can be addressed using marketing analytics:

- What is the likely impact of a 15 percent increase in our social media expenditure next year?
- What is the return-on-investment of influencer marketing programs? Why is the ROI of one campaign higher than another?
- What is the relative impact of offline versus online marketing expenditures on sales revenue growth in the past three years? What will happen if we shift the budget to spend more money in online than offline channels next year?

Answers to questions such as the ones outlined above can help allow companies to align their brand health with financial returns, leading to improved metrics as well as learning.[20]

The impact of such dashboards on corporate profitability can be profound; one study suggested that an increase in use of marketing analytic dashboards contributed to an 8 percent increase in return-on-assets.[21] Another study showed that adding marketing analytics to a single new department can result in a .35 percent increase in profitability.[22]

However, one challenge with the use of marketing analytics within organizations is that of communication. Only 10 percent of respondents in a survey believed that they were communicating and activating insights (rather than generating insights). In situations when companies did communicate insights to the right end-users within the organization, significant benefits accrued. The case study on Taco Bell in Branding Brief 9-2 below describes how the company utilized its mobile app to generate insights about customers.

BRANDING BRIEF 9-2

How Taco Bell Uses Data-Driven Social Media Marketing to Engage Its Customers

One of the best examples of using analytics to drive social media strategy is with Taco Bell. In fact, Taco Bell is frequently listed as a top social media strategist, based on overall social and digital performance within the restaurant sector. Taco Bell launched its mobile app in 2015, and within a few months was receiving nearly 75 percent of its orders via the app. The mobile strategy was based on a beta test in which Taco Bell added a number of features based on feedback received from the testing phase of the mobile app. Another key to its success is the integration of mobile with other parts of the marketing campaign including television spots, and promotions offered within its restaurants.

By using data analytics, Taco Bell has been able to identify brands which resonate well with their target audiences. In doing so, Taco Bell has been able to develop their social media strategy by engaging with big brands on Twitter and striking up conversations with these brands and their social media handles (see the figure for examples of Taco Bell and Netflix).

Taco Bell has also leveraged data analytics to improve its location-based mobile targeting. For example, the brand

Netflix US @netflix · May 21
Sorry @TacoBell , but Bruiser's a vegetarian. #tbt #LegallyBlonde and #LegallyBlonde2 pic.twitter.com/tOW5711Zca

128   454

Taco Bell @tacobell · May 22
@netflix Vegetarian options are endless at Taco Bell.

143   503

Netflix US @netflix · May 22
@tacobell Perfect. Bruiser will take a veggie cantina burrito, Elle Woods style. pic.twitter.com/qCV19fezcx

119   397

Taco Bell ✅
@tacobell

Following

@netflix So, Taco Bell and Netflix date tonight?

RETWEETS	FAVORITES
321	542

4:31 PM - 22 May 2015

Taco Bell and Netflix Tweet at Each Other

Sources: Amy Gesenhues, "A CMO's View: Taco Bell's Chris Brandt Makes Mobile a Priority and It Has Paid Off with Nearly 2M App Downloads," *Marketing Land*, January 21, 2015, https://marketingland.com/cmos-view-taco-bells-chris-brandt-talks-mobile-114988, accessed November 21, 2017; http://rsmindex.com/brand-rank.

recently conducted a campaign meant to raise money for a college scholarship program. The campaign leveraged geolocation data to both target consumers near its locations, and also gauge which audiences (based on location) were reacting favorably. This "Location for Good" campaign encouraged recipients of the personalized mobile ad to visit a local Taco Bell and purchase a Doritos Locos Taco. A portion of these proceeds were to be donated to a scholarship fund. The success of this campaign allowed the restaurant chain to donate $500,000 to a scholarship fund meant for students whose interests fell outside traditional athletic or academic categories. Another innovative twist to Taco Bell's mobile strategy was to partner with the ride-hailing company Lyft and create a setting in its mobile app called "Taco mode," allowing passengers to stop at a Taco Bell restaurant drive-through during the ride. This resulted in an 8 percent increase in customer weekend visits, following the campaign.

Recently, Taco Bell has utilized its data-driven approach to tackle employee turnover at its company. Using statistical analysis along with employee-generated insights, Taco Bell was able to reduce its employee turnover. Overall, Taco Bell's recent campaigns have demonstrated the value of adopting analytics and data-driven strategies, to optimize various corporate goals ranging from reducing employee turnover to maximizing brand campaign performance.

Sources: Amy Gesenhues, "A CMO's View: Taco Bell's Chris Brandt Makes Mobile a Priority and It Has Paid Off with Nearly 2M App Downloads," *Marketing Land*, January 21, 2015, https://marketingland.com/cmos-view-taco-bells-chris-brandt-talks-mobile-114988, accessed November 21, 2017; Restaurant Social Media Index, http://rsmindex.com/brand-rank, accessed November 7, 2018; Genevieve Douglas, "Taco Bell Tackles Turnover Through Data Analytics," *Bloomberg BNA*, May 16, 2017, https://www.bna.com/taco-bell-tackles-m73014451006/, accessed November 21, 2017; Robert Williams, "Taco Bell Boosts Store Traffic with Location-Based Mobile Targeting," *Mobile Marketer*, www.mobilemarketer.com/news/taco-bell-boosts-store-traffic-with-location-based-mobile-targeting/506103/, accessed November 21, 2017; Mark Ritson, "Brand Tracking: Try It and You'll Never Look Back," *Marketing Week*, February 5, 2014, www.marketingweek.com/2014/02/05/brand-tracking-try-it-and-youll-never-look-back/; WARC, "Samsung Taps Power of 'True Insights,'" November 6, 2017, www.warc.com/newsandopinion/news/samsung_taps_power_of_%E2%80%98true_insights/39554, accessed November 20, 2017; Geoffrey Precourt, "How MillerCoors Connects in an Explosive Marketing EcoSystem," *Warc*, www.warc.com/content/article/A103223_How_MillerCoors_connects_in_an_explosive_marketing_ecosystem/103223, accessed 20 November 2017.

ESTABLISHING A BRAND EQUITY MANAGEMENT SYSTEM

Brand tracking studies, as well as brand audits, can provide a huge reservoir of information about how best to build and measure brand equity. To get the most value from these research efforts, firms need proper internal structures and procedures to capitalize on the usefulness of the brand equity concept and the information they collect about it. Although a brand equity measurement system does not ensure that managers will always make good decisions about the brand, it should increase the likelihood they do, and, if nothing else, decrease the likelihood of bad decisions.

Embracing the concept of branding and brand equity, many firms constantly review how they can best factor it into the organization. Interestingly, perhaps one of the biggest threats to brand equity comes from *within* the organization, and the fact that too many marketing managers remain on the job for only a limited period of time. As a result of these short-term assignments, marketing managers may adopt a short-term perspective, leading to an over-reliance on quick-fix sales-generating tactics such as line and category extensions, sales promotions, and so forth. Because these managers lack an understanding and appreciation of the brand equity concept, some critics maintain, they are essentially running the brand "without a license."

To counteract these and other potential forces within an organization that may lead to ineffective long-term management of brands, as we noted in Chapter 2, many firms have made internal branding a top priority. As part of these efforts, they must put a brand equity management system into place. A **brand equity management system** is a set of organizational processes designed to improve the understanding and use of the brand equity concept within a firm. Three major steps help to implement a brand equity management system: creating brand charters or bibles, assembling brand equity reports, and defining brand equity responsibilities. The following subsections discuss each of these steps. Branding Brief 9-3 describes how the Mayo Clinic developed its brand equity measurement and management system.

BRANDING BRIEF 9-3

Understanding and Managing the Mayo Clinic Brand

Mayo Clinic was founded in the late 1800s by Dr. William Worral Mayo and his two sons, who later pioneered the "group practice of medicine" by inviting other physicians to work with them in Rochester, Minnesota. The Mayos believed that "two heads are better than one, and three are even better." From this beginning on the frontier, Mayo Clinic grew to be a worldwide leader in patient care, research, and education and became renowned for its world-class specialty care and medical research. In addition to the original facilities in Rochester, Mayo later built clinics in Jacksonville, Florida, and Scottsdale, Arizona, during the 1980s. More than 500,000 patients are cared for in Mayo's inpatient and outpatient practice annually.

In 1996, Mayo undertook its first brand equity study and since then has conducted regular, national qualitative and quantitative studies. Mayo Clinic has eight values which epitomize its corporate mission, including respect, compassion, integrity, healing, teamwork, excellence, innovation, and stewardship. The commitment to these values has allowed Mayo Clinic to become one of the most trusted hospital brands in the world. Although some of these values also characterize other high-quality medical centers, teamwork or integration and integrity are more nearly unique to Mayo.

In terms of teamwork or integration, respondents described Mayo as bringing together a wealth of resources to provide the best possible care. They perceived Mayo to be efficient, orga-nized, harmonious, and creating a sense of participation and partnership. For example, one person described Mayo as "A well conducted symphony . . . works harmoniously . . . One person can't do it alone . . . Teamwork, cooperation, compatibility." For integrity, respondents placed great value on the fact that Mayo is noncommercial and committed to health and healing over profit. One participant said, "The business element is taken out of Mayo . . . Their ethics are higher . . . which gives me greater faith in their diagnosis."

Although none of Mayo Clinic's brand attributes are solely negative, perceptions of exclusivity pose some specific challenges. This attribute was sometimes described positively, in perceptions that Mayo offers the highest quality care and elite doctors, but inaccurate beliefs that it serves only the rich and famous and the sickest of the sick were emotionally distancing and made Mayo appear to be inaccessible.

As these comments suggest, however, one of the main rea-sons that Mayo Clinic has been successful is how they treat all their patients. To build their brand, Mayo Clinic keeps the focus on their patients, even if it does not make sense from a financial standpoint. This relentless focus on the patient and on quality is seen throughout the organization, from the heart surgeon down to the cleaning staff. Not only does the Mayo Clinic speak to their patients and keep them at the heart of every decision, they also keep track of patients through their recent alliance with United Health Group called Optum, which created an open innovation center to support data-driven research on important health care issues. A data-driven approach to technology allows Mayo Clinic to keep track of health care outcomes and costs.[23]

Another key to Mayo's success is integration across prac-tice, education and research. Much of their 600-million-dollar research budget is funded by the National Institutes of Health. Their researchers work closely with physicians to understand the key issues. The patient-centric model of research allows Mayo clinic to integrate discovery-based research, translational research, and clinical outcomes research, with a focus on creating solutions or treatment for patients.

In order to better serve its patient, Mayo Clinic reengineered their process for caring for those with chronic kidney disease. They utilized a variety of patient metrics such as hospitalization rate, patient satisfaction, etc., to measure progress. Further, they segmented their patients into eight groups based on their behav-iors, needs, goals, motivations, and expectations. By understand-ing how these patient types differed in terms of factors such as their health status, psychological factors, and values, Mayo Clinic was able to generate novel insights into patient decision-making, which, in turn, allowed them to develop a new approach. This new approach to patient management is credited with reducing hospital stay by 1,000 days between 2011 and 2013. The perso-nas that they developed helped them identify gaps in their service delivery to patients.[24]

The above showcases just one approach that Mayo Clinic utilizes in understanding its patients. Another way in which they aim to proactively improve the patient experience is through the Patient Experience Subcommittee (PES), which is an in-house resource to provide Mayo Clinic staff with feedback on the patient experience. This committee is credited with ensuring that the voice of the Mayo patient is heard throughout the organiza-tion, and has been instrumental in creating a service-focused cul-ture through various educational classes and consultations with departments, health care providers, and care teams. The Patient

Mayo Clinic knows the importance and value of its brand and carefully monitors and manages its image and equity.
Source: Used by permission of Mayo Foundation for Medical Education and Research. All rights reserved.

Experience Subcommittee (PES) has pioneered service improve-ment projects within Mayo Clinic that help manage the patient journey across Mayo Clinic.

Another key to Mayo Clinic's success is their investment in digital marketing, which is now nearly two-thirds of their budget. According to John Weston, Mayo Clinic's CMO, digital market-ing allows healthcare organizations to meet consumers where they are. One example of how they leverage digital marketing is their ability to connect patients with useful content. By using their extensive library of online content, Mayo Clinic can deliver relevant content that patients can readily access. By allowing patients to conduct their online research via one of their doctor-approved articles, Mayo establishes a bond with its patients as a trustworthy brand.[25]

Mayo Clinic also utilizes social media to promote health edu-cation and literacy. This allows Mayo Clinic to provide informa-tion to consumers on health care questions that arise, thereby allowing them to gain access to information.[26] Mayo Clinic's YouTube channel has 1.75 million followers on Twitter and more than 1,000,000 Facebook followers. Mayo also offers blogs and podcasts surrounding different types of diseases to offer support to their patients and updated information based on the latest scientific evidence. Additionally, *Sharing Mayo Clinic* is a blog which allows patients and employees to tell stories about their Mayo Clinic experience.

Mayo Clinic's brand strength is evident in the percentage of patients who are loyal to the brand, and willing to refer the brand to others. Ninety-five percent of Mayo Clinic patients indicated that they would recommend and praise the clinic to others, and that each speaks to more than 40 people. By converting patients into evangelists for the brand, Mayo Clinic has found an alternative to traditional advertising—its patients do the advertising.[27]

From its research, Mayo Clinic understands that its brand "is precious and powerful." Mayo realized that, while it had an overwhelmingly positive image, it was vital to develop guidelines to protect the brand. In 1999, the clinic created a brand management infrastructure to be the "institutional clearinghouse for ongoing knowledge about external perceptions of Mayo Clinic and its related activities." Mayo Clinic also established guidelines for applying the brand to products and services. Its brand management measures work to ensure that the clinic preserves its brand equity, as well as allowing Mayo to continue to accomplish its mission: "To inspire hope and contribute to health and well-being by providing the best care to every patient through integrated clinical practice, education and research."

Sources: Thanks to Mayo Clinic's John La Forgia, Kent Seltman, Scott Swanson, and Amy Davis for assistance and cooperation, including interviews in October 2011; The Mayo Clinic, www.mayoclinic.org; "Mayo Clinic Brand Management," internal document, 1999; Leonard L. Berry and Neeli Bendapudi, "Clueing in Customers," *Harvard Business Review* 81, no. 2 (February 2003): 100–106; Paul Roberts, "The Agenda—Total Teamwork," *Fast Company*, April 1999, 148; Leonard L. Berry and Kent D. Seltman, *Management Lessons from Mayo Clinic: Inside One of the World's Most Admired Service Organizations* (New York: McGraw Hill, 2008); Max Nisen, "Mayo Clinic CEO: Here's Why We've Been The Leading Brand in Medicine for 100 Years," *Business Insider*, February 23, 2013, www.businessinsider.com/how-mayo-clinic-became-the-best-brand-in-medicine-2013-2, accessed November 12, 2017; Sandhya Pruthi, Dawn Marie R. Davis, Dawn L. Hucke, Francesca B. Ripple, Barbara S. Tatzel, James A. Dilling, Paula J. Santrach, Jeffrey W. Bolton, and John H. Noseworthy, "Vision, Mission, and Values: From Concept to Execution at Mayo Clinic," *Patient Experience Journal* 2, no. 2 (2015): 169–173; Bloom Creative, "5 Key Things That Make Mayo Clinic a Marketing Machine," July 11, 2016, http://bloomcreative.com/5-key-things-that-make-mayo-clinic-a-marketing-machine/, accessed November 12, 2016; Joan Justice, "The Big Brand Theory: How the Mayo Clinic Became the Gold Standard for Social Media in Healthcare," May 21, 2013, www.socialmediatoday.com/content/big-brand-theory-how-mayo-clinic-became-gold-standard-social-media-healthcare, accessed November 12, 2017; Mark Schaefer, "Lessons from a Horrible Social Media Strategy," May 20, 2012, www.businessesgrow.com/2012/05/20/lessons-from-a-horrible-social-media-strategy/, accessed November 12, 2017; Leonard L. Berry and Kent D. Seltman, "Building a Strong Services Brand: Lessons from Mayo Clinic." *Business Horizons* 50 (3) (2007): 199–209.

Brand Charter or Bible

The first step in establishing a brand equity management system is to formalize the company view of brand equity into a document, the ***brand charter***, or brand bible as it is sometimes called, that provides relevant guidelines to marketing managers within the company as well as to key marketing partners outside the company such as marketing research suppliers or ad agency staff. This document should crisply and concisely do the following:

Define the firm's view of branding and brand equity and explain why it is important.

Describe the scope of key brands in terms of associated products and the manner by which they have been branded and marketed (as revealed by historical company records as well as the most recent brand audit).

Specify what the actual and desired equity is for brands at all relevant levels of the brand hierarchy, for example, at both the corporate and the individual product level (as outlined in Chapter 12). The charter should define and clarify points-of-parity, points-of-difference, and the brand mantra.

- Explain how brand equity is measured in terms of the tracking study and the resulting brand equity report (described shortly).
- Suggest how marketers should manage brands with some general strategic guidelines, stressing clarity, consistency, and innovation in marketing thinking over time.
- Outline how to devise marketing programs along specific tactical guidelines, satisfying differentiation, relevance, integration, value, and excellence criteria. Guidelines for specific brand management tasks such as advertising campaign evaluation and brand name selection may also be offered.
- Specify the proper treatment of the brand in terms of trademark usage, design considerations, packaging, and communications. As these types of instructions can be long and detailed, it is often better to create a separate brand or corporate identity style manual or guide to address these more mechanical considerations
- Although parts of the brand charter may not change from year to year, the firm should nevertheless update it on an annual basis to provide decision makers with a current brand profile and to identify new opportunities and potential risks for the brand. As marketers introduce new products, change brand programs, and conduct other marketing initiatives, they should reflect these adequately in the brand charter. Many of the in-depth insights that emerge from brand audits also belong in the charter.

Skype's brand bible provides important guidelines about how the brand should look and behave.
Source: Skype

Skype's brand bible, for example, outlines the branding and image of its products and services.[28] The document clearly states how Skype wants to be viewed by consumers, how the firm uses its branding to achieve that, and why this is important. It also explains how Skype's logo of clouds and the vivid blue color are designed to make clean lines and foster a creative and simple look. The brand bible explains the "dos and don'ts" of marketing Skype's products and services and the dangers for the company image of working outside the brand guidelines.

Brand Equity Report

The second step in establishing a successful brand equity management system is to assemble the results of the tracking survey and other relevant performance measures for the brand into a brand equity report or scorecard to be distributed to management on a regular basis (weekly, monthly, quarterly, or annually). Recall how "analytic dashboards" were described above as a way of combining brand metrics with overall performance metrics. Much of the information relevant to the brand equity report can be derived from such analytic dashboards. The brand equity report attempts to summarize the contents of analytic dashboard information, with a view to aid decision-making.[29]

Contents.   The brand equity report should describe *what* is happening with the brand as well as *why* it is happening. It should include all relevant internal measures of operational efficiency and effectiveness and external measures of brand performance and sources and outcomes of brand equity.[30]

In particular, one section of the report should summarize consumers' perceptions of key attribute or benefit associations, preferences, and reported behavior as revealed by the tracking study. Another section of the report should include more descriptive market-level information such as the following:

• Product shipments and movement through channels of distribution
• Retail category trends
• Relevant cost breakdowns
• Price and discount schedules where appropriate
• Sales and market share information broken down by relevant factors (such as geographic region, type of retail account, or customer)
• Profit assessments

These measures can provide insight into the market performance component of the brand value chain. Management can compare them to various frames of reference—performance last month, quarter, or year—and color code them green, yellow, or red, depending on whether the trends are positive, neutral, or negative, respectively. Internal measures might focus on how much time, money, and labor was being spent on various marketing activities.[31]

Brand Equity Responsibilities

To develop a brand equity management system that will maximize long-term brand equity, managers must clearly define organizational responsibilities and processes with respect to the brand. Brands need constant, consistent nurturing to grow. Weak brands often suffer from a lack of discipline, commitment, and investment in brand building. In this section, we consider internal issues of assigning responsibilities and duties for properly managing brand equity, as well as external issues related to the proper roles of marketing partners. The Science of Branding 9-2 describes some important principles in building a brand-driven organization.

THE SCIENCE OF BRANDING 9-2
Maximizing Internal Branding

Internal branding doesn't always receive as much time, money, or effort as external branding programs receive. But although it may require significant resources, it generates a number of benefits. Internal branding creates a positive and more productive work environment. It can also be a platform for change and help foster an organization's identity. For example, KPMG's "Purpose Program" launched in 2014, which asked employees to provide entries addressing the "meaning" that their job provided to them. The company received nearly 42,000 entries via its employee intranet, with staff creating posters that included a personal testimonial relaying the "meaning" they derived from their job including "I advance science" to "I help farms grow." The program was a success, and the company went on to have its most profitable year in its 118-year history.

Branding expert Scott Davis offers a number of insights into what it takes to make a brand-driven organization. According to Davis, for employees to become passionate brand advocates, they must understand what a brand is, how it is built, what their organization's brand stands for, and what their role is in delivering on the brand promise. Formally, he sees the process of helping an organization's employees assimilate the brand as three stages:

1. *Hear it:* How do we best get it into their hands?
2. *Believe it:* How do we best get it into their heads?
3. *Live it:* How do we best get it into their hearts?

Davis also argues that six key principles should guide the brand assimilation process within an organization, offering the following examples.

1. *Make the brand relevant.* Each employee must understand and embrace the brand meaning. Nordstrom, whose brand relies on top-notch customer service, empowers sales associates to approve exchanges without manager approval.

2. *Make the brand accessible.* Employees must know where they can get brand knowledge and answers to their brand-related questions. Ernst & Young launched "The Branding Zone" on its intranet to provide employees easy access to information about its branding, marketing, and advertising programs.

3. *Reinforce the brand continuously.* Management must reinforce the brand meaning with employees beyond the initial rollout of an internal branding program. Southwest Airlines continually reinforces its brand promise of "a symbol

Southwest Airlines demonstrates how important it is to strengthen your internal brand as it has a positive impact on subsequent customer service.

of freedom" through ongoing programs and activities with a freedom theme.

4. *Make brand education an ongoing program.* Provide new employees with inspiring and informative training. Ritz-Carlton ensures that each employee participates in an intensive orientation called "The Gold Standard" that includes principles to improve service delivery and maximize guest satisfaction.

5. *Reward on-brand behaviors.* An incentive system to reward employees for exceptional support of the brand strategy should coincide with the roll-out of an internal branding program. Prior to its merger with United, Continental Airlines rewarded employees with cash bonuses each month that the airline ranked in the top five of on-time airlines.

6. *Align hiring practices.* Human resources and marketing must work together to develop criteria and screening procedures to ensure that new hires are good fits for the company's brand culture. Pret A Manger sandwich shops has such a carefully honed screener that only 20 percent of applicants end up being hired.

Davis also emphasizes the role of senior management in driving internal branding, noting that the CEO ultimately sets the tone and compliance with a brand-based culture and determines whether proper resources and procedures are put into place.

Sources: Scott M. Davis, *Building the Brand-Driven Business: Operationalize Your Brand to Drive Profitable Growth* (San Francisco, CA: Jossey-Bass, 2002); Scott M. Davis, "Building a Brand-Driven Organization," in *Kellogg on Branding*, eds. Alice M. Tybout and Tim Calkins (Hoboken, NJ: John Wiley & Sons, 2005); Scott M. Davis, *The Shift: The Transformation of Today's Marketers into Tomorrow's Growth Leaders* (San Francisco, CA: Jossey-Bass, 2009); Becki Hall, "5 Ways to Build Your Internal Branding Strategy," June 23, 2016, www.interact-intranet.com/5-ways-build-internal-branding-strategy/, accessed November 25, 2016.

Overseeing Brand Equity. To provide central coordination, the firm should establish a position responsible for overseeing the implementation of the brand charter and brand equity reports, to ensure that product and marketing actions across divisions and geographic boundaries reflect their spirit as closely as possible and maximize the long-term equity of the brand. A natural place to house such oversight duties and responsibilities is in a corporate marketing group that has a senior management reporting relationship.

Scott Bedbury, who helped direct the Nike and Starbucks brands during some of their most successful years, is emphatic about the need for "top-down brand leadership."[32] He advocates the addition of a chief brand officer (CBO) who reports directly to the CEO of the company and who:

- *Is an omnipresent conscience whose job is to champion and protect the brand—the way it looks and feels—both inside and outside the company.* The CBO recognizes that the brand is the sum total of everything a company does and strives to ensure that all employees understand the brand and its values, creating "brand disciples" in the process.
- *Is an architect and not only helps build the brand but also plans, anticipates, researches, probes, listens, and informs.* Working with senior leadership, the CBO helps envision not just what works best for the brand today but also what can help drive it forward in the future.
- *Determines and protects the voice of the brand over time by taking a long-term (two to three years) perspective.* The CBO can be accountable for brand-critical and corporate-wide activities such as advertising, positioning, corporate design, corporate communications, and consumer or market insights.

Bedbury also advocates periodic brand development reviews (full-day meetings quarterly, or even half-day meetings monthly) for brands in difficult circumstances. As part of a brand development review, he suggests the following topics and activities:[33]

- *Review brand-sensitive material:* For example, review brand strength monitors or tracking studies, brand audits, and focus groups, as well as less formal personal observations or "gut feelings."
- *Review the status of key brand initiatives:* Because brand initiatives include strategic thrusts to either strengthen a weakness in the brand or exploit an opportunity to grow the brand in a new direction, customer perceptions may change, and marketers therefore need to assess them.
- *Review brand-sensitive projects:* For example, evaluate advertising campaigns, corporate communications, sales meeting agendas, and important human resources programs (recruitment, training, and retention that profoundly affect the organization's ability to embrace and project brand values).
- *Review new product and distribution strategies with respect to core brand values:* For example, evaluate licensing the brand to penetrate new markets, forming joint ventures to develop new products or brands, and expanding distribution to nontraditional platforms such as large-scale discount retailers.
- *Resolve brand positioning conflicts:* Identify and resolve any inconsistencies in positioning across channels, business units, or markets.

Even strong brands need careful watching to prevent managers from assuming that it is acceptable to "make one little mistake" with brand equity or to "let it slide." A number of top companies like Colgate-Palmolive, Canada Dry, Quaker Oats, Pillsbury, Coca-Cola, and Nestlé Foods have created brand equity gatekeepers for some or all of their brands at one time.[34]

One of senior management's important roles is to determine marketing budgets and decide where and how to allocate company resources within the organization. The brand equity management system must be able to inform and provide input to decision makers so that they can recognize the short-term and long-term ramifications of their decisions for brand equity. Decisions about which brands to invest in, and whether to implement brand-building marketing programs or leverage brand equity through brand extensions instead, should reflect the current and desired state of the brand as revealed through brand tracking and other measures.

Organizational Design and Structures.   The firm should organize its marketing function to optimize brand equity. Several trends have emerged in organizational design and structure that reflect the growing recognition of the importance of the brand and the challenges of managing brand equity carefully. For example, an increasing number of companies are embracing brand management. Companies from more and more industries—such as the automobile, health care, pharmaceutical, and computer software and hardware industries—are introducing brand managers into their organizations. Often, they have hired managers from top packaged-goods companies, adopting some of the same brand marketing practices as a result.

Interestingly, packaged-goods companies, such as Procter & Gamble, continue to evolve the brand management system. Procter & Gamble's marketing directors became brand directors, with four functions including brand management, consumer and marketing knowledge, communications and design—thus, creating a "single-point responsibility for the strategies, plans and results for the brands."[35] With category management, manufacturers offer retailers advice about how to best stock their shelves. An increasing number of retailers are also adopting category management principles. Although manufacturers functioning as category captains can improve sales, experts caution retailers to exercise their own insights and values to retain their distinctiveness in the marketplace.

Many firms are thus attempting to redesign their marketing organizations to better reflect the challenges faced by their brands. At the same time, because of changing job requirements and duties, the traditional marketing department is disappearing from a number of companies that are exploring other ways to conduct their marketing functions through business groups, multidisciplinary teams, and so on.[36] In the context of the digital revolution, with its emphasis on data analytics and hypertargeting, many companies have reorganized their marketing departments to become more agile and data-driven.[37]

For example, Clorox made the following changes to adapt to the digital revolution in marketing: (1) it increased its investment in digital media and analytics; (2) it partnered with digital advertising agencies; and (3) it changed its marketing organization to allow for faster reaction to marketplace changes.[38] Further, the skills needed to succeed in marketing are changing with a greater emphasis on understanding of how data can be structured and used in order to succeed in the digital world.

The goal in these new organizational structures and new marketing skills is to improve internal coordination and efficiencies as well as external focus on retailers and consumers, in the fast-changing digital era. Although these are laudable goals, clearly one of the challenges with these new designs is to ensure that brand equity is preserved and nurtured, and not neglected due to a lack of oversight. With a multiple-product, multiple-market organization, the difficulty often lies in making sure that both product and place are in balance. As in many marketing and branding activities, achieving the proper balance is the goal, in order to maximize the advantages and minimize the disadvantages of both approaches.

Managing Marketing Partners.   Because the performance of a brand also depends on the actions taken by outside suppliers and marketing partners, firms must manage these relationships carefully. Increasingly, firms have been consolidating their marketing partnerships and reducing the number of their outside suppliers. As noted above with regard to Clorox, a number of companies are consolidating their advertising with a single digital advertising agency (e.g., Clorox has partnered with FCB and McGarryBowen), with a significant expertise across multiple social media and digital channels.

Factors like cost efficiencies, organizational leverage, and creative diversification affect the number of outside suppliers the firm will hire in any one area. From a branding perspective, one advantage of dealing with a single major supplier such as an ad agency is the greater consistency in understanding and treatment of a brand that can result.

Other marketing partners can also play an important role. For example, Chapter 5 described the importance of channel members and retailers in enhancing brand equity and the need for cleverly designed push programs. One important function of having a brand charter or bible is to inform and educate marketing partners so that they can provide more brand-consistent support.

REVIEW

A brand equity measurement system is defined as a set of research procedures designed to provide timely, accurate, and actionable information for marketers regarding brands so that they can make the best possible tactical decisions in the short run as well as strategic decisions in the long run. Implementing a brand equity measurement system involves three steps: conducting brand audits, designing brand tracking studies, and establishing a brand equity management system. Further, with the advent of the digital revolution, a brand's digital assets must be considered in creating and assessing the brand inventory. Continuous tracking systems which also utilize the vast troves of available social media data can also be leveraged to generate deeper insights on an ongoing basis.

A brand audit is a consumer-focused exercise to assess the health of the brand, uncover its sources of brand equity, and suggest ways to improve and leverage its equity. It requires understanding brand equity from the perspective of both the firm and the consumer. The brand audit consists of two steps: the brand inventory and the brand exploratory.

The purpose of the brand inventory is to provide a complete, up-to-date profile of how all the products and services sold by a company are marketed and branded. Profiling each product or service requires us to identify the associated brand elements as well as the supporting marketing program. The brand exploratory is research activity directed to understanding what consumers think and feel about the brand to identify sources of brand equity.

Brand audits can be used to set the strategic direction for the brand. As a result of this strategic analysis, a marketing program can be put into place to maximize long-term brand equity. Tracking studies employing quantitative measures can then be conducted to provide marketers with current information as to how their brands are performing on the basis of a number of key dimensions identified by the brand audit.

Tracking studies involve information collected from consumers on a routine basis over time and provide valuable tactical insights into the short-term effectiveness of marketing programs and activities. Whereas brand audits measure "where the brand has been," tracking studies measure "where the brand is now" and whether marketing programs are having their intended effects.

Three major steps must occur as part of a brand equity management system. First, the company view of brand equity should be formalized into a document, the brand charter. This document serves a number of purposes: It chronicles the company's general philosophy with respect to brand equity; summarizes the activity and outcomes related to brand audits, brand tracking, and so forth; outlines guidelines for brand strategies and tactics; and documents proper treatment of the brand. The charter should be updated annually to identify new opportunities and risks and to fully reflect information gathered by the brand inventory and brand exploratory as part of any brand audits.

Second, the results of the tracking surveys and other relevant outcome measures should be assembled into a brand equity report that is distributed to management on a regular basis (monthly, quarterly, or annually). The brand equity report should provide descriptive information as to *what* is happening to a brand as well as diagnostic information as to *why* it is happening. These reports are often being displayed in marketing dashboards for ease of review. Marketing analytic dashboards are increasingly being used to help with continuous tracking of a brand's performance.

Finally, senior management must be assigned to oversee how brand equity is treated within the organization. The people in that position would be responsible for overseeing the implementation of the brand charter and brand equity reports to make sure that, as much as possible, product and marketing actions across divisions and geographic boundaries are performed in a way that reflects the spirit of the charter and the substance of the report to maximize the long-term equity of the brand.

DISCUSSION QUESTIONS

1. What do you see as the biggest challenges in conducting a brand audit? What steps would you take to overcome them?
2. Pick a brand. See if you can assemble a digital brand asset inventory for it, by consulting various social media channels (e.g., Facebook, Instagram, Twitter). What does your exercise reveal about the consistency of the brand's presence across its multiple touchpoints?

3. Consider the Starbucks tracking survey presented in Branding Brief 9-1. What might you do differently? What questions would you change or drop? What questions might you add? How might this tracking survey differ from those used for other products?
4. Can you develop a tracking survey for the Mayo Clinic? How might it differ from the Starbucks' tracking survey?
5. Critique the Rolex brand audit in Brand Focus 9.0. How do you think it could be improved?

BRAND FOCUS 9.0
Sample Rolex Brand Audit

For over a century, Rolex has remained one of the most recognized and sought-after luxury brands in the world. In 2017, the BrandZ Top 100 Most Valuable Global Brands (which is a ranking by Kantar Millward Brown, or KMB), the world's most valuable watch brand is Rolex, which has an estimated brand value of $8.053 billion.[39] The estimate is based on a complicated formula combining financial information and consumer surveys. KMB interviews three million consumers in more than 50 global markets about 100,000 different brands. It uses data from Bloomberg and Kantar Worldpanel to analyze companies' financial and business performance.

To be clear, Rolex is not among KMB's Top 100 brands. (A brand needed a value of at least $11.3 billion to make that list.) Rolex appears in the report on the BrandZ Luxury Top 10 list, where it holds the #5 position (see table below). Rolex is the only one of the top 10 luxury brands whose sole product is watches. No other watches-only brand is included in the BrandZ report.

A thorough audit can help pinpoint opportunities and challenges for Rolex, whose brand equity has been historically strong, as much is at stake.

"The name of Rolex is synonymous with quality. Rolex—with its rigorous series of tests that intervene at every stage—has redefined the meaning of quality."

—**www.rolex.com**

BACKGROUND
History

Rolex was founded in 1905 by a German named Hans Wilsdorf and his brother-in-law, William Davis, as a watch-making company, Wilsdorf & Davis, with headquarters in London, England. Wilsdorf, a self-proclaimed perfectionist, set out to improve the mainstream pocket watch right from the start. By 1908, he had created a timepiece that kept accurate time but was small enough to be worn on the wrist. That same year, Wilsdorf trademarked the name "Rolex" because he thought it sounded like the noise a watch made when it was wound. Rolex was also easy to pronounce in many different languages.

In 1912, Rolex moved its headquarters to Geneva, Switzerland, and started working on improving the reliability of its watches. Back then, dust and moisture could enter the watch case and cause damage to the movement or internal mechanism of the watch. As a result, Wilsdorf invented a screw crown and waterproof casebook mechanism that revolutionized the watch industry. In 1914, the Rolex wristwatch obtained the first Kew

"A" certificate after passing the world's toughest timing test, which included testing the watch at extreme temperature levels.

Twelve years later, Wilsdorf developed and patented the now-famous Oyster waterproof case and screw crown. This mechanism became the first true protection against water, dust, and dirt. To generate publicity for the watch, jewelry stores displayed fish tanks in their windows with the Oyster watch completely submerged in it. The Oyster was put to the test on October 7, 1927, when Mercedes Gleitze swam the English Channel wearing one. She emerged 15 hours later with the watch functioning perfectly, much to the amazement of the media and public. Gleitze became the first of a long list of "ambassadors" that Rolex has used to promote its wristwatches.

Over the years, Rolex has pushed innovation in watches to new levels. In 1931, the firm introduced the Perpetual self-winding rotor mechanism, eliminating the need to wind a watch. In 1945, the company invented the first watch to display a number date at the 3 o'clock position and named it the Datejust. In 1953, Rolex launched the Submariner—the first diving watch that was water-resistant and pressure-resistant to 100 meters. The sporty watch appeared in various James Bond movies in the 1950s and became an instant symbol of prestige and durability.

For decades, Swiss-made watches owned the middle and high-end markets, remaining virtually unrivaled until the invention of the quartz watch in 1969. Quartz watches kept more accurate time, were less expensive to make, and quickly dominated the middle market. Within 10 years, quartz watches made up approximately half of all watch sales worldwide.[40] Joe Thompson, editor of *Modern Jeweler*, a U.S. trade publication, explained, "By 1980, people thought the mechanical watch was dead."[41]

Rolex proved the experts wrong. The company would not give in to the quartz watch rage. In order to survive, however, Rolex was forced to move into the high-end market exclusively—leaving the middle to the quartz people—and create a strategy to defend and build its position there. More recently, the watch industry has undergone a significant change with the introduction of smart watches, e.g., Apple Watch, which combine the functionality of a watch with many features of a smartphone. Although Rolex is seen as the most valuable luxury brand of watches, Apple watches has a larger sales revenue than Rolex watches.[42]

Private Ownership

Rolex is a privately owned company and has been controlled by only three people in its 100-year history. Before Wilsdorf died,

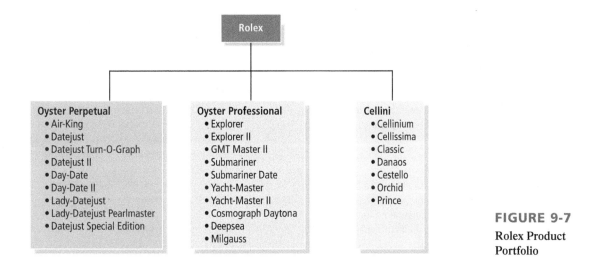

FIGURE 9-7
Rolex Product
Portfolio

he set up the Hans Wilsdorf Foundation, ensuring that some of the company's income would go to charity, and that control of the company lay with the foundation.[43] This move was a critical step toward the long-term success of Rolex as a high-end brand. Over the years, many luxury brands have been forced to affiliate with conglomerates in order to compete, but by staying an independent entity, Rolex has remained focused on its core business. André Heiniger, managing chairman of Rolex through the 1980s, explained, "Rolex's strategy is oriented to marketing, maintaining quality, and staying out of fields where we are not prepared to compete effectively."

Brand Portfolio

Rolex includes several sub-brands of wristwatches, called "collections"; each has a subset of brands (see Figure 9-7).

- The *Oyster Perpetual Collection* includes the "traditional" Rolex wristwatch, and has eight sub-brands that are differentiated by features and design. The Perpetual Collection targets affluent men and women.

- The *Professional Collection* targets specific athletic and adventurer user groups through its features and imagery.

- The *Cellini Collection* focuses on formal occasions through its elegant designs, and encompasses seven sub-brands. These

watches incorporate fashion and style features like colored leather bands and an extensive use of diamonds.

In addition to these collections, Rolex owns a separate "fighter" brand called Tudor, developed in 1946 to stave off competition from mid-range watches such as Tag Heuer, Citizen, and Rado. Tudor has its own range of family brands, or collections, namely Prince, Princess, Monarch, and Sport, each of which encompasses a number of sub-brands. Tudor watches are sold at own-brand specialty stores and through the network of exclusive Rolex dealers. Although they are no longer for sale in the United States, there are many outlets in Europe and Asia. Tudor targets younger consumers and offers watches at a lower price range. The brand is distinctly separate, and the Rolex name does not appear on Tudor watches.

Brand Inventory

Rolex's success as the largest single luxury watch brand can be credited to several factors. The company not only produces extremely high-quality timepieces, but also tightly controls how its watches are sold, ensuring high demand and premium prices. In addition, Rolex's sophisticated marketing strategy has created an exclusive and premium brand that many aspire to own. The brand inventory will describe each of these factors in more depth.

Rolex's brand portfolio includes a wide range of luxury wristwatches called "collections," which provide a number of options to the consumer.
Source: geogphotos/Alamy Stock Photo

Brand Elements

Rolex's most distinguishable brand element is its Crown logo. Trademarked in 1925, the Crown made its appearance on the watches in 1939. The logo has undergone few revisions, keeping its signature five-point crown intact over the years. Rolex watches feature the name "Rolex" on the dial, a tradition dating to 1926. This development initially helped increase brand recognition. Many Rolex watches also have a distinct look, including a big round face and wide wrist band.

Product

Throughout the years, Rolex timepieces have maintained the high quality, durability, and prestige on which the company built its name. In particular, the firm has maintained a keen focus on delivering a highly accurate watch of superior craftsmanship, using only the finest premium materials such as gold, platinum, and jewels. It continually works on improving the functionality of its watches with better movements and new, sophisticated features. As a result, Rolex watches are complex mechanisms compared to most mass-produced watches. A quartz watch, for example, has between 50 and 100 parts; a Rolex Oyster chronometer has 220.[44]

Each Rolex watch consists of 10 unique features identified as the company's "10 Golden Rules:"

1. A waterproof case
2. The Perpetual rotor
3. The case back
4. The Oyster case
5. The winding crown
6. The finest and purest materials
7. Quality control
8. Rolex self-winding movement
9. Testing from the independent Controle Official Suisse des Chronometres
10. Rolex testing

The company does not license its brand or produce any other product besides watches. Its product portfolio is clear, concise, and focused.

Rolex spends more time and money than any other watch company fighting counterfeiters. Today, it is often hard to spot the differences between a $25 counterfeit and a $10,000 authentic Rolex watch. The global counterfeiting industry is said to be valued at $461 billion dollars, and Rolex (along with Nike, Ray-Ban and Louis Vuitton) are among the brands with the most knockoffs.[45]

Pricing

By limiting production to approximately 2,000 watches a day, Rolex keeps consumer demand high and prices at a premium. Prices start around $2,500 for the basic Oyster Perpetual and can reach $200,000, depending on the specific materials used such as steel, yellow gold, or platinum. Scarcity also helps positively influence the resale value of Rolex watches. One report indicated that "almost all older Rolex models are valued above their initial selling price."[46]

Distribution

Rolex carefully monitors how its timepieces are sold, distributing them only through its approximately 60,000 "Official Rolex Dealers" worldwide. Official dealers must meet several criteria, including a high-end image, adequate space, attractive location, and outstanding service. In addition, a large secondary market exists for Rolex, both through online auction sites such as eBay and at live auctions run by Christie's, and Sotheby's.

Communications

Rolex's marketing and communications strategy strives to create a high-quality, exclusive brand image. The company associates itself with "ambassadors"—established artists, top athletes, rugged adventurers, and daring explorers—to help create this imagery. Rolex also sponsors various sports and cultural events as well as philanthropy programs to help align with targeted demographics as well as create positive associations in consumers' minds.

Advertising. Rolex is the number-one watch advertiser in the world. In 2015, the firm spent over $56 million on advertising, more than any other watch brand.[47] One of the company's largest expenditures is for magazine advertising. Rolex's print ads are often simple and austere, usually featuring one of its many brand ambassadors or a close-up photo of one of its watches with the tagline "Rolex. A Crown for Every Achievement." Rolex does not advertise extensively on television but does sponsor some events that are televised.

More recently, Rolex has begun using digital marketing techniques to connect with its customers, although its efforts have been very measured and carefully thought out. Rolex started a Facebook page, and has adopted a content marketing strategy with a careful emphasis on providing high-quality content, rather than focus on quantity of content.[48] Previously, it also had launched a YouTube channel in 2012 and used it as a platform to launch in-house documentaries about topics of interest to its consumers including Himalayan expeditions and deep-sea missions to investigate the polar ice caps. The brand also used social media platforms (e.g., Facebook) to communicate quirky features that are typical of the Rolex brand. For example, Rolex launched a "Did You Know" series to explain why Rolex uses IIII, the "Clockmaker's Four," instead of IV. These communications on social media were aimed at maintaining the interest of a loyal customer base along with clarifying the brand's values to its customers.

Ambassadors. Rolex's celebrity endorsers are continuously added and dropped depending on their performance. These ambassadors fall into four categories: athletes, artists, explorers, and yachtsmen (see Figure 9-8). Aligning with acclaimed artists symbolizes the pursuit of perfection. Association with elite sports figures is meant to signify the company's quest for excellence. Its support of sailing events—for example, highlights the company's core values: excellence, precision, and team spirit.[49] Explorers also test the excellence and innovation of Rolex's watches at extreme conditions. Rolex ambassadors have scaled Mount Everest, broken the speed of sound, reached the depths of the ocean, and traveled in space. A print ad will usually feature one ambassador and one specific watch, with the goal of targeting a very specific demographic or consumer group.

In 2011, much to the surprise of industry experts, Rolex signed golfer Tiger Woods as a Rolex ambassador. Rolex's sponsorship marked the golfer's first celebrity endorsement since 2009. After Tiger Woods' reputation fell following a sex scandal, Rolex also signed on other brand ambassadors, including professional golfers and star athletes such as Jason Day, Phil Mickelson, and Arnold Palmer, among others.[50]

Artists	Explorers	Golfers	Racing
Cecilia Bartoli	David Doubilet	Paul Casey	Sir Jackie Stewart
Michael Buble	Sylvia Earle	Luke Donald	Tom Kristensen
Placido Domingo	Alain Hubert	Ricky Fowler	Rolex 24 at Daytona
Gustavo Dudamel	Jean Troillet	Retief Goosen	Goodwood Revival
Renee Fleming	Ed Viesturs	Charles Howell	24 Hours at Le Mans
Sylvie Guillem	Chuck Yeager	Trevor Immelman	
Jonas Kaufmann	Setting Out to Conquer the World	Martin Kaymer	Tennis
Diana Krall	Deepsea Under the Pole	Matteo Manassero	Roger Federer
Yo-Yo Ma	The Deep	Phil Mickelson	Justine Henin
Anoushka Shankar	The Deepest Dive	Jack Nicklaus	Ana Ivanovic
Bryn Terfel		Lorena Ochoa	Zheng Jie
Rolando Villazon	Yachting	Arnold Palmer	Juan Martín del Potro
Yuja Wang	Robert Scheidt	Gary Player	Li Na
Royal Opera House	Paul Cayard	Adam Scott	Jo-Wilfried Tsonga
Teatro Alla Scalla	Rolex Sydney Hobart	Annika Sorenstam	Caroline Wosniacki
Wiener Philharmoniker	Maxi Yacht Rolex Cup	Camilo Villegas	Wimbledon
	Rolex Fastnet Race	Tom Watson	Australian Open
	Rolex Farr 40 World Championship	U.S. Open Championship	Monte-Carlo Rolex Masters
	Rolex Swan Cup	The Open Championship	Shanghai Rolex Masters
		The Ryder Cup	
	Equestrian	The President's Cup	Skiing
	Rodrigo Pessoa	Evian Masters	Hermann Maier
	Gonzalo Pieres, Jr.	The Solheim Cup	Lindsay Vonn
			Carlo Janka
			The Hahnenkamm Races

FIGURE 9-8
2011 Rolex Ambassadors

Sports and Culture.   Rolex sponsors a variety of elite athletic and cultural events to reinforce the same messages, values, and associations as it does through its ambassador endorsements. These include a quest for excellence, pursuit of perfection, teamwork, and ruggedness. Rolex sponsors sporting events in golf (U.S. Open Championship, the Open Championship, and the Ryder Cup), tennis (Wimbledon and the Australian Open), skiing (the Hahnenkamm Races), racing (Rolex 24 at Daytona), and equestrian events.

Rolex also sponsors several sailing races, including the Rolex Sydney, Rolex Fastnet Race, and Maxi Yacht Rolex Cup. The company has partnered with extreme exploration expeditions, including The Deepest Dive and Deepsea Under the Pole. It is a major contributor to establishments such as the Royal Opera House in London and the Teatro alla Scala in Milan to align with a more cultural audience.

Philanthropy.   Rolex gives back through three established philanthropic programs:

1. The *Awards for Enterprise* program (www.rolexawards.com/) supports individuals whose work focuses on benefiting their communities and the world. These projects are focused on science and health, applied technology, exploration and discovery, the environment, and cultural heritage.[51]

2. The *Young Laureates Programme* (www.rolexawards.com/40/laureates-2016) is part of the Awards for Enterprise program, providing support for outstanding innovators between the ages of 18 and 30.[52]

3. The *Rolex Mentor and Protégé Arts Initiative* (www.rolexmentorprotege.com/) seeks out extraordinarily gifted young artists

around the world and pairs them with established masters. Young artists have been paired with accomplished filmmakers, dancers, artists, composers, and actors.[53]

BRAND EXPLORATORY
Consumer Knowledge

Rolex has successfully leveraged its history and tradition of excellence along with innovation to become the most powerful and recognized watchmaker in the world. Some positive consumer brand associations for Rolex might be the following: sophisticated, prestigious, exclusive, powerful, elegant, and high quality. Some negative brand associations that some consumers may link to the brand could include flashy or snobby. Figure 9-9 displays a hypothetical Rolex mental map.

In one report by the Luxury Institute research group in New York, consumers had positive attitudes in terms of purchase intent toward Rolex. Wealthy people said they were more likely to buy a Rolex than any other brand for their next watch. The Rolex brand was far more recognizable (84 percent knew it) than Bulgari (39 percent) and even Cartier (63 percent), although several rivals outranked Rolex for perceived quality and exclusivity.[54]

A 2008 Mintel survey on the watch industry revealed that "women are still likely to view watches as an accessory, with many buyers choosing their watch based on looks alone. However, at the top end of the luxury market, there is a growing number of women who are interested in mechanical watches. The study also found that women are increasingly choosing androgynous or unisex watches."[55]

Many older, affluent people place a high value on owning a Rolex, whether new or collectible. In 2017, at a New York auction

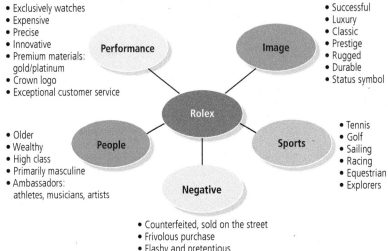

- Exclusively watches
- Expensive
- Precise
- Innovative
- Premium materials: gold/platinum
- Crown logo
- Exceptional customer service

- Successful
- Luxury
- Classic
- Prestige
- Rugged
- Durable
- Status symbol

- Older
- Wealthy
- High class
- Primarily masculine
- Ambassadors: athletes, musicians, artists

- Tennis
- Golf
- Sailing
- Racing
- Equestrian
- Explorers

- Counterfeited, sold on the street
- Frivolous purchase
- Flashy and pretentious

FIGURE 9-9

Rolex Mental Map

house Phillips, a bidder agreed to pay $17.8 million for a Rolex Daytona that used to belong to actor Paul Newman, setting a new world record for a wristwatch sold at auction. The watch was given to Newman by his wife, at the time when he was filming an auto racing movie called "Winning."[56]

While the brand and product line seem to resonate well with older, wealthy individuals, Rolex struggles somewhat to connect with younger consumers. In a NPD Group poll, 36 percent of people under the age of 25 did not wear a watch.[57] Another study by Piper Jaffray revealed that 59 percent of teenagers said they never wear a watch, and 82 percent said they did not plan to buy one in the next six months. The advent of smartwatches, and the entry of Apple Watch into the fray in 2015 has certainly given the traditional watch industry a lot to be concerned about. With an approximate price of $400, a smartwatch offers many benefits to a consumer that traditional watches do not offer, such as the ability to monitor health and fitness metrics via the smartwatch, communications and messaging, as well as access to mobile apps.

Brand Resonance Pyramid

The Rolex brand resonance model pyramid (see Chapter 3) is equally strong on the left-hand and right-hand sides. There is great synergy between the two sides of the pyramid; the functional and emotional benefits Rolex strives to deliver are in harmony with consumers' imagery and feelings about the brand. The pyramid is also strong from bottom to top, enjoying the highest brand awareness of any luxury brand as well as high repeat purchase rates and high customer loyalty. Rolex has successfully focused on both the superior product attributes and the imagery associated with owning and wearing a Rolex. Figure 9-10 highlights some key aspects of the Rolex brand resonance pyramid.

Competitive Analysis

Rolex has many competitors in the $26.5 billion watch industry; however, only a few brands compete in the very high-end market.[58] Through its pricing and distribution strategies, Rolex has positioned itself as a high-end luxury watch brand. On the lower end of the spectrum, it competes with companies such as TAG Heuer and OMEGA, and on the high end with brands such as Patek Philippe, maker of the world's most expensive wristwatch.

TAG Heuer. A leader in the luxury watch industry, the Swiss firm TAG Heuer distinguishes itself by focusing on extreme chronograph precision in its watches and on sports and auto-racing sponsorship in its advertising. Founded by Edouard Heuer in 1876, TAG Heuer has been a mainstay in the luxury watch business. In 1887, the firm created the first oscillating pinion, a technology that significantly improved the chronograph industry and is still used in many of its watches today. In 1895, it developed and patented the first water-resistant case for pocket watches. TAG Heuer expanded into the United States in 1910, introduced a chronograph wristwatch in 1914, and has continued to focus on chronograph innovation ever since.

TAG's image and positioning is inextricably connected to chronograph precision. Its timepieces were the official stopwatches of the Olympic Games in 1920, 1924, and 1928. The firm was a Ferrari team sponsor of Formula 1 from 1971 to 1979 and was part of the TAG-McLaren racing team from 1985 to 2002. It was also the official timekeeper of the F-1 race series for much of the 1990s and early 2000s.[59] TAG Heuer has sponsored numerous Americas Cup teams and other yacht racing teams over the years, and has also sponsored the English Premier League football

TAG Heuer uses officially licensed retailers to sell its watches both in stores and online. These licensed retailers range from exclusive jewelers to department stores such as Nordstrom and Macy's. The watchmaker generates brand awareness through brand ambassadors and sponsoring sporting events and advertises extensively in magazines. In 1999, TAG Heuer was purchased by luxury goods conglomerate LVHM.

OMEGA. Founded in 1848 by Louis Brandt, OMEGA has long prided itself on the precision of its watches and timing devices. It built what was Amelia Earhart's watch of choice during one of her transatlantic flights and has been involved in aviation and athletic timing ever since. OMEGA was the time equipment selected for the 1936 Winter Olympics, which saw the first use of synchronized chronographs. By 1937, the company had launched its first waterproof wristwatch, and in 1967, it invented the first underwater touchpad timing equipment, which was used in Olympic swimming competitions. OMEGA watches accompanied the expedition to locate the exact position of the North Pole, and boarded the Apollo 11 mission to become the first and only

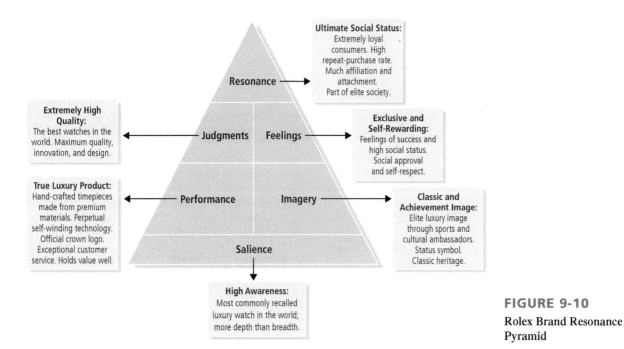

FIGURE 9-10

Rolex Brand Resonance Pyramid

watch ever to land on the moon. OMEGA is now owned by watch conglomerate Swatch Group.

Like Rolex and TAG Heuer, OMEGA employs ambassadors to generate brand awareness, including athletes Michelle Wei, Sergio Garcia, astronaut Buzz Aldrin, and actor Daniel Craig. Since 1995, OMEGA has been the official watch of the *James Bond* film franchise.

OMEGA watches are offered in both women's and men's styles in four different collections: Globemaster, Constellation, Seamaster, Speedmaster, and De Ville. Prices vary greatly even within individual collections. Watches in the De Ville collection range from $1,650 to more than $100,000.

Patek Philippe.   In 1839, Antoine Norbert de Patek and François Czapek started a Swiss-based watch company built upon 10 values: independence, innovation, tradition, quality and workmanship, rarity, value, aesthetics, service, emotion, and heritage. After several name changes during its formative years, the company was finally named Patek Philippe. The innovator of many technologies found in today's high-end watch, it represents the absolute pinnacle of luxury timepieces. In particular, the firm prides itself on creating many of the world's most complicated watches through innovations with split-second chronograph and perpetual date technology.

Unlike other leading luxury watchmakers, Patek Philippe does not rely on event sponsorship or brand ambassadors to generate name recognition. However, since 1851, the firm has made watches for royalty throughout Europe. Its watches are only sold through authorized retailers, of which there are 600 worldwide. In 1996, the brand started its "Generations" campaign, building on its values of heritage and tradition and featuring the tagline, "You Never Actually Own a Patek Philippe, You Merely Look After It for the Next Generation."

Patek Philippe evaluates every authorized dealer's storefront to ensure that it meets the watchmaker's quality standards. It also separates itself from other watchmakers on price, with its least expensive non-customized watch retailing at $11,500 and its most expensive at over $600,000.

STRATEGIC RECOMMENDATIONS
Positioning

Figure 9-11 summarizes some positioning analysis and possible points-of-parity and points-of-difference, as described below.

Points-of-Parity.   Rolex is similar to other watchmakers in the high-end luxury watch market on several levels. They all make their watches in Switzerland, which is renowned for superior craftsmanship in watch making, and they all deliver high quality. All pride themselves on their attention to detail and ongoing innovation in the watch industry.

Points-of-Difference.   Rolex separates itself from the competition in several ways. One, Rolex watches have a distinct look with their Crown logo, big face, and wide band. Two, Rolex has kept a strategically tight control on its distribution channel and production levels, creating a sense of prestige, importance, and exclusivity in the minds of consumers. Three, it has kept the brand pure, remaining focused only on watches and never licensing its name. Through careful selection of event sponsorships and brand ambassadors, Rolex has cut through the clutter, resonated with consumers around the world, and maintained an air of prestige.

Brand Mantra:
"Classic Designs, Timeless Status"

Points-of-Parity	Points-of-Difference
• Swiss watchmaker	• Innovative products
• Durable	• Unique appearance
• Fine materials	Big face; wide wrist band
• Quality craftsmanship	• Iconic crown logo
• Accurate	• Exclusive, prestigious imagery
• Attractive	• Rich history and heritage
	• Enduring premium value

FIGURE 9-11

Possible Rolex Brand Positioning

Brand Mantra. Rolex has been extremely successful in building a global name through clever marketing and communications, without compromising the integrity of the brand. It has nurtured the belief that acquiring a Rolex represents a milestone in one's life and has built a well-known brand recognized for its elegance and status throughout the entire world. A brand mantra that captures these ideas might be, "Classic Designs, Timeless Status."

TACTICAL RECOMMENDATIONS

The Rolex brand audit proved that Rolex is a very strong brand with significant brand equity. It also identified a few opportunities and challenges:

Leverage the Company's Independent, Continuous Heritage and Focus

- Rolex is the largest and most successful watch company in the world. As a result, many consumers don't realize it is privately owned and competes against major conglomerates such as TAG Heuer's parent company, LVMH, and OMEGA's parent company, Swatch Group. While being privately owned is a good thing for many reasons, it also brings up several challenges. For example, Rolex has to compete against companies that are 10 times its size. Larger companies have lower labor costs, wider distribution, and significant advertising synergies.

- Rolex may want to leverage and promote the fact that in some ways it has to work harder to succeed. It is doing what it has done for 100 years—making durable, reliable, premium watches on its own. Due to the currently popular anti-Wall-Street vibe, this positioning may resonate well with consumers.

Leverage the Company's Elite Craftsmanship and Innovation

- Research from the Luxury Institute group suggested that consumers do not consider Rolex the top brand in quality and exclusivity. History has proved that Rolex watches are, in fact, leaders in both craftsmanship and innovation, and Rolex may want to run a campaign focused more on these aspects.

Connect with the Female Consumer

- Women make up the majority of jewelry and watch purchases. However, as Mintel's 2008 study revealed, women are more and more interested in purchasing unisex mechanical watches rather than feminine-styled watches. This is a great opportunity for Rolex, whose watches are primarily masculine in design. The firm could move away from its decorative, jeweled watches and introduce more powerful, gender-neutral watches. Its 2009 Oyster Perpetual Datejust Rolesor 36 mm is one example—robust, with large utilitarian numbers, and waterproof to a depth of 100 meters.[60] However, its floral dial design and diamond-set bezel possibly give it an unnecessary feminine angle.

- Rolex may want to tweak its female ambassador list to coincide with a more unisex product line. Women who have succeeded in a male-dominated environment such as Condoleezza Rice or Katie Couric could be powerful brand endorsers.

Attack the Online Counterfeit Industry

- Counterfeits damage the company's brand equity and present a huge risk to the brand. The boom in e-commerce has taken counterfeit Rolexes from the street corner to the Internet, where fakes can reach far more consumers. Consequently, the age-old problem of counterfeiting is a bigger threat than ever before. To maintain its limited distribution, Rolex does not authorize any of its watches to be sold on the Internet. In order to combat the online sale of counterfeits, Rolex might consider building an exclusive online store, or an exclusive distribution site to which all official e-retailers must link. In fact, Rolex dedicates extensive resources to fight the illegal use of the brand, including sponsoring the International Anti-Counterfeiting Coalition and suing companies that allow the sale of counterfeit Rolexes.

Use Marketing to Reach Younger Consumers

- Research has shown that younger consumers do not value watches the same way older generations did. As a result, Rolex should be researching the questions: How will prestige be defined in the twenty-first century? Who or what symbolizes prestige, ruggedness, precision? Will the same formula work for the millennial generation as they age and move into the Rolex target market? As noted previously, the introduction of smartwatches has given the traditional watch industry a jolt. Rolex needs to consider how best it will incorporate some of these features of smartwatches. Alternatively, Rolex may want to expand its brand to include a variety of fashion products beyond watches, so as to minimize its reliance on traditional watches alone.

Reach Consumers Using Digital and Social Media Channels

- Unlike many other brands, Rolex has adopted a more careful wait-and-watch approach with regard to its use of digital marketing techniques. This was probably wise given that it wanted to ensure that its efforts on the digital front would not diminish its legacy or its loyal fans. However, with marketing increasingly relying on digital marketing, Rolex needs to make some dramatic changes in its approach and reach, particularly to reach younger audiences.

Communicate Long-Term Value

- Rolex competes for a share of the luxury buyer's wallet with a host of other types of goods, such as clothes, shoes, and handbags. Many are less durable over time than a Rolex watch and are susceptible to falling out of fashion. Rolex should leverage its superior value retention—both in its resale value and in its "heirloom" quality—in order to better compete for luxury spending with brands outside its category.

- Swiss luxury watch competitor Patek Philippe used print advertising to communicate the heirloom quality of its watches. Rolex could pursue a similar approach, perhaps using its more visible ambassadors, to communicate its own heirloom quality.

NOTES

1. Frederick E. Webster Jr., Alan J. Malter, and Shankar Ganesan, "Can Marketing Regain Its Seat at the Table?" *Marketing Science Institute Report* No. 03–113, Cambridge, MA, 2003. See also Frederick E. Webster Jr., Alan J. Malter, and Shankar Ganesan, "The Decline and Dispersion of Marketing Competence," *MIT Sloan Management Review* 46, no. 4 (Summer 2005): 35–43.

2. Patrick LaPointe, *Marketing by the Dashboard Light— How to Get More Insight, Foresight, and Accountability from Your Marketing Investment* (New York: Association of National Advertisers, 2005).

3. Forbes and Neustar, "Marketing Accountability," https:// cmo-practice.forbes.com/wp-content/uploads/2017/10 /Forbes-Marketing-Accountability-Executive-Summary-10.2.17.pdf, accessed July 10, 2018.

4. Clyde P. Stickney, Roman L. Weil, Katherine Schipper, and Jennifer Francis, *Financial Accounting: An Introduction to Concepts, Methods, and Uses* (Mason, OH: Southwestern Cengage Learning, 2010).

5. Phillip Kotler, William Gregor, and William Rogers, "The Marketing Audit Comes of Age," *Sloan Management Review* 18, no. 2 (Winter 1977): 25–43.

6. Laurel Wentz, "Brand Audits Reshaping Images," *Ad Age International* 67, no. 37 (September 1996): 38–41.

7. Grand Ogilvy Winner, "Pizza Turnaround: Speed Kills. Good Taste Counts," *Journal of Advertising Research* 51, no. 3 (September 2011): 463–466; Seth Stevenson, "Like Cardboard," *Slate*, January 11, 2010; Ashley M. Heher, "Domino's Comes Clean with New Pizza Ads," *Associated Press*, January 11, 2010; Bob Garfield, "Domino's Does Itself a Disservice by Coming Clean About Its Pizza," *Advertising Age*, January 11, 2010; James F. Peltz, "Domino's Pizza Stock Is Up 5,000% Since 2008. Here's Why," *Los Angeles Times*, May 15, 2017.

8. Thomas Hobbs, "Domino's Pizza: We Have a Much Clearer Identity than Many of Our Fast-Food Rivals," *Marketing Week*, March 23, 2016, www .marketingweek.com/2016/03/23/dominos-pizza-our-fast-food-rivals-have-lost-their-sense-of-identity/.

9. Private correspondence with Chris Grams and John Adams from Red Hat.

10. Stefan Deeran, "Content Marketing 101: Auditing Your Digital Assets," *Huffington Post*, June 17, 2013, www .huffingtonpost.com/stefan-deeran/content-marketing-101-aud_b_3093146.html.

11. Sidney J. Levy, "Dreams, Fairy Tales, Animals, and Cars," *Psychology and Marketing* 2, no. 2 (Summer 1985): 67–81.

12. Deborah Roeddder John, Barbara Loken, Kyongheui Kim, and Alokparna Basu Monga, "Brand Concept Maps: A Methodology for Identifying Brand Association Networks," *Journal of Marketing Research* 43, no. 4 (November 2006): 549–563.

13. Expert Commentator, "What Should an Online Brand Audit Include," *Smart Insights*, September 30, 2014, www.smartinsights.com/online-brand-strategy/ brand-development/brand-audit/.

14. Keith Quesenberry, "Conducting a Social Media Audit," *Harvard Business Review*, accessed November 23, 2017, https://hbr.org/2015/11/conducting-a-social-media-audit.

15. John Roberts, professor of marketing, Australian National University, personal correspondence, June 23, 2011.

16. WARC, "McDonald's Wins Back Millennials," *WARC*, October 17, 2016, www.warc.com/NewsAndOpinion/ News/37580.

17. Matt Ariker, Alejandro Diaz, Christine Moorman, and Mike Westover, "Quantifying the Impact of Marketing Analytics," *Harvard Business Review*, November 5, 2015, https://hbr.org/2015/11/quantifying-the-impact-of-marketing-analytics.

18. Ibid.

19. Referenced in Koen Pauwels, (2014), "It's Not the Size of the Data—It's How You Use It: Smarter Marketing with Analytics and Dashboards," HarperCollins Publishers.

20. Ibid.

21. Ibid.

22. Matt Ariker, Alejandro Diaz, Christine Moorman, and Mike Westover, "Quantifying the Impact of Marketing Analytics," *Harvard Business Review*, November 5, 2015, https://hbr.org/2015/11/quantifying-the-impact-of-marketing-analytics.

23. Max Nisen, "Mayo Clinic CEO: Here's Why We've Been the Leading Brand in Medicine for 100 Years," *Business Insider*, February 23, 2013, www .businessinsider.com/how-mayo-clinic-became-the-best-brand-in-medicine-2013-2.

24. Sandhya Pruthi, Dawn Marie R. Davis, Dawn L. Hucke, Francesca B. Ripple, Barbara S. Tatzel, James A. Dilling, Paula J. Santrach, Jeffrey W. Bolton, and John H. Noseworthy, "Vision, Mission, and Values: From Concept to Execution at Mayo Clinic," *Patient Experience Journal* 2, no. 2 (2015): 169–173.

25. Bloom Creative, "5 Key Things That Make Mayo Clinic a Marketing Machine," *Bloom Creative*, July 11, 2016, http://bloomcreative.com/5-key-things-that-make-mayo-clinic-a-marketing-machine/.

26. Joan Justice, "The Big Brand Theory: How the Mayo Clinic Became the Gold Standard for Social Media in Healthcare," *Social Media Today*, May 21, 2013, www.socialmediatoday.com/content/big-brand-theory-how-mayo-clinic-became-gold-standard-social-media-healthcare.

27. Leonard L. Berry and Kent D. Seltman, "Building a Strong Services Brand: Lessons from Mayo Clinic," *Business Horizons* 50, no. 3, (2007): 199–209.

28. Skype, "Skype Brand Book," *Skype* 2017, https://secure.skypeassets.com/content/dam/scom/pdf/skype_brand_guidelines.pdf.

29. Joel Rubinson, "Brand Strength Means More Than Market Share," paper presented at the ARF Fourth Annual Advertising and Promotion Workshop, New York, 1992.

30. Tim Ambler, *Marketing and the Bottom Line,* 2nd ed. (London: FT Prentice Hall, 2004).

31. Michael Krauss, "Marketing Dashboards Drive Better Decisions," *Marketing News*, 36, no. 16 (October 2005): 7.

32. Scott Bedbury, *A New Brand World* (New York: Viking Press, 2002).

33. Ibid.

34. Betsy Spethman, "Companies Post Equity Gatekeepers," *Brandweek,* May 2, 1994, 5.

35. Michael Lee, "Does P&G's Reorganized Marketing Department Go Far Enough?, *Forbes*, July 8, 2014, https://www.forbes.com/sites/michaellee/2014/07/08/does-pgs-reorganized-marketing-department-go-far-enough/#5a4f3fac5e88, accessed July 11, 2018.

36. The Economist (US), "Death of the Brand Manager (Consumer-Goods Firms Re-engineering of Marketing Departments)," *The Economist*, April 9, 1994, https://www.highbeam.com/doc/1G1-15110919.html, accessed November 7, 2018.

37. Steve Olenski, "Why a Major Brand Felt the Need to Change Its Marketing Department," *Forbes*, July 18. 2016, https://www.forbes.com/sites/steveolenski/2016/07/18/why-a-major-brand-felt-the-need-to-change-its-marketing-department/#57b3015915fa.

38. Ibid.

39. Joe Thompson, "The World's Most Valuable Watch Brand," *Bloomberg*, October 2, 2017, www.bloomberg.com/news/articles/2017-10-02/rolex-is-the-world-s-most-valuable-watch-brand.

40. David Liebeskind, "What Makes Rolex Tick?," *Stern Business*, Fall/Winter 2004, http://w4.stern.nyu.edu/sternbusiness/fall_winter_2004/rolex.html, accessed July 11, 2018.

41. Peter Passell, "Watches That Time Hasn't Forgotten," *The New York Times*, November 24, 1995, https://www.nytimes.com/1995/11/24/business/watches-that-time-hasn-t-forgotten.html, accessed November 7, 2018.

42. Joe Thompson, "The World's Most Valuable Watch Brand," *Bloomberg,* October 2, 2017, www.bloomberg.com/news/articles/2017-10-02/rolex-is-the-world-s-most-valuable-watch-brand.

43. Gene Stone, *The Watch* (New York: ABRAMS, 2006).

44. David Liebeskind, "What Makes Rolex Tick?" *Stern Business*, Fall/Winter 2004, https://w4.stern.nyu.edu/sternbusiness/fall_winter_2004/rolex.html, accessed November 7, 2018.

45. Alana Petroff, "The 'Fakes' Industry Is Worth $461 Billion," *CNN*, April 18, 2016, http://money.cnn.com/2016/04/18/news/economy/fake-purses-shoes-economy-counterfeit-trade/index.html.

46. Ibid.

47. Español Русский, "Who Are the Biggest Spenders in the Watch World?" *Europa Star WorldWatchWeb*, July 2015, www.europastar.com/news/1004088088-who-are-the-biggest-spenders-in-the-watch-world.html.

48. Eli Epstein, "Rolex: How a 109-Year-Old Brand Thrives in the Digital Age," *Mashable*, accessed November 25, 2017, http://mashable.com/2014/04/17/rolex-marketing-strategy/#dAzYZRIgMPqa.

49. ROLEX, "History of Rolex," https://www.rolex.com/rolex-history.html, accessed November 7, 2018.

50. Instagram photo, www.instagram.com/p/-bS4kDmA43/.

51. ROLEX, "History of Rolex," https://www.rolex.com/rolex-history.html, accessed November 7, 2018.

52. Ibid.

53. Ibid.

54. Christina Binkley, "Fashion Journal: Celebrity Watch: Are You a Brad or a James?" *The Wall Street Journal*, January 11, 2007, D1.

55. Jemima Sissons, "Haute Couture Takes on Horlogerie: Fashion's Big Guns Continue to Impress in the Battle for Women's Wrists," *The Wall Street Journal*, March 19, 2010.

56. Rob McLean and Jethro Mullen, "Most Expensive Wristwatch Ever Auctioned Just Fetched $17.8 million," *CNN*, October 27, 2017, http://money.cnn.com/2017/10/27/news/paul-newman-rolex-auction-record/index.html.

57. Harry Hurt, "The 12-Watches-a-Year Solution," *New York Times*, July 1, 2006, C5.

58. Women's Wear Daily, July 2005, https://wwd.com; Federation of the Swiss Watch Industry, http://www.fhs.swiss/eng/homepage.html.

59. F1 Scarlet Pit Crew, "History of TAG Heuer in Formula 1," *F1Scarlet*, http://www.f1scarlet.com/historyoftag_f1.html, accessed November 7, 2018.

60. Jemima Sissons, "Haute Couture Takes On Horlogerie: Fashion's Big Guns Continue to Impress in the Battle for Women's Wrists," *The Wall Street Journal* (Online), March 19, 2010.

Measuring Sources of Brand Equity: Capturing Customer Mind-Set

10

Learning Objectives

After reading this chapter, you should be able to

1. Describe effective qualitative research techniques for tapping into consumer brand knowledge.

2. Identify effective quantitative research techniques for measuring brand awareness, image, responses, and relationships.

3. Outline how big data can help with understanding brand perceptions and brand positioning.

4. Explain the role of social media monitoring "control rooms" as a marketing research tool.

5. Profile and contrast some popular brand equity models.

Marketers develop new products based on a variety of inputs from consumers, derived from both quantitative and qualitative marketing research.

PREVIEW

Understanding the current and desired brand knowledge structures of consumers is vital to effectively building and managing brand equity. Ideally, marketers would be able to construct detailed "mental maps" to understand exactly what exists in consumers' minds—all their thoughts, feelings, perceptions, images, beliefs, and attitudes toward different brands. These mental blueprints would then provide managers with insights to develop a solid brand positioning with the right points-of-parity and points-of-difference and the strategic guidance to help them make good brand decisions. Unfortunately, such brand knowledge structures are not easily measured because they reside only in consumers' minds.

Nevertheless, effective brand management requires us to thoroughly understand the consumer. Often a simple insight into how consumers think of or use products and the particular brands in a category can help create a profitable change in the marketing program. That is why many large companies conduct exhaustive research studies (or brand audits, as described in Chapter 9) to learn as much as possible about consumers.

A number of detailed, sophisticated research techniques and methods now exist to help marketers better understand consumer knowledge structures. A host of primary and secondary data sources exist online. Many industry or company studies can be accessed. Surveys can be efficiently distributed and collected. This chapter highlights some of the important considerations critical to the measurement of brand equity.[1] Figure 10-1 outlines general considerations in understanding consumer behavior, and Branding Brief 10-1 describes the lengths to which marketers have gone in the past to learn about consumers.

According to the brand value chain, sources of brand equity arise from the customer mind-set. In general, measuring sources of brand equity requires that the brand manager fully understand how customers shop for and use products and services and, most important, what customers know, think, and feel about and act toward various brands. In particular, measuring sources of customer-based brand equity requires us to measure various aspects of brand awareness and brand image that can lead to the differential customer response making up brand equity.

Consumers may have a holistic view of brands that is difficult to divide into component parts. Many times we can isolate perceptions and assess them in greater detail. The remainder of this chapter describes qualitative and quantitative approaches to identifying potential sources of brand equity—that is, capturing the customer mind-set.

QUALITATIVE RESEARCH TECHNIQUES

There are many different ways to uncover the types of associations linked to the brand and their corresponding strength, favorability, and uniqueness. *Qualitative research techniques* often identify possible brand associations and sources of brand equity. These are relatively unstructured measurement approaches that permit a range of both questions and answers and so can often be a useful first step in exploring consumer brand and product perceptions.

FIGURE 10-1

Understanding Consumer Behavior

Source: Based on a list from George Belch and Michael Belch, *Advertising and Communication Management,* 3rd ed. (Homewood, IL: Irwin, 1995).

Who buys our product or service?
Who makes the decision to buy the product?
Who influences the decision to buy the product?
How is the purchase decision made? Who assumes what role?
What does the customer buy? What needs must be satisfied?
Why do customers buy a particular brand?
Where do they go or look to buy the product or service?
When do they buy? Any seasonality factors?
What are customers' attitudes toward our product?
What social factors might influence the purchase decision?
Does the customers' lifestyle influence their decisions?
How is our product perceived by customers?
How do demographic factors influence the purchase decision?

BRANDING BRIEF 10-1
Digging Beneath the Surface to Understand Consumer Behavior

Because the consumer behavior we observe can differ from the behavior consumers report in surveys, useful marketing insights sometimes emerge from unobtrusively observing consumers rather than talking to them. For example, Hoover became suspicious when people claimed in surveys that they vacuumed their houses for an hour each week. To check, the company installed timers in certain models and exchanged them for the same models in consumers' homes. The timers showed that people actually spent only a little over *half* an hour vacuuming each week. One researcher analyzed household trash to determine the types and quantities of food people consumed, finding that people do not have a very good idea of how much and what types of food they eat. Similarly, much research has shown that people report they eat healthier food than would appear to be the case if you opened their cabinets!

The right behavioral insights can have important marketing implications. DuPont commissioned marketing studies to uncover personal pillow behavior for its Dacron polyester unit, which supplies filling to pillow makers and sells its own Comforel brand (now part of INVISTA). One challenge: people don't give up their old pillows. Thirty-seven percent of one sample described their relationship with their pillow as like "an old married couple," and an additional 13 percent characterized their pillow like a "childhood friend." The researchers found that people fell into distinct groups in terms of pillow behavior: stackers (23 percent), plumpers (20 percent), rollers or folders (16 percent), cuddlers (16 percent), and smashers, who pound their pillows into a more comfy shape (10 percent). Women were more likely to plump, while men were more likely to fold. The prevalence of stackers led the company to sell more pillows packaged as pairs, as well as to market different levels of softness or firmness.

Much of this type of research has its roots in *ethnography*, the anthropological term for the study of cultures in their natural surroundings. The intent behind these in-depth, observational studies is for consumers to drop their guard and provide a more realistic portrayal of who they are rather than who they would like to be. On the basis of ethnographic research that uncovered consumers' true feelings, ad campaigns have been created for various brands.

For example, Benylin's "Take a Benylin Day" was an ad campaign developed based on a key customer insight that having a cold really makes the consumer feel bad enough, but trying to fight through it and getting to work can just make them feel even worse. Many cough medicines were advertising their medicines to ensure their customers were back at work when they were really looking to take time off to recover. Benylin used this key customer insight and designed an ad campaign giving consumers "permission" to take the day off and rest.

Another interesting campaign inspired by a key observational insight with customers was when the U.K.-based mobile company Three designed an ad campaign HolidaySpam, based on a customer insight into how people behave while on vacation. It featured customers talking about their vacations and featuring an apology to those receiving photos of sandy beaches and gorgeous sunsets (called *holiday spam* by some)[2] from friends vacationing in sunny places. The ad featured the mobile company Three's offer allowing customers to use their mobile phones abroad at

DuPont commissioned a marketing study to learn about different "pillow behaviors". This study resulted in a redesigning of pillows to meet the needs of different types of consumers.

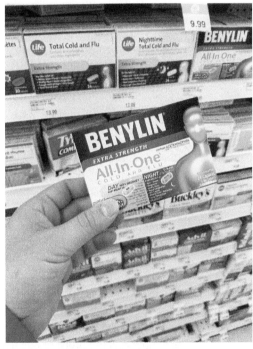

Benylin's "Take a Benylin Day" ad campaign was the result of a key customer insight that taking a day off from work to recover from a cough actually made consumers feel better.

Intel used in-depth insights from ethnographic research to make technology more accessible. Intel's China Home Learning PC is an example of this.

no extra cost. This campaign became a viral success, garnering a 90 percent increase in social conversation volume.

In another example of ethnographic research, Intel utilized ethnographic insights to develop new collaborations to make technology more accessible. For instance, Dr. Genevieve Bell, Intel's anthropologist "tech intellectual," interviewed Chinese parents who were frustrated with the distractions computers created in their children's school work. Bell helped develop a "China Home Learning PC" that gave parents a key to prevent games. Additionally, upon digging up the contents of people's cars around the world, she found that many people were ignoring the technology already built into their cars. Based on that research, Intel has collaborated with Jaguar and Toyota to develop better ways for consumers to sync their devices to the built-in technology in their automobiles.

Sources: Russell Belk, ed., *Handbook of Qualitative Research Method in Marketing* (Northampton, MA: Edward Elgar Publishing, 2006); Eric J. Arnould and Amber Epp, "Deep Engagement with Consumer Experience:

Listening and Learning with Qualitative Data," in *The Handbook of Marketing Research: Uses, Misuses, and Future Advances*, eds. Rajiv Grover and Marco Vriens (Thousand Oaks, CA: Sage Press, 2006): 51–58; Jennifer Chang Coupland, "Invisible Brands: An Ethnography of Households and the Brands in Their Kitchen Pantries," *Journal of Consumer Research* 32, no. 1 (June 2005): 106–118; John Koten, "You Aren't Paranoid If You Feel Someone Eyes You Constantly," *The Wall Street Journal*, March 29, 1985, p. 1, 22; Susan Warren, "Pillow Talk: Stackers Outnumber Plumpers; Don't Mention Drool," *The Wall Street Journal*, January 8, 1998, B1; Natasha Singer, "Intel's Sharp-Eyed Social Scientist," *The New York Times*, February 15, 2014, www.nytimes.com/2014/02/16/technology/intels-sharp-eyed-social-scientist.html?mcubz=0, accessed October 5, 2017; Lorna Keane, "5 Ad Campaigns Inspired by Powerful Consumer Insights," April 3, 2017, http://blog.globalwebindex.net/marketing/powerful-consumer-insights/, accessed October 7, 2017; Graham Robertson, "How to Find Amazing Consumer Insights to Help your Brand," http://beloved-brands.com/2013/11/126/consumer-insight/, November 12, 2013, accessed October 5, 2017; Video of three campaign ads can be seen here: www.youtube.com/watch?v=1a1cL4TIMMc&feature=youtu.be www.youtube.com/watch?v=Wz7YbGCeWPA&feature=youtu.be.

Qualitative research has a long history in marketing. Ernest Dichter, one of the early pioneers in consumer psychoanalytic research, first applied these research principles in a study for Plymouth automobiles in the 1930s.[3] His research revealed the important—but previously overlooked—role that women played in the automobile purchase decision. Based on his consumer analysis, Plymouth adopted a new print advertising strategy that highlighted a young couple gazing admiringly at a Plymouth automobile under the headline "Imagine Us in a Car Like That." Dichter's subsequent work had an important impact on a number of different ad campaigns.[4]

Some of his assertions were fairly controversial. For example, he equated convertibles with youth, freedom, and the secret wish for mistresses; argued that women used Ivory soap to wash away their sins before a date; and maintained that baking was an expression of femininity and pulling a cake or loaf out of an oven for women was "in a sense like giving birth." His suggested tagline "Putting a Tiger in the Tank" for Exxon resulting in a long-running and successful ad campaign, however.[5]

This section next reviews several qualitative research techniques for identifying sources of brand equity such as brand awareness, brand attitudes, and brand attachment. These techniques also can identify outcomes of brand equity such as price elasticities, brand choice, and preference.

Free Association

The simplest and often the most powerful way to profile brand associations is free association tasks, in which subjects are asked what comes to mind when they think of the brand, without any more specific probe or cue than perhaps the associated product category. Examples include: "What does the Rolex name mean to you?" or "Tell me what comes to mind when you think of Rolex watches." Marketers can use the resulting associations to form a rough mental map for the brand (see Figure 10-2 for a sample mental map for State Farm).

Marketers use free association tasks mainly to identify the range of possible brand associations in consumers' minds, but free association may also provide some rough indication of the relative strength, favorability, and uniqueness of brand associations.[6] Coding free association responses in terms of the order of elicitation—whether they are early or late in the sequence—at least gives us a rough measure of their strength.[7] For example, if many consumers mention "fast and convenient" as one of their first associations when given "McDonald's restaurants" as a probe, then the association is probably a relatively strong one and likely able to affect consumer decisions. Associations later in the list may be weaker and thus, more likely to be overlooked during consumer decision-making. Comparing associations with those elicited for competitive brands can also tell us about their relative uniqueness. Finally, we can discern even favorability, to some extent, by how consumers phrase their associations.

Answers to free-association questions help marketers clarify the range of possible associations and assemble a brand profile.[8] To better understand the favorability of associations, we can ask consumers follow-up questions about the favorability of associations they listed or, more

generally, what they like best about the brand. Similarly, we can ask them follow-up questions about the uniqueness of associations they listed or, more generally, about what they find unique about the brand. Useful questions include the following:

1. What do you like best about the brand? What are its positive aspects or advantages?
2. What do you like least about the brand? What are its negative aspects or disadvantages?
3. What do you find unique about the brand? How is it different from other brands?

These simple, direct measures can be extremely valuable for determining core aspects of a brand image. To elicit more structure and guidance, consumers can be asked further follow-up questions about what the brand means to them in terms of classic journalism "who, what, when, where, why, and how" questions:

1. Who uses the brand? What kind of person?
2. What types of situations do they use the brand?
3. When and where do they use the brand?
4. Why do people use the brand? What do they get out of using it?
5. How do they use the brand? What do they use it for?

Guidelines.   The two main issues to consider in conducting free association tasks are what types of probes to give to subjects, and how to code and interpret the resulting data. In order not to bias results, it is best to move from general considerations to more specific considerations, as we illustrated earlier. Thus, ask consumers first what they think of the brand as a whole without reference to any particular category, followed by specific questions about particular products and aspects of the brand image.

Consumers' responses to open-ended probes can be either oral or written. The advantage of oral responses is that subjects may be less deliberate and more spontaneous in their reporting. In terms of coding the data, divide the protocols that each consumer provides into phrases and aggregate them across consumers in categories. Because of their more focused nature, responses to specific probes and follow-up questions are naturally easier to code.

The Science of Branding 10-1 below describes an approach to assembling brand associations using social media data and computer-science-based network and language-processing techniques.

THE SCIENCE OF BRANDING 10-1
Using Text Mining to Uncover Brand Associations and Positioning

The increased availability of large quantities of user-generated data (e.g., reviews, ratings, and comments in online discussion forums) from digital and online channels has spurred considerable interest in applying text-mining methods to generate insights that are relevant to marketing. For example, Lee and Bradlow analyzed reviews for digital cameras between 2004 and 2008 to uncover consumer-defined product attributes. Netzer, Feldman, Goldenberg, and Fresko used data from an online discussion forum subjected to text-mining algorithms to better understand the market structure and to construct a brand positioning map. Tirunillai and Tellis applied natural language processing approaches from computer science to analyze product reviews from 15 firms over a four-year period to generate key inferences regarding consumer satisfaction and quality and its underlying dimensions.

Another interesting approach to developing brand positioning involves analyzing "tags" or keywords generated by users to describe the content of online discussions and articles. Nam and Kannan utilized these user-generated social tags as proxies for diverse concepts and associations that were connected to a given brand. Research has also examined how to classify brands into different groups based on the unique language features associated with a given brand in social media.

Using a technique called Differential Language Analysis, Swaminathan, Schwartz, and Hill conducted a large-scale analysis of messages on Twitter. Their approach helped to identify different clusters of words (or topics) linked to brands as a way of determining unique language features associated with brands. In addition to text, Liu, Dzyabura, and Mizik and other researchers

have also begun examining how images contained in social media can be analyzed effectively to generate deeper insights into brand associations and brand positioning.

As data availability and computational social science-based methods become increasingly important, all of these different approaches hold great promise to marketers and marketing researchers going forward.

Sources: Nikolay Archak, Anindya Ghose, and Panagiotis G. Ipeirotis. "Deriving the Pricing Power of Product Features by Mining Consumer Reviews," *Management Science* 57, no. 8 (August 2011): 1485–1509; Abhishek Borah and Gerard J. Tellis, "Halo (Spillover) Effects in Social Media: Do Product Recalls of One Brand Hurt or Help Rival Brands?" *Journal of Marketing Research*, 53, no. 2 (April 2016): 143–160; Thomas Y. Lee and Eric T. Bradlow, "Automated Marketing Research Using Online Customer Reviews," *Journal of Marketing Research*, 48, no. 5 (2011): 881–894; Liu Liu, Daria Dzyabura, and Natalie Mizik, "Visual Listening In: Extracting Brand Image Portrayed on Social Media," revised October 1, 2018, https://ssrn.com/abstract=2978805 or http://dx.doi.org/10.2139/ssrn.2978805, accessed November 11, 2018; Hyoryung Nam, Yogesh V. Joshi, and P. K. Kannan, "Harvesting Brand Information from Social Tags," *Journal of Marketing*, 81, no. 4: 88–108; Oded Netzer, Ronen Feldman, Jacob Goldenberg, and Moshe Fresko, "Mine Your Own Business: Market-Structure Surveillance Through Text Mining," *Journal of Marketing Science*, 31, no. 3 (May 2012): 521–543; Seshadri Tirunillai and Gerard J. Tellis, "Mining Marketing Meaning from Online Chatter: Strategic Brand Analysis of Big Data Using Latent Dirichlet Allocation," *Journal of Marketing Research*, 51, no. 4 (August 2014): 463–479; Vanitha Swaminathan, Andy Schwartz, and Shawndra Hill "The Language of Brands in Social Media," working paper, 2016; Anbang Xu, Yuheng Hu, David Gal, Rama Akkiraju, and Vibha Sinha, "Modeling Brand Personality with Social Media," working paper, 2018.

Projective Techniques

For marketers to succeed in uncovering the sources of brand equity, they must profile consumers' brand knowledge structures as accurately and completely as possible. Unfortunately, under certain situations, consumers may feel that it would be socially unacceptable or undesirable to express their true feelings—especially to an interviewer they do not even know! As a result, they may find it easier to fall back on stereotypical, pat answers they believe would be acceptable or perhaps even expected by the interviewer.

Consumers may be particularly unwilling or unable to reveal their true feelings when marketers ask about brands characterized by a preponderance of imagery associations. For example, it may be difficult for consumers to admit that a certain brand name product has prestige and enhances their self-image. They may instead refer to some particular product feature as the reason they like or dislike the brand. Or they may simply find it difficult to identify and express their true feelings when asked directly, even if they attempt to do so. For either of these reasons, it might be impossible to obtain an accurate portrayal of brand knowledge structures without some rather unconventional research methods.

Projective techniques are diagnostic tools to uncover the true opinions and feelings of consumers when they are unwilling or otherwise unable to express themselves on these matters.[9] Marketers present consumers with an incomplete stimulus and ask them to complete it, or they give consumers an ambiguous stimulus and ask them to make sense of it. The idea is that in the process consumers will reveal some of their true beliefs and feelings. Thus, projective techniques can be especially useful when deeply rooted personal motivations or personally or socially sensitive subjects are at issue. In a **Rorschach test**, experimenters present ink blots to subjects and ask them what the ink blots remind them of; these tests can be used to assess the memories that a person has on a topic.[10]

Projective techniques have a long history in marketing, beginning with the motivation research of the late 1940s and 1950s.[11] A classic example is an experiment exploring hidden feelings toward instant coffee conducted by Mason Haire in the late 1940s, summarized in Branding Brief 10-2.[12] Although projective techniques do not always yield results as powerful as in that example, they often provide useful insights that help to assemble a complete picture of consumers and their relationships with brands. Many kinds of projective techniques are possible. We highlight a few here.[13]

BRANDING BRIEF 10-2

Once Upon a Time . . . You Were What You Cooked

One of the most famous applications of psychographic techniques was made by Mason Haire in the 1940s. The purpose of the experiment was to uncover consumers' true beliefs and feelings toward Nescafé instant coffee.

The impetus for the experiment was a survey conducted to determine why the initial sales of Nescafé instant coffee were so disappointing. The majority of the people who reported they did not like the product stated that the reason was the flavor. On the basis of consumer taste tests, however, Nescafé's management knew consumers found the taste of instant coffee acceptable when they didn't know what type of coffee they were drinking. Suspecting that consumers were not expressing their true feelings, Haire designed a clever experiment to discover what was really going on.

Haire set up two shopping lists containing the same six items. Shopping List 1 specified Maxwell House drip ground coffee, whereas Shopping List 2 specified Nescafé instant coffee, as follows:

Marketers of Nescafé used a novel psychographic technique to help uncover consumers' true feelings and thoughts about the brand, by comparing the brand to perceptions of its competitor Maxwell House.

Shopping List 1	Shopping List 2
Pound and a half of hamburger	Pound and a half of hamburger
2 loaves Wonder bread	2 loaves Wonder bread
Bunch of carrots	Bunch of carrots
1 can Rumford's Baking Powder	1 can Rumford's Baking Powder
Maxwell House coffee (drip ground)	Nescafé instant coffee
2 cans Del Monte peaches	2 cans Del Monte peaches
5 lbs. potatoes	5 lbs. potatoes

After coding the responses into frequently mentioned categories, Haire found that two starkly different profiles emerged:

	List 1 (Maxwell House)	List 2 (Nescafé)
Lazy	4%	48%
Fails to plan household purchases and schedules well	12%	48%
Thrifty	16%	4%
Not a good wife	0%	16%

Two groups of matched subjects were each given one of the lists and asked to "Read the shopping list. Try to project yourself into the situation as far as possible until you can more or less characterize the woman who bought the groceries." Subjects then wrote a brief description of the personality and character of that person.

Haire interpreted these results as indicating that instant coffee represented a departure from homemade coffee and traditions with respect to caring for one's family. In other words, at that time, the "labor-saving" aspect of instant coffee, rather than being an asset, was a liability in that it violated consumer traditions. Consumers were evidently reluctant to admit this fact when asked directly but were better able to express their true feelings when asked to project to another person.

The strategic implications of this new research finding were clear. Based on the original survey results, the obvious positioning for instant coffee with respect to regular coffee would have been to establish a point-of-difference on "convenience" and a point-of-parity on the basis of "taste." Based on the projective test findings, however, it was obvious that there also needed to be a point-of-parity on the basis of user imagery. As a result, a successful ad campaign was launched that promoted Nescafé coffee as a way for housewives to free up time so they could devote additional time to more important household activities!

Sources: Mason Haire, "Projective Techniques in Marketing Research," *Journal of Marketing* 14, no. 5 (April 1950): 649–652; J. Arndt, "Haire's Shopping List Revisited," *Journal of Advertising Research* 13, no. 5 (1973): 57–61; George S. Lane and Gayne L. Watson, "A Canadian Replication of Mason Haire's 'Shopping List' Study," *Journal of the Academy of Marketing Science* 3, no. 1 (December 1975): 48–59; William L. Wilkie, *Consumer Behavior*, 3rd ed. (New York: John Wiley and Sons, 1994).

Completion and Interpretation Tasks.   Classic projective techniques use incomplete or ambiguous stimuli to elicit consumer thoughts and feelings. One approach is "bubble exercises," which depict different people buying or using certain products or services. Empty bubbles, as in cartoons, are placed in the scenes to represent the thoughts, words, or actions of one or more of the participants. Marketers then ask consumers to "fill in the bubble" by indicating what they believe is happening or being said in the scene. The stories and conversations told this way can be especially useful for assessing user and usage imagery for a brand.

Comparison Tasks.   Another useful technique is comparison tasks, in which we ask consumers to convey their impressions by comparing brands to people, countries, animals, activities, fabrics, occupations, cars, magazines, vegetables, nationalities, or even other brands.[14] For example, we might ask consumers, "If Dannon yogurt were a car, which one would it be? If it were an animal, which one might it be? Looking at the people depicted in these pictures, which ones do you think would be most likely to eat Dannon yogurt?" In each case, we would ask a follow-up question about why subjects made the comparison they did. The objects people choose to represent the brand and their reasons can provide glimpses into the psyche of the consumer with respect to a brand, particularly useful in understanding imagery associations. By examining the answers to probes, researchers may be better able to assemble a rich image for the brand, for example, identifying key brand personality associations.

Zaltman Metaphor Elicitation Technique

One interesting approach to better understand how consumers view brands is the Zaltman Metaphor Elicitation Technique (ZMET).[15] ZMET is based on a belief that consumers often have subconscious motives for their purchasing behavior. "A lot goes on in our minds that we're not aware of," said former Harvard Business School professor Gerald Zaltman. "Most of what influences what we say and do occurs below the level of awareness. That's why we need new techniques to get at hidden knowledge—to get at what people don't know they know."

To access this hidden knowledge, he developed the Zaltman Metaphor Elicitation Technique. As described in its U.S. patent, ZMET is "a technique for eliciting interconnected constructs that influence thought and behavior." The word *construct* refers to "an abstraction created by the researcher to capture common ideas, concepts, or themes expressed by customers." For example, the construct "ease of use" might capture the statements "simple to operate," "works without hassle," and "you don't really have to do anything."

ZMET stems from knowledge and research from varied fields such as cognitive neuroscience, neurobiology, art critique, literary criticism, visual anthropology, visual sociology, semiotics, art therapy, and psycholinguistics. The technique is based on the idea that most social communication is nonverbal and, as a result, approximately two-thirds of all stimuli received by the brain are visual. Using ZMET, Zaltman teases out consumers' hidden thoughts and feelings about a particular topic, which often can be expressed best using metaphors.

Zaltman argues that metaphors can be very useful to us in that they are "the representation of one thing in terms of another [and can] often help us express the way we feel about or view a particular aspect of our lives." ZMET focuses on surface, thematic, and deep metaphors. Some common deep metaphors include transformation, container, journey, connection, and sacred and profane.

A ZMET study starts with a group of participants who are asked in advance to think about the research topic at hand and collect a set of images from their own sources (the Internet, magazines, catalogs, and family photo albums) that represent their thoughts and feelings about the research topic.

The participants bring these images with them for a personal one-on-one 2-hour interview with a trained ZMET interviewer, who uses advanced interview techniques to explore the images with the participant and reveal their deep ideas, archetypes, themes, and emotions through a "guided conversation."

The interview consists of a series of steps, each with a specific purpose in mind:

1. *Storytelling:* Exploring individual visual metaphors
2. *Expand the Frame:* Expanding the metaphoric meaning of images
3. *Sensory Metaphor:* Eliciting metaphors about the research topic from each sensory modality
4. *Vignette:* Using the mind's eye to create a short story about the research topic
5. *Digital Image:* Integrating the images to create a visual summary of the research topic

Cisco's Human Network Campaign was developed based on research—conducted using ZMET—into consumers' thoughts and feelings about Cisco Systems and its role in their lives.

Once the participants' interviews have been completed, researchers identify key themes or constructs, code the data, and assemble a consensus map of the most important constructs. Quantitative analyses of the data can provide information for advertising, promotions, and other marketing decisions.

The Zaltman Metaphor Elicitation Technique (ZMET) has been applied in a variety of different ways, including as a means to help understand consumers' images of brands, products, and companies. Marketers can employ ZMET for a variety of consumer-insight research topics. ZMET is useful in understanding consumers' images of brands, products, companies, brand equity, product concepts and designs, product usage and purchase experiences, life experiences, consumption context, and attitudes toward business.

An interesting case study involves Cisco Systems' use of ZMET to research how IT professionals and business decision makers viewed the brand. The purpose of the study was to find out if these segments had an emotional connection to a seemingly rational brand and service. ZMET was used to uncover deeper answers to the question, "What are your thoughts and feelings about Cisco Systems and its role in your life?" As it turned out, there were strong emotional connections to the brand including the peace-of-mind and calmness of knowing that Cisco was there for you, but also the anxiety and fear of what could happen if there were no longer a Cisco. Cisco used the deep metaphor of "connection" to highlight the positive emotions that the brand delivered to customers. Much like the archetypical "father figure," customers felt safe and protected by Cisco, even if much of what Cisco provided was unseen behind the Internet infrastructure. This discovery contributed to the development of a rebranding initiative around Cisco as "The Human Network," helping to bring an emotional face to the network product and services from the company. The rebranding led to significant increases in brand recognition and brand value.

Neural Research Methods

Taking ZMET one step further to dig even deeper into the subconscious, some marketing researchers are bypassing any verbal response from consumers to literally get inside the minds of consumers through various neural research methods. **Neuromarketing** is the study of how the brain responds to marketing stimuli, including brands.[16] For example, some firms are applying sophisticated techniques such as EEG (electroencephalogram) technology to monitor brain activity and better gauge consumer responses to marketing. Still others use functional magnetic resonance imaging (fMRI) to track the brain's blood flow to understand how participants in the research are responding to various stimuli. Although more expensive than EEG—for example, a single fMRI can cost $1,000 per machine per hour—fMRI can help researchers get deeper insights into how the brain responds to various outside stimuli.[17] For example, PayPal used neuromarketing research to redesign their ad campaign and focused on speed and convenience, rather than safety and security.

Neurological research has been applied many other ways in marketing.[18] Companies such as Campbell's Soup and Frito-Lay have used neuromarketing to understand consumer responses to packaging, including color, fonts, and images. Frito-Lay discovered that the types of bags used in packaging could impact consumer responses. Based on this research, they replaced their shiny bags with matte bags. Frito-Lay also used neuromarketing to get inside the minds of consumers as

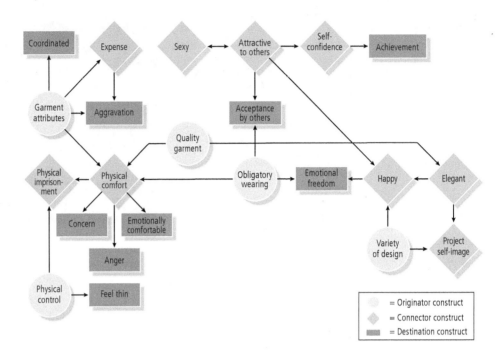

FIGURE 10-3

Application of ZMET to Intimate Apparel Market

they reacted to Cheetos cheese-flavored snacks. Scanning the brains of a carefully chosen group of consumers revealed that their most powerful responses were to the product's messy outer coating. The research study's insight led to an award-winning ad campaign, which made the orange coating of Cheetos the focus of the ad campaign.[19]

Neuromarketing has also been used to measure the type of emotional response consumers exhibit when presented with marketing stimuli. For instance, marketers have studied how marketing actions can influence the neural representation of experienced pleasantness or pleasure.[20] Others have explored how neuromarketing can help answer marketing questions that cannot be readily solved through traditional marketing methods. For example, marketers could expose consumers to a commercial and then measure consumers' responses using blood oxygenation level-dependent measurement.[21] Neurological research has shown that people activate different regions of the brain in assessing the personality traits of people than they do when assessing brands.

One major research finding to emerge from neurological consumer research is that many purchase decisions appear to be characterized less by the logical weighing of variables and more "as a largely unconscious habitual process, as distinct from the rational, conscious, information-processing model of economists and traditional marketing textbooks." Even basic decisions, such as the purchase of gasoline, seem to be influenced by brain activity at the subrational level.

Given the complexity of the human brain, however, many researchers caution that neurological research should not form the sole basis for marketing decisions. These research activities have not been universally accepted. The measurement devices to capture brain activity can be highly obtrusive, such as with skull caps studded with electrodes, creating artificial exposure conditions. Others question whether they offer unambiguous implications for marketing strategy. Brian Knutson, a professor of neuroscience and psychology at Stanford University, compares the use of EEG to "standing outside a baseball stadium and listening to the crowd to figure out what happened."

PayPal used neuromarketing research to redesign their ad campaign and focused on speed and convenience rather than safety and security.

Brand Personality and Values

As defined in Chapter 2, brand personality is the human characteristics or traits that consumers can attribute to a brand. We can measure it in different ways. Perhaps the simplest and most direct way is to solicit open-ended responses to a probe such as the following:

> If the brand were to come alive as a person, what would it be like? What would it do? Where would it live? What would it wear? Who would it talk to if it went to a party (and what would it talk about)?

If consumers have difficulty getting started in their descriptions, an easily understood example or prompt serves as a guide. For example, if Campbell's Soup were to be described as a person, one possible response might be as follows:[22]

> Mrs. Campbell is a rosy-cheeked and plump grandmother who lives in a warm, cozy house and wears an apron as she cooks wonderful things for her grandchildren.

Other means are possible to capture consumers' points of view. For example, marketers can give consumers a variety of pictures or a stack of magazines and ask them to assemble a profile of the brand. Ad agencies often conduct "picture sorting" studies to clarify who are typical users of a brand.

As Chapter 3 noted, brand personality and user imagery may not always agree. When *USA Today* was first introduced, a research study exploring consumer opinions of the newspaper indicated that the benefits readers and nonreaders perceived were highly consistent. Perceptions of the *USA Today* brand personality—as colorful, friendly, and simple—were also highly related. User imagery, however, differed dramatically: Nonreaders viewed a typical *USA Today* reader as a shallow "air head"; readers, on the other hand, saw a typical *USA Today* reader as a well-rounded person interested in a variety of issues. Based on these findings, an advertising campaign was introduced to appeal to nonreaders that showed how prominent people endorsed the newspaper.[23]

A consumer research study of *USA Today* revealed stark differences in user imagery among readers and non-readers, even though perceptions of the brand's personality were consistent.

The Big Five. We can assess brand personality more definitively through adjective checklists or ratings. Stanford's Jennifer Aaker conducted a research project that provides an interesting glimpse into the personality of some well-known brands, as well as a methodology to examine the personality of any one brand. Based on an extensive data collection of ratings of 114 personality traits on 37 brands in various product categories by more than 600 individuals representative of the U.S. population, she created a brand personality scale that reflected the following five factors (with underlying facets) of brand personality:[24]

1. Sincerity (down-to-earth, honest, wholesome, and cheerful)
2. Excitement (daring, spirited, imaginative, and up-to-date)
3. Competence (reliable, intelligent, and successful)
4. Sophistication (upper class and charming)
5. Ruggedness (outdoorsy and tough).

Figure 10-4 depicts the specific trait items that make up the Aaker brand personality scale. Respondents in her study rated how descriptive each personality trait was for each brand according to a seven-point scale (1 = not at all descriptive; 7 = extremely descriptive). Aaker averaged responses to provide summary measures. Some brands tend to be strong on one particular factor; some brands like Nike are high on more than one factor; some brands score poorly on all factors.

Brand personality has been shown to impact brand outcomes in various ways. A meta-analysis of brand personality research aimed to connect the various dimensions of brand personality with different outcome measures including brand attitudes and commitment. The researchers found that sincerity and competence dimensions were more impactful on brand attitude and commitment; excitement and ruggedness had the weakest impact. Further, they found brand personality exerted the greatest impact on brands in the maturity stage of their life cycle compared with brands in an early life-cycle stage.[25]

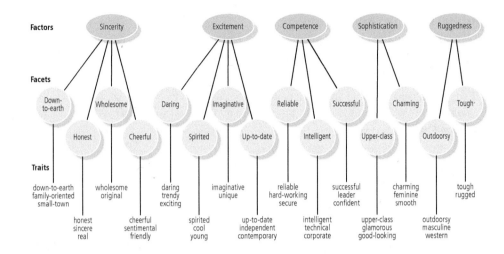

FIGURE 10-4

Brand Personality Scale Measures

Ethnographic and Experiential Methods

More than ever, researchers are working to improve the effectiveness of their qualitative approaches, as well as to go beyond traditional qualitative techniques to research consumers in their natural environment.[26] The rationale is that no matter how clever the research design, consumers may not be able to fully express their true selves as part of a formalized research study. By tapping more directly into consumers' actual home, work, or shopping behaviors, researchers might be able to elicit more meaningful responses.[27] As markets become more competitive and many brand differences are threatened, any insight that helps to support a stronger brand positioning or create a stronger link to consumers is valuable (see Branding Brief 10-3).

BRANDING BRIEF 10-3

Making the Most of Consumer Insights

Consumer research plays a significant role in uncovering information valuable to consumer-focused companies. David Taylor, the founder of the Brand Gym consultancy, cautions that not all findings from consumer research can be considered insights. He defines insight as "a penetrating, discerning understanding that unlocks an opportunity."

According to Taylor, an insight holds far more potential than a finding. Using Microsoft as an example, Taylor draws the contrast between the finding that "people need to process more and more information and data" and the insight that "information is the key to power and freedom." This insight might help Microsoft develop products that appeal to a larger consumer base than if the company relied solely on the finding.

Taylor developed a set of criteria to evaluate insights:

- *Fresh:* An insight might be obvious and, in fact, be overlooked or forgotten as a result. Check again.

- *Relevant:* An insight when played back to other target consumers should strike a chord.

- *Enduring:* By building on a deep understanding of consumers' beliefs and needs, a true consumer insight should have the potential to remain relevant over time.

- *Inspiring:* All the team should be excited by the insight and see different but consistent applications.

Insights can come from consumer research such as focus groups, but also from using what Taylor describes as the "core insight drills." A sample of these drills follows:

- How could the brand or category do more to help improve people's lives?

- What do people really value in the category? What would they not miss?

- What conflicting needs do people have? How can these tradeoffs be solved?

- What bigger market is the brand really competing in from a consumer viewpoint? What could the brand do more of to better meet these higher-order needs?

- What assumptions do people make about the market that could be challenged?

- How do people think the product works, and how does it work in reality?

- How is the product used in reality? What other products are used instead of the brand, where the brand could do a better job?

These drills can help companies unearth consumer insights that lead to better products and services, and ultimately, to stronger brands.

Source: David Taylor, "Drilling for Nuggets: How to Use Insight to Inspire Innovation," *Brand Strategy*, March 2000. Used with permission of Brand Strategy, www.brandstrategy.co.uk.

We've noted that much of this type of research has its roots in ethnographic research origi-nally used by anthropologists. Ethnographic research uses "thick description" based on participant observation. In marketing, the goal of ethnographic research is to extract and interpret the deep cultural meaning of events and activities through various research techniques such as consumer immersion, site visits, shop-alongs, embedded research, and so on.[28]

Advocates of the ethnographic approach have sent researchers to consumers' homes in the morning to see how they approach their days, given business travelers digital cameras and diaries to capture their feelings when in hotel rooms, and conducted "beeper studies" in which partici-pants are instructed to write down what they are doing when they are paged or texted.[29]

Marketers such as Procter & Gamble seek consumers' permission to spend time with them in their homes to see how they actually use and experience products. Some of the many other compa-nies that have used ethnographic research to study consumers include Best Western (to learn how seniors decide when and where to shop), Moen (to observe over an extended time how customers really use their shower devices), and Intel (to understand how people use mobile communications in moving around a city).[30] A comprehensive ethnographic research study for JCPenney on their wedding registry resulted in a complete makeover at all levels.[31] The Branding Brief 10-4 below describes how a technique of ethnography applied to digital environments (i.e., netnography, can be beneficial to brands).

In addition to the business-to-consumer applications of ethnography and netnography, busi-ness-to-business firms can also benefit from company visits that help to cement relationships and supplement research efforts. Technology firms—such as Hewlett-Packard—use cross-functional customer visits as a market research tool to gain a competitive advantage. Figure 10-5 offers advice from one expert on the subject, Ed McQuarrie, about best practices for an outbound or inbound customer visit.[32]

BRANDING BRIEF 10-4
Netnography as a Digital Research Technique

Recently, with our social interactions increasingly taking place in digital environments, an ethnographic technique for digital environments called *netnography* has become popular as a mar-keting research tool. Two types of data can be gathered to con-duct research in online forums: (1) the actual communications in online communities, and (2) researchers' observations regarding interactions among community members.

Netnography involves six stages, as follows: (1) developing a research plan; (2) establishing entrée; (3) collecting and triangulating data; (4) analyzing and interpreting data; (5) ensuring ethical stan-dards; and (6) reporting on research finding and associated insights.

One application of netnography to Starbucks Coffee was conducted by the company, NetBase. It resulted in various inter-pretations of the brand based on comments posted on various Web sites. Positive themes which emerged included its vari-ants, the instant coffee, the taste of coffee, and the stimulant effects of coffee. An example comment was "I love Starbucks; it's so yummy! When I grow up, I want my bedroom to smell like Starbucks coffee!" In contrast, negative themes revolve around its premium pricing, its taste, and poor quality. Other negative themes include side effects and the coffee house experience.

There are some pros and cons of netnography. Like ethnog-raphy, netnography studies human behavior in a descriptive way. Similar to ethnographic methods, netnography also utilizes mul-tiple approaches, can be adapted to varying contexts, and can provide deep insights due to its immersive nature. Netnography has certain benefits over other qualitative research tools—such as focus groups or in-depth interviews—in that it is less obtrusive and is conducted at a lower cost.

However, one downside of netnographic approaches is it is limited to research pertaining to digital environments, and there-fore, is not applicable to consumers who do not have access or do not participate in social media. The findings may be subject to biases that are typical of online research conducted on consumers who have self-selected themselves into a study, and therefore, must be carefully scrutinized for sample selection biases. Never-theless, there is certainly supporting evidence that ethnography applied to online forums (i.e., netnography) can yield valuable insights to brands and companies.

Sources: Robert V. Kozinets, *Netnography: Doing Ethnographic Research Online* (Thousand Oaks, CA: Sage Publications, 2010); Robert V. Kozinets, "The Field Behind the Screen: Using Netnography for Marketing Research in Online Communities," *Journal of Marketing Research* 39, no. 1 (2002): 61–72; Hope Ngyuyen, "Starbucks Netnography," January 4, 2012, www.netbase.com/blog/starbucks-netnography/, accessed October 8, 2017. Gigi DeVault, "Netnography: Obtaining Social Media Insight," February 28, 2017, www.thebalance.com/investigate-social-media-like-an-anthropologist-2297153, accessed November 6, 2017. Daiuchuu Ginga, "In the Footsteps of Kozinets: Towards a New Netnographic Taxonimization," *Journal of Internet Appreciation*, (2013): 418–419; Robert V. Kozinets (1998), "On Netnography Initial Reflections on Consumer Research Investigations of Cyberculture," in *Advances in Consumer Research*, Volume 25, eds. Joseph Alba and Wesley Hutchinson (Provo, UT: Association for Consumer Research, 1998), 366–371.

1. Send an advance letter of confirmation with an agenda so customers know what to expect and can be prepared.
2. Send small cross-functional teams.
3. Select customers according to a plan and visit at least a dozen.
4. Don't keep going back to the same small group of favorite customers.
5. Interview people at each site who represent each stage of the purchasing decision.
6. Get support from local account management.
7. Use a two- to three-page discussion guide in outline form.
8. Assign roles to team members (moderator, listener, note taker, etc.).
9. Use open-ended questions.
10. Don't ask customers to give solutions—get them to identify problems.
11. Don't talk too much and don't show off your expertise.
12. Probe deeper by using follow-up questions.
13. Debrief immediately.
14. Highlight verbatim quotes in reports.
15. A summary report should emphasize big news and be organized by major themes.
16. Archive the report online with other marketing research and intelligence.

FIGURE 10-5

Tips for Conducting
Good Customer Visits

The show *Undercover Boss* is an American television series in which a person who is a senior-level executive goes undercover as an entry-level employee in an effort to uncover problems or issues with the company. Similarly, service companies often employ mystery shoppers, paid researchers who pose as customers to learn about the service experience provided by a company. Sometimes the results can be eye-opening. When the president of Office Depot decided to pose as a mystery shopper himself, he found that employees were spending too much time keeping stores clean and well-stocked and not enough time building relationships with customers. As a result, the company reduced the size of stores, retrained and incentivized employees to focus more on customers, and added other products and services that customers wanted that were not currently available.[33]

Through the years, companies have changed the way they gain customer insights. Microsoft employs ethnographic research with in-depth studies of consumer online search attitudes and behavior. Observing consumers inside and outside the home in a series of research studies, the company learned of changes over time in the way consumers explore and learn about new things online. The German company Miele used ethnographic research to uncover how consumers who suffered from allergies engaged in constant cleaning of their homes. They designed a vacuum cleaner with a traffic-light indicator to show when a surface is dust-free.[34]

Lead users of a product are of special research importance to many consumers. Many firms ask online groups of their most progressive consumers to give feedback via instant messages or chat rooms. Alternatively, companies may design contests to generate new product design ideas from their most engaged consumers. This type of consumer-designed product or ad campaign has become a popular way by which companies engage their customers. For example, Frito-Lay has introduced several flavors for its Lay's potato chip brand based on the annual "Do Us a Flavor" contest, which enlists chip fans to identify new flavors. The three finalist flavors in 2017 included Everything Bagel, Fried Green Tomatoes, and Tacos.[35] Another company, Procter & Gamble, has a number of innovations that resulted from its customer insights, as we outline in the Branding Brief 10-5 below.

Despite its many advantages, two of the more significant downsides to ethnographic research are that it is time-consuming and expensive. Compact video cameras make capturing participants' words and actions easier, and short films are often part of the research output that is reported to help bring the research to life.[36] Moreover, because it is based on subjective interpretation, multiple points of view may prevail. Every research method, however, has its advantages and disadvantages.[37]

BRANDING BRIEF 10-5
How P&G Innovates Using Qualitative Research Data

Procter & Gamble has learned the value of combining quantitative with qualitative data in managing its brands. When P&G's baby care group was receiving quantitative and qualitative information that was contradictory about its Pampers diaper brand, P&G collected qualitative data to shed further light on *why* there was consumer attrition, by following 12 mothers. Participants in the study had to answer questions about their diaper changing behaviors, and what products they bought. The moms completed shopping assignments, answered surveys and uploaded pictures on various sizes. Based on nearly 600 pages of consumer feedback, they found that the lack of good diaper fit sometimes caused moms to switch to a different brand or adapt to a much larger size. Based on this insight, P&G was able to create a new diaper size and improve their communications regarding diaper sizes on their packaging.

P&G's blockbuster product Swiffer is also the result of a customer insight derived from ethnographic methods. Through qualitative research, P&G understood the value of a clean home to the consumer. Many homeowners viewed their clean floors as a reflection of themselves, and therefore, exerted a lot of their time and effort on this household chore. To conduct their research, a team of researchers entered 18 homes to understand the process of mopping and cleaning. They found that more than half the time that was devoted to this household chore was being used to clean the mop itself. This insight led to the design of the Swiffer. By using disposable cloths at the end of a broom, the Swiffer product eliminates the need for cleaning the mop. The Swiffer product

P&G's blockbuster product, Swiffer, is the result of a customer insight derived from qualitative marketing research.

was a huge blockbuster hit for P&G, and the case study helps demonstrate the value of qualitative insight to developing new products that solve a real customer problem.

Sources: Elise Dupre, "P&G Solves Diaper Dilemma with Qualitative Research," November 26, 2013, www.dmnews.com/dataanalytics/pg-solves-diaper-dilemma-with-qualitative-research/article/322357/, accessed October 8, 2017; Jo Bowman, "The Rise of People-Watching Research Carried Out by Brands," September 1, 2016, www.raconteur.net/business/the-rise-of-people-watching-research-carried-out-by-brands, accessed October 8, 2017; Eric Butterman "Mopping the Floor with the Status Quo," December 2012, www.asme.org/engineering-topics/articles/product-planning/mopping-floor-the-status-quo, accessed October 8, 2017.

Qualitative research techniques are a creative means of ascertaining consumer perceptions that may otherwise be difficult to uncover. The range of possible qualitative research techniques is limited only by the creativity of the marketing researcher.

However, qualitative research also has its drawbacks. The in-depth insights that emerge have to be tempered by the realization that the samples are often very small and may not necessarily generalize to broader populations. Moreover, given the qualitative nature of the data, there may be questions of interpretation. Different researchers examining the same results from a qualitative research study may draw different conclusions.

QUANTITATIVE RESEARCH TECHNIQUES

Although qualitative measures are useful in identifying the range of possible associations with a brand and some initial insights into their strength, favorability, and uniqueness, marketers often want a more definitive portrait of the brand to allow them to make more confident and defensible strategic and tactical recommendations.

Some say qualitative research strives to uncover and discover, while quantitative research aims to prove or disprove. Whereas qualitative research typically elicits some type of verbal response from consumers, **quantitative research** typically employs various types of scale questions from which researchers can draw numerical representations and summaries.

Quantitative measures of brand knowledge can help to more definitively assess the depth and breadth of brand awareness; the strength, favorability, and uniqueness of brand associations; the positivity of brand judgments and feelings; and the extent and nature of brand relationships. Quantitative measures are often the primary ingredient in tracking studies that monitor brand knowledge structures of consumers over time, as we discussed in Chapter 9.

Brand Awareness

Recall that brand awareness is related to the strength of the brand in memory, as reflected by consumers' ability to identify various brand elements like the brand name, logo, symbol, character, packaging, and slogan under different conditions. Brand awareness describes the likelihood that a brand will come to mind in various situations, and the ease with which it does so given distinct types of cues.

Marketers use several measures of awareness of brand elements.[38] Choosing the right one is a matter of knowing the relative importance of brand awareness for consumer behavior in the category and the role it plays in the success of the marketing program, as we discussed in Chapter 2. Let's look at some of these awareness issues.

Recognition. Brand recognition requires consumers to identify the brand under a variety of circumstances and can rest on the identification of any of the brand elements. The most basic recognition test gives consumers a set of individual items visually or orally and asks them whether they think they have previously seen or heard of these items. To provide a more sensitive test, it is often useful to include decoys or lures—items consumers could not possibly have seen. In addition to "yes" or "no" responses, consumers can also rate how confident they are in their recognition of an item.

Other, somewhat subtler, recognition measures test perceptually degraded versions of the brand, which are masked or distorted in some way or shown for an extremely brief duration. For example, we can test brand name recognition with missing letters. Figure 10-6 tests your ability to recognize brand names with less than full information. These subtler measures may be particularly important for brands that have a high level of recognition, in order to provide more sensitive assessments.[39]

Brand recognition is especially important for packaging, and some marketing researchers have used creative means to assess the in-store visibility of package design. As a starting point, they consider the benchmark or "best case" of the visibility of a package when a consumer (1) with 20–20 vision, (2) is face-to-face with a package, (3) at a distance of less than five feet, and (4) under ideal lighting conditions.

A key question then is whether the package design is robust enough to be still recognizable if one or more of these four conditions are not present. Because shopping is often not conducted under ideal conditions, such insights are important. For example, many consumers who wear eyeglasses do not wear them when shopping in a supermarket. Is the package still able to effectively communicate to consumers under such conditions?

A brand name with a high level of awareness will be recognized under less than ideal conditions. Consider the following list of incomplete names (i.e., word fragments). Which ones do you recognize? Compare your answers to the answer key in the footnote to see how well you did.

1. D _ _ N E _
2. K O _ _ K
3. D U _ A C _ _ _
4. H Y _ T _
5. A D _ _ L
6. M _ T _ E L
7. D _ L T _
8. N _ Q U _ L
9. G _ L L _ T _ _
10. H _ _ S H _ Y
11. H _ L L _ _ R K
12. M _ C H _ _ I N
13. T _ P P _ R W _ _ E
14. L _ G _
15. N _ K _

FIGURE 10-6

Don't Tell Me, It's On the Tip of my Tongue

Answers: (1) Disney; (2) Kodak; (3) Duracell; (4) Hyatt; (5) Advil; (6) Mattel; (7) Delta; (8) NyQuil; (9) Gillette; (10) Hershey; (11) Hallmark; (12) Michelin; (13) Tupperware; (14) Lego; (15) Nike.

Research methods using tachistoscopes (T-scopes) and eye tracking techniques exist to test the effectiveness of alternative package designs according to a number of specific criteria:

- Degree of shelf impact
- Impact and recall of specific design elements
- Perceived package size
- Copy visibility and legibility
- Distance at which the package can first be identified
- Angle at which the package can first be identified
- Speed with which the package can be identified.

These additional measures can provide more sensitive measures of recognition than simple "yes" or "no" tasks. By applying these direct and indirect measures of brand recognition, marketers can determine which brand elements exist in memory, and, to some extent, the strength of their association. One advantage that brand recognition measures have over recall measures is the chance to use visual recognition. It may be difficult for consumers to describe a logo or symbol in a recall task; it's much easier for them to assess the same elements visually in a recognition task.

Nevertheless, brand recognition measures provide only an approximation of *potential* recallability. To determine whether consumers will actually recall the brand elements under various circumstances, we need measures of brand recall.

Recall.   To demonstrate brand recall, consumers must retrieve the actual brand element from memory when given some related probe or cue. Thus, brand recall is a more demanding memory task than brand recognition because consumers are not just given a brand element and asked to say whether they have seen or heard it before.

Different measures of brand recall are possible depending on the type of cues provided to consumers. *Unaided recall* on the basis of "all brands" provided as a cue is likely to identify only the very strongest brands. *Aided recall* uses various types of cues to help consumer recall. One possible sequence of aided recall might use progressively narrower cues—such as product class, product category, and product type labels—to provide insight into the organization of consumers' brand knowledge structures.

For example, if recall of the Porsche 911—a high-performance German sports car—in non-German markets were of interest, recall probes could begin with all cars and move to more and more narrowly defined categories, such as sports cars, foreign sports cars, or even high-performance German sports cars. Marketers could ask consumers: When you think of foreign sports cars, which brands come to mind?

Other types of cues can help measure brand recall. For example, marketers can ask about product attributes (When you think of chocolate, which brands come to mind?) or usage goals (If you were thinking of having a healthy snack, which brands come to mind?). Often, to capture the breadth of brand recall and to assess brand salience, we might need to examine the context of the purchase decision or consumption situation, such as different times and places. The stronger the brand associations to these nonproduct considerations, the more likely it is that consumers will recall them when given those situational cues.

When combined, measures of recall based on product attribute or category cues and situational or usage cues indicate breadth and depth of recall. We can further distinguish brand recall according to the order as well as the latency or speed of recall. In many cases, people will recognize a brand when it is shown to them and will recall it if they are given a sufficient number of cues. Thus, potential recallability is high. The more important issue is the salience of the brand: Do consumers think of the brand under the right circumstances, for example, when they could be either buying or using the product? How quickly do they think of the brand? Is it automatically or easily recalled? Is it the first brand they recall?

Corrections for Guessing.   Any research measure must consider the issue of consumers making up responses or guessing. That problem may be especially evident with certain types of aided awareness or recognition measures for the brand. Spurious awareness occurs when consumers erroneously claim they recall something they really don't and that may not even exist.

From a marketing perspective, the problem with spurious awareness is that it may send misleading signals about the proper strategic direction for a brand. For example, Oxtoby-Smith reported that one of its clients was struggling with a 5 percent market share even though 50 percent of survey respondents reported they were aware of the brand. On the surface, it would seem a good idea to improve the image of the brand and attitudes toward it in some way. Upon further examination, marketers determined that spurious awareness account for *almost half* the survey respondents who reported brand awareness, suggesting that a more appropriate solution to the true problem would be first to build awareness to a greater degree. Marketers should be sensitive to the possibilities of misleading signals because of spurious brand awareness, especially with new brands or ones with plausible-sounding names.

Strategic Implications. The advantage of aided recall measures is that they yield insight into how brand knowledge is organized in memory and what kind of cues or reminders may be necessary for consumers to be able to retrieve the brand from memory. Understanding recall when we use different levels of product category specificity as cues is important, because it has implications for how consumers form consideration sets and make product decisions.

For example, again consider the Porsche 911. Assume consumer recall of this particular car model was fairly low when all cars were considered but very high when foreign sports cars were considered. In other words, consumers strongly categorized the Porsche 911 as a prototypical sports car but tended to think of it in only that way. If that were the case, for more consumers to entertain the possibility of buying a Porsche 911, we might need to broaden the meaning of Porsche so that it has a stronger association to cars in general. Of course, such a strategy risks alienating existing customers who had been initially attracted by the purity and strong identification of the Porsche 911 as a sports car. The choice of an appropriate strategy would depend on the relative costs and benefits of targeting the two different segments.

The point is that the category structure that exists in consumers' minds—as reflected by brand recall performance—can have profound implications for consumer choice and marketing strategy. The insights gleaned from measuring brand recall are also valuable for developing brand identity and integrated marketing communication programs, as we showed in Chapters 4 and 6. For example, we can examine brand recall for each brand element to explore the extent to which any one of these (name, symbol, or logo) suggests any other. Are consumers aware of all the different brand elements and how they relate?

We also need a complete understanding of brand image, as covered in the following section.

Brand Image

One vitally important aspect of the brand is its image, as reflected by the associations that consumers hold for it. It is useful for marketers to make a distinction between lower-level considerations, related to consumer perceptions of specific performance and imagery attributes and benefits, and higher-level considerations related to overall judgments, feelings, and relationships. There is an obvious connection between the two levels, because consumers' overall responses and relationship with a brand typically depend on perceptions of specific attributes and benefits of that brand. This section considers some issues in measuring lower-level brand performance and imagery associations.

Beliefs are descriptive thoughts that a person holds about something (for instance, that a particular software package has many helpful features and menus and is easy to use).[40] Brand association beliefs are those specific attributes and benefits linked to the brand and its competitors.

In Chapter 2, we provided a structured set of measures to tap into performance and imagery associations. The qualitative research approaches we described earlier are useful in uncovering the different types of specific brand associations making up the brand image. To better understand their potential ability to serve as the basis for brand positioning and how they might contribute to brand equity, we can assess belief associations by one or more of the three key dimensions—strength, favorability, and uniqueness—making up the sources of brand equity.

As a first cut, we can use open-ended measures that tap into the strength, favorability, and uniqueness of brand associations, as follows:

1. What are the strongest associations you have to the brand? What comes to mind when you think of the brand? (Strength)

1. To what extent do you feel the following product characteristics are descriptive of Lipton iced tea (where 1 = strongly disagree and 7 = strongly agree)?

   _____ convenient
   _____ refreshing and thirst quenching
   _____ real and natural
   _____ good tasting
   _____ contemporary and relevant
   _____ used by young professionals

2. How good or bad is it for iced tea to have the following product characteristics (where 1 = very bad and 7 = very good)?

   _____ convenient
   _____ refreshing and thirst quenching
   _____ real and natural
   _____ good tasting
   _____ contemporary and relevant
   _____ used by young professionals

3. How unique is Lipton iced tea in terms of the following product characteristics (where 1 = not at all unique and 7 = highly unique)?

   _____ convenient
   _____ refreshing and thirst quenching
   _____ real and natural
   _____ good tasting
   _____ contemporary and relevant
   _____ used by young professionals

FIGURE 10-7

Example of Brand Association Ratings

2. What is good about the brand? What do you like about the brand? What is bad about the brand? What do you dislike about the brand? (Favorability)
3. What is unique about the brand? What characteristics or features does the brand share with other brands? (Uniqueness)

To gain more specific insights, we could rate these belief associations according to strength, favorability, and uniqueness, as Figure 10-7 illustrates with Lipton iced tea. Indirect tests also can assess the derived importance and favorability of these brand associations (through multivariate regression techniques).

Other Approaches.   A more complicated quantitative technique to assess overall brand uniqueness is multidimensional scaling or perceptual maps. ***Multidimensional scaling (MDS)*** is a procedure for determining the perceived relative images of a set of objects, such as products or brands. MDS transforms consumer judgments of similarity or preference into distances represented in perceptual space. For example, if Brands A and B are judged by respondents to be the most similar of a set of brands, the MDS algorithm will position Brands A and B so that the distance between them in multidimensional space is smaller than the distance between any other two pairs of brands. Respondents may base their similarity between brands on any basis—tangible or intangible.[41]

Figure 10-8 displays a hypothetical perceptual map of restaurants in a particular market. Segment 1 is more concerned with health than taste and is well targeted by Brand B; segment 2 is more concerned with taste and is well targeted by Brand C. Brand A is trapped in the middle. It either must improve taste to provide a healthy alternative to Brand C for segment 2, or it must improve healthiness to prove a tastier alternative to Brand B for segment 1.

The next section outlines recent developments in social media listening, as companies have built sophisticated algorithms to understand how social media can provide clues about consumers' thoughts and perceptions. This provides a way of measuring and monitoring brand image by leveraging social media conversations, which can be accessed by brand marketers on a continuous basis at a relatively low cost.

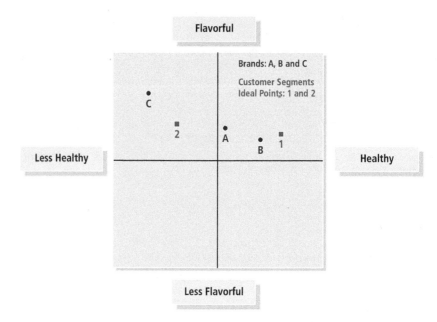

FIGURE 10-8

Hypothetical Restaurant
Perceptual Map

SOCIAL MEDIA LISTENING AND MONITORING

Social media monitoring is a fast-growing and increasingly specialized area of marketing research. Firms use social media monitoring services to track brand and product mentions across various online social media sources, such as online social networking platforms exemplified by Facebook and Twitter, as well as blogs and online discussion forums. These services typically provide firms with two types of brand-level time series data: *volume*, which counts the number of times a given brand (or keyword, more generally) is mentioned in various social media sources, and *valence*, which quantifies the extent to which these brand mentions are positive or negative (i.e., sentiment) and is indicative of the liking toward the brand.

A summary of key statistics associated with a brand is often referred to as a dashboard, which may consist of the following: (1) number of engagements (e.g., Facebook Likes or Twitter Re-tweets) of brand messages across various social media platforms; (2) sentiment (positive versus negative) associated with social media messages; (3) topics that are related to a brand; (4) lists of keywords that are associated with a brand. This information is further contextualized by examining trends over time or contrasting these across a brand's key competitors.[42] Figure 10-9 provides an example of a social media dashboard.

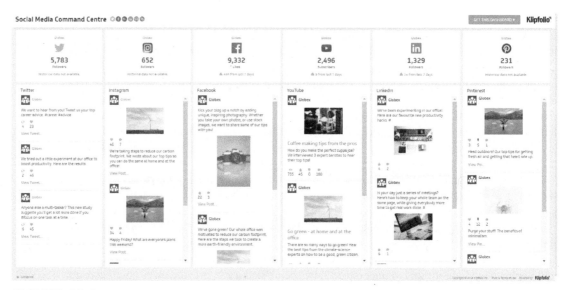

FIGURE 10-9

Social Media Dashboard
A social media dashboard offers a quick snapshot of a brand's social media presence and can be a useful tool for managing a digital brand.

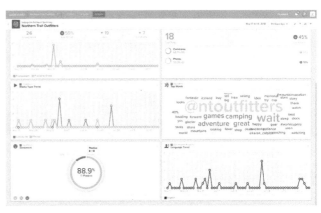

The social monitoring and listening industry consists of a number of leading companies such as Crimson Hexagon, which provide a number of services to assist brands in listening to customers on social media channels.

Salesforce Social Cloud is an important tool for social media listening.

The social monitoring and listening industry has evolved to include several well-known players such as Crimson Hexagon, Oracle's Social Cloud, Sysomos, Salesforce' Social Cloud, and BrandWatch.[43] These companies offer social media monitoring services and social media analytics to brand marketers to enable them to keep track of social media conversations surrounding their brands. Compared to traditional marketing research methods for tracking brands over time (e.g., surveys), social media monitoring data has the advantage of being observational and unobtrusive and also tends to be cheaper to collect. The obvious disadvantage is that direct probes and queries are not possible as is possible with other methods like focus groups or surveys. The Branding Brief 10-6 below describes how one leading brand—Gatorade—uses its social listening facility to keep track of consumers' thoughts and perceptions regarding the brand and its marketing.

BRANDING BRIEF 10-6

Gatorade's Social Media Command Center

Gatorade's Social Media Command Center inside its Chicago headquarters is often seen as one of the prime examples of how a marketer can utilize social media listening tools to improve their marketing and brand strategy. The company has partnered with Crimson Hexagon for its social monitoring, and its control room features six big monitors and displays some data visualizations. The visualizations could present information such as the number of tweets that are relevant to Gatorade, the key terms that consumers are using in conjunction with the brand name, and the trending topics relevant to athletes and sports nutrition-linked topics. The monitors also display the key topics that are being discussed on various blogs and summarizes the sentiment linked to the brand itself.

The listening center allows the brand to optimize their landing page and ensure that followers see the most relevant content, a tactic which enabled the brand to increase its engagement by 250 percent. Other important ways by which Gatorade uses its listening center includes: (1) identifying key concerns that customers may have and ensuring these concerns are addressed; (2) improving the accuracy of the targeting of promotional offers and measuring their effectiveness; and (3) examining the impact of different advertising campaigns. Broader trends relevant to sports nutrition may also emerge

from understanding and tracking customer conversations relevant to the brand.

It was because of the listening center that they caught on to the key customer insight that the song that was used in a Gatorade commercial, "Evolve," generated a lot of customer interest, so much so, customers were asking on social media "Where can I get that song?" In response, Gatorade made the song (by David Banner) available for a free download on their Web site, thereby generating more traffic to it. This type of quick response was possible because of the social listening platform, which provided continuous feedback on what customers were thinking and talking about. The listening center has also helped Gatorade identify customer service issues and resolve them quickly.

The need for social listening is particularly acute as Gatorade has invested in various novel and unconventional advertising campaigns (e.g., using virtual reality and augmented reality). For example, in 2015, Gatorade used virtual reality to allow fans to experience hitting a baseball into the stands from the perspective of major baseball star player, Bryce Harper. The user is placed in the position of waiting for a final throw to come in, and they get to experience the rush that comes with clubbing a home run. The ad uses YouTube 360 which allows viewers to explore different angles of videos by dragging their mouse.

Gatorade's Social Media Command Center offers continuous feedback to managers on what customers are thinking or talking about.

Along a similar vein, in partnership with Snapchat, the Gatorade digital dunk was another innovation that Gatorade experimented with to generate social media buzz and raise awareness. "We figured with the success we had last year, why not give it another try with a little bit of a twist," said Kenny Mitchell, head of consumer engagement at Gatorade. The campaign allowed users to superimpose a Gatorade bath over their video selfies using Snapchat's library of animated filters. The campaign—which took place during the run-up to the 2017 Super Bowl—featured Serena Williams and other celebrities, and garnered a staggering 165 million impressions. The campaign also allowed Gatorade to reach audiences on Snapchat on a massive scale, with an interactive experience that was tied specifically to Gatorade. With Gatorade experimenting with novel augmented reality and social media-based campaigns, it is no wonder that its social listening offers the brand a good way of keeping track of whether Gatorade's campaigns are a hit or a miss.

Sources: Adam Ostrow, "Inside Gatorade's Social Media Command Center," *Mashable.com*, June 15, 2010, http://mashable.com/2010/06/15/gatorade-social-media-mission-control/#BrTi2hww28qZ, accessed October 17, 2017; Fiona Saluk, "Taking a Look at the Most Impressive Command Centers," January 23, 2015, www.brandwatch.com/blog/taking-look-impressive-command-centers/, accessed October 17, 2017; Garett Sloane, "Gatorade Is Reprising the Super Bowl Dunk on Snapchat," February 3, 2017, http://adage.com/article/special-report-super-bowl/gatorade-reprising-super-bowl-dunk-snapchat/307844/, accessed October 17, 2017; E.J. Schultz, "Gatorade Lets Viewers Step Up to Bat with Virtual Reality Campaign," *AdAge*, September 16, 2015, http://adage.com/article/digital/gatorade-puts-viewers-bat-virtual-reality-campaign/300384/, accessed October 31, 2017; Kenny Mitchell, Head of Customer Engagement, Gatorade, personal correspondence, October 5, 2017.

As we described above with regard to social media monitoring, the communications environment has shifted and customers are engaged in conversations with each other, to a larger degree than ever before. With the proliferation of social media and digital communications options, one concern of brand marketers everywhere is understanding the return-on-investment (ROI) of each communication channel. We describe this focus on attribution modeling in the Branding Brief 10-7.

Brand Responses

The purpose of measuring more general, higher-level considerations is to find out how consumers combine all the more specific, lower-level considerations about the brand in their minds to form different types of brand responses and evaluations. Chapter 2 provided examples of measures of key brand judgments and feelings. Here we delve into more detail.

BRANDING BRIEF 10-7
Understanding Attribution Modeling

With the proliferation of consumer touchpoints based on social media and digital channels, marketers are increasingly interested in understanding the return-on-investment of social media and digital marketing. Which social media channels have contributed most to awareness, engagement or sales? This focus—called attribution modeling—has been defined by Google's Analytics software as "the rule, or set of rules, that determines how credit for sales and conversions is assigned to touchpoints in conversion paths." Allocating credit across multiple touchpoints is a significant problem for marketers.

There are three broad challenges involved in attribution modeling. One challenge is how to make attributions regarding the offline impact of online marketing and advertising activities, and vice versa. To illustrate this, imagine evaluating the return-on-investment of paid search advertising. The volume of search for a given brand depends on consumers' interest in the brand name; however, the search queries may be driven by offline marketing efforts including television advertising, magazine advertising or outdoor ads. Therefore, it is challenging to disentangle the impact of paid advertising alone from the indirect impact of these other forms of marketing and promotions.

A second challenge is assigning attributions for marketing efforts across multiple devices, including laptops, smartphones, and televisions. Such cross-device shopping involving more than one device accounts for nearly 40 percent of all e-commerce transactions. For example, one digital marketer of a large online clothing retailer may examine their online transactions by device and find that many of their purchases are resulting from desktop computers. However, a more careful look at activities preceding the last click might show that consumers typically used a tablet or smartphone to browse for clothes earlier in the path-to-purchase, before completing the purchase on a desktop computer. This type of cross-device behavior can add a layer of complexity into media planning and buying yet is critically important to the planning process. Understanding the intricacies of the cross-device behavior of consumers can help ensure the success of digital marketing campaigns.

The third challenge with attribution models is to ensure accurate evaluation of the effectiveness of different digital marketing channels (social, display, YouTube, referral, e-mail, search, others)

in contributing to conversions. Many standard analytics packages such as Google Analytics or SiteCatalyst are used to identify the path length and portfolio of media options that are responsible for driving conversions. However, assigning credit to each media option can still be a challenging issue. The most common ways of attributing conversions are by using first-touch or last-touch methods. First-touch attribution models assign credit to the first touch point that initiated an interaction. In contrast, last-touch attribution models give credit to the touch point and interaction driving the ultimate conversion. For example, the Last Interaction model in Google Analytics assigns credit to the final touchpoints (i.e., clicks) that immediately precede sales or conversions. Another option is linear attribution, which splits the contribution for a given conversion equally across all channels. The issue with linear attribution is that it does not take into consideration the varying impacts of the different touchpoints in the path-to-purchase. More complex attribution models, while increasing accuracy, may also be more time-consuming and data-intensive. Given these challenges, coming up with accurate and easy-to-use attribution models may continue to be the Holy Grail of digital marketers for many years to come.

Sources: Kohki Yamaguchi, "3 Challenges of Attribution Modeling: The Bad, the Bad and the Ugly," September 25, 2014, https://marketingland.com/3-challenges-attribution-modeling-bad-bad-ugly-101257, accessed November 7, 2017; Criteo, "The State of Mobile Commerce," September 13, 2016, www.criteo.com/resources/mobile-commerce-report/, accessed November 7, 2017; Google Support, Analytics Help, "Attribution Modeling Overview," https://support.google.com/analytics/answer/1662518?hl=en, accessed October 11, 2017; Avinash Kaushik, "Multi-Channel Attribution Modeling: The Good, Bad and Ugly Models," Occam's Razor, August 12, 2013, https://www.kaushik.net/avinash/multi-channel-attribution-modeling-good-bad-ugly-models/, accessed November 11, 2018; Eva Anderl, Ingo Becker, Florian Von Wangenheim, and Jan Hendrik Schumann, "Mapping the Customer Journey: Lessons Learned from Graph-Based Online Attribution Modeling," *International Journal of Research in Marketing* 33, no. 3 (2016): 457–474; P. K. Kanna, Werner Reinartz, and Peter C. Verhoef, "The Path to Purchase and Attribution Modeling: Introduction to Special Section," *International Journal of Research in Marketing* 33, no. 3 (2016): 449–456.

Purchase Intentions.   Another set of measures closely related to brand attitudes and consideration looks at purchase intentions and focus on the likelihood of buying the brand or of switching to another brand.[44] Research in psychology suggests that purchase intentions are most likely to be predictive of actual purchase when there is correspondence between the two in the following dimensions:[45]

- Action (buying for own use or to give as a gift)
- Target (specific type of product and brand)
- Context (in what type of store based on what prices and other conditions)
- Time (within a week, month, or year).

In other words, when asking consumers to forecast their likely purchase of a product or a brand, we want to specify *exactly* the circumstances—the purpose of the purchase, the location of the purchase, the time of the purchase, and so forth. For example, we could ask consumers:

"Assume your refrigerator broke down over the next weekend and could not be inexpensively repaired. If you went to your favorite appliance store and found all the different brands competitively priced, how likely would you be to buy a General Electric refrigerator?"

Tesla rates very high on a key metric of customer satisfaction called Net Promoter Score, which captures a customer's willingness to recommend a product to a friend.

Consumers could indicate their purchase intention on an 11-point probability scale that ranges from 0 (definitely would not buy) to 10 (definitely would buy).

Likelihood to Recommend. Bain's Frederick Reichheld suggests there is only one customer question that really matters: "How likely is it that you would recommend this product or service to a friend or colleague?" According to Reichheld, a customer's willingness to recommend results from all aspects of a customer's experience.[46]

Reicheld uses answers to this question to create what he calls a Net Promoter Score (NPS). Specifically, in a survey, customers are asked to rate their likelihood to recommend on a 0–10-point scale. Marketers then subtract *detractors* (those who gave a 0–6) from *promoters* (those who gave a 9 or 10) to arrive at the NPS score. Customers who rate the brand with a 7 or 8 are deemed *passively satisfied* and are not included. A typical set of NPS scores falls in the 10–30 percent range, but world-class companies can score over 50 percent. Some firms with top NPS scores include Tesla Motors (80 percent), USAA (89 percent), Apple (77 percent), Amazon (61 percent), Intel (52 percent), and Jeep (59 percent).[47]

Several companies have seen benefits from adopting NetPromoter scores as a means of tracking brand health. When the European unit of GE Healthcare overhauled its call center and put more specialists in the field, GE Healthcare's Net Promoter scores jumped 10–15 points. BearingPoint found clients who gave it high Net Promoter scores showed the highest revenue growth. When Intuit applied Net Promoter to its TurboTax product, feedback revealed dissatisfaction with the software's rebate procedure. After Intuit dropped the proof-of-purchase requirement, sales jumped 6 percent.

Despite its simplicity and the anecdotal evidence surrounding its merits, no conclusive study exists to prove the superiority of NPS over other available metrics for tracking customer experiences and satisfaction. NPS is certainly not without its limitations. Some have argued that NPS may be increased by sacrificing other aspects such as firm profitability.[48] Others have argued that more diagnostic information is needed to unpack a low NPS score.[49] Regardless of these stated limitations, it can be worthwhile using NPS as part of a broader set of actions taken by a company to ensure advocacy by their promoters, and to promote an organizational culture which is customer-centric.

Brand Relationships

Chapter 2 characterized brand relationships in terms of brand resonance and offered possible measures for each of the four key dimensions: behavioral loyalty, attitudinal attachment, sense of community, and active engagement. This section includes additional considerations with respect to each of those four dimensions. Figure 10-10 displays a scale that, although originally developed by its authors to measure overall brand engagement, could easily be adapted to measure brand

FIGURE 10-10

A Brand Engagement Scale

Source: David Sprott, Sandor Czellar, and Eric Spangenberg, "The Importance of a General Measure of Brand Engagement on Market Behavior: Development and Validation of a Scale," *Journal of Marketing Research* 46, no. 1 (February 2009): 92–104.

1. I have a special bond with the brands I like.
2. I consider my favorite brands to be part of myself.
3. I often feel a personal connection between my brands and me.
4. Part of me is defined by important brands in my life.
5. I feel as if I have a close personal connection with the brands I most prefer.
6. I can identify with important brands in my life.
7. There are links between the brands that I prefer and how I view myself.
8. My favorite brands are an important indication of who I am.

resonance by replacing mentions of brands with a specific brand. For example, instead of saying, "I have a special bond with the brands I like," it could say, "I have a special bond with my Saab automobile," and so on.

Behavioral Loyalty.   To capture reported brand usage and behavioral loyalty, we could ask consumers several questions directly. Or we could ask them what percentage of their last purchases in the category went to the brand (past purchase history), and what percentage of their planned next purchases will go to the brand (intended future purchases). For example, the marketers or brand managers of Duracell batteries might ask the following questions:

Duracell batteries can measure brand loyalty and usage by asking consumers various questions about the brands they typically buy and the ones that they intend to purchase in the future.

- Which brand of batteries do you usually buy?
- Which brand of batteries did you buy last time?
- Do you have any batteries on hand? Which brand?
- Which brands of batteries did you consider buying?
- Which brand of batteries will you buy next time?

These types of questions can provide information about brand attitudes and usage for Duracell, including potential gaps with competitors and the names of other brands that might be in the consideration set at the time of purchase.

Marketers can make their measures open-ended, force consumers to choose one of two brands, or offer multiple choice or rating scales. They can compare the answers with actual measures of consumer behavior to assess whether consumers are accurate in their predictions. For example, if 30 percent of consumers reported, on average, that they thought they would take their vitamins daily over the next two weeks, but only 15 percent of consumers reported two weeks later that they had done so during that period, then Centrum brand managers might need to devise strategies to better convert intentions to actual behavior.

In a business-to-business setting, Narayandas advocates analyzing sales records, talking to sales teams, and conducting surveys to assess where customers stand on a "loyalty ladder."[50]

Attitudinal Attachment.   Several different approaches have been suggested to measure the second component of brand resonance—brand attachment.[51] Some researchers like to characterize it in terms of brand love.[52] One study proposed a brand love scale that consists of 10 items: (1) This is a wonderful brand; (2) This brand makes me feel good; (3) This brand is totally awesome; (4) I have neutral feelings about this brand (reverse-coded item); (5) This brand makes me very happy; (6) I love this brand; (7) I have no particular feelings about this brand (reverse-coded item); (8) This brand is a pure delight; (9) I am passionate about this brand; and (10) I am very attached to this brand.[53]

Another study found 11 dimensions that characterized brand love:[54]

1. Passion (for the brand).
2. Duration of the relationship (the relationship with the brand exists for a long time).
3. Self-congruity (congruity between self-image and product image).
4. Dreams (the brand favors consumer dreams).
5. Memories (evoked by the brand).
6. Pleasure (that the brand provides to the consumer).
7. Attraction (feel toward the brand).
8. Uniqueness (of the brand and/or of the relationship).
9. Beauty (of the brand).
10. Trust (the brand has never disappointed).
11. Declaration of affect (feel toward the brand).

One promising approach defines brand attachment in terms of two underlying constructs— brand-self connections and brand prominence—where each of those two dimensions has two subdimensions, suggesting the following sets of measures:[55]

1. Brand-Self Connection

    a. *Connected:* "To what extent do you feel that you are personally connected to (brand)?"
    b. *Part of Who You Are:* "To what extent is (brand) part of you and who you are?"

2. Brand Prominence

   a. *Automatic:* "To what extent are your thoughts and feelings toward (brand) often automatic, coming to mind seemingly on their own?"
   b. *Naturally:* "To what extent do your thoughts and feelings toward (brand) come to you naturally and instantly?"

Sense of Community.   Although measuring behavioral loyalty and attitudinal attachment may require a fairly structured set of questions, both sense of community and active engagement could call for more varied measures because of their diverse set of issues.

One interesting concept that has been proposed with respect to the community is *social currency*, developed by brand consultants Vivaldi Partners. They define social currency as "the extent to which people share the brand or information about the brand as part of their everyday social lives at work or at home." Figure 10-11 displays the different dimensions that make up the social currency concept according to Vivaldi Partners.

Active Engagement.   According to the brand resonance model, *active engagement* for a brand is defined as the extent to which consumers are willing to invest their own personal resources—time, energy, money, and so on—on the brand beyond those resources expended during the purchase or consumption of the brand.

For example, in terms of engagement, in-depth measures could explore word-of-mouth behavior, online behavior, and so forth. For online behavior, measures could explore the extent of customer-initiated versus firm-initiated interactions, the extent of learning and teaching by the customer versus by the firm, the extent of customers teaching other customers, and so on.[56]

The key to such metrics is the qualitative nature of the consumer-brand interaction and how well it reflects the intensity of feelings. One mistake many firms made in the early days of the Internet was to put too much emphasis on "eyeballs" and "stickiness"—the number and duration of page views at a Web site, respectively. The depth of the underlying brand relationships of the customers making those visits, however, and the manner in which those relationships manifest themselves in brand-beneficial actions, will typically be more important.

Accordingly, researchers are attempting to determine the brand value of different online and social media activities.[57] For example, how important is a "like" from a user on Facebook? One firm estimated that bringing a user on as a fan could be worth between 44 cents and $3.60 in equivalent media value from increased impressions generated from the Facebook newsfeed. Critics of the study, however, pointed out that not all fans are created equal.[58]

Several different specific approaches have been suggested to measure brand engagement. The Science of Branding 10-2 provides a detailed breakdown of the concept.

Fournier's Brand Relationship Research.   Boston University's Susan Fournier argues that brands can and do serve as viable relationship partners, and she suggests a reconceptualization of the notion of brand personality within this framework.[59] Specifically, she maintains that the everyday execution of marketing mix decisions constitutes a set of behaviors enacted on the

FIGURE 10-11

Vivaldi Partners Social Currency Model

Source: Used with permission from Erich Joachimsthaler at Vivaldi Partners.

Dimension	Key Question	Value of Dimension
Conversation	What share of your brand users recognizes and stirs buzz?	Customers proactively talk about a brand.
Advocacy	How many act as disciples and stand up for your brand?	Customers are willing to tell others about a brand or recommend it further.
Information	How many feel they exchange fruitful information with others?	The more information customers have about a brand, the more likely they are to develop preferences for the brand.
Affiliation	What share of users has a sense of community?	Value of brand is closely related to sense of community it creates among other like-minded people.
Utility	How much value do consumers derive from interacting with others?	Social exchange with others involving a brand is an integral part of people's lives.
Identity	How many of your users can identify with other users?	Customers develop strong sense of identity and ability to express themselves to others by using a brand.

THE SCIENCE OF BRANDING 10-2
Understanding Brand Engagement

Recall that we defined and outlined a model for online brand engagement in Chapter 7. There are several different ways to think of brand engagement. *Actual brand engagement* is the activities with which the consumer currently is engaged with the brand and is typically what is measured with the brand resonance model. Two other approaches provide interesting contrasts. *Ideal brand engagement* is the activities the brand consumer wishes they could do with the brand. *Market brand engagement* is the activities the consumer believes other consumers are doing with the brand.

Market brand engagement will be closely related to measures of *brand momentum*—how much progress the brand appears to be making with consumers in the marketplace. Both sets of measures deal with consumer perceptions of how other consumers are connecting to a brand.

Measures of actual brand engagement can take two forms— more general, macro measures or more specific, micro measures. Macro measures focus on the types of resources expended, for example:

Time: "It is worth spending more time on the brand (or going out of the way for it)."

Energy: "It is worth investing extra effort on the brand."

Money: "It is worth spending more money on the brand."

Micro sets of measures focus on specific categories of brand-related activities. These activities fall into three categories depending on whether they relate to: (1) collecting brand information, (2) participating in brand marketing activities, or (3) interacting with other people and having a sense of community. Here are some possible questions.

Collecting Brand Information

I like learning about this brand.

If this brand has any new products or services, I tend to notice it.

If I see a newspaper or magazine article about this brand, I tend to read it.

If I hear a TV or radio story about this brand, I tend to listen to it.

If I see a news story online about this brand, I tend to open and read it.

I like to visit this brand's Web site.

I like to read online blogs about this brand.

Participating in Brand Marketing Activities

If I notice an ad for this brand, I tend to pay attention to it.

If I notice a sales promotion from this brand, I tend to pay attention to it.

If I get something in the mail from this brand, I tend to open it.

If this brand sponsors a sports, entertainment or arts event, I tend to notice it.

If I see a billboard or any outdoor type ad for this brand, I tend to notice it.

If this brand has a display or demonstration in the store, I tend to notice it.

If this brand shows up in a movie or television show, I tend to notice it.

If I get a chance to sample one of this brand's new products, I tend to try it.

I like to buy licensed products from this brand.

Interacting with Other People

I like to talk to others about this brand.

I like to talk to people at work about this brand.

I like to talk to my friends and family about this brand.

I like to seek out others who use this brand.

I have joined or would like to join an online community with other users of this brand.

I have joined or would like to join an online community with others who like this brand.

I have joined or would like to join an online community with people from the company who makes this brand.

I am active in a loyalty program for this brand.

I tend to notice when other people are using this brand.

These are only some representative examples of the types of survey measures that could be employed to assess brand engagement. Depending on the category and circumstances, a variety of other questions could be devised and fruitfully applied.

---

part of the brand. These actions trigger a series of inferences regarding the implicit *contract* that appears to guide the engagement of the consumer and brand, and, hence, the type of relationship formed.

Brand personality as conceptualized within this framework describes the *relationship role* enacted by the brand in its partnership capacity. For example, if the brand expresses behaviors that signal a commitment to the consumer, and further, if it sends gifts as symbols of affection, the consumer may infer a courtship or marriage type of engagement with the brand.

Fournier identifies a typology of 15 different relationship types characterizing consumers' engagement with brands (see Figure 10-12). Fournier argues that this relationship role view of brand personality provides more actionable guidance to managers who wish to create and manage

Relationship Form	Case Examples
Arranged marriage: Nonvoluntary union imposed by preferences of third party. Intended for long-term, exclusive commitment.	Karen's husband's preferred brands (e.g., Mop'n Glo, Palmolive, Hellman's); Karen's Esteé Lauder, imposed through gift-giving; Jean's use of Murphy's Oil Soap as per manufacturer recommendation.
Casual friend/buddy: Friendship low in affect and intimacy, characterized by infrequent or sporadic engagement and few expectations of reciprocity or reward.	Karen and her household cleaning brands.
Marriage of convenience: Long-term, committed relationship precipitated by environmental influence rather than deliberate choice, and governed by satisfying rules.	Vicki's switch to regional Friend's Baked Beans brand from favored B&M brand left behind; Jean's loyalty to DeMoulas salad dressing brand left behind by client at the bar.
Committed partnership: Long-term, voluntarily imposed, socially supported union high in love, intimacy, trust, and commitment to stay together despite adverse circumstances. Adherence to exclusivity rules expected.	Jean and virtually all her cooking, cleaning, and household appliance brands; Karen and Gatorade.
Best friendship: Voluntary union based on reciprocity principle, the endurance of which is ensured through continued provision of positive rewards. Characterized by revelation of true self, honesty, and intimacy. Congruity in partner images and personal interests common.	Karen and Reebok running shoes; Vicki and Crest or Ivory.
Compartmentalized friendship: Highly specialized, situationally confined, enduring friendship characterized by lower intimacy than other friendship forms but higher socio-emotional rewards and interdependence. Easy entry and exit.	Vicki and her stable of shampoos, perfumes, and lingerie brands.
Kinship: Nonvoluntary union with lineage ties.	Vicki's preferences for Tetley tea or Karen's for Ban, Joy, and Miracle Whip, all of which were inherited through their mothers.
Rebound relationship: Union precipitated by desire to replace prior partner, as opposed to attraction to replacement partner.	Karen's use of Comet, Gateway, and Success Rice.
Childhood friendship: Infrequently engaged, affective relation reminiscent of childhood times. Yields comfort and security of past self.	Jean and Jell-O pudding.
Courtship: Interim relationship state on the road to committed partnership contract.	Vicki and her Musk scent brands.
Dependency: Obsessive, highly emotional, selfish attractions cemented by feeling that the other is irreplaceable. Separation from other yields anxiety. High tolerance of other's transgressions results.	Karen and Mary Kay; Vicki and Soft 'n Dry.
Fling: Short-term, time-bounded engagement of high emotional reward. Devoid entirely of commitment and reciprocity demands.	Vicki's trial-size shampoo brands.
Enmity: Intensely involving relationship characterized by negative affect and desire to inflict pain or revenge on the other.	Karen and her husband's brands, postdivorce; Jean and her other-recommended-but-rejected brands (e.g., ham, peanut butter, sinks).
Enslavement: Nonvoluntary relationship union governed entirely by desires of the relationship partner.	Karen and Southern Bell, Cable Vision. Vicki and Playtex, a bra for large-breasted women.
Secret affair: Highly emotive, privately held relationship considered risky if exposed to others.	Karen and the Tootsie Pops she sneaks at work.

FIGURE 10-12

A Typology of Consumer-Brand Relationships

their brand personalities in line with marketing actions than does the trait-based view, which identifies general personality tendencies that might or might not be connected to marketing strategies and goals.

Fournier has conducted fascinating research that reframes the conceptualization and measurement of brand strength strictly in relationship terms. It defines a brand's strength in terms of the strength, depth, and durability of the consumer-brand relational bond using the multifaceted concept of **brand relationship quality**, or BRQ. Extensive validation work supported a multifaceted hierarchical structure for the BRQ construct that includes six main dimensions of relationship strength, many with important subfacets. The main facets are (1) interdependence, (2) self-concept connection, (3) commitment, (4) love/passion, (5) intimacy, and (6) brand partner quality.

Fournier argues that these facets and their subfacets (such as trust within the partner quality facet or consumer-to-firm and firm-to-consumer intimacy) have superior diagnostic value over competing strength measures, and she suggests they have greater managerial utility in their application. In her experience, BRQ measures have been successfully incorporated in brand tracking studies, where they provide profiles of brand strength versus competitors, useful ties to marketplace performance indicators, and specific guidance for the enhancement and dilution of brand equity through managerial actions in the marketplace. Although brand relationship quality shares some characteristics with brand resonance, it provides valuable additional perspectives and insights.

The six main facets of brand relationship quality are as follows:

- *Interdependence:* The degree to which the brand is ingrained in the consumer's daily course of living, both behaviorally (frequency, scope, and strength of interactions) and cognitively (longing for and preoccupation with anticipated brand interactions). At its extremes, interdependence becomes dependency and addiction.
- *Self-concept connection:* The degree to which the brand delivers on important identity concerns, tasks, or themes, thereby expressing a significant part of the self-concept, both past (including nostalgic references and brand memories) and present, and personal as well as social. In its extreme form, self-connection reflects the integration of concepts of brand and self.
- *Commitment:* Dedication to continued brand association and betterment of the relationship, despite circumstances foreseen and unforeseen. Commitment is not defined solely by sunk costs and irretrievable investments that pose barriers to exit.
- *Love or passion:* Affinity toward and adoration of the brand, particularly concerning other available alternatives. Love includes the belief that the brand is irreplaceable and uniquely qualified as a relationship partner.
- *Intimacy:* A sense of deep familiarity with and understanding of both the essence of the brand as a partner in the relationship and the nature of the consumer-brand relationship itself. Intimacy is a two-dimensional concept: the consumer develops an intimate knowledge of the brand, and also feels a sense of intimacy exhibited on the part of the brand toward the individual as a consumer.
- *Partner quality:* Perceived partner quality involves a summary judgment of the caliber of the role enactments performed by the brand in its partnership role.

COMPREHENSIVE MODELS OF CONSUMER-BASED BRAND EQUITY

The customer-based brand equity model presented in this text provides a comprehensive, cohesive overview of brand building and brand equity. Other researchers and consultants have also put forth consumer-based brand equity models that share some of the same principles and philosophy as the CBBE model, although developed differently. Brand Focus 10.0 presents a detailed account of arguably the most successful and influential industry branding model, Young and Rubicam's Brand Asset Valuator.

REVIEW

According to the brand value chain, sources of brand equity arise from the customer mind-set. In general, measuring sources of brand equity requires that the brand manager fully understand how customers shop for and use products and services, and, most important, what customers know, think, and feel about various brands. In particular, measuring sources of customer-based brand equity requires measuring various aspects of brand awareness and brand image that lead to the customer response that creates brand equity.

I. **Qualitative Research Techniques**
   Free association
   Adjective ratings and checklists
   Projective techniques
   Photo sorts
   Bubble drawings
   Story telling
   Personification exercises
   Role playing
   Experiential methods

II. **Quantitative Research Techniques**
   A. Brand Awareness
      Direct and indirect measures of brand recognition
      Aided and unaided measures of brand recall
   B. Brand Image
      Open-ended and scale measures of specific brand attributes and benefits
         Strength
         Favorability
         Uniqueness
      Overall judgments and feelings
      Overall relationship measures
         Intensity
         Activity

FIGURE 10-13

Summary of Qualitative and Quantitative Measures

This chapter described both qualitative and quantitative approaches to measure consumers' brand knowledge structures and identify potential sources of brand equity—that is, measures to capture the customer mind-set. Qualitative research techniques are a means to identify possible brand associations. Quantitative research techniques are a means to better approximate the breadth and depth of brand awareness; the strength, favorability, and uniqueness of brand associations; the favorability of brand responses; and the nature of brand relationships. Because of their unstructured nature, qualitative measures are especially well-suited to provide an in-depth glimpse of what brands and products mean to consumers. To obtain more precise and generalizable information, however, marketers typically use quantitative scale measures. We reviewed some novel approaches to brand monitoring that have become available thanks to the proliferation of social media channels. As machine learning algorithms become more sophisticated, many of the existing approaches may be supplanted with brand image analyses based on widely available, low-cost, social media data.

Figure 10-13 summarizes some of the different types of measures that were discussed in the chapter.

DISCUSSION QUESTIONS

1. Pick a brand. Employ projective techniques to attempt to identify sources of its brand equity. Which measures work best? Why?
2. Run an experiment to see whether you can replicate Mason Haire's instant coffee experiment (see Branding Brief 10-2). Do the same attributions still hold? If not, can you replace coffee with a brand combination from another product category that would produce pronounced differences?
3. Pick a product category. Can you profile the brand personalities of the leading brands in the category using Aaker's brand personality inventory?
4. Describe how social media data can be utilized in understanding brand perceptions.
5. Describe how social media monitoring is changing how brands can monitor consumers' thoughts and perceptions regarding a brand. What are the implications of this trend for brand management as a whole?
6. Describe what attribution modeling is. Why is it important in today's communication environment?
7. Think of your brand relationships. Can you find examples of brands that fit into Fournier's different categories?

BRAND FOCUS 10.0
Young & Rubicam's Brand Asset Valuator

This appendix summarizes the Brand Asset® Valuator (BAV), originally developed by Young & Rubicam, now overseen and expanded by The BAV Group.[60] It is the world's largest database of consumer-derived information on brands. The BAV model is developmental in that it explains how brands grow, how they get into trouble, and how they recover.

The BAV measures brands on four fundamental measures of brand equity plus a broad array of perceptual dimensions.* It provides comparative measures of the equity value of thousands of brands across hundreds of different categories, as well as a set of strategic brand management tools for planning: brand positioning, brand extensions, joint branding ventures, and other strategies designed to assess and direct brands and their growth. The BAV is also linked to financial metrics and is used to determine a brand's contribution to a company's valuation.

Since 1993, the BAV has researched nearly 1,200,000 consumers in 52 countries, enabling BAV to identify truly global brand trends. Consumers' perceptions of approximately 56,000 brands have been collected across the same set of 75 dimensions, including 48 image attributes, usage, consideration, and cultural and customer values. These elements are incorporated into a specially developed set of brand loyalty measures.

The BAV represents a unique brand equity research tool. Unlike most conventional brand image surveys that adhere to a narrowly defined product category, respondents evaluate brands in a category-agnostic context. Brands are percentile ranked against *all* brands in the study for each brand metric. Thus, by comparing brands across as well as within categories, the BAV can draw the broadest possible conclusions about how consumer-level brand equity is created and built—or lost. In the United States, data

has been collected quarterly from an 18,000-person panel, which enables the identification and analysis of short-term branding trends and phenomena.

Four Pillars

There are four key components of brand health in BAV (see Figure 10-14), referred to as "Brand Pillars." Each pillar is derived from various measures that relate to different aspects of consumers' brand perceptions. Taken together, the four pillars trace the progression of a brand's development.

- *Energized Differentiation* measures the degree to which a brand is seen as different from others, and captures the brand's direction and momentum. This is a necessary condition for profitable brand building. It relates to pricing power and is often the key brand pillar in explaining valuation multiples like market value to sales.

- *Relevance* measures the appropriateness of the brand to consumers and the overall size of a brand's potential franchise or penetration.

- *Esteem* measures how well the brand is regarded and respected—in short, how well it's liked. Esteem is related to loyalty.

- *Knowledge* measures how intimately familiar consumers are with a brand and is related to the saliency of the brand. Interestingly, high knowledge is inversely related to a brand's potential.

Relationship Among the Pillars

Examining the relationships between these four dimensions—a brand's "pillar patterns"—reveals much about a brand's current

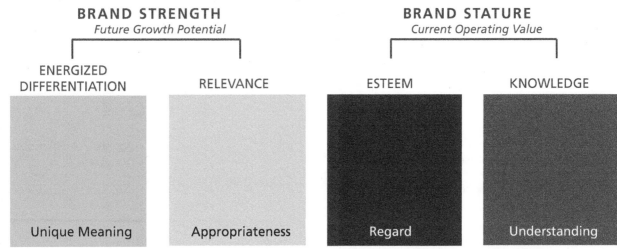

BRAND EQUITY PILLARS

BRAND STRENGTH		BRAND STATURE	
Future Growth Potential		*Current Operating Value*	
ENERGIZED DIFFERENTIATION	RELEVANCE	ESTEEM	KNOWLEDGE
Unique Meaning	Appropriateness	Regard	Understanding
Relates to margins, loyalty, cultural currency	*Relates to market penetration*	*Relates to perception of quality & respect*	*Relates to consumer experience*

FIGURE 10-14

Four Pillars Assess Brand Health, Development, and Momentum

---

* In Chapter 11, we discuss five BAV dimensions, with energy being listed as a separate dimension. Young and Rubicam has combined energy and differentiation dimensions and now call it energized differentiation.

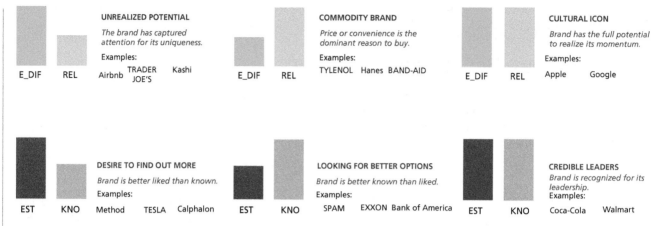

FIGURE 10-15

Pillar Patterns Tell a Story

Source: BrandAsset Consulting. Used with permission.

and future status (see Figure 10-15). It is not enough to look at each brand pillar in isolation; it is the relationships between the pillars that tell a story about brand health and opportunities. Here are some key relationships:

- When Energized Differentiation is greater than Relevance, the brand is standing out and receiving attention in the marketplace. It now has the potential to channel this point of difference and energy into building meaningfulness for consumers by driving Relevance.

- But if a brand is more Relevant than Differentiated, this suggests commoditization. While the brand is appropriate and meaningful within the lives of consumers, it is perceived as interchangeable with other players in the category. Therefore, consumers will not go out of their way for this brand, remain loyal to it, or pay a premium for it, since it lacks that special something we quantify as Energized Differentiation. Convenience, habit, and price become drivers of brand choice in this scenario.

- Leadership brands are strong on both pillars, resulting in consumer passion as well as market penetration.

Brands often strive to build awareness, but if the brand's pillars are not in the proper alignment, then consumer knowledge of a brand becomes an obstacle that may need to be surmounted before the brand can continue to build healthy momentum.

- When a brand's Esteem is greater than its Knowledge, consumers like what they know about the brand so far, and typically want to find out more, suggesting growth potential.

- However, if a brand's Knowledge is greater than its Esteem, then consumers may feel that they know more than enough about the brand, and they are not interested in getting to know it any better. In this case, Knowledge is an impediment that the brand must try to overcome if it wishes to attract more consumers.

The PowerGrid

The Brand Asset® Valuator has integrated the two macro dimensions of Brand Strength (Energized Differentiation and Relevance) and Brand Stature (Esteem and Knowledge) into a visual analytical representation known as the PowerGrid (see Figure 10-16). The PowerGrid depicts the stages in the cycle of brand development—each with its characteristic pillar patterns—in successive quadrants.

Brands generally begin their life in the lower left quadrant, where they first need to develop Relevant Differentiation and establish their reason for being. Some brands get "stuck" in this quadrant because of their commodity image or specialized marketing, like Lincoln Financial and Marvin Windows. Most often, the movement from there is "up" into the top left quadrant. Increased Differentiation, followed by Relevance, initiates growth in Brand Strength. These developments occur before the brand has acquired significant Esteem or is widely known.

This quadrant represents two types of brands. For brands destined for a mass target, like Method, illy, and Apple Pay, this is the stage of emerging potential. Specialized or narrowly targeted brands, however, tend to remain in this quadrant (when viewed from the perspective of a mass audience) and can use their strength to occupy a profitable niche. This includes brands like Square, Kimpton, and Snapchat. From the point of view of brand leaders, new potential competitors will emerge from this quadrant.

The upper right quadrant, the Leadership Quadrant, is populated by brand leaders—those that have high levels of both Brand Strength and Brand Stature. Both older and relatively new brands can be in this quadrant, meaning that brand leadership is truly a function of the pillar measures, not of longevity. When properly managed, a brand can build and maintain a leadership position indefinitely. Examples of brands in the leadership position include Apple, the NFL, and Disney.

Although declining brand equity is not inevitable, brands for whom strength has declined (usually driven by declining Energized Differentiation) can also be seen in this same quadrant. Brands whose Strength has started to dip below the level of their Stature display the first signs of weakness, which may well be masked by their still-buoyant sales and wide penetration. Examples include such brands as Macy's, V8, and Visa.

Brands that fail to maintain their Brand Strength—their Relevant Differentiation—begin to fade and move "down" into the bottom right quadrant. These brands become vulnerable not just to existing competitors, but also to the depredations of discount price brands, and they frequently end up being drawn into heavy and continuous price promotion in order to defend their consumer franchise and market share: American Airlines, Citibank, ExxonMobil, and Kmart fall into this category.

A PowerGrid can also be used to measure a brand's equity among different constituencies. Figure 10-17 depicts *The Wall Street Journal's* brand equity among various usage or demographic

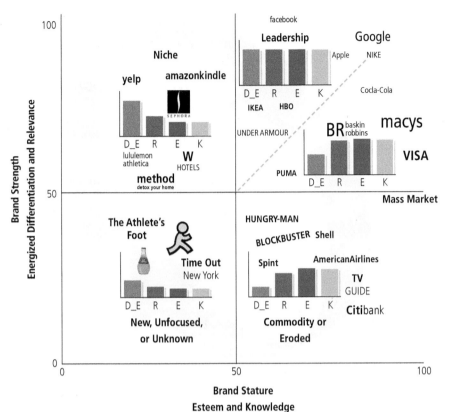

FIGURE 10-16

Brand Development Cycle as Illustrated by the PowerGrid

Source: BrandAsset Consulting. Used with permission.

cuts including gender, age, income and political views. The Wall Street Journal is generally an established brand with high Brand Stature, but depending on the audience, Brand Strength differs. The Wall Street Journal is more differentiated and relevant among readers, Republicans, men, and individuals of age 55+ and income $100K+. This is a powerful tool to identify opportunities and target audiences for brands.

Significant investigations have been done on relating the BAV metrics to financial performance and stock price. First, the position of a brand on the PowerGrid indicates the level of intangible value (market value of a brand or company-invested capital) per dollar of sale. The leadership quadrant produces brands with the largest intangible value per dollar of sale. Next, through extensive modeling, the BAV has shown that a change in brand assets impacts stock price. From a macro perspective, two-thirds of the change in brand assets directly impacts stock price and the expectation for future returns. One-third of the change in brand assets impacts current earnings. The importance of brand assets on stock price and company valuation is highly dependent on the category or economic sector.

Applying BAV to Google

The best way to understand the BAV model is to apply it to a brand and category. Google is a dramatic example. Google achieved leadership status faster than any other brand measured in the BAV. Google built each brand pillar, beginning with Energized Differentiation, both quickly and strongly. After rapidly establishing Energized Differentiation, Google built the other three pillars. It took only three years for Google's percentile-ranking on all four pillars to reach the high 90s.

At the same time, AOL began to falter, losing first Energized Differentiation, then Relevance and Esteem. For a period, AOL's Knowledge remained high, but with declining Relevance, eroding

Differentiation and less Esteem, consumers began to lose interest until finally, AOL's Knowledge pillar followed the other pillars and began to decline. Figure 10-18 displays the sharp contrast in brand development between the two.

How has Google developed and maintained brand leadership? From the BAV perspective, there are three main contributing factors: (1) consistently strong brand attributes that translate into competitive advantages, (2) successful brand extensions into new categories, and (3) successful expansion into global markets building on differentiation to become a leadership brand.

Competitive Advantages on Brand Attributes

Google's leadership is supported by competitive advantages on the key attributes to driving the pillars and loyalty. The BAV uses 48 emotional attributes to see through the eyes of consumers when considering Google and its competitive set.

As shown in Figure 10-19, Google is stronger than the competitive average on *innovative* and *visionary*. These elements build Google's Energized Differentiation. Google's advantage on *trustworthy* and *helpful* helps keep the Relevance pillar strong, and Google's strength on *reliable* and *leader* supports both the Relevance and the Esteem pillars.

Successful Category Extensions

Google has done a masterful job of entering new categories with sub-brands. In many of these categories—such as Google Docs, Chrome, and Gmail—the Google entrant has become the category leader. Most of the sub-brands also have very high Brand Strength, which helps replenish the Brand Strength of the Google corporate brand (see Figure 10-20). In this way, the leadership of the sub-brands helps support the parent brand, a common theme among strong parent brands with sub-brands.

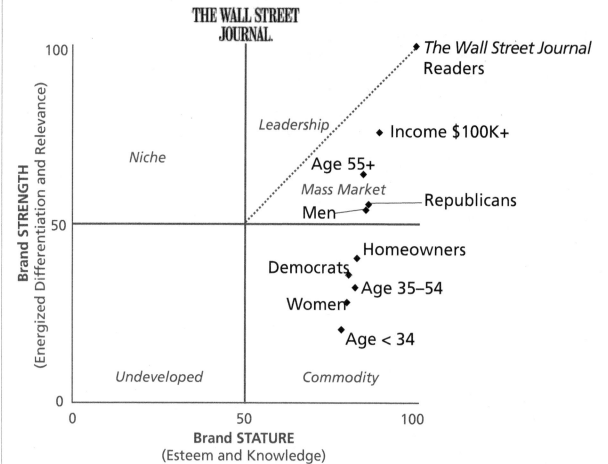

FIGURE 10-17

Profile of *The Wall Street Journal*

Source: BrandAsset Consulting. Used with permission.

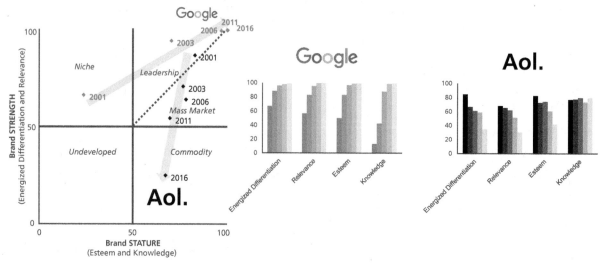

FIGURE 10-18

Google vs. AOL Brand Development

Source: BrandAsset Consulting. Used with permission.

GOOGLE'S TOP ATTRIBUTES

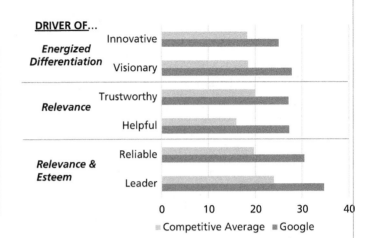

FIGURE 10-19

Google's Top Attributes

Source: BrandAsset Consulting. Used with permission.

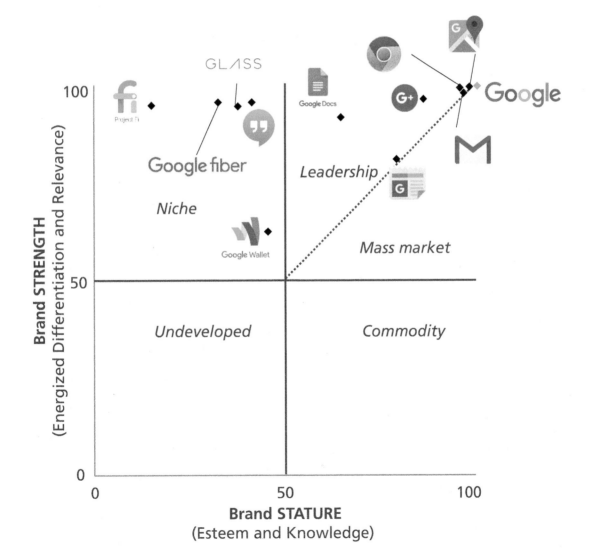

FIGURE 10-20

Google's Successful New Product Introductions

Source: BrandAsset Consulting. Used with permission.

The significant strength of Google's image profile has made entrance into new categories easier. Google does not face the entrance issues that weaker brands have when their image profiles are not robust enough to create differentiation in the new category, a key condition for a successful extension.

Successful Global Expansion

The Brand Asset® Valuator (BAV) metrics uniquely gauge the nature of international marketing opportunities. The BAV shows global brands must build consistently strong Brand Strength, Brand Stature, and meaning *in each market*. Specifically, financial analysis of global brands has shown that brands that have consistently high Brand Strength and consistently high common meaning will deliver better margin growth rates and are more efficient at producing higher pretax margins.

Google has achieved leadership status in global markets the same way it achieved leadership status in the United States—by quickly outperforming competitors on Brand Strength and Brand Stature. In all countries recently surveyed, Google is a super-leadership brand on the PowerGrid (see Figure 10-21). Reviewing the key imagery across countries shows that Google ranks consistently high on reliable and intelligent, *according to consumers in each local market*. This is true consistency and a great strategic base from which to build.

Summary

There is much commonality between the basic BAV model and the brand resonance model. The four factors in the BAV model can easily be related to specific components of the brand resonance model:

- BAV's Differentiation relates to brand superiority.
- BAV's Relevance relates to brand consideration.
- BAV's Esteem relates to brand loyalty.
- BAV's Knowledge relates to brand resonance.

Note that brand awareness and familiarity are handled differently in the two approaches. The brand resonance framework maintains that brand salience, and breadth and depth of awareness is a necessary first step in building brand equity. The BAV model treats familiarity more effectively—almost in a warm feeling or friendship sense—and thus see it as the *last* step in building brand equity, more akin to the resonance component itself.

The main advantage of the BAV model is that it provides rich category-agnostic descriptions and profiles across a large number of brands. It also provides focus on four key branding dimensions. It provides a brand landscape in which marketers can see where their brands stand relative to other prominent brands in many different markets.

The descriptive nature of the BAV model does mean, however, that there is potentially less insight as to exactly *how* a brand could rate highly on specific attributes. Because the measures underlying the four pillars have to be relevant across a very disparate range of product categories, the measures (and, consequently, the pillars) tend to be abstract in nature and not related directly to product attributes and benefits, or more specific marketing concerns. Nevertheless, the BAV model represents a landmark study regarding its ability to enhance marketers' understanding of what drives top brands and where their brands fit in a vast brandscape.

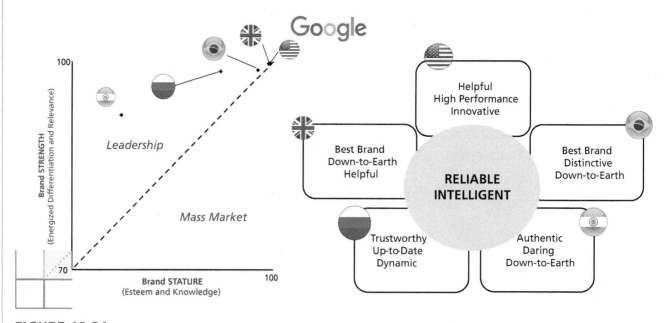

FIGURE 10-21

Google Is Consistently a Global Brand Leader

Source: BrandAsset Consulting. Used with permission.

NOTES

1. Some leading textbooks in this area are J. Paul Peter and Jerry C. Olson, *Consumer Behavior and Marketing Strategy*, 8th ed. (Homewood, IL: McGraw-Hill/Irwin, 2007); Wayne D. Hoyer and Deborah J. Mac Innis, *Consumer Behavior*, 5th ed. (Mason, OH: SouthWestern, 2010); and Michael R. Solomon, *Consumer Behavior: Buying, Having, and Being*, 9th ed. (Upper Saddle River, NJ: Prentice Hall, 2011).

2. Videos of Three UK's campaign ads can be seen here: Three UK, "TV Ad | Prepare yourself for #holidayspam; Austrialia | Three" YouTube video, 1:00, posted by "Three UK," January 17, 2015, http://www.youtube.com/watch?v=1a1cL4TIMMc&feature=youtube.; Three UK, "TV Ad | We're sorry for #holidayspam | Three" YouTube video, 1:00, posted by "Three UK," July 4, 2014, www.youtube.com/watch?v=Wz7YbGCeWPA&feature=youtube.

3. John Motavalli, "Probing Consumer Minds," *Adweek*, December 7, 1987, 4–8.

4. Ernest Dichter, *Handbook of Consumer Motivations* (New York: McGraw-Hill, 1964).

5. The Economist, "Retail Therapy: How Ernest Dichter, An Acolyte of Sigmund Freud, Revolutionised Marketing," *The Economist*, December 17, 2011, 120, https://www.economist.com/christmas-specials/2011/12/17/retail-therapy, accessed November 11, 2018.

6. H. Shanker Krishnan, "Characteristics of Memory Associations: A Consumer-Based Brand Equity Perspective," *International Journal of Research in Marketing* 13, no. 4 (October 1996): 389–405; Geraldine R. Henderson, Dawn Iacobucci, and Bobby J. Calder, "Using Network Analysis to Understand Brands," in *Advances in Consumer Research* 29, eds. Susan M. Broniarczyk and Kent Nakamoto (Valdosta, GA: Association for Consumer Research, 2002): 397–405.

7. J. Wesley Hutchinson, "Expertise and the Structure of Free Recall," in *Advances in Consumer Research* 10, eds. Richard P. Bagozzi and Alice M. Tybout (Ann Arbor, MI: Association of Consumer Research, 1983): 585–589; see also Chris Janiszewski and Stijn M. J. van Osselaer, "A Connectionist Model of Brand—Quality Associations," *Journal of Marketing Research* 37, no. 3 (August 2000): 331–350.

8. Yvan Boivin, "A Free Response Approach to the Measurement of Brand Perceptions," *International Journal of Research in Marketing* 3, no. 1 (1986): 11–17; Jeffrey E. Danes, Jeffrey S. Hess, John W. Story, and Keith Vorst, "On the Validity of Measuring Brand Images by Rating Concepts and Free Associations," *Journal of Brand Management*, (2012) 19, 289–303, http://www.academia.edu/4641496/On_the_validity_of_measuring_brand_images_by_rating_concepts_and_free_associations, accessed November 11, 2018.

9. Jean Bystedt, Siri Lynn, and Deborah Potts, *Moderating to the Max* (Ithaca, NY: Paramount Market Publishing, 2003).

10. For an application in marketing, see Kathryn A. Braun-LaTour, Michael S. LaTour, and George M. Zinkhan, "Using Childhood Memories to Gain Insight into Brand Meaning," *Journal of Marketing* 71, no. 2 (April 2007): 45–60.

11. Sydney J. Levy, "Dreams, Fairy Tales, Animals, and Cars," *Psychology and Marketing* 2, no. 2 (1985): 67–81.

12. Mason Haire, "Projective Techniques in Marketing Research," *Journal of Marketing* 14, no. 5 (April 1950): 649–656. Interestingly, a follow-up study conducted several decades later suggested that instant coffee users were no longer perceived as psychologically different from drip grind users. See Frederick E. Webster Jr. and Frederick Von Pechmann, "A Replication of the 'Shopping List' Study," *Journal of Marketing* 34, no. 2 (April 1970): 61–63.

13. Sydney J. Levy, "Dreams, Fairy Tales, Animals, and Cars," *Psychology and Marketing* 2, no. 2 (1985): 67–81.

14. Jeffrey Durgee and Robert Stuart, "Advertising Symbols and Brand Names That Best Represent Key Product Meanings," *Journal of Consumer Marketing* 4, no. 3 (1987): 15–24.

15. Gerald Zaltman and Robin Higie, "Seeing the Voice of the Customer: Metaphor-Based Advertising Research," *Journal of Advertising Research* (July/August 1995): 35–51; Daniel H. Pink, "Metaphor Marketing," *Fast Company*, March 31, 1998, https://www.fastcompany.com/33672/metaphor-marketing, accessed November 11, 2018; Gerald Zaltman, "Metaphorically Speaking," *Marketing Research* 8, no. 2 (Summer 1996): 13–20, https://www.hbs.edu/faculty/Pages/item.aspx?num=4106; Gerald Zaltman, "How Customers Think: Essential Insights into the Mind of the Market," *Harvard Business School Press* (2003); Wendy Melillo, "Inside the Consumer Mind: What Neuroscience Can Tell Us About Marketing," *Adweek*, January 16, 2006, https://www.adweek.com/brand-marketing/inside-consumer-mind-83549/, accessed November 11, 2018; Torsten Ringberg, Gaby Odekerken-Schröder, and Glenn L. Christensen, "A Cultural Models Approach to Segmenting Consumer Recovery Expectations," *Journal of Marketing* 71, no. 3 (July 2007): 194–214; Gerald Zaltman and Lindsay Zaltman, *Marketing Metaphoria: What Deep Metaphors Reveal About the Minds of Consumers* (Boston: Harvard Business School Press, 2008).

16. For some provocative research, see Carolyn Yoon, Angela H. Gutchess, Fred M. Feinberg, and Thad A. Polk, "A Functional Magnetic Resonance Imaging Study of Neural Dissociations between Brand and Person Judgments," *Journal of Consumer Research* 33, no. 1 (June 2006): 31–40; Samuel M. McClure, Jian Li, Damon Tomlin, Kim S. Cypert, Latané M. Montague, and P. Read Montague, "Neural Correlates of Behavioral Preference for Culturally Familiar Drinks," *Neuron* 44, no. 2 (October 2004): 379–387; Hilke Plassmann, Carolyn Yoon, Fred M. Feinberg, and Baba Shiv, "Consumer Neuroscience," in *Wiley International Encyclopedia of Marketing, Volume 3: Consumer Behavior*, eds. Richard P. Bagozzi and Ayalla Ruvio (West Sussex, UK: John

Wiley, 2010). Martin Lindstrom, *Buyology: Truth and Lies About Why We Buy* (New York: Doubleday, 2008).

17. Erica Dube, "Neuromarketing 101: What Is Neuromarketing and How Are Companies Using It?," *Impact*, September 7, 2017, www.impactbnd.com/blog/neuromarketing-101.

18. For foundational research, see Giovanna Egidi, Howard C. Nusbaum, and John T. Cacioppo, "Neuroeconomics," in *The Handbook of Consumer Psychology*, eds. Curtis Haugvedt, Paul Herr, and Frank Kardes, Vol. 57 (Mahwah, NJ: Lawrence Erlbaum Associates, 2007): 1177–1214.

19. Adam Penenberg, "NeuroFocus Uses Neuromarketing to Hack Your Brain," *Fast Company*, September 8, 2011, www.fastcompany.com/1769238/neurofocus-uses-neuromarketing-hack-your-brain.

20. Nick Lee, Amanda J. Broderick, and Laura Chamberlain, "What Is 'Neuromarketing'? A Discussion and Agenda for Future Research," *International Journal of Psychophysiology* 63, no. 2 (2007): 199–204; Hilke Plassman, John O'Donerty, Baba Shiv, and Antonio Rangel, "Marketing Actions Can Modulate Neural Representations of Experienced Pleasantness," *PNAS Proceedings* 105, no. 3, (2007): 1050–1054.

21. Dan Ariely and Gregory S. Berns "Neuromarketing: The Hope and Hype of Neuroimaging in Business," *Nature*, 11, no. 4 (April 2010): 284–292.

22. Jennifer Aaker, "Dimensions of Brand Personality," *Journal of Marketing Research* 34, no. 8 (1997): 347–356.

23. Jay Dean, "A Practitioner's Perspective on Brand Equity," in *Proceedings of the Society for Consumer Psychology*, eds. Wes Hutchinson and Kevin Lane Keller (Clemson, SC: CtC Press, 1994), 56–62.

24. Jennifer Aaker, "Dimensions of Brand Personality." See also Jennifer Aaker, "The Malleable Self: The Role of Self-Expression in Persuasion," *Journal of Marketing Research* 36, no. 2 (1999): 45–57; Joseph T. Plummer, "Brand Personality: A Strategic Concept for Multinational Advertising," in *Marketing Educators' Conference* (New York: Young & Rubicam, 1985): 1–31.

25. Martin Eisend and Nicola E. Stokburger-Sauer, "Brand Personality: A Meta-analytic Review of Antecedents and Consequences," *Marketing Letters* 24, no. 3 (2013): 205–216.

26. Gil Ereaut and Mike Imms, "'Bricolage': Qualitative Market Research Redefined," *Admap*, Issue 434 (December 2002): 16–18.

27. Jennifer Chang Coupland, "Invisible Brands: An Ethnography of Households and the Brands in Their Kitchen Pantries," *Journal of Consumer Research* 32, no. 1 (June 2005): 106–118; Mark Ritson and Richard Elliott, "The Social Uses of Advertising: An Ethnographic Study of Adolescent Advertising Audiences," *Journal of Consumer Research* 26, no. 3 (December 1999): 260–277.

28. Donna Kelly and Michael Gibbons, "Ethnography: The Good, the Bad, and the Ugly," *Journal of Medical Marketing* 8, no. 4 (2008): 279–285; Caroline Hayter Whitehill, "Introduction to IJMR Special Issue on Ethnography," *International Journal of Market Research* 49, no. 6 (November 2007): 687–689.

29. Melanie Wells, "New Ways to Get into Our Heads," *USA Today*, March 2, 1999, B1–B2.

30. Gerry Kermouch, "Consumers in the Mist," *Business Week*, February 26, 2001, 92–94, https://www.bloomberg.com/news/articles/2001-02-25/consumers-in-the-mist, accessed November 11, 2018; Alfred Hermida, "Bus Ride to the Future," *BBC*, December 3, 2011, http://news.bbc.co.uk/2/hi/sci/tech/1684773.stm, accessed November 11, 2018.

31. Eric J. Arnould and Amber Epp, "Deep Engagement with Consumer Experience: Listening and Learning with Qualitative Data," in *The Handbook of Marketing Research: Uses, Misuses, and Future Advances*, eds. Rajiv Grover and Marco Vriens (Thousand Oaks, CA: Sage Press, 2006): 51–58.

32. Edward F. McQuarrie, "Taking a Road Trip," *Marketing Management* 3 (Winter 1995): 9–21; Edward F. McQuarrie, *Customer Visits: Building a Better Market Focus*, 3rd ed. (Armonk, NY: M. E. Sharpe, 2008); Edward F. McQuarrie, "How to Conduct Good Customer Visits: 16 Tips from Ed McQuarrie," *The Management Roundtable*, http://events.roundtable.com/Event_Center/CustomerVisits/GoodCustomerVisits-McQuarrieTips.pdf, accessed November 11, 2018.

33. Kevin Peters, "Office Depot's President on How "Mystery Shopping" Helped Spark a Turnaround," *Harvard Business Review*, November 2011 Issue, 47–50, https://hbr.org/2011/11/office-depots-president-mystery-shopping-turnaround, accessed November 11, 2018.

34. David Burrows, "How to Use Ethnography for In-Depth Consumer Insight," *Marketing Week*, May 9, 2014, www.marketingweek.com/2014/05/09/how-to-use-ethnography-for-in-depth-consumer-insight/.

35. Pauline Lacsamana, "Lay's Introduces 3 New Chip Flavors in 'Do Us a Flavor' Contest," *The Daily Meal.com*, July 21, 2017, www.thedailymeal.com/news/eat/lay-s-introduces-3-new-chip-flavors-do-us-flavor-contest/072117.

36. Russell W. Belk and Robert V. Kozinets, "Videography in Marketing and Consumer Research," *Qualitative Market Research* 8, no. 2 (2005): 128–142.

37. Louella Miles, "Market Research: Living Their Lives," CampaignLive, December 11, 2003, https://www.campaignlive.com/article/market-research-living-lives/197919, accessed November 11, 2018.

38. Judith A. Howard and Daniel G. Renfrow, "Social Cognition," in *Handbook of Social Psychology*, ed. John Delamater (New York: Springer Science+Business, 2006), 259–282; Robert S. Wyer, "The Role of Information Accessibility in Cognition and Behavior: Implications for Consumer Information Processing," in *The Handbook of Consumer Psychology*, eds. Curtis Haugvedt, Paul Herr, and Frank Kardes, Vol. 57 (Mahwah, NJ: Lawrence Erlbaum Associates, 2007), 31–76; Barbara Loken, Larry Barsalou, and Christopher Joiner, "Categorization Theory and Research in Consumer Psychology: Category Representation and Category-Based Inference," in *The Handbook of Consumer Psychology*, eds. Curtis Haugvedt, Paul Herr, and Frank Kardes, Vol. 57 (Mahwah, NJ: Lawrence Erlbaum Associates, 2007), 453–485.

39. For an interesting related topic, see Henrik Hagtvedt, "The Impact of Incomplete Typeface Logos on Perceptions of the Firm," *Journal of Marketing* 75, no. 3 (July 2011): 86–93.

40. Philip Kotler and Kevin Lane Keller, *Marketing Management: Analysis, Planning, Implementation, and Control*, 14th ed. (Upper Saddle River, NJ: Prentice Hall, 2012).

41. Joseph F. Hair Jr., Rolph E. Anderson, Ronald Tatham, and William C. Black, *Multivariate Data Analysis*, 4th ed. (Englewood Cliffs, NJ: Prentice Hall, 1995); James Lattin, Douglas Carrol, and Paul Green, *Analyzing Multivariate Data*, 5th ed. (Pacific Grove, CA: Duxbury Press, 2003).

42. Brandon Olson, "How to Monitor Multiple Social Media Metrics in a Single Dashboard," *Social Media Examiner*, August 8, 2016, www.socialmediaexaminer.com/how-to-monitor-multiple-social-media-metrics-in-a-single-dashboard, accessed July 14, 2018.

43. Jill Bowers, "The Best Social Media Monitoring of 2017," *Top Ten Reviews*, December 18, 2017, www.toptenreviews.com/services/internet/best-social-media-monitoring/socialclout-review/.

44. J. Scott Armstrong, Vicki G. Morwitz, and V. Kumar, "Sales Forecasts for Existing Consumer Products and Services: Do Purchase Intentions Contribute to Accuracy?" *International Journal of Forecasting* 16, no. 3, (2000): 383–397.

45. Icek Ajzen and Martin Fishbein, *Understanding Attitudes and Predicting Social Behavior* (Englewood Cliffs, NJ: Prentice Hall, 1980); Vicki G. Morwitz, Joel Steckel, and Alok Gupta, "When Do Purchase Intentions Predict Sales?" *International Journal of Forecasting* 23, no. 3, (2007): 347–364; Pierre Chandon, Vicki G. Morwitz, and Werner J. Reinartz, "Do Intentions Really Predict Behavior? Self-Generated Validity Effects in Survey Research," *Journal of Marketing* 69, no. 2 (April 2005): 1–14.

46. Fred Reichheld, *Ultimate Question: For Driving Good Profits and True Growth* (Cambridge, MA: Harvard Business School Press, 2006); Jena McGregor, "Would You Recommend Us?" *BusinessWeek*, 71, no. 3 January 30, 2006, 94–95; Kathryn Kranhold, "Client-Satisfaction Tool Takes Root," *The Wall Street Journal*, Eastern Edition, July 10, 2006, B3; Timothy L. Keiningham, Bruce Cooil, Tor Wallin Andreassen, and Lerzan Aksoy, "A Longitudinal Examination of Net Promoter and Firm Revenue Growth," *Journal of Marketing* 71, no. 3 (July 2007): 39–51; Neil A. Morgan and Lopo Leotte Rego, "The Value of Different Customer Satisfaction and Loyalty Metrics in Predicting Business Performance," *Marketing Science* 25, no. 5 (September–October 2006): 426–439; Timothy L. Keiningham, Lerzan Aksoy, Bruce Cooil, and Tor W. Andreassen, "Linking Customer Loyalty to Growth," *MIT Sloan Management Review* 49, no. 4 (Summer 2008): 51–57.

47. NPS Benchmarks, Net Promoter Score, "Companies," https://npsbenchmarks.com/companies, accessed November 11, 2018.

48. Neil T. Bendle and Charan K. Bagga, "The Metrics That Marketers Muddle," *MIT Sloan Management Review* 57, no. 3 (2016): 73.

49. David Ensing, "NPS: Using It Correctly," *Business 2 Community*, October 17, 2017, www.business2community.com/customer-experience/nps-using-correctly-01939678#e4XigUe3AIp1VO4B.97.

50. Das Narayandas, "Building Loyalty in Business Markets," *Harvard Business Review* 83, no. 9 (September 2005): 131–138.

51. For a more general discussion of consumer attachment, see Susan S. Kleine and Stacy M. Baker, "An Integrative Review of Material Possession Attachment," *Academy of Marketing Science Review* 8, no. 4 (2004): 1–39; Rosellina Ferraro, Jennifer Edson Escalas, and James R. Bettman, "Our Possessions, Our Selves: Domains of Self-Worth and the Possession-Self Link," *Journal of Consumer Psychology* 21, no. 2 (2011): 169–177.

52. See, for example, Lars Bergkvist and Tino Bech-Larsen, "Two Studies of Consequences and Actionable Antecedents of Brand Love," *Journal of Brand Management* 17, no. 7 (June 2010): 504–518.

53. Barbara A. Carroll and Aaron C. Ahuvia, "Some Antecedents and Outcomes of Brand Love," *Marketing Letters* 17, no. 2 (2006): 79–89.

54. Rajeev Batra, Aaron Ahuvia, and Richard P. Bagozzi, "Brand Love," *Journal of Marketing* 76, no. 2 (March 2012): 1–16, https://www.ama.org/publications/JournalOfMarketing/documents/jm.09.0339_web_appendix.pdf, accessed November 11, 2018.

55. C.W. Park, Deborah J. Macinnis, Joseph Priester, Andreas B. Eisingerich, and Dawn Iacobucci, "Brand Attachment and Brand Attitude Strength: Conceptual and Empirical Differentiation of Two Critical Brand Equity Drivers," *Journal of Marketing* 74, no. 6 (November 2010): 1–17.

56. Vikas Mittal and Mohanbir S. Sawhney, "Managing Customer Retention in the Attention Economy," working paper, University of Pittsburgh, 2001.

57. For a broad overview, Brittany Darwell, "2011: The Year in Facebook Advertising," *Adweek*, December 28, 2011, https://www.adweek.com/digital/the-year-in-facebook-advertising/; "Digital Marketing: Special Advertising Section," *Adweek*, October 28, 2011.

58. Jon Bruner, "What's a 'Like' Worth?," *Forbes*, August 8, 2011, Vol. 188, Issue 2, 28–30; Brian Morrisey, "Value of a 'Fan' on Social Media: $3.60," *Adweek*, April 13, 2010, accessed July 14, 2018, https://www.adweek.com/digital/value-fan-social-media-360-102063/ http://www.vitrue.com.

59. Susan M. Fournier, "Consumers and Their Brands: Developing Relationship Theory in Consumer Research," *Journal of Consumer Research* 24, no. 4 (March 1998): 343–373; Susan M. Fournier, Susan Dobscha, and David G. Mick, "Preventing the Premature Death of Relationship Marketing," *Harvard Business Review* 76, no. 1 (January–February 1998): 42–51; Susan M. Fournier and Julie L. Yao, "Reviving Brand Loyalty: A Reconceptualization Within the Framework of Consumer–Brand Relationships," *International Journal of Research in Marketing* 14, no. 5 (1997): 451–472; Susan Fournier, "Lessons Learned About Consumers' Relationships with Their Brands," in *Handbook of Brand Relationships*, eds. Joseph Priester, Deborah MacInnis, and C. W. Park (New York: Society for Consumer Psychology and M.E. Sharp, 2009), 5–23; Susan Fournier, Michael Breazeale, Marc Fetscherin, and T. C. Melewar, eds., *Consumer–Brand Relationships: Theory and Practice* (London: Routledge Taylor & Francis Group, 2012).

60. This section greatly benefited from helpful and insightful contributions by Michael Sussman, Anne Rivers, and Eunjin Koh.

11

Measuring Outcomes of Brand Equity: Capturing Market Performance

Learning Objectives

After reading this chapter, you should be able to

1. Recognize the multidimensionality of brand equity and the importance of multiple methods to measure it.

2. Contrast different comparative methods to assess brand equity.

3. Explain the basic logic of how conjoint analysis works.

4. Review different holistic methods for valuing brand equity.

5. Describe the relationship between branding and finance.

Intel uses a price premium approach to track its brand strength relative to competition.

PREVIEW

Ideally, to measure brand equity, we would create a "brand equity index"—one easily calculated number that summarizes the health of the brand and completely captures its brand equity. Just as a thermometer measuring body temperature provides only one indication of how healthy a person is, so does any one measure of brand equity provide only one indication of the health of a brand. Brand equity is a multidimensional concept, and complex enough to require many different types of measures. Applying multiple measures increases the diagnostic power of marketing research and the likelihood that managers will better understand what is happening to their brands, and, perhaps more important, why.[1]

In arguments suggesting that researchers should employ multiple measures of brand equity, writers have drawn interesting comparisons between measuring brand equity and assessing the performance of an aircraft in flight or a car on the road; for example:

> The pilot of the plane has to consider a number of indicators and gauges as the plane is flown. There is the fuel gauge, the altimeter, and a number of other important status indicators. All of these dials and meters tell the pilot different things about the health of the plane. There is no one gauge that summarizes everything about the plane. The plane needs the altimeter, compass, radar, and the fuel gauge. As the pilot looks at the instrument cluster, he has to take all of these critical indicators into account as he flies.[2]

The dashboard of a car or the gauges on the plane, which together measure its health while being driven or flown, are analogous to the multiple measures of brand equity necessary to assess the health of a brand.

The preceding chapter described different approaches to measuring brand knowledge structures and the customer mind-set that marketers can use to identify and quantify potential sources of brand equity. By applying these measurement techniques, we should gain a good understanding of the depth and breadth of brand awareness; the strength, favorability, and uniqueness of brand associations; the positivity of brand responses; and the nature of brand relationships for their brands. As we described in Chapters 1 and 2, a product with positive brand equity can enjoy the following six important customer-related benefits:

1. Perception of better product or service performance
2. Greater loyalty and less vulnerability to competitive marketing actions and marketing crises
3. Larger margins and more inelastic responses to price increases and elastic responses to price decreases
4. Greater trade cooperation and support
5. Increased marketing communication effectiveness
6. Opportunity for successful licensing and brand extension.

The customer-based brand equity model maintains that these benefits, and the ultimate value of a brand, depend on the underlying components of brand knowledge and sources of brand equity. As Chapter 10 described, we can measure these individual components; however, to provide more direct estimates, we still must assess their resulting value in some way. This chapter examines measurement procedures to assess the effects of brand knowledge structures on these and other measures that capture market performance for the brand.[3]

First, we review comparative methods, which are meant to better assess the effects of consumer perceptions and preferences on consumer response to the marketing program and the specific benefits of brand equity. Next, we look at holistic methods, which attempt to estimate the overall or summary value of a brand.[4] Some of the interplays between branding and financial considerations are included in Brand Focus 11.0.

COMPARATIVE METHODS

Comparative methods are research studies or experiments that examine consumer attitudes and behavior toward a brand to directly estimate specific benefits arising from having a high level of awareness and strong, favorable, and unique brand associations. There are two types of comparative methods.

- *Brand-based comparative approaches* use experiments or analyses in which one group of consumers responds to an element of the marketing program or some marketing activity when it is attributed to the target brand, and another group responds to that same element or activity when it is attributed to a competitive or fictitiously named brand.
- *Marketing-based comparative approaches* use experiments or analyses in which consumers respond to changes in elements of the marketing program or marketing activity for the target brand or competitive brands.

The brand-based approach holds the marketing program fixed and examines consumer response based on changes in the brand identification, whereas the marketing-based approach holds the brand fixed and examines consumer response based on changes in the marketing program. We will look at each of these two approaches in turn and then describe conjoint analysis as a technique that, in effect, combines the two.

Brand-Based Comparative Approaches

Competitive brands can be useful benchmarks in brand-based comparative approaches. Although consumers may interpret marketing activity for a fictitiously named or unnamed version of the product or service in terms of their general product category knowledge, they may also have a particular brand, or *exemplar*, in mind. This exemplar may be the category leader or some other brand that consumers feel is representative of the category, like their most preferred brand. Consumers may make inferences to supply any missing information based on their knowledge of this particular brand. Thus, it may be instructive to examine how consumers evaluate a proposed new advertising campaign, new promotion offering, or new product when it is also attributed to one or more major competitors.

In a blind test of different types of inexpensive beers, "Natty Light" was the surprising winner, even though it was the most inexpensive beer that was tested.

Applications.   The classic example of the brand-based comparative approach is blind testing research studies in which different consumers examine or use a product with or without brand identification. Invariably, differences emerge. For example, in one small-sample study conducted by *Business Insider*, people were asked to "blind test" different brands of cheap, inexpensive beer. To much surprise, on this unbranded basis, it was Natural Light ("Natty Light"), the cheapest beer tested, that actually received the highest rating amongst the participants.[5]

One natural application of the brand-based comparative approach is product purchase or consumption research for new or existing products, as long as the brand identification can be hidden in some way for the "unbranded" control group. Brand-based comparative approaches are also useful to determine brand equity benefits related to price margins and premiums.

T-MOBILE

Deutsche Telecom invested much time and money in building its T-Mobile mobile communication brand. However, in the United Kingdom, the company leased or shared its network lines with competitor Virgin Mobile. As a result, the audio quality of the signal that a T-Mobile customer received in making a call should have been virtually identical to the audio quality of the signal for a Virgin Mobile customer. After all, the same network was being used to send the signal. Despite that fact, research showed that Virgin Mobile customers rated their signal quality significantly higher than did T-Mobile customers. The strong Virgin brand image appeared to cast a halo over its different service offerings, literally causing consumers to change their impressions of product performance.[6]

Virgin Mobile customers rated their signal quality significantly higher than did T-Mobile customers, even though the same network was used, indicating the power of Virgin Mobile's brand equity.

Critique.   The main advantage of a brand-based comparative approach is that because it holds all aspects of the marketing program fixed for the brand, it isolates the value of a brand in a very real sense. Understanding exactly how knowledge of the brand affects consumer responses to prices, advertising, and so forth is extremely useful in developing strategies in these different areas. At the same time, we could study an almost infinite variety of marketing activities, so what we learn is limited by the number of different applications we examine.

Brand-based comparative methods are particularly applicable when the marketing activity under consideration represents a change from past marketing activities of the brand, for example, a new sales or trade promotion, ad campaign, or proposed brand extension. If the marketing activity under consideration is already strongly identified with the brand—such as an ad campaign that has been running for years—it may be difficult to attribute some aspect of the marketing program to a fictitiously named or unnamed version of the product or service in a believable fashion.

Thus, a crucial consideration with the brand-based comparative approach is the realism we can achieve in the experiment or analyses. For example, brand-based comparative approaches may highlight the particular product characteristics enough to make them more salient than they would otherwise be, thus distorting the results. An alternative is the marketing-based comparative approach, which is described next.

Marketing-Based Comparative Approaches

Marketing-based comparative approaches hold the brand fixed and examine consumer response based on changes in the marketing program.

Applications.   There is a long academic and industry tradition of exploring price premiums using marketing-based comparative approaches. In the mid-1950s, Edgar Pessemier developed a dollar-metric measure of brand commitment that relied on a step-by-step increase in the price difference between the brand normally purchased and an alternative brand.[7] To reveal brand-switching and loyalty patterns, Pessemier plotted the percentage of consumers who switched from their regular brand as a function of the brand price increases.

Some marketing research suppliers have adopted variations of this approach to derive similar types of demand curves, and many firms now try to assess price sensitivity and willingness-to-pay thresholds for different brands.[8] For example, Intel would routinely survey computer shoppers to find out how much of a discount they would require before switching to a personal computer that did not have an Intel microprocessor in it (say, an AMD chip) or, conversely, what premium they would be willing to pay to buy a personal computer that did have an Intel microprocessor in it.

We can apply marketing-based comparative approaches in other ways, assessing consumer response to different advertising strategies, executions, or media plans through multiple test markets. For example, IRI's electronic test markets and similar research methodologies can permit tests of different advertising weights or repetition schedules as well as ad copy tests. By controlling for other factors, we can isolate the effects of the brand and product. One increasingly common example of the marketing-based comparative approach online is A/B testing. With A/B testing, digital marketers utilize split testing of different versions of a marketing program or activity—for example, two different versions of a Web site, Version A and Version B. Visitors to a Web site can be shown either Web page A or B, and the version with a better conversion rate is selected.

Marketers can also explore potential brand extensions by collecting consumer evaluations of a range of concept statements describing brand extension candidates. For example, the results of a consumer survey conducted at one time examined reactions to hypothetical extensions of the Planters nuts brand. Contrasting those extensions provides some indication of the equity of the brand. Figure 11-1 displays the results of a consumer survey conducted at one time to examine reactions to hypothetical extensions of the Planters nuts brand. Contrasting those extensions provides some indication of the equity of the brand.

In this example, the survey results suggested that consumers expected any Planters brand extension to be nut-related. Appropriate product characteristics for a possible Planters brand extension seemed to be crunchy, sweet, salty, spicy, and buttery. In terms of where in the store consumers would have expected to find new Planters products, the snack and candy sections seemed most likely. On the other hand, consumers did not seem to expect to find new Planters products in the breakfast food aisle, bakery product section, refrigerated section, or frozen food section. Consistent with these survey results, Planters sells a variety of nuts (cashews, peanuts, pistachios, almonds, and mixed nuts) which are marketed as delicious-tasting and nutritious snacks. Planters has also added dessert-inspired mixes—such as Planters chocolate peanut butter brownie mix—to its snack offerings, thereby combining its perceived associations with both snack and candy aisles within a store.

Critique. The main advantage of the marketing-based comparative approach is ease of implementation. We can compare virtually any proposed set of marketing actions for the brand. At the

Digital marketers test different versions of a marketing program using A/B testing and the version with a better conversion rate is selected.

Average Scale Rating[*]	Proposed Extensions
10	Peanuts
9	Snack mixes, nuts for baking
8	—
7	Pretzels, chocolate nut candy, caramel corn
6	Snack crackers, potato chips, nutritional granola bars
5	Tortilla chips, toppings (ice cream/dessert)
4	Lunchables/lunch snack packs, dessert mixes (cookie/cake/brownie)
3	Ice cream/ice cream bars, toppings (salad/vegetable)
2	Cereal, toaster pastries, Asian entrees/sauces, stuffing mix, refrigerated dough, jams/jellies
1	Yogurt

[*]Consumers rated hypothetical proposed extensions on an 11-point scale anchored by 0 (definitely would *not* expect Planter's to sell it) and 10 (definitely would expect Planter's to sell it).

FIGURE 11-1

Reactions to Proposed Planters Extensions

same time, the main drawback is that it may be difficult to discern whether consumer responses to changes in the marketing stimuli are being caused by brand knowledge or by more generic product knowledge. In other words, it may be that for *any* brand in the product category, consumers would be willing to pay certain prices, accept a particular brand extension, and so forth. One way to determine whether consumer response is specific to the brand is to conduct similar tests of consumer response with competitive brands. A statistical technique well-suited to do just that is described next.

Conjoint Analysis

Conjoint analysis is a survey-based multivariate technique that enables marketers to profile the consumer decision process concerning products and brands.[9] Specifically, by asking consumers to express preferences or choose among a number of carefully designed product profiles, researchers can determine the trade-offs consumers are making between various brand attributes, and the importance they are attaching to them.[10]

Each profile consumers see is made up of a set of attribute levels chosen on the basis of experimental design principles to satisfy certain mathematical properties. The value consumers attach to each attribute level, as statistically derived by the conjoint formula, is called a ***part worth***. We can use the part worth in various ways to estimate how consumers would value a new combination of the attribute levels. For example, one attribute is the brand name. The part worth for the brand name attribute reflects its value.

One classic study of conjoint analysis, reported by Green and Wind, examined consumer evaluations of a spot-remover product on five attributes: package design, brand name, price, *Good Housekeeping Seal*, and money-back guarantee.[11] These same authors also applied conjoint analysis in a landmark research study to arrive at the design that became the Courtyard by Marriott hotel chain.[12] Conjoint analysis has since been applied in a variety of industries ranging from bar soaps to lawn chemicals, to cameras, and to apartment design. It has also been used in the design of health insurance policies and hotel design.[13]

Applications. Conjoint analysis has a number of possible applications. In the past, the Ogilvy & Mather advertising agency used a brand and price trade-off methodology as a means of assessing advertising effectiveness and brand value.[14] Brand and price trade-off is a simplified version

Conjoint analysis was applied to arrive at the design that became the Courtyard by Marriott hotel chain.

of conjoint measurement with just two variables—brand and price. Consumers make a series of simulated purchase choices between different combinations of brands and prices. Each choice triggers an increase in the price of the selected brand, forcing the consumer to choose between buying a preferred brand and paying less. In this way, consumers reveal how much their brand loyalty is worth, and, conversely, which brands they would relinquish for a lower price. Academic researchers have employed conjoint techniques to show how extendible brand names are, to evaluate the effectiveness of corporate image programs and to identify relevant attributes driving consumer preferences.[15]

Critique.   The main advantage of the conjoint-based approach is that it allows us to study different brands and different aspects of the product or marketing program (product composition, price, distribution outlets, and so on) simultaneously. Thus, we can uncover information about consumers' responses to different marketing activities for both the focal and competing brands.

One of the disadvantages of conjoint analysis is that marketing profiles may violate consumers' expectations based on what they already know about brands. Thus, we must take care that consumers do not evaluate unrealistic product profiles or scenarios. It can also be difficult to specify and interpret brand attribute levels, although some useful guidelines have been put forth to more effectively apply conjoint analysis to brand positioning.[16]

HOLISTIC METHODS

We use comparative methods to approximate the specific benefits of brand equity. *Holistic methods* place an overall value on the brand in either abstract utility terms or concrete financial terms. Thus, holistic methods attempt to "net out" various considerations to determine the unique contribution of the brand. The *residual approach* examines the value of the brand by subtracting consumers' preferences for the brand—based on physical product attributes alone—from their overall brand preferences. The *valuation approach* places a financial value on brand equity for accounting purposes, mergers and acquisitions, or other such reasons. After an example from Liz Claiborne, we'll look at each of these approaches.

Similar to Liz Claiborne, it is not unusual for brand names to trade hands multiple times over their lifetime. Each time there is a potential bidder, the potential acquirer may subject the brand to a major valuation exercise, using one of the many approaches suggested in this chapter. The goal of these valuation estimates is to ensure that a fair price is paid to the target firm to acquire the brand name.

LIZ CLAIBORNE

A company that found great success selling popular fashions to working women in the 1980s—generating $2 billion in annual sales by the early 1990s—Liz Claiborne found itself in serious trouble two decades later when sales started to cool. A brand transformation that eliminated some slower-selling older lines to focus on younger customers failed to turn the business around. Aging core customers deserted the brand, and department stores began to replace it with their own private labels. The company was posting annual losses by 2006, and sales dropped by half over the next five years. Management decided to retrench in 2011 and focus its resources on its faster-selling brands—Kate Spade, Lucky Brand Jeans, and Juicy Couture. The Claiborne and Monet brands were sold to JCPenney for $288 million, and as part of the sales agreement, Liz Claiborne was given one year to change its name. The firm was making another financial bet on a new brand strategy it hoped would prove successful, while JCPenney was betting there was life left in the Liz Claiborne brand.[17] Liz Claiborne subsequently rebranded its company as Kate Spade & Company in 2012, and was later acquired by Coach in 2017 for $2.4 billion.[18]

Kate Spade, initially known as Liz Claiborne Inc., rebranded itself and was later acquired by Coach.

Residual Approaches

The rationale behind residual approaches is the view that brand equity is what remains of consumer preferences and choices after we subtract physical product effects. The idea is that we can infer the relative valuation of brands by observing consumer preferences and choices *if* we take into account as many sources of measured attribute values as possible. Several researchers have defined brand equity as the incremental preference over and above what would result without brand identification. In this view, we can calculate brand equity by subtracting preferences for objective characteristics of the physical product from overall preference.[19]

Scanner Panel. Some researchers have focused on the analysis of brand value based on data sets from supermarket scanners of consumer purchases. In an early study, Kamakura and Russell proposed a measure that employs consumer purchase histories from supermarket scanner data to estimate brand equity through a residual approach.[20] Specifically, their model explains the choices observed from a panel of consumers as a function of the store environment (actual shelf prices, sales promotions, displays), the physical characteristics of available brands, and a residual term dubbed brand equity. By controlling for other aspects of the marketing mix, they estimate that aspect of brand preference that is unique to a brand and not currently duplicated by competitors.

More recently, a variation proposed by Ailawadi, Lehmann, and Neslin employs actual retail sales data to calculate a "revenue premium" as an estimate of brand equity by calculating the difference in revenues between a brand and a generic or private label in the same category.[21] Sriram, Balachandar, and Kalwani similarly use store-level scanner data to track brand equity and key drivers of brand equity over time.[22]

Choice Experiments. Swait, Erdem, and colleagues have proposed a related approach to measuring brand equity with choice experiments that account for brand names, product attributes, brand image, and differences in consumer sociodemographic characteristics and brand usage.[23] They define the *equalization price* as the price that equates the utility of a brand to the utilities that could be attributed to a brand in the category where no brand differentiation occurred. We can consider equalization price a proxy for brand equity.[24]

Multi-Attribute Attitude Models. Srinivasan, Park, and Chang have proposed a comprehensive residual methodology to measure brand equity based on the multi-attribute attitude model.[25] Their approach reveals the relative sizes of different bases of brand equity by dividing brand equity into three components: brand awareness, attribute perception biases, and nonattribute preference.

- The *attribute-perception based component* of brand equity is the difference between subjectively perceived attribute values and objectively measured attribute values. Objectively measured attribute values come from independent testing services such as *Consumer Reports* or acknowledged experts in the field.
- The *nonattribute preference component* of brand equity is the difference between subjectively perceived attribute values and overall preference. It reflects the consumers' overall appraisal of a brand that goes beyond the utility of individual product attributes.

The researchers also incorporate the effects of enhancing brand awareness and preference on consumer pull and the brand's availability. They propose a survey procedure to collect information for estimating these different perception and preference measures.

Dillon and his colleagues have presented a model for decomposing attribute ratings of a brand into two components: (1) brand-specific associations, meaning features, attributes, or benefits that consumers link to a brand, and (2) general brand impressions based on a more holistic view of a brand.[26]

Critique. Residual approaches provide a useful benchmark for interpreting brand equity, especially when we need approximations of brand equity or a financially oriented perspective on it. The disadvantage of residual approaches is that they are most appropriate for brands with a lot of product-related attribute associations, because these measures are unable to distinguish between different types of nonproduct-related attribute associations. Consequently, the residual approach's diagnostic value for strategic decision-making in other cases is limited.

Generally, residual approaches take a fairly static view of brand equity by focusing on consumer preferences. This contrasts sharply with the process view advocated by the customer-based brand equity framework. The brand-based and marketing-based comparative approaches stress looking at consumer response to the marketing of a brand and attempting to uncover the extent to which that response is affected by brand knowledge.

This distinction is also relevant for the issue of separability in brand valuation that various researchers have raised. For example, imagine that a brand becomes known for providing extraordinary customer service because of certain policies and favorable advertising, publicity, or word-of-mouth (e.g., Singapore Airlines, Ritz Carlton hotels). These favorable perceptions of customer service and the attitudes they engender could create customer-based brand equity by affecting consumer response to a price policy (consumers would be willing to pay higher prices), a new ad campaign (consumers would accept an ad illustrating customer satisfaction), or a brand extension (customers would become interested in trying a new type of retail outlet).

Valuation Approaches

Based on several different analyses, a widely held belief is that much of the corporate value of many companies are wrapped up in the value of their brands. One estimate suggests that

$8 trillion or nearly half of the $17.9 trillion market capitalization of the S&P 500 index is on account of intangible assets.[27] Furthermore, brands are an important component of these intangible assets and may account for 30 percent or more of the stock market value of companies in the S&P 500.[28]

A survey done by the World Economic Forum reinforced this idea of the importance of brands—roughly three-fifths of CEOs of global corporations believe that their corporate brand and reputation represents more than 40 percent of their company's market's capitalization.[29] Table 11-1 demonstrates the role of brand value as a percentage of the overall value of a firm,

Table 11–1 Brand Value as a Percentage of Firms' Market Value*

Company	Brand Value (in $ billions)*	Total Value (in $ billions)**	Brand Value as a Percentage of Overall Value
Apple	184.1	868.88	21%
Google	141.7	729.1	19%
Microsoft	79.9	659.9	12%
Coca-Cola	69.7	195.5	36%
Amazon	64.7	563.5	11%
Samsung #	56.2	300	19%
Toyota	50.3	188.2	27%
Facebook	48.2	420.8	11%
Mercedes	47.8	79.3	60%
IBM	46.8	142	33%

*Source: Data are for 2017; http://interbrand.com/best-brands/best-global-brands/2017/ranking/

**Source: Market capitalization information based on data from CRSP Monthly

Samsung market capitalization converted to US currency from South Korean won

Apple is the most valuable brand name in the world.

based on 2017 data. As can be seen, there are wide variations in the percentages of valuation accounted for by brand names; however, it also supports the idea that brands are a key source of value to a firm.

The recognition of the important role of brand names has spurred much research on valuation. The ability to put a specific price tag on a brand's value is useful for a number of reasons:

- *Mergers and acquisitions:* Both to evaluate possible purchases as well as to facilitate disposal.
- *Brand licensing:* Internally for tax reasons and to third parties.
- *Fund-raising:* As collateral on loans or for sale or leaseback arrangements; to establish to current and future investors how the firm's efforts have resulted in valuation creation, as demonstrated by the valuations of the brands owned by the firm.
- *Brand portfolio decisions:* To develop the brand strategy of a portfolio of brands based on their brand valuation.
- *Internal resource allocation decisions and understanding the return on investment (ROI):* Capital allocation decisions within a firm could revolve around the valuations of different brands. The valuation of brand names could help in establishing the return on investment of marketing expenditures.

To help illuminate the issues relating to the valuation of brands, we first provide a brief overview of the issues relevant to the accounting of the firm's assets.

Accounting Background.   The assets of a firm can be either tangible or intangible. **Tangible assets** include property, plant, and equipment; current assets (inventories, marketable securities, and cash); and investments in stocks and bonds. We can estimate the value of tangible assets using accounting book values and reported estimates of replacement costs.

Intangible assets are any factors of production or specialized resources that permit the company to earn cash flows in excess of the return on tangible assets. In other words, intangible assets augment the earning power of a firm's physical assets. They are typically lumped under the heading of **goodwill** and include things such as patents, trademarks, and licensing agreements, as well as softer considerations such as the skill of the management team and customer relations.

In an acquisition, the goodwill item often includes a premium paid to gain control, which, in certain instances, may even exceed the value of tangible and intangible assets. Brand assets are intangible assets and are governed by the same accounting principles that involve reporting of intangible assets. Paradoxically, in the United States, brands developed in-house are not valued explicitly in the balance sheet; however, brand acquisitions are reported on the balance sheet because there is a defined cost of purchase associated with an acquired brand, which can be reported as an expense. This contributes to an anomaly in accounting for brands, such that brands acquired from outside via a merger or acquisition are explicitly recognized on the balance sheet, whereas internally developed brands are ignored. The Financial Accounting Standards Board (FASB) standards in the United States (and International Accounting Standards as well) state that,

> Expenditure on internally generated brands . . . cannot be distinguished from the cost of developing the business as a whole. Therefore, such items are not recognized as intangible assets.

It is worth comparing how intangible assets are viewed by the FASB (in its Generally Accepted Accounting Principles or GAAP) in the United States relative to International Financial Reporting Standards. In the United States, based on GAAP, intangible assets are recognized at fair market value and nothing more. In contrast, International Financial Reporting Standards (IFRS) takes into account future economic benefits that could be derived from intangible assets.[30] This fundamental difference in philosophy provides the basis for why brands as intangible assets are viewed differently in the United States and overseas.

Compounding the lack of guidance from the accounting standards boards is the fact that the valuation of brands itself can be complicated and challenging for a variety of reasons. First, brand valuations are based at least in part on consumers' perceptions, which can be notoriously fickle and difficult to measure. Second, brands are one among many intangible assets of a firm, and the valuation of brands could vary based on assumptions driving the methodology and the relative value of other intangible assets (e.g., patents, goodwill, etc.).

A third reason why brands are not reported on the balance sheet is that brand value on balance sheets may be subject to impairment.[31] In the event of negative publicity or loss of reputation, such impairment could be difficult to quantify and reconcile on the balance sheet. Accountants have been reluctant to revise the brand value that is reported on the balance sheet, resulting in a phenomenon which has been called the "moribund effect."[32] As an example, Gillette was acquired by P&G for $24 billion in 2005. However, its brand value has not changed since the acquisition, even though P&G's overall market capitalization has changed significantly since the acquisition.

In the United States, according to the FASB, private companies can amortize goodwill for book purposes, over a 10-year period, or less (i.e., over their useful life). This policy requires a test for impairment on an annual basis (called the goodwill impairment test). It has been noted that the FASB cannot allow brand equity in financial reporting because of the "absence of verifiable costs, inability to verify a certain transaction or series of transactions (lagged effect of advertising), and uniqueness of each intangible brand and resulting difficulty in establishing criteria for relevancy and reliability."[33] Despite these concerns, valuation has tremendous managerial significance, and there have been many significant efforts to quantify the value of brands.

P&G's acquisition of Gillette showcases the importance of brand valuation, as well as difficulties associated with reporting a brand's value on the balance sheet.

Historical Perspectives.   Brand valuation's more recent past started with Rupert Murdoch's News Corporation, which included a valuation of some of its magazines on its balance sheets in 1984, as permitted by Australian accounting standards. In the United Kingdom, Grand Metropolitan was one of the first British companies to place a monetary value on the brands it owned and to put that value on its balance sheet. British firms used brand values to boost their balance sheets and have argued that this effort helps bring their shareholder funds nearer to the market capitalization of the firm. Certain other countries (including Canada, Germany, and Japan) have permitted some or all of the goodwill (including that arising from brand names) in an acquisition to be deducted for tax purposes.

General Approaches.   In determining the value of a brand in an acquisition or merger, firms can choose from three main approaches: the cost, market, and income approaches.[34]

The cost approach maintains that brand equity is the amount of money that would be required to reproduce or replace the brand (including all costs for research and development, test marketing, advertising, etc.). One common criticism of approaches relying on historical or replacement cost is that they reward past performance in a way that may bear little relation to future profitability—for example, many brands with expensive introductions have been unsuccessful. On the other hand, for brands that have been around for decades (such as Heinz, Kellogg's, and Chanel), it would be virtually impossible to find out what the investment in brand development was—and largely irrelevant as well.

It is also obviously easier to estimate costs of tangible assets than intangible assets, but the latter often may lie at the heart of brand equity. Similar problems exist with a replacement cost approach; for example, the cost of replacing a brand depends a great deal on how quickly the process would occur and what competitive, legal, and logistical obstacles might be encountered.

According to the second approach, the market approach, we can think of brand equity as the present value of the future economic benefits to be derived by the owner of the asset. In other words, it is the amount an active market would allow so that the asset would exchange between a willing buyer and willing seller. The main problems with this approach are the lack of open market transactions for brand name assets, and the fact that the uniqueness of brands makes extrapolating from one market transaction to another problematic.

The third approach to determining the value of a brand, the income approach, argues that brand equity is the discounted future cash flow from the future earnings stream for the brand. Three such income approaches are as follows:

1. Capitalizing royalty earnings from a brand name (when these can be defined)
2. Capitalizing the premium profits that are earned by a branded product (by comparing its performance with that of an unbranded product)
3. Capitalizing the actual profitability of a brand after allowing for the costs of maintaining it and the effects of taxation.

For example, as an example of the first income approach, brand consultancy Brand Finance uses a Royalty Relief methodology for brand valuation. Their approach is based on the premise that brand value can be thought of in terms of what a company avoids in paying a license fee from actually owning the trademark. Their rationale is that such an approach has much credibility with accountants, lawyers, and tax experts because it calculates brand values on the basis of comparable third-party transactions. They use the publicly available information to estimate future, post-tax royalties of a brand, and thus, its net present value and overall brand value.[35] We next describe some of the major and influential valuation approaches.

BRAND VALUATION: A REVIEW OF MAJOR APPROACHES

There have been many approaches suggested by academic researchers to systematically value brands. One seminal academic research study proposed a technique for estimating a firm's brand equity derived from financial market estimates of brand-related profits.[36] The methodology defined brand equity as the incremental cash flows accruing to branded products over and above the cash flows that would result from the sale of unbranded products. This fundamentally assumed that the market value of the firm's securities would provide an unbiased estimate of the future cash flows attributable to all the firm's assets. Further, brand equity was regarded as an intangible asset contributing to firm value. By taking into consideration factors such as the age of the brand, order of entry in the category, and current and past advertising share, the approach was able to estimate brand equity. Aside from such academic approaches, there are a few well-established brand valuation approaches that derive from industry, and we review three of them here. All three approaches—Interbrand, BrandZ, and Brand Finance—combine brand equity measurement and financial valuation in deriving estimates of brand value. A detailed description of these brand valuation approaches is given next.

Interbrand

One of the leading brand valuation firms is Interbrand. Recall that we provided a list of the most valuable global brands according to Interbrand in Table 11-1. Interbrand's approach takes into account different ways in which a brand benefits an organization both internally and externally—from attracting and retaining talent to delivering on customer expectations. There are three key components of Interbrand's brand value assessment: (1) financial forecast, (2) role of brand; and (3) strength analysis.[37]

Financial Forecast. The basic principle underlying this step is that the worth of brands—like any other asset owned by a firm or the firm's overall value—can be calculated based on the estimates of the present value of its future cash flows. For each of the segments identified as important to a brand, the valuation process involves identifying and forecasting the net revenues (or potential cash flows). The calculation of economic profit involves three further adjustments to the net revenues generated by a brand: (1) operating costs, to arrive at net operating profit; (2) subtracting taxes from net operating profit; and (3) subtracting a capital charge to account for the capital used to generate the brand's revenues. The economic profit that is calculated is then multiplied by the role of brand (a percentage, as described below) to determine the branded earnings that contribute to the valuation total.

Role of Brand. Role of brand measures the portion of the customer decision to purchase that is attributable to the brand—exclusive of other purchase drivers such as price or product features. Conceptually, role of brand reflects the portion of demand for a branded product or service that exceeds what the demand would be for the same product or service if it were unbranded. Interbrand determines the role of brand in different ways, including primary research, by assessing the roles of brands across companies within that industry and through an expert panel assessment. They multiply the percentage for the role of brand by the economic profit of the branded products or services to determine the amount of branded earnings that contribute to the overall valuation.

Strength Analysis.   Brand strength measures the ability of the brand to secure the delivery of expected future earnings. Brand strength is reported on a scale of 0 to 100 based on an evaluation across 10 dimensions of internal and external aspects. The internal dimensions include clarity, commitment, governance, and responsiveness. The external dimensions include authenticity, relevance, differentiation, consistency, presence, and engagement. According to Interbrand, these 10 dimensions combine to provide an assessment of the strength of a brand. Performance in these dimensions is generally judged relative to other brands in the industry, and relative to other global brands. The brand strength inversely determines brand risk in terms of a discount rate through a proprietary algorithm. The key idea is that increases in brand strength can translate into varying discount rates that could apply to the streams of cash flows. The estimated discount rate is used to discount branded earnings back to a present value, based on the likelihood that the brand will be able to withstand challenges and deliver the expected earnings.

BrandZ

BrandZ's approach to brand equity measurement is based on the Meaningfully Different Framework that suggests that brands can create value if they offer three key benefits: (1) they are meaningful (they meet customer needs); (2) they are different (they are unique and they set trends); and (3) they are salient (they are top of mind).[38] These benefits translate into power (by increasing sales), premium (by commanding a high price), and potential (by helping to sustain future growth). Their findings indicate that meaningfully different brands capture significantly higher volume (five times as much), have a 13 percent price premium, and are more likely to increase their share of value.[39] The key steps in the BrandZ valuation are as follows.

Calculating Financial Value.   The first step in the Brand Valuation process is to apportion the earnings of the corporation across a portfolio of brands. By analyzing financial information from annual reports and other sources, the Attribution Rate is determined. This approach then multiplies Corporate Earnings by the Attribution Rate to arrive at Branded Earnings, the amount of Corporate Earnings attributed to a particular brand. They must then determine prospects for future earnings. Information supplied by Bloomberg data helps in calculating a Brand Multiple, a component that assesses future earnings prospects as a multiple of current earnings. BrandZ takes the Branded Earnings and multiplies that number by the Brand Multiple to arrive at the Financial Value.[40]

BrandZ's approach to financial valuation indicates that meaningfully different brands capture significantly higher volume, have a price premium, and are more likely to increase their share of value.

Calculating Brand Contribution. Following the estimate of financial value from the previous step, the methodology seeks to isolate the value of the brand itself—that intangible asset that exists in the minds of consumers—from other drivers of in-market or logistical factors that may drive the value of branded business, such as availability, distribution, or price. This involves calculating the brand contribution or ability of brand associations in consumers' minds to deliver sales by predisposing consumers to choose the brand or pay more for it. BrandZ's approach relies on extensive data collected on a large sample of consumers worldwide—involving 2 million consumers and more than 10,000 brands—to assess the brands' perceptions by consumers on a category-by-category and country-by-country basis.[41] As noted previously, the BrandZ approach focuses on three aspects of brands that they have found make people buy more and pay more for brands: being Meaningful, being Different, and being Salient. The approach identifies the purchase volume and any extra price premium delivered by these brand associations. This unique role played by brands is called the Brand Contribution.

Calculating Brand Value. BrandZ uses the calculated Financial Value and multiplies it by Brand Contribution, which is expressed as a percentage of Financial Value. Brand Value is the dollar amount a brand contributes to the overall value of a corporation.

Brand Finance

Brand Finance's approach to brand equity measurement is based on the "relief from royalty" approach.[42] With this approach, a brand's value is based on the royalties that a company would have paid for licensing that brand from a third party, assuming it was not the brand owner. The net present value of the projected royalty stream becomes the estimate of brand value. The approach can be summarized as follows. First, Brand Finance calculates the brand strength on a scale of 1 to 100 using data from the Brand Asset Valuator database (described in Chapter 10), which results in a Brand Strength Index (or BSI score).[43] Second, the methodology involves assessing the brand royalty rate by applying the BSI score to the royalty rates that apply to a given industry. These industry-specific royalty rates are identified through databases containing comparable licensing agreements. For example, if the industry royalty rates range between 1 to 5 percent, and the brand has a strength score of 80 out of 100, the appropriate royalty rate for the brand in this industry would be 4 percent.[44] Third, these royalty rates, when applied to forecasted revenues, help determine brand value. Revenue forecasts are further generated based on a combination of historical revenues, equity analyst forecasts as well as economic growth rates. Finally, brand value is determined by discounting forecasted revenues to net present value terms.

Comparing the Major Brand Valuation Approaches

Comparing the three methods, some similarities and differences are worth highlighting.

1. All three approaches are based on some variation of the income-based approach to brand valuation in that they are based on projections of income from brands into the foreseeable future. Both Interbrand and BrandZ adopt the economic profit method, whereas Brand Finance adopts the relief from royalty method.

The three major approaches to brand valuation (Interbrand, BrandZ, and Brand Finance) rely on the income-based approach to brand valuation.

2. All three methods compute the present value of projected future earnings based on an estimate of brand strength and an application of a discount rate, although the specific way they do so differ. While Interbrand and Brand Finance use a discount rate, BrandZ uses a brand multiple.

3. All three approaches use available financial and market data and compute the economic value added. Interbrand assesses the role of brand to extract brand-linked earnings from the projected income stream. BrandZ isolates the role of brand from other in-market factors that could influence brand value, and uses extensive consumer research data to understand the unique brand associations as a key driver of brand value. Brand Finance extracts brand earnings by applying brand strength to the royalty rates appropriate to a given sector.

4. The types of data used to measure brand perceptions vary across the three approaches. Interbrand's brand strength score relies on data collected from consumers over a sample of global brands. BrandZ's approach relies heavily on consumer research collected across a large sample of consumers and over a large number of brands. Brand Finance's methodology relies on brand strength data derived from Brand Asset Valuator. It also utilizes secondary data to determine royalty rates.[45]

Despite having some similarities in their approaches, the three methods have enough differences to produce some fairly significant differences in estimates of brand value for the same brand, causing considerable criticism regarding the validity of these approaches. The comparisons of the three valuation approaches for a sample of 68 brands for which real financial transaction data was available revealed significant anomalies, with all approaches overestimating value by nearly two or three times.[46] Further, these approaches are also inconsistent with each other. A comparison of the three approaches—and the variations in their assessments of brand value—for five major brands are shown in Table 11-2.

Why are these discrepancies so high, and why do inconsistencies exist across the approaches? With a proliferation of different methodologies and definitions, sometimes the underlying assumptions made by the approaches could contribute to variations. Sampling variations and types of brands that are incorporated could tilt the valuations across the approaches. For example, one criticism of Interbrand is that its approach is limited to large, high-profile brands with multinational operations. According to the criteria indicated by Interbrand, in order to be included in the study, brands must be global—that is, 30 percent of the brand's revenue must be from outside of the brand's home region, and it must have a presence in emerging markets.[47] Brand Finance's valuations are based on "relief from royalty" approach, and can, therefore, be applied to brands for which some information on royalties is available. BrandZ considers smaller, low-profile brands, and those operating in a single country. BrandZ covers retailer brands and sector-wise rankings, allowing for easy comparison across competitors.

At the heart of much of the criticism of all brand valuation approaches is the issue of separability that we identified earlier. An *Economist* editorial put it this way: "Brands can be awkward to separate as assets. With Cadbury's Dairy Milk, how much value comes from the name Cadbury? How much from Dairy Milk? How much merely from the product's (replicable) contents or design?"[48] To draw a sports analogy, extracting brand value may be as difficult as determining the value of the coach to a team's performance. And the way a brand is managed can have a large effect, positive or negative, on its value.

In summary, brand valuation and the brands on the balance sheet debate are controversial subjects. There is no one universally agreed-upon approach.[49] Many marketing experts feel it

Table 11–2 Comparisons of Brand Values in 2016 ($ millions)

	Interbrand	**BrandZ**	**Brand Finance**
Google	133,252	245,581	109,470
Apple	178,119	234,671	107,141
Amazon	50,338	139,286	106,396
Coca-Cola	73,102	78,142	31,885
Toyota	53,580	28,660	46,255

Separating the value of a brand from related assets may be as difficult a task as separating the value of a sports coach from the value of the entire team.

is impossible to reduce the richness of a brand to a single, meaningful number, and that any formula that tries to do so is an abstraction and arbitrary. To mitigate some of these issues, ISO 10668 was established as a "meta-standard" specified by the International Organization for Standardization (ISO) to develop standard procedures and methods of measuring brand value, and was first published in September 2010.[50] Also, to address some of the criticisms and limitations surrounding brand valuations, the Marketing Accountability Standards Board (MASB) has been established, and one of its goals is to develop a single, unified approach to brand valuation. The Science of Branding 11-1 describes the goals and brand valuation approach of the MASB next.

THE SCIENCE OF BRANDING 11-1
Understanding Brand Valuation

The Marketing Accountability Standards Board (MASB) is an initiative launched in 2007 by both industry professionals and academics. The goal of the MASB is to increase the contribution of the marketing function within an organization by proposing standards for marketing performance measurement and to identify processes that would link marketing activities with financial performance.

One of the MASB's projects involves creating an established set of standards for brand valuation. The organization conducted an 18-month tracking study in which it brought together leading academics, marketing, and finance practitioners from various companies. The study of 120 brands helped identify a key brand strength metric, and showed how to link this measure to market share and cash flows. The brand strength—measured using brand preference—explained 77 percent of the variation in unit shares across 120 brands. According to the MASB researchers, the estimate of market share can be transformed into brand valuation by multiplying the share with price, and making assumptions about the cost of production and category size/category penetration. The model, which links consumer brand strength to financial performance, is based on the following assumptions:

1. Brand strength drives market share.

2. Market share drives velocity (the flow of money into a business).

3. Velocity and market share together determine operating cash flow.

4. Real options (the ability to leverage a brand's strength across categories and countries) together with operating cash flow drive brand value.

In summary, according to the MASB, brand preference drives the net present value of a brand's cash flows, and the value of a brand is driven by the preference towards the brand—that is, the percent of consumers who choose the brand across a set of competitors. In line with this idea, Professor David Stewart, previously the chair of MASB, noted that linking brand choice or preference to metrics—such as market share, price premium, and distribution coverage—can help generate estimates of future operating cash flow, allowing for brand value estimation. Taken together, MASB's approach attempts to connect the dots across various factors that drive the value of a brand by providing a systematic framework to help companies value their brands. In the future, reporting the brand value on its balance sheet may be a standard for companies everywhere.

The Marketing Accountability Standards Board (MASB) is an initiative launched in 2007 by both industry professionals and academics to develop criteria and implement standards for marketing performance measurement.

Sources: Frank Findley, "Brand Investment and Valuation: A New, Empirically-Based Approach," MASB White Paper & Presentation at ARF RE!think Conference, March 2016; Jack Neff, "One Marketing Metric to Rule Them All? Group Believes It Has One. Lengthy Test Across 100 Brands Is a Step Toward Linking Marketing to Cash Flow," *Advertising Age*, November 23, 2015, http://adage.com/article/cmo-strategy/marketing-accountability-group-finds-simple-metric-predicts-market-share/301464/, accessed October 29, 2017.

REVIEW

This chapter considered the two main ways to measure the benefits or outcomes of brand equity: comparative methods (a means to better assess the effects of consumer perceptions and preferences on aspects of the marketing program) and holistic methods (attempts to come up with an estimate of the overall value of the brand). Figure 11-2 summarizes the different, but complementary, approaches. Understanding the particular range of benefits for a brand on the basis of comparative methods may be useful as an input in estimating the overall value of a brand by holistic methods.

Combining these outcome measures with the measures of sources of brand equity from Chapter 10 as part of the brand value chain can provide insight into the effectiveness of marketing actions. Nevertheless, assessing the return on investment of marketing activities remains a challenge.[51] Here are four general guidelines for creating and measuring ROI from brand marketing activities:

1. *Spend wisely—focus and be creative.* To be able to measure ROI, we need to be earning a return to begin with! Investing in distinctive and well-designed marketing activities increases the chance for a more positive and discernible return on investment.
2. *Look for benchmarks—examine competitive spending levels and historical company norms.* It is important to get the lay of the land in a market or category in order to understand what we may expect.
3. *Be strategic—apply brand equity models.* Use models such as the brand resonance model and the brand value chain to provide discipline and a structured approach to planning, implementing, and interpreting marketing activity.
4. *Be observant—track both formally and informally.* Qualitative and quantitative insights can help us understand brand performance.

Perhaps the dominant theme of this chapter and the preceding chapter on measuring sources of brand equity is the importance of using multiple measures and research methods to capture the richness and complexity of brand equity. No matter how carefully we apply them, single measures of brand equity provide at best a one- or two-dimensional view of a brand and risk missing important dimensions of brand equity. Recall the problems encountered by Coca-Cola from its overreliance on blind taste tests, described in Branding Brief 1-1.

No single number or measure fully captures brand equity.[52] Rather, we should think of the brand equity as a multidimensional concept that depends on what knowledge structures are present in the minds of consumers, and what actions a firm takes to capitalize on the potential that these knowledge structures offer.

Comparative methods: Use experiments that examine consumer attitudes and behavior toward a brand, to more directly assess the benefits arising from having a high level of awareness and strong, favorable, and unique brand associations.

- *Brand-based comparative approaches:* Experiments in which one group of consumers responds to an element of the marketing program when it is attributed to the brand, and another group responds to that same element when it is attributed to a competitive or fictitiously named brand.

- *Marketing-based comparative approaches:* Experiments in which consumers respond to changes in elements of the marketing program for the brand or competitive brands.

- *Conjoint analysis:* A survey-based multivariate technique that enables marketers to profile the consumer buying decision process with respect to products and brands.

Holistic methods: Attempt to place an overall value on the brand in either abstract utility terms or concrete financial terms. Thus, holistic methods attempt to "net out" various considerations to determine the unique contribution of the brand.

- *Residual approach:* Examines the value of the brand by subtracting out from overall brand preferences consumers' preferences for the brand based on physical product attributes alone.

- *Valuation approach:* Places a financial value on the brand for accounting purposes, mergers and acquisitions, or other such reasons.

FIGURE 11-2

Measures of Outcomes of Brand Equity

There are many different sources of, and outcomes from, brand equity, depending on the marketers' skill and ingenuity. Firms may be more or less able to maximize the potential value of a brand according to the type and nature of their marketing activities. As Wharton's Peter Fader says:

> The actual value of a brand depends on its fit with buyer's corporate structure and other assets. If the acquiring company has manufacturing or distribution capabilities that are synergistic with the brand, then it might be worth paying a lot of money for it. Paul Feldwick, a British executive, makes the analogy between brands and properties on the Monopoly game board. You're willing to pay a lot more for Marvin Gardens if you already own Atlantic and Ventnor Avenues![53]

The customer-based brand equity framework, therefore, emphasizes employing a range of research measures and methods to fully capture the multiple potential sources and outcomes of brand equity.

DISCUSSION QUESTIONS

1. Choose a product. Conduct a branded and unbranded experiment. What do you learn about the equity of the brands in that product class?
2. Can you identify any other advantages or disadvantages of the comparative methods?
3. Pick a brand and conduct an analysis similar to that done with the Planters brand. What do you learn about its extendibility as a result?
4. Go to Interbrand's Web site (www.interbrand.com). Compare the top 10 brands from the current year to the list from the previous year. What brands entered the top 10, and which ones left the top 10? What contributed to these shifts in brand value? Which brands showed the most increases or decreases in brand value? Why?
5. Select a brand from Interbrand's top 100 brand names (one which you know is publicly traded on a stock exchange). Go to a finance Web site (e.g., Google Finance or Yahoo Finance) and locate its market capitalization. Determine how much of the brand's value is as a percentage of its market capitalization. Describe what this percentage means, and how it relates to brand valuation.

BRAND FOCUS 11.0

Financial Perspectives on Brands and the Brand Value Chain

Brands can be seen as a key link in a value-creation chain, beginning with the raw materials and production and ending in firm value. As described in Chapter 3, brand and brand equity contribute in different ways to this value chain.[54] The corresponding brand value chain consists of four components or stages: (1) What companies do; (2) what customers think and feel; (3) what customers do; and (4) how financial markets react. The following is an overview of some of the research that has been linked to different aspects of this brand value chain.

Brand Quality Information

Information about brand quality helps move stock prices as it allows investors to gain better knowledge about a firm's value that was not captured by accounting measures.[55] Aaker and Jacobson examined the association between yearly stock returns and yearly brand changes (as measured by EquiTrend's perceived quality rating of brand equity for 34 companies, and the changes in current-term ROI. They found that brand attitude changes were associated with stock return changes, and the gains in stock returns averaged nearly 30 percent, whereas declines were linked to average losses of 10 percent in stock market returns.

Brand quality information can impact the risk of a firm's stock returns. There are two types of risk. Idiosyncratic risk refers to the volatility of stock returns, whereas the systematic risk is the extent to which a firm's returns shifts in tandem with the entire stock market. Bharadwaj and colleagues found that changes in brand quality are related directly to stock returns, and increases in quality can lower the idiosyncratic risk associated with a firm. They tested these findings using a sample of 132 firms from 2000 to 2005. They found that unanticipated changes in quality could also increase the perceptions of systematic risk.[56] This was particularly true in highly competitive markets and when the firm's performance (earnings) in the short-term increases.

> *Key Takeaways:* Information about brand quality moves stock prices and increases stock market returns; improvements in quality can lower firm risk or volatility of stock returns (i.e., idiosyncratic risk).

Brand Quality and Rating Dispersions

In addition to average quality ratings, a factor worth considering is how variable the quality ratings are across consumers. To address this, Xueming Luo and colleagues conducted a large-scale study of 960 brands from the United States, the United Kingdom, and Germany, using the Brand Index dataset from YouGov from 2008 to 2011. They uncovered that it was both good and bad to have dispersion—a Janus-like effect—when it comes to brand quality rating dispersions.

While rating dispersion can lower the returns associated with a brand, it can also lower firm risk.[57] The maximum stock returns of 5.6 percent were seen when average ratings increased while dispersion decreased. Further, an increase in dispersion (by one standard deviation) could cost an average firm with $36.9 billion market capitalization, a loss of $2.2 million after 10 days. These findings demonstrate that there are consequences to average quality ratings as well as the

dispersion (or variance) of those ratings across consumers. Managers would, therefore, be wise to look at how consumers are distributed in their quality perceptions of a brand, rather than to look at the averages alone.

> *Key Takeaway:* Dispersion of brand quality ratings can lower the stock market returns and lower the risk.

Dimensions of Brand Equity and Stock Market Valuation and Returns

Mizik and Jacobson examined how different dimensions of brand equity influenced stock market returns. Recall the various dimensions of brand equity as proposed by Young & Rubicam's Brand Asset Valuator (BAV) Model (described in Chapter 10). Mizik and Jacobson used the BAV dimensions to demonstrate its effect on a company's stock market returns. Using a dataset of 890 observations from 1998 to 2004, they found that relevance and energy dimensions of brand equity significantly impacted stock market returns.[58] They found that relevance had a stronger impact than energy—a unit increase in relevance contributing to an 8.2 percent increase in stock returns on average, and a unit increase in energy contributing to a 6 percent increase in stock returns. Esteem and knowledge were more directly influential in accounting measures, and differentiation impacted accounting performance in a subsequent time-period. In sum, different BAV brand equity dimensions were shown to have varying roles, with relevance and energy showing the most effect.[59]

One key concern of managers is how to value brands, particularly in a merger and acquisition setting. Sometimes, the valuation may be seen as excessive. For example, although the car brand Ferrari was valued at $9.8 billion, some believe that is overvalued. How much is too much for Ferrari?[60] Further, using brand equity dimensions such as with BAV, can a firm construct specific multipliers which can improve the accuracy of valuing a firm?

Research by Mizik and Jacobson on 200 brands belonging to mono-brand firms (i.e., firms with a single brand accounting for a majority of the sales) in the years 2000–2006 showed some interesting patterns. They used an expanded version of BAV with a fifth dimension of energy included in addition to differentiation, relevance, esteem, knowledge, and energy and showed a firm could improve the valuation accuracy by about 16 percent, relative to predictions based on accounting variables (e.g., return on investment) alone[61]

> *Key Takeaways:* Dimensions of brand equity—particularly BAV's relevance and energy—can increase stock market returns. Using all dimensions of brand equity can help firms improve the accuracy with which they conduct valuations, particularly in the case of mergers and acquisitions where accurate valuations are the key to success.

Brand Equity and Risk

Rego, Billet, and Morgan examined the role of brand equity on two types of firm risk—systematic and idiosyncratic (as defined above) for 252 firms between 2000 and 2006. They found that brand equity had a substantial impact on lowering idiosyncratic risk, and also in lowering downside systematic risk. They concluded that brand equity can lower the risk facing a firm.

Key Takeaway: Brand equity can lower the risk facing a firm.

Negative News (e.g., Recalls) and Performance of Competitors

Borah and Tellis analyzed daily traffic, topic, and sentiment on more than 1,000 automotive Web sites following recall announcements for about 16 months. They found that recall events increased negative chatter even among competitors, particularly in the same country, and led to a lowering of competitors' sales as well as stock market performance. Online chatter surrounding a recall amplified the negative impact of recalls on sales by nearly 4.5 times.[62]

Key Takeaway: Negative news about a brand can spill over and impact closely-related competitors' perceptions and their stock market performance as well.

Brand Portfolio Characteristics

Morgan and Rego analyzed how aspects of a brand's portfolio—for example, the number of brands owned, number of segments marketed, how brands compete, and customer perceptions of quality and price—impact outcomes such as marketing and financial performance. They conducted this analysis on 72 public firms over a 10-year period (1994–2003). They looked at the effect on seven performance outcomes including: (1) consumer loyalty; (2) market share; (3) marketing efficiency (ratio of advertising spending to sales; (4) ratio of selling, general, and administrative expenses to sales; (5) financial performance (Tobin's q, as defined below); (6) cash flow; and (7) cash flow variability. They showed that several portfolio characteristics helped explain the performance outcomes. For example, larger portfolios of brands can increase financial performance and can reduce cash flow variability. Brand portfolios with higher quality positioning enjoy higher performance; in contrast, those with high-price positioning have lower financial performance.

Key Takeaway: The characteristics of the brand's portfolios can impact firm performance and stock market outcomes.

Brand Architecture

Research by Rao and colleagues contrasted the impact of three types of brand architecture strategies (branded house versus house of brands versus mixed branding) on Tobin's q, which is one way of capturing a firm's stock market performance.[63] Tobin's q is a forward-looking measure of intangible assets and is measured as follows:[64]

$$\frac{Market\ Value\ of\ Equity\ +\ Liquidating\ Value\ of\ a\ Firm's\ Outstanding\ Preferred\ Stock\ +\ Debt}{Book\ Value\ of\ Total\ Assets}$$

A mixed branding strategy is when a firm had both corporate names for some products (a la branded house) and individual names for others (a la house of brands).

With their sample, corporate branding had higher Tobin's q whereas mixed branding had lower Tobin's q. One of the key benefits of corporate branding is that it increases the ability of firms to engage in cross-selling of products within its portfolio, thus, enhancing the efficiency with which it utilizes its brand name across a variety of categories. This effect was shown to hold true in both business-to-business and business-to-consumer contexts, although it was stronger in a business-to-business setting.

Later research examined the implications of these brand architecture strategies by examining the effects of a broader range of branding strategies including sub-branding and endorsed branding strategies on both stock market returns as well as stock market risk. This research found that brand architecture strategies can have significant implications for a variety of different types of risk associated with a firm and can be related to impact on reputation, dilution, cannibalization, and brand stretch.[65]

Key Takeaway: The type of brand strategy and brand architecture can influence stock market returns.

Marketing Expenditures

In a review of almost 83 prior studies, Edeling and Fischer examined how much changes in marketing expenditures and brand relationships influenced firm value. They found that, on average, changes in brand relationships were significant in their impact on firm value.[66] Often, marketing managers and finance managers do not appear to speak the same language or work towards the same goals. Marketing is focused on sales impact, whereas finance executives tend to focus on financial outcomes (e.g., cost of capital). Firms should find ways of connecting these two functional areas. Researchers Fischer and Himme[67] looked at how marketing and financial metrics interact. They found that advertising increased customer-based brand equity, which, in turn, impacted how the financial leverage and credit spread, later contributed to higher financial resources. Therefore, the researchers concluded that finance and marketing goals are highly interconnected.

Key Takeaway: Given that finance and marketing goals are closely related, it may be a good idea for managers to demonstrate the relationships between marketing and finance goals, to strengthen cross-functional coordination within a firm.

Brand Extensions

Lane and Jacobson showed that the stock market's reactions to brand extension announcements depended a great deal on brand attitude and familiarity.[68] For instance, they found that the stock market response was most favorable when extensions involved high-esteem, high-familiarity brands (e.g., Hershey, Coca-Cola) as well as low-esteem, low-familiarity brands (perhaps because there was less risk in these extensions). The stock market reaction was unfavorable or even negative for brand extensions when consumers were highly familiar with the brand but did not have high regard, or vice versa.

Horsky and Swyngedouw found that name changes for firms produced positive returns, particularly in industrial goods sectors or when prior performance was poor; also, researchers have shown that when firms with high marketing investments undergo a corporate name change, they experience more rewards from the stock market reactions.[69]

Key Takeaway: Stock market reactions to brand extensions and name changes could vary based on how much prior brand equity is involved; typically, when prior brand equity is high, both extensions and name changes could elicit a more positive reaction from investors.

Brand Alliances and Marketing Agreements

Imagine a marketing agreement between Coca-Cola and Nike, or a marketing alliance between Apple and Lego for children's video games. Such alliances could be seen as positive developments, and could contribute to higher stock market returns. However, research has shown that these benefits could vary based on circumstances surrounding the introduction, as well as the characteristics of the companies themselves.

Research by Swaminathan and Moorman used a sample of 230 marketing alliance announcements in the high-tech industry (1988–2005 time period).[70] They showed that, on average, 1.4 percent positive increase in stock market returns occurs (with an average capitalization of companies within the sample of $49 billion), translating to $600 million average increase in firm value, following announcements of marketing alliances. They also showed the positive role of networks of alliance partners in strengthening outcomes. When a firm announcing an alliance had a strong network of previous partners, those alliance networks could also profit from a given marketing alliance. For example, when Angry Birds and Star Wars announced a new video game, the new customers may also purchase other video games of Angry Birds, thus benefiting the network as a whole.

Research by Cao and Sorescu[71] focused on co-branded partnerships and the impact on the firm's value. They found that, on average, the stock market reaction to the announcement of co-branded products are 1 percent. Also, when firms enter into co-branded agreements,[72] the consistency of the brand image of the two partners, whether or not the agreement was exclusive to the partners, and how innovative the product was, could strengthen the value of co-branded partnerships.

Key Takeaways: Investors are generally positive when a firm enters into a marketing alliance or co-branded partnership. However, these stock market returns could vary based on characteristics of networks surrounding a given firm, exclusivity of the partnership, and how innovative the products of the partnership may be.

Brand Mergers and Brand Acquisitions

Research typically examine conditions surrounding brand acquisitions or brand mergers which either increase the stock market reaction or weaken it. Newmeyer, Swaminathan, and Hulland examined this issue using a dataset of 138 acquisitions over a 20-year period. They found that the stock market returns, on average, increased 1.2 percent to announcements of both brand and product acquisitions. Brand acquisitions, in general, had higher returns than product acquisitions without explicit mention of brand names being acquired. Also, they showed that when both target and acquirer had strong marketing capabilities, and when brand portfolio diversity was high, the value of the target firm's brands was higher.[73] The more related a target and acquirer firm's product offerings were, the higher the value a brand acquisition had.[74]

When firms acquire brands whose price and quality positioning is higher than their existing portfolio, then the acquirer can see stronger benefits regarding stock market returns.[75] Wiles, Morgan, and Rego investigated brand acquisitions and disposals over a 15-year period between 1994 and 2008. Their findings indicated that acquirers' abnormal returns were, on average,

.75 percent (approximately $137 million in shareholder value), whereas, disposals were around .88 percent of additional abnormal stock returns ($283 million dollars on average in shareholder value). This is perhaps one reason why luxury brand acquisitions have been popular, with Coach acquiring Kate Spade and Michael Kors acquiring Jimmy Choo.[76] Or perhaps entering a higher price point using an internally developed brand name is a challenging task, and therefore, acquisitions of these types of brands are viewed positively by investors.

Key Takeaways: Both acquisitions of brands and disposals are big events from an investors' standpoint. Under the right conditions, both could strengthen the stock market value of the acquirer or target firm.

Brand Equity and Customer Acquisition or Retention

Using the traditional four pillars of BAV (differentiation, relevance, esteem and knowledge), Stahl, Heitmann, Lehmann, and Neslin[77] examined its relationship with customer acquisition, customer retention, and the lifetime value associated with customers for a set of automobile brands. Their findings showed that differentiation is a very key element, leading to higher customer profitability and lower acquisition and retention rates. Thus, differentiation could be a double-edged sword. The other dimension of knowledge has a strong and positive impact on customer acquisition, customer retention, and customer profitability.

Key Takeaway: Brand equity dimensions could enhance customer retention and acquisition, along with customer profitability.

Marketing Expenditures on Social Media and Consumer Mind-Set Metrics

Research has also explored how social media expenditures impact shareholder value through its impact on customer mind-set metrics such as brand awareness, purchase intent, and customer satisfaction. Earned social media was found to impact brand awareness and purchase intent but not customer satisfaction; owned social media impacted brand awareness and customer satisfaction. Both purchase intent and customer satisfaction, in turn, were found to influence shareholder value.[78]

Other research by DeVries, Gensler, and Leeflang showed the relative impact of traditional advertisements and social media ads on Facebook and consumer-to-consumer conversations on brand building and customer acquisition. Firm performance was shown to be optimal when companies leveraged traditional advertising for brand building and customer acquisition and leveraged social media to improve the impact of traditional ads.[79]

Key Takeaway: Marketing expenditures can impact firm performance and stock market valuation through its impact on brands and customers.

NOTES

1. C. B. Bhattacharya and Leonard M. Lodish, "Towards a System for Monitoring Brand Health," *Marketing Science Institute Working Paper Series* (00–111) (July 2000).

2. Richard F. Chay, "How Marketing Researchers Can Harness the Power of Brand Equity," *Marketing Research* 3, no. 2 (1991): 10–30.

3. For an interesting approach, see Martin R. Lautman and Koen Pauwels, "Metrics That Matter: Identifying the Importance of Consumer Needs and Wants," *Journal of Advertising Research* 49, no. 3 (September 2009): 339–359.

4. Peter Farquhar and Yuji Ijiri have made several other distinctions in classifying brand equity measurement procedures. Peter H. Farquhar, Julia W. Han, and Yuji Ijiri, "Recognizing and Measuring Brand Assets," *Marketing Science Institute Report* 28, no. 2 (1991): 91–119. They describe two broad classes of measurement approaches to brand equity: separation approaches and integration approaches. Separation approaches view brand equity as the value added to a product. Farquhar and Ijiri categorize separation approaches into residual methods and comparative methods. Residual methods determine brand equity by what remains after subtracting physical product effects. Comparative methods determine brand equity by comparing the branded product with an unbranded product or an equivalent benchmark. Integration approaches, on the other hand, typically define brand equity as a composition of basic elements. Farquhar and Ijiri categorize integration approaches into association and valuation methods. Valuation methods measure brand equity by its cost or value as an intangible asset for a particular owner and intended use. Association methods measure brand equity in terms of the favorableness of brand evaluations, the accessibility of brand attitudes, and the consistency of brand image with consumers. The previous chapter described techniques that could be considered association methods. This chapter considers techniques related to the other three categories of methods.

5. Darren Weaver, "We Did a Blind Taste Test of Bud, Coors, Miller and Natty Light—Here's the Verdict," *Business Insider*, December 31, 2016, http://www.businessinsider.com/blind-taste-test-bud-coors-miller-natty-light-beers-2016-12.

6. Julian Clover, "Virgin Connects Mobile Network with Orange," *Broadband TV News*, October 10, 2011, https://www.broadbandtvnews.com/2011/10/10/virgin-connects-mobile-network-with-orange/; Chris Martin, "Virgin Media Mobile Customers Will Get Orange Network Coverage," *The Inquirer*, October 7, 2011, https://www.theinquirer.net/inquirer/news/2115502/virgin-media-mobile-customers-orange-network-coverage.

7. Edgar Pessemier, "A New Way to Determine Buying Decisions," *Journal of Marketing* 24, no. 2 (1959): 41–46.

8. Björn Höfer and Volker Bosch, "Brand Equity Measurement with GfK Price Challenger, *Yearbook of Marketing and Consumer Research* 5 (2007): 21–39.

9. Paul E. Green and V. Srinivasan, "Conjoint Analysis in Consumer Research: Issues and Outlook," *Journal of Consumer Research* 5, no. 2 (1978): 103–123; Paul E. Green and V. Srinivasan, "Conjoint Analysis in Marketing: New Developments with Implications for Research and Practice," *Journal of Marketing* 54, no. 4 (1990): 3–19; David Bakken and Curtis Frazier, "Conjoint Analysis: Understanding Consumer Decision Making," Chapter 15 in *Handbook of Marketing Research: Uses, Misuses, and Future Advances*, eds. Rajiv Grover and Marco Vriens (Thousand Oaks, CA: Sage Publications, 2006): 288–311.

10. For more details, see Betsy Sharkey, "The People's Choice," *Adweek* 30 (November 27, 1989): 6–10.

11. Paul E. Green and Yoram Wind, "New Ways to Measure Consumers' Judgments," *Harvard Business Review* 53 (July–August 1975): 107–117.

12. Jerry Wind, Paul E. Green, Douglas Shifflet, and Marsha Scarbrough, "Courtyard by Marriott: Designing a Hotel Facility with Consumer-Based Marketing Models," *Interfaces* 19, no. 1 (January–February 1989): 25–47.

13. V. R. Rao, *Applied Conjoint Analysis* (Berlin: Springer Science & Business Media, 2014).

14. Max Blackstone, "Price Trade-Offs as a Measure of Brand Value," *Journal of Advertising Research* 30, no. 4 (August/September 1990): RC3–RC6.

15. Arvind Rangaswamy, Raymond R. Burke, and Terence A. Oliva, "Brand Equity and the Extendibility of Brand Names," *International Journal of Research in Marketing* 10, no. 1 (March 1993): 61–75. See also Moonkyu Lee, Jonathan Lee, and Wagner A. Kamakura, "Consumer Evaluations of Line Extensions: A Conjoint Approach," *Advances in Consumer Research*, Vol. 23 (Ann Arbor, MI: Association of Consumer Research, 1996), 289–295; Howard Barich and V. Srinivasan, "Prioritizing Marketing Image Goals under Resource Constraints," *Sloan Management Review*, 34, no. 4 (Summer 1993): 69–76; Sebastián Maldonado, Ricardo Montoya, and Richard Weber, "Advanced Conjoint Analysis Using Feature Selection Via Support Vector Machines," *European Journal of Operational Research* 241, no. 2 (2015): 564–574.

16. Marco Vriens and Curtis Frazier, "The Hard Impact of the Soft Touch: How to Use Brand Positioning Attributes in Conjoint," *Marketing Research* (Summer 2003): 23–27.

17. Nicholas Rubino, Letter to the Editor, "McComb Played a Bad Hand Well," *The Wall Street Journal*, October 20, 2011, https://www.wsj.com/articles/SB10001424052970204479504576639272311225918, accessed November 15, 2018; Dana Mattioli, "Liz Claiborne Must Say Adieu to Liz," *The Wall Street Journal*, October 13, 2011, https://www.wsj.com/articles/SB10001424052970203914304576626711202553884, accessed November 15, 2018.

18. Noah Kirsch, "Why Kate Spade Won't See a Penny of the $2.4 Billion Sale to Coach," *Forbes*, May 8, 2017, www.forbes.com/sites/noahkirsch/2017/05/08/why-kate-spade-wont-see-a-penny-of-the-2-4-billion-sale-to-coach/#64b52b5f5b2b.

19. V. Srinivasan, "Network Models for Estimating Brand-Specific Effects in Multi-Attribute Marketing Models," *Management Science* 25, no. 1 (January 1979): 11–21; V. Srinivasan, Chan Su Park, and Dae Ryun Chang, "An Approach to the Measurement, Analysis, and Prediction of Brand Equity and Its Sources," *Management Science* 51, no. 9 (September 2005): 1433–1448.

20. Wagner A. Kamakura and Gary J. Russell, "Measuring Brand Value with Scanner Data," *International Journal of Research in Marketing* 10, no. 1 (1993): 9–22.

21. Kusum Ailawadi, Donald R. Lehmann, and Scott A. Neslin, "Revenue Premium as an Outcome Measure of Brand Equity," *Journal of Marketing* 67, no. 4 (October 2003): 1–17. See also Avi Goldfarb, Qiang Lu, and Sridhar Moorthy, "Measuring Brand Value in an Equilibrium Framework," *Marketing Science* 28, no. 1 (January–February 2009): 69–86; C. Whan Park, Deborah J. MacInnis, Xavier Dreze, and Jonathan Lee, "Measuring Brand Equity: The Marketing Surplus & Efficiency (MARKSURE)–Based Brand Equity Measure," in *Brands and Brand Management: Contemporary Research Perspectives*, eds. Barbara Loken, Rohini Ahluwalia, and Michael J. Houston (London: Taylor and Francis Group Publishing, 2010), 159–188.

22. S. Sriram, Subramanian Balachander, and Manohar U. Kalwani, "Monitoring the Dynamics of Brand Equity

Using Store-level Data," *Journal of Marketing* 71, no. 2 (April 2007): 61–78.

23. Joffre Swait, Tülin Erdem, Jordan Louviere, and Chris Dubelar, "The Equalization Price: A Measure of Consumer-Perceived Brand Equity," *International Journal of Research in Marketing* 10, no. 1 (1993): 23–45; Tülin Erdem and Joffre Swait, "Brand Equity as a Signaling Phenomenon," *Journal of Consumer Psychology* 7, no. 2 (1998): 131–157; Tülin Erdem, Joffre Swait, and Ana Valenzuela, "Brands as Signals: A Cross-Country Validation Study," *Journal of Marketing* 70, no. 1 (January 2006): 34–49; Joffre Swait and Tülin Erdem, "Characterizing Brand Effects on Choice Set Formation and Preference Discrimination Under Uncertainty," *Marketing Science* 26 (September–October 2007): 679–697.

24. See also Eric L. Almquist, Ian H. Turvill, and Kenneth J. Roberts, "Combining Economic Analysis for Breakthrough Brand Management," *Journal of Brand Management* 5, no. 4 (1998): 272–282.

25. V. Srinivasan, Chan Su Park, and Dae Ryun Chang, "An Approach to the Measurement, Analysis, and Prediction of Brand Equity and Its Sources," *Management Science* 51, no. 9 (September 2005): 1433–1448. See also Chan Su Park and V. Srinivasan, "A Survey-Based Method for Measuring and Understanding Brand Equity and Its Extendability," *Journal of Marketing Research* 31, no. 2 (May 1994): 271–288; see also Na Woon Bong, Roger Marshall, and Kevin Lane Keller, "Measuring Brand Power: Validating a Model for Optimizing Brand Equity," *Journal of Product and Brand Management* 8, no. 3 (1999): 170–184; Randle Raggio and Robert P. Leone, "Producing a Measure of Brand Equity by Decomposing Brand Beliefs into Brand and Attribute Sources," in "Brand Equity Measurement: Concepts and Applications," ICFAI Press, 2007.

26. William R. Dillon, Thomas J. Madden, Amna Kirmani, and Soumen Mukherjee, "Understanding What's in a Brand Rating: A Model for Assessing Brand and Attribute Effects and Their Relationship to Brand Equity," *Journal of Marketing Research* 38, no. 4 (November 2001): 415–429.

27. Vipal Monga, "Accounting's 21st Century Challenge: How to Value Intangible Assets," *The Wall Street Journal*, March 21, 2016, www.wsj.com/articles/accountings-21st-century-challenge-how-to-value-intangible-assets-1458605126.

28. The Economist, "What Are Brands For?," *The Economist*, August 30, 2014, www.economist.com/news/business/21614150-brands-are-most-valuable-assets-many-companies -possess-no-one-agrees-how-much-they.

29. Margaret Molloy, "Brand Counts: Strategic Metrics Bear Out Clear Value," *CMO*, September 2, 2016, www.cmo.com/opinion/articles/2016/9/1/why-brand-counts.html#gs.foOqu0w.; Alexander Brigham, "Your Brand Reputational Value Is Irreplaceable. Protect It!", *Forbes*, February 1, 2010, www.forbes .com/2010/02/01/brand-reputation-value-leadership-managing-ethisphere.html.

30. Intuit Firm of the Future Team, "Top 10 Differences Between IFRS and GAAP Accounting," https://www .firmofthefuture.com/content/top-10-differences-between-ifrs-and-gaap-accounting/, accessed November 15, 2018; The International Financial Reporting Standards Foundation (IFRS), "IAS 38 Intangible Assets," https:// www.ifrs.org/issued-standards/list-of-standards/ias-38-intangible-assets/, accessed November 15, 2018.

31. An impaired asset is one whose market value is lower than that listed on the company's balance sheet.

32. Roger Sinclair and Kevin Lane Keller, "Brand Value, Accounting Standards, and Mergers and Acquisitions: 'The Moribund Effect,'" *Journal of Brand Management,* 24 (2) (2017), doi:10.1057/s41262-016-0025-1.

33. Vince Howe, William H. Sackley, Frederika Spencer, David Mautz, and Justin Freed, "'Accounting' for Brand Equity—Value Relevance and Reliability: A Marketing and FASB Dilemma," *Society for Marketing Advances Proceedings*, November 2013, http://bit.ly/2rirB1I).

34. Lew Winters, "Brand Equity Measures: Some Recent Advances," *Marketing* Research 3, no. 4 (December 1991): 70–73; Gordon V. Smith, *Corporate Valuation: A Business and Professional Guide* (New York: John Wiley & Sons, 1988), 70–73.

35. *Brand Finance*, http://www.brandfinance.com, accessed November 15, 2018.

36. Investors put capital into a company to ensure it can operate on a day-to-day basis. This money does not come free, as investors expect a return on their investment. While accountants are happy to accept the difference between revenue and expenses as the company's profit, economists believe that true profit is accounting profit less the expected return on the company's capital employed: the investors' funds.

37. Interbrand, "Best Global Brands," https://www.interbrand .com, accessed November 15, 2018.

38. Ken Schept, "Brandz Top 100 Most Valuable Brands 2017," Brandz, accessed October 29, 2017, http://brandz .com/admin/uploads/files/BZ_Global_2017_Report.pdf.

39. MB Global, "Meaningfully Different Framework," http://www.millwardbrown.com/Mb-Global/What-We-Do/Brand/Brand-Equity/Meaningfully-Different-Framework, accessed November 15, 2018.

40. BrandZ, "Global 100 | BrandZ Brand Valuation Methodology," http://brandz.com/article/global-100—methodology-134, accessed November 15, 2018. http:// brandz.com/article/global-100--methodology-134.

41. Ibid.

42. R. Harish, "Brand Valuation—A Comparative Study of the Methods Adopted by Interbrand, Millward Brown and Brand Finance," working paper.

43. BrandFinance, "Global 500 2017: The Annual Report on the World's Most Valuable Brands," http:// brandfinance.com/images/upload/global_500_2017_ locked_website.pdf, accessed November 15, 2018.

44. Brand Finance, "Explanation of the Methodology," http://brandirectory.com/methodology, accessed November 15, 2018.

45. R. Harish, "Brand Valuation—A Comparative Study of the Methods Adopted by Interbrand, Millward Brown and Brand Finance," working paper.

46. Mark Ritson, "Brand Valuations Do Not Always Tell the Full Story," *Marketing Week*, September 29, 2011, www .marketingweek.co.uk/sectors/industry/brand-valuations-do-not-always-tell-the-full-story/3030524.article.; Mark Ritson, "What Is the Point of Brand Valuations If Those Doing the Valuing Are So Off Target," *Marketing Week*, April 22, 2015, www.marketingweek.com/2015/04/22/

what-is-the-point-of-brand-valuations-if-those-doing-the-valuing-are-so-off-target/.

47. Interbrand, "Methodology," https://www.interbrand.com/best-brands/best-global-brands/methodology/, accessed November 15, 2018.

48. The Economist, "On the Brandwagon: Valuing Brands on Corporate Balance Sheets Adds More Fog to the Murky Art of Accounting," https://www.highbeam.com/doc/1G1-8349877.html, accessed November 15, 2018.

49. For example, brand characteristics have been shown to improve brand valuation accuracy. See Natalie Mizik and Robert Jacobson, "Valuing Branded Businesses," *Journal of Marketing* 73, no. 6 (November 2009): 137–153.

50. International Organization for Standardization, Technical Committee, "Brand Valuation: Requirements for Monetary Brand Valuation," https://www.iso.org/standard/46032.html, accessed November 15, 2018.

51. Koen Pauwels and Martin Lautman, "What Is Important? Identifying Metrics That Matter," *Journal of Advertising Research* 49, no. 3 (September 2009), 339–359.

52. For an interesting empirical application, see Manoj K. Agarwal and Vithala Rao, "An Empirical Comparison of Consumer-Based Measures of Brand Equity," *Marketing Letters* 7, no. 3 (1996): 237–247.

53. Fader, course notes.

54. Kevin Lane Keller and Donald R. Lehmann, "Brands and Branding: Research Findings and Future Priorities," *Marketing Science* 25, no. 6 (2006): 740–759.

55. David A. Aaker and Robert Jacobson, "The Financial Information Content of Perceived Quality," *Journal of Marketing Research* 31, no. 2 (1994): 191–201.

56. Sundar G. Bharadwaj, Kapil R. Tuli, and Andre Bonfrer, "The Impact of Brand Quality on Shareholder Wealth," *Journal of Marketing* 75, no. 5 (2011): 88–104.

57. Xueming Luo, Sascha Raithel, and Michael A. Wiles, "The Impact of Brand Rating Dispersion on Firm Value," *Journal of Marketing Research* 50, no. 3 (2013): 399–415.

58. As noted previously, the BAV dimensions previously included energy and differentiation as separate dimensions. They have since been combined into a single dimension called *energized differentiation*.

59. Natalie Mizik and Robert Jacobson, "The Financial Value Impact of Perceptual Brand Attributes," *Journal of Marketing Research* 45, no. 1 (2008): 15–32.

60. Michael J. de la Merced, "$9.8 Billion Valuation for Ferrari," *The New York Times*, October 20, 2015, https://www.nytimes.com/2015/10/21/business/dealbook/9-8-billion-valuation-for-ferrari.html?mcubz=1, accessed November 15, 2018.

61. Natalie Mizik and Robert Jacobson, "Valuing Branded Businesses," *Journal of Marketing* 73, no. 6 (2009): 137–153.

62. Abhishek Borah and Gerard J. Tellis, "Halo (Spillover) Effects in Social Media: Do Product Recalls of One Brand Hurt or Help Rival Brands?," *Journal of Marketing Research* 53, no. 2 (2016): 143–160.

63. Vithala R. Rao, Manoj K. Agarwal, and Denise Dahlhoff, "How Is Manifest Branding Strategy Related to the Intangible Value of a Corporation?," *Journal of Marketing* 68, no. 4 (2004): 126–141.

64. Kee H. Chung and Stephen W. Pruitt, "A Simple Approximation of Tobin's q," *Financial Management* 23, no. 3 (1994): 70–74.

65. Liwu Hsu, Susan Fournier, and Shuba Srinivasan, "Brand Architecture Strategy and Firm Value: How Leveraging, Separating, and Distancing the Corporate Brand Affects Risk and Returns," *Journal of the Academy of Marketing Science* 44, no. 2 (2016), 261–280.

66. Alexander Edeling and Marc Fischer, "Marketing's Impact on Firm Calue: Generalizations from a Meta-analysis," *Journal of Marketing Research* 53, no. 4 (2016): 515–534.

67. Marc Fischer and Alexander Himme, "The Financial Brand Value Chain: How Brand Investments Contribute to the Financial Health of Firms." *International Journal of Research in Marketing* 34, no. 1 (2017): 137–153.

68. Vicki Lane and Robert Jacobson, "Stock Market Reactions to Brand Extension Announcements: The Effects of Brand Attitude and Familiarity." *The Journal of Marketing* 59, no. 1 (January 1995): 63–77.

69. Dan Horsky and Patrick Swyngedouw, "Does It Pay to Change Your Company's Name? A Stock Market Perspective," *Marketing Science* 6, no. 4 (1987): 320–335; Saim Kashmiri and Vijay Mahajan, "The Name's the Game: Does Marketing Impact the Value of Corporate Name Changes?" *Journal of Business Research* 68, no. 2 (2015): 281–290.

70. Vanitha Swaminathan and Christine Moorman, "Marketing Alliances, Firm Networks, and Firm Value Creation," *Journal of Marketing* 73, no. 5 (2009): 52–69.

71. Zixia Cao and Alina Sorescu, "Wedded Bliss or Tainted Love? Stock Market Reactions to the Introduction of Cobranded Products." *Marketing Science* 32, no. 6 (2013): 939–959.

72. Ibid.

73. Sundar G. Bharadwaj, Kapil R. Tuli, and Andre Bonfrer, "The Impact of Brand Quality on Shareholder Wealth," *Journal of Marketing* 75, no. 5 (2011): 88–104.

74. Casey E. Newmeyer, Vanitha Swaminathan, and John Hulland, "When Products and Brands Trade Hands: A Framework for Acquisition Success," *Journal of Marketing Theory and Practice* 24, no. 2 (2016): 129–146.

75. Michael A. Wiles, Neil A. Morgan, and Lopo L. Rego, "The Effect of Brand Acquisition and Disposal on Stock Returns," *Journal of Marketing* 76, no. 1 (2012): 38–58.

76. Paula N. Danziger, "Luxury Brand Mergers and Acquisitions Set to Explode," *Forbes*, August 16, 2017, https://www.forbes.com/sites/pamdanziger/2017/08/16/luxury-brand-mergers-and-acquisitions-set-to-explode/#6c2d820d9c0f, accessed November 15, 2018.

77. Florian Stahl, Mark Heitmann, Donald R. Lehmann, and Scott A. Neslin, "The Impact of Brand Equity on Customer Acquisition, Retention, and Profit Margin," *Journal of Marketing* 76, no. 4 (2012): 44–63.

78. Anatoli Colicev, Ashwin Malshe, Koen Pauwels, and Peter O'Connor, "Improving Consumer Mind-Set Metrics and Shareholder Value through Social Media: The Different Roles of Owned and Earned," *Journal of Marketing* 82, no. 1 (2017); Dominique M. Hanssens and Koen H. Pauwels. "Demonstrating the Value of Marketing," *Journal of Marketing* 80, no. 6 (2016): 173–190; Koen Pauwels, Zeynep Aksehirli, and Andrew Lackman. "Like the Ad or the Brand? Marketing Stimulates Different Electronic Word-of-Mouth Content to Drive Online and Offline Performance," *International Journal of Research in Marketing* 33, no. 3 (2016): 639–655.

79. Lisette de Vries, Sonja Gensler, and Peter S. H. Leeflang, "Effects of Traditional Advertising and Social Messages on Brand-Building Metrics and Customer Acquisition," *Journal of Marketing* 81, no. 5 (2017): 1–15.

Designing and Implementing Brand Architecture Strategies

12

Learning Objectives

After reading this chapter, you should be able to

1. Define the key components of brand architecture.
2. Define a brand-product matrix.
3. Outline the principles of a good brand portfolio.
4. Assemble a basic brand hierarchy for a brand.
5. Describe how a corporate brand is different from a product brand.
6. Explain the role of brand architecture in strengthening a brand's value and a firm's performance.
7. Understand how sustainability initiatives, corporate social responsibility and green marketing can enhance a brand.

Luxury brands such as Gucci are adopting a careful approach to extending their brands, after early strategic moves highlighted the pitfalls of extending into too many categories.

PREVIEW

Parts II, III, and IV of this book examined strategies for building and measuring brand equity. Part V takes a broader perspective and considers how to sustain, nurture, and grow brand equity under various situations and circumstances.

The successful launch of new products and services is of paramount importance to firms' long-term financial prosperity. Firms must maximize brand equity across all the different brands and products and services they offer. The brand architecture strategy determines which brand elements they apply to their new and existing products and services. It is the means that help consumers understand those products and services and organize them in their minds.

Many firms employ complex brand architecture strategies that are reflected in brand names which consist of multiple brand-name elements (e.g., Canon EOS 5D Mark IV camera), and each element may signify an important aspect of the brand's architecture. What is the best way to characterize a firm's brand architecture strategy? What guidelines exist for choosing the right combinations of brand names and other brand elements to best manage brand equity across the entire range of a firm's products?

We begin by outlining a three-step process to develop an effective brand architecture strategy. We next describe two important strategic tools—brand portfolios and brand hierarchies—that, by defining various relationships among brands and products, help characterize and formulate brand architecture strategies. We then consider corporate branding strategies. After outlining corporate image dimensions, we examine three specific issues in managing a corporate brand: corporate social responsibility, corporate image campaigns, and corporate name changes. Brand Focus 12.0 devotes special attention to the topic of corporate social responsibility and its important role in a successful brand strategy.

DEVELOPING A BRAND ARCHITECTURE STRATEGY

The firm's **brand architecture strategy** helps marketers determine which products and services to introduce, and which brand names, logos, symbols, and so forth to apply to new and existing products. As we describe later, it defines both the brand's breadth or boundaries and its depth or complexity. Which different products or services should share the same brand name? How many variations of that brand name should we employ? The role of brand architecture is twofold:

- *To clarify brand awareness:* Improve consumer understanding and communicate similarity and differences between individual products and services.
- *To improve brand image:* Maximize transfer of equity between the brand and individual products and services to improve trial and repeat purchase.

An overview of the chapter is given in Figure 12-1.

We outline the key ideas in this chapter across three specific themes, which are core to developing a brand architecture strategy. These are the following:

Step 1: Defining brand potential in terms of a market footprint
Step 2: Identifying brand extension opportunities or selecting the product and service extensions that will allow the brand to achieve that potential, and
Step 3: Branding new products and services including deciding on the branding elements and positioning.

Although we introduce all three topics here, this chapter concentrates on insights and guidelines into the first and third topics. Chapter 13 exclusively focuses on the second topic and how to launch successful brand extensions. The Science of Branding 12-1 describes a useful tool to help depict brand architecture strategies for a firm.

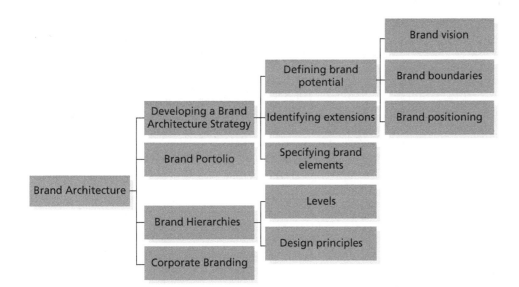

FIGURE 12-1

A Map of Brand Architecture Strategies and Decisions

THE SCIENCE OF BRANDING 12-1
The Brand–Product Matrix

To characterize the brand architecture strategy of a firm, one useful tool is the **brand–product matrix**, a graphical representation of all the brands and products sold by the firm. The matrix (or grid) has the firm's brands as rows and the corresponding products as columns (see Figure 12-2).

- The rows of the matrix represent **brand–product relationships**. They capture the firm's brand-extension strategy in terms of the number and nature of products sold under its different brands. A **brand line** consists of all products—original as well as line and category extensions—sold under a particular brand. Thus, a brand line is one row of the matrix. We want to judge a potential new product extension for a brand on how effectively it leverages existing brand equity from the parent brand to the new product, as well as how effectively the extension, in turn, contributes to the equity of the parent brand.

- The columns of the matrix represent **product–brand relationships**. They capture the brand portfolio strategy in terms of the number and nature of brands to be marketed in each category. The **brand portfolio** is the set of all brands and brand lines that a particular firm offers for sale to buyers in a particular category. Thus, a brand portfolio is one column of the matrix. Marketers design and market different brands to appeal to various market segments.

We can characterize a firm's brand architecture strategy according to its *breadth* (in terms of brand–product relationships and brand extension strategy) and its *depth* (in terms of product–brand relationships and the brand portfolio or mix). For example, a brand architecture strategy is both deep and broad if the firm has a large number of brands, many of which have been extended into various product categories.

Several other terms are useful to understanding how to characterize the brand architecture strategies of a firm.

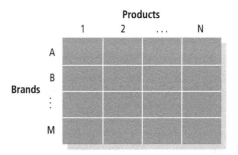

FIGURE 12-2

Brand-Product Matrix

- A **product line** is a group of products within a product category that are closely related because they function in a similar manner, are sold to the same customer groups, are marketed through the same type of outlets, or fall within given price ranges. A product line may include different brands, a single family brand, or individual brand that has been line extended. Campbell's makes a variety of different soup products, varying in flavor, type, sizes, and so on.

- A **product mix** (or product assortment) is the set of all product lines and items that a particular seller makes available to buyers. Thus, product lines represent different sets of columns in the brand–product matrix that, in total, make up the product mix. In addition to soup, Campbell's sells tomato sauces, salsa, vegetable juices, and cookies and crackers.

- A **brand mix** (or brand assortment) is the set of all brand lines that a particular seller makes available to buyers. Campbell's brand lines include Prego, Pace, V8, and Pepperidge Farm.

A firm, such as Campbell's, has to make strategic decisions about how many different product lines it should carry (the breadth of the product mix), as well as how many variants to offer in each product line (the depth of the product mix).

Understanding the brand–product matrix and developing the right brand architecture strategy is key to success for many large firms. In defining a company's "market footprint," there are three decisions that a firm has to make. This involves deciding what areas of the business and associated target segments will receive focus, how to tailor brand architecture to suit the needs of the predefined target market, and how to divest areas of the business that are not selected as focus areas. As an example of these strategic decisions, consider Nestlé—the biggest producer of food in the world, with more than 90 billion Swiss Francs in revenue and 2 to 4 percent growth rate in 2016. Nestlé evolved its organization and architecture as follows:

- *Defining (and Redefining) Areas of Focus:* Nestlé's areas of focus have changed over time, although it has retained many of its core businesses throughout its history. Recently, the company decided to focus more on products relating to consumer health and well-being, thus adopting a narrower product mix to offer to its customers. To support this strategic focus, Nestlé's brand mix comprised of brand names such as Optisource, Novasource, and Isosource, which offered nutritional supplements to individuals being treated for various ailments.

- *Customizing Brands Based on Target Market:* Nestlé's brand mix changes based on the type of market it serves, and may feature unique brands to appeal to local tastes in foreign markets. For example, Nestlé India features Nestlé Everyday with six natural spice flavors—including cardamom, ginger, black pepper, clove, cinnamon, and bay leaf—that are suited to Indian consumer tastes. In China, Nestlé Yiyang introduced a milk powder with added ingredients to appeal to China's aging population.

- *Divestments of Nonfocal Areas:* A key part of adapting the brand architecture include strategically divesting businesses that are not contributing to growth of the overall company, as Nestlé recently has done with its confectionary business.

Overall, Nestlé has had success with managing its brand architecture by continually adapting its product and brand mix over time to stay abreast of changes in the marketplace.

Sources: Phillip Kotler and Kevin Lane Keller, *Marketing Management*, 14th ed. (Upper Saddle River, NJ: Prentice Hall, 2012); Beth Kowitt, "Nestle: Tailoring Products to Local Niches," *Fortune*, July 2, 2010, http://archive.fortune.com/2010/07/02/news/companies/nestle_refreshes_brand.fortune/index.htm, accessed November 20, 2018; Ralph Atkins, "Nestle Sales Growth Continues to Fall Short," *Financial Times*, October 20, 2016, www.ft.com/content/abce2c4e-99bb-3c74-86cc-7cd0bed19b3a; Phillip Kotler and Kevin Lane Keller, *Marketing Management*, 14th ed. (Upper Saddle River, NJ: Prentice Hall, 2012); Bloomberg, "Nestle Launches YIYANG Powder to Target China's Ageing Population," May 31, 2017, www.business-standard.com/article/international/nestle-launches-yiyang-powder-to-target-china-s-ageing-population-117053101870_1.html, accessed November 19, 2018.

Step 1: Defining Brand Potential

The first step in developing an architecture strategy is to define the brand potential by considering three important characteristics:

A. Brand vision
B. Brand boundaries
C. Brand positioning

Articulating the Brand Vision.   *Brand vision* is management's view of the brand's long-term potential. It is influenced by how well the firm is able to recognize the current and possible future brand equity. Many brands have latent brand equity that is never realized because the firm is unable or unwilling to consider all that the brand could and should become.

A key aspect of a changing brand architecture is the shifting boundaries of the brand, and many brands have transcended their initial market boundaries to become much more. This is also a key takeaway from various examples of large companies and brands that have redefined their boundaries. We will subsequently describe how Nestlé modified its architecture to keep up with changes taking place in the marketplace. Another example, Starbucks has at times discussed transforming itself from a coffee company to more of a lifestyle company, offering a broader range of products. While Starbucks has successfully transitioned beyond coffee, some of its

Crayola's brand meaning has broadened over time through various brand extensions, and it is summarized as "colorful arts and crafts for kids."

more-removed extensions have been unsuccessful (e.g., beer and wine sales through its stores, Teavana tea),[1] and may have cost the company loss of shareholder value. Perhaps in recognition of its risk, Starbucks has reverted to a greater focus on its core business of coffee and coffee experiences. The issue with Starbucks was the extension beyond coffee and a coffeehouse culture and experience did not entirely succeed within the parameters of the existing brand.

Sometimes, marketers adopt a sequential approach to extending their brand, thereby gradually expanding brand meaning. For example, Crayola, known for its crayons, first sought to expand its brand meaning by making some fairly direct brand extensions into other drawing and coloring implements, such as markers, pencils, paints, pens, brushes, and chalk. The company further expanded beyond coloring and drawing into arts and crafts with extensions such as Crayola Chalk, Crayola Clay, Crayola Dough, Crayola Glitter Glue, and Crayola Scissors. These extensions established a new brand meaning for Crayola as "colorful arts and crafts for kids." Crayola says its brand essence is to find the "what if" in each child. The Branding Brief 12-1 on Google summarizes its brand architecture dilemma as it extended beyond search engines.

BRANDING BRIEF 12-1
Google: Expanding Beyond Search

Google is a prominent technology brand, but began primarily as a search engine and has dominated the search industry for more than a decade, overcoming strong competition from Yahoo!, Microsoft's Bing, and so on. Google's proprietary search algorithm was at the heart of its success as a search engine. However, Google's footprint now encompasses various sub-brands that are linked to the corporate brand name (such as Google Earth, Google Maps, and Google Play), as well as a long list of individual brands that have resulted from various acquisitions. In 2016, Google unveiled a series of products that included a Google-branded smartphone, a virtual-reality headset, a voice-activated home assistant, and a Wi-Fi router.

Google's brand architecture has utilized a hybrid approach. In addition to the corporate branded house (BH) approach, Google also simultaneously employed a portfolio comprising many different brand names, which we later define as a "house of brands (HOB)" strategy, where the Google brand itself is not a part of the brand name (such as with Nest, Calico, and Fiber). As the brand moved beyond its core business and began exploring various risky ventures, the brand name's lack of relevancy across these disparate areas became a challenge.

In 2016, Google reorganized itself by creating a new parent company, Alphabet. The creation of Google's parent company Alphabet made sense as it allowed Google to work in disparate areas—such as driverless cars and curing diseases using separate company names and entities—without compromising the meaning of the Google brand name. The infographic summarizes the timeline of Google's evolution into a technology megabrand.

In line with its rapid growth across diverse areas, Google remains one of the most successful technology brands in history. Its success across many product lines has helped strengthen the value of the Google brand name. As of 2017, Interbrand listed Google as the second largest brand globally with a brand value of $141.7 billion.

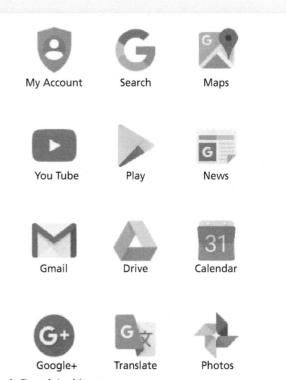

Google Brand Architecture

Sources: Marty Swant, "Google Debuts New Hardware, Including Smartphone and VR Headset, With AI at the Core." *Adweek*, accessed October 04, 2016. http://www.adweek.com/digital/google-debuts-tv-spots-new-smartphone-and-virtual-reality-headset-173894/; K@W Strategic Management, "A

Tale of Two Brands: Yahoo's Mistakes vs. Google's Mastery" Knowledge@ Wharton, February 23, 2016, accessed April 17, 2017. http://knowledge .wharton.upenn.edu/article/a-tale-of-two-brands-yahoos-mistakes-vs-googles-mastery/; Marketwatch, "Yahoo! vs. Google Signals Return of the Portal Wars," *Marketwatch: Technology* 3, no. 7: 8. Business Source Complete, EBSCOhost (accessed April 16, 2017); Lauren Johnson, "Here's Everything You Need to Know About Mobile Payments." *Adweek*, March 05, 2015, accessed May 02, 2017. http://www.adweek.com/digital/heres-everything-you-need-know-about-mobile-payments-163269/; Martin Reeves, "Google Couldn't Survive with One Strategy," https://hbr.org/2015/08/ google-couldnt-survive-with-one-strategy, August 18, 2015, accessed April 23, 2017; Ian Morris, "Google Is Sitting on a Timebomb with Its Nest Disaster," *Forbes*, April 6, 2016, accessed April 23, 2017; 2015, Jonathan Gordon, "How Google Breaks Through" *McKinsey Quarterly*, February 2015; Nicholas Carlson, "A List of Products Larry Page Has Google Working On

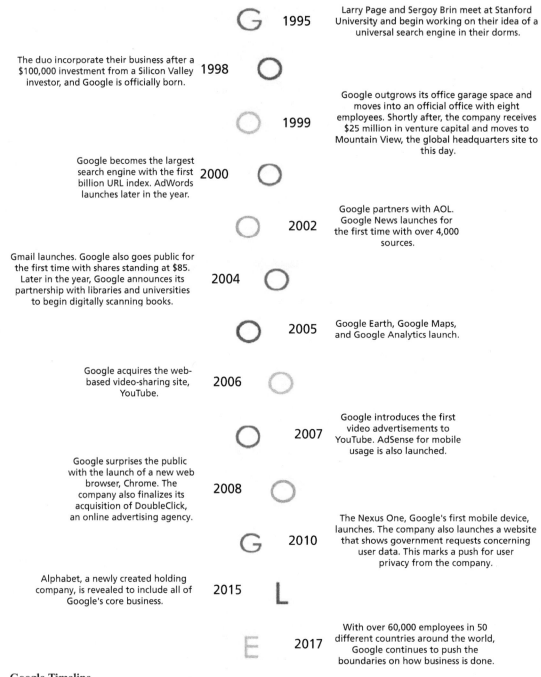

Google Timeline

Other Than Search, Such as Spoons," September 22, 2014, *Business Insider*, http://www.businessinsider.com/a-list-of-google-products-2014-9, accessed July 14, 2018; Wikipedia, "List of Google Products," https://en.wikipedia. org/wiki/List_of_Google_products; Kevin Lane Keller, "The Branding Logic Behind Google's Creation of Alphabet," July 5, 2017; http://interbrand.com/best-brands/best-global-brands/2017/ranking/.

Without a clear understanding of its current equity, however, it is difficult to understand what a brand could be built on. As shown previously with the many changes that took place in the case of the Google brand, a good strategy has to account for the past as well as the future by articulating a sufficiently broad vision for the brand. Brand vision obviously needs to be aspirational, so the brand has room to grow and improve in the future, yet it cannot be unobtainable. The trick is to strike the right balance between what the brand is and what it could become, and to identify the right steps to get it there.

Fundamentally, brand vision relates to the higher-order purpose of the brand, based on keen understanding of consumer aspirations and brand truths. It transcends the brand's physical product category descriptions and boundaries. P&G's legendary former CMO Jim Stengel maintains that successful brands have clear ideals—such as "eliciting joy, enabling connection, inspiring exploration, evoking pride, or impacting society"—and a strong purpose of building customer loyalty and driving revenue growth.[2]

Defining the Brand Boundaries.   Some of the world's strongest brands, such as General Electric (GE), Virgin, and Apple, have been stretched across multiple categories. Defining brand boundaries thus means—based on the brand vision and positioning—identifying the products or services the brand should offer, the benefits it should supply, and the needs it should satisfy.

Although many product categories may seem to be good candidates for a brand extension, as we will develop in Chapter 13, marketers would be wise to heed the "Spandex Rule" espoused by Scott Bedbury, former advertising vice president for Nike and marketing vice president for Starbucks: "Just because you can . . . doesn't mean you should!" Marketers must evaluate extending their brand carefully and launch new products selectively.

A *broad* brand is one with an abstract positioning that is able to support a higher-order promise applicable in multiple product settings. It often has a transferable point-of-difference, thanks to a widely relevant benefit supported by multiple reasons-to-believe or supporting attributes. For example, Delta Faucet Company has taken its core brand associations—stylish and innovative—and successfully expanded the brand from faucets to a variety of kitchen and bathroom products and accessories.

Nevertheless, all brands have boundaries. It would be very difficult for Delta Faucet to introduce a car, tennis racquet, or lawnmower. Japanese carmakers Honda, Nissan, and Toyota chose to introduce their luxury brands in North America under new brand names, Acura, Infiniti, and Lexus, respectively. Even considering its own growth, Nike chose to purchase Cole Haan to sell into the dressier, more formal shoe market.

To improve market coverage, companies target different segments with multiple brands in a portfolio. They have to be careful to not over-brand, however, or attempt to support too many brands. The trend among many top marketing companies in recent years has been to focus on fewer, stronger brands. Each should be clearly differentiated and appeal to a sizable enough market segment to justify its marketing and production costs.

Crafting the Brand Positioning.   Brand positioning puts some specificity into a brand vision. Chapter 2 reviewed brand positioning considerations in detail; the four key ingredients are: (1) competitive frame of reference, (2) points-of-difference, (3) points-of-parity, and (4) brand mantra. The brand mantra, in particular, can be very useful in establishing product boundaries or brand guardrails. It should offer rational and emotional benefits and be sufficiently robust to permit growth, relevant enough to drive consumer and retailer interest, and differentiated enough to sustain longevity.

Step 2: Identifying Brand Extension Opportunities

Determining the brand vision, boundaries, and positioning in Step 1 helps define the brand potential and provides a clear sense of direction for the brand. Step 2 is to identify new products and services to achieve that potential through a well-designed and implemented brand extension strategy.

A brand extension is a new product introduced under an existing brand name. We differentiate between **line extensions**, new product introductions within existing categories (Tide Pods or Tide Total Care laundry detergent), and **category extensions**, new product introductions outside existing categories (Tide Dry Cleaners retail outlets).

It is important to carefully plan the optimal sequence of brand extensions to achieve brand potential. The key is to understand equity implications of each extension in terms of points-of-parity and points-of-difference. By adhering to the brand promise and growing the brand carefully through little steps, marketers can ensure that brands cover a lot of ground.

For example, through a well-planned and well-executed series of new product introductions in the form of category extensions over a 25-year period, Nike evolved from a company selling running, tennis, and basketball shoes to mostly males between the ages of 12 and 29 in North America in the mid-1980s, to a company now selling athletic shoes, clothing, and equipment across a range of sports to men and women of all ages in virtually all countries. It also has embraced technology to improve fitness, by co-branding with Apple to introduce the Nike+iPod activity tracking device and mobile app.

Launching a brand extension is harder than it might seem. Given that the vast majority of new products are extensions, and the vast majority of new products fail, the clear implication is that too many brand extensions fail. An increasingly competitive marketplace will be even more unforgiving to poorly positioned and marketed extensions in the years to come. To increase the likelihood of success, marketers must be rigorous and disciplined in their analysis and development of brand extensions. Chapter 12 provides detailed guidelines for successful brand extension strategies.

Step 3: Specifying Brand Elements for Branding New Products and Services

The final step in developing the brand architecture is to decide on the specific brand elements to use for any particular new product or service associated with the brand. New products and services must be branded in a way to maximize the brand's overall clarity and understanding to consumers and customers. What names, looks, and other branding elements are to be applied to the new and existing products for any one brand?

One way we can distinguish brand architecture strategies is by looking at whether a firm is employing an umbrella corporate or family brand for all its products, known as a *branded house*, or a collection of individual brands all with different names, known as a *house of brands*.

- Firms largely employing a BH strategy include many business-to-business industrial firms, such as SAP, Siemens, Oracle, and Goldman Sachs.
- Firms largely employing a HOB strategy include consumer product companies, such as Procter & Gamble, Unilever, and ConAgra.

The reality is that most firms adopt a strategy somewhere between these two end points, often employing various types of sub-brands. ***Sub-brands*** are an extremely popular form of brand extension in which the new product carries both the parent brand name and a new name (Apple iPad, Ford Fusion, and American Express Blue card).

A good sub-branding strategy can tap associations and attitudes about the company or family brand as a whole, while also allowing for the creation of new brand beliefs to position the extension in the new category. For example, Hershey's Kisses taps into the quality, heritage, and familiarity of the Hershey's brand, but at the same time has a much more playful and fun brand image. Similarly, FedEx imbues its various sub-brands with separate identities and unique color schemes (see the figure). As noted previously, Google has also a variety of sub-brands that it has launched over the years (as shown in the figure).

Sub-brands play an important brand architecture role by signaling to consumers to expect similarities *and* differences in the new product. To realize these benefits, however, sub-branding typically requires significant investments and disciplined and consistent marketing to establish the proper brand meanings with consumers. In the absence of such financial commitments, marketers may be well advised to adopt the simplest brand hierarchy possible, such as using a BH approach with the company or a family brand name with product descriptors. Marketers should employ sub-branding only when there is a distinctive, complementary benefit; otherwise, they should just use a product descriptor to designate the new product or service.

Summary

The three steps we outlined provide a careful and well-grounded approach to developing a brand architecture strategy. To successfully execute this process, marketers should use brand portfolio analysis for determining brand potential (Step 1), and brand hierarchy analysis for defining brand boundaries and identifying brand elements for branding particular products and services (Steps 2 and 3). We describe both tools next.

BRAND PORTFOLIOS

A ***brand portfolio*** includes all brands sold by a company in a product category. We judge a brand portfolio by its ability to maximize brand equity: Any one brand in the portfolio should not harm or decrease the equity of the others. Ideally, each brand maximizes equity in combination with all other brands in the portfolio.

Why might a firm have multiple brands in the same product category? The primary reason is market coverage. Although multiple branding was originally pioneered by General Motors, Procter & Gamble is widely recognized as popularizing the practice. P&G became a proponent of multiple brands after introducing its Cheer detergent brand as an alternative to its already successful Tide detergent, resulting in higher combined product category sales.

Firms introduce multiple brands because no one brand is viewed equally favorably by all the distinct market segments the firm would like to target. Multiple brands allow a firm to pursue various price segments, a variety of distribution channels, different geographic boundaries, and so forth.[3]

In designing the optimal brand portfolio, marketers must first define the relevant customer segments. How much overlap exists across segments, and how well can products be cross-sold?[4] Branding Brief 12-2 describes how Marriott has introduced different brands and sub-brands to attack different markets.

Other reasons for introducing multiple brands in a category include the following:[5]

- To increase shelf presence and retailer dependence in the store
- To attract consumers seeking variety who may otherwise switch to another brand
- To increase internal competition within the firm
- To yield economies of scale in advertising, sales, merchandising, and physical distribution

Marketers generally need to trade off market coverage and these other considerations with costs and profitability. A portfolio is too big if profits can be increased by dropping brands; it is not big enough if profits can be increased by adding brands. Brand lines with poorly differentiated brands are likely to be characterized by much cannibalization and require appropriate pruning.[6]

The basic principle in designing a brand portfolio is to *maximize market coverage* so that no potential customers are being ignored, but *minimize brand overlap* so that brands are not competing among themselves to gain the same customer's approval. Each brand should have a distinct target market and positioning.[7]

For example, over the last 10 years or so, Procter & Gamble has sought to maximize market coverage and minimize brand overlap by pursuing organic growth from existing core brands rather than introducing a lot of new brands. The company has focused its innovation efforts on its core "billion dollar" brands—those with more than $1 billion in revenue. Numerous successful market-leading brand and line extensions followed, such as Crest whitening products, Tide Pods, Gillette Fusion razors, and Pampers Swaddlers.[8]

Besides these considerations, brands can play a number of specific roles as part of a brand portfolio. Figure 12-3 summarizes some of them, which we review next.

Flankers.   Certain brands act as protective flanker or "fighter" brands.[9] The purpose of flanker brands typically is to create stronger points-of-parity with competitors' brands so that more important (and more profitable) flagship brands can retain their desired positioning. In particular, as

1. To attract a particular market segment not currently being covered by other brands of the firm
2. To serve as a flanker and protect flagship brands
3. To serve as a cash cow and be milked for profits
4. To serve as a low-end entry-level product to attract new customers to the brand franchise
5. To serve as a high-end prestige product to add prestige and credibility to the entire brand portfolio
6. To increase shelf presence and retailer dependence in the store
7. To attract consumers seeking variety who may otherwise have switched to another brand
8. To increase internal competition within the firm
9. To yield economies of scale in advertising, sales, merchandising, and physical distribution

FIGURE 12-3

Possible Special Roles of Brands in the Brand Portfolio

BRANDING BRIEF 12-2

Expanding the Marriott Brand

Marriott International grew to an international hospitality giant from its humble roots as a single root beer stand (started by John and Alice Marriott in Washington, D.C.), during the 1920s. The Marriotts added hot food to their root beer stand and renamed their business the Hot Shoppe. As the number of regional restaurants called Hot Shoppes grew, Marriott expanded into in-flight catering by serving food on Eastern, American, and Capital Airlines, beginning in 1937. Hot Shoppes subsequently began its food service management business and later opened its first hotel in Arlington, Virginia, named the Twin Bridges Marriott Motor Hotel. Hot Shoppes, which was renamed Marriott Corporation in 1967, grew nationally and internationally by making strategic acquisitions and entering new service categories; by 1977, sales topped $1 billion.

In pursuit of more growth, Marriott continued to diversify its business. Determining that its high penetration in the traditional hotel market did not offer many opportunities for growth, the company initiated a segmented marketing strategy by introducing the moderately priced Courtyard by Marriott brand in 1983. Moderately priced hotels constituted the largest segment of the U.S. lodging industry, filled with established competitors such as Holiday Inn, Ramada, and Quality Inn. Marriott's research registered the greatest consumer dissatisfaction in this segment, so Courtyard hotels were designed to offer travellers greater convenience and amenities, such as balconies and patios, large desks and sofas, and pools and spas.

Early success with Courtyard prompted Marriott to expand further. In 1984, the company entered the vacation timesharing business by acquiring American Resorts Group. The following year, it purchased Howard Johnson Company, selling the hotels and retaining the restaurants and rest stops. The first JW Marriott luxury hotel was opened on Pennsylvania Avenue in Washington, D.C., as a tribute to the founder.

In 1987, Marriott added three new chains to their portfolio to target different segments and to fuel growth in the process: Marriott Suites, full-service suite accommodations; Residence Inn, extended-stay rooms for business travelers; and Fairfield Inn, an economy hotel brand.

In 1993, Marriott Corporation split in two, forming Host Marriott to own the hotel properties, and Marriott International to manage them and franchise its brands. Marriott International bought a stake in the Ritz-Carlton luxury hotel group and expanded again in 1997 by acquiring the Renaissance Hotel Group. The Marriott brand further expanded to include TownePlace Suites, Fairfield Suites, and Marriott Executive Residences. Marriott added a new hotel brand in 1998 with the introduction of SpringHill Suites, which provide moderately priced suites that are 25 percent larger than standard hotel rooms. The following year, the company acquired corporate housing specialist ExecuStay Corporation and formed ExecuStay by Marriott, now a franchise business.

A new century saw new growth. The launch in 2007 of stylish EDITION hotels put Marriott in the luxury boutique market. Each property was distinctive and designed by famed hotel developer Ian Schrager. The Autograph Collection was also introduced in 2011, a diverse collection of high-personality, upper-upscale independent hotels. AC Hotels by Marriott was another lifestyle hotel entry in 2011, an upper-moderate tier brand targeting design-conscious younger travellers in Europe with stylish, urban properties.

Today, Marriott International is one of the leading hospitality companies in the world, with 600 properties in 122 countries and territories worldwide that brought in almost $17 billion in global revenues in 2017, and a market capitalization of $35 billion. Marriott's growth over the years has been aided by various acquisitions including Protea Hospitality Group (2014), Delta Hotels and Resorts (2015), and more recently Starwood Hotels (2016). Marriott International developed a formal brand architecture that it shared with prospective guests on its Web sites to aid them in their lodging decisions (see Figure 12-4; https://hotel-development.marriott.com/brands-dashboard/). As 2016 approached, the Marriott Hotel's gross bookings increased 57 percent, totalling more than $3 billion. In 2016, Marriott acquired Starwood hotels and resorts for $13 billion, thereby becoming the world's largest hotel chain. The juxtaposition of Starwood offerings and Marriott offerings suggests many ways in which the merger completes the Marriott architecture, although there are opportunities for some of the hotels within each brand to be merged and consolidated. Overall, Marriott has approached its brand architecture decisions in a systematic way, ensuring market coverage and minimizing overlap, which has ensured its success in the industry.

Brand Category	Brands
Iconic Luxury	Bvlgari The Ritz-Carlton The Ritz-Carlton Destination Club
Luxury	JW Marriott
Lifestyle | Collections	Edition Autograph Collection Renaissance Hotels AC Hotels
Signature	Marriott Hotels and Resorts
Modern Essentials	Courtyard SpringHill Suites Fairfield Inn and Suites
Extended Stay	Residence Inn TownePlace Suites ExecuStay Marriott Executive Apartments
Vacation Clubs	Marriott Vacation Club Grand Residences

FIGURE 12-4

Marriott International Portfolio Architecture
Source: Marriott International, Inc. Used with permission.

Sources: Marriott International, www.marriott.com; Kim Clark, "Lawyers Clash on Timing of Marriott's Plan to Split," *Baltimore Sun*, September 27, 1994, http://articles.baltimoresun.com/1994-09-27/business/1994270134_1_marriott-corp-host-marriott-marriott-executive, accessed November 20, 2018; Neil Henderson, "Marriott Gambles on Low-Cost, Classy 'Corporate History,'" *Factbook*, n.d; "Suburban Motels," *The Washington Post*, June 18, 1994; Neil Henderson, "Marriott Bares Courtyard Plans," *The Washington Post*, June 12, 1984; Elizabeth Tucker, "Marriott's Recipe for Corporate Growth," *The Washington Post*, June 1, 1987; Paul Farhi, "Marriott to Sell 800 Restaurants," *The Washington Post*, December 19, 1989; Stephane Fitch, "Soft Pillows and Sharp Elbows," *Forbes*, May 10, 2004, 66; Associated Press (2016), "Marriott Closes $13-Billion Purchase of Starwood to Become World's Largest Hotel Chain," September 23, 2016, www.latimes.com/business/la-fi-marriott-starwood-20160923-snap-story.html, accessed November 20, 2018.

we noted in Chapter 5, many firms are introducing discount brands as flankers, to better compete with store brands and private labels and to protect their higher-priced brand companions. A good example of such a strategy is when Qantas (in Australia) launched Jetstar airlines as a discount fighter brand to compete with the recently introduced low-priced Virgin Blue airlines—which was meeting with much success—and to protect its flagship premium Qantas brand. Firms have also either repositioned existing brands or acquired new brands to serve as flankers within the portfolio. For example, Wyndham hotels purchased Days Inn to appeal to the value segment and recently purchased AmericInn to gain a foothold in the midscale segment of the market.[10]

Flanker brands can have an important strategic role to play in protecting the main brands, and the lack of flankers can also pose a threat to a core brand. For example, Gillette's higher-priced razors posed an opportunity for the low-cost Dollar Shave Club—and others—to enter the market at the low end. Dollar Shave Club gained 5 percent market share and cost Gillette significantly in terms of lost sales. The introduction of a flanker brand at a lower price point might have helped the Gillette brand mitigate the competitive threat at the lower end of the market. As an example, P&G repositioned its Luvs diaper brand to serve as a price fighter against private labels and store brands to protect the premium Pampers brand.

In designing fighter brands, marketers walk a fine line. Fighters must not be so attractive that they take sales away from their higher-priced comparison brands or referents. At the same time, if they are connected to other brands in the portfolio in any way (say, through a common branding strategy), they must not be designed so cheaply that they reflect poorly on these other brands.

Cash Cows.   Some brands may be kept around despite dwindling sales because they still manage to hold on to a sufficient number of customers and maintain their profitability with virtually no marketing support. Marketers can effectively milk these cash cows by capitalizing on their reservoir of existing brand equity. For example, even while technological advances have moved much of the sales to streaming, Netflix still offers a DVD service to around 4.3 million diehard fans who prefer to receive a DVD via mail and watch these via DVD players. Contrast this with the 93 million subscribers to the streaming service.[11] Netflix does not spend any money in promoting the DVD service. Thus, the DVD business acts as a cash cow with an operating profit of 50 percent. Given the loyalty of DVD subscribers to the format, withdrawing the DVD service does not make economic sense as it may not necessarily switch customers to another type of product, for example, streaming. Therefore, as is typical of a cash cow strategy, Netflix profits more by retaining the traditional DVD business than withdrawing from the business.

Low-End, Entry-Level, or High-End, Prestige Brands.   Many brands introduce line extensions or brand variants in a certain product category that vary in price and quality. These sub-brands leverage associations from other brands while distinguishing themselves on price and quality. In this case, the end points of the brand line often play a specialized role.

The role of a relatively low-priced brand in the brand portfolio often may be to attract customers to the brand franchise. Retailers like to feature these traffic builders because they often are able to trade up customers to a higher-priced brand. For example, Verizon Wireless plans allow customers to upgrade their old, sometimes cheaper cell phones to newer versions that are more expensive but still cheaper than retail.

BMW introduced certain models into its 3-series automobiles in part as a means of bringing new customers into its brand franchise, with the hope of moving them up to higher-priced models when they traded their cars in. As the 3 series gradually moved up-market, BMW introduced the 1 series in 2004, which was built on the same production line as the 3 series and priced between the 3 series and the MINI.

On the other hand, the role of a relatively high-priced brand in the brand family is often to add prestige and credibility to the entire portfolio. For example, one analyst argued that the real value to Chevrolet of its Corvette high-performance sports car was "its ability to lure curious customers into showrooms and, at the same time, help improve the image of other Chevrolet cars. It does not mean a hell of a lot for GM profitability, but there is no question that it is a traffic builder."[12] Corvette's technological image and prestige cast a halo over the entire Chevrolet line.

Summary.   Multiple brands can expand coverage, provide protection, extend an image, or fulfill a variety of other roles for the firm. In all brand portfolio decisions, the basic criteria are simple, even though their application can be quite complicated: to minimize overlap and get the most from the portfolio, each brand-name product must have (1) a well-defined role to fulfill for the firm and, thus, (2) a well-defined positioning indicating the benefits or promises it offers consumers. As Chapter 12 reveals, many firms find that due to product proliferation through the years, they now can cut the number of brands and product variants they offer and still profitably satisfy consumers.

BRAND HIERARCHIES

A ***brand hierarchy*** is a useful means of graphically portraying a firm's branding strategy by displaying the number and nature of common and distinctive brand elements across the firm's products, revealing their explicit ordering. It is based on the realization that we can brand a product in different ways depending on how many new and existing brand elements we use and how we combine them for any one product.

For example, a Dell Latitude E7450 computer consists of three different brand name elements, "Dell," "Latitude," and "E7450." Some of these may be shared by many different products; others are limited. Dell uses its corporate name to brand many of its products, but Latitude designates a certain type of computer ("highly secure, manageable and reliable" laptops and notebooks for business users), and E7450 identifies a particular model of Latitude ("a premium thin and light notebook with superior performance and premium features").

We can construct a hierarchy to represent how (if at all) products are nested with other products because of their common brand elements. Figure 12-5 displays a simple characterization of Apple's brand hierarchy. As the figure shows, a brand hierarchy can include multiple levels.

Dell's computer models are uniquely identified via a sub-brand name and a model number which together provide information about the distinct features of each model.

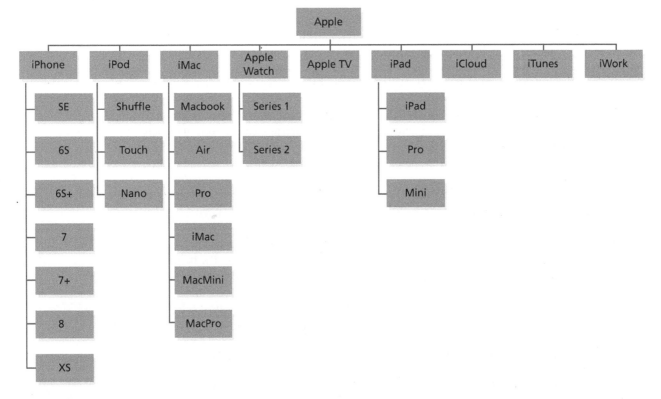

FIGURE 12-5

Apple Brand Hierarchy

There are different ways to define brand elements and levels of the hierarchy. Perhaps the simplest representation from top to bottom might be:

1. Corporate or company brand (General Motors)
2. Family brand (Buick)
3. Individual brand (Regal)
4. Modifier (designating item or model) (GS)
5. Product description (midsize luxury sport sedan automobile).

Levels of a Brand Hierarchy

Different levels of the hierarchy have different issues, as we review in turn.

Corporate or Company Brand Level.   The highest level of the hierarchy technically always consists of one brand—the ***corporate or company brand***. For simplicity, we refer to corporate and company brands interchangeably, recognizing that consumers may not necessarily draw a distinction between the two or know that corporations may subsume multiple companies.

For legal reasons, the company or corporate brand is almost always present somewhere on the product or package, although the name of a company subsidiary may appear instead of the corporate name. For example, Fortune Brands has, over the years, owned many different companies, such as Moen, Master Lock, Jim Beam whiskey, Vox vodka, and El Tesoro tequila, but it does not use its corporate name on any of its lines of business.

For some firms such as General Electric and Hewlett-Packard, the corporate brand is virtually the only brand. Conglomerate Siemens's varied electrical engineering and electronics business units are branded with descriptive modifiers, such as Siemens Mobility. In other cases, the company name is virtually invisible and, although technically part of the hierarchy, receives virtually no attention in the marketing program. Black & Decker does not use its name on its high-end DeWalt professional power tools.

As we detail later, we can think of a ***corporate image*** as the consumer associations to the company or corporation making the product or providing the service. Corporate image is particularly relevant when the corporate or company brand plays a prominent role in the branding strategy.

Family Brand Level.   At the next-lower level, a ***family brand***, also called a ***range brand*** or ***umbrella brand***, is used in more than one product category but is not necessarily the name of the company or corporation. For example, ConAgra's Healthy Choice family brand appears on a wide spectrum of food products, including packaged meats, soups, pasta sauces, breads, popcorn, and ice cream. Some other notable family brands for companies that generate more than $1 billion in sales include Purina and Kit Kat (Nestlé); Mountain Dew, Doritos, and Quaker Foods (PepsiCo); and Oreo, Cadbury, and Maxwell House (Mondelez International).

Because a family brand may be distinct from the corporate or company brand, company-level associations may be less salient. Most firms typically support only a handful of family brands. If the corporate brand is applied to a range of products, then it functions as a family brand too, and the two levels collapse to one for those products.

Marketers may apply family brands instead of corporate brands for several reasons. As products become more dissimilar, it may be harder for the corporate brand to retain any product meaning or to effectively link the disparate products. Distinct family brands, on the other hand, can evoke a specific set of associations across a group of related products.[13]

Family brands can be an efficient means to link common associations to multiple, but distinct, products. The cost of introducing a related new product can be lower and the likelihood of acceptance higher when marketers apply an existing family brand to a new product.

On the other hand, if the products linked to the family brand and their supporting marketing programs are not carefully considered and designed, the associations to the family brand may become weaker and less favorable. Moreover, the failure of one product may hurt other products sold under the same brand.

Individual Brand Level.   Individual brands are restricted to essentially one product category, although multiple product types may differ on the basis of model, package size, flavor, and so forth. For example, in the salty snack product class, Frito-Lay offers Fritos corn chips, Doritos and Tostitos tortilla chips, SunChips multigrain chips, Lays and Ruffles potato chips, and Rold

Gold pretzels. Each brand has had a dominant position in its respective product category within the broader salty snack product class.

The main advantage of creating individual brands is that we can customize the brand and all its supporting marketing activity to meet the needs of a specific customer group. Thus, the name, logo, and other brand elements, as well as product design, marketing communication programs, and pricing and distribution strategies, can all focus on a certain target market. Moreover, if the brand runs into difficulty or fails, the risk to other brands and the company itself is minimal. The disadvantages of creating individual brands, however, are the difficulty, complexity, and expense of developing separate marketing programs to build sufficient levels of brand equity.

Modifier Level.   Regardless of whether marketers choose corporate, family, or individual brands, they must often further distinguish brands according to the different types of items or models. A *modifier* is a means to designate a specific item or model type or a particular version or configuration of the product. Land O'Lakes offers whipped, unsalted, and regular versions of its butter. Yoplait yogurt comes as light, custard style, and original flavors.

Adding a modifier often can signal refinements or differences between brands related to factors such as quality levels (Johnnie Walker Red Label, Black Label, and Gold Label Scotch whiskey), attributes (Wrigley's Spearmint, Doublemint, Juicy Fruit, and Winterfresh flavors of chewing gum), function (Dockers Relaxed Fit, Classic Fit, Straight Fit, Slim Fit, and Extra Slim Fit pants), and so forth.[14] Thus, one function of modifiers is to show how one brand variation relates to others in the same brand family.

Modifiers help make products more understandable and relevant to consumers or even to the trade. They can even become strong trademarks if they are able to develop a unique association with the parent brand—only Uncle Ben's has "Converted Rice," and only Orville Redenbacher sells "Gourmet Popping Corn."[15]

Product Descriptor.   Although not considered a brand element per se, the product descriptor for the branded product may be an important ingredient of branding strategy. The product descriptor helps consumers understand what the product is and does and also helps define the relevant competition in consumers' minds.

In some cases, it may be hard to describe succinctly what the product is, a new product with unusual functions or even an existing product that has dramatically changed. For instance, public libraries are no longer about checking out books or taking a preschooler to story time. A full-service modern public library serves as an educational, cultural, social, and recreational community center.

In the case of a truly new product, introducing it with a familiar product name may facilitate basic familiarity and comprehension, but perhaps at the expense of a richer understanding of how the new product is different from closely related products that already exist.

Yoplait yogurt uses a combination of different brand elements to distinguish across types and flavors of yogurt.

Orville Redenbacher's "Gourmet Popping Corn" demonstrates the value of using a modifier in a brand name to develop a unique brand association.

Designing a Brand Hierarchy

Given the different possible levels of a brand hierarchy, a firm has a number of branding options available, depending on whether and how it employs each level. Designing the right brand hierarchy is crucial. Branding Brief 12-3 describes how Netflix has made adjustments over time to adjust its brand architecture to broaden its appeal and enhance profitability.

BRANDING BRIEF 12-3

Netflix: Evolving a Brand Architecture to Grow the Brand

A media darling for much of his company's meteoric rise, Reed Hastings, founder and CEO of Netflix, seemingly could do no wrong. Founded in 1997, Netflix pioneered the DVD-by-mail category, successfully challenging traditional video stores and driving industry leader Blockbuster into bankruptcy in the process. Netflix's bold formula for success included flawless service delivery combined with a state-of-the-art movie recommendation engine for users. The company even famously sponsored a contest with a $1 million prize to anyone who could make its recommendation algorithm work better.

Netflix's business philosophy was captured by two credos found on its corporate Web site: "Avoid 'barnacles' that can slow down a fast-growing business," and "Make tough decisions without agonizing and focus on great results rather than process." Hard-charging and constantly seeking to innovate, Netflix dove in head first as streaming technology evolved online and quickly found a receptive audience ready to instantaneously download and view videos. That's also where the trouble began.

The difference in gross profit margins between mail order (37 percent) and streaming rentals (65 percent) was significant. In part to better account for these revenue differences, management decided

Netflix's foray into original programming has resulted in many hit shows such as *Stranger Things*.

in April 2011 to split the company into two brands and businesses. As the first step, customers were told on July 12, 2011, that they would begin to be charged $7.99 for each form of rental instead of $9.99 for both forms, in effect, a 60 percent price increase for the 24 million subscribers who wanted to use both physical discs and streaming. In an unfortunate coincidence, at roughly the same time, cable channel Starz very publicly ended negotiations with Netflix to renew a key online deal to supply movies and TV shows.

Perceiving that they would be paying more for less, customers were decidedly unhappy. More than 600,000 terminated their accounts in the following months, catching Netflix off guard.

The company compounded its problems when Hastings announced that the company's movies-by-mail service would be rebranded Qwikster and would add video games to its catalog, while the Netflix brand would be devoted to streaming video only. Once again, consumer response was emphatically negative—to the strategy and even to the new name. After several weeks of negative criticism and publicity, the company reversed course and announced that the company would no longer split its services in two.

Although, Netflix's brand architecture problems slowed down the momentum the company had achieved in the marketplace, it was quick to fix the problems as they arose. Soon, the company stabilized, and analysts were cautiously optimistic that Netflix would be able to put its problems behind it.

The analysts were proven correct. Despite its missteps regarding pricing, Netflix has been deliberate and strategic in strengthening its brand over the years through carefully executed brand extensions. Its foray into original programming represents a successful strategy, and it has launched numerous shows that have received critical acclaim and have delivered strong audience numbers. For instance, one of its hit shows is *House of Cards*, which was first released in 2013. The series has been a huge success and went on to win multiple Primetime Emmy Awards. Netflix also felt this success when its stock tripled in value. Netflix also introduced many original television shows and movies, including *Orange is the New*

Black and *Stranger Things*. In 2014 and 2015, Netflix expanded into several new countries until it became available worldwide in 2016.

Taken together, despite the problematic pricing change, which threatened to substantially impact the brand and negate its achievements, Netflix has proven its ability to learn quickly from failures, by reversing its course when faced with failure. It has also simultaneously strengthened its brand presence in the entertainment category through carefully executed brand extensions, which have reaffirmed its position as a strong brand.

Sources: Netflix Media Center, "About Netflix," https://media.netflix.com/en/about-netflix, accessed November 20, 2018; Michael V. Copeland, "Reed Hastings: Leader of the Pack," *Fortune*, December 6, 2010, 121–130; Ronald Grover and Cliff Edwards, "Can Netflix Find Its Future by Abandoning the Past?," *Bloomberg BusinessWeek*, September 22, 2011, https://www.bloomberg.com/news/articles/2011-09-22/can-netflix-find-its-future-by-abandoning-the-past, accessed November 20, 2018; Cliff Edwards and Ronald Grover, "Can Netflix Regain Lost Ground?," *Bloomberg Businessweek*, October 20, 2011, https://www.bloomberg.com/news/articles/2011-10-19/can-netflix-regain-lost-ground, accessed November 20, 2018; John D. Sutter, "Netflix Whiplash Stirs Angry Mobs—Again," CNN, October 10, 2011, https://www.kshb.com/money/business-news/netflix-whiplash-stirs-angry-mobs-again, accessed November 20, 2018; Doug Gross, "Customers Fume Over Netflix Changes," September 21, 2011, https://www.cnn.com/2011/09/20/tech/web/netflix-reaction/index.html, accessed November 20, 2018; Logan Burruss and David Goldman, "Netflix Abandons Plan for Qwikster DVD Service," October 10, 2011, https://money.cnn.com/2011/10/10/technology/netflix_qwikster/index.htm, accessed November 20, 2018; Stu Woo and Ian Sherr, "Netflix Recovers Subscribers," *The Wall Street Journal*, January 26, 2012, https://www.wsj.com/articles/SB10001424052970203806504577183303393083214, accessed November 20, 2018.

Brand elements at each level of the hierarchy may contribute to brand equity through their ability to create awareness as well as foster strong, favorable, and unique brand associations and positive responses. The challenge in setting up a brand hierarchy is to decide:

1. The specific products to be introduced for any one brand.
2. The number of levels of the hierarchy to use.
3. The desired brand awareness and image at each level.
4. The combinations of brand elements from different levels of the hierarchy, if any, to use for any one particular product.
5. The best way to link any one brand element, if at all, to multiple products.

The following discussion reviews these five decisions. Figure 12-6 summarizes guidelines in each of these areas to assist in the design of brand hierarchies.

Specific Products to Introduce.   Consistent with discussions in other chapters about what products a firm should introduce for any one brand, we can note three principles here: that is, *principle of growth, principle of survival*, and *principle of synergy*.

The *principle of growth* maintains that investments in market penetration or expansion versus product development for a brand should be made according to ROI opportunities. In other words, firms must make cost–benefit calculations for investing resources in selling more of a brand's existing products to new customers versus launching new products for the brand. As an example, in seeing its traditional networking business slow down, Cisco decided to bet big on new Internet video products. The other two principles address the dynamics of brand extension success, as developed in great detail in Chapter 13. The *principle of survival* states that brand extensions must achieve brand equity in their categories. In other words, "me too" extensions must be avoided. The *principle of synergy* states that brand extensions should also enhance the equity of the parent brand.

Number of Levels of the Brand Hierarchy.   Given product boundaries and an extension strategy in place for a brand, the first decision to make in defining a branding strategy is, broadly, which level or levels of the branding hierarchy to use. Most firms choose to use more than one

1. **Decide on which products are to be introduced.**
   * *Principle of growth:* Invest in market penetration or expansion vs. product development according to ROI opportunities.
   * *Principle of survival:* Brand extensions must achieve brand equity in their categories.
   * *Principle of synergy:* Brand extensions should enhance the equity of the parent brand.

2. **Decide on the number of levels.**
   * *Principle of simplicity:* Employ as few levels as possible.
   * *Principle of clarity:* Logic and relationship of all brand elements employed must be obvious and transparent.

3. **Decide on the levels of awareness and types of associations to be created at each level.**
   * *Principle of relevance:* Create abstract associations that are relevant across as many individual items as possible.
   * *Principle of differentiation:* Differentiate individual items and brands.

4. **Decide on how to link brands from different levels for a product.**
   * *Principle of prominence:* The relative prominence of brand elements affects perceptions of product distance and the type of image created for new products.

5. **Decide on how to link a brand across products.**
   * *Principle of commonality:* The more common elements products share, the stronger the linkages.

FIGURE 12-6

Guidelines for Brand Hierarchy Decisions

level, for two main reasons. Each successive branding level allows the firm to communicate additional, specific information about its products. Thus, developing brands at lower levels of the hierarchy allows the firm flexibility in communicating the uniqueness of its products. At the same time, developing brands at higher levels of the hierarchy is obviously an economical means

GATORADE

First created by researchers at the University of Florida in the mid-1960s—whose nickname for its sports teams, the "Gators," gave the product its name—Gatorade was a carbohydrate-electrolyte beverage designed to replace what the school's athletes would lose from sweating in the intense Gainesville heat. Pioneering the sports drink market, Gatorade became an on-court and off-court staple for athletes everywhere. PepsiCo bought Quaker Oats and the brand in 2000, but after a decade of ownership, sales began to slump. A slew of new water and energy drink competitors helped erode Gatorade's sales. The "What is G?" ad campaign failed to reignite sales in 2009. That year, Pepsi marketers decided to launch the innovative new "G series" to reconnect with competitive athletes and to ensure that Gatorade was not seen as "the sports drink of my father." The G series was designed to "fuel the body before, during, and after practice, training, and competition." It consisted of three product groupings:

* *Prime 01*, pre-game fuel in the form of four-ounce beverage pouches packed with carbohydrates, sodium, and potassium to be consumed before athletic activity.

* *Perform 02*, the traditional Thirst Quencher and G2 beverage lines used to hydrate and refresh during periods of heavy exertion, exercise, or competition.

* *Recover 03*, a protein-packed beverage to aid hydration and muscle recovery after exercise.

Other versions of G Series were also launched. G Series Pro was initially available only for professional athletes but was later broadened to target the more serious amateur; G Series Natural contained natural ingredients like sea salt, fruit flavors, and natural sweeteners. G Series Fit was a healthier and low-calorie version of the product line to be used before, during, and after personal workouts. Further, Gatorade has invested in the Gatorade Sports Science Institute (GSSI) as a way of ensuring that it continually develops and introduces new products that will help retain and solidify its leadership position in the sports beverages sector.

Sources: Natalie Zmuda, "Another Gatorade Product Line, Another Dedicated Ad Blitz," *Advertising Age*, May 2, 2011; Natalie Zmuda, "Gatorade Planning Another Facelift, New Products in 2010," *Advertising Age*, December 14, 2009; Beverage Industry, "Sports Drink Sales Get Into Shape," July 12, 2011, https://www.bevindustry.com/articles/84828-sports-drink-sales-get-into-shape, accessed November 20, 2018; Gatorade Sports Science Institute, "About GSSI," accessed July 2, 2017, http://www.gssiweb.org/en/about/about-gssi.

of communicating common or shared information and providing synergy across the company's operations, both internally and externally.

As we noted earlier, the practice of combining an existing brand with a new brand is called sub-branding, because the subordinate brand is a means of modifying the superordinate brand. A sub-brand, or hybrid branding, strategy can also allow for the creation of specific brand beliefs. Pepsi is working hard to create a number of sub-brands for its Gatorade brand.

Sub-branding thus creates a stronger connection to the company or family brand and all the associations that come along with that. At the same time, developing sub-brands also allows for the creation of brand-specific beliefs. This more detailed information can help customers better understand how products vary and which particular product may be the right one for them.

Sub-brands also help organize selling efforts so that salespeople and retailers have a clear picture of how the product line is organized and how best to sell it. For example, one of the main advantages to Nike of continually creating sub-brands in its basketball line with Air Max Lebron, Nike Zoom Kobe, as well as the very popular Jordan line, is to generate retail interest and enthusiasm. These sub-brands have helped Nike retain its leadership position within the athletic footwear market. As of 2016, Nike owned 31 percent of the percent share of the global athletic footwear market,[16] and within the basketball category, controls 90 percent of the U.S. market.[17]

Marketers can employ a host of brand elements as part of a sub-brand, including name, product form, shape, graphics, color, and version. By skillfully combining new and existing brand elements, they can effectively signal the intended similarity or fit of a new extension with its parent brand.

The ***principle of simplicity*** is based on the need to provide the right amount of branding information to consumers—no more and no less. The desired number of levels of the brand hierarchy depends on the complexity of the product line or product mix, and thus on the combination of shared and separate brand associations the company would like to link to any one product.

With relatively simple low-involvement products—such as light bulbs, batteries, and chewing gum—the branding strategy often consists of an individual or perhaps a family brand combined with modifiers that describe differences in product features. For example, for years, GE marketed three main brands of general-purpose light bulbs (Edison, Reveal, and Energy Smart) combined with designations for basic functionality (Standard, Reader, and three-way), aesthetics (soft white and daylight), and performance (40, 60, and 100 watts). With the advent of the LED technological revolution, GE has released a slew of new products, including a new type of light bulb that specializes in lighting for your life and sleep. C by GE is a Smart Bulb that connects with consumers' smartphones to enable them to control the lighting in the room. The C-Life bulb is specialized for every room in the house, to provide the optimal levels of brightness. C-Sleep, on the other hand, supports the body's natural sleep cycle by providing dimmer lights. Overall, GE has expanded their brand offerings to include generalized and specialized products for consumers, depending on their needs and wants.[18]

A complex set of products—such as automobiles, computers, or other durable goods—requires more levels of the hierarchy. Thus, Samsung has family brand names such as Galaxy to denote one set of smartphone products and Gear to denote smartwatches and fitness trackers. A company with a strong corporate brand selling a relatively narrow set of products, such as luxury automobiles, can more easily use nondescriptive alphanumeric product names because consumers strongly identify with the parent brand, as Acura found out.

ACURA

Honda grew from humble origins as a motorcycle manufacturer to become a top automobile import competitor in the United States. Recognizing that future sales growth would come from more upscale customers, it set out in the early 1980s to compete with European luxury cars. Since Honda's image of dependable, functional, and economical cars did not have the cachet to appeal to this segment, the company created the new Acura division. However, after meeting initial success, sales began to drop. Research revealed part of the problem: Acura's Legend, Integra, and Vigor sub-brand names did not communicate luxury and order in the product line as well as the alphanumeric branding scheme of competitors BMW, Mercedes, Lexus, and Infiniti. Honda decided that the strength of the brand should lie in the Acura name. Thus, despite the fact that it had spent nearly $600 million on advertising Acura sub-brands over the previous eight years to build their equity, the firm announced a new alphanumeric branding scheme in the winter of 1995: the 2.5 TL and 3.2 TL (for Touring Luxury) sedan series, the 3.5 RL, the 2.2 CL, and 3.0 CL, and the RSX series. By 2017, all Acura cars are coded by a three letter combination, an "L" representing their line of sedans, a "D" representing their Sport Utility models and an "S" to signify their sport car. All of these three letter combinations end in an "X", like the NSX super-car for example. Acura spokesperson Mike Spencer said, "It used to be that people said they owned or drove a Legend . . . . Now they say they drive an Acura, and that's what we wanted." Introducing new models with new names paid off, and sales subsequently rose. Although Acura solved its branding problems, a perceived lack of styling has plagued the brand, and in recent years, the company has struggled to keep up with its luxury compatriots.

Acura's brand name features an alphanumeric branding scheme to distinguish across multiple luxury models.

Sources: David Kiley, "I'd Like to Buy a Vowel, Drivers Say," *USA Today*, August 9, 2000; Fara Werner, "Remaking of a Legend," *Brandweek*, April 25, 1994, 23–28; Neal Templin, "Japanese Luxury-Car Makers Unveiling Cheaper Models in Bid to Attract Buyers," *The Wall Street Journal*, February 9, 1995; T. L. Stanley and Kathy Tryer, "Acura Plays Numbers Game to Fortify Future," *Brandweek*, February 20, 1995, 3; Michelle Krebs, "Acura: Can Style Save Honda's Luxury Brand," *Edmunds Auto Observer*, March 20, 2008; Alan Ohnsman, "Honda Hopes New Acura ILX Helps Keep Gen-Y Out of Lexus, BMW," *Bloomberg News*, December 12, 2011; Richard Bremner, "BMW Mulls New Naming Strategies for Car Brands," www.insideline.com, July 28, 2011; Stefan Constantinescu, "Nokia to Change How They Name Devices Yet Again, Switching to BMW-like 500/600/700 Series Model Numbers," www.intomobile.com, June 28, 2011.

It is difficult to brand a product with more than three levels of brand names without overwhelming or confusing consumers. A better approach might be to introduce multiple brands at the same level (multiple family brands) and expand the depth of the branding strategy.

Desired Awareness and Image at Each Hierarchy Level. How much awareness and what types of associations should marketers create for brand elements at each level? Achieving the desired level of awareness and strength, favorability, and uniqueness of brand associations may take some time and call for a considerable change in consumer perceptions. Assuming marketers use some type of sub-branding strategy for two or more brand levels, two general principles—*relevance and differentiation*—should guide them at each level of the brand knowledge creation process.

The *principle of relevance* is based on the advantages of efficiency and economy. Marketers should create associations that are relevant to as many brands nested at the level below as possible, especially at the corporate or family brand level. The greater the value of an association in the firm's marketing, the more efficient and economical it is to consolidate this meaning into one brand linked to all these products.[19] For example, Nike's slogan ("Just Do It") reinforces a key point-of-difference for the brand—performance—that is relevant to virtually every product it sells.

The more abstract the association, the more likely it is to be relevant in different product settings. Thus, benefit associations are likely to be extremely advantageous because they can cut across many product categories. For brands with strong product category and attribute associations, however, it can be difficult to create a brand image robust enough to extend into new categories.

For example, Blockbuster struggled to expand its meaning from "a place to rent videos" to "your neighborhood entertainment center" in hopes of creating a broader brand umbrella with greater relevance to more products. However, Blockbuster did not move to expand its brand meaning fast enough as it eventually declared bankruptcy before being acquired via auction by satellite television provider Dish Network in April 2011.[20] As of 2017, Blockbuster only had a few stores operating within the United States.

The ***principle of differentiation*** is based on the disadvantages of redundancy. Marketers should distinguish brands at the same level as much as possible to ensure consumers and retailers can clearly see the distinctions; otherwise, brand variations can easily get out of control.[21] One of the criticisms of marketing at General Motors was that the company had failed to adequately distinguish its family brands of automobiles, perhaps ultimately leading to the demise of the Oldsmobile, Pontiac, and Saturn brands. To better control its inventory and avoid brand proliferation, Procter & Gamble discontinued more than 60 brands, and cash flows improved as a result.[22]

A ***flagship product*** is one that best represents or embodies the brand to consumers. It is often the first product by which the brand gained fame, a widely accepted best seller, or a highly admired or award-winning product. For example, although other products are associated with their brands, flagship products might be soap for Ivory, credit cards for American Express, and cake mix for Betty Crocker.[23] A key issue in designing a brand hierarchy is thus choosing which product should be the core or flagship product.

Flagship products play a key role in the brand portfolio in that marketing them can have short-term benefits (increased sales), as well as long-term benefits (improved brand equity). Recently, Viacom announced its intention to unify its efforts around six flagship brands including MTV, Nickelodeon, Nick Jr., Comedy Central, BET, and Paramount.[24] Sometimes, combining a few products under a single brand umbrella can offer significant efficiencies—for example, Hershey's recently announced its masterbrand strategy, in which it would unify all its advertising under the Hershey masterbrand. This is in tune with what Coca-Cola did recently as well with their various Coke variants and their "Taste the Feeling" campaign. Previously, Chrysler put a lot of marketing effort behind selected models when they were hot sellers, even though they made up only 22 percent of the brand's total sales, because the 300 selected models also appeared to provide a halo over the rest of the Chrysler line. At a time when General Motors sales were declining by 4 percent, Chrysler's sales shot up 10 percent.[25]

Combining Brand Elements from Different Levels.   If we combine multiple brand elements from different levels of the brand hierarchy, we must decide how much emphasis to give each. For example, if we adopt a sub-brand strategy, how much prominence should we give individual brands at the expense of the corporate or family brand?

Principle of Prominence.   The ***prominence*** of a brand element is its relative visibility compared with other brand elements. Prominence depends on several factors, such as order, size, and appearance, as well as semantic associations. A name is generally more prominent when it appears first, is larger, and looks more distinctive. When a brand like Nike adopts a sub-branded strategy, and combines its corporate family brand name Nike with a new individual brand name like Air Max, the relative emphasis on Nike and Air Max helps either the Nike name as the dominant brand name on packaging or Air Max. If the Air Max is more prominent—for example, Air Max by Nike—it would shift the emphasis to the sub-brand name rather than the family name.

The ***principle of prominence*** states that the relative prominence of the brand elements determines which become the primary one(s) and which the secondary one(s). Primary brand elements should convey the main product positioning and points-of-difference. Secondary brand elements convey a more restricted set of supporting associations such as points-of-parity or perhaps an additional point-of-difference. A secondary brand element may also facilitate awareness.

According to the principle of prominence, the more prominent a brand element, the more emphasis consumers will give it in forming their brand opinions. The relative prominence of the individual and the corporate brands will be viewed very literally by consumers, and will therefore affect perceptions and image created for a new product. For example, "Marriott's Courtyard" would be seen as much more of a Marriott hotel than "Courtyard by Marriott" by virtue of having the corporate name first. With a more prominent corporate or family brand, however, feedback effects will be more evident.

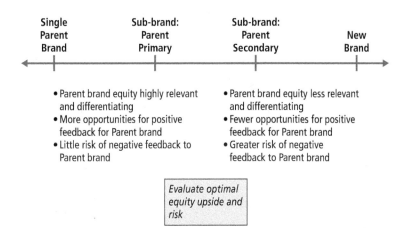

FIGURE 12-7

Branding Strategy
Screen

In some cases, the brand elements may not be explicitly linked at all. In a ***brand endorsement strategy***, a brand element—often the corporate brand name or logo—appears on the package, signage, or product appearance in some way but is not directly included as part of the brand name. For example, General Mills places its "Big G" logo on its cereal packages, but retains distinct brand names such as Cheerios, Wheaties, and Lucky Charms. The brand endorsement strategy presumably establishes the maximum distance between the corporate or family brand and the individual brands, suggesting that it would yield the smallest transfer of brand associations to the new product but, at the same time, minimize the likelihood of any negative feedback effects.

Branding Strategy Screen.   Marketers can use the branding strategy screen displayed in Figure 12-7 to dial up or dial down different brand elements. If a potential new product or service is strongly related to the parent brand such that there is a high likelihood of parent brand equity carryover, and if there is little equity risk, a product descriptor or parent-brand-first sub-brand may make sense.[26]

On the other hand, if a potential new product or service is more removed from the parent brand such that there is a lower likelihood of parent brand equity carryover, or if there is higher equity risk, then a parent-brand-second sub-brand or even a new brand may be more appropriate. In these latter cases, the parent brand may just be used as an endorser.

These pros and cons help determine whether a BH or HOB is the more appropriate strategy. What consumers know about and want from the brand, and how they will actually use it, are also important.

Linking Brand Elements to Multiple Products.   So far, we have highlighted how to apply different brand elements to a particular product—the vertical aspects of the brand hierarchy. Next, we consider how to link any one brand element to multiple products—the horizontal aspects. The ***principle of commonality*** states that the more common brand elements products share, the stronger the linkages between them.

The simplest way to link products is to use the brand element *as is* across them. Adapting the brand, or some part of it, offers additional possibilities for making the connection.

- Hewlett-Packard capitalized on its highly successful LaserJet computer printers to introduce a number of new products using the "Jet" suffix—for example, the DeskJet, PaintJet, ThinkJet, and OfficeJet printers.
- McDonald's has used its "Mc" prefix to introduce a number of products, such as Chicken McNuggets, Egg McMuffin, and the McRib sandwich.
- Donna Karan's DKNY brand, Calvin Klein's CK brand, and Ralph Lauren's Double RL brand rely on initials.
- Apple uses the *i* prefix to unify the brand across a range of products such as the iPod, iPhone, and iPad.

We can also create a relationship between a brand and multiple products with common symbols. For example, corporate brands like Nabisco often place their corporate logo more prominently on their products than their name, creating a strong brand endorsement strategy.

TABLE 12–1 Summary of Brand Architecture Design Principles

Design Objective/Goal	Principle	Definition
Specifying products to introduce	Growth	Investments made in market or product development should be made according to ROI opportunities.
Specifying products to introduce	Survival	Brand extensions must achieve brand equity in their categories
Specifying products to introduce	Synergy	Brand extensions must enhance the equity of the parent brand
Number of levels in hierarchy	Simplicity	Provide the right amount of branding information at each level in hierarchy, balancing the number of shared and separate associations
Achieving awareness and image at each level	Relevance	Create associations at each level that are relevant to as many brands nested at the level below
Achieving awareness and image at each level	Differentiation	Distinguish brands at the same level as much as possible to ensure lack of overlap
Combining elements from different levels	Prominence	Relative visibility of a brand element determines its importance in consumers' perceptions
Combining elements from different levels	Commonality	The more common brand elements products share, the stronger the linkages between them.

Finally, it's often a good idea to logically order brands in a product line to communicate how they are related and to simplify consumer decision making. We can communicate the order through colors (American Express offers Red, Blue, Green, Gold, Platinum, and Black or Centurion cards), numbers (BMW offers its 3-, 5-, and 7-series cars), or other means. This strategy is especially important in developing brand migration pathways for customers to switch among the brands offered by the company. The relative position of a brand within a brand line may also affect consumer perceptions and preferences.[27] A summary of the various design principles provided in this section is summarized in Table 12-1.

CORPORATE BRANDING

Given its fundamental importance in brand architecture, we will go into greater detail on corporate branding. A corporate brand is distinct from a product brand in that it can encompass a much wider range of associations. As detailed in the following paragraphs, a corporate brand name may be more likely to evoke associations of common products and their shared attributes or benefits, people and relationships, programs and values, and corporate credibility.

These associations can have an important effect on the brand equity and market performance of individual products. For example, one research study revealed that consumers with a more favorable corporate image of DuPont were more likely to respond favorably to the claims made in an ad for Stainmaster carpet, and therefore, actually buy the product.[28]

Building and managing a strong corporate brand, however, can necessitate that the firm keep a high public profile, especially to influence and shape some of the more abstract types of associations. The CEO or managing director, if associated with a corporate brand, must also be willing to maintain a more public profile to help communicate news and information, as well as perhaps provide a symbol of current marketing activities. At the same time, a firm must also be willing to subject itself to more scrutiny and be extremely transparent in its values, activities, and programs. Corporate brands have to be comfortable with a high level of openness.

A corporate brand offers a host of potential marketing advantages, but only if corporate brand equity is carefully built and nurtured—a challenging task. Many marketing winners in the coming years will, therefore, be those firms that properly build and manage corporate brand equity. Branding Brief 12-4 describes a closely related concept—corporate reputation—and how we can look at it from the perspective of consumers and other firms.[29]

Corporate brand equity is the differential response by consumers, customers, employees, other firms, or any relevant constituency to the words, actions, communications, products, or services provided by an identified corporate brand entity. In other words, positive corporate brand equity occurs when a relevant constituency responds more favorably to a corporate ad campaign,

BRANDING BRIEF 12-4

Corporate Reputations: The Most Admired U.S. Companies

Two annual surveys offer insights into corporate reputation. Every year, *Fortune* magazine conducts a comprehensive survey of business perceptions of the companies with the best corporate reputations. The 2017 survey included the 1,500 largest U.S. and non-U.S. companies in 64 industry groups. Approximately 3,800 senior executives, outside directors, and financial analysts were asked to select the 10 companies they admired most, regardless of industry. To create industry lists, respondents rated companies in their industry on nine criteria: (1) quality of management; (2) quality of products or services; (3) innovativeness; (4) long-term investment value; (5) financial soundness; (6) ability to attract, develop, and keep talented people; (7) responsibility to the community and the environment; (8) wise use of corporate assets; and (9) global competitiveness.

Since the 2010 ranking, many of the companies have changed. Some companies, however, such as Apple, have remained in the top 10 for years. *Fortune's* top 10 most admired companies from 2017 and their rankings are as follows:

Rank	Company	Rank	Company
1	Apple	6	Alphabet
2	Amazon.com	7	General Electric
3	Starbucks	8	Southwest Airlines
4	Berkshire Hathaway	9	Facebook
5	Disney	10	Microsoft

Another informative survey, the RQ 2017 study of corporate reputations, conducted each year since 1999 by Harris

Interactive and the Reputation Institute, demonstrated both the enduring character of corporate reputations but their ability to change quickly at the same time. Researchers determine which companies should be rated on the basis of a preliminary sampling of more than 30,000 members of the U.S. general public, utilizing the proprietary Harris Poll online panel. Respondents are asked first to identify the 60 most visible companies and then to rate them on 20 different attributes that make up the Reputation Quotient (RQ) instrument. The attributes are then grouped into six different reputation dimensions: emotional appeal, products and services, social responsibility, vision and leadership, workplace environment, and financial performance. The study also includes a number of questions that help provide a comprehensive understanding of how the public perceived firms' reputations. The 2017 rankings are as follows:

Rank	Company	Rank	Company
1	Amazon	6	UPS
2	Wegmans	7	Walt Disney
3	Publix	8	Google
4	Johnson & Johnson	9	Tesla
5	Apple	10	3M Company

Sources: Fortune, "World's Most Admired Companies," http://fortune.com/worlds-most-admired-companies/, accessed November 20, 2018; "Corporate Reputation Is Politically Polarized: The Reputation of America's 100 Most Visible Companies," *The Harris Poll,* N.D.

THE SCIENCE OF BRANDING 12-2

Brand Architecture Strategies: House of Brands or Branded House?

As noted earlier, two types of brand architecture strategies are typically used by firms. One is branded house (BH), in which a single corporate brand name is used across all entities in the portfolio (e.g., GE, 3M, IBM); house of brands (HOB), wherein distinct brands not linked to the corporate brand are cultivated for specific market segments (e.g., P&G with Tide and Cheer); and a mixed architecture that combines all other alternatives. In one study, researchers found that BH generated the highest financial values (using stock market returns) and concluded that markets might not value HOB appropriately, as investors may underappreciate that a multitude of brands distributes risk over more brands.

Later research examined the implications of these brand architecture strategies by examining the effects of a broader range of branding strategies including sub-branding and endorsed branding strategies on both stock market returns as well as stock market risk. Their research found that brand architecture strategies can have significant implications for a variety of different types of risk associated with a firm and can be

related to impact on reputation, dilution, cannibalization, and brand stretch. Sub-branding may cause a brand to overextend, thereby exacerbating the risk associated with a firm. Therefore, a brand such as FedEx may stand to gain from having a number of sub-brands, but should also be mindful of potential risks to the brand name associated with over extension or dilution.

Researchers have also examined how characteristics of a brand portfolio might impact marketing and financial performance of firms, including: (1) number of brands owned; (2) number of segments in which they are marketed; (3) degree to which the brands in the firm's portfolio compete with one another; and (4) consumer perceptions of the quality and price of the brands in the firm's portfolio. This research has shown that these characteristics can have a significant impact on a variety of metrics capturing a firm's effectiveness in the market place, its efficiency of marketing spending, and overall financial performance.

Taken together, managers should be mindful that brand architecture strategies that they employ may impact the stock returns accruing to the firm as well as the volatility and exposure (i.e., risk) associated with those returns. The BH seems to provide significant efficiencies that investors value, and this translates into higher stock market returns. The impact of brand architecture (e.g., use of sub-branding strategies) on risk to a brand name also impacts overall stock market risk of a firm. Finally, context factors (e.g., size of target audiences) should be kept in mind to assess the impact of a brand on overall firm performance and stock market valuation. These insights are, in large part, due to the valuable role of brands in shaping the future potential of a firm, and the brand architecture strategy can signal to investors how valuable or risky a firm's brand assets are.

Sources: Vithala R. Rao, Manoj K. Agarwal, and Denise Dahlhoff. "How Is Manifest Branding Strategy Related to the Intangible Value of a Corporation?," *Journal of Marketing* 68, no. 4 (2004): 126–141; Liwu Hsu, Susan Fournier, and Shuba Srinivasan, "Brand Architecture Strategy and Firm Value: How Leveraging, Separating, and Distancing the Corporate Brand Affects Risk and Returns," *Journal of the Academy of Marketing Science* 44, no. 2 (2016): 261–280; Neil A. Morgan and Lopo L. Rego, "Brand Portfolio Strategy and Firm Performance," *Journal of Marketing* 73, no. 1 (2009): 59–74.

a corporate-branded product or service, a corporate-issued PR release, and so on than if the same offering were attributed to an unknown or fictitious company.

A corporate brand can be a powerful means for firms to express themselves in a way that is not tied to their specific products or services. The Science of Branding 12-2 describes how brand architecture decisions can play an important role in firm performance, both in terms of returns from stock market, as well as riskiness of the firm.

Corporate Image Dimensions

A corporate image will depend on a number of factors, such as the products a company makes, the actions it takes, and the manner in which it communicates to consumers. This section highlights some of the different types of associations that are likely to be linked to a corporate brand and that can affect brand equity (see Figure 12-8).[30]

Common Product Attributes, Benefits, or Attitudes.   Like individual brands, a corporate or company brand may evoke in consumers a strong association to a product attribute (Hershey with chocolate), type of user (BMW with yuppies), usage situation (Club Med with fun times), or overall judgment (3M with innovation).

If a corporate brand is linked to products across diverse categories, then some of its strongest associations are likely to be those intangible attributes, abstract benefits, or attitudes that span each of the different product categories. For example, companies may be associated with products or services that solve particular problems (Black & Decker), bring excitement and fun to certain activities (Nintendo), are built with the highest quality standards (Motorola), contain advanced or innovative features (Rubbermaid), or represent market leadership (Hertz).

Two specific product-related corporate image associations—high quality and innovation—deserve special attention.

A *high-quality corporate image association* creates consumer perceptions that a company makes products of the highest quality. A number of different organizations like J.D. Power, *Consumer*

Common Product Attributes, Benefits, or Attitudes
Quality
Innovativeness

People and Relationships
Customer orientation

Values and Programs
Concern with environment
Social responsibility

Corporate Credibility
Expertise
Trustworthiness
Likability

FIGURE 12-8

Some Important Corporate Image Associations

3M's corporate brand name stands for innovation.

Reports, and various trade publications for automobiles rate products. Nowadays, a number of reviews and ratings Web sites provide quality scores for products and services. For example, Yelp and Travelocity provide valuable ratings information for the restaurant and travel sectors, respectively. Quality is one of the most important, if not *the* most important, decision factors for consumers.

An ***innovative corporate image association*** creates consumer perceptions of a company as developing new and unique marketing programs, especially with respect to product introductions or improvements. Keller and Aaker experimentally showed how different corporate image strategies—being innovative, environmentally concerned, or involved in the community—could affect corporate credibility and strategically benefit the firm by increasing the acceptance of brand extensions.[31] Interestingly, consumers viewed a company with an innovative corporate image as not only expert but also trustworthy and likable. Being innovative is seen as being modern and up-to-date, investing in research and development, employing the most advanced manufacturing capabilities, and introducing the newest product features.

An image priority for many Japanese companies—from consumer product companies such as Kao to more technically oriented companies such as Canon—is to be perceived as innovative.[32] Perceived innovativeness is also a key competitive weapon and priority for firms in other countries. Michelin ("A Better Way Forward") describes how its commitment to the environment, security, value, and driving pleasure has been spurring innovation. Branding Brief 12-5 describes how 3M has developed an innovative culture and image.

People and Relationships.   Corporate image associations may reflect characteristics of the employees of the company. Although focusing on employees is a natural positioning strategy for service firms like Southwest Airlines, Avis car rental, and Ritz-Carlton hotels

BRANDING BRIEF 12-5
Corporate Innovation at 3M

3M has fostered a culture of innovation and improvisation from its very beginnings. In 1904, the company's directors were faced with a failed mining operation, but they turned the leftover grit and waste into a revolutionary new product: sandpaper. Today, 3M makes more than 50,000 products, including adhesives, contact lenses, and optical films. Over the last century, some of its noteworthy product launches include Scotch masking and transparent tape, Scotchgard fabric protector, and Post-it Notes.

Each year, 3M launches scores of new products, regularly ranking among the top 10 U.S. companies each year in patents received. Under new Chief Technology Officer Ashish Khandpur, 3M has raised their R&D spending budget from 5.5 percent of revenue in 2012 to 6 percent by 2017, an increase that represents about $160 million annually. The firm is able to consistently produce innovations in part because it promotes a corporate environment that facilitates new discoveries:

- 3M encourages everyone, not just engineers, to become product champions. The company's "15 percent time" lets all employees spend up to 15 percent of their time working on projects of personal interest. A culture of healthy competition among highly motivated peers helps 3M innovate and create.

- Each promising new idea is assigned to a multidisciplinary venture team headed by an executive champion. 3M hands Golden Step awards each year to the venture teams whose new products earned more than $2 million in U.S. sales or $4 million in worldwide sales within three years of commercial introduction.

- 3M expects some failures and uses them as opportunities to learn how to make products that work. It is also very selective

about acquisitions, seeing them as only supplementary to organic growth and internal innovations and developments.

- Starting in 2010, 3M has introduced social networks into its innovation process, inviting 75,000 global employees and more than 1,200 other people to participate in its annual Markets of the Future brainstorming session. More than 700 new ideas have been generated, leading to nine new markets for the company to explore.

Some of the innovations that 3M focused on in 2017 include utilizing Information and Communications Technologies (ICTs) to foster innovation, economic growth, and progress, helping Western Europe achieve the Industry 4.0 plan which will make the manufacturing sector more efficient through further computerization, and increasing sustainability throughout their organization's infrastructure.

Sources: 3M 2010 Annual Report, www.3m.com; Chuck Salter, "The Nine Passions of 3M's Mauro Porcini," *Fast Company*, October 10, 2011, https://www.fastcompany.com/1777592/nine-passions-3ms-mauro-porcini, accessed November 20, 2018; Kaomi Goetz, "How 3M Gave Everyone Days Off and Created an Innovation Dynamo," *Fast Company Design*, February 1, 2011, https://www.fastcompany.com/1663137/how-3m-gave-everyone-days-off-and-created-an-innovation-dynamo, accessed November 20, 2018; Trefis Team, "What Trends Will Ensure Growth for 3M in Western Europe in the Future?," *Forbes*, June 9, 2017, accessed June 19, 2017, https://www.forbes.com/sites/greatspeculations/2017/06/09/what-trends-will-ensure-growth-for-3m-in-western-europe-in-the-future/#6156c5ea1548; Lewis Krauskopf, "3M's New Technology Chief Has a Bigger Budget, Bigger Goal," *Reuters*, June 1, 2015, accessed June 19, 2017, http://www.reuters.com/article/us-3m-research-idUSKBN0OH3BV20150601.

as well as retailers like L.L.Bean and Nordstrom, manufacturing firms like DuPont and others have also used it in the past. Their rationale is that the traits that employees exhibit will directly or indirectly influence consumers about the products the firm makes or the services it provides. Conversely, the lack of employee satisfaction could work against a strong corporate image. Recently, the high-flying technology company, Uber, has been the focus of significant controversy because of accusations of a "toxic office culture" in which female employees are allegedly subject to harassment.

Consumers may themselves form more abstract impressions of a firm's employees, especially in a services setting. One major public utility company was described by customers as "male, 35–40 years old, middle class, married with children, wearing a flannel shirt and khaki pants, who would be reliable, competent, professional, intelligent, honest, ethical, and business-oriented." On the downside, these same customers also described the utility as "distant, impersonal, and self-focused," suggesting an important area for improvement in its corporate brand image.

Retail stores also derive brand equity from their employees. For example, from its origins as a small shoe store, Seattle-based Nordstrom has become one of the nation's leading fashion specialty retailers through a commitment to quality, value, selection, and, especially, service. Legendary for its personalized touch and willingness to go to extraordinary lengths to satisfy its customers, Nordstrom creates brand equity largely through the efforts of its salespeople and the relationships they develop with customers.

Thus, a ***customer-focused corporate image association*** creates consumer perceptions of a company as responsive to and caring about its customers. Consumers believe their voice will be heard and that the company has their best interests in mind. Often, this philosophy is reflected throughout the marketing program and communicated through advertising.

Values and Programs.   Corporate image associations may reflect company values and programs that do not always directly relate to the products. Firms can run corporate-image ad campaigns to describe to consumers, employees, and others their philosophy and actions with respect to organizational, social, political, or economic issues.

For example, many recent corporate advertising campaigns have focused on environmental issues and social responsibility. A ***socially responsible corporate image association*** portrays the company as contributing to community programs, supporting artistic and social activities, and generally attempting to improve the welfare of society as a whole. An ***environmentally concerned corporate image association*** projects a company whose products protect or improve the environment and make more effective use of scarce natural resources. We consider corporate responsibility in more detail later, and Brand Focus 12.0 looks at the broader issue of cause marketing, in which British Airways has been a pioneer.

BRITISH AIRWAYS

An innovative cause marketer, British Airways has successfully introduced several noteworthy cause programs. It first partnered with UNICEF in 1994 for the cleverly titled "Change for Good" campaign, based on a very simple idea: foreign coins are particularly difficult to exchange at banks and currency exchanges. So passengers were asked to place any surplus coins—or bills, for that matter—in envelopes provided by British Airways, which donated them directly to UNICEF. British Airways advertised the program on the backs of seat cards, during an in-flight video, and with in-flight announcements with such success that fellow international carriers in the Oneworld Alliance began to participate. In June 2010, the program was replaced with the Flying Start program. This new program was a partnership with Comic Relief UK, a successful charity started by comedians whose aim is to "bring about positive and lasting change in the lives of poor and disadvantaged people." To publicize the new program, the airlines teamed up with Guinness World Records for the "Highest Stand-Up Comedy Gig in the World." Three comedians entertained 75 lucky passengers for a two-and-a-half-hour champagne flight. Flying Start was structured like Change for Good—donations were collected in-flight as well as online and at Travelex currency exchange locations in U.K. airports—but had a stronger local angle. The program raised almost $3 million in its first year, with a goal to "improve the lives of hundreds of thousands of children living in the U.K. and in some of the poorest countries across the world."[33] In 2017, British Airways was named favorite brand in the U.K. for the fourth year in a row.[34]

British Airways cemented its reputation as a reputable global corporate brand through various cause-related marketing programs.

Corporate Credibility.   A particularly important set of abstract brand associations is corporate credibility. As defined in Chapter 2, corporate credibility measures the extent to which consumers believe a firm can design and deliver products and services that satisfy their needs and wants. It is the reputation the firm has achieved in the marketplace. Corporate credibility—as well as success and leadership—depends on three factors:

1. *Corporate expertise:* The extent to which consumers see the company as able to competently make and sell its products or conduct its services.
2. *Corporate trustworthiness:* The extent to which consumers believe the company is motivated to be honest, dependable, and sensitive to customer needs.
3. *Corporate likability:* The extent to which consumers see the company as likable, attractive, prestigious, dynamic, and so forth.

While consumers who perceive the brand as credible are more likely to consider and choose it, a strong and credible reputation can offer additional benefits.[35] L.L.Bean is a company with much corporate credibility.

A highly credible company may be treated more favorably by other external constituencies, such as government or legal officials. It also may be able to attract better-qualified employees and motivate existing employees to be more productive and loyal. As one Shell Oil employee remarked as part of some internal corporate identity research, "If you're really proud of where you work, I think you put a little more thought into what you did to help get them there."

A strong corporate reputation can help a firm survive a brand crisis and avert public outrage that could otherwise depress sales or block expansion plans. As Harvard's Stephen Greyser notes, "Corporate reputation . . . can serve as a capital account of favorable attitudes to help buffer corporate trouble."

L.L.BEAN

A brand seen as highly credible, outdoors product retailer L.L.Bean attempts to earn its customers' trust every step of the way—by providing pre-purchase advice, secure transactions, best-in-class delivery, and easy returns and exchanges. Founded in 1912, L.L.Bean backs its efforts with a 100-percent satisfaction guarantee as well as its Golden Rule: "Sell good merchandise at a reasonable profit, treat your customers like human beings, and they will always come back for more." Now a billion-dollar brand that celebrated its 100th anniversary in 2012, the company retains its original image of being passionate about the outdoors and believing profoundly in honesty, product quality, and customer service.

L.L.Bean is a credible, trustworthy brand that promises best-in-class service.

Summary.   Many intangible brand associations can transcend the physical characteristics of products, providing valuable sources of brand equity and serving as critical points-of-parity or points-of-difference.[36] Companies have a number of means—indirect or direct—of creating these associations. But they must "talk the talk" and "walk the walk" by communicating to consumers and backing up claims with concrete programs that consumers can easily understand or even experience.

Managing the Corporate Brand

A number of specific issues arise in managing a corporate brand. Here we consider three: corporate social responsibility, corporate image campaigns, and corporate name changes.

Corporate Social Responsibility.   Some marketing experts believe consumers are increasingly using their perceptions of a firm's role in society in their purchase decisions. For example, consumers want to know how a firm treats its employees, shareholders, local neighbors, and other stakeholders or constituents.[37] As the head of a large advertising agency put it: "The only sustainable competitive advantage any business has is its reputation."[38]

Consistent with this reasoning, 91 percent of respondents in a large global survey of financial analysts and others in the investment community agreed that a company that fails to look after its reputation will endure financial difficulties. Moreover, 96 percent said the CEO's reputation was fairly, very, or extremely important in influencing their ratings.[39]

The realization that consumers and others may be interested in issues beyond product characteristics and associations has prompted much marketing activity to establish the proper corporate image.[40] Some firms are putting corporate social responsibility at the very core of their existence.[41] Ben & Jerry's has created a strong association as a "do-gooder" by using Fair Trade ingredients and donating 7.5 percent of its pre-tax profits to various causes. Its annual Social and Environmental Assessment Report details the company's main social mission goals and spells out how it is attempting to achieve them.

TOMS Shoes used cause marketing to launch its brand.

TOMS SHOES

When entrepreneur and former reality-show contestant Blake Mycoskie visited Argentina in 2006, he saw masses of children who suffered health risks and interrupted schooling due to a simple lack of shoes. Once home, Mycoskie started TOMS Shoes, whose name conveys "Shoes for a Better Tomorrow." The company started with a simple vision, provide one pair of shoes to a child in need with every pair purchased. The shoes themselves are based on the classic *alpargata* style found in Argentina. They are sold online and through top retailers such as Whole Foods, Nordstrom, and Neiman Marcus. TOMS's donated shoes—black, unisex canvas slip-ons with a sturdy sole—can now be found on the feet of more than 35 million children in developing countries such as Argentina and Ethiopia.[42] TOMS also has a strong social media presence with almost 4 million likes on Facebook. By 2017, Mycoskie has expanded TOMS to giving not only shoes on a One for One model, but now has campaigns to give the gifts of sight, water, safe birth, and kindness to those in the developing world.

Toms Shoes' "One for One" campaign began in 2006, when the company's founder saw that Argentinian children did not have adequate shoes to protect their feet.

Brand Focus 12.0 outlines the advantages of cause marketing, the obstacles they face, and how to successfully design a successful campaign, with particular emphasis on green marketing.

Corporate Image Campaigns. **Corporate image campaigns** are designed to create associations to the corporate brand as a whole; consequently, they tend to ignore or downplay individual products or sub-brands.[43] As we would expect, some of the biggest spenders on these kinds of campaigns are well-known firms that use their company or corporate name prominently in their branding strategies, such as Apple, Google, GE, Toyota, British Telecom, IBM, Novartis, and Deutsche Bank.

Corporate image campaigns have been criticized as an ego-stroking waste of time, and they can be easy for consumers to ignore. However, a strong campaign can provide invaluable marketing and financial benefits by allowing the firm to express itself and embellish the meaning of its corporate brand and associations for its individual products, as Philips did.

PHILIPS

In recent years, Philips has focused on simplifying not only the products it produces, but also how the business is run. In November 2013, the brand unveiled a new, streamlined shield logo to keep in line with its overall outlook of innovation through simplicity. With that redesign, Philips also unveiled its new slogan "Innovation and You" highlighting the company's mission of improving people's lives through meaningful innovation.[44] One of its latest products, Norelco OneBlade, furthers the mission of innovation through simplicity with the slogan, "You only need OneBlade." To reposition itself as a more consumer-friendly brand, Philips Consumer Electronics originally launched a global corporate advertising campaign in 2004 that ran for a number of years. Centered on the company's new tagline, "Sense and Simplicity," that replaced the nine-year-old "Let's Make Things Better." The ads showcased innovative Philips products like the Flat TV with Ambilight, the HDRW720 DVD recorder with built-in hard disk, and the Sonicare Elite toothbrush, all fitting in effortlessly with users' sophisticated lifestyles. Philips president and CEO Gerard Kleisterlee described the repositioning campaign by saying, "Our route to innovation isn't about complexity—it's about simplicity, which we believe will be the new cool."[45]

Philips has focused on innovation and simplicity as the two key pillars of its brand positioning as a consumer-friendly brand.

To maximize the probability of success, however, marketers must clearly define the objectives of a corporate image campaign *and* carefully measure results against them.[46] A number of different objectives are possible in a corporate brand campaign:[47]

- Build awareness of the company and the nature of its business.
- Create favorable attitudes and perceptions of company credibility.
- Link beliefs that can be leveraged by product-specific marketing.
- Make a favorable impression on the financial community.
- Motivate present employees and attract better recruits.
- Influence public opinion on issues.

In terms of building customer-based brand equity, the first three objectives are particularly critical. A corporate image campaign can enhance awareness and create a more positive image of the corporate brand that will influence consumer evaluations and increase the equity associated with individual products and any related sub-brands. In certain cases, however, the latter three objectives can take on greater importance.[48]

A corporate image campaign may be useful when mergers or acquisitions transform the company. Consolidation in the financial services industry has caused firms like Zurich and UBS to develop and implement strong corporate branding strategies.

Like product advertising, corporate image campaigns are becoming more creative and often include digital strategies as an integral component. Many of these campaigns include a philanthropic component to strengthen their appeal to consumers, for example, ConAgra Foods' campaign to end child hunger and Johnson & Johnson's "Care to Recycle" campaign.

Unlike a corporate image campaign that presents the brand in abstract terms with few, if any, references to specific products, **brand line campaigns** promote a range of products associated with a brand line. By showing consumers the different uses or benefits of the multiple products offered by a brand, brand line ads or promotions can be particularly useful in building brand awareness, clarifying brand meaning, and suggesting additional usage applications. Sometimes a brand line campaign will emphasize a common thread running through all the products for a brand, as was the case with General Mills.

GENERAL MILLS

In 2004, General Mills elected to make all its cereals with 100 percent whole grains so that each provided at least half a serving (8 grams) in every bowl. Despite the many benefits of whole grains, including lowered risks of chronic diseases such as heart disease, certain cancers, and diabetes, only 5 percent of U.S. consumers at that time got the minimum three daily servings recommended by the U.S. Dietary Guidelines for Americans. Much consumer confusion existed about what whole grains were and why it mattered. Based on research showing that consumers read their cereal boxes an average of 2.7 times, General Mills decided to promote the health benefits of 100 percent whole-grain cereal on all its product packaging, using the U.S. Department of Agriculture food guide pyramid. An advertising campaign also touted the switch to whole grains. The program met with much success, essentially adding 1.5 billion servings of whole grains to the U.S. diet each year. In 2011, General Mills partnered with Dr. Travis Stork, host of a popular daytime talk show, to donate 1 million servings of whole grain to families in need.[49] In 2015, General Mills further pledged to remove artificial flavors and colors from all of its cereals, with a goal of having all-natural ingredients in all its cereals within a two-year period.[50]

Corporate Name Changes.   Corporate names may have to change for many reasons, but they should be the right reasons pursued in the right way.

Rationale.   A merger or acquisition is often the impetus to reevaluate naming strategies and weigh the existing and potential equity of each brand in its new context.[51]

- A new corporate name arising from a merger or acquisition may be based on some combination of two existing names, if they are strong. For example, when FedEx and Kinko's merged into a single entity, they created a joint FedExKinko's brand. J.P. Morgan & Co. and Chase Manhattan Corporation became JPMorgan Chase after their merger.
- If there is an imbalance in brand equity, the firm typically chooses the name with more inherent brand equity and relegates the other to a sub-brand role or eliminates it altogether. When Citicorp merged with Travelers, the latter's name was dropped, although its familiar red umbrella symbol was retained as part of the new Citigroup brand look. Similarly, United's name was combined with Continental's globe logo when those two air carriers merged.
- Finally, if neither name has the desired brand equity, a completely new name can signal new capabilities.

Clearly, there are many nuances to identifying brand names for acquisition, the naming strategy for the newly acquired brand, and significant considerations in managing a newly acquired brand. The Science of Branding 12-3 section, which follows, outlines what researchers have uncovered about brand acquisitions.

THE SCIENCE OF BRANDING 12-3
When Brands Trade Hands

The world of marketing is rife with examples of brands trading hands. Building products and brands internally can be slow and costly, and new product failure rates are high. One important implication is that a brand has different growth prospects depending on which firm owns it. This is particularly a concern in a merger or acquisition context. Many firms acquire brands from external sources to improve their competitive strength or to establish a presence in a new market or segment. For example, Estee Lauder announced that it had acquired *By Kilian*, a Paris-based prestige fragrance brand, for an undisclosed sum. Nantucket Nectars, currently owned by Dr. Pepper Snapple Group, was acquired from Cadbury Schweppes PLC. Cadbury Schweppes PLC, in turn, had acquired the brand from Ocean Spray. Some high-profile acquisitions from the past few years are listed in Table 12-2, along with the acquisition price. As brand acquisitions are increasing in frequency and scope, a series of academic research papers have explored issues surrounding such acquisitions.

A key question that arises is whether these acquisitions benefit the acquiring firm by increasing its market share and by adding shareholder value. If so, under what conditions?

Researchers have found that when the acquiring firm's marketing capabilities overall were higher, investors increased how they valued the brand acquisition. One study collected stock market data on brand and product acquisition announcements in multiple business-to-consumer industries over a 20-year-period to see how shareholders reacted to the announcement of an acquisition. Their findings implied that managers should carefully consider the nature of the resources available internally to ensure successful transfer of brands from the target to the acquiring firm. According to these researchers, managers should ensure that the following conditions are present to achieve successful transfer: (1) a strong target brand with significant brand equity, (2) strong organizational marketing management capability within the acquiring firm, and (3) a low level of acquiring firm diversification. The potential for brand name change is also a factor in the success of an acquisition, as investors realize that there are significant risks to a brand's equity when an acquired brand undergoes a significant name change.

Taken together, brand acquisitions represent a viable alternative to organic growth, particularly for managers faced with high new product development costs and high rates of failure. The success of an acquisition depends a great deal on maintaining focus and dedicating resources to the acquired brand. Many brands, even after acquisition, can become neglected or forgotten, especially if the firm has an expansive set of brands. In addition to focus and resources, the impact on brand architecture

TABLE 12–2   Selected List of Major Acquisitions Over the Years

Year	Acquirer	Target	Acquisition Price ($)
2000	General Mills	Pillsbury	10.5 billion
2005	Procter & Gamble	Gillette	57 billion
2006	Johnson & Johnson	Pfizer	16.6 billion
2007	Coca-Cola	Vitaminwater	4.1 billion
2010	General Mills	Mountain High yogurt	84.8 million
2013	Fairfax Financial	Blackberry	5 billion
2016	Microsoft	LinkedIn	28.1 billion

and potential for name change should be carefully considered along with the acquiring firm's marketing and brand capabilities to ensure success in acquisitions.

Sources: Kevin Lane Keller and Don Lehmann, "Assessing Brand Potential," in special issue, "Brand Value and Valuation," of *Journal of Brand Management* 17, eds. Randall Raggio and Robert P. Leone (September 2009): 6–17; Kevin Lane Keller and David A. Aaker, "The Effects of Sequential Introduction of Brand Extensions," *Journal of Marketing Research* 29 (February 1992): 35–50; Randle Raggio and Robert P. Leone, "The Theoretical Separation of Brand Equity and Brand Value: Managerial Implications for Strategic Planning," *Journal of Brand Management* 14 (May 2007): 380–395; Yana Damoiseau, William C. Black, and Randle D. Raggio, "Brand Creation vs. Acquisition in Portfolio Expansion Strategy," *Journal of Product & Brand Management* 20, no. 4 (2011): 268–281; Michael A. Wiles, Neil A. Morgan, and Lopo L. Rego, "The Effect of Brand Acquisition and Disposal on Stock Returns," *Journal of Marketing* 76, no. 1, (2012): 38–58; S. Cem Bahadir, Sundar G. Bharadwaj, and Rajendra K. Srivastava (2008), "Financial Value of Brands in Mergers and Acquisitions: Is Value in the Eye of the Beholder?," *Journal of Marketing* 72 (November) 49–64; Casey Newmeyer, Vanitha Swaminathan, and John Hulland (2016), "When Products and Brands Trade Hands: A Framework for Acquisition Success," *Journal of Marketing Theory and Practice* 24 (2), 129–146.

Mergers and acquisitions may necessitate brand name changes, but other factors may also prompt name changes including brand divestitures, leveraged buyouts, or the sale of assets. When Andersen Consulting was allowed to separate from Arthur Andersen following an arbitrator's ruling in 2000, it was required to stop using its old name by the end of the year. After an extensive naming search and rebranding project, the firm was renamed "Accenture"—an employee suggestion meant to connote an "accent on the future." Having a new name proved especially fortuitous when Arthur Andersen was convicted of obstruction of justice in 2002 in the wake of the Enron scandal and ceased to operate as a business. Some residual negative perceptions from Arthur Andersen would likely have transferred to the Andersen Consulting brand.

Significant shifts in corporate strategy may necessitate name changes. U.S. Steel changed its name to USX to downplay the importance of steel and metal in its product mix. Allegheny Airlines changed its name to USAir when it moved from being a regional to a national carrier, and then later to USAirways when it wanted to be seen as an international carrier. Finally, the desire to create distance from scandal can also motivate a name change. A new name cannot repair a company's damaged reputation, though, and experts advise against making a switch in the midst of bad publicity; otherwise the stigma and suspicion will follow the new name. The Lance Armstrong Foundation changed its name to the Livestrong Foundation to distance itself from its disgraced cyclist former ambassador.

Guidelines.   Although renaming can yield growth opportunities, experts recommend a cautious approach. Name changes are typically complicated, time-consuming, and expensive, and firms should undertake them only when compelling marketing or financial considerations prevail, and a proper supporting marketing program can be put into place. A new corporate name cannot hide product or other deficiencies, and it requires extensive legal and URL vetting to make sure it is available and appropriate. Rebranding campaigns also usually forfeit the brand recognition and loyalty attached to the old name.

Many of the branding issues we discussed in Chapter 4 are relevant in choosing or changing a corporate name. Given the corporate branding strategy and marketing objectives, firms should evaluate candidate names in terms of memorability, meaningfulness, likability, protectability, adaptability, and transferability. If the consumer market is the primary objective, the name may reflect or be suggestive of certain product characteristics, benefits, or values. Consolidated Foods Corporation switched to Sara Lee Corporation, Blue Ribbon Sports changed its name to Nike, Starbucks Coffee to Starbucks, and Apple Computers to Apple. Alternatively, a name change can help clarify strategic direction for a company. In 2015, Google announced that it would reorganize under a parent company called Alphabet that would include all of the holding companies linked to Google under one entity. This also allowed Google to separate the management of its core businesses from the new ventures that it was launching.

Once the firm has chosen the new name, the substantial task of introducing it to employees, customers, suppliers, investors, and the public begins—often with the launch of a new marketing campaign and the opportunity to work with a blank canvas. Corporate rebranding is a time- and resource-intensive process that demands a company's total commitment to succeed.

It is also important not to move too fast in rebranding. In updating brand architecture in any way, the goal is to at least preserve if not actually enhance brand equity as much as possible. For example, when Macy's acquired May Department Stores and Chicago retailing icon Marshall Field's in August 2005, its rebranding efforts did not resonate well with its customers. Initial reaction to rebranding is almost always negative, simply because people resist change. Sometimes, however, an especially harsh reception will cause a firm to abandon a new name. Gap tried to change its logo to give it a modern look. The new logo was criticized for looking too bland, cheap and tacky. Within a week, Gap reverted to its original look.

When UAL, the parent company of United Airlines, decided a new name was necessary to reflect the one-stop travel options that resulted from its acquisitions of Hertz car rental and Westin and Hilton International hotels, it chose the name "Allegis," a compound of "allegiance" and "aegis." Public reaction was decidedly negative. Critics maintained that the name was difficult to pronounce, sounded pretentious, and had little connection with travel services. Donald Trump, formerly a major UAL shareholder, said the new name was "better suited to the next world-class disease." After six weeks and $7 million in research and promotion expenditures, the company decided to shed its car rental and hotel businesses and rename the surviving company United Airlines, Inc.[52]

Over time, though, if properly chosen and handled, new names gain familiarity and acceptance. Guidelines that encourage uniformity and consistency in the brand's appearance and usage help make the implementation effective; these rules should be part of a revised brand charter (see Chapter 8).

BRAND ARCHITECTURE GUIDELINES

Brand architecture is a classic example of the art and science of marketing. It is important to establish rules and conventions and be disciplined and consistent. Yet, at the same time, it is also important to be flexible and creative. There rarely are pure solutions to a brand architecture challenge, and no uniform agreement exists on the one type of branding strategy that all firms should adopt for all products. Even within a firm, hybrid strategies often prevail, and marketers may adopt various branding strategies for different products.

For example, although Miller has long used its name across its different types of beer, with various sub-brands like Miller High Life, Miller Lite, and Miller Genuine Draft, it carefully branded its no-alcohol beer substitute as Sharp's, its ice beer as Icehouse, and its low-priced beer as Milwaukee's Best, with no overt Miller identification. The assumption was that the corporate family brand name would not be relevant to or valued by the target market in question.

The brand hierarchy may not be symmetric. Corporate objectives, consumer behavior, or competitive activity may sometimes dictate significant deviations in branding strategy and the way the brand hierarchy is organized for different products or for different markets.

Brand elements may receive more or less emphasis, or not be present at all, depending on the particular products and markets. For example, in an organizational market segment where the DuPont brand name may be more valuable, that element might receive more emphasis than associated sub-brands. In appealing to a consumer market segment, a sub-brand such as Teflon may be more meaningful; thus, it receives relatively more emphasis when DuPont is targeting that market.

In evaluating a brand architecture strategy, we should ask a number of questions, such as:

- For the brand portfolio, do all brands have defined roles? Do brands collectively maximize coverage and minimize overlap?
- For the brand hierarchy, does the brand have extension potential? Within the category? Outside the category? Is the brand overextended?
- What positive and negative brand equity implications will transfer from the parent brand to individual products? What feedback exists from the individual products to the parent brands in turn?
- What profit streams result from different branding arrangements? How much revenue does each brand generate? At what cost? What other cross-selling opportunities exist between brands?

In answering these questions and in devising and implementing the optimal brand architecture strategy, marketers should keep the following five guidelines in mind.

1. *Adopt a strong customer focus.* Recognize what customers know and want, and how they will behave.
2. *Create broad, robust brand platforms.* Strong umbrella brands are highly desirable. Maximize synergies and flow.
3. *Avoid overbranding and having too many brands.* For example, high-tech products are often criticized for branding every ingredient, so the overall effect is like a NASCAR race car with logos and decals everywhere.
4. *Selectively employ sub-brands.* Sub-brands can communicate relatedness *and* distinctiveness and are a means of complementing and strengthening brands.
5. *Selectively extend brands.* As Chapter 13 explains, brand extensions should establish new brand equity and enhance existing brand equity.
6. *Ensure brand acquisitions mesh well with current brand architecture.* Sudden efforts to rebrand an acquisition could have negative consequences which may result in loss of customers.

REVIEW

A key aspect of managing brand equity is adopting the proper branding strategy. Brand names of products typically consist of a combination of different names and other brand elements. A brand architecture strategy for a firm identifies which brand elements a firm chooses to apply across the various products or services it sells. Several tools aid in developing a brand architecture strategy. Combining the brand–product matrix, the brand portfolio, and the brand hierarchy with customer, company, and competitive considerations can help a marketing manager formulate the optimal brand architecture strategy.

The brand–product matrix is a graphical representation of all the firm's brands and products, with brands as rows and the corresponding products as columns. The rows represent brand–product relationships and capture the firm's brand extension strategy. Marketers should judge potential extensions by how effectively they leverage existing brand equity to a new product, as well as how effectively the extension, in turn, contributes to the equity of the existing parent brand. The columns of the matrix represent product–brand relationships and capture the brand portfolio strategy in terms of the number and nature of brands to be marketed in each category.

We characterize a brand architecture strategy according to its breadth in terms of brand–product relationships and brand extension strategy, and its depth in terms of product–brand relationships and the brand portfolio or mix. Breadth describes the product mix and which products the firm should manufacture or sell. Depth deals with the brand portfolio and the set of all brands and brand lines that a particular seller offers.

A firm may offer multiple brands in a category to attract different—and potentially mutually exclusive—market segments. Brands also can take on very specialized roles in the portfolio: as flanker brands to protect more valuable brands, as low-end entry-level brands to expand the customer franchise, as high-end prestige brands to enhance the worth of the entire brand line, or as cash cows from which to milk all potentially realizable profits. Companies must be careful to understand exactly what each brand should do for the firm and, more important, what they want it to do for the customer.

A brand hierarchy reveals an explicit ordering of all brand names by displaying the number and nature of common and distinctive brand name elements across the firm's products. By capturing the potential branding relationships among the different products sold by the firm, a brand hierarchy graphically portrays a firm's branding strategy. One simple representation of possible brand elements, and thus, of potential levels of a brand hierarchy, is (from top to bottom): corporate (or company) brand, family brand, individual brand, and modifier.

In designing a brand hierarchy, marketers should define the number of different levels of brands (generally two or three) and the relative emphasis that brands at different levels will receive when combined to brand any one product. One common strategy to brand a new product is to create a sub-brand, combining an existing company or family brand with a new individual brand. When marketers use multiple brand names, as with a sub-brand, the relative visibility of each brand element determines its prominence. Brand visibility and prominence will depend on factors such as the order, size, color, and other aspects of the brand's physical appearance. To provide structure and content to the brand hierarchy, marketers must make clear to consumers the specific means by which a brand applies across different products and, if different brands are used for different products, the relationships among them.

In designing the supporting marketing program in the context of a brand hierarchy, marketers must define the desired awareness and image at each level of the brand hierarchy for each product. In a sub-branding situation, the desired awareness of a brand at any level will dictate the relative prominence of the brand and the extent to which associations linked to the brand will transfer to the product. In terms of building brand equity, we should link associations at any one level based on principles of relevance and differentiation. In general, we want to create associations relevant to as many brands nested at the level below as possible and to distinguish any brands at the same level.

Corporate or family brands can establish a number of valuable associations to differentiate the brand, such as common product attributes, benefits, or attitudes; people and relationships; programs and values; and corporate credibility. A corporate image will depend on a number of factors, such as the products a company makes, the actions it takes, and the manner in which it communicates to consumers. Communications may focus on the corporate brand in the abstract or on the different products making up the brand line. Any corporate name changes and rebranding efforts need to be done carefully. In a brand acquisition or merger context, name changes can result in a sudden loss of brand equity. This is true of customers and also investors who tend to pay attention (and accordingly penalize brands) due to the risks inherent in such name changes that take place after an acquisition.

An area of increasing importance for many brands is corporate social responsibility. Firms are becoming more aware of the environmental, economic, and social impact of their words and actions. Many now employ cause-marketing programs designed to align their brands with a cause of importance to their customers. Many consumers are also becoming much more aware of the environmental aspect of the products and services of a firm and how they are produced and disposed.

DISCUSSION QUESTIONS

1. Pick a company. As completely as possible, characterize its brand portfolio and brand hierarchy. How would you improve the company's branding strategies?
2. How do technology companies leverage their brand name, and what key characteristics of their brand architecture do they typically follow? For example, contrast the brand architecture of Google and Yahoo! over the years.
3. Contrast the branding strategies and brand portfolios of market leaders in two different industries. For example, contrast the approach by Anheuser-Busch and its Budweiser brand with that of Kellogg's in the ready-to-eat cereal category.

4. What are some of the product strategies and communication strategies that General Motors could use to further enhance the level of perceived differentiation between its divisions? How can online digital marketing and social media be utilized to strengthen the distinctions across brands within a particular portfolio?

5. Identify a company that has organized its brand architecture using multiple levels in the hierarchy. Review the design principles summarized in Table 12-1, and describe whether the brand architecture successfully follows these design principles. If not, how would you improve the brand architecture?

6. Scan recent news stories for an announcement concerning an acquisition of a brand. Provide a justification for the acquisition from the acquirer's standpoint. Describe pros and cons of the acquisition.

7. Consider the companies listed in Branding Brief 12-3 as having strong corporate reputations. By examining their Web sites, can you determine why they have such strong corporate reputations?

BRAND FOCUS 12.0

CORPORATE SOCIAL RESPONSIBILITY AND BRAND STRATEGY

Corporate Social Responsibility and Brand Strategy

In recent years, a key initiative that many firms have embraced is the rise of corporate social responsibility (CSR). Fortune 500 companies in the United States and United Kingdom are spending more than $15 billion on corporate social responsibility initiatives.[53] Many companies—such as Google, Microsoft, Oracle, Merck, Johnson & Johnson—are particularly well-known for their CSR activities. CSR activities can increase consumers' preferences for a firm's goods by providing a signal of quality, and it can also create a halo effect that consumers value.[54] This has significant implications for corporate brand image building as well. However, before we begin to explore these implications, it is worth defining what corporate social responsibility is.

At the broadest level, CSR has been defined as the impact of business behavior on society.[55] More specifically, CSR is defined as "an organization's obligation to maximize its positive impact and minimize its negative impact on society."[56] Thus, CSR activities are broadly defined and encompass several related activities including cause-related marketing, green marketing, sustainability, etc. Many reasons for engaging in CSR have been proposed previously. Globally, a 2015 Nielsen report suggested that 66

percent are willing to spend more on a brand which engages in sustainability efforts and 73 percent of millennials were willing to spend on products engaging in corporate social responsibility efforts.[57] Some reasons why CSR activities improve brand perceptions are given in the following list:

- *Increasing Legitimacy.* CSR provides firms with legitimacy in consumers' eyes. Consumers prefer to interact with firms who have high ethical and moral standards, and brands that incorporate cause marketing are rewarded with greater awareness and consideration. For example, Tide detergent incorporated cause marketing in its "Loads of Hope" program, which was meant to raise funds for disaster relief. For example, in the wake of Hurricane Katrina, Tide helped provide loads of clean laundry to hundreds of New Orleans residents. Tide has expanded the program to help in more than 20 natural disasters globally by 2017. The Tide Loads of Hope Clothing Drive helped collect, renew, and donate clothing to people in local communities, generating considerable positive publicity for the Tide detergent and strengthening the brand's perceptions in consumers' eyes.[58]

- CSR could affect multiple dimensions of credibility, because consumers may think of a firm willing to invest in CSR as caring more about customers and being more dependable than

Tide's "Loads of Hope" program has helped collect, renew, and donate clothing to people in local communities, generating positive publicity for the Tide brand.

other firms, at least in a broad sense, as well as being likable for doing the right things. Whirlpool generated much goodwill with its "More Than Houses" cause program with Habitat for Humanity, in which it donated a range and refrigerator for each new home built. In 16 years, the program has donated more than $85 million; has more than 8,000 company volunteers; and has helped more than 100,000 families.[59]

- *Building brand awareness:* Because of the nature of the brand exposure, CSR programs can be a means of improving recognition for a brand, although not necessarily recall. Like sponsorship and other indirect forms of brand-building communications, most CSR programs may be better suited to increasing exposure to the brand rather than to tying the brand to specific consumption or usage situations, because it can be difficult or inappropriate to include product-related information. At the same time, repeated or prominent exposure to the brand as a result of the CSR program can facilitate brand recognition.

- *Enhancing brand image:* Because most CSR programs do not include much product-related information, we would not expect them to have much impact on more functional, performance-related considerations. On the other hand, we can link two types of abstract or imagery-related associations to a brand via CSR: user profiles—CSR may allow consumers to develop a positive image of brand users to which they also may aspire in terms of being kind, generous, and doing good things; and personality and values—CSR could clearly bolster the sincerity dimension of a brand's personality such that consumers would think of the people behind the brand as caring and genuine.

- *Evoking brand feelings:* Two categories of brand feelings that seem particularly applicable to CSR are social approval and self-respect. In other words, CSR may help consumers justify their self-worth to others or to themselves. CSR programs may need to provide consumers with external symbols to explicitly advertise or signal their affiliation to others—for example, bumper stickers, ribbons, buttons, and T-shirts. They can also give people the notion that they are doing the right thing and should feel good about themselves for having done so. External symbols in this case may not be as important as the creation of "moments of internal reflection," during which consumers are able to experience these feelings. Communications that reinforce the positive outcomes associated with the cause program—and how consumer involvement contributed to that success—could help trigger these types of experiences. To highlight the consumer contribution, it may be necessary to recommend certain actions or outcomes such as having consumers donate a certain percentage of income or a designated amount.

- *Creating a sense of brand community:* CSR and a well-chosen cause can serve as a rallying point for brand users and a means for them to connect to or share experiences with other consumers or employees of the company itself.[60] One place where communities of like-minded users exist is online. Marketers may be able to tap into the many close-knit online groups that have sprung up around cause-related issues (for instance, medical concerns such as Alzheimer's disease, cancer, and autism). The brand might even serve as the focal point or ally for these online efforts to be seen in a more positive light. One CSR campaign which went viral is the ALS Ice Bucket Challenge.

ALS ICE BUCKET CHALLENGE

The Ice Bucket Challenge was a campaign involving a unique activity of the dumping of a bucket of ice and water over a person's head. This campaign was conducted in 2015 (and also 2016) to promote awareness of the disease amyotrophic lateral sclerosis (ALS, also known as motor neuron disease and in the United States as Lou Gehrig's disease) and encourage donations to research. In mid-2014, the Ice Bucket Challenge was a viral sensation on social media, and many people, celebrities, politicians, and athletes were posting videos of themselves online and on TV participating in the event. As noted in an article in *The New York Times*, people shared more than 1.2 million videos on Facebook between June 1 and August 13 and mentioned the phenomenon more than 2.2 million times on Twitter between July 29 and August 17. Within weeks of the challenge going viral, *The New York Times* reported that the ALS Association had received $41.8 million in donations from more than 739,000 new donors from July 29 until August 21, more than double the $19.4 million the association received during the year that ended January 31, 2013. This case illustrates the impact of social media in helping with socially relevant causes, which may provide valuable insights for companies engaged in CSR initiatives as well.

The ALS "Ice Bucket Challenge" helped raise more that $40 million in donations and demonstrates the important role of social media in building awareness.

- *Eliciting brand engagement:* Participating in a cause-related activity as part of a CSR program for a brand is certainly one means of eliciting active engagement. As part of any of these activities, customers themselves may become brand evangelists and ambassadors and help communicate about the brand and strengthen the brand ties of others. A CSR program of strategic volunteerism, whereby corporate personnel volunteer their time to help administer the nonprofit program, could actively engage consumers with both the cause and the brand.

Perhaps the most important benefit of cause-related marketing is that by humanizing the firm, it may help consumers develop a strong, unique bond with the firm that transcends normal marketplace transactions. A striking success story is McDonald's, whose franchises have long been required to stay close to their local communities. Ronald McDonald House Charities provides comfort and care to sick children and their families by supporting around 365 Ronald McDonald Houses and 50 Ronald McDonald Care Mobiles in communities around the world and by making grants to other not-for-profit organizations whose programs help children in need. Ronald McDonald Houses effectively leverage the company's Ronald McDonald character and its identification with children to concretely symbolize the firm's "do-good" efforts. This well-branded cause program enhances McDonald's reputation as caring and concerned for customers.

Designing Cause-Marketing Programs

Cause marketing comes in many forms related to education, health, the environment, the arts, and so on. Some firms have used cause marketing very strategically to gain a marketing advantage.[61] Toyota has run corporate advertising for years—most recently its "Moving Forward" campaign—showing it has roots in local U.S. communities. For Toyota, this campaign may go beyond cause marketing to become a means to help create a vital point-of-parity with respect to domestic car companies on "country of origin."

A danger is that the promotional efforts behind a cause-marketing program could backfire if cynical consumers question the link between the product and the cause and see the firm as self-serving and exploitive as a result. To realize brand equity benefits, firms must brand their cause-marketing efforts in the right manner. In particular, consumers must be able to make some kind of connection from the cause to the brand.[62] Alternatively, there is a chance that companies are seen as hypocritical if their CSR efforts contradict with other negative publicity that the company is eliciting for neglecting a particular aspect of either their employees, community or the environment. Researchers have studied this idea of corporate hypocrisy[63] and showed that its perceptions of hypocrisy could weaken a company's CSR efforts by weakening consumers' attitudes towards the firm.

The hope is that cause marketing strikes a chord with consumers and employees, improving the image of the company and energizing these constituents to act. With near-parity products, some marketers feel that a strongly held point-of-difference on the basis of community involvement and concern may in some cases be the best way—and perhaps the only way—to uniquely position a product.

Green Marketing

A special case of cause marketing is *green marketing*. Although environmental issues have long affected marketing practices, especially in Europe, companies are increasingly recognizing that the environment is an important issue to their customers and shareholders and, therefore, to their bottom lines. Research shows the environment is one of the top five issues that youth care most about.

One survey revealed that two-thirds of leaders of major brands believe sustainability initiatives were critical to stay competitive. Firms like Kimberly-Clark, HP, and GE stated that it was a key priority. "For us now, it's about looking at the full spectrum of sustainability," said one senior executive at Kimberly-Clark, who noted the firm is seeking to generate 25 percent of 2015 net sales from sustainable products in its fast-moving consumer goods (FMCG) group.[64] Here is what GE is doing.

GE

Despite its industrial past, GE views eco-friendly products as a high-growth business. Spurred by environmental concerns voiced by its customers, GE and CEO Jeffrey Immelt launched Ecomagination in 2005, the name of which is a play on its ongoing corporate campaign "Imagination at Work." The initiative focused on how to effectively and efficiently "create, connect to, and use power and water" and committed $1.5 billion in annual investment to research and technology into cleaner technologies. Some of its goals were to double GE revenue from sales of products and services that provide environmental advantages, and to reduce greenhouse gas emissions and improve the energy efficiency of operations. GE built an Ecomagination advertising campaign that targeted business-to-business customers, investors, employees, and consumers. In a 2011 letter to investors, customers, and other stakeholders to mark its progress, the company was able to note these achievements in the first five years of the program:

- $5 billion of clean-tech research and development
- $85 billion in revenue from Ecomagination products and solutions
- 22 percent reduction in greenhouse gas emissions
- 30 percent reduction in water use
- $130 million in energy efficiency savings.

GE also launched a Smart Grid initiative— "a vision for a smarter, more efficient, and sustainable electrical energy grid that GE technology is helping to bring to life."[65] GE's Ecomagination and Smart Grid initiatives have transformed the company into one of the world's top green brands. By investing millions of dollars in initiatives—such as wind and solar power—the company altered its reputation and became known as a forward-thinking and transparent company that was able to inspire its external stakeholders (e.g., customers, investors) and also its customers.[66]

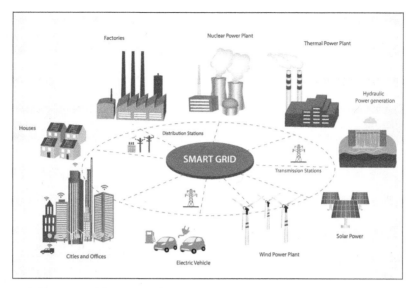

GE's Smarter Grid Initiative has transformed it into one of the world's top brands.

On the corporate side, a host of marketing initiatives have been undertaken by a wide variety of firms with environmental overtones. The auto industry is responding to the dual motivators of concerned consumers and rising oil prices by introducing gas-saving and emission-reducing hybrid models. McDonald's has introduced a number of well-publicized environmental initiatives through the years, such as moving to unbleached paper carry-out bags and replacing polystyrene foam sandwich clamshells with paper wraps and lightweight recyclable boxes.

From a branding perspective, however, green marketing programs have not always been entirely successful.[67] What obstacles have they encountered?

Overexposure and Lack of Credibility.
So many companies have made environmental claims that the public has sometimes become skeptical of their validity. What does it mean when a product claims it is organic, fair trade, or eco-friendly? Government investigations into some green claims, such as the degradability of trash bags, and media reports of the spotty environmental track records behind others have only increased consumers' doubts. This backlash has led many consumers to consider environmental claims to be marketing gimmicks.

Efforts to provide consumers with more information have sometimes only complicated the situation. Hundreds of different product labels have been introduced, for instance. Seeking to serve as an environmental leader, Walmart announced a Sustainability Index in 2009 to grade suppliers and products on a range of environmental and sustainable factors. The company found it hard to actually implement such a formal rating, however, and later announced it was committed only to providing more product information to consumers.[68]

The challenge is that producing and consuming products always requires trade-offs—all products, regardless of how *green* they appear or claim to be, affect the environment in some way. To understand the full environmental impact of any one product, we need to understand the entire production and consumption process, from raw material inputs to ultimate disposal.

And the results of green actions are not always obvious. Gary Hirshberg, founder and CEO of Stonyfield Farm, notes that although many see the use of recyclable packaging as environmentally friendly, Stonyfield further reduced its carbon footprint by switching to yogurt cups that were *not* recyclable, and meant to be thrown away. These cups, made from plants that are disposed into landfills, generate far fewer greenhouse gas emissions than recycled plastic containers.

Similarly, when Patagonia examined the environmental impact of the fibers in its outdoor apparel lines, it found the most harmful one was cotton—not petroleum-based synthetics—because growing cotton requires the use of pesticides. The company switched to organic cotton, but that has its own drawbacks because it uses so much water. Manufacturing a single pair of jeans can require 1,200 gallons of water![69]

Deciphering environmental claims is thus very tricky. To help provide some clarity, the U.S. government has stepped in and demanded that companies be more specific and substantiate environmental claims. A *recycled* claim must specify how much of the product or package is recycled and whether it is *postconsumer* (previously used goods) or *preconsumer* (manufacturing waste). The Federal Trade Commission (FTC) is leading the charge, cracking down on vague, unsubstantiated claims by requiring independent product testing. For example, firms cannot use the government's Energy Star logo on their products unless third-party testing proves they are more efficient than comparable regular products.[70]

Consumer Behavior.
Like many well-publicized social trends, corporate environmental awareness is often fairly complex in reality and does not always fully match public perceptions. Several studies help put consumer attitudes toward the environment in perspective.

Although consumers often assert that they would like to support environmentally friendly products, their behavior doesn't always match their intentions.[71] In most segments, they appear unwilling to give up the benefits of other options to choose green products. For example, some consumers dislike the performance, appearance, or texture of recycled paper and household products. Others are unwilling to give up the convenience of disposable products like diapers.

Poor Implementation.   In jumping on the green marketing bandwagon, many firms initially did a poor job. Products were poorly designed, overpriced, and inappropriately promoted. Once product quality improved, advertising sometimes still missed the mark, being overly aggressive or not compelling. One research study found that assertive environmental messages were most effective for important environmental causes; otherwise, a softer touch was more beneficial.[72]

Possible Solutions.   The environmental movement in Europe and Japan has a longer history and firmer footing than in the United States. In Europe, many of Procter & Gamble's basic household items, including cleaners and detergents, are available in refills that come in throw-away pouches. P&G says U.S. customers probably would not take to the pouches. In the United States, firms continue to strive to meet the wishes of consumers concerning the environmental benefits of their products, while maintaining necessary profitability.

NOTES

1. George Anderson, "Starbucks Knows How to Fail Fast, Just Like Amazon," *Forbes*, January 18, 2017, https://www.forbes.com/sites/retailwire/2017/01/18/starbucks-knows-how-to-fail-fast-just-like-amazon/#5529eaba7ea2.

2. Jim Stengel, *Grow: How Ideals Power Growth and Profitability at the World's Greatest Companies* (New York: Crown Business, 2011); WARC Staff, "Ideals Key for Top Brands," *WARC*, January 4, 2012, https://www.warc.com/NewsAndOpinion/news/Ideals_key_for_top_brands/d4ce6d0c-1461-4860-bc28-597ea599a6d1, Data sourced from Financial Times; additional content by Warc staff; Jack Neff, "Just How Well-Defined Is Your Brand's Ideal?," *Advertising Age*, January 16, 2012.

3. Neil A. Morgan and Lopo Leotte do Rego, "Brand Portfolio Strategy and Firm Performance," *Journal of Marketing* 73, no. 1 (January 2009): 59–74.

4. Bharat N. Anand and Ron Shachar, "Brands as Beacons: A New Source of Loyalty to Multiproduct Firms," *Journal of Marketing Research* 41 (May 2004): 135–150.

5. Philip T. Kotler and Kevin Lane Keller, *Marketing Management*, Pearson; Patrick Barwise and Thomas Robertson, "Brand Portfolios," *European Management Journal* 10, no. 3 (September 1992): 277–285.

6. For a methodological approach for assessing the extent and nature of cannibalization, see Charlotte H. Mason and George R. Milne, "An Approach for Identifying Cannibalization within Product Line Extensions and Multi-brand Strategies," *Journal of Business Research* 31, no. 2–3 (1994): 163–170. For an analytical exposition, see Preyas S. Desai, "Quality Segmentation in Spatial Markets: When Does Cannibalization Affect Product Line Design," *Marketing Science* 20, no. 3 (Summer 2001): 265–283.

7. Jack Trout, *Differentiate or Die: Survival in Our Era of Killer Competition* (New York: Wiley, 2000).

8. Patricia Sellers, "P&G: Teaching an Old Dog New Tricks," *Fortune*, May 31, 2004, 166–172; Jennifer Reingold, "CEO Swap: The $79 Billion Plan," *Fortune*, November 20, 2009, http://archive.fortune.com/2009/11/19/news/companies/procter_gamble_lafley.fortune/index.htm.

9. Mark Ritson, "Should You Launch a Fighter Brand?," *Harvard Business Review* 87 (October 2009): 65–81.

10. Nick Hatler, "Wyndham Buying Chanhassen-Based AmericInn Hotel Brand for $170M," *Minneapolis/St. Paul Business Journal*, July 18, 2017, https://www.bizjournals.com/twincities/news/2017/07/18/wyndham-buying-chanhassen-based-americinn-hotel.html.

11. Mike Wehner, "Here's How Many People Still Rent Netflix DVDs By Mail, and Why Netflix Loves It," *Boy Genius Report*, January 20, 2017, http://bgr.com/2017/01/20/netflix-dvd-rentals-subscribers/.

12. Paul W. Farris, "The Chevrolet Corvette," Case UVA-M-320 (Charlottesville, VA: Darden Graduate Business School Foundation, University of Virginia, 1995).

13. Zeynep Gurhan-Canli, "The Effect of Expected Variability of Product Quality and Attribute Uniqueness on Family Brand Evaluations," *Journal of Consumer Research* 30, no. 1 (June 2003): 105–114.

14. Much of this section—including examples—is based on an excellent article by Peter H. Farquhar, Julia Y. Han, Paul M. Herr, and Yuji Ijiri, "Strategies for Leveraging Master Brands," *Marketing Research* 4, no. 3 (September 1992): 32–43.

15. Peter H. Farquhar, Julia Y. Han, Paul M. Herr, and Yuji Ijiri, "Strategies for Leveraging Master Brands," *Marketing Research* 4, no. 3 (September 1992): 32–43.

16. "Statistic Brain Research Company, "Nike Company Statistics 2016," http://www.statisticbrain.com/nike-company-statistics/, accessed July 27, 2018.

17. Drew Harwell, "Sneaker Wars: How Basketball Shoes Became a Billion-Dollar Business," *The Washington Post*, March 17, 2015, https://www.washingtonpost.com/news/business/wp/2015/03/17/how-sneaker-kings-are-fighting-to-win-the-war-for-americas-feet/?utm_term=.f0871fcda934.

18. "A-Series Lighting Control Panel," A-Series Lighting Control Panel | GE Industrial Solutions, July 13, 2017,

19. Tulin Erdem and Baohung Sun, "An Empirical Investigation of the Spillover Effects of Advertising and Sales Promotions in Umbrella Branding," *Journal of Marketing Research* 39, no. 4 (November 2002): 408–420.

20. Ben Fritz, "Dish Network Wins Bidding for Assets of Bankrupt Blockbuster," *Los Angeles Times*, April 7, 2011, http://articles.latimes.com/2011/apr/07/business/la-fi-ct-dish-blockbuster-20110407.

21. Emily Nelson, "Too Many Choices," *The Wall Street Journal*, April 20, 2001, B1, B4.

22. Simon Eskow, "What Is SKU Rationalization and Why Is Everybody Doing It?," *Cin7*, November 3, 2016, https://www.cin7.com/sku-rationalization-everybody-doing/.

23. Deborah Roedder John, Barbara Loken, and Christopher Joiner, "The Negative Impact of Extensions: Can

Flagship Products Be Diluted?," *Journal of Marketing* 62, no. 1 (January 1998): 19–32.

24. Georg Szalai, "Viacom Unveils Focus on Flagship Brands, 'Deeper Integration' of Paramount Pictures," *The Hollywood Reporter*, February 9, 2017, http://www.hollywoodreporter.com/news/viacom-unveils-focus-flagship-networks-deeper-integration-paramount-pictures-973795.

25. Derrick Daye and Brad VanAuken, "Creating the Brand Halo Effect," *Branding Strategy Insider*, September 21, 2009, www.brandingstrategyinsider.com/2009/09/building-a-brand-halo-effect.html#.W1d_xGevKLU.

26. Guido Berens, Cees B.M. van Riel, and Gerrit H. van Bruggen, "Corporate Associations and Consumer Product Responses: The Moderating Role of Corporate Brand Dominance," *Journal of Marketing* 69, no. 3 (July 2005): 35–48.

27. France Leclerc, Christopher K. Hsee, and Joseph C. Nunes, "Narrow Focusing: Why the Relative Position of a Good Within a Category Matters More Than It Should," *Marketing Science* 24, no. 2 (Spring 2005): 194–206.

28. "DuPont: Corporate Advertising," Case 9-593-023 (Boston: Harvard Business School, 1992); John B. Frey, "Measuring Corporate Reputation and Its Value," presentation given at Marketing Science Conference, Duke University, March 17, 1989.

29. Charles J. Fombrun, *Reputation* (Boston: Harvard Business School Press, 1996).

30. Several thoughtful reviews of corporate images are available. See, for example, James R. Gregory, *Marketing Corporate Image: The Company as Your Number One Product* (Lincolnwood, IL: NTC Business Books, 1999); Grahame R. Dowling, *Creating Corporate Reputations: Identity, Image and Performance* (Oxford, UK: Oxford University Press, 2001).

31. Kevin Lane Keller and David A. Aaker, "The Effects of Sequential Introduction of Brand Extensions," *Journal of Marketing Research* 29, no. 1 (February 1992): 35–50. See also Thomas J. Brown and Peter Dacin, "The Company and the Product: Corporate Associations and Consumer Product Responses," *Journal of Marketing* 61, no. 1 (January 1997): 68–84.

32. Masashi Kuga, "Kao's Strategy and Marketing Intelligence System," *Journal of Advertising Research* 30 (April/May 1990): 20–25.

33. John Williams, "British Airways Launch Flying Start in Partnership with Comic Relief," UK Business News, February 16, 2011; "BA and Comic Relief Launch Global Children's Charity," *Travel Weekly*, June 30, 2010; http://www.ba-flyingstart.com/; https://www.comicrelief.com/partners/british-airways-flying-start, accessed November 20, 2018.

34. R.L. Team, British Airways Remains UK's Favourite Consumer Brand," *Research Live*, July 19, 2017, https://www.research-live.com/article/news/british-airways-remains-uks-favourite-consumer-brand/id/5019143.

35. Tulun Erdem and Joffre Swait, "Brand Credibility, Brand Consideration and Choice," *Journal of Consumer Research* 31, no. 1 (June 2004): 191–198; Marvin E. Goldberg and Jon Hartwick, "The Effects of Advertiser Reputation and Extremity of Advertising Claim on Advertising Effectiveness," *Journal of Consumer Research* 17, no. 2 (September 1990): 172–179.

36. Majken Schultz, Mary Jo Hatch, and Mogens Holten Larsen, eds., *The Expressive Organization: Linking Identity, Reputation, and the Corporate Brand* (New York: Oxford University Press, 2000); Mary Jo Hatch and Majken Schultz, "Are the Strategic Stars Aligned for Your Corporate Brand?" *Harvard Business Review* (February 2001): 129–134; Mary Jo Hatch and Majken Schultz, *Taking Brand Initiative: How Companies Can Align Strategy, Culture, and Identity Through Corporate Branding* (San Francisco, CA: Jossey-Bass, 2008). See also James Gregory, *Leveraging the Corporate Brand* (Chicago: NTC Press, 1997); Lynn B. Upshaw and Earl L. Taylor, *The Masterbrand Mandate* (New York: John Wiley & Sons, 2000).

37. For some broad discussion, see Bhaskar Chakravorti, Special Issue on Stakeholder Marketing, *Journal of Public Policy and Marketing* 29, no. 1 (April 2010): https://journals.sagepub.com/doi/full/10.1509/jppm.29.1.97, accessed November 20, 2018.

38. Laurel Cutler, vice-chairman of FCB/Leber Katz Partners, a New York City advertising agency, quoted in Susan Caminit, "The Payoff from a Good Reputation," *Fortune*, March 6, 1995, 74. See also Michael E. Porter and Mark R. Kramer, "The Competitive Advantage of Corporate Philanthropy," *Harvard Business Review* 80 (December 2002): 56–69; Steve Hoeffler, Paul Bloom, and Kevin Lane Keller, "Understanding Stakeholder Responses to Corporate Citizenship Initiatives: Managerial Guidelines and Research Directions," *Journal of Public Policy & Management* 29, no. 1 (Spring 2010): 78–88; Frank Huber, Frederik Meyer, Johannes Vogel, and Stefan Vollman, "Corporate Social Performance as Antecedent of Consumer's Brand Perception," *Journal of Brand Management* 19, no. 3 (December 2011): 228–240.

39. Hill & Knowlton, Return on Reputation Study, March 2006.

40. Tillmann Wagner, Richard J. Lutz, and Barton A. Weitz, "Corporate Hypocrisy: Overcoming the Treat of Inconsistent Corporate Social Responsibility Perceptions," *Journal of Marketing* 73, no. 6 (November 2009): 77–91.

41. Raj Sisodia, David B. Wolfe, and Jag Sheth, *Firms of Endearment: How World-Class Companies Profit from Passion and Purpose* (Upper Saddle River, NJ: Wharton School Publishing, 2007); John A. Quelch and Katherine E. Jocz, *Greater Good: How Good Marketing Makes for Better Democracy* (Boston, MA: Harvard Business School Press, 2007).

42. TOMS.com, LLC, "What We Give," https://www.toms.com/what-we-give, accessed November 20, 2018. TOMS.com, LLC "Gift of Shoes," https://www.toms.com/what-we-give-shoes, accessed November 20, 2018.

43. For a review of current and past practices, see David W. Schumann, Jan M. Hathcote, and Susan West, "Corporate Advertising in America: A Review of Published Studies on Use, Measurement, and Effectiveness," *Journal of Advertising* 20, no. 3 (September 1991): 35–56. See also Zeynep Gürhan-Canli and Rajeev Batra, "When Corporate Image Affects Product Evaluations: The Moderating Role of Perceived Risk," *Journal of Marketing Research* 41, no. 2 (May 2004): 197–205.

44. "Philips Unveils New Brand Direction Centered Around Innovation and People," *Philips*, November 13, 2013, https://www.usa.philips.com/a-w/about/news/archive/standard/news/press/2013/20131113-Philips-unveils-new-brand-direction-centered-around-innovation-and-people.html.

45. "Sense and Simplicity: Philips Is Spending 80 Million [Euro] on a Rebranding Strategy That Will Emphasize Simplicity and Give Consumers What They Want," *ERT Weekly*, September 23, 2004; John Zerio, "Philips: Sense and Simplicity," Thunderbird Case # A12-07-013; accessed February 27, 2012, www.philips.com.

46. David M. Bender, Peter Farquhar, and Sanford C. Schulert, "Growing from the Top: Corporate Advertising Nourishes the Brand Equity from Which Profits Sprout," *Marketing Management* 4, no. 4 (1996): 10–19; Nicholas Ind, "An Integrated Approach to Corporate Branding," *Journal of Brand Management* 5, no. 5 (1998): 323–329; Cees B. M. Van Riel, Natasha E. Stroker, and Onno J. M. Maathuis, "Measuring Corporate Images," *Corporate Reputation Review* 1, no. 4 (1998): 313–326.

47. Gabriel J. Biehal and Daniel A. Shenin, "Managing the Brand in a Corporate Advertising Environment," *Journal of Advertising* 28, no. 2 (1998): 99–110.

48. Mary C. Gilly and Mary Wolfinbarger, "Advertising's Internal Audience," *Journal of Marketing* 62, no. 1 (January 1998): 69–88.

49. Bruce Horovitz, "General Mills Cereals Go Totally Whole Grain," *USA Today*, September 30, 2004; Loraine Heller, "General Mill's Whole Grain Cereal Conversion in Retrospect," *FoodNavigator-USA*, September 19, 2006, www.foodnavigator-usa.com; MPR News, "General Mills Chief Marketing Officer Mark Addicks on How Marketing Can Make a Better World," January 25, 2011, https://www.mprnews.org/story/2011/01/20/bright-ideas-with-mark-addicks; General Mills, "General Mills Donates 1 Million Servings of Whole Grain," *General Mills*, February 10, 2011, https://www.generalmills.com/en/News/NewsReleases/Library/2011_archive/February/GeneralMillsDonatesWholeGrainCereals.

50. Hadley Malcolm, "General Mills to Ax Artificial Flavors from Cereals," *USA Today*, June 22, 2015, https://www.usatoday.com/story/money/2015/06/22/general-mills-artificial-ingredients-cereal/29101165/.

51. Richard Ettenson and Jonathan Knowles, "Merging the Brand and Branding the Merger," *MIT Sloan Management Review* (Summer 2006): 39–49; Lucinda Shen, "These Are the 12 Biggest Mergers and Acquisitions of 2016," *Fortune*, June 13, 2016, http://fortune.com/2016/06/13/12-biggest-mergers-and-acquisitions-of-2016/

52. "Allegis: A $7 Million Name Is Grounded," *San Francisco Examiner*, June 16, 1987, C9.

53. Alison Smith, "Fortune 500 Companies Spend More Than $15bn on Corporate Responsibility," *Financial Times*, October 12, 2014, https://www.ft.com/content/95239a6e-4fe0-11e4-a0a4-00144feab7de.

54. Elaine Wong, "Tide's Charitable Makeover," *Adweek*, April 10, 2009, http://www.adweek.com/brand-marketing/tides-charitable-makeover-105580/.

55. The Economist, "Corporate Social Responsibility: The Halo Effect," *The Economist*, June 25, 2015, https://www.economist.com/news/business/21656218-do-gooding-policies-help-firms-when-they-get-prosecuted-halo-effect.

56. Alison Smith, "Fortune 500 Companies Spend More Than $15bn on Corporate Responsibility," *Financial Times*, October 12, 2014, https://www.ft.com/content/95239a6e-4fe0-11e4-a0a4-00144feab7de.

57. Sarah Landrum, "Millenials Driving Brands to Socially Responsible Marketing," *Forbes*, March 17, 2017, https://www.forbes.com/sites/sarahlandrum/2017/03/17/millennials-driving-brands-to-practice-socially-responsible-marketing/#70305f634990.

58. Lee E. Preston, "Business and Public Policy," *Journal of Management* 12, no. 2 (1986): 261–275.

59. William M. Pride and O. C. Ferrell, *Marketing* (International edition). (1995).

60. Matt Walker, "4 Ways Agencies Can Add Meaning to Corporate Social Responsibility Programs," *Adweek*, August 30, 2016, http://www.adweek.com/brand-marketing/4-ways-agencies-can-add-meaning-corporate-social-responsibility-programs-173191/.

61. Leon Kaye, "Whirlpool and Habitat for Humanity Partnership: True Corporate Giving," *TriplePundIt*, April 14, 2015, http://www.triplepundit.com/special/disrupting-short-termism/whirlpool-and-habitat-for-humanity-partnership-true-corporate-giving/.

62. T. Wagner, R. J. Lutz, and B. A. Weitz, "Corporate Hypocrisy: Overcoming the Threat of Inconsistent Corporate Social Responsibility Perceptions," *Journal of Marketing* 73, no. 6 (2009): 77–91.

63. Alexander Haldermann, "GE's Ecomagination Turns 10: How a Brand Can Be a Driver for Change," *Huffington Post*, http://www.huffingtonpost.com/dr-alexander-haldemann/startup-slideshow-test_b_7181672.html, September 16, 2016.

64. Sankar Sen, Shuili Du, and C. B. Bhattacharya, "Building Relationships through Corporate Social Responsibility," in *Handbook of Brand Relationships*, eds. Joseph Priester, Deborah MacInnis, and C.W. Park (New York: M. E. Sharp, 2009): 195–211; C.B. Bhattacharya, Sankar Sen, and Daniel Korschun, "Using Corporate Social Responsibility to Win the War for Talent," *MIT Sloan Management Review* 49 (January 2008): 37–44; Xueming Luo and C. B. Bhattacharya, "Corporate Social Responsibility, Customer Satisfaction, and Market Value," *Journal of Marketing* 70, no. 4 (October 2006): 1–18; Pat Auger, Paul Burke, Timothy Devinney, and Jordan J. Louviere, "What Will Consumers Pay for Social Product Features?" *Journal of Business Ethics* 42, no. 3 (February 2003): 281–304; Dennis B. Arnett, Steve D. German, and Shelby D. Hunt, "The Identity Salience Model of Relationship Marketing Success: The Case of Nonprofit Marketing," *Journal of Marketing* 67, no. 2 (April 2003): 89–105; C. B. Bhattacharya and Sankar Sen, "Consumer-Company Identification: A Framework for Understanding Consumers' Relationships with Companies," *Journal of Marketing* 67, no. 2 (April 2003): 76–88; Sankar Sen and C. B. Bhattacharya, "Does Doing Good Always Lead to Doing Better? Consumer Reactions to Corporate Social Responsibility," *Journal of Marketing Research* 38, no. 2 (May 2001): 225–244; Xiaoli Nan and Kwangjun Heo, "Consumer Responses to Corporate Social Responsibility (CSR)

Initiatives: Examining the Role of Brand-Cause Fit in Cause-Related Marketing," *Journal of Advertising* 36, no. 2 (Summer 2007): 63–74.

65. David Kiron, Nina Kruschwitz, Knut Haanaes, Martin Reeves, and Ingrid von Streng Velken, "Sustainability Nears a Tipping Point," *MIT Sloan Management Review* (January 2012): 69–74, https://sloanreview.mit.edu/ projects/sustainability-nears-a-tipping-point/, accessed November 21, 2018.

66. Geoff Colvin, "Grading Jeff Immelt," *Fortune Magazine*, 163, no. 3 (February 2011): 75–80, http:// archive.fortune.com/magazines/fortune/fortune_ archive/2011/02/28/toc.html, accessed November 21, 2018; Beth Comstock, Ranjay Gulati, and Stephen Liguori, "Unleashing the Power of Marketing," *Harvard Business Review* (October 2010): 90–98, https:// hbr.org/2010/10/unleashing-the-power-of-marketing, accessed November 21, 2018; Bob Sechler, "GE's 'Green' Effort Fails to Strike Investors' Imagination," *Chicago Tribune,* July 6, 2008, 8; Anne Fisher, "America's Most Admired Companies," *Fortune Magazine*, March 19, 2007, 88–94, http://archive.fortune.com/magazines/fortune/fortune_archive/2007/03/19/8402323/index.htm, accessed November 21, 2018; Daniel Fisher, "GE Turns Green," *Forbes*, August 15, 2005, 80–85, https://www.forbes.com/forbes/2005/0815/080 .html#1b1593ff2389, accessed November 21, 2018; Mark Egan, "Ecomagination Ten Years Later: Proving That Efficiency and Economics Go Hand-in-Hand," GE Reports, October 29, 2015, https://www.ge.com/reports/ ecomagination-ten-years-later-proving-efficiency-economics-go-hand-hand/, accessed November 21, 2018.

67. Alexander Haldemann, "GE's Ecomagination Turns 10: How a Brand Can Be a Driver for Change, *Huffington Post*, September 16, 2015, updated September 16, 2016, https://www.huffingtonpost.com/dr-alexander-haldemann/startup-slideshow-test_b_7181672.html, accessed November 21, 2018.

68. Joanne Lipman, "Environmental Theme Hits Sour Notes," *The Wall Street Journal*, May 3, 1990, B6.

69. Stephanie Rosenbloom, "Wal-Mart Unveils Plan to Make Supply Chain Greener," *The New York Times*, February 25, 2010, https://www.nytimes.com/2010/02/26/ business/energy-environment/26walmart.html, accessed November 21, 2018.

70. Wendy Koch, "Green, Green, It's Green They Say," *USA Today*, April 21, 2011.

71. Katherine White, Rhiannon MacDonnell, and John H. Ellard, "Belief in a Just World: Consumer Intentions and Behaviors Toward Ethical Products," *Journal of Marketing* 76, no. 1 (January 2012): 103–118; Remi Trudel and June Cotte, "Does It Pay to Be Good?," *Sloan Management Review* 50 (January 2009): 61–68, https://sloanreview.mit .edu/article/does-it-pay-to-be-good/, accessed November 21, 2018; Michael G. Luchs, Rebecca Walker Naylor, Julie R. Irwin, and Rajagopal Raghunathan, "The Sustainability Liability: Potential Negative Effects of Ethicality on Product Preference, *Journal of Marketing* 74, no. 5 (September 2010): 18–31.

72. Ann Krorod, Amir Grinstein, and Luc Wathieu, "Go Green! Should Environmental Messages Be So Assertive?," *Journal of Marketing* 76 (January 2012): 95–102, https://www.ama.org/documents/environmental_ messages_assertive.pdf, accessed November 21, 2018.

13

Introducing and Naming New Products and Brand Extensions

Learning Objectives

After reading this chapter, you should be able to

1. Define the different types of brand extensions.
2. List the main advantages and disadvantages of brand extensions.
3. Summarize how consumers evaluate extensions and how extensions contribute to parent brand equity.
4. Outline the key assumptions and success criteria for brand extensions.

After too many extensions began to harm its image, Gucci retrenched and adopted a more careful approach to stretching its brand that met with greater success.
Source: Lou Linwei/Alamy Stock Photo

PREVIEW

Chapter 12 introduced the concept of brand architecture and described a process by which marketers can develop it. An important part of the process is the introduction of new products to help a brand grow and achieve its potential. Thus, this chapter considers in more detail the role of product strategy in creating, maintaining, and enhancing brand equity. Specifically, we will develop guidelines to improve the introduction and naming of new products and brand extensions.

Let us start with a little historical perspective. For years, firms tended to follow the lead of Procter & Gamble, Unilever, and other major consumer goods marketers that essentially avoided introducing any new products using an existing brand name. Over time, tight economic conditions, a need for growth, and competitive realities forced firms to rethink their "one brand–one product" policies. Recognizing that brands are among their most valuable assets, many firms have since decided to leverage that value by introducing a host of new products under some of their strongest brand names.

Many firms seek to build power or mega brands that establish a broad market footprint, appealing to multiple customer segments with multiple products all underneath one brand umbrella. Unilever's Dove brand has made successful forays from its roots in soap into a range of skin care and body care products, backed by its "Real Beauty" media campaign. At the same time, marketers are also realizing that too many product variations can be counterproductive, and ill-advised brand proliferation may actually repel consumers.

We've previously learned about the best-practice management of brand extensions. This chapter begins by describing brand extensions and outlining their advantages and disadvantages. Then, we present a simple model of how consumers evaluate brand extensions and offer managerial guidelines for introducing and naming new products and brand extensions. We conclude with a comprehensive summary of some of the key academic research findings on brand extensions. Brand Focus 13.0 provides a detailed case study of Apple's brand extension and growth strategies through the years.

NEW PRODUCTS AND BRAND EXTENSIONS

As background, first consider the sources of growth for a firm. One useful perspective is Ansoff's product and market expansion grid, also known as the *growth matrix*. As in Figure 13-1, we can categorize growth strategies according to whether they rely on existing or new products, and whether they target existing or new customers or markets. Branding Brief 13-1 describes McDonald's growth strategies along these lines.

Although existing products can further penetrate existing customer markets or push into additional ones (the focus of Chapter 14), new product introductions are often vital to the long-run success of a firm. A discussion of all the issues in effectively managing the development and introduction of new products is beyond the scope of this chapter. Here we simply address some brand equity implications of new products.[1]

First, we will establish some terminology. When a firm introduces a new product, it has three approaches for branding it:

1. It can develop a new brand, individually chosen for the new product.
2. It can apply one of its existing brands.
3. It can use a combination of a new brand and an existing brand.

	Current Products	**New Products**
Current Markets	Market Penetration Strategy	Product Development Strategy
New Markets	Market Development Strategy	Diversification Strategy

FIGURE 13-1
Ansoff's Growth Matrix

BRANDING BRIEF 13-1
Growing the McDonald's Brand

Over the last decade, McDonald's has faced a challenging marketing environment. A major challenge has been the growing awareness regarding health issues posed by fast food which is causing consumers to switch to healthier food options. Added to this is market saturation and economic uncertainty, both of which have posed additional challenges to the growth of this brand. To overcome these, the company has employed a number of different growth strategies that we can classify using the Ansoff growth matrix. As a result of these strategies, the company's financial fortunes have largely remained steady, even in the face of challenges and uncertainties. The brand has even been credited with producing a "halo effect"—that is "driving growth for the entire quick-service restaurant category." McDonald's differentiates itself through cost leadership, providing value meals for low income families. Facing fierce competition, McDonald's continues to provide new products to match consumer needs as well as focus on cutting costs through refranchising and cutting SG&A expenses.

McDonald's snack wraps and smoothies help attract a new type of customer—one who is looking for a quick snack between meals.

Market Penetration

For a long time, McDonald's increased its market penetration just by introducing hundreds of new outlets each year. By 2002, markets had become saturated and sales had slumped. On becoming CEO in 2004, James Skinner adopted a new corporate motto, "Better, not bigger." Rather than trying to grow by adding new restaurants, McDonald's would grow by generating greater returns from the ones it had.

Thus, instead of investing in new real estate, the firm made huge investments in upgrading the facilities and operations of existing stores. One important way McDonald's made it easier for its customers to spend more money was by expanding to 24-hour service at many stores. To accommodate the longer hours, the menu is constantly fine-tuning the offerings to suit any meal or snack opportunity.

Breakfast has become an essential part of the McDonald's revenue equation. A quarter of its domestic revenue—more than $6 billion—and half its profits come from breakfast, which includes the highly successful McMuffin and McGriddle breakfast sandwiches. In 2015, McDonald's began offering breakfast items all 24 hours a day. Surveys report one-third of customers who bought breakfast items outside of breakfast hours had not patronized the restaurant in the previous month. The all-day breakfast continued to bring in sales and revenue growth through its sales of all-day Egg McMuffin or hash browns for lunch or other parts of the day.

Snack Wraps and smoothies entice customers between meals. Snack Wraps are ideal for drive-thru customers (which accounts for 60 percent of sales of this product) who need to have one hand on the steering wheel. McDonald's decade-long "I'm Lovin' It" global advertising campaign has served as the perfect vehicle to support new product launches and enhance loyalty. Translated into a number of languages worldwide, it replaced some 20 different ad platforms that had been running in different regions.

Market Development

McDonald's has made concerted efforts to expand globally through the years, and its progress has been astounding. There are more than 33,000 restaurants worldwide in 119 different countries today, and 1.5 million employees serve 69 million customers daily in the United States, Europe, the Middle East, the Asia-Pacific region, Africa, Canada, and Latin America.

One key to its global success has been McDonald's willingness to adapt its menu to different cultural preferences and regional tastes. The chain offers specialized menu items, such as the Teriyaki Burger in Japan and Vegetable McNuggets in England. In India—where beef is not consumed because cows are sacred—it introduced the Maharaja Mac, made from mutton. The company also developed spicy sauces, such as McMasala and McImli.

McDonald's targets different demographic and psychographic market segments as well. The product offerings in Happy Meals have been tweaked through the years to appeal to both children and their parents. More recently, McDonald's sought to develop a new U.S. market by attracting 20- and 30-year-old females with premium salads served with Newman's Own dressing, and other lighter menu options. McDonald's rapidly became the number-one salad brand in the United States.

Product Development

McDonald's found its popularity in its core markets under threat as international concern grew about the role of fast food in poor health and obesity, highlighted by the 2001 book *Fast Food Nation* and the 2004 movie *Super Size Me*, among other critiques. In response, the company began to focus on healthier options such as salads and whole wheat wraps that were meant to appeal to health-conscious consumers.

The shift in focus toward healthy eating and physical activity was emphasized by McDonald's recasting of Ronald McDonald as its

"Chief Happiness Officer," a sports enthusiast who donned a more athletic version of his traditional yellow-and-red clown suit and snowboarded, skateboarded, and juggled fruit in a new TV spot.

The company also tapped into the growing premium-coffee trend in the United States by launching McDonald's Premium Roast coffee, which retails for about 35 percent less than a cup of Starbucks coffee. McDonald's also introduced a new line of premium hamburger and chicken sandwiches—signature crafted recipes including Pico Guacamole and Maple Bacon Dijon burgers. The marketing campaign for these burgers included the introduction of the "frork"—a fork made of fries to scoop up all of the toppings on the new burgers. The 20-piece Chicken McNuggets offering allowed the company to enter the shared-meals segment dominated by KFC.

Diversification

Although McDonald's has largely focused on expansion through market penetration, market development, and product development, it has done some diversification to target new customers with new service offerings. It extended its brand in 2001 with the opening of its first domestic McCafé, a gourmet coffee shop inspired by the success of Starbucks that had debuted in Portugal and Austria. After the initial success, McDonald's is now focusing on expanding McCafé into its restaurants and retail chains as well as opening additional stand-alone McCafés internationally. With more premium coffee being sold in the United States and with McDonald's family-oriented restaurants, they believe they can take market share from Starbucks. Another diversification offering is McTreat, an ice cream and dessert shop.

While several Golden Arch Hotels in Switzerland failed to make it and were sold off, experimentation continues. In Hong Kong, three McDonald's locations offer wedding packages for loyal couples. The basic Warm and Sweet Wedding Package for 50 guests goes for under $1,300. An additional $165 covers a rented "gown" of pearly white balloons.

Sources: Joanna Doonar, "Life in the Fast Lane," *Brand Strategy*, 186 (October 2004): 20–23; Gina Piccolo, "Fries with That Fruit?" *Los Angeles Times*, July 18, 2005, F1; Pallavi Gogoi and Michael Arndt, "Hamburger Hell," *BusinessWeek*, March 3, 2003, 104; Kate MacArthur, "Big Mac's Back," *Advertising Age*, December 13, 2004, S1; Michael Arndt, "McDonald's 24/7," *Bloomberg BusinessWeek*, February 5, 2007; "McDonald's to Diversify into 'Shared Meals' Segment," www.room54.co, February 13, 2011; Dan Malovany and Maria Pilar Clark, "McSmart and McSnackable: McDonald's New Product Strategy Boosts Bottom Line," *Stagnito's New Products Magazine*, June 2007; Stefan Michel, "McDonald's Failed Venture in Hotels," www.knowledgenetwork.thunderbird.edu, July 11, 2008; Hillary Brenhouse, "Want Fries with That Ring? McDonald's Offers Weddings," *Time*, March 7, 2001; Trefis Team, "Here's Why McDonald's Is Increasing Focus On McCafe," Nasdaq, December 7, 2016, https://www.nasdaq.com/article/heres-why-mcdonalds-is-increasing-focus-on-mccafe-cm718236, accessed November 22, 2018; Sarah Whitten, "McDonald's Invents 'Supremely Superfluous' Frork Utensil to Pitch Its New Burgers," CNBC, May 1, 2017, https://www.cnbc.com/2017/05/01/mcdonalds-invents-the-frork-to-pitch-its-new-burgers.html, accessed November 22, 2018; Gene Marcial, "McDonald's Turnaround Signals Accelerating Long-Term Growth," *Forbes*, January 31, 2017, www.forbes.com/sites/genemarcial/2017/01/31/mcdonalds-turnaround-signals-accelerating-long-term-growth/#794d3d4e6c84; Michal Addady, "McDonald's All-Day Breakfast Is Succeeding," *Fortune*, December 9, 2015, http://fortune.com/2015/12/09/mcdonalds-all-day-breakfast-sales/, accessed May 21, 2017; Team Trefis, "'Healthy' Food Options in the Core Menu Can Drive Revenues for McDonald's, www.forbes.com/sites/greatspeculations/2016/07/25/healthy-food-options-in-the-core-menu-can-drive-revenues-for-mcdonalds/#7726f3e17726, accessed May 31, 2017; Craig Smith, "42 Interesting McDonald's Facts and Statistics (October 2018)," DMR Business Statistics, https://expandedramblings.com/index.php/mcdonalds-statistics/, accessed November 22, 2018; John Kell, "McDonald's Struggles to Repeat Success of All-Day Breakfast Launch," *Fortune Magazine*, January 23, 2017, http://fortune.com/2017/01/23/mcdonalds-us-sales-slow/, accessed November 22, 2018.

A **brand extension** occurs when a firm uses an established brand name to introduce a new product (approach 2 or 3). As we noted in Chapter 12, when a new brand is combined with an existing brand (approach 3), the brand extension can also be a **sub-brand**. An existing brand that gives birth to a brand extension is the **parent brand**. If the parent brand is already associated with multiple products through brand extensions, then it may also be called a **family brand**.

Brand extensions fall into two general categories:[2]

- *Line extension:* Marketers apply the parent brand to a new product that targets a new market segment within a product category the parent brand currently serves. A line extension often adds a different flavor or ingredient variety, a different form or size, or a different application for the brand. In 2017, Apple's introduction of the iPhone 8 with new features is an example of a line extension. Starbucks introduced cold coffee beverages as a line extension within the coffee category.

- *Category extension:* Marketers apply the parent brand to enter a different product category from the one it currently serves. For example, Oprah Winfrey leveraged the success of her show to introduce the successful publication called *O, The Oprah Magazine*. Oreos extended its brand from cookies into ice cream bars.

Among all the new product introductions in any given year, 80 to 90 percent of these introductions are typically line or brand extensions.[3] Both in Europe and in the United States, the rates of product failure in the consumer goods sector range are around 80 percent.[4] In identifying reasons for product failure, the lack of a well-established brand name has surfaced as a key factor. For example, in a global survey of consumers conducted by AC Nielsen, nearly 60 percent mentioned that they prefer line extensions because of recognition of and familiarity with the brand.[5] Some notable launches in recent times in consumer-packaged goods include both line and brand extensions such as Clorox Toilet Bowl cleaners, Old Spice Hydro Wash body wash, and Tide Stain Remover pens.[6] In other categories as well, numerous extensions can be found, including iTunes Radio, Adidas watches, and Samsung's gaming monitor. All these new products were launched as extensions.[7] Nevertheless, many new products are still introduced each year as new brands. A slew of new technology brands have recently begun to make their mark, such as the SurveyMonkey online survey tool, the Spotify music Web site, Lookout mobile's security software, and the Twilio voice and text messaging application facilitator.

Even in a product category as simple and established as hamburgers, a number of competitors in the category have attained prominence in recent years including In-N-Out Burger, Five Guys, Big Boy, Smashburger, Fatburger, and Shake Shack. Each of these chains has claimed a unique niche. For instance, Shake Shack's updated "roadside burger stand" continues to be successful by featuring a mix of high-quality natural ingredients, cooking food to order, and emphasizing the happiness of its customers and employees.[8]

As described previously, most new products are branded and launched as extensions. To understand why, we'll next outline some of the main advantages and disadvantages of brand extensions.

ADVANTAGES OF EXTENSIONS

For most firms, the question is not *whether* to extend the brand, but when, where, and how to extend it. Well-planned and well-implemented extensions offer a number of advantages that we can broadly categorize as those that facilitate new-product acceptance and those that provide feedback benefits to the parent brand or company as whole (see Figure 13-2).

Facilitate New-Product Acceptance

The high failure rate of new products has been well documented. Marketing analysts estimate that only 2 of 10 new products will be successful, or maybe even as few as 1 of 10. Brand extensions can certainly suffer some of the same shortcomings as any new product. Nevertheless, a new product introduced as a brand extension may be more likely to succeed, at least to some degree, because the advantages—that we describe later—work to increase acceptance.

Improve Brand Image. As we saw in Chapter 2, one of the advantages of a well-known and well-liked brand is that consumers form expectations of its performance over time. They can form similar inferences and expectations about the likely composition and performance of a brand extension, based on what they already know about the brand itself and the extent to which they feel this information is relevant to the new product.[9]

These inferences may improve the strength, favorability, and uniqueness of the extension's brand associations. For example, when Microsoft first introduced the Xbox video gaming console, consumers may have been more likely to feel comfortable with its anticipated performance because of their experience with and knowledge of other Microsoft products.

Facilitate New Product Acceptance

Improve brand image
Reduce risk perceived by customers
Increase the probability of gaining distribution and trial
Increase efficiency of promotional expenditures
Reduce costs of introductory and follow-up marketing programs
Avoid cost of developing a new brand
Allow for packaging and labeling efficiencies
Permit consumer variety-seeking

Provide Feedback Benefits to the Parent Brand and Company

Clarify brand meaning
Enhance the parent brand image
Bring new customers into brand franchise and increase market coverage
Revitalize the brand
Permit subsequent extensions

FIGURE 13-2
Advantages of Brand Extension

Reduce Risk Perceived by Customers.   One research study found that the most important factor for predicting initial trial of a new product was the extent to which it connected to a known family brand.[10] Extensions from well-known brands such as 3M, Amazon, Google, Apple, or others may communicate longevity and sustainability. Although corporate brands can lack specific product associations because of the breadth of products attached to their name, their established reputation for introducing high-quality products and standing behind them may be an important risk-reducer for consumers.[11]

Perceptions of corporate credibility—in terms of the firm's expertise and trustworthiness—can be valuable associations in introducing brand extensions.[12] Similarly, although widely extended supermarket family brands—such as Kellogg's, Kraft, and Pepperidge Farm—may lack specific product meaning, they may still stand for product quality in the minds of consumers and, by reducing perceived risk, facilitate the adoption of brand extensions.

Increase the Probability of Gaining Distribution and Trial.   The potential for increased consumer demand for a new product introduced as an extension may convince retailers to stock and promote it. One study indicated that brand reputation was a key screening criteria of gatekeepers making new-product decisions at supermarkets.[13]

Increase Efficiency of Promotional Expenditures.   From a marketing communications perspective, one obvious advantage of introducing a new product as a brand extension is that the introductory campaign does not have to create awareness of both the brand and the new product but instead can concentrate on only the new product itself.[14]

Several research studies document this benefit. One comprehensive study found that the average advertising-to-sales ratio for brand extensions was 10 percent, compared with 19 percent for new brands, thereby confirming prior findings.[15] The following example of movie sequels makes the case for how extensions can lead to efficient use of advertising dollars.

MOVIE SEQUELS AS LINE EXTENSIONS

Successful movies often introduce sequels that are intended to capitalize on the sales of the original hit movie. The success and popularity of sequels is evident in the fact that top box office revenue is increasingly derived from sequels (see this trend summarized in Figure 13-3). The arguments are much the same as those made for typical brand and line extensions. Movie studies typically leverage the existing awareness of the storyline and characters, thereby reducing the risk associated with launching a new movie. Given the decline in movie studio audiences, and the high potential for failure, this risk mitigation approach may offer significant advantages.

Moreover, the expenditures on promoting a sequel are typically much lower than a new movie, as seen in the advertising-to-sales ratio of movie sequels. In 2015, *Star Wars Episode VII: The Force Awakens* was a sequel that had among the highest sales revenue to advertising ratio of all movies during that year, and earned $25.4 million in domestic revenue for every dollar spent on advertising. This ad-sales ratio was closely

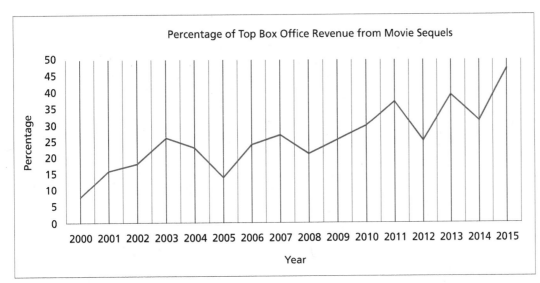

FIGURE 13-3

Percentage of Box Office Revenue from Movie Sequels

followed by *Jurassic World* with $15.8 million in domestic revenue for every dollar spent on advertising. Their successes reinforce the notion that movie sequels can lead to cost savings. If a sequel is able to effectively tap into the success factors from earlier films to deliver on the brand promise of the franchise, highly favorable advertising-to-sales ratios can result from the increased efficiencies (i.e., lower costs) associated with promoting the movie. Sequels may also benefit the DVD sales associated with the original film, thus demonstrating significant spillover effects, as shown by researchers Henning-Thurau, Houson, and Heitjans.

All sequels are not the same, obviously, and there are differences in how sequels are marketed. Academic researchers Sood and Drèze have suggested that numbered sequels (e.g., Daredevil 2) are more influenced by similarity to the parent (original film) than named sequels (*Daredevil: Taking It to the Streets).*

Despite their overall popularity, sequel success is not a guarantee. Sequels associated with smaller hit productions are often not financially lucrative, thus belying the faith that Hollywood places in these sequels. When it comes to sequels and other artistic productions, it is worthwhile conducting an in-depth assessment of the extension opportunity using a similar set of guidelines, as in the case of product or service extensions.

Sources: boxofficemojo, jackdaw research; Dawson, Jan "Hollywood Clings to Sequels Despite Diminishing Returns," June 7, 2016. http://variety.com/2016/film/features/hollywood-franchises-sequels-box-office-1201789704/. Accessed June 3, 2017. [1] Sanzo, Nick, "May the Force Be With Your Sequels". Kantar Media. 14 January 2016. www.kantarmedia.com/us/thinking-and-resources/blog/may-the-force-be-with-your-sequels. Accessed May 21, 2017. Thorsten Hennig-Thurau, Mark B. Houston, and Torsten Heitjans, "Conceptualizing and Measuring the Monetary Value of Brand Extensions: The Case of Motion Pictures," *Journal of Marketing* 73 (November 2009): 167–183. Sood, Sanjay, and Xavier Drèze. "Brand extensions of experiential goods: Movie sequel evaluations." *Journal of Consumer Research* 33, no. 3 (2006): 352–360.

Reduce Costs of Introductory and Follow-Up Marketing Programs. Because of these push and pull considerations in distribution and promotion, it has been estimated that a firm can save 40 to 80 percent on the estimated $30 to $50 million it can cost to launch a new supermarket product nationally in the United States. Other efficiencies can result after the launch. For example, when a brand becomes associated with multiple products, advertising can be more cost-effective for the family brand as a whole.

Avoid Cost of Developing a New Brand. Developing new brand elements is an art and a science. To conduct the necessary consumer research and employ skilled personnel to design high-quality brand names, logos, symbols, packages, characters, and slogans can be quite expensive, and there is no assurance of success. As the number of available—and appealing—brand names keeps shrinking, legal conflicts grow more likely. To avoid these, a global trademark search is a must for any major new brand launch or rebranding, and it can cost millions of dollars.

Allow for Packaging and Labeling Efficiencies. Similar or identical packages and labels for extensions can result in lower production costs, and, if coordinated properly, more prominence in the retail store where they can create a "billboard" effect. For example, Campbell's soup offers a variety of soups and flavors in visually similar packaging, which increases their visibility when they are stocked together in the freezer. Coca-Cola soft drinks and Gerber's baby food achieve a similar effect.

Permit Consumer Variety-Seeking. If marketers offer a portfolio of brand variants within a product category, consumers who need a change—because of boredom or satiation—can switch without having to leave the brand family. A company that seems to offer something for everyone is L'Oréal.

L'ORÉAL

Concentrating solely on beauty and personal care since its founding in 1907, L'Oréal has become a global powerhouse through its extensive brand portfolio. The firm has products for virtually every channel, price point, and market. Garnier is its fast-growing mass brand. L'Oréal Paris is at the higher end of the mass range, combining sophisticated cosmetics at accessible price points. Lancôme is the premium luxury brand. L'Oréal adheres to a strict channel exclusivity strategy. Professional products (Matrix and Redken) are sold at hair salons, consumer product brands (Maybelline and Garnier) at retail stores, including drug stores and food stores, luxury products (Biotherm and Lancôme) at specialty stores or department stores, and active cosmetic brands (La Roche-Posay) at dispensing dermatologists and pharmacies. L'Oréal also owns two retail chain brands—Kiehl's and the Body Shop. Geographically, the company casts a wide net. Many of its brands are sold in as many as 130 countries; Lancôme is sold in 160 countries. Recently, L'Oréal has placed much importance on emerging markets, China and India in particular, and it aims to double its existing customer base of 1 billion customers worldwide by 2021. The firm invests heavily in research and development (earmarking approximately 3 percent of net sales) in the belief that science and technology and the quality of its products are the keys to success. Roughly 15 to 20 percent of the product lines turn over in any given year due to product improvements or the launch of new products. L'Oréal is also putting more emphasis on digital and mobile strategies to engage customers but without abandoning the traditional magazine print ads that have served beauty brands well through the years.[16] The company, partnering with Automat Technologies, is jumping into artificial intelligence, launching a Facebook Messenger bot that converses with consumers. L'Oréal's focus has been strongly set on technology to expand products and services, and its ecommerce business grew 32 percent in 2016.[17]

L'Oréal has an extensive portfolio of brands involving many different price points, markets, and channels.

Provide Feedback Benefits to the Parent Brand

Besides facilitating acceptance of new products, brand extensions can also provide positive feedback to the parent brand in a number of ways.

Clarify Brand Meaning.   Extensions can help clarify the meaning of a brand to consumers and define the kinds of markets in which it competes, an important first step in the brand architecture process. Thus, through brand extensions, Dove means "personal care," Johnson & Johnson means "baby care," Prada means "luxury," and Lego stands for "creativity, imagination, fun." Figure 13-4 shows how various brands that have introduced multiple brand extensions have broadened their meaning to consumers.

As Chapter 12 noted, broader brand meaning often is necessary so that firms avoid "marketing myopia" and do not mistakenly draw narrow boundaries around their brand, either missing market opportunities or becoming vulnerable to well-planned competitive strategies. Thus, as Harvard's Ted Levitt pointed out in a pioneering article, railroads are not just in the "railroad" business, but are also in the "transportation" business.[18]

Thinking more broadly about product meaning can easily inspire different marketing programs and new product opportunities. For example, when Xerox introduced the slogan, "The Document Company," it broadened its business definition to include not only copiers but digital printing, document services, and so on. Similarly, GE broadened its business mission to

Brand	Original Product	Extension Products	New Brand Meaning
Weight Watchers	Fitness centers	Low-calorie foods	Weight loss and maintenance
Sunkist	Oranges	Vitamins, juices	Good health
Kellogg's	Cereal	Nutri-Grain bars, Special K bars	Healthy snacking
Aunt Jemima	Pancake mixes	Syrups, frozen waffles	Breakfast foods

FIGURE 13-4

Expanding Brand Meaning through Extensions

shift away from industrial products such as turbines and engines to digital services that would help their customers deliver better services to their end users.[19] In the Indian context, Titan Company Limited (owned by the famous Tata Group, and known for manufacturing watches, jewelry, and eyewear) widened its footprint in the personal lifestyle segment with the launch of the SKINN Titan range of fine fragrances.[20] By changing their business mission to stay in tune with fundamental shifts in their respective industries, Xerox, GE, and the Indian brand Titan broadened their meaning to customers, thereby opening the way to introducing future line and brand extensions.

In some cases, it is advantageous to establish a portfolio of related products that completely satisfy consumer needs in a certain area. For example, many specific-purpose cleaning products have broadened their meaning to being viewed as multipurpose, including Clorox, Method, Lysol, Comet, and Mr. Clean.

Enhance the Parent Brand Image.   According to the customer-based brand equity model, one desirable outcome of a successful brand extension is that it may enhance the parent brand image by strengthening an existing brand association, improving the favorability of an existing brand association, adding a new brand association, or a combination of these.

One common way a brand extension affects the parent brand image is by helping to clarify its core brand values and associations. Core brand associations, as we defined them in Chapter 3, are those attributes and benefits that come to characterize all the products in the brand line and, as a result, are those with which consumers often have the strongest associations. For example, Nike has expanded from running shoes to other athletic shoes, athletic clothing, and athletic equipment, strengthening its associations to peak performance and sports in the process.

Another type of association that successful brand extensions may improve is consumer perceptions of the company's credibility. For example, one research study showed that a successful corporate brand extension led to improved perceptions of the expertise, trustworthiness, and likability of the company.[21]

Bring New Customers into the Brand Franchise and Increase Market Coverage.   Line extensions can benefit the parent brand by expanding market coverage, such as by offering a product benefit whose absence may have prevented consumers from trying the brand. For example, by offering a chewable tablet, Tylenol was able to offer a product for children who had difficulty swallowing tablets and might have otherwise avoided the brand.

Creating news and bringing attention to the parent brand may benefit the family brand as a whole. Through the skillful introduction of extensions, Tide as a family brand has managed to maintain its market leadership and actual market share—roughly 40 percent in the United States—from the 1950s to the present.[22] Another example of using an extension to tap into a new market is the introduction of Coke Zero by Coca-Cola in 2005.

COKE ZERO

This extension of a low-calorie, zero-sugar, cola targeted for men became among the most successful extensions launched by Coca-Cola.[23] In order to attract this newer segment of the market, Coke Zero leveraged social media to build a loyal following. For example, in 2010, the Coke Zero Facial Profiler Facebook app was introduced to help followers find lookalikes by utilizing a novel face detection technology. The brand also had a tie-in with the James Bond movie *Skyfall*. The viral video for Coke Zero was watched more than 11 million times.[24] A giant billboard was set up during the 2015 NCAA Final Four in which the massive billboard dispensed ice cold Coke Zero from a bottle supported by 4,500 feet of tubing. Viewers of a commercial for the brand were encouraged to download a Shazam app, which showed a glass filling up with Coke Zero as it was being poured in the TV commercial. Overall, the Coke Zero introduction was a success for the brand and resulted in the brand being a top 10 brand in the carbonated beverage category with a market share of 1.8 percent in 2014.[25] The success of this extension was due to a well-thought-out segmentation, targeting, and positioning for the Coke Zero brand, and an effective set of marketing mix tactics to support the introduction. The introduction of this extension allowed Coke to reassert its dominance in the carbonated beverages category and helped mitigate the threat of competition from both Diet Pepsi and newer competitors (e.g., juice drinks).

Revitalize the Brand.   Sometimes brand extensions can be a means to renew interest in and liking for the brand. The introduction of the sleek CTS sedan and muscular Escalade SUV completely transformed the once dowdy Cadillac brand image.

Permit Subsequent Extensions.   One benefit of a successful extension—especially a category extension—is that it may serve as the basis for subsequent extensions. For example, when Apple introduced the iPod, it quickly became a market leader, representing one of the company's most successful new products ever. It also provided a halo effect that significantly boosted sales for the company's existing computer and software products. Finally, it made it easier for the company to introduce the iPhone smartphone and perhaps even the iPad tablet computer (see Brand Focus 13.0 for a more in-depth analysis of Apple's brand strategy).

DISADVANTAGES OF BRAND EXTENSIONS

Despite their potential advantages, brand extensions have a number of disadvantages (see Figure 13-5).

Can Confuse or Frustrate Consumers

Different varieties of line extensions may confuse and perhaps even frustrate consumers about which version of the product is the right one for them. For example, one study found that consumers were more likely to make a purchase after sampling a product (and being given a coupon) when there were six product flavors to sample than when there were 24.[26] So, in some situations, greater product variety may induce shoppers to buy less. Consumers may reject new extensions for tried and true favorites or all-purpose versions that claim to supersede more specialized product versions. This is reflected in the success of Colgate Total, which positions itself as an inclusive product that contains all the necessary or desirable toothpaste benefits.

Many retailers do not have enough shelf or display space to stock the large number of new products and brands continually being introduced even if they wanted to. So some consumers may be disappointed when they are unable to find an advertised brand extension because a retailer is unable or unwilling to stock it. If a firm launches extensions that consumers deem inappropriate, they may question the integrity and competence of the brand.

Can Encounter Retailer Resistance

The number of consumer packaged-goods stock-keeping units (SKUs) outpaces the growth of retail space in year-on-year percentage growth. Own-brand or private-label goods also continue to grow as a percentage of total grocery sales. Many brands now come in a multitude of different forms. For example, Campbell's has introduced a number of different lines of soup—including Campbell's Go, Condensed, Home Cookin', Chunky, Healthy Request, Select, Simply Home, Ready-to-Serve Classic, Oriental, and portable Soup at Hand—and many flavors within each type.

As a result, it has become virtually impossible for a grocery store or supermarket to offer all the different varieties available across all the various brands in any one product category. Moreover, retailers often feel that many line extensions are merely "me-too" products that duplicate existing brands in a product category and should not be stocked even if there is space. Walmart, the biggest retailer in the United States, attempts to stock the items that sell best, dropping as many as 20 percent of slow-moving items from its shelves annually.[27]

Can confuse or frustrate consumers
Can encounter retailer resistance
Can fail and hurt parent brand image
Can succeed but cannibalize sales of parent brand
Can succeed but diminish identification with any one category
Can succeed but hurt the image of parent brand
Can dilute brand meaning
Can cause the company to forgo the chance to develop a new brand

FIGURE 13-5

Disadvantages of Brand Extension

Can Fail and Hurt Parent Brand Image

The worst possible scenario for an extension is not only to fail, but to harm the parent brand image in the process. Unfortunately, these negative feedback effects can sometimes happen.

Even if an extension initially succeeds, by linking the brand to multiple products, the firm increases the risk that an unexpected problem or even a tragedy with one product in the brand family can tarnish the image of some or all the remaining products. The Audi is a classic example. A number of years ago, perceived driving problems with the Audi 5000 "spilled over" and tarnished the image of the Audi 4000, although the more distinctly branded and positioned Audi Quattro was not hurt as much.

Understanding when unsuccessful brand extensions may damage the parent brand is important, and later in the chapter we'll develop a conceptual model to address the topic and describe some important findings. On a more positive note, however, one reason an unsuccessful brand extension may not necessarily damage the parent brand is the very reason the extension may have been unsuccessful in the first place—hardly anyone may even have heard of it! Thus, the silver lining when a brand extension fails to achieve sufficient brand awareness or distribution is that the parent brand is more likely to survive unscathed. As we'll argue later, product failures in which the extension is found to be inadequate on the basis of performance are more likely to hurt perceptions of the parent brand than these market failures.

Can Succeed but Cannibalize Sales of Parent Brand

Even if sales of a brand extension are high and meet targets, success may result merely from consumers switching from existing offerings of the parent brand—in effect cannibalizing it. Line extensions designed to establish points-of-parity with current offerings in the parent brand category particularly may result in cannibalization. In the carbonated beverages category, Diet Coke's point-of-parity of good taste and point-of-difference of low calories undoubtedly took some sales from regular Coke drinkers. In fact, although U.S. sales of Coca-Cola's cola products have held steady since 1980, sales in 1980 came from Coke alone, whereas sales today include significant contributions from Diet Coke, Coke Zero, Cherry Coke, and uncaffeinated and flavored forms of Coke. Without the introduction of those extensions, however, some of Coke's sales might have gone to competing Pepsi products or other soft drinks or beverages instead.

Sometimes, however, such intrabrand shifts in sales are not undesirable; we can think of them as a form of preemptive cannibalization. In other words, without the introduction of the line extension, consumers might have switched to a competing brand instead. This alternative view of preemptive cannibalization as a positive outcome was also echoed by Steve Jobs, co-founder of Apple, who famously said "cannibalize yourself (before someone else does)."[28]

Can Succeed, but Diminish Identification with Any One Category

One risk of linking multiple products to a single brand is that the brand may not be identified enough with any one product. Thus, brand extensions may obscure the brand's identification with its original categories, reducing brand awareness.[29] For example, when Gillette introduced Venus (a razor for women), it may have diminished its identification with the target audience of men.

Some notable—and fascinating—counterexamples to these dilution effects exist, however, in firms that have branded a heterogeneous set of products and still achieved a reasonable level of perceived quality for each. As we saw in Chapter 11, many Japanese firms have adopted a corporate branding strategy with a very broad product portfolio. For example, Yamaha developed a strong reputation selling an extremely diverse brand line that includes motorcycles, guitars, and pianos. Mitsubishi uses its name to brand a bank, cars, and aircraft. Canon has successfully marketed cameras, photocopiers, and office equipment.

Along a similar vein, the founder of Virgin Records, Richard Branson, has conducted an ambitious, and perhaps risky, brand extension program (see Branding Brief 13-2). In all these cases, it seems the brand has been able to secure a dominant association to quality in the minds of consumers without strong product identification that might otherwise limit it.

BRANDING BRIEF 13-2

Are There Any Boundaries to the Virgin Brand Name?

Perhaps the most extensive brand extension program in recent years has been undertaken by Richard Branson with his Virgin brand. Virgin's brand strategy is to go into categories where consumer needs are not well met and do different things—and do them differently—to better satisfy consumers.

Branson founded the Virgin record label at the age of 21, and in 1984, he launched Virgin Atlantic Airways. Later, he made millions on the sale of his record label, his Virgin record retail chain, and his Virgin computer games business. After licensing the use of the Virgin name to European startup airlines that were flying the London–Athens and London–Dublin routes, Branson decided to expand the range of products carrying the Virgin brand.

Branson has since licensed the Virgin name for use on personal computers and set up joint ventures in 1994 to market Virgin Vodka and Virgin Cola. In 1997, he took over six of the United Kingdom's government rail lines and established Virgin Rail. In 1999, he launched Virgin Mobile, a wireless company that provides cellular service through a partnership with Deutsche Telecom. He branched into e-commerce that same year with the debut of Virgin.com, a portal where consumers can purchase every product or service offered by the Virgin brand.

Today, the Virgin Group employs more than 71,000 people, spans 35 countries, and contains more than 60 branded companies marketing such diverse product areas as travel, lifestyle, media and mobile, money, people and planet, music, health care, and alcohol. Virgin had 2016 revenues of an estimated £15 billion, and Branson's personal fortune was estimated at £4.9 billion in 2016.

- *Travel:* Virgin Australia, Virgin Atlantic Airways, Virgin Holidays, Virgin Holidays + Hip Hotels, Virgin Holidays Cruises, Virgin Limited Edition, Virgin Vacations, Virgin Galactic, Virgin Books, Virgin Limobike, Virgin Trains
- *Lifestyle:* Virgin Active UK, Virgin Active Australia, Virgin Active Italia, Virgin Active Portugal, Virgin Active South Africa, Virgin Active Spain, Virgin Experience Days, Virgin Racing, Virgin Balloon Flights, The Virgin Voucher, Virgin Sports
- *Money:* Virgin Money UK, Virgin Money Australia, Virgin Money South Africa, Virgin Money Giving, Virgin Gift Card, Virgin Startup
- *People and Planet:* Virgin Earth Challenge, Virgin Green Fund, Virgin Unite
- *Telecom and Tech:* Virgin Connect, Virgin Media, Virgin Business, Virgin Mobile
- *Music:* Virgin Megastore, Virgin Radio International, Virgin Festivals
- *Health Care:* Virgin Health Bank, Virgin Pulse, Virgin Care, Virgin Pure
- *Alcohol:* Virgin Wines Australia, Virgin Wines UK, Virgin Wines US.

The Virgin brand name has expanded to many different categories, resulting in a debate about the limits of its brand extension strategy.

Virgin's growth and expansion has sparked debate about Branson's seemingly undisciplined extension of the brand. One branding expert criticized Virgin's rapid expansion: "Virgin makes no sense; it's completely unfocused." When Virgin ventures are poorly received, as Virgin Cola, Virgin Vodka, Virgin PCs, Virgin Jeans, Virgin Brides, and Virgin Clothing were in recent years, experts worry about the cumulative negative effect of these unsuccessful brands on the company's overall equity. One marketing executive illustrated the risk of launching an unsuccessful brand by saying, "When I'm delayed on a Virgin train, I start wondering about Virgin Atlantic. Every experience of a brand counts, and negative experiences count even more."

Some critics believe Virgin consumer products will do little more than generate publicity for Virgin airlines. They also warn of overexposure, even with the young, hip audience the Virgin brand has attracted. For example, one advertising agency wondered if there was a risk that the Virgin brand name would be overextended to the point that it lost its core meaning. In Branson's view, as long as a new brand adds value for the consumer, and the consumer benefits, there should be no reason to shy away from launching new products and extending the brand name.

Among the new products Branson is launching are Virgin Oceanic for oceanic exploration and Virgin Galactic for space tourism on rocket ships. Yet, Virgin has become more disciplined about its expansion in recent years: The company now states that it pursues new businesses only if they are expected to generate more than $150 million in sales within three years. Virgin is also placing great emphasis on sustainability and the environment. Its Web site describes its mission as "to contribute to creating happy and fulfilling lives which are also sustainable." Virgin also attempts to minimize damage to its brand from failed extensions through swift actions when an extension no longer provides any financial value or brand value to strengthen its position as bold and innovative.

Sources: Andy Pasztor, "Virgin Galactic's Flights Seen Delayed Yet Again," *The Wall Street Journal*, October 26, 2011; Jenny Wilson, "Virgin Oceanic: Just the Latest in Richard Branson's Massive Ventures," *Time*, April 6, 2011; Alan Deutscham, "The Gonzo Way of Branding," *Fast Company*, October 2004, 91; Melanie Wells, "Red Baron," *Forbes*, July 3, 2000; Quentin Sommerville, "High-Flying Brand Isn't All It Appears," *Scotland on Sunday*, December 24, 2000; Roger Crowe, "Global—A Brand Too Far?," *GlobalVue*, October 28, 1998; Virgin, "Our Purpose," https://www.virgin.com/virgingroup/content/our-purpose-0, accessed November 22, 2018; Media Network Blog, "Smart Brand Extension Allows Virgin to Keep Up Appearances," October 23, 2014, https://www.theguardian.com/media-network/media-network-blog/2014/oct/23/virgin-success-brand-extension-easygroup, accessed November 22, 2018; Virgin, "About Us," https://www.virgin.com/virgingroup/content/about-us, accessed November 22, 2018.

Can Succeed, but Hurt the Image of the Parent Brand

If customers see the brand extension's attribute or benefit associations as inconsistent or even conflicting with the corresponding associations for the parent brand, they may change their perceptions of the parent brand as a result. Although Coach originally began as a maker of luxury leather handbags, it subsequently introduced (line and brand) extensions in a range of categories including women's and men's leather accessories, among others. They also began to sell more of their products in their own outlet stores and in department stores who often aggressively discounted the brand. Although these products and their prices attracted consumers in the "affordable luxury" segment, it also hurt the image of Coach as a luxury brand. Brand perception suffered some as a result. In recent years, the company has deliberately moved away from those channels to restore margins and their image as a true luxury brand. [30]

Can Dilute Brand Meaning

The potential drawbacks of a brand extension's lack of identification with any one category and a weakened image may be especially evident with high-quality or prestige brands. Consider how Gucci ran into the hazards of overexpansion.

GUCCI

In its prime, the Gucci brand symbolized luxury, status, elegance, and quality. By the 1980s, however, the label had become tarnished by sloppy manufacturing, countless knock-offs, and even a family feud among the managing Gucci brothers. The product line consisted of 22,000 items, distributed extensively across all types of department stores. Not only were there too many items, but some did not even fit the Gucci image—for example, a cheap canvas pocketbook with the double-G logo that was easily counterfeited and sold on the street for $35. Sales recovered only when Gucci refocused the brand, paring the product line to 7,000 high-end items and selling them through its own company-owned outlets. The strategy helped

Gucci has introduced many brand extensions that are symbolic of luxury, high quality, and status.

propel Gucci to the height of the fashion business. With revenue of $4.3 billion in 2016, Gucci is consistently ranked in the world's top 50 brands in value by Interbrand.[31]

To protect their brands from dilution, many up-and-coming fashion companies and designers seeking to establish their brand through a family of brand extensions are now forging exclusive licensing partnerships with a single retailer. Target started with exclusive deals with architect and designer Michael Graves. Target also entered into an agreement with the legendary Italian fashion house Missoni for a limited-edition collection of apparel and accessories for women, men, girls, and babies, as well as home goods including bedding, dinnerware, stationery, and décor.[32] These exclusive licenses enable the licensor to better control the inventory, avoid discounts, and, most importantly, protect the brand.

Can Cause the Company to Forego the Chance to Develop a New Brand

One easily overlooked disadvantage of brand extensions is that by introducing a new product as a brand extension, the company forgoes the chance to create a new brand, with its own unique image and equity. For example, consider the benefits of Amazon's runaway success with Kindle, which gave Amazon the ability to go beyond its traditional arena of online retailing and offer a unique product to consumers.

These brands all created their own associations and image and tapped into markets completely different from those that currently existed for other brands sold by the company. Thus, introducing a new product as a brand extension can have significant and potentially hidden costs in terms of the lost opportunities of creating a new brand franchise. The extension's brand positioning may be less flexible, too, given that it has to live up to the parent brand's promise and image. The positioning of a new brand, in contrast, could be introduced and updated in the most competitively advantageous way possible.

UNDERSTANDING HOW CONSUMERS EVALUATE BRAND EXTENSIONS

What determines whether a brand extension is able to capitalize on potential advantages and avoid, or at least minimize, potential disadvantages? Figure 13-6 displays some examples of successful and unsuccessful brand extensions through the years. Note how even leading marketing companies have sometimes failed despite their best intentions when launching a brand extension.

This section examines how consumers evaluate brand extensions and develops some ideas to help marketing managers better forecast and improve the odds for success of a brand extension.[33]

Successful Category Extensions	Unsuccessful Category Extensions
Dove shampoo and conditioner	Campbell's tomato sauce
Vaseline Intensive Care skin lotion	LifeSavers chewing gum
Hershey's chocolate milk	Cracker Jack cereal
Jell-O Pudding Pops	Harley-Davidson wine coolers
Visa traveler's checks	Hidden Valley Ranch frozen entrees
Sunkist orange soda	Ben-Gay aspirin
Colgate toothbrushes	Kleenex diapers
Mars ice cream bars	Clorox laundry detergent
Arm and Hammer toothpaste	Levi's Tailored Classics suits
Bic disposable lighters	Nautilus athletic shoes
Honda lawn mowers	Domino's fruit-flavored bubble gum
Mr. Clean Auto Dry car wash system	Smucker's ketchup
Fendi watches	Fruit of the Loom laundry detergent
Porsche coffee makers	Coors Rocky Mountain Spring Water
Jeep strollers	Cadbury soap

FIGURE 13-6

Examples of Category Extensions

Managerial Assumptions

To analyze potential consumer response to a brand extension, let's start with a baseline case in which consumers are evaluating the brand extension based only on what they already know about the parent brand and the extension category, and before any advertising, promotion, or detailed product information is available. This baseline case provides the cleanest test of the extension concept itself, and it gives managers guidance about whether to proceed with an extension concept and, if so, what type of marketing program they might need.

Under these baseline conditions, we can expect consumers to use their existing brand knowledge, as well as what they know about the extension category, to try to infer what the extension product might be like. For these inferences to result in favorable evaluations of an extension, four basic conditions must generally hold true:

1. *Consumers have some awareness of and positive associations about the parent brand in memory.* Unless they have positive associations about the parent brand, consumers are unlikely to form favorable expectations of an extension.
2. *At least some of these positive associations will be evoked by the brand extension.* A number of different factors will determine which parent brand associations are evoked, but, in general, consumers are likely to infer associations similar in strength, favorability, and uniqueness to the parent brand when they see the brand extension as similar or close in fit to the parent.
3. *Negative associations are not transferred from the parent brand.* Ideally, any negative associations that do exist for the parent brand will be left behind and not play a prominent role in consumers' evaluation of the extension.
4. *Negative associations are not created by the brand extension.* Finally, any parent-brand attributes or benefits that consumers view positively—or at least neutrally—must not be seen as negative for the extension. Consumers must also not infer any new attribute or benefit associations that did not characterize the parent brand but which they see as a potential drawback to the extension.

If any assumption does not hold true, problems can follow. Now we'll examine some factors that influence the validity of these assumptions and consider in more detail how a brand extension, in turn, affects brand equity.

Brand Extensions and Brand Equity

An extension's ultimate success will depend on its ability to both achieve some of its own brand equity in the new category and contribute to the equity of the parent brand.

Creating Extension Equity.   For the brand extension to create equity, it must have a sufficiently high level of awareness and achieve necessary and desired points-of-parity and points-of-difference. Brand awareness will depend primarily on the marketing program and resources devoted to spreading the word about the extension. As Chapter 12 described, it will also obviously depend on the type of branding strategy adopted. The more prominently we use an existing brand that has already achieved a certain level of awareness and image to brand an extension, the easier it should be to create awareness of and an image for the extension in memory.

Initially, whether we can create a positive image for an extension will depend on three consumer-related factors:

1. How *salient* parent brand associations are in the minds of consumers in the extension context; that is, what information comes to mind about the parent brand when consumers think of the proposed extension, and the strength of those associations.
2. How *favorable* any inferred associations are in the extension context; that is, whether this information suggests the type of product or service the brand extension would be, and whether consumers view these associations as good or bad in the extension context.
3. How *unique* any inferred associations are in the extension category, that is, how these perceptions compare with those about competitors.

As with any brand, successful brand extensions must achieve desired points-of-parity and points-of-difference. Without essential points-of-difference, the brand risks becoming an undistinguished "me-too" entry, vulnerable to well-positioned competitors.[34] Tauber refers to "competitive leverage" as the set of advantages that a brand conveys to an extended product in the new category, that is, "when the consumer, by simply knowing the brand, can think of important ways that they perceive that the new brand extension would be better than competing brands in the category."[35]

PayPal launched its mobile payments solutions (PayPal Here) in the category of mobile payment processing after the launch of Square and PayAnywhere. PayPal leveraged its brand recognition, its ease of use, wide installed base of users, and financial resources to make this foray into mobile payments a success.

At the same time, marketers must also establish any required points-of-parity. The more dissimilar the extension product is to the parent brand, the more likely that points-of-parity will become a positioning priority, and the more important it is to make sure that category POPs are sufficiently well-established. Consumers might have a clear understanding of the extension's intended point-of-difference because it uses an existing brand name. What they often need reassurance about, however—and what should often be the focus of the marketing program—is whether the extension also has the necessary points-of-parity.

For example, Nivea became a leader in the skin cream category by creating strong points-of-difference on the benefits of "gentle," "mild," "caring," and "protective," which consumers value in many categories. Through skillful product development and marketing, the Nivea brand was successfully expanded across a wide variety of skin care and personal care product categories. When it leveraged its brand equity into categories such as deodorants, shampoos, and cosmetics, Nivea found it necessary to establish category points-of-parity before it could promote its points-of-difference. These were of little value unless consumers believed its deodorant was strong enough, its shampoo would produce beautiful enough hair, and its cosmetics would be colorful enough. Once points-of-parity were established, Nivea's core brand associations could be introduced as compelling points-of-difference.

Contributing to Parent Brand Equity. To contribute to parent brand equity, an extension must strengthen or add favorable and unique associations to the parent brand and not diminish the strength, favorability, or uniqueness of any existing associations. The effects of an extension on consumer brand knowledge will depend on four factors:

1. How *compelling* the evidence is about the corresponding attribute or benefit association in the extension context—that is, how attention-getting and unambiguous or easily interpretable the information is. Strong evidence is attention-getting and unambiguous. Weak evidence may be ignored or discounted.
2. How *relevant* or diagnostic the extension evidence is for the attribute or benefit for the parent brand, that is, how much consumers see evidence on product performance or imagery in one category as predictive of product performance or imagery for the brand in other categories. Evidence will affect parent brand evaluations only if consumers feel extension performance is indicative of the parent brand in some way.
3. How *consistent* the extension evidence is with the corresponding parent brand associations. Consistent extension evidence is less likely to change the evaluation of existing parent brand associations. Inconsistent extension evidence creates the potential for change, with the direction and extent of change depending on the relative strength and favorability of the evidence. Note, however, that consumers may discount or ignore highly inconsistent extension evidence if they do not view it as relevant.[36]
4. How *strongly* existing attribute or benefit associations are held in consumer memory for the parent brand, that is, how easy an association might be to change.

Feedback effects that change brand knowledge are thus most likely when consumers view information about the extension as equally revealing about the parent brand, and when they hold only a weak and inconsistent association between the parent brand and that information.[37] Note that negative feedback effects are not restricted to product-related performance associations. As we saw earlier, if a brand has a favorable prestige image association, then consumers may disapprove or even resent a vertical extension (a new version of the product at a lower price). As the Apple case description at the end of this chapter demonstrates, a successful brand expansion strategy could involve introducing a series of well-planned and executed category and line extensions to ensure growth and profitability over time.

The Science of Branding 13-1 provides a framework for scoring brand extensions based on guidelines emanating from prior research on brand extensions. The related research findings are summarized later in the chapter.

Vertical Brand Extensions

We have seen that brand extensions can expand market coverage and bring new consumers into the brand franchise. Vertical brand extensions, which extend the brand up into more premium market segments or down into more value-conscious segments, are a common means of attracting new groups of consumers. The central logic here is that the equity of the parent brand can be transferred in either direction to appeal to consumers who otherwise would not consider it.

THE SCIENCE OF BRANDING 13-1
Scoring Brand Extensions

When identifying and evaluating brand extensions, it is helpful to have a summary tool to judge their viability. The following checklist along with the steps summarized in Figure 13-7 can provide some guidance:

1. Does the parent brand have strong equity?
2. Is there a strong basis of extension fit?
3. Will the extension have necessary points-of-parity and points-of-difference?
4. How can marketing programs help enhance extension equity?
5. What implications will the extension have on parent brand equity and profitability?
6. How should feedback effects best be managed?

It is also useful to employ a more systematic analysis of proposed extensions. The Brand Extendibility Scorecard is designed to help marketers conduct thoughtful, thorough analysis of brand extensions (see Figure 13-8). Like any marketing tool or framework, however, it serves as a means to an end and is designed to inform decision-making, not to provide black-and-white "go or no-go" decisions.

On the scorecard, three of its four main criteria follow the classic "3 Cs" perspectives to judge brand positioning—the consumer, company, and competitive point of view. The fourth criterion is unique to the scorecard and measures brand equity feedback.

Within each criterion, there are two major factors and one minor factor. Major factors are scored on a 10-point scale; minor factors, on a 5-point scale. Maximum points are awarded if the extension candidate is clearly ideal on that factor, using either company or industry measures.

When we are scoring extensions, relative performance is important as absolute performance. Ranking extension candidates by their scores can provide a clear sense of priority, but we may also want to set cutoff points to guide decisions about potential extensions, perhaps by first scoring recent successful and unsuccessful extensions for the brand and even for competitors. This step also allows the marketing team to become more familiar with the scorecard.

1. Define actual and desired consumer knowledge about the brand (e.g., create a mental map and identify key sources of equity).
2. Identify possible extension candidates on the basis of parent brand associations and overall similarity or fit of extension to the parent brand.
3. Evaluate the potential of the extension candidate to create equity according to the three-factor model:
   - Salience of parent brand associations
   - Favorability of inferred extension associations
   - Uniqueness of inferred extension associations
4. Evaluate extension candidate feedback effects according to the four-factor model:
   - How compelling the extension evidence is
   - How relevant the extension evidence is
   - How consistent the extension evidence is
   - How strong the extension evidence is
5. Consider possible competitive advantages as perceived by consumers and possible reactions initiated by competitors.
6. Design marketing campaign to maximize the likelihood of success and potential positive feedback effects.
7. Evaluate extension success and effects on parent brand equity.

FIGURE 13-7

Steps in Successfully Introducing Brand Extensions

Allocate points according to how well the new product concept rates on the specific dimensions in the following areas:

Consumer Perspectives: Desirability

10 pts. _____ Product category appeal (size, growth potential)

10 pts. _____ Equity transfer (perceived brand fit)

5 pts. _____ Perceived consumer target fit

Company Perspectives: Deliverability

10 pts. _____ Asset leverage (product technology, organizational skills, marketing effectiveness via channels and communications)

10 pts. _____ Profit potential

5 pts. _____ Launch feasibility

Competitive Perspectives: Differentiability

10 pts. _____ Comparative appeal (many advantages, few disadvantages)

10 pts. _____ Competitive response (likelihood, immunity or invulnerability from)

5 pts. _____ Legal/regulatory/institutional barriers

Brand Perspectives: Equity Feedback

10 pts. _____ Strengthens parent brand equity

10 pts. _____ Facilitates additional brand extension opportunities

5 pts. _____ Improves asset base

TOTAL _____ pts

FIGURE 13-8

Brand Extendibility Scorecard

Pros and Cons.   Vertical extensions can confer a number of advantages. An upward extension can improve brand image, because a premium version of a brand often brings positive associations with it. Extensions in either direction can offer consumers variety, revitalize the parent brand, and permit further extensions in a given direction.

Yet, vertical extensions are also susceptible to many of the disadvantages of brand extensions. A vertical extension to a new price point, whether higher or lower, can confuse or frustrate consumers who have learned to expect a certain price range from a brand. If the upward extension is sub-branded on the basis of a new attribute addition, then competitive brands sharing that attribute may enter the picture, and the parent brand may suffer in comparison.[38] Consumers may reject the extension, and the parent brand's image will suffer. For prestige brands in particular, firms must often maintain a balance between availability and scarcity such that people always aspire to be a customer and do not feel excluded.

Even a successful downward extension has the possibility of harming the parent's brand image by introducing associations common to lower-priced brands, such as inferior quality or reduced service. Interestingly, however, research has shown that higher-quality extensions are likely to improve evaluations of the parent brand more than lower-quality extensions might harm it.[39]

One of the biggest risk factors of a vertical extension, particularly a downward one, is that it will succeed but cannibalize sales of a parent brand. It may bring new consumers to the brand franchise, but it may also bring a greater number of existing customers of the parent brand.

In the technology context, another type of vertical extension that is frequently observed is that of a company offering a basic version of software for free and later introducing a line extension with additional features for a significant price. The *freemium* model has been very successful across a range of software products. For example, Dropbox, the cloud storage platform, offered a free plan for up to 2 GB of space, and later on, upgraded users to the Pro plan with significantly larger amounts of storage for a price of $9.99 per month.[40] This type of vertical extension only works when there are significant benefits associated with creating a large user base who interact regularly with the free product. These users can then be targeted for upselling the higher-priced extensions of the base product.

TESLA 3 is a lower-priced Tesla meant to appeal to a larger audience.

Examples.   Despite the problems inherent in vertical extensions, many companies have succeeded in extending their brands to enter new markets across a range of price points. These companies have made sure that clear differentiation existed between brand extensions, minimizing the potential for brand overlap and accompanying consumer confusion and brand cannibalization. Each extension also lived up to the core promise of the parent brand, thus reducing the possibility that any would hurt the parent's image. Consider how vertical extensions have helped these two brands appeal to a broader audience.

- As part of a plan to upgrade, Holiday Inn Worldwide broke its domestic hotels into five separate chains to tap into five different benefit segments: the upscale Crowne Plaza, the traditional Holiday Inn, the budget Holiday Inn Express, and the business-oriented Holiday Inn Select (although soon to be phased out) and Holiday Inn Hotel & Suites. Different branded chains received different marketing programs and emphasis.
- Tesla is a major automaker that introduced the Model S in 2012 as a luxury electric sedan. This very successful electric car in 2017 was priced at $68,000. Capitalizing on the success of this car, Tesla introduced the Tesla Model X as a full-size SUV at a retail price of US $132,000. The Tesla Model 3 has a price of $35,000 and is aimed to offer the eco-friendly brand to a larger audience.

Naming Strategies.   Firms often adopt sub-branding strategies to distinguish their lower-priced entries. For example, the retail outlet, Nordstrom Rack offers cheaper merchandise and discounted clothing and is typically priced lower than the parent retailer, Nordstrom, which offers higher-priced merchandise. Such extension introductions clearly must be handled carefully; typically, the parent brand plays a secondary role.

An even more difficult vertical extension is an upward brand stretch. In general, it is difficult to change people's impressions of the brand enough to justify a significant upward extension. Concern about the unwillingness of consumers to update their brand knowledge was what led Honda, Toyota, Hyundai, and Nissan to introduce their luxury car models as separate nameplates (Acura, Lexus, Equus, and Infiniti, respectively). As it turns out, product improvements to the upper ends of their brand lines since the introduction of these new car nameplates may have made it easier to bridge the gap into the luxury market with their brands.

At the same time, it is possible to use certain brand modifiers to signal a noticeable, although presumably not dramatic, quality improvement—for example, iPhone SE, Ultra Dry Pampers, Extra Strength Tylenol, or PowerPro Dustbuster Plus. These indirect extensions, or "super-brands," may be less risky than direct extensions when moving a master brand up-market.

To avoid the potential difficulties associated with vertical extensions, however, companies sometimes elect to use new and different brand names to expand vertically. The Gap has employed a three-tier approach, using the Banana Republic brand to command a 40 percent price premium that the Gap would likely never attain on its own and launching the Old Navy brand to offer 40 percent discounts.

By developing unique brand names, companies pursuing vertical expansion can avoid a negative transfer of equity from a lower brand to a higher brand, but they sacrifice some ability to transfer positive associations. Yet, when the parent brand makes no secret of its ownership of the vertical brands, as is the case with both the Gap and Toyota, some associations may be transferred because the parent acts as a "shadow endorser" of the new brand.[41]

Branding Brief 13-3 illustrates how Levi Strauss & Co. has been able to expand its market coverage and attract new consumers through vertical extensions.

BRANDING BRIEF 13-3
Levi's Extends Its Brand

Levi Strauss & Co. is an iconic U.S. brand, best known for the distinctive red tab on the back pocket of its jeans. Founded in 1853 by Bavarian immigrant Levi Strauss, the company grew to one of the world's largest apparel companies, with more than $6 billion in revenue and cachet as the cool jeans teens aspired to wear. During the late 1990s, Levi faced declining sales and growing debt. Its long tradition of producing durable jeans became a liability for its fashion image, and the firm remained private despite pressure to take all or part of it public to pay down debt.

For years, market power had been shifting away from suppliers like Levi and toward retailers. Mass merchants were selling about one-third of all jeans in the United States, and their share of the market was growing. The advent of discount stores made many consumers more price-sensitive. In 1999, Levi Strauss adopted a segmentation strategy to convince different types of retailers (department stores, specialty chains, upscale boutiques, and mass merchants) to carry its products.

Levi's has a number of line extensions that appeal to different segments, and include discount brand DENIZEN; Levi's 501 has introduced CT (customized and tapered) jeans, 501 Stretch, and 501 Skinny.

Under the segmentation strategy, Levi's brands ranged from a relatively inexpensive discount line to $150-and-up vintage designs. Levi already sold to JCPenney and Sears, Roebuck and Co., and those choices had alienated some major retail customers who preferred the brand to remain exclusive and slightly more upscale. Despite management concerns about potential reputation damage, Levi created the Signature by Levi Strauss & Co. brand to sell at mass merchants and began selling to Walmart in 2003.

Signature, positioned as a premium mass brand, carried new labels and styles manufactured from less-expensive fabric. The Levi Strauss & Co. name appeared in cursive; gone were the red tab and traditional Levi pocket stitching and logo. At that time, Levi priced Signature jeans at $23—more than other mass brands but below its $29 regular brand.

Initially, the segmentation strategy created rough spots for other Levi brands. As Levi's executives struggled to appease Walmart and find the right price point for mass retailers, other parts of the business suffered. Orders from department stores slipped, and sales of regular Levi's, which had finally steadied leading up to the launch of the Signature brand, resumed their decline. Furthermore, a new high-fashion line called Type 1 failed.

In 2006, however, Walmart's price-chopping move ultimately proved effective, and Signature jeans began to sell more quickly. The company also added lines of Signature baby clothing, bags and wallets, and men's khaki pants, selling to other mass retailers such as Kmart and Meijer.

Around the same time, Levi attempted to expand into premium segments, selling premium lines such as Levi's Capital E to Bloomingdales and Barney's New York. The upward stretch has proven to be more challenging. Levi recently consolidated several premium subbrands under just two names: Made & Crafted, a premium denim line featuring better fabrics and fit, and Levi's Vintage Clothing, offering reproductions of items from the brand's historical archives.

The biggest launch, however, was another discount brand, DENIZEN from Levi's, first introduced into Asia in 2010. The name was chosen because it means "inhabitant" or someone belonging to a community of family and friends. After being launched in China, India, Mexico, Pakistan, Singapore, and South Korea, DENIZEN from Levi's was introduced into the U.S. market, initially sold exclusively at Target for $17.99 to $29.99. Levi's has continued to innovate through the introduction of line extensions of the 501 brand. For example, in 2015 and 2016, it launched CT (customised and tapered) jean, 501 Stretch, 501 Skinny which retail for $80. By making several styles available online, Levi's has bypassed traditional retail channels.

Sources: Levi Strauss & Co., "About Us," https://www.levi.com/US/en_US/features/about-us, accessed November 22, 2018; Sandra O'Loughlin, "Levi Strauss Seeing Green with Signature Blues," *Brandweek*, July 25, 2005; "In Bow to Retailer's New Clout, Levi Strauss Makes Alterations," *The Wall Street Journal*, June 17, 2004, A1; Robert Guy Matthews, "Levi Strauss Brushes Up On Its Shakespeare," *The Wall Street Journal*, January 14, 2005; Jacques Chevron, "Tacit Messages: A Lesson from Levi's," *Brandweek*, February 6, 2006; "Strauss & Co.; On the Record: Phil Marineau," *San Francisco Chronicle*, March 6, 2006, https://www.sfgate.com/business/ontherecord/article/LEVI-STRAUSS-CO-On-the-Record-Phil-Marineau-2521804.php, accessed November 22, 2018; Rachel Dodes, "Levi's Shoots for the High-End Hipster," *The Wall Street Journal*, April 14, 2010, https://www.wsj.com/articles/SB10001424052702303695604575182252816707936, accessed November 22, 2018; Purvita Chatterjee, "Levi's Takes on Private Labels with Denizen," *The Hindu Business Line*, May 23, 2011; Denizen, "dENiZEN Jeans from the Levi's Brand Arrive Exclusively at Target," July 19, 2011, https://www.prnewswire.com/news-releases/denizen-jeans-from-the-levis-brand-arrive-exclusively-at-target-125813583.html, accessed November 22, 2018; Barney Jopson and Patti Waldmeir, "Levi's Denizen Brand Poised for U.S. Launch," *Financial Times*, April 11, 2011, https://www.ft.com/content/2345e5c2-648a-11e0-a69a-00144feab49a, accessed November 22, 2018; Vanessa Friedman, "Levi's Responds to Challengers with Revamped Women's Jeans," *The New York Times*, July 7, 2015, https://www.nytimes.com/2015/07/09/fashion/levis-responds-to-challengers-with-revamped-womens-jeans.html, accessed November 22, 2018.

EVALUATING BRAND EXTENSION OPPORTUNITIES

Academic research and industry experience have revealed a number of principles governing successful brand extensions. Marketers must consider their strategies carefully by systematically following the steps listed in Figure 13-9 and using managerial judgment and marketing research to help make *each* of these decisions.

1. Successful brand extensions occur when the parent brand is seen as having favorable associations, and there is a perception of fit between the parent brand and the extension product.
2. There are many bases of fit: product-related attributes and benefits as well as non-product-related attributes and benefits related to common usage situations or user types.
3. Depending on consumer knowledge of the product categories, perceptions of fit may be based on technical or manufacturing commonalities or more surface considerations such as necessary or situational complementarity.
4. High-quality brands stretch farther than average-quality brands, although both types of brands have boundaries.
5. A brand that is seen as prototypical of a product category can be difficult to extend outside the category.
6. Concrete attribute associations tend to be more difficult to extend than abstract benefit associations.
7. Consumers may transfer associations that are positive in the original product class but become negative in the extension context.
8. Consumers may infer negative associations about an extension, perhaps even based on other inferred positive associations.
9. It can be difficult to extend into a product class that is seen as easy to make.
10. A successful extension can not only contribute to the parent brand image but also enable a brand to be extended even farther.
11. An unsuccessful extension hurts the parent brand only when there is a strong basis of fit between the two.
12. An unsuccessful extension does not prevent a firm from backtracking and introducing a more similar extension.
13. Vertical extensions can be difficult and often require sub-branding strategies.
14. The most effective advertising strategy for an extension is one that emphasizes information about the extension (rather than reminders about the parent brand).
15. Individual differences can affect how consumers make an extension decision, and will moderate extension effects.
16. Cultural differences across markets can influence extension success.

FIGURE 13-9

Brand Extension Guidelines Based on Academic Research

Define Actual and Desired Consumer Knowledge about the Brand

It is critical for marketers to fully understand the depth and breadth of awareness of the parent brand, and the strength, favorability, and uniqueness of its associations. Moreover, marketers must know what is to be the basis of positioning and core benefits satisfied by the brand. Profiling actual and desired brand knowledge structures helps identify possible brand extensions as well as guide decisions that contribute to their success. In evaluating an extension, a company must understand where it would like to take the brand in the long run. Because the introduction of an extension can change brand meaning, it can affect consumer response to all subsequent marketing activity as well (see Chapter 14).

Identify Possible Extension Candidates

Chapter 12 described a number of consumer, firm, and competitor criteria for choosing which products and markets a firm should enter. With respect to consumer factors, marketers should consider parent brand associations—especially as they relate to brand positioning and core benefits—and product categories that might seem to fit with that brand image in the minds of consumers.[42] Although consumers are generally better able to react to an extension concept than to suggest one, it still may be instructive to ask consumers what products the brand should consider offering if it were to introduce a new product. Brainstorming is another way to generate category extension candidates, along with consumer research.

One or more associations can often serve as the basis of fit. Allegra is a well-known allergy medication which extended its brand to introduce Allegra Anti-Itch Cooling Relief and Anti-Itch Intensive Relief. These products leveraged the success of the Allegra product and utilized a similar color scheme on their packaging. Tyson's brand of breakfast sausages, Jimmy Dean, introduced a new line of products designed for lunch and dinner by leveraging its association with frozen foods.[43] As these examples help illustrate, identifying key brand associations can become the starting point of identifying potential brand extension opportunities.

Evaluate the Potential of the Extension Candidate

In forecasting the success of a proposed brand extension, marketers should assess—through judgment and research—the likelihood that the extension will realize the advantages and avoid the disadvantages of brand extensions, as summarized in Figures 13-2 and 13-4. As with any new product, analysis of the 3 Cs—consumer, corporate, and competitive factors—as well as category factors can be useful.

Consumer Factors. To evaluate the potential of a proposed brand extension, we assess its ability to achieve its own brand equity, as well as the likelihood that it can affect the parent brand's existing brand equity. First, marketers must forecast the strength, favorability, and uniqueness of *all* associations to the brand extension. In other words, what will be the salience, favorability, or uniqueness of parent brand associations in the proposed extension context? Similarly, what will

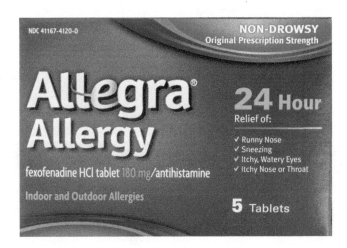

Allegra extended its popular allergy product to introduce new products for anti-itch relief, using the same color scheme on their packaging to unify the brand's identity across the products.

be the strength, favorability, and uniqueness of any other inferred associations? The three-factor model of extension evaluations and the four-factor model of extension feedback effects can provide guidance in studying consumer reactions.

To narrow down the list of possible extensions, we often need consumer research (see Chapter 10 for a review). We can ask consumers directly for their brand permission (How well does the proposed extension fit with the parent brand? Would you expect such a new product from the parent brand?). We can even ask what products they believe are currently attached to the brand. If a majority of consumers believe a proposed extension product is already being sold under the brand, there would seem to be little risk in introducing it, at least based on initial consumer reaction.

To understand consumers' perceptions of a proposed extension, we can use open-ended associations (What comes into your mind when you think of the brand extension? What are your first impressions on hearing that the parent brand is introducing the extension?), as well as ratings scales based on reactions to concept statements. An interesting statistical approach uses Bayesian factor analysis to separate brand and category effects to better assess brand fit.[44]

Common pitfalls include failing to take all consumers' brand knowledge structures into account. Often marketers mistakenly focus on one or perhaps a few brand associations as a potential basis of fit and ignore other, possibly more important, brand associations in the process.

Another major mistake in evaluating brand extensions is overlooking how literal consumers can be in evaluating brand extensions. Although consumers ultimately care about benefits, they often notice and evaluate attributes—especially concrete ones—in reacting to an extension. Brand managers, though, tend to focus on perceived benefits in predicting consumer reactions, and, as a result, they may overlook some potentially damaging attribute associations.

BIC

By emphasizing inexpensive, disposable products, the French company Société Bic was able to create markets for nonrefillable ballpoint pens in the late 1950s, disposable cigarette lighters in the early 1970s, and disposable razors in the early 1980s. It unsuccessfully tried the same strategy in marketing Bic perfumes in the United States and Europe in 1989. The perfumes—two for women ("Nuit" and "Jour") and two for men ("Bic for Men" and "Bic Sport for Men")—were packaged in quarter-ounce glass spray bottles that looked like fat cigarette lighters and sold for $5 each. The products were displayed on racks in plastic packages at checkout counters throughout Bic's extensive distribution channels, which included 100,000 or so drugstores, supermarkets, and other mass merchandisers. At the time, a Bic spokeswoman described the new products as extensions of the Bic heritage—"high quality at affordable prices, convenient to purchase, and convenient to use."[45] The brand extension was launched with a $20 million advertising and promotion campaign containing images of stylish people enjoying themselves with the perfume and using the tagline "Paris in Your Pocket." Nevertheless, Bic was unable to overcome its lack of cachet and negative image associations; failing to achieve a critical point-of-parity, the extension fell short. Other brand extensions by Bic (e.g., Bic disposable underwear) although leveraging the association of Bic with disposable products, were also seen as brand extension failures.

Although Bic has pioneered a variety of successful brand extensions which are of a disposable nature, its perfume brand extension was less well received.

Corporate and Competitive Factors.   Marketers must take not only a consumer perspective in evaluating a proposed brand extension, but also a broader corporate and competitive perspective. How effectively are the corporate assets leveraged in the extension setting? How relevant are existing marketing programs, perceived benefits, and target customers to the extension? What are the competitive advantages to the extension as consumers perceive them, and possible reactions initiated by competitors as a result?

One of the biggest mistakes marketers make in launching extensions is failing to properly account for competitors' actions and reactions.[46] Too many extension products and too strongly entrenched competition can put a strain on company resources. Arm & Hammer's brand extension program met major resistance in categories such as deodorants when existing competitors fought back.

Brand counterextensions—whereby a competing brand in the extension category chooses to launch its own extension into the parent brand's category—can pose a significant threat. The introduction of Hershey's strawberry syrup was followed by Smucker's chocolate syrup; Dixie paper plates was followed by Chinet paper cups. A successful extension can reduce the perceived fit between categories, making it easier for a brand to counterattack.[47]

Category Factors.   Marketers must determine the optimal product line strategy for their brand. To do so, they need a clear understanding of the market and the cost interdependencies between products.[48] This, in turn, means examining the percentage of sales and profits contributed by each item in the product line and its ability to withstand competition and address consumer needs.

A product line is too short if the manager can increase long-term profits by adding items; the line is too long if the manager can increase profits by dropping items.[49] Increasing the length of the product line by adding new variants or items typically expands market coverage, and therefore, market share, but it also increases costs. From a branding perspective, longer product lines may decrease the consistency of the associated brand image if all items use the same brand.

Reddy, Holak, and Bhat studied the determinants of line extension success using data on 75 line extensions of 34 cigarette brands over a 20-year period.[50] Their major findings indicate that:

- Line extensions of strong brands are more successful than extensions of weak brands.
- Line extensions of symbolic brands enjoy greater market success than those of less symbolic brands.
- Line extensions that receive strong advertising and promotional support are more successful than those extensions that receive meager support.
- Line extensions entering earlier into a product subcategory are more successful than extensions entering later, but only if they are extensions of strong brands.
- Firm size and marketing competencies also play a part in an extension's success.
- Earlier line extensions have helped in the market expansion of the parent brand.
- Incremental sales generated by line extensions may more than compensate for the loss in sales due to cannibalization.

Despite the pitfalls of line extensions and the many considerations necessary to properly manage extensions, the allure of line extensions for companies remains strong, primarily due to the cost and risk incurred in launching an entirely new brand. One report showed that line extensions take half as long to develop, cost far less to market, and enjoy twice the success rate of major new brand launches.[51]

Design Marketing Programs to Launch Extension

Too often, companies use extensions as a shortcut means of introducing a new product and pay insufficient attention to developing a branding and marketing strategy that will maximize the equity of the brand extension as well as enhance the equity of the parent brand. As is the case with a new brand, building brand equity for a brand extension requires choosing brand elements, designing the optimal marketing program to launch the extension, and leveraging secondary associations.

Choosing Brand Elements.   By definition, brand extensions retain one or more elements from an existing brand. They do not have to leverage only the brand name but can use other brand elements too. For example, Heinz and Campbell's have implemented package designs that distinguish different line extensions or brand types, but reveal their common origin at the same time.[52]

Sometimes packaging is such a critical component of brand equity that it is hard to imagine an extension without it. Brand managers are in a real dilemma in such cases, because if they choose the same type of packaging, they run the risk that the extension will not be well distinguished. If they use different packaging, they may leave a key source of brand equity behind.

A brand extension can retain or modify one or more brand elements from the parent brand as well as adopt its own brand elements. In creating new brand elements for an extension, marketers should follow the same guidelines of memorability, meaningfulness, likeability, protectability, adaptability, and transferability that we described in Chapter 4 for the development of any brand.

New brand elements are often necessary to help distinguish the brand extension and build awareness and image. As Chapter 12 noted, the relative prominence of existing parent brand elements and new extension brand elements will dictate the strength of transfer from the parent brand to the extension, as well as the feedback from the extension to the parent brand.

Designing an Optimal Marketing Program.   The marketing program for a brand extension must consider the same guidelines in building brand equity that we described in Chapters 5 and 6. Consumer perceptions of value must guide pricing decisions, distribution strategies must blend push and pull considerations, and the firm must integrate marketing communications by mixing and matching communication options.

When it comes to positioning, the less similar the extension is to the parent brand, the more important it typically is to establish necessary and competitive points-of-parity. The points-of-difference for a category extension in many cases directly follow from the points-of-difference for the parent brand, and consumers readily perceive them. Thus, when Nivea extended into shampoos and conditioners, deodorants, and cosmetics and other beauty products, its key "gentleness" point-of-difference transferred relatively easily. With line extensions, on the other hand, marketers have to create a new association that can serve as an additional point-of-difference and help distinguish the extension from the parent brand too.

For line extensions, consumers must also understand how the new product relates to existing products in order to minimize possible cannibalization or confusion.

Leveraging Secondary Brand Associations.   Brand extensions will often leverage the same secondary associations as the parent brand, although competing in the extension category may require some additional fortification like linking to other entities. A brand extension differs in that, by definition, there is always some leveraging of another brand or company. The extent to which these other associations become linked to the extension, however, depends on the branding strategy the firm adopts and how it brands the extension. As we've seen, the more common the brand elements and the more prominence they receive, the more likely it is that parent brand associations will transfer.

Evaluate Extension Success and Effects on Parent Brand Equity

The final step in evaluating brand extension opportunities is to assess the extent to which an extension is able to achieve its own equity as well as contribute to the equity of the parent brand. To help measure its success, we can use brand tracking based on the customer-based brand equity model or other key measures of consumer response centered on both the extension and the parent brand as a whole. A simple checklist and a more detailed scorecard to help in evaluating brand extension opportunities follows.

EXTENSION GUIDELINES BASED ON ACADEMIC RESEARCH

Now we turn to some specific guidance about brand extensions. Fortunately, much academic research has focused on this strategy. We summarize some of the important conclusions in Figure 13-9 and describe them in detail in this section.

1. *Successful brand extensions occur when the parent brand has favorable associations, and consumers perceive a fit between the parent brand and the extension product.* To better understand the process by which consumers evaluate a brand extension, many academic researchers have adopted a categorization perspective. Categorization research suggests that people usually evaluate a stimulus in terms of whether they can classify it as a member of a previously defined mental category.

We could argue that consumers use their categorical knowledge of brands and products to simplify, structure, and interpret their marketing environment.[53] For example, consumers may see brands as categories that, over time, have acquired a number of specific attributes based on their individual members.[54] As Method has expanded its range of cleaning products, consumers might develop stronger brand associations to modern designs and environmental friendliness.

In this categorization perspective, if consumers saw a brand extension as closely related or similar to the brand category, they could easily transfer their existing attitude about the parent brand to the extension. If they were not as sure about the similarity, they might evaluate the extension in a more detailed, piecemeal fashion. In this case, the strength, favorability, and uniqueness of salient brand associations would determine how they viewed the extension.[55]

Consistent with these notions, Aaker and Keller collected consumer reactions to 20 proposed extensions from six well-known brands and found that both a perception of fit between the original and extension product categories and a perception of high quality for the parent brand led to more favorable extension evaluations.[56]

A number of subsequent studies have explored the generalizability of these findings to markets outside the United States. Based on a comprehensive analysis of 131 brand extensions from seven such replication studies around the world, Bottomly and Holden concluded that this basic model clearly generalized, although cross-cultural differences influenced the relative importance attached to the model components.[57]

Thus, in general, brand extensions are more likely to be favorably evaluated by consumers if they see some basis of fit or congruity between the proposed extension and parent brand.[58] Interestingly, moderately incongruent extensions can evoke more favorable extension evaluations than highly congruent extensions under certain specialized situations, such as when consumers are highly involved, and the extension is otherwise undifferentiated from competitors.[59]

2. *There are many bases of fit; both product-related and non-product-related attributes and benefits may influence extension fit.* Any association about the parent brand that consumers hold in memory may serve as a potential basis of fit. Most academic researchers assume consumers' judgments of similarity are a function of salient shared associations between the parent brand and the extension product category. Specifically, the more common and the fewer distinctive associations that exist, the greater the perception of overall similarity, whether based on product- or non product-related attributes and benefits.[60]

To demonstrate how fit does not have to be based on product-related associations alone, Park, Milberg, and Lawson showed how the more prestige-oriented Rolex brand could more easily extend into categories such as grandfather clocks, bracelets, and rings than the more function-oriented Timex brand; however, Timex could more easily extend into categories such as stopwatches, batteries, and calculators.

Broniarczyk and Alba provide another compelling demonstration of the importance of recognizing salient brand associations.[61] They showed that a perceived lack of fit between the parent brand's product category and the proposed extension category could be overcome if key parent brand associations were salient and relevant in the extension category. For example, Froot Loops cereal—that has strong brand associations to sweet, flavor, and kids—was better able to extend to dissimilar product categories—such as lollipops and popsicles than to similar product categories such as waffles and hot cereal—because of the relevance of its brand associations in the dissimilar extension category.

Thus, extension fit is more than just the number of common and distinctive brand associations between the parent brand and the extension product category.[62] These research studies and others demonstrate the importance of taking a broader perspective of categorization and fit. For example, Bridges, Keller, and Sood refer to *category coherence* as members that "hang together" and "make sense." Based on this concept of category coherence, physically dissimilar toy, bath care, and car seat products in the Fisher-Price product line can be linked together as "products for children."[63]

Researchers have also explored other, more specific, aspects of fit, and have found that the use of specific contexts could influence judgments of fit. For example, Bush provided experimental data that suggests that when fit is judged in the context of a specific brand name ("*Time* magazine is like *Time* books"), judgments of fit are different than when fit is judged with only category labels (e.g., magazines and books). Smith and Andrews surveyed industrial goods marketers and found that the relationship between fit and new product evaluations was influenced by customers' confidence that a firm could provide a proposed new product.[64]

3. *Depending on their knowledge of the product categories, consumers may perceive fit based on technical or manufacturing commonalities, or on surface considerations such as necessary or situational complementarity.* Consumers can also base fit on considerations other than attributes or benefits. Taking a demand-side and supply-side perspective of consumer perceptions, Aaker and Keller showed that perceived fit between the parent brand and the extension product could be related to the economic notions of substitutability and complementarity in product use (from a demand-side perspective), as well as to the firm's perceived grasp of the skills and assets necessary to make the extension product (from a supply-side perspective).

   Thus, Honda's perceived expertise in making motors for lawn mowers and cars may help perceptions of fit for any other machinery with small motors that Honda might want to introduce. The Food Network leveraged its expertise in foods to introduce Food Network cookware. On the other hand, some extension examples have little manufacturing compatibility but greater usage complementarity, such as Colgate's extension from toothpaste to toothbrushes or Duracell's extension from batteries to flashlights. Harley Davidson clothing and Coppertone sunglasses are extension products which leverage the particular usage occasions in which their respective parent brands are used (i.e., motorcycles and sunscreen). In other cases, extensions may leverage a similar target audience, as in the case of Visa traveler's checks.

   These perceptions of fit, however, may depend on how much consumers know about the product categories. As Muthukrishnan and Weitz demonstrated, expert consumers are more likely to use technical or manufacturing commonalities to judge fit, whereas less knowledgeable novice consumers are more likely to use superficial, perceptual considerations, such as common package, shape, color, size, and usage.[65] Zhang and Sood showed a similar pattern of knowledge effects based on age. Children were more likely to evaluate extensions on the basis of surface cues (such as brand name linguistic characteristics of an extension, for example whether a brand name rhymed or not) while adults were more likely to use deep cues (like category similarity between the parent brand and extension category).[66]

   Fit perceptions also vary across different types of consumers and how they view product extensions. Yorkston, Nunes, and Matta demonstrated that those consumers who believe that the personality traits of a brand are malleable (i.e., *incremental theorists*), are more accepting of brand extensions than consumers who believe that a brand's traits are fixed (i.e., *entity theorists*). Another set of findings by Cutright, Bettman, and Fitzsimmons show that when feelings of *personal control* are low for consumers, they may be more likely to reject brand extensions that do not seem to fit well with a parent brand. Finally, researchers Monga and Gurhan-Canli found that mating mind-sets (thinking about a mate) can increase perceptions of extension fit particularly for moderately dissimilar extensions because it induces something called *relational processing*.[67]

4. *High-quality brands stretch farther than average-quality brands, although both types have boundaries.* Consumers often see high-quality brands as more credible, expert, and trustworthy. As a result, even if they believe a relatively distant extension does not really fit with the brand, they may be more willing to give a high-quality brand the benefit of the doubt than a brand they see as average in quality.[68]

   Thus, one important benefit of building a strong brand is that it can extend more easily into more diverse categories.[69] Fedorikhin, Park, and Thomson found that if consumers had a high degree of attachment with a brand, they were willing to pay more for an extension, recommend it to others, and forgive any mishaps.[70] Similarly, Yeung and Wyer showed that if a brand evokes a strong positive emotional reaction, consumers are likely to be less influenced by the fit of the extension.[71]

   Regardless, all brands have boundaries, as a number of observers have persuasively argued by pointing out ridiculous, and even comical, hypothetical brand extension possibilities. As Tauber once noted, few consumers would want Jell-O shoelaces or Tide frozen entrees!

5. *A brand that consumers see as prototypical for a product category can be difficult to extend outside the category.* As a caveat to the earlier conclusion, if consumers see a brand as exemplifying a category too strongly, it may be difficult for them to think of it in any other way.

Numerous examples exist of category leaders that have failed in introducing brand extensions.[72] For example, Bayer, a brand synonymous with aspirin, ran into a stumbling block introducing the Bayer Select line of specialized nonaspirin painkillers.[73] Perhaps the most extreme examples are brands that lost their trademark distinctiveness and became a generic term for the category, such as Thermos and Kleenex. To illustrate the difficulty a prototypical brand may have in extending, consider the experiences of Clorox.

CLOROX

Clorox is a well-known brand whose name is virtually synonymous with bleach. In 1988, Clorox took on consumer goods giants Procter & Gamble and Unilever by introducing the first bleach with detergent. After pouring $225 million into the development and distribution of its detergent products over three years, Clorox was able to achieve only a 3 percent market share. Despite being beaten to market, P&G subsequently introduced Tide with Bleach and was able to achieve a 17 percent share. Reluctantly, Clorox chose to exit the market. Its failure can certainly be attributed in part to the fact that consumers could think of Clorox only in a very limited sense as a bleach product. In a combined "laundry detergent with bleach" product, too, they see laundry detergent as the primary ingredient and bleach as secondary. As a result, in this market, we might expect a laundry detergent extension such as Tide with Bleach to have an advantage over a bleach extension such as Clorox. On the other hand, Clorox has successfully extended its brand into a wide variety of household cleaning products like toilet bowl cleaners, where the bleach ingredient is seen as more relevant.[74]

The relationship between primary and secondary ingredients Clorox may have encountered might also explain why Aunt Jemima was successful in introducing a pancake syrup extension from its well-liked pancake mix product, but syrup maker Log Cabin was less successful in introducing a pancake mix extension: pancake mix is seen as a more dominant ingredient than pancake syrup in breakfast pancakes.

6. *Concrete attribute associations tend to be more difficult to extend than abstract benefit associations.* The limits to market leaders' extension boundaries may be more rigid because many market leaders have strong concrete product attribute associations. These may even be reinforced by their names, like Liquid Paper, Cheez Whiz, and Shredded Wheat.[75] La-Z-Boy, for example, has struggled some to expand its strong usage imagery outside the narrow product line of recliners.

Concrete attribute associations thus may not transfer as broadly to extension categories as more abstract attribute associations.[76] For example, the Aaker and Keller study showed that consumers dismissed a hypothetical Heineken popcorn extension as potentially tasting bad or like beer, and a hypothetical Crest chewing gum extension as tasting unappealing or like toothpaste. More abstract associations, on the other hand, may be more relevant across a wide set of categories because of their intangible nature.

We should note several caveats, however. First, parent brands' concrete attributes *can* transfer to some product categories.[77] A concrete attribute that is highly valued in the extension category because it creates a distinctive taste, ingredient, or component can often make the extension successful. According to Farquhar and Herr, such extensions might include Tylenol sinus medication, Oreo cookies and cream ice cream, and Arm & Hammer carpet deodorizer.[78]

Second, abstract associations may not always transfer easily. This second caveat emerged from a study conducted by Bridges, Keller, and Sood, who examined the relative transferability of product-related brand information when it was represented either as an abstract brand association or as a concrete brand association. Although these authors expected the abstract brand representation to fare better, they found that, for several reasons, the two types of brand images extended equally well into a dissimilar product category—handbags. Perhaps the most important reason was that consumers did not believe the abstract benefit would have the same meaning in the extension category (durability does not necessarily transfer because durability for a watch is not the same as durability for a handbag).[79]

Finally, Joiner and Loken, in a demonstration of the inclusion effect in a brand extension setting, showed that consumers often generalized possession of an attribute from a specific category (like Sony televisions) to a more general category (say, all Sony products) more readily than they generalized the attribute from the specific category (Sony televisions) to another specific category (Sony bicycles). The effect was greater the more the specific extension category was typical of the general category (Sony cameras are more typical than Sony bicycles).[80]

7. *Consumers may transfer associations that are positive in the original product class but become negative in the extension context.* Because they have different motivations or use the product differently in the extension category, consumers may not value a brand association as highly as the original product. For example, when Campbell's test-marketed a tomato sauce with the Campbell's name, it flopped. Apparently, Campbell's strong associations to soup signaled to consumers that the new product would be watery. To give the product more credibility, Campbell changed the name to the Italian-sounding "Prego," and the product has gone on to be a long-term success.

8. *Consumers may infer negative associations about an extension, perhaps even based on other inferred positive associations.* Even if consumers transfer positive associations from the parent brand to the extension, they may still infer other negative associations. For example, the Bridges, Keller, and Sood study showed that consumers who thought a proposed handbag extension from a hypothetical maker of durable watches also would be durable also assumed it would not be fashionable, helping to contribute to low extension evaluations.[81]

9. *It can be difficult to extend into a product class that consumers see as easy to make.* Aaker and Keller showed that consumers may dismiss some seemingly appropriate extensions if they see the product as comparatively easy to make and brand differences are hard to come by. Then a high-quality brand may seem incongruous; alternatively, consumers may feel the extension will attempt to command an unreasonable price premium and be too expensive.

    When consumers see the extension category as difficult to make, on the other hand, such that brands can vary a great deal in quality, an extension has a greater opportunity to differentiate itself, although consumers may also be less sure what the exact quality level of the extension will be.[82]

10. *A successful extension can not only contribute to the parent brand image but also enable a brand to extend even farther.* An extension can help the image of the parent brand by improving the strength, favorability, or uniqueness of its associations.[83] For example, Swaminathan, Fox, and Reddy showed that when consumers did not already have strongly held attitudes, the successful introduction of a brand extension improved their choice and evaluations of a parent brand they originally perceived to be of only average quality.

    If an extension changes the image and meaning of the brand, subsequent extensions that otherwise might not have seemed appropriate to consumers may make more sense and appear to be a better fit. Keller and Aaker showed that by taking little steps, that is, by introducing a series of closely related but increasingly distant extensions, marketers may insert brands into product categories that would have been much more difficult, or perhaps even impossible, to enter directly.[84]

    A successful extension thus helps brands grow in three important ways:

    1. By establishing a new market for the brand,
    2. By strengthening existing markets for the brand, and
    3. By opening up the possibility of additional new markets for the brand to subsequently enter.

    For example, when Toyota launched the successful Prius hybrid gasoline–electric car, it not only cast a positive halo on the Toyota corporate brand as a whole as innovative and environmentally concerned, but it also paved the way for the introduction of a whole family of four different Prius models.

    Different factors affect the success of multiple extensions. Boush and Loken found that consumers evaluated far extensions from a broad brand with extensions already in many different categories more favorably than from a narrow brand who had not been so widely extended.[85] Dacin and Smith have shown that if the perceived quality levels of different members of a brand portfolio are more uniform, then consumers tend to make higher, more confident evaluations of a proposed new extension.[86] It is as if consumers in this case think, "Whatever this company does, it tends to do well."

    In an empirical study of 95 brands in 11 nondurable consumer goods categories, Sullivan found that, in terms of stages of the product category life cycle, early-entering brand extensions did not perform as well, on average, as either early-entering new-name products or late-entering brand extensions.[87]

Shine, Park, and Wyer demonstrate an interesting brand synergy effect of multiple extensions. The simultaneous introduction of two brand extensions (e.g., two digital cameras) had an effect on consumer evaluations of the extensions independent of their similarity or fit to the parent brand (e.g., Xerox). Consumers appear to view a related set of products from a single manufacturer as inherently appealing.[88] Mao and Krishnan point out that consumers may form their perceptions of extension fit very differently when a brand operates in multiple product domains.[89]

11. *An unsuccessful extension hurts the parent brand only when there is a strong basis of fit between the two.* The general rule of thumb emerging from academic research and industry experience is that an unsuccessful brand extension can damage the parent brand only when there is a high degree of similarity or fit—for example, in the case of a failed line extension in the same category.

Roedder John and Loken found that perceptions of quality for a parent brand in the health and beauty aids area decreased with the hypothetical introduction of a lower-quality extension in a similar product category (shampoo). Quality perceptions of the parent brand were unaffected, however, when the proposed extension was in a dissimilar product category (facial tissue).[90]

Similarly, Keller and Aaker, as well as Romeo, found that unsuccessful extensions in dissimilar product categories did not affect evaluations of the parent brand.[91] Roedder John, Loken, and Joiner found that dilution effects were less likely to be present with flagship products; they occurred with line extensions but were not always evident for more dissimilar category extensions.[92]

Gürhan-Canli and Maheswaran extended the results of these studies by considering the moderating effect of consumer motivation and extension typicality.[93] In high-motivation conditions, they found that incongruent extensions were scrutinized in detail and led to the modification of family brand evaluations, regardless of the typicality of the extensions. In low-motivation conditions, however, brand evaluations were more extreme in the context of high (than low) typicality. Because consumers considered the less typical extension an exception, it had reduced impact.

Consistent with these high-motivation findings, Milberg and colleagues found that negative feedback effects were present when (1) consumers perceived extensions as belonging to product categories dissimilar from those associated with the family brand, and (2) extension attribute information was inconsistent with image beliefs that consumers associated with the family brand.[94]

In terms of individual differences, Lane and Jacobson found some evidence of a negative reciprocal impact from brand extensions, especially for high-need-for-cognition subjects, but did not explore extension similarity differences.[95] Kirmani, Sood, and Bridges found dilution effects with owners of prestige-image automobiles when low-priced extensions were introduced, but not with owners of nonprestige automobiles or nonowners of either automobile.[96] Finally, Morrin revealed that exposing consumers to brand extension information strengthened rather than weakened parent brand associations in memory, particularly for parent brands that were dominant in their original product category.[97]

12. *An unsuccessful extension does not prevent a firm from backtracking and introducing a more similar extension.* The Keller and Aaker study also showed that unsuccessful extensions do not necessarily prevent a company from retrenching and later introducing a more similar extension. For example, the introduction of Levi's Tailored Classics by Levi Strauss & Co. was initially unsuccessful, as there were problems with the chosen target market, distribution channels, and product design. Perhaps the most fundamental problem was the lack of fit between the Levi's informal, rugged, outdoor image and the image the company sought from its three-piece suits. Despite the ultimate withdrawal of the product, Levi Strauss later was able to execute one of the most successful apparel launches ever—Dockers pants—an extension much closer in fit and more strongly sub-branded.[98]

As these experiences with brand extensions illustrate, failure does not doom a firm *never* to be able to introduce any extensions—certainly not for a brand with as much equity as Levi's. An unsuccessful extension does, however, create a perceptual boundary of sorts, in that it reveals the limits of the brand in the minds of consumers that may need to be overcome. In fact, Parker and his colleagues showed that if an unsuccessful extension managed to change and broaden the brand concept in the process, it could help to fuel more dissimilar extensions over time.[99]

13. *A co-branded brand extension can leverage the success and equity of two brands.* As noted in Chapter 7, co-branding can create positive effects for a stock brand, both in terms of consumer perceptions and financial performance. A study by Park, Youl Jun, and Shocker suggested that having a co-branded brand extension can strengthen brand attitude by leveraging the strengths of multiple brands.[100] For example, a co-branded extension like the Angry Birds Star Wars mobile game leverages the popularity of both Star Wars and Angry Birds brands in a joint (co-branded) extension. Cao and Sorescu found that the stock market reacted favorably to announcements of new co-branding arrangements.[101]

14. *Both similar and dissimilar brands can partner successfully in a co-branded extension to achieve greater synergies.* A study by Swaminathan et al. showed that co-branded extensions can be equally successful when even highly similar brands (those with similar brand images) join together, by leveraging their similarity of image and appeal. In contrast, complementary brands (with varying strengths), can combine together to compensate for their relative weaknesses of the other brand and create a more successful jointly branded extension in the process. Thus, both similar and complementary extensions can succeed, although their relative success depends on how the information about the co-branded product is processed by consumers.[102] If the brands are dissimilar on the basis of how well-known they are, however, the less well-known brand must be careful that it is not overshadowed by the more well-known brand.[103]

15. *Vertical extensions can be difficult and often require sub-branding strategies.* Some academic research has investigated vertical extensions. For instance, researchers Randall, Ulrich, and Reibstein found that brand price premium was positively correlated with the quality of the lowest-quality model in the product line for the lower-quality segments of the market; for the upper-quality segments of the market, brand price premium was also significantly positively correlated with the quality of the highest-quality model in the product line.[104]

Hamilton and Chernev showed that upscale extensions increased the price image of a brand, and downscale extensions decreased its price image when consumers were browsing or just looking around, but that did not necessarily apply when consumers were actively looking to make a purchase. In the latter case, the effects could even be reversed: upscale extensions may actually decrease price image, and downscale extensions increase it, if consumers have an explicit buying goal.[105]

Kirmani, Sood, and Bridges examined the ownership effect—whereby owners have more favorable responses than nonowners to brand extensions—in the context of brand line stretches. They found that the ownership effect occurred for upward and downward stretches of nonprestige brands (such as Acura) and for upward stretches of prestige brands (such as Calvin Klein and BMW). For downward stretches of prestige brands, however, the ownership effect did not occur because of owners' desires to maintain brand exclusivity. In this situation, a sub-branding strategy protected owners' parent brand attitudes from dilution.[106]

16. *The most effective advertising strategy for an extension is one that emphasizes information about the extension (rather than reminders about the parent brand).* A number of studies have shown that the information provided about brand extensions, by triggering selective retrieval from memory, may frame the consumer decision process and affect extension evaluations. In general, the most effective strategy appears to be one that recognizes the type of information already salient for the brand in the minds of consumers when they first consider the proposed extension, and that highlights additional information they would otherwise overlook or misinterpret.

Aaker and Keller found that elaborating briefly on specific extension attributes about which consumers were uncertain or concerned led to more favorable evaluations. Bridges, Keller, and Sood—as well as Klink and Smith—found that providing information could improve perceptions of fit when consumers perceived low fit between the brand and the extension, either by reinforcing an overlooked basis of fit or by addressing a distracting negative association.[107] Lane found that repeating an ad that evoked primarily benefit brand associations could overcome negative perceptions of a highly incongruent brand extension.[108]

Research has also explored several other aspects of extension marketing programs. Sood and Keller found that branding effects—in terms of inferences based on parent brand knowledge—operated both in the absence and presence of product experience with an extension, although they were less pronounced, or, in the case of an unambiguous negative experience, even nonexistent.[109]

In considering the effects of retailer displays, Buchanan, Simmons, and Bickart found that evaluations of a high-equity brand could be diminished by an unfamiliar competitive brand when (1) a mixed display structure led consumers to believe the competitive brand was relevant and useful for judging the high-equity brand, (2) the precedence given to one brand over another in the display made expectations about brand differences or similarities more evident to consumers, and (3) the unfamiliar competitive brand disconfirmed these expectations.[110]

17. *Individual differences can affect how consumers make an extension decision and will moderate extension effects.* Consumers vary in their short-term or long-term motivation, ability, and opportunity to evaluate an extension in a number of important ways. Researchers have shown how these differences can affect extension fit and evaluations, as follows.

Monga and John demonstrate that one important individual difference in extension evaluations is whether consumers are analytical (those who focus on comparing particular attributes) or holistic thinkers (those who focus more on comparing overall attitudes and judgments of the parent brand and extension). Analytical and holistic thinkers both gave prestige brands permission to extend widely, but holistic thinkers gave functional brands much greater permission to extend than analytical thinkers.[111]

Similarly, Yorkston, Nunes, and Matta show that consumers known as *incremental theorists*, who believe the personality traits of a brand are malleable, are more accepting of brand extensions than consumers known as *entity theorists*, who believe a brand's traits are fixed.[112]

Another important individual difference relates to *self-construal*, or how people view and make sense of life and their life.[113] A person with an *independent self-construal* is more concerned with the uniqueness of individuals. A person with an *interdependent self-construal* is more concerned with relationships between and among individuals.

In a branding context, Ahluwalia posited that a consumer with an interdependent self-construal should be better able to uncover the possible relationships among a brand extension and its parent brand and thus, have higher perceptions of extension fit and favorability, particularly when interdependents were sufficiently motivated.[114]

Similarly, Puligadda, Ross, and Grewal argue that *brand-schematic* consumers are more likely than others to process or organize information according to their brand knowledge. *Brand-aschematic* consumers, on the other hand, use other information such as product characteristics or attributes as a frame of reference. Brand schematic consumers were shown to be more likely to see the similarity in a brand extension concept.[115]

Another important individual difference between consumers is what academics call *regulatory focus*. This deals with motivation and how people go about pursuing their goals. Individuals with a *prevention focus* are concerned with negative outcomes and avoiding losses via safety, security, responsibility, and so on. Individuals with a *promotion focus* are concerned with positive outcomes, seeking gains and pleasure, and avoiding missed opportunities.[116]

Yeo and Park showed that consumers who are focused on prevention tend to judge dissimilar extensions less favorably than consumers who focus on promotion, due to their different interpretations of risk.[117] Relatedly, Chang, Lin, and Chang showed that promotion-focused consumers are more likely to focus abstractly on the overlap in benefits in judging an extension, whereas prevention-focused consumers are more likely to focus concretely on sheer category similarity.[118]

Temporal factors can affect extension evaluations. Barone, Miniard, and Romeo experimentally demonstrated that positive mood led consumers to think more positively of extensions they viewed as moderately similar to a brand they valuated favorably (as opposed to very similar or dissimilar).[119]

18. *Cultural differences across markets can influence extension success.* Building in part on branding research on individual differences, much recent research has explored how various cultures respond differently to brand extensions. Monga and John, as well as Ng and Houston, have shown that consumers from Eastern cultures (such as China) have a more holistic style of thinking and perceive higher levels of extension fit than do consumers from Western cultures (such as the United States), who have a more analytical style of thinking.[120]

Dilution effects for a typical or similar extension that fails also can vary by culture and consumer motivation. Consumers from Eastern cultures exhibit significantly greater dilution when their motivation is high; consumers from Western cultures exhibit significantly greater dilution when their motivation is low.[121]

Additionally, Torelli and Ahluwalia show that cultural congruency can aid culturally consistent brand extensions over and beyond the effects of perceived fit. They note that a cultural congruent brand extension might be something like Sony electric car; a culturally incongruent car might be something like Sony cappuccino-macchiato maker. According to the research, beyond the inherent levels of fit that any electronic manufacturer might enjoy with an electric car, Sony would be expected to get an extra boost in fit and evaluations because of its Japanese country of origin and Japan's strong association with electronics.[122]

REVIEW

Brand extensions occur when a firm uses an established brand name to introduce a new product. We can distinguish them by whether the new product is being introduced in a product category currently served by the parent brand (a line extension) or in a completely different product category (a category extension). Brand extensions can come in all forms. They offer many potential benefits but also can pose many problems.

The basic assumptions behind brand extensions are that consumers have some awareness of and positive associations about the parent brand in memory, and that the brand extension will evoke at least some of these. Moreover, marketers assume that negative associations will not be transferred from the parent brand or created by the brand extension.

The brand extension's ability to establish its own equity will depend on the salience of consumers' associations with the parent brand in the extension context and the favorability and uniqueness of any associations they infer. The brand extension's ability to contribute to parent brand equity will depend on how compelling is the evidence about the corresponding attribute or benefit association in the extension context, how relevant or diagnostic the extension evidence is about the attribute or benefit for the parent brand, and how strong consumers' existing attribute or benefit associations are for the parent brand.

To evaluate brand extension opportunities, marketers need to carefully consider brand extension strategies by applying managerial judgment and consumer research to the following steps: define actual and desired consumer knowledge about the brand, identify possible extension candidates, evaluate the potential of extension candidates, design marketing programs to launch extensions, and evaluate extension success and effects on parent brand equity. Finally, a number of important research findings deal with factors affecting the acceptance of a brand extension, as well as the nature of feedback to the parent brand.

DISCUSSION QUESTIONS

1. Pick a brand extension. Use the models presented in the chapter to evaluate its ability to achieve its own equity as well as contribute to the equity of a parent brand. If you were the manager of that brand, what would you do differently?
2. Do you think Virgin's brand is overextended? What are the arguments for or against?
3. How successful do you predict these recently proposed extensions will be? Why?
   a. Mont Blanc (famous for pens): fragrances and other accessories (watches, cufflinks, sunglasses, and pocket knives)
   b. Evian (famous for water): high-end spas
   c. Starbucks (famous for coffee): film production and promotion
   d. A company such as LinkedIn which enables networking for employment opportunities: a business magazine

4. Consider the following brands, and discuss the extendibility of each:
   a. Harley-Davidson
   b. Red Bull
   c. Tommy Hilfiger
   d. Whole Foods
   e. Netflix
   f. U.S. Marines
   g. Grey Goose Vodka
   h. LEGO
   i. BlackBerry
   j. Las Vegas
   k. Kate Spade
   l. Game of Thrones
   m. ESPN

5. There are four fake brand extensions among the following list; the other six were marketed at one point. Can you identify the four fakes?[123]
   a. Ben-Gay Aspirin: Pain Relief That Comes with a Warm Glow
   b. Burberry Baby Stroller: For Discriminating Newborns
   c. Smith & Wesson Mountain Bikes: Ride without Fear
   d. Atlantic City Playing Cards: Talcum-Coated for Easy Shuffling
   e. Pond's Toothpaste: Reduces the Appearance of Fine Wines
   f. Slim Jim Beef-Flavored Throat Lozenges: For Meat Lovers Who Like to Sing Karaoke
   g. Frito-Lay Lemonade: A Tangy, Crunchy Thirst Quencher
   h. Cosmo Yogurt: Spoon It Up, Slim Down Those Thighs
   i. Richard Simmons Sneakers: Shake Your Cute Little Booty to the Oldies
   j. Madonna Condoms: For Men Who Are Packing

BRAND FOCUS 13.0

Apple: Creating a Tech Megabrand

A Brief History

Apple was co-founded by Steve Jobs and Steve Wozniak in 1976, and was initially a manufacturer of personal computers (e.g., Apple II, Macintosh). The company subsequently entered the laptop segment in the 1990s. The company's successful foray into smaller consumer electronics began with the launch of the iPod in 2001. The iTunes music store in 2003 heralded Apple's entry into digital distribution, and during this period, Apple signaled its broader focus by dropping the "Computer" from its name. Apple's highly successful expansion into smartphone and tablet computer categories, with its launch of the iPhone and iPad, solidified its presence as a market leader.

Apple further strengthened its broad consumer electronics focus with the introduction of the Apple Watch in 2014, and expanded the focus through the introduction of Apple Pay in the same year. Apple's SIRI (speech interpretation and recognition interface), was launched in 2011 as an intelligent personal assistant to enhance the ability of users to interact with their devices through voice-activated commands. Apple's app store added to its appeal—as of March 2016, the App Store had more than one million apps for the iPad. By June 2017, Apple had the highest market capitalization of any public company of $810 billion, and its annual profitability in net income terms was $45 billion.[124]

Throughout, Apple has maintained its consistent focus on quality, design, and ease of use, and has sequentially extended its brand name into multiple categories, ranging from phones to tablets, to its apps, and its operating system. Apple's ability to seamlessly integrate between hardware and software, along with the availability of vast digital content in the form of Apple Music, iTunes, iBooks, the apps, all of which are easily accessed via a range of mobile devices, have enabled Apple to provide exceptional value to its customers.

Apple's Brand Image

Apple's mission has evolved from being a computer manufacturer to a broader mission of being a "mobile devices company." Apple's one-time advertising tagline of "Think Different" appears to be more than a mere slogan. It also embodies a culture, and serves as a guide to Apple regarding what their product offerings should be. The reasoning behind the slogan has been applied with great success across many of its products and indicates that Apple will seek to avoid introducing products that lack distinctiveness. Combined with its mission of being a mobile devices company, it demarcates, at least for now, the products that Apple would be likely to focus on, and its positioning within those categories.

A critical success factor of the Apple brand is the user's ability to switch across Apple devices with ease and the availability of identical features across multiple devices. For example, the Share button on the iPhone (a rectangle with an upward arrow), is consistently used in various interfaces. Another success factor is the ability of devices to seamlessly connect to each other. For example, a Mac user can access the Internet through the Instant Hotspot feature, which shows up if there is an Apple iPhone in the vicinity. Much of this is the outcome of Apple's co-founder Steve Jobs' vision of a tightly integrated set of Apple offerings from devices that consumers would use every day.

Apple's ability to integrate across devices is also supported by its consistent use of brand elements such as typeface, logos, etc. This idea has been described in Chapter 12 as the *principle of commonality*. For example, Apple's choice of font (typically, a font known as Apple Garamond) has been consistently used for product names as well as in many ads.[125] All of Apple's products feature the same distinctive logo and product names are signified by a lower case *i* (e.g., iMac, iPad, iPhone). The logo changed colors but retained the same image through the years.

Apple's brand image is inextricably linked to the personality of Steve Jobs, who presided over much of Apple's success. He emphasized excellence, innovation, and quality, and these values are central to Apple's corporate culture. In addition to exceptional quality, Apple also has a premium brand image. Apple products, due to their high quality and high price, are synonymous with luxury and act as symbols of status.

Apple's personality of innovation and lifestyle has been reinforced via its advertising over the years, which has featured edgy comparative advertising (PC versus Mac commercials). Incidentally, these commercials sparked a series of counter-campaigns on YouTube by both PC and Mac users—and inspired a Microsoft "I am a PC" counter-campaign. Many of its other advertising are straightforward and typically feature the magical ability of the devices to enable the user to do many things that were previously either difficult or impossible to do. They also emphasize the futuristic nature of these devices. Apple has also created buzz through its advertising campaigns. For instance, its recent "Shot on iPhone" campaign, which features photographs taken by everyday users on their iPhone cameras, generated significant social media buzz.

Apple Brand Strategy Over Time and Across Categories

Using the Ansoff matrix, we can identify four types of growth strategies that Apple has followed over time to strengthen its brand and its profitability.

1. *Existing products–existing markets.* Apple has successfully leveraged its existing customer base by offering them upgrades of existing products such as the iPhone and iPad almost annually. These upgrades feature better (larger or smaller) screens, faster processor speeds, better cameras, and so on. Despite the longevity of Macs or iPhones, consumers are encouraged to upgrade their devices every three or four years. In upgrading existing products, Apple's current users are encouraged to spend more to keep up with the latest and most advanced features that their product has to offer.

2. *Existing products–new markets.* Apple has sequentially lowered the prices of high-end products over time, and offered several line extensions so as to appeal to newer market segments for the same products. Its vertical extension strategy with the iPod (iPod, Classic followed by iPod Touch, iPod Nano, and iPod Shuffle) is one example of this. The iPod shuffle is a version of the iPod, but its small and rugged nature makes it suitable for lower end uses and price-sensitive customers.

A notable aspect of Apple's line extension strategy is that some amount of cannibalization across the various extensions is expected and seen as a part of the strategy. For example, the introduction of the iPhone potentially cannibalized sales of an iPod. Likewise, the iPad introduction cannibalized sales from the iPhone and the MacBook. Even within the product, sales of the smaller iPad mini (priced at $329) potentially cannibalized sales of the larger iPad (priced at $499). Despite these issues of cannibalization, the switching taking place between Apple products have benefited the Apple brand overall, suggesting that some cannibalization within the portfolio is acceptable and even desirable. Apple's CEO Tim Cook has noted, "I see cannibalization as a huge opportunity for us. One, our base philosophy is to never fear cannibalization."

3. *New products–existing markets.* Apple has also offered new complementary products to its existing users. For example, current users of the iPhone can use Apple Pay to make mobile payments in an easier and more secure manner. Apple Music provides the ability to listen to music on various Apple devices. Currently, the installed base of iPhones is a remarkable 600 million customers, offering Apple several opportunities for cross-selling various products under the Apple brand. (See Figure 13-10.) Even the Apple iPad, a relatively recent entrant, has an installed customer base of 300 million

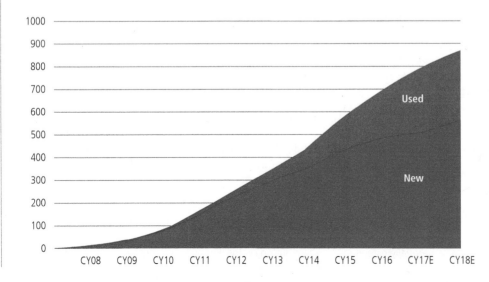

FIGURE 13-10

Apple iPhone Installed Customer Base (in Millions) and Growth Over Time

Source: P. Elmer-DeWitt (2017), *Apple: A Deep Dive into the iPhone Installed Base.*

users, which provides opportunities for growth through sales of complementary products.

4. *New products–new markets.* Apple's diversification into software (e.g., iTunes) in the earlier years when it was primarily offering hardware was seen as a risky move. However, its seemingly unrelated venture into digital content via iTunes is now seen as an important step in creating an ecosystem of Apple products which deliver exceptional value to their users. Apple's foray into retail was also seen as a diversification away from consumer electronics, but it has successfully leveraged its retail outlets to build brand presence and deliver customer service.

Collectively, the four approaches summarize how Apple has achieved significant growth over time. The systematic introduction of complementary products and the growth of a significant user base have created positive spillover of the hardware sales on software sales, and vice versa. For example, as the available digital content accessible via the iTunes store grew, it further spurred the success of devices such as the iPhone, which provided a means to access this content. Likewise, the success of online gaming in recent years has been linked to the growth of the mobile device industry; conversely, the availability of numerous gaming apps has increased the usefulness of iPads for gaming and entertainment purposes.

MARKETING PROGRAMS AND ACTIVITIES
Product

Apple's product strategy involves entering into new markets with technologically advanced products that often set the bar extremely high both in terms of performance, as well as design and aesthetics. Apple also believes in continuous innovation and introduces updates to its various products almost on an annual basis. For example, Apple introduced new iPhones and iPads with smaller screen sizes to appeal to consumers in untapped markets but also to appeal to its core customers.

Pricing

Apple has used premium pricing approaches and has employed its skimming strategy successfully. For instance, when the iPhone was first introduced, Apple priced it at a relatively high price to appeal to the high-end users. Over time, the average price of the iPhone has decreased through a series of line extensions, thereby making it available to a broader audience. Apple also has successfully pursued a vertical extension strategy by introducing line extensions both at the high end and at the low end to flank the competition. The vertical extension strategy is evident in the case of its iPod launches. The iPod was initially introduced as a high-end product, and Apple priced it at $249 to $349. Subsequently, Apple introduced the iPod Touch at the high end ($299 to $399) and Nano and Shuffle at the low end ($149 to $199 for the Nano and $79 for the Shuffle). In doing so, Apple was able to minimize competitive threats while at the same time broadening the appeal of the iPod across various customer segments.

Marketing Communications

Apple limits its advertising through traditional mass media. However, its previous ad campaigns have been inspirational. Its initial ad campaign "Think Different" was created by ad agency TBWA\Chiat\Day and featured black-and-white footage of various iconic personalities, including Albert Einstein, Bob Dylan, and Martin Luther King, Jr. Recently, Apple launched the "Shot on iPhone" campaign[126] that featured 10,000 billboards across 25 countries showcasing photographs taken by real people using their iPhones.

Distribution

Apple distributes its products across both online and brick-and-mortar retail stores. Although a majority of its sales takes place online, Apple's retail stores are an important component of its image and a key touchpoint with their customers; the stores also feature the clean layout and design that are typical of all other Apple products.

Apple Brand Hierarchy and Extension Strategy

A summary of Apple's brand architecture is provided in Figure 13-11. As can be seen, Apple's line and brand extensions over time have resulted in a product portfolio that is high in breadth, length, and depth.

Brand and Line Extension Strategy

Even though the product categories that Apple has extended into are seen as a set of disparate categories, Apple always focused on a key set of associations to support each and every extension that it introduced. These PODs included reinvention, innovation, and offering an exceptional user experience. Apple's extensions have offered spillover effects. The introduction of the iPhone allowed smartphone users to purchase a range of related, complementary products from Apple, including downloads from the iTunes store, apps from the App store, and so on. Further, the iPhone introduction allowed Apple to become a credible mobile devices company, and paved the way for introduction of tablets, watches, and so on.

FUTURE CHALLENGES FOR THE APPLE BRAND
Sales Growth

Despite its product proliferation, Apple's top three product lines, iPhone, iPad, and Mac, representing nearly 90 percent of Apple's total sales, are all falling. The decrease in growth of the iPad and the slower growth of iPhones present challenges for Apple going into the future.

Competition

Despite its success, competition from Alphabet Google (with its Android operating system competing against Apple operating system), Microsoft Windows (Windows operating system competing against Apple operating system), Samsung's Galaxy and Motorola's Moto Z smartphones (competing with iPhones), and Fire Tablets (competing with iPad) have posed challenges for the Apple brand. Apple has also been engaged in a patent infringement lawsuit against Samsung over patented design elements, and will continue to find it difficult to prevent competitors from adapting and incorporating successful design elements into their own products.[127] Apple's operating system is seen as less customizable and versatile than Android, which also limits the extent to which software developers choose to focus on Apple's operating system, relative to the ability of developers to create new features and themes to run on devices that have the Android operating system.[128] The high prices of Apple's products make it harder for newer segments of customers (especially those in developing countries who cannot afford the high prices) to adopt the product, thereby limiting the future growth of Apple.

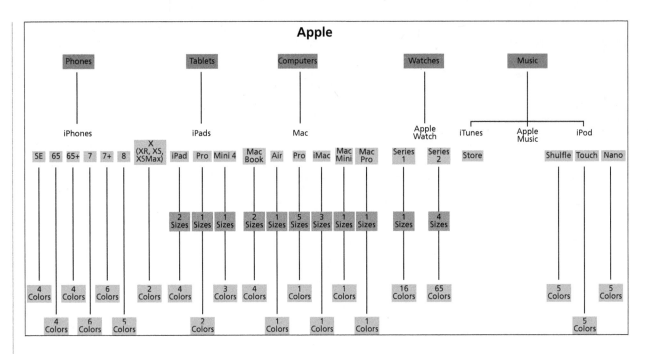

FIGURE 13-11

Apple Brand Hierarchy Reflects the Breadth, Depth, and Length of Its Portfolio

Antibrand Activism

Despite the success of the Apple brand, it has its share of detractors and anti-brand activists. This polarization of the brand landscape is particularly a consequence of how much digital devices are closely linked to consumers' identities as individuals. The rise of Android—as an alternative to iOS—has spurred a dislike for Apple among many Android fans.

Conclusion

Despite these challenges, Apple's strategy has ensured the growth and success of Apple as a mobile devices company. Interbrand has ranked Apple as the largest brand in the world with a brand value of $178 billion.[129] A key feature of the Apple brand is its duality—its ability to appeal both rationally and emotionally to its customers. This duality is an outcome of its quality products and well-executed creative advertising campaigns, which have struck an emotional chord with its audience. This, along with its aesthetically pleasing user-interfaces and elegant simplicity, has caused many consumers to develop a deep, emotional connection (i.e., brand resonance) with their Apple products.

Sources: From annual reports, Apple Inc. *Form 10-K 2015*, page 24; From annual reports, Apple Inc. *Form 10-K 2016*, page 23; Last two rows from https://arstechnica.com/apple/2017/01/apple-sets-revenue-and-iphone-sales-records-in-q1-of-2017/; Andrew Cunningham, "Apple Sets Revenue and iPhone Sales Records in Q1 of 2017," January 31, 2017, https://arstechnica.com/apple/2017/01/apple-sets-revenue-and-iphone-sales-records-in-q1-of-2017/, accessed May 23, 2017; Marketing Minds, Case Study, "Apple's Branding Strategy, http://www.marketingminds.com.au/apple_branding_strategy.html, accessed November 22, 2018; Ashraf Eassa, "Why Apple Inc. Is So Profitable," *The Motley Fool*, March 23, 2017, https://www.fool.com/investing/2017/03/23/why-apple-inc-is-so-profitable.aspx, accessed

November 22, 2018; Farhad Manjoo, "Apple Strengthens Pull of Its Orbit with Each Device," *The New York Times*, October 22, 2014, https://www.nytimes.com/2014/10/23/technology/personaltech/devices-with-yosemite-and-ios-8-operating-systems-seamlessly-connect-in-apples-ecosystem.html, accessed November 22, 2018; Wikipedia, "Typography of Apple Inc."; Rob Janoff, "Apple Logo Story," http://robjanoff.com/applelogo/, accessed November 22, 2018; Top 10 Iconic Apple Ads https://www.youtube.com/watch?v=ilarNBQHevA; Susan Fournier and Lara Lee, "Getting Brand Communities Right, *Harvard Business Review*, April 2009 Issue, https://hbr.org/2009/04/getting-brand-communities-right, accessed November 22, 2018; Albert M. Muniz Jr. and Hope Jensen Schau, "Religiosity in the Abandoned Apple Newton Brand Community," *Journal of Consumer Research* 31, no. 4 (March 2005): 737–747; Luke Dormehl, "Apple Reveals How Long Its Devices Typically Last," Cult of Mac, April 15, 2016, https://www.cultofmac.com/423304/apple-reveals-how-long-its-devices-typically-last/, accessed November 22, 2018; Zachary M. Seward, "Yes, the iPad Mini Is Cannibalizing Sales of the Larger iPad," Quartz, January 23, 2013, https://qz.com/47265/apple-ipad-mini-is-cannibalizing-sales-of-the-larger-ipad/, accessed November 22, 2018; Ben Bajarin, "Apple's Uncharted Territory," Recode, May 3, 2016, https://www.recode.net/2016/5/3/11634186/apples-uncharted-territory, accessed November 22, 2018; MacDailyNews, "Apple's iPad Has an Installed Base of Over 300 Million, Far Larger Than the Mac's User Base," March 24, 2017, http://macdailynews.com/2017/03/24/apples-ipad-has-an-installed-base-of-over-300-million-far-larger-than-the-macs-user-base/, accessed November 22, 2018; Dean Takahashi, "Mobile Games Hit $40.6 Billion in 2016, Matching World Box Office Numbers," VentureBeat, February 1, 2017, https://venturebeat.com/2017/02/01/superdata-mobile-games-hit-40-6-billion-in-2016-matching-world-box-office-numbers/, accessed November 22, 2018; DawnNews, "Apple Cuts Prices, Screen Sizes for New iPhone, iPad," March 22, 2016, https://www.dawn.com/news/1247119, accessed November 22, 2018; Brittany A. Roston, "These Magazine Covers Were Swith the iPhone 7 Plus," Slash Gear, April 18, 2017, https://www.slashgear.com/these-magazine-covers-were-shot-with-the-iphone-7-plus-18482648/, accessed November 22, 2018; Dan Moren, "Analysis: Apple's Ads Let Products Speak for Themselves," *Macworld*, April 4, 2011, https://www.macworld .com/article/1159004/apple_advertising.html, accessed November 22, 2018; Li Justi, "Apple's Challenge: Where Is the Future?," Deakin Business School, April 25, 2016, https://mpk732t12016clustera .wordpress.com/2016/04/25/apples-challenge-where-is-the-future/, accessed November 22, 2018; Camila Domonoske, "Supreme Court Sides with Samsung, Against Apple in Patent Infringement Fight," National Public Radio, December 6, 2016, https://www.npr.org/ sections/thetwo-way/2016/12/06/504545297/supreme-court-sides-with-samsung-against-apple-in-patent-infringement-fight, accessed November 22, 2018; Josh Smith, "Android vs. iPhone: 14 Reasons Android Is Still Better," GottaBeMobile.com, February 7, 2018, https://www .gottabemobile.com/android-vs-iphone-android-better/, accessed November 22, 2018; Mike Elgan, "Why Does Apple Inspire So Much Hate?," Cult of Mac, June 9, 2012, https://www.cultofmac.com/172428/ why-does-apple-inspire-so-much-hate/, accessed November 22, 2018.

NOTES

1. For a more comprehensive treatment, see Glen Urban and John Hauser, *Design and Marketing of New Products,* 2nd ed. (Upper Saddle River, NJ: Prentice Hall, 1993).

2. Peter Farquhar, "Managing Brand Equity," *Marketing Research* 1, no. 3 (September 1989): 24–33.

3. Kurt Schroeder, "Why So Many New Products Fail (and It's Not the Product)," *The Business Journals*, May 14, 2017, www.bizjournals.com/bizjournals/how-to/ marketing/2017/03/why-so-many-new-products-fail-and-it-s-not-the.html.

4. The Nielsen Company, "Looking to Achieve New Product Success?," *Nielsen*, June 23, 2015, www.nielsen.com/ us/en/insights/reports/2015/looking-to-achieve-new-product-success.html.

5. Mark Dolliver, "Brand Extensions Set the Pace in 2009," *Adweek*, March 22, 2010, https://www.adweek .com/brand-marketing/brand-extensions-set-pace-2009-101891/.

6. Information Resources, Inc., "IRI Announces the Most Successful New Brands of 2009," IRI, March 22, 2010, https://www.businesswire.com/news/ home/20100322006486/en/IRI-Announces-Successful-New-Brands-2009, accessed November 23, 2018.

7. Craig Smith, "42 Interesting McDonald's Facts and Statistics (March 2018)," *DMR*, March 30, 2018, http:// expandedramblings.com/index.php/mcdonalds-statistics/.

8. Roy Brunner, "How Shake Shack Leads The Better Burger Revolution," *Fast Company*, June 22, 2015, www.fastcompany.com/3046753/shake-shack-leads-the-better-burger-revolution, accessed May 21, 2017.

9. Byung-Do Kim and Mary W. Sullivan, "The Effect of Parent Brand Experience on Line Extension Trial and Repeat Purchase," *Marketing Letters* 9, no. 2 (1998): 181–193.

10. Henry J. Claycamp and Lucien E. Liddy, "Prediction of New Product Performance: An Analytical Approach," *Journal of Marketing Research* 6, no. 4 (November 1969): 414–420.

11. Kevin Lane Keller and David A. Aaker, "The Effects of Sequential Introduction of Brand Extensions," *Journal of Marketing Research* 29, no. 1 (February 1992): 35–50; John Milewicz and Paul Herbig, "Evaluating the Brand Extension Decision Using a Model of Reputation Building," *Journal of Product & Brand Management* 3, no. 1 (1994): 39–47.

12. See also Jonlee Andrews, "Rethinking the Effect of Perceived Fit on Customers' Evaluations of New Products," *Journal of the Academy of Marketing Science* 23, no. 1 (1995): 4–14.

13. David B. Montgomery, "New Product Distribution: An Analysis of Supermarket Buyer Decisions," *Journal of Marketing Research* 12, no. 3 (1978): 255–264.

14. Tülin Erdem and Baohong Sun, "An Empirical Investigation of the Spillover Effects of Advertising and Sales Promotions in Umbrella Branding," *Journal of Marketing Research* 39, no. 4 (November 2002): 408–420.

15. Mary W. Sullivan, "Brand Extensions: When to Use Them," *Management Science* 38, no. 6 (June 1992): 793–806; Daniel C. Smith, "Brand Extension and Advertising Efficiency: What Can and Cannot Be Expected," *Journal of Advertising Research* 32, no. 6 (November/December 1992): 11–20. See also Daniel C. Smith and C. Whan Park, "The Effects of Brand Extensions on Market Share and Advertising Efficiency," *Journal of Marketing Research* 29, no. 3 (August 1992): 296–313.

16. Jack Neff, "Speichert Looks for Big Growth Bets as First CMO," *Advertising Age*, February 21, 2011, https://adage.com/print/148915, accessed November 23, 2018; Jack Neff, "Zigging Where Others Zagged, L'Oréal Focuses on U.S.—to Beautiful Effect," *Advertising Age*, November 7, 2011, http://adage.com/article/ special-report-marketer-alist/marketer-a-list-l-oreal-focuses-u-s-market-beautiful-effect/230833/; "L'Oréal Shifts Marketing Model," *WARC*, October 25, 2010; K@W, "Why L'Oreal's Jean-Paul Agon Believes He Is on the Winning Team," *Knowledge@Wharton*, March 30, 2005, http://knowledge.wharton.upenn.edu/article/ why-loreals-jean-paul-agon-believes-he-is-on-the-winning-team/.

17. Leonie Roderick, "L'Oréal on Why Artificial Intelligence Is 'a Revolution as Big as the Internet'," *Marketing Week (Online Edition)*, April 24, 2017, https://www.marketingweek.com/2017/04/24/ loreal-artificial-intelligence/.

18. Theodore Levitt, "Marketing Myopia," *Harvard Business Review* 38, no. 4 (July–August 1960): 45–46.

19. Jason Bloomberg, "Transformation at Scale at General Electric: Digital Influencer Bill Ruh," *Forbes*, July 25, 2016, www.forbes.com/sites/jasonbloomberg/2016/07/25/

digital-transformation-at-scale-at-general-electric-digital-influencer-bill-ruh/#3cebdf46a2fe.

20. TataWorld, "Titan Company Launches SKINN Range of Perfumes," *Tata*, September 16, 2013, www.tata.com/company/releasesinside/zoEU8Oa7AFs=/TLYVr3YPkMU.

21. K. L. Keller and D.A. Aaker, "The Effects of Sequential Introduction of Brand Extensions," *Journal of Marketing Research* 29, no. 1 (1992): 35–50.

22. Demitrios Kalogeropoulos, "The Procter & Gamble Company's Best Product in 2015," *The Motley Fool*, December 27, 2015, www.fool.com/investing/general/2015/12/27/the-procter-gamble-companys-best-product-in-2015.aspx. Robert Klara, "Chances are, the Clothes You're Wearing Right Now Have Been Washed in Tide: How the detergent has reigned for 68 years,"*AdWeek*, December 1, 2014, www.adweek.com/brand-marketing/why-clothes-youre-wearing-right-now-have-probably-been-washed-tide-161643.

23. Jay Moye, "How Coke Zero Became a Hero: 10 Facts to Mark the Brand's 10th Birthday," *Coca-Cola*, June 30, 2015, www.coca-colacompany.com/stories/how-coke-zero-became-a-hero-10-facts-to-mark-the-brands-10th-birthday.

24. Mark J. Miller, "Coca-Cola Woos James Bond Fans with Coke Zero Skyfall Tie-In," *Brand Channel*, September 12, 2012, http://brandchannel.com/2012/09/12/coca-cola-woos-james-bond-fans-with-coke-zero-skyfall-tie-in/.

25. Ben Reynolds, "Pepsi Overtakes Diet Coke as #2 Soda in U.S.—Which Is Best Investment?," SureDividend Blog, March 28, 2015, http://www.talkmarkets.com/content/stocks--equities/pepsi-overtakes-diet-coke-as-2-soda-in-us--which-is-best-investment?post=61756, accessed November 23, 2018.

26. Laura Shanahan, "Designated Shopper," *Brandweek* 42, no. 10 (March 2001): 26.

27. Ibid.

28. Interview with James Allworth, "Why You Should Cannibalize Your Company," interview with James Allworth, *Harvard Business Review*, November 2012, https://hbr.org/2012/11/why-you-should-cannibalize-you.

29. Maureen Morrin, "The Impact of Brand Extensions on Parent Brand Memory Structures and Retrieval Processes," *Journal of Marketing Research* 36, no. 4 (1999): 517–525.

30. Nathan Bomey, "Coach to Acquire Kate Spade for $2.4 Billion," *Forbes*, May 8, 2017, www.forbes.com/sites/greatspeculations/2017/05/09/coachs-acquisition-of-kate-spade-finally-comes-to-fruition/#2a9d90173e26; Based on Insights from Timothy Calkins, "Reviving a Brand That's Lost Its Luster," *Kellogg Insight*, November 2, 2016, https://insight.kellogg.northwestern.edu/article/reviving-a-brand-thats-lost-its-luster.

31. Alessandra Galloni, "Inside Out: At Gucci, Mr. Polet's New Design Upends Rules for High Fashion," *The Wall Street Journal,* August 9, 2005, A1; Interbrand, "Best Global Brands," www.interbrand.com/en/best-global-brands/Best-Global-Brands-2011.aspx.

32. Macala Wright, "Mid-Tier to Luxury Fashion Brands Open Their Doors to Licensing," October 16, 2011, www.macalawright.com/2011/10/fashion-licensing-deals/; Jessica Wohl, "Target Hopes Exclusive Designer Deals Boost Sales," *Reuters*, August 2, 2011, https://www.reuters.com/article/target-exclusives/target-hopes-exclusive-designer-deals-boost-sales-idUS-N1E7700FA20110802.

33. For some reviews of the brand extension literature, see Sandor Czellar, "Consumer Attitude Toward Brand Extensions: An Integrative Model and Research Propositions," *International Journal of Research in Marketing* 20, no. 3 (2003): 97–115; Barbara Loken, Rohini Ahluwalia, and Michael J. Houston, eds., *Brands and Brand Management: Contemporary Research Perspectives* (New York: Psychology Press, 2010); Franziska Volkner and Henrik Sattler, "Drivers of Brand Extension Success," *Journal of Marketing* 70, no. 2 (April 2006): 18–34.

34. Kalpesh Kaushik Desai, Wayne D. Hoyer, and Rajendra Srivastava, "Evaluation of Brand Extension Relative to the Extension Category Competition: The Role of Attribute Inheritance from Parent Brand and Extension Category," working paper, State University of New York at Buffalo, 1996.

35. Edward M. Tauber, "Brand Leverage: Strategy for Growth in a Cost-Control World," *Journal of Advertising Research* 28 (August/September 1988): 26–30.

36. Barbara Loken and Deborah Roedder John, "Diluting Brand Beliefs. When Do Brand Extensions Have a Negative Impact?" *Journal of Marketing* 57, no. 7 (1993): 71–84.

37. For another conceptual point of view, see Abishek Dwivedi, Bill Merrilees, and Arthur Sweeney, "Brand Extension Feedback Effects: A Holistic Framework," *Journal of Brand Management* 17, no. 5 (March 2010): 328–342.

38. Fabio Caldieraro, Ling-Jing Kao, and Marcus Cunha, Jr., "Harmful Upward Line Extensions: Can the Launch of Premium Products Result in Competitive Disadvantages?" *Journal of Marketing* 79, no. 6 (November 2015): 50–70.

39. Timothy B. Heath, Devon DelVecchio, and Michael S. McCarthy, "The Asymmetric Effects of Extending Brands to Lower and Higher Quality," *Journal of Marketing* 75, no. 4 (July 2011): 3–20.

40. Sujan Patel, "7 Examples of Freemium Products Done Right," *Forbes*, April 29, 2015, www.forbes.com/sites/sujanpatel/2015/04/29/7-examples-of-freemium-products-done-right/3/#6c4867e82576.

41. Peter H. Farquhar, Julia Y. Han, Paul M. Herr, and Yuji Ijiri, "Strategies for Leveraging Master Brands," *Journal of Marketing Research* 4, no. 3 (September 1992): 32–43.

42. Gillian Oakenfull, Edward Blair, Betsy Gelb, and Peter Dacin, "Measuring Brand Meaning," *Journal of Advertising Research* 40, no. 5 (September–October 2000): 43–53.

43. Erik Oster, "Jimmy Dean Moves Beyond Breakfast in New Ads Campaign" *Adweek*, September 8, 2014, www.adweek.com/brand-marketing/jimmy-dean-moves-beyond-breakfast-new-ads-159972/.

44. Rajeev Batra, Peter Lenk, and Michel Wedel, "Brand Extension Strategy Planning: Empirical Estimation of Brand-Category Personality Fit and Atypicality,"

Journal of Marketing Research 47, no. 2 (April 2010): 335–347.

45. Andrea Rothman, "France's Bic Bets U.S. Consumers Will Go for Perfume on the Cheap," *The Wall Street Journal,* January 12, 1989, B6; Deborah Wise, "Bic Counts on a New Age for Spray Perfume," *The New York Times,* October 17, 1988, https://www.nytimes.com/1988/10/17/business/international-report-bic-counts-on-a-new-age-for-spray-perfume.html; David A. Aaker, *Managing Brand Equity* (New York: Free Press, 1991).

46. Sandra J. Milberg, Francisca Sinn, and Ronald C. Goodstein, "Consumer Reactions to Brand Extensions in a Competitive Context: Does Fit Still Matter?," *Journal of Consumer Research* 37, no. 3 (October 2010): 543–553.

47. Piyush Kumar, "Brand Counterextensions: The Impact of Extension Success Versus Failure," *Journal of Marketing Research* 42, no. 2 (May 2005): 183–194. See also Piyush Kumar, "The Impact of Cobranding on Customer Evaluation of Brand Counterextensions," *Journal of Marketing* 69, no. 3 (July 2005): 1–18.

48. Glen L. Urban and Steven H. Star, *Advanced Marketing Strategy: Phenomena, Analysis, and Decisions* (Englewood Cliffs, NJ: Prentice Hall, 1991).

49. Kotler and Keller, *Marketing Management.*

50. Srinivas K. Reddy, Susan L. Holak, and Subodh Bhat, "To Extend or Not to Extend: Success Determinants of Line Extensions," *Journal of Marketing Research* 31, no. 2 (May 1994): 243–262. For some conceptual discussion, see Kalpesh Kaushik Desai and Wayne D. Hoyer, "Line Extensions: A Categorization and an Information Processing Perspective," in *Advances in Consumer Research,* Vol. 20 (Provo, UT: Association for Consumer Research, 1993), 599–606.

51. Jack Neff, "Small Ball: Marketers Rely on Line Extensions," *Advertising Age,* April 11, 2005, 10, https://adage.com/article/news/small-ball-marketers-rely-line-extensions/102862/, accessed November 23, 2018.

52. Murphy, *Brand Strategy.*

53. Mita Sujan, "Nature and Structure of Product Categories," working paper, Pennsylvania State University, 1990; Joan Myers-Levy and Alice M. Tybout, "Schema Congruity as a Basis for Product Evaluation," *Journal of Consumer Research* 16, no. 18 (June 1989): 39–54.

54. Deborah Roedder John and Barbara Loken, "Diluting Brand Equity: The Impact of Brand Extensions," *Journal of Marketing,* 57, no. 3 (July 1993): 71–84.

55. David Boush and Barbara Loken, "A Process Tracing Study of Brand Extension Evaluations," *Journal of Marketing Research* 28, no. 1 (February 1991): 16–28; Cathy L. Hartman, Linda L. Price, and Calvin P. Duncan, "Consumer Evaluation of Franchise Extension Products: A Categorization Processing Perspective," *Advances in Consumer Research,* Vol. 17 (Provo, UT: Association for Consumer Research, 1990), 120–126.

56. David A. Aaker and Kevin Lane Keller, "Consumer Evaluations of Brand Extensions," *Journal of Marketing* 54, no. 1 (January 1990): 27–41.

57. Paul A. Bottomley and Stephen J. S. Holden, "Do We Really Know How Consumers Evaluate Brand Extensions? Empirical Generalizations Based on Secondary Analysis of Eight Studies," *Journal of Marketing Research* 38, no. 4 (November 2001): 494–500. See also Jörg Hensler, Csilla Horváth, Marko Sarstedt, and Lorenz Zimmerman, "A Cross-Cultural Comparison of Brand Extensions Success Factors: A Meta-Study," *Journal of Brand Management* 18, no. 1 (2010): 5–20.

58. David Boush, Shannon Shipp, Barbara Loken, Ezra Gencturk, et al., "Affect Generalization to Similar and Dissimilar Line Extensions," *Psychology and Marketing* 4, no. 3 (Fall 1987): 225–241.

59. Specifically, applying Mandler's congruity theory, Meyers-Levy and her colleagues showed that products associated with moderately incongruent brand names could be preferred over ones that were associated with either congruent or extremely incongruent brand names. They interpreted this finding in terms of the ability of moderately incongruent brand extensions to elicit more processing from consumers that could be satisfactorily resolved (assuming consumers could identify a meaningful relationship between the brand name and the product). See Joan Meyers-Levy, Therese A. Louie, and Mary T. Curren, "How Does the Congruity of Brand Names Affect Evaluations of Brand Name Extensions?" *Journal of Applied Psychology* 79, no. 1 (1994): 46–53. See also Eyal Maoz and Alice M. Tybout, "The Moderating Role of Involvement and Differentiation in the Evaluation of Brand Extensions," *Journal of Consumer Psychology* 12, no. 2 (2002): 119–131; Hyeong Min Kim, "Evaluations of Moderately Typical Products: The Role of Within- Versus Cross-Manufacturer Comparison," *Journal of Consumer Psychology* 16, no. 1 (2006): 70–78.

60. Deborah MacInnis and Kent Nakamoto, "Cognitive Associations and Product Category Comparisons: The Role of Knowledge Structures and Context," working paper, University of Arizona, 1990.

61. Susan M. Broniarczyk and Joseph W. Alba, "The Importance of the Brand in Brand Extension," *Journal of Marketing Research* 31, no. 2 (May 1994): 214–228. Incidentally, although a Crest toothbrush was not available at the time that this study was conducted, one was later in fact introduced as Crest Complete.

62. Tammo H. A. Bijmolt, Michel Wedel, Rik G. M. Pieters, and Wayne S. DeSarbo, "Judgments of Brand Similarity," *International Journal of Research in Marketing* 15 (3) (1998): 249–268.

63. Sheri Bridges, Kevin Lane Keller, and Sanjay Sood, "Explanatory Links and the Perceived Fit of Brand Extensions: The Role of Dominant Parent Brand Associations and Communication Strategies," *Journal of Advertising* 29, no. 4 (2000): 1–11.

64. Daniel C. Smith and Jonlee Andrews, "Rethinking the Effect of Perceived Fit on Customers' Evaluations of New Products," *Journal of the Academy of Marketing Science* 23, no. 1 (1995): 4–14.

65. A. V. Muthukrishnan and Barton A. Weitz, "Role of Product Knowledge in Brand Extensions," in *Advances in Consumer Research,* Vol. 18, eds. Rebecca H. Holman and Michael R. Solomon (Provo, UT: Association for Consumer Research, 1990), 407–413. See also Susan M. Broniarczyk and Joseph W. Alba, "The Importance of the Brand in Brand Extension," *Journal of Marketing Research* 31, no. 2 (May 1994): 214–228.

66. Shi Zhang and Sanjay Sood, "'Deep' and 'Surface' Cues: Brand Extension Evaluations by Children and Adults," *Journal of Consumer Research* 29, no. 1 (June 2002): 129–141.

67. E. A. Yorkston, J. C. Nunes, and S. Matta, "The Malleable Brand: The Role of Implicit Theories in Evaluating Brand Extensions," *Journal of Marketing* 74, no.1 (2010): 80–93; K. M. Cutright, J. R. Bettman, and G. J. Fitzsimons, "Putting Brands In Their Place: How a Lack of Control Keeps Brands Contained," *Journal of Marketing Research* 50, no. 3 (2013): 365–377; A. B. Monga and Z. Guhan-Canli, "The Influence of Mating Mind-sets on Brand Extension Evaluation," *Journal of Marketing Research* 49, no. 4 (2013): 581–593.

68. Kevin Lane Keller and David A. Aaker, "The Effects of Sequential Introduction of Brand Extensions," *Journal of Marketing Research* 29, no. 1 (1992), 35–50; Susan M. Broniarczyk and Andrew D. Gershoff, "The Reciprocal Effects of Brand Equity and Trivial Attributes," *Journal of Marketing Research* 40, no. 2 (May 2003): 161–175.

69. See also Arvind Rangaswamy, Raymond Burke, and Terence A. Oliva, "Brand Equity and the Extendibility of Brand Names," *International Journal of Research in Marketing* 10, no. 1 (1993): 61–75. See also Zeynep Gürhan-Canli, "The Effect of Expected Variability of Product Quality and Attribute Uniqueness on Family Brand Evaluations," *Journal of Consumer Research* 30, no. 1 (June 2003): 105–114; Julio J. Rotenberg, "Expected Firm Altruism, Quality Provision, and Brand Extensions," *Marketing Science* 32, no. 2 (March–April 2013): 325–341.

70. Alexander Fedorikhin, C. Whan Park, and Matthew Thomson, "Beyond Fit and Attitude: The Effect of Emotional Attachment on Consumer Responses to Brand Extensions," *Journal of Consumer Psychology* 18, no. 4 (2008): 281–291.

71. Catherine W. M. Yeung and Robert S. Wyer, Jr., "Does Loving a Brand Mean Loving Its Products? The Role of Brand-Elicited Affect in Brand Extension Evaluations," *Journal of Marketing Research* 42, no. 4 (November 2005): 495–506; H. H. Chun, C. W. Park, A.B. Eisingerich, and D. J. MacInnis, "Strategic Benefits of Low Fit Brand Extensions: When and Why?," *Journal of Consumer Psychology* 25, no. 4 (2015): 577–595.

72. See, for example, Peter H. Farquhar and Paul M. Herr, "The Dual Structure of Brand Associations," in *Brand Equity and Advertising: Advertising's Role in Building Strong Brands*, eds. David A. Aaker and Alexander L. Biel (Hillsdale, NJ: Lawrence Erlbaum Associates, 1993), 263–277.

73. Ian M. Lewis, "Brand Equity or Why the Board of Directors Needs Marketing Research," paper presented at the ARF Fifth Annual Advertising and Promotion Workshop, February 1, 1993.

74. Robert D. Hof, "A Washout for Clorox?" *BusinessWeek,* July 9, 1990, 32–33; Alicia Swasy, "P&G and Clorox Wade into Battle over the Bleaches," *The Wall Street Journal,* January 16, 1989, 5; Maria Shao, "A Bright Idea That Clorox Wishes It Never Had," *BusinessWeek,* June 24, 1991, 118–119.

75. Peter H. Farquhar, Julia Y. Han, Paul M. Herr, and Yuji Ijiri, "Strategies for Leveraging Master Brands," *Marketing Research* 4, no. 3 (September 1992): 32–43.

76. Alokparna Basu Monga and Deborah Roedder John, "What Makes Brands Elastic? The Influence of Brand Concept and Styles of Thinking on Brand Extension Evaluation," *Journal of Marketing Research* 74, no. 3 (May 2010): 80–92; Tom Meyvis and Chris Janiszewski, "When Are Broader Brands Stronger Brands? An Accessibility Perspective on the Success of Brand Extensions," *Journal of Consumer Research* 31, no. 2 (September 2004): 346–357; Stijn M. J. Van Osselaer and Joseph W. Alba, "Locus of Equity and Brand Extensions," *Journal of Consumer Research* 29, no. 4 (March 2003): 539–550; Henrik Hagtvedt and Vanessa M. Patrick, "The Broad Embrace of Luxury: Hedonic Potential as a Driver of Brand Extendibility," *Journal of Consumer Psychology* 19, no. 4 (2009): 608–618.

77. Peter H. Farquhar, Julia Y. Han, Paul M. Herr, and Yuji Ijiri, "Strategies for Leveraging Master Brands," *Marketing Research* 4, no. 3 (1992).

78. Ibid.

79. S. Bridges, K. L. Keller, and S. Sood, "Communication Strategies for Brand Extensions: Enhancing Perceived Fit by Establishing Explanatory Links," *Journal of Advertising* 29, no. 4 (2000): 1–11.

80. Christopher Joiner and Barbara Loken, "The Inclusion Effect and Category-Based Induction: Theory and Application to Brand Categories," *Journal of Consumer Psychology* 7, no. 2 (1998): 101–129.

81. S. Bridges, K. L. Keller, and S. Sood, "Communication Strategies for Brand Extensions: Enhancing Perceived Fit by Establishing Explanatory Links," *Journal of Advertising* 29, no. 4 (2000): 1–11.

82. Frank Kardes and Chris Allen, "Perceived Variability and Inferences about Brand Extensions," in *Advances in Consumer Research,* Vol. 18, eds. Rebecca H. Holman and Michael R. Solomon (Provo, UT: Association for Consumer Research, 1990), 392–398; Babu John Mariadoss, Raj Echambadi, Mark J. Arnold, and Vishal Bindroo, "An Examination of the Effects of Perceived Difficulty of Manufacturing the Extension Product on Brand Extension Attitudes," *Journal of the Academy of Marketing Science* 38, no. 6 (2010): 704–719.

83. Vanitha Swaminathan, Richard J. Fox, and Srinivas K. Reddy, "The Impact of Brand Extension Introduction on Choice," *Journal of Marketing* 65, no. 4 (October 2001): 1–15; Subramanian Balachander and Sanjay Ghose, "Reciprocal Spillover Effects: A Strategic Benefit of Brand Extensions," *Journal of Marketing* 67, no. 1 (January 2003): 4–13; Sridhar Moorthy, "Can Brand Extension Signal Product Quality?," *Marketing Science* 31, no. 5 (September–October 2012): 756–770.

84. Sandy D. Jap, "An Examination of the Effects of Multiple Brand Extensions on the Brand Concept," in *Advances in Consumer Research,* Vol. 20 (Provo, UT: Association for Consumer Research, 1993), 607–611.

85. David M. Boush and Barbara Loken, "A Process-Tracing Study of Brand Extension Evaluation," *Journal of Marketing Research* 28, no. 1 (1991): 16–28.

86. Peter Dacin and Daniel C. Smith, "The Effect of Brand Portfolio Characteristics on Consumer Evaluations of

Brand Extensions," *Journal of Marketing Research* 31, no. 2 (May 1994): 229–242. See also David M. Boush and Barbara Loken, "A Process-tracing Study of Brand Extension Evaluation," Journal of Marketing Research 28, no. 1 (1991): 16–28; and Niraj Dawar, "Extensions of Broad Brands: The Role of Retrieval in Evaluations of Fit," *Journal of Consumer Psychology* 5, no. 2 (1996): 189–207.

87. Mary W. Sullivan, "Brand Extensions: When to Use Them," *Management Science* 38, no. 6 (1992): 793–806; Patrick DeGraba and Mary W. Sullivan, "Spillover Effects, Cost Savings, R&D and the Use of Brand Extensions," *International Journal of Industrial Organization* 13, no. 2 (1995): 229–248.

88. Byung Chul Shine, Jongwon Park, and Robert S. Wyer, Jr., "Brand Synergy Effects in Multiple Brand Extensions," *Journal of Marketing Research* 44, no. 4 (November 2007): 663–670; Ryan Rahinel and Joseph P. Redden, "Brands as Product Coordinators: Matching Brands Make Joint Consumption Experiences More Enjoyable," *Journal of Consumer Research* 39, no. 6 (June 2013), 1290–1299.

89. Huifang Mao and H. Shanker Krishnan, "Effects of Prototype and Exemplar Fit on Brand Extension Evaluations: A Two-Process Contingency Model," *Journal of Consumer Research* 33, no. 1 (June 2006): 41–49. See also Ujwal Kayande, John H. Roberts, Gary L. Lilien, and Duncan K. H. Fong, "Mapping the Bounds of Incoherence: How Far Can You Go and How Does It Affect Your Brand?," *Marketing Science* 26, no. 4 (July–August 2007): 504–513.

90. Deborah Roedder John and Barbara Loken, "Diluting Brand Beliefs: When Do Brand Extensions Have a Negative Impact?," *Journal of Marketing* 57, no. 4 (Summer 1993): 71.

91. Jean B. Romeo, "The Effect of Negative Information on the Evaluation of Brand Extensions and the Family Brand," in *Advances in Consumer Research*, Vol. 18, eds. Rebecca H. Holman and Michael R. Solomon (Provo, UT: Association for Consumer Research, 1990), 399–406.

92. Deborah Roedder John, Barbara Loken, and Christopher Joiner, "The Negative Impact of Extensions: Can Flagship Products Be Diluted?," *Journal of Marketing* 62, no. 1 (January 1998): 19–32.

93. Zeynep Gürhan-Canli and Durairaj Maheswaran, "The Effects of Extensions on Brand Name Dilution and Enhancement," *Journal of Marketing Research* 35, no. 11 (1998): 464–473.

94. Sandra J. Milberg, C. W. Park, and Michael S. McCarthy, "Managing Negative Feedback Effects Associated with Brand Extensions: The Impact of Alternative Branding Strategies," *Journal of Consumer Psychology* 6, no. 2 (1997): 119–140.

95. Vicki R. Lane and Robert Jacobson, "Stock Market Reactions to Brand Extension Announcements: The Effects of Brand Attitude and Familiarity," *Journal of Marketing* 59, no. 1 (1995): 63–77.

96. Amna Kirmani, Sanjay Sood, and Sheri Bridges, "The Ownership Effect in Consumer Responses to Brand Line Stretches," *Journal of Marketing* 63, no. 1 (1999): 88–101.

97. Maureen Morrin, "The Impact of Brand Extensions on Parent Brand Memory Structures and Retrieval Processes," *Journal of Marketing Research* 36, no. 4 (1999): 517–525.

98. David A. Aaker, Managing Brand Equity (New York: Free Press, 1991; Jean-Noel Kapferer, Strategic Brand Management, 2nd ed. (New York: Free Press, 2005); Not By Jeans Alone video, PBS Enterprise, 1983.

99. Jeffrey Parker, Donald Lehmann, Kevin Lane Keller, and Martin Schleicher, "Building a Multi-Category Brand: When Should Dissimilar Products Be Introduced?," *Journal of the Academy of Marketing Science*, 46 (2), 300–316; Timothy B. Heath, Subimal Chatterjee, Suman Basuroy, Thorsten Hennig-Thurau, and Bruno Kocher, "Innovation Sequences Over Iterated Offerings: A Relative, Innovation, Comfort, and Stimulation Framework of Consumer Responses," *Journal of Marketing* 79, no. 6 (November 2015): 71–93.

100. C. Whan Park, Sung Youl Jun, and Allan D. Shocker, "Composite Branding Alliances: An Investigation of Extension and Feedback Effects," *Journal of Marketing Research November* 79, no. 6 (1996): 453–466.

101. Zixia Cao and Alina Sorescu, "Wedded Bliss or Tainted Love? Stock Market Reactions to the Introduction of Cobranded Products," *Marketing Science* 32, no. 6 (November–December 2013): 939–959.

102. Vanitha Swaminathan, Zeynep Gürhan-Canli, Umut Kubat, and Ceren Hayran, "How, When, and Why Do Attribute-Complementary Versus Attribute-Similar Cobrands Affect Brand Evaluations: A Concept Combination Perspective," *Journal of Consumer Research* 42, no. 1 (June 2015): 45–58; Ralf van der Lans, Bram Van den Bergh, and Evelien Dieleman, "Partner Selection in Brand Alliances: An Empirical Investigation of the Drivers of Brand Fit," *Marketing Science* 33, no. 4 (July–August 2014): 551–566.

103. Marcus Cunha, Jr., Mark R. Forehand, and Justin W. Angle, "Riding Coattails: When Co-Branding Helps versus Hurts Less-Known Brands," *Journal of Consumer Research* 41, no. 5 (February 2015): 1284–1300.

104. Taylor Randall, Karl Ulrich, and David Reibstein, "Brand Equity and Vertical Product Line Extent," *Marketing Science* 17, no. 4 (1998): 356–379.

105. Ryan Hamilton and Alexander Chernev, "The Impact of Product Line Extensions and Consumer Goals on the Formation of Price Image," *Journal of Marketing Research* 47, no. 1 (February 2010): 51–62.

106. Amna Kirmani, Sanjay Sood, and Sheri Bridges, "The Ownership Effect in Consumer Responses to Brand Line Stretches," *The Journal of Marketing* 63, no. 1 (1999): 88–101.

107. Sheri Bridges, Kevin Lane Keller, and Sanjay Sood, "Explanatory Links and the Perceived Fit of Brand Extensions: The Role of Dominant Parent Brand Associations and Communication Strategies," *Journal of Advertising* 29, no. 4 (2000): 1–11; Richard R. Klink and Daniel C. Smith, "Threats to the External Validity of Brand Extension Research," *Journal of Marketing Research* 38, no. 3 (August 2001): 326–335.

108. Vicki R. Lane, "The Impact of Ad Repetition and Ad Content on Consumer Perceptions of Incongruent Extensions," *Journal of Marketing* 64, no. 4 (2000): 80–91.

109. Sanjay Sood and Kevin Lane Keller, "The Effects of Product Experience and Branding Strategies on Parent Brand Evaluations and Brand Equity Dilution," *Journal of Marketing Research* (2012).

110. Lauranne Buchanan, Carolyn J. Simmons, and Barbara A. Bickart, "Brand Equity Dilution: Retailer Display and Context Brand Effects," *Journal of Marketing Research* 36, no. 8 (1999): 345–355.

111. Alokparna Basu Monga and Deborah Roedder John, "What Makes Brands Elastic? The Influence of Brand Concept and Styles of Thinking on Brand Extension Evaluation," *Journal of Marketing Research* 74, no. 3 (May 2010): 80–92. See also Hakkyun Kim and Deborah Roedder John, "Consumer Response to Brand Extensions: Construal Level as a Moderator of the Importance of Perceived Fit," *Journal of Consumer Psychology* 18, no. 2 (2008): 116–126.

112. Eric A. Yorkston, Joseph C. Nunes, and Shashi Matta, "The Malleable Brand: The Role of Implicit Theories in Evaluating Brand Extensions," *Journal of Marketing* 74, no. 1 (January 2010): 80–93.

113. Hazel R. Markis and Shinobu Kitayama, "Culture and the Self: Implications for Cognition, Emotion, and Motivation," *Psychological Review* 98, no. 2 (April 1991): 224–253; Angela Y. Lee, Jennifer L. Aaker, and Wendi L. Gardner, "The Pleasures and Pains of Distinct Self-Construals: The Role of Interdependence in Regulatory Focus," *Journal of Personality and Social Psychology* 78, no. 6 (June 2000): 1122–1134; Angela Y. Lee, Punam Anand Keller, and Brian Sternthal, "Value from Regulatory Construal Fit," *Journal of Consumer Research* 36, no. 5 (February 2010): 735–747.

114. Rohini Ahluwalia, "How Far Can a Brand Stretch? Understanding the Role of Self-Construal," *Journal of Marketing Research* 45, no. 3 (June 2008): 337–350.

115. Sanjay Puligadda, William T. Ross, Jr., and Radeep Grewal, "Individual Differences in Brand Schematicity," *Journal of Marketing Research* 49, no. 1 (February 2012): 115–130; Jochim Hansen, Florian Kutzner, and Michaela Wänke, "Money and Thinking: Reminders of Money Trigger Abstract Construal and Shape Consumer Judgments," *Journal of Consumer Research*, 39, no. 6 (April 2013): 1154–1166.

116. Edward T. Higgins, "Beyond Pleasure and Pain," *American Psychologist* 52, no. 12 (December 1997): 1280–1300; Edward T. Higgins, "How Self-Regulation Creates Distinct Values: The Case of Promotion and Prevention Decision Making," *Journal of Consumer Psychology* 12, no. 3 (2002): 177–191.

117. Junsang Yeo and Jongwon Park, "Effects of Parent-Extension Similarity and Self-Regulatory Focus on Evaluations of Brand Extensions," *Journal of Consumer Psychology* 16, no. 3 (2006): 272–282.

118. Chung-Chau Chang, Bo-Chi Lin, and Shin-Shin Chang, "The Relative Advantages of Benefit Overlap Versus Category Similarity in Brand Extension Evaluation: The Moderating Role of Self-Regulatory Focus," *Marketing Letters* 22, no. 4 (November 2011): 391–404.

119. Michael J. Barone, Paul W. Miniard, and Jean B. Romeo, "The Influence of Positive Mood on Brand Extension Evaluations," *Journal of Consumer Research* 26, no. 4 (December 2000): 386–400.

120. Alokparna Basu Monga and Deborah Roedder John "Cultural Differences in Brand Extension Evaluation: The Influence of Analytic versus Holistic Thinking," *Journal of Consumer Research* 33, no. 4 (March 2007): 529–536; Sharon Ng and Michael Houston, "Exemplars or Beliefs? The Impact of Self-View on the Nature and Relative Influence of Brand Associations," *Journal of Consumer Research* 32, no. 4 (March 2006): 519–529.

121. Sharon Ng, "Cultural Orientation and Brand Dilution: Impact of Motivation Level and Extension Typicality," *Journal of Marketing Research* 47, no. 1 (February 2010): 186–198.

122. Carlos J. Torelli and Rohini Ahluwalia, "Extending Culturally Symbolic Brands: A Blessing or Curse?," *Journal of Consumer Research* 38, no. 5 (February 2012): 933–947.

123. The fakes are Burberry Baby Stroller, Atlantic City Playing Cards, Slim Jim Beef Jerky Throat Lozenges, and Richard Simmons Sneakers.

124. Ashraf Essa, "Why Apple Inc. Is So Profitable," *Fool*, March 23, 2017, www.fool.com/investing/2017/03/23/why-apple-inc-is-so-profitable.aspx.

125. Wikipedia, "Typography of Apple Inc.," https://en.wikipedia.org/wiki/Typography_of_Apple_Inc., accessed July 20, 2018.

126. Brittnay A. Roston, "These Magazine Covers Were Shot with the iPhone 7 Plus," *Slash Gear*, April 18, 2017, www.slashgear.com/these-magazine-covers-were-shot-with-the-iphone-7-plus-18482648/.

127. Camila Domonoske, "Supreme Court Sides with Samsung, Against Apple in Patent Infringement Fight," *National Public Radio*, December 6, 2016, www.npr.org/sections/thetwo-way/2016/12/06/504545297/supreme-court-sides-with-samsung-against-apple-in-patent-infringement-fight.

128. Josh Smith, "Android vs iPhone: 14 Reasons Android Is Still Better," *Gotta Be Mobile*, February 7, 2018, www.gottabemobile.com/android-vs-iphone-android-better/.

129. Interbrand, "Best Global Brands 2016 Rankings," accessed July 20, 2018, http://interbrand.com/best-brands/best-global-brands/2016/ranking/.

Managing Brands Over Time

14

Learning Objectives

After reading this chapter, you should be able to

1. Understand the important considerations in brand reinforcement.
2. Describe the range of brand revitalization options available to a company.
3. Outline the various strategies to improve brand awareness and brand image.
4. Define the key steps in managing a brand crisis.

Some companies like Barnes & Noble have found it difficult to maintain market leadership in the face of strong competition and the sweeping changes taking place due to online retailing.

PREVIEW

One of the obvious challenges in managing brands is constant change in the marketing environment. Shifts in consumer behavior, competitive strategies, government regulations, technological advances, and other areas can profoundly affect the fortunes of a brand. Besides these external forces, the firm's own strategic focus may force minor or major adjustments in the way it markets its brands. Effective brand management thus requires proactive strategies designed to at least maintain—if not actually enhance—customer-based brand equity in the face of all these different forces.

Consider the fate of these four brands: Myspace, Yahoo!, Blockbuster, and Barnes & Noble. In the mid-2000s, each enjoyed a strong market position, if not outright leadership. In just a few short years, however, each was struggling for survival as Facebook, Google, Netflix, and Amazon, respectively, raced past them to establish market superiority. Although there are many explanations, the way these brands were managed certainly contributed to the outcomes.

This chapter considers how to best manage brands over time. Any marketing action a firm takes today can change consumers' brand awareness or brand image and have an indirect effect on the success of future marketing activities (see Figure 14-1). For example, the frequent use of temporary price decreases as sales promotions may create or strengthen a discount association to the brand, with potentially adverse implications on customer loyalty and responses to future price changes or nonprice-oriented marketing communication efforts.[1]

Unfortunately, marketers may have a particularly difficult time trying to anticipate future consumer responses; if the new knowledge structures that will influence future consumer responses do not exist until the short-term marketing actions actually occur, how can they realistically simulate future consumer responses to permit accurate predictions?

The main assertion of this chapter is that marketers must actively manage brand equity over time by reinforcing the brand meaning, and, if necessary, by making adjustments to the marketing program to identify new sources of brand equity. In considering these two topics, we will look at a number of different brand reinforcement issues and brand revitalization strategies. The Brand Focus 14.0 at the end of the chapter considers how to deal with a marketing crisis, with specific emphasis on Johnson & Johnson's experiences with the Tylenol brand through the years.

REINFORCING BRANDS

How should we reinforce brand equity over time? How can marketers make sure consumers have knowledge structures that support brand equity for their brands? Generally, we reinforce brand equity by marketing actions that consistently convey the meaning of the brand to consumers in terms of brand awareness and brand image. As we have discussed before, questions marketers should consider are as follows:

- *What products does the brand represent, what benefits does it supply, and what needs does it satisfy?* Nutri-Grain has expanded from cereals into granola bars and other products, cementing its reputation as "makers of healthy breakfast and snack foods." Disney has been continually updating its portfolio through a series of high-profile acquisitions. In 2005, Disney acquired Pixar, and Disney bought Marvel in 2009. Disney acquired Lucasfilm and the entire Star Wars franchise for $4 billion. These acquisitions have helped Disney maintain its competitive edge and expand its appeal to its audiences.
- *How does the brand make those products superior? What strong, favorable, and unique brand associations exist in the minds of consumers?* Through product development and the successful introduction of brand extensions, Black & Decker is now seen as offering innovative designs in its small appliance products.

Both these issues—brand meaning in terms of products, benefits, and needs, as well as in terms of product differentiation—depend on the firm's general approach to product development, branding strategies, and other strategic concerns, as we discussed in Chapters 12 and 13.

This section on brand reinforcement examines three key issues: (1) advantages of maintaining brand consistency; (2) importance of protecting sources of brand equity; and (3) and trade-offs between fortifying and leveraging brands. If there is one rule for modern branding, however, it is that brands can never stand still. Brands must be constantly moving forward. A vivid example is the way Coldplay chose to launch their latest album.

COLDPLAY

Having sold 55 million albums in their careers, British rock band Coldplay might find the release of a new album to be nothing special. After all, their fourth album *Viva la Vida or Death and All His Friends* sold 2.8 million units in the United States alone, and their U.S. tour grossed more than $126 million.

When launching their fifth album, *Mylo Xyloto*, however, Chris Martin, lead singer and front man for the band, noted how aggressively they had to approach the release. "Because of the speed of media and entertainment, with every album you have to think like a new act," noted Martin. "Just because they liked *A Rush of Blood to the Head* doesn't mean they're gonna like this one. So we start again." Before launching a worldwide tour in 2012—that was scheduled to last over a year—the band made 60 appearances of various sorts in 2011 to help promote the album; a video shoot in South Africa; a live-streamed *Amex Unstaged* launch show in Madrid shot by famed video and film director Anton Corbijn, and so on. Performances of new songs appeared on YouTube and elsewhere. The band also created a viral campaign to generate fan interest and involvement. Leaving nothing to chance paid off for the band. *Mylo Xyloto* went to No. 1 in album sales in 17 countries, and most venues for the world tour sold out in minutes. The band did not stand still with respect to their world tour, either. In a concert first, each concertgoer received a RF-driven Xyloband flashing wristband that changed colors for different songs after receiving a signal.[2]

Coldplay has managed to remain relevant to their audiences through a series of music albums featuring their hit songs and spectacular concert performances.

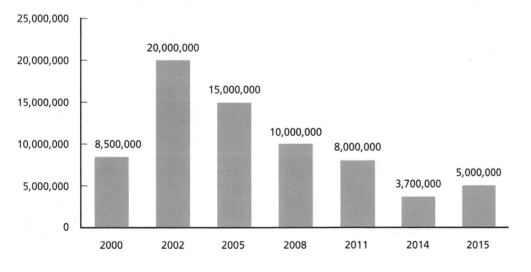

FIGURE 14-1
Coldplay Album Sales Across Years

Overall, a series of carefully executed strategies has helped Coldplay effectively manage its brand over time, and this has helped with improving their album sales over time (see Figure 14-2). For their sixth album, *Ghost Stories*, Coldplay reversed direction and chose to book only six performances in more intimate settings.[3] The promotional mix included a scavenger hunt where lyrics to the nine songs on the album were

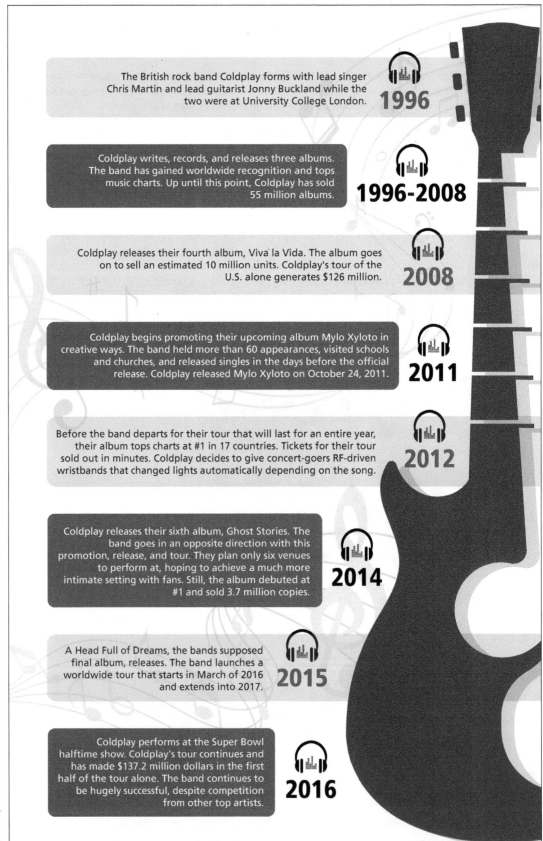

FIGURE 14-2

Coldplay Timeline Coldplay's timeline highlights key milestones in the band's twenty-year history.

included in ghost story books over the world.[4] For the seventh and potentially final album, *A Head Full of Dreams*, released in December 2015, Coldplay launched a world tour beginning in 2016. The long-term success of this band based on well-thought-out product and marketing strategy has resulted in long-term success. This type of success is somewhat rare in the music industry, where music bands have a relatively short existence.[5]

Maintaining Brand Consistency

Maintaining consistency involves two key aspects: (1) consistency of marketing support; and (2) consistency of brand associations. Without question, the most important consideration in reinforcing brands is consistency in the nature and amount of marketing support the brand receives. Brand consistency is critical to maintaining the strength and favorability of brand associations. Another way to achieve a consistent appeal is through retro-marketing, or convincing consumers that heritage brands have nostalgic appeal that can help consumers connect with their past, as outlined in a section that follows.

Consistent Marketing Support for Market Leader Brands. Inadequate marketing support is an especially dangerous strategy when combined with price increases. An example of failure to adequately support a brand occurred in the kitchen and bath fixtures market.

DELTA FAUCET

Delta Faucet, the first company to advertise faucets on television in the 1970s, was the market leader in the 1980s with more than 30 percent market share. Beginning in the 1990s, however, two major factors contributed to a decline in market share. First, whereas Delta had built a strong business model based on the loyalty of professional plumbers, the advent of hardware superstores and online shopping empowered consumers to make their own choices and repairs. Second, Delta's support for its brand through innovation and advertising diminished during this time. These factors combined to give rival Moen an opportunity to gain market share, and by 2005, each company held 25 percent of the U.S. faucet market. That same year, Delta countered by raising its advertising budget 60 percent and conducting thousands of interviews and other forms of consumer research to feed R&D efforts.[6]

Lost market share can be difficult to regain. In 2015, it was estimated that 17.9 percent of U.S. construction firms use Delta faucets.[7] Overall, they commanded a market share in the low 20 percent area, giving them the second largest share.[8] In an effort to gain market share, Delta Faucet tried various approaches. For instance, it was a key partner for five 5k Warrior Dash mud runs in 2015, where it provided showers for runners after the race and set a Guinness World Record for the most people simultaneously showering at a single venue. Providing a photo booth for the runners who were unable to carry their cell phones through the mud and subsequently e-mailing the photos generated more than 50 percent opt-ins to receive additional information about Delta Faucet.[9]

Even a cursory examination of the brands that have maintained market leadership for the last 50 or 100 years or so testifies to the advantages of staying consistent. Brands such as Disney, McDonald's, Mercedes Benz, and others have been remarkably true to their strategies once they achieved a preeminent market leadership position.

Perhaps an even more compelling demonstration of the benefits of consistency is the fortunes of brands that have constantly repositioned or changed ad agencies.

Consistency and Change. Being consistent does not mean, however, that marketers should avoid making any changes in the marketing program. On the contrary, managing brand equity with consistency may require making numerous tactical shifts and changes in order to maintain the strategic thrust and direction of the brand. The most effective tactics for a particular brand at any one time can certainly vary. Prices may move up or down, product features may be added or dropped, ad campaigns may employ different creative strategies and slogans, and different brand extensions may be introduced or withdrawn to create the same desired knowledge structures in consumers' minds.

Nevertheless, the strategic positioning of many leading brands has been kept remarkably uniform over time by the retention of key elements of the marketing program and the preservation of the brand meaning. In fact, many brands have kept a key creative element in their marketing communication programs over the years and, as a result, have effectively created some "advertising equity." As the Branding Brief 14-1 illustrates, Patagonia has continually refined its vision and mission of sustainability.

As the next segment on nostalgic brands suggests, brands sometimes return to their roots to remind existing or lapsed customers or to attract new ones. Such efforts to refresh awareness obviously can make sense. At the same time, marketers should be sure that these old advertising elements or marketing appeals have enduring meaning with older consumers but are also relevant to younger consumers. They should examine the entire marketing program to determine which elements are making a strong contribution to brand equity and must therefore be protected.

BRANDING BRIEF 14-1

Patagonia

Patagonia is a brand whose mission and values are focused on sustainability. The company stated aims are as follows: "We design and sell things made to last and be useful. But we ask our customers not to buy from us what you don't need or can't really use. Everything we make—everything anyone makes—costs the planet more than it gives back." This ethos runs through everything that the company does, and it has built its entire brand image on socially and environmentally responsible business practices. Doing so has helped the brand resonate with its customers. As one marketing observer noted, "Patagonia's audience trusts the brand, admires its values, and aspires to live by the same principles. Very few brands can compete on quality and price alone."

Patagonia has refined its business practices to reflect its sustainability mission. Since its beginning in 1973 as an outdoor clothing and gear company, the company has communicated its commitment to sustainability and environmental causes. For example, in 1986, the company began donating 10 percent of its profits each year to small grassroots environmental protection groups. In 1993, the company began making recycled polyester from plastic soda bottles and was the first outdoor clothing manufacturer to transform trash into fleece. In 1994, the company conducted its first environmental impact assessment report and subsequently began an exclusive use of organically grown cotton in all cotton products. In 2002, Yvon Chouinard co-founded One Percent for the Planet, whose goal was to encourage businesses to donate 1 percent of sales to help protect the environment.

In 2007, Fortune named Patagonia the "Coolest Company on the Planet." That same year, the company introduced the Footprint Chronicles, a Web site that explained its social and environmental practices and told stories of its products' origins. In 2008, the company began sharing strategies for "greening" supply chain with Walmart for free and also began working with Walmart to build a sustainability index for its products. In a major effort to strengthen its sustainability efforts, Patagonia, in coordination with Walmart, founded the Sustainable Apparel Coalition, standardizing sustainability metrics for the industry. Soon after, Patagonia began collaborating with its competitors REI and North Face, agreeing to use Bluesign Technologies to grade dyeing and finishing by textile suppliers.

In 2011, Patagonia launched its "Don't Buy This Jacket" campaign asking consumers to consider purchasing used jackets. Soon after, the company launched its "Worn Wear" program to repair used items to keep them out of landfills. Patagonia also launched its new hexagonal packaging using 100 percent post-consumer waste corrugate and later launched "The New Localism" campaign,

a call to take action in standing up for environmental causes. More recently, when PETA released video footage of cruelty on Ovis 21 farms, Patagonia dropped them as a wool supplier. To further reinforce their sustainability mission and vision, Patagonia released a set of new wool principles that guide the treatment of animals as well as land-use practices and sustainability. In 2017, Patagonia announced it will accept used clothing for store credit, repairing and reselling the used items as Worn Wear. Overall, Patagonia has been successful at maintaining a consistent brand positioning around the theme of social and environmental responsibility, but has leveraged this positioning in multiple ways by sponsoring various sustainability initiatives.

Patagonia's Common Threads Initiative spotlights its commitment to sustainability.

Sources: Ashley Lutz, "A Clothing Company Discourages Customers from Buying Its Stuff—And Business Is Booming," *Business Insider*, September 8, 2014, https://www.businessinsider.com/patagonia-business-strategy-2014-9, accessed November 24, 2018; Monte Burke, "Wal-Mart, Patagonia Team to Green Business," *Forbes Magazine*, May 6, 2010, https://www.forbes.com/forbes/2010/0524/rebuilding-sustainability-eco-friendly-mr-green-jeans.html#5a3e71d74299, accessed November 24, 2018; Marc Gunther, "The Patagonia Adventure: Yvon Chouinard's Stubborn Desire to Redefine Business," B the Change, September 6, 2016, https://bthechange.com/the-patagonia-adventure-yvon-chouinards-stubborn-desire-to-redefine-business-f60f7ab8dd60, accessed November 24, 2018; Megan Michelson, "Want Ethically Sourced Wool? Buy from Patagonia," Outside Online, July 29, 2016, https://www.outsideonline.com/2101871/want-ethically-sourced-wool-buy-patagonia, accessed November 24, 2018; People for the Ethical Treatment of Animals (PETA), "Patagonia's 'Sustainable Wool' Supplier Exposed: Lambs Skinned Alive, Throats Slit, Tails Cut Off," https://investigations.peta.org/ovis-lamb-slaughter-sheep-cruelty/, accessed November 24, 2018; Poonkulali Thangavelu, "The Success of Patagonia's Marketing Strategy," Investopedia, https://www.investopedia.com/articles/personal-finance/070715/success-patagonias-marketing-strategy.asp, accessed November 24, 2018.

1973	Founded by Yvon Chouinard.
Early **1980s**	Patagonia begins to gain popularity with technical new fabrics and vivid colored clothing, while ramping up R&D.
1985 – 1986	Patagonia shift entire line of polypropylene underwear to Capilene; sales soar. Company commits to donate 10% of profits each year to small environmental protection groups.
1993	Company begins making recycled polyester from plastic soda bottles–the first manufacturer to transform trash into fleece.
1994	Company conducts its first environmental impact assessment report.
1996	Patagonia opens distribution center in Reno, NV, achieving 60% reduction in energy usage. Company begins exclusively using organic cotton in all cotton products.
2002	Couhinard co-founds One Percent for the Planet, encouraging businesses to donate 1% of sales to protect the environment. Introduces Down products.
2005	Company is criticized by PETA for wool sourced from Australian farm requiring mulesing. Chouinard's book "Let My People Go Surfing" published.
2007	Fortune names Patagonia "Coolest Company on the Planet." Company introduces Footprint Chronicles, explaining its social and environmental practices as well as stories of products' origins.
2008 – 2009	Patagonia begins sharing strategies for "greening" supply chain with Walmart. Company co-founds the Sustainable Apparel Coalition with Walmart, standardizing sustainability metrics for industry.
2010	Patagonia begins collaborating with competitors REI and North Face, agreeing to use Bluesign Technologies to grade dyeing and finishing by textile suppliers.
2011	Company launches "Don't Buy This Jacket" campaign asking consumers to buy used jackets instead. Revenues increase 30%.
2012	Company becomes California certified B Corp. Chouinard's account of operating a responsible business, "The Responsible Company: What We've Learned from Patagonia's First 40 Years" published.
2013	Patagonia introduces new hexagonal packaging using 100% post consumer waste corrugate. Company begins "Worn Wear" program to reuse items and keep used items out of landfills while also introducing Traceable Down products.
2014	Patagonia launches The New Localism campaign, a call to stand up for environmental causes. Patagonia branded film DamNation premieres at SXSW.
2015	PETA releases video footage of cruelty on wool supplier Ovis 21 farms; company drops them as supplier. Chouinard named to Marketing Hall of Fame.
2016	Company releases new wool principles, guiding treatment of animals along with land-use practices and sustainability.

patagonia

FIGURE 14-3

Patagonia's Timeline
Patagonia's timeline highlights how the brand's sustaintability initiatives over the years have played an important role in its success.

Brand Flashbacks.   Older, heritage brands can reach into their past in different ways to develop successful new marketing campaigns. One way is to revisit well-known and loved past ad campaigns, perhaps giving them a twist and updating them in the process.

Dubbed *retro-branding, retro-advertising,* or *nostalgia marketing* by some marketing pundits, the tactic is a means to tie in with past advertising that was, and perhaps could still be, a key source of brand equity. Demonstrating the latent value of past advertising is the return of such advertising icons as Colonel Sanders for KFC, who reappeared in new advertising and packaging focused on the restaurant's Southern roots, albeit with a thinner face and a red apron instead of the classic three-piece suit, and a very different attitude!

Retro-branding can activate and strengthen brand associations that would be virtually impossible to recreate with new advertising today. In some cases, a key point-of-difference for the brand may just turn out to be heritage or nostalgia rather than any product-related difference. Heritage can be a powerful point-of-difference—at least as long as it conveys expertise, longevity, and experience and not just age.

Anniversaries and milestones of longevity can be excellent opportunities to launch a campaign to celebrate. Marketers should focus as much on the future of the brand as on its past, of course, perhaps emphasizing how all that the brand has gone through will benefit its customers in the future.

Oreo's 100-year anniversary (which took place in 2012) was marked by the popular "celebrate the kid inside" campaign. The advertising featured many spots highlighting how Oreos can liven up an otherwise dull bus ride or morning commute with kids serving adults Oreos. The ads and in-store contests created a birthday party atmosphere and focused on the "Twist, Lick, and Dunk" method of eating Oreos with milk. The marketing campaign also included a 100-day "Daily Twist" promotion that paired the brand with various cultural images and icons. The Oreo birthday page received 25 million likes, and sales increased 25 percent, making it one of the most successful brand pages. Oreo also adapted this campaign for the global marketplace. In a variation of the 'Twist, Lick, and Dunk" campaign, Oreo also created ads featuring shared moments of togetherness between family members, and featured a father and son in the "twist, lick, dunk" ritual. It also encouraged parents to sign a "Oreo Togetherness Pledge" promising to spend more quality time with their children. In addition, in the India market, an Oreo Togetherness Bus roamed various cities across the country providing a platform for parents and children to catch fun family moments.[10]

Research shows that nostalgic advertising can positively influence consumers. One empirical study confirmed that intentionally nostalgic advertisements yielded favorable attitudes toward the advertisement and the brand. Another study identified a potential source of nostalgic purchase behavior, called "intergenerational influence," or the influence of a parent's purchase behavior and brand attitudes on a child's behavior and attitudes.

The nostalgic connection evoked by the mobile game Pokémon GO was a key factor accounting for the runaway success of this game.[11] The characters featured on the Pokémon GO mobile game were identical to the ones featured in the cards when they were first introduced. A number of millennials enjoyed playing a game that allowed them to reconnect with the characters that were familiar to them and brought back memories of their youth.

Some brands attempt to make the case that their enduring appeal is still relevant for lapsed users today. Kraft Macaroni and Cheese Dinner, long sold to parents as a meal favorite for children, turned the tables on grown-ups to remind them, "You Know You Love It." A $50 million campaign featuring TV, print and online ads, billboards, a Web site (www.youknowyouloveit .com), and social media communications on Facebook and Twitter supported the entire product line. The Branding Brief 14-2 describes how Pabst has retained its appeal over the years.

BRANDING BRIEF 14-2
Pabst

Heritage appeals do not necessarily have to use advertising though, as Pabst Blue Ribbon (PBR) beer shows. The brand was born in 1882, when the Pabst Brewing Company began tying silk ribbons to bottles of its Select beer. The company became one of the major U.S. beer brands and remained so through 1977, when sales peaked at 18 million barrels. As competition from Budweiser and Miller increased, however, the PBR brand suffered as a consequence of price cuts, quality problems, and ownership changes.

After years of decline, sales of PBR suddenly spiked in the Portland, Oregon area in 2001. Management investigated and discovered that young trendsetters were adopting the beer as a "blue-collar, Americana" alternative to the big brands and craft beers favored by their parents. Rather than using above-the-line advertising, which it had not done since the 1970s, Pabst sought to capitalize on this market through word-of-mouth, on-premise promotions, and event sponsorships, primarily of local bands and concerts, and licensed merchandise aimed at "hipsters."

Pabst regained its market presence through a combination of word-of-mouth, on-premise promotions, and event sponsorships.

By letting the brand's image be created as much by consumers as by the company itself and by keeping it local, hip, and organic, Pabst increased sales over the next nine years. With the Metropoulus family as new owners, other Pabst brands became candidates for revitalization—including Schlitz, Schaefer, Stroh's, and Falstaff. A total of 5 of the top 10 brands—from 1973! More recently, Pabst has been entering into partnerships with various craft breweries to improve its market presence against the large, national breweries such as Anheuser-Busch InBev and MillerCoors.

Sources: Bruce Horovitz, "Southern Finger-Lickin' Roots Help KFC Revamp," *USA Today*, April 20, 2005, 3B; Darrel D. Muehling and David E. Sprott, "The Power of Reflection: An Empirical Examination of Nostalgia Advertising Effects," *Journal of Advertising* 33, no. 3 (Autumn 2004): 25–35; Elizabeth S. Moore, William L. Wilkie, and Richard J. Lutz, "Passing the Torch: Intergenerational Influences as a Source of Brand Equity," *Journal of Marketing* 66, no. 2 (April 2002): 17–37; Stephen Brown, Robert V. Kozinets, and John F. Sherry Jr., "Teaching Old Brands New Tricks: Retro Branding and the Revival of Brand Meaning," *Journal of Marketing* 67, no. 3 (July 2003): 19–33; Katherine E. Loveland, Dirk Smeesters, and Naomi Mandel, "Still Preoccupied with 1995: The Need to Belong and Preference for Nostalgic Products," *Journal of Consumer Research* 37, no. 3 (October 2010): 393–408; Jenn Abelson, "L.L.Bean Marks 100 Years with 'Bootmobile'," *Boston Globe*, January 18, 2012, https://www.bostonglobe.com/business/2012/01/18/bean-marks-years-with-bootmobile-tour/ToAo57TJgsb6NWYi9bOFAN/story.html, accessed November 24, 2018; Stuart Elliott, "Kraft Hope to Encourage Adults to Revert to a Childhood Favorite," *The New York Times*, May 26, 2010, https://www.nytimes.com/2010/05/27/business/media/27adco.html, accessed November 24, 2018; Jeremy Mullman, "Schlitz Tries to Revive '50s Heyday," *Advertising Age*, April 17, 2006, 8; Ann Cortissoz, "Not Your Father's Beer: Your Grandfather's," *Boston Globe*, October 20, 2004, F1, http://archive.boston.com/ae/food/articles/2004/10/20/not_your_fathers_beer_your_grandfathers/, accessed November 24, 2018; Matt Schwartz, "Can This Stay Cool? A Jet-Setting Family Takes Over a Blue Collar Brand," *Bloomberg BusinessWeek*, September 20, 2010; E. J. Schultz, "A Tiger at 60: How Kellogg's Tony Is Changing for a New Age," *Advertising Age*, August 29, 2011, https://adage.com/article/news/kellogg-s-tony-tiger-60-changing-a-age/229493/, accessed November 24, 2018; Lauren Friedman, "Why Nostalgia Marketing Works So Well with Millennials, and How Your Brand Can Benefit," *Forbes Magazine*, August 2, 2016, https://www.forbes.com/sites/laurenfriedman/2016/08/02/why-nostalgia-marketing-works-so-well-with-millennials-and-how-your-brand-can-benefit/#423ed3e93636, accessed November 24, 2018; Jason Notte, "How Pabst Is Taking on Big Beer, Craft Beer and Imported Beer All at Once," MarketWatch, January 10, 2017, https://www.marketwatch.com/story/how-pabst-is-taking-on-big-beer-craft-beer-and-imported-beer-all-at-once-2017-01-10, accessed November 24, 2018.

Protecting Sources of Brand Equity

Consistency thus guides strategic direction and does not necessarily prescribe the particular tactics of the supporting marketing program for the brand at any one point in time. Unless some change in either consumer behavior, competition, or the company makes the strategic positioning of the brand less powerful, there is likely little need to deviate from a successful positioning.

Although brands should always look for potentially powerful new sources of brand equity, a top priority is to preserve and defend those that already exist. Often brands can be the subject of scandals and transgressions which may cause irreparable harm. As the Volkswagen Branding Brief 14-3 illustrates, firms have to monitor and recover their reputation in the aftermath of a scandal.

Brand Crises.   Regardless of how strong a brand is, crises incidents are unavoidable. These crises could range from product or service failures resulting in product recalls to moral transgressions which may lead consumers to question a company's values. For example, in 2009, Toyota experienced a major crisis when its faulty brake pedals caused its cars to suddenly accelerate. The Toyota brand crisis resulted in the largest recall of its history, with nearly 9 million vehicles being recalled from 2004 to 2010.[12]

How do these crises incidents impact a brand's reputation, and how can a brand recover? Researchers have examined brand crises (or transgressions) with a view to explaining how they can impact consumers' perceptions and preferences. Some key findings are highlighted in The Science of Branding 14-1. Following that, Branding Brief 14-3 describes how the Volkswagen diesel emissions scandal played out in social media. What are some strategies for brands to recover from such crises? The section that follows highlights specific recovery strategies for brands to recover from such crises and provides examples of each of these approaches.

Recovering from a Brand Crisis or Scandal.   Firms resort to many approaches to recover their brand reputation following a crisis or a scandal. However, there are two principles to keep in mind as you craft a response: swiftness and sincerity. The response to a brand crisis must be swift. The longer it takes a firm to respond to a marketing crisis, the more likely that customers will form negative impressions based on unfavorable media coverage or word-of-mouth. Perhaps worse, they may decide they do not really like the brand after all and permanently switch to alternatives. In the context of the Volkswagen diesel emissions crisis, VW adopted a strategy of apologizing for the incident. While this is a good response to an unfolding crisis—some viewed this as too little, too late—the company wavered in the initial days of the crisis. Swift actions must also come across as sincere. Public acknowledgment of the severity of the impact on consumers and willingness to take whatever steps are necessary and feasible to solve the crisis reduce the chance that consumers will form negative attributions for the firm's behavior.

BRANDING BRIEF 14-3
Volkswagen

In September 2015, the Environmental Protection Agency found that many Volkswagen cars sold in the United States were equipped with software that could falsely improve the performance of diesel engines on emissions tests. This cheating was subsequently acknowledged by the car manufacturer. Among the many issues at stake for the company was one of public perception. Anecdotal evidence at the time of the incident suggested irreparable harm to the Volkswagen brand. So could Volkswagen recover in the short-term in this regard? And more broadly, how did brand perception towards Volkswagen change during the scandal, particularly in an era where social media can cause negative news to proliferate and reverberate over time?

Academic researchers conducted extensive analysis of the Volkswagen scandal using data from Twitter. They analyzed periods aligned with some of the key events relating to the scandal, and also representing periods during and following the scandal. Specifically, they examined how customers were reacting to information about the scandal based on three factors: (1) frequency of mentions of the Volkswagen brand name; (2) the sentiment towards the brand; and (3) topics that dominated the conversation at various points in time.

They found that the frequency of mentions varied dramatically day by day, and the mentions seemed to parallel specific actions taken by Volkswagen in order to issue apologies or by regulatory agencies in order to place responsibility or issue punishments. In terms of topics that were discussed, initially the focus was on cheating itself, but later gave way to discussions of specific models—for example, Beetle and Jetta that were the focus of the recall. Their findings suggested that while sentiment towards the brand was extremely negative at the beginning of the scandal, over time, the daily percentage of negative mentions decreased and the sentiment became more neutral. To a large extent, recovering a brand reputation depends on the recovery strategies that a company employs in the aftermath of a brand crisis. Table 14–1 summarizes and provides examples of different types of recovery efforts that a firm could use to overcome the negative consequences of a reputational crisis.

Source: Vanitha Swaminathan and Suyun Mah, "What 100,000 Tweets About the Volkswagen Scandal Tell Us About Angry Customers," *Harvard Business Review*, September 2, 2016, https://hbr.org/2016/09/what-100000-tweets-about-the-volkswagen-scandal-tell-us-about-angry-customers, accessed November 24, 2018.

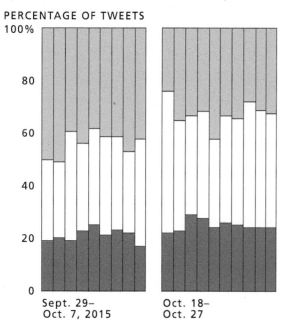
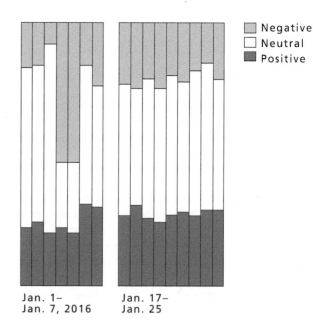

FIGURE 14-4

Volkswagen on Twitter

Volkswagen's emissions scandal was reflected in increased negative sentiment towards the brand in social media, and the negative sentiment became more neutral over time.

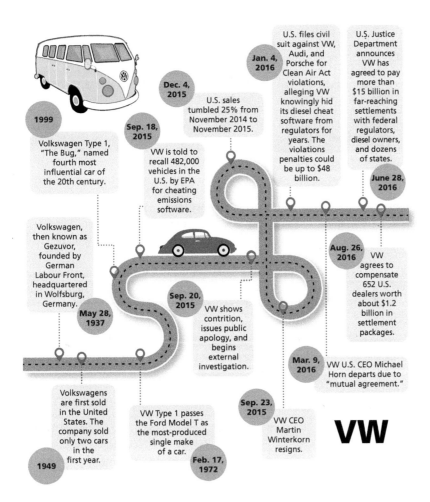

1999
Volkswagen Type 1, "The Bug," named fourth most influential car of the 20th century.

Sep. 18, 2015
VW is told to recall 482,000 vehicles in the U.S. by EPA for cheating emissions software.

Dec. 4, 2015
U.S. sales tumbled 25% from November 2014 to November 2015.

Jan. 4, 2016
U.S. files civil suit against VW, Audi, and Porsche for Clean Air Act violations, alleging VW knowingly hid its diesel cheat software from regulators for years. The violations penalties could be up to $48 billion.

U.S. Justice Department announces VW has agreed to pay more than $15 billion in far-reaching settlements with federal regulators, diesel owners, and dozens of states.

June 28, 2016

May 28, 1937
Volkswagen, then known as Gezuvor, founded by German Labour Front, headquartered in Wolfsburg, Germany.

Sep. 20, 2015
VW shows contrition, issues public apology, and begins external investigation.

Aug. 26, 2016
VW agrees to compensate 652 U.S. dealers worth about $1.2 billion in settlement packages.

Mar. 9, 2016
VW U.S. CEO Michael Horn departs due to "mutual agreement."

1949
Volkswagens are first sold in the United States. The company sold only two cars in the first year.

Feb. 17, 1972
VW Type 1 passes the Ford Model T as the most-produced single make of a car.

Sep. 23, 2015
VW CEO Martin Winterkorn resigns.

VW

FIGURE 14-5
Volkswagen's Emissions Scandal: Timeline of Events

THE SCIENCE OF BRANDING 14-1

UNDERSTANDING BRAND CRISES

1. There are various research articles that have shed light on the impact of brand crises on brand equity and reputation. Some brand types and some consumers react more negatively to brand crises. Researchers Aaker, Fournier, and Brasel found that certain types of brands (e.g., brands like Campbell's soup which have a sincere brand personality) are likely to be affected more when a crisis occurs.

2. Some consumers are more likely to punish brands for transgressions, especially those consumers who have strong relationships with brands, but this effect is only seen when the consumer directly experiences the crisis. In these situations, consumers may experience a sense of injustice or betrayal.

3. In other cases, when consumers have strong relationships with brands, and the crisis does not impact them directly, they are more willing to forgive the brand. Researchers have found an interesting phenomenon called counter-argumentation which occurs when consumers are highly committed to a brand, in which consumers actually produce arguments why their brand is not responsible or accountable for the crisis.

Consumers are known to resort to counter-argumentation when negative information is seen as a direct challenge to their self and identity, causing them to want to defend their brand.

4. Crises involving related brands can spill over and impact the reputation of a parent brand as well, particularly when the brand has line extensions and brand extensions carrying the same brand name.

5. Brand crises could also provide opportunities to strengthen relationships with customers. The Brand Focus 14.0 on Tylenol's crisis is an excellent example of this. If handled well, companies can institute recovery efforts such as apology or compensation that may cause some consumers to feel even more positive towards a brand.

In most cases, crises incidents can be very detrimental to a brand's reputation. This is more so today with social media acting as an amplifier of information about brands. Branding Brief 14-3 outlined how the diesel emissions crisis harmed the reputation of the Volkswagen brand, and how the crisis played out in social media.

Sources: Yany Gregoire, Thomas M. Tripp, and Renaud Legoux, "When Customer Love Turns Into Lasting Hate: The Effects of Relationship Strength and Time on Customer Revenge and Avoidance," *Journal of Marketing* 73, no. 6 (2009): 18–32; Rohini Ahluwalia, Robert E. Burnkrant, and H. Rao Unnava, "Consumer Response to Negative Publicity: The Moderating Role of Commitment," *Journal of Marketing Research* 37, no. 2 (2000): 203–214; Rohini Ahluwalia, "Examination of Psychological Processes Underlying Resistance to Persuasion," *Journal of Consumer Research* 27, no. 2 (2000): 217–232; Niraj Dawar and Madan M. Pillutla, "Impact of Product Harm Crises on Brand Equity: The Moderating Role of Consumer Expectations," *Journal of Marketing Research* 37, no. 2 (2000): 215–226; Vanitha Swaminathan, Karen L. Page, and Zeynep Gurhan-Canli, "'My' Brand or 'Our' Brand: The Effects of Brand Relationship Dimensions and Self-Construal on Brand Evaluations," *Journal of Consumer Research* 34, no. 2 (2007): 248–259; Mary Sullivan, "Measuring Image Spillovers in Umbrella-Branded Products," *The Journal of Business* 63, no. 3 (July 1990): 309–329; Matthew Thomson, Jodie Whelan, and Allison R. Johnson, "Why Brands Should Fear Fearful Consumers: How Attachment Style Predicts Retaliation," *Journal of Consumer Psychology* 22, no. 2 (2012): 289–298.

As Table 14–1 illustrates, a variety of recovery strategies have been employed by firms in the aftermath of a scandal. Before selecting a particular approach, firms must carefully examine the nature of the crisis itself.[13] The severity and likely causes of the crisis will dictate the appropriate recovery effort.

Ideally, the key sources of brand equity are of enduring value. Unfortunately, marketers can easily overlook that value as they attempt to expand the meaning of their brands and add new product-related or nonproduct-related brand associations. The next section considers these types of trade-offs.

Table 14-1   Recovery Strategies for Brand Crises

Recovery Approach	What Is It?	Example
Apology and admission	Accepting responsibility for the scandal or crisis	On April 9, 2017, millions watched as passenger Dr. David Dao, of Kentucky, was violently dragged off a United flight by Chicago Aviation Department security officers. Cell phone videos captured the disturbing incident, and social media quickly disseminated the video to millions of viewers, prompting public outrage and corporate backpedaling by United officials. The airline said the incident was a consequence of over booking, and the seat occupied by the passenger was needed by one of its employees. This sparked calls for a boycott and even parody adverts from rival companies. Overall, this incident turned into a public relations disaster for United Airlines and caused severe harm to the brand name. Even with the United Airlines CEO issuing an apology, United Airlines lost $250 million in market value in the immediate aftermath.*
Bolstering brand image	The bolstering response involves companies countering the negative publicity with some positive publicity.	When Maggi Noodles (a company owned by Nestle which marketed a brand of instant noodles called Maggi) was the subject of negative publicity in the India market, it countered the negative effects by embarking on an advertising campaign to win its customers back. Chipotle attempted to win back customers after an *E. coli* outbreak threatened its brand reputation. The outbreak affected a number of people across various states, and Chipotle doubled the amount of food that was given away at its restaurants in an effort to retain its customers (see enclosed video links).
Not just me	This response is useful to provide consumers with the big picture regarding why the transgression may not be limited to only a single brand.	In 2013, Southwest Airlines was forced to acknowledge flight delay problems. Now at least Southwest is admitting the error of its ways: "Looking back, the changes we made were too aggressive and impacted our overall performance—putting us behind on on-time (performance) by around 10 minutes." The carrier managed to put some of the blame for its recent poor performance on the weather, saying the adjustments it made earlier in connect and turn times were exacerbated by challenging weather and high holiday load factors in late 2013. This is an example of how Southwest was partially resorting to a "Not just me" response to mitigate the fallout from the negative publicity.
Downplaying the crisis	Downplaying the crisis involves explaining the reasons or mitigating factors for a crisis and trying to downplay the damage from the incident itself. Sometimes this may involve finger-pointing and blame shifting.	Samsung pointed to problems with its supplier in order to mitigate blame from the Galaxy 7 phones which overheated, and caught on fire when batteries exploded.

Recovery Approach	What Is It?	Example
Limit damage	When there is no way of avoiding the scandal entirely, some companies try to limit the damage to certain makes, models, products, or to a given geographic region.	When Ford Explorer SUVs were subject to recalls due to rollover incidents, Ford tried to limit damage to only those vehicles which were equipped with Firestone tires.
Flat-out denial	Categorically denying that the scandal is true.	Tommy Hilfiger was falsely accused of being racist and he issued a flat-out denial as follows: "We had heard that I was supposedly on "Oprah," and I had told her that if I had known black people were going to buy my clothes, I wouldn't have been a designer. I had never been on "Oprah," and I had never said that. And I would never believe that anyway, nor would I ever say that anyway [. . .] It was a rumor and a myth. Oprah invited me [to be on the show to deal with it]."
Counterattack or attack the accuser	A brand or company could undertake an offensive attack against the accuser, with a view to discrediting the source of negative information.	Hewlett-Packard and Xerox had filed patent infringement lawsuits against each other, and both brands were subject to negative publicity.

*The recovery strategies are adapted from Gita V. Johar, Matthias Birk, and Sabine Einwiller, "Brand Recovery: Communication in the Face of Crisis, Columbia Case Works," April 1, 2010.

Fortifying versus Leveraging

Chapters 4–7 described a number of different ways to raise brand awareness and create strong, favorable, and unique brand associations in consumer memory to build customer-based brand equity. In managing brand equity, marketers face trade-offs between activities that fortify brand equity and those that leverage or capitalize on existing brand equity to reap some financial benefit.

Marketers can design marketing programs that mainly try to capitalize on or maximize brand awareness and image—for example, by reducing advertising expenses, seeking increasingly higher price premiums, or introducing numerous brand extensions. The more marketers pursue this strategy, however, the easier it is to neglect and perhaps diminish the brand and its sources of equity. Without its sources of brand equity, the brand itself may not continue to yield such valuable benefits. Just as failure to properly maintain a car eventually affects its performance, so too can neglecting a brand, for whatever reason, catch up with marketers.

Fine-Tuning the Supporting Marketing Program

Marketers are more likely to change the specific tactics and supporting marketing program for the brand than its basic positioning and strategic direction. They should make such changes, however, only when it is clear the marketing program and tactics are no longer making the desired contributions to maintaining or strengthening brand equity. The way brand meaning is reinforced may depend on the nature of brand associations. We next look at specific considerations in terms of product-related performance and nonproduct-related imagery associations.

Product-Related Performance Associations.   For brands whose core associations are primarily product-related performance attributes or benefits, innovation in product design, manufacturing, and merchandising is especially critical to maintaining or enhancing brand equity.

For companies in categories as diverse as high technology, toys and entertainment products, personal care products, and insurance, innovation is critical to success. For example, Progressive has become one of the most successful auto insurers, in part due to consistent innovations in service. A pioneer in direct sales of insurance online, the firm was the first to offer prospective customers the ability to instantly compare price quotes from up to three other insurers.

Failure to innovate can have dire consequences. Smith Corona, after struggling to sell its typewriters and word processors in a booming personal computer market, finally filed for bankruptcy. As one industry expert observed, "Smith Corona never realized they were in the document business, not the typewriter business. If they had understood that, they would have moved into software."[14] Blockbuster, the video rental company, encountered a similar fate when its retail locations' based model of renting videos and DVDs was quickly replaced by subscription-based streaming services. Netflix seized the opportunity to transform the business by introducing a subscription-based services model and effectively moved past its well-entrenched rival, Blockbuster.[15]

Product innovations are, therefore, critical for performance-based brands whose sources of equity reside primarily in product-related associations. In some cases, product advances may include brand extensions based on a new or improved product ingredient or feature. In fact, in many categories, a strong family sub-brand has emerged from product innovations associated with brand extensions (such as Wilson Hammer wide-body tennis racquets).

At the same time, it is important not to change products too much, especially if the brand meaning for consumers is wrapped up in the product design or makeup. Recall the strong consumer resistance encountered by New Coke, described in Chapter 1. In making product changes to a brand, marketers want to reassure loyal consumers that it is a better product, but not necessarily a *different* one. The timing of the announcement and the introduction of a product improvement are also important: if the brand improvement is announced too soon, consumers may stop buying existing products; if too late, competitors may already have taken advantage of the market opportunity with their own introductions.

Nonproduct-Related Imagery Associations. For brands whose core associations are primarily nonproduct-related attributes and symbolic or experiential benefits, relevance in user and usage imagery is especially critical. Because of their intangible nature, nonproduct-related associations may be easier to change, for example, through a major new advertising campaign that communicates a different type of user or usage situation. MTV is a brand that has worked hard to stay relevant with young consumers.

Nevertheless, ill-conceived or too-frequent repositionings can blur the image of a brand and confuse or perhaps even alienate consumers. It is particularly dangerous to flip-flop between product-related performance and nonproduct-related imagery associations because of the fundamentally different marketing and advertising approaches each entails. Heineken has sometimes been accused of flip-flopping too much between product-focused advertising ("It's All About the Beer") and more user-focused advertising ("Give Yourself a Good Name"). The JCPenney repositioning case study offers a cautionary tale to marketers who wish to change their brand image.

JCPENNEY: REPOSITIONING A RETAIL BRAND

JCPenney is an example of a brand that tried to drastically change its positioning. Until 2013, JCPenney was a well-known retailer, and famous for its periodic sales and for offering coupons to consumers at various points during the year. The company tried to reposition itself and move away from issuing coupons throughout

JC Penney's repositioning involved doing away with coupons and moving towards an everyday low price.

the year to a steady pricing model. In addition to becoming an everyday low price retailer, JCPenney tried to redesign its stores to emulate the Apple retail experience. Having steady prices and a better store environment implied an entirely different type of consumer that JCPenney was not catering to. Further, doing away with sales coupons altogether deprived JCPenney of the fundamental appeal of its brand—that is, consumers who liked to share stories about deals that they received with their friends and family. Therefore, this shift in positioning did not appeal to JCPenney's target consumers, and sales continued to decline.[16] More recently, JCPenney reversed its strategy and went back to offering coupons, but it is still difficult to recoup its lost sales and stem the sales decline. The retail giant is part of a growing trend of consumers who are purchasing increasingly online. While it has made efforts to change its product assortment to better appeal to consumers within stores, it is hard to say whether these efforts will pay off for the brand.[17]

Significant repositionings may be dangerous for other reasons, too. Brand images can be extremely sticky, and once strong associations have formed, they may be difficult to change. Consumers may choose to ignore or simply be unable to remember the new positioning when strong, but different, brand associations already exist in memory.[18] Club Med has attempted for years to transcend its image as a vacation romp for swingers to attract a broader cross-section of people.

For dramatic repositioning strategies to work, marketers must present convincing new brand claims in a compelling fashion.

Summary.   Reinforcing brand equity requires consistency in the amount and nature of the supporting marketing program for the brand. Although the specific tactics may change, marketers should preserve and amplify the key sources of equity for the brand where appropriate. Product innovation and relevance are paramount in maintaining continuity and expanding the meaning of the brand.

At the end of every day, week, month, quarter, and year, marketers should ask themselves, What have we done to innovate our brand and its marketing and make them more relevant? A weak answer can have adverse consequences. One-time industry icons Blockbuster and Yahoo! have both desperately struggled in recent years to catch up as the markets they were in have gone through remarkable technological and marketing transformations.[19] On a more positive note, Branding Brief 14-6 describes how the British brand Burberry remade itself in the world of fashion. Next, we consider what to do when brands find themselves in situations in which more drastic brand actions are needed.

REVITALIZING BRANDS

In virtually every product category are examples of once prominent and admired brands that have fallen on hard times or even completely disappeared. Nevertheless, a number of brands have managed to make impressive comebacks in recent years, as marketers have breathed new life into their customer franchises.[20] Recently, brands such as Microsoft, GE, and Old Spice are examples of brands which have successfully repositioned their brands.

For a successful turnaround, brands sometimes have to return to their roots to recapture lost sources of equity. In other cases, the brand meaning has had to fundamentally change to recapture market leadership. Regardless of approach, brands on the comeback trail must make more *revolutionary* than *evolutionary* changes to reinforce brand meaning.

Often, the first place to look in turning around the fortunes of a brand is the original sources of brand equity. In profiling brand knowledge structures to guide repositioning, marketers need to accurately and completely characterize the breadth and depth of brand awareness; the strength, favorability, and uniqueness of brand associations and brand responses held in consumer memory; and the nature of consumer–brand relationships. A comprehensive brand equity measurement system as outlined in Chapter 9 should help reveal the current status of these sources of brand equity. If not, or to provide additional insight, a special brand audit may be necessary.

Of particular importance is the extent to which key brand associations are still adequately functioning as points-of-difference or points-of-parity to properly position the brand. Are positive associations losing their strength or uniqueness? Have negative associations become linked to the brand—for example, because of some change in the marketing environment?

Marketers must next decide whether to retain the same positioning or create a new one, and, if the latter, which positioning to adopt. The positioning considerations outlined in Chapter 3 can provide useful insights as to the desirability, deliverability, and differentiability of possible positions based on consumer, company, and competitive considerations.

Revitalization strategies obviously run along a continuum, with pure back-to-basics at one end and pure reinvention at the other. In some cases, the positioning is still appropriate, but the marketing program is the source of the problem because it is failing to deliver on it. In these instances, a back-to-basics strategy may make sense. As is described in Branding Brief 14-4, Harley-Davidson rode this "back to basics" strategy to icon status. At the other extreme, a complete repositioning is needed. The Mountain Dew example (Branding Brief 14-5) provides an illustration of this approach. A moderate approach which falls in between these two extremes is illustrated in the Burberry example (Branding Brief 14-6).

Finally, note that *market* failures, in which insufficient consumers are attracted to a brand, are typically much less damaging than *product* failures, in which the brand fundamentally fails to live up to its consumer promise. In the latter case, strong, negative associations may be difficult to overcome. With market failures, a relaunch can sometimes prove successful.

BRANDING BRIEF 14-4
Harley-Davidson Motor Company

Harley-Davidson is one of the few companies in the world that can claim a legion of fans so dedicated to the brand that some of them get tattoos of the logo. Even more impressive is the fact that the company attracted such a loyal customer base with a minimum of advertising. Founded in 1903 in Milwaukee, Wisconsin, it has twice narrowly escaped bankruptcy and is today one of the most recognized brands in the world.

In recovering from its financial downfalls, Harley-Davidson realized its product needed to better live up to the brand promise. Quality problems plagued the product line in the 1970s. Although consumers loved what the brand represented, they hated the constant need for repairs. The joke was that you needed to have two Harleys because one was always in the shop!

Harley's back-to-basics approach to revitalization centered on improving factories and production process to achieve higher levels of quality. The company also dialed up marketing efforts to better sell its products. Establishing a broader access point with consumers to make the brand relevant to more people, Harley was able to attract a diverse customer base that went way beyond the traditional biker image. The company also changed the way it went to market.

Before the 1980s, Harley-Davidson relied almost exclusively on word-of-mouth endorsements and the image of its user group to sell its motorcycles. In 1983, the company established an owners' club, the Harley Owners Group (HOG), which sponsors bike rallies, charity rides, and other motorcycle events. Every Harley owner becomes a member for free by signing up at the www.hog.com Web site. In its first year, HOG had 33,000 members. Now, it has more than one million in 1,400 chapters throughout the world.

In the early 1980s, Harley-Davidson began a licensing program to protect its trademarks and promote the brand. Early efforts primarily supported the riding experience with products like T-shirts, jewelry, small leather goods, and other products appealing to riders. Currently, the primary target for licensed products is existing customers through the Harley dealer network. To attract new customers, though, Harley-Davidson has licensed children's clothing, toys, games, and many other items aimed at children and sold beyond the dealer network. In the world of licensing, Harley-Davidson is considered an evergreen brand and earns the company tens of millions in revenue annually.

Motorcycle riding gear has been around almost as long as motorcycles. As business grew, Harley-Davidson created Harley-Davidson MotorClothes to produce traditional riding gear along with men's and women's casual sportswear and accessories to reach an ever-expanding and diverse customer base of riders and nonriders. Harley MotorClothes is a key facet of the company's General Merchandise division, whose revenues nearly doubled from $151 million in 2000 to $274 million in 2011.

Harley-Davidson continues to promote its brand with grassroots marketing efforts. Many employees and executives at the company own Harleys and often ride them with customers, making traditional advertising almost unnecessary. As ever, Harley's highly visible contingent of riders provides invaluable promotions and endorsements free of cost. Many other marketers seek to borrow the Harley cachet and use the bikes in their ads, giving the company free product placement.

One of the newest growth areas is its target audience of women. For women and smaller riders, Harley offers Sportster motorcycles that are built low to the ground with narrower seats, softer clutches, and adjustable handlebars and windshields. Several times a year, Harley dealers hold garage parties for women to help them learn about their bikes. Five hundred such events in March 2010 attracted 27,000 women, almost half of whom were at a Harley dealer for the first time, leading to 3,000 new bikes sold. After making up only 2 percent of Harley owners in 1995, women now represent about 12 percent of sales.

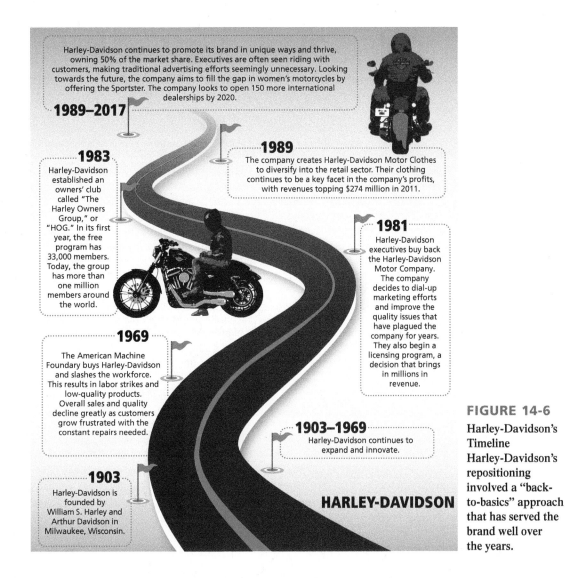

1989–2017
Harley-Davidson continues to promote its brand in unique ways and thrive, owning 50% of the market share. Executives are often seen riding with customers, making traditional advertising efforts seemingly unnecessary. Looking towards the future, the company aims to fill the gap in women's motorcycles by offering the Sportster. The company looks to open 150 more international dealerships by 2020.

1983
Harley-Davidson established an owners' club called "The Harley Owners Group," or "HOG." In its first year, the free program has 33,000 members. Today, the group has more than one million members around the world.

1989
The company creates Harley-Davidson Motor Clothes to diversify into the retail sector. Their clothing continues to be a key facet in the company's profits, with revenues topping $274 million in 2011.

1981
Harley-Davidson executives buy back the Harley-Davidson Motor Company. The company decides to dial-up marketing efforts and improve the quality issues that have plagued the company for years. They also begin a licensing program, a decision that brings in millions in revenue.

1969
The American Machine Foundary buys Harley-Davidson and slashes the workforce. This results in labor strikes and low-quality products. Overall sales and quality decline greatly as customers grow frustrated with the constant repairs needed.

1903–1969
Harley-Davidson continues to expand and innovate.

1903
Harley-Davidson is founded by William S. Harley and Arthur Davidson in Milwaukee, Wisconsin.

HARLEY-DAVIDSON

FIGURE 14-6

Harley-Davidson's Timeline Harley-Davidson's repositioning involved a "back-to-basics" approach that has served the brand well over the years.

While Harley-Davidson maintains about a 50 percent market share of motorcycles in the United States, its market share in Europe is around 10 percent. In 2015, they opened 40 new international dealerships with plans of adding 150 more by 2020. However, 2015 was also plagued by recalls that are reminiscent of their brand troubles in the 1970s. Revenues that year saw a decrease of 3.7 percent in 2014. Revenues as well as stock prices dipped in early 2016, but Harley continues to rebound with increasing revenues and stock prices. The introduction of their new Milwaukee-Eight Engines, based on customer interviews about what they wanted to see in a new touring bike, has given the company confidence that sales will remain strong. Relying on Harley-Davidson's strength, the new engine provides more power, more comfort, a smoother ride, and less engine noise. These changes may be part of the reason that the company is the largest seller of on-road motorcycles to young adults, women, African Americans, and Hispanic Americans.

Sources: Bill Tucker, Terry Keenan, and Daryn Kagan, "In the Money," *CNNfn*, January 20, 2000; "Harley-Davidson Extends MDI Entertainment License for Lotteries' Hottest Brand," *Business Wire*, May 1, 2001; Glenn Rifkin, "How Harley-Davidson Revs Its Brand," *Strategy & Business*, October 1, 1997, https://www.strategy-business.com/article/12878?gko=ffaa3, accessed November 24, 2018; Joseph Weber, "He Really Got Harley Roaring," *BusinessWeek*, March 21, 2005, 70, https://www.bloomberg.com/news/articles/2005-03-20/commentary-he-really-got-harley-roaring, accessed November 24, 2018; Rick Barrett, "From the Executive Suite to the Saddle," *Chicago Tribune*, August 1, 2004, CN3; Clifford Krauss, "Harley Woos Female Bikers," *The New York Times*, July 25, 2007; Mark Clothier, "Why Harley Is Showing Its Feminine Side," *Bloomberg BusinessWeek*, September 30, 2010, https://www.bloomberg.com/news/articles/2010-09-30/why-harley-is-showing-its-feminine-side, accessed November 24, 2018; Richard D'Aveni, "How Harley Fell Into the Commoditization Trap," *Forbes*, March 17, 2010, https://www.forbes.com/2010/03/17/harley-davidson-commoditization-leadership-managing-competition.html#706481635e87, accessed November 24, 2018; "Harley Motorcycle Sales Up in 2011," *Classic American Iron*, January 25, 2012; Harley-Davidson MotorClothes, https://motorclothes.harley-davidson.eu/education/heritage/, accessed November 24, 2018.

BRANDING BRIEF 14-5

A New Morning for Mountain Dew

Mountain Dew was launched in 1969. PepsiCo initially marketed it with a rural folksy image, exemplified by the countrified tagline "Yahoo Mountain Dew! It'll Tickle Your Innards." Since then, the drink has far outgrown its provincial roots, though an unsuccessful attempt to bring urban teenagers to the brand in the early 1980s by advertising on MTV left it on the brink of deletion. The company decided to switch its ad focus to outdoors action scenes, and by the late 1980s, Mountain Dew had begun to show signs of life again.

The brand really hit its stride in the 1990s, experiencing phenomenal, double-digit growth. Mountain Dew was the fastest-growing major U.S. soft drink for much of the decade, rising to a market share of 7.2 percent in 2000 from a mere 2.7 percent back in 1980. Growth was fueled by some edgy advertising from PepsiCo's long-time ad agency BBDO that was funny and fast-paced, featuring a rotating group of guys—the Dew dudes—engaged in action sports such as skydiving, skateboarding, and snowboarding to up-tempo music. The tagline "Do the Dew," was a strong call to action, and the ads were a high-energy blast of adrenalin.

The next decade saw much product expansion, introduction of nontraditional marketing, and a pioneering digital strategy. In 2000, PepsiCo launched Mountain Dew Code Red, the brand's first line extension since Diet Mountain Dew debuted in 1988. The bright red cherry-flavored drink was supported by a national advertising campaign that employed grassroots marketing as well as high-profile media buys. The launch was an unqualified success.

To better connect with its core teen audience, Mountain Dew increased its sponsorship of the Mix Tape street basketball tour and the Dew Action Sports Tour. The company also launched the Dew U loyalty program, in which drinkers exchanged codes printed under bottle caps for a variety of goods available on the Dew U Internet site.

In 2005, Mountain Dew launched another brand extension, a highly caffeinated energy drink called MDX aimed at the estimated 180 million video game players, by introducing it as the official soft drink of the E3 Electronics Entertainment Expo. Prior to the launch, the company invited gamers to "beta test" the product in order to refine the recipe and name.

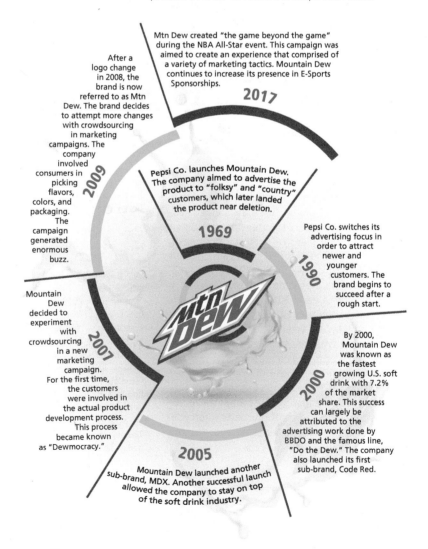

FIGURE 14-7

Mountain Dew's Timeline Mountain Dew's timeline highlights the brand's ability to makeover its image every few years, as a way of maintaining the brand's appeal to its target audiences.

All these actions helped Mountain Dew remain the number-four carbonated U.S. beverage in terms of sales throughout the decade. A logo change on the packaging occurred in 2008, as the company chose the simpler "Mtn Dew." An even bigger change was a viral marketing experiment in crowdsourcing that put customers into the actual product development process. The initial "Dewmocracy" campaign began in 2007 and included an online game in which players designed a new drink.

The follow-up Dewmocracy campaign in 2009 raised the stakes. Mountain Dew marketers put the bulk of their marketing budget online to allow consumers to select three new flavors to be distributed nationwide. The campaign began with 50 contest winners receiving home-tasting kits of seven potential flavors. They were instructed to share their tasting experiences via video on YouTube. Next, consumers helped pick the colors, names, packaging, and even the ad agency! Enormous buzz followed—much of it generated by the actual product users, as intended.

During NBA All-Star 2017, Mountain Dew created a "the game beyond the game" fan experience. The experience comprised of a variety of marketing activations including the launch of The Courtside Project at Courtside HQ, which brings together NBA players and trendsetters across style, art, and music, and a basketball game for elite amateur players featuring NBA All-Stars Russell Westbrook and Kyrie Irving as honorary general managers. Russell Westbrook's involvement worked perfectly as he also starred in an advertising spot with a new rallying cry: "Don't Do 'They'—Do You."

Mountain Dew increased its presence in E-Sports Sponsorship by creating an amateur E-Sports League in partnership with ESL and the Entertainment E-Sports Association (ESEA). The league allows players to participate through a league called the Mountain Dew Pro League, with a chance to enter the ESP Pro League.

Sources: Theresa Howard, "Being True to Dew," *Brandweek*, April 24, 2000, 28–31; Greg Johnson, "Mountain Dew Hits New Heights to Help Pepsi Grab a New Generation," *Los Angeles Times*, October 6, 1999, http://articles.latimes.com/1999/oct/06/business/fi-19312, accessed November 24, 2018; Michael J. McCarthy, "Mountain Dew Goes Urban to Revamp Country Image," *The Wall Street Journal*, April 19, 1989; John D. Sicher, "Beverage Digest/Maxwell Ranks Soft Drink Industry for 2000," Beverage Online, February 15, 2001, https://www.beverageonline.com/doc/beverage-digestmaxwell-ranks-soft-drink-indus-0001, accessed November 24, 2018; Kate MacArthur, "Mountain Dew Gives Gamers More Caffeine," *Advertising Age*, September 26, 2005, 6; Gregg Bennett, Mauricio Ferreora, Jaedeock Lee, and Fritz Polie, "The Role of Involvement in Sports and Sports Spectatorship in Sponsor's Brand Use: The Case of Mountain Dew and Action Sports Sponsorship," *Sports Marketing Quarterly*, 18 (March 2009): 14–24; Natalie Zmuda, "Why Mtn Dew Let Skater Dudes Take Control of Its Marketing," *Advertising Age*, February 22, 2010, https://adage.com/article/special-report-digital-alist-2010/digital-a-list-2010-mtn-dew-lets-skaters-control-marketing/142201/, accessed November 24, 2018; Simon Landon, "Mountain Dew® Takes Hoops Culture to New Heights During NBA All-Star 2017," PR Newswire, February 13, 2017, www.prnewswire.com/news-releases/mountain-dew-takes-hoops-culture-to-new-heights-during-nba-all-star-2017-300406010.html; Jacob Wolf, "Mountain Dew Launches CS:GO League, Allows Amateur Teams to Qualify for ESL Pro League," ESPN, July 13, 2016, www.espn.com/esports/story/_/id/17050356/mountain-dew-launches-csgo-league-allows-amateur-teams-qualify-esl-pro-league.

BRANDING BRIEF 14-6
Remaking Burberry's Image

Burberry, founded in 1856 by 21-year-old Thomas Burberry, was a veritable fashion disaster in the mid-1990s. It was known to many as a stodgy throwback brand making raincoats for the middle-aged, "far off the radar screens of the fashion world." Yet, within a span of several years, with the help of contemporary designs and updated marketing, the brand shrugged off its staid image and became fashionable again. The company instituted a new motto—"Never stop designing"—that encapsulated its new approach to establishing and maintaining relevance with the fickle fashion consumer.

Burberry's repositioning strategy is an excellent example of how best to improve a brand's image through product innovation and marketing strategy.

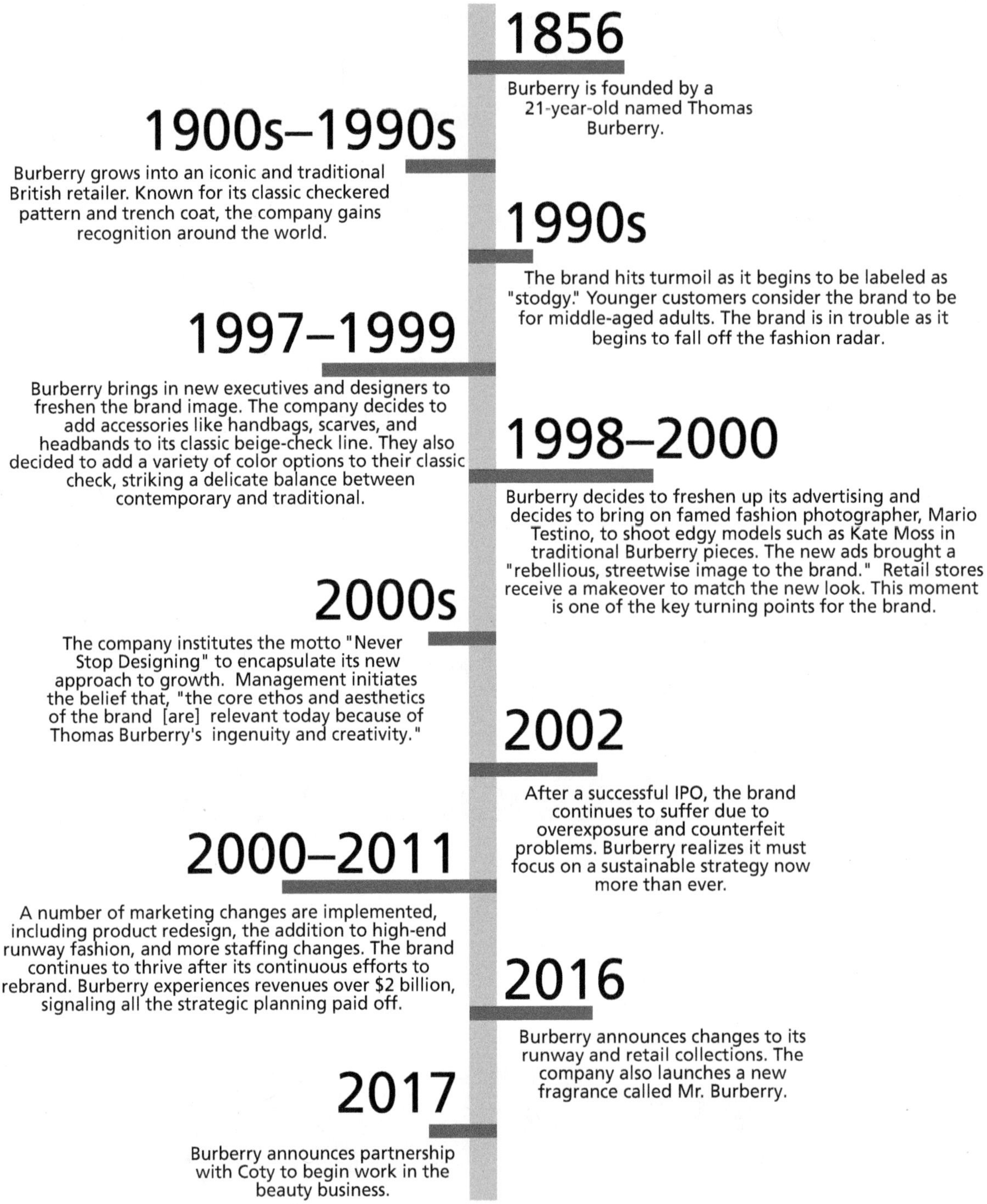

1856

Burberry is founded by a 21-year-old named Thomas Burberry.

1900s–1990s

Burberry grows into an iconic and traditional British retailer. Known for its classic checkered pattern and trench coat, the company gains recognition around the world.

1990s

The brand hits turmoil as it begins to be labeled as "stodgy." Younger customers consider the brand to be for middle-aged adults. The brand is in trouble as it begins to fall off the fashion radar.

1997–1999

Burberry brings in new executives and designers to freshen the brand image. The company decides to add accessories like handbags, scarves, and headbands to its classic beige-check line. They also decided to add a variety of color options to their classic check, striking a delicate balance between contemporary and traditional.

1998–2000

Burberry decides to freshen up its advertising and decides to bring on famed fashion photographer, Mario Testino, to shoot edgy models such as Kate Moss in traditional Burberry pieces. The new ads brought a "rebellious, streetwise image to the brand." Retail stores receive a makeover to match the new look. This moment is one of the key turning points for the brand.

2000s

The company institutes the motto "Never Stop Designing" to encapsulate its new approach to growth. Management initiates the belief that, "the core ethos and aesthetics of the brand [are] relevant today because of Thomas Burberry's ingenuity and creativity."

2002

After a successful IPO, the brand continues to suffer due to overexposure and counterfeit problems. Burberry realizes it must focus on a sustainable strategy now more than ever.

2000–2011

A number of marketing changes are implemented, including product redesign, the addition to high-end runway fashion, and more staffing changes. The brand continues to thrive after its continuous efforts to rebrand. Burberry experiences revenues over $2 billion, signaling all the strategic planning paid off.

2016

Burberry announces changes to its runway and retail collections. The company also launches a new fragrance called Mr. Burberry.

2017

Burberry announces partnership with Coty to begin work in the beauty business.

FIGURE 14-8

Burberry's Timeline

One of Burberry's first moves to freshen the brand was to leverage its classic beige-check plaid in a series of accessories that quickly became best sellers, including handbags, scarves, and headbands. Another was rejuvenating the check itself by using different colors, patterns, sizes, and materials. Burberry was careful to maintain a balance between the contemporary and the traditional, since tradition still resonated with modern consumers. It also sought to leverage other iconic imagery, such as the trench coat and the Prorsum horse insignia. The use of these brand icons reflected management's belief that, "the core ethos and aesthetics of the brand were relevant today because of Thomas Burberry's ingenuity and creativity."

Another key to Burberry's turnaround was refreshing its advertising. The company hired famed fashion photographer Mario Testino to shoot a spread featuring edgy supermodels, such as Kate Moss, wearing iconic Burberry raincoats. The ads were credited with bringing a "rebellious, streetwise image to the brand." The company gave its retail stores a makeover as well to match the contemporary feel of the new designs.

Collectively, these efforts turned the company's fortunes around—but almost too well. One of the challenges in any brand revitalization is sustaining momentum, and Burberry was no exception. After peaking in 2002 with a successful IPO, the brand began to suffer from overexposure and a slew of counterfeit products. Following a holiday sales slump in 2004, the company knew it had to set a different course.

Several marketing changes were implemented. The trademark Burberry plaid was dialed down and made more discreet, appearing on only 10 percent of the brand's different items. More emphasis was placed on high-margin accessories—nonapparel accounts for one-third of revenue—and high-end fashions. The pricey Prorsum collections made up only 5 percent of the brand's sales, but they became the label's fashion flag-bearer and source of creative credibility.

Benefiting from vibrant emerging markets such as China, a constantly updated new product pipeline, and one of the most advanced digital strategies of any luxury brand, Burberry found itself in 2011 with annual revenues over $2 billion, far exceeding financial forecasts. In 2015, Burberry launched a 40-piece capsule collection called Burberry XO Barneys New York in partnership with Barneys New York. The collection was inspired by the spirit of its Prorsum collection. The collection launched with a feature on Barneys microsite, as well as a digital lookbook and an Instagram initiative. Burberry has also invested significantly in mobile marketing through a partnership with Apple and WeChat. Overall, Burberry has continually reinvented itself to stay abreast of changes in consumers' fashion and tastes, and this approach has yielded significant benefits to the brand. (The corresponding timeline summarizes Burberry's strategic shifts over time.)

Sources: Sally Beatty, "Plotting Plaid's Future," *The Wall Street Journal*, September 9, 2004, B1; Mark Tungate, "Fashion Statement," *Marketing*, July 27, 2005, 28; Sharon Wright, "The Tough New Yorker Who Transformed a UK Institution Gets Her Reward," *The Express*, August 5, 2004, 17; Kate Norton, "Burberry, Plaid in Check, Is Hot Again," *Bloomberg BusinessWeek*, April 16, 2007, https://www.bloomberg.com/news/articles/2007-04-16/burberry-plaid-in-check-is-hot-againbusinessweek-business-news-stock-market-and-financial-advice, accessed November 24, 2018; Kathy Gordon, "Global Demand Buoys Burberry," *The Wall Street Journal*, July 13, 2011, https://www.wsj.com/articles/SB10001424052702304911104576443122620649828, accessed November 24, 2018; Nancy Hass, "Earning Her Stripes: Burberry CEO Angela Ahrendts Balances Life and Work," *WSJ Magazine*, September 9, 2010, http://magazine.wsj.com/features/the-big-interview/earning-her-strips/, accessed November 24, 2018.

With an understanding of the current and desired brand knowledge structures in hand, we can again look to the customer-based brand equity framework for guidance about how to best refresh old sources of brand equity or create new ones to achieve the intended positioning. According to the model, we have two strategic options:

1. Expand the depth or breadth of brand awareness, or both, by improving consumer recall and recognition of the brand during purchase or consumption settings.
2. Improve the strength, favorability, and uniqueness of the brand associations making up the brand image. This may require programs directed at existing or new brand associations.

By enhancing brand salience and brand meaning in these ways, we can achieve more favorable responses and greater brand resonance.

Tactically, we can refurbish lost sources of brand equity and establish new ones in the same three ways we create sources of brand equity to start with: by changing brand elements, changing the supporting marketing program, or leveraging new secondary associations. Next, we consider several alternative strategies to achieve these goals.

FEBREZE

When P&G introduced Febreze household odor eliminators, it adopted the classic problem–solution pattern that characterizes much of its brand advertising. But there was one flaw—people didn't think they had a problem! They had become accustomed to odors from cigarettes, pets, and cooking, no matter what others might say. When the problem–solution ads fell flat, P&G's marketers conducted in-depth research, prompting a relaunch that focused on Febreze as a finishing touch and a way to celebrate that a room was really clean. The new positioning connected, and sales exploded. With revenues now exceeding a billion dollars, Febreze has been successfully extended into air fresheners, candles, and laundry detergents.[21] Febreze's first Super Bowl in 2017 ad was a huge success.[22] The ad featured a half-time bathroom break based on a study done relating water usage to the Super Bowl half-time. The ad introduces Febreze's new OdorClean technology and rallies around a "unifying moment." A part of Febreze's "Odor Odes" marketing campaign, which states that the things people love most can also stink, there are more extensions available after the Super Bowl.[23]

Expanding Brand Awareness

With a fading brand, often *depth* of awareness is not the problem—consumers can still recognize or recall the brand under certain circumstances. Rather, the *breadth* of brand awareness is the stumbling block—consumers tend to think of the brand only in very narrow ways. As we suggested in Chapter 3, one powerful means of building brand equity is to increase the breadth of brand awareness, making sure consumers do not overlook the brand.

Assuming a brand has a reasonable level of consumer awareness and a positive brand image, perhaps the most appropriate starting point is to increase usage. This approach often does not require difficult and costly changes in brand image or positioning, but rather relatively easier changes in brand salience and awareness.

We can increase usage either by increasing the level or the quantity of consumption (how *much* consumers use the brand), or by increasing the frequency of consumption (how *often* they use it). It is probably easier to increase the number of times a consumer uses the product than to actually change the amount he or she uses at any one time. (A possible exception is impulse-purchase products like soft drinks and snacks, whose usage increases when the product is more available.) Increasing frequency of use is particularly attractive for category leaders with large market share; it requires either identifying new opportunities to use the brand in the same basic way or identifying completely new and different ways to use it. Let's look at both approaches.

Identifying Additional or New Usage Opportunities. To identify additional or new opportunities for consumers to use the brand more—albeit in the same basic way—marketers should design a marketing program to include both of the following:

- Communications about the appropriateness and advantages of using the brand more frequently in existing situations or in new situations
- Reminders to consumers to actually use the brand as close as possible in time to those situations for which it could be used

For many brands, increasing usage may be as simple as improving top-of-mind awareness through reminder advertising (as V8 vegetable juice did with its classic "Wow! I Could Have Had a V8" ad campaign). In other cases, more creative retrieval cues may be necessary. Consumers often adopt functional fixedness with a brand, which makes it easy to ignore in nontraditional consumption settings.

For example, consumers see some brands as appropriate only for special occasions. As the Chobani Greek Yogurt example suggests, an effective strategy is to identify new occasions and highlight these using novel social media and digital marketing techniques.

Another opportunity to increase frequency of use occurs when consumers' *perceptions* of their usage differ from the reality. For many products with relatively short life spans, consumers may fail to buy replacements soon enough or often enough.[24] Here are two possible solutions:

- Tie the act of replacing the product to a certain holiday, event, or time of year. For example, several brands, such as Oral-B toothbrushes, have run promotions tied in with the springtime switch to daylight saving time.
- Provide consumers with better information about either (1) when they first used the product or need to replace it, or (2) the current level of product performance. For example, batteries offer built-in gauges that show how much power they have left, and toothbrushes and razors have color indicators to indicate when they have worn out.

Finally, perhaps the simplest way to increase usage occurs when it is at less than the optimal or recommended level. Here, we want to persuade consumers of the merits of more regular usage and overcome any potential hurdles to increased usage, such as by making product designs and packaging more convenient and easier to use.

CHOBANI

Chobani, a market leader in Greek Yogurt, is one of the most successful brands launched in recent years.[25] The founder Hamdi Ulukaya introduced the first Greek Yogurt as a novel alternative to American yogurt brands including Dannon and Yoplait in 2005. By launching a unique product based on a new recipe, the brand was able to carve out a presence in the yogurt category. Their keys to success included a focus on broad distribution through grocery stores, their emphasis on taste as well as packaging. This strategy brought them considerable success as sales reached $1 billion by 2010 only a few years after the brand was launched. Chobani Flip was introduced as a line extension and positioned as an afternoon snack yogurt with various new flavors. This was a successful introduction and contributed significantly to sales increases. Further, Chobani extended its brand beyond Greek Yogurt by introducing Chobani Meze dips (resembling hummus or salsa).[26]

Chobani has also evolved various unique approaches to utilizing in-store promotions, aimed at increasing the usage occasions that the brand would become a part of. For example, Chobani Greek Yogurt utilized the

Chobani Greek Yogurt is among the most successful new brand introductions in recent times, and it has effectively capitalized on consumers' desire for healthy alternatives to traditional snacks.

power of online social influencers to generate buzz and identify special ways of using their brand. The company sponsored a "Smoothie Week" challenge where social influencers were challenged to create novel recipes by utilizing Chobani Greek Yogurt flavors. The unique recipes created by the social influencers allowed Chobani to expand its usage as an important ingredient in a range of healthy smoothie options. The campaign resulted in over 33K engagements from 22 blog posts and a return on investment on marketing that was more than 200 percent of the marketing expenditure for the campaign.[27] For campaigns like this to work, however, the brand has to retain its primary brand association (e.g., healthiness in the case of Chobani)—a key source of equity—while convincing consumers to adopt broader usage habits at the same time.

COACH

Coach has played a key role over the past decade in getting U.S. women to buy more handbags; most now make three new purchases annually. Coach's strategy was to fill "usage voids"—situations where existing bag options were not appropriate—with a plethora of different bag options for almost every occasion, including evening bags, backpacks, satchels, totes, briefcases, coin purses, and duffels. Rather than owning a small number of bags suitable for a limited number of uses, women were encouraged to treat handbags as "the shoes of the twenty-first century: a way to frequently update wardrobes with different styles without shelling out for new clothes." When the recession of 2008 challenged many providers of luxury fashion

Coach's marketing strategy involves promoting handbags as a key fashion accessory.

accessories, who began to introduce steep discounts, Coach was an exception. The company maintained prices on its regular product lines and instead introduced new low-priced items. Coach always conducts much research, and here, it engaged with consumers to confirm two facts. First, the new products would not cheapen or damage its image. Second, the resulting decreases in margin would be more than offset by increases in volume. Through renegotiated deals with suppliers, new sources of leather, fabric, and hardware, and other steps, the company assured itself the handbags could have the proper designs at the necessary price points. Thus, the youthful and somewhat eclectic Poppy line was launched with an average price of $260, about 20 percent less than the typical Coach purse. The percentage of sales of low-priced handbags increased from about one-third to one-half of sales as a result of the shift in consumer willingness to pay. Handbags make up almost two-thirds of Coach's sales.[28]

Coach's successes in product strategy over time are outweighed by some problems with their pricing and channel strategies. For instance, Coach is currently finding itself in a predicament where they have been increasing the number of retail and department stores, but same store sales growth has been declining.[29] Although sales increased in 2016 for North American stores, customers have become used to discounted prices on their handbags, potentially hurting Coach's brand image as a luxury brand. Introducing a new high-end line resulted in handbags priced at $400+ to make up 4 percent of sales, up 30 percent from 2015. "The move comes as Coach tries to position itself as more of a luxury brand, after years of over expansion and discounting that hurt its image. The company is also scaling back online outlet flash sales, closing underperforming stores, and introducing new products with better quality and higher prices."[30] The handbag category has shown minimal growth recently, but there is success with limited edition and higher-priced, higher-quality products.[31]

Identifying New and Completely Different Ways to Use the Brand.   The second approach to increasing frequency of use is to identify completely new and different applications. Food product companies have long advertised new recipes that use their branded products in entirely different ways. Perhaps the classic example of finding creative new applications is Arm & Hammer baking soda, whose deodorizing and cleaning properties have led to a number of new uses.

Other brands have taken a page from Arm & Hammer's book: Clorox has run ads stressing the many benefits of its bleach, such as how it eliminates kitchen odors; Wrigley's chewing gum advertising touts it as a substitute for smoking; and Tums promotes its antacid's benefits as a calcium supplement.

New usage applications may require more than just new advertising campaigns or merchandising approaches. Sometimes they can arise from new packaging. For example, Arm & Hammer introduced a "Fridge-Freezer Pack" (with "freshflo vents") for its natural baking soda that was specially designed to freshen and deodorize refrigerators and freezers better.

Improving Brand Image

Although changes in brand awareness are probably the easiest means of creating new sources of brand equity, more fundamental changes are often necessary. We may need to create a new marketing program to improve the strength, favorability, and uniqueness of brand associations making up the brand image. As part of this repositioning—or recommitment to the existing positioning—we may need to bolster any positive associations that have faded, neutralize any negative associations that have been created, and create additional positive associations. These repositioning decisions require us to clearly specify the target market and the nature of the competition to set the competitive frame of reference.

Identifying the Target Market.   Marketers often focus on taking action with one or more of four key target market segments as part of a brand revitalization strategy:

1. Retaining vulnerable customers
2. Recapturing lost customers
3. Identifying neglected segments
4. Attracting new customers.

There is a clear hierarchy in these strategic targeting options. In an attempt to turn sales around, some firms mistakenly focus initially on the fourth one, chasing after new customers. This is the riskiest option. If it fails, two bad things can happen: the firm may fail to attract any new customers, but even worse, it may lose existing ones.

When Talbots, seller of women's suits, blouses, and dresses in roughly 580 predominately suburban locations, ran into sales troubles after the 2008 recession, it decided to expand its target market. Bold jewelry and metallic suits appeared next to classic pearls and seasonal sweaters in an attempt to reach a younger audience than its traditional, older than 35-year-old women. The result was a disaster that confused existing customers as well as hoped-for new prospects, and sales plunged. Asia's leading chain of low-priced casual wear, Uniqlo, ran into the exact same predicament when stores began to stock too many fashion-forward items at the expense of popular basics.[32]

To avoid this double whammy and steady the course in the face of a sales decline, it is often best to try to halt the erosion first and ensure that no more customers are lost in the short run before chasing after new ones. Some of the same marketing efforts to retain existing customers can also help recapture lost customers who are no longer using the brand. This may mean simply reminding consumers of the virtues of a brand they have forgotten about or begun to take for granted. Recall how the New Coke debacle described in Chapter 1—although not intended to do so—accomplished just that, in a roundabout way. Kellogg's Corn Flakes once ran a successful ad campaign with the slogan "Try Them Again for the First Time."

The third approach—segmenting on the basis of demographic variables or other means and identifying neglected segments—is the next-most viable brand revitalization option. Of course, the final strategic targeting option for revitalizing a fading brand is simply to more or less abandon the consumer group that supported it in the past to target a completely new market segment.

Many firms have reached out to new customer groups to build brand equity. The Home Shopping Network (HSN) found success in going after fashion-oriented power shoppers by dumping a slew of unknown brands with me-too products to make the cable channel more designer-friendly to celebrities such as Badgley Mischka, Sean "Diddy" Combs, Stefani Greenfield, and Serena Williams.[33]

Market segments the firm currently serves with other products may represent potential growth targets for the brand. Effectively targeting these segments, however, typically requires some changes or variations in the marketing program, especially in advertising and other communications, and the decision whether to do so ultimately depends on the outcome of a cost–benefit analysis.

Attracting a new market segment can be deceptively difficult. Brands such as Gillette, Harley-Davidson, and ESPN have worked hard for years to find the right blend of products and advertising to make their masculine-image brands relevant and attractive to women. Creating marketing programs to appeal to women has become a priority of makers of products from cars to computers.

TOMMY HILFIGER

One of the hottest fashion brands in the 1990s—when its worldwide sales peaked at $2 billion—Tommy Hilfiger was overexposed and struggling to stay relevant by the early 2000s. Other labels such as Phat Farm, FUBU, Sean John, and Ecko had drawn customers away by better executing the young urban, hip-hop style on which Hilfiger had built its 1990s success. Bloomingdale's reduced the number of Hilfiger boutiques from 23 to 1, and Hilfiger closed all but 7 of its 44 own-brand specialty shops in 2003. To recover, the firm essentially cut all ties with the style that had made it popular—oversized apparel, even more oversized logos, and an edgy urban aura—even going so far as to remove the stylized U.S. flag logo from many of its clothing products. Hilfiger struck out in a new direction with classic preppy styles more closely associated with the brand's original roots, although perhaps with a twist. One set of styles was inspired by the sun

Tommy Hilfiger is known for transforming its runway into an entertainment experience.

and surf, for instance. An exclusive distribution deal with Macy's in 2008 allowed the company to focus its marketing efforts, and by 2010, the brand was being sold in 1,000 retail locations in 65 countries. Hilfiger tailored its offerings in many of these markets. For example, German consumers preferred darker colors, whereas Spanish consumers wanted lighter and brighter shades. In many overseas markets such as China, India, and parts of Europe, the brand was seen as high status. All these revitalizing efforts were validated when the Hilfiger brand was purchased for $3 billion by Phillips-Van Heusen.[34] With the brand back on its feet, Tommy Hilfiger embraced new technology and other means to bring innovation and relevance to the brand to keep it moving. Tommy Hilfiger also launched a fashion line for children with disabilities in partnership with the nonprofit Runway of Dreams. The designers created clothing that eased the process of getting dressed for children with disabilities. Tommy Hilfiger creates a Virtual Reality immersive runway show experience for its customers. Through the Samsung GearVR device, viewers were able to view the football-themed fashion show. The show included behind the scenes looks at the fashion show. This push for digital improved the shopping experience at one of Tommy Hilfiger's flagship retail locations.[35]

Tommy Hilfiger has recently been retooling its brand for fashion immediacy by developing items that are available for immediate purchase on Tommy.com and at retail locations. The brand has successfully generated buzz by transforming its runway into an entertainment experience. Fashion shows are abuzz with amusement parks complete with carnival rides, flamethrowers, and live musical performances. Fashion runways shows utilize online social influencers to generate online buzz about their offerings. In these ways, Tommy Hilfiger has become known as the fashion industry's "de facto showman."[36]

Marketers have also introduced programs targeted to different racial and ethnic groups, age groups, and income groups. These cultural market segments may require different messages, creative strategies, and media. They can be fickle, however, as Tommy Hilfiger discovered, forcing the brand to implement a back-to-basics revitalization strategy, which then was further refined into a positioning focused on fashion immediacy.

Repositioning the Brand.   Regardless of the type of target market segment, repositioning the brand sometimes requires us to establish more compelling points-of-difference. At other times, we need to reposition a brand to establish a point-of-parity on some key image dimension.

A common problem for marketers of established, mature brands is to make them more contemporary by creating relevant usage situations, a more contemporary user profile, or a more modern brand personality. Heritage brands that have been around for years may be seen as trustworthy but also boring, uninteresting, and not that likable.

Updating a brand may require some combination of new products, new advertising, new promotions, and new packaging. Reaching its 100th birthday in 2013, Clorox is a heritage brand that must constantly take steps to update itself. To reach young parents on the go, it developed the myStain smartphone app dedicated to stain removal. Family-oriented images, such as photos of kids' faces covered with spaghetti sauce, were included to make the app more accessible and fun. Many solutions offered convenient alternatives to Clorox products, such as seltzer water as a stain treatment in a restaurant.[37]

Changing Brand Elements.   Often we must change one or more brand elements either to convey new information or to signal that the brand has taken on new meaning because the product or some other aspect of the marketing program has changed. The brand name is typically the most important brand element, and it's often the most difficult to change. Nevertheless, we can drop names or combine them into initials to reflect shifts in marketing strategy or to ease pronounceability and recall. Shortened names or initials can also minimize potentially negative product associations.

For example, Federal Express chose to officially shorten its name to FedEx and introduce a new logo to acknowledge what consumers were actually calling the brand.[38] In an attempt to convey a healthier image, Kentucky Fried Chicken abbreviated its name to the initials KFC. The company also introduced a new logo incorporating the character of Colonel Sanders as a means of maintaining tradition but also modernizing its appeal. When the company began to emphasize grilled chicken and sandwiches in its national advertising over the traditional bone-in fried offerings though, some franchisees actually sued, saying the brand had strayed too far from its roots.[39]

It is easier to change other brand elements, and we may need to, especially if they play an important awareness or image function. Chapter 4 described how to modify and update packaging, logos, and characters over time. We noted there that changes generally should be moderate and evolutionary, and marketers must take great care to preserve the most salient aspects of the brand elements.

ADJUSTMENTS TO THE BRAND PORTFOLIO

Managing brand equity and the brand portfolio requires taking a long-term view and carefully considering the role of different brands in the portfolio and their relationships over time. Sometimes, a brand refresh just requires cleaning up the brand architecture.

When P&G saw sales slump for its $3-billion-in-revenue Pantene hair care brand during the recession of 2008, the company engaged in a massive research and development process to improve and revamp the product line. Extensive consumer testing and technologies typically employed for medical and space research were used to examine how different ingredients interacted with various hair types to develop new and improved products. P&G reduced the number of its shampoos, conditioners, and styling aids by one-third and reorganized and color-coded the entire product line around four specific hair types: color-treated, curly, fine, and medium-to-thick.[40]

Migration Strategies

The *brand migration strategy* helps consumers understand how various brands in the portfolio can satisfy their needs as they change over time, or as the products and brands themselves change over time. Managing brand transitions is especially important in rapidly changing, technologically intensive markets. Ideally, brands will be organized in consumers' minds so they know at least implicitly how they can switch among them as their needs or desires change.

A corporate or family branding strategy in which brands are ordered in a logical manner could provide the hierarchical structure in consumers' minds to facilitate brand migration. Automobile companies are quite sensitive to this issue, and brands such as BMW—with its 3-, 5-, and 7-series numbering systems to denote increasingly higher levels of quality—are good examples.

Acquiring New Customers

All firms face trade-offs between attracting new customers and retaining existing ones. In mature markets, trial is generally less important than building loyalty and retaining existing customers. Nevertheless, some customers inevitably leave the brand franchise—even if only from natural causes. Thus, firms must proactively develop strategies to attract new customers, especially younger ones. The marketing challenge here, however, often lies in making a brand seem relevant to vastly different generations and cohort groups or lifestyles. The challenge is greater when the brand has a strong personality or user image associations that tie it to one particular consumer group.

Unfortunately, even as younger consumers age, there is no guarantee they will have the same attitudes and behaviors as the older consumers who preceded them. In 2011, the first wave of post–World War II baby boomers celebrated their 65th birthdays and officially entered the senior citizen market. Many experts forecast that this group will insist companies embrace their own unique values in marketing products and services. As one demographic expert says, "Nothing could be further from the truth than saying boomers will be like their parents."

The response to the challenge of marketing across generations and cohort groups has taken all forms. Some marketers have attempted to cut loose from the past, as Tommy Hilfiger did by renouncing the urban styles it had come to embody in the 1990s. Other brands have attempted to develop more inclusive marketing strategies to encompass both new and old customers. For example, Brooks Brothers has worked hard to upgrade its merchandise mix, renovate its fleet of stores, expand the franchise into overseas markets, and introduce its first designer label, Black Fleece, to retain the loyalty of older customers but attract new, younger customers at the same time. The company also engaged in an exclusive partnership with Nordstrom to sell a selected set of its more contemporary offerings.[41]

Retiring Brands

Because of dramatic or adverse changes in the marketing environment, some brands are just not worth saving. Their sources of brand equity may have essentially dried up, or, even worse, damaging and difficult-to-change new associations may have been created. At some point, the size of the brand franchise—no matter how loyal—fails to justify support. In the face of such adversity, decisive management actions are necessary to properly retire or milk the brand.

Several options are possible. A first step in retrenching a fading brand is to reduce the number of its product types (package sizes or variations). Such actions reduce the cost of supporting the brand and allow it to put its best foot forward so it can more easily hit profit targets. If a sufficiently large and loyal enough customer base exists, eliminating marketing support can be a means to milk or harvest profits from these cash cows.

An *orphan brand* is a once-popular brand with diminished equity that a parent company allows to decline by withdrawing marketing support. Typically, these orphan brands have a customer base too small to warrant advertising and promotional expenditures. For example, Take 5 was a once-popular Hershey's salty-sweet chocolate brand, originally launched in 2004. In 2011, the brand, despite being popular, was targeted by Hershey's for withdrawal of marketing support.[42] Despite its withdrawing support for the Take 5 brand, its continued popularity with consumers caused Hershey's to reverse its decision. The brand was relaunched in 2016 with a new packaging and a new marketing campaign targeting the millennial population.

Finally, a permanent solution is to discontinue the product altogether. The marketplace is littered with brands that either failed to establish an adequate level of brand equity or saw their sources of brand equity disappear because of changes in the marketing environment. Toyota recently made the decision to discontinue the Scion model, in 2016, 13 years after its launch. This young-oriented car brand was not able to keep up with shifting attitudes of young buyers towards the Toyota brand name, and many of the millennials in the Scion's target market did not view the brand favorably.[43] Companies sometimes spin off their orphan brands when sales drop too far, as Campbell did with Vlasic pickles and Swanson frozen dinners. Other companies sell brands if they are not directly aligned with their strategic goals and focus areas. For instance, P&G sold its beauty brands (including well-known brands such as (Covergirl, Clairol, and Wella) to Coty for $12.5 billion in order to focus on other, larger brands within its portfolio.[44] Similarly, P&G also sold its Duracell battery brand to Berkshire Hathaway and its Iams pet food brand to Mars. In divesting these brands, P&G was able to eliminate its slow-growing and declining brands, thereby freeing up resources to focus on the high-performing brands.[45]

Harvard professor Nancy Koehn explains that old brands retain some value because consumers often remember them from childhood. "There's at least an unconscious link," says Koehn.[46] Perhaps this fact helps explain the success of a Web site called www.mybrands.com, which offers hundreds of exotic orphan brands such as Chupa Chups Cremosa Lollipops. Other brands such as Fruitopia from Coca-Cola are still being sold overseas in Australia and Germany. As long as orphan brands remain popular with a core audience, it seems that companies are willing to sell them.[47]

Obsoleting Existing Products

Technological changes and shifting consumer tastes can often spell trouble for brands that have not kept up with changes in the marketplace. In this context, companies can be faulted for *not* discontinuing products fast enough. Discontinuing such brands (or deliberate obsoleting) can often be a bold move, but one which can pave the way for the introduction of innovative new brands. In 2016, Blackberry decided to stop manufacturing its once-famous cell phones, as it had failed to keep up with changes such as touchscreen technology, while its competitors (e.g., Apple iPhone) had forged ahead with innovative features.[48] Kodak faced significant challenges, as consumers shifted to digital cameras, and Kodak still remained focused on selling traditional film (despite having the technology and investment in digital cameras). Its shift to digital technologies did not happen quickly enough, and Fuji quickly seized the opportunities for creating and introducing new digital products, thereby moving ahead of Kodak. Thus, obsoleting existing products can sometimes be an essential strategy in fast-paced technology industries.[49] The decision to retire a brand depends on a number of factors.

Fundamentally, the issue is the existing and latent equity of the brand. As the former head of consumer packaged-goods giant Unilever commented in explaining his company's decision to review about 75 percent of its brands and lines of businesses for possible sell-offs, "If businesses aren't creating value, we shouldn't be in them. It's like having a nice garden that gets weeds. You have to clean it up, so the light and air get in to the blooms which are likely to grow the best."[50]

REVIEW

Effective brand management requires taking a long-term view and recognizing that any changes in the supporting marketing program for a brand may, by changing consumer knowledge, affect the success of future marketing programs. A long-term view also dictates proactive strategies designed to maintain and enhance customer-based brand equity over time, in the face of external changes in the marketing environment and internal changes in a firm's marketing goals and programs.

Marketers reinforce brand equity by actions that consistently convey the meaning of the brand—what products the brand represents, what core benefits it supplies, what needs it satisfies, how it makes products superior, and which strong, favorable, and unique brand associations should exist in consumers' minds. The most important consideration in reinforcing brands is consistency in the nature and amount of marketing support. Consistency does not mean marketers should avoid making any changes in the marketing program; in fact, many tactical changes may be necessary to maintain the brand's strategic thrust and direction. Unless there is some change in the marketing environment or shift in strategic direction, however, there is little need to deviate from a successful positioning. The critical points-of-parity and points-of-difference that represent sources of brand equity should then be vigorously preserved and defended.

The strategy for reinforcing brand meaning depends on the nature of the brand association. For brands whose core associations are primarily product-related attributes and functional benefits, innovation in product design, manufacturing, and merchandising is especially critical to maintaining or enhancing brand equity. For brands whose core associations are primarily nonproduct-related attributes and symbolic or experiential benefits, relevance in user and usage imagery is especially critical to maintaining or enhancing brand equity.

In managing brand equity, managers have to make trade-offs between those marketing activities that fortify the brand and reinforce its meaning, and those that attempt to leverage or borrow from its existing brand equity to reap some financial benefit. At some point, failure to fortify the brand will diminish brand awareness and weaken brand image. Without these sources of brand equity, the brand itself may not continue to yield valuable benefits. Figure 14-9 summarizes brand reinforcement strategies.

Revitalizing a brand requires marketers to either recapture lost sources of brand equity or establish new ones. According to the CBBE framework, two general approaches are possible: (1) expand the depth or breadth (or both) of brand awareness by improving brand recall and recognition by consumers during purchase or consumption settings; and (2) improve the strength, favorability, and uniqueness of brand associations making up the brand image. This latter approach may require programs directed at existing or new brand associations.

With a fading brand, the depth of brand awareness is often not a problem as much as the breadth; that is, consumers tend to think of the brand in very narrow ways. Although changing brand awareness is probably the easiest means of creating new sources of brand equity, we may often have to create a new marketing program to improve the strength, favorability, and uniqueness of brand associations.

As part of this repositioning, target markets should be analyzed carefully. It is often best to first retain new customers and then try to attract lapsed users or neglected segments before attempting to attract wholly different segments. The challenge in all these efforts to modify the brand image is not to destroy the equity that already exists. Figure 14-10 summarizes brand revitalization strategies.

Managers must also consider the role of different brands in the portfolio and their relationships over time. In particular, a brand migration strategy should ensure that consumers understand how various brands in the portfolio can satisfy their needs as they change or as the products and brands themselves change over time. Strategies exist to retire those brands whose sources of brand equity have essentially dried up or that have acquired damaging and difficult-to-change associations.

If a brand encounters a crisis, being swift and sincere are of paramount importance. Companies that come across as unresponsive or uncaring with their customers inevitably encounter problems. In the context of social media, there is a significant risk of company reputations being destroyed within days of a crisis incident going viral. Companies should be carefully reviewing and utilizing various recovery strategies to combat any negative publicity surrounding their brands.

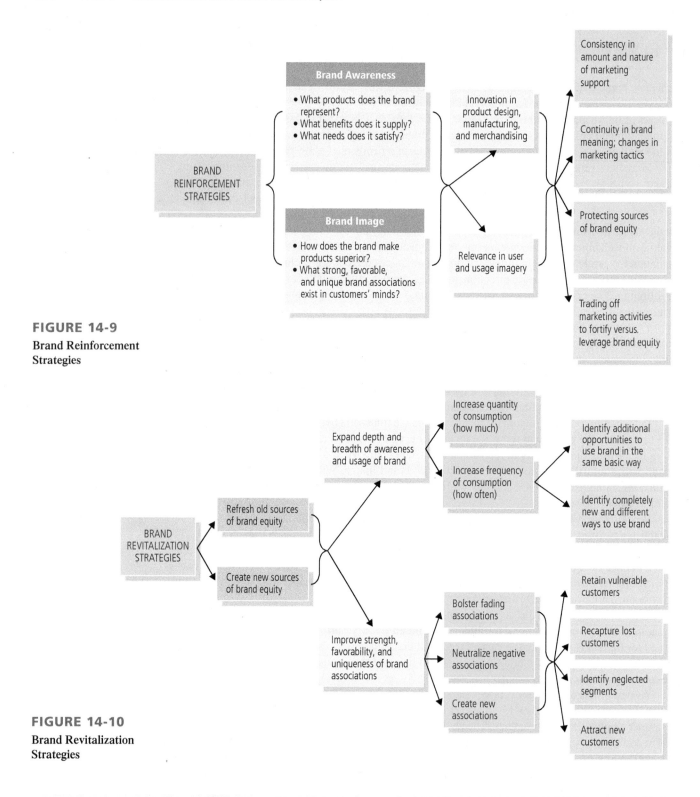

FIGURE 14-9

Brand Reinforcement
Strategies

FIGURE 14-10

Brand Revitalization
Strategies

DISCUSSION QUESTIONS

1. Pick a brand. Assess its efforts to manage brand equity in the last five years. What actions has it taken to be innovative and relevant? Can you suggest any changes to its marketing program?

2. Pick a product category. Examine the histories of the leading brands in that category over the last decade. How would you characterize their efforts to reinforce or revitalize brand equity?

3. Identify a fading brand. What suggestions can you offer to revitalize its brand equity? Try to apply the different approaches suggested in this chapter. Which strategies would seem to work best?

4. Try to think of additional examples of brands that adopted either a back-to-basics or a reinvention revitalization strategy. How well did the strategies work?

5. Choose a brand that has recently experienced a marketing crisis. How would you evaluate the marketers' response? What did they do well? What did they not do well? How did the company utilize social media to control the crisis incident? Which of the recovery approaches used by the company worked well, particularly in social media?

BRAND FOCUS 14.0

Responding to a Brand Crisis

Tylenol has been a true marketing success story.[51] Originally introduced by McNeil Laboratories as a liquid alternative to aspirin for children, Tylenol achieved nonprescription status when McNeil was bought by Johnson & Johnson (J&J) in 1959. J&J's initial marketing plan promoted a tablet form of the product for physicians to prescribe as a substitute for aspirin when allergic reactions occurred. Tylenol consists of acetaminophen, a drug as effective as aspirin in the relief of pain and fever but without the stomach irritation that often accompanies aspirin use.

Backed by this selective physician push, sales for the brand grew slowly but steadily over the course of the next 15 years. By 1974, sales reached $50 million, or 10 percent of the analgesic market. In defending its turf from Bristol-Myers's low-priced but heavily promoted entry Datril, J&J recognized the value of advertising Tylenol directly to consumers.

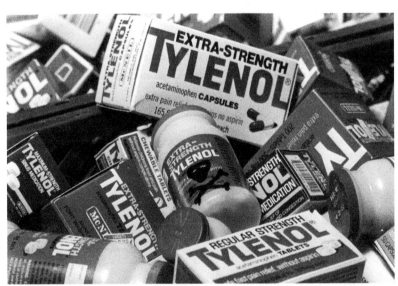

Tylenol's response to a product tampering incident provides a great example of how a great crisis response can avert damage to a brand's image.

Thanks also to the successful introduction of a line extension, Extra-Strength Tylenol in tablet and capsule form, the brand's market share had risen to 37 percent of the pain reliever market by 1982. As the largest single brand in the history of health and beauty aids, Tylenol was used by 100 million U.S. consumers. It contributed 8 percent to J&J's sales but almost twice that percentage in net profits.

Advertising support for the brand was heavy. A $40 million media campaign for 1982 used two different messages. The "hospital campaign" employed testimonials from people who had been given Tylenol in the hospital and had grown to trust it. The ad concluded with the tagline, "Trust Tylenol—hospitals do." The "hidden camera" campaign showed subjects who had been unobtrusively filmed while describing the symptoms of their headache, trying Extra-Strength Tylenol as a solution, and vowing to use it again based on its effectiveness. These advertisements concluded with the tagline, "Tylenol . . . the most potent pain reliever you can buy without a prescription."

The Tylenol Product Tampering Crisis

All this success came crashing to the ground in the first week of October 1982, with the news that seven people had died in the Chicago area after taking Extra-Strength Tylenol capsules that turned out to contain cyanide poison. Although it quickly became evident that the problem was restricted to that area of the country and had almost certainly been the work of some deranged person outside the company, consumer confidence was severely shaken.

Most marketing experts believed the damage to the brand's reputation was irreparable, and that Tylenol would never fully recover. Well-known advertising guru Jerry Della Femina was quoted in *The New York Times* as saying, "On one day, every single human being in the country thought that Tylenol might kill them. I don't think there are enough advertising dollars, enough marketing men, to change that . . . You'll not see the name Tylenol in any form within a year." Tylenol's comeback from these seemingly insurmountable odds has become a classic example of how best to handle a marketing crisis.

The Tylenol Product Tampering Recovery

Within the first week of the crisis, Johnson & Johnson issued a worldwide alert to the medical community, set up a 24-hour toll-free telephone number, recalled and analyzed sample batches of the product, briefed the Food and Drug Administration, and offered a $100,000 reward to apprehend the culprit of the tampering. During the week of October 5, the company began a voluntary withdrawal of the brand by repurchasing 31 million bottles with a retail value of $100 million. It stopped advertising, and all communications with the public were in the form of press releases.

To monitor consumer response to the crisis, J&J started to conduct weekly tracking surveys with 1,000 consumer respondents. Ultimately, the company spent a total of $1.5 million for marketing research in the fourth quarter of 1982. The following week of October 12, it introduced a capsule exchange offer, promoted in half-page press announcements in 150 major markets across the country, that invited the public to mail in bottles of capsules and receive tablets in exchange. Although well intentioned, this offer met with poor consumer response.

During the week of October 24, J&J made its return to TV advertising with the goals of convincing Tylenol users they could continue to trust the safety of Tylenol products and encouraging the use of the tablet form until tamper-resistant packaging was available. The spokesperson for the ad was Dr. Thomas N. Gates, the company's medical director, whose deep, reassuring voice exuded confidence and control. Looking calmly straight into the camera, he stated:

> You're all aware of the recent tragic events in which Extra-Strength Tylenol capsules were criminally tampered with in limited areas after they left our factories. This act damages all of us—you the American public, because you have made Tylenol a trusted part of your healthcare, and we who make Tylenol because we've worked hard to earn that trust. We will now work even harder to keep it. We have voluntarily withdrawn all Tylenol capsules from the shelf. We will reintroduce capsules in tamper-resistant containers as quickly as possible. Until then, we urge all Tylenol capsule users to use the tablet form and we have offered to replace your capsules with tablets. Tylenol has had the trust of the medical profession and 100 million Americans for over 20 years. We value that trust too much to let any individual tamper with it. We want you to continue to trust Tylenol.

The heavy media schedule for this ad ensured that 85 percent of the market viewed it at least four times during this week.

On November 11, 1982, six weeks after the poisonings and after intense behind-the-scenes activity, the chairman of J&J held a live teleconference with 600 news reporters throughout the United States to announce the return of Tylenol capsules to the market in a new, triple-sealed package that was regarded as virtually tamperproof. To get consumers to try the new packaging, the company undertook the largest program of couponing in commercial history.

On November 28, 1982, 60 million coupons offering a free Tylenol product (valued up to $2.50) were distributed in Sunday newspapers nationwide. Twenty million more coupons were distributed the following Sunday. By the end of December, 30 percent of the coupons had been redeemed. J&J also engaged in a number of activities to enlist the support of retailers in the form of trade promotions, sales calls, and so forth.

Convinced that market conditions were now stable enough to commence regular advertising, J&J's ad agency developed three ad executions using the testimony of loyal Tylenol users with the goal of convincing consumers that they could continue to use Tylenol with confidence. The first ad execution contained excerpts of consumers' reaction to the tampering incident, the second ad brought back a Tylenol supporter from an ad campaign run before the tampering incident to reassert her trust in Tylenol, and the third ad used the testimony of a Tylenol user who reasoned that she could still trust the product because hospitals still used it. The recall scores for two of the commercials were among the highest ever recorded by ASI, a well-known marketing research firm that conducted the ad testing for J&J. The return to advertising was accompanied by additional coupon promotional offers to consumers.

Incredibly, by February 1983, sales for Tylenol had almost fully returned to the lofty pretampering sales levels the brand had enjoyed six months earlier. Clearly, J&J's skillful handling of an extremely difficult situation was a major factor in the brand's comeback. Another important factor, however, was the equity of the brand and its strong and valuable trust association built up over the years prior to the incident. The feelings of trust the brand engendered helped speed its recovery, a fact certainly evident to J&J (note how often the word *trust* appears in the initial Gates ad—five times).

Johnson & Johnson and McNeil Consumer Healthcare's remarkable recovery from the brink of disaster allowed the company to reap the benefits of market leadership. A $1 billion brand, Tylenol was successfully extended into cough and cold remedies, nighttime pain relievers, and children's versions. The next-largest pain reliever competitor had only half the market share.

The tide began to turn in the 1990s, however, as the possibility of liver damage and even death from taking more than the recommended dosage of Tylenol was found. Some analysts felt J&J should have been more forthcoming about the possible product dangers in its labeling. This health issue persisted over the next two decades as research continued to uncover consumers' lack of understanding of proper dosing and dangers of side effects. The government continued to weigh its regulatory options.

Tylenol's Quality Control Crises

Concerns about dosage were exacerbated by a series of disastrous quality-control scandals and problems. During 2009 to 2011, the brand came under a flood of negative publicity and harsh criticism from government regulators. Unlike the tampering incidents, these wounds were self-inflicted, and although no deaths occurred, the care, comfort, and confidence of Tylenol customers were at stake, making Johnson & Johnson's actions—or inactions, in some cases—highly troubling.

The problems seemed to arise in cutbacks in quality control and compliance at some of McNeil Consumer Healthcare's manufacturing facilities. Cost-cutting and a change in oversight procedures let several defective products fall through the cracks, while errors in judgment after the fact only compounded the problems.

In one of the first incidents, J&J recalled two dozen varieties of its Children's Tylenol in 2009 because of possible bacterial contamination at one of its manufacturing facilities. Additional problems emerged in the same plant the following year, and government regulators expressed their displeasure at the company's lack of progress in dealing with the problem.

In January 2010, J&J recalled several hundred batches of Tylenol, Motrin, Benadryl, and St. Joseph's Aspirin, 20 months after it reportedly first began to receive consumer complaints about moldy-smelling bottles that made some people feel ill. The FDA faulted the company for not conducting a timely, comprehensive investigation; not quickly identifying the source of the problem; and not notifying authorities of the problem, all of which prolonged consumer vulnerability.

The culprit was the breakdown of a chemical used to treat wood pallets that transported and stored product packaging in a Las Piedras, Puerto Rico facility. A few months later, in April 2010, J&J also recalled millions of bottles of Tylenol, Benadryl, Zyrtec, and Motrin because excessively high levels of an active drug, metal specks, or ingredients that had failed testing requirements led to possible safety violations. Ever-higher levels of scrutiny of the company followed, revealing that back in 2009, McNeil Consumer Healthcare had hired private contractors to buy scores of bottles of defective Motrin in a stealth recall. Because there was no actual safety risk, the company maintained that a formal recall

was not necessary. Once again, federal regulators disagreed with its handling of a problem.

These unprecedented quality-control miscues cost the company $1 billion in sales, and, perhaps more importantly, the trust, respect, and admiration of the public it had worked so hard to preserve back in 1982. After much criticism contrasting his handling of the quality control problems with the product tampering crisis, CEO William Weldon stepped down in April 2012.

Other controversies, however, continued to challenge Tylenol. Despite these additional reasons to question the brand, consumers appear to still trust it and continue to buy it, and the Tylenol brand was still valued at $200 million in 2013. The strength of its brand has gotten Tylenol through many crises, and the size of the market helps keep sales at a high level, but competition is strong. Tylenol remains the #4 brand of analgesic tablets after private labels, Advil, and Aleve. Aleve has overtaken Tylenol because of its ease of use, requiring only 2 tablets for 24 hours.[52]

NOTES

1. Leonard M. Lodish and Carl F. Mela, "If Brands Are Built Over Years, Why Are They Managed Over Quarters?," *Harvard Business Review* 85, no. 7/8 (July–August 2007): 104–112.

2. Craig McLean, "Q Live: Coldplay," *Q*, March 2012, 123–125; Ben Sisario, "Chris Martin of Coldplay Asks: What Would Bruce Do?," *The New York Times*, October 13, 2011; Ray Waddell, "Coldplay: The Billboard Cover Story," *Billboard*, August 12, 2011.

3. IFPI Digital Music Report 2015: Charting the Path to Sustainable Growth (PDF), *International Federation of the Phonographic Industry*, http://www.ifpi.org/downloads/Digital-Music-Report-2015.pdf, accessed July 17, 2018.

4. Megan Gibson, "Coldplay Launches Lyric Treasure Hunt for Ghost Stories Album," *Time*, April 29, 2014, http://time.com/80732/coldplay-treasure-hunt-ghost-stories, accessed July 17, 2018.

5. MTN News, "Pollstar's 2017 Mid-Year Report: World's Best Venues and Tours," July 18, 2017, Top 100 Worldwide Tours," *Pollstar*, https://www.mountainproductions.com/blog/2017/07/18/pollstars-2017-mid-year-report-worlds-best-venues-and-tours/, accessed July 17, 2018.

6. J. K. Wall, "Delta Opens Faucet on Marketing with New Ads," *USA Today*, May 4, 2005, 6B; Brooke Capps, "Delta Faucet Co. Names Y&L AOR," *Advertising Age*, February 1, 2007, https://adage.com/article/small-agency-news/delta-faucet-names-y-1-aor/114682/, accessed November 24, 2018; Bridget A. Otto, "Interior News & Notes: Street of Dreams News; High-Tech Bathroom," *The Oregonian*, August 23, 2011, https://www.oregonlive.com/hg/index.ssf/2011/08/interior_news_notes_street_of.html.

7. Statista, "Faucets Used the Most by Construction Firms in the United States in 2015," https://www.statista.com/statistics/307423/most-used-faucets-brands-in-the-us/, accessed November 24, 2018.

8. Marilyn Alva, "Fortune Brands May Buy What Home Products Next?," *Investor's Business Daily*, August 17, 2015, www.investors.com/research/the-new-america/fortune-brands-sales-rising-on-acquisitions/.

9. Patricia Odell, "Delta Faucet Brand Manager on Events as Part of the Mix," *Promotional Marketing*, http://www.chiefmarketer.com/delta-faucet-brand-manager-events-part-mix/, accessed July 17, 2018.

10. Shirley Brady, "Oreo Turns 100 with 25 Million Facebook Licks and Global Celebration," *Brand Channel*, February 28, 2012, http://brandchannel.com/2012/02/28/oreo-turns-100-with-25-million-facebook-licks-and-global-celebration/; Kylie Jane Wakefield, "Oreo Is One Smart Cookie on Facebook," *Contently*, May 9, 2012, https://contently.com/strategist/2012/05/09/oreo-is-one-smart-cookie-on-facebook/; Candid Marketing, "Oreo Togetherness Bus," http://www.candidmarketing.com/case_study/42/Oreo-Togetherness-Bus, accessed November 24, 2018.

11. Quentin Hardy, "Pokémon Go, Millennials' First Nostalgia Blast," *The New York Times*, July 13, 2016, www.nytimes.com/2016/07/14/technology/pokemon-go-millennials-first-nostalgia-blast.html?_r=0; Marina Villenueve, "'It's Really Nostalgic for Me': Millennials Live Childhood Dreams With 'Pokemon Go,'" *NBC Chicago*, July 20, 2016, www.nbcchicago.com/news/national-international/Millennials-Childhood-Dreams-Pokemon-Go-387700191.html.

12. Scott Evans and Angus MacKenzie, "The Toyota Recall Crisis: A Chronology of How the World's Largest and Most Profitable Automaker Drove into a PR Disaster," *Motor Trend*, January 27, 2010, www.motortrend.com/news/toyota-recall-crisis/.

13. Gita V. Johar, Matthias M. Birk, and Sabine A. Einwiller, "How to Save Your Brand in the Face of Crisis," *MIT Sloan Management Review*, June 11, 2010, https://sloanreview.mit.edu/article/how-to-save-your-brand-in-the-face-of-crisis/, accessed November 24, 2018.

14. Jonathan Auerbach, "Smith Corona Seeks Protection of Chapter 11," *The Wall Street Journal*, July 6, 1995, A4.

15. Greg Satell, "A Look Back at Why Blockbuster Really Failed and Why It Didn't Have To," *Forbes*, September 5, 2014, www.forbes.com/sites/gregsatell/2014/09/05/a-look-back-at-why-blockbuster-really-failed-and-why-it-didnt-have-to/2/#3044a11cbe4a.

16. Panos Mourdoukoutas, "A Strategic Mistake That Haunts JC Penney," *Forbes*, September 27, 2013, www.forbes.com/sites/panosmourdoukoutas/2013/09/27/a-strategic-mistake-that-haunts-j-c-penney/#3215b0c0134c.

17. Tony Garcia, "J.C. Penney Upgraded on Turnaround Strategy That Steers Away from Apparel," *Marketing Watch*, May 17, 2016, www.marketwatch.com/story/jc-penney-upgraded-on-turnaround-strategy-that-steers-away-from-apparel-2016-05-16.

18. Susan Heckler, Kevin Lane Keller, and Michael J. Houston, "The Effects of Brand Name Suggestiveness on Advertising Recall," *Journal of Marketing* 62, no. 1 (January 1998): 48–57.

19. Matthew Lynn, "The Fallen King of Finland," *Bloomberg BusinessWeek*, September 20, 2010; Diane Brady and Hugo Miller, "Failure to Communicate," *Bloomberg BusinessWeek*, October 11, 2010, Issue No. B4196; Elizabeth Woyke, "BlackBerry Battles Back," *Forbes Magazine*, February 9, 2011, https://www.forbes.com/forbes/2011/0228/technology-apple-google-android-rim-blackberry-battles-back.html#27cccbd84b11, accessed November 24, 2018.

20. Larry Light and Joan Kiddon, *Six Rules for Brand Revitalization* (Upper Saddle River, NJ: Pearson Education, 2009).

21. Charles Duhigg, "How Companies Learn Your Secrets," *The New York Times*, February 16, 2012, https://www.nytimes.com/2012/02/19/magazine/shopping-habits.html; Ellen Byron, "Febreze Joins P&G's $1 Billion Club," *The Wall Street Journal*, March 9, 2011, https://www.wsj.com/articles/SB10001424052748704076804576180683371307932; Karl Greenberg, "P&G: Febreze Makes Scents That Make Happiness," *Marketing Daily*, July 10, 2011, https://www.mediapost.com/publications/article/153781/pg-febreze-makes-scents-that-make-happiness.html, accessed November 24, 2018.

22. Ace Metric, "Ace Metric Names Lightheartedness the Key to Super Bowl LI Advertising Success," Media Coverage, Ace Metrix, www.acemetrix.com/about-us/company-news/media-coverage/ace-metrix-names-lightheartedness-the-key-to-super-bowl-li-advertising-success/, accessed July 17, 2018.

23. Julien Rath, "People Are Loving Febreze's Ad About Needing to Take a Super Bowl Half-time Bathroom Break," *Business Insider*, February 5, 2017, www.businessinsider.com/people-are-loving-febrezes-ad-super-bowl-half-time-bathroom-break-2017-2; Barrett J. Brunsman, "P&G Reveals Super Bowl Ad Linked to 'National Movement'," *Cincinnati Business Courier*, January 30, 2017, www.bizjournals.com/cincinnati/news/2017/01/30/p-g-reveals-super-bowl-ad-linked-to-national.html.

24. John D. Cripps, "Heuristics and Biases in Timing the Replacement of Durable Products," *Journal of Consumer Research* 21, no. 2 (September 1994): 304–318.

25. Hamdi Ulukaya, "Chobani's Founder on Growing a Start-Up without Outside Investors," *Harvard Business Review*, 91, no. 10 (October 2013): 45–48.

26. Jessica Wohl, "Chobani Makes Its First Move Beyond the Dairy Case," *Advertising Age*, June 20, 2016, http://adage.com/article/cmo-strategy/chobani-offers-unique-home-move-dairy-aisle/304553/.

27. Colleen Vaughan, "The Power of New Usage Occasions for Products," *Collective Bias*, October 31, 2016, http://collectivebias.com/blog/2016/10/power-new-usage-occasions-products/.

28. Ellen Byron, "How Coach Won a Rich Purse by Inventing New Uses for Bags," *The Wall Street Journal*, November 17, 2004, A1; Kevin Lamiman, "Coach, Inc.," *Better Investing*, 60, no. 2 (October 2010): 26; Susan Berfield, "Coach's Poppy Line Is Luxury for Recessionary Times," *Bloomberg BusinessWeek*, June 18, 2009, https://www.bloomberg.com/news/articles/2009-06-18/coachs-poppy-line-is-luxury-for-recessionary-times, accessed July 17, 2018.

29. Phalguni Soni, "Transformative Change Is Coming to Coach," Premium Brand Power: An Investor's Guide to Coach," *Market Realist*, posted January 16, 2015, http://marketrealist.com/2015/01/transformative-change-coming-coach-inc/.

30. Suzanne Kapner and Joshua Jamerson, "Coach's Sales Slowed by Shift Away from Department Stores," *The Wall Street Journal*, November 1, 2016, www.wsj.com/articles/coach-posts-same-store-sales-growth-amid-turnaround-effort-1478002268.

31. Marie Driscoll, "Coach, Kors & Kate: The Handbag Wars," November 15, 2016, https://www.therobinreport.com/coach-kors-kate-the-handbag-wars/, accessed July 14, 2018.

32. Jenn Abelson, "A Makeover for Talbots," *Boston Globe*, December 11, 2011, https://www.bostonglobe.com/business/2011/12/11/makeover-for-talbots/k30V7AdfcrCNwm5mNsvCyJ/story.html, accessed November 24, 2018; Ashley Lutz, "How Talbots Got the Girl—and Lost the Woman," *Bloomberg BusinessWeek*, June 20, 2011, 31–32; Sean Gregory, "J. Crew and Talbots: Can Michelle Obama Save Fashion Retailing?," *Time Magazine*, May 6, 2009, http://content.time.com/time/business/article/0,8599,1895631,00.html, accessed November 24, 2018; Naoko Fujimura and Shunichi Ozasa, "Asia's Top Clothier Is Back to Basics," *Bloomberg BusinessWeek*, January 10, 2011, 20.

33. Susan Berfield, "The New Star of Sellavision," *Bloomberg BusinessWeek*, May 24, 2010, 60–63,

34. Tracie Rozhon, "Reinventing Tommy: More Surf, Less Logo," *The New York Times*, March 16, 2003, 1; Michael Barbaro, "Macy's and Hilfiger Strike Exclusive Deal," *The New York Times*, October 26, 2007, https://www.nytimes.com/2007/10/26/business/26retail.html; Ali McConnon, "Tommy Hilfiger's Upscale Move to Macy's," *Bloomberg BusinessWeek*, October 22, 2008; Michael J. de la Merced, "Why Phillips-Van Heusen Is Buying Tommy Hilfiger," *The New York Times*, March 15, 2010, https://dealbook.nytimes.com/2010/03/15/behind-phillips-van-heusens-deal-for-tommy-hilfiger/;

K@W, "'Keep the Heritage of the Brand Intact': Tommy Hilfiger on Weathering the Ups and Downs of Retail Fashion," *Knowledge @ Wharton*, March 17, 2010, http://knowledge.wharton.upenn.edu/article/keep-the-heritage-of-the-brand-intact-tommy-hilfiger-on-weathering-the-ups-and-downs-of-retail-fashion/.

35. Leanna Garfield, "Tommy Hilfiger Just Launched an Adorable Fashion Line for Disabled Kids," *Business Insider*, February 23, 2016, www.businessinsider.com/tommy-hilfiger-making-clothing-for-disabled-kids-2016-2/#these-changes-can-make-a-world-of-difference-becausethe-identity-of-the-clothing-remains-the-samescheier-says-the-crux-of-it-is-that-were-not-recreating-the-wheel-were-modifying-the-wheel-to-fit-on-all-other-parts-4; Sharon Edelson, "Tommy Hilfiger's Virtual Reality Play," *Women's Wear Daily*, October 20, 2015, http://wwd.com/business-news/retail/tommy-hilfigers-virtual-reality-play-10265078/; Lauren Sherman, "How Tommy Hilfiger Is Rewiring For Fashion Immediacy," *The Business of Fashion*, September 6, 2016, www.businessoffashion.com/articles/intelligence/tommy-hilfiger-gigi-hadid-fashion-immediacy-direct-to-consumer.

36. BOF Team, "#TommyNow Takes Venice Beach," *The Business of Fashion*, February 9, 2017, www.businessoffashion.com/articles/fashion-show-review/tommynow-takes-venice-beach.

37. Christine Birkner, "Mama's Got the Magic of Mobile, Too," *Marketing News*, September 15, 2011, 12–13.

38. Tim Triplett, "Generic Fear to Xerox Is Brand Equity to FedEx," *Marketing News*, August 15, 1994, 12–13.

39. Burt Helm, "At KFC, a Battle Among the Chicken-Hearted," *Bloomberg BusinessWeek*, August 16, 2010, 19.

40. Mark Clothier, "Procter & Gamble's Root-to-End Pantene Makeover," *Bloomberg BusinessWeek*, May 20, 2010, https://www.bloomberg.com/news/articles/2010-05-20/procter-and-gambles-root-to-end-pantene-makeover, accessed November 24, 2018.

41. Jean E. Palmieri, "Man in the News: I, Claudio," *Menswear*, April 2011.

42. Christopher Steiner, "The Most Undervalued Brand in the World," *Forbes*, May 20, 2013, https://www.forbes.com/sites/christophersteiner/2013/05/20/the-most-undervalued-brand-in-the-world/; Kate Taylor, "Hershey Is Relaunching a Cult Classic That Has Been Called 'Most Undervalued Brand in the World'," *Business Insider*, January 20, 2016, www.businessinsider.com/hershey-is-relaunching-the-take-5-bar-2016-1.

43. Autoweek Editors, "Toyota Dumps Scion: Toyota's Youth-Oriented Sub-Brand Is Put Out of Its Misery," *Autoweek*, February 3, 2016, http://autoweek.com/article/car-news/toyota-dumps-scion.

44. Phil Wahba, "Procter & Gamble Selling Beauty Brands Like Clairol, Covergirl to Coty for $12.5 Billion," *Fortune*, July 9, 2015, http://fortune.com/2015/07/09/procter-gamble-coty/.

45. Alexander Coolidge, "P&G to Spin Off 43 Beauty Brands Including CoverGirl, *USA Today*, July 9, 2015, https://www.usatoday.com/story/money/business/2015/07/09/procter-and-gamble-cover-girl-wella/29903833/, accessed July 14, 2018.

46. Nancy F. Koehn, *Brand New: How Entrepreneurs Earned Consumers' Trust from Wedgwood to Dell* (Boston: Harvard Business School Press, 2001).

47. Betsy McKay, "Why Coke Indulges (the Few) Fans of Tab," *The Wall Street Journal*, April 13, 2001, B1; Devon Spurgeon, "Aurora Bet It Could Win by Fostering Neglected Foods," *The Wall Street Journal*, April 13, 2001, B1; Jim Hopkins, "Partners Turn Decrepit Detergent into Boffo Start-Up," *USA Today*, June 20, 2001, 6B; Matthew Swibel, "Spin Cycle," *Forbes*, April 2, 2001, 118.

48. Paul R. La Monica, "End of an Era: BlackBerry Will Stop Making Its Own Phones," *CNN Tech*, September 28, 2016, http://money.cnn.com/2016/09/28/technology/blackberry-outsource-phones/.

49. Scott Anthony, "Kodak's Downfall Wasn't About Technology," *Harvard Business Review*, July 15, 2016, https://hbr.org/2016/07/kodaks-downfall-wasnt-about-technology.

50. Tara Parker-Pope, "Unilever Plans a Long-Overdue Pruning," *The Wall Street Journal*, September 3, 1996, A13.

51. The section on Tylenol is based on a series of articles and papers: John A. Deighton, "Features of Good Integration: Two Cases and Some Generalizations," in *Integrated Communications: The Search for Synergy in Communication Voices*, eds. J. Moore and E. Thorsen (Hillsdale, NJ: Lawrence Erlbaum Associates, 1996); O. C. Ferrell and Linda Ferrell, "Tylenol Continues Its Battle for Success," Daniel Funds Ethics Initiative, University of New Mexico, Anderson School of Management, Highlighted Cases and Case Studies, 2011, https://danielsethics.mgt.unm.edu/teaching-resources/highlighted-cases-and-case-studies.asp, accessed November 24, 2018; Mina Kimes, "Why J&J's Headache Won't Go Away," *Fortune*, September 6, 2010, 100; Parija Kavilanz, "Johnson & Johnson CEO: 'We Made a Mistake'," *CNN Money*, September 30, 2010, https://money.cnn.com/2010/09/30/news/companies/hearing_johnson_fda_drug_recalls/index.htm, accessed November 24, 2018; Jonathan D. Rockoff and Joann S. Lublin, "J&J CEO Weldon Is Out," *The Wall Street Journal*, February 22, 2012, https://www.wsj.com/articles/SB10001424052970204909104577237642041667180, accessed November 24, 2018.

52. Sean Williams, "The Surprising Over-the-Counter Pain Reliever Consumers Are Least Loyal To," *The Motley Fool*, September 6, 2014, www.fool.com/investing/general/2014/09/06/the-surprising-over-the-counter-pain-reliever-cons.aspx.

15 Managing Brands Over Geographic Boundaries and Market Segments

Learning Objectives

After reading this chapter, you should be able to

1. Understand the role of a regional marketing strategy with a focus on marketing based on geodemographics, ethnicity, and age.

2. Understand the rationale for developing a global brand.

3. Outline the main advantages and disadvantages of developing a global marketing program.

4. Define a global brand and describe the strategic steps in developing a global brand positioning.

5. Describe how to tailor different marketing mix elements to global markets.

6. Describe some of the unique characteristics of brand building in emerging growth markets such as China.

KFC is among the most popular fast-food brands in China, and has more than 5,000 restaurants across the country.

PREVIEW

In earlier chapters, we have considered how and why marketers (1) create brand portfolios to satisfy different market segments and (2) develop brand migration strategies to attract new and retain existing customers. This chapter looks at managing brand equity in different types of market segments, both in domestic markets and international markets.

We begin by examining market segments within the U.S. market to showcase brand management issues over regional, demographic, and cultural market segments. Given their unique characteristics and strategic relevance to marketers, we provide an in-depth look at millennials as a demographic group.

Next, we will pay particular attention to international issues and global branding strategies. After reviewing the basic rationale for taking brands into new international markets, we consider the broader issues in developing a global brand strategy. We will also look at some of the pros and cons of developing a standardized global marketing program. In the remainder of the chapter, we concentrate on specific strategic and tactical issues in building global customer-based brand equity, organized around the concept of the "Ten Commandments of Global Branding." To illustrate these guidelines, we will rely on global brand pioneers such as Coca-Cola. Brand Focus 15.0 addresses branding issues in the exploding Chinese market.[1]

REGIONAL MARKET SEGMENTS

Regionalization seems to run counter to globalization. Marketers are more interested in regional marketing today than previously because there is high-quality data available about purchasing behavior both in-store and online. For example, online platforms such as Facebook and Google include geotargeting as a key feature, which can identify and track consumers down to their specific location. These targeting options make it possible to target different customer segments with different offerings by dynamically varying product attributes and pricing based on what consumers are seeking. Syndicated data made available by companies such as AC Nielsen provides insights about where consumers live, where they shop, and what media they use. Therefore, a regional targeting strategy can make a brand more relevant and appealing to any one individual. Regionalization can have downsides. Marketing efficiency may suffer, and costs may rise with regional marketing. Moreover, regional campaigns may force local producers to become more competitive or blur a brand's national identity. The upside, however, is that marketing can have a stronger impact. The following box describes how using Nielsen's Spectra data, brand marketers can develop an in-depth understanding of regional segments.

UNDERSTANDING BEHAVIORSTAGES AND LIFESTYLES OF CONSUMERS USING NIELSEN'S SPECTRA

Spectra is a consumer segmentation and targeting tool owned by AC Nielsen. Spectra provides segmentation and targeting information based on scanner panel data as well as data from retailers. AC Nielsen augments this information with data from the U.S. Census to provide the "most comprehensive understanding of their consumers" that will provide brand managers the ability to accurately assess the demand potential of various segments. In addition, the Spectra Lifestyle and BehaviorStage segments offer companies the ability to track the most effective marketing programs that can be useful to drive growth. For instance, one analysis revealed that the older bustling family segment was critical to drive growth. This segment only accounted for 10 percent of the population of U.S. households, but was shown to spend 33 percent more than the average household and have larger basket sizes.

Spectra's 10 behavior stages are based on family groups and the number and age of children within the household. For example, the start-up family consists of households with young children under the age of 6, whereas the senior singles group consists of one-person households with individuals older than 65 who have no children in the household. Spectra's lifestyle segments include cosmopolitan centers, struggling urban cores, and so on, and they provide an assessment of where a given brand's customers may live and shop. For example, consumers in affluent suburban spreads have average incomes much higher than those in cosmopolitan centers or comfortable country areas.

SPECTRA LIFESTYLES DEFINITIONS

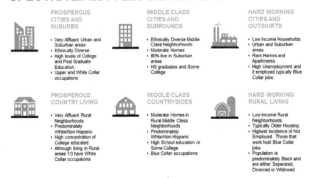

SPECTRA BEHAVIORSTAGE DEFINITIONS

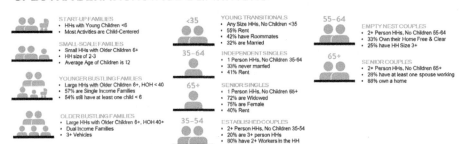

Nielsen's Spectra Segmentation characterizes consumers based on BehaviorStages, which describes consumer segments based on a variety of demographic variables. Nielsen's Spectra segmentation also integrates information about consumer lifestyles.

Source: https://www.nielsen/com/us/en/solutions/capabilities/spectra.html, accessed December 18, 2018.

How Spectra Can Help Brand Managers

One way in which brand managers can utilize Spectra data is to identify high- and low-potential segments for focusing their marketing and advertising dollars. For instance, a brand like Iams dog food can evaluate the Spectra data and identify a segment, such as cosmopolitan centers and older bustling families, as having a high customer demand. Further, they may evaluate the extent to which consumers in this segment are loyal to other competing brands. A competitor to Iams may not be as popular in this same segment, which provides useful insights to brand managers as to where to invest their marketing expenditures. Also, Spectra can help in identifying gaps in the brand portfolio if there are segments with high demand for the pet food category as a whole, but for which no strong brand presence is present. This would indicate an important opportunity for either brand extensions or line extensions. This type of analysis can also point out potential overlaps, particularly if there are multiple brands that are serving the needs of a given segment. Spectra can also help identify other products that the current customers of a brand are likely to buy, thereby identifying opportunities for co-branding or co-promotions. It can also help identify sales gaps and pinpoint particular stores to target for in-store promotions and demonstrations.[2] This allows brand managers to evolve specific strategies that can vary by geodemographic segments, thereby allowing for customized brand messages and offerings across various customer segments.

OTHER DEMOGRAPHIC AND CULTURAL SEGMENTS

Any market segment—however we define it—may be a candidate for a specialized marketing and branding program. For example, demographic dimensions such as age, income, gender, ethnicity, and race—as well as psychographic considerations—often relate to more fundamental differences in shopping behaviors or attitudes about brands. These differences can often serve as the rationale for a separate branding and marketing program. The decision ultimately rests on the costs and benefits of customized marketing efforts versus those of a less targeted focus.

Marketing Based on Age

Chapter 14 described how important it is for marketers to consider age segments, and how younger consumers can be brought into the consumer franchise. Of particular interest to marketers in recent years is the segment of millennials. These are consumers who were born after 1980[3] and have

Table 15-1 Marketing to Millennials

Key Traits	Characteristics of Millennials
Size	Millennials consist of 83 million individuals or more than a quarter of the U.S. population.
Traits	Some of the traits that distinguish millennials include environmentally conscious, idealistic, tolerant, entrepreneurial, wasteful, self-absorbed, cynical, greedy.
Use of Technology	The millennial population is seen as very tech savvy. A majority of them have a social media presence (more than 80 percent have a Facebook page)[4], and a majority (75 percent) of them own and use a smartphone. They regularly use text messaging to communicate (44 percent). They are twice as likely as nonmillennials to use smartphones to research products. Paradoxically, 83 percent of millennials prefer brick-and-mortar stores to online shopping.
Education	Millennials place high value on college education (63 percent) and plan on getting a college degree.
Diversity	Millennials are extremely diverse and have a higher concentration of bilinguals (38 percent) relative to English-dominant (31 percent) or Spanish-dominant (31 percent) individuals.
Spending	Millennials spend $600 billion annually. It is predicted that by 2020, millennial spending power will reach $1.4 trillion.
Family and Home Values	A number of millennials are postponing family obligations until later, and fewer millennials are likely to own their own home, relative to other cohorts (e.g., Generation X or Baby Boomers). 60 percent of millennials rent their homes. Millennials are highly fitness- and health-focused. A high percentage (more than 70 percent) disapprove of smoking and drinking. They invest in their health and spend a lot on athletic gear.
Brands	Millennials seek out high-quality products (75 percent), and 89 percent of millennials also indicated that they would like brands to incorporate socially responsible practices.
Shopping Influences	Millennials are more influenced by word-of-mouth from peers and friends while shopping for products and brands. They are skeptical of traditional advertising, but 50 percent of them are willing to try products with celebrity endorsers, if the celebrity is liked by them. 68 percent of them are influenced to try a product or brand based on a friend's social media post.

various distinct traits that single them out from a marketing standpoint. The Marketing Memo highlights some of these distinguishing features of the millennial generation and spotlights how Campbell's Soup has evolved a campaign focused on this segment.

Marketing Based on Ethnicity

Why is marketing to different ethnic groups an effective strategy? Different ethnicities have unique characteristics, tastes, and preferences such that brands which are customized tend to be more appealing. We next describe each sub group in turn. Table 15-2 provides a summary of key characteristics of major ethnic segments in the United States.

African Americans. Although much marketing has targeted baby boomers, millennials, Hispanics, and other demographic and psychographic groups, many critics argue that firms have not effectively targeted the African American market.

Because almost all African Americans speak English as their first language and watch much network television, many companies rely on general marketing campaigns to reach them. But unique attitudes and behaviors distinguish this audience. Black media executives such as Thomas Burrell, founder and chairman emeritus of Burrell Advertising in Chicago, the largest black-owned agency in the United States, says: "Black people aren't dark-skinned white people. We have different preferences and customs, and we require special effort." Many observers note the important role of religion, church, and family. As a result of their historical experiences, African Americans are often thought to exhibit a strong togetherness and pride in their heritage. They are also seen as style leaders who set fashion trends, especially among younger people. Marketers are increasingly focusing on this group, and ad dollars focusing on African-American audiences almost tripled between 2011 and 2015.[8]

The challenge for building brand equity among African Americans is to create relevant marketing programs and communication campaigns that accurately portray brand personality and avoiding fostering stereotypes, offending sensibilities, or lumping market segments together. The president of one black-owned agency says the formula for marketing to blacks consists of

CAMPBELL'S SOUP

Campbell's Soup is a brand that is a classic and traditional brand, but it had to deal with a challenge of marketing its traditional brand in a very old-fashioned product category (i.e., soups) to the millennial target audience. To address this challenge, the company created a new product line with global tastes incorporating Caribbean, Middle Eastern, and African flavors and used this to appeal to the multicultural cuisine preferences of millennials. Their redesigned packaging was based on microwaveable pouches that fit into millennials' need for convenience and portability. Further, the company used an edgy advertising campaign, which leveraged a newly redesigned Web site, and encouraged consumers to make Spotify playlists based on soup flavors.[5] Campbell's Soup also initiated the Communal Tables program which involved inviting millennials in select cities such as New York and Chicago to gather around the Campbell's Go Communal Tables, which are hosted by an influential and well-known celebrity, to enjoy a meal and discuss a topic. In these ways, a traditional brand such as Campbell's Soup reinvigorated its brand to appeal to a youthful millennial audience with unique tastes and characteristics.[6]

Campbell's Go Soup (targeted to millenials) featured new flavors and redesigned packaging.

Table 15-2   Ethnic Segments in the United States[7]

Ethnic Group	Population (United States)	Purchasing Power ($)	Best Marketing Practices
African Americans	46.3 million	1.2 trillion	Use ads featuring African Americans, particularly using TV, radio, and social media Use of African American influencers to speak directly to consumers
Hispanics and Latino-Americans	56.6 million	1 trillion	Use bilingual advertising Use pop culture influencers to represent Hispanic and Latino pride Identify regional differences
Asian Americans	21 million	962 billion	Focus on distinct sub segments (e.g., Chinese Americans, Indian Americans) Leverage the influence of online Asian celebrities

relevance, recognition, and respect. As with global brand programs in general, marketers should blend standardization and customization as appropriate.[9]

Hispanics and Latinos.   The term Hispanic refers to persons of Spanish-speaking origin or ancestry, and Latinos references those who are of Latin-American origin, including those who are Portuguese speakers (e.g., Brazilians). We broadly combine these groups for the current description of Hispanics and Latinos. Numerous companies have devised unique marketing and advertising strategies specifically targeting this group. For instance, Toyota's Más Que Un Auto (More Than a Car) campaign featuring car owners with personalized nameplates for their cars, leverages the Hispanic tradition of naming their vehicles with descriptive names that reflect the car's attributes. Research shows that unique ads that are developed for a specific ethnic group—for example, Hispanic Americans, are judged three times more effective as those that were translated into Spanish (from English).[10]

Social networking has special resonance for Hispanics and Latinos in the United States as a way to keep in touch with family members elsewhere. A recent study conducted regarding Facebook usage showed that 48 percent of U.S. Latino and Hispanics' Facebook friends were family members, relative to 36 percent among U.S. Facebook users in general.[11] The average Hispanic and Latino spends more than eight hours watching online videos each month—more than 90 minutes longer than the U.S. average. Despite these important differences, the Hispanic and Latino market, particularly with regard to digital marketing and advertising spends, remains under served. According to Marla Skiko, senior vice president and director of digital innovation at SMG Multicultural, "Many marketers may think they [U.S. Hispanics/ Latinos] trail the so-called general market in adoption of new tech, when in fact they are far ahead and should be among the first prospects for marketers seeking to grow their consumer base."[12] In order to better appeal to this segment, some companies such as Moët Hennessy have partnered with hip-hop artists such as Nas and Manny Pacquiao to increase their appeal to Latino and Hispanic youth. Others have turned to digital channels such as MiTu (a multichannel YouTube network) and Young California (a West Coast network of DJs and content creators focused on hip-hop) to appeal to millennial Latinos and Hispanics.[13]

Asian Americans.   The Asian-American group is also among the fastest growing groups in the United States (growth rate of 3.4 percent in 2015), relative to Hispanics (growth rate of 2.2 percent), African Americans (growth rate of 1.3 percent), and Caucasians (growth rate of 0.5 percent). Some unique aspects of Asian American households include the larger-than-average ownership of Internet devices, and a greater emphasis on marriage, parenthood, hard work, and career success.[14] A number of companies—for example, Costco and Toyota—have developed marketing campaigns specifically targeting this ethnic group. Some best practices for marketing to various ethnic groups are highlighted in Table 15-2.

It is worth highlighting a key downside of targeting specific ethnic or cultural groups—the potential that this may backfire. Marketing critics say that some consumers may not like being targeted on the basis of being different, since that only reinforces their image as outsiders or a minority. Moreover, consumers not in the targeted segment may feel alienated or distanced from the company and brand as a result.[15]

GLOBAL BRANDING

We organize this section on global branding to answer the following three questions:

1. *Why* should a brand focus on global markets? What are the advantages and disadvantages of expanding internationally?
2. *What* is the definition of a global brand? What are some factors which contribute to global brand equity?
3. What are some *pros* and *cons* of standardizing versus customizing brand offerings? *How* should a brand effectively customize various aspects of marketing mix?

We conclude with a discussion of China as a global market, given its size and strategic importance in the global marketplace.

BRANDING BRIEF 15-1
Marketing to Ethnic Groups

African Americans: Verizon effectively appealed to this audience through its annual festival called "How Sweet the Sound." This campaign was effective because it aligned Verizon with something that holds important and unique meaning to that community: gospel music. The campaign included lush drawings of performers in print ads, and these looked like vibrant paintings of African Americans. Verizon saw a 14 percent increase in sales in the cities where the program was implemented.

CoverGirl cosmetics was successful in targeting African Americans with unique colors in their make-up line. This campaign was effective because African-American audiences of all ages and income brackets respond more positively to marketing where their ethnicity is highlighted, and where it is an integral part of the marketing effort.

Hispanic Americans and Latinos: Buchanan's Whisky is an example of a brand which effectively targeted Hispanics and Latinos. Their campaign was centered around the theme of "It's Our Time," Es Nuestro Momento in Spanish. The campaign partnered with global Latin music superstar, J Balvin, and aimed to empower a new generation of Latinos with the belief that their cultural pride was key to unlocking true greatness. Balvin embodied the brand's belief that true greatness comes from embracing who you are and where you come from.

Asian Americans: Toyota launched a campaign targeting Asian Americans. Hoping to capitalize on actor Lee Min Ho's popularity among Asian Americans, Toyota's American marketing team tapped the celebrity to appear in a web series, *The One & Only*. *The One & Only* was successful in winning over consumers from its three key markets: Chinese, Vietnamese, and Korean immigrants living in America. Asian Americans surveyed saw the car as "smart" and that they attributed "smart" as attractive. Toyota was successful because it selected a celebrity the Asian demographic sees as both attractive and smart, the dual attributes it wants to be associated with the Camry brand.

Verizon appealed to African-American target audiences with its annual music festival called "How Sweet the Sound."

CoverGirl introduced bold new colors into its makeup line, enhancing its brand's appeal to African-American target audiences.

Sources: Esther Franklin, "Multicultural Marketing Requires a Whole-Market Approach," *Adweek*, July 1, 2014, https://www.adweek.com/brand-marketing/multicultural-marketing-requires-whole-market-approach-158613/, accessed November 25, 2018; César Melgoza, "Multicultural Marketing Is All About the Metrics," *Entrepreneur*, January 22, 2016, https://www.entrepreneur.com/article/254347, accessed November 25, 2018; SKULocal, "How to Effectively Target Multicultural Audiences in Your Marketing," January 14, 2016, http://www.skulocal.com/insights/how-to-effectively-target-multicultural-audiences-in-your-marketing/, accessed November 25, 2018; www.multivu.com/players/English/7947751-buchanans-es-nuestro-momento-j-balvin/, accessed February 28, 2017; The Nielsen Co., "The Multicultural Edge: Rising Super Consumers," March 18, 2015, https://www.nielsen.com/us/en/insights/reports/2015/the-multicultural-edge-rising-super-consumers.html, accessed November 25, 2018; www.ana.net/blogs/show/id/30414 accessed February 28, 2017; http://mashable.com/2015/07/24/multicultural-marketing-tactics/#XxeYQ1fpHGqL, accessed February 28, 2017; Glenn Llopis, "5 Steps to Capturing the Hispanic Market: The Last True Growth Opportunity," *Forbes Magazine*, September 3, 2013, https://www.forbes.com/sites/glennllopis/2013/09/03/5-steps-to-capturing-the-hispanic-market-the-last-true-growth-opportunity/#50707ab63406, accessed November 25, 2018; Glenn Llopis, "Don't Sell to Me! Hispanics Buy Brands That Empower Their Cultural Relevancy," *Forbes Magazine*, May 14, 2012, https://www.forbes.com/sites/glennllopis/2012/05/14/dont-sell-to-me-hispanics-buy-brands-that-empower-their-cultural-relevancy/#60427f1c661c, accessed November 25, 2018; www.ahaa.org/Portals/0/Research/Marketing%20&%20Advertising%20Trends/2014%

Buchanan's Whisky's "Es Neustro Momento" (It's Our Time) campaign in Spanish showcased how marketing to ethnic groups should incorporate a deep understanding of the values and beliefs of different cultural and ethnic segments.

Toyota Camry featured Asian-American celebrities and actors in their advertising targeting this ethnic group.

20Hispanic%20Fact%20Pack/2014%20Hispanic%20Fact%20Pack. pdf, accessed March 5, 2017; Hispanic Market Works, "Coca Cola Launches New "Orgulloso De Ser" Campaign, September 13, 2015, http://www.hispanicmarketworks.org/newsletter/coca-cola-launches-new-orgulloso-de-ser-campaign/, accessed November 25, 2018; Lisa Gevelber, "Your Next Big Opportunity: The U.S. Hispanic Market," Think with Google, July 2014, https://www.thinkwithgoogle.com/ consumer-insights/us-hispanic-market-digital/, accessed November 25, 2018; Claudia "Havi" Goffan, "Hispanic Market Trends Forecast," Target Latino, https://targetlatino.com/hispanic-market-trends-forecast/, accessed November 25, 2018; U.S. Census Bureau, "Facts for Features: Hispanic Heritage Month 2015," September 14, 2015, https:// www.census.gov/newsroom/facts-for-features/2015/cb15-ff18.html, accessed November 25, 2018; Eliana Murillo, "New Research Shows How to Connect with U.S. Hispanics Online," Think with Google, June 2015, https://www.thinkwithgoogle.com/consumer-insights/new-research-shows-how-to-connect-with-digital-hispanics-online/, accessed November 25, 2018; Pew Research Center Hispanic Trends, "Hispanic Population and Origin in Select U.S. Metropolitan Areas, 2014," September 6, 2016, http://www.pewhispanic.org/interactives/hispanic-population-in-select-u-s-metropolitan-areas/, accessed November 25, 2018; www.ahaa.org/Portals/0/Research/The%20Hispanic%20 Consumer/Power,%20Influence%20&%20Behavior/The%20Growing %20Hispanic%20Population%202011.pdf, accessed March 5, 2017; Journey Staff, "#OrgullosoDeSer: Coke's Hispanic Heritage Month Campaign Embraces Latino Pride," Coca-Cola Journey, September 16, 2015, https://www.coca-colacompany.com/stories/orgullosodeser-cokes-hispanic-heritage-month-campaign-embraces-latino-pride, accessed

November 25, 2018; Roy E. Kokoyachuk, "Advertising and the Bilingual Brain," ThinkNow Research, September 8, 2015, https://thinknowresearch .com/blog/advertising-and-the-bilingual-brain/, accessed November 25, 2018; Kristina Monllos, "Here's Why Brands Are Speaking Spanish in General Market Ads," *Adweek*, June 24, 2014, https://www.adweek.com/ brand-marketing/heres-why-brands-are-speaking-spanish-general-market-ads-158448/, accessed November 25, 2018; MP Mueller, "Marketing Tips for Reaching Hispanic Americans," *The New York Times*, February 1, 2013, https://boss.blogs.nytimes.com/2013/02/01/marketing-tips-for-reaching-hispanic-americans/?mtrref=www.google.com&gwh=F25BD 0442EB9439DCAE2F14AA52BC914&gwt=pay, accessed November 25, 2018; Samantha Masunaga, "Target Takes Aim at Latinos with New Marketing Campaign," *Los Angeles Times*, April 18, 2015, https://www .latimes.com/business/la-fi-target-latino-marketing-20150418-story .html, accessed November 25, 2018; Kim Souza, "Wal-Mart to Focus More On Hispanic Shoppers," Talk Business & Politics, March 21, 2013, https://talkbusiness.net/2013/03/wal-mart-to-focus-more-on-hispanic-shoppers-2/, accessed November 25, 2018; Consumer Insights, "African-American Digital Consumers Infographic," Think with Google, October 2011, https://www.thinkwithgoogle.com/consumer-insights/african-american-digital-consumers-infographic/, accessed November 25, 2018; Janie Boschma, "Black Consumers Have 'Unprecedented Impact' in 2015," *The Atlantic*, February 2, 2016, https://www.theatlantic.com/ politics/archive/2016/02/black-consumers-have-unprecedented-impact-in-2015/433725/, accessed November 25, 2018; The Nielsen Co., "Connecting Through Culture: African-Americans Favor Diverse Advertising," October 20, 2014, https://www.nielsen.com/us/en/insights/news/2014/ connecting-through-culture-african-americans-favor-diverse-advertising .html, accessed November 25, 2018; The Nielsen Co., "Meet the Fastest-Growing Multicultural Segment in the U.S.: Asian-Americans," June 11, 2015, https://www.nielsen.com/us/en/insights/news/2015/meet-the-fastest-growing-multicultural-segment-in-the-us-asian-americans.html, accessed November 25, 2018; Jacob M. Chacko, "Targeting Asian-Indian American Consumers," http://www.aabri.com/manuscripts/08126.pdf, accessed November 25, 2018; MarketingMag, "How Toyota Won Over the Asian American Market with a Korean Web Series," http://marketingmag .ca/uncategorized/how-toyota-won-over-the-asian-american-market-with-a-korean-web-series-75175/, accessed November 25, 2018; Bill Duggan, "Marketing to Asian Americans and Insights from the 3AF Conference," ANA, May 21, 2012, https://www.ana.net/blogs/show/id/23552, accessed November 25, 2018; Luxury Daily, "Gucci Uses Actress Endorsement for China-Area Accessories Campaign," April 25, 2012, https://www .luxurydaily.com/gucci-appeals-to-chinese-consumers-in-latest-accessories-campaign/, accessed November 25, 2018; Gravity Media, "Asian-Americans Represent Significant Opportunities for Hotels and Beverage Brands," February 1, 2016, http://www.mediagravity.com/ blog/asian-americans-represent-significant-opportunities-hotels-and-beverage-brands, accessed November 25, 2018.

Why Should a Brand Focus on Global Markets?

A number of well-known global brands such as Apple, Google, Coca-Cola, Microsoft, and Toyota have derived their sales and profits from international markets. This has encouraged many firms to market their brands internationally, for the following reasons:

- Perception of slow growth and increased competition in domestic markets
- Belief in enhanced overseas growth and profit opportunities
- Desire to reduce costs from economies of scale
- Need to diversify risk
- Recognition of global mobility of customers.

In more product categories, the ability to establish a global profile is becoming a prerequisite for success. Ideally, the marketing program for a global brand consists of one product formulation, one package design, one advertising program, one pricing schedule, one distribution plan, and so on that would prove the most effective and efficient option for every country in which the brand is sold. Unfortunately, such a uniformly optimal strategy is rarely possible.

Next, let's consider the advantages and disadvantages of creating globally standardized marketing programs for brands.

Advantages of Global Marketing

A number of potential advantages attach to a global marketing program (see Figure 15-1).[16]

Economies of Scale in Production and Distribution.   From a supply-side or cost perspective, the primary advantages of a global marketing program are the manufacturing efficiencies and lower costs that derive from higher volumes in production and distribution. The more that strong experience curve effects exist—driving down the cost of making and marketing a product with increases in production—the more economies of scale in production and distribution from a standardized global marketing program will prevail.[17]

Lower Marketing Costs.   Another set of cost advantages arises from uniformity in packaging, advertising, promotion, and other marketing communication activities. The more uniform, the greater the potential savings. Branding experts maintain that using one name can save a business tens of millions of dollars a year in marketing costs.[18]

Power and Scope.   A global brand profile can communicate credibility.[19] Consumers may believe that selling in many diverse markets is an indication that a manufacturer has gained much expertise and acceptance, meaning the product is high quality and convenient to use. An admired global brand can also signal social status and prestige[20] and enable consumers to signal their identity,[21] particularly as global citizens.

Consistency in Brand Image.   Maintaining a common marketing platform all over the world helps maintain consistency of the brand and company image; this is particularly important where customers move often, or media exposure transmits images across national boundaries. Services often desire to convey a uniform image due to consumer movements. For example, American Express communicates the prestige and utility of its card worldwide.

FIGURE 15-1

Advantages of Global
Marketing Programs

Economies of scale in production and distribution
Lower marketing costs
Power and scope
Consistency in brand image
Ability to leverage good ideas quickly and efficiently
Uniformity of marketing practices

Ability to Leverage Good Ideas Quickly and Efficiently.   Not having to develop strictly local versions speeds a brand's market entry. Marketers can leverage good ideas across markets as long as the right knowledge transfer systems are put into place. MasterCard's corporate marketing group helps facilitate information and best practices across the organization.[22]

Uniformity of Marketing Practices.   Finally, a standardized global marketing program may simplify coordination and provide greater control of communications in different countries. By keeping the core of the marketing program constant, marketers can pay greater attention to making refinements across markets and over time to improve its effectiveness.

Disadvantages of Global Marketing

Perhaps the most compelling disadvantage of standardized global marketing programs is that they often ignore fundamental differences of various kinds across countries and cultures (see Figure 15-2). Critics claim that designing one program for all possible markets results in unimaginative and ineffective strategies geared to the lowest common denominator. Possible differences across countries come in a host of forms, as we discuss next.

Differences in Consumer Needs, Wants, and Usage Patterns for Products.   Differences in cultural values, economic development, and other factors across nationalities lead customers to behave very differently. For example, the per capita consumption of alcoholic beverages varies dramatically from country to country: in liters consumed per capita annually, the Czech Republic (8.51) and Ireland (7.04) drink the most beer; France (8.14) and Portugal (6.65) drink the most wine; and South Korea (9.57) and Russia (6.88) drink the most distilled spirits.[23]

The Science of Branding 15-1 describes some of the research providing concrete evidence of key differences in consumers across cultures.

One consequence of the differences is that strategies that work in one country may not work in another. Here is an example highlighting the importance of understanding the local culture and customs prior to launching a global brand. When Krispy Kreme doughnuts crossed the Atlantic from the United States to the United Kingdom in 2003, it was faced with a market in the United Kingdom that was unfamiliar with doughnuts. Rather than introduce Krispy Kreme as a breakfast food, the company decided to leverage the British tradition of bringing cakes to work for special occasions. It positioned Krispy Kreme doughnuts as a communal experience that could be purchased in bulk and shared with coworkers. It also launched a gift card that would give holders a dozen doughnuts in a box, to support the idea of sharing. This novel approach to the UK market allowed Krispy Kreme to overcome potential hurdles associated with launching an unfamiliar breakfast food.[24]

Differences in Consumer Response to Branding Elements.   Linguistic differences across countries can twist or change the meaning of a brand name. Sound systems that differ across dialects can make a word problematic in one country but not another. Cultural context is key. Customers may actually respond well to a name with potentially problematic associations. The questions are how widespread the association is, how immediate it is, and how problematic it actually would be.

Differences in consumer needs, wants, and usage patterns for products
Differences in consumer response to branding elements
Differences in consumer response to marketing mix elements
Differences in brand and product development and the competitive environment
Differences in the legal environment
Differences in marketing institutions
Differences in administrative procedures

FIGURE 15-2

Disadvantages of Global Marketing Programs

When Krispy Kreme launched its doughnuts in the UK market, it devised a novel marketing strategy to overcome the barriers to consuming doughnuts as a breakfast food.

Well-known brand consultancy Lexicon employs linguists to help make these assessments for clients.[25] The agency has uncovered names that would have been a sexual insult in Colombian Spanish, been sacrilegious in Hindi, conveyed impotence in Japanese, and translated as "prostitute" in Hebrew.[26] Given this, it is perhaps not surprising that researchers have found differences in the ways Chinese- and English-speaking consumers processed brand names. In one study, results showed that mental representations of verbal information are coded mainly visually among Chinese and in a phonological manner among English speakers. Another study showed that more positive brand attributes resulted when peripheral features of a brand name ("script" aspects, such as the type of font employed, or "sound" aspects, such as the way the name is pronounced) matched the associations or meaning of the brand. Chinese native speakers were affected primarily by script matching, whereas English native speakers' attitudes were primarily affected by sound matching.

Differences in Consumer Responses to Marketing Mix Elements. Consumers in different parts of the world feel differently about marketing activity.[27] U.S. consumers tend to be fairly cynical toward advertising, whereas Japanese view it much more positively. Differences also exist in advertising style: Japanese ads tend to be softer and more abstract in tone, whereas U.S. ads are often richer in product information. There are also major differences in how consumers use social media. Latin America is the fourth largest mobile market, and more than half the smartphones are used to access social media.[28] In Argentina, where 62 percent of the population use social media, companies reap rich rewards from social media campaigns. Burger King conducted a social media campaign on Snapchat to "flame grill" competitors' burgers, by asking participants to draw grill marks (e.g., Snap-King) on competitors' burger patties in return for free vouchers. The campaign earned the company 4.1 million new fans on the Snapchat platform.[29] Overall, digital marketing techniques (e.g., search engine marketing) is seen as a cost-effective alternative to traditional marketing in Latin America.

Other than advertising and social media usage, price sensitivity, promotion responsiveness, sponsorship support, and other activities all may differ by country, and these differences can motivate consumers' behavior and decision-making.

Differences in Brand and Product Development and the Competitive Environment. Products may be at various stages of their life cycle in different countries. For example, consider the detergent category and how P&G modified its strategy for its detergent brand Tide. When entering the India market, P&G had to grapple with the fact that only 10 percent of India's

THE SCIENCE OF BRANDING 15-1
Key Insights Regarding Global Brand Strategies Based on Research Findings

1. **Cultures place varying emphasis on the *self* versus the *group*, with implications for consumer-brand relationships:** Academic researchers have also focused on how cultural dimensions that define a culture could impact how consumers form relationships with brands. One important dimension on which cultures are different is whether the emphasis is on the independent self (or a focus on the individual rather than the group) or whether the culture focuses on the interdependent self (focus on the group as opposed to the individual). Researchers have shown that consumers in independent cultures may use brands because it strengthens their individual identity, whereas consumers in interdependent cultures may use brands because it strengthens their relationship with their social group. Perhaps attuned to these differences, Harley-Davidson (which has a brand personality associated with ruggedness and individualism) in Japan organizes a number of rallies and get-togethers to provide a sense of fun and community for their riders.

2. **Vertical and horizontal cultural contexts cause differences in how consumers relate to high-status brands:** Cross-cultural differences based on power-distance can also play a role in how consumers react to brands. The power distance dimension is defined as the extent to which society accepts inequality in power distribution and reflects the hierarchical or vertical nature of society. When power distance is larger, each individual has a unique social status, and comparisons with those in higher or lower social status are more common. In high power distance cultures, global brands—such as Armani and Mercedes—can help consumers reflect social status. In contrast, research findings reveal that those in horizontal cultures place a great deal of emphasis on equality. This could lead to a differential preference for brand names that convey uniqueness without being of high status (e.g., Abercrombie and Fitch, and Hollister).

3. **Brands can be symbolic of culture, and this has strategic implications for managers:** Brands can be symbolic of cultural identity, and such symbolism can influence global brand strategy. For example, brands such as Budweiser and Levi's are more symbolic of the American culture, whereas New Balance and JanSport are examples of brands that are neutral in cultural symbolism. Academic researchers have found that culturally symbolic brands are preferred when consumers had a high level of cultural identification with a given culture, or when their social identity was threatened. Research also shows that a brand's cultural symbolism (or the degree to which a brand symbolizes a cultural group) is an important contextual factor influencing how individuals react to advertising using multiple languages (i.e., bilingual advertising).

4. **Brands have different personalities across cultures:** An important finding is that consumers project their own personality preferences in various cultures onto global brands. One large cross-national study have suggested that meanings derived from brands and brand personalities are culture-specific with "ruggedness" traits being more specific to the United States, "peacefulness" in Japan, and "passion" in Spain.

Sources: J. B. Nezlek, K. Kafetsios, and V. Smith, "Emotions in Everyday Social Encounters," *Journal of Cross-Cultural Psychology* 39, no. 4, (2008): 366–372; Marieke de Mooij and Geert Hofstede, "Cross-Cultural Consumer Behavior: A Review of Research Findings," *Journal of International Consumer Marketing* 23, no. 3–4, (2011): 181–192; Vanitha Swaminathan, Karen Page, and Zeynep Gürhan-Canli, "My Brand or Our Brand: Individual- and Group-Based Brand Relationships and Self-Construal Effects on Brand Evaluations," *Journal of Consumer Research* 34, no. 2 (2007): 248–259; Chris Betros, "Harley-Davidson Gains Popularity in Japan," *Japan Today*, August 10, 2009, www.japantoday.com/category/executive-impact/view/harley-davidson-gains-popularity-in-japan; Sara Loughran Dommer, Vanitha Swaminathan, and Rohini Ahluwalia, "Using Differentiated Brands to Deflect Exclusion and Protect Inclusion: The Moderating Role of Self-Esteem on Attachment to Differentiated Brands," *Journal of Consumer Research* 40, no. 4, 657–675.; Angela Y. Lee and Carlos J. Torelli, "Crosscultural Issues in Consumer Behavior," *Frontiers of Social Psychology* (2008): 227; Sharon Shavitt, Carlos J. Torelli, and Jimmy Wong, "Identity-Based Motivation: Constraints and Opportunities in Consumer Research," *Journal of Consumer Psychology* 19, no. 3 (2009): 261; Marieke De Mooij and Geert Hofstede, "The Hofstede Model: Applications to Global Branding and Advertising Strategy and Research," *International Journal of Advertising* 29, no. 1 (2010): 85–110; Theodore M. Singelis, Harry C. Triandis, Dharm PS Bhawuk, and Michele J. Gelfand, "Horizontal and Vertical Dimensions of Individualism and Collectivism: A Theoretical and Measurement Refinement," *Cross-Cultural Research* 29, no. 3 (1995): 240–275; H. C. Triandis, *Individualism and Collectivism* (Boulder, CO: Westview, 1995); Michelle R. Nelson and Sharon Shavitt, "Horizontal and Vertical Individualism and Achievement Values: A Multimethod Examination of Denmark and the United States," *Journal of Cross-Cultural Psychology* 33, no. 5 (2002): 439–458; Carlos J. Torelli and Rohini Ahluwalia, "Extending Culturally Symbolic Brands: A Blessing or a Curse?," *Journal of Consumer Research* 38, no. 5 (2012): 933–947; Umut Kubat and Vanitha Swaminathan, "Crossing the Cultural Divide through Bilingual Advertising: The Moderating Role of Brand Cultural Symbolism," *International Journal of Research in Marketing* 32, no. 4 (2015): 354–362; C. J. Torelli, H. T. Keh, and C. Y. Chiu, "Cultural Symbolism of Brands," in *Brands and Brand Management: Contemporary Research Perspectives*, B. Loken, R. Ahluwalia, and M. J. Houston (Eds.) (Psychology Press, 2009); Jennifer Aaker, Veronica Benet-Martinez, and Jordi Garolera, "Consumption Symbols as Carriers of Culture: A Study of Japanese and Spanish Brand Personality Constructs," *Journal of Personality and Social Psychology* 81, no. 3 (2001): 492–508.

consumers have access to a washing machine.[30] Most consumers wash their clothes with detergent bars and water.

Tide targeted the middle-class consumer who preferred to wash clothes on their own, even though Tide detergent is a washing machine-based detergent in many developed markets. Tide

Tide's variants are modified to suit local market tastes.

also introduced variants with local appeal (e.g., Jasmine and Rose-scented detergent), and Tide Naturals was launched to appeal to consumers who preferred a lower price point. Due to these changes in local market strategy, Tide became a market leader in the detergents category in India, even though the category was dominated by other well-entrenched competitors.[31] This example highlights the importance of understanding the stage of development of a given product category prior to launching a global brand. Moreover, the perceptions and positions of particular brands may also differ considerably across countries, based on local market conditions. For example, McDonald's and KFC are regarded as inexpensive fast food restaurants in the United States, but in India and China they have a premium positioning.[32]

The nature of competition may also differ, and brand managers must be prepared to reexamine their competitive positioning carefully for each country and devise a plan to account for unexpected rivals in the marketplace.

Differences in the Legal Environment. One of the challenges in developing a global advertising campaign is the maze of constantly changing legal restrictions from country to country. For example, Canada banned prescription drug advertising on television. Poland required commercial lyrics to be sung in Polish. Sweden prohibited advertising to children, and Brazil recently instituted similar laws. Malaysia did not allow lawyers or law firms to advertise. Advertising restricts the use of children in commercials in Austria, comparative ads in Singapore, and product placement on public television channels in Germany.

In the context of social media advertising, the U.S. Federal Trade Commission requires that paid testimonials and endorsements made by a consumer or any third party for a brand or company on social media be clearly revealed, a rule which is also found in other countries (e.g., Singapore).[33] Many data privacy laws have been instituted in the European Union, which may impact the ability of marketers to utilize individual consumer-level data to develop and implement digital marketing strategies.[34]

Although some of these laws have been challenged or are being relaxed, numerous legal differences still exist.

Differences in Marketing Institutions. Channels of distribution, retail practices, media availability, and media costs all may vary significantly from country to country, making implementation of the same marketing strategy difficult. Foreign companies struggled for years to break into Japan's rigid distribution system that locks out many foreign goods. The prevalence of online shopping, smartphones, supermarkets, and so on may also vary considerably, especially in developing countries.

Differences in Administrative Procedures.   In practice, it may be difficult to achieve the control necessary to implement a standardized global marketing program. Local offices may resist having their autonomy threatened. Local managers may suffer from the "not invented here" syndrome and raise objections—rightly or wrongly—that the global marketing program misses some key dimension of the local market. Local managers who feel their autonomy reduced may lose motivation and feel doomed to failure.

STRATEGIES FOR CREATING & MANAGING GLOBAL BRANDS

We previously showed the rationale associated with global markets along with the pros and cons of a global marketing program. We next describe a set of key principles to building global brand equity. Before we dive into strategic considerations, it may be worthwhile defining a global brand. Although many definitions exist, most experts agree that, to be regarded as a *successful* global brand, you should derive at least half your revenue outside their domestic market and have much of their growth derived from these global markets.[35]

Creating Global Brand Equity

A brand can create strong global brand equity using the same approaches to creating brand resonance as in Chapter 3. Global brand equity can be built by achieving the following for each global market:

1. Establishing breadth and depth of brand awareness
2. Creating points-of-parity and points-of-difference
3. Eliciting positive, accessible brand responses
4. Forging intense, active brand relationships

In each and every market in which marketers sell the brand, they must consider how to achieve brand salience, brand performance, brand imagery, brand judgments, brand feelings, and brand resonance, which are the key building blocks associated with achieving the previously outlined goals. For example, brand managers should be aware of how the sequential timing of introduction can impact *brand salience* and brand perceptions across different markets. Different orders of introduction can profoundly affect consumer perceptions about what products the brand offers, the benefits supplied, and the needs satisfied. *Brand imagery* associations may vary considerably across markets because of variations in brand history and heritage. Further, in crafting brand image strategies, it is important to remember that a desirable brand personality in one market may be less desirable in another. Nike's competitive, aggressive user imagery proved a detriment in its introduction into European markets in the early 1990s. The company achieved greater success when it dialed down its image somewhat and emphasized team concepts more.

Brand judgments must be positive in new markets—consumers must find the brand to be of good quality, credible, worthy of consideration, and superior. Finally, achieving *brand resonance* in new markets means that consumers must have sufficient opportunities and incentives to buy and use the product, interact with other consumers and the company itself, and actively learn and experience the brand and its marketing. Digital marketing and social media communications can be deployed to strengthen brand resonance. Nevertheless, digital efforts cannot completely replace grassroots marketing efforts that help connect the consumer with the brand.

Global Brand Positioning

To best capture differences in consumer behavior, and to guide our efforts in revising the marketing program, it is highly recommended that companies evolve a global brand positioning which derives from a deep understanding of how brands must be positioned across various markets. Recall that brand positioning means creating mental maps, defining core brand associations, identifying points-of-parity and points-of-difference, and crafting a brand mantra. Many companies have a global brand positioning document that typically addresses a number of questions. The answers to these questions will guide how to structure a global brand positioning and will help identify which aspects of a brand's positioning can be modified based on local considerations. These questions include:

1. How valid is the brand's mental map based in the home market relevant to a new market? How appropriate is the positioning? What is the existing level of awareness? How valuable are the core brand associations, points-of-parity, and points-of-difference?
2. What changes should we make to the positioning? Do we need to create any new associations? Should we *not* recreate any existing associations? Should we modify any existing associations?
3. How should we create this new mental map? Can we still use the same marketing activities? What changes should we make? What new marketing activities are necessary?

In evolving a brand's global positioning, we need to define a hierarchy of brand associations in the global context that defines which associations we want consumers in all countries to hold, and which we want consumers only in certain countries to have. We have to determine how to create these associations in various markets to account for diverse consumer perceptions, tastes, and environments. Thus, we must be attuned to similarities and differences across markets. Häagen-Dazs provides a good example of a global brand positioning which is then executed using locally relevant strategies. We follow that up with a brief set of recommendations for how a brand can modify different aspects of its marketing mix to improve its appeal to various global markets.

HÄAGEN-DAZS GLOBAL BRAND: MANY FLAVORS OF INDULGENCE

Häagen-Dazs, a well-known brand of ice cream, is in more than 50 markets and has sales revenue of $2.09 trillion. Häagen-Dazs is owned by General Mills and marketed by Nestlé in some markets.[36] Its global advertising campaign leverages its super-premium image, and has a unified global positioning around three key themes: indulgence, affordable luxury, and intense sensuality. This standardized positioning strategy globally is combined with customized flavors and line extensions as well as diversified advertising executions around the world. For example, the brand uses distinctive flavors in different countries, including Green Tea in Asia, Banana Caramel Crêpe and Macadamia Nut Brittle in France, Mooncakes in China, and different flavors for various European markets. In China (which is among the largest global markets for ice cream, along with Brazil), you will find sushi ice cream, consisting of ice cream scoops wrapped in chocolate and served like sushi. Soft serves at the Shanghai store cost seven times that of the nearby McDonald's, reaffirming Häagen-Dazs position as a super-premium ice cream that is meant for only those who crave its indulgence. As this discussion suggests, although firms are increasingly adopting an international marketing perspective, numerous aspects of the marketing strategy need to be adapted to suit local market conditions. Before providing some specific tactical guidelines on how to build global

Häagen-Dazs introduced a new ice cream bar in a variety of flavors to suit local market tastes.

customer-based brand equity, we highlight the debate regarding standardization versus c
next. As an example, the Branding Brief 15-2 on Coca-Cola provides an overview of how to b
branding with local execution.

BRANDING BRIEF 15-2
Coca-Cola's Global Brand Strategy with Local E

The most recognized brand name in the world got its start in an Atlanta pharmacy, where it sold for five cents a glass. The name Coca-Cola was registered as a trademark on January 31, 1893. The drink soon became a national phenomenon; by 1895, the company had established syrup plants in Chicago, Dallas, and Los Angeles.

In the 1920s, Coca-Cola pursued aggressive global branding, finding such creative placements for its logo on dogsleds in Canada and on the walls of bullfighting arenas in Spain. Its popularity throughout the world was fueled by colorful and persuasive advertising that cemented its image as the "all-American" beverage. Coca-Cola's early moves into formerly restricted markets, such as China in 1978 and the Soviet Union in 1979, bolstered its image as a global company. By 1988, Coca-Cola was voted the best known and most admired brand in the world.

Coca-Cola's hybrid marketing strategy for global markets involved a global marketing strategy combined with local market activations.

Perhaps the most consistently standardized element of Coca-Cola is its product appearance. Coke essentially keeps the same basic look and packaging of the product everywhere (except in countries where laws dictate use of the local language). The company simultaneously stresses that the brand be relevant and well positioned against the competition. To keep it relevant, Coca-Cola uses different advertising agencies in different countries in order to make the brand feel local.

In 1999, Coca-Cola's new global marketing mantra became "Think Local. Act Local"—an important twist on its old mantra, "Think Global. Act Local." Intended to get Coca-Cola back to the basics, the strategy meant hiring more local staff and allowing field managers to tailor marketing to their regions. The results of this hyperlocal focus were missed sales targets and local advertising that, in some cases, did not fit with the carefully crafted Coke image, such as an Italian ad featuring skinny-dippers running along a beach. The company scrapped the "Think Local. Act Local" mantra in favor of a hybrid strategy, in which a global marketing network of local executives took direction from Coke's Atlanta headquarters, with some room for interpretation at the local level.

In 2016, Coca-Cola announced a unified creative campaign titled "Taste the Feeling" which underscores that Coca-Cola is a simple pleasure which makes everyday moments special. The ad campaign focuses on authentic moments in a consumer's life. Coca-Cola has an international network of advertising agencies to bring this campaign theme to life in various ways in different local markets via TV commercials, digital advertising, print, and shopper materials.

Today, Coca-Cola conducts business with more than 400 brands in more than 200 countries. About three-quarters of its revenues come from outside the United States. For example, while Coca-Cola sells Coke to a growing group of consumers in Asia, it also sells local brands there, such as the hugely successful Georgia iced coffee in Japan, which actually outsells Coke, as well as new drinks, such as Ayataka green tea. In India, a big seller for Coca-Cola is Thums Up, an indigenous variant that it purchased. In South America, Coca-Cola test-marketed a new flavor called Coca-Cola Life, which was then launched in Argentina and expanded to Chile, United Kingdom, and to some outlets in the United States. This was in response to studies which showed that Argentineans demonstrated concern for the environment. The Coca-Cola Life brand contains a mix of sugar and stevia (an indigenous herb) and is a reduced-calorie beverage which is in a recyclable bottle. Since its launch, Coca-Cola Life has garnered a large following, as seen in the number of Twitter followers, Facebook likes, and YouTube views. Its combination of local and global brands enables Coca-Cola to exploit the benefits of global branding and global trends in tastes while tapping into traditional domestic markets at the same time.

Sources: Duane Stanford, "Africa: Coke's Last Frontier," *Bloomberg BusinessWeek,* October 28, 2010, https://www.bloomberg.com/news/articles/2010-10-28/africa-cokes-last-frontier, accessed November 25, 2018; Mehul Srivastava, "For India's Consumers, Pepsi Is the Real Thing," *Bloomberg BusinessWeek,* September 16, 2010, https://www.bloomberg.com/news/articles/2010-09-16/for-indias-consumers-pepsi-is-the-real-thing, accessed November 25, 2018; "Coke Profit Fails to Meet Expectations," *The New York Times,* April 20, 2010; "The Story of Coca-Cola," www.coca-cola.com;

Betsy McKay, "Coca-Co
Asian Wall Street Jou
$400M to Fix It,"
"Coca-Cola H
6, 2001, 6B
Asia," *T*
for M

Restructuring Effort Has Yet to Prove Effective," *~nal*, March 2, 2001; Kate MacArthur, "Coke Commits ~*Advertising Age*, November 15, 2004; Theresa Howard, ~pes Taking New Path Leads to Success," *USA Today*, March ~, Michael Flagg, "Coca-Cola Adopts Local-Drinks Strategy in ~*e Wall Street Journal*, July 30, 2001; Dylan Kissane, "Four Tips ~arketing to Australians," DOZ.com, January 27, 2016, https://www.doz ~m/marketing-resources/tips-marketing-australian, accessed November 25, 2018; The Coca-Cola Company, "Coca-Cola Announces "One Brand" Global Marketing Approach," January 19, 2016, https://www.coca-colacompany .com/press-center/press-releases/coca-cola-announces-one-brand-global-marketing-approach, accessed November 25, 2018; Kristin Kovner, "6 Marketing Lessons Learned in Argentina," Mashable, April 15, 2015, https://mashable .com/2015/04/15/marketing-argentina/#7MzggoonhOqf, accessed November 25, 2018; Yuri Kageyama, "Coca-Cola No. 1 in Japan with Drinks Galore, But Not Coke," December 1, 2016, https://japantoday.com/category/features/food/coca-cola-no-1-in-japan-with-drinks-galore-but-not-coke, accessed November 25, 2018; Kent Landers, "Coke VP on Assignment in Japan Gushes About Vending Variety," The Coca-Cola Co., September 17, 2014, https:// www.coca-colacompany.com/stories/coke-vp-on-assignment-in-japan-gushes-about-vending-variety, accessed November 25, 2018; Campaign Asia, "Coke Tightens Grip on Drinks Market," February 16, 2001, https://www .campaignasia.com/article/coke-tightens-grip-on-drinks-market/180665, accessed November 25, 2018; The Coca-Cola Co., "2012 Per Capita Consumption of Company Beverage Products," www.coca-colacompany.com/ cs/tccc-yir2012/pdf/2012-per-capita-consumption.pdf; Soni Satpathy-Singh, "A Big 'Thums Up' to India's Beloved Cola: A Brief History and Recipe," April 1, 2016, https://www.india.com/food-2/a-big-thums-up-to-indias-beloved-cola-a-brief-history-and-recipe-1058524/; Coca-Cola India, "Maaza Mango Juice," www.coca-colaindia.com/our-products/product-list-descriptions/maaza/; Statista, "Annual Per Capita Consumption of Coca-Cola Company's Beverage Products from 1991 to 2012 (in servings of 8-fluid ounce beverages)," www.statista.com/statistics/271156/per-capita-consumption-of-soft-drinks-of-the-coca-cola-company-by-country/.

CUSTOMIZING MARKETING MIX ELEMENTS IN LOCAL MARKETS FOR GLOBAL BRANDS

Many brands need to customize specific aspects of the marketing mix to better appeal to local market conditions. We next review the four major elements of a marketing program—product, communications, distribution, and pricing strategies—in terms of adaptation issues.

Product Strategy

One reason so many companies ran into trouble initially going overseas is that they unknowingly—or perhaps even deliberately—overlooked differences in consumer behavior. Because of the relative expense and lack of a developed marketing research industry in smaller markets, many companies chose to forgo basic consumer research and put products on the shelf to see what would happen. As a result, they sometimes became aware of consumer differences only after the fact. To avoid these types of mistakes, marketers may need to conduct research into local markets. For instance, Nestlé's Kit Kat has researched and developed more than 300 flavors, many of which are unique to the Japanese market.[37]

In many cases, however, marketing research reveals that product differences are not justified for certain countries. At one time, Palmolive soap was sold globally with 22 different fragrances, 17 packages, nine shapes, and numerous positionings. After conducting marketing analyses to reap the benefits of global marketing, the company chose to employ just seven fragrances, one core packaging design, and three main shapes, all executed around two related positionings (one for developing markets and one for developed markets).[38]

Nestle's Green Tea-flavored Kit Kat in Japan illustrates how products can be customized to appeal to consumers in different international markets.

From a corporate perspective, one obvious solution to the trade-off between global and local brands is to sell both types of brands as part of the brand portfolio in a category. Even companies that have succeeded with global brands maintain that standardized international marketing programs work with only some products, in some places, and at some times, and will never totally replace brands and ads with local appeal.[39] Thus, despite the trend toward globalization, it seems that there will always be opportunities for good local brands.

Communication Strategy

Advertising is one area of marketing communications in which many firms face challenges internationally. Although the brand positioning may be the same in different countries, creative strategies in advertising may have to differ to some degree. Different countries can be more or less receptive to different creative styles. For example, humor is more common in U.S. and U.K. ads than, say, in German ads. European countries such as France and Italy are more tolerant of sex appeal and nudity in advertising.[40] In India, many ads feature family and "mother-child" themes, because family orientation and belongingness are a cornerstone of the collectivistic Indian culture. For example, Horlicks, a brand from Smithkline Beecham, used the "mother-child" relationship in its advertisements to drive its proposition of nurturing the all-around growth of children ("taller, stronger, and sharper").[41]

With the growth of social media and digital marketing, companies should carefully evaluate their options for communicating with consumers using online media. A common misconception is that many consumers in lower income levels do not have access to the Internet. However, the proliferation of smartphones has made the Internet more accessible. For example, the World Bank reported that by 2012, 98 percent of the Latin American population had access to a mobile cell signal, and most households had subscribed to some form of a mobile service plan. Further, Internet kiosks, community access centers, and multimedia communication booths in countries such as Peru, Mexico, and Ecuador have increased access to the Internet.[42]

The penetration of satellite and cable TV has expanded broadcast media options, making it easier to simultaneously air the same television commercial in many different countries. U.S. cable networks such as CNN, MTV, ESPN, and the Cartoon Network, and other networks such as Sky Broadcasting from the United Kingdom, and Star/Zee TV in Asia have increased advertisers' global reach.

Each country has its own unique media challenges and opportunities. When Colgate-Palmolive decided to further penetrate the market of the 630 million or so people who lived in rural India, the company had to overcome the fact that more than half of all Indian villagers are illiterate, and only one-third live in households with television sets. Its solution was to create half-hour infomercials carried through the countryside in video vans.[43] Sponsorship programs have a long tradition in many countries outside the United States because of a historical lack of advertising media there. Increasingly, marketers can execute sponsorship on a global basis. For example, FIFA World Cup Soccer has a long list of prominent partners and sponsors including global brands such as Adidas, Coca-Cola, Hyundai, Sony, and Visa. Entertainment and sports sponsorships can be an especially effective way to reach a younger audience.

Distribution Strategy

Distribution channels present challenges to many firms because there are few global retailers, especially supermarkets and grocery stores.[44] There are many distribution challenges, particularly in continents such as Africa where consumers live in urban and rural areas. To address distribution challenges, Weetabix, a UK-based brand of breakfast cereal, has adopted a unique distribution system in Kenya. It employs a sales force that distributes small sachets comprising only two biscuits to retail shops via bicycle. These efforts have paid off, as Weetabix enjoys 70 percent of the market share of the cereal market in Kenya.[45] Similarly, in East Africa, Coca-Cola has developed a network of micro distribution centers (MDCs) which provide distribution to thousands of small, rural outlets which are poorly connected via roads. The MDC owners use handcarts to transport Coca-Cola products to smaller, rural outlets in their region. Coca-Cola says that its MDC network handles the distribution of more than 80 percent of its business in some East African countries, providing employment for 13,500 people.[46]

Pricing Strategy

When it comes to designing a global pricing strategy, the value-pricing principle from Chapter 5 still generally applies. Marketers need to understand in each country what consumer perceptions of the value of the brand are, their willingness to pay, and their elasticities with respect to price changes. Sometimes differences in these considerations permit variations in pricing strategies.

Brands such as Levi's, Heineken, and Perrier have been able to command a much higher price outside their domestic market because in other countries they have a distinctly different brand image—and thus, sources of brand equity—that consumers value. But setting drastically different prices across countries can be difficult.[47] Pressures for international price alignment have arisen, in part because of the increasing numbers of legitimate imports and exports and the ability of retailers and suppliers to exploit price differences through "gray imports" across borders. There are three options for varying prices offered in different global markets. The first is to create an international "price corridor" that takes into account both the inherent differences between countries and alignment pressures. Specifically, the corridor is calculated by company headquarters and its country subsidiaries by considering market data for the individual countries, price elasticities in the countries, parallel imports resulting from price differentials, currency exchange rates, costs in countries and arbitrage costs between them, and data on competition and distribution. No country is then allowed to set its price outside the corridor. The second is to introduce different brands in high-price, high-income countries and in low-price, low-income countries, depending on the relative cost trade-offs of standardization versus customization.[48] Third, developing a completely new product for a local market using indigenous materials is another way to provide competitive offerings. For instance, in order to offer an affordable alternative to hospitals, GE Healthcare developed a portable ultrasound machine, which is significantly cheaper than existing alternatives, for emerging markets.[49]

MARKETING TO CONSUMERS IN DEVELOPING AND DEVELOPED MARKETS

Perhaps the most basic distinction we make between the countries that global brands enter is whether they are developing or have developed markets. The distinction between developing and developed markets is increasingly blurring, as some markets such as China have a large GDP, even though their infrastructure and resources are limited, relative to their more developed counterparts. Some of the most important developing markets are captured by the acronym BRICS (for Brazil, Russia, India, China, and South Africa).[50] A few interesting facts about consumers in emerging and developing markets are the following:

1. Eighty percent of consumers in emerging markets buy their products from tiny bodegas, stalls, kiosks, and mom-and-pop stores not much bigger than a closet.
2. Smaller packaging and lower sales prices are often critical when incomes and housing spaces are limited.
3. Many companies (e.g., Procter & Gamble and Unilever) have devised cheaper, clever ways to make the right kinds of products to suit consumer demand.
4. Mobile and digital strategies may take on greater importance given the relatively high smart phone penetration.

TEN COMMANDMENTS TO BUILDING GLOBAL CUSTOMER-BASED BRAND EQUITY

In designing and implementing a global brand marketing program, marketers want to realize the advantages while suffering as few of the disadvantages as possible.[51] This section explores in more detail how to tactically build strong global brands, relying on the "Ten Commandments of Global Branding" (see Figure 15-3).

FIGURE 15-3

The Commandments of Global Branding

1. Understand similarities and differences in the global branding landscape.
2. Do not take shortcuts in brand building.
3. Establish marketing infrastructure.
4. Embrace integrated marketing communications.
5. Cultivate brand partnerships.
6. Balance standardization and customization.
7. Balance global and local control.
8. Establish operable guidelines.
9. Implement a global brand equity measurement system.
10. Leverage brand elements.

1. **Understand Similarities and Differences in the Global Branding Landscape**

    The first—and most fundamental—guideline is to recognize that international markets can vary in terms of brand development, consumer behavior, marketing infrastructure, competitive activity, legal restrictions, and so on. Virtually every top global brand and company adjusts its marketing program in some way across some markets but holds the parameters fixed in other markets. The best examples of global brands often retain a thematic consistency and alter specific elements of the marketing mix in accordance with consumer behavior and the competitive situation in each country. Marketers should also resist the attempt to view a single continent or country as a unified market with similar tastes. For example, Latin America consists of many country-specific and regional differences. Many companies such as McDonald's, Coca-Cola, and Puma have realized the benefits of local and regional campaigns when it comes to Latin-American markets.[52]

2. **Do Not Take Shortcuts in Brand Building**

    In terms of building global customer-based brand equity, many of the basic tactics we discussed in Part II of the text still apply. In particular, we must create brand awareness and a positive brand image in each country in which a brand is sold. The means may differ from country to country, or the actual sources of brand equity themselves may vary. Nevertheless, it is critically important to have sufficient levels of brand awareness and strong, favorable, and unique brand associations to provide sources of brand equity in each country. Volkswagen has struggled to gain a strong foothold in the U.S. market because, unlike its Asian import competitors, it has been less willing to modify its designs for U.S. buyers. Although it has ambitious goals for global auto supremacy, one industry analyst noted, "They need to spend much more time understanding the U.S. consumer."[53]

    Building a brand in new markets must be done from the bottom up. Strategically, that means concentrating on building awareness first, before the brand image. Tactically, or operationally, it means determining how to best create sources of brand equity in new markets. Distribution, communication, and pricing strategies may not be appropriate in any two markets, even if the same overall brand image is desired in both. If the brand is at an earlier stage of development, rather than alter it or the advertising to conform to local tastes, marketers will try to influence local behavior to fit the established uses of the brand. Consumer education then accompanies brand-development efforts.

    This guideline suggests the need for patience, and the possibility of backtracking on brand development, to engage in a set of marketing programs and activities that the brand has long since moved beyond in its original markets. Marketers sometimes fail to realize that in their own country, they are building on a foundation of perhaps decades of carefully compiled associations in customers' minds. Although the period needed to build the brand in new markets may be compressed, it will still take some time.

    The temptation—and often the mistake—is to export the current marketing program because it seems to work. Although that may be the case, the fact that a marketing program can meet with acceptance or even some success doesn't mean it is the best way to build strong, sustainable, global brand equity. An important key to success is to understand each consumer, recognize what he or she knows or could value about the brand, and tailor marketing programs to his or her desires.

3. **Establish Marketing Infrastructure**

    A critical success factor for many global brands is their manufacturing, distribution, and logistical advantages. These brands have created the appropriate marketing infrastructure, from scratch if necessary, and adapted to capitalize on the existing marketing infrastructure in other countries. We noted that channels especially vary in their stages of development. Chain grocers have a 50 percent share in China, 40 percent in Russia, but only 15 percent in India.[54] Concerned about poor refrigeration in European stores, Häagen-Dazs ended up supplying thousands of free freezers to retailers across the continent.[55]

    Companies go to great lengths to ensure consistency in product quality across markets. McDonald's gets more than 90 percent of its raw materials from local suppliers and will even expend resources to create the necessary inputs if they are not locally available. Hence, investing to improve potato farms in Russia is standard practice because French fries are one of McDonald's core products and a key source of brand equity. More often, however, companies have to adapt production and distribution operations, invest in foreign partners, or both in order to succeed abroad. General Motors's success in Brazil—in the 1990s, after years of mediocre performance—came about in part because of its concerted efforts to develop a lean manufacturing program and a sound dealership strategy to create the proper marketing infrastructure.[56]

4. **Embrace Integrated Marketing Communications**

   Many top global firms have introduced extensive integrated marketing communications programs. Overseas markets do not have the same advertising opportunities as the expansive, well-developed U.S. media market. As a result, U.S.-based marketers have had to embrace other forms of communication in those markets—such as sponsorship, promotions, public relations, merchandising activity, and so on—to a much greater extent.

   To help make the quintessentially Vermont brand Ben & Jerry's more locally relevant in Britain, the company ran a contest to create the "quintessential British ice cream flavor." Finalists covered the gamut of the British cultural spectrum and included references to royalty (Cream Victoria and Queen Yum Mum), rock and roll (John Lemon and Ruby Chewsday), literature (Grape Expectations and Agatha Crispie), and Scottish heritage (Nessie's Nectar and Choc Ness Monster). Other finalists included Minty Python, Cashew Grant, and James Bomb. The winning flavor, Cool Britannia, was a play on the popular British military anthem *Rule Britannia* and consisted of vanilla ice cream, English strawberries, and chocolate-covered Scottish shortbread.[57]

   A global firm can utilize an integrated marketing communications approach to address the needs of multilingual populations. For instance, many Hispanic-American households speak a mix of Spanish and English. While there are potential pitfalls of appealing to multiple ethnic and cultural identities with a single ad, this approach can also yield rich rewards. In Branding Brief 15-3, we showcase some research on marketing to bicultural consumers using communications that are bilingual, which highlights the importance of this approach.

5. **Cultivate Brand Partnerships**

   Most global brands have marketing partners of some form in their international markets, ranging from joint venture partners, licensees or franchisees, and distributors, to advertising

BRANDING BRIEF 15-3
Marketing to Bicultural Consumers Using Bilingual Advertising

Consider María Perez who lives in New York City with her husband and two young children under two. María and her husband Miguel both moved from Mexico when they were in their teens and speak fluent Spanish. They watch the Spanish-language television network, Univision, and stay in touch with their extended family in Mexico via Facebook. The multicultural consumer landscape comprising individuals like María and Miguel is large, makes up nearly 40 percent of the U.S. population, and globally, includes nearly 232 million people living outside their home countries. This population poses a unique challenge to companies.

In deciding how to advertise to multiculturals, the first consideration is that members of these ethnically diverse populations may be at different stages of assimilation into the host culture, meaning they will have varying degrees of receptiveness to bicultural marketing efforts. Bicultural people are those who identify equally with both their home and host cultures, and bilingual advertisements—ads involving the blending of words from the home language—can be extra appealing to the bicultural population under certain circumstances.

However, it is important to realize that bilingual ads only work when paired with the right type of brand, or brands which do not have strong monocultural connotations. For example, McDonald's and Coca-Cola are strong cultural symbols of the American

identity; when people see McDonald's and Coca-Cola, they are reminded of what it means to be "American." In contrast, Coors Brewing Co. and GAP clothing are neutral in cultural symbolism. Research has identified sharp contrasts in how biculturals living in the United States responded to advertising. Advertisements with bilingual messaging fell flat among these consumers when used with brands with high cultural symbolism, and they were better received when paired with less culturally symbolic brands.

In essence, marketing to a bicultural audience means appealing to two identities, and it is important to ensure the associations of the brand mesh well with the themes of the bilingual or multicultural advertising. It is also important to evolve an integrated communications approach which incorporates bilingual and multicultural themes across a range of marketing activations including traditional advertising, sponsorships, promotions and online digital and social media advertising.

Sources: "Number of International Migrants Rises Above 23 Million, UN Reports," *UN News,* September 11, 2013, www.un.org/appsnewsstory .aspNewsID=45819#.VeRmS5eYFSN; Umut Kubat and Vanitha Swaminathan, "Crossing the Cultural Divide through Bilingual Advertising: The Moderating Role of Brand Cultural Symbolism," *International Journal of Research in Marketing* 32, no. 4 (2015): 354–362.

agencies and other marketing support people. Barwise and Robertson identify three alternative ways to enter a new global market:[58]

1. By exporting existing brands of the firm into the new market (introducing a "geographic extension")
2. By acquiring existing brands already sold in the new market but not owned by the firm
3. By creating some form of brand alliance with another firm (joint ventures, partnerships, or licensing agreements)

The choice of entry strategy depends in part on how the resources and objectives of the firm match up with each strategy's costs and benefits. Procter & Gamble would enter new markets in categories in which it excels (diapers, detergents, and sanitary pads), building its infrastructure and then bringing in other categories such as personal care or health care. Heineken's sequential strategy was slightly different. The company first entered a new market by exporting to build brand awareness and image. If the market response was deemed satisfactory, the company licensed its brands to a local brewer in hopes of expanding volume. If that relationship were successful, Heineken might then take an equity stake or forge a joint venture, piggybacking sales of its high-priced brand with an established local brand.[59] As a result, Heineken is the world's third-largest brewer in volume, selling in more than 170 countries with a product portfolio of more than 250 brands. With brewing operations in about 70 countries and export activities all over the world, Heineken is the most international brewery group in the world.[60]

One common reason for establishing brand partnerships is to gain access to distribution. When Starbucks made its entry into the India market, it entered into a joint venture with the India's conglomerate Tata. Tata Starbucks Ltd. is a 50:50 joint venture company, co-owned by both Tata Global Beverages and Starbucks Corporation, that jointly owns and operates Starbucks outlets in India. This is one example of how involving a local partner (Tata) helped Starbucks use their partner's extensive distribution expertise and knowledge to enter into the India market.[61]

Another goal of partnerships could be to leverage the partner's equity and associations to establish brand presence in a foreign market. For example, Under Armour replaced Puma in supplying footwear and equipment to Tottenam Hotspur, which is a well-known professional football club based in North London. This was launched in 2012 as a five-year campaign and helped Under Armour gain immediate brand recognition.

Companies are sometimes legally required to partner with a local company, as in many Middle Eastern countries, or when entering certain markets, such as insurance and telecoms in India. In other cases, companies elect to establish a joint venture with a corporate partner as a fast and convenient way to enter complex foreign markets. Joint ventures have been popular in Japan, where convoluted distribution systems, tightly knit supplier relationships, and

TATA Global Beverages and Starbucks Corporation formed a joint venture called
TATA-Starbucks Private Limited to own and operate Starbucks retail outlets in India.

close business–government cooperation have long encouraged foreign companies to link up with knowledgeable local partners.[62] Sometimes, the mode of entry could involve a merger.

As these examples illustrate, different entry strategies have been adopted by different firms, by the same firm in different countries, or even in combination by one firm in the same country. Entry strategies can also evolve over time. Branding Brief 15-4 describes how global brand powerhouse Nestlé has entered new markets.

6. Balance Standardization and Customization

As we discussed earlier, one implication of similarities and differences across international markets is that marketers need to blend local and global elements in their marketing programs. The challenge, of course, is to get the right balance—to know which elements to customize or adapt and which to standardize. Some of the factors often suggested in favor of a more standardized global marketing program include the following:

- Common customer needs
- Global customers and channels
- Favorable trade policies and common regulations
- Compatible technical standards
- Transferable marketing skills

BRANDING BRIEF 15-4
Managing Global Nestlé Brands

For about 15 years, starting in 1984, Nestlé spent more than $30 billion on acquisitions in different countries, including such major brands as Carnation dairy (and other) products (United States), Perrier (France) and San Pellegrino (Italy) mineral water, Stouffer's frozen foods (United States), Rowntree confectionery (United Kingdom), Ralston Purina pet food (United States), and Buitoni-Perugina pasta and chocolate (Italy). Thus, major acquisitions yielded valuable economies of scale to Nestlé in developed markets.

In less-developed markets, however, the company adopted a different strategy. Its entry strategy there was to manipulate ingredients or processing technology for local conditions and then apply the appropriate brand name—existing brands like Nescafé coffee, in some cases, and new brands, such as Bear brand condensed milk in Asia, in others. Nestlé strove to get into markets first and was patient; it negotiated for more than a decade to enter China. To limit risks and simplify its efforts in new markets, the company attacked with a handful of labels selected from a set of strategic brand groups. Then, it concentrated its advertising and marketing money on just two or three brands.

Nestlé attempts to balance global and local control in managing its brands. Some decisions, such as branding, follow strict corporate guidelines. The company has six *strategic corporate brands*—Nestlé, Nescafé, Nestea, Maggi, Buitoni, and Purina. There are 70 different *strategic international brands*, including Nesquik line of chocolate milk products, as well as product brands Kit Kat, Friskies, and Perrier. There are 83 *strategic regional brands*, including Aquarel and Contrex. Finally, there are a host of *local brands* that are only important to particular countries. Their portfolio strategy is one that has a strong focus on nutrition, health, and wellness.

Nestlé had used a decentralized management approach, in which most decisions—apart from decisions about the worldwide and corporate brands—were primarily made by the local managers. In 1997, following many acquisitions, a new CEO determined

that Nestlé needed more formal central and regional control. The company consolidated factory management by region and combined oversight of similar products into strategic business units. Still, local managers retained the decision-making power necessary to adapt products to local tastes. For example, Nestlé continued to make 200 different varieties of its Nescafé instant coffee, each tuned to local palates.

Nestlé's more centralized management approach enabled the company to focus on growing its core brands at each level. From 1999 to 2003, organic growth (excluding acquisitions) was 5.1 percent, almost double competitor Unilever's organic growth rate of 2.7 percent. The rest of the decade saw Nestlé enjoy even more above-average market performance. Despite tough economic conditions, the company experienced organic growth of approximately 4.2 percent in 2015.

Sources: Carla Rapoport, "Nestlé's Brand Building Machine," *Fortune,* September 19, 1994, 147–156; The Economist, "Nestle: Daring, Defying, To Grow," August 5, 2004, https://www.economist.com/special-report/2004/08/05/daring-defying-to-grow, accessed November 25, 2018; Laura MacInnis, "Nestlé Outshines Peers, Expects Stronger 2010," *Reuters,* February 19, 2010, https://uk.reuters.com/article/us-nestle/nestle-outshines-peers-expects-stronger-2010-idUSTRE61I1MK20100219, accessed November 25, 2018; Nestle Press Release, "Full Year 2011: 7.5% Organic Growth, +60 Basis Points Margin Improvement," February 16, 2012, https://www.nestle.com/media/pressreleases/allpressreleases/full-year-results-2011, accessed November 25, 2018; Jean-Nöel Kapferer, *The New Strategic Brand Management: Advanced Insights and Strategic Thinking,* 5th ed. (London: Kogan-Page, 2012); www.nestle.com/asset-library/documents/library/documents/annual_reports/2015-annual-review-en.pdf; Corinne Gretler, "Nestle Sales Beat Estimates on Coffee as Competition Heats Up," *Bloomberg Businessweek,* April 14, 2016, Nestle Press Release, "Nestle Nine-Month Sales: 3.3% Organic Growth, 2.5% Real Internal Growth | Full-Year Outlook: Organic Growth Around 3.5% with Margin Improvement," October 20, 2016, www.nestle.com/media/pressreleases/allpressreleases/nine-month-sales-2016.

What types of products are likely to sell through standardized global marketing programs? The following are likely candidates for global campaigns that retain a similar marketing strategy worldwide:

1. **High-technology products with strong functional images:** Examples are computers, watches, digital cameras, and automobiles.
2. **High-image products with strong associations to fashionability, sensuality, wealth, or status:** Examples are cosmetics, clothes, jewelry, and liquor.
3. **Services and business-to-business products that emphasize corporate images in their global marketing campaigns:** Examples are airlines and banks.
4. **Retailers that sell to upper-class individuals or that specialize in a salient but unfulfilled need:** By offering a wide variety of toys at affordable prices, Toys"R"Us transformed the European toy market, getting Europeans to buy toys for children at any time of the year, not just Christmas, and forcing competitors to level prices across countries.[63]
5. **Brands positioned primarily on the basis of their country of origin:** An example is Australia's Foster's beer, which ran the "How to Speak Australian" ad campaign for years in the United States.
6. **Products that do not need customization or other special products to be able to function properly:** ITT Corporation found that stand-alone products such as heart pacemakers could easily be sold the same way worldwide, but that integrated products such as telecommunications equipment have to be tailored to function within local phone systems.[64]

7. **Balance Global and Local Control**
Building brand equity in a global context must be a carefully designed and implemented process. A key decision in developing a global marketing program is choosing the most appropriate organizational structure for managing global brands. In general, there are three main approaches to organizing for a global marketing effort:

1. Centralization at home office or headquarters
2. Decentralization of decision making to local foreign markets
3. Some combination of centralization and decentralization.

In general, firms tend to adopt a combination of centralization and decentralization to better balance local adaptation and global standardization.[65] Organizationally, Kimberly-Clark created mechanisms which facilitated information sharing across regions, including the creation of a global marketing Web site which provides information about best practices within the organization across various regions. Further, they also instituted a Global Marketing University which brought together executives from various regions and was also a method to enhance sharing of knowledge and best practice information. The overall approach was to provide autonomy to subsidiaries while at the same time utilizing centralized approaches to strengthen brand consistency.

In a similar approach to Kimberly-Clark, Lexus also overhauled its global marketing approach.[66] Its NX compact crossover and RC sporty coupe were launched using a new unified global approach. Previously, ad and brand messages were developed separately in each country. For the NX and RC launches, however, brand positioning was developed jointly by global marketers to ensure consistency of theme and message. The shared strategy and creative executions also resulted in significant efficiencies. Lexus U.S. sales results rose 19 percent in 2014 and exceeded BMW and Mercedes, despite lagging behind these rivals earlier in the year.

Some firms such as GE, Intel, and AstraZeneca have adopted a T-shaped country organization that localizes customer-facing operations to allow for fast, detailed marketing actions while at the same distributing back-end activities (manufacturing, product development, R&D) across countries.[67] Cost and revenue should be the primary considerations in deciding which elements of the marketing program will be adapted for which country.

Many global companies divide their markets into five or so regions—for example, Europe, Asia, Latin America, North America, and Africa/Middle East. A key theme is the need to balance global and local control. Coca-Cola, for example, distinguishes between local marketing activities that would appear to dilute brand equity and those that are not as effective as desired. Headquarters would stop the first from occurring but would not stop the latter, leaving the activity's appropriateness to the local manager's judgment but also holding him or her responsible for its success. Similarly, Levi Strauss & Co. has balanced global and local control with a "thermometer" model. Marketing elements below the "freezing point" are fixed: "brand soul" (akin to brand essence or mantra) and logos are standardized worldwide. Above the freezing point, product quality, pricing, advertising, distribution, and promotions are all fluid, meaning each international division can handle thc marketing mix elements in any way that it feels is appropriate for its region.

8. **Establish Operable Guidelines**

   Brand definitions and guidelines must be established, communicated, and properly enforced so marketers in different regions have a good understanding of what they are and are not expected to do. The goal is for everyone within the organization to understand the brand's meaning and be able to translate it to satisfy local consumer preferences. Brand definition and communication often revolve around two related issues. First, some sort of document, such as a brand charter or a global brand positioning statement document, should detail what the brand is and what it is not. Second, the product line should reflect only those products consistent with the brand definition

   As an example of deriving product strategy from a brand definition, consider Disney. Everyone at the company is exposed to the Disney brand mantra, "fun family entertainment" (see Branding Brief 2-4). To establish global guidelines, Disney's centralized marketing group worked with members of the consumer products group for months to assign virtually every possible product to one of three categories:

   - Acceptable to license without permission (such as T-shirts)
   - Not permissible to ever license (such as toilet paper)
   - Requires validation from headquarters to license (about 20 categories, including air fresheners)

   Finally, for all this planning to work, there must be effective lines of communication. Coca-Cola stresses the importance of having people on the ground who can effectively manage the brand in concert with headquarters in Atlanta. To facilitate coordination, much training occurs at the company's headquarters; a sophisticated communication system is in place; and global databases are available. The goal of this heavily integrated information system is to facilitate the local manager's ability to tap into what constitutes "relevance" in any particular country and then communicate those ideals to headquarters.

9. **Implement a Global Brand Equity Measurement System**

   As the guidelines in Chapter 9 indicate, a global brand equity measurement system is a set of research procedures designed to provide timely, accurate, and actionable information for marketers on brands, so they can make the best possible tactical decisions in the short run and strategic decisions in the long run in all relevant markets. As part of this system, a global brand equity management system defines the brand equity charter in a global context, outlining how to interpret the brand positioning and resulting marketing program in different markets, as suggested by the previous global branding commandment.[68] With the global brand strategy template in place, brand tracking can assess progress, especially in terms of creating the desired positioning, eliciting the proper responses, and developing brand resonance.

LEVI STRAUSS

Levi Strauss & Co. continually monitors its brand equity among consumers in most of its key markets around the world. The company developed "Brand Value Propositions" for each of its major brands. These are a set of enduring strategies that define each brand and differentiate it from competition. They succinctly list the brand's global positioning (including frame of reference and point-of-difference), its global character, and its global "building blocks" or desired state regarding consumer wants and needs. The Brand Value Propositions drive all brand strategies and actions and provide a globally consistent platform for regionally relevant product and marketing execution. In tracking each brand's equity via ongoing consumer surveys, Levi Strauss & Co. monitors the consumer's perceptions and interactions with its brands; the impact that its clothes, retail distribution, marketing, and other touchpoints are having on consumers; and whether the results of its efforts are in line with its Brand Value Propositions. Through these efforts, Levi Strauss & Co. is able to tailor brand strategies to ensure each brand is meeting consumer needs while being true to its essence.

10. Leverage Brand Elements

Proper design and implementation of brand elements can often be critical to the successful building of global brand equity. As Figure 15-2 showed, a number of brands have encountered resistance because of difficulty in translating their name, packaging, slogans, or other brand elements to another culture. In general, nonverbal brand elements such as logos, symbols, and characters are more likely to directly transfer well—at least as long as their meaning is visually clear—than verbal brand elements that may need to be translated into another

1. Understand similarities and differences in the global branding landscape.
- Have you tried to find as many commonalities as possible across markets?
- Have you identified what is unique about different markets?
- Have you examined all aspects of the marketing environment (e.g., stages of brand development, consumer behavior, marketing infrastructure, competitive activity, legal restrictions)?
- Have you reconciled these similarities and differences in the most cost-effective and brand-building manner possible?

2. Do not take shortcuts in brand building.
- Have you ensured that the brand is being built from the bottom up strategically by creating brand awareness first before crafting the brand image?
- Have you ensured that the brand is being built from the bottom up tactically by determining the appropriate marketing programs and activity for the brand in each market given the particular strategic goals?

3. Establish marketing infrastructure.
- Have you created the appropriate marketing infrastructure—in terms of manufacturing, distribution, and logistics—from scratch, if necessary?
- Have you adapted to capitalize on the existing marketing infrastructure in other countries?

4. Embrace integrated marketing communications.
- Have you considered nontraditional forms of communication that go beyond conventional advertising?
- Have you ensured that all communications are integrated in each market and are consistent with the brand's desired positioning and heritage?

5. Cultivate brand partnerships.
- Have you formed partnerships with global and local partners to improve possible deficiencies in your marketing programs?
- Have you ensured that all partnerships avoid compromising the brand promise and do not harm brand equity in any way?

6. Balance standardization and customization.
- Have you been careful to retain elements of marketing programs that are relevant and add value to the brand across all markets?
- Have you sought to find local adaptations and additions that complement and supplement these global elements to achieve greater local appeal?

7. Balance global and local control.
- Have you established clear managerial guidelines as to principles and actions that all global managers must adhere to?
- Have you carefully delineated the areas in which local managers are given discretion and autonomy in their decision making?

8. Establish operable guidelines.
- Have you explicated brand management guidelines in a clear and concise fashion in a document to be used by all global marketers?
- Have you established means of seamless communication between headquarters and local and regional marketing organizations?

9. Implement a global brand equity measurement system.
- Do you conduct brand audits when appropriate in overseas markets?
- Have you devised a brand tracking system to provide timely, accurate, and actionable information on brands in relevant markets?
- Have you established a global brand equity management system with brand equity charters, brand equity reports, and brand equity overseers?

10. Leverage brand elements.
- Have you checked the relevance of brand elements in global markets?
- Have you established visual brand identities that transfer across market boundaries?

FIGURE 15-4

Self-Evaluation Ratings for the 10 Commandments of Global Branding language. Nonverbal brand elements are more likely to be helpful in creating brand awareness than brand image, however, which may require more explicit meaning and direct statements. If the meaning of a brand element is visually clear, it can be an invaluable source of brand equity worldwide. Even Web sites dedicated to brands can be an important source of brand equity, and standardizing some aspects of the Web site, while varying others, is an important consideration in managing a brand for a global market.

REVIEW

Increasingly, marketers must properly define and implement a global branding strategy. Some advantages of a global marketing program are economies of scale in production and distribution, lower marketing costs, communication of power and scope, consistency in brand image, an ability to leverage good ideas quickly and efficiently, and uniformity of marketing practices, and thus, greater competitiveness. The more standardized the marketing program, in general, the more the firm can actually realize these different advantages.

At the same time, the primary disadvantages of a standardized global marketing program are that it may ignore important differences across countries in various areas: consumer needs, wants, and usage patterns for products; consumer response to marketing mix elements; product development and the competitive environment; the legal environment; marketing institutions; and administrative procedures.

In developing a global marketing program, marketers attempt to obtain as many of these advantages as possible while minimizing any possible disadvantages. Building global customer-based brand equity means creating brand awareness and a positive brand image in each country in which the brand is sold.

Marketers are blending global objectives with local or regional concerns. The means by which brand equity is built may differ from country to country, or the actual sources of brand equity themselves may vary across countries in terms of specific attribute or benefit associations. Nevertheless, there must be sufficient levels of brand awareness and strong, favorable, and unique brand associations in each country in which the brand is sold to provide sources of brand equity.

Some of the biggest differences in global marketing occur between developed and developing or emerging markets. Because of the extremely low incomes and differences in consumer behavior in developing markets, marketers must fundamentally rethink every aspect of their marketing program.

In general, in entering a new market of any kind, it is necessary to identify differences in consumer behavior (how consumers purchase and use products and what they know and feel about brands) and adjust the branding program accordingly (through the choice of brand elements, nature of the supporting marketing program, and leverage of secondary associations).

Figure 15-4 lists the "Ten Commandments of Global Branding" along with a series of questions that can be asked to help guide effective global brand management.

DISCUSSION QUESTIONS

1. Pick a product category. How are different leading brands targeting different geodemographic market segments? How are brands targeting different ethnic groups with their advertising?
2. Pick a brand marketed in more than one country. Assess the extent to which the brand is marketed on a standardized versus customized basis. (Note: An excellent resource to identify global brands is the annual global brand survey from Interbrand, accessed via www.interbrand.com).
3. Pick a product category. Consider the strategies of market leaders in different countries. How are they the same, and how are they different?
4. Identify how consumers' usage of social media and digital marketing channels varies across markets. How can a brand manager utilize this information to improve their brand presence in different global markets?

BRAND FOCUS 15.0
China's Global Brand Ambitions

Growth at Home

China, the world's most populous country, with more than 1.3 billion people, was essentially closed to the West during the period from the Communist overthrow of the government in 1949 until gradual economic reforms began in 1978, culminating with China's admission into the World Trade Organization in 2001. Since reforms began, China has industrialized at a remarkable rate and is now the world's second-largest economy, a manufacturing giant boasting a record $41 billion trade surplus in 2016.[69]

The statistics of China's production are staggering. China accounts for 25 percent of all manufacturing worldwide; further, it produces about 80 percent of the world's air conditioners, 70 percent of its mobile phones, and 60 percent of its shoes.[70] The primary reason for China's manufacturing prowess is its remarkably cheap labor pool. Recently, due to labor shortages and strikes, there has been a push to increase wages. In the financial capital of Shanghai, which has the highest minimum wage in China, the monthly rate increased from 1,120 yuan in 2010 to 2,190 yuan (US $327) in 2016.[71] The following sections will illustrate the successes and difficulties that characterize modern China.

A Growing Consumer Class

China's rise to a global economic superpower enriched many of its citizens; it has the world's largest number of billionaires, and nearly four million are now millionaires.[72] With this newfound wealth came an interest in consuming conspicuously, which precipitated a windfall for foreign luxury-goods manufacturers. With a rapidly expanding middle class, China went from consuming 1 percent of the world's luxury goods in 2001 to 20 percent in 2015, making the country the world's largest luxury market.[73] Roughly half these luxuries are being bought on the mainland; the other half, abroad.[74] China's vast population of only children—called "Little Emperors" for the way many are doted on by their parents—are expected to drive demand for luxury goods for years to come.[75]

Luxury brands have flocked to China to try to cash in. L'Oréal purchased the country's most popular cosmetics brand, Yue Sai, and bought bargain brand Mininurse, with an enviable distribution network of more than 250,000 small stores. L'Oréal also invested in a 32,000-square-foot laboratory in Pudong to develop products specific to the Chinese market and containing local ingredients such as ginkgo leaf and ginseng. One of the company's big challenges in China was educating consumers about the benefits of different cosmetic products. "In other countries, women learn how to use cosmetics from the mom," said Paolo Gasparrini, president of L'Oréal China. "That's not the case in China. We have to substitute [for the] mom." Still, L'Oréal experienced double-digit sales increases for 11 years, approaching $2.3 billion in sales in 2015.[76] L'Oréal also effectively leveraged digital marketing strategies to catapult its sales. Most Chinese consumers use mobile phones to search for information (80 percent of Baidu's searches take place on mobile devices), buy products, or even get food delivered. L'Oréal leveraged this by creating a unique app called Makeup Genius (https://youtu.be/iSdU9jmscBg), in which women can try on makeup products virtually and wait for the "Magic" (the name of a L'Oréal brand) to happen.[77]

Despite the fortunate wealthy few, vast numbers of urban and (especially) rural poor have been left behind. Rural workers earn half the average salary of urban factory workers, often not

Lenovo, a brand which originated in China, is the largest PC manufacturer in terms of market share worldwide.

enough to send their children to school. Consequently, rural Chinese are migrating to cities in search of better-paying jobs, increasing urban congestion and unemployment rates. By 2016, an estimated 55 percent of the population lived in cities, aggravating these problems.[78] Despite the concerns generated by this wealth polarization, China's consumer class still harbors enough purchasing power to attract foreign brands, as the next section describes.

A number of foreign brands have entered the Chinese market. Popular U.S. brands include General Motors' automobile brands such as Chevrolet, Buick, and Cadillac. GM China (co-owned by Shanghai Automotive Industry Corp) had 15 percent market share and sold more than 3.6 million cars in China.[79] Another dominant brand in China is Apple with 83 percent market share of the tablet category. Starbucks currently has 2,300 stores in China but is expected to increase to more than 5,000 stores by 2021. In the words of Howard Schultz, ex-CEO and chairman of Starbucks," There's no doubt at some point China will exceed the U.S."[80] The next section highlights the strength of one Chinese brand, Lenovo, which effectively competes with and beats foreign competition.

Lenovo in China

If you were to visit Zhongguancun—the electronics district in Beijing—you would find a Lenovo store at every turn. It is no wonder that the ubiquitous Lenovo (with more than 100 stores in this electronics district) is the number one PC seller in China, with a network of more than 15,000 stores, an international workforce of 27,000 employees (including 4,000 engineers worldwide as of 2017), 10 international laboratories, and a global presence in more than 160 countries. Worldwide, Lenovo is the largest PC manufacturer with nearly 19 percent of the worldwide market share. It recently introduced a gaming laptop (called Legion) in countries like Korea, Taiwan, Thailand, and India where there is a large consumer demand for gaming. In addition to PCs, laptops (ThinkPad), and phones (Motorola smartphones), it also has a series of products such as the VR headset and Lenovo Smart Assistant that show that it has diversified into related categories. The Lenovo Smart Assistant (expected to be sold for $129 and launched in 2017) is part of a line of new products called Smart Home. Overall, Lenovo's product portfolio demonstrates its readiness to maintain its leadership position in PCs and other electronics.

Founder Liu Chuanzhi (Chairman Liu) in 1984 started the Chinese Academy of Sciences Computer Technology Research Institute New Technology Development Co., which formed a partnership with AST. The company was reorganized in 1990, and by 1997, Lenovo was the top selling PC maker in China. In 2005, Lenovo paid $1.75 billion for IBM's PC business, an acquisition which made Liu a national hero. Speed of decision-making is key to the company's success. "Fu pan" (which translates to replaying the chess board), or the emphasis on examining every strategic move with a view toward improving it, is a key to their success. They also examine every strategic move of their competitors such as Dell and HP in an effort to improve their success. Their global approach includes meetings of top 100 executives from various countries.

Their ad campaign was built around the slogan, "For Those Who Do," and features computers as "do machines" that empower people to use them in different ways. Various markets featured different executions of the same theme. For Japan, the advertising campaign turned laptop into a Japanese train terminal, while in Indonesia, billboards featured a Lenovo-branded climbing wall that "doers" could use.

Overall, Lenovo approaches its global market with a great deal of care and caution, identifying the right markets for its products and deploying its global advertising strategy with a mix of local executions. This "protect and attack" approach has yielded rich rewards and will likely secure Lenovo's future.

Sources: http://economictimes.indiatimes.com/magazines/panache/motorola; Gartner, Inc., "Gartner Says Worldwide PC Shipments Declined 9.6 Percent in First Quarter of 2016," April 11, 2016, www.gartner.com/newsroom/id/3280626; Patrick Moorhead, "Lenovo Enters the Smart Home, Gets Aggressive in Gaming, AR and Premium X1 Line at CES 2017," *Forbes Magazine*, January 3, 2017, www.forbes.com/sites/partrickmoorhead/2017/01/03/lenovo-enters-the-smart-home-gets-aggressive-in-gaming-ar-and-premium-x1-line-at-ces2017/#6f93f23c2471; Chuck Salter, "Protect and Attack: Lenovo's New Strategy," *Fast Company*, November 22, 2011, Issue 161, pp. 116–155, https://www.fastcompany.com/1793529/protect-and-attack-lenovos-new-strategy, accessed November 25, 2018.

NOTES

1. For a more detailed discussion of branding in Asia, see Pierre Xiao Lu, *Elite China: Luxury Consumer Behavior in China* (Singapore: John Wiley & Sons, 2008); Martin Roll, *Asian Brand Strategy: How Asia Builds Strong Brands* (London: Palgrave Macmillan, 2005); and Paul Temporal, *Branding in Asia: The Creation, Development, and Management of Asian Brands for the Global Market* (New York: John Wiley & Sons, 2001).

2. AC Nielsen, "Spectra: Powerful Insights for Consumer Targeting," *Nielson*, accessed April 16, 2017, www.nielsen.com/content/dam/nielsen/en_us/documents/pdf/Fact%20Sheets/Nielsen%20Spectra%20Overview%20.

3. Pew Research Center, "Millennials," http://www.pewresearch.org/topics/millennials/, accessed November 26, 2018.

4. Shannon Greenwood, Andrew Perrin, and Maeve Duggan, "Social Media Update 2016," Pew Research Center, November 11, 2016, http://www.pewinternet.org/2016/11/11/social-media-update-2016/, accessed November 26, 2018.

5. Michael Del Gigante, "Campbell's Soup Goes 'All In' on Marketing to Millennials," MDG Advertising, March 2, 2013, https://www.mdgadvertising.com/marketing-insights/campbells-soup-goes-all-in-on-marketing-to-millennials/, accessed November 26, 2018.

6. Campbell Soup Company, "Campbell's Go™ Sets the Table for Millennials with Communal Table Events in New York City and Chicago," Press Release, November 13, 2012, https://www.campbellsoupcompany.com/newsroom/press-releases/campbells-go-sets-the-table-for-millennials-with-communal-table-events-in-new-york-city-and-chicago/, accessed November 26, 2018.

7. Laurel Wentz, "Ad Age's 2016 Hispanic Fact Pack Is Out Now," AdvertisingAge, August 2, 2016, https://adage.com/article/ad-age-graphics/ad-age-s-2016-hispanic-fact-pack/305259/, accessed November 26, 2018; Sam Fahmy, "Despite Recession, Hispanic and Asian Buying Power Is Expected to Surge, According to Annual UGA Selig Center Multicultural Economy Study," *Terry College of Business*, November 4, 2010, https://news.uga.edu/despite-recession-hispanic-and-asian-buying-power-expected-to-surge-in-u-s/; Tom Tindle, "Advertising Strategies for Targeting U.S. Hispanics," *comScore*, October 26, 2011, www.comscore.com/ita/Insights/Blog/Advertising-Strategies-for-Targeting-U.S.-Hispanics.

8. The Nielsen Co. Press Release, "Nielsen 2016 Report: Black Millennials Close The Digital Divide," *Press Room*, October 17, 2016, www.nielsen.com/us/en/press-room/2016/nielsen-2016-report-black-millennials-close-the-digital-divide.html.

9. Based on material from Marlene L. Rossman, *Multicultural Marketing: Selling to a Diverse America* (New York: AMACOM, 1994); and Barbara Lloyd, *Capitalizing on the American Dream: Marketing to America's Ethnic Minorities,* Stanford Business School independent study, 1990; Richard C. Morais, "The Color of Beauty," *Forbes,* November 27, 2000, 170–176, https://www.forbes.com/forbes/2000/1127/6614170a.html#592dc3ac51ec, accessed November 26, 2018; Marcia Pledger, "There's No Debating One Thing: Hair Care Is a Healthy Business," *Cleveland Plain Dealer,* October 27, 2009, http://blog.cleveland.com/pdextra/2009/10/theres_no_debating_one_thing_h.html, accessed August 23, 2018; "Buying Power Among African Americans to Reach $1.1 Trillion by 2012," *Reuters,* February 6, 2008, https://www.huffingtonpost.com/2011/11/10/black-buying-power-to-rea_n_1086369.html, accessed August 23, 2018; Mike Beirne, "Has This Group Been Left Behind?," *Brandweek,* March 14, 2005, 46, no. 11 (2005): 33–36; Natalie Zmuda, "How Coke Is Targeting Black Consumers: Q&A with Yolanda White, Assistant VP of African-American Marketing," *Advertising Age,* July 1, 2009, http://adage.com/article/the-big-tent/marketing-coke-targeting-african-american-consumers/137716/, accessed August 23, 2018; Vernellia R. Randall, "Targeting of African Americans," in *Dying While Black* (Seven Principles Press, 2006).

10. Tom Tindle, "Advertising Strategies for Targeting U.S. Hispanics," *comScore*, October 26, 2011, www.comscore.com/ita/Insights/Blog/Advertising-Strategies-for-Targeting-U.S.-Hispanics, accessed February 22, 2017.

11. eMarketer.com, "Hispanics Make Social a Crucial Part of Digital Lives," *eMarketer*, May 28, 2015, www.emarketer.com/Article/Hispanics-Make-Social-Crucial-Part-of-Digital-Lives/1012534#sthash.8OnL3DA8.dpuf, accessed February 22, 2017.

12. Lisa Gevelber, "Your Next Big Opportunity: The U.S. Hispanic Market," Think with Google, accessed February 20, 2017, www.thinkwithgoogle.com/articles/us-hispanic-market-digital.html.

13. Macala Wright, "4 New Rules for Multicultural Marketing," *Mashable*, July 24, 2015, http://mashable.com/2015/07/24/multicultural-marketing-tactics/#.37eZ9LsjPqx.

14. The Nielsen Co., "Asian-Americans: Culturally Diverse and Expanding Their Footprint," *Nielson*, May 19, 2016, www.nielsen.com/us/en/insights/reports/2016/asian-americans-culturally-diverse-and-expanding-their-footprint.html; Pew Research Center, "Asian Americans: A Diverse and Growing Population," accessed November 26, 2018, www.pewsocialtrends.org/asianamericans-graphics/.

15. Jennifer L. Aaker, Anne M. Brumbaugh, and Sonya A. Grier, "Nontarget Markets and Viewer Distinctiveness: The Impact of Target Marketing on Advertising Attitudes," *Journal of Consumer Psychology* 9, no. 3 (2000): 127–140; Sonya A. Grier and Rohit Deshpande, "Social Dimensions of Consumer Distinctiveness: The Influence of Social Status on Group Identity and Advertising Persuasion," *Journal of Marketing Research* 38, no. 2 (May 2001): 216–224.

16. Shaoming Zou and S. Tamer Cavusgil, "The GMS: A Broad Conceptualization of Global Marketing Strategy and Its Effect on Firm Performance," *Journal of Marketing* 66, no. 4 (October 2002): 40–56.

17. Interbrand, "Best Global Brands 2017 Rankings," https://www.interbrand.com/best-brands/best-global-brands/2017/ranking/, accessed November 26, 2018.

18. David Kiley, "One World, One Car, One Name," *Bloomberg BusinessWeek*, March 13, 2008.

19. Dana L. Alden, Jan-Benedict E. M. Steenkamp, and Rajeev Batra, "Brand Positioning Through Advertising in Asia, North America, and Europe: The Role of Global Consumer Culture," *Journal of Marketing* 63, no. 1 (January 1999): 75–87.

20. Rakeev Batra, Venkatram Ramaswamy, Dana L. Alden, Jan-Benedict E. M. Steenkap, and S. Ramachander, "Effects of Brand Local and Nonlocal Origin on Consumer Attitudes in Developing Countries," *Journal of Consumer Psychology* 9, no. 2 (2000): 83–95; Jan-Benedict E. M. Steenkamp, Rajeev Batra, and Dana L. Alden, "How Perceived Globalness Creates Brand Value," *Journal of International Business Studies* 34, no. 1 (2003): 53–65.

21. Yuliya Strizhakova, Robin A. Coulter, and Linda L. Price, "Branding in a Global Marketplace: The Mediating Effects of Quality and Self-Identity Brand Signals," *International Journal of Research in Marketing* 28, no. 4 (2011): 342–351.

22. Corporate Executive Board, "Overcoming Executional Challenges in Global Brand Management," Marketing Leadership Council, Case Book, March 2001; Bernard L. Simonin and Segül Özsomer, "Knowledge Processes and Learning Outcomes in MNCs: An Empirical Investigation of the Role Of HRM Practices in Foreign Subsidiaries," *Human Resource Management* 48, no. 4 (July–August 2009): 505–530.

23. "World Health Organization Report," *World Health Organization*, accessed March 24, 2012, www .wh.int.

24. Jane Galvez, "Krispy Kreme Introduces the Double Hundred Dozen Doughnuts," *Franchise Herald*, September 23, 2014, www.franchiseherald.com/articles/ 7169/20140923/krispy-kreme.htm.

25. Emma Jacobs, "No Faux Pas in Any Language," *Financial Times*, February 17, 2012, https://www.ft.com/ content/d77459ae-57bc-11e1-b089-00144feabdc0, Accessed August 23, 2018.

26. CBC News, "GM Faces Car-Name Conundrum," October 2, 2009, https://www.cbc.ca/news/gm-faces-car-name-conundrum-1.775246, accessed November 26, 2018.

27. For example, see Niraj Dawar and Philip Parker, "Marketing Universals: Consumers' Use of Brand Name, Price, Physical Appearance, and Retailer Reputation as Signals of Quality," *Journal of Marketing* 58, no. 4 (April 1994): 81–95; and Ayşegül Özsomer, "The Interplay Between Global and Local Brands: A Closer Look at Perceived Brand Globalness and Local Iconness," *Journal of International Marketing*, 2012.

28. Nataly Kelly, "How Marketing Is Evolving in Latin America," *Harvard Business Review*, June 1, 2015, https:// hbr.org/2015/06/how-marketing-is-evolving-in-latin-america, accessed March 18, 2017; Ruth Reader, "More Than Half of All Smartphone Users in Latin America Use Twitter, Study Claims," *Venture Beat*, February 16, 2015, http://venturebeat.com/2015/02/16/more-than-half-of-all-smartphone-users-in-latin-america-use-twitter-study-claims/.

29. Digital Training Academy, "Snapchat Case Study: Burger King 'Grills' Competitors with Lenses Competition," May 2016, http://www.digitaltrainingacademy .com/casestudies/2016/05/snapchat_case_study_ burger_king_grills_competitors_with_lenses_ competition.php, accessed November 26, 2018.

30. Statista, "Household Penetration Rate of Home Appliances in India in 2013," accessed January 9, 2017, www .statista.com/statistics/370635/household-penetration-home-appliances-india/.

31. Laura Wood, Research and Markets, "India Detergent Market Overview 2016–2021," March 14, 2016, https://www.businesswire.com/news/ home/20160314006184/en/India-Detergent-Market-Overview-2016-2021---Research, accessed November 26, 2018; Rajni Pandey, "Small Is Big," IndianRetailer, July 2011, https://www.indianretailer.com/magazine/ 2011/july/Small-is-big.m47-2-3/, accessed November 26, 2018.

32. Nitish Singh, "A Localized Global Marketing Strategy," *Brand Quarterly*, June 25, 2012, http://www.brandquarterly .com/localized-global-marketing-strategy, accessed November 26, 2018.

33. Martin Beck, "FTC Puts Social Media Marketers on Notice with Updated Disclosure Guidelines,"*Marketing Gland*, June 12, 2015, http://marketingland.com/ftc-puts-social-media-marketers-on-notice-with-updated-disclosure-guidelines-132017; Marketing Interactive, "ASAS Issues New Guidelines for Digital and Social Media Marketing," *Maximize Social Business*, accessed April 16, 2017, https://www.marketing-interactive .com/asas-issues-new-guidelines-for-online-and-social-media-marketing/.

34. Ronan Shields, "What Does Shake-Up of EU Data Laws Mean for Marketers," *The Drum*, April 14, 2016, www.the-drum.com/news/2016/04/14/what-does-shake-cu-data-laws-mean-marketers-0.

35. Douglas B. Holt, John A. Quelch, and Earl L. Taylor, "How Global Brands Compete," *Harvard Business Review* 82, no. 9 (2004): 68–75; Ayşegül Özsomer, "The Interplay between Global and Local Brands: A Closer Look at Perceived Brand Globalness and Local Iconness," *Journal of International Marketing* 20, no. 2 (2012): 72–95; Jan-Benedict Steenkamp, *Global Brand Strategy World-Wise Marketing in the Age of Branding*, (Palgrave MacMillan, UK, 2017).

36. Yehong Zhu, "The World's Top-Selling Ice Cream Brands," *Forbes*, June 21, 2016, www.forbes.com/ sites/yehongzhu/2016/06/21/the-worlds-top-selling-ice-cream-brands-2/#66ecbae66a24.

37. Danny Kichi, "Did You Know There Are Over 300 Flavors of Japanese Kit Kat?," *Dramafever*, September 20, 2016, www.dramafever.com/news/did-you-know-there-are-over-300-flavors-of-japanese-kit-kat/.

38. Maureen Marston, "Transferring Equity Across Borders," paper presented at the ARF Fourth Annual Advertising and Promotion Workshop, February 12–13, 1992.

39. Joanne Lipman, "Marketers Turn Sour on Global Sales Pitch Harvard Guru Makes," *The Wall Street Journal*, May 12, 1988, 1.

40. Martin S. Roth, "The Effects of Culture and Socioeconomics on the Performance of Global Brand Image Strategies," *Journal of Marketing Research* 32, no. 2 (May 1995): 163–175.

41. Arun Bhattacharyya, Ramesh Kumar, and Vanitha Swaminathan, "Cultural Context and Advertising Appeals: The Indian Context," in *Perspectives on Indian Consumer Behavior*, eds. Durairaj Maheswaran and Thomas Puliyel (India: Oxford University Press, 2017).

42. Nicole Tufts, "Latin American Social Media 2015," *The Spark Group*, June 24, 2015, https:// thesparkgroup.com/latin-american-social-media/; eMarketer.com, "Latin America Loves Facebook," March 2, 2016, https://www.emarketer.com/Article/ Latin-America-Loves-Facebook/1013651, accessed November 26, 2018. Arun Bhattacharyya, Ramesh Kumar, and Vanitha Swaminathan, "Cultural Context and Advertising Appeals: The Indian Context," in *Perspectives on Indian Consumer Behavior*, eds. Durairaj Maheswaran and Thomas Puliyel (India: Oxford University Press, 2017).

43. Miriam Jordan, "In Rural India, Video Vans Sell Toothpaste and Shampoo," *The Wall Street Journal*, January 10, 1996, B1, B5.

44. Jim Prevor, "Tesco's Problem with Fresh & Easy—Why Is It So Hard for Retailers to Cross the Pond?," *Perishable Pundit*, September 9, 2011, http://www.perishable-pundit.com/index.php?hot=tesco, accessed November 26, 2018.

45. Weetabix East Africa, http://www.weetabixea.com/, accessed November 26, 2018.

46. Ashutosh Dekhne, "Winning Supply Chain Strategies for African Markets," *Supply Chain*, 2015, www.supplychainquarterly.com/topics/Strategy/20150331-winning-supply-chain-strategies-for-african-markets/.

47. Hermann Simon, "Pricing Problems in a Global Setting," *Marketing News,* October 9, 1995, 4.

48. See also Robert J. Dolan and Hermann Simon, *Power Pricing: How Managing Price Transforms the Bottom Line* (New York: Free Press, 1996).

49. Jeffrey R. Immelt, Vijay Govindarajan, and Chris Trimble, "How GE Is Disrupting Itself," *Harvard Business Review* 87, no. 10 (2009): 56–65.

50. Ruben Farzad, "The BRIC Debate: Drop Russia, Add Indonesia?," *Bloomberg BusinessWeek*, November 18, 2010, https://www.bloomberg.com/news/articles/2010-11-18/the-bric-debate-drop-russia-add-indonesia, accessed August 23, 2018.

51. For more information on global marketing and branding strategies, see George S. Yip, *Total Global Strategy* (Englewood Cliffs, NJ: Prentice Hall, 1996); Johny K. Johansson, *Global Marketing: Foreign Entry, Local Marketing, and Global Management*, 5th ed. (Burr Ridge, IL: McGraw-Hill-Irwin, 2009); Nigel Hollis, *The Global Brand: How to Create and Develop Lasting Brand Value in the World Market* (New York: Palgrave Macmillan, 2010).

52. IMS, "For Marketers, 'One-Size-Fits-All' Doesn't Fit in Latin America," *Mashable*, May 13, 2014, http://mashable.com/2014/05/13/brand-marketing-latam/#96dqIF6Y7Oq3.

53. Alex Taylor III, "VW's Grand Plan," *Fortune*, October 18, 2010, 162.

54. Bill Johnson, "The CEO of Heinz on Powering Growth in Emerging Markets," *Harvard Business Review*, October 2011 Issue, https://hbr.org/2011/10/the-ceo-of-heinz-on-powering-growth-in-emerging-markets, accessed November 26, 2018.

55. Mark Maremont, "They're All Screaming for Häagen-Dazs," *BusinessWeek,* October 4, 1991, 121.

56. Peter Fritsch and Gregory L. White, "Even Rivals Concede GM Has Deftly Steered Road to Success in Brazil," *The Wall Street Journal,* February 25, 1999, A1, A8.

57. William Wells, "Global Advertisers Should Pay Heed to Contextual Variations," *Marketing News,* February 13, 1987, 18.

58. Patrick Barwise and Thomas Robertson, "Brand Portfolios," *European Management Journal* 10, no. 3 (September 1992): 277–285.

59. Julia Flynn, "Heineken's Battle To Stay Top Bottle," *Bloomberg BusinessWeek* 3383 (1994): 60–62.

60. "Michael De Carvalho—On the Rise of the Heineken Empire," *Business Today,* Fall 2011.

61. Piyush Pandey, "Tate, Starbucks to Extend Their Partnership Beyond India," *The Hindu,* June 27, 2016, www.thehindu.com/business/Industry/Tata-Starbucks-to-extend-their-partnership-beyond-India/article14404953.ece.

62. David P. Hamilton, "United It Stands. Fuji Xerox Is a Rarity in World Business: A Joint Venture That Works," *The Wall Street Journal,* September 26, 1996, R19.

63. "Toys"R"Us, Inc. Expands Presence in Europe with Market Entry into Poland," *Business Wire*, October 26, 2011, https://www.toysrusinc.com/press/toysrus-inc-expands-presence-in-europe-with-market-entry-into-poland, Accessed August 23, 2018.

64. George Anders, "Ad Agencies and Big Concerns Debate World Brands' Value," *The Wall Street Journal,* June 14, 1984, 33.

65. For an in-depth examination of how Kimberly-Clark implements its global brand management strategy, see Tandadzo Matanda and Michael T. Ewing, "The Process of Global Brand Strategy Development and Regional Implementation," *International Journal of Research in Marketing* 29, no. 1 (March 2012): 5–12.

66. Hans Greimel, "Lexus Tries Unified Front for Global Marketing," *AdAge,* August 12, 2014, http://adage.com/article/cmo-strategy/lexus-unified-front-global-marketing/294553/, accessed July 7, 2017.

67. Nirmalya Kumar and Phanish Puranam, "Have You Restructured for Global Success?," *Harvard Business Review* 89, no. 10 (October 2011): 123–128.

68. For an examination of brand equity measures across the Chinese and American markets, see Don Lehmann, Kevin Lane Keller, and John Farley, "The Structure of Survey-Based Brand Metrics," in special issue, "Branding in the Global Market-place," of *Journal of International Marketing* 16, no. 4 (December 2008): 29–56.

69. "China's Trade Surplus May Be Gone in Two Years, Adviser Says," *Bloomberg BusinessWeek*, November 21, 2011, www.tradingeconomics.com/china/balance-of-trade.

70. The Economist, "Global Manufacturing: Made In China?," Print Edition, March 12, 2015, March 12, 2015, www.economist.com/news/leaders/21646204-asias-dominance-manufacturing-will-endure-will-make-development-harder-others-made.

71. China Labour Bulletin, "Employment and Wages." A version of this article was first published in 2008. It was last updated in June 2018: https://clb.org.hk/content/employment-and-wages, accessed November 26, 2018.

72. Lucy Westcott, "China Adds 1 Million Millionaires in 2014," *Newsweek,* June 15, 2015, www.newsweek.com/china-adds-one-million-new-millionaires-2014-343175.

73. Yuval Atsmon, Vinay Dixit, and Cathy Wu, "Tapping China's Luxury-Goods Market," *McKinsey Quarterly*, April 2011, www.mckinsey.com/business-functions/marketing-and-sales/our-insights/tapping-chinas-luxury-goods-market.

74. Wang Zhuoqiong, "Chinese Snap Up Luxury Products," *China Daily*, February 7, 2012, http://www.chinadaily.com.cn/m/hangzhou/e/2012-02/07/content_14635962.htm, accessed November 26, 2018.

75. Clay Chandler, "Little Emperors," *Fortune,* October 4, 2004, 138, https://money.cnn.com/magazines/fortune/fortune_archive/2004/10/04/8186784/, accessed November 26, 2018.

76. Tu Lei, "China Now No. 2 Market for L'Oreal After U.S.," *Global Times*, February 25, 2016, www.globaltimes.cn/content/970486.shtml.

77. Olivier Verot "The Digital Strategy of L'Oreal in China," July 21, 2016, http://marketingtochina.com/powerful-digital-strategy-loreal/, accessed January 9, 2017.

78. AP News, "More Than 55 Percent of Chinese Now Live in Urban Areas," *AP News*, April 21, 2016, https://apnews.com/7238b70e4e7f48a0bdf8a5fb11fcb244

79. David E. Zoia, "Some Market Pressures, But GM China Expects Continued Growth," Wards Auto, April 29, 2016, https://www.wardsauto.com/industry/some-market-pressures-gm-china-expects-continued-growth, accessed November 26, 2018.

80. Rami Grunbaum, "Starbucks CEO Schultz Sees China Market Passing U.S.," *The Seattle Times*, October 19, 2016, www.scattletimes.com/business/starbucks/starbucks-ceo-schultz-sees-china-market-surpassing-us/.

Closing Observations

16

Learning Objectives

After reading this chapter, you should be able to

1. Understand the six future brand imperatives.
2. Identify the ten criteria for the brand report card.
3. Outline the seven deadly sins of brand management.

Strategic brand management needs to be a well thought out, carefully conducted process, helped by tools such as The Brand Report Card.

549

PREVIEW

This final chapter provides some closing observations concerning strategic brand management. First, we will briefly review the customer-based brand equity (CBBE) framework. Next, we highlight managerial guidelines and key themes that emerged in previous chapters and summarize some success factors for branding. Toward that goal, we will present the brand report card to help brand managers understand and rate their brands' performance on key branding dimensions, as well as the seven deadly sins of brand management. We conclude by considering specific applications of branding in different types of industries in Brand Focus 16.0.

STRATEGIC BRAND MANAGEMENT GUIDELINES

Summary of Customer-Based Brand Equity Framework

Strategic brand management includes the design and implementation of marketing programs and activities to build, measure, and manage brand equity. Before we review some guidelines for strategic brand management, let's briefly summarize—one last time!— the customer-based brand equity framework.

The rationale behind the framework is to recognize the importance of the customer in the creation and management of brand equity. As one top marketing executive put it, "Consumers own brands, and your brand is what consumers will permit you to have." Consistent with this view, we defined customer-based brand equity in Chapter 2 as the differential effect that consumers' brand knowledge has on their response to the marketing of that brand. A brand has positive customer-based brand equity if customers react more favorably to a product and the way it is marketed when the brand is identified than when the product carries a fictitious name or no name.

The basic premise of customer-based brand equity is thus that the power of a brand lies in the minds and hearts of consumers, and what they have experienced, learned, and felt about the brand over time. More formally, we described brand knowledge in Chapter 2 in terms of an associative network memory model, in which the brand is like a node in memory with a variety of different types of associations linked to it. As summarized in Figure 16-1, brand knowledge has two components: brand awareness and brand image.

Brand awareness is related to the strength of the brand node or trace in memory, as reflected by consumers' ability to recall or recognize the brand under different conditions. Brand awareness has depth and breadth. Depth describes the likelihood that consumers can recognize or recall the brand. Breadth describes the variety of purchase and consumption situations in which the brand comes to mind.

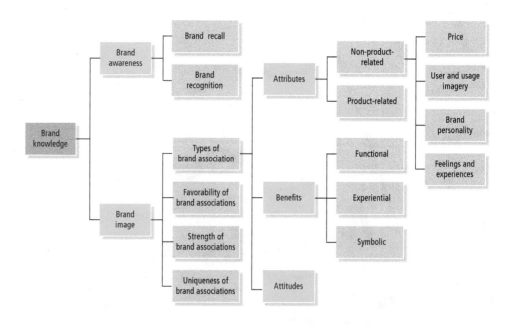

FIGURE 16-1

Summary of Brand Knowledge

Brand image is consumer perceptions of and preferences for a brand, measured by the various types of brand associations held in memory. Although brand associations come in many forms, we can usefully distinguish between product-related or performance-related versus non-product-related or imagery-related attributes. A useful distinction with benefits is between functional (intrinsic product advantages), symbolic (extrinsic product advantages), or experiential (product consumption advantages) benefits. Some of these attribute and benefit associations may be more rational or cognitive in nature; others, more emotional or affective.

Sources of Brand Equity.   Customer-based brand equity occurs when the consumer has a high level of awareness and familiarity with the brand and holds some strong, favorable, and unique brand associations in memory. In some cases, brand awareness alone is sufficient to result in more favorable consumer response—for example, in low-involvement decision settings in which consumers lack motivation or ability and are willing to base their choices merely on familiar brands. In other cases, the strength, favorability, and uniqueness of the brand associations help determine the differential response making up the brand equity. The dimensions of brand associations depend on three factors:

1. **Strength:** The strength of a brand association is a function of both the amount, or quantity, of processing that information initially receives, and the nature, or quality, of the processing. The more deeply a person thinks about brand information and relates it to existing brand knowledge, the stronger the resulting brand associations. The personal relevance of the information and the consistency with which the consumer sees it over time both strengthen the association.
2. **Favorability:** Favorable associations for a brand are those that are desirable to customers, successfully delivered by the product, and conveyed by the supporting marketing program. They can relate to the product or to intangible, non-product-related aspects like usage or user imagery. However, consumers will not deem all brand associations important or view them all favorably, nor will they value them equally across different purchase or consumption situations.
3. **Uniqueness:** To create the differential response that leads to customer-based brand equity, marketers need to associate unique, meaningful points-of-difference (PODs) to the brand that provide a competitive advantage and a reason why consumers should buy it. For other brand associations, however, being comparable or roughly equal in favorability to competing associations might be enough. The brand's associations function as points-of-parity in consumers' minds to establish category membership and negate potential points-of-difference for competitors. In other words, they are designed to provide no reason why not to choose the brand.

Figure 16-2 summarizes these broad conceptual guidelines for creating desired brand knowledge structures.

---

1. **Depth of brand awareness:** Determined by the ease of brand recognition and recall.
2. **Breadth of brand awareness:** Determined by the number of purchase and consumption situations for which the brand comes to mind.
3. **Strong brand associations:** Created by marketing programs that convey relevant information to consumers in a consistent fashion at any one point in time, as well as over time.
4. **Favorable brand associations:** Created when marketing programs effectively deliver product-related and non-product-related benefits that are desired by consumers.
5. **Unique brand associations:** Strong and favorable associations create points of difference that distinguish the brand from other brands. Brand associations that are not unique, however, can create valuable points-of-parity to establish necessary category associations or to neutralize competitive points-of-difference.

FIGURE 16-2

Determinants of Desired
Brand Knowledge
Structures

Brand-Building Tools and Objectives ⟶ Consumer Knowledge Effects ⟶ Branding Benefits

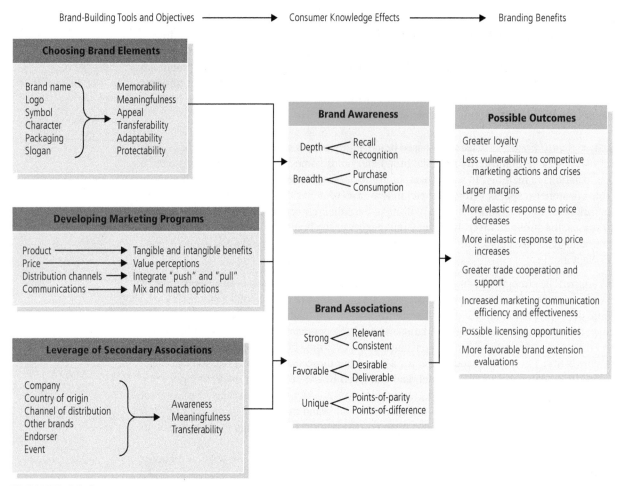

FIGURE 16-3 Building Customer-Based Brand Equity

Outcomes of Brand Equity.   Assuming we can create a positive brand image, with marketing programs that register the brand in memory and link it to strong, favorable, and unique associations, we can realize a number of benefits for the brand, as follows:

- Improved perceptions of product performance
- Greater customer loyalty
- Less vulnerability to competitive marketing actions
- Less vulnerability to marketing crises
- Higher margins
- More inelastic consumer response to price increases
- More elastic consumer response to price decreases
- Greater trade cooperation and support
- Increased marketing communication effectiveness
- Possible licensing opportunities
- Additional brand extension opportunities
- Improved attraction and retention of employees.

Tactical Guidelines

Chapter 1 highlighted the chief ingredients of the CBBE framework in terms of how to build, measure, and manage brand equity. The specific themes and recommendations we developed in subsequent chapters are as follows.

Building Brand Equity.   Tactically, we can build brand equity in three major ways: (1) through the initial choice of the brand elements making up the brand, (2) through marketing activities and the design of the marketing program, and (3) through the leverage of secondary associations that link the brand to other entities like a company, geographic region, channel of distribution, other brand, person, or event. Guidelines emerged in Chapters 4 to 7 for each of these approaches, as summarized in Figures 16-3 and 16-4.

1. Mix and match brand elements—brand names, logos, symbols, characters, slogans, jingles, and packages—by choosing different brand elements to achieve different objectives and by designing brand elements to be as mutually reinforcing as possible.

2. Ensure a high level of perceived quality and create a rich brand image by linking tangible and intangible product-related and non-product-related associations to the brand.

3. Adopt value-based pricing strategies to set prices and guide discount pricing policies over time that reflect consumers' perceptions of value and willingness to pay a premium.

4. Consider a range of direct and indirect distribution options and blend brand-building push strategies for retailers and other channel members with brand-building pull strategies for consumers.

5. Mix marketing communication options by choosing a broad set of communication options based on their differential ability to affect brand awareness and create, maintain, or strengthen favorable and unique brand associations. Match marketing communication options by ensuring consistency and directly reinforcing some communication options with other communication options. Effectively leverage the power of digital marketing and social media channels to connect with your customers.

6. Leverage secondary associations to compensate for otherwise missing dimensions of the marketing program by linking the brand to other entities such as companies, channels of distribution, other brands, characters, spokespeople or other endorsers, or events that reinforce and augment the brand image.

FIGURE 16-4
Guidelines for Building Brand Equity

Themes.   A dominant theme across many of these various ways to build brand equity is the importance of complementarity and consistency. Ensuring *complementarity* means choosing a variety of brand elements and supporting marketing activities so that the potential contribution to brand equity of one compensates for the shortcomings of others. For example, some brand elements may primarily enhance awareness through a memorable brand logo, whereas others may facilitate the linkage of brand associations with a meaningful brand name or a clever slogan. Similarly, an ad campaign might create a certain point-of-difference association, whereas a retail promotion creates a vital point-of-parity association. Finally, we can link certain other entities to the brand to leverage secondary associations, provide other sources of brand equity, or further reinforce existing associations.

Thus, it is important to put into place a varied set of brand elements and marketing activities and programs in order to create the desired level of awareness and type of image that leads to brand equity. At the same time, a high degree of *consistency* across these elements helps create the highest level of awareness and the strongest and most favorable associations possible. Consistency ensures that diverse brand and marketing mix elements share a common core meaning, perhaps by conveying the same information, such as a benefit association that is reinforced by a highly integrated, well-branded marketing communications program.

Measuring Brand Equity.   We can gauge brand equity indirectly by measuring its potential sources, and directly by measuring its possible outcomes. This means measuring aspects of brand awareness and brand image leading to the differential customer response that creates brand equity: breadth and depth of brand awareness; the strength, favorability, and uniqueness of brand associations; the valence of brand responses; and the nature of brand relationships. Measuring outcomes requires us to estimate the various benefits from creating these sources of brand equity. The brand value chain depicts this relationship more broadly by considering how marketing activity affects these sources of brand equity, and how the resulting outcomes influence the investment community, as well as how various filters or multipliers intervene between the stages.

Marketers need to properly design and implement a *brand equity measurement system*, a set of research procedures designed to provide timely, accurate, and actionable information for marketers about their brands. Implementing a brand equity measurement system has three

1. Formalize the firm's view of brand equity into a document, the brand equity charter, that provides relevant branding guidelines to marketing managers.

2. Conduct brand inventories to profile how all of the products sold by a company are branded and marketed, and conduct brand exploratories to understand what consumers think and feel about a brand as part of periodic brand audits to assess the health of brands, understand their sources of brand equity, and suggest ways to improve and leverage that equity.

3. Conduct consumer tracking studies on a routine basis to provide current information as to how brands are performing with respect to the key sources and outcomes of brand equity as identified by the brand audit.

4. Assemble results of tracking survey and other relevant outcome measures into a brand equity report to be distributed on a regular basis to provide descriptive information as to what is happening with a brand as well as diagnostic information as to why it is happening.

5. Establish a person or department to oversee the implementation of the brand equity charter and brand equity reports to make sure that, as much as possible, product and marketing actions across divisions and geographic boundaries are done in a way that reflects the spirit of the charter and the substance of the report to maximize the long-term equity of the brand.

FIGURE 16-5

Guidelines for Measuring Brand Equity

steps: (1) conducting brand audits, (2) designing brand tracking studies, and (3) establishing a brand equity management system.

Guidelines for each of these areas are summarized in Figure 16-5.

Themes.   The dominant theme in measuring brand equity is the need to employ a full complement of research techniques and processes that capture as much as possible the richness and complexity of brand equity. We need multiple techniques and measures to tap into all the various sources and outcomes of brand equity, to help interpret brand equity research, and to ensure that we get actionable information at the right time. With social media listening growing in importance, some of the traditional brand audit and tracking activities could employ social media listening and other digital research tools as a substitute or complement to existing efforts.

Managing Brand Equity.   Finally, managing brand equity requires taking a broad, long-term perspective of brands. A broad view of brand equity is critically important, especially when firms are selling a wide variety of products and brands in multiple markets. Here, brand hierarchies must define common and distinct brand elements among various nested products. New product and brand extension strategies also must ensure that we have optimal brand and product portfolios. Finally, we need to manage these brands and products effectively over geographic boundaries and target market segments by creating brand awareness and a positive brand image in each market in which the brand is sold.

We need a long-term view of brand equity because changes in current marketing programs and activities and in the marketing environment can affect consumers' brand knowledge structures, and thus, their response to future marketing programs and activities. Managing brands over time requires reinforcing the brand meaning and adjusting the branding program as needed. For brands whose equity has eroded over time, we rely on a number of revitalization strategies. Figures 16-6 and 16-7 highlight some important guidelines for managing brand equity.

Themes.   The dominant themes in managing brand equity are the importance of maintaining balance in marketing activities and of making moderate levels of change in the marketing program over time. Without some modifications of the marketing program, a brand runs the risk of becoming obsolete or irrelevant to consumers. At the same time, dramatic shifts back and forth

1. Define Brand Hierarchy

  A. *Principle of Simplicity:* Employ as few levels as possible.
  B. *Principle of Clarity:* Logic and relationship of all brand elements employed must be obvious and transparent.
  C. *Principle of Relevance:* Create abstract associations relevant to as many products as possible.
  D. *Principle of Differentiation:* Differentiate individual products and brands.
  E. *Principle of Growth:* Investments in market penetration or expansion vs. product development should be made according to ROI opportunities.
  F. *Principle of Survival:* Brand extensions must achieve brand equity in their categories.
  G. *Principle of Synergy:* Brand extensions should enhance the equity of the parent brand.
  H. *Principle of Prominence:* Adjust prominence to affect perceptions of product distance.
  I. *Principle of Commonality:* Link common products through shared brand elements.

2. Define Brand–Product Matrix

  A. *Brand Extensions:* Establish new equity and enhance existing equity.
  B. *Brand Portfolio:* Maximize coverage and minimize overlap.

3. Enhance Brand Equity over Time

  A. *Brand Reinforcement:* Innovation in product design, manufacturing, and merchandising. Relevance in user and usage imagery.
  B. *Brand Revitalization:* "Back to basics" strategy. "Reinvention" strategy.

4. Establish Brand Equity over Market Segments

  A. *Identify Differences in Consumer Behavior:* How they purchase and use products. What they know and feel about different brands.
  B. *Adjust Branding Program:* Choice of brand elements. Nature of supporting marketing program. Leverage of secondary associations.

FIGURE 16-6
Managing Customer-Based Brand Equity

1. Define the brand hierarchy in terms of the number of levels to use and the relative prominence that brands at different levels will receive when combined to brand any one product.
2. Create brand associations relevant to as many brands nested at the level below in the hierarchy as possible but sharply differentiate brands at the same level of the hierarchy.
3. Introduce brand extensions that complement the product mix of the firm, leverage parent brand associations, and enhance parent brand equity.
4. Clearly establish the roles of brands in the brand portfolio, adding, deleting, and modifying brands as necessary.
5. Reinforce brand equity over time through marketing actions that consistently convey the meaning of the brand in terms of what products the brand represents, what benefits it supplies, what needs it satisfies, and why it is superior to competitive brands.
6. Enhance brand equity over time through innovation in product design, manufacturing, and merchandising and continued relevance in user and usage imagery.
7. Identify differences in consumer behavior in various market segments, and adjust the branding program accordingly on a cost-benefit basis.

FIGURE 16-7
Guidelines for Managing Brand Equity

in brand strategies can confuse or alienate consumers. Thus, a consistent thread of meaning—which consumers can recognize—should run through the marketing program and reflect the key sources of equity for the brand and its core brand associations.

WHAT MAKES A STRONG BRAND?

To create a strong brand and maximize brand equity, marketing managers must:

- Understand brand meaning and market the company's products and services in an appropriate manner.
- Properly position the brand.
- Provide superior delivery of desired benefits.
- Employ a full range of complementary brand elements, supporting marketing activities, and secondary associations.
- Embrace integrated marketing communications and communicate with a consistent voice.
- Measure consumer perceptions of value and develop a pricing strategy accordingly.
- Establish credibility and appropriate brand personality and imagery.
- Maintain innovation and relevance for the brand.
- Strategically design and implement a brand architecture strategy.
- Implement a brand equity management system to ensure that marketing actions properly reflect the brand equity concept.

Branding Brief 16-1 provides more detail on these requirements for successful brand management in the form of the brand report card.[1]

BRANDING BRIEF 16-1

The Brand Report Card

The brand report card can reveal how well you are managing your brand. Rate your brand on a scale of 1 to 10 (1 = extremely poor; 10 = extremely good) for each of the following characteristics. Create a similar report card for your major competitors. Compare and contrast the results with all the relevant participants in the management of your brand. Doing so should help you identify where you excel, pinpoint areas that need improvement, and learn more about how your particular brand is configured. Be brutally honest in answering the questions—approach them as an outsider and from a consumer's perspective.

Score

1. _____ **Managers understand what the brand means to consumers.**

- Have you created detailed, research-driven mental maps of your target customers?
- Have you attempted to define a brand mantra?
- Have you outlined customer-driven boundaries for brand extensions and guidelines for marketing programs?

2. _____ **The brand is properly positioned.**

- Have you established category, competitive, and correlational points-of-parity?
- Have you established desirable, deliverable, and differentiated points-of-difference?

3. _____ **Customers receive superior delivery of the benefits they value most.**

- Have you attempted to uncover unmet consumer needs and wants?
- Do you relentlessly focus on maximizing your customers' product and service experiences?

4. _____ **The brand takes advantage of the full repertoire of branding and marketing activities available to build brand equity.**

- Have you strategically chosen and designed your brand name, logo, symbol, slogan packaging, signage, URL, and other brand elements to build brand awareness and image?
- Have you implemented integrated push and pull strategies that target intermediaries and end customers, respectively?

5. _____ **Marketing and communications efforts are seamlessly integrated (or as close to it as humanly possible). The brand communicates with one voice.**

- Have you considered all the alternative ways to create brand awareness and link brand associations?
- Have you ensured that common meaning is contained throughout your marketing communication program?
- Have you capitalized on the unique capabilities of each communication option?

- Have you been careful to preserve important brand values in your communications over time?
- Have you leveraged digital and social media channels optimally to communicate your intended message to the target audience?
- Have you utilized the capabilities of mobile marketing to communicate with your desired target audience at a time, place, and manner that are most appropriate?

6. _____ **The brand's pricing strategy is based on consumer perceptions of value.**

- Have you estimated the added value perceived by customers?
- Have you optimized price, cost, and quality to meet or exceed consumer expectations?

7. _____ **The brand uses appropriate imagery to support its personality.**

- Have you established credibility by ensuring that the brand and the people behind it are seen as expert, trustworthy, and likable?
- Have you established appropriate user and usage imagery?
- Have you crafted the right brand personality?

8. _____ **The brand is innovative and relevant.**

- Have you invested in product and marketing improvements that provide improved benefits and better solutions for your customers?

- Have you stayed up-to-date and in touch with your customers?

9. _____ **For a multiproduct, multibrand company, the brand architecture is strategically sound.**

- For the brand hierarchy, are associations at the highest levels relevant to as many products as possible at the next lower levels, and are brands well-differentiated at any one level?
- For the brand portfolio, do the brands maximize market coverage while minimizing their overlap at the same time?

10. _____ **The company has a system in place to monitor brand equity and performance.**

- Have you created a brand charter that defines the meaning and equity of the brand and how it should be treated?
- Do you conduct periodic brand audits to assess the health of your brands and to set strategic direction?
- Do you conduct routine tracking studies to evaluate current marketing performance?
- Do you regularly distribute brand equity reports that summarize all brand-relevant research and information to assist marketing decision making?
- Have you assigned people within the organization the responsibility of monitoring and preserving brand equity?

On the flip side of the coin, what common branding mistakes prevent firms from creating strong, powerful brands? The seven deadly sins of brand management include the following (see Figure 16-8):[2]

1. **Failure to fully understand the meaning of the brand:** Given that consumers "own" brands, it is critical to understand what they think and feel about them and then plan and implement marketing programs accordingly. Too often, managers convince themselves of the validity of marketing actions—for example, a new brand extension, ad campaign, or price hike—based on a mistaken belief about what consumers know or what marketers would like them to know about the brand. Managers often ignore the full range of associations—both tangible and intangible—that may characterize the brand.

2. **Failure to live up to the brand promise:** A brand should be a promise and a commitment to consumers, but too often, that promise is broken. A common mistake is to set brand expectations too high and then fail to live up to them in the marketing program. By overpromising and not delivering, a firm is worse off in many ways than if it had not set expectations at all.

1. Failure to fully understand the meaning of the brand
2. Failure to live up to the brand promise
3. Failure to adequately support the brand
4. Failure to be patient with the brand
5. Failure to adequately control the brand
6. Failure to properly balance consistency and change with the brand
7. Failure to understand the complexity of brand equity measurement and management

FIGURE 16-8

Seven Deadly Sins of Brand Management

3. **Failure to adequately support the brand:** Creating and maintaining brand knowledge structures requires marketing investments. Too often, managers want to get something for nothing by building brand equity without providing proper marketing support or, once brand equity has been built, by expecting the brand to remain strong despite the lack of further investments.

4. **Failure to be patient with the brand:** Brand equity must be carefully and patiently built from the ground up. A firm foundation requires that consumers have the proper depth and breadth of awareness and strong, favorable, and unique associations in memory. Managers should avoid taking shortcuts that bypass more basic branding considerations—such as achieving the necessary level of brand awareness—to concentrate on flashier aspects of brand building related to its image.

5. **Failure to adequately control the brand:** All employees of the firm must understand brand equity, and the firm's actions must reflect a broader corporate perspective as well as a more specific product perspective. Firms sometimes make decisions haphazardly, without a true understanding of the current and desired brand equity or recognition of the impact these decisions have on other brands or brand-related activities. Given the possibility of a social media crisis that almost every brand seemingly faces, it is important that company personnel across different functional areas (marketing, PR, sales) be prepared to launch a coordinated communications effort in the aftermath of a social media crisis to ensure that the public relations fallout does not harm the brand's equity in the long run.

6. **Failure to properly balance consistency and change with the brand:** Managing a brand necessitates striking the delicate, but crucial, balance between maintaining continuity in marketing activities and keeping the product or image of a brand up-to-date. If managers do not make adjustments in their marketing program to reflect changes in the marketing environment, they can be left behind. Or they may make so many changes that the brand becomes a moving target without any meaning to consumers.

7. **Failure to understand the complexity of brand equity measurement and management:** Effective brand management requires discipline, creativity, focus, and the ability to make hundreds of decisions in the best possible manner. Sometimes marketers oversimplify the process and try to equate success in branding with taking one particular action or approach. Brand equity is not optimized as a result.

Historically, one of the most skilled brand builders is Procter & Gamble (P&G). Branding Brief 16-2 describes some of the ways it has changed its marketing processes and philosophy in recent years to reflect new marketing challenges and realities.

BRANDING BRIEF 16-2
Reinvigorating Branding at Procter & Gamble

Procter & Gamble has been a leader in marketing for much of its 160-plus years of existence. It has been referred to as the single greatest marketing company in the world. Already the world's largest consumer packaged-goods company, P&G became even larger with the $57 billion acquisition of Gillette in 2005. Despite its overall success, P&G has been struggling to maintain its leadership status due to the dramatic shifts taking place in marketing. In order to adapt to these changes, P&G is trying to blend the best of their old practices with new practices to create a modern blueprint for successful brand management in the coming years. There were many changes made to branding strategies by the leadership of P&G—first by Bob McDonald (CEO until 2013) and then by David Taylor who became the CEO in 2015. These changes have allowed P&G to evolve with the changes taking place in marketing. The priorities of P&G in recent years are described in the following section:

Building category growth: Changing consumer habits could be key to category growth, and a key feature of P&G's strategy is to fundamentally rethink how consumers are interacting with products in a given category. For instance, their blockbuster product Swiffer was based on a deep understanding of how consumers cleaned their homes, and the amount of time consumers spent on cleaning the mops themselves—an insight which led to the creation of the Swiffer product. In this way, P&G has approached each category in which they do business with a view to finding novel approaches to generating category growth.

Streamlining its product portfolio: P&G has been aggressively pruning its product portfolio and also re-evaluating its presence in many businesses. For example, it decided to divest many of its beauty brands including CoverGirl, Clairol, and Wella by selling these brands to Coty. By divesting these brands,

Products such as Tide PODS, Febreze, and Head & Shoulders Smooth and Silky 3 Action Formula, are examples of recent innovations from P&G which have been highly successful.

P&G was able to rid itself of those categories where they felt challenged to develop winning strategies, which represented a drag on its profitability and growth, thus, allowing it to be more focused and nimble with other, more promising categories.

Driving innovation and new products: New product development continues to be an important focus for P&G. While it has been credited with highly successful innovations such as Head and Shoulders' new Smooth and Silky 3 Action Formula and Tide PODS, P&G has also been successful in innovating in smaller categories. For example, Febreze odor eliminators became a member of P&G's "billion dollar revenue club" based on innovating in a relatively small product category.

Embracing new communications strategies: P&G increasingly balances online and offline communication channels to promote their brands. The company's "Like a Girl" ad campaign for their Always brand struck a chord with its target audiences by taking what was previously seen as a patronizing remark—the phrase "like a girl"—and making it into a statement of strength that would provide encouragement and confidence to young girls everywhere. While the campaign has leveraged traditional media efforts (including advertising during the Super Bowl), it has also effectively utilized social media advertising including creating a hashtag (#LikeAGirl), which garnered a large online following, along with numerous female athletes endorsing the campaign. While P&G has embraced new digital media to communicate

with its audiences, it also has done so carefully, to ensure that its brand's positioning and appeal are not compromised. For example, in 2017, P&G announced a cut of nearly $150 million in digital ads, citing concerns over brand safety—that is, brands were not being placed in media platforms or vehicles consistent with their intended positioning. Another feature of P&G's digital strategy is to focus on search and to ensure digital ad placement in online retail Web sites such as Amazon and brick-and-mortar retailers' Web sites. This thoughtful and results-driven approach to the use of digital media is likely to continue to be a feature of P&G's digital strategy.

Adopting a new brand management structure: P&G reorganized its marketing function in 2014 and replaced its marketing organization (and the titles of marketing directors) with a brand management structure. While previously, P&G's focus in marketing was on revenue generation and promotional spending, the switch to brand management was meant to increase focus on developing brand identity and enhancing brand valuation. P&G's marketing directors became brand directors. A key part of this shift is that P&G was reorganized around four major divisions including baby, feminine and family care, homecare, beauty, health and grooming And brands that are closely aligned in terms of their target audiences as well as competitors were organized within the same division. The changes helped create a single-point responsibility for the strategies, plans and results for the brands, thus, making way for faster decision-making, and allowing for better execution of their strategy.

Sources: Sofia Pitt, "One Year Later: How P&G Has Changed under New CEO David Taylor," October 27, 2016, https://www.cnbc.com/2016/10/27/one-year-later-how-pg-has-changed-under-new-ceo-david-taylor.html; Jack Neff, "P&G Makes It Official with Beauty Divestiture to Coty," July 9, 2015, http://adage.com/article/adroll/p-g-makes-official-beauty-divestiture-coty/299408/; Leonie Roderick, "P&G: We Need to Build Stronger Brand Identities Online," July 27, 2017, https://www.marketingweek.com/2017/07/27/pg-digital-investment/; Michael Lee, "Does P&G's Reorganized Marketing Department Go Far Enough?," July 8, 2014, www.forbes.com/sites/michaellee/2014/07/08/does-pgs-reorganized-marketing-department-go-far-enough/#6441b62c5e88; Jack Neff, "It's the End of 'Marketing' as We Know It at Procter & Gamble," June 30, 2014, http://adage.com/article/cmo-strategy/end-marketing-procter-gamble/293918/.

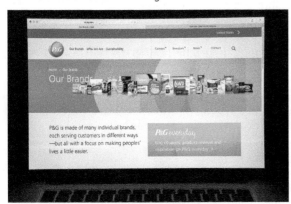

P&G balances online and offline communication channels to promote its brands.

FUTURE BRAND PRIORITIES

Our journey to better understand strategic brand management is about over, but it's worth considering a few final questions. How will branding change in the coming years? What are the biggest branding challenges? What will make a successful twenty-first-century brand?

The importance of branding seems unlikely to change for one critical reason: Consumers will continue to value the functions that brands provide. In an increasingly complex world, well-managed brands can simplify, communicate, reassure, and provide important meaning to consumers.[3] Brands have survived for centuries because they serve a very fundamental purpose. At their best, they allow consumers to reduce risk and gain greater satisfaction in their lives. Strong brands can make consumers' lives a little—or sometimes even a lot—better. The role and functions of brands are so fundamentally pervasive and valued by consumers that it is difficult to see their *potential* importance diminishing.

However, managing brands to achieve that potential is as challenging as ever.[4] The marketing environment always changes, but the pace of change has greatly accelerated in the past decade. Consumers are increasingly diverse, enlightened, and empowered. Virtually every market has experienced heightened competition as a result of the entrance of global firms, private labels, and megabrands from related categories. Rapidly changing technology has profoundly affected how consumers live and shop, and how marketers learn about consumer needs and wants and manage their brands. Finally, serious environmental, community, and social concerns exist all over the world.

As a result, the rules of the branding game have changed.[5] Marketers are rethinking—and sometimes fundamentally altering—their branding policies and practices. Using the principles reflected in the brand report card and avoiding the seven deadly sins of brand management reviewed earlier should help in the pursuit of brand management. Building on prior concepts and examples from the book, this final section highlights six branding imperatives to help managers navigate the challenges of brand management in the years to come, as summarized in Figure 16-9.[6]

Fully and Accurately Factor the Consumer into the Branding Equation

One of the most important rules of branding is *the consumer owns the brand*. The power of consumer perceptions and beliefs to make or break brands has been demonstrated time and again in the lab and in the real world. From the New Coke debacle to the modern challenges some companies face in convincing consumers of the quality of their products in the face of negative reviews, consumer sovereignty rules.

Nowadays, the growth of social media platforms as a stage for customer-to-customer interactions increases the power of customers to express positive sentiment towards a brand (through

FIGURE 16-9

Future Brand
Imperatives

1. **Fully and accurately factor the consumer into the branding equation.**
   Focus on the consumer and recognize what they know and don't know about brands and what they want and don't want from brands. Engage in "participation marketing" in the process.

2. **Go beyond product performance and rational benefits.**
   Craft well-designed products and services that provide a full set of rational and emotional benefits.

3. **Make the whole of the marketing program greater than the sum of the parts.**
   Develop fully integrated channel and communication strategies that optimally blend their strengths and weaknesses.

4. **Understand where you can take a brand (and how).**
   Design and implement a new product development and brand architecture strategy that maximizes long-term growth across product offerings, customer segments, and geographical markets.

5. **Do the "right thing" with brands.**
   Embrace corporate social responsibility and manage brands for the long run.

6. **Take a big picture view of branding effects. Know what is working (and why).**
   Justify brand investments and achieve deeper understanding of the power of brands.

sharing of positive word-of-mouth) or detract from or even completely destroy a brand (through sharing of negative word-of-mouth). Such unprecedented power in consumers' hands has shifted the equation for brand managers considerably. They have to view consumers as potential producers of brand meaning and incorporate their interpretations of the brand into their strategic thinking regarding the brand.

From a managerial perspective, it is beneficial to incorporate the consumer voice in every branding decision. To illustrate, consider brand architecture decisions. Managers frequently err in naming new products by taking an internal company perspective and arriving at overly complicated solutions with many different layers and levels of branding. Consumers then try to simplify the branding, or worse, they may move to a competitor with a straightforward, more easily grasped set of offerings. Part of the appeal of Colgate Total has undoubtedly been that its name suggests a very simple solution to navigating the toothpaste aisle, a section of the store consumers often find bewildering.

In naming products and services—and in developing marketing programs and activities to build those brands—managers must fully incorporate a consumer point of view. This requires illuminating consumer research and a sharp marketing mind-set to properly interpret and act on the findings. The best marketers use consumer insights to skillfully manage customers and brands and to maximize brand equity and customer equity. Brands serve as the bait that retailers and other channel intermediaries use to attract customers from whom they extract value. Customers serve as the tangible profit engine for marketers to monetize their brand value.

However, for even the most customer-centric companies, the increasing diversity and empowerment of customers offer significant branding challenges.

Customer Diversity. Multiple segments and subsegments of consumers typically make up a customer franchise for a brand. We define these segments using many dimensions; some of the most challenging are cultures and geographies. A multicultural perspective in branding is a necessity in today's diverse world in order to directly affect all types of target consumers or groups. It also helps marketers focus on the *overall* relevance of their brand and how they can effectively adapt it to all segments in their target market. As we showed in Chapter 15, there are many ways that brands try to adapt their offerings to suit the needs of different types of target segments.

In recognition of customer diversity and increasing segmentation, marketing pundits have introduced concepts such as permission marketing, one-to-one marketing, brand journalism, and digital personalization. These concepts all reinforce the fact that any brand franchise has multiple constituents we need to understand and address in the marketplace.

We need to apply these concepts with care, however. Brand journalism, for example, suggests that—just as journalists tell many facets of a story to capture the interests of diverse groups of readers—marketers should communicate different messages to different market segments. Digital personalization involves using vast troves of data on consumers' browsing history and online buyer behavior to offer a set of benefits uniquely suited to individual customers. However, while these trends may provide the basis for highly distinctive branding segmentation and differentiation, the common core of the brand promise is found in virtually all aspects of the marketing program. Ritz-Carlton's brand mantra of "ladies and gentlemen serving ladies and gentlemen" affects how the hotel chain delivers service to *all* its guests as they come into contact with the brand.

Macrumors.com provides a place for customers to discuss issues relevant to consumers of all Apple products.

Web sites such as Twitch are a live streaming video platform which allows for video game live streaming and broadcasts of eSports competitions. It is a platform that enables avid video gamers to learn about and discuss new video games.

Customer Empowerment.   Much has been made of the newly empowered consumer. One of the driving factors behind this trend is the greater transparency that now prevails in the marketing environment. The emergence of the Internet and social media—as well as the expansion and pervasiveness of traditional media—have given consumers the ability, for better or worse, to seek information and arrive at what they feel is "the truth" about products, services, and brands like never before. By merely being observant or proactive, consumers can find out and judge how well a product or service works or what a company is doing (or not doing) to the environment or their local community. Information and opinions can now travel around the world in mere minutes. Marketers must anticipate that any actions they take or claims they make will be scrutinized, deemed truthful or not, and shared with others almost instantaneously.

With this new transparency, consumers can undoubtedly be more actively involved in the fortunes of brands than ever before. But the reality is that only *some of the consumers* want to get involved with *some of the brands* they use and, even then, only *some of the time.* For consumers who do choose to become engaged at a deeper level, marketers must do everything they can to encourage them with social media and other marketing tools. But many consumers will choose *not* to do so, and it is crucially important to understand how to best market a brand given such diversity in consumer propensities, interests, and activity levels.

Moreover, even consumers who choose to become more engaged with a brand have undefined, ambiguous, or even conflicting preferences. They may need guidance and assistance in forming and conveying their preferences to firms. "Participation marketing" may then be a more appropriate concept for marketers to employ, because marketers and consumers need to work together to find out how the firm can best satisfy consumer goals. In participation marketing, consumers and firms freely exchange information to arrive at mutually beneficial solutions.[7] A highly successful premium brand, King Arthur Flour, has created a loyal online brand community by recognizing that baking is an activity consumers want to learn about and discuss with other consumers and company experts.

Go Beyond Product Performance and Rational Benefits

At the heart of a great brand is a great product or service. This is even more true in today's highly transparent world. Many firms make the design aspects of products and services an increasingly crucial component of their value proposition, including adept marketers such as Apple, Nike, Ritz-Carlton, Singapore Airlines, and Samsung. Developing better-designed products and services, however, requires a clear, comprehensive, up-to-date understanding of consumers and how they purchase and use products and services and think and feel about brands.

Product design encompasses not only how a product works, but also how it looks, feels, and even sounds and smells. Similarly, service design is a function of all sensory aspects that consumers encounter and experience with a brand. Designing products and services that can more efficiently and effectively deliver the full range of category benefits is still of paramount importance and provides a powerful means to gain competitive advantage. This is true even in many mature categories, as illustrated by P&G's recent success with brands such as Tide, Swiffer, and Venus.

Great product and service design comes from keen consumer insight and inspired, creative solutions. A well-designed brand offers advantages in product and service performance, and in the imagery that creates significant functional and psychological benefits. Emotional benefits will be most impactful, in particular, when they are directly linked to a functional benefit.

Consider P&G's successful repositioning of its Pampers brand. The disposable diaper had been positioned for years on the basis of dryness and absorbency via classic product comparison advertising. As a result of insights gained from consumer research, the company leveraged those functional product benefits to create a powerful emotional benefit. It based the new Pampers positioning on consumers' beliefs that: (1) a dry baby sleeps better, and (2) a well-rested baby will play and learn more the next day. In other words, to parents, the functional benefit "dryness" leads directly to the emotional benefit of "caring for your baby." The new positioning thus celebrated Pampers as "caring for baby's development"—the emotional payoff from the brand's rational product benefits.

Design considerations will increasingly drive the innovation pipeline. Competitive advantages and brand strength will come from having better-designed products and services than competitors, providing a wider range of compelling consumer benefits as a result.

King Arthur Flour has built a loyal online brand community among consumers highly involved with baking. It also uses online video tutorials to help address customers' issues related to baking.

Make the Whole of the Marketing Program Greater Than the Sum of the Parts

The diversity of means to communicate about and sell products and services to consumers has grown exponentially in recent years. Major shifts in the media industry have emerged due to a number of factors: the rise of digital media channels, fragmentation of TV viewership, the growing use of streaming services, video gaming, the increasing use of mobile phones, the explosion of social media, online blogs and social communities, and the greater importance of events, experience, and buzz marketing.

These developments have fundamentally affected how companies communicate about their products and services. Firms now have a host of ways to distribute and sell their products online or offline, directly or indirectly. Marketers are embracing different types of personal and mass media and combining digital marketing techniques, real-world experiential communications, and traditional mass media practices. They are also merging online and offline channels to maximize coverage and impact. In turn, digital brands are embracing ways of connecting with consumers in offline worlds—including such tactics as popup stores, delivery services, and so on—while also acquiring brick-and-mortar outlets.

The challenge for top brands is assembling the best set of channel and communication options to maximize sales in the short run and brand equity in the long run. The art and science of integrated marketing is to optimally design and implement any one channel or communication activity so that it creates not only direct effects, but also indirect effects that increase the impact of other channel or communication options. A breathtaking TV ad may change a viewer's opinions of a brand, but it may also make that viewer more likely to visit the branded Web site or respond more favorably to a tweet posted by a brand on Twitter, or a company's Facebook post.

As a result of the increasingly diverse communications options available to companies today, consumers have different channel and communications histories, and, as a result, very different levels of brand knowledge. This creates a challenge—and an opportunity—for the wise brand marketer. Ideally, a channel or communication option or activity would be versatile enough to work effectively regardless of consumer history or past experience. Indeed, one advantage of a well-designed Web site is that, because of its interactivity, it can successfully communicate and sell to consumers regardless of their personal shopping or communications history.

For example, Nike's amazing marketing success is partly due to its combination of a broad range of distribution channels with an extensive online and offline communication program, as relevant to the world's elite athletes looking to excel in their sport as it is to the average person who just wants to incorporate Nike into everyday recreational life.

Digital Communications.   As more consumers spend more time on the Internet, it is crucial to use online, interactive communications to affect consumers directly at all stages of the consumer decision funnel, and thus, to reinforce offline marketing efforts. An online, interactive communications program typically includes some or all of the following: a well-designed Web site (with customer-generated content and feedback) linked to a solid search engine optimization strategy; search advertising; e-mail marketing; banner ads and rich media; video ads; and social media advertising. Of these, the newest and most challenging component is social media.

Social media programs—encompassing social media advertising including Facebook, Twitter, Instagram, YouTube, and so on, along with other outlets such as online communities (e.g., Facebook groups), utilizing blogs (including sponsored blogging)—provide an effective means to creating active customer engagement and involvement. By offering

P&G was successful in repositioning Pampers on the emotional benefits of "caring for your baby."

The growing use of event sponsorships and branded experiences shows the transformation of media and marketing.

Brands such as Gap, Volkswagen, United Airlines, Pepsi, Adidas, and Uber were all at the receiving end of social media attacks.

Technologies such as geofencing and location-based advertising enable companies to send coupons to customers as they approach (or are in close proximity to) a retail outlet.

the right online information, experiences, and platforms for brands, marketers can help consumers learn from each other about a brand as well as express their brand loyalty and observe that of others. However, engaging and involving consumers brings potential dangers as well, such as subversive behavior by a small group of consumers or undeservedly negative feedback. Undesirable branding effects can occur with or without a social media campaign, of course, although being online and providing a positive point of view may help counterbalance or even overcome them. Adopting a "thick-skin" stance online is imperative, given that a caustic comment or unpleasant review is only one consumer click away, and some negativity is to be expected and tolerated.

Mobile platforms allow marketers to connect with consumers and provide the right brand information at the right time and right place. Similarly, companies use technologies such as geofencing and location-based advertising to send coupons and promotions to customers as they are in close proximity to a retail outlet. Further, mobile messaging is available to consumers around the world and is a powerful tool for sending branded offers to consumers. One innovative use of mobile marketing is an app offered by Home Depot which was launched in collaboration with The Weather Channel. Based on the weather in a given region, Home Depot would change the recommended do-it-yourself projects, tailoring the projects and advice to the weather in a given location. The Weather Channel interactive app—with more than 10 million consumers—has the ability to segment its audiences and is able to target its audiences in a precise fashion, making it highly attractive to advertisers.[8]

Location-based marketing uses mobile devices to make offers available to consumers at the right time and right place. Fortunately, an increasingly robust and detailed set of online metrics exist by which marketers can track the nature, extent, and valence of public sentiment. By monitoring online buzz and activities in this way, marketers can more effectively assess and determine the proper response to any potentially damaging online or even offline episode. Dove was subjected to backlash on social media when it decided to redesign its shampoo bottles to reflect different body types, which inadvertently seemed to suggest that there was an optimal body type.[9] This example points to the importance of paying close attention to unfolding crises (if they were to occur) and to make sure that the social media and public relations teams are able to respond to these crises in an appropriate manner.

Understand Where You Can Take a Brand (and How)

For long-term financial prosperity, the successful launch of new products and services and the entry of existing products and services into new markets and customer segments are of paramount importance. From a branding standpoint, growth requires a well-thought-out and well-implemented brand architecture strategy that clarifies three key issues: (1) the potential of a brand in terms of the breadth of its market footprint; (2) the types of product and service extensions that would allow a brand to achieve that potential; and (3) the brand elements, positioning, and images that identify and are associated with all the offerings of a brand in different markets and to different consumers.

Brand Potential.   A good brand architecture defines brand boundaries: What products or services the brand could represent; what benefits it could supply; and what needs it could satisfy. It provides guardrails for appropriate—and inappropriate—line and category extensions. It clarifies the meaning and promise of the brand to consumers and helps consumers choose the right version of the product or service for themselves.

Understanding the brand promise and how it should best be translated and adapted to different products and markets is challenging, but critical. Every product or service sharing the brand name should deliver on the unique brand promise. If you can replace the specific brand in any of its marketing with a competitive brand, and its marketing would still essentially make sense and work with consumers, then the marketing is probably not aligned sharply enough with the brand promise and meaning.

By adhering to the brand promise and growing the brand carefully through little steps, marketers can cover a lot of ground. Take Lego, which illustrates the value of a well-thought-out brand strategy to expand a brand and allow it to better reach its potential. Their success with *The Lego Movie* opened up a new source of revenue through theatrical entertainment, while also increasing sales of the Lego brand by around 25 percent.[10] The movie helped reinforce the brand's key associations including creativity, joy, and fun, thereby deepening the target customer's affinity for the brand.

Brand Extensions.   The vast majority of new products are extensions, and the vast majority of new products fail. In other words, too many brand extensions fail. Why? They are not creating sufficient relevance and differentiation in their new product or service categories. An increasingly competitive marketplace will be even more unforgiving to poorly positioned and marketed extensions in the years to come. To succeed, marketers must be rigorous and disciplined in analyzing and developing brand extensions.

We've looked at some of the academic research on brand extensions. Based on this and other inputs, Figure 13-8 presented a scorecard with criteria for evaluating a proposed brand extension. The specifications there are intended to offer a starting point; particular items or the weights applied to them can be adjusted to the specific marketing context. The key point is that, by adopting some type of formal model or scorecard, we can apply systematic thinking to judging the merits of a proposed extension and increase its likelihood of success.

Brand Elements.   The third aspect in a brand architecture strategy encompasses the name, look, and other branding elements applied to new products. A key concept here is the proper use of sub-branding. By combining new brand elements with existing parent brand elements, we can use sub-branding effectively to signal the intended similarity or fit of a new extension with its parent brand. Consumers are very literal. For example, putting the parent brand name before a new, individual name makes it more like the parent brand than putting it second. Marriott's Courtyard is seen as much more of a Marriott hotel than Courtyard by Marriott by having the corporate name first.

A good sub-branding strategy can facilitate access to associations and attitudes to the company or family brand as a whole, while allowing for the creation of new brand beliefs to position the extension in the new category. Moreover, subbranding can also help protect or shield the parent brand from any negative feedback that might be associated with an

Tide PODS is a successful line extension by the Tide laundry detergent brand.

General Mills' "Box Tops for Education" program has benefitted schools and raised engagement with participating brands such as Cheerios cereal.

extension. In a carefully researched study, the sudden acceleration problems experienced by the Audi 5000 a number of years ago were found to significantly hurt the sales of its sibling Audi 4000, but they had a much less pronounced effect on sales of the Audi Quattro, in part because of its more distinctive sub-branding.

To realize the benefits of association, however, sub-branding typically requires significant investments and disciplined and consistent marketing to establish the proper brand meanings with consumers. Without such financial commitments, marketers may be well advised to adopt the simplest brand hierarchy possible, such as using the company or family brand name with product descriptors.[11]

Do the "Right Thing" with Brands

Increased media coverage of business has brought greater transparency and awareness of companies' internal and external actions and statements. Many consumers believe companies should have a higher purpose that would somehow benefit local communities, society as a whole, or the broader natural environment. At the same time, heightened scrutiny from the investment community has caused many companies to adopt an overly myopic short-term planning horizon for their brands. Brand marketers need to address both these marketplace realities.

Cause Marketing. Brand marketers must embrace social responsibility and ethically and morally proper behavior at all times. In particular, they need to find win–win solutions with cause marketing programs and other activities that allow them to enhance the welfare of consumers, society, or the environment while still profitably running their businesses. Effective cause marketing programs can accomplish a number of objectives for a brand: build brand awareness, enhance brand image, establish brand credibility, evoke brand feelings, create a sense of brand community, and elicit brand engagement. A good long-running example of a successful cause marketing program is General Mills' "Box Tops for Education" program, which has benefitted schools by raising nearly $800 million since 1996.[12]

Protecting Brand Equity. Doing the right things with brands sometimes means doing something even simpler and more straight forward: protecting and respecting the brand promise and meaning to consumers. Even a simple typeface or font change can create massive negative sentiment among consumers, as brands such as Twitter and The Gap have found out, suggesting the sensitive nature of consumers' relationships with their brands. Problems arise when managers engage in overexposing, overextending, overmodernizing, and overdiscounting, and in doing so, take advantage of a brand. The best and most widely admired marketers treat their brands with understanding and respect and a clear sense of commercial and social purpose. They take their brands on a well-mapped-out journey that allows them to profitably grow while preserving close bonds with consumers and benefits to society as a whole. Disney launched an internal brand mantra of "fun family entertainment" to help employees judge whether any marketing or other action was "on brand." The worry was not that any single decision would be fatal or even damaging to the brand, but that a number of little concessions and compromises would eventually add up to significantly erode the equity of the Disney brand.

Take a Big Picture View of Branding Effects. Know What Is Working (and Why)

Justifying Brand Investments. Increasingly, marketers have had to do more with less in their marketing budgets and persuasively justify all marketing expenditures. One challenge in achieving brand accountability is that brand marketing activities are intended to have long-term, broad, and varied effects. Any particular marketing activity may increase the breadth or depth of brand awareness; establish or strengthen performance-related or imagery-related brand associations; elicit positive judgments or feelings; create stronger ties or bonds with the brand; initiate brand-related actions such as search, word-of-mouth, and purchase; or many or even all the above. And its effects may be enduring as well as short-term.

Marketers must adopt comprehensive, cohesive, and actionable models to help them develop ROI insights and interpretations. As an example, three linked, interlocking models in Chapters 2 and 3 that marketers can use in brand planning, tracking, and measurement are:

1. The *brand positioning model* describes how to establish competitive advantages via points-of-difference (associations unique to the brand that are also strongly held and favorably evaluated by consumers) and points-of-parity (associations shared with other brands that are designed to negate competitors' points-of-difference, overcome perceived vulnerabilities of the brand, or establish category credentials).

2. The *brand resonance model* considers how intense, active loyalty relationships are created with customers. The basic premise is that building a strong brand requires a series of steps as part of a "branding ladder" and a set of logically constructed "brand-building blocks." Brand resonance occurs when consumers feels completely "in sync" with the brand. The second level of the model is where the output from the brand positioning model appears, in terms of which points-of-parity and points-of-difference are to be created with which performance and/or imagery associations.

3. The *brand value chain model* describes how to trace the value creation process to better understand the financial impact of marketing expenditures and investments. The model examines four different stages in the value creation process for a brand. It considers how marketing activities affect the customer mind-set—as measured by all the building blocks in the brand resonance model—which, in turn, creates various marketplace outcomes and ultimately shareholder value.

The specific components of these three models are not as important as their purpose and scope. The models can both assist planning and measurement, and they can capture a full range of marketing activities for any type of brand. In particular, by tracing the effects of marketing activities through the customer mind-set, and on to various marketplace outcomes such as price premiums, loyalty, sales, market share, and profitability, marketers can gain a clearer picture of how well their marketing is doing and why.

Achieving Deeper Brand Understanding.   Branding is clearly a complex marketing endeavor. To better grasp all its dimensions, we adopt a multidisciplinary view to interpret branding effects and more completely understand brands, the value they have created, and how they should be managed as a result. We can develop marketing guidelines for branding from a variety of different perspectives, including economic, psychological, and sociological.

Fundamentally, marketing should help create or enhance the equity and value of a brand to all its various constituents. The stronger the brand, the more power brand marketers have with distributors and retailers, and the easier it is to implement marketplace programs to capitalize on brand equity. Extracting proper price premiums that reflect the value of the brand—and not over- or underpricing—is one of the most critical financial considerations for branding.

Finding the Branding Sweet Spot

Given their substantial intangible value, brands are likely to remain a top priority for organizations. The branding area continues to receive intense research attention, as researchers tackle old problems and address new challenges in important ways. Successful branding in the twenty-first century requires new areas of emphasis and new skills as described in the preceding six imperatives. We conclude by discussing one broad theme that cuts across all six: achieving balance in managing brands by finding the branding sweet spot.

Brand Balance.   To find the branding sweet spot, managers must reconcile trade-offs in brand management and strike the balance between simplicity and complexity in all brand decision-making and activity. Trade-offs are pervasive in marketing a brand—short-run sales versus long-run

Old Spice used a video ad campaign to engage younger audiences with the brand.

brand equity, global control versus local customization, retaining versus acquiring customers, and investing in online versus offline advertising, to name just a few.

The art and science of modern brand marketing is to fully understand and creatively address these significant branding trade-offs. To do so, companies have employed a variety of strategies: breakthrough product or service innovations, improved business models, expanded or leveraged resources, enhanced or embellished marketing, perceptual framing to overcome misperceptions, or just sheer creativity and inspiration.

For example, the trade-off between sales-generating and brand-building activities requires that marketing communications affect both the short run (sales) and the long run (brand building). Firms have addressed this in different ways. Some classic examples include: California's "Got milk?" campaign that entertained consumers and sold milk; P&G's Ivory promotional campaign challenged consumers to find one of the few bars that was weighted to sink in the bathtub, reinforcing the key attribute of floating; Old Spice's video ad campaign featuring the ad "The Man Your Man Could Smell Like" was a viral sensation. With Old Spice, P&G followed it up with an interactive video asking fans to post questions, and this interactive approach to marketing resulted in more than 65 million views. The Old Spice campaign is an excellent example of how to engage younger audiences in your brand.[13]

Another trade-off focuses on points-of-difference and points-of-parity. To be effectively positioned, the brand must have points-of-difference where it excels, and at least points-of-parity versus competitors where it may be seen as inferior. Volvo and Southwest Airlines approached this challenge by developing unique PODs (safety and low price/value, respectively), as well as parity with competitors on key points (for Volvo, style; for Southwest Airlines, good service, on-time arrivals). When the first Apple computer launched, it was so easy to use, the market thought it must not be powerful. Apple reframed that negative perception by redefining the idea of power: power is not what is inside the computer, but what you can do with it.

In developing solutions to achieve balance in branding, it is important: (1) not to oversimplify branding so that all the richness is stripped away, but, at the same time; (2) not to overcomplicate branding such that marketers and other employees are overwhelmed by the complexity. The optimal branding approach recognizes that many different aspects of branding matter; the imperatives we've previously discussed point the way to the most critical.

New Capabilities for Brand Marketers

Brand management is undergoing a transformation, and the chapters in this book have shone a spotlight on various aspects of brand management and the shifting roles of brand managers. Many of the skills that are needed to manage brands are also skills that are required in leadership roles within companies and organizations. We highlight a few of these critical skills:

1. **Analytical and quantitative capabilities:** As we have discussed throughout the book, brand management is increasingly data-driven. Managers of brands should have the capacity to interface with data scientists, statistical modelers, and computational social scientists in order to generate insights from data. Data can provide useful guidance to brand managers who wish to personalize their brands to suit individual customers' needs and wants. To do so, the brand manager of the future should be able to envision what types of data they need to improve their customer interface, and liaison with the data scientists to ensure access to the right types of metrics and data. Chapter 7 provides a broad overview of the types of tools and techniques that brand managers would use in the context of digital marketing and social media.

2. **Storytelling and creativity:** Consumers use brands as a way of communicating with others and for performing key roles in their lives. The brand story is thus a critical factor in its appeal. Brand managers should be creative in articulating a value proposition

that captivates customers' attention. Chapters 2 to 4 highlight several examples of brands that have created equity and resonance with their consumers, and Chapter 7 outlines the various channel options to communicate the brand story.

3. **Collaboration and teamwork:** Brand management is all about coordination and collaboration. Be it with sales personnel, ad agencies, digital marketing partners, R&D, supply chain, production, or consumers, brand managers are typically mini-CEOs whose role is to manage the profit-and-loss statement for a given brand. Thus, collaboration and teamwork are integral to this role. In the future, brand management may be incorporated in various C-level jobs such as chief experience officer, chief design officer, and so on. Many digital-only companies now have a chief experience officer who is tasked with managing the customer experience from beginning to end, and this

Chief experience officer and chief design officer are some of the new designations in organizations that provide support for brand management roles and responsibilities.

role may interface with more traditional brand management functions to help strengthen a company's customer interactions. Chapters 5 and 6 discuss how brand managers can implement marketing programs to build brand equity, and better leverage communication channel options.

4. **Strategic thinking, understanding current and future trends:** Success in brand management requires staying abreast of customer trends and modifying brands to incorporate these new trends. In fact, successful brands will be those that can successfully interpret trends and incorporate these insights into brand attributes and benefits. Brand managers should be able to see the big picture and evolve brand strategy to keep up with changing times. Chapters 12 to 15 describe how brands can be managed strategically and leverage marketplace trends effectively.

5. **Empathy and understanding:** A key role of brand managers is to acquire and retain customers. Customer retention, in particular, depends on satisfying customer needs, and resolving complaints, in a satisfactory way. Brand managers of the future should have empathy and deep understanding of issues from a customer perspective in order to maximize customer experiences and generate the highest customer satisfaction. Key account managers and sales personnel are often customer-facing, and brand managers should be able to work well with sales to improve a brand's appeal to the customer or end-consumer. Chapters 8 to 10 describe ways of measuring outcomes in the marketplace, so that brand managers can keep track of customer satisfaction and brand equity.

6. **Digital marketing and technological and computing skills:** Given the shift in advertising to digital and social media channels, advertising is increasingly becoming algorithmic in nature. Large companies are increasingly automating the process of placing advertisements on various digital, social and mobile platforms. Using search engine optimization/search engine advertising requires a great deal of skill in social media application programming interfaces (APIs) to understand analytics reports and so on. Further, brand managers should be nimble and respond quickly to changes in the digital and social marketing landscape. Brand managers should be knowledgeable about the functions performed by these entities and also effectively liaison with them. Chapter 7, in particular, showcases the role of digital marketing and social media, and across all the other chapters, we highlight various examples of brands that are reinventing themselves.

Developments in digital marketing offer great promise and pose significant challenges to brand managers in the future.

REVIEW

The challenges and complexities of the modern marketplace make efficient and effective marketing an imperative. The businesses that win in the twenty-first century will be those whose marketers successfully build, measure, and manage brand equity. This final chapter reviewed some of the important guidelines put forth in this text to help in that endeavor.

Effective brand management requires consistent application of these guidelines across all aspects of the marketing program. Nevertheless, to some extent, rules are made to be broken, and the guidelines can be only a point of departure in the challenging process of creating a world-class brand. Each branding situation and application is unique and requires careful scrutiny and analysis about how best to apply, or perhaps in some cases ignore, these various recommendations and guidelines. Smart marketers will capitalize on every tool at their disposal—and devise new ones—in their relentless pursuit of brand preeminence.

DISCUSSION QUESTIONS

1. What do you think makes a strong brand? Can you add any criteria to the list provided?
2. Consider the deadly sins of brand management. Do you see anything missing from the list of seven in Figure 16-8?
3. Pick one of the special applications of branding and choose a representative brand within that category. How well do the five guidelines for that category apply? Can you think of others not listed?
4. What do you see as the future of branding? How will the roles of brands change? What different strategies might emerge for building, measuring, and managing brand equity in the coming years? What do you see as the biggest challenges? How have the advent of social media and the availability of digital marketing tools changed brand management?
5. Consider the trade-offs involved with achieving marketing balance. Can you identify a company that has excelled in achieving balance on various trade-offs?

BRAND FOCUS 16.0

Special Applications

In Chapter 1, we deliberately defined **product** as encompassing not only physical goods, but also services, retail stores, people, organizations, places, and ideas. While the themes and guidelines for building, measuring, and managing brand equity that we have presented are appropriate for virtually all types of products, here, we'll consider in greater detail some specific issues for some less conventional types of products—online brands, industrial and business-to-business products, high-technology products, services, retailers, and small businesses.

ONLINE

Creating a brand online brings a special set of challenges. Many of the guidelines for business-to-business, high-tech, retailing, and small businesses—identified in the following discussion—will apply, but a few others are worth reinforcing (as summarized in Figure 16-10).

Don't forget the brand-building basics. Remember brand-building basics such as establishing points-of-parity (convenience,

FIGURE 16-10

Additional Guidelines
for Online Brands

1. Don't forget the brand-building basics.
2. Create strong brand identity.
3. Generate strong consumer pull.
4. Selectively choose brand partnerships.
5. Maximize relationship marketing.

price, and variety) and points-of-difference (customer service, credibility, and personality). As we noted in earlier chapters, one mistake of many failed dot-com brands was being impatient to build their brands and failing to build from the bottom up.

Research undertaken to understand *online service quality*, defined as the extent to which a Web site facilitates efficient and effective shopping, purchasing, and delivery, has shown that it is driven by four types of factors, that is, Web site design, fulfillment, customer service, and security.[14] Lands' End became a top-selling company online by treating its online operations as a digital translation of its successful catalog, ensuring that merchandise was presented properly, and excellent customer service prevailed.

Create strong brand identity. Given that consumers aren't physically confronted by brands online as they are in a store, brand awareness and recall are critical. Choosing the best URL and devising an effective search term strategy are therefore critical. Keep the basic brand element criteria in mind, perhaps with greater emphasis on brand recall as an objective (1-800-FLOWERS took its brand directly to the Web). A simple but evocative name can also be useful, like Amazon Mom, an information and commerce Web site providing content on pregnancy and babies to young parents who are current customers of Amazon.

Generate strong consumer pull. An important lesson for online brands was the need to create demand off-line in order to drive consumers online. Online marketers must introduce the best possible integrated marketing communication program, using sampling and other trial devices, as well as social media; public relations; sponsorships; and television, radio, and print advertising.

Selectively choose brand partnerships. Brand partnerships that satisfy brand-building and profit criteria can drive traffic, signal credibility, and help enhance image. In Australia, Seniors Club Online, which caters to consumers aged 60-plus with various entertainment and promotional offers, partnered with *Reader's Digest* magazine to offer free issues.[15]

Maximize relationship marketing. Finally, to leverage the advantages of customization and interactivity, marketers must engage in one-to-one, participatory, experiential, and other forms of relationship marketing. Creating a strong online brand community between the consumer and the brand, as well as with other consumers, through blogs, online contests, and social media can help achieve brand resonance. Online brands can offer much potentially relevant customer information; for example, Amazon provides professional and customer reviews, purchase circles and overall sales rankings, text samples, and personalized recommendations.

INDUSTRIAL AND BUSINESS-TO-BUSINESS PRODUCTS

Industrial goods and business-to-business marketing sometimes call for different branding practices.[16] Here are some basic branding guidelines (see Figure 16-11).

Adopt a corporate or family branding strategy, and create a well-defined brand hierarchy. Because companies selling industrial goods often carry a large and complex number of product lines and variations, marketers should devise a logical and well-organized brand hierarchy. Given the breadth and complexity of their product mix, companies selling industrial goods—like GE, Hewlett-Packard, IBM, BASF, and John Deere—are more likely to emphasize corporate or family brands. Thus, a particularly effective branding strategy for industrial goods is to create sub-brands by combining a well-known and respected corporate name with descriptive product modifiers.

Link non-product-related imagery associations. Programs to build brand equity for industrial goods can be different from those for consumer goods, because, given the nature of the organizational buying process, product-related associations may play a relatively more important role than non-product-related associations. Industrial brands often emphasize functionality and cost–benefit comparisons. Nevertheless, even non-performance-related associations can be useful for forming other perceptions of the firm, such as prestige or the type of companies that use its products.

Corporate or family brands must convey credibility and possess favorable overall associations. Corporate credibility is often a primary risk reduction heuristic adopted by industrial buyers. For years, one of the key sources of brand equity for IBM was the perception that "you'll never get fired for buying IBM." Once that special cachet faded, the brand found itself in a much more competitive situation. Creating a feeling of security for industrial buyers can thus be an important source of brand equity. Many industrial firms distinguish themselves on the basis of the customer service they provide, in addition to the quality of their products.

Employ a full range of marketing communication options. Another difference between industrial and consumer products is the way they are sold (see Figure 16-12). Industrial marketing communications tend to convey more detailed product information in a more direct or face-to-face manner. Thus, personal selling plays an important role. At the same time, other communication options can enhance awareness or the formation of brand associations. One effective industrial marketing communication approach is to combine direct hard-sell messages with indirect image-related messages that convey who and what the company is all about.

---

1. Adopt a corporate or family branding strategy and create a well-defined brand hierarchy.
2. Link non-product-related imagery associations.
3. Employ a full range of marketing communication options.
4. Leverage equity of other companies that are customers.
5. Segment markets carefully and develop tailored branding and marketing programs.

FIGURE 16-11

Additional Guidelines for Industrial Products

Media advertising (TV, radio, newspaper, magazines)

Trade journal advertising

Directories

Direct mail

Brochures and sales literature

Audiovisual presentation tapes

Giveaways

Sponsorship or event marketing

Exhibitions, trade shows, and conventions

Publicity or public relations

FIGURE 16-12

Alternative Communication
Options: Business-to-Business
Market

Leverage equity of other companies that are customers. Industrial brands can leverage secondary associations differently; for example, identifying other companies that are customers for their products or services conveys credibility. The challenge in advertising that fact, however, is ensuring these other companies do not distract from the message about the advertised company and its brands.

Segment customers carefully, and develop tailored branding and marketing programs. Finally, as for any brand, understand how different customer segments view products and brands. For industrial goods, different customer segments such as engineers, accountants, and purchasing managers may exist within, as well as across, organizations and have different associations that serve as sources of brand equity. It may be particularly important to achieve points-of-parity with these different constituencies, so that key points-of-difference can come into play.

Marketing programs must reflect the role of individuals in the buying center, or the process-initiator, influencer, purchaser, user, and so on. Some individuals within the organization may be more concerned with developing a deep relationship with the company, and therefore, place greater value on trustworthiness and corporate credibility; others may seek merely to make transactions, and therefore, place greater value on product performance and expertise.

HIGH-TECH PRODUCTS

One special category of physical goods, in both consumer and industrial markets, is technologically intensive or high-tech products. The distinguishing feature of high-tech products is that they change rapidly over time because of innovations and R&D breakthroughs. Technology isn't limited to computer-related products: it has played an important role in the branding and marketing of

products as diverse as razor blades for Gillette and athletic shoes for Nike.

The short product life cycles for high-tech products have several significant branding implications (see Figure 16-13 for specific guidelines).

Establish brand awareness and a rich brand image. Many high-tech companies have learned the hard way the importance of branding their products and not relying on product specifications alone to drive their sales. It's typically not true that "if you build a great product, they will come." You need well-designed and well-funded marketing programs to create brand awareness and a strong brand image. Non-product-related associations concerning brand personality or other imagery may be important, especially in distinguishing near-parity products.

Create corporate credibility associations. One implication of rapid product turnover is the need to create a corporate or family brand with strong credibility associations. Because of the often-complex nature of high-tech products and the continual introduction of new products or modifications of existing products, consumer perceptions of the expertise and trustworthiness of the firm are particularly important. In a high-tech setting, trustworthiness also relates to consumers' perceptions of the firm's longevity and staying power. For technology companies, the president or CEO often is a key component of the brand and performs an important brand-building and communication function, in some cases as an advocate of the technology. Consider the late Steve Jobs, for example.

Leverage secondary associations of quality. Lacking the ability to judge the quality of high-tech products, consumers may use brand reputation as a means to reduce risk. This means secondary associations may better communicate

FIGURE 16-13

Additional Guidelines
for High-Tech Products

1. Establish brand awareness and a rich brand image.
2. Create corporate credibility associations.
3. Leverage secondary associations of quality.
4. Avoid overbranding products.
5. Selectively introduce new products as new brands, and clearly identify the nature of brand extensions.

product quality, such as third-party endorsements from top companies, leading consumer magazines, or industry experts. To garner these endorsements, however, products need to achieve demonstrable differences in product performance, suggesting the importance of innovative product development over time.

Avoid overbranding products. One mistake high-tech firms often make is to "overbrand" products by using too many ingredient and endorser brands. In a kind of "NASCAR effect," so many brands and logos are present for all the different product ingredients that the consumer can be overwhelmed or confused, and no individual brand element adds much value.

Selectively introduce new products as new brands, and clearly identify brand extensions. Short product life cycles in high-tech industries make well-designed brand portfolios and hierarchies even more important. With new products continually emerging, it would be prohibitively expensive to brand them with new names in each case. Typically, names for new products include modifiers from existing products—for example, alphabetical (Microsoft Xbox One X), numerical (Tesla Model 3), time-based (Intuit Premier Desktop 2018 Accounting Software), or other schemes. A new name for a new product signals a major departure that is significantly different from prior versions.

Thus, family brands are an important means of grouping products. Marketers must clearly distinguish individual items or products within those brand families, however, and define brand migration strategies that reflect product introduction strategies and consumer market trends. When high-tech firms continually introduce totally new sub-brands, it grows difficult for consumers to develop product or brand loyalty to any one brand.

SERVICES

We noted in Chapter 1 that the level of sophistication in service branding has greatly increased in recent years, as suggested by the following guidelines (see Figure 16-14).

Maximize service quality by recognizing the myriad ways to affect consumer service perceptions. It is challenging to develop brands for intangible services. Consumers may have difficulty forming their quality evaluations, and may, therefore, base them on considerations other than their own service experience.

Researchers have identified a number of dimensions of service quality:[17]

- **Tangibles:** Physical facilities, equipment, and appearance of personnel
- **Reliability:** Ability to perform the promised service right the first time (standardized facilities and operations)
- **Responsiveness:** Willingness to help customers and provide customer service
- **Competence:** Knowledge and skill of employees
- **Trustworthiness:** Believability and honesty (ability to convey trust and confidence)
- **Empathy:** Caring, individualized attention
- **Courtesy:** Friendliness of customer contact
- **Communication:** Keeping customers informed in language they can understand and listening to what they say.

Thus, service quality perceptions depend on a number of specific associations that vary in how directly they relate to the actual service experience.[18]

Employ a full range of brand elements to enhance brand recall and signal more tangible aspects of the brand. Because consumers often make service decisions away from the actual service location itself (say, at home or at work), brand recall, preferably aided by an easy-to-remember and easy-to-pronounce brand name, becomes critically important. Product packaging is not really relevant, although the physical facilities of the service provider—primary and secondary signage, environmental design and reception area, apparel, collateral material—serve as external packaging for the service.

Other brand elements—logos, symbols, characters, and slogans—must pick up the slack and complement the brand name to build awareness and image. These elements can help make the service and some of its key benefits more tangible—for example, the "friendly skies" of United, the "good hands" of Allstate, and the "bullish" nature of Merrill Lynch. All aspects of the service delivery process can be branded, which is why Allied Moving Lines is concerned about the appearance of its drivers and laborers, why UPS has developed such strong equity with the brown color of its trucks, and why Doubletree hotels offer warm, fresh-baked cookies to symbolize the company's caring and friendliness.

Create and communicate strong organizational associations. Organizational associations are particularly important in creating perceptions of service quality. Relevant associations are company credibility and the perceived expertise, trustworthiness, and likability of the people who make up the organization and provide the service.

1. Maximize service quality by recognizing the myriad ways to affect consumer service perceptions.
2. Employ a full range of brand elements to enhance brand recall and signal more tangible aspects of the brand.
3. Create and communicate strong organizational associations.
4. Design corporate communication programs that augment consumers' service encounters and experiences.
5. Establish a brand hierarchy by creating distinct family brands or individual brands as well as meaningful ingredient brands.

FIGURE 16-14

Additional Guidelines for Services

Design communication programs that augment consumers' service encounters and experiences. Service firms must design marketing communications so consumers learn more about the brand than what they glean from service encounters alone. Advertising, direct mail, and online communications are particularly effective at helping develop the brand personality. The communication programs should be fully integrated and evolve over time. Citigroup walked away from a strong credibility position for its retail brand when it dropped its "Citi Never Sleeps" ad campaign, although it later returned to it during some tough economic times.

Establish a brand hierarchy by creating distinct family brands or individual brands as well as meaningful ingredient brands. Finally, services also must consider developing a brand hierarchy and brand portfolio that allow them to position and target different market segments on the basis of price and quality. Such vertical extensions often require sub-branding strategies that combine the corporate name with an individual brand name or modifier. Delta Airlines brands its business class service as Business Elite, its frequent flier program as SkyMiles, and its short-haul East Coast flights as Delta Shuttle. Hilton Hotel introduced Hilton Garden Inns to target budget-conscious business travelers and compete with the popular Courtyard by Marriott chain.

RETAILERS

Chapters 5 and 8 reviewed how retailers and other channel intermediaries can affect the brand equity of the products they sell, as well as creating their own brand equity, by establishing awareness and associations to their product assortment (breadth and depth), pricing and credit policy, and quality of service. Walmart has made itself a top U.S. retail brand by becoming the low-price, high-value provider of a host of everyday consumer products. The following are several guidelines relevant for building brand equity for a retailer (see Figure 16-15).

Create a brand hierarchy by branding the store as a whole, as well as individual departments, classes of service, or any other noteworthy aspects of the retail service or shopping experience. Establishing a brand hierarchy helps create synergies in brand development, including for retailers. Walmart introduced Sam's Club to tap into the growing discount or warehouse retail market. Similarly, individual departments can take on unique sets of associations that appeal to a particular target market. Nordstrom has a number of clothing departments, each designed with distinct images and positions, such as tbd for the latest women's trends, BP

for teen girls, and Encore for plus-size women. The retailer may brand these departments or even use them as "ingredient brands," designed and supported by a national manufacturer (such as Polo shops in major department stores that sell only that Ralph Lauren brand).

Enhance manufacturer's brand equity. Retailers should exploit as much as possible the brand equity of the manufacturer brands they sell, by communicating and demonstrating their points-of-difference and other strong, favorable, and unique brand associations. By cooperating with, and perhaps even enhancing, manufacturers' push strategies, retailers should be able to sell products at higher prices and margins.

Establish brand equity at all levels of the brand hierarchy by offering added value in the selection, purchase, or delivery of product offerings. Retailers must create their own strong, favorable, and unique associations that go beyond the products they sell. Victoria's Secret has gained popularity as a provider of stylish feminine clothing. Costco has created a strong discount association. To communicate these broader associations, image campaigns often focus on the advantages to consumers of shopping at and buying from the stores in general, rather than on promotions for specific sale items. For example, Ace Hardware advertises itself as the helpful hardware place.

Embrace omnichannel shopping behavior. Consumers shop across a range of different types of channels, and often may search for information in one channel, but make purchases in another. Retailers are also engaged in sales in a variety of channels, such as physical stores, catalogs, and online Web sites. Regardless of the channel, consumers must have rewarding shopping experiences in searching, choosing, paying for, and receiving products. In some cases, these experiences may turn out to be valuable points-of-difference, or at least necessary points-of-parity, with respect to competitors.

Avoid overbranding. Finally, if a retailer is selling its own private labels, it is important not to employ too many brands. Retailers are particularly susceptible to bottom-up branding, in which each department creates its own set of brands. Nordstrom found itself supporting scores of various brands across its different departments, sometimes with little connection among them. Recall from Chapter 5 that one advantage of store brands, however, is that they often represent associations that transfer across categories. The more an abstract association like value or fashionability is desirable and deliverable across categories, the more likely that the marketer can gain efficiencies by concentrating on a few major brands.

---

1. Create a brand hierarchy by branding the store as a whole, as well as individual departments, classes of service, or any other aspects of the retail service or shopping experience.
2. Enhance manufacturers' brand equity by communicating and demonstrating their points-of-difference and other strong, favorable, and unique brand associations.
3. Establish brand equity at all levels of the brand hierarchy by offering added value in the selection, purchase, or delivery of product offerings.
4. Create multichannel shopping experiences.
5. Avoid overbranding.

FIGURE 16-15

Additional Guidelines for Retailers

Small Businesses

Building brands is a challenge for small businesses because of their limited resources and budgets. They usually do not have the luxury of making mistakes and must design and implement marketing programs much more carefully.[19] Nevertheless, many entrepreneurs have built their brands into powerhouses essentially from scratch.

Online footwear retailer Zappos, founded by Tony Hsieh, has become a top brand in a little over a decade because of its relentless customer focus and strong corporate culture. With free shipping and returns, 24/7 customer service, and fast turnaround on a wide selection of 200,000 styles of shoes from 1,200 makers, Zappos finds that three-fourths of its purchases during any one day are from repeat customers. Bought by Amazon in 2009 for a reported $850 million, but still run separately, the company now also sells clothing, handbags, and accessories.[20]

Because there are usually limited resources behind a small-business brand, marketing focus and consistency are critically important. Creativity is also paramount for finding new ways to market ideas about products to consumers. Figure 16-16 displays some specific branding guidelines for small businesses.

Emphasize building one or two strong brands. Given fewer resources, strategically, it may be necessary to emphasize building one or two strong brands. A corporate branding strategy can be an efficient means to build brand equity, although the focus may just be on a few family brands. For example, Intuit concentrated its marketing efforts on building the Quicken brand name of software.

Focus the marketing program on one or two key associations. Small businesses often must rely on only one or two key associations as points-of-difference, consistently reinforcing them across the marketing program and over time. Former Navy SEAL Alden Mills created the Perfect Pushup, adding rotation to the classic U-shaped push-up stands to provide more natural movement and engage more muscles while going easy on the joints. Sales-generating print ads, direct-response TV ads, and a Web site hammered home the founder's exemplary Navy SEAL credentials and the significant fitness benefits of the product's unique design.[21]

Employ a well-integrated set of brand elements. Tactically, it is important for small businesses to maximize the contribution of each of the three main ways to build brand equity. First, a distinctive, well-integrated set of brand elements will enhance both brand awareness and brand image, as suggested by Smartfood popcorn. The company introduced its first product without any advertising, using a unique package that served as a strong visual symbol on the shelf and an extensive sampling program that encouraged trial. Proper

Online footwear retailer Zappos rose to prominence within the last decade because of its focus on offering exceptional customer service.

names or family names that often characterize small businesses can provide distinctiveness, but if they lack pronounceability, meaningfulness, memorability, and other branding considerations, founders should explore other brand names and brand elements.

Design creative brand-building push campaigns and consumer-involving pull campaigns that capture attention and generate demand. Small businesses must design creative push and pull programs that capture the attention of consumers and other channel members alike. Clearly, this is a sizable challenge on a limited budget. Unfortunately, without a strong pull campaign creating product interest, retailers may not feel enough motivation to stock and support the brand. Conversely, without a strong push campaign that convinces retailers of the merits of the product, the brand may fail to achieve adequate support or even be stocked at all. Thus, creative and cost-effective push and pull marketing programs must increase the visibility of the brand and get both consumers and retailers talking about it.

Because small businesses often must rely on word-of-mouth to create strong, favorable, and unique brand associations, public relations and low-cost promotions and sponsorship can be inexpensive means to enhance brand awareness and brand image. The use of referral programs can transform a small business into an industry leader. Dropbox grew 3,900 percent through a referral program between 2008 and 2017. The referral program allowed it to double its user base in the initial years, focused on offering free space to anyone who offered a referral. Dropbox made the referral process extremely simple by allowing users to post invitations on social media.[22]

1. Emphasize building one or two strong brands.
2. Focus the marketing program on one or two key associations.
3. Employ a well-integrated set of brand elements that enhances both brand awareness and brand image.
4. Design creative brand-building push campaigns and consumer-involving pull campaigns that capture attention and generate demand.
5. Leverage as many secondary associations as possible.

FIGURE 16-16

Additional Guidelines for Small Business

Dropbox used a referral program to double its customer base.
Source: Valentin Wolf/imageBROKER/Alamy Stock Photo

Marketers of the PowerBar, a nutrient-rich, low-fat energy bar, used selective sponsorship of top marathon runners, cyclists, and tennis players, and events like the Boston Marathon to raise awareness and improve image. Selective distribution that targets opinion leaders can also be a cost-effective means to implement a push strategy. Perrier bottled water and Paul Mitchell and Nexus shampoo were initially introduced to a carefully selected set of outlets before broadening distribution.

Content marketing is another approach that small businesses can use to build their reputation and to establish themselves as a leader in an area. Content marketing efforts may involve creating various forms of content, including videos, e-books, Infographics, white papers and reports, and survey data, to engage the target audience. Content marketing is among the best approaches available for small businesses to generate Web site traffic and build awareness.[23]

Leverage as many secondary associations as possible. Finally, another way for small businesses to build brand equity is to leverage as many secondary associations as possible. Consider any entity with potentially relevant associations—a highly regarded location, a well-known set of customers or any prestigious awards—especially those that help signal quality or credibility. Along those lines, to make the company appear bigger than it really is, a well-designed Web site can be invaluable.

NOTES

1 Kevin Lane Keller, "The Brand Report Card," *Harvard Business Review* 78, no. 1 (January 2000): 147–157.
2. Ibid.
3. Allen P. Adamson, *Brand Simple* (New York: Palgrave Macmillan, 2006); Francis J. Kelly and Barry Silverstein, *The Breakaway Brand* (New York: McGraw-Hill, 2005).
4. John Gerzema and Ed Lebar, *The Brand Bubble* (New York: Jossey-Bass, 2008).
5. For some practical tools, see Mark Sherrington, *Added Value: The Alchemy of Brand-Led Growth* (Hampshire,

UK: Palgrave Macmillan, 2003); David Taylor, *The Brand Gym*, 2nd ed. (Chichester, UK: John Wiley & Sons, 2010).
6. For some in-depth reviews, see Tim Calkins and Alice M. Tybout, *Kellogg on Branding* (New York: John Wiley & Sons, 2001); Rita Clifton and John Simmon, eds., *The Economist on Branding*, 2nd ed. (New York: Bloomberg Press, 2009); Barbara Loken, Rohini Ahluwalia, and Michael J. Houston, eds., *Brands and Brand Management: Contemporary Research Perspectives* (New York: Taylor & Francis, 2010).

7. For some provocative discussion, see Deborah J. MacInnis, C. Whan Park, and Joseph R. Priester, eds., *Handbook of Brand Relationships* (Armonk, NY: M. E. Sharpe, 2009).

8. Mobilemarketer.com (2018), "Home Depot, Weather Channel Expand Partnership to Mobile," www .mobilemarketer.com/ex/mobilemarketer/cms/news/ content/2738.html, accessed September 6, 2018; Lauren Wishom, "Unlikely Biz Collaborations: Home Depot & The Weather Channel— Part 2," August 28, 2016, www .drlaureen.com/unlikely-biz-collaborations-home-depot-the-weather-channel-part-2/.

9. Jason DeMers, "The 7 Biggest Social Media Fails of 2017—So Far," May 30, 2017, www.entrepreneur.com/ article/294925#.

10. Kristina Monllos, "Meet the Man Responsible for Protecting the LEGO Brand as It Became a Mega Movie Franchise," *Adweek.com*, March 10, 2017, www.adweek .com/brand-marketing/meet-the-man-responsible-for-protecting-the-lego-brand-as-it-became-a-mega-movie-franchise/, accessed September 6, 2018.

11. Mary Jo Hatch and Majken Schultz, *Taking Brand Initiative* (San Francisco: Jossey-Bass, 2008).

12. Raja Rajamannar, "Here's How Cause Marketing Can Make a Difference," *Forbes,* July 10, 2017, www.forbes .com/sites/onmarketing/2017/07/10/heres-how-cause-marketing-can-make-a-difference/#50bef57838d4.

13. D&AD, "Case Study: Old Spice Response Campaign," February 2010, www.dandad.org/en/d-ad-old-spice-case-study-insights/, accessed December 27, 2017.

14. Markus Blut, Nivriti Chowdhry, Vikas Mittal, and Christian Brock, "E-service Quality: A Meta-analytic Review," *Journal of Retailing* 91, no. 4 (2015): 679–700; Valarie A. Zeithaml, Parsu Parasuraman, and Arvind Mal-hotra, "Understanding e-Service Quality," presentation made at MSI Board of Trustees Meeting, "Marketing Knowledge in the Age of e-Commerce," November 2000; William Boulding, Ajay Kalra, and Richard Staelin, "A Dynamic Process Model of Service Quality: From Expectations to Behavioral Intentions," *Journal of Marketing Research* 30, no. 1 (February 1993): 7–27; Joel E. Collier and Carol C. Bienstock, "Measuring Service Quality in E-Retailing," *Journal of Service Research* 8, no. 3, (February 2006): 260–275.

15. Reader's Digest, http://www.readersdigestcom.au, accessed September 6, 2018.

16. Kevin Lane Keller and Frederick E. Webster, Jr., "A Roadmap for Branding in Industrial Markets," *Journal of Brand Management* 11, no. 5 (May 2004): 388–402. See also Mark S. Glynn and Arch G. Woodside, eds., "Business-to-Business Brand Management: Theory, Research, and Executive Case Study Exercises," in *Advances in Business Marketing & Purchasing* series,

Vol. 15 (Bingley, UK: Emerald Group Publishing, 2009); Philip Kotler and Waldemar Pfoertsch, *B2B Brand Management* (Berlin, Germany: Springer, 2006).

17. A. Parasuraman, Valarie A. Zeithaml, and Leonard L. Berry, "A Conceptual Model of Service Quality and Its Implications for Future Research," *Journal of Marketing* (Fall 1985): 41–50; Michael K. Brady and J. Joseph Cronin Jr., "Some New Thoughts on Conceptualizing Perceived Service Quality: A Hierarchical Approach," *Journal of Marketing* 65, no. 3 (July 2001): 34–49.

18. Leonard L. Berry, A. Parasuraman, and Valarie A. Zeithaml, "Ten Lessons for Improving Service Quality," MSI Report 93–104 (Cambridge, MA: Marketing Science Institute, 1993).

19. Adam Morgan, *Eating the Big Fish*, 2nd ed. (Hoboken, NJ: John Wiley & Sons, 2009).

20. Helen Coster, "A Step Ahead," *Forbes Magazine,* May 23, 2008, https://www.forbes.com/global/2008/ 0602/064.html#5849a0eb2efd, accessed November 27, 2018; Paula Andruss, "Delivering Wow Through Service," *Marketing News*, October 15, 2008, 10, https://archive.ama.org/archive/ResourceLibrary/ MarketingNews/Pages/2008/42/17/DeliveringWow .aspx, accessed November 27, 2018; Jeffrey M. O'Brien, "Zappos Knows How to Kick It," *Fortune Magazine* 159, no. 2 (February 2009): 55–60; Brian Morrissey, "Amazon to Buy Zappos," *Adweek*, July 22, 2009, https://www.adweek.com/brand-marketing/amazon-buy-zappos-99916/, accessed November 27, 2018; Christopher Palmeri, "Zappos Retails Its Culture," December 30, 2009, https://www.bloomberg.com/news/ articles/2009-12-30/zappos-retails-its-culture, accessed November 27, 2018.

21. Inc. Magazine, Courtesy Company, "How I Did It: Alden Mills of Perfect Fitness," September 1, 2009, https://www.inc.com/magazine/20090901/how-i-did-it-alden-mills-of-perfect-fitness.html, accessed November 27, 2018.

22. Inside Viral Loops, "How Dropbox Grew 3900% with a Simple Referral Program," June 26, 2018, https://viral-loops.com/blog/dropbox-grew-3900-simple-referral-program/, accessed November 27, 2018.

23. Megan Totka, "4 Reasons Your Small Business Needs Content Marketing," September 27, 2017, https://smallbi-ztrends.com/2017/01/ways-to-use-content-marketing .html, accessed November 27, 2018; Jason DeMers, "3 Steps to Creating a Killer Small Business Content Marketing Strategy," September 2, 2016, www .forbes.com/sites/jaysondemers/2016/09/02/3-steps-to-creating-a-killer-small-business-content-marketing-strategy/#418654d82be4, accessed November 27, 2018.

INDEX